University Casebook Series

December, 1980

ACCOUNTING AND THE LAW, Fourth Edition (1978), with Problems Pamphlet (Successor to Dohr, Phillips, Thompson & Warren)

George C. Thompson, Professor, Columbia University Graduate School of Business.
Robert Whitman, Professor of Law, University of Connecticut.
Ellis L. Phillips, Jr., Member of the New York Bar.
William C. Warren, Professor of Law Emeritus, Columbia University.

ACCOUNTING FOR LAWYERS, MATERIALS ON (1980)

David R. Herwitz, Professor of Law, Harvard University.

ADMINISTRATIVE LAW, Seventh Edition (1979), with 1979 Problems Supplement (Supplement edited in association with Paul R. Verkuil, Dean and Professor of Law, Tulane University)

Walter Gellhorn, University Professor Emeritus, Columbia University.
Clark Byse, Professor of Law, Harvard University.
Peter L. Strauss, Professor of Law, Columbia University.

ADMIRALTY, Second Edition (1978), with Statute and Rule Supplement

Jo Desha Lucas, Professor of Law, University of Chicago.

ADVOCACY, see also Lawyering Process

ADVOCACY, INTRODUCTION TO, Third Edition (1981)

Board of Student Advisers, Harvard Law School.

AGENCY, see also Enterprise Organization

AGENCY-ASSOCIATIONS-EMPLOYMENT-PARTNERSHIPS, Second Edition (1977)

Abridgement from Conard, Knauss & Siegel's Enterprise Organization.

ANTITRUST AND REGULATORY ALTERNATIVES (1977), Fifth Edition

Louis B. Schwartz, Professor of Law, University of Pennsylvania.
John J. Flynn, Professor of Law, University of Utah.

ANTITRUST SUPPLEMENT—SELECTED STATUTES AND RELATED MATERIALS (1977)

John J. Flynn, Professor of Law, University of Utah.

BIOGRAPHY OF A LEGAL DISPUTE, THE: An Introduction to American Civil Procedure (1968)

Marc A. Franklin, Professor of Law, Stanford University.

BUSINESS ORGANIZATION, see also Enterprise Organization

BUSINESS PLANNING (1966), with 1980 Supplement

David R. Herwitz, Professor of Law, Harvard University.

BUSINESS TORTS (1972)

Milton Handler, Professor of Law Emeritus, Columbia University.

CIVIL PROCEDURE, see Procedure

CLINIC, see also Lawyering Process

COMMERCIAL AND CONSUMER TRANSACTIONS, Second Edition (1978)

William D. Warren, Dean of the School of Law, University of California, Los Angeles.
William E. Hogan, Professor of Law, Cornell University.
Robert L. Jordan, Professor of Law, University of California, Los Angeles.

COMMERCIAL LAW, CASES & MATERIALS ON, Third Edition (1976)

E. Allan Farnsworth, Professor of Law, Cornell University.
John Honnold, Professor of Law, University of Pennsylvania.

COMMERCIAL PAPER, Second Edition (1976)

E. Allan Farnsworth, Professor of Law, Columbia University.

COMMERCIAL PAPER AND BANK DEPOSITS AND COLLECTIONS (1967), with Statutory Supplement.

William D. Hawkland, Professor of Law, University of Illinois.

COMMERCIAL TRANSACTIONS—Text, Cases and Problems, Fourth Edition (1968)

Robert Braucher, Professor of Law Emeritus, Harvard University, and
The late Arthur E. Sutherland, Jr., Professor of Law, Harvard University.

COMPARATIVE LAW, Fourth Edition (1980)

Rudolf B. Schlesinger, Professor of Law, Hastings College of the Law.

COMPETITIVE PROCESS, LEGAL REGULATION OF THE, Second Edition (1979), with Statutory Supplement

Edmund W. Kitch, Professor of Law, University of Chicago.
Harvey S. Perlman, Professor of Law, University of Virginia.

CONFLICT OF LAWS, Seventh Edition (1978), with 1980 Supplement

Willis L. M. Reese, Professor of Law, Columbia University, and
Maurice Rosenberg, Professor of Law, Columbia University.

CONSTITUTIONAL LAW, Fifth Edition (1977), with 1980 Supplement

Edward L. Barrett, Jr., Professor of Law, University of California, Davis.

CONSTITUTIONAL LAW, Tenth Edition (1980)

Gerald Gunther, Professor of Law, Stanford University.

CONSTITUTIONAL LAW, INDIVIDUAL RIGHTS IN, Third Edition (1981)

Gerald Gunther, Professor of Law, Stanford University.

CONTRACT LAW AND ITS APPLICATION, Second Edition (1977)

Addison Mueller, Professor of Law Emeritus, University of California, Los Angeles.
Arthur I. Rosett, Professor of Law, University of California, Los Angeles.

CONTRACT LAW, STUDIES IN, Second Edition (1977)

Edward J. Murphy, Professor of Law, University of Notre Dame.
Richard E. Speidel, Professor of Law, University of Virginia.

CONTRACTS, Third Edition (1977)

John P. Dawson, Professor of Law Emeritus, Harvard University, and
William Burnett Harvey, Professor of Law and Political Science, Boston University.

CONTRACTS, Third Edition (1980), with Statutory Supplement

E. Allan Farnsworth, Professor of Law, Columbia University.
William F. Young, Professor of Law, Columbia University.

CONTRACTS, Second Edition (1978), with Statutory and Administrative Law Supplement (1978)

Ian R. Macneil, Professor of Law, Cornell University.

COPYRIGHT, Unfair Competition, and Other Topics Bearing on the Protection of Literary, Musical, and Artistic Works, Third Edition (1978)

Benjamin Kaplan, Professor of Law Emeritus, Harvard University, and
Ralph S. Brown, Jr., Professor of Law, Yale University.

CORPORATE FINANCE, Second Edition (1979), with 1980 New Developments Supplement

Victor Brudney, Professor of Law, Harvard University.
Marvin A. Chirelstein, Professor of Law, Yale University.

CORPORATE READJUSTMENTS AND REORGANIZATIONS (1976)

Walter J. Blum, Professor of Law, University of Chicago.
Stanley A. Kaplan, Professor of Law, University of Chicago.

CORPORATION LAW, BASIC, Second Edition (1979), with Documentary Supplement

Detlev F. Vagts, Professor of Law, Harvard University.

CORPORATIONS, see also Enterprise Organization

CORPORATIONS, Fifth Edition—Unabridged (1980)

William L. Cary, Professor of Law, Columbia University.
Melvin Aron Eisenberg, Professor of Law, University of California, Berkeley.

CORPORATIONS, Fifth Edition—Abridged (1980)

William L. Cary, Professor of Law, Columbia University.
Melvin Aron Eisenberg, Professor of Law, University of California, Berkeley.

CORPORATIONS, THE LAW OF: WHAT CORPORATE LAWYERS DO (1976)

Jan G. Deutsch, Professor of Law, Yale University.
Joseph J. Bianco, Professor of Law, Yeshiva University.

CORPORATIONS COURSE GAME PLAN (1975)

David R. Herwitz, Professor of Law, Harvard University.

CREDIT TRANSACTIONS AND CONSUMER PROTECTION (1976)

John Honnold, Professor of Law, University of Pennsylvania.

CREDITORS' RIGHTS, see also Debtor-Creditor Law

UNIVERSITY CASEBOOK SERIES—Continued

CRIMINAL JUSTICE, THE ADMINISTRATION OF, Second Edition (1969)

Francis C. Sullivan, Professor of Law, Louisiana State University.
Paul Hardin III, Professor of Law, Duke University.
John Huston, Professor of Law, University of Washington.
Frank R. Lacy, Professor of Law, University of Oregon.
Daniel E. Murray, Professor of Law, University of Miami.
George W. Pugh, Professor of Law, Louisiana State University.

CRIMINAL JUSTICE ADMINISTRATION AND RELATED PROCESSES, Successor Edition (1976), with 1980 Supplement

Frank W. Miller, Professor of Law, Washington University.
Robert O. Dawson, Professor of Law, University of Texas.
George E. Dix, Professor of Law, University of Texas.
Raymond I. Parnas, Professor of Law, University of California, Davis.

CRIMINAL JUSTICE, LEADING CONSTITUTIONAL CASES ON (1980)

Lloyd L. Weinreb, Professor of Law, Harvard University.

CRIMINAL LAW, Second Edition (1979)

Fred E. Inbau, Professor of Law Emeritus, Northwestern University.
James R. Thompson, Professor of Law Emeritus, Northwestern University.
Andre A. Moenssens, Professor of Law, University of Richmond.

CRIMINAL LAW, Third Edition (1980)

Lloyd L. Weinreb, Professor of Law, Harvard University.

CRIMINAL LAW AND ITS ADMINISTRATION (1940), with 1956 Supplement

Jerome Michael, late Professor of Law, Columbia University, and
Herbert Wechsler, Professor of Law, Columbia University.

CRIMINAL LAW AND PROCEDURE, Fifth Edition (1977)

Rollin M. Perkins, Professor of Law Emeritus, University of California, Hastings College of the Law.
Ronald N. Boyce, Professor of Law, University of Utah.

CRIMINAL PROCEDURE, Second Edition (1980)

Fred E. Inbau, Professor of Law Emeritus, Northwestern University.
James R. Thompson, Professor of Law Emeritus, Northwestern University.
James B. Haddad, Professor of Law, Northwestern University.
James B. Zagel, Chief, Criminal Justice Division, Office of Attorney General of Illinois.
Gary L. Starkman, Assistant U. S. Attorney, Northern District of Illinois.

CRIMINAL PROCEDURE, CONSTITUTIONAL (1977), with 1980 Supplement

James E. Scarboro, Professor of Law, University of Colorado.
James B. White, Professor of Law, University of Chicago.

CRIMINAL PROCESS, Third Edition (1978), with 1979 Supplement

Lloyd L. Weinreb, Professor of Law, Harvard University.

DAMAGES, Second Edition (1952)

Charles T. McCormick, late Professor of Law, University of Texas, and
William F. Fritz, late Professor of Law, University of Texas.

DEBTOR-CREDITOR LAW (1974), with 1978 Case-Statutory Supplement

William D. Warren, Dean of the School of Law, University of California, Los Angeles.
William E. Hogan, Professor of Law, Cornell University.

DECEDENTS' ESTATES (1971)

Max Rheinstein, late Professor of Law Emeritus, University of Chicago.
Mary Ann Glendon, Professor of Law, Boston College.

DECEDENTS' ESTATES AND TRUSTS, Fifth Edition (1977)

John Ritchie, Professor of Law Emeritus, University of Virginia.
Neill H. Alford, Jr., Professor of Law, University of Virginia.
Richard W. Effland, Professor of Law, Arizona State University.

DECEDENTS' ESTATES AND TRUSTS (1968)

Howard R. Williams, Professor of Law, Stanford University.

DOMESTIC RELATIONS, see also Family Law

DOMESTIC RELATIONS, Third Edition (1978) with 1980 Supplement

Walter Wadlington, Professor of Law, University of Virginia.
Monrad G. Paulsen, Dean of the Law School, Yeshiva University.

DYNAMICS OF AMERICAN LAW, THE: Courts, the Legal Process and Freedom of Expression (1968)

Marc A. Franklin, Professor of Law, Stanford University.

ELECTRONIC MASS MEDIA, Second Edition (1979)

William K. Jones, Professor of Law, Columbia University.

ENTERPRISE ORGANIZATION, Second Edition (1977), with 1979 Statutory and Formulary Supplement

Alfred F. Conard, Professor of Law, University of Michigan.
Robert L. Knauss, Dean of the School of Law, Vanderbilt University.
Stanley Siegel, Professor of Law, University of California, Los Angeles.

EQUITY AND EQUITABLE REMEDIES (1975)

Edward D. Re, Adjunct Professor of Law, St. John's University.

EQUITY, RESTITUTION AND DAMAGES, Second Edition (1974)

Robert Childres, late Professor of Law, Northwestern University.
William F. Johnson, Jr., Professor of Law, New York University.

ESTATE PLANNING PROBLEMS (1973), with 1977 Supplement

David Westfall, Professor of Law, Harvard University.

ETHICS, see Legal Profession, and Professional Responsibility

EVIDENCE, Fourth Edition (1981)

David W. Louisell, late Professor of Law, University of California, Berkeley.
John Kaplan, Professor of Law, Stanford University.
Jon R. Waltz, Professor of Law, Northwestern University.

EVIDENCE, Sixth Edition (1973), with 1980 Supplement

John M. Maguire, late Professor of Law Emeritus, Harvard University.
Jack B. Weinstein, Professor of Law, Columbia University.
James H. Chadbourn, Professor of Law, Harvard University.
John H. Mansfield, Professor of Law, Harvard University.

EVIDENCE (1968)

Francis C. Sullivan, Professor of Law, Louisiana State University.
Paul Hardin, III, Professor of Law, Duke University.

FAMILY LAW, see also Domestic Relations

FAMILY LAW (1978), with 1981 Supplement

Judith C. Areen, Professor of Law, Georgetown University.

FAMILY LAW: STATUTORY MATERIALS, Second Edition (1974)

Monrad G. Paulsen, Dean of the Law School, Yeshiva University.
Walter Wadlington, Professor of Law, University of Virginia.

FEDERAL COURTS, Sixth Edition (1976), with 1980 Supplement

Charles T. McCormick, late Professor of Law, University of Texas.
James H. Chadbourn, Professor of Law, Harvard University, and
Charles Alan Wright, Professor of Law, University of Texas.

FEDERAL COURTS AND THE FEDERAL SYSTEM, Hart and Wechsler's Second Edition (1973), with 1981 Supplement

Paul M. Bator, Professor of Law, Harvard University.
Paul J. Mishkin, Professor of Law, University of California, Berkeley.
David L. Shapiro, Professor of Law, Harvard University.
Herbert Wechsler, Professor of Law, Columbia University.

FEDERAL PUBLIC LAND AND RESOURCES LAW (1981)

George C. Coggins, Professor of Law, University of Kansas.
Charles F. Wilkinson, Professor of Law, University of Oregon.

FEDERAL RULES OF CIVIL PROCEDURE, 1980 Edition

FEDERAL TAXATION, see Taxation

FOOD AND DRUG LAW (1980)

Richard A. Merrill, Dean of the School of Law, University of Virginia.
Peter Barton Hutt, Esq.

FUTURE INTERESTS (1958)

Philip Mechem, late Professor of Law Emeritus, University of Pennsylvania.

FUTURE INTERESTS (1970)

Howard R. Williams, Professor of Law, Stanford University.

FUTURE INTERESTS AND ESTATE PLANNING (1961), with 1962 Supplement

W. Barton Leach, late Professor of Law, Harvard University.
James K. Logan, formerly Dean of the Law School, University of Kansas.

GOVERNMENT CONTRACTS, FEDERAL (1975), with 1980 Supplement

John W. Whelan, Professor of Law, Hastings College of the Law.
Robert S. Pasley, Professor of Law Emeritus, Cornell University.

HOUSING—THE ILL-HOUSED (1971)

Peter W. Martin, Professor of Law, Cornell University.

INJUNCTIONS (1972)

Owen M. Fiss, Professor of Law, Yale University.

INSTITUTIONAL INVESTORS, 1978

David L. Ratner, Professor of Law, Cornell University.

INSURANCE (1971)

William F. Young, Professor of Law, Columbia University.

INTERNATIONAL LAW, see also Transnational Legal Problems and United Nations Law

INTERNATIONAL LEGAL SYSTEM (1973), with Documentary Supplement

Noyes E. Leech, Professor of Law, University of Pennsylvania.
Covey T. Oliver, Professor of Law, University of Pennsylvania.
Joseph Modeste Sweeney, Professor of Law, Tulane University.

INTERNATIONAL TRADE AND INVESTMENT, REGULATION OF (1970)

Carl H. Fulda, late Professor of Law, University of Texas.
Warren F. Schwartz, Professor of Law, University of Virginia.

INTERNATIONAL TRANSACTIONS AND RELATIONS (1960)

Milton Katz, Professor of Law, Harvard University, and
Kingman Brewster, Jr., Professor of Law, Harvard University.

INTRODUCTION TO LAW, see also Legal Method, On Law in Courts, and Dynamics of American Law

INTRODUCTION TO THE STUDY OF LAW (1970)

E. Wayne Thode, late Professor of Law, University of Utah.
Leon Lebowitz, Professor of Law, University of Texas.
Lester J. Mazor, Professor of Law, University of Utah.

JUDICIAL CODE and Rules of Procedure in the Federal Courts with Excerpts from the Criminal Code, 1981 Edition

Henry M. Hart, Jr., late Professor of Law, Harvard University.
Herbert Wechsler, Professor of Law, Columbia University.

JURISPRUDENCE (Temporary Edition Hardbound) (1949)

Lon L. Fuller, Professor of Law Emeritus, Harvard University.

JUVENILE COURTS (1967)

Hon. Orman W. Ketcham, Juvenile Court of the District of Columbia.
Monrad G. Paulsen, Dean of the Law School, Yeshiva University.

JUVENILE JUSTICE PROCESS, Second Edition (1976), with 1980 Supplement

Frank W. Miller, Professor of Law, Washington University.
Robert O. Dawson, Professor of Law, University of Texas.
George E. Dix, Professor of Law, University of Texas.
Raymond I. Parnas, Professor of Law, University of California, Davis.

LABOR LAW, Eighth Edition (1977), with Statutory Supplement, and 1979 Case Supplement

Archibald Cox, Professor of Law, Harvard University, and
Derek C. Bok, President, Harvard University.
Robert A. Gorman, Professor of Law, University of Pennsylvania.

LABOR LAW (1968), with Statutory Supplement and 1974 Case Supplement

Clyde W. Summers, Professor of Law, University of Pennsylvania.
Harry H. Wellington, Dean of the Law School, Yale University.

UNIVERSITY CASEBOOK SERIES—Continued

LAND FINANCING, Second Edition (1977)

Norman Penney, Professor of Law, Cornell University.
Richard F. Broude, of the California Bar.

LAW AND MEDICINE (1980)

Walter Wadlington, Professor of Law and Professor of Legal Medicine, University of Virginia.
Jon R. Waltz, Professor of Law, Northwestern University.
Roger B. Dworkin, Professor of Law, Indiana University, and Professor of Biomedical History, University of Washington.

LAW, LANGUAGE AND ETHICS (1972)

William R. Bishin, Professor of Law, University of Southern California.
Christopher D. Stone, Professor of Law, University of Southern California.

LAWYERING PROCESS (1978), with Civil Problem Supplement and Criminal Problem Supplement

Gary Bellow, Professor of Law, Harvard University.
Bea Moulton, Professor of Law, Arizona State University.

LEGAL METHOD

Harry W. Jones, Professor of Law Emeritus, Columbia University.
John M. Kernochan, Professor of Law, Columbia University.
Arthur W. Murphy, Professor of Law, Columbia University.

LEGAL METHODS (1969)

Robert N. Covington, Professor of Law, Vanderbilt University.
E. Blythe Stason, late Professor of Law, Vanderbilt University.
John W. Wade, Professor of Law, Vanderbilt University.
Elliott E. Cheatham, late Professor of Law, Vanderbilt University.
Theodore A. Smedley, Professor of Law, Vanderbilt University.

LEGAL PROFESSION (1970)

Samuel D. Thurman, Dean of the College of Law, University of Utah.
Ellis L. Phillips, Jr., Professor of Law, Columbia University.
Elliott E. Cheatham, late Professor of Law, Vanderbilt University.

LEGISLATION, Third Edition (1973)

Horace E. Read, late Vice President, Dalhousie University.
John W. MacDonald, Professor of Law Emeritus, Cornell Law School.
Jefferson B. Fordham, Professor of Law, University of Utah, and
William J. Pierce, Professor of Law, University of Michigan.

LEGISLATIVE AND ADMINISTRATIVE PROCESSES (1976)

Hans A. Linde, Professor of Law, University of Oregon.
George Bunn, Professor of Law, University of Wisconsin.

LOCAL GOVERNMENT LAW, Revised Edition (1975)

Jefferson B. Fordham, Professor of Law, University of Utah.

MASS MEDIA LAW (1976), with 1979 Supplement

Marc A. Franklin, Professor of Law, Stanford University.

MENTAL HEALTH PROCESS, Second Edition (1976)

Frank W. Miller, Professor of Law, Washington University.
Robert O. Dawson, Professor of Law, University of Texas.
George E. Dix, Professor of Law, University of Texas.
Raymond I. Parnas, Professor of Law, University of California, Davis.

UNIVERSITY CASEBOOK SERIES—Continued

MUNICIPAL CORPORATIONS, see Local Government Law

NEGOTIABLE INSTRUMENTS, see Commercial Paper

NEW YORK PRACTICE, Fourth Edition (1978)

Herbert Peterfreund, Professor of Law, New York University.
Joseph M. McLaughlin, Dean of the Law School, Fordham University.

OIL AND GAS, Fourth Edition (1979)

Howard R. Williams, Professor of Law, Stanford University
Richard C. Maxwell, Professor of Law, University of California, Los Angeles.
Charles J. Meyers, Dean of the Law School, Stanford University.

ON LAW IN COURTS (1965)

Paul J. Mishkin, Professor of Law, University of California, Berkeley.
Clarence Morris, Professor of Law Emeritus, University of Pennsylvania.

OWNERSHIP AND DEVELOPMENT OF LAND (1965)

Jan Krasnowiecki, Professor of Law, University of Pennsylvania.

PARTNERSHIP PLANNING (1970) (Pamphlet)

William L. Cary, Professor of Law, Columbia University.

PERSPECTIVES ON THE LAWYER AS PLANNER (Reprint of Chapters One through Five of Planning by Lawyers) (1978)

Louis M. Brown, Professor of Law, University of Southern California.
Edward A. Dauer, Professor of Law, Yale University.

PLANNING BY LAWYERS, MATERIALS ON A NONADVERSARIAL LEGAL PROCESS (1978)

Louis M. Brown, Professor of Law, University of Southern California.
Edward A. Dauer, Professor of Law, Yale University.

PLEADING AND PROCEDURE, see Procedure, Civil

POLICE FUNCTION (1976) (Pamphlet)

Chapters 1–11 of Miller, Dawson, Dix & Parnas' Criminal Justice Administration, Second Edition.

PREVENTIVE LAW, see also Planning by Lawyers

PROCEDURE—Biography of a Legal Dispute (1968)

Marc A. Franklin, Professor of Law, Stanford University.

PROCEDURE—CIVIL PROCEDURE, Second Edition (1974), with 1979 Supplement

James H. Chadbourn, Professor of Law, Harvard University.
A. Leo Levin, Professor of Law, University of Pennsylvania.
Philip Shuchman, Professor of Law, University of Connecticut.

PROCEDURE—CIVIL PROCEDURE, Fourth Edition (1978), with 1980 Supplement

Richard H. Field, late Professor of Law, Harvard University.
Benjamin Kaplan, Professor of Law Emeritus, Harvard University.
Kevin M. Clermont, Professor of Law, Cornell University.

PROCEDURE—CIVIL PROCEDURE, Third Edition (1976), with 1978 Supplement

Maurice Rosenberg, Professor of Law, Columbia University.
Jack B. Weinstein, Professor, of Law, Columbia University.
Hans Smit, Professor of Law, Columbia University.
Harold L. Korn, Professor of Law, Columbia University.

UNIVERSITY CASEBOOK SERIES—Continued

PROCEDURE—PLEADING AND PROCEDURE: State and Federal, Fourth Edition (1979)

David W. Louisell, late Professor of Law, University of California, Berkeley.
Geoffrey C. Hazard, Jr., Professor of Law, Yale University.

PROCEDURE—FEDERAL RULES OF CIVIL PROCEDURE, 1980 Edition

PROCEDURE PORTFOLIO (1962)

James H. Chadbourn, Professor of Law, Harvard University, and
A. Leo Levin, Professor of Law, University of Pennsylvania.

PRODUCTS LIABILITY (1980)

Marshall S. Shapo, Professor of Law, Northwestern University.

PRODUCTS LIABILITY AND SAFETY (1980), with Statutory Supplement

W. Page Keeton, Professor of Law, University of Texas.
David G. Owen, Professor of Law, University of South Carolina.
John E. Montgomery, Professor of Law, University of South Carolina.

PROFESSIONAL RESPONSIBILITY (1976), with 1979 Problems, Cases and Readings, Supplement, 1980 Statutory (National) Supplement, and 1980 Statutory (California) Supplement

Thomas D. Morgan, Professor of Law, University of Illinois.
Ronald D. Rotunda, Professor of Law, University of Illinois.

PROPERTY, Fourth Edition (1978)

John E. Cribbet, Dean of the Law School, University of Illinois.
Corwin W. Johnson, Professor of Law, University of Texas.

PROPERTY—PERSONAL (1953)

S. Kenneth Skolfield, late Professor of Law Emeritus, Boston University.

PROPERTY—PERSONAL, Third Edition (1954)

Everett Fraser, late Dean of the Law School Emeritus, University of Minnesota.
Third Edition by Charles W. Taintor, late Professor of Law, University of Pittsburgh.

PROPERTY—INTRODUCTION, TO REAL PROPERTY, Third Edition (1954)

Everett Fraser, late Dean of the Law School Emeritus, University of Minnesota.

PROPERTY—REAL PROPERTY AND CONVEYANCING (1954)

Edward E. Bade, late Professor of Law, University of Minnesota.

PROPERTY—FUNDAMENTALS OF MODERN REAL PROPERTY (1974), with 1980 Supplement

Edward H. Rabin, Professor of Law, University of California, Davis.

PROPERTY—PROBLEMS IN REAL PROPERTY (Pamphlet) (1969)

Edward H. Rabin, Professor of Law, University of California, Davis.

PROSECUTION AND ADJUDICATION (1976) (Pamphlet)

Chapters 12–16 of Miller, Dawson, Dix & Parnas' Criminal Justice Administration, Successor Edition.

PUBLIC REGULATION OF DANGEROUS PRODUCTS (paperback) (1980)

Marshall S. Shapo, Professor of Law, Northwestern University.

UNIVERSITY CASEBOOK SERIES—Continued

PUBLIC UTILITY LAW, see Free Enterprise, also Regulated Industries

REAL ESTATE PLANNING (1980), with 1980 Problems, Statutes and New Materials Supplement

> Norton L. Steuben, Professor of Law, University of Colorado.

RECEIVERSHIP AND CORPORATE REORGANIZATION, see Creditors' Rights

REGULATED INDUSTRIES, Second Edition, 1976

> William K. Jones, Professor of Law, Columbia University.

RESTITUTION, Second Edition (1966)

> John W. Wade, Professor of Law, Vanderbilt University.

SALES (1980)

> Marion W. Benfield, Jr., Professor of Law, University of Illinois.
> William D. Hawkland, Chancellor, Louisiana State University Law Center.

SALES AND SALES FINANCING, Fourth Edition (1976)

> John Honnold, Professor of Law, University of Pennsylvania.

SECURITY, Third Edition (1959)

> John Hanna, late Professor of Law Emeritus, Columbia University.

SECURITIES REGULATION, Fourth Edition (1977), with 1980 Selected Statutes Supplement and 1980 Cases and Releases Supplement

> Richard W. Jennings, Professor of Law, University of California, Berkeley.
> Harold Marsh, Jr., Member of the California Bar.

SENTENCING AND THE CORRECTIONAL PROCESS, Second Edition (1976)

> Frank W. Miller, Professor of Law, Washington University.
> Robert O. Dawson, Professor of Law, University of Texas.
> George E. Dix, Professor of Law, University of Texas.
> Raymond I. Parnas, Professor of Law, University of California, Davis.

SOCIAL WELFARE AND THE INDIVIDUAL (1971)

> Robert J. Levy, Professor of Law, University of Minnesota.
> Thomas P. Lewis, Dean of the College of Law, University of Kentucky.
> Peter W. Martin, Professor of Law, Cornell University.

TAX, POLICY ANALYSIS OF THE FEDERAL INCOME (1976)

> William A. Klein, Professor of Law, University of California, Los Angeles.

TAXATION, FEDERAL INCOME (1976), with 1980 Supplement

> Erwin N. Griswold, Dean Emeritus, Harvard Law School.
> Michael J. Graetz, Professor of Law, University of Virginia.

TAXATION, FEDERAL INCOME, Second Edition (1977), with 1979 Supplement

> James J. Freeland, Professor of Law, University of Florida.
> Stephen A. Lind, Professor of Law, University of Florida.
> Richard B. Stephens, Professor of Law Emeritus, University of Florida.

TAXATION, FEDERAL INCOME, Volume I, Personal Income Taxation (1972), with 1979 Supplement; Volume II, Taxation of Partnerships and Corporations, Second Edition (1980)

> Stanley S. Surrey, Professor of Law, Harvard University.
> William C. Warren, Professor of Law Emeritus, Columbia University.
> Paul R. McDaniel, Professor of Law, Boston College Law School.
> Hugh J. Ault, Professor of Law, Boston College Law School.

UNIVERSITY CASEBOOK SERIES—Continued

TAXATION, FEDERAL WEALTH TRANSFER (1977)

Stanley S. Surrey, Professor of Law, Harvard University.
William C. Warren, Professor of Law Emeritus, Columbia University, and
Paul R. McDaniel, Professor of Law, Boston College Law School.
Harry L. Gutman, Instructor, Harvard Law School and Boston College Law
School.

TAXATION OF INDIVIDUALS, PARTNERSHIPS AND CORPORATIONS, PROBLEMS in the (1978)

Norton L. Steuben, Professor of Law, University of Colorado.
William J. Turnier, Professor of Law, University of North Carolina.

TAXES AND FINANCE—STATE AND LOCAL (1974)

Oliver Oldman, Professor of Law, Harvard University.
Ferdinand P. Schoettle, Professor of Law, University of Minnesota.

TORT LAW AND ALTERNATIVES: INJURIES AND REMEDIES, Second Edition (1979)

Marc A. Franklin, Professor of Law, Stanford University.

TORTS, Sixth Edition (1976)

William L. Prosser, late Professor of Law, University of California, Hastings
College.
John W. Wade, Professor of Law, Vanderbilt University.
Victor E. Schwartz, Professor of Law, American University.

TORTS, Third Edition (1976)

Harry Shulman, late Dean of the Law School, Yale University.
Fleming James, Jr., Professor of Law Emeritus, Yale University.
Oscar S. Gray, Professor of Law, University of Maryland.

TRADE REGULATION (1975), with 1979 Supplement

Milton Handler, Professor of Law Emeritus, Columbia University.
Harlan M. Blake, Professor of Law, Columbia University.
Robert Pitofsky, Professor of Law, Georgetown University.
Harvey J. Goldschmid, Professor of Law, Columbia University.

TRADE REGULATION, see Antitrust

TRANSNATIONAL LEGAL PROBLEMS, Second Edition (1976), with Documentary Supplement

Henry J. Steiner, Professor of Law, Harvard University.
Detlev F. Vagts, Professor of Law, Harvard University.

TRIAL, see also Lawyering Process

TRIAL ADVOCACY (1968)

A. Leo Levin, Professor of Law, University of Pennsylvania.
Harold Cramer, of the Pennsylvania Bar.
Maurice Rosenberg, Professor of Law, Columbia University, Consultant.

TRUSTS, Fifth Edition (1978)

George G. Bogert, late Professor of Law Emeritus, University of Chicago.
Dallin H. Oaks, President, Brigham Young University.

TRUSTS AND SUCCESSION (Palmer's), Third Edition (1978)

Richard V. Wellman, Professor of Law, University of Georgia.
Lawrence W. Waggoner, Professor of Law, University of Michigan.
Olin L. Browder, Jr., Professor of Law, University of Michigan.

UNIVERSITY CASEBOOK SERIES—Continued

UNFAIR COMPETITION, see Competitive Process and Business Torts

UNITED NATIONS IN ACTION (1968)

Louis B. Sohn, Professor of Law, Harvard University.

UNITED NATIONS LAW, Second Edition (1967), with Documentary Supplement (1968)

Louis B. Sohn, Professor of Law, Harvard University.

WATER RESOURCE MANAGEMENT, Second Edition (1980)

Charles J. Meyers, Dean of the Law School, Stanford University.
A. Dan Tarlock, Professor of Law, Indiana University.

WILLS AND ADMINISTRATION, 5th Edition (1961)

Philip Mechem, late Professor of Law, University of Pennsylvania.
Thomas E. Atkinson, late Professor of Law, New York University.

WORLD LAW, see United Nations Law

University Casebook Series

EDITORIAL BOARD

COPYRIGHT, PATENT, TRADEMARK

AND

RELATED STATE DOCTRINES

CASES AND MATERIALS ON

THE LAW

OF

INTELLECTUAL PROPERTY

SECOND EDITION

By

PAUL GOLDSTEIN

Professor of Law
Stanford University

Mineola, New York

THE FOUNDATION PRESS, INC.

1981

Library of Congress Cataloging in Publication Data

Main entry under title:

Copyright, patent, trademark, and related state
  doctrines.

  (University casebook series)
  Includes index.
  1. Intellectual property—United States—Cases.
I. Goldstein, Paul, 1943-   . II. Series.
KF2978.C66   1981   346.7304'8   81–3201
                         347.30648   AACR2

ISBN 0-88277-029-2

Goldstein Cs. Law Intell. Prop. 2d Ed. UCB

To

My Mother and Father

*

PREFACE

At a meeting of the American Bar Association's Section on Patents, Trademarks and Copyrights, a seasoned copyright practitioner introduced his remarks with the observation that Section members "are exposed to many occupational hazards . . . One of the less serious ones—but still an obstacle faced almost daily—is the fact that most people do not understand the difference between patents, trademarks and copyrights. This applies to clients, other lawyers and at times even judges. When I tell a general practitioner that I am a copyright lawyer, he immediately corrects me: 'You mean patents!' He then says: 'Well, anyway, as a patent lawyer, you can copyright a name for me can't you?' " [a]

Why so much confusion between copyright, patent and trademark? Doubtless one reason is that the three laws occupy a common ground, each seeking to stimulate investment in information by awarding property rights to products of the mind. The types of information produced—and the specific intellectual property rights that attach to each—are sometimes hard to separate. Adding to the confusion is the fact that the three federal laws also have state law counterparts—the law of ideas, common law copyright, trade secrets, unfair competition and the newly emerging right of publicity.

Because these laws occupy a common field, they invite comparison. One aim of this book is to encourage you to compare each body of intellectual property law with the others to assess mechanical and policy malfunctions. How, and how efficiently, does each law allocate costs among the producers, distributors and consumers of information? To what extent should the state law systems, largely judge-made, be modelled after their more refined federal statutory counterparts? Benjamin Kaplan's wise counsel, that certain of common law copyright's interstices might properly be filled by reference to counterpart aspects of the federal copyright statutes,[b] applies equally to the relationship between trade secret and patent law and between unfair competition and trademark law.

In taking all of intellectual property law as its embrace, this book also recognizes that the combination fits comfortably with the realities of law practice, particularly general practice. Presented with a raw idea that his or her client is interested in marketing, a lawyer can sometimes rely on contract protection alone. But if the idea is to be developed, the lawyer must decide whether common law copyright, trade secret or unfair competition protection is called for and, at some

---

a. Latman, Preliminary Injunctions in Patent, Trademark and Copyright Cases, 60 Trademark Rep. 506 (1970).

b. Kaplan, Publication in Copyright Law: The Question of Phonograph Records, 103 U.Pa.L.Rev. 469, 487–488 (1955).

point, whether the federal copyright, patent or trademark machinery should be engaged. The lawyer must be prepared to pick out for the client's project not only a single thread of protection (one consisting, say, of contract, common law copyright and statutory copyright) but possibly a more ample fabric (a combination, perhaps, of contract, common law copyright, statutory copyright, unfair competition and trademark law). And, whatever the form of protection sought, the lawyer must be alert to the possibility that the client's project will infringe the intellectual property rights of others. The centrality of these counselling considerations is implicit in the book's organization. Treatment of idea protection, placed first, is followed by the specialized state intellectual property laws, then the federal laws. Some transactional topics—tax, antitrust and international law—appear last.

Although the lawyer piecing together the needed threads of protection moves easily from state to federal law, the lines between, like so many other lines in a federal system, bristle with conflict. Aspects of this conflict, often possessing a constitutional dimension, have occupied the Supreme Court's attention several times in recent years. Federal system conflicts, analyzed in the first part of the book, are also noted throughout the text.

*　　*　　*

Stanford Law School, where I completed the first edition of this book, continued to provide a congenial setting for work on the second. I am particularly indebted to Dean Charles J. Meyers and Associate Deans Joseph Leininger and J. Keith Mann for their generous support throughout, and to the staff of the Robert Crown Law Library for helping so many times in so many ways. I am grateful to John Barlow and Diana Van Etten, students at the Law School, for lightening many of the necessary technical burdens. Their work was supported by the Stanford Legal Research Fund, made possible by a bequest from the estate of Ira S. Lillick and by gifts from Roderick E. and Carla A. Hills and other friends of the Stanford Law School. I am also indebted to my secretary, Marjorie Wright, for typing the manuscript with her usual grace and care.

Finally, my thanks to Stephen Kahn, Esq. for reviewing and commenting on the patent chapter of the book, and to Jan Thompson for providing advice and encouragement well beyond her calling as an artist and art historian.

A Note on Style. The articles and many of the cases appearing in these pages have been edited. The deletion of sentences and paragraphs is indicated by ellipses. The deletion of string citations is not indicated. Most footnotes have been excised. Those that remain have not been renumbered. Parallel citation to federal, state and regional reporters and the United States Patent Quarterly has been employed where appropriate.

P. G.

Stanford, California
April, 1981

SUMMARY OF CONTENTS

		Page
PREFACE		xix
TABLE OF CASES		xxvii

PART ONE: THE ROLE OF INTELLECTUAL PROPERTY LAW

I.	A Constitutional View	1
II.	Some Functional Views	9
	A. Copyright	9
	B. Patent	15
	C. Trademark	19

PART TWO: STATE LAW OF INTELLECTUAL PROPERTY

I.	Rights in Undeveloped Ideas	33
	A. Theories of Protection	45
	B. Limits of Protection: The Place of Ideas in the Competitive Plan	64
II.	Unfair Competition	71
	A. Theory of Protection	71
	B. Limits of Protection	118
III.	Trade Secrets	141
	A. Theory of Protection	141
	B. Limits of Protection	162
IV.	Common Law Copyright	195
	A. Theory of Protection	197
	B. Limits of Protection	213
V.	Right of Publicity	242
	A. Theory of Protection	242
	B. Limits of Protection	259

PART THREE: FEDERAL LAW OF INTELLECTUAL PROPERTY

I.	Trademark Law	276
	A. Requirements for Protection	279
	B. Administrative Procedures	355
	C. Rights and Remedies	359
	D. Infringement	395
	E. Rights Beyond Trademark: Lanham Act § 43(a)	418
II.	Patent Law	430
	A. Requirements for Protection	432
	B. Administrative Procedures	557

II. Patent Law—Continued   **Page**
    C. Rights and Remedies ---------------------------------- 576
    D. Infringement --- 633

III. Copyright Law --- 652
    A. Requirements for Protection -------------------------- 654
    B. Rights and Remedies --------------------------------- 713
    C. Infringement -- 830
    D. Rights Beyond Copyright: Moral Right ---------------- 855

PART FOUR: INTELLECTUAL PROPERTIES IN THE MARKETPLACE

I. Antitrust -- 872
    A. Patents --- 872
    B. Copyrights -- 881
    C. Trademarks -- 886

II. Federal Income Taxation ------------------------------------- 897
    A. Patents --- 897
    B. Copyrights -- 907
    C. Trademarks -- 915

PART FIVE: INTERNATIONAL PROTECTION: THE CONVENTIONS

I. Copyright -- 918
II. Patent -- 933
III. Trademark -- 943
Index --- 957

TABLE OF CONTENTS

Page

PREFACE xix

TABLE OF CASES xxvii

PART ONE: THE ROLE OF INTELLECTUAL PROPERTY LAW

I. A Constitutional View 1

II. Some Functional Views 9
    A. Copyright 9
    B. Patent 15
    C. Trademark 19

PART TWO: STATE LAW OF INTELLECTUAL PROPERTY

I. Rights in Undeveloped Ideas 33
    A. Theories of Protection 45   #2
    B. Limits of Protection: The Place of Ideas in the Competitive Plan 64

II. Unfair Competition 71
    A. Theory of Protection 71
        1. Traditional Elements 71   #3
        2. New Directions 96   #4
            a. Zone of Expansion 96
            b. Dilution 101
            c. Misappropriation 107
    B. Limits of Protection 118
        1. Personal Interests: Rights in Names 118
        2. Economic Interests: The Place of Unfair Competition in the Competitive Plan 128

III. Trade Secrets 141
    A. Theory of Protection 141
    B. Limits of Protection 162   #5
        1. Personal Interests: Restraints on Postemployment Competition 162
        2. Economic Interests: The Place of Trade Secrets in the Competitive Plan 175

IV. Common Law Copyright 195
    A. Theory of Protection 197
    B. Limits of Protection 213
        1. Economic Interests: The Preemption of Common Law Copyright 213
        2. Personal Interests: The Right of Privacy 232

Page

V. Right of Publicity --- 242
   A. Theory of Protection ----------------------------------- 242
   B. Limits of Protection ----------------------------------- 259

PART THREE: FEDERAL LAW OF INTELLECTUAL PROPERTY

I. Trademark Law -- 276
   A. Requirements for Protection --------------------------- 279
      1. Use and Use in Commerce ----------------------- 279
      2. Distinctiveness ------------------------------------ 293
         a. Common Law Theory ------------------------ 293
         b. Statutory Variations on the Common Law Theme 308
            (*i.*) "Merely Descriptive" ---------------------- 308
            (*ii.*) "Primarily Geographically Descriptive" ---- 311
            (*iii.*) "Primarily Merely a Surname" ----------- 318
      3. Statutory Subject Matter --------------------------- 325
         a. Types of Marks ------------------------------- 325
            (*i.*) Trademarks and Service Marks ----------- 325
            (*ii.*) Certification Marks and Collective Marks -- 331
         b. Content -------------------------------------- 339
   B. Administrative Procedures ---------------------------- 355
   C. Rights and Remedies --------------------------------- 359
      1. Rights -- 359
         a. Geographic Boundaries --------------------- 360
         b. Product Boundaries: Dilution ---------------- 369
      2. Remedies --- 387
   D. Infringement --------------------------------------- 395
   E. Rights Beyond Trademark: Lanham Act § 43(a) ------- 418

II. Patent Law -- 430
   A. Requirements for Protection --------------------------- 432
      1. Statutory Standards ------------------------------- 432
         a. Section 103: Nonobviousness ---------------- 432
         b. Section 102: Novelty and the Statutory Bars --- 454
         c. Sections 102 and 103 in Concert: What is Prior Art? --------------------------------- 478
         d. Utility --------------------------------------- 485
         e. Originality ---------------------------------- 494
      2. Statutory Subject Matter --------------------------- 497
         a. Utility Patents ------------------------------- 497
         b. Design Patents ------------------------------ 526
         c. Plant Patents ------------------------------- 543
   B. Administrative Procedures --------------------------- 557
      1. Application -------------------------------------- 557
         a. Claims ------------------------------------- 558
         b. Specification ------------------------------- 559
         c. Drawings ---------------------------------- 561
      2. Prosecution -------------------------------------- 562
      3. Judicial Review ---------------------------------- 568

II. Patent Law—Continued   **Page**
- C. Rights and Remedies --------------------------------- 576
  - 1. Statutory Rights --------------------------------- 576
  - 2. Patents in the Marketplace --------------------- 592
  - 3. Remedies --- 619
- D. Infringement --------------------------------------- 633

III. Copyright Law -- 652
- A. Requirements for Protection ---------------------- 654
  - 1. Formalities ------------------------------------- 654
    - a. Notice -- 654
    - b. Registration and Deposit -------------------- 658
  - 2. Originality ------------------------------------- 669
  - 3. Statutory Subject Matter --------------------- 684
- B. Rights and Remedies ------------------------------- 713
  - 1. Rights --- 713
    - a. The Nature of Copyright -------------------- 713
    - b. Statutory Rights ----------------------------- 737
    - c. Fair Use -------------------------------------- 763
    - d. Duration, Ownership and Transfer ---------- 786
  - 2. Remedies -- 811
- C. Infringement --------------------------------------- 830
  - 1. Literature --------------------------------------- 831
  - 2. Music -- 836
  - 3. Visual Arts -------------------------------------- 842
- D. Rights Beyond Copyright: Moral Right ------------- 855

PART FOUR: INTELLECTUAL PROPERTIES IN THE MARKETPLACE

I. Antitrust --- 872
- A. Patents -- 872
- B. Copyrights -- 881
- C. Trademarks --------------------------------------- 886

II. Federal Income Taxation ------------------------------ 897
- A. Patents -- 897
- B. Copyrights -- 907
- C. Trademarks --------------------------------------- 915

PART FIVE: INTERNATIONAL PROTECTION: THE CONVENTIONS

I. Copyright --- 918

II. Patent --- 933

III. Trademark --- 943

Index --- 957

*

TABLE OF CASES

The principal cases are in italic type. Cases cited or discussed are in roman
type. References are to Pages.

A & M Records, Inc. v. M. V. C. Distributing Corp., 228
Adams, United States v., 448
Addison-Wesley Pub. Co. v. Brown, 117
Adkins v. Lear, Inc., 617
Aero Spark Co. v. B. G. Corp., 647
Alberto-Culver Co. v. Andrea Dumon, Inc., 710
Algren Watch Findings Co. v. Kalinsky, 630
Allen v. Standard Crankshaft & Hydraulic Co., 451
Allied Maintenance Corp. v. Allied Mechanical Trades, Inc., 101, 115
Allis Chalmers Mfg. Co. v. Continental Aviation & Engineering Corp., 172
Alva Studios, Inc. v. Winninger, 680, 681
American Enka Corp. v. Marzall, 349
American Home Products Corp. v. Johnson & Johnson, 426
American Metropolitan Enterprises of New York, Inc. v. Warner Bros. Records, Inc., 829
American Steel Foundries v. Robertson, 277
American Trading Co. v. Heacock Co., 277
American Travel & Hotel Directory Co. v. Gehring Pub. Co., 851
American Washboard Co. v. Saginaw Mfg. Co., 71, 89, 91, 304, 425
Amex Holding Corp., In re, 349
Amsterdam v. Triangle Publications, Inc., 682, 683
Anderson's-Black Rock, Inc. v. Pavement Salvage Co., 449
Andrews v. Guenther Pub. Co., 683
Anthony, In re, 494
Anti-Monopoly, Inc. v. General Mills Fun Group, Inc., 305
Application of (see name of party)
Arc Music Corp. v. Lee, 850
Arnesen v. Raymond Lee Organization, Inc., 428
Arnstein v. Porter, 830, 849
Aro Corp. v. Allied Witan Co., 619

Aro Mfg. Co. v. Convertible Top Replacement Co., 588
Aronson v. Quick Point Pencil Co., 6, *64, 70,* 136, 193, 617, 619
Atlas v. Eastern Airlines, Inc., 476
Automatic Radio Mfg. Co. v. Hazeltine Research, Inc., 617
Avco Corp. v. Precision Air Parts, Inc., 224

Baker v. Selden, 713, 732
Barbed Wire Patent, The, 452
Barofsky v. General Elec. Corp., 542
Bartok v. Boosey & Hawkes, Inc., 808
Basic Chemicals, Inc. v. Benson, 173
Bass, In re, 484, 485
Batlin & Son, Inc., L. v. Snyder, 680, 681
Bayer, In re, 474
Bayer v. United Drug Co., 306, 663
Beatrice Foods Co., In re, 379, 380
Beech-Nut Packing Co. v. P. Lorillard Co., 381
Belcher v. Tarbox, 711, 712
Bell & Co., Alfred v. Catalda Fine Arts, Inc., 681
Bennett v. Halahan, Aronsen & Lyon, 493
Benny v. Loew's, 780, 781
Berlin v. E. C. Publications, Inc., 767
Bernard Food Indus. v. Dietene Co., 426
Best Lock Corp. v. Schlage Lock Co., 351
Bicentennial Comm'n of Pennsylvania v. Olde Bradford Co., 223
Bissell, Inc. v. Easy Day Mfg. Co., 380
Blaustein v. Burton, 56
Bleistein v. Donaldson Lithographing Co., 670, 680, 681, 708
Blisscraft of Hollywood v. United Plastics Co., 541
Blonder-Tongue Laboratories, Inc. v. University of Illinois Foundation, 649, 650
Blue Bell, Inc. v. Farah Mfg. Co., 279, 287
Blue Bell, Inc. v. Jaymar-Ruby, Inc., 287
Bobbs-Merrill Co. v. Straus, 759

Bookbinder's Restaurant, Inc., Application of, 291

Booth v. Colgate-Palmolive Co., 258

Booth v. Haggard, 666

Borden Ice Cream Co. v. Borden's Condensed Milk Co., 114

Borden, Inc., 384

Borst, Application of, 454, 473, 477

Boutell v. Volk, 650

Bouve v. 20th Century Fox Film Corp., 668

Breffort v. I Had A Ball Co., 823

Brenner v. Manson, 486, 493

Bristol v. Equitable Life Assur. Soc'y of United States, 33, 42

Broadcast Music, Inc. v. Columbia Broadcasting System, Inc., 810

Broadview Chem. Corp. v. Loctite Corp., 619, 629, 631

Brooks v. Stoffel Seals Corp., 452

Bros, Inc. v. Browning Mfg. Co., 473

Bros, Inc. v. W. E. Grace Mfg. Co., 473

Brose v. Sears, Roebuck & Co., 632

Brown Chem. Co. v. Meyer, 125, 126

Brown Sheet Iron & Steel Co. v. Brown Steel Tank Co., 125, 126

Brulotte v. Thys, 70, 616, 617

Brunner v. Stix Baer & Fuller Co., 61

Burgess Battery Co., In re, 339, 346

Burmel Handkerchief Corp. v. Cluett, Peabody & Co., 350

Burroughs Corp. v. Cimakasky, 173

Calmar, Inc. v. Cook Chem. Co., 448, 557, 568, *569*

Canal Co. v. Clark, 293, 304

Capitol Records, Inc. v. Mercury Records Corp., 227

Carrier-Call & Television Corp. v. Radio Corp. of America, 495

Carson, In re, 325

Carson Products Co. v. Califano, 162

Carter Products, Inc. v. Colgate-Palmolive Co., 475

Castleton China, Inc., In re, 284, 292

Catalin Corp. of America v. Catalazuli Mfg. Co., 649

Certain Steel Toy Vehicles, In re, 574

Champion Spark Plug Co. v. Gyromat Corp., 450

Champion Spark Plug Co. v. Sanders, 93

Chanel, Inc. v. Smith, 94

Charcoal Steak House of Charlotte, Inc. v. Staley, 83

Chrysler Corp. v. Brown, 162

Clairol, Inc. v. Boston Discount Center of Berkley, Inc., 94

Clairol, Inc. v. Cody's Cosmetics, Inc., 93

Clairol, Inc. v. Peekskill Thrift Drug Corp., 93

Clairol, Inc. v. Sarann Co., 93

Classic Film Museum, Inc. v. Warner Bros., Inc., 211, 212

Clemens, In re, 484

Coastal Chem. Co. v. Dust-A-Way, Inc., 379, 380

Coca-Cola Co. v. Dixi-Cola Laboratories, Inc., 95

Coca-Cola Co. v. Gemini Rising, Inc., 383

Coca-Cola Co. v. The Koke Co. of America, 324

Coca-Cola Co. v. Victor Syrup Corp., 394

Coffee v. Guerrant, 493

Cole v. Phillips H. Lord, Inc., 56

Colgate-Palmolive Co. v. Carter Products Co., 452

Colgate-Palmolive Co. v. Cook Chem. Co., 448, 569

Colligan v. Activities Club of New York, Ltd., 428

Columbia Broadcasting System, Inc. v. American Soc'y of Composers, Authors & Publishers, 810

Columbia Broadcasting System, Inc. v. DeCosta, 713, 734, 735

Columbia Broadcasting System, Inc. v. Documentaries Unlimited, Inc., 140, 227

Columbia Broadcasting System, Inc. v. Zenith Radio Corp., 650

Columbia Pictures Corp. v. National Broadcasting Co., 782, 783

Compco Corp. v. Day-Brite Lighting, Inc., 70, *133,* 136–140, 191, 223, 224, 227–229, 267, 352, 426, 617, 735

Conmar Products Corp. v. Universal Slide Fastener Co., 158, 193

Consumer's Union of United States, Inc. v. Theodore Hamm Brewing Co., 426

Crescent Tool Co. v. Kilborn & Bishop Co., 128, 138

Crossbow, Inc. v. Dan-Dee Imports, Inc., 426

Cuno Corp. v. Automatic Devices Corp., 453

Dallas Cowboys Cheerleaders, Inc. v. Pussycat Cinema, Ltd., 384

Davies v. Carnation Co., 63

Davies v. Krasna, 59

Davis v. General Foods Corp., 64

Dawn Donut Co. v. Hart's Food Stores, Inc., 360, 377, 378, 382, 393

Dawson Chem. Co. v. Rohm & Haas Co., 597, 616, 617

De Acosta v. Brown, 852

TABLE OF CASES

De Sylva v. Ballentine, 807, 808
DeCosta v. Columbia Broadcasting System, Inc., 735
Deepsouth Packing Co. v. Laitram Corp., 576, 588, 590
DeJonge & Co. v. Breuker & Kessler Co., 666, 667, 829
Dellar v. Samuel Goldwyn, Inc., 763
Denys Fisher (Spirograph) Ltd. v. Louis Marx & Co. of West Virginia, 272
DeSilva Constr. Corp. v. Herrald, 209
Desny v. Wilder, 56, 58
Diamond v. Chakrabarty, 497, 526
Diamond v. Diehr, 507, 525
Donahue v. Ziv Television Programs, Inc., 57
Donald v. Zack Meyer's T.V. Sales & Serv., 675, 680, 681, 682
Donaldson v. Beckett, 211
Downey v. General Foods Corp., 53, 58, 59
Dubilier Condenser Corp., United States v., 173
Dunhill, Ltd., Alfred v. Interstate Cigar Co., 427
Dunhill of London, Alfred v. Dunhill Shirt Shop, 114, 115
Duo-Tint Bulb & Battery Co. v. Moline Supply Co., 138, 139
duPont deNemours & Co., E. I. v. Christopher, 150, 156, 191
Dymow v. Bolton, 850

Edison v. Thomas A. Edison, Jr. Chem. Co., 125, 126
Egbert v. Lippmann, 476
Eibel Process Co. v. Minnesota & Ontario Paper Co., 451
Electric Smelting & Aluminum Co. v. Carborundum Co., 628
Elsmere Music, Inc. v. National Broadcasting Co., 782
Ely-Norris Safe Co. v. Mosler Safe Co., 76, 425
Encyclopedia Britannica Educational Corp. v. Crooks, 767, 780
Engelhard Indus., Inc. v. Research Instrumental Corp., 649
Erie R. Co. v. Tompkins, 115, 274, 275
Esquire, Inc. v. Ringer, 699, 709
Estate of (see name of party)
Ex parte (see name of party)
Eyre v. Higbee, 240

F. T. C. v. Formica Corp., 307
Factors Etc., Inc. v. Pro Arts, Inc., 256, 267

Federal-Mogul-Bower Bearings, Inc. v. Azoff, 421, 425
Ferris v. Frohman, 209
Fields v. Schuyler, 540
Findlay, Inc., David B. v. Findlay, 118, 125, 126
Fisher Controls Co. v. Control Components, Inc., 575
Fisher Music Co., Fred v. M. Witmark & Sons, 807, 808
Fleischer Studios, Inc. v. Ralph A. Freundlich, Inc., 736
Fleischmann Distilling Corp. v. Maier Brewing Co., 394
Flexitized, Inc. v. National Flexitized Corp., 137
Flintkote Co. v. Tizer, 416
Florida Citrus Comm'n, In re, 331
Folsom v. Marsh, 239, 241, 763, 766
Food Center, Inc. v. Food Fair Stores, Inc., 114
Forest Laboratories, Inc. v. Formulations, Inc., 141, 155
Forest Laboratories, Inc. v. Pillsbury Co., 155, 156, 158, 159
Foster, Application of, 478, 483, 485
Foster, Ex parte, 555
Fotomat Corp. v. Cochran, 351
Fotomat Corp. v. Photo Drive-Thru, Inc., 351
Fox-Stanley Photo Products, Inc. v. Otaguro, 394
Franklin Knitting Mills, Inc. v. Fashionit Sweater Mills, Inc., 297
Franklin Mint Corp. v. National Wildlife Art Exchange, Inc., 851
Frantz Mfg. Co. v. Phenix Mfg. Co., 483
Frey Ready-Mixed Concrete v. Pine Hill Concrete Mix Corp., 766
Friend v. H. A. Friend & Co., 126
Frito Co., The v. Buckeye Foods, Inc., 381

Galt House, Inc. v. Home Supply Co., 84, 89, 95
Gastown, Inc., Application of, 291
General Drafting Co. v. Andrews, 851
General Foods Corp. v. Struthers Scientific & Int'l Corp., 272
General Instrument Corp. v. Hughes Aircraft Co., 648
General Shoe Corp. v. Rosen, 298, 304
Georgia Pacific Corp. v. United States Plywood Corp., 451
Gershwin Pub. Corp. v. Columbia Artists Management, Inc., 854
Gibson-Stewart Co. v. William Bros. Boiler & Mfg. Co., 473

Goldstein Cs. Law Intell.Prop. 2d Ed. UCB—2

xxix

Gilliam v. American Broadcasting Companies, Inc., *859*, 870, 871

Girl Scouts of the United States of America v. Personality Posters Mfg. Co., 427

Gold Seal Co. v. Weeks, 324

Golding v. R. K. O. Pictures, Inc., 56

Goldstein v. California, 6, 70, 136, 140, 227, 228, 230, 267

Goodrich Co., B. F. v. Wohlgemuth, 174

Goodyear Tire & Rubber Co. v. Ray-O-Vac Co., 452

Gorham Mfg. Co. v. White, 541

Gottschalk v. Benson, 525

Graham v. John Deere Co., *432*, 448, 449, 450, 452, 569, 650

Graver Tank & Mfg. Co. v. Linde Air Products Co., *634*, 649

Great American Ins. Co., Ex parte, 349

Gross v. Seligman, *848*

Grove Press, Inc. v. Greenleaf Pub. Co., 212, *723*, 733, 735

Haelan Laboratories Inc. v. Topps Chewing Gum, Inc., 255, 256

Haig & Haig Ltd., Ex parte, 350, 351

Hamilton Nat'l Bank v. Belt, 60

Hamilton, United States v., 683

Handmacher-Vogel, Inc., Ex parte, *328*

Hanover Star Milling Co. v. Metcalf, 114

Hanson v. Alpine Val. Ski Area, Inc., 450

Harms Co., T. B. v. Eliscu, 269, 271

Harrington v. Mure, 270, 271

Hartop, In re, 494

Hassenfeld Bros., Inc. v. Mego Corp., 851

Hazeltine Research, Inc. v. Brenner, *481*, 483-485, 618

Head Ski Co. v. Kam Ski Co., 158, 172

Healy & Son, Inc., J. T. v. James A. Murphy & Son, Inc., 157

Hemingway, Estate of v. Random House, Inc., *234*, 238-241

Hepperle, In re, 354

Herschensohn v. Hoffman, 450

Heyman v. Commerce & Industry Ins. Co., 766

Higgins v. Keuffel, 710

High v. Trade Union Courier Pub. Corp., 58

Hildreth v. Mastoras, 493

Hill v. Whalen & Martell, Inc., 736

Hillerich & Bradsby, Application of, 347

Hirsch v. S. C. Johnson & Son, Inc., *242*, 258

Hoehling v. Universal City Studios, 684

Hollister v. Benedict & Burnham Mfg. Co., 453

Hollywood Brands, Inc., Application of, 322

Hollywood Brands, Inc., Ex parte, 322

Hollywood Jewelry Mfg. Co. v. Dushkin, 682

Honeywell, Inc., Application of, 353

Hotchkiss v. Greenwood, 453

Hurn v. Oursler, 273, 274

Illinois Foundation, Univ. of v. Blonder-Tongue Laboratories, Inc., 474

Imperial Homes Corp. v. Lamont, 733

In re (see name of party)

International News Serv. v. Associated Press, 115, 140

Irons & Sears v. Dann, 194

Isenstead v. Watson, 494

Ives Laboratories, Inc. v. Darby Drug Co., 137, 426

Jennings v. Kibbe, 541

Jet Spray Cooler, Inc. v. Crampton, 159, 160

Jewel Music Pub. Co. v. Leo Feist, Inc., *836*

Johnson v. Duquesne Light Co., 525

K & G Oil Tool & Serv. Co. v. G & G Fishing Tool Serv., 158

Kamin v. Kuhnau, 157

Kaufman, Inc., P. v. Rex Curtain Corp., 664

Kellogg Co. v. National Biscuit Co., 297, 306, 352

Kepner-Tregoe, Inc. v. Carabio, 851, 852

Kewanee Oil Co. v. Bicron Corp., 6, 7, 136, 140, *178*, 191-193, 228, 267

King v. Mister Maestro, Inc., 209, 210

King-Seeley Thermos Co. v. Aladdin Indus., Inc., *300*, 323

Kinkade v. New York Shipbuilding Corp., 173

Kleinman v. Betty Dain Creations, Inc., 273, 274

Kleinman v. Kobler, 451

Kolbe Co., H. M. v. Armgus Textile Co., 667

Kotzin, In re, 347, 348

Krahmer v. Luing, *206*, 208-210, 212

Kraly v. National Distillers & Chem. Corp., 618

Kress Co., S. H. v. Aghnides, 452

Krimmel, In re, 494

Kurlan v. Columbia Broadcasting System, Inc., 56

Lahr v. Adell Chem. Co., Inc., 257, 258

L'Aiglon Apparel, Inc. v. Lana Lobell, Inc., *418*, 425, 426, 428, 429

Lear v. Adkins, 70, 451, 574, 617-619, 650

Lee v. Runge, 682

Leon v. Pacific Tel. & Tel. Co., 782

Leschen & Sons Rope Co., A. v. American Steel & Wire Co., 278

Leschen & Sons Rope Co., A. v. Broderick & Bascom Rope Co., 347

Letter Edged in Black Press, Inc. v. Public Bldg. Comm'n of Chicago, *197*, 208-210

Levi Strauss & Co., In re, 348

Levitt Corp. v. Levitt, 126, 128

Ling-Tempco-Vought, Inc. v. Kollsman Instrument Corp., 452

Lionel Corp. v. De Filippis, 632

Lipman v. Massachusetts, 241

Loeb Pipes, Inc., In re Charles S., 311

Loew's, Inc. v. Columbia Broadcasting System, Inc., 782, 783

Lombardo v. Doyle, Dane & Bernbach, Inc., 255

Lowell v. Lewis, 485, 492

Luckett v. Delpark, Inc., 271

Lueddecke v. Chevrolet Motor Co., 45, 59, 64

Lugosi v. Universal Pictures, 255-257

Lyon v. Lyon, 126

McGregor-Doniger Inc. v. Drizzle, Inc., 401

McKenzie v. Cummings, 493

Malachowski, Application of, 494

Maltina Corp. v. Cawy Bottling Co., 387, 393

Marcalus Mfg. Co. v. Watson, 347

Marcus Advertising, Inc. v. M. M. Fisher Associates, Inc., 43

Masline v. New York, N. H. & H. R. Co., 50, 52, 57, 58

Mastro Plastics Corp. v. Emenee Indus., Inc., 117

Matarese v. Moore-McCormack Lines, 59

Maternally Yours, Inc. v. Your Maternity Shop, Inc., 274, 275

Mathey v. United Shoe Machine Corp., 630

Mayne, Ex parte, 525

Mazer v. Stein, 691, 708, 709, 712

Meeropol v. Nizer, 763

Meier Co., Joshua v. Albany Novelty Mfg. Co., 425

Memphis Development Foundation v. Factors Etc., Inc., 257

Metallizing Engineering Co. v. Kenyon Bearing & Auto Parts Co., 459

Metropolitan Opera Ass'n Inc. v. Wagner-Nichols Recorder Corp., 107, 115, 227

Meyer & Wenthe, Inc., In re, 322

Millar v. Taylor, 211

Miller v. Universal City Studios, Inc., 684

Miller Music Corp. v. Charles N. Daniels, Inc., 807, 808

Milprint, Inc. v. Curwood, Inc., 272

Minerals Separation, Ltd. v. Hyde, 451

Mink Breeders Ass'n v. Lou Nierenberg Corp., 426

Minnesota Mining & Mfg. Co., Ex parte, 350

Mitchell v. Penton/Industrial Pub. Co., 218

Mitchell Bros. Film Group v. Cinema Adult Theatre, 710-712

Mogen David Wine Corp., Application of, 352, 353

Monolith Portland Midwest Co. v. Kaiser Aluminum & Chem. Corp., 159

Morell & Co., John v. Reliable Packing Co., 385

Morse v. Fields, 850

Morseburg v. Balyon, 225

Morton v. New York Eye Infirmary, 526

Mosler Safe Co. v. Ely-Norris Safe Co., 78, 89, 91

Motschenbacher v. R. J. Reynolds Tobacco Co., 258

Mueller Brass Co. v. Reading Indus., 496

Muller, Ex parte, 526

Mura v. Columbia Broadcasting Corp., 759, 760

Musher Foundation v. Alba Trading Co., 273

Musto v. Meyer, 852

National Comics Publications, Inc. v. Fawcett Publications, Inc., 664, 735

National Football League Properties, Inc. v. Consumer Enterprises, Inc., 136

National Geographic Soc'y v. Classified Geographic, 760

Nelson v. Bowler, 494

Nerney v. New York, N. H. &. H. R. Co., 625, 628

New York Times Co. v. Roxbury Data Interface, Inc., 786

Nichols v. Universal Pictures Corp., 831

Nickerson v. The Bearfoot Sole Co., 649

Northam Warren Corp. v. Universal Cosmetic Co., 417

Norwich Pharmacal Co. v. International Brokers, Inc., 629

Novelty Textile Mills, Inc. v. Joan Fabrics Corp., 842

Nutt v. National Institute, Inc. for the Improvement of Memory, 209

Occumpaugh v. Norton, 477

Official Airlines Schedule Information Serv., Inc. v. Eastern Air Lines, Inc., 60

Otto v. Koppers Co., 451

Package Devices, Inc. v. Sun Ray Drug Co., 483

Palmer v. Orthokinetics, Inc., 450

Parker v. Flook, 525

Patou, Inc., Jean v. Jacqueline Cochran, Inc., 382

Paula Co., C. M. v. Logan, 760

Perceval v. Phipps, 241

Peter Pan Fabrics, Inc. v. Martin Weiner Corp., 654, 662–664

Picard v. United Aircraft Corp., 1

Pikle-Rite Co. v. Chicago Pickle Co., 395, 416, 417

Plastic Container Corp. v. Continental Plastics of Oklahoma, Inc., 450

Poncy v. Johnson & Johnson, 381

Pope v. Curl, 241

Prater, In re, 525

Prestonettes, Inc. v. Coty, 92, 93

Price v. Hal Roach Studios, Inc., 256

Procter & Gamble Co. v. Jacqueline Cochran, Inc., 290

Puddu v. Buonamici Statuary, Inc., 665

Ransburg Electro-Coating Corp. v. Ford Motor Co., 628

Reddy Communications, Inc. v. Environmental Action Foundation, 383

Reed, Roberts Associates, Inc. v. Strauman, 168, 193

Reeves Bros. Inc. v. United States Laminating Corp., 452

Republic Indus., Inc. v. Schlage Lock Co., 450

Republic Pictures Corp. v. Security-First Nat'l Bank of Los Angeles, 270

Richter v. Westab, Inc., 36, 42, 43

Rickard v. Du Bon, 492

Ricordi & Co., G. v. Paramount Pictures, Inc., 212, 733

River Mills, Inc., Dan v. Danfra Ltd., 381

Riverbank Canning Co., In re, 353

Robbins v. Frank Cooper Associates, 60

Rohauer v. Killiam Shows, Inc., 797, 805

Rolls-Royce Motors Ltd. v. Custom Cloud Motors, Inc., 115, 230

Rosemont Enterprises, Inc. v. Random House, Inc., 764, 765

Rosenthal Jewelry Corp., Herbert v. Grossbardt, 665

Royalty Control Corp. v. Sanco, Inc., 271

Rushton Co. v. Vitale, 829

Russell Box Co. v. Grant Paper Box Co., 630

Ryan Associates, Inc., How. J. v. Century Brewing Ass'n, 43

S. C. M. v. Langis Foods Ltd., 288, 290

Sakraida v. Ag Pro, Inc., 443, 449, 450, 453, 526, 588

Sample, Inc., The v. Porrath, 96, 113, 115

Sampson-United Corp. v. F. A. Smith Mfg. Co., 630

Samson Cordage Works v. Puritan Cordage Mills, 139

Sarkar, Application of, 194

Scarves by Vera, Inc. v. Todo Imports Ltd., 369, 377, 378

Scarves by Vera, Inc. v. United Merchants & Mfrs., Inc., 666

Schlegel Mfg. Co. v. U. S. M. Corp., 618

Scholz Homes, Inc. v. Maddox, 732

Schonwald v. F. Burkart Mfg. Co., 52

Schriber-Schroth v. Cleveland Trust Co., 648

Schulenburg v. Signatrol, Inc., 158

Schwinn Bicycle Co. v. Goodyear Tire & Rubber Co., 526, 540, 541

Screen Gems-Columbia Music, Inc. v. Mark-Fi Records Inc., 854

Searle & Co., In re G. D., 322

Sears, Roebuck & Co. v. Allstate Driving Sch., 411, 417, 426

Sears, Roebuck & Co. v. Stiffel Co., 6, 7, 70, *130,* 136–140, 191, 192, 223, 224, 227–229, 267, 352, 617, 735

Selchow & Righter Co. v. McGraw-Hill Book Co., 308

Servo Corp. of America v. Electro-Devices, Inc., 380

Servo Corp. of America v. Kelsey-Hays Co., 380

Shapiro, Bernstein & Co. v. H. L. Green Co., 854

Sheldon v. Metro-Goldwyn Pictures Corp., 669, 681, *816,* 829

Shellmar Products Co. v. Allen-Qualley Co., 158

Shenango Ceramics, Inc., In re, 351, 352

Sid & Marty Krofft Television Productions, Inc. v. McDonald's Corp., 829

Silenus Wines, Inc., Application of, 291

Sims v. Mack Truck Corp., 450

Sinatra v. Goodyear Tire & Rubber Co., 258

Singer Mfg. Co. v. June Mfg. Co., 306, 352

Singer Mfg. Co. v. Redlich,. 307

Skinner & Sons, William, Ex parte, 349

Smith v. Chanel, Inc., 94

Smith v. Recrion Corp., 58

Smith v. Whitman Saddle Co., 541

Societe Comptoir De L'Industrie Cotonniere Etablissements Boussac v. Alexander's Dept. Stores, 427

Solomons v. United States, 173

Standard Elektrik Lorenz Aktiengesellschaft, In re, 318

Stanley v. Columbia Broadcasting System Inc., 51, 56

Starkes Tarzian, Inc. v. Audio Devices, Inc., 156

Stauffer v. Exley, 429

Sterling Brewing, Inc. v. Cold Spring Brewing Corp., 378

Stevens v. National Broadcasting Co., 117

Stigwood Group Ltd., Robert v. O'Reilly, 829

Stoddard & Co., A. F. v. Dann, 496

Strachman v. Palmer, 272

Straus v. Notaseme Hosiery Co., 394

Straussler v. United States, 641

Sullivan v. Ed Sullivan Radio & T. V., Inc., 123, 126

Sun Oil Co., In re, 308

Sutter Products Co. v. Pettibone Mulliken Corp., 484

Sweetheart Plastics, Inc. v. Illinois Tool Works, Inc., 632

Swift v. Tyson, 275

Swift & Co., In re, 341, 346

Synercom Technology, Inc. v. University Computing Co., 140

Syntex Laboratories, Inc. v. Norwich Pharmacal Co., 416

Tabor v. Hoffman, 175, 192, 212

Tee-Pak, Inc. v. St. Regis Paper, 483

Telephone Cases, The, 477

Telex Corp. v. International Business Mach. Corp., 160

Tenney, In re, 474

Theis, In re, 464, 476

Tiffany & Co. v. Tiffany Productions, 114, 115

Tillamook County Creamery Ass'n v. Tillamook Cheese & Dairy Ass'n, 385

Time, Inc. v. Bernard Geis Associates, 767

Trade Mark Cases, 1, 277

Transmatic, Inc. v. Gulton Indus., Inc., 532

Triangle Publications, Inc. v. Knight-Ridder Newspapers, Inc., 786

Triangle Publications, Inc. v. Rohrlich, 418

Trio Process Corp. v. L. Goldstein's Sons, Inc., 630

Triplett v. Lowell, 649, 650

Troxel Mfg. Co. v. Schwinn Bicycle Co., 618

Truck Equipment Serv. Co. v. Fruehauf Corp., 139, 426

Twentieth Century Music Corp. v. Aiken, 742, 758

Union Carbide Corp. v. Ever-Ready, Inc., 385

Union Carbide Corp. v. Graver Tank & Mfg. Co., 630, 647, 648

Uniroyal Inc. v. Daly-Herring Co., 629

United Drug Co. v. Theodore Rectanus Co., 359, 377

United States v. ⸺ (see opposing party)

Universal City Studios, Inc. v. Sony Corp. of America, 786

University of Illinois Foundation v. Blonder-Tongue Laboratories, Inc., 479

Upton v. Ladd, 493

USM Corp. v. Marson Fastener Corp., 157

Vacheron & Constantin-Le Coultre Watches, Inc. v. Benrus Watch Co., 669

Van Products Co. v. General Welding & Fabricating Co., 192

Vocational Personnel Servs., Inc. v. Statistical Tabulating Corp., 95

Wainwright Securities, Inc. v. Wall Street Transcript Corp., 785

Walker Process Equipment, Inc., In re, 349

Wall v. Rolls-Royce of America, 114

Walt Disney Productions v. Air Pirates, 734, 777, 780–782, 785

Walters v. Shari Music Pub. Corp., 272

Warne & Co., Frederick v. Book Sales, Inc., 735

Warner & Co., William R. v. Eli Lilly & Co., 80, 89, 90

Warner Bros. Pictures, Inc. v. Columbia Broadcasting System, Inc., 718, 734, 735

Warner-Jenkinson Co. v. Allied Chem. Corp., 618

Warner-Lambert Pharmaceutical Co. v. John J. Reynolds, Inc., 192, 193

Washingtonian Pub. Co. v. Pearson, 658, 662, 668

Wearly v. FTC, 161

Weiner King, Inc. v. Wiener King Corp., 380

Weitzenkorn v. Lesser, 56

Wexler v. Greenberg, 162, 173

Wheaton v. Peters, 210, 211

Wilbur-Ellis Co. v. Kuther, 585, 588, 590

Williams v. Weisser, 241

Williams & Wilkins Co. v. United States, 780

Wilson & Co., Thomas v. Irving J. Dorfman Co., 829

Winans v. Denmead, 647

Winston Research Corp. v. Minnesota Mining & Mfg. Co., 159

Winthrop-Stearns, Inc. v. Milner Products Co., 348

Worden v. California Fig Syrup Co., 323

Worden v. Fisher, 495, 496

Yadkoe v. Fields, 63

Yoder Bros., Inc. v. California-Florida Plant Corp., 543, 555

Zacchini v. Scripps-Howard Broadcasting Co., 259, 267, 268

Zenie Bros. v. Miskind, 632

Zippo Mfg. Co. v. Rogers Imports, Inc., 138

Zotos Int'l, Inc. v. Kennedy, 162

COPYRIGHT, PATENT, TRADEMARK
AND
RELATED STATE DOCTRINES

Part One

THE ROLE OF INTELLECTUAL PROPERTY LAW

I. A CONSTITUTIONAL VIEW

UNITED STATES CONSTITUTION, Article 1, Section 8

"The Congress shall have power . . .

(3) To regulate Commerce with foreign Nations, and amo; g the several States, and with the Indian Tribes . : .

(8) To promote the Progress of Science and useful Arts, by se-curing for limited Times to Authors and Inventors the exclusive Right to their respective Writings and Discoveries . . . ."

NOTES

1. Clause 3, which describes the congressional commerce power, is the constitutional basis for federal trademark legislation. Clause 8 is the source of federal copyright and patent legislation.

Courts and commentators have on occasion sought to escape the straitjacket of the traditional view, suggesting, for example, that clause 8's implicit limitation of congressional power can be eluded by resting copyright and patent legislation on clause 3. See, M. Nimmer, Copyright § 1.09 (1980); Picard v. United Aircraft Corp., 128 F.2d 632, 643 n. 22, 53 U.S.P.Q. 563 (2d Cir. 1942). And in the *Trade-mark Cases,* discussed at p. 277, below, the government sought unsuc-cessfully to avoid the requirements of clause 3 by adducing "the like-ness which property in the use of trade-marks bears to that in pat-ents and copyrights" for its argument that "the power of Congress over them might be derived from the same source"—clause 8. 100 U. S. 82, 86, 25 L.Ed. 550 (1879).

2. Colonial usage and syntax suggest that the Constitution's framers, in speaking of "Science" in clause 8, were referring to the work of authors, and by "useful Arts" meant the work of inventors.

Structurally the clause is a balanced sentence—a style common to the period—and can be reworked to read:

(8) (a) To promote the Progress of Science . . . by securing for limited Times to Authors . . . the exclusive
Right to their . . . Writings.

(b) To promote the Progress of . . . useful Arts, by securing for limited Times to . . . Inventors the exclusive Right to their . . . Discoveries.

3. Clauses 3 and 8 predicate a federal system. The terms "Writings" and "Discoveries" describe the matter that is subject to Congress's copyright and patent powers. By negative implication, these terms also describe the ambit of state jurisdiction—over non-Writings and non-Discoveries. This state power is in turn limited by the operation of the supremacy clause of article 6, with the effect that exercises of state jurisdiction, even within an initially legitimate ambit, may be struck down if they interfere with the workings of federal power. The line between state and federal jurisdiction over the copyright and patent interests is a frequent source of problems. Although the line between state and federal jurisdiction over the trademark interest can be more easily drawn, it, too, is problematic.

GOLDSTEIN, THE COMPETITIVE MANDATE: FROM SEARS TO LEAR

59 Calif.L.Rev. 873–875; 878–880; 895–896; 898–899; 903–904 (1971).*

The Supreme Court has in recent years renewed its attention to the economy's governing competitive principles. The Court's approach to these principles has been most explicit, and most problematic, in a series of cases involving administration of the monopolies effected by the state law of trade secrets, common law copyright, unfair competition and contract. In each case the Court's concern was whether the state law in question interfered with competitive needs generally and with either of two federal law monopolies, patent and copyright, specifically. The question posed by the Court for decision in Sears, Roebuck & Co. v. Stiffel Co.[a] typifies its method of inquiry: "whether a State's unfair competition law can, consistently with the federal patent laws, impose liability for or prohibit the copying of an article which is protected by neither a federal patent nor a copyright." In each case, *Sears*, Lear v. Adkins,[b] and Brulotte v. Thys Co.,[c] the Court answered by striking down or severely restricting the state law.

Probably because the Court's answers lack the closely reasoned premises necessary for consistent and principled decision, they have

* Copyright © 1971, California Law Review, Inc. Reprinted by permission.

a. Set out beginning at page 130 of the text.

b. Discussed at page 617, below.

c. Discussed at page 616, below.

been largely misapplied, circumscribed or ignored by state and lower federal courts and have stirred no little confusion among scholars. The absence from the decisions of neutral and broadly applicable principles is specifically attributable to the Court's failure to grasp or, at least, explicate fully two important contextual implications. First, these decisions are rooted in the nation's historic commitment to a competitive economy and in the modern premise that competition can be maintained only through government interference in enterprise conduct. One relevant and particularly traditional method of interference has been the government's provision for artificial incentive through the grant of legal monopolies—patent, copyright, trademark, trade secrets, common law copyright and unfair competition. Second, the Court failed to discern the similarity between these cases and contemporary decisions involving constitutional review generally, decisions in which, for example, state laws and practices governing criminal procedure or regulating individual speech have been tested to determine their consonance with federal constitutional standards.

Combined, these contextual perspectives provide a series of three premises that make resolution of the questions involved in *Sears, Lear,* and *Brulotte* as easy a matter as 1, 2, 3: 1, there is a constitutional mandate for a competitive economy and this mandate is paramount to the federal and state law monopolies; 2, the federal law monopolies are implements designed to assist in meeting the competitive mandate; and 3, the state law monopolies, though cruder than their federal law counterparts, are also designed to meet the competitive mandate and, for this reason, the federal law monopolies can be employed as models for refinement of the state laws.

The Mandate for a Competitive Economy

The federal constitutional mandate for a competitive economy occupies a small but decisive corner in American law's general commitment to competitive principles. This commitment predicates that the nation's interests in the equitable distribution of income, in the promotion of technological advance and in the dedication of resources to their most productive possible uses will be best advanced by a market economy. Whether a competitive system can serve these interests and whether, in fact, competition occupies a predominant place in the present American economy, are questions aside from the present point. The relevant fact is that legislatures and courts, and the Supreme Court particularly, have largely assumed the centrality of a market economy and have, with equal consistency, committed their energies to promoting competitive principles. . . .

The operation of federal patent, copyright and trademark laws is assumed to advance the federal competitive mandate. Each law grants a proprietary monopoly over subject matter that, but for the grant, would lie in the public domain. The Constitution's authorization to Congress to grant patent and copyright protection represents a judgment that, although short-range competitive interests would benefit from immediate and free public access to technological and artistic innovation, to permit such access would destroy incentive to innovate; new products and works would not be introduced into the market and consequently the long-range competitive situation would decline. The patent and copyright statutes, each in its own way, strike a balance between these long- and short-range competitive interests. By identifying the monopoly holder with the long-range interest in incentive and the alleged infringer with the short-range interest in access, they assure that both aspects of the competitive interest will be represented in any infringement action. The trademark monopoly, although it differs from patent and copyright in many vital respects, shares their fundamental balance between long- and short-range competitive interests and, for this reason, can be grouped with them with respect to the competitive mandate.

There is another group of law-created monopolies that, as implements of the competitive mandate, has attracted comparatively little attention. The monopolies effected by state laws governing trade secrets, common law copyright, and unfair competition, which generically embrace the subject matter of patent, copyright, and trademark, respectively, reflect a state determination that competitive interests will be advanced by their enforcement. Although the relationship between each state monopoly and its federal counterpart—between trade secret and patent law, for example—is by no means symmetrical, the state laws are, like the federal laws, administered on the basis of a balance struck between long- and short-range competitive needs. The law of trade secrets, for example, mediates between long- and short-range interests in subject matter that is either being developed to the stage necessary for a patent application or for which no patent application is contemplated. The trade secret holder, like the patent owner, can be identified with the long range competitive interest, and the trade secret infringer, like the patent infringer, can be identified with the short-range interest in immediate access.

The federal mandate for a competitive economy can, then, be partially implemented by select, balanced monopolies. Conversely, the legitimacy of a monopoly's balance can be gauged in terms of its capacity to advance the mandate. That the federal law monopolies —patent, copyright, and trademark—are intended to implement the mandate has been clear from their inception. On the other hand, the implemental nature of the state law monopolies—trade secrets, common law copyright, and unfair competition—has not been so clearly perceived by the courts. .   .   .

Each state system, like its federal counterpart, is designed to advance the competitive mandate. Because they are the products of ad hoc decision and tend in some respects to be crude or indecisive, the state systems presumably fulfill the mandate less precisely than do their federal counterparts which, formed by statute, are comparatively structured and articulate. The federal patent, copyright, and trademark systems can, for this reason, serve as models for the refinement of their counterpart state laws. When, in any case involving a state law monopoly, there is, for lack of clear guidelines, indecision as to how the balance between incentive and access ought to be struck, the counterpart federal law monopoly can be referred to for guidance, as good evidence of the sorts of balanced monopolies that are capable of advancing the competitive mandate.   .   .   .

The ease with which the federal patent, copyright, and trademark laws can be employed in the design of state law monopolies should not obscure two critical limitations on their use. First, the interests that underlie the state law monopolies may differ in vital respects from the interests that underlie the federal law monopolies. So long as effectuation of these discrete state interests does not contradict the competitive mandate, they should not be subordinated through unexamined adherence to the federal models. The constitutional requirement, for example, that federal patent and copyright protection be for "limited times" is not applicable to the states which may, as a consequence, grant perpetual protection through their trade secret and common law copyright doctrines. Although the federal requirement is good evidence that some durational limit is necessary to a properly set balance between incentive and access, independent state interests may require protection in perpetuity. Thus, to the extent that state common law copyright incidentally protects individual interests in privacy, perpetuity may be a valid expression of state interests. Perpetuity in this context should be overridden only upon a showing both that vindication of the competitive mandate requires the result and that other constitutional interests—in this example, the interest in the integrity of individual personality—coincide with or can properly be subordinated to the competitive mandate.

Second, although state and federal law monopolies are easily compared, the fundamental comparison is between the state law monopolies and the constitutional mandate for a competitive economy. The comparative function of the federal monopolies is strictly modular; they suggest how a legal monopoly over the subject matter in question can be structured to advance the competitive mandate. In particular, the federal models should not be used to preempt the introduction, by proprietor and infringer respectively, of empirical data addressed to the capacity or incapacity of the state law monopoly in question to perform its single function of advancing the competitive mandate.   .   .   .

Questions of the legitimate scope of any state or federal law monopoly should be resolved by comparing the effect of its rules and doctrines with the requirements of the competitive mandate. The Supreme Court's explicit adoption of this comparative method, implicitly espoused for federal monopolies in all cases and for state monopolies in *Lear,* would advance a number of interests. State and lower federal courts, troubled since *Sears* by the Court's recondite and sometimes aimless criteria, would no doubt benefit from the formulation of a clear, sound method for resolution of these recurrent questions. Clarification would also inject a significant measure of certainty into business planning for the management of intellectual properties, a process particularly unsettled by dicta in *Lear.*   .   .   .

That the task of accommodating state doctrines to the competitive mandate may be prolonged is no argument against either its propriety or manageability. The judicial and legislative chore need be no less tractable than the one imposed by the Court's decisions governing the administration of criminal procedure; unlike its desegregation and reapportionment decisions, which required the design of entirely new systems, these decisions call only for the adjustment of existing doctrine.

Indeed, prolongation may represent a third, more lasting, benefit of the comparative method. Underlying the decision in every case involving a state or federal law monopoly is the determination that the competitive mandate requires either expansion or curtailment of the monopoly in suit. For the state law monopolies, this determination can to some extent be made through comparison with the federal law monopolies that presumably strike the correct balance between the competing needs of incentive and access. But, to a more profound extent, and in the case of federal law as well as state law monopolies, this determination will have to be rested upon a hard and sustained empirical look at the effects upon innovation and competition of the decision for expansion or curtailment. The judicial and legislative judgments produced—conceivably, for example, judgments that to reduce the duration of the patent or copyright term by half would not diminish technological or artistic incentive one whit—would mark a worthy return to first principles.

NOTES

1. In 1973, the Supreme Court began what was to become a nearly full retreat from its decision in *Sears*. Goldstein v. California, 412 U.S. 546, 93 S.Ct. 2303, 37 L.Ed.2d 163, 178 U.S.P.Q. 129 (1973), marked the first step away from *Sears'* harsh preemptive method and toward a method closer to the one advanced in the article excerpted above. The Court there upheld California's record piracy law against claims of preemption, reasoning that "the State of California has exercised a power which it retained under the Constitution, and that the challenged statute, as applied in this case, does not intrude into an area which Congress has, up to now, pre-empted." 412 U.S. 546, 571, 93 S.Ct. 2303, 2319.

The next step in the retreat came in Kewanee Oil Co. v. Bicron Corp., 416 U.S. 470, 94 S.Ct. 1879, 40 L.Ed.2d 315, 179 U.S.P.Q. 321 (1974), set out at page 178, below. There the Court validated state trade secret protection for unpatentable subject matter despite the claim that the state law violated the supremacy of federal patent law. Aronson v. Quick Point Pencil Co., 440 U.S. 257, 99 S.Ct. 1096, 59 L. Ed.2d 296, 201 U.S.P.Q. 1 (1979), set out at page 64, below, further confirmed the retreat from *Sears* by upholding state contract protection for an unpatentable idea on the ground that "[p]ermitting inventors to make enforceable agreements licensing the use of their inventions in return for royalties provides an additional incentive to invention." 440 U.S. 257, 262, 99 S.Ct. 1096, 1099.

The impact of these decisions on state rules governing idea protection, unfair competition, trade secrets, common law copyright and the right of publicity is considered in the chapters on state law that follow. For an introductory analysis of the evolution away from *Sears,* see Goldstein, Kewanee Oil Co. v. Bicron Corp: Notes on a Closing Circle, 1974 Sup.Ct.Rev. 81.

2. At the same time that the Supreme Court was turning away from *Sears* and toward reinvigorated state intellectual property doctrines, efforts to deplete these doctrines were emerging from another quarter. After protracted consideration, Congress in 1976 passed a new copyright law to replace the 1909 Act. One of the new Act's central changes, embodied in section 301, is to eliminate common law copyright and other state doctrines equivalent to copyright. The Act's framers justified the preemption of common law copyright as a necessary incident to the Act's larger plan to bring United States copyright law into line with the copyright laws of other nations. But they also recognized that preemption would eliminate many troublesome questions that over the previous two centuries had clouded the line between state and federal copyright powers. See H.R. No. 94–1476, 94th Cong., 2d. Sess. 129–130 (1976).

The problem with section 301 lies not so much in its rationale as in its wording. The section abolishes not only common law copyright but also "all legal or equitable rights that are equivalent to any of the exclusive rights within the general scope of copyright . . . in works of authorship that are fixed in a tangible medium of expression and come within the subject matter of copyright." Read literally, this section could preempt large areas of unfair competition law and laws protecting ideas, trade secrets and the right to publicity. Section 301, and some possible solutions to the dilemmas it creates, are considered at pages 223–232, below.

3. The concept of "public domain" plays an important and shifting role in intellectual property law. The term is sometimes used to describe material that is unprotectable because it falls outside a particular law's constitutional or statutory subject matter. Thus, copyright law declares ideas to be in the public domain and patent law places discoveries and natural principles there. The term may also describe subject matter that, though of a protectable type, fails to meet some formal or qualitative test for protection. Untimely patent applications and nondistinctive trademarks are in the public domain for these reasons. Or the term may describe subject matter that, having once enjoyed the law's protection, is now free for all to use because the statutory term has expired.

Courts frequently obscure the basis for their decisions by saying merely that a work is in the public domain, and not indicating which specific public domain rationale dictated the result. Consider, for example, the assertion in *Kewanee,* "That which is in the public domain cannot be removed therefrom by action of the States." 416 U.S. 470, 481, 94 S.Ct. 1879, 1886. Does this mean that states have no competence to protect subject matter that has, for one or another of several reasons, failed to qualify for copyright, patent or trademark protection? That was covered by a copyright or patent whose term has expired, or a trademark that was abandoned? Does it imply that states cannot define the public domain that surrounds their own systems of intellectual property law—idea protection, trade secrets, common law copyright, unfair competition and right to publicity?

As you read the materials in the next section on the functions served by intellectual property systems, you might try to shape a concept of public domain that will effectively accommodate the described functions as well as any countervailing public policies. And, as you encounter the term "public domain" in cases throughout this book, you may find it instructive to ask how the court is using the term and whether in the circumstances the use is proper. Two guidelines may aid your analysis. First, instead of treating public domain as a general phrase, you might start by viewing it as a specific concept whose shape and content will vary with the state or federal law with which it is associated in any case. Second, it may help to consider that subject matter is in the public domain not because some brooding omnipresence has declared it to be there, but only because a court or legislature has determined that it should be there. Ideas, for example, are free as air not because they are naturally fugitive, but because Congress, state legislatures and courts have decided that they should go unprotected.

II. SOME FUNCTIONAL VIEWS

A. COPYRIGHT

MACAULAY, SPEECH DELIVERED IN
THE HOUSE OF COMMONS
5 FEBRUARY 1841

Macaulay, Prose and Poetry 731, 733–737 (G. Young Ed. 1967).

. . . The advantages arising from a system of copyright are obvious. It is desirable that we should have a supply of good books: we cannot have such a supply unless men of letters are liberally remunerated; and the least objectionable way of remunerating them is by means of copyright. You cannot depend for literary instruction and amusement on the leisure of men occupied in the pursuits of active life. Such men may occasionally produce compositions of great merit. But you must not look to such men for works which require deep meditation and long research. Works of that kind you can expect only from persons who make literature the business of their lives. Of these persons few will be found among the rich and the noble. The rich and the noble are not impelled to intellectual exertion by necessity. They may be impelled to intellectual exertion by the desire of distinguishing themselves, or by the desire of benefiting the community. But it is generally within these walls that they seek to signalise themselves and to serve their fellow creatures. Both their ambition and their public spirit, in a country like this, naturally take a political turn. It is then on men whose profession is literature, and whose private means are not ample, that you must rely for a supply of valuable books. Such men must be remunerated for their literary labour. And there are only two ways in which they can be remunerated. One of those ways is patronage; the other is copyright.

There have been times in which men of letters looked, not to the public, but to the government, or to a few great men, for the reward of their exertions. It was thus in the time of Maecenas and Pollio at Rome, of the Medici at Florence, of Lewis the Fourteenth in France, of Lord Halifax and Lord Oxford in this country. Now, Sir, I well know that there are cases in which it is fit and graceful, nay, in which it is a sacred duty to reward the merits or to relieve the distresses of men of genius by the exercise of this species of liberality. But these cases are exceptions. I can conceive no system more fatal to the integrity and independence of literary men than one under which they should be taught to look for their daily bread to the favour of ministers and nobles. I can conceive no system more certain to turn those minds which are formed by nature to be the blessings and ornaments of our species into public scandals and pests.

9

We have, then, only one resource left. We must betake ourselves to copyright, be the inconveniences of copyright what they may. . . . Thus, then, stands the case. It is good that authors should be remunerated; and the least exceptionable way of remunerating them is by a monopoly. Yet monopoly is an evil. For the sake of the good we must submit to the evil; but the evil ought not to last a day longer than is necessary for the purpose of securing the good.

Now, I will not affirm, that the existing law is perfect, that it exactly hits the point at which the monopoly ought to cease; but this I confidently say, that the existing law is very much nearer that point than the law proposed by my honorable and learned friend. For consider this; the evil effects of the monopoly are proportioned to the length of its duration. But the good effects for the sake of which we bear with the evil effects are by no means proportioned to the length of its duration. A monopoly of sixty years produces twice as much evil as a monopoly of thirty years, and thrice as much evil as a monopoly of twenty years. But it is by no means the fact that a posthumous monopoly of sixty years gives to an author thrice as much pleasure and thrice as strong a motive as a posthumous monopoly of twenty years. On the contrary, the difference is so small as to be hardly perceptible.

. . . I will take an example. Dr. Johnson died fifty-six years ago. If the law were what my honorable and learned friend wishes to make it, somebody would now have the monopoly of Dr. Johnson's works. Who that somebody would be it is impossible to say; but we may venture to guess. I guess, then, that it would have been some bookseller, who was the assign of another bookseller, who was the grandson of a third bookseller, who had bought the copyright from Black Frank, the Doctor's servant and residuary legatee, in 1785 or 1786. Now, would the knowledge that this copyright would exist in 1841 have been a source of gratification to Johnson? Would it have stimulated his exertions? Would it have once drawn him out of his bed before noon? Would it have once cheered him under a fit of the spleen? Would it have induced him to give us one more allegory, one more life of a poet, one more imitation of Juvenal? I firmly believe not. I firmly believe that a hundred years ago, when he was writing our debates for the Gentleman's Magazine, he would very much rather have had twopence to buy a plate of shin of beef at a cook's shop underground. Considered as a reward to him, the difference between a twenty years' term and a sixty years' term of posthumous copyright would have been nothing or next to nothing. But is the difference nothing to us? I can buy Rasselas for sixpence; I might have had to give five shillings for it. I can buy the Dictionary, the entire genuine Dictionary, for two guineas, perhaps for less; I might have had to give five or six guineas for it. Do I grudge this to a man like Dr. Johnson? Not at all. Show me that the prospect of this boon roused him to any vigorous effort, or sustained his spirits under depressing circumstances, and I am quite willing to pay the price of such an object, heavy as that price is. But what I do complain of is that my circumstances are to be worse, and Johnson's none the better; that I am to give five pounds for what to him was not worth a farthing.

BREYER, THE UNEASY CASE FOR COPYRIGHT: A STUDY OF COPYRIGHT IN BOOKS, PHOTOCOPIES, AND COMPUTER PROGRAMS

84 Harv.L.Rev. 281, 292–302 (1970).*

I. Would the Abolition of Copyright Protection Seriously Injure Book Production?

To abolish copyright protection would allow publishers to compete in the production and sale of an individual title. The proponents of copyright protection would argue strongly that even if such competition sometimes brings the reader books at lower prices, it may often prevent him from obtaining a book at all. A subsequent publisher could copy and sell a particular book at lower costs than those incurred by the initial publisher. If competition immediately forced that book's price down to the copier's costs, the initial publisher could not recover his fixed costs or pay the author. The fear of such a result in a world without copyright would, it is claimed, discourage publishers from publishing and authors from writing. To evaluate the importance of this economic claim for copyright protection, we must appraise the impact of possible copying on initial publishers' revenues and the possible harm that could flow from any such revenue loss.

(a) Would Competition in the Production of Individual Titles Seriously Threaten Book Publishers' Revenues?

(i) The Copying Publisher's Cost Advantage.—A copying publisher could produce a copy for considerably lower cost than an initial publisher, for the initial publisher incurs many costs that a subsequent publisher would not have to bear. The initial publisher must edit the book and he must pay various fixed manufacturing expenses, such as those of composing type into pages, making corrections, and designing plates for the jacket. A copying publisher can avoid many of these costs simply by photographing the pages of the completed book and using the photographs for printing purposes. He can also escape a portion of the selling, promotion, and overhead costs that an initial publisher must bear. And he might not pay the author a royalty.

Because a copier's cost advantage will vary considerably, depending upon the title and the number of copies that the book sells, one can more easily discuss the extent of the advantage in terms of specific dollar examples, rather than percentages. The following example is constructed to illustrate the typical extent of the cost advantage. The example shows the differing costs to the initial publisher and to a copier of producing an unillustrated 400-page college text that is expected to sell about 5000 copies.[d]   It will be sold to booksellers for $4.80.   The booksellers will retail it for $6.00.   (The example is based upon average cost figures contained in the American Education Publishers' Institute Annual Survey of the textbook publishing industry for 1968.   Since textbook publishers accounting for more than ninety percent of all textbooks sold provided detailed cost information for that survey, the average cost figures are reasonably representative.)

The copier's cost advantage is fairly large.   To produce an edition of 5,000 copies would cost him less than two-thirds what it would cost the initial publisher.   The result is that the book's initial publisher must sell 3,700 copies before he begins to earn a profit whereas a copying publisher selling the book at the same price will begin to earn a profit after selling 1,400 copies.   Moreover, if the copier expects to sell 2,500 copies, he could set a price to the retailer of $3.20 instead of $4.80 and still earn a small profit.   And the retailer could sell the text for $4.40 instead of $6.00 while earning no less than before.

The copier's cost advantage may be larger in the case of many complicated textbooks but smaller for many bestselling tradebooks. In general, editing, illustrations, footnotes, tables, and indices raise a book's fixed manufacturing costs, increasing the copier's advantage.

Fixed Costs	First Publisher	Copier
Plant	$4,500	$900
Editorial	1,440	500
Other overhead	2,880	2,000
Selling	1,000	1,000
Promotion	700	350
Total fixed cost	$10,520	$4,750

Variable Costs		
Manufacturing	$.80 per copy	$.80 per copy
Warehouse and shipping	.16 " "	.16 " "
Royalty to author	.70 " "	.00 " "
Selling	.20 " "	.20 " "
Promotion	.14 " "	.07 " "
Publishers' total variable cost	2.00 " "	1.23 " "
Retailers' markup *	1.20 " "	1.20 " "
Total variable cost	3.20 " "	2.43 " "

d.   "*Textbooks* account for the single largest portion (about thirty-five percent) of all publishing revenues. They comprise books used in colleges and books used in elementary or high schools (known in the industry as "elhi" texts).   *Tradebooks* include the novels and popular nonfiction that ordinarily spring to mind when copyright is discussed.   Adult tradebooks (both hardbound and paperback) sold by booksellers account for only about ten percent of all publishing revenue. If we add in children's books, tradebooks sold through book clubs, and pulp novels, the figure rises to about twenty-seven percent."   Pp. 292–293.

* Retailers' markup is the difference between the $6.00 price and $4.80, which the retailer pays for the book. This $4.80 figure includes the publisher's profit.

A large number of sales reduces that advantage by spreading fixed costs over a large number of copies.

The copier's cost advantage today is somewhat greater than copiers enjoyed in previous generations. In the nineteenth century copiers could not photograph a book's pages and thus had to bear the heavy cost of composing type for printing; nor did they benefit much from promotional expenditures, for publishers then seem to have advertised much less than now. More importantly the copier's cost advantage may decline somewhat in the near future. With the aid of computers, printers may be able to make printing plates directly from a typed manuscript, eliminating the cost of retyping copy on, for example, a linotype machine. Computers may also lower inventory costs by making possible the printing of books "on demand."

In any event, one cannot deny the existence of a fairly large cost advantage at present. The advantage shows that copying publishers could sell books profitably at prices that will prove unremunerative for initial publishers—a fact that may lead some to copy books soon after they appear on the market. On the other hand, the cost difference does not prove by itself that copying publishers will be able to drive a book's price low enough soon enough to prevent its initial publisher from earning a profit; nor does it show by itself that several publishers will often attempt to sell the same book.

(ii) Countervailing Forces: The Initial Publisher's Advantages of Lead Time and the Threat of Retaliation.—A book's initial publisher will ordinarily enjoy several advantages that may partially offset a copier's lower production costs. For one thing, his book will reach the market first. To obtain this "lead time" in the nineteenth century an American publisher would often agree to pay a popular English novelist, such as Sir Walter Scott, substantial royalties for early proofs of a new novel. The proofs would be rushed to America before any other publisher could compete by obtaining a copy of the book's English edition. Books were sold with sufficient speed that a few days lead time could spell the difference between profit and loss. In fact, lead time was important enough that many English writers earned more from the sale of advance proofs to American publishers (despite lack of copyright protection in America) than from the copyright royalties on their English sales.

Lead time should still prove advantageous to publishers of tradebooks. Publishers expect a tradebook to begin to return a profit within a few months of publication if it is ever to do so. By the time a copier chooses a book, prints it, and distributes it to retailers, he may be six to eight weeks behind, by which time the initial publisher will have provided retailers with substantial inventories. It is unlikely that a price difference of less than a dollar will lead many retailers or customers to wait for a cheaper edition, for hardbound book customers do not seem to respond readily to price reductions. They are not willing, after all, to wait for a cheaper paperbound edition. And, if the copier tries to cut his competitor's lead by rushing publication, he will incur special costs that will cut into his price advantage. In the case of textbooks, however, lead time, while helpful, should prove less important, for college texts often take a year or more before they begin to earn a profit, and elhi texts may not begin to earn a return for two or three years.

Second, the copier will be somewhat constrained by fear of retaliation by the initial publisher. Publishers in the past protected themselves from copying by producing punitive "fighting editions," which they would sell below the copier's cost. Even if the fear of antitrust action makes the modern publisher hesitate to set a price that is lower than that of the copier, the antitrust laws should not prevent him from *meeting* the copier's price. And at equivalent prices he will benefit from marginal advantages, such as somewhat better quality reproduction, more fully developed channels of distribution, or an ability to proclaim his the "authorized" edition. When, for example, a copying publisher recently put out an $8.50 edition of a book about ancient houses, the book's original publisher responded with a new edition priced at $4.00 and, because of his better established distribution channels, drove the copier from the market.

A copying publisher, faced with the problems of "lead time" and "retaliation" is unlikely to see much profit in copying low-volume titles. It seems unlikely, for example, that a publisher thinking of copying the type of tradebook that now sells about 4,000 copies, would count on selling the 2,000 or more copies needed to earn a profit. Nor would a publisher seem likely to compete in the production of a low-volume text as long as its initial publisher is not earning unusually high profits from its sale. Indeed, pre-1958 British books, which are often in the public domain in America, are rarely copied—I should think because their market is too small to make copying attractive.

A copier is more likely to compete in the sale of those tradebooks (variously estimated at ten to fifteen percent of total tradebooks) that sell more than a few thousand copies. Yet the copier's cost advantage is smaller for such higher volume books. And with only one or a few copies we may find that price competition is not sufficiently fierce to force initial publishers to incur a loss; "duopoly" or "oligopoly" pricing may leave a profit for all publishers on books worth copying. That competition in the sale of such books is feasible is suggested by existing competition in the sale of popular government documents, such as the *Warren Report*, or of classics in the public domain, and by the fact that publishers paid popular nineteenth-century English writers substantial royalties despite the lack of copyright protection.

Nonetheless, to introduce competition and lower the return that a "best-seller" earns may make tradebook publishers less willing to run the risk of publishing books of unpredictable future popularity. Moreover, copiers are likely to compete in the production of popular texts or reference books. These books, unlike "best-selling" novels, may involve heavy fixed costs which the original publisher does not expect to recoup for two or three years or more. Such books present the strongest examples for those who fear that the threat of competition will make publishers hesitate to produce books. Yet publishers will continue to produce them as long as they can earn a reasonable profit on their sale; and copyright would be unnecessary even in this category if it proved possible to assure them this profit by developing currently underutilized marketing techniques for channeling money from reader to publisher—techniques that we shall now discuss.

B. PATENT

"TO PROMOTE THE PROGRESS OF . . . USEFUL ARTS"

Report of the President's Commission on the Patent System 1–3 (1966).

The United States patent system is an institution as old as the Nation itself. Stemming from a Constitutional mandate, patent acts were passed in 1790, 1793, and 1836. The Act of 1836 established the pattern for our present system by providing statutory criteria for the issuance of patents and requiring the Patent Office to examine applications for conformance thereto. Although the law has been amended on numerous occasions—and even rewritten twice since 1836—no basic changes have been made in its general character in the succeeding one hundred and thirty years.

However, during this period of few statutory changes, major developments have occurred in the social and economic character of the country. The United States has undergone a dramatic transformation, creating and utilizing an enormously complex technology, to emerge as the world's most productive industrial community. . . .

Agreeing that the patent system has in the past performed well its Constitutional mandate "to promote the progress of . . . useful arts," the Commission asked itself: What is the basic worth of a patent system in the context of present day conditions? The members of the Commission unanimously agreed that a patent system today is capable of continuing to provide an incentive to research, development, and innovation. They have discovered no practical substitute for the unique service it renders.

First, a patent system provides an incentive to invent by offering the possibility of reward to the inventor and to those who support him. This prospect encourages the expenditure of time and private risk capital in research and development efforts.

Second, and complementary to the first, a patent system stimulates the investment of additional capital needed for the further development and marketing of the invention. In return, the patent owner is given the right, for a limited period, to exclude others from making, using, or selling the invented product or process.

Third, by affording protection, a patent system encourages early public disclosure of technological information, some of which might otherwise be kept secret. Early disclosure reduces the likelihood of duplication of effort by others and provides a basis for further advances in the technology involved.

Fourth, a patent system promotes the beneficial exchange of products, services, and technological information across national boundaries by providing protection for industrial property of foreign nationals.

MACHLUP, AN ECONOMIC REVIEW OF THE PATENT SYSTEM

Study No. 15, Subcommittee on Patents, Trademarks and Copyrights, Senate Committee on the Judiciary, 85th Cong., 2d Sess., 44–45, 50–52, 54–55 (1958).

Patents, by giving their owners exclusive rights to the commercial exploitation of inventions, secure to these owners profits (so-called "quasi rents") which are ultimately collected from consumers as part of the price paid for goods and services. The consumers pay; the patent owners receive. Are the consumers—the non-patent-owning people—worse off for it?

"No; they are not," says one group of economists. Patents are granted on inventions which would not have been made in the absence of a patent system; the inventions make it possible to produce more or better products than could have been produced without them; hence, whatever the consumers pay to the patent owners is only a part of the increase in real income that is engendered by the patent-induced inventions.

"Wrong," says another group of economists. Many of the inventions for which patents are granted would also be made and put to use without any patent system. The consumers could have the fruits of this technical progress without paying any toll charges. Even if *some* inventions are made and used thanks only to the incentives afforded by the patent system, consumers must pay for *all* patented inventions and, hence, lose by the bargain. Moreover, if patents result in monopolistic restrictions which hold down production and hinder the most efficient utilization of resources, it is possible that total real income is less than what it would be without the patent system. Of course, there is impressive technical progress and a substantial growth of national income under the patent system, yet perhaps less so than there would be without patents.

This is but one of the fundamental conflicts in the economics of the patent system. There is another, which is quite independent of any profits collected by the patent owners and of any monopolistic restrictions imposed on production. This second basic problem relates to the overall allocation of productive resources in a developing economy, and to the question whether at any one time the allocation to industrial research and development is deficient, excessive, or just right. . . .

Competition among rival firms which takes the form of a race between their research teams—a race, ultimately, to the patent office —may have various objectives: (a) To be the first to find a patentable solution to a problem posed by the needs and preferences of the customers—a better product—or by the technological needs and hopes of the producers—better machines, tools, processes; (b) after a competitor has found such a solution and has obtained exclusive patent rights in its exploitation, to find an alternative solution to the same problem in order to be able to compete with him in the same market—in other words, to "invent around" the competitor's patent; and (c) after having found and patented the first solution, to find and patent all possible alternative solutions, even inferior ones, in order to "block" the competitor's efforts to "invent around" the first patent.

These forms of "competitive research" were described and discussed by antipatent economists during the patent controversy of the 19th century. Concerning the first form, there was much complaint that other inventors who discovered practically simultaneously "the same utility," but were not the first in the race to the patent office, had to forego their "natural privilege of labor" and were barred from using their own inventions. The fact that there was competition in making new inventions was found to be healthy. But that he who lost the race to the patent office should be barred from using his own invention, and should have to search for a substitute invention, was found to be absurd.

What may appear absurd to a disinterested observer, or unjust and unfair to one who lost the right to use the fruit of his own labor and investment, must to an economist appear as sheer economic waste. Of course, one may regard this as an incidental expense of an otherwise beneficial institution, an unfortunate byproduct, an item of social cost, which, perhaps, is unavoidable and must be tolerated in view of the social advantages of the system as a whole. However, from merely defending the need of "inventing around a patent" as a minor item of waste, the discussion has recently proceeded to eulogize it as one of the advantages of the system, indeed as one of its "justifications."

The advantage is seen in the additional "encouragement" to research. If the competitors were given licenses under the patent of the firm that won the race, they would have to pay royalties but would not be compelled to "invent around" it. Exclusivity, however, forces some of them to search for a "substitute invention." But why should this be regarded as an advantage? The idea is probably that, if industrial research is desirable, more research is more desirable, and that it does not matter what kind of knowledge the research effort is supposed to yield. From an economic point of view, research is costly since it absorbs particularly scarce resources which could produce other valuable things. The production of the knowledge of how to do in a somewhat different way what we have already learned to do in a satisfactory way would hardly be given highest priority in a rational allocation of resources.

This same, or a still lower, evaluation must be accorded to the third form of "competitive research"—inventive effort for the purpose of obtaining patents on all possible alternatives of an existing patented invention just in order to "block" a rival from "inventing around" that patent. In this case inventive talent is wasted on a project which, even (or especially) if it succeeds exactly in achieving its objective, cannot possibly be as valuable as would be other tasks to which the talent might be assigned. When thousands of potential inventions are waiting to be made—inventions which might be of great benefit to society—how can one seriously justify the assignment of a research force to search for inventions that are not intended for use at all—but merely for satisfying a dog-in-a-manger ambition?

There is, however, another "justification" for this kind of "competitive research": it can be summarized in the colorful word "serendipity." This means "the faculty of making happy and unexpected discoveries by accident." The idea is that the research teams engaged in "inventing around patents," or in inventing to obtain patents to "block" other people's efforts to "invent around patents," might by sheer accident hit upon something really useful. In other words, the work of these research forces is justified by the possibility or probability that they might find something which they did not set out to find.

There is no doubt that these happy accidents occur again and again. But can one reasonably let an effort to produce something without social value take the credit for accidental byproducts that happen to be useful? Can one reasonably assert that research not oriented toward important objectives is more likely to yield useful results than are research efforts that are so oriented? Is it easier to find the important by seeking the unimportant? . . .

The most perplexing and disturbing confusions occur in discussions about the "value of patents." This is no wonder, what with the large number of possible meanings in the minds of the writers on the subject: they may be talking about (a) the value of patents to their owners, (b) the value of patents to society, (c) the value of the patent system to society, (d) the value of patented inventions to their users, (e) the value of patented inventions to society, (f) the value of patent-induced inventions to society. But even this is not all, because the social value of inventions may depend on the degree to which they are used, and the value of patents to their owners on the way they are exploited.

Singling out, from this long list, (b) the value of patents to society—and making quite sure that this refers neither to the social benefits of the patent system nor to the social value of the inventions, which are altogether different matters—it is worth pointing out that existing domestic patents held by domestic owners cannot be reasonably regarded as parts of the national wealth or as sources of real national income. To regard them so is as fallacious as it would be to include in national wealth such things as the right of a businessman to exclude others from using his trade name, or the right of a (domestic) creditor to collect from his (domestic) debtors, or to include such things as (domestic) money, securities, damage claims, and lottery tickets. The right of a person to keep others from doing something is no social asset and, again, somebody's right to keep others from using his invention should not be confused with the invention itself. To confuse an important invention with the patent that excludes people from using it is like confusing an important bridge with the tollgates that close it to many who might want to use it. No statistics of national wealth would ever include (domestic) "patent property." And the "destruction of patent property"—though it may affect the future performance of the economy—would leave the Nation's wealth, as it is now understood in social accounting, unimpaired. (An exception must be noted concerning foreign patent rights. One may regard domestic holdings of foreign patents as claims to future royalties and profits earned abroad and, hence, as assets; of course, foreign holdings of domestic patents, establishing foreign rights to future royalties and profits earned here, would then have to be counted among the liabilities and, therefore, as deductions from national wealth.)

C. TRADEMARK

BACKMAN, THE ROLE OF TRADEMARKS IN OUR COMPETITIVE ECONOMY

58 Trademark Rep. 219–220; 226–229 (1968).*

The trademark or brand name has become a key element in marketing many products, particularly consumers goods. It is the means of identifying products of consistent quality and the firms which produce those products. The major role played by the brand name has been caught in the slogan "You Can Be *Sure* If It's Westinghouse."

Paradoxically, the brand name has been described as a monopolistic device although it is a vital ingredient in many competitive markets. Trademarks are intimately tied in with advertising since they provide the identification of the advertised products. Within an industry there may be many competing brands, each seeking to preempt a share of the market. But few, if any, market positions remain impregnable, as new brands seek the favor of consumers or as existing brands are revitalized or refurbished.

Some idea of the multiplication of advertised brands is indicated by the following compilation prepared by *Drug Trade News*. It found advertising expenditures for:

22 brands of vitamins;

78 brands of cough and cold products;

17 brands of headache remedies;

59 brands of ointments, liniments, and other external medication;

33 brands of antacids, laxatives, and stomach sweeteners.

This was not a complete tabulation of all of the brands available. For example, included in the 17 headache remedies were only 5 brands of aspirin. The tabulation did not include Squibb, Norwich, Rexall, McKesson, and the numerous private brands that are readily available. Nor did the tabulation include the many ethical products that often compete with proprietaries.

Many products may be differentiated in some way from competing products even though functionally they may be substitutable. Differentiated products usually have brands so that the product may be easily identified by the consumer. This places a premium on quality, since the consumer can readily blame—or give credit—to the manufacturer. Of course, the existence of a brand does not assure demand by consumers. As in all sectors of our economy, the demand for products covered by some brands may be expanding while in other instances it may be stable or contracting.

It sometimes seems to be assumed that advertisers can sell any product to the public. However, there are many illustrations to show that large-scale advertising by a well-known firm does not assure that a new product can be launched successfully or that existing products will hold their market shares. Perhaps the outstanding demonstration of this point in recent years was the failure of Ford to secure public acceptance of the Edsel as against the public's acceptance of the Mustang. The public must desire a product and be convinced of its superior quality before it will make large-scale purchases.

The multiplication of brands has been criticized because " . . . much product differentiation consists of minor variations in ingredients, shape, color, or the like." But what is the alternative in a competitive economy? Shall we allocate special sectors of the market to different companies as is done under cartels? Or shall we prohibit the introduction of new brands which are not "genuinely new products," however that term is to be defined? Clearly there are inefficiencies inherent in the competitive process. These must be incurred if the benefits of competition are to be realized. Competition is not without its costs as well as its benefits, but its net efficiency cannot be denied. . . .

Competition and Market Shares

Does product differentiation, through the establishment of brands, make it possible for a company to insulate itself against com-

petitive pressures and hence to establish some degree of monopoly?
By building brand loyalty can a company preempt part of a market
to itself even if its product is higher in price than a competitive one?
Some critics of advertising answer these questions in the affirmative.

Practically every market situation combines elements of monopoly and of competition. A brand gives a product an identification
which differentiates it from those of its competitors. The company
that owns the brand has a "monopoly" of its use.

The basic question is which is more powerful: the monopoly of
the brand or the competitive pressures exerted by the alternative
products available? The answer is found in the history of market
shares. If the brand is the dominant factor, then the product should
be able to maintain or even increase its share of the market over
time. On the other hand, if competitive pressures overcome and
hence outweigh the "market power" of a brand, market shares should
change. And the more overpowering the competitive pressures, the
more dramatic the changes in market shares.

Companies recognize their inability to develop complete brand
loyalty when they offer a diversity of brands for similar products in
order to appeal to different groups and to attract the patronage of
those who are constantly experimenting or who are dissatisfied with
other brands. The significant changes in the shares accounted for by
brands in many product markets is a familiar phenomenon.

Actual experience indicates that the "market power" associated
with brands usually is not very potent. Even where brand loyalty is
developed, it does not determine the buying habits of all purchasers.
Varying proportions of the purchasers of all categories of products
have weak brand loyalties. Let me cite a few illustrations.

Soaps and Detergents—Tide's share increased from 13% in 1948
to 35% in 1952 and then declined to 15% in 1967. Rinso, Super-Suds
and Oxydol accounted for 46% of the market in 1948 and less than
9% in 1960 despite their conversion to detergents.

Cigarettes—Between 1956 and 1966, the shares of Camel, Lucky
Strike and Chesterfield each fell by seven percentage points or more,
Pall Mall remained about unchanged, and large increases took place
for Winston, Salem and Kent. These trends were undoubtedly influenced by the cancer publicity.

Dentifrices—Between 1961 and 1965, the first and second brands
switched places and the fifth largest brand in 1961 was no longer in
the Big Five in 1966.

Ready-To-Eat-Cereals—Two of the five largest brands in 1961
had been replaced by 1965; the second largest seller in 1965 was not
in the Big Five in 1961.

Soft Drink Industry—Between 1950 and 1964, the share of
Coca-Cola was cut by ten percentage points while Pepsi-Cola and
Royal Crown each moved forward sharply.

Dry Soups—Between 1962 and 1966, the share of Campbell's Red Kettle brand fell from 16% to 6%; in 1966 it was discontinued. Wyler's moved up from fourth to second place with a rise from 7% to 16%.

Consumers shift their purchasing in response to price differentials, to more effective advertising, to dissatisfaction with a product, to health scares, and to the desire to experiment.

The proliferation of brands has reflected dynamic competition and has resulted in significant changes in market shares. These developments indicate that the degree of market power which supposedly accompanies product differentiation identified by brand name and implemented by large-scale advertising is much weaker than contended.

Against this background of dynamic competition, the conclusions of two intensive studies I have made of price trends in the post-World War II years and of profit rates are not surprising.

Advertising and Price Changes

The price behavior of brand name products, whether heavily advertised or not, differs from that of standardized products such as wheat. Prices for brands tend to be more rigid, neither advancing as much nor declining as much as those for other products, with price changes tending to lag behind those in other industries.

Much of the charge concerning monopoly prices is related to the insulation of these prices from immediate response to changes in supply or demand. That the prices of branded items are not always completely rigid is illustrated by the price specials periodically offered for some products.

Sometimes, this price competition develops through private brands or by the development of new brands. Nevertheless, prices of brand name products tend to be more rigid. Nonprice competition (e. g. improved products, advertising and other promotion, quality changes, etc.), rather than price competition, characterizes these products—as is true for most goods and services whether heavily advertised or not.

The most intensively advertised categories of products have tended to show smaller increases in price than less heavily advertised categories during the post-World War II price inflation. The postwar record of changes in wholesale and retail prices for broad groups of products and for selected foods and proprietary drugs reveals that there has been no relationship between the intensity of advertising expenditures and the magnitude of price increases.

These data show that heavy advertising expenditures did not create a degree of market power which gave the affected industries the freedom to raise prices substantially during this period of general price inflation. It may be asserted that these data merely show that the market power was unexerted but remains a threat in the future.

However, the earlier discussion indicated that the theory that brands create excessive market power is a myth. The price experience reinforces this conclusion.

Advertising and Profit Rates

A study of the relationship between intensity of advertising and profits as a percent of invested capital indicates that in 1964 and 1965, about one-tenth of the difference in profit rates was attributable to relative differences in advertising-sales ratios. The average return earned by the 102 manufacturers with the largest dollar expenditures for advertising was 14.7% as compared with the 13.8% return earned by 2,298 leading manufacturing companies reported by The First National City Bank of New York.

Companies with relatively high advertising-sales ratios tended to have somewhat higher profit rates than less intensive advertisers. These higher profits appear to reflect the larger volume resulting from successful advertising rather than the exercise of market power to charge high monopolistic prices.

KAYSEN & TURNER, ANTITRUST POLICY

69–70 (1965).*

The appropriateness of expenditures on selling and promotion is the other aspect of performance in this class. We seek to determine whether an industry, or some of the firms in it, spends "too much" resources in this way. Although we cannot define "too much," we are not entirely without some guide lines. In the first place, resource expenditure on pure deception or misinformation can clearly be called wasteful. However, much advertising and other selling effort conveys no information at all, strictly speaking, and it is not possible to determine whether this is wasteful in the same sense. "It is better" is a phrase with no specific content, but whether or not the expenditure of resources on repeating it in print or on the air waves is useful, it cannot be called deceptive. Secondly, promotional expenditures by rival sellers which are mutually self-canceling, so that the demand curves of the sellers are the same after the expenditures as they would have been without them, can also be termed clearly wasteful. But it is difficult to determine which expenditures are self-canceling in this respect, and which do alter the pattern of relative demands.

In conceptual terms, we can analyze the results of sales promotion efforts into three components: the provision of "useful information," the test of which, conceptually, is that buyers would be willing to pay for it if it was provided and priced separately rather than tied to the goods promoted; the influencing of tastes, usually in nonrational ways, so that the ultimate pattern of tastes is different than it would be in the absence of all sales promotion efforts except those of the first class; and, finally, the purely mutually stultifying efforts of rival sellers, whose net effects are zero. But in general we have no way of dividing the effects of specific sales promotion activities according to this scheme. Chesterfield advertising may be canceled by Lucky Strike advertising, but together they may increase the demand for cigarettes relative to that for liquor or food. If this is so, the separation of the third class of effects from the second is difficult. Since consumer tastes are essentially nonrational, we cannot logically apply purely rational criteria—that is, usefulness, in the sense defined above—to make a division between what is wasteful and what is not. Even misinformation may be effective in changing consumer tastes; if we define it as wasteful, it is rather on the ground that if the consumer knew the truth he would reject the influence of the promotional effort, but this is perhaps an overly rational assumption about actual behavior.

BROWN, ADVERTISING AND THE PUBLIC INTEREST: LEGAL PROTECTION OF TRADE SYMBOLS

57 Yale L.J. 1165, 1180–85, 1187, 1189–90 (1948).*

Defenders of the institution have two additional lines of defense. The first is that persuasive advertising creates a cluster of values, no less real because they are intangible. The second, related to the first, argues that the sovereign consumer has made a free election between those values and the austerities of price competition.

These considerations bring us to the consumer as an individual. As an individual, instead of a faceless component of mass purchasing power, he is a creature of infinite diversity, with, moreover, a soul. To make a complete analysis of what he gets from advertising, the relations of material rewards and spiritual values, as affected by advertising, would have to be considered. That task we must leave to the philosophers and the psychologists. As was indicated earlier, they have not yet performed it. The only arena which is at all adequately staked out is that of the economic conflict between seller and buyer. The agreed goal is the maximum satisfaction of each consumer, as determined by his free choice in disposing of his income. In a roundabout way, problems of aggregate output and investment, already discussed, bear on the same goal. Now we have to consider how persuasive advertising adds to or subtracts from the sum of the individual's satisfied wants.

What are the intangible values? One is said to be the assurance of reliability, because the advertiser wants to build up repeat sales, and cannot afford to sell patently unsatisfactory goods. Admitting, for the sake of getting on, that unadvertised brands offer a greater

* Copyright 1948 by The Yale Law Journal Co., Inc. Reprinted by permission of The Yale Law Journal Company and Fred B. Rothman & Company from The Yale Law Journal, Vol. 57, pp. 1165, 1180–1185, 1187, 1189–1190.

opportunity for "hit-and-run" frauds, the difficulty with this contention is that the hope of continued custom is quite unrelated to the magnitude of persuasive advertising. Nothing more than information as to source is necessary for the consumer to be able to repeat a satisfactory purchase.

Other values derive from the proposition that cheapness is not enough. The buyer of an advertised good buys more than a parcel of food or fabric; he buys the pause that refreshes, the hand that has never lost its skill, the priceless ingredient that is the reputation of its maker. All these may be illusions, but they cost money to create, and if the creators can recoup their outlay, who is the poorer? Among the many illusions which advertising can fashion are those of lavishness, refinement, security, and romance. Suppose the monetary cost of compounding a perfume is trivial; of what moment is this if the ads promise, and the buyer believes, that romance, even seduction, will follow its use? The economist, whose dour lexicon defines as irrational any market behavior not dictated by a logical pecuniary calculus, may think it irrational to buy illusions; but there is a degree of that kind of irrationality even in economic man; and consuming man is full of it.

The taint of irrationality may be dispelled by asserting flatly that the utility of a good, that is, its capacity to satisfy wants, is measured exactly by what people will pay for it. If, as is undeniably the case, consumers will pay more for an advertised brand than for its unheralded duplicate, then consumers must get more satisfaction out of the advertised brand. The nature of the satisfaction is of concern only to the moralist. Though this argument can easily be pushed to absurdity—suppose it was to the interest of the advertisers to consume half the national product in persuasion?—it seems plausible if it is based on the dogma of consumer autonomy. Then anyone who questions the untrammelled use of influence by the seller and its uncoerced acceptance by the buyer is at best a Puritan, at worst a Fascist. The debate seems to end in a defense of freedom, for the advertiser as well as for the consumer.

But does the sovereign consumer have real freedom of choice? The first requisite of choice is an adequate presentation of alternatives. The classical economists who enthroned the consumer never dreamed that he would make his decisions under a bombardment of stupefying symbols. He should be informed, and willing to pay the necessary price for information. But the most charitable tabulations reveal relatively little information in advertising directed to consumers outside the classified columns and local announcements. National advertising is dominated by appeals to sex, fear, emulation, and patriotism, regardless of the relevance of those drives to the transaction at hand. The purchase of many advertised articles, then, has a raw emotional origin. Many others are compelled by the endless reiteration of the advertisers' imperative: eat lemons, drink milk, wear hats. Pseudo-information fills any gaps. It takes many forms. There is the bewildering manipulation of comparatives and superlatives: "No other soap washes cleaner"; "The world's most wanted pen." In the atomic age, precise scientific data are helpful. Bayer's Aspirin tells us that the tablet dissolves in two seconds. Whether the analgesic effect is then felt in one hour or two hours will no doubt be explained in time. Buick lists among its features such well-understood engineering terms as "Dynaflow Drive, Taper-thru Styling, Vibra-Shielded Ride, Hi-Poised Fire-ball Power." The reader, after ten minutes with a magazine or the radio, can select his own examples of the types of influence that are thought to move the sovereign consumer. . . .

Advertising has two main functions, to inform and to persuade. With qualifications that need not be repeated, persuasive advertising is, for the community as a whole, just a luxurious exercise in talking ourselves into spending our incomes. For the individual firm, however, it is a potent device to distinguish a product from its competitors, and to create a partial immunity from the chills and fevers of competition. The result of successful differentiation is higher prices than would otherwise prevail. The aim, not always achieved, is higher profits. Whether persuasive advertising enhances the total flow of goods by promoting cost reductions is disputable. Whether it swells the flow of investment by the lure of monopoly profits is doubtful.

For the consumer who desires to get the most for his money, persuasive advertising displays a solid front of irrelevancy. The alternatives to what the advertisers offer are not adequately presented, and the choice among advertised products is loaded with a panoply of propaganda for which the buyer pays, whether he wants it or not. However, both buyer and seller profit from informative advertising. In a complex society, it is an indispensable adjunct to a free traffic in goods and services. The task before the courts in trade symbol cases, it may therefore be asserted, should be to pick out, from the tangle of claims, facts, and doctrines they are set to unravel, the threads of informative advertising, and to ignore the persuasive. The two functions are very much intertwined in trade symbols, how confusingly will appear when we try to separate them. . . .

By trade symbols we mean the devices classified in law as trade-marks, trade names, or distinctive appearance of goods. In the marketer's vocabulary, branding and packaging embrace like operations. For present purposes, brand names, trade-marks, or trade names are functional equivalents, and any technical differences may be ignored. They refer to words or phrases used in connection with goods and services to identify and to distinguish them. Non-verbal symbols used for the same purposes, such as colors, shapes, pictures, and designs, have no generally understood label. The word "appearance" when used herein is to be understood as referring to them.

Trade symbols are a species of advertising; their special characteristics are brevity and continuity in use, both of which are essential to their symbolic function. These characteristics make them easy to imitate, unlike most advertising, which may be diffuse and changing.

Consequently, attempts to appropriate advertising values do not usually undertake to copy extensive advertising, but only brand names or appearance. The occasions when the law will prevent or punish any such appropriations presumably have an important bearing on the value of advertising to the advertiser. But the role of the law should not be appraised in terms of the advertiser's interest alone. And from what has been said earlier, it is clear that a distinction must be attempted between the informative and persuasive functions of trade symbols.

The Informative Function

The informative job of trade symbols is conventionally considered to be identification of source; and it is this capacity which courts traditionally have protected. If, by using *A*'s mark, *B* confuses buyers who mean to buy from *A* and rely on the mark to denote *A*'s goods, *A* is injured and can claim protection against the diversion of trade caused by *B*'s appropriation. Besides making *A* whole, the remedies given him are thought to help the misled consumer, whose own action for deceit is practically useless. The buyer should be able to assign praise or blame to the true source; equally, if it adds to his satisfaction to buy goods of specific origin, he should be able to do so. These obvious interests correspond to those of the injured seller, and thus, because of its informational value, the function of identification is a clear case for protecting trade symbols against confusing imitation. . . .

The informative functions of trade symbols outlined above, though they would be independently useful, rarely exist except as part of a larger campaign of persuasion to divert demand toward a particular advertised article. One of the problems of persuasion is the difficulty of concentrating it on a single brand. A rhapsody to toothpaste is likely to benefit the entire cause of overpriced dental hygiene unless it is focused on the advertised product intensely enough to direct a purchase of that product rather than any other dentifrice. Trade symbols are the distinguishing devices which set one brand of toothpaste apart from the other ninety-and-nine. They not only reach over the shoulders of the retailer; they reach from a radio program on Sunday to a compulsive purchase on Friday. The function is still, in a sense, one of identification. But now it is identification not with source, nor with prior purchases. It is identification with advertising. If the advertising is successful, it directs demand to the article bearing the symbol. The symbol itself then becomes a vital link. It is a narrow bridge over which all the traffic powered by the advertising must pass. If an imitator can seize the bridge, he can collect the rich toll; and so it is commonplace that the more highly advertised is a branded product, the more attractive is its symbol to imitators.

With time, the symbol comes to be more than a conduit through which the persuasive power of the advertising is transmitted, and acquires a potency, a "commercial magnetism," of its own.

To recapitulate, we have now seen that trade symbols may serve as a bridge between advertising and purchase, and that they may themselves be the vehicle of persuasion, either because of extensive repetition and embellishment apart from their use on goods, or because the advertiser has selected and somehow appropriated to his exclusive use a symbol which independently predisposes the customer to buy. These characteristics are usually thoroughly intermingled; in any combination they add up to a distinct category which should be called the persuasive advertising function of trade symbols. Others have simply labelled it the advertising function, but we will call it the persuasive function, in contrast to the informative or identification function. The latter comprehends the accepted legal doctrine of identification of the source, and the emerging doctrine of identification of goods (misnamed the guarantee function), which serve generally the same purposes as other informative advertising.

From what has been said earlier about the economic waste and distortion of consumer choice growing out of large-scale persuasive advertising, it should be clear that the persuasive function of trade symbols is of dubious social utility. There seems little reason why the courts should recognize or protect interests deriving from it.

NOTES

1. The object of all intellectual property laws, state and federal, is to attract private investment to the production of specified information. The method employed is a proprietary monopoly enabling investors to appropriate to themselves some part of the value of the information that their investment produced. Copyright attracts investment to the production and distribution of expressive information by promising investors exclusive rights for a limited period. Patent law takes the same approach to stimulate private investment in new, useful and nonobvious technological information. Trademark law encourages firms to invest in symbolic information about their goods and services by prohibiting competitors from using the same symbols on their own wares. Common law copyright, trade secrets and unfair competition have historically served an auxiliary function, protecting information until it has been sufficiently developed to qualify for federal protection under the copyright, patent or trademark laws.

The fact that information is intangible gives special reason for legal protection. Much information has little value to its producer unless it is salable. But few prospective buyers will pay for information until they have had the opportunity to inspect and evaluate it. The dilemma, of course, is that having once examined the information, the prospective buyer possesses it as surely as if he had created it himself. He might be forced to hand back the pages or the device that embody the information, but he cannot be compelled to return the information itself. Within this framework, only a system of property rights that limits others' freedom to use protected information will give the producer any substantial hope for return on his investment.

The intangibility of its subject matter also explains some features of intellectual property law that are not present in real and personal property law. Because information can be used anywhere, unobtrusively, infringements of intellectual property are more difficult to detect and to prove than trespasses on real property or conversion of personal property. Special rules on contributory infringement, vicarious liability and proof of infringement have evolved to secure the proprietor's position against elusive incursions. At the same time, because information can be used endlessly, universally and by unlimited numbers of people, and because no one's use of the information will interfere with the owner's physical dominion over it, courts tend to tolerate far more extensive inroads into intellectual property than they would if it were land or goods that were being taken. Also, courts tend in close cases to side with the user rather than the producer because they know that no further incentive is needed to produce the information in suit. What they wrongly ignore are their decisions' effects on incentives to produce information that is still unknown.

Another distinction from the law of land and goods is that copyright, patent and trademark law each establish threshold standards that information must meet before it will be cloaked with property protection. The imposition of these qualitative standards stems in large part from the concern that, without them, the marketplace of ideas will be clogged with monopolies over the most obvious, unoriginal and common information.

2. Professor Breyer's uneasy case for copyright is carefully examined in Tyerman, The Economic Rationale for Copyright Protection for Published Books: A Reply to Professor Breyer, 18 U.C.L.A. L.Rev. 1100 (1971). One point Tyerman questions is whether the initial publisher will have the lead time advantages claimed by Breyer. "Advances in book publishing technology have seriously diminished the time (and cost) that would be required to copy a given book." Further, "the alleged price insensitivity of book *consumers* may be largely irrelevant since to a great degree it is book *distributors* . . . who actually determine the character of the retail market for most books. Thus, if a copier could offer copies of a particular book at a price significantly below that offered by the initial publisher, many retailers would be willing to tolerate a slight delay in stocking that book in return for the prospect of a greater profit margin on the eventual sale to the public." Pp. 1109–1111. (Emphasis in original.)

As to the fear of retaliation, Tyerman notes that "any stigma that might once have attached to book 'pirating' would probably be removed by the legislature's act of repealing copyright protection. Under these circumstances, it is unlikely that 'fighting editions' would prove to be the significant deterrent to book copying that they might have been in the nineteenth century." In his view, the important question is "how many times could a publisher sell drastically below his costs to drive out a copier and still remain financially solvent?" In a world without copyright, "there would be no safe haven in which the initial publisher could produce a book free from competition in that title and make the profits necessary to finance the production and sale of 'fighting editions' of other titles." P. 1113.

Is it relevant that, at least in the case of best-selling fiction, a principal source of profit lies in the sale of subsidiary rights—rights to serialization, condensation, paperback publication and motion picture production, among others? What effect would the elimination of copyright in books have on returns from subsidiary uses?

3. Both the Breyer and Tyerman articles focus on copyright's connection to the *quantity* of books produced. What about copyright's effects on the *quality* of published books? Does copyright assure the "supply of good books" promised by Macaulay? What is copyright's impact on the different kinds of writings—literary or technical—that may be embodied in books? On the production of musical works and works of visual art?

The quality of works produced under copyright is significantly connected to copyright law's guiding principle that expressions are protected but not their underlying ideas—elemental plots, themes and designs. Because copyright does not protect ideas, it offers no incentive to invest in their production or dissemination, and producers will focus instead on new ways of expressing old ideas. The result is a marketplace crowded with works that, though different in their expressions, are redundant in their ideas. Is this result desirable in the case of fiction, musical composition, paintings and graphics? In the case of technical works, maps and computer programs?

On the economics of copyright generally, see Hurt & Schuchman, The Economic Rationale of Copyright, 56 Am.Econ.Rev. 421 (1966); Plant, The Economic Aspects of Copyright in Books, 1 Economica 167 (1934).

4. Debates over waste in advertising, and the consequent need to distinguish between trademarks' informative and persuasive functions, belong very much to the twentieth century. Yet they also coincide with a doctrinal split that has marked trademark law from its beginnings. Is trademark law a tort system, aimed at protecting consumers from deception as to the source or quality of goods? Or is trademark law a property system, aimed at encouraging producers to invest in the selection, design and promotion of trade symbols?

The first concept, which stems from trademark law's original and continuing alliance with the law of fraud, deceit and passing off, underpins the informative function of trademarks. By identifying the source or quality of goods, trademarks offer consumers accurate and useful information; by prohibiting passing off, trademark law bars competitors from providing erroneous information and making wasteful expenditures. The second concept, that trademarks are property, expands the trademark monopoly from one that is effective only against competitors to one that prohibits anyone from using the mark, without regard for deception as to source or quality. The property rationale, because it enables the mark to transcend the boundaries of a single product or service, offers fertile possibilities for investment in a mark's persuasive functions.

It is impossible in trademark law's day-to-day adminstration to draw a sharp line between the two concepts. Property concepts inevitably creep into even the most blatant passing off cases, and a concern for deceit, however attenuated, is always present in decisions that treat trademark law as a property system. Although the property rationale has been more heavily emphasized in recent years, the evolution away from tort has by no means been uninterrupted. For a superb treatment of trademark law's legal, intellectual and economic history, see McClure, Trademarks and Unfair Competition: A Critical History of Legal Thought, 69 Trademark Rep. 305 (1979).

5.   Patent law, like copyright law, denies protection to abstract ideas. "Surely," notes one writer, "it would be intolerable to give a patent on most of the fundamental ideas that arise from basic research." Turner, The Patent System and Competitive Policy, 44 N. Y.U.L.Rev. 450, 457 (1969). Patent law's threshold standards for protection—nonobviousness, novelty and utility—are far more rigorous than copyright's. The result of these rules is that patent law steers private investment in research and development away from the discovery of fundamental ideas, and away from inventions that make only obvious or non-novel leaps from the prior art. These two pressures, away from fundamental discoveries and merely incremental advances, clearly define patent law's incentive structure. But patent law's intermediate place is by no means an easy one. Indeed, most of the judicial decisions invalidating patents do so on the ground that the patent was granted to too basic an idea or, more frequently, to too trivial a technological advance.

For an interesting analysis of patent law's place in the research and development continuum, see Kitch, The Nature and Function of the Patent System, 20 J. Law & Econ. 265 (1977). Among the general studies of the patent system's operation, in addition to the Machlup monograph excerpted above, are Plant, The Economic Theory Concerning Patents for Inventions, 1 Economica 30 (n. s.) (1934); W. Nordhaus, Invention, Growth and Welfare: A Theoretical Treatment of Technological Change (1969); Polanvi, Patent Reform, 11 Rev.Econ.Stud. 61 (1943); Canadian Department of Consumer & Corporate Affairs, Working Paper on Patent Law Revision (June, 1976).

6.   What are the alternatives to intellectual property for stimulating the production of desired information? The most prominent answer today is government subsidy, both as an alternative and supplement to intellectual property. Much of the basic research conducted in universities, government institutes and even private firms is directly supported by cash from the federal government. Subsidies do not end with basic research and may also be paid to encourage pro-

ducers to implement inventions and consumers to acquire them. Agriculture and instructional technology are two fields in which consumers have been unwilling themselves to undertake the risk and expense associated with adopting new technologies. Government subsidies in the form of county agents and regional educational laboratories have been deployed to overcome the last hurdles to innovation represented by consumer ignorance or indifference. For an analysis of the role of intellectual property and federal subsidy programs in the research, development and dissemination of instructional technology, see P. Goldstein, Changing the American Schoolbook: Law, Politics and Technology (1978).

Subsidies may also be awarded in the form of prizes. One bill before the United States Senate would have authorized a National Science and Technology Awards Council to publish annually a list of no more than ten "most wanted scientific breakthroughs," and to award prizes ranging from $5,000 to $150,000 to the first person to meet the performance criteria established by the Council for each category. S. 1480, 94th Cong. 1st Sess., 121 Cong.Rec. 10832–10834 (1975). Tax incentives can also be used. One method is to allow investors to treat research and development costs as deductible current expenses, rather than as expenditures that must be capitalized and then amortized over the life of the invention. See, for example, Internal Revenue Code § 174. But see, Treas.Reg. § 1.174–2(a)(1) (1974).

7. Where government has subsidized research that is later developed into patentable or copyrightable subject matter, should the developer be denied a patent or copyright on the ground that, since the research was publicly financed, its fruits belong to the public without charge? Is it unfair or inefficient to give monopoly rewards to a private entrepreneur who has paid nothing for the basic research, and to require the public to pay for it twice—first in the tax revenues allocated to the research program, and a second time in increased prices paid for the goods produced? See Leontief, On Assignment of Patent Rights in Inventions Made Under Government Research Contracts, 77 Harv.L.Rev. 492 (1964). Note that some expenditure, private or public, will always be necessary to put an invention into practice. This means that the public will pay a second time, in any event, either through higher prices paid for private distribution or for subsidies to dissemination. Is the real question, then, whether the private or public sector is in the circumstances the most efficient vehicle for dissemination? See generally P.L. 96–517, 94 Stat. 3015 (1980) in the *Statute Supplement*.

Part Two

STATE LAW OF INTELLECTUAL PROPERTY

I. RIGHTS IN UNDEVELOPED IDEAS

BRISTOL v. EQUITABLE LIFE ASSUR. SOC'Y OF UNITED STATES, 132 N.Y. 264, 30 N.E. 506 (1892). LANDON, J.: Assuming, without deciding, that if the defendant has wrongfully appropriated or converted to its own use the plaintiff's property, or infringed upon his property rights or privileges, and has without right made use of them, it ought to respond to the plaintiff for such use, and should render an account to him respecting the same, the question arises upon this complaint whether the subject of the appropriation and use constituted property or property rights of the plaintiff. The plaintiff does not allege that he was the exclusive possessor of the system. His letter to the defendant instances several companies which have used it to advantage, and states that "underlying the whole system is a common-sense plan of advertising." Its use seems to be its disclosure. He does not complain of the use that the defendant has made of it, but seeks to recover for it, as if defendant had used his property. His case is unlike those in which the injunctive process of the court is sought to restrain the disclosure of a secret or the publication of a letter which may prove injurious to business or character. Nor is his case like that of one who writes a tale or treatise or play, or composes a piece of music, or paints a picture, or makes an invention. In such cases there is a production which can by multiplying copies be put to marketable use, and its exclusive ownership be easily preserved and protected. Whoever infringes takes benefits or profits which otherwise would naturally come to the producer. Here the defendant has taken from the plaintiff no profits, nor diverted them from him. Without denying that there may be property in an idea or trade secret or system, it is obvious that its originator or proprietor must himself protect it from escape or disclosure. If it cannot be sold or negotiated or used without a disclosure, it would seem proper that some contract should guard or regulate the disclosure; otherwise, it must follow the law of ideas, and become the acquisition of whoever receives it. The allegation of the complaint that the plaintiff disclosed the system in confidence to the defendant is vague. It does not necessarily mean that the defendant agreed not to use it. It may mean something else. Defendant is at liberty to conduct its business in its own way. It obtained a valuable hint from

33

the plaintiff, and assumed no legal obligation to pay the plaintiff if it should conclude to act upon it. Plaintiff communicated his system without marketing it. It was valuable to the defendant. But what has plaintiff lost thereby? He alleges nothing more than the loss of the sale to a single party who refused to buy. The system, we may assume, was valuable to those who had insurance to sell. Plaintiff does not allege that he had any to sell. He does not allege that his system was marketable, or might have been made so but for the use made of it by defendant. A. wishes to sell his house and lot. B. tells him in confidence that C. desires to buy it, and B. solicits employment to negotiate the sale. A. declines, but, acting upon B.'s communication, meets C., and himself negotiates and closes the contract of sale. B. has no cause of action against A. He had information which he hoped to market, but he parted with it without finding any market. The plaintiff himself communicated his system to the defendant to induce it to employ him, and thus used it as an attractive adjunct to his own self-commendation or in corroboration of it. He could not induce the defendant to "adopt this system and the writer with it." Yet as the defendant acted upon the hint the plaintiff gave to it, and found it profitable to do so, the plaintiff asks the defendant to pay him a percentage of its profits. We do not think the complaint states a cause of action. Judgment should be affirmed. All concur, except VANN, J., not sitting.

OLSSON, DREAMS FOR SALE

23 Law & Contemp.Prob. 34–35, 54–55 (1958).*

Idea submission claims have been a real plague for many years, but, as an attorney writing about idea submitters and advertisers has observed, things have taken a turn for the worse in the past quarter century, as courts now have a tendency to allow recovery where they would not earlier have done so. Consequently, reward is being given prematurely to those who otherwise might turn their mere "ideas" into finished works, and the commercial users of ideas are exposed to danger by the law in some American jurisdictions if they depart from well-worn idea channels. The battlefield in these cases is generally that of the submitted idea for which the submitter later claims that compensation is due him as the result of a use allegedly made by the recipient of the idea.

Such a claim takes one of several guises: that the recipient expressly promised to pay the submitter if he used the idea; that he impliedly promised to pay if he used the idea; that the law imposes an obligation to pay on quasi-contractual unjust enrichment grounds if the idea is used; that the recipient took a property—the idea—belonging to the submitter and used it, thus committing a tort in the nature of a conversion; or, finally, that a fiduciary relationship was violated by the recipient.

Occasionally, the claim is made seriously that a statutory or common law copyright infringement has been committed by the recipient; but copyright lawyers, as we shall see, have had little difficulty, except for a time in opportunity-rich California, in disposing of that contention. It is sometimes claimed that the act of use constitutes unfair competition; and in this area, all lawyers have difficulty, for unfair competition has been made the bridge between law and morality, and all sorts of baggage has been trundled across it since the historic International News Service v. Associated Press case [248 U.S. 215, 39 S.Ct. 68, 63 L.Ed. 211 (1918)] . . . .

Some Statistics

Robert W. Sarnoff, president of National Broadcasting Company, recently said: "In the year now ending, NBC headquarters, its stations, its field offices, its artists, and its producers will have received some three million letters from the viewing public. In New York alone, we will have had more than 41,000 telephone calls praising or criticising our shows, and more than 100,000 telegrams." Dore Schary, one of the motion picture industry's outstanding producers, told recently on a television program that a large studio receives 20,000 stories or ideas a year, of which but twenty are made into motion pictures.

Of the three national TV networks, one, NBC, currently is receiving 30,000 to 40,000 suggestions of all types every year. These figures include everything from letter outlines to pilot films. One department alone received from 7,000 to 10,000 "approaches" a year. From 2,000 to 3,000 get some serious study. Ten thousand story submissions of all types are offered. The effect of this tremendous influx is obvious. At the present time, the idea-submission lawsuits confronting the networks probably account for sixty-five percent of all suits against them in the area of copyright, defamation, right of privacy, and unfair competition.

The extraordinary and multiple claims that result from idea protection are perhaps illustrated best by citing a case of a new program coming on the air and what happened to the network—NBC in this case—that put it on:

On March 1, 1954 the program "Home" was first presented on the NBC Television Network. Prior to its date of first broadcast, NBC had received six idea submission claims relating thereto. The six claims were entirely independent of one another, and each claimant claimed that his idea submission would form the basis of the series to be broadcast. Advance publicity about the program, the only information probably available on which each of the claims could have been based, said little more than that "Home" would be a service-type (as opposed to entertainment-type) program, like a magazine-of-the-air. But this was not the end of our trouble, for following the first broadcast of the program three more claims came in. Two of them became lawsuits. The program went off the air following its broadcast on August 9, 1957. Two of the three idea submission lawsuits concerning it are still pending. As late as July 31, 1957, a motion was noticed for an order enjoining the series three days prior to its going off the air.

The fact that the idea was old was no deterrent to the claims made regarding the "Home" program. A brief search of the exhaustive files maintained by NBC revealed that the network had received submissions of the basic "home" idea since 1929—prior to the earliest of the nine claimants' alleged submissions.

RICHTER v. WESTAB, INC.

United States Court of Appeals, Sixth Circuit, 1976.
529 F.2d 896, 189 U.S.P.Q. 321.

WEICK, Circuit Judge.

The plaintiff-appellants sued the defendants in the District Court to recover damages in the amount of $2,500,000, for breach of contract to develop a fashion design for loose leaf notebook covers and binders manufactured and sold by Westab, Inc., a subsidiary of Mead Corporation. Jurisdiction was based on diversity of citizenship, and the case is admittedly governed by Ohio law.

The case was tried before the District Court without a jury. The facts are set forth at length in the Memorandum Decision of the District Judge, and will be referred to only briefly here in our discussion of the issues.

Plaintiffs were partners in the firm of Richter & Mracky Design Associates, which created and developed designs for products and marketing concepts. In 1964 Mark Seitman, an employee of Richter & Mracky, observed that the school supplies industry was characterized by drabness and a lack of attractiveness in the various product lines. He believed that a school supply firm could improve its sales by using on notebook covers and binders fashion designs and fabrics which matched clothing being advertised in young women's fashion magazines; that such fashion-oriented supplies could be matched as a package so that the fashion-conscious buyer could purchase all items from one company; and that these lines of school supplies could be advertised in fashion magazines rather than in trade journals as had been the practice with school supplies in the past.

Seitman solicited Westab and arranged a meeting for February 10, 1965, with its officers. Westab was the largest manufacturer of school supplies in the country. At this meeting Seitman presented his concept, which resulted in authorization for Richter & Mracky to produce tentative designs and samples for presentation to Westab sales officials. During the meeting a Westab officer suggested that the notebook binders in the fashion line have interchangeable covers, and Richter & Mracky was also authorized to develop this idea.

After the meeting Seitman discussed with Edgar Stovall, Vice-President of Westab, the matter of compensation which included a royalty of five percent of Westab's sale price, to be paid on specific designs submitted by Richter & Mracky and used by Westab. It did not include royalties on the mere concept of fashion design.

During the summer of 1965 Richter & Mracky worked to perfect interchangeable binder covers and to produce fashion designs which it named "Fashion Goes To School." Samples were submitted to Westab. The interchangeable covers became loose when the notebook was opened, and were not practical. The "Fashion Goes To School" concept was submitted at a meeting of Westab's salesmen; it called for a retail price of $4.95 for the package.

None of the designs was acceptable to Westab, and the project was rejected in October 1965 when Westab marketing officials balked at the projected retail price of $4.95 for the package. Westab then paid Richter & Mracky for shop expenses and asked that the work product not be given to competitors.

The concept was then presented to Sears, Roebuck and Company by Richter & Mracky, proposing that the binders would be purchased from Westab. Westab agreed to furnish the binders, but Sears declined to purchase the concept.

In 1965 Westab's research and marketing personnel independently developed a package of school supplies with matching plaid covers, packed together in a transparent shrink wrapper, and called "Campus Mates." This package was a success. In 1967 Westab introduced paisley-patterned binder covers. In 1968 more paisley patterns and stripe patterns were introduced in the "Girl Talk" line, promoted by advertisements in the magazine *Seventeen*. In 1969 Westab coordinated binder fabrics with fashion trends in "The Wet Look" and "The Leather Look" lines. In 1970 the fashion binder lines were promoted in fashion magazines as clothing accessories: "Think of a notebook as something you wear"; "Westab's got notebook ensembles to go along with all those sharp new clothes you've just bought this fall." These fashion lines generated sales revenues in excess of $4.6 million in the years 1966–1969.

In 1969 Seitman first noticed that Westab's marketing strategy resembled the concept which he had presented to Westab in 1965. In 1971 the present suit was brought to recover five percent royalties on all sales by Westab of fashion-coordinated school supplies.

Two theories of recovery were presented: breach of express contract and breach of implied contract arising from the use of a trade secret. The District Court found that an express contract, partly oral and partly in writing, existed but had not been breached; that the contract did not contain the provisions claimed by Richter & Mracky; and that the concept could not be protected as a trade secret because it did not fit within the definition of a trade secret under Ohio law.

THE EXPRESS CONTRACT

Richter & Mracky challenges the finding of the District Court that an express contract existed, the terms of which were not breached. This finding must be affirmed if supported by substantial evidence in the record, and can be reversed only if clearly erroneous.

If the contract called for Westab to pay a five percent royalty only on binders carrying specific designs furnished by Richter & Mracky no breach of contract occurred. There was substantial evidence to support the finding that the contract required Richter & Mracky to submit specific designs and to be paid only for use of the designs so submitted.

On cross-examination of Seitman the following exchange occurred:

Q Tell us what you said?

A How is this to be compensated for us, there is outside work, and you ask how it should be billed for it, and as far as the items that come from the concept Mr. Stovall had clearly said, and I had clearly said, that we would receive a royalty on them.

Q Let me ask you to do this. If you would, consider yourself a tape recorder, could you play back what you said to Mr. Stovall at that meeting of February 10, 1965 concerning the contract, and what you were to do?

A Let's take the next step as per the excitement, let's develop these products.

Q Is that what you said?

A Yes. You are asking what I said to the man.

Q Go ahead, tell all that you said to him.

A He said that we would receive a five percent royalty. I said we would develop the products that showed interest, that there was interest in, we would develop different approaches to the vision as you have expressed in it, as everybody was excited about, and on anything that is used we are to get five percent royalty, and on any work you ask us to do we should bill you outside costs.

That's what I said to him, and that's what he agreed upon. (A. 108–09)

This testimony supports the terms of the contract found by the District Court. In addition, the letters exchanged between the parties in April and May of 1965 can be fairly construed to indicate that a five percent royalty was to be paid for a particular line of binders called "Fashion Back To School," which was to be designed by Richter & Mracky, but which was rejected by Westab's sales managers in October. Finally, Stovall testified that the agreement made between himself and Seitman called for Richter & Mracky to be paid a royalty on sales of items designed by Richter & Mracky.

We conclude that the District Court's finding that an express contract existed calling for Richter & Mracky to be paid a royalty for specific designs submitted by them was supported by substantial evidence, including the finding that such contract was not breached. We further conclude that such findings were not clearly erroneous.

THE TRADE SECRET THEORY

An alternate theory of recovery claimed was that an implied contract arises to pay for use of a trade secret when the secret is divulged as part of a confidential relationship. Even if this principle is a correct statement of Ohio law it cannot create an implied contract in Ohio because the fashion coordinating concept is not a trade secret as defined in B. F. Goodrich Co. v. Wohlgemuth, 117 Ohio App. 493, 498–99, 192 N.E.2d 99, 104 (1963):

> A trade secret may consist of any formula, pattern, device or compilation of information which is used in one's business, and which gives him an opportunity to obtain an advantage over competitors who do not know or use it. It may be a formula for a chemical compound, a process of manufacturing, treating or preserving materials, a pattern for a machine or other device, or a list of customers. . . . A trade secret is a process or device for continuous use in the operation of the business. Generally it relates to the production of goods, as, for example, a machine or formula for the production of an article. . . .

This definition does not include a marketing concept or a new product idea. Trade secret law is designed to protect a continuing competitive advantage, which a company enjoys due to confidential information it possesses, from destruction due to disclosure by a departed former employee. A marketing concept does not by confidentiality create a continuing competitive advantage because once it is implemented it is exposed for the world to see and for competitors to legally imitate.

This conclusion is even more compelling because Richter & Mracky is asking for compensation to cover periods when fashion binders were widely sold on the market by Westab's competitors as well as by Westab. Even if Westab had been paying Richter & Mracky to use the concept, it would have ceased being a trade secret upon introduction of the products, and Richter & Mracky thereafter would have no legal right to the concept.

Any competitive advantage to be gained from use of this concept would last only until a competitor could place similar items on the market. Richter & Mracky would have no remedy against Westab's competitors for their use of the concept.

Prior to sending samples to Westab plaintiffs had disclosed its concept to editorial personnel of fashion magazines, to potential suppliers of fabrics, and to an assistant professor of art at the University of California. When defendant declined to accept plaintiffs' "Fashion Goes To School" concept plaintiffs disclosed the alleged secret to Sears, Roebuck and Company.

THE LEGAL PROTECTION OF IDEAS

We must recognize that firms which sell ideas as their product should be able to protect their right to ask for and to receive compensation for their products just as any other business can. These firms have traditionally been protected by patent and copyright laws. However, intangible concepts which are being sold by many consultants today cannot be protected by patent or copyright statutes.

Richter & Mracky suggests that legal protection is sometimes given to advertising slogans, marketing concepts, and television program concepts. This is true, but such relief is not found under the law of trade secrets. The logical means to protect a marketing concept is a tort action for conversion of intellectual property, or a quasi-contract action for wrongful appropriation of intellectual property. Such a cause of action is quite rare in Ohio.

The general rule of law is that ideas are not the property of anyone under federal law unless patented or copyrighted. Lear, Inc. v. Adkins, 395 U.S. 653, 668, 89 S.Ct. 1810, 23 L.Ed.2d 610 (1969).

If an idea cannot meet the requirements of patent or copyright laws which entitle it to protection, the states can not render such requirements nugatory by affording such ideas protection under state law. Sears, Roebuck & Co. v. Stiffel Co., 376 U.S. 225, 231, 84 S.Ct. 784, 11 L.Ed.2d 661 (1964). There are exceptions to this rule: state protection of trade secrets is considered to be not inconsistent with patent laws. Kewanee Oil Co. v. Bicron Corp., 416 U.S. 470, 94 S.Ct. 1879, 40 L.Ed.2d 315 (1974), (upholding Ohio law of trade secrets).

With respect to ideas which are colorably patentable the law seems clear that states are limited in their ability to protect items not meeting patent criteria. However, with respect to literary property the failure to meet the criteria for copyright protection does not necessarily preclude protection under state common law. This is particularly true of unfinished program concepts presented to the broadcast media. The reason for this toleration of state law copyrighting is that the federal copyright statutes antedate the development of modern marketing concepts and the broadcast media. The need for legal protection of unfinished marketing and broadcast program concepts has not been met by amendment of the copyright laws, so the common law has once again served to meet new legal problems by finding protection for such concepts.

Ohio law recognizes the existence of a common law copyright which protects unpublished works from appropriation when exposed in confidence to another.

Common law copyright protection has been held in other jurisdictions to protect not only polished manuscripts but also advertising slogans and program concepts. However, when protection is to be afforded to a concept rather than to a specific expression, the concept must be both novel and concrete.

The idea of fashion-coordinated designs on binder covers does not appear to meet the test of novelty required in Stevens v. Continental Can Co., 308 F.2d 100 (6th Cir. 1962). There the plaintiff's concept was to place a wood grain design on paper plates and cups. We held that even if wood grain patterns had never been used before on paper plates and cups the idea was not novel because the wood grain design was not novel. The idea of using a design on a particular item is abstract. The design to be used is concrete; but if the design to be used is not novel then no legal protection is available.

In the case at bar Richter & Mracky suggested that Westab apply to their school supplies designs already seen on clothing fashions. Since the designs to be used were not originated by Richter & Mracky, the suggestion lacks novelty according to *Stevens,* supra, and the idea that the designs be placed on binders, standing alone, also lacks concreteness.

While there is authority in other jurisdictions for permitting recovery on an implied contract theory for use of an idea which is neither novel nor concrete in the legal sense, an implied contract theory is inappropriate here because an express contract has been found to exist.

The law does not favor the protection of abstract ideas as the property of the originator. An idea should be free for all to use at least until someone is able to translate such idea into a sufficiently useful form that it may be patented or copyrighted. Thus competition in the use of ideas is a social good, hastening the process of invention.

When a design firm suggests that a particular product be decorated with thematic designs, this act of suggesting should not establish an exclusive right to exploit the idea. Perhaps the design firm will not be sufficiently competent to produce good designs based upon the concept. A concept is of little use until solidified into a concrete application. The idea of fashion designs is useless unless good designs are obtained. If the design firm is incapable of producing good designs the public should not be denied the benefit of the idea if another designer could produce good designs. Thus the principle denying legal protection to abstract ideas has important social interests behind it.

In spite of this policy, firms which specialize in selling abstract concepts may protect their work product by contract. If Richter & Mracky had made a contract with Westab which required Westab to pay a royalty on all fashion binders sold by Westab, the contract would have been enforceable in the courts. Likewise, if the parties had made an agreement in advance of the meeting that any sale arising from the use of concepts presented at the meeting would require royalty payments to Richter & Mracky, the facts here would probably require a judgment for plaintiffs.

We doubt that Westab would ever enter into such a contract, preferring to hear the presentation, or to see the proposed designs, before agreeing to a contract for their use. Such action would merely reflect the fact that an abstract idea has little commercial value until translated into a specific utilization.

Here the contract between the parties called for Richter & Mracky to submit the specific designs called for in the concept, and to be compensated for their acceptance and use. Similarly, when those designs proved to be unsatisfactory, it was the design department of Westab which gave the idea commercial value by developing its own designs which would utilize the concept.

The abstract concept of fashion designs on binders was a sales tool for Richter & Mracky, not a product. Richter & Mracky wished to sell designs, not the concept. The concept was necessary to the firm because it enabled the firm to solicit contracts for the purchase of its designs from a new market, the manufacturers of school supplies. Richter & Mracky obtained value for the idea, and opened up a new market for its design services. However, its design services were not sufficiently superior to the skills of Westab's own designers to cause Westab to purchase Richter & Mracky's product. Westab's own designers produced designs which attracted a significant volume of business, and the company was rewarded by the market for its efforts. The public benefited from this system which permitted competition to develop the best utilization for an abstract idea.

Denying the existence of a legal interest in abstract ideas disclosed in confidence will not as a practical matter impede the flow of ideas between companies. In this case Richter & Mracky never intended to sell its concept of fashion binders; it intended to sell designs to the school supplies industry. The disclosure of the concept was made in soliciting a contract to design binder covers. This disclosure would have occurred regardless of the legal status of the idea disclosed.

We do not find in the circumstances of this case any basis under which Richter & Mracky, or its members, would be entitled to compensation for use by Westab of the fashion design concept.

Affirmed.

NOTES

1. Is *Westab* correct that a "concept is of little use until solidified into concrete application"? Which do you suppose played a greater role in Westab's profits—the marketing idea to emblazon notebooks with fabric designs or the specific designs themselves?

What assumptions does *Westab* make about the efficient division of labor in information industries? Is it correct to assume that workers who come up with the best ideas are also best placed to execute them? That those who are well placed to execute ideas are also well placed to originate them? Does it follow from decisions like *Bristol* and *Westab* that division of labor between idea origination and idea development will occur only within firms? Can contracts effectively bridge the efforts of idea originators and idea developers?

What are the effects of a rule that denies property protection to ideas? Will the denial of protection spur firms both to originate and develop new ideas, or will firms merely take old ideas and develop them into new, concrete forms? Note that the elaboration of an idea into concrete form will not gain protection for the idea itself, but only for the specific form in which it is elaborated.

For a thoughtful analysis of organizational problems surrounding the development of ideas, and some suggestions for institutional innovation, see Udell, The Essential Nature of the Idea Brokerage Function, 57 J.P.O.S. 642 (1975).

2. Should recovery for use of an idea ever turn on whether the submitter is an amateur or, as in *Westab,* a professional? What are the respective expectations, bargaining positions and long-run interests of amateur and professional idea submitters?

Doubtless, the law implies a duty to compensate in the ordinary lawyer-client and doctor-patient relationships. Although the item compensated may be characterized as services rendered, is it clear that these services are really anything other than submitted ideas? The distinction between services rendered and ideas submitted is well illustrated by cases involving an advertising agency's submission of a commercial slogan to its client. Some courts will focus on the act of submission and permit recovery on the basis of professional services rendered, without regard for the slogan's novelty or concreteness. See, for example, How. J. Ryan Associates, Inc. v. Century Brewing Ass'n, 185 Wash. 600, 55 P.2d 1053 (1936). Other courts will ignore the service aspect, weigh the slogan's novelty and concreteness, and deny recovery if these requisites are not met. See, for example, Marcus Advertising, Inc. v. M. M. Fisher Associates, Inc., 444 F.2d 1061, 170 U.S.P.Q. 244 (7th Cir. 1971). Generally, cases in the first, services rendered, category involve established, professional advertising agencies while those in the second category involve amateur submitters. See generally, Havighurst The Right to Compensation for an Idea, 49 Nw.U.L.Rev. 295 (1954).

3. Two marketing professors at the University of Oregon have studied the treatment of unsolicited ideas in a wide variety of firms. Most firms that participated in the survey said that they will evaluate an unsolicited idea, particularly if the idea looks promising. Slightly under one-half of the respondents indicated that they require the submitter to sign a waiver before they will examine an unsolicited idea. Approximately one-half of the firms said that they ignore unsolicited ideas at least in some cases. One firm responded with unusual candor: "most of these [unsolicited ideas] are thrown in the waste basket after we examine them. If we are interested, we proceed [to secure a waiver]."

Some companies receiving unsolicited ideas return the submitted materials together with a waiver form:

Your letter was opened in our mail department. It apparently pertains to a new product suggestion. It is the policy of our company not to accept suggestions from outside sources without first receiving a signed copy of our disclosure form.

Enclosed you will find the material you submitted as well as a copy of our policy statement on unsolicited ideas. A disclosure agreement form is also enclosed for your use if you wish to submit your idea to our company under the terms stated in the enclosed policy statement.

Other companies retain the idea while awaiting receipt of an executed waiver form:

> I do not have a technical background, and one of the obligations of my position is to insure that any information submitted such as yours is neither reviewed by me nor presented for review to anyone else in the company unless and until we have received the non-confidential disclosure agreement I have referred to above. I trust that you will sign the agreement and return it, at which point I will forward the material you sent me to the appropriate personnel for evaluation. Otherwise those materials will be returned to you by me without having been examined or reviewed by anyone. . . .

The waiver forms themselves contain a variety of conditions: that review of the idea imposes no obligation of any kind on the firm; that any review and offer to negotiate is not an admission of novelty, priority or originality; that review of the idea does not impair the firm's right to contest existing or future patents on the idea; that acceptance and review of an idea does not create a confidential relationship; and that the submitter waives all rights except those that may be acquired under patent law.

The study is reported in Hawkins & Udell, Corporate Caution and Unsolicited New Product Ideas: A Survey of Corporate Waiver Requirements, 58 J.P.O.S. 375 (1976).

4. Disillusioned by corporate rebuffs and stymied by inhospitable legal doctrine, idea originators have turned in large numbers to professional idea brokers and invention promoters who for a fee, and sometimes part of the profits, agree to develop the idea and place it with an appropriate manufacturer. One count in 1974 revealed "about 250 idea brokers in the United States, doing about $100 million in business and servicing approximately 100,000 hopeful inventors annually." Udell, The Essential Nature of the Idea Brokerage Function, 57 J.P.O.S. 642, 643 (1975).

Few of these would-be inventors enjoy any success. One promoter disclosed that for every 586 of its customers only four received more income from their inventions than they paid in fees. Another indicated a success rate of two out of 3,200, and another, 3 out of 30,000. Thomas, Invention Development Services and Inventors: Recent Inroads on Caveat Inventor, 60 J.P.O.S. 355, n. 3 at 355–356 (1978). Although client cupidity doubtless contributed to this dismal record, promoter overreaching, puffing and false advertising also played a role. See Abrams, For Inventors: Mostly Promises, N.Y. Times, June 12, 1977, section 3 at 1, col. 5; Shaffer, Caveat Inventor: Concerns that Promise to Assist Gadgeteers are Disappointing Many, Wall Street J., Nov. 30, 1973, at 1, col. 1.

By the mid-1970's, the widespread perception of abuses sparked a fusillade of regulatory efforts. State attorneys general went after promoters for deceptive advertising practices and unauthorized practice of law in advising on the patentability of submitted ideas. The Federal Trade Commission's investigation of the industry culminated in consent decrees or litigation with several major firms. See, generally, Udell & O'Neil, The FTC in the Matter of IRD, Inc.: An Analysis of Recent FTC Action Against Invention Promoters, 58 J.P. O.S. 442 (1976). State legislatures also acted. California passed a pioneer law regulating invention development contracts. The act requires developers to maintain a bond of at least $25,000 and provides for cancellation by either party within seven days of the contract's execution; clear and conspicuous disclosure of fees; and recovery of treble damages, or at least $3,000, by injured customers. Cal.Bus. & Prof.Code §§ 22370 et seq. (West.Supp.1980).

For an excellent overview of practices and regulation in the invention development industry, see Thomas, Invention Development Services and Inventors: Recent Inroads on Caveat Inventor, 60 J.P. O.S. 355 (1978).

5. Idea submissions typically fall into one of four postures: (a) X submits his idea to Y upon Y's express solicitation; (b) X informs Y that he would like to submit an idea of possible value to Y and Y does nothing to block the submission; (c) X thrusts upon Y a full disclosure of his idea before Y has the opportunity to block the submission; (d) X makes no submission at all but charges that Y has copied his idea.

Courts usually act as if these distinctions in posture make no difference when deciding which theory of action to apply to the facts before them. As you read the materials in the next section outlining the theories on which recovery for the use of ideas can be based—express contract, implied in fact contract, quasi contract, property—consider whether one of the four theories is particularly well suited to resolve the interests at stake under each of the four postures.

A. THEORIES OF PROTECTION

LUEDDECKE v. CHEVROLET MOTOR CO.

United States Circuit Court of Appeals, Eighth Circuit, 1934.
70 F.2d 345.

WOODROUGH, Circuit Judge.

Mr. H. W. Lueddecke brought this action at law, as plaintiff, against Chevrolet Motor Company and other corporations (all referred to herein as companies), as defendants, to recover on an alleged implied contract on the part of the defendant companies to pay plaintiff the reasonable value of an idea and suggestion which he alleges he furnished to them. Demurrers were interposed to the petition and were sustained. Plaintiff having declined to plead further, the case was dismissed, and the plaintiff appeals.

The petition alleges that the plaintiff sent the following letter to the companies:

"Dear Sirs: As the proud owner of a Chevrolet Sedan, and also with the knowledge of a man who knows automobiles, I am asking you a few questions and then making you a proposition.

"Do you know that a very serious error has been made in the general location of several of the individual units or mechanisms of the Chevrolet car? Do you also know that within another year or so this very error (unless corrected) will reduce Chevrolet sales by possibly a million or even several million dollars? And again, while I, as well as many others, have had and will still have this error of your designers overcome at considerable expense, it will within a short space of time possibly cause some other low-priced car to become more popular than the Chevrolet.

"While many car owners have gone to the trouble of correcting this defect, I have found neither an owner nor a mechanic who was able to discover the cause of the defect. And, unless corrected, the defect will mean considerable annual expense to the owner of the car, for which there is really no excuse at all.

"The cost of overcoming this defect in a car should not be over 20¢ to 30¢ to you as you build the car if you take the easiest and shortest way out of the difficulty. To the owner who has purchased his car the cost will vary from $3.00 to $7.00 depending on where he lives, in city or country.

"The best way out of the difficulty, however, would necessitate a change of design as suggested above, and that can be done without great expense or without sacrificing the essential features of the design of the car.

"Now, I shall not ask you for a one-eighth royalty on $500,000 or $1,000,000 of sales, but I would like to have you make me an offer stating what such information would be worth to you—or how much you could offer and would pay for the same. Upon receipt of your reply, if your offer is satisfactory, I will give you complete information of the above mentioned changes for the Chevrolet car.

"An early reply will be appreciated.

"Yours truly,"

That reply was made as follows:

"Dear Sir: Your letter of June 27, to the Chevrolet Motor Company, regarding your suggestion to change the design of Chevrolet cars, has been forwarded to the New Devices Committee for attention.

"We have this Committee in General Motors, composed of some of our most important executives and engineers, to review all new inventions submitted direct to the Corporation or through any of its divisions or executives.

"It is against the policy of the Corporation to make any agreement for inventions until we know exactly what they are and have sufficient information to place them before the New Devices Committee for consideration.

"If you care to send us drawings and a description of your ideas, the Committee will be very glad to examine them and let you know whether or not General Motors is interested.

"We always insist, however, that everything submitted to us be protected in some way and would suggest, if you have not applied for patents, that you establish legal evidence of ownership and priority of your idea by having your original drawing signed, dated and witnessed by two or more competent persons or notarized.

"We assure you that, if we find the design of sufficient interest to warrant further investigation, some mutually satisfactory agreement will be made.

> "Yours very truly,
> "New Devices Committee."

That plaintiff then answered:

"Dear Sirs: I have Mr. T. O. Richards' reply (dated July 15th) to my letter of June 27th. Referring to my previous letter you will find that I said that your designers of the Chevrolet car had made a very serious blunder in the location of several of the individual units of the car. I also stated that many car owners have gone to the trouble of correcting the defect, either temporarily or permanently, at considerable expense to themselves. But I have never found either a mechanic or a car owner who knew the cause of the trouble drivers were having with their cars. Because of this fact I thought it expedient and profitable to take the matter up directly with your company.

"Now the matter that I have to present is this: You will find that the body of *all* Chevrolet cars that have been driven 200 miles or more is from one inch to three inches lower on the left side of the driver than on his right side. Because of this the left rear fender especially, in driving over fairly rough or wavy streets or in rounding corners to the right, will quite often strike against the tires. This has been the cause of tearing up tires or of suddenly slowing down the car—thereby making accidents likely. The experience is also annoying to the driver and occupants of the car.

"Many drivers seem to think that the springs on the left side were naturally weak and not so good; others seem to think that they struck a bad place in the road and that the springs lost their elasticity as a result. But the fact of the case is that the car is not properly balanced—right side against left side. On the left side you have the steering mechanism, the starter, the generator, and the storage battery. This, together with a one hundred fifty pound (150#) driver, when one drives by himself, throws approximately three hundred pounds (300#) more weight on the left side than on the right side of the car.

"After I had driven my car about 2,800 miles the body was exactly two and three-quarters inches lower on the left side than on the right side. In order to level the body of the car I had an extra spring leaf put into both the front and rear springs on the left side, and that straightened the body up perfectly. My plan is that you either put in this extra spring leaf in both front and rear springs on the left side of the car when you build the car, or else you should change the location of some of the individual units—shifting those units which could be most conveniently moved to the right side of the car or motor. It is my idea that the battery should be moved from the left side to the right side. This would take about fifty pounds from the heavy side and add it to the light side. Then either or both the starter and generator should be moved to the right side of the motor—they would just about balance the weight of the steering unit and the usual excess weight of the driver over his front seat mate.

"The facts given above cannot be denied, and the remedy is simple and clear. I hope you will find them of profit to your firm. I would appreciate a reply at your earliest convenience.

"Respectfully submitted."

To which the New Devices Committee replied:

"Dear Sir: This will acknowledge your letter of July 22 regarding a system for balancing the weight of cars.

"The Committee, at its last meeting, thoroughly discussed your suggestion but decided, unfortunately, that it would not be advisable to redesign our springs in this manner at the present time. We cannot therefore, see our way clear to go into the matter with you further.

"We appreciate your interest in General Motors and regret that we cannot reply to you more favorably.

"Yours very truly,
"New Devices Committee."

It is then alleged in the petition that the plaintiff, by and through these letters, did sell and convey to the defendants ideas as to how to balance a Chevrolet car so that the fenders would not strike the wheels, and more particularly to balance the car so that the weight would be more evenly divided on both sides, and that he forwarded his ideas in the form that defendants had requested, and that thereafter the defendants had put into force and effect the ideas so submitted by the plaintiff, or a portion thereof, and that the defendants had, since the plaintiff's ideas were presented to them, used the same or substantial portions thereof on all Chevrolet motorcars manufactured by the defendants, and by the defendants' request that the plaintiff forward his ideas to them, and by using the same, or portions thereof, there was an implied contract on the part of the defendants to pay to the plaintiff the reasonable value of said ideas, which said reasonable value it is alleged was $2,500,000.

We are of the opinion that the demurrers were properly sustained by the trial court. In the first place we are not persuaded that the idea communicated in the letters of the plaintiff was a novel and useful idea in which plaintiff could successfully assert a property right. In the second place, the correspondence and alleged conduct of the companies controvert the claim that there was a promise to pay plaintiff for the ideas or suggestions which he transmitted, and there are no circumstances presented from which the law implies such a promise.

It appears from plaintiff's first letter to the companies that it was then known to many others besides the plaintiff that there was a defect in the Chevrolet car as it was being manufactured and sold. Plaintiff did not claim to be the discoverer of this defect in the car. He says: "I, as well as many others, have had and will still have this error of your designers to overcome at considerable expense." "Many car owners have gone to the trouble of correcting this defect." The plaintiff's second letter discloses that the defect he had in mind was that the body of the car was not held suspended in balance by the springs with sufficient strength to maintain a constant equilibrium, but that when the car was used the body would sag down on the left side. The remedy availed of by himself and others was to reinforce the springs on the side where the body sagged. This much of the idea being generally known and common property, the only other idea which the plaintiff conveyed to the defendants is in the suggestion that the defendants relocate some of the individual units contained in the body of the car with reference to the center of gravity of the car, "Shift those units which could be most conveniently moved to the right side of the car or motor." Plaintiff says: "It is my idea that the battery should be moved from the left side to the right side. This would take about fifty pounds from the heavy side and add it to the light side. Then either or both the starter and generator should be moved to the right side of the motor—they would just about balance the weight of the steering unit and the usual excess weight of the driver over his front seat mate."

From these statements it is apparent that the plaintiff did not claim to know just what shifting of individual units from one side of the car to the other would be necessary or practicable to effect the proper balance of the car in use. He recognizes cases when "one is driving by himself and thereby puts the weight of his body on one side of the car." He reflects the thought that there is a "usual excess weight of the driver over his front seat mate." In other words, that, when several passengers are riding in a car, the weight may not bear evenly on both sides of the center of gravity of the body of the vehicle. Plaintiff's suggestion really was that the companies should make experiments in redisposing some of the readily movable units mounted on the car body and in shifting them from the left to the right side of the car until a balance was effected which would turn out to be enduring in use. The plaintiff said, in effect: It is known that your car body sags lopsidedly to the left when it is being used. I suggest that you try shifting the units which can be most conveniently moved until you get a better balance.

Plaintiff did not say that he had made any such experiments himself or that he knew through experiments what the effect of the suggested shifting of units would be upon a car when the car was used. Plaintiff alleges that what the companies did after they got this letter was to shift the battery from the left side to the right side of the car and also other equipment as set out in the letter "or a portion thereof." That is, the defendants, knowing as others knew that the body of their car when the car was used sagged lopsidedly to the left, transposed fifty pounds of batteries to the opposite side and such other movable equipment as they found from experiment (or engineering calculations) sufficed to produce a more effective balance of the car body when the car was in use. The matter would be no clearer or simpler if we had to do with spring wagons or buggies rather than Chevrolet automobiles. The springs of either vehicle have to be strong enough to offset some uneven disposal of weights on the body. The mere idea of experimenting with the disposal of the weights was not novel and useful, and plaintiff had no property right therein.

In Masline v. New York, etc., R. Co., 95 Conn. 702, 112 A. 639, 641, the court stated: "An idea may undoubtedly be protected by contract. But it must be the plaintiff's idea. Upon communication to the defendant it at once did appear that the idea was not original with the plaintiff, but was a matter of common knowledge, well known to the world at large. He had thought of nothing new, and had therefore no property right to protect which would make his idea a basis of consideration for anything. His valuable information was a mere idea, worthless so far as suggesting anything new was concerned, known to every one, to the use of which the defendant had an equal right with himself."

In the second place, the letter of the New Devices Committee of the companies to the plaintiff contains no promise to pay for any mere suggestion or idea which the plaintiff might choose to send them. They said it was against the policy of the companies to make any agreement for inventions until they knew exactly what they were. They suggested that plaintiff establish legal evidence of his ownership of his ideas by having his original drawing notarized. In the first letter plaintiff said: "I, as well as many others, have had and will still have this error of your designers overcome at considerable expense." "The best way out of the difficulty would necessitate a change of design." And, therefore, the committee suggested that plaintiff send drawings and a description of his ideas, and that he establish legal evidence of ownership and priority of his ideas by having his original drawing signed or notarized, and that, if they found the design of sufficient interest to warrant further investigation, some mutually satisfactory agreement would be made.

The clear implication is that the companies did not make any agreement to pay for merely pointing out some defect in the Chevrolet car or for any mere suggestion that they perfect the car by experimentation or improvement of their own working out, but if the plaintiff should submit a design with drawings and descriptions of his ideas, then, if the design was of sufficient interest to warrant investigation, an agreement would be made. As the plaintiff did not submit any "design" or "drawings and description of his ideas" or bring himself within the committee's proposal or offer, he cannot successfully claim a contract, even if he had an idea in which he had a property right and which he could make a subject of barter and sale. The correspondence shows that the minds of the parties never met on any proposed sale of plaintiff's ideas. The law will not imply a promise on the part of any person against his own express declaration. Municipal Waterworks Co. v. City of Ft. Smith (D.C.) 216 F. 431; Landon v. Kansas City Gas Co., 300 F. 351 (D.C.); Boston Ice Co. v. Potter, 123 Mass. 28, 25 Am.Rep. 9; Earle v. Coburn, 130 Mass. 596. In the latter case it is stated: "As the law will not imply a promise, where there was an express promise, so the law will not imply a promise of any person against his own express declaration; because such declaration is repugnant to any implication of a promise."

If, in fact, the defendants did derive benefit from the plaintiff's ideas that the units on their Chevrolet car should be shifted, and if their subsequent redisposal of some of the units to the other side of the car body was in any wise inspired by the plaintiff's idea, nevertheless, they are not indebted to the plaintiff, because they did not offer to make any agreement to pay for such mere suggestion as the plaintiff made, and their correspondence did not invite such a suggestion. When plaintiff voluntarily divulged his mere idea and suggestion, whatever interest he had in it became common property, and, as such, was available to the defendants. In Bristol v. Equitable Life Assur. Soc'y [132 N.Y. 264, 267, 30 N.E. 506, 507] the court stated: "Without denying that there may be property in an idea or trade secret or system, it is obvious that its originator or proprietor must himself protect it from escape or disclosure. If it cannot be sold or negotiated or used without a disclosure, it would seem proper that some contract should guard or regulate the disclosure; otherwise, it must follow the law of ideas, and become the acquisition of whoever receives it."

The judgment is affirmed.

STANLEY v. COLUMBIA BROADCASTING SYSTEM, INC., 35 Cal.2d 653, 674–76, 221 P.2d 73, 86 U.S.P.Q. 520 (1950). TRAYNOR, J., dissenting: The policy that precludes protection of an abstract idea by copyright does not prevent its protection by contract. Even though an idea is not property subject to exclusive ownership, its disclosure may be of substantial benefit to the person to whom it is disclosed. That disclosure may therefore be consideration for a promise to pay. Unlike a copyright, a contract creates no monopoly; it is effective only between the contracting parties; it does not withdraw the idea from general circulation. Any person not a party to the contract is free to use the idea without restriction.

Even though the idea disclosed may be "widely know [sic] and generally understood," Schonwald v. F. Burkart Mfg. Co., 356 Mo. 435, 202 S.W.2d 7, 13, it may be protected by an express contract providing that it will be paid for regardless of its lack of novelty. An implied-in-fact contract differs from an express contract only in that the promise is not expressed in language but implied from the promisor's conduct. It is not a reasonable assumption, however, in the absence of an express promise, or unequivocal conduct from which one can be implied, that one would obligate himself to pay for an idea that he would otherwise be free to use. Even an express contract to pay for "valuable information" to be submitted by the plaintiff does not carry the implication of a promise to pay if it is found upon disclosure to be common knowledge. Masline v. New York, New Haven & Hartford R. Co., 95 Conn. 702, 708, 112 A. 639. If the idea is not novel, the evidence must establish that the promisor agreed expressly or impliedly to pay for the idea whether or not it was novel.

The gravamen of plaintiff's cause of action is not the unauthorized use of his idea, since ideas may be freely borrowed, but the breach of an agreement to pay for its use. If the evidence discloses that there is no express or implied-in-fact contract there can be no recovery. It is urged that even in the absence of express or implied contract recovery may be predicated upon a quasi-contract, or implied-in-law promise to pay the reasonable value of the idea if it is used. Quasi-contractual liability, however, is based, not upon any evidence of consensual agreement but in the absence of such agreement, upon the theory that the defendant would be unjustly enriched if he were allowed to use the idea without paying for it. A defendant who makes use of an abstract idea that is common property is not unjustly enriched thereby, since he has taken nothing to which the plaintiff or any other person has the right of exclusive ownership. Given the principle that abstract ideas are free, there is no more right to recovery for their use in an action in quasi-contract than in an action for infringement of copyright. It has been consistently held that an action in quasi-contract for the use of an idea is governed by the same principles that control a tort action for copyright infringement: the idea must be embodied in a concrete form attributable to plaintiff's own ingenuity, and the form as distinguished from the abstract idea must be used by the defendant. In either case the plaintiff must prove that property was taken that was his. His choice of alternative actions is analogous to that of a plaintiff whose personal property has been converted and who may elect between a tort action for the value of the converted property and an action based upon an implied-in-law contract to pay the reasonable value of its use. The plaintiff's election will govern the nature of his recovery, but it does not affect the basic elements of his cause of action.

DOWNEY v. GENERAL FOODS CORP.

Court of Appeals of New York, 1972.
31 N.Y.2d 56, 286 N.E.2d 257, 175 U.S.P.Q. 374.

FULD, Chief Judge.

The plaintiff, an airline pilot, brought this action against the defendant General Foods Corporation to recover damages for the alleged misappropriation of an idea. It is his claim that he suggested that the defendant's own gelatin product, "Jell-O," be named "Wiggley" or a variation of that word, including "Mr. Wiggle," and that the product be directed towards the children's market; that, although the defendant disclaimed interest in the suggestion, it later offered its product for sale under the name "Mr. Wiggle." The defendant urges —by way of affirmative defense—that the plaintiff's "alleged 'product concept and name' was independently created and developed" by it. The plaintiff moved for partial summary judgment "on the question of liability" on 5 of its 14 causes of action and the defendant crossmoved for summary judgment dismissing the complaint. The court at Special Term denied both motions, and the Appellate Division affirmed, 37 A.D.2d 250, 323 N.Y.S.2d 578, granting leave to appeal to this court on a certified question.

The plaintiff relies chiefly on correspondence between himself and the defendant, or, more precisely, on letters over the signature of a Miss Dunham, vice-president in charge of one of its departments. On February 15, 1965, the plaintiff wrote to the defendant, stating that he had an "excellent idea to increase the sale of your product JELL-O . . . making it available for children". Several days later, the defendant sent the plaintiff an "Idea Submitted Form" (ISF) which included a form letter and a space for explaining the idea.[2] In that form, the plaintiff suggested, in essence, that the product "be packaged & distributed to children under the name 'WIG-L-E' (meaning wiggly or wiggley) or 'WIGGLE-E' or 'WIGGLE-EEE'. or 'WIGLEY.'" He explained that, although his children did not "get especially excited about the Name JELL-O, or wish to eat it", when referred to by that name, "the kids really took to it fast" when his wife "called it 'wiggle-y,'" noting that they then "associate[d] the name to the 'wiggleing' dessert." Although this is the only recorded proof of his idea, the plaintiff maintains that he sent Miss

---

2. The form letter—signed and returned by the plaintiff—recited that "I submit this suggestion with the understanding, which is conclusively evidenced by my use and transmittal to you of this form, that this suggestion is not submitted to you in confidence, that no confidential relationship has been or will be established between us and that the use, if any, to be made of this suggestion by you and the compensation to be paid therefor, if any, if you use it, are matters resting solely in your discretion."

Dunham two handwritten letters in which he set forth other variations of "Wiggiley," including "Mr. Wiggley, Wiggle, Wigglee." [3]

A letter, dated March 8, 1965, over the signature of Miss Dunham, acknowledged the submission of the ISF and informed the plaintiff that it had no interest in promoting his suggestion. However, in July, the defendant introduced into the market a Jell-O product which it called "Mr. Wiggle." The plaintiff instituted the present action some months later. In addition to general denials, the answer contains several affirmative defenses, one of which, as indicated above, recites that the defendant independently created the product's concept and name before the plaintiff's submission to it.

In support of its position, the defendant pointed to depositions taken by the plaintiff from its employees and from employees of Young & Rubicam, the firm which did its advertising. From these it appears that the defendant first began work on a children's gelatin product in May, 1965—three months after the plaintiff had submitted his suggestion—in response to a threat by Pillsbury Company to enter the children's market with a product named "Jiggly." Those employees of the defendant in charge of the project enlisted the aid of Young & Rubicam which, solely on its own initiative, "came up with the name 'Mr. Wiggle' ". In point of fact, Miss Dunham swore in her deposition that she had had no knowledge whatever of the plaintiff's idea until late in 1966, shortly before commencement of his suit; that ideas submitted by the general public were kept in a file by an assistant of hers "under lock and key"; and that no one from any other of the defendant's departments ever asked to research those files. The assistant, who had alone handled the correspondence with the plaintiff over Miss Dunham's signature—reproduced by means of a signature duplicating machine—deposed that she had no contact whatsoever with Young & Rubicam and had never discussed the name "Wiggle" or "Mr. Wiggle" with any one from that firm.

In addition to the depositions of its employees and the employees of its advertising agency, the defendant submitted documentary proof of its prior use of some form of the word "wiggle" in connection with its endeavor to sell Jell-O to children. Thus, it submitted (1) a copy of a report which Young & Rubicam furnished it in June of 1959 proposing "an advertising program directed at children as a means of securing additional sales volume"; (2) a copy of a single dimensional reproduction of a television commercial, prepared in 1959 and used thereafter by the defendant in national and local television broadcasts, which contained the phrase, "ALL THAT WIGGLES IS NOT JELL-O"; and (3) a copy of a newspaper advertisement that appeared in 1960, depicting an Indian "squaw" puppet and her "papoose" preparing Jell-O—the "top favorite in every American tepee"—and suggesting to mothers that they "[m]ake a wigglewam of Jell-O for your tribe tonight!"

---

3. Neither of these letters was found in the defendant's files, nor did the plaintiff have the originals or exact copies.

The critical issue in this case turns on whether the idea suggested by the plaintiff was original or novel. An idea may be a property right. But, when one submits an idea to another, no promise to pay for its use may be implied, and no asserted agreement enforced, if the elements of novelty and originality are absent, since the property right in an idea is based upon these two elements. (See Soule v. Bon Ami Co., 201 App.Div. 794, 796, 195 N.Y.S. 574, 575, affd. 235 N.Y. 609, 139 N.E. 754; Bram v. Dannon Milk Prods., 33 A.D.2d 1010, 307 N.Y.S.2d 571.) The *Bram* case is illustrative; in reversing Special Term and granting summary judgment dismissing the complaint, the Appellate Division made it clear that, despite the asserted existence of an agreement, the plaintiff could not recover for his idea if it was not original and had been used before (33 A.D.2d, at p. 1010, 307 N.Y.S.2d 571): "The idea submitted by the plaintiff to the defendants, the concept of depicting an infant in a highchair eating and enjoying yogurt, was lacking in novelty and had been utilized by the defendants . . . prior to its submission. Lack of novelty in an idea is fatal to any cause of action for its unlawful use. In the circumstances a question of fact as to whether there existed an oral agreement between the parties would not preclude summary judgment."

In the case before us, the record indisputably establishes, first, that the idea submitted—use of a word ("wiggley" or "wiggle") descriptive of the most obvious characteristic of Jell-O, with the prefix "Mr." added—was lacking in novelty and originality and, second, that the defendant had envisaged the idea, indeed had utilized it, years before the plaintiff submitted it. As already noted, it had made use of the word "wiggles" in a 1959 television commercial and the word "wigglewam" in a 1960 newspaper advertisement. It was but natural, then, for the defendant to employ some variation of it to combat Pillsbury's entry into the children's market with its "Jiggly." Having relied on its own previous experience, the defendant was free to make use of "Mr. Wiggle" without being obligated to compensate the plaintiff.

It is only necessary to add that, in light of the complete pretrial disclosure in this case of every one who had any possible connection with the creation of the name, the circumstance, adverted to by the courts below, that the facts surrounding the defendant's development of the name were within the knowledge of the defendant and its advertising agency does not preclude a grant of summary judgment. In the present case, it was shown beyond peradventure that there was no connection between Miss Dunham's department and the defendant's other employees or the employees of the advertising outfit who took part in the creation of "Mr. Wiggle." In exhaustive discovery proceedings—which included examinations of all parties concerned either with that name or the defendant's idea files—the plaintiff was furnished with every conceivable item of information in the defendant's possession bearing on the privacy and confidentiality of such files and on the absence of access to them by those outside of Miss

Dunham's department. The hope expressed by the plaintiff that he may be able to prove that the witnesses who gave testimony in examinations before trial lied, is clearly insufficient to create an issue of fact requiring a trial or defeat the defendant's motion for summary judgment.

The order appealed from should be reversed, without costs, the question certified answered in the negative and the defendant's motion for summary judgment dismissing the complaint granted.

BURKE, SCILEPPI, BERGAN, BREITEL, JASEN and GIBSON, JJ., concur.

Order reversed, without costs, and case remitted to Special Term for further proceedings in accordance with the opinion herein. Question certified answered in the negative.

NOTES

1. *Property.* "*In the first place we are not persuaded that the idea communicated in the letters of the plaintiff was a novel and useful idea in which plaintiff could successfully assert a property right.*" [*Lueddecke*, p. 347.]

Idea submitters rarely succeed on a property theory. Any expression of an idea that is sufficiently novel and concrete to qualify on the property ground could probably also qualify for protection under one of the more developed and traditional intellectual property systems like trade secret or patent law. Thus, when courts invoke property doctrine in idea cases it is usually as a gentle way of telling the submitter that recovery will not be allowed.

Yet, from time to time and in special circumstances, property doctrine is applied to allow recovery. At one time, the California Supreme Court took a maverick route, actively giving property protection to ideas. So long as the idea was "novel and reduced to concrete form prior to its appropriation by the defendant," it could in the court's opinion qualify for property as well as contract protection. See, for example, Golding v. R. K. O. Pictures, Inc., 35 Cal.2d 690, 221 P.2d 95, 86 U.S.P.Q. 537 (1950); Stanley v. Columbia Broadcasting System, Inc., 35 Cal.2d 653, 221 P.2d 73, 86 U.S.P.Q. 529 (1950). The court later returned to the mainstream, substantially adopting the approach suggested by Justice Traynor in his *Stanley* dissent excerpted above. See Kurlan v. Columbia Broadcasting System, Inc., 40 Cal.2d 799, 256 P.2d 962, 97 U.S.P.Q. 556 (1953); Weitzenkorn v. Lesser, 40 Cal.2d 778, 256 P.2d 947, 97 U.S.P.Q. 545 (1953). But just three years later, in Desny v. Wilder, 46 Cal.2d 715, 299 P.2d 257, 110 U.S.P.Q. 433 (1956), the court intimated that the property ground was not completely moribund. See also, Blaustein v. Burton, 9 Cal. App.3d 161, 88 Cal.Rptr. 319, 168 U.S.P.Q. 779 (1970), which draws extensively on *Desny* and, incidentally, provides a fascinating glimpse of customs in the motion picture industry.

Can trade custom create property rights in ideas? Consider the following passage from Cole v. Phillips H. Lord, Inc., 262 App.

Div. 116, 117, 120, 28 N.Y.S.2d 404, 50 U.S.P.Q. 490, 491–492 (1st Dept.1941), in which plaintiff, who had conceived and communicated to defendant production company the format for a radio series, "Racketeer and Co.," sought to recover a share of the profits from defendant's sale of the series idea under the title, "Mr. District Attorney," to a radio network:

> Plaintiff's testimony and that of the witness Titterton, who was not only disinterested but might have been partial to the defendant by reason of the fact that his employer, National Broadcasting Company, had purchased the rights to defendant's alleged creation, established that in the radio field there is a well recognized right to an original idea or combination of ideas, set forth in a formula for a program. Such program contemplates an indefinite number of broadcasts in a series. Each broadcast has a script which represents a dialogue and 'business' of that particular broadcast. The idea or the combination of ideas formulated into a program remains constant whereas, of course, the script varies in each separate broadcast.

> That a property right exists with respect to a combination of ideas evolved into a program as distinguished from rights to particular scripts, finds support in defendant's own course of conduct. When it transferred any rights to Mr. District Attorney, it sold not scripts but the basic idea.

Special trade assumptions can, of course, also be construed to permit recovery on a more orthodox contract basis. See, for example, Donahue v. Ziv Television Programs, Inc., 245 Cal.App.2d 593, 54 Cal.Rptr. 130, 151 U.S.P.Q. 657 (1966).

2. *Express Contract.* *"He had thought of nothing new, and had therefore no property right to protect which would make his idea a basis of consideration for anything."* [*Lueddecke,* p. 348, quoting from Masline v. New York, N. H. & H. R. Co., 95 Conn. 702, 112 A. 639 (1921).]

Under the facts of *Masline,* plaintiff, a brakeman and baggage-master on defendant's line, informed defendant "that he had information of value in the operation of the defendant's road by which, if applied by the defendant, it could earn at least $100,000 a year therefrom without any expense on the part of the defendant, and that the plaintiff would furnish the defendant this information for a valuable consideration." Subsequently, plaintiff and defendant orally "agreed that, if the plaintiff would submit his proposition, and if said proposition was adopted and acted upon by the defendant, the plaintiff should receive as compensation for imparting such information," five percent of the receipts. Plaintiff then disclosed the idea that defendant sell advertising space in its cars and railway depots. Defendant promptly implemented the idea but refused to compensate plaintiff. Although the court found that, before plaintiff's disclosure, defendant had never used this type of plan, it found, too, that the idea "was not new . . . but was perfectly obvious to all men." From this, the court reasoned, the idea "could have no market value so as to form the consideration for a contract . . . and that the idea was not property nor did it constitute consideration for a promise." 112 A. 639–640.

Should the fact that an idea is insufficiently novel and concrete to qualify as property also disqualify it as contract consideration? Could consideration have been found in plaintiff's bargained-for act of disclosure? High v. Trade Union Courier Pub. Corp., 31 Misc.2d 7, 69 N.Y.S.2d 526 (Sup.Ct.1946) states what appears to be the New York position: "While the idea disclosed may be common or even open to public knowledge, yet such disclosure, if protected by contract, is sufficient consideration for the promise to pay." 69 N.Y.S. 2d 526, 529. Does the emphasis in Downey v. General Foods on proof of "novelty and originality" suggest that New York may be slipping into the *Masline* approach?

Would the *Masline* court have better reached the same result by implying into the contract a condition that compensation would be paid only if the disclosed idea were concrete and novel? By finding that defendant had acted not on plaintiff's disclosure but rather on its own general knowledge and initiative?

If an idea recipient first agrees to pay for an idea after it has been disclosed to him, will the contract fail for lack of consideration? Smith v. Recrion Corp., 91 Nev. 666, 541 P.2d 663, 191 U.S.P.Q. 397 (1975) held that if the recipient subsequently promised compensation, "the promise would be unenforceable for the reason that it would have been unsupported by consideration. Past consideration is the legal equivalent of no consideration." 91 Nev. 666, 669, 541 P.2d 663, 665. Compare Desny v. Wilder, 46 Cal.2d 715, 738, 299 P.2d 257, 269, 110 U.S.P.Q. 433, 442 (1956) ("where an idea has been conveyed with the expectation by the purveyor that compensation will be paid if the idea is used, there is no reason why the producer who has been the beneficiary of the conveyance of such an idea, and who finds it valuable and is profiting by it, may not then for the first time, although he is not at that time under any legal obligation so to do, promise to pay a reasonable compensation for that idea—that is, for the past service of furnishing it to him—and thus create a valid obligation.").

3. *Contract Implied in Fact.* "*The correspondence shows that the minds of the parties never met on any proposed sale of plaintiff's ideas. The law will not imply a promise on the part of any person against his own express declaration.*" [*Lueddecke*, p. 348].

The relationship of the parties is the fact most often examined in determining whether a contract is to be implied. If the submitter can show a confidential relationship with the recipient, he has gone far toward making out a case for recovery. Proof of confidential relationship forms the basis for a series of inferences that can lead logically to implication of a contract: disclosure of an idea within a confidential relationship indicates that the idea is disclosed in confidence; that the idea is disclosed in confidence indicates that the originator does not intend to divest his rights in it by publication, at least not without compensation; acceptance of the idea by the recipient in confidence suggests his understanding that he is not to publish or otherwise use it without the originator's consent, at least not without compensating him for the use.

Are actions for breach of confidence respecting disclosed ideas properly classified as actions for breach of implied contract or as tort actions for breach of confidential relationship?　The distinction may be critical when it comes to determining the appropriate statute of limitations.　See, for example, Davies v. Krasna, 14 Cal.3d 502, 121 Cal.Rptr. 705, 535 P.2d 1161 (1975).

4.　*Quasi Contract*.　*"If, in fact, the defendants did derive benefit from the plaintiff's ideas* . . . *nevertheless, they are not indebted to the plaintiff because they did not offer to make any agreement to pay for such mere suggestion as the plaintiff made* . . ."
[*Lueddecke*, p. 348.]

Compare Matarese v. Moore-McCormack Lines, 158 F.2d 631, 71 U.S.P.Q. 311 (2d Cir. 1946), which raised the issue "whether a corporation may be required to pay the reasonable value of the use of certain inventive ideas disclosed by an employee to an agent of the corporation in the expectation of payment where an express contract fails for want of proof of the agent's authority."　158 F.2d 631, 632. The court answered in the affirmative.　The agent's "promise of compensation, the specific character, novelty and patentability of plaintiff's invention, the subsequent use made of it by defendants, and the lack of compensation given the plaintiff—all indicate that the application of the principle of unjust enrichment is required."　158 F.2d 631, 634.　The court was careful to distinguish *Lueddecke*: "Courts have justly been assiduous in defeating attempts to delve into the pockets of business firms through spurious claims for compensation for the use of ideas.　Thus to be rejected are attempts made by telephoning or writing vague general ideas to business corporations and then seizing upon some later general similarity between their products and the notions propounded as a basis for damages . . . See *Lueddecke v. Chevrolet Motors*. . . . "　158 F.2d 631, 634.

5.　The words "novel and concrete" appear in virtually all idea cases and have taken on almost talismanic significance.　The terms have nonetheless gained little specific content.　Presumably, "novel" means the opposite of "common" or, perhaps, "old."　"Concrete" is probably the antithesis of "abstract," and also implies that, to be protectable, the ideas must be reduced to tangible form.　Beyond this, the decisions offer nothing definitive.

Novelty.　Why did the court find that the idea in Downey v. General Foods was not novel and original?　Because it did little more than reflect the tendency of defendant's product to wiggle?　Because it consisted of no more than two words in common use?　Because no substantial investment was needed to produce the idea?　Because defendant had previously considered, but shelved, the possible use of the term? Because somebody else, somewhere, had probably coined the phrase previously?

To the extent that the term "novel" is intended to refer to a specific attribute, such as newness, how well equipped are courts to measure the attribute? Patent law uses the term "novel" in a very precise sense, and assumes that novelty will be determined through systematic searches of prior art in the Patent and Trademark Office and in the relevant technical literature. See pages 454 to 477. Are similar searches possible, or desirable, in the context of submitted ideas?

Concreteness. "The law shies away from according protection to vagueness, and must do so especially in the realm of ideas with the obvious dangers of a contrary rule." Hamilton Nat'l Bank v. Belt, 210 F.2d 706, 708, 99 U.S.P.Q. 388 (D.C.Cir. 1953). Plaintiff in *Hamilton* sought to recover for the bank's use of an idea he had submitted for organizing and sponsoring radio broadcasts of student talent shows. In the court's view, "If the idea had been merely to broadcast programs of selected student talent it would have been too general and abstract and perhaps would also have lacked newness and novelty. On the other hand, had the plan been accompanied with a script for each broadcast it would have been sufficiently concrete." 210 F.2d 706, 709. The court observed that plaintiff's submission fell somewhere between these two poles and affirmed a judgment for plaintiff: "where the plan is for a series of broadcasts the contents of which depend upon selection of talent at different times, a detailed program cannot be presented at the preliminary stages of negotiation." 210 F.2d 706, 709.

A finding that the submitted idea is novel and concrete does not guarantee recovery even if the other required property or contract elements are found. For the submitter to recover, the court must also find that the recipient used the idea in its concrete form. Thus, Hamilton Bank probably would have escaped liability if it had used Belt's basic idea—a weekly broadcast of student talent—but had varied the trappings from those described in Belt's presentation. See Official Airlines Schedule Information Serv., Inc. v. Eastern Air Lines, Inc., 333 F.2d 672, 141 U.S.P.Q. 546 (5th Cir. 1964) (affirming grant of motion to dismiss plaintiff's complaint that its idea for "Plane Facts"—an hourly, joint airline radio broadcast of flight schedule information—which had been submitted to defendant in 1961, was appropriated when, in 1962, defendant began its hourly "Flite Facts" program broadcasting information concerning its flights only).

6. At least in the abstract, the theory of action pursued will determine the measure of damages for idea appropriations. If an express contract is proved, its terms on compensation will govern. For a factually implied contract the measure will be what the defendant is presumed to have agreed to pay, or the reasonable value of the material. If recovery is based on quasi contract, the damage is defendant's unjust enrichment—what it actually profited from the use of the material. See Robbins v. Frank Cooper Associates, 19 A.D.2d

242, 244, 241 N.Y.S.2d 259 (1st Dept. 1963), rev'd 14 N.Y.2d 913, 252 N.Y.S.2d 318 (1964).

Because there is no fluent market for undeveloped ideas, and because the recipient who must pay the award is typically the only one who has used the idea, recovery will frequently be measured by evidence of the idea's value to the recipient. The main problem of measurement lies in identifying the extent to which the submitted idea contributed to the recipient's profits.

In Brunner v. Stix, Baer & Fuller Co., 352 Mo. 1225, 181 S.W.2d 643 (1944), the court found that defendant department store had successfully employed plaintiff's plan to promote the store's charge account operation. As to damages, the court ruled: "The complaint against plaintiff's instruction No. 2 is directed to that portion which authorized the jury to 'consider net results, if any, secured for defendant by said plan,' in that it failed to take into account the part defendant's employees took without any aid from plaintiff in the execution of the plan it used; and in failing to confine 'net results to those attributable to plaintiff's plan,' left the jury to roam at large as to the reasonable value of the plan. Under plaintiff's petition and proof, it was the reasonable value of the plan to defendant for which it was obligated to pay. .   .   .

" .   .   . On the last submission of this cause we held the verdict to be excessive, and to that view we are constrained to adhere. By appellant's own admission, 2,592 new charge accounts were secured as a result of the contest in question, the total cost of which was $2,863.18 or $1.03 per account. Earlier in the same year defendant had carried on a direct mail campaign under which 79 new accounts were added, at a net cost of $13.15 each. Concerning the latter, defendant's witness Wolfort was asked the direct question if 'the results were not pretty poor,' to which he answered, 'Yes, on numbers.' From this it is argued, with some plausibility, that the jury might infer that the direct mail plan was not objectionable on the score of excessive cost, but was unsatisfactory only as to the quantity produced. From the foregoing, it appears that the difference in cost per account under the two methods was $12.12. The plaintiff, therefore, argues that the jury would have been justified in returning a verdict for such difference, or an aggregate of $31,415.04. It was developed on the cross-examination of one of defendant's witnesses, who qualified as an expert in department store advertising, that between 3½ and 4% is the allowable percentage of gross sales for the acquisition of new business. Moreover, there was evidence tending to show that from 1930 to 1938 the average purchase on each of the store's charge accounts (averaging approximately 65,000) was $1,074.59. There was, however, no substantial evidence showing the average life of defendant's charge accounts, the nearest approach being the testimony of one of the vice-presidents that while he did not know the average life of such accounts, he was sure that they 'had accounts with the grandmother, mother and daughter. I know some of them have had charge accounts in our place ever since we have been in business [45 years].' Another witness testified to such accounts having been on defendant's books for 10 years. We do not think it can be said, nor did the jury find, that plaintiff was entitled to be compensated at the rate of $12.12 per account, which, as indicated, represents the difference in the expense of procurement under the two systems above-referred to. The amount actually allowed was on the basis of approximately $7.70 per account, a sum which we regard as disproportionate to the loss sustained by reason of defendant's breach of its contract. We have concluded that $10,000 is the maximum sum for which the judgment should be permitted to stand, under the proof adduced, but in so saying, we are not to be understood as holding that plaintiff cannot, in any event, recover in excess of said amount. If plaintiff will, within ten days, enter a remittitur of $10,000, the judgment will be affirmed, as reduced; otherwise, it will be reversed, and the cause remanded." 352 Mo. 1225, 1241–43, 181 S.W.2d 643, 651–653.

7.   Since rights to an idea may be lost upon its unguarded communication, an idea submitter is well advised to obtain, prior to disclosure, the recipient's agreement to compensate for use of the idea. Recipients are, however, also—and more often—well advised. If they encourage the submission of ideas at all, they typically condition receipt upon a release from any obligation to pay for the ideas, whether used or not. Competing considerations of insulation from suit and good public relations make drafting the relevant documents a particularly sensitive task. Consider how one layman botched the job:

43 Bock Ave. Aug. 8th 1938

Newark, J. J., Newark, N. J.

Mr. W. C. Fields:

Dear Bill:

Enclosed find a radio script which I think suits your inimitable style of super-comedy.

To say that I rate you as the greatest of comedians is putting it mildly you old rascal you.

There isn't a greater master of mimicry, buffoonery, or what have you on the stage, radio, or screen.

When you open up your hocus pocus, hipper dipper, strong men weep and pay their income tax.

When I read in a daily paper that a medico tried to limit your liquid refreshment I knew the millenium was here.

Bill without his nourishment.

Egad! What next? Is there no Justice? Gazooks! Must an old Indian fighter turn squaw.

When Goofus, Gufus, Hoofus and Affadufus are allegedly doing comedy on the "air," your very absence and silence is "funny."

You "Old Reprobate."

When are you coming back to us over the "ether" without an operation except on our funny bone.

What's that?   "Bill Cody" Fields has retired from the "Fields" of comedy.

Preposterous! Idiotic! Fantastic! Whatever you think the enclosed radio script is worth is O.K. with me "Bill."

Pardon a young man's brashness in addressing you so familiarly, but I know you'll understand.

With sincerest best wishes to you for a long life and happy days.

I remain

Sincerely yours,
Harry Yadkoe
43 Bock Ave.
Newark, N. J.
September 9, 1938

To which Fields replied:

Mr. Harry Yadkoe
43 Bock Ave.
Newark, N. J.

Dear Harry Yadkoe:

I liked your wheezes and your treatment, which follows along the line I have been giving our dear customers. Thanks for your gay compliments and thanks for the snake story. I shall use it in conjunction with one I have either on the radio or in a picture. I am about to embark on a new radio series and if you would like to submit a couple of scripts gratis and I am able to use them, who knows, both parties being willing, we might enter into a contract. My reason for injecting the vile word "gratis" is that we get so many letters from folks who if we even answer in the negative, immediately begin suit for plagiarism. Whilst we have never had to pay off, they sometimes become irritating no end.

Very truly yours,
W. C. Fields (signed)
W. C. Fields
c/o Beyer & MacArthur Agents
Taft Bldg.,
Cor. Hollywood Blvd. & Vine
Sts., Hollywood Calif.

Plaintiff, who claimed that Fields used several of the submitted gag ideas, was awarded an $8,000 judgment for breach of an implied contract to pay for the reasonable value of the use of his material. Appropriately enough, the movie in which plaintiff's material was used was "You Can't Cheat an Honest Man." Yadkoe v. Fields, 66 Cal. App.2d 150, 151 P.2d 906, 63 U.S.P.Q. 103 (1944).

Language more satisfactory from the viewpoint of the recipient appears in Davies v. Carnation Co., 352 F.2d 393, 147 U.S.P.Q. 350

(9th Cir. 1965) and Davis v. General Foods Corp., 21 F.Supp. 445 (S. D.N.Y.1937). For a more extensive release form see Olsson, Dreams for Sale, 23 Law & Contemp.Prob. 34, 55–59 (1958). Reread the form letter involved in Lueddecke v. Chevrolet Motor Co., above, and consider whether, as house counsel for defendant, you would have approved its attempt at courtesy—"it would not be advisable to redesign our springs in this manner at the present time."

8. The legal theories that can be employed to recover for use of submitted ideas are canvassed in Jack, The Legal Protection of Abstract Ideas: A Remedies Approach, 18 IDEA 7 (1976). California courts have been singularly preoccupied with idea submission cases, particularly those involving ideas for motion pictures and television programs. The evolution of California's idea jurisprudence has attracted considerable commentary. See Kaplan, Implied Contract and the Law of Literary Property, 42 Calif.L.Rev. 28 (1954); Kaplan, Further Remarks on Compensation for Ideas in California, 46 Calif. L.Rev. 699 (1958); Gershon, Contractual Protection for Literary or Dramatic Material: When, Where and How Much?, 27 So.Calif.L. Rev. 290 (1954); Nimmer, The Law of Ideas, 27 So.Calif.L.Rev. 119 (1954). Comment, Television Formats—The Search for Protection, 58 Calif.L.Rev. 1169 (1970), explores the law outside, as well as within California.

B. LIMITS OF PROTECTION: THE PLACE OF IDEAS IN THE COMPETITIVE PLAN

ARONSON v. QUICK POINT PENCIL CO.

Supreme Court of the United States, 1979.
440 U.S. 257, 99 S.Ct. 1096, 59 L.Ed.2d 296, 201 U.S.P.Q. 1.

Mr. Chief Justice BURGER delivered the opinion of the Court.

We granted certiorari to consider whether federal patent law pre-empts state contract law so as to preclude enforcement of a contract to pay royalties to a patent applicant, on sales of articles embodying the putative invention, for so long as the contracting party sells them, if a patent is not granted.

(1)

In October 1955 the petitioner Mrs. Jane Aronson filed an application, Serial No. 542677, for a patent on a new form of keyholder. Although ingenious, the design was so simple that it readily could be copied unless it was protected by patent. In June 1956, while the patent application was pending, Mrs. Aronson negotiated a contract with the respondent, Quick Point Pencil Company, for the manufacture and sale of the keyholder.

The contract was embodied in two documents. In the first, a letter from Quick Point to Mrs. Aronson, Quick Point agreed to pay Mrs. Aronson a royalty of 5% of the selling price in return for "the exclusive right to make and sell keyholders of the type shown in your application, Serial No. 542677." The letter further provided that the parties would consult one another concerning the steps to be taken "[i]n the event of any infringement."

The contract did not require Quick Point to manufacture the keyholder. Mrs. Aronson received a $750 advance on royalties and was entitled to rescind the exclusive license if Quick Point did not sell a million keyholders by the end of 1957. Quick Point retained the right to cancel the agreement whenever "the volume of sales does not meet our expectation." The duration of the agreement was not otherwise prescribed.

A contemporaneous document provided that if Mrs. Aronson's patent application was "not allowed within five (5) years, Quick Point Pencil Co. [would] pay two and one half percent (2½%) of sales . . . so long as you [Quick Point] continue to sell same."

In June 1961, when Mrs. Aronson had failed to obtain a patent on the keyholder within the five years specified in the agreement, Quick Point asserted its contractual right to reduce royalty payments to 2½% of sales. In September of that year the Board of Patent Appeals issued a final rejection of the application on the ground that the keyholder was not patentable, and Mrs. Aronson did not appeal. Quick Point continued to pay reduced royalties to her for 14 years thereafter.

The market was more receptive to the keyholder's novelty and utility than the Patent Office. By September 1975 Quick Point had made sales in excess of seven million dollars and paid Mrs. Aronson royalties totalling $203,963.84; sales were continuing to rise. However, while Quick Point was able to pre-empt the market in the earlier years and was long the only manufacturer of the Aronson keyholder, copies began to appear in the late 1960's. Quick Point's competitors, of course, were not required to pay royalties for their use of the design. Quick Point's share of the Aronson keyholder market has declined during the past decade.

(2)

In November 1975 Quick Point commenced an action in the United States District Court for a declaratory judgment, pursuant to 28 U.S.C.A. § 2201, that the royalty agreement was unenforceable. Quick Point asserted that state law which might otherwise make the contract enforceable was preempted by federal patent law. This is the only issue presented to us for decision.

Both parties moved for summary judgment on affidavits, exhibits, and stipulations of fact. The District Court concluded that the "language of the agreement is plain, clear and unequivocal and has no relation as to whether or not a patent is ever granted." Accordingly, it held that the agreement was valid, and that Quick Point was obliged to pay the agreed royalties pursuant to the contract for so long as it manufactured the keyholder.

The Court of Appeals reversed, one judge dissenting. It held that since the parties contracted with reference to a pending patent application, Mrs. Aronson was estopped from denying that patent law principles governed her contract with Quick Point. Although acknowledging that this Court had never decided the precise issue, the Court of Appeals held that our prior decisions regarding patent licenses compelled the conclusion that Quick Point's contract with Mrs. Aronson became unenforceable once she failed to obtain a patent. The court held that a continuing obligation to pay royalties would be contrary to "the strong federal policy favoring the full and free use of ideas in the public domain," Lear Inc. v. Adkins, 395 U.S. 653, 674, 89 S.Ct. 1902, 1913, 23 L.Ed.2d 610 (1969). The court also observed that if Mrs. Aronson actually had obtained a patent, Quick Point would have escaped its royalty obligations either if the patent were held to be invalid, see id., at 674, 89 S.Ct. at 1913, or upon its expiration after 17 years, see Brulotte v. Thys Co., 379 U.S. 29, 85 S. Ct. 176, 13 L.Ed.2d 99 (1964). Accordingly, it concluded that a licensee should be relieved of royalty obligations when the licensor's efforts to obtain a contemplated patent prove unsuccessful.

(3)

On this record it is clear that the parties contracted with full awareness of both the pendency of a patent application and the possibility that a patent might not issue. The clause de-escalating the royalty by half in the event no patent issued within five years makes that crystal clear. Quick Point apparently placed a significant value on exploiting the basic novelty of the device, even if no patent issued; its success demonstrates that this judgment was well founded. Assuming, *arguendo*, that the initial letter and the commitment to pay a 5% royalty was subject to federal patent law, the provision relating to the 2½% royalty was explicitly independent of federal law. The cases and principles relied on by the Court of Appeals and Quick Point do not bear on a contract that does not rely on a patent, particularly where, as here, the contracting parties agreed expressly as to alternative obligations if no patent should issue.

Commercial agreements traditionally are the domain of state law. State law is not displaced merely because the contract relates to intellectual property which may or may not be patentable; the states are free to regulate the use of such intellectual property in any manner not inconsistent with federal law. Kewanee Oil Co. v. Bicron Corp., 416 U.S. 470, 479, 94 S.Ct. 1879, 1885, 40 L.Ed.2d 315 (1974); see Goldstein v. California, 412 U.S. 546, 93 S.Ct. 2303, 37 L.Ed.2d 163 (1973). In this as in other fields, the question of whether federal law pre-empts state law "involves a consideration of whether that law 'stands as an obstacle to the accomplishment and execution of the full purposes and objectives of Congress.' Hines v. Davidowitz, 312 U.S. 52, 67 (1941)." *Kewanee Oil Co.*, supra. If it does not, state law governs.

In *Kewanee Oil Co.*, supra, 416 U.S. at 480–481, 94 S.Ct. at 1885–1886, we reviewed the purposes of the federal patent system. First, patent law seeks to foster and reward invention; second, it promotes disclosure of inventions, to stimulate further innovation and to permit the public to practice the invention once the patent expires; third, the stringent requirements for patent protection seek to assure that ideas in the public domain remain there for the free use of the public.

Enforcement of Quick Point's agreement with Mrs. Aronson is not inconsistent with any of these aims. Permitting inventors to make enforceable agreements licensing the use of their inventions in return for royalties provides an additional incentive to invention. Similarly, encouraging Mrs. Aronson to make arrangements for the manufacture of her keyholder furthers the federal policy of disclosure of inventions; these simple devices display the novel idea which they embody wherever they are seen.

Quick Point argues that enforcement of such contracts conflicts with the federal policy against withdrawing ideas from the public domain and discourages recourse to the federal patent system by allowing states to extend "perpetual protection to articles too lacking in novelty to merit any patent at all under federal constitutional standards," Sears, Roebuck & Co. v. Stiffel Co., 376 U.S. 225, 232, 84 S.Ct. 784, 789, 11 L.Ed.2d 661 (1964).

We find no merit in this contention. Enforcement of the agreement does not withdraw any idea from the public domain. The design for the keyholder was not in the public domain before Quick Point obtained its license to manufacture it. In negotiating the agreement, Mrs. Aronson disclosed the design in confidence. Had Quick Point tried to exploit the design in breach of that confidence, it would have risked legal liability. It is equally clear that the design entered the public domain as a result of the manufacture and sale of the keyholders under the contract.

Requiring Quick Point to bear the burden of royalties for the use of the design is no more inconsistent with federal patent law than any of the other costs involved in being the first to introduce a new product to the market, such as outlays for research and development and marketing and promotional expenses. For reasons which Quick Point's experience with the Aronson keyholder demonstrate, innovative entrepreneurs have usually found such costs to be well worth paying.

Finally, enforcement of this agreement does not discourage anyone from seeking a patent. Mrs. Aronson attempted to obtain a patent for over five years. It is quite true that had she succeeded, she would have received a 5% royalty only on keyholders sold during the 17-year life of the patent. Offsetting the limited terms of royalty payments, she would have received twice as much per dollar of Quick Point's sales, and both she and Quick Point could have licensed any others who produced the same keyholder. Which course would have produced the greater yield to the contracting parties is a matter of speculation; the parties resolved the uncertainties by their bargain.

(4)

No decision of this Court relating to patents justifies relieving Quick Point of its contract obligations. We have held that a state may not forbid the copying of an idea in the public domain which does not meet the requirements for federal patent protection. Compco Corp. v. Day-Brite Lighting, Inc., 376 U.S. 234, 84 S.Ct. 779, 11 L. Ed.2d 669 (1964); Sears, Roebuck & Co. v. Stiffel Co., 376 U.S. 225, 84 S.Ct. 784, 11 L.Ed.2d 661 (1964). Enforcement of Quick Point's agreement, however, does not prevent anyone from copying the key-holder. It merely requires Quick Point to pay the consideration which it promised in return for the use of a novel device which enabled it to preempt the market.

In Lear, Inc. v. Adkins, 395 U.S. 653, 89 S.Ct. 1902, 23 L.Ed.2d 610 (1969), we held that a person licensed to use a patent may challenge the validity of the patent, and that a licensee who establishes that the patent is invalid need not pay the royalties accrued under the licensing agreement subsequent to the issuance of the patent. Both holdings relied on the desirability of encouraging licensees to challenge the validity of patents, to further the strong federal policy that only inventions which meet the rigorous requirements of patentability shall be withdrawn from the public domain. Accordingly, neither the holding nor the rationale of *Lear* controls when no patent has issued, and no ideas have been withdrawn from public use.

Enforcement of the royalty agreement here is also consistent with the principles treated in Brulotte v. Thys Co., 379 U.S. 29, 85 S. Ct. 176, 13 L.Ed.2d 99 (1964). There, we held that the obligation to pay royalties in return for the use of a patented device may not extend beyond the life of the patent. The principle underlying that holding was simply that the monopoly granted *under a patent* cannot lawfully be used to "negotiate with the leverage of that monopoly." The Court emphasized that to "use that leverage to project those royalty payments beyond the life of the patent is analogous to an effort to enlarge the monopoly of a patent . . . ." Id., at 33, 85 S.Ct., at 179. Here the reduced royalty which is challenged, far from being negotiated "with the leverage" of a patent, rested on the contingency that no patent would issue within five years.

No doubt a pending patent application gives the applicant some additional bargaining power for purposes of negotiating a royalty agreement. The pending application allows the inventor to hold out the hope of an exclusive right to exploit the idea, as well as the threat that the other party will be prevented from using the idea for 17 years. However, the amount of leverage arising from a patent application depends on how likely the parties consider it to be that a valid patent will issue. Here, where no patent ever issued, the record is entirely clear that the parties assigned a substantial likelihood to that contingency, since they specifically provided for a reduced royalty in the event no patent issued within five years.

This case does not require us to draw the line between what constitutes abuse of a pending application and what does not. It is clear that whatever role the pending application played in the negotiation of the 5% royalty, it played no part in the contract to pay the 2½% royalty indefinitely.

Our holding in *Kewanee Oil Co.*, supra, puts to rest the contention that federal law pre-empts and renders unenforceable the contract made by these parties. There we held that state law forbidding the misappropriation of trade secrets was not preempted by federal patent law. We observed:

> "Certainly the patent policy of encouraging invention is not disturbed by the existence of another form of incentive to invention. In this respect the two systems [patent and trade secret law] are not and never would be in conflict." Id., 416 U.S., at 484, 94 S.Ct., at 1887.

Enforcement of this royalty agreement is even less offensive to federal patent policies than state law protecting trade secrets. The most commonly accepted definition of trade secrets is restricted to confidential information which is not disclosed in the normal process of exploitation. See Restatement of Torts § 757, comment b (1939). Accordingly, the exploitation of trade secrets under state law may not satisfy the federal policy in favor of disclosure, whereas disclosure is inescapable in exploiting a device like the Aronson keyholder.

Enforcement of these contractual obligations, freely undertaken in arm's length negotiation and with no fixed reliance on a patent or a probable patent grant, will:

> "encourage invention in areas where patent law does not reach, and will prompt the independent innovator to proceed with the discovery and exploitation of his invention. Competition is fostered and the public is not deprived of the use of valuable, if not quite patentable, invention." [Footnote omitted.] Id., at 485, 94 S.Ct., at 1888.

The device which is the subject of this contract ceased to have any secrecy as soon as it was first marketed, yet when the contract was negotiated the inventiveness and novelty were sufficiently apparent to induce an experienced novelty manufacturer to agree to pay for the opportunity to be first in the market. Federal patent law is not a barrier to such a contract.

Reversed.

Mr. Justice BLACKMUN, concurring in the result.

For me, the hard question is whether this case can meaningfully be distinguished from Brulotte v. Thys Co., 379 U.S. 29, 85 S.Ct. 176, 13 L.Ed.2d 99 (1964). There the Court held a patent licensor could not use the leverage of its patent to obtain a royalty contract that extended beyond the patent's 17-year term. Here Mrs. Aronson has used the leverage of her patent application to negotiate a royalty contract which continues to be binding even though the patent application was long ago denied.

The Court asserts that her leverage played "no part" with respect to the contingent agreement to pay a reduced royalty if no patent issued within five years. Yet it may well be that Quick Point agreed to that contingency in order to obtain its other rights that depended on the success of the patent application. The parties did not apportion consideration in the neat fashion the Court adopts.

In my view, the holding in *Brulotte* reflects hostility toward extension of a patent monopoly whose term is fixed by statute, 35 U.S. C.A. § 154. Such hostility has no place here. A patent application which is later denied temporarily discourages unlicensed imitators. Its benefits and hazards are of a different magnitude from those of a granted patent that prohibits all competition for 17 years. Nothing justifies estopping a patent application licensor from entering into a contract whose term does not end if the application fails. The Court points out that enforcement of this contract does not conflict with the objectives of the patent laws. The United States, as *amicus curiae*, maintains that patent application licensing of this sort is desirable because it encourages patent applications, promotes early disclosure, and allows parties to structure their bargains efficiently.

On this basis, I concur in the Court's holding that federal patent law does not pre-empt the enforcement of Mrs. Aronson's contract with Quick Point.

NOTES

1. Lear v. Adkins, discussed in the *Aronson* opinion, is considered at page 617 and Brulotte v. Thys is considered at page 616. Kewanee v. Bicron appears at page 178. Goldstein v. California is discussed at page 228. *Sears* and *Compco* appear at pages 130, 133.

2. Does *Aronson* represent a blanket endorsement of state idea protection? What if, instead of express contract, the state law ground for recovery had been contract implied in fact? Quasi contract? Property? What are the different market effects of each of these theories? Did the Court indicate a line between those state doctrines whose market effects are tolerable and those that are not?

II. UNFAIR COMPETITION

A. THEORY OF PROTECTION

1. TRADITIONAL ELEMENTS

AMERICAN WASHBOARD CO. v. SAGINAW MFG. CO.

United States Circuit Court of Appeals, Sixth Circuit, 1900.
103 F. 281.

DAY, Circuit Judge. This cause is in this court on appeal from an order of the circuit court denying an injunction as prayed for in the bill, and also to reverse the decree sustaining a demurrer to the bill, and dismissing the same. A perusal of the bill discloses a case which invokes the equitable jurisdiction of the court because of the interference of the defendant with the trade and good will of complainant in the manufacture and sale of certain aluminum washboards, for which complainant claims to have adopted as a trade-name the word "Aluminum," stamped upon the washboards. It may be stated at the outset that the case is not one for the protection of a trade-mark. It is well settled that a name merely descriptive of an article of trade, of its qualities, ingredients, or characteristics, cannot be employed as a trade-mark, and the exclusive use of it entitled to legal protection. It was said by the supreme court, in Lawrence Mfg. Co. v. Tennessee Mfg. Co., 138 U.S. 547, 11 S.Ct. 400, 34 L.Ed. 1003:

> Nothing is better settled than that an exclusive right to the use of letters, words, or symbols to indicate merely the quality of the goods to which they are affixed cannot be acquired.

To the same effect is the case of Chemical Co. v. Meyer, 139 U.S. 542, 11 S.Ct. 626, 35 L.Ed. 248, in which it was said:

> The general proposition is well established that words which are merely descriptive of the character, qualities, or composition of an article, or of the place where it is manufactured or produced, cannot be monopolized as a trade-mark.

Indeed, we do not understand that the learned counsel who represents appellant in this case makes any claim that his client is entitled to protection upon the ground that it has adopted the word "Aluminum" as a technical trade-mark. In the brief for appellant it is stated that the case is one of unlawful competition in trade, and it has been argued upon that basis. A brief summary of the bill shows that it contains the following statements: That the complainant is engaged in the manufacture and sale of washboards. That its goods en-

joy a high reputation in the market of the United States and elsewhere, having been sold in large quantities. That the superior quality of the washboard so manufactured and sold by complainant had
acquired a high reputation with the public. That the complainant, at
some date prior to the date of the wrongs complained of in the bill
(the exact time not being stated), had devised and manufactured a
washboard, the rubbing face of which was made of aluminum. That
said metal, on account of its cost, was regarded as one of the precious
metals. That its capacity and adaptability to said purpose was unknown up to and at the time complainant adopted it, and by a trial
and test showed its adaptability for that purpose. That, the word
"Aluminum" never having been used in connection with or applied to
a washboard, complainant adopted the word as a trade-mark or
trade-name for its aluminum washboards, but did not then go into the
business of making and selling said washboards, but, owing to the
high price of sheet aluminum, its use was at that time, from a commercial standpoint, practically prohibitive, for which reason complainant suspended the manufacture of such washboards. Afterwards
the selling price of aluminum became materially reduced, and though
the defendant, about that time, made and sold aluminum washboards,
—perhaps 50 or 100,—and represented that it had adopted the word
"Aluminum" as a trade-mark or trade-name, defendant never engaged generally in the business and did not secure any rights to said
name. That the selling price of aluminum became so low that it was
profitable to resume the manufacture of aluminum washboards,
which complainant did, and stenciled the name on each washboard,
which trade-mark or trade-name it has since continuously used to its
great benefit and advantage. The public has recognized the fitness of
the name, the exclusive right of complainant thereto, and said complainant has made large sales of boards thus branded, and has demonstrated the capability of such washboards. Complainant made only
the rubbing face of such washboards of pure aluminum, so that purchasers have come to know or distinguish them by that name; and,
but for the illegal acts of defendant, washboards so branded would be
recognized as containing a rubbing face of pure aluminum. That
complainant, upon entering upon the manufacture of such washboards, made a contract with the Pittsburg Reduction Company,
which is a large producer of aluminum, and the only producer of said
metal in the United States, whereby it contracted for and purchased
and has acquired and will continue to acquire the entire output of
sheet aluminum suitable for forming the rubbing sheets of washboards produced or on sale in the United States. That by extensive
advertising it built up its present business. That it has expended
large sums of money and much time in introducing such washboard
under such trade-name. Complainant avers that defendant, well
knowing the facts set forth in the bill, has been and now is engaged
in the manufacture of washboards in the Eastern district of Michigan
and elsewhere, which are branded "Aluminum," advertised by said
defendant as aluminum, and sold under that name. That said wash-

boards are not made of aluminum in any part. That in fact no ascertainable quantity is used in the manufacture, particularly in the rubbing sheet thereof. That, being thus branded with the word "Aluminum," and so advertised, purchasers and users are induced to believe that the rubbing sheet is made of aluminum, and induced to buy them from that belief. The fact is that the rubbing sheet of said washboard is made of zinc, long used for such purpose and containing no aluminum. The washboards manufactured by defendant are approximately the same size and shape as complainant's, and being branded with the word "Aluminum" further tends to mislead purchasers, "so that, when intending to purchase a genuine article (of which complainant is the sole manufacturer), they are led to purchase a fraudulent and falsely branded article of defendant's manufacture, to the great and irreparable injury of your orator therein, as also to the great and lasting injury of the public." And further complainant says it has a right to represent truthfully the quality of its manufacture by the word "Aluminum"; that so long as it continues to be the sole manufacturer of washboards made of pure aluminum, as it expects to continue to be, it has a right to the exclusive use of said name as a trade-mark or trade-name for a washboard, especially as against defendant's misleading use of the same word. The bill prays for the protection of complainant's alleged exclusive right.

The question presented is, is the case thus stated one which entitles complainant to a remedy by injunction and accounting against the defendants? There are numerous cases in the reports upon the subject of unfair competition in trade. From the general principle running through them all it may be said that when one has established a trade or business in which he has used a particular device, symbol, or name so that it has become known in trade as a designation of such person's goods, equity will protect him in the use thereof. Such person has a right to complain when another adopts this symbol or manner of marking his goods so as to mislead the public into purchasing the same as and for the goods of complainant. Plaintiff comes into a court of equity in such cases for the protection of his property rights. The private action is given, not for the benefit of the public, although that may be its incidental effect, but because of the invasion by defendant of that which is the exclusive property of complainant. . . .

Applying this doctrine to the allegations of complainant's bill, we do not find it anywhere averred that the defendant, by means of its imitation of complainant's trade-mark, is palming off its goods on the public as and for the goods of complainant. The bill is not predicated upon that theory. It undertakes to make a case, not because the defendant is selling its goods as and for the goods of complainant, but because it is the manufacturer of a genuine aluminum board, and the defendant is deceiving the public by selling to it a board not made of aluminum, although falsely branded as such, being in fact a board made of zinc material; that is to say, the theory of the case seems to be that complainant, manufacturing a genuine aluminum board, has a right to enjoin others from branding any board "Aluminum" not so in fact, although there is no attempt on the part of such wrongdoer to impose upon the public the belief that the goods thus manufactured are the goods of complainant. We are not referred to any case going to the length required to support such a bill. It loses sight of the thoroughly established principle that the private right of action in such cases is not based upon fraud or imposition upon the public, but is maintained solely for the protection of the property rights of complainant. It is true that in these cases it is an important factor that the public are deceived, but it is only where this deception induces the public to buy the goods as those of complainant that a private right of action arises. .   .   .

If the doctrine contended for by complainant in this case was to be carried to its legitimate results, we should, as suggested by Mr. Justice Bradley in the case of New York & R. Cement Co. v. Coplay Cement Co. (C.C.) 44 Fed. 277, open a Pandora's box of litigation. A person who undertook to manufacture a genuine article could suppress the business of all untruthful dealers, although they were in no wise undertaking to pirate his trade. Says Mr. Justice Bradley:

> The principle for which counsel for complainant contends would enable any crockery merchant of Dresden or elsewhere interested in the particular trade to sue a dealer of New York or Philadelphia who should sell an article as Dresden china, when it is not Dresden china. .   .   . A dry-goods merchant selling an article of linen as Irish linen could be sued by all the haberdashers of Ireland and all the linen dealers of the United States.

Take the metal which is the subject-matter of the controversy in this case. Many articles are now being put upon the market under the name of aluminum, because of the attractive qualities of that metal, which are not made of pure aluminum, yet they answer the purpose for which they are made and are useful. Can it be that the courts have the power to suppress such trade at the instance of others starting in the same business who use only pure aluminum? There is a wide-spread suspicion that many articles sold as being manufactured of wool are not entirely made of that material. Can it be that a dealer who should make such articles only of pure wool could invoke the equitable jurisdiction of the courts to suppress the trade and business of all persons whose goods may deceive the public? We find no such authority in the books, and are clear in the opinion that, if the doctrine is to be thus extended, and all persons compelled to deal solely in goods which are exactly what they are represented to be, the remedy must come from the legislature, and not from the courts. A class of cases is cited and much relied upon wherein geographical names have been sustained as trade-names in cases of unfair competition in trade, although not technically trade-marks. These cases seem to establish the doctrine that geographical names, such as "Minneapolis," applied to flour, may be adopted as a trade-name, so that one who undertakes to pirate the trade of another who has established among purchasers this designation of his goods will be entitled to an injunction against one who seeks to avail himself of the reputation thus acquired by imposing upon the public his goods as the goods of complainant. An examination of these cases shows that they are based upon the doctrine which we have already shown to be the basis of equitable interference. The doctrine is well stated in the syllabus of the case of Gage-Downs Co. v. Featherbone Corset Co. (C.C.) 83 Fed. 213:

> One making corset waists at Chicago, and selling them as "Chicago Waists" so that this designation has come to denote among purchasers the goods made by him, is entitled to an injunction against another who makes similar waists in a different state and city, and sells them as "Chicago Waists," with the manifest intent of availing himself of the reputation acquired by the other's goods.

As was said by Judge Severens in that case (page 214):

> The circumstances vary greatly, but the underlying principle which is effective in the solution of such cases is that a party may not adopt a mark or symbol which has been employed by another manufacturer, and by long use and employment on the part of that other has come to be recognized by the public as denoting the origin of the manufacture, and thus impose upon the public by inducing them to believe that the goods which this new party thus offers are the goods of the original party. In other words, it is a fundamental principle that a man cannot make use of a reputation which another manufacturer has acquired in a trade-mark or trade-name, and, by inducing the public to act upon a misapprehension as to the source of the origin, deprive the other party of the good will and reputation which he has acquired, and to which he is entitled.

Nor do we find anything in the allegations of the bill as to complainant's monopoly in the use of the metal aluminum for washboard purposes which would extend its rights. We are not referred to any case, nor can we think of any reason why one who has obtained a monopoly in the material of which his goods are made should have any broader rights in protecting his trade-name than another who is engaged in competition in the same line of business. The intended adoption of the word "Aluminum" as a trade-mark prior to its use in the manufacture and sale of washboards fails to strengthen the case of complainants, as was said by Judge Coxe in George v. Smith (C.C.) 52 Fed. 830:

> It is the party who uses it first as a brand for his goods, and builds up a business under it, who is entitled to protection, and not the one who first thought of using it on similar goods, but did not use it. The law deals with acts, not intentions.

The allegations of complainant's bill in this case show that it did not establish its right to use the trade-name "Aluminum" until after the manufacture of boards by defendant. Upon the whole case we are of opinion that complainant's bill lacks the essential allegations necessary to make the case entitling to it the relief sought, and we are of opinion that the demurrer to the bill was properly sustained. This decision makes it unnecessary to pass upon the ruling on the motion for a preliminary injunction. If the bill was demurrable, it cannot authorize the granting of an injunction, and therefore the ruling of the court below was correct in that respect. The decree and order of the court will be affirmed.

ELY–NORRIS SAFE CO. v. MOSLER SAFE CO.

United States Circuit Court of Appeals, Second Circuit, 1925.
7 F.2d 603, reversed 273 U.S. 132, 47 S.Ct. 314, 71 L.Ed. 578.

Appeal from the District Court of the United States for the Southern District of New York.

Suit in equity by the Ely-Norris Safe Company against the Mosler Safe Company. From decree of dismissal, plaintiff appeals. Reversed.

The jurisdiction of the District Court depended upon diverse citizenship, and the suit was for unfair competition. The bill alleged that the plaintiff manufactured and sold safes under certain letters patent, which had as their distinctive feature an explosion chamber, designed for protection against burglars. Before the acts complained of, no one but the plaintiff had ever made or sold safes with such chambers, and, except for the defendant's infringement, the plaintiff has remained the only manufacturer and seller of such safes. By reason of the plaintiff's efforts the public has come to recognize the value of the explosion chamber and to wish to purchase safes containing them. Besides infringing the patent, the defendant has manufactured and sold safes without a chamber, but with a metal band around the door, in the same place where the plaintiff put the chamber, and has falsely told its customers that this band was employed to cover and close an explosion chamber. Customers have been thus led to buy safes upon the faith of the representation, who in fact wished to buy safes with explosion chambers, and would have done so, but for the deceit.

The bill prayed an injunction against selling safes with such metal bands, and against representing that any of its safes contained an explosion chamber. From the plaintiff's answers to interrogatories it appeared that all the defendant's safes bore the defendant's name and address, and were sold as its own. Furthermore, that the defendant never gave a customer reason to suppose that any safe sold by it was made by the plaintiff.

Before HOUGH, MANTON, and HAND, Circuit Judges.

HAND, Circuit Judge (after stating the facts as above). This case is not the same as that before Mr. Justice Bradley in New York & Rosendale Co. v. Coplay Cement Co. (C.C.) 44 F. 277, 10 L.R.A. 833. The plaintiffs there manufactured cement at Rosendale, N. Y., but it did not appear that they were the only persons making cement at that place. There was no reason, therefore, to assume that a customer of the defendant, deceived as to the place of origin of the defendant's cement, and desiring to buy only such cement, would have bought of the plaintiffs. It resulted that the plaintiffs did not show any necessary loss of trade through the defendant's fraud upon its own customers. We agree that some of the language of the opinion goes further, but it was not necessary for the disposition of the case.

American Washboard Co. v. Saginaw Mfg. Co., 103 F. 281 (C.C. A.6), 43 C.C.A. 233, 50 L.R.A. 609, was, however, a case in substance like that at bar, because there the plaintiff alleged that it had acquired the entire output of sheet aluminum suitable for washboards. It necessarily followed that the plaintiff had a practical monopoly of this metal for the articles in question, and from this it was a fair inference that any customer of the defendant, who was deceived into buying as an aluminum washboard one which was not such, was a presumptive customer of the plaintiff, who had therefore lost a bargain. This was held, however, not to constitute a private wrong, and so the bill was dismissed.

Furthermore, we do not agree with the plaintiff that cases like Federal Trade Commission v. Winsted Hosiery Co., 258 U.S. 483, 42 S.Ct. 384, 66 L.Ed. 729, and our decision in Royal Baking Powder Co. v. Federal Trade Commission, 281 F. 744, are in his favor. These arose under the Federal Trade Commission Act (Comp.St. §§ 8836a– 8836k) where it is only necessary to show that the public interest has been affected. The defendant's customers in such cases had an undoubted grievance, and this was thought to be enough to justify the intervention of the Federal Trade Commission. It by no means follows from such decisions that a competing manufacturer has any cause of suit.

We must concede, therefore, that on the cases as they stand the law is with the defendant, and the especially high authority of the court which decided American Washboard Co. v. Saginaw Mfg. Co., supra, makes us hesitate to differ from their conclusion. Yet there is no part of the law which is more plastic than unfair competition, and what was not reckoned an actionable wrong 25 years ago may have become such today. We find it impossible to deny the strength of the plaintiff's case on the allegations of its bill. As we view it, the question is, as it always is in such cases, one of fact. While a competitor may, generally speaking, take away all the customers of another that he can, there are means which he must not use. One of these is deceit. The false use of another's name as maker or source of his own goods is deceit, of which the false use of geographical or descriptive terms is only one example. But we conceive that in the end the questions which arise are always two: Has the plaintiff in fact lost customers? And has he lost them by means which the law forbids? The false use of the plaintiff's name is only an instance in which each element is clearly shown.

In the case at bar the means are as plainly unlawful as in the usual case of palming off. It is as unlawful to lie about the quality of one's wares as about their maker; it equally subjects the seller to action by the buyer. Indeed, as to this the case of Federal Trade Commission v. Winsted Hosiery Co., supra, is flatly in point, if authority be needed. The reason, as we think why such deceits have not been regarded as actionable by a competitor, depends only upon his inability to show any injury for which there is a known remedy. In an open market it is generally impossible to prove that a customer, whom the defendant has secured by falsely describing his goods, would have bought of the plaintiff, if the defendant had been truthful. Without that, the plaintiff, though aggrieved in company with other honest traders, cannot show any ascertainable loss. He may not recover at law, and the equitable remedy is concurrent. The law does not allow him to sue as a vicarious avenger of the defendant's customers.

But, if it be true that the plaintiff has a monopoly of the kind of wares concerned, and if to secure a customer the defendant must represent his own as of that kind, it is a fair inference that the customer wants those and those only. Had he not supposed that the defendant could supply him, presumably he would have gone to the plaintiff, who alone could. At least, if the plaintiff can prove that in fact he would, he shows a direct loss, measured by his profits on the putative sale. If a tradesman falsely foists on a customer a substitute for what the plaintiff alone can supply, it can scarcely be that the plaintiff is without remedy, if he can show that the customer would certainly have come to him, had the truth been told.

Yet that is in substance the situation which this bill presents. It says that the plaintiff alone could lawfully make such safes, and that the defendant has sold others to customers who asked for the patented kind. It can make no difference that the defendant sold them as its own. The sale by hypothesis depended upon the structure of the safes, not on their maker. To be satisfied, the customer must in fact have gone to the plaintiff, or the defendant must have infringed. Had he infringed, the plaintiff could have recovered his profit on the sale; had the customer gone to him, he would have made that profit. Any possibilities that the customers might not have gone to the plaintiff, had they been told the truth, are foreclosed by the allegation that the plaintiff in fact lost the sales. It seems to us merely a corollary of Federal Trade Commission v. Winsted Hosiery Co., supra, that, if this can be proved, a private suit will lie.

Decree reversed.

MOSLER SAFE CO. v. ELY–NORRIS SAFE CO.

Supreme Court of the United States, 1927.
273 U.S. 132, 47 S.Ct. 314, 71 L.Ed. 578.

Mr. Justice HOLMES delivered the opinion of the Court.

This is a bill in equity brought by a corporation of New Jersey against a corporation of New York alleging unfair competition. It was treated below as a suit by the only manufacturer of safes containing an explosion chamber for protection against burglars. It seeks an injunction against selling safes with a metal band around the door in the place where the plaintiff put the chamber, or falsely representing that the defendant's safes contain an explosion chamber. The plaintiff admitted that the defendant's safes bore the defendant's name and address and that the defendant never gave any customer reason to believe that its safes were of the plaintiff's make. The District Court, following American Washboard Co. v. Saginaw Manufacturing Co., (C.C.A.) 103 F. 281, 50 L.R.A. 609, held that representations such as were sought to be enjoined did not give a private cause of action. The Circuit Court of Appeals held that if, as it took it to be alleged, the plaintiff had the monopoly of explosion chambers and the defendant falsely represented that its safes had such chambers, the plaintiff had a good case, and that since the decision above cited the law had grown more liberal in granting relief. It therefore reversed the decree below. In view of the conflict between the Circuit Courts of Appeals a writ of certiorari was granted by this Court.

At the hearing below all attention seems to have been concentrated on the question passed upon and the forcibly stated reasons that induced this Court of Appeals to differ from that for the Sixth Circuit. But, upon a closer scrutiny of the bill than seems to have been invited before, it does not present that broad and interesting issue. The bill alleges that the plaintiff has a patent for an explosion chamber as described and claimed in said Letters Patent; that it has the exclusive right to make and sell safes containing such an explosion chamber; that no other safes containing such an explosion chamber could be got in the United States before the defendant, as it is alleged, infringed the plaintiff's patent, for which alleged infringement a suit is pending. It then is alleged that the defendant is making and selling safes with a metal band around the door at substantially the same location as the explosion chamber of plaintiff's safes, and has represented to the public that the said metal band was employed to cover or close an explosion chamber by reason of which the public has been led to purchase defendant's said safes as and for safes containing an explosion chamber, such as is manufactured and sold by the plaintiff herein. It is alleged further that sometimes the defendant's safes have no explosion chamber under the band but are bought by those who want safes with a chamber and so the defendant has deprived the plaintiff of sales, competed unfairly and damaged the plaintiff's reputation. The plaintiff relies upon its patent suit for relief in respect of the sales of safes alleged to infringe its rights. It complains here only of false representations as to safes that do not infringe but that are sold as having explosion chambers although in fact they do not.

It is consistent with every allegation in the bill and the defendant in argument asserted it to be a fact, that there are other safes with explosion chambers beside that for which the plaintiff has a patent. The defendant is charged only with representing that its safes had an explosion chamber, which, so far as appears, it had a perfect right to do if the representation was true. If on the other hand the representation was false as it is alleged sometimes to have been, there is nothing to show that customers had they known the facts would have gone to the plaintiff rather than to other competitors in the market, or to lay a foundation for the claim for a loss of sales. The bill is so framed as to seem to invite the decision that was obtained from the Circuit Court of Appeals, but when scrutinized is seen to have so limited its statements as to exclude the right to complain.

Decree reversed.

WILLIAM R. WARNER & CO. v. ELI LILLY & CO.

Supreme Court of the United States, 1924.
265 U.S. 526, 44 S.Ct. 615, 68 L.Ed. 1161.

Mr. Justice SUTHERLAND delivered the opinion of the Court.

Respondent is a corporation engaged in the manufacture and sale of pharmaceutical and chemical products. In 1899 it began and has ever since continued to make and sell a liquid preparation of quinine, in combination with other substances, including yerba-santa and chocolate, under the name of Coco-Quinine.

Petitioner also is a pharmaceutical and chemical manufacturer. The Pfeiffer Chemical Company, Searle & Hereth Company and petitioner are under the same ownership and control. The first named company in 1906 began the manufacture of a liquid preparation which is substantially the same as respondent's preparation and which was put upon the market under the name of Quin-Coco. Two years later the Searle & Hereth Company engaged in the manufacture of the preparation, which ever since has been sold and distributed by petitioner.

This suit was brought in the Federal District Court for the Eastern District of Pennsylvania by respondent to enjoin petitioner from continuing to manufacture and sell the preparation if flavored or colored with chocolate; and also from using the name Quin-Coco, on the ground that it was an infringement of the name Coco-Quinine, to the use of which respondent had acquired an exclusive right. The District Court decided against respondent upon both grounds. On appeal the Court of Appeals ruled with the District Court upon the issue of infringement but reversed the decree upon that of unfair competition.

The entire record is here and both questions are open for consideration.

First. We agree with the courts below that the charge of [trademark] infringement was not sustained. The name Coco-Quinine is descriptive of the ingredients which enter into the preparation. The same is equally true of the name Quin-Coco. A name which is merely descriptive of the ingredients, qualities or characteristics of an article of trade cannot be appropriated as a trademark and the exclusive use of it afforded legal protection. The use of a similar name by another to truthfully describe his own product does not constitute a legal or moral wrong, even if its effect be to cause the public to mistake the origin or ownership of the product.

Second. The issue of unfair competition, on which the courts below differed, presents a question of more difficulty. The testimony is voluminous, more than two hundred witnesses having been examined; but, since the question with which we are now dealing is primarily one of fact, we have found it necessary to examine and consider it. Nothing is to be gained by reviewing the evidence at length, and we shall do no more than summarize the facts upon which we have reached our conclusions.

The use of chocolate as an ingredient has a three-fold effect: It imparts to the preparation a distinctive color and a distinctive flavor, and, to some extent, operates as a medium to suspend the quinine and prevent its precipitation. It has no therapeutic value; but it supplies the mixture with a quality of palatability for which there is no equally satisfactory substitute. Respondent, by laboratory experiments, first developed the idea of the addition of chocolate to the preparation for the purpose of giving it a characteristic color and an agreeable flavor. There was at the time no liquid preparation of quinine on the market containing chocolate, though there is evidence that it was sometimes so made up by druggists when called for. There is some evidence that petitioner endeavored by experiments to produce a preparation of the exact color and taste of that produced by respondent; and there is evidence in contradiction. We do not, however, regard it as important to determine upon which side lies the greater weight. Petitioner, in fact, did produce a preparation by the use of chocolate so exactly like that of respondent that they were incapable of being distinguished by ordinary sight or taste. By various trade methods an extensive and valuable market for the sale of respondent's preparation already had been established when the preparation of petitioner was put on the market. It is apparent, from a consideration of the testimony, that the efforts of petitioner to create a market for Quin-Coco were directed not so much to showing the merits of that preparation as they were to demonstrating its practical identity with Coco-Quinine, and, since it was sold at a lower price, inducing the purchasing druggist, in his own interest, to substitute, as far as he could, the former for the latter. In other words, petitioner sought to avail itself of the favorable repute which had been established for respondent's preparation in order to sell its own. Petitioner's salesmen appeared more anxious to convince the druggists with whom they were dealing that Quin-Coco was a good substitute for Coco-Quinine and was cheaper, than they were to independently demonstrate its merits. The evidence establishes by a fair preponderance that some of petitioner's salesmen suggested that, without danger of detection, prescriptions and orders for Coco-Quinine could be filled by substituting Quin-Coco. More often, however, the feasibility of such a course was brought to the mind of the druggist by pointing out the identity of the two preparations and the enhanced profit to be made by selling

Quin-Coco because of its lower price. There is much conflict in the testimony; but on the whole it fairly appears that petitioner's agents induced the substitution, either in direct terms or by suggestion or insinuation. Sales to druggists are in original bottles bearing clearly distinguishing labels and there is no suggestion of deception in those transactions; but sales to the ultimate purchasers are of the product in its naked form out of the bottle; and the testimony discloses many instances of passing off by retail druggists of petitioner's preparation when respondent's preparation was called for. That no deception was practiced on the retail dealers, and that they knew exactly what they were getting is of no consequence. The wrong was in designedly enabling the dealers to palm off the preparation as that of the respondent. One who induces another to commit a fraud and furnishes the means of consummating it is equally guilty and liable for the injury.

The charge of unfair competition being established, it follows that equity will afford relief by injunction to prevent such unfair competition for the future. Several acts of unfair competition having been shown, we are warranted in concluding that petitioner is willing to continue that course of conduct, unless restrained. It remains to consider the character and extent of this relief.

Respondent has no exclusive right to the use of its formula. Chocolate is used as an ingredient not alone for the purpose of imparting a distinctive color, but for the purpose also of making the preparation peculiarly agreeable to the palate, to say nothing of its effect as a suspending medium. While it is not a medicinal element in the preparation, it serves a substantial and desirable use, which prevents it from being a mere matter of dress. It does not merely serve the incidental use of identifying the respondent's preparation, and it is doubtful whether it should be called a non-essential. The petitioner or anyone else is at liberty under the law to manufacture and market an exactly similar preparation containing chocolate and to notify the public that it is being done. But the imitator of another's goods must sell them as his own production. He cannot lawfully palm them off on the public as the goods of his competitor. The manufacturer or vendor is entitled to the reputation which his goods have acquired and the public to the means of distinguishing between them and other goods; and protection is accorded against unfair dealing whether there be a technical trademark or not. The wrong is in the sale of the goods of one manufacturer or vendor as those of another. If petitioner had been content to manufacture the preparation and let it make its own way in the field of open and fair competition, there would be nothing more to be said. It was not thus content, however, but availed itself of unfair means, either expressly or tacitly, to impose its preparation on the ultimate purchaser as and for the product of respondent.

Nevertheless, the right to which respondent is entitled is that of being protected against unfair competition, not of having the aid of a decree to create or support, or assist in creating or supporting, a monopoly of the sale of a preparation which everyone, including petitioner, is free to make and vend. The legal wrong does not consist in the mere use of chocolate as an ingredient, but in the unfair and fraudulent advantage which is taken of such use to pass off the product as that of respondent. The use dissociated from the fraud is entirely lawful, and it is against the fraud that the injunction lies. But respondent being entitled to relief, is entitled to effective relief; and any doubt in respect of the extent thereof must be resolved in its favor as the innocent producer and against the petitioner, which has shown by its conduct that it is not to be trusted. Clearly, the relief should extend far enough to enjoin petitioner, and its various agents from, directly or indirectly, representing or suggesting to its customers the feasibility or possibility of passing off Quin-Coco for Coco-Quinine. The Court of Appeals held that petitioner should be unconditionally enjoined from the use of chocolate. We think this goes too far; but, having regard to the past conduct of petitioner, the practices of some druggists to which it has led, and the right of respondent to an effective remedy, we think the decree fairly may require that the original packages sold to druggists shall not only bear labels clearly distinguishing petitioner's bottled product from the bottled product of respondent, but that these labels shall state affirmatively that the preparation is not to be sold or dispensed as Coco-Quinine or be used in filling prescriptions or orders calling for the latter. With these general suggestions, the details and form of the injunction can be more satisfactorily determined by the District Court. The decree of the Court of Appeals is reversed and the cause remanded to the District Court for further proceedings in conformity with this opinion.

Reversed.

CHARCOAL STEAK HOUSE OF CHARLOTTE, INC. v. STALEY, 263 N.C. 199, 139 S.E.2d 185, 144 U.S.P.Q. 241 (1964). SHARP, J.: Although a generic word or a geographic designation cannot become an arbitrary trademark, it may nevertheless be used deceptively by a newcomer to the field so as to amount to unfair competition, and the prohibition against any right to the exclusive use of such a word or designation has been modified by the "secondary meaning" doctrine. This was fashioned to protect the public from deception, and is but one facet of the law of unfair competition.

When a particular business has used words publici juris for so long or so exclusively or when it has promoted its product to such an extent that the words do not register their literal meaning on the public mind but are instantly associated with one enterprise, such words have attained a secondary meaning. This is to say, a secondary meaning exists when in addition to their literal, or dictionary, meaning, words connote to the public a product *from a unique source*. It has been suggested, however, that when a descriptive word or phrase has come to mean a particular entrepreneur, the term *secondary meaning* is inaccurate because, in the field in which the phrase has acquired its new meaning, its so-called secondary meaning has become its primary, or natural, meaning.

The law will afford protection against the tortious appropriation of trade names and trademarks alike. To establish a secondary meaning for either, a plaintiff must show that it has come to stand for his business in the public mind, that is, "that the primary significance of the term in the minds of the consuming public is not the product but the producer." Kellogg Co. v. Nat. Biscuit Co., 305 U.S. 111, 118, 59 S.Ct. 109, 113, 83 L.Ed. 73, 78, 39 U.S.P.Q. 296, 299. But even though generic, or descriptive, words, when used alone, have come to have a secondary meaning, "a competitor may nevertheless use them if he accompanies their use with something which will adequately show that the first person or his product is not meant." Union Oyster House v. Hi Ho Oyster House, supra, 316 Mass. at 544, 55 N.E.2d at 943, 62 U.S.P.Q. at 218.

GALT HOUSE, INC. v. HOME SUPPLY CO.

Court of Appeals of Kentucky, 1972.
483 S.W.2d 107, 174 U.S.P.Q. 268.

REED, Judge.

The plaintiff, Galt House, Inc., instituted this action to enjoin the defendants, Home Supply Company, and its principal officer and stockholder, Al J. Schneider, from operating a new hotel in Louisville, Kentucky, under the assumed trade name "Galt House." The trial judge refused to enjoin the use of the name at the plaintiff's behest. We affirm that decision for the reasons later discussed. No other issue involved in the pending litigation in the trial court is decided. We confine our consideration to the sole issue presented by this appeal.

In February 1964, the plaintiff, Galt House, Inc., incorporated under the laws of this state. In its articles of incorporation it adopted as its corporate name the term "Galt House." The articles required and specified that the minimum capital with which plaintiff would commence business would be the sum of $1,000. This amount has never been paid in. The plaintiff has no assets and no liabilities; neither does it have corporate books or records. Plaintiff's president and sole shareholder is Arch Stallard, Sr., a real estate broker in Louisville, Kentucky, who specializes in hotels and motel real estate. Mr. Stallard has on occasions since the date of the filing of plaintiff's articles of incorporation made a few sporadic inquiries concerning possible locations for a hotel and considered engaging in an enterprise by which a franchise operation would be effected. These few efforts came to naught and Mr. Stallard testified that because of illness and death in his family he had been "laying dormant."

The defendant, Home Supply Company, is a Kentucky corporation organized sometime prior to 1950. The defendant, Al J. Schneider, is its president and controlling shareholder. Home Supply Company is active in the business of constructing and operating hotels in this state. It presently operates a hotel on the Kentucky State Fair Board property under the assumed name "Executive Inn." It is presently engaged in the construction and completion of a high-rise hotel on riverfront-development property belonging to an agency of the City of Louisville.

In April 1969, Home Supply Company, through its president Schneider, submitted to the city agency plans of a hotel bearing the name Galt House. This name had been recommended to Schneider by the then mayor of the City of Louisville, Kenneth Schmied, and the chairman of the Riverfront Development Commission, Archibald Cochran. The trial judge found from the evidence that throughout discussions leading up to the bidding, the new hotel was referred to as the Galt House and has been so referred to since. Home Supply Company was the successful bidder, was awarded the contract, and construction commenced in May 1970. A new hotel, 26 stories in height with 714 rooms, is now nearly completed and has affixed a sign bearing the name "The Galt House." The hotel already has scheduled future conventions and room reservations, although it will not open until after May 1972. In April 1971, Home Supply Company applied for and received from the Secretary of State of Kentucky a registration and service mark of the name "The Galt House."

Plaintiff filed suit in August 1971, seeking to enjoin the defendants from any use of the name Galt House. Evidence was taken in the form of depositions and written interrogatories. In February 1972, the trial judge entered a judgment that was made final for purposes of appeal; the judgment was based on findings of fact and conclusions of law set forth in two written opinions. The trial judge concluded in substance that the plaintiff did not by mere incorporation acquire property rights in the name "Galt House" and that the plaintiff had not performed sufficient acts since incorporation to acquire property rights in and to that name. Accordingly, the trial judge reasoned that the plaintiff was not entitled to injunctive relief against the defendants' use of the contested name. Plaintiff then appealed to this court and asserts several grounds on which it bases its contention that the trial court was in error in not granting it an injunction against the defendant. We shall deal with these contentions subsequently herein, but first a bit of history of the particular name that is the subject of controversy will be briefly related.

During the Nineteenth Century the Galt House Hotel was a famous hostelry in Louisville with an excellent and widely recognized reputation. In 1838 the barroom at the Galt House was the scene of a killing as a result of which an attorney and judge and his two companions were indicted for murder. They were tried and acquitted. The trial was held at Harrodsburg, Kentucky, to which venue had been transferred because of the intense public sentiment in Louisville against the defendants who were prominent citizens of Mississippi. The victims of the affray were Louisville residents. The trial itself is famous in the annals of Kentucky history.

In 1842 Charles Dickens toured America. In his account in "American Notes," he was characteristically uncomplimentary in his description of Louisville; he was impressed, however, with the Galt House. He wrote: "We slept at the Galt House; a splendid hotel; and were as handsomely lodged as though we had been in Paris, rather than hundreds of miles beyond the Alleghanies (sic)." In 1858 Charles Mackay, an English writer, passed through Louisville. In his account in "Life and Liberty in America" he remarked: ". . . we crossed in the steamer to Louisville, and once more found ourselves in a land of plenty and comfort, in a flourishing city, in an excellent hotel—the Galt House, one of the best conducted establishments in America; . . .."

The Galt House, located on Main Street at Second Street, occupied separate buildings during its existence as a hotel. The second Galt House was destroyed by fire in January 1865 at a reported loss of $1,000,000. The third Galt House, a magnificent structure in its day, was abandoned as a hotel and ceased operations in 1920. Belknap Hardware Company thereafter occupied the site of the last Galt House.

Thus, it would appear that since 1920 there has been no use of the name Galt House in connection with or to describe a hotel. The name doubtless strikes interest when used in the presence of history buffs and among those familiar with the folklore of Louisville. Among such cognoscenti the name encourages remembrance of things past.

As found by the circuit judge, the corporation which operated the last Galt House was formed in 1911 and its formal corporate existence expired in 1961. From 1920 to 1961, however, it did not engage in the hotel business. Therefore, the name Galt House had not been used in connection with a going business for 49 years when defendants undertook to use it as the name of their new hotel in 1969.

The primary argument asserted by the plaintiff actually rests upon a premise that by mere incorporation under a corporate name it retains the right to exclude others from the use of that name so long as the corporation legally exists. In Covington Inn Corp. v. White Horse Tavern, Inc., Ky., 445 S.W.2d 135, 163 U.S.P.Q. 438 (1969), we considered the effect of KRS 271.045, a part of the corporation law of this state, and held that its provision that a corporate name shall not be the same as "nor deceptively similar to" the name of other corporations, constituted an expression by the legislature that stated a policy conforming to the common law of "unfair competition" as applied in Kentucky. Thus, when under subsection (4) of the same statute an equity action is authorized to enjoin the doing of business under a name adopted in violation of this statute, the common law of unfair competition prescribes the standards which the court applies in determining whether to enjoin.

In that same opinion we remarked that perhaps this statute could be reasonably construed to extend to an assumed name of a corporation. That is the situation in this case. The defendant Home Supply Company has undertaken to do business under the assumed trade name Galt House, which is the same as plaintiff's adopted corporate name. In Meredith v. Universal Plumbing & Construction Co., 272 Ky. 283, 114 S.W.2d 94 (1938), we held that under our corporate statutes and other statutory laws applicable to transacting business under an assumed name there was no legal impediment to a corporation using an additional trade name that was different from its adopted corporate name. The pertinent statutes read the same now as they did then. Hence, there is no legal impediment to the defendant Home Supply Company's adoption of the trade name "Galt House", unless the plaintiff by the mere act of incorporation of the same name has precluded this defendant's right to adopt and use the name.

Surely the plaintiff acquires no standing to enjoin under the accepted principles of the law of unfair competition. Under the modern extended scope of the doctrine of unfair competition, its present outer limits afford protection and relief against the unjust appropriation of, or injury to, the good will or business reputation of another, even though he is not a competitor. Plaintiff is concededly a nonuser of the contested name. Plaintiff has no customers, conducts no real or substantial business and has never held its name out to the public in connection with any going business. Therefore, by its inaction, it could not have established either a good will or reputation which the defendants could be legitimately accused of pirating as a competitor or otherwise. Therefore, if plaintiff has standing to enjoin, its status must rest upon the acquisition of a protectable right by its act of incorporation under the contested name.

In Lawyers Title Ins. Co. v. Lawyers Title Ins. Corporation, 71 App.D.C. 120, 109 F.2d 35, 43 U.S.P.Q. 166 (1939), Mr. Justice Rutledge, writing for the Circuit Court of Appeals for the District of Columbia, considered the problem. This opinion is characterized by Fletcher as a leading case. See Volume 6, Fletcher Cyc. Corp. (1968 Perm. Ed.), Sec. 2425, page 55. That case and the prior case of Waterman Co. v. Modern Pen Co., 235 U.S. 88, 45 S.Ct. 91, 59 L.Ed. 142 (1914), established clearly that mere incorporation under a particular name does not create the right to have such name protected against use by another. Mr. Justice Holmes said in Waterman:

> "While it very well may be true that the transfer of a name without a business is not enough to entitle the transferee to prevent others from using it, it still is a license that may be sufficient to put the licensee on the footing of the licensor as against the plaintiff."

The plaintiff, however, relies upon the case of Drugs Consolidated v. Drug Incorporated, 16 Del.Ch. 240, 144 A. 656 (1929). In our view the opinion in that case undertakes to prove too much. There is dictum that the corporation statutes of Delaware, which are substantially similar to the corporation statutes of Kentucky so far as the present point is concerned, assure a right to have the corporate name distinguished from other corporations of like kind subsequently created and that this right does not depend on showing of actual use, in business, of the name, but the right exists as soon as corporate existence is brought into being and as long as it continues; the specific factual findings in the opinion, however, demonstrate that the plaintiff corporation, although it was not yet actually engaged in the business of manufacturing and marketing drugs, had, nevertheless, been engaged in promoting the objects and purposes of its incorporation. Therefore, if this opinion represents a holding that a nonuser of a corporate name retains the right to pre-empt that name during the period of its formal corporate existence without ever having engaged in carrying on any of the objects and purposes of the corporation, it is contrary to the weight of authority concerning that proposition and does not, in our opinion, represent the generally accepted view.

The Drugs Consolidated opinion was cited with approval by the Mississippi Supreme Court in Meridian Yellow Cab Co. v. City Yellow Cabs, 206 Miss. 812, 41 So.2d 14 (1949). In this case, however, the plaintiff who first incorporated had actually commenced operations at the time it sought to enjoin the defendant who had later incorporated under a similar name. Although the plaintiff did not commence business until after the defendant, it, nevertheless, did actually start active operations in the taxicab business within three years of the date of its incorporation and within two months after the defendant actually operated taxicabs; whether the plaintiff was theretofore engaged in activities to promote the objects and purposes of the corporation is not mentioned. However misplaced that court's reliance on the Drugs Consolidated case may have been, its decision, which granted the plaintiff injunctive relief, does not militate against our conclusion in this case that the plaintiff's act of incorporation in a particular name pre-empts the use of that name by a subsequent user only for a reasonable period in which to allow plaintiff's business to begin. To this extent, incorporation and registration take the place of user in the case of a trade name. Pre-emption for a reasonable period of time in which to allow the business to begin is not the equivalent of a perpetual monopoly of the trade name without use in trade. Upon this rationale, the case of Pacific Northwest Bell Telephone Co. v. Rivers, 88 Idaho 240, 398 P.2d 63 (1964), also cited by plaintiff, is readily distinguishable from the instant case. . . .

The judgment from which the appeal was prosecuted is affirmed.

All concur.

NOTES

1. The history of unfair competition law is summarized in Chafee, Unfair Competition, 53 Harv.L.Rev. 1289 (1940) and is treated exhaustively in F. Schechter, The Historical Foundations of the Law Relating to Trade-Marks (1925). For a brief, comparative view, see Comment, Unfair Competition: A Comparative Study of its Role in Common and Civil Law Systems, 53 Tul.L.Rev. 164 (1978).

2. In its traditional design, unfair competition law protects (a) the first to use a name, brand or other symbol in connection with the sale of goods or services against (b) a competitor whose own use of

the symbol (c) confuses, or is likely to confuse, consumers into believing that the first user, rather than the competitor, is the source of the goods or services. The formula seeks to accommodate the interests of competitors in choosing and investing in symbols that will capture their good will and the interests of consumers in being free from confusion as to the source of goods and services.

(a) *First user.* What was there about the word "aluminum," that made the court in *American Washboard* withhold trademark protection? Say that plaintiffs had used the term exclusively for several years so that substantial secondary meaning had accrued and consumers identified "aluminum" washboards as coming from plaintiff. Would, and should, the court have protected plaintiff in these circumstances? Say that the *Warner* plaintiff's formula for Coco-Quinine had been patented. Would there be any reason to deny plaintiff the benefits of secondary meaning that accrued to the product and its name during the patent's seventeen-year term?

Even if plaintiff has a monopoly over its product, is it correct to assume, as apparently the circuit court did in *Mosler*, that every sale made by the false advertiser is one that otherwise would have been made by the plaintiff? If, as often happens, the false advertiser offers its wares at a lower price than the truthful advertiser, is it possible that this is the highest price that some group of consumers is willing to pay? Was it appropriate for the Supreme Court in *Mosler* to act as if *no* sales had been diverted? If diversion is relevant, at all, is it not best measured by calculating the number of competitors and the probabilities of consumer choice? Problems of proof aside, why should diversion be an important element of plaintiff's cause of action, either in false advertising or passing off cases?

(b) *Competitors.* If *American Washboard* refused to give plaintiff trademark rights in the descriptive term, "aluminum" because competitors should be free to use commonly accepted descriptive terms to describe their wares, does it follow that competitors should be free to use the descriptive term to *mis*describe their products? Since defendant's washboard was made of zinc, not aluminum, what stood in the way of defendant obtaining trademark rights in the term "aluminum" as applied to zinc washboards?

Say that plaintiff in *Galt* began operating a Galt House Hotel after the defendant announced plans for its hotel, but before defendant opened for business. Would the court have enjoined defendant? On a counterclaim, would it have given defendant an injunction against plaintiff? Did the court properly attend to the fact that the name, "Galt House," possessed considerable historic significance in Louisville? Does the fact that neither party to the action was responsible for the name's historic appeal mean that neither should have any exclusive rights in it? That neither should be allowed to use it? Is "Galt House" in this sense like the term "aluminum"?

(c) *Consumers.* Would consumers be better off if the rules of *American Washboard* and *Mosler* were altered to give merchants an action against misleading statements by competitors? How well placed are consumers to discover and protect themselves against deceptions of the sort involved in these two cases? How well placed are they to discover and protect themselves against deception of the sort involved in *Warner*? Would consumers ever know that Searle & Hereth, not Eli-Lilly, had produced the flavored quinine that they imbibed?

3. Unfair competition's three operative elements—the first user's investment in goodwill, the competitor's deceptive acts, and the consumer's confusion as to source—are obviously matters of degree. Somewhat less obvious is that each of the three elements reciprocates the other two. For example, the need for direct proof of consumer confusion will decrease as the distinctiveness of the first user's name or symbol, and the extent of its replication by the competitor, increase.

Three typical unfair competition cases will illustrate the workings of this reciprocal relationship. In one case, the first user's symbol or device has, because of its descriptiveness or brevity of use, acquired no secondary meaning, no capacity to identify the first user as a source. For the first user to prevail, it must prove that the competitor actively palmed off its goods or services as coming from the first user, and deceived consumers as to source by word or deed. It must show, too, that as a consequence of this conduct, consumers were in fact confused as to the source of the goods or services.

In the second situation, the first user's symbol or device, though descriptive or otherwise common, also possesses secondary meaning. Neither a conscious intent to deceive nor actual deception of consumers need be shown here, only the likelihood that the competitor's use of the symbol or device will deceive consumers as to source. In the third case, the first user has adopted a distinctive, nondescriptive symbol or device that functions exclusively to identify it. Here, courts will conclusively presume that the competitor's use of the symbol was intended to, and did, cause consumer confusion. Given the infinite variety of symbols and other insignia available for adoption by the competitor, courts assume that the competitor's use of the facsimile could only have been motivated by an intent to deceive and was in fact successful in accomplishing the deception.

In any of these three situations, the symbol or device used by the competitor need not be absolutely identical to the first user's. The closer the similarity between the two, however, the greater is the probability that a court will infer deception.

4. *Unfair Competition and Trademarks.* Doctrinally, trademark law is part of unfair competition law. Unfair competition embraces a broad continuum of competitive conduct likely to confuse consumers as to the source of goods and services—from the appropriation of relatively nondistinctive symbols accompanied by acts of passing off, to the appropriation of distinctive symbols in which case confusion is presumed. Trademark law occupies only the last part of

this continuum, protecting distinctive, arbitrary or otherwise strong marks against appropriation by competitors and requiring no proof that consumers have actually been deceived.

Although trademark and unfair competition law differ in degree rather than kind, some categorical distinctions can be made. Unfair competition law is entirely circumstantial. In determining whether a defendant's conduct is unfair, courts will look at the aggregate effect of all the elements employed in plaintiff's and defendant's respective marketing efforts. Among the elements that will be considered are the nature of the product, the color, shape and size of its package, the configuration of the label and any insignia, terms and names appearing on the label, and the nature, media and content of any surrounding advertising. If a comparison of the total images created by the first user and its competitor indicates that consumer confusion is likely, the court will enter a decree requiring the defendant to modify its marketing effort to avoid confusion.

The method of trademark law, by contrast, is to focus exclusively on each discrete element in the plaintiff's marketing image. If the element meets trademark's distinctiveness standards, it will be protected. If not, the element will not be considered further. Defendant's appropriation of each protected element will be enjoined, with little if any concern paid to surrounding circumstances. The injunction will typically be absolute, even though a conditional decree or a requirement of labeling would suffice to dispel confusion. See generally, Handler & Pickett, Trade-Marks and Trade Names—An Analysis and Synthesis, (pts. 1 & 2) 30 Colum.L.Rev. 168, 759 (1930).

The most consequential distinction between trademark and unfair competition law is jurisdictional. Although there is some overlap, trademarks are administered largely under the federal Trademark Act and unfair competition under state common law and statute. While many states also provide by statute for the registration of trademarks used within their borders, these statutes are of limited substantive consequence. Part 3, Chapter I covers the federal law of trademarks and their statutory companions—service marks, collective marks and certification marks.

5. Section 43(a) of the Lanham Trade-Mark Act, 15 U.S.C.A. § 1125(a), effectively reverses the rule of *American Washboard* as a matter of federal law. It imposes liability for the use "in connection with any goods or services" of "any false description or representation." See page 418, below.

As a matter of state law, *Mosler's* approach quickly found a home in the first Restatement of Torts (1939):

Section 761. *False Advertising—Liability to Competitor.* One who diverts trade from a competitor by fraudulently representing that the goods which he markets have ingredients or qualities which in fact they do not have but which the goods of the competitor do have is liable to the competitor for the harm so caused, if,

(a) when making the representation he intends that it should, or knows or should know that it is likely to, divert trade from the competitor, and

(b) the competitor is not marketing his goods with material fraudulent misrepresentations about them.

After debating an alternative formulation for the second Restatement, the American Law Institute decided to drop the matter altogether as part of its larger decision not to cover interference with business relations comprehensively. See Introductory Note, Restatement of Torts, Second, Vol. 4, Division 9, 1–2 (1979).

As a practical matter, what incentives do firms have to misrepresent the quality of their wares? How great a need is there for actions by competitors and for government intervention? See Jordan & Rubin, An Economic Analysis of the Law of False Advertising, 8 J. Leg.Stud. 527, 551 (1979).

6. Can merchants refer to the goods they sell by the trademark or trade name applied to the goods by their manufacturer? Before giving the easy and obvious answer, remember that there is a large market for secondhand, repaired, and reconstructed goods, and that the conditions of this market may make the question of collateral trademark use problematic.

In Prestonettes, Inc. v. Coty, 264 U.S. 359, 44 S.Ct. 350, 68 L.Ed. 731 (1924), Coty sought to "restrain alleged unlawful uses of the plaintiff's registered trademarks, 'Coty' and 'L'Origan' upon toilet powders and perfumes. The defendant purchases the genuine powder, subjects it to pressure, adds a binder to give it coherence and sells the compact in a metal case. It buys the genuine perfume in bottles and sells it in smaller bottles." The district court decree would have permitted a truthful allusion to Coty—a label on the compacts, for example, reading, "Prestonettes, Inc., not connected with Coty, states that the compact of face powder herein was independently compounded by it from Coty's—(giving the name) loose powder and its own binder. Loose powder—per cent, Binder—per cent," with "every word to be in letters of the same size, color, type and general distinctiveness."

The circuit court concluded that the district court's decree did not sufficiently protect Coty and absolutely enjoined all use of its marks by defendants on the ground that, "to permit the plaintiff's name and trade-mark to be used on other than his original packages should be forbidden, as the value of his name and trade-mark would be endangered through the deterioration of his product due to the action of unauthorized and unsupervised persons in changing the perfumes from the receptacles in which they were originally placed into others which may be wholly unfit even though the perfumes remain unadulterated." 285 F. 501, 513 (2d Cir. 1922).

The Supreme Court, in an opinion by Mr. Justice Holmes, reversed and ordered the district court decree reinstated. Since "The plaintiff could not complain of its [defendant's] stating the nature of the component parts and the source from which they were derived if it did not use the trademark in doing so," the fact that its trademark was involved added nothing to plaintiff's rights: "When the mark is used in a way that does not deceive the public we see no such sanctity in the word as to prevent its being used to tell the truth. It is not taboo." As to the possible deterioration in the product's quality and consequent impairment of the manufacturer's name, Justice Holmes concluded, "it might be a misfortune to the plaintiff, but the plaintiff would have no cause of action, as the defendant was exercising the rights of ownership and only telling the truth." 264 U.S. 359, 368, 44 S.Ct. 350, 351.

Twenty-three years later, in Champion Spark Plug Co. v. Sanders, 331 U.S. 125, 67 S.Ct. 1136, 91 L.Ed. 1386, 73 U.S.P.Q. 133 (1947), which involved defendant's repair, reconditioning, and sale of spark plugs bearing the mark of their original manufacturer, the Court affirmed an order permitting collateral use of the plaintiff's mark so long as the plugs also bore the word "Repaired" or "Used." Recognizing that, unlike *Prestonettes*, this case involved questions of unfair competition as well as trademark infringement, the court nonetheless followed the *Prestonettes* reasoning and result. In dicta, however, it cautioned that "Cases may be imagined where the reconditioning or repair would be so extensive or basic that it would be a misnomer to call the article by its original name, even though the words 'used' or 'repaired' were added."

That the last word on these matters is not the Supreme Court's is well evidenced by a triad of cases: Clairol, Inc. v. Peekskill Thrift Drug Corp., 141 U.S.P.Q. 147 (N.Y.Sup.Ct.1964); Clairol, Inc. v. Sarann Co., 146 U.S.P.Q. 726 (Pa.Ct.Com.Pl.1965); Clairol, Inc. v. Cody's Cosmetics, Inc., 353 Mass. 385, 231 N.E.2d 912 (1967). The facts, roughly the same in all three cases, were these: Plaintiff sold its hair coloring product, "Miss Clairol," under a dual pricing system so that the professional trade—jobbers for beauty salons—was able to buy the goods at about one-half the price charged to the retail trade —drug and cosmetic wholesalers. The products distributed through these two channels were identical, the only difference being in the method of packaging. The retail trade received individually boxed single application bottles, and the professional trade received single application bottles in six-packs. An instruction sheet containing several warnings as to the dangers of misusing the product, and advice on how to avoid them, was enclosed in each retail carton but not in the professional six-pack. Every professional carton bore the legend, "Professional Use Only." Defendants, drug and cosmetic retailers, purchased professional six-packs at the substantial discount and sold the bottles individually, without cartons, to their retail customers. To these bottles defendants attached mimeographed instruction sheets which in all three cases omitted vital information, given in Clairol's retail instruction sheet, on the methods and dangers of use.

Clairol's action to enjoin defendants from selling "Miss Clairol" in any form other than the complete Clairol retail package succeeded in New York and Pennsylvania. In the New York action, plaintiff's proof that defendant's conduct was "likely to injure plaintiff's goodwill and business reputation" was held sufficient to warrant relief under the state's broad unfair competition statute, General Business Law § 368–d. Lacking the statutory authority available in New York, the Pennsylvania court rested its decision on two common-law grounds. First, conceding that no passing off had been shown, the court concluded that defendant's conduct nonetheless constituted unfair competition: "the consumer will attribute any unsatisfactory performance from 'Miss Clairol' to plaintiff, and not to defendant. Defendant thus used plaintiff's goodwill to make sales, but acts in a manner which can only decrease plaintiff's goodwill, thus damaging an important property interest of plaintiff." Second, the court concluded: "plaintiff, by placing on the bottle of 'Miss Clairol' destined for professional use the legend 'Professional Use Only,' has placed an equitable servitude or restriction on the bottle, thus preventing defendant from acting in violation of that restriction."

Clairol did not fare nearly as well in Massachusetts. Refusing to extend unfair competition beyond its basic passing off formula, and clearly rejecting the equitable servitude argument, the court concluded that the injury to consumers was only incidental and that the essential injury was to "an effective marketing and advertising device." Recognizing that there was some danger that consumers would suffer injury from uninstructed use, the court did enjoin defendant from selling the professional bottles without a legible, printed statement containing appropriate warnings. See also, Clairol, Inc. v. Boston Discount Center of Berkley, Inc., 608 F.2d 1114, 204 U.S.P.Q. 89 (6th Cir. 1979) (approving the unfair competition complaint and rejecting defendant's antitrust counterclaim and defenses).

7. Can one who has lawfully copied a product refer to the product's trademark in his own advertising for the purpose of identifying the product he has copied? In Smith v. Chanel, Inc., 402 F.2d 562, 159 U.S.P.Q. 388 (9th Cir. 1968), the court held that appellant, who advertised his less costly fragrance as an exact duplicate of plaintiff's "Chanel No. 5", could use the trademark for this purpose "and that such advertising may not be enjoined under either the Lanham Act, 15 U.S.C.A. § 1125(a), or the common law of unfair competition, so long as it does not contain misrepresentations or create a reasonable likelihood that purchasers will be confused as to the source, identity, or sponsorship of the advertiser's product." 402 F.2d 562, 563. On remand, however, the district court found that defendant's fragrance was not in fact an exact duplicate of Chanel No. 5 and concluded that his advertising thus involved a misrepresentation. Chanel, Inc. v. Smith, 178 U.S.P.Q. 630, (N.D.Cal.1973), aff'd 528 F.2d 284 (9th Cir. 1976).

8. Injunctions against unfair competition are limited only by the judicial imagination. At one end is outright prohibition of any use of plaintiff's trade insignia. At the other is a requirement only that defendant include in its labels and advertising explanatory mate-

rial as to the source of its goods or services. Vocational Personnel Services, Inc. v. Statistical Tabulating Corp., 305 F.Supp. 701, 163 U. S.P.Q. 55 (D.Minn.1969), made a more intricate use of the remedy. Defendant there was ordered to instruct the local telephone company to delete his confusingly similar name from its future directories and to have intercepts placed on his present telephone number so that telephone company operators could query callers as to whether they were interested in the services of plaintiff or defendant, and to relay the calls accordingly.

Although proof of defendant's fraudulent or other ill intent is not necessary for an injunction to issue, it may affect the injunction's scope. See, for example, Coca-Cola Co. v. Dixi-Cola Laboratories, Inc., 155 F.2d 59, 69 U.S.P.Q. 360 (4th Cir. 1946), cert. denied, 329 U.S. 773, 67 S.Ct. 192, 91 L.Ed. 665.

9. The two principal monetary remedies, damages and accounting of profits, are generally awarded only if defendant's conduct is willful or fraudulent. The formula for each is relatively straightforward. Under the accounting measure, plaintiff is entitled to all profits made by defendant as a consequence of its unfair conduct. Defendant has the burden of apportioning its total profits between those that were consequential and those that were earned independent of its unfair conduct, and of proving deductions from profits—costs of manufacturing, selling and other items of overhead. Under the damages measure, plaintiff bears the burden of proving its losses attributable to defendant's conduct—losses, for example, resulting from reduction in business or prices, or from injury to the plaintiff's business reputation. The general rule, that if a plaintiff is entitled to one of these measures it is entitled to both, has created some problems. Where plaintiff and defendant are direct competitors, to award plaintiff defendant's profits as well as damages for its lost profits would effect a punitive double recovery. Recognizing this, courts have in these cases allowed the accounting but confined damages to items independent of lost sales, such as price reductions and advertising outlays required to combat defendant's activity. In cases in which defendant's conduct has been notably oppressive, punitive damages may be awarded.

Monetary awards in the two leading commercial jurisdictions are discussed in Note, Monetary Awards for Unfair Competition in New York, 35 N.Y.U.L.Rev. 1068 (1960) and Note, Monetary Awards for Unfair Competition in California, 34 S.Calif.L.Rev. 283 (1961).

10. As *Galt* makes clear, unfair competition law traditionally requires that, to gain and maintain protection, a firm must actually use its name or other symbol in its business. The use requirement means that names cannot be reserved for future use. It also means that a firm can have no exclusive rights in geographic, product or service markets that it has not yet entered. At least originally, it was thought that the use requirement adequately balanced the interests of first users, their competitors and their consumers. Since, pre-

sumably, the first user's name or symbol did not identify it in markets it had not yet entered, the use of the name or symbol in those markets by competitors would not confuse consumers as to source nor divert trade from the first user. Indeed, as a consequence of the use requirement, it was the competitor who would gain exclusive rights to the symbol in these markets.

How can the use requirement be administered in a world of highly mobile consumers carrying the memory of symbols, goods and services from one region to another? In a world in which firms, seeking to capitalize on the symbols and goodwill associated with one line of goods or services, use the same symbol in their carefully timed introduction of different products or services? These questions lie at the source of unfair competition's newer directions, considered next.

2. NEW DIRECTIONS

a. ZONE OF EXPANSION

THE SAMPLE, INC. v. PORRATH

Supreme Court of New York, Appellate Division, Fourth Department, 1973.
41 A.D.2d 118, 341 N.Y.S.2d 683, 178 U.S.P.Q. 365, aff'd on opinion
below 33 N.Y.2d 961, 353 N.Y.S.2d 733, 309 N.E.2d 133,
181 U.S.P.Q. 850.

GOLDMAN, Presiding Justice.

In this action appellants, The Sample, Inc. and The Sample of Buffalo, Inc., appeal from a judgment denying their application for a declaratory judgment permitting them to use the trade name "Sample" in connection with a proposed new retail outlet in the Town of Wheatfield, Niagara County, New York. The order denying appellants this requested relief granted the respondents, Theresa Porrath, Samuel Porrath, Dorothy Gellman and Samuel Gellman, copartners doing business under the firm name of The Sample Shop, a permanent injunction restraining appellants from using the name "Sample" in any business operation to be conducted within the City of Niagara Falls and the Towns of Niagara, Wheatfield, Lewiston and Porter in the County of Niagara.

The history of the business activities of the parties, their methods of operation, the territorial markets they serve and much pertinent data were fully presented to the trial court. It appears from the proof that the Buffalo based "The Sample, Inc." was established in 1929 and has advertised in Buffalo papers under the trade name "The Sample" since its founding. In its early days it specialized in the sale of women's apparel but over the years has expanded greatly the variety of merchandise offered for sale and now includes men's as well as women's clothing and in addition thereto operates other departments such as jewelry, ladies' shoes and fabrics, children's wear and many other commodities. "The Sample, Inc." opened its first branch store outside of Buffalo in the City of Lockport, Niagara County, in 1946 and now operates in nine locations in Western New York, two of which are in Niagara County. Each branch store is a separate, wholly-owned subsidiary corporation. The parent corporation had net sales in 1971 in excess of $10,600,000 with more than $1,350,000 produced by the two Niagara County stores. Over 61,500 persons hold charge accounts with "The Sample, Inc." and 7,200 of these customers live in Niagara County. Appellants have spent $2,165,461 for advertising under the name "The Sample", spending almost as much in 1971 as respondents have in the last 23 years. This advertising has appeared primarily in two large Buffalo newspapers, which have a circulation of over 25,000 in Niagara County and appellants have also advertised extensively in the Lockport Union Sun and Journal and the Tonawanda News, both of which are largely distributed throughout Niagara County.

Respondents operate two stores, the first of which was opened in 1934 in Niagara Falls under the name "Sample Dress Shop". These stores which had net sales of $678,000 in 1971 stock primarily women's apparel and do not offer for sale such items as men's wear and the various other merchandise which is sold in "The Sample, Inc." stores. Since 1948 respondents have spent a total of $311,000 in advertising, almost entirely in the Niagara Falls Gazette. The primary market of the two stores is in the City of Niagara Falls and the four towns surrounding the city.

The store which appellants desire to open would be located in the Summit Park Mall in the Town of Wheatfield in Niagara County, one and a half miles from one of respondents' stores. They propose to name it "The Sample Shop of Buffalo, Inc.". Appellants have offered to call the store by any other name, which includes the word "Sample", such as the "Bunis (family name of principal stockholders) Sample Shop", or any reasonable and distinguishing name so long as it includes the word "Sample". Appellants have demonstrated a willingness to select a name which will eliminate any conflict with respondents' "The Sample Shop".

An in-depth market survey by National Marketing Associates, Inc. was put into evidence by appellants. It indicates that women in the 18–50 years age group who live within a five mile radius of the Summit Park Mall are more likely to associate the word "Sample" with a store operated by appellants than one owned by respondents. The market data contained in the survey clearly show that a substantial majority of persons interviewed, when asked to identify a store operated under the names "The Sample" or "Sample Shops", responded by indicating the store owned by appellants.

The trial court found that respondents' name, "The Sample Shop", has "acquired a secondary meaning identifying in the minds of the public" the two stores operated by respondents in the City of Niagara Falls. It further found "that the public would be confused and deceived by plaintiffs' use of the word 'Sample'" and that there "is a likelihood of dilution of the distinctive quality of defendants' trade name by plaintiffs' use of the word 'Sample' as a part of a corporate or assumed name". The trial court concluded from its findings that appellants are not entitled to judgment declaring their right to operate the new store under the name "The Sample of Buffalo, Inc." and granted judgment to respondents restraining and enjoining appellants from the "use of the word 'Sample' as part of a corporate or assumed name". We find this determination to be against the weight of the evidence.

The preponderance of the evidence supports appellants' contention that a majority of potential customers of both parties are more likely to associate the word "Sample" with a store operated by appellants rather than one operated by respondents. The uncontradicted data of the market survey and the history of the business activities of both parties show that respondents' business name has not acquired a secondary meaning and that the greater likelihood is that appellants' name, "The Sample, Inc.", has gained such a secondary meaning in the minds of the purchasing public.

In the determination of the issue here presented, the overriding objective is to promote and protect the concept of commercial fairness. Unfair competition and trademark infringement are all unique in their particular factual patterns and each case should be decided "on its facts", and because of incompatibility there cannot be strict adherence to precedents.

The principle of commercial fairness is well enunciated by the United States Court of Appeals of the First Circuit in Food Center v. Food Fair Stores, 356 F.2d 775, 148 U.S.P.Q. 621. In that case a Massachusetts retail supermarket carried on business under the name "New England Food Fair". It sought to enjoin the defendant, the nation's fifth largest chain of grocery supermarkets operating in 15 States under the name "Food Fair", from operating under its name in the Massachusetts area. The District Court found that the plaintiff's name had acquired a secondary meaning in greater Boston and to some extent in other parts of Eastern Massachusetts. In vacating the judgment of the District Court the Circuit Court said "In attempting to apply principles and precedents to the facts of this case, we recognize at the outset that the field of protection of trade names is part of the wider domain of the law relating to unfair competition, where the overriding objective of courts and legislatures is that of commercial fairness". As in the case at bar in the use of the word "Sample", the court found that the name "Food Fair" was not of the strongest order of originality. The Federal court concerned itself, as we should, that the public be not disadvantaged by confusion of names and set forth specific recommendations as to territory and operation to avoid confusion. In the case at bar all that is required is the adoption of a name by appellants which will clearly identify appellants' store and distinguish it, in the minds of the public, from respondents' stores. This we believe is accomplished by using the word "Buffalo" in appellants' name.

Succinctly stated, the paramount question is whether the acts complained of are fair or unfair. No longer is it the law that the protection of a business name depends primarily upon whether that name has acquired a secondary meaning. International News Serv. v. Assoc. Press, 248 U.S. 215, 235, 237, 39 S.Ct. 68, 63 L.Ed. 211. If it is demonstrable and clear from the record that the acts of one charged with usurpation of another's commercial name are actually unfair, equitable principles become operative. What equity will not tolerate is the appropriation of another's business name together with the exploitation and the grasping for enjoyment of the benefits of another's labor and effort, when the latter has culminated in a special quality being attached to the particular name. Tiffany & Co. v. Tiffany Prods., 147 Misc. 679, 681, 264 N.Y.S. 459, 461–462, affd. 237 App.Div. 801, 260 N.Y.S. 821, affd. 262 N.Y. 482, 188 N.E. 130; Miles Shoes of New York v. Niles Bootery, Inc., 235 App.Div. 575, 257 N. Y.S. 790, app. dsmd. 260 N.Y. 566, 184 N.E. 95; Long's Hat Stores Corp. v. Long's Clothes, Inc., 224 App.Div. 497, 231 N.Y.S. 107.

The issue of trade name infringement was not decided by the trial court because neither party had taken any action concerning the matter for many years. The court found that there were two separate and distinct market areas; that the trade name of both parties had acquired a secondary meaning in their particular area; each entity was entitled to protection in its own specialized area; the public would be confused and deceived by the appellants' use of the word "Sample" at the store at Summit Park Mall; there was a likelihood of diluting the distinctive quality of the respondents' trade name; there would be little disadvantage to the appellants if they were unable to use the word "Sample" in the name of their new store; and by using the name the appellants would be taking advantage of the goodwill associated with the word "Sample" and established by the respondents.

Secondary meaning has been defined as the trade meaning which may attach to a particular market because its user has expended time and money in the promotion of the market. Where a business name acquires a special significance pointing to only one business enterprise in a certain locality, it is protected from use by another in the same area. The concept of secondary meaning is that a name has become so identified with a particular business that it exclusively signifies only that one particular business. Priority of use alone is not equivalent to acquisition of that special significance which entitles a trade name to protection against infringement.

The respondents have not met the burden of establishing the existence of a secondary meaning for their trade name "The Sample Shop" and this they must do in order to restrain appellants from using that trade name. The results of the consumer attitude study conducted at the request of appellants are entitled to probative weight. This study demonstrated that many more consumers were aware of the appellants' name than that of the respondents. This awareness no doubt emanates from the considerable advertising carried on by the appellants in and by all of the media. This awareness also mitigates against a finding that the business name of respondents has acquired a secondary meaning either in the respondents' limited geographical area or within the metropolitan area constituting Buffalo and Niagara Falls in Erie and Niagara Counties.

The finding that the appellants will be taking advantage of the goodwill associated with the name "Sample" and established by the respondents is not supported by the record. The consumers in the Summit Park Mall area relate the name "Sample" to the Buffalo based retail stores more than to the Niagara Falls based stores. This identification probably stems from the advertising of the word "Sample" in connection with appellants as early as 1929.

The record fails to establish that the appellants' use of the word "Sample" would deceive the public and dilute the distinctive quality of respondents' name. The facts are that the public identifies the name "Sample" with the appellants rather than with the respondents or at least it cannot be said on this record that the identification is more in favor of respondents than appellants.

Finally, a finding that the use of a different name would result in little disadvantage to appellants is not valid. The name associated with the Buffalo stores has acquired singular significance through substantial advertising expenditures. That the new store would be deprived of that name is of no little consequence and would be detrimental to successful operation.

There is no inkling of bad faith on the part of the appellants or of any intention to deceive and confuse the public and to identify the respondents' products with the appellants.

Of course, an injunction will issue to prevent any activity calculated to impair the value of a trade name or to deceive the public. The appellants are not attempting to trade on the goodwill of the respondents' distinctive name so that there is a misappropriation of a property right belonging to another. There may possibly be some confusion as a result of the use of appellants' name in the Summit Park Mall but we must look at the over-all picture, and it is quite clear that neither party has any manifestly superior claim to the name "Sample". The most equitable solution to this controversy is to allow the use of similar but not identical names so that both stores may use the word "Sample". By such a disposition the interests of all parties will be protected and commercial fairness will be achieved.

The judgment below should be reversed and judgment entered declaring that the appellants may operate a retail store in the Summit Park Mall, in the Town of Wheatfield, Niagara County, New York, under the name "The Sample of Buffalo, Inc.".

b. DILUTION

ALLIED MAINTENANCE CORP. v. ALLIED MECHANICAL TRADES, INC.

Court of Appeals of New York, 1977.
42 N.Y.2d 538, 399 N.Y.S.2d 628, 369 N.E.2d 1162, 198 U.S.P.Q. 418.

JASEN, Judge.

We are called upon today to decide whether the trade name "Allied Maintenance" is entitled to protection pursuant to section 368–d of the General Business Law—commonly referred to as the anti-dilution statute.

The plaintiff, Allied Maintenance Corporation, has been in business, in one form or another, since 1888. Throughout the many years since its inception, Allied Maintenance has concentrated the scope of its services upon the cleaning and maintenance of large office buildings. The defendant, Allied Mechanical Trades, Inc., a corporation organized in 1968 as a successor to Controlled Weather Corporation, is engaged primarily in the installation and repair of heating, ventilating and air-conditioning equipment.

Alleging that the defendant performed maintenance services identical to those it performed, Allied Maintenance brought this action to enjoin Allied Mechanical from operating under the name "Allied" or "Allied Mechanical Trades, Inc." or using the word "Allied" in any way in connection with its business. The trial court granted the injunction, finding that the parties were actual and potential competitors in the cleaning and maintenance industry in the metropolitan New York City area and that the auditory and visual similarity between their names created a likelihood of confusion. On this basis, the court concluded that defendant's use of the name Allied Mechanical would result in irreparable injury to plaintiff's reputation, good will, and proprietary business interests, and would thus constitute unfair competition. The Appellate Division reversed, however, finding an absence of either competition or confusion, actual or potential. The court concluded that "no user of the services of either party has been or may probably be confused or deceived by any similarity in the names of the parties." (55 A.D.2d 865, 866, 390 N.Y.S.2d 101, 102.)

In addition to the protection of trademarks and trade names afforded by the traditional actions for trademark infringement and unfair competition, New York, as well as a number of other states,[1] has

---

1. Ark.Stat.Ann., § 70–550 (Cum.Supp. 1976); Cal.Bus. & Prof.Code, § 14330 (West 1974); Conn.Gen.Stat.Ann., § 35–11i(c) (West 1969); Del.Code, tit. 6, § 3313 (Cum.Supp.1976); Fla.Stat. Ann., § 495.151 (1974); Idaho Code, § 48–512 (Cum.Supp.1976); Ill.Rev. Stat., ch. 140, § 22 (1975); Iowa Code Ann., § 548.11(2) (West 1975); Mass. Gen.Laws Ann., ch. 110b, § 12 (West Supp.1975–1976); Mo.Ann.Stat., § 417.061 (Vernon Supp.1975); Neb. Rev.Stat., § 87–122 (1971); N.H.Rev. Stat.Ann., § 350–A:12 (Supp.1973); N.M.Stat.Ann., § 49–4–11.2 (Supp. 1975); Ore.Rev.Stat., § 647.107 (1975); R.I.Gen.Laws, § 6–2–12 (Supp.

adopted an anti-dilution statute. (General Business Law, § 368–d.) This statute provides: "Likelihood of injury to business reputation or of dilution of the distinctive quality of a mark or trade name shall be ground for injunctive relief in cases of infringement of a mark registered or not registered or in cases of unfair competition, *notwithstanding the absence of competition between the parties or in the absence of confusion as to the source of goods or services.*" (Emphasis added.) The purpose behind the enactment of this statute was the prevention of trademark or trade name dilution—i. e., "the whittling away of an established trademark's selling power and value through its unauthorized use by others upon dissimilar products." (N.Y.Legis.Ann., 1954, p. 49.) In the absence of a statute of this nature, a plaintiff seeking to prohibit the use of a trade name by another would be required to frame his complaint within the strictures of an action for either trademark infringement or unfair competition. A brief review of the elements of these actions is useful in interpreting the legislative intent behind the enactment of section 368–d.

Historically, two causes of action have existed to protect the user of a trademark or trade name from its improper use by another— viz., trademark infringement and unfair competition. Trademark infringement developed as the remedy designed to protect technical trademarks—i. e., those marks which were arbitrary, fanciful or coined. Trademarks such as "Kodak", "Xerox", "Exxon" and "Coke" would fall within this category. As the law evolved, the protection provided by an action for trademark infringement was supplemented by the formulation of a broader remedy—an action for unfair competition. This remedy was intended to protect nontechnical, common law trademarks—marks used although not registered—as well as trade names.

Today, in an action for trademark infringement brought pursuant to either New York (General Business Law, § 368–b) or Federal law (Lanham Act, § 32[1], 15 U.S.C.A. § 1114[1]), it is necessary to show that the defendant's use of the trademark is likely to cause confusion, mistake or to deceive; actual confusion need not be shown. Similarly, it has been held that in an action for unfair competition a showing of a likelihood of confusion, rather than actual confusion, is all that is required to state a cause of action.

Since an action for infringement as well as an action for unfair competition both require a showing that the public is likely to confuse the defendant's product or service with that of the plaintiff, relief may be difficult to secure in situations in which the parties are not in competition, nor produce similar products or perform similar services. It is for this reason that section 368–d specifically provides that an injunction may be obtained *notwithstanding the absence of competition or confusion.*

1975). Although minor differences in wording exist, each of these statutes is a substantive duplicate of New York's anti-dilution statute.

Generally, courts which have had the opportunity to interpret an anti-dilution statute have refused to apply its provisions literally. New York courts, state and federal, have read into the statute a requirement of some showing of confusion, fraud or deception.

Judicial hesitance to enforce the literal terms of the anti-dilution statute has not been limited to New York. In Illinois, for example, some courts have gone so far as to declare the statute inapplicable where the parties are competitors and a likelihood of confusion does exist. These decisions were premised upon the belief that a plaintiff who can frame his complaint under a theory of infringement or unfair competition—albeit unsuccessfully perhaps—should not succeed under a dilution theory. However, one court in Illinois has interpreted the anti-dilution statute literally, reasoning that unless recovery for dilution is permitted in the absence of competition or confusion the statute adds nothing to existing law. (Polaroid Corp. v. Polaraid, Inc., 319 F.2d 830, 836–837, 138 U.S.P.Q. 265, 270–271.) This approach has also been taken in Massachusetts. (See, e. g., Tiffany & Co. v. Boston Club, Inc., 231 F.Supp. 836, 844, 143 U.S.P.Q. 2, 8; Clairol, Inc. v. Cody's Cosmetics, Inc., 353 Mass. 385, 391, 231 N.E.2d 912.)

Notwithstanding the absence of judicial enthusiasm for the anti-dilution statutes, we believe that section 368–d does extend the protection afforded trademarks and trade names beyond that provided by actions for infringement and unfair competition. The evil which the Legislature sought to remedy was not public confusion caused by similar products or services sold by competitors, but a cancer-like growth of dissimilar products or services which feeds upon the business reputation of an established distinctive trademark or name. Thus, it would be of no significance under our statute that Tiffany's Movie Theatre is not a competitor of, nor likely to be confused with Tiffany's Jewelry. (See N.Y.Legis.Ann., 1954, p. 50, citing Tiffany & Co. v. Tiffany Prods., Inc., 147 Misc. 679, 264 N.Y.S. 459, affd. 237 App.Div. 801, 260 N.Y.S. 821, affd. 262 N.Y. 482, 188 N.E. 30.) The harm that section 368–d is designed to prevent is the gradual whittling away of a firm's distinctive trademark or name. It is not difficult to imagine the possible effect which the proliferation of various non-competitive businesses utilizing the name Tiffany's would have upon the public's association of the name Tiffany's solely with fine jewelry. The ultimate effect has been appropriately termed dilution.

Although section 368–d does not require a showing of confusion or competition to obtain an injunction, it does require a "likelihood of injury to business reputation or of dilution of the *distinctive quality* of a mark or trade name. . . ." (Emphasis added.) The statute prohibits any use of a name or mark likely to dilute the *distinctive quality* of a name in use. To merit protection, the plaintiff must possess a strong mark—one which has a distinctive quality or has acquired a secondary meaning which is capable of dilution. Courts interpreting Massachusetts' anti-dilution statute—applying its terms literally—have required a showing that the trademark or name to be protected is either unique or has acquired a secondary meaning before issuing an injunction.

Turning to the case before us, it is quite apparent that the name "Allied" is a weak trade name. Rather than being distinctive, arbitrary, fanciful or coined, it is, in essence, generic or descriptive. Although the name "Allied" bespeaks of more originality than "maintenance", it is nevertheless a common word in English usage today. There is nothing in the name "Allied Maintenance" itself which indicates that it is an inherently strong trade name susceptible to dilution. Nor can it be said that the name Allied Maintenance has acquired a secondary meaning. Plaintiff seeks to prevent the defendant from using the word "allied" in any connection with its business. To establish secondary meaning it must be shown that through exclusive use and advertising by one entity, a name or mark has become so associated in the mind of the public with that entity or its product that it identifies the goods sold by that entity and distinguishes them from goods sold by others. A quick glance at the New York City phone directories will reveal the existence of at least 300 business entities in the metropolitan area incorporating the word "allied" in their trade name. In light of the large number of business entities using the generic term allied in their trade name, it cannot be said that the name "allied" has acquired a secondary meaning. We remain unconvinced that the public associates the word "allied" with the plaintiff's cleaning and maintenance service.

In sum, although section 368–d should be interpreted literally to effectuate its intended purpose—protection against dilution—only those trade names which are truly of *distinctive* quality or which have acquired a secondary meaning in the mind of the public should be entitled to protection under the anti-dilution statute. "Allied Maintenance" cannot be said to have attained this stature.

Accordingly, the order of the Appellate Division should be affirmed.

COOKE, Judge, dissenting.

I dissent, voting for a reversal of the Appellate Division order and reinstatement of the judgment of trial term granting an injunction in favor of plaintiff.

The majority's analysis of General Business Law § 368–d, it is respectfully submitted, imposes a narrow, overly-technical gloss on its terms and, in effect, dilutes the "anti-dilution" statute. For the reason that future litigants may suffer from this interpretation, a broader view is needed and, in my opinion, was intended.

In interpreting this legislation, the Court should not overemphasize the importance of a memorandum in support of this statute (see N.Y.Legis.Ann., 1954, pp. 49–51). That writing describes the author's view of the purpose of the proposed legislation and enumerates various problems in the area of dilution of a trade name or trademark. Dilution of a trade name through sales of dissimilar products is illustrated by somewhat fanciful examples such as "Buick aspirin tablets", "Schlitz varnish", "Kodak pianos", and "Bulova gowns" (id. p. 49). Indeed, that dilution can occur even in the case of dissimilar products, as the memorandum notes (id. p. 50), has long been recognized by our common law which granted the right to enjoin the use of another's name even in the absence of competition. Nevertheless, if the statute was intended to "codify the State common law concerning dilution" (N.Y.Legis.Ann., 1954, p. 49, supra; see also 3 N.Y.Law Forum, 313, 316), there is no basis for restricting its application in the manner suggested by the majority.

Dilution does not occur only in the case of a name that is widely known. To be sure, the name Tiffany would be diluted if many non-competing businesses used that name. However, a less well-known name can also be diluted, perhaps in a more harmful and direct manner. And dilution can occur in instances where there is competition, though in that instance a more appropriate remedy will ordinarily be found under general principles of unfair competition. The difficult case is where a specialized business, with a generic name used in other unrelated businesses, is used by a relatively small segment of the public who rely on its name. The problem occurs when that business is confronted with a newer company, bearing the same or a similar name, engaging in a field that, while perhaps non-competing, is so closely related to that of the more established business that its customers will identify its name with the newcomer. This is such a case.

It is asserted that the legislative intent was to remedy "not public confusion caused by similar products or services sold by competitors, but a cancer-like growth of dissimilar products or services which feeds upon the business reputation of an established distinctive trademark or name." It is then concluded that Allied is not sufficiently distinctive but rather is "a weak trade name." But the terms of the statute do not require this interpretation and the protection it affords should be available to plaintiff based on the facts of this case.

While the trial court determined that plaintiff and defendant are actual and potential competitors, the Appellate Division majority found that the parties are not competitors in their own peculiar specialities nor are they likely to be. Whichever view of the facts one takes, however, it is apparent that the businesses are closely related. There is no basis in the statutory language for concluding that the enactment was not intended to provide a remedy for confusion caused by similar (though perhaps not actually competing) services such as these. The statute provides a remedy "notwithstanding the absence of competition" but does not mandate that in order to benefit from its provisions there must be no competition or dissimilar services, as urged to the contrary. Therefore, if plaintiff's name is of a distinctive quality, it is entitled to a remedy under the anti-dilution statute.

It is wrong to conclude that the name Allied Maintenance is not "an inherently strong trade name susceptible to dilution." Of course its name is not as unique as other names held capable of dilution, but it is, to a limited audience, as distinctive as many others. The word Allied is a generic term but, as the trial court determined, that name has long been associated by the public, including customers and competitors in the building cleaning and maintenance industry, with plaintiff and its subsidiaries. Even a generic or descriptive name may acquire a secondary meaning in a given circumstance. That plaintiff's name is not distinctive enough to allow it to prevent its use by others in non-competing industries should not be a ground for allowing one in a closely-related business to dilute the distinctive quality of its name in its field.

The majority opinion may be read as limiting the statute in question to the protection of only the most well-known names, such as Tiffany, of which there are few, from dilution by non-competing products or services. The common law of the State has not so narrowed the protection afforded to less unique names and the fact that the statute operates even in the absence of competition does not, as noted, mean that it should have no effect where there is potential, if not actual, competition. A good illustration of this point is Long's Hat Stores Corp. v. Long's Clothes (224 App.Div. 497, 231 N.Y.S. 107). There, the plaintiff conducted a business of selling retail hats and haberdashery and, although it had discontinued its sales of clothing, it declared an intention to resume that branch of its business. The plaintiff there had developed a trade name and had a number of retail stores to which customers were attracted by the name "Long's". Some 22 years later, an individual engaged in the retail clothing business incorporated a business which maintained a retail clothing shop called "Long's Clothing". In granting an injunction to protect plaintiff's name, the Appellate Division reasoned:

> In this case the plaintiff is damaged because the articles sold by the defendant are so closely related to those presently sold by the plaintiff and so identical with those which the plaintiff has sold and intends to sell in the future, that there is direct appropriation of the plaintiff's good will. In the enjoyment of its trade name the plaintiff is to be protected not only with respect to the merchandise it presently sells, but also with respect to that which the public would believe, through the deception practiced by the defendant, that the plaintiff was selling. When a trade mark has been used by the owner and by another on goods of the same class, "though different in species, the question whether they are so closely related—so near akin—as to be regarded as having the 'same descriptive properties' arises." (Rosenberg Bros. & Co. v. Elliott, 3 Cir., 7 F.[2d] 962, 964.)

The circumstances here are closely analogous. The name Allied, like the name Long's, is not so unique that all would know its business, but it is known to a segment of the public that makes use of the service of cleaning and maintenance of buildings. After plaintiff was in business for many years, defendant entered into a related area and, depending upon whether one accepts the view of the Appellate Division majority or the Trial Court, may provide in some instances the same services. The use of a name associated with a particular business by one in a closely-related field is a dilution of a less well-known name and is of no less significance to the particular plaintiff than use of an extremely well-known trade name by a totally unrelated business. This is the rationale underlying the holding in Long's (supra), a case that has been regarded as a forerunner of the anti-dilution theory. General Business Law § 368–d was intended to codify cases such as Long's and that is why the statute should be applicable here.

Plaintiff should be granted the relief it seeks because, as a result of the similarity of names, those using defendant's services may well be confused as to the source. But the cause of action would not necessarily fail even if the two could be distinguished. Under the statute recovery is allowed even "in the absence of confusion" and, despite any suggestion to the contrary, this State's appellate courts have not expressed acceptance of any reading into the statute of a requirement of some showing of confusion.

To conclude, prior to enactment of the statute in question, in cases of this sort it was not determinative that a generic or descriptive name was so commonly used that the plaintiff could not prevent its use by unrelated businesses. For example, an injunction was granted against another business' use of the name Columbia, a word that, like Allied, is commonly found in the title of many businesses. Moreover, the pre-statutory cases recognized that a trade name should be protected from businesses that offer similar products or services and that is the situation faced by plaintiff in this matter. General Business Law § 368–d was intended to make clear the broad reach of our State's case law, which protected trade names even in the absence of competition, but, as noted in the memorandum relied on by the majority as indicative of the legislative intent, the statute is "essentially a codification of the common law" (N.Y.Legis.Ann., 1954, p. 50, supra). Therefore, interpreting the statute in light of the State's common law, it is submitted that under the circumstances of this case plaintiff is entitled to the relief it seeks. Accordingly, for the reasons stated, the order of the Appellate Division should be reversed.

c. MISAPPROPRIATION

METROPOLITAN OPERA ASS'N, INC. v. WAGNER–NICHOLS RECORDER CORP.

Supreme Court of New York County, 1950.
199 Misc. 786, 101 N.Y.S.2d 483, 87 U.S.P.Q. 173, aff'd 279
App.Div. 632, 107 N.Y.S.2d 795.

GREENBERG, Justice.

The plaintiffs Metropolitan Opera Association, Inc. (hereinafter referred to as "Metropolitan Opera"), and American Broadcasting Company, Inc. (hereinafter referred to as "American Broadcasting"), and the intervening plaintiff, Columbia Records, Inc. (hereinafter referred to as "Columbia Records"), move for a preliminary injunction to restrain the defendants from recording, advertising, selling or distributing musical performances of Metropolitan Opera broadcast over the air, and from using the name "Metropolitan Opera" or any similar name which is calculated to mislead the public into believing that the records sold by the defendants are records of performances made or sold under the control or supervision or with the consent of the plaintiffs. . . .

The complaints of the plaintiffs allege in substance:

Metropolitan Opera is an educational membership corporation. Over a period of sixty years it has, by care, skill and great expenditure, maintained a position of pre-eminence in the field of music and grand opera. By reason of this skill and pre-eminence it has created a national and worldwide audience and thereby a large market for radio broadcasts and phonograph recordings of its performances. Metropolitan Opera has sold the exclusive right to broadcast its performances and the exclusive right to record its performances, as set forth below, and uses the proceeds to defray part of its operating expenses.

It has sold the exclusive right to make and sell phonograph records of its operatic performances and to use the names "Metropolitan Opera Orchestra," "Metropolitan Opera Chorus" and any other names identified with Metropolitan in connection with these phonograph records to Columbia Records, which has acquired a reputation and good will of great value. This contract is for a five-year period ending December 31, 1951. The exclusive nature of these rights is of the essence of the contract. In payment for these exclusive rights Metropolitan Opera receives royalties on records sold, with a guaranteed minimum of $125,000 during the five-year term of the contract. Columbia Records is required to pay the entire cost of each performance of an opera which it records. Metropolitan Opera has reserved to itself the right to approve all phonograph records of its performances before they may be offered for sale to the public.

Pursuant to this contract Metropolitan Opera's performances of three operas have been recorded and are now being offered for sale and sold. Columbia Records has incurred very substantial expenses in making these recordings and in preparing for the recording of additional operas, and it has extensively advertised the records and its exclusive right to record Metropolitan Opera performances.

Metropolitan Opera has sold the exclusive right to broadcast its opera performances during the 1949–50 season to American Broadcasting, for which Metropolitan Opera receives $100,000. Under this contract American Broadcasting is prohibited from making recordings of such performances except for certain limited purposes related to broadcasting. Negotiations for a similar contract for the 1950–51 and 1951–52 opera seasons are in progress. Under the contract for the 1949–50 season, American Broadcasting broadcast Metropolitan Opera performances of eighteen operas between November 26, 1949, and March 25, 1950.

Since November 26, 1949, the defendants have recorded these broadcast performances of Metropolitan Opera and have used their master recordings to make phonograph records of Metropolitan Opera performances. The defendants have advertised and sold these records as records of broadcast Metropolitan Opera performances. By reason of this publicity and the reputation of Metropolitan Opera, these records have aroused wide interest. Since the defendants, unlike Columbia Records, pay no part of the cost of the performance of the operas and are held to no standard of artistic or technical excellence, they incur only the very small cost of recording these performances "off the air." The quality of their recordings is inferior to that of Columbia Records and is so low that Metropolitan Opera would not have approved the sale and release of such records to the general public. By reason of their negligible costs, defendants are able in competition with Columbia Records to sell their records at considerably less than those of the latter, with a consequent loss of revenue to Columbia Records and Metropolitan Opera. . . .

The defendants urge that the complaints fail to state a cause of action in that they do not allege the defendants are "palming off" their recordings as those of plaintiffs, or that plaintiffs are in competition with the defendants. They further urge that plaintiffs have no property right in the broadcast performances and that the defendants are therefore free to record these performances and sell their recordings.

The defendants' cross-motion attacking the complaints must necessarily be considered first.

In passing upon the question of the sufficiency of a complaint alleging unfair competition it is helpful to bear in mind the origin and evolution of this branch of law. It originated in the conscience, justice and equity of common-law judges. It developed within the framework of a society dedicated to freest competition, to deal with business malpractices offensive to the ethics of that society. The theoretic basis is obscure, but the birth and growth of this branch of law is clear. It is an outstanding example of the law's capacity for growth in response to the ethical as well as the economic needs of society. As a result of this background the legal concept of unfair competition has evolved as a broad and flexible doctrine with a capacity for further growth to meet changing conditions. There is no complete list of the activities which constitute unfair competition.

The statement of a sufficient cause of action in unfair competition, in the last analysis, is therefore dependent more upon the facts set forth and less upon technical requirements than in most causes of action. This may best be illustrated by a consideration of the objections raised by the defendants.

The defendants contend that no cause of action is stated due to the absence of an allegation of "palming off." One of the inferences which may fairly be drawn from the allegations of the complaint and the prayers for relief is that the activities of the defendants appropriate and trade on the name and reputation of Metropolitan Opera and tend to mislead the public into believing the recordings are made with the co-operation of Metropolitan Opera and under its supervision. However, even in the absence of such an inference the failure to allege "palming off" would not be a fatal defect. The early cases of unfair competition in which relief was granted were cases involving "palming off"—that is, the fraudulent representation of the goods of the seller as those of another. The early decisions condemning this practice were based on the two wrongs inflicted thereby: (1) The deceit and fraud on the public; and (2) the misappropriation to one person of the benefit of a name, reputation or business good will belonging to another.

With the passage of those simple and halcyon days when the chief business malpractice was "palming off" and with the development of more complex business relationships and, unfortunately, malpractices, many courts, including the courts of this state, extended the doctrine of unfair competition beyond the cases of "palming off." The extension resulted in the granting of relief in cases where there was no fraud on the public, but only a misappropriation for the commercial advantage of one person of a benefit or "property right" belonging to another.

The courts have used various formulae in making this extension. Many of the earlier of such decisions relied on the presence of special elements: For example, inducing breach of trust or breach of contract in misappropriating the property. However, in Fonotipia, Limited v. Bradley, C.C., 171 F. 951, the Circuit Court, after reviewing these decisions, found there was unfair competition in a case of misappropriation even in the absence of any of the special factors. In that case the plaintiff had engaged artists and made recordings of their musical performance for sale to the public. The defendant obtained some of these recordings, mechanically reproduced them and sold the copies in competition with plaintiff's records at much lower prices. The court posed the question as follows 171 F. at page 959: ". . . whether the taking of property in the shape of valuable ideas and products, by mechanical imitation or reproduction, is susceptible of notice by a court of equity, and whether any remedy therefor can exist apart from the questions of patent, trade-mark, and intentional deception or imitation and deceitful substitution of the product." It held, at page 964: "It cannot now be determined how far such appropriation of ideas could be prevented; but it would seem that where a product is placed upon the market, under advertisement and statement that the substitute or imitating product is a duplicate of the original, and where the commercial value of the imitation lies in the fact that it takes advantage of and appropriates to itself the commercial qualities, reputation, and salable properties of the original, equity should grant relief."

Subsequently, in 1918, the Supreme Court of the United States laid down a similar principle in International News Service v. Associated Press, 248 U.S. 215, 39 S.Ct. 68, 63 L.Ed. 211. In that case the

Associated Press sued to enjoin International News Service, among other things, from copying its news from bulletin boards and early editions of member newspapers and selling it bodily or in rewritten form to International News Service customers. The case presented particular difficulty because of the great public interest in the freest dissemination of the news. However, the court recognized that, as between the parties, even news was quasi-property.

In granting an injunction to the Associated Press against the pirating of its news the court held 248 U.S. at page 239 et seq., 39 S.Ct. at page 72, 63 L.Ed. 211. "The right of the purchaser of a single newspaper to spread knowledge of its contents gratuitously, for any legitimate purpose not unreasonably interfering with complainant's right to make merchandise of it, may be admitted; but to transmit that news for commercial use, in competition with complainant— which is what defendant has done and seeks to justify—is a very different matter. In doing this, defendant, by its very act, admits that it is taking material that has been acquired by complainant as the result of organization and the expenditure of labor, skill, and money, and which is salable by complainant for money, and that defendant in appropriating it and selling it as its own is endeavoring to reap where it has not sown, and by disposing of it to newspapers that are competitors of complainant's members is appropriating to itself the harvest of those who have sown. Stripped of all disguises, the process amounts to an unauthorized interference with the normal operation of complainant's legitimate business precisely at the point where the profit is to be reaped, in order to divert a material portion of the profit from those who have earned it to those who have not; with special advantage to defendant in the competition because of the fact that it is not burdened with any part of the expense of gathering the news. The transaction speaks for itself and a court of equity ought not to hesitate long in characterizing it as unfair competition in business. . . . It is said that the elements of unfair competition are lacking because there is no attempt by defendant to palm off its goods as those of the complainant, characteristic of the most familiar, if not the most typical, cases of unfair competition. . . . But we cannot concede that the right to equitable relief is confined to that class of cases. In the present case the fraud upon complainant's rights is more direct and obvious. Regarding news matter as the mere material from which these two competing parties are endeavoring to make money, and treating it, therefore, as quasi-property for the purposes of their business because they are both selling it as such defendant's conduct differs from the ordinary case of unfair competition in trade principally in this that, instead of selling its own goods as those of complainant, it substitutes misappropriation in the place of misrepresentation, and sells complainant's goods as its own."

The significance and limits of this decision have been widely discussed. That it extended the doctrine of unfair competition to cases based on misappropriation of property has been accepted by the leading authorities. Chief Justice Hughes in A. L. A. Schechter Poultry

Corporation et al. v. United States, 295 U.S. 495, at page 531, 55 S.Ct. 837 at page 844, 79 L.Ed. 1570, stated: ". . . 'Unfair competition,' as known to the common law, is a limited concept. Primarily, and strictly, it relates to the palming off of one's goods as those of a rival trader. . . . In recent years, its scope has been extended. It has been held to apply to misappropriation as well as misrepresentation, to the selling of another's goods as one's own—to misappropriation of what equitably belongs to a competitor. International News Service v. Associated Press, 248 U.S. 215, 241, 242, 39 S.Ct. 68, 63 L.Ed. 211."

The doctrine of extending unfair competition beyond cases of "palming off" has similarly been recognized and applied by the courts of this state. Thus an allegation of "palming off" is not essential to a cause of action for unfair competition.

The defendants also raise the objection that the complaint does not include an allegation that the parties are actual competitors. This objection is rendered untenable by the intervention of Columbia Records. However, again, the existence of actual competition between the parties is no longer a prerequisite. Tiffany & Co. v. Tiffany Productions, Inc., 147 Misc. 679, 264 N.Y.S. 459, affirmed without opinion 237 App.Div. 801, 260 N.Y.S. 821, affirmed without opinion 262 N.Y. 482, 188 N.E. 30; Long's Hat Stores Corp. v. Long's Clothes, Inc., 224 App.Div. 497, 231 N.Y.S. 107.

The modern view as to the law of unfair competition does not rest solely on the ground of direct competitive injury, but on the broader principle that property rights of commercial value are to be and will be protected from any form of unfair invasion or infringement and from any form of commercial immorality, and a court of equity will penetrate and restrain every guise resorted to by the wrongdoer. The courts have thus recognized that in the complex pattern of modern business relationships, persons in theoretically non-competitive fields may, by unethical business practices, inflict as severe and reprehensible injuries upon others as can direct competitors. That defendants' piratical conduct and practices have injured and will continue to injure plaintiffs admits of no serious challenge, and possible money damages furnishes no adequate remedy. That such practices constitute unfair competition both with Metropolitan Opera and Columbia Records is made abundantly clear by the record. Plaintiff Metropolitan Opera derives income from the performance of its operatic productions in the presence of an audience, from the broadcasting of those productions over the radio, and from the licensing to Columbia Records of the exclusive privilege of making and selling records of its own performances. Columbia Records derives income from the sale of the records which it makes pursuant to the license granted to it by Metropolitan Opera. Without any payment to Metropolitan Opera for the benefit of its extremely expensive performances, and without any cost comparable to that incurred by Columbia Records in making its records, defendants offer to the public recordings of Metropolitan Opera's broadcast performances. This constitutes unfair competition.   International News Service v. Associated Press, 248 U.S. 215, 39 S.Ct. 68, 63 L.Ed. 211.

The New York courts have applied the rule in the International News Service case in such a wide variety of circumstances as to leave no doubt of their recognition that the effort to profit from the labor, skill, expenditures, name and reputation of others which appears in this case constitutes unfair competition which will be enjoined.

.   .   .

The defendants raise the further objection that the complaints fail to state a cause of action in that they set forth no property rights of the plaintiffs.   Clearly, some property rights in the plaintiffs and interference with and misappropriation of them by defendants are necessary to a cause of action.   However, "property rights," as has often been pointed out, are rights which are recognized and protected by the courts by excluding others therefrom.   The designation is therefore more in the nature of a legal conclusion than a description.

.   .   .

The Court of Appeals in Fisher v. Star Company, 231 N.Y. 414, 428, 132 N.E. 133, 137, 19 A.L.R. 937, quoted with approval the broad definition of property rights laid down by the Supreme Court of the United States in the International News Service case, supra, 231 N.Y. at page 429, 132 N.E. at page 137, 19 A.L.R. 937: " '.   .   .   The rule that a court of equity concerns itself only in the protection of property rights treats any civil right of a pecuniary nature as a property right.   .   .   .   And the right to acquire property by honest labor or the conduct of a lawful business is as much entitled to protection as the right to guard property already acquired.   .   .   . It is this right that furnishes the basis of the jurisdiction in the ordinary case of unfair competition.' "

The right to the exclusive use of one's own name and reputation has long been recognized by the courts, as evidenced by the early protection of trade marks and trade names, and the "palming off" cases.

The law has also, as Justice Brandeis points out in his dissent in the International News Service case, supra, protected the creative element in intellectual productions—that is, the form or sequence of expression, the new combination of colors, sounds or words presented by the production.   The production of an opera by an opera company of great skill, involving as it does, the engaging and development of singers, orchestra, the training of a large chorus and the blending of the whole by expert direction into a finished interpretative production would appear to involve such a creative element as the law will recognize and protect against appropriation by others.

NOTES

1.   Did the fact in *Sample* that "many more consumers were aware of the appellants' name than that of the respondents," necessarily mean that respondent's name had acquired *no* secondary meaning, even in its own limited geographical area?   If so, would appel-

lants have succeeded in an action to enjoin respondents from using the "Sample" name on their present stores? If not, would appellant's use of the "Sample" name in the Summit Park Mall necessarily produce some consumer confusion?

In Food Center, Inc. v. Food Fair Stores, Inc., relied on in *Sample*, the First Circuit Court of Appeals observed that "as for the public, there would be confusion in areas served by both enterprises, but, at least at present, we see no evidence that it would suffer in quality of service or that the reputation of either party would suffer in the process." 356 F.2d 775, 782. What relief would, or should, be available to the parties and to the public in the event that the quality of either firm's goods and services later declined?

Should a firm ever have rights to a region in which it does no business? In which its name has no secondary meaning? Under the so-called "zone of expansion" doctrine, traditionally identified with dicta in Hanover Star Milling Co. v. Metcalf, 240 U.S. 403, 36 S.Ct. 357, 60 L.Ed. 713 (1916), a prior user can preempt the exclusive right to use its name and symbols in territories "that would probably be reached by the prior user in the natural expansion of his trade." 240 U.S. 403, 420, 36 S.Ct. 357, 363. *Food Fair*, and to some extent *Sample*, suggest that larger, more aggressive firms will be given more commodious zones of expansion than smaller firms. Is it relevant that large retailers have been known to fail? That small firms are sometimes acquired by larger ones?

2. Dilution is commonly asserted to occur when a name or symbol used by a merchant in connection with one line of goods or services is used without his authority in connection with noncompeting goods or services. Borden Ice Cream Co. v. Borden's Condensed Milk Co., 201 F. 510 (7th Cir. 1912), reflects the early view that such noncompetitive poaching is not actionable. An injunction against defendant's use of the name, "Borden," in connection with the sale of ice cream was denied to plaintiff, condensed milk company, on the ground that it was not engaged in the ice cream business. But, soon after, the Tiffany jewelry people, the Rolls-Royce automobile people and the Dunhill pipe people were respectively held entitled to injunctive relief against defendants who had used the name, "Tiffany" in connection with motion pictures, "Rolls-Royce" in connection with radio tubes, and "Dunhill" in connection with shirts. Tiffany & Co. v. Tiffany Productions, 147 Misc. 679, 264 N.Y.S. 459 (Sup.Ct.1932), aff'd 262 N.Y. 482, 188 N.E. 30; Wall v. Rolls-Royce of America, 4 F.2d 333 (3d Cir. 1925); Alfred Dunhill of London v. Dunhill Shirt Shop, 3 F.Supp. 487 (S.D.N.Y.1929).

Decisions for plaintiff in dilution cases are typically rationalized on a deception ground. Where, as in *Rolls-Royce*, there is some likelihood that consumers will believe that plaintiff manufactured defendant's goods, the deception relied on is of the usual passing-off variety. Where, as in *Dunhill*, the likelihood of confusion as to source is more attenuated, confusion of sponsorship may be employed as the ground for decision. Where, however, as in *Tiffany*, the likelihood of confusion as to source or sponsorship is hardly colorable, courts tend to avoid the deception ground entirely and to rely instead upon the appropriation ground.

In *Allied*, were Judges Jasen and Cooke each talking about a different kind of dilution—Jasen, about dilution of the type that occurred in *Tiffany*, and Cooke about dilution of the type that occurred in *Rolls-Royce* and *Dunhill*? Is there anything in Judge Jasen's opinion to suggest that the majority would have relaxed the distinctiveness requirement if consumer confusion had been shown? If the parties' services had been more closely competitive?

Underlying all dilution decisions is the question whether one party should have rights in a product or service market it has not yet entered. How, if at all, does this question differ from the question that underlies zone of expansion cases, like *Sample*, in which the battleground is unoccupied geographic, rather than product or service, markets? Does Metropolitan Opera v. Wagner-Nichols suggest that New York's already established unfair competition jurisprudence offered the *Allied* court an easier, alternative ground for decision?

Allied is noted at 46 Fordham L.Rev. 1315 (1978). Schechter, The Rational Basis of Trademark Protection, 40 Harv.L.Rev. 813 (1927), is the seminal essay on dilution. See also, Callmann, Unfair Competition Without Competition? 95 U.Pa.L.Rev. 443 (1947); Middleton, Some Reflections on Dilution, 42 Trademark Rep. 175 (1952); Derenberg, The Problem of Trademark Dilution and the Antidilution Statutes, 44 Calif.L.Rev. 439 (1956).

3. In discarding the deception requirement, International News Serv. v. Associated Press, 248 U.S. 215, 39 S.Ct. 68, 63 L.Ed. 211 (1918), and its progeny like *Metropolitan Opera*, represent the highwater mark of the modern emphasis upon the misappropriation component of unfair competition. Although it has been argued that little credence is due *I.N.S.*—that subsequent decisions have limited it to the news context and that it belongs to the federal common law obliterated by the Court's decision in Erie R. Co. v. Tompkins twenty years later—the decision has enjoyed a broad and continuing acceptance in New York. Good early discussions of *I.N.S.* appear in Notes, 18 Colum.L.Rev. 257 (1918); 32 Harv.L.Rev. 566 (1919) and 28 Yale L.J. 387 (1919). More recent discussion appears *passim* in Goldstein, Federal System Ordering of the Copyright Interest, 69 Colum.L.Rev. 49 (1969).

Because misappropriation has always been an element in unfair competition's traditional passing off formula, most jurisdictions weigh it in combination with the formula's other elements, particularly deception. Like the question of deception, the question of appropriation is one of degree. In situations involving a high degree of appropriation and a low degree of deception, or vice-versa, plaintiff will probably prevail. Where proof of both appropriation and deception is weak, or slightly under middling, victory is improbable. This suggests that the distinction between New York decisions, which endorse misappropriation as an independent ground for recovery, and decisions in other states may only be nominal. While New York courts would tend to characterize a case involving a high degree of appropriation and a low degree of deception as one of misappropriation, other states may classify it as just another instance of passing off.

4. The label, "unfair competition" embraces conduct outside the basic appropriation-competition-deception formula. Among the types of conduct proscribed under the general head of unfair competition are false advertising, misrepresentation of one's own goods, misrepresentation or disparagement of another's goods, trade boycotts, inducement to breach contract, price wars and molestation or physical interference with another's business.

The term "unfair competition" has also been applied to a multitude of unrelated and sometimes exotic commercial wrongs. Consider whether defendant's conduct was—should have been—held actionable in the following situations. [Answers appear on the next page.]

    a.   Plaintiffs are the publisher and authors of a set of physics textbooks that contain problems to be used by instructors in classroom exercises, examinations, and homework assignments. Defendants publish a book with ready-made solutions to these problems. Plaintiffs seek to restrain the sale and distribution of the answer book on the ground that it will destroy the market for their textbooks.

    b.   In the course of setting up his own business, defendant solicits the trade of customers he serviced when he was employed by plaintiff.

    c.   Defendant buys bongo drums from plaintiff, removes plaintiff's trademarks and other identifying characteristics, replaces them with defendant's own insignia, and uses the drums as a sample to the trade of its own brand of bongos. Plaintiff seeks an injunction and damages.

    d.   Local storekeepers in a small city, greatly disturbed by their loss of business to large mail-order houses, announce a children's show with excellent performers to be held in the local theatre. The only admission ticket required is the surrender of the family Sears, Roebuck catalogue. Sears, Roebuck seeks to have the practice enjoined.

    e.   Plaintiff, producer-director of a motion picture that has been licensed for television broadcast, seeks to enjoin the network licensee from inserting commercials in the broadcast in a manner that will tend to impair the film's artistic integrity.

Answers to questions in note 4:

a. Actionable unfair competition: "The trend of the law today is to enforce higher standards of fairness and morality in trade, depending upon the character and nature thereof." Addison-Wesley Pub. Co., Inc. v. Brown, 207 F.Supp. 678, 133 U.S.P.Q. 647 (E.D.N.Y. 1962).

b. Sometimes actionable, sometimes not. See generally, Hays, Unfair Competition—Another Decade, 51 Calif.L.Rev. 51 (1963).

c. Not actionable. "The use of its own trademark amounted to a representation that defendant and not the plaintiff stood behind the sample chattel and behind the chattels bought in reliance on the sample. This is the antithesis of palming off and the plaintiff demonstrates no actionable rights in the defendant's use of its own trademark on a product it bought to use in promoting its own products." Mastro Plastics Corp. v. Emenee Industries, Inc., 16 App.Div.2d 420, 228 N.Y.S.2d 514 (1st Dept.), aff'd 12 N.Y.2d 826, 187 N.E.2d 360 (1960). The complaint, as subsequently amended to allege a violation of Lanham Act section 43(a), 15 U.S.C.A. § 1125(a), was upheld against defendant's motion to dismiss: "The Act defines a new civil wrong and the prior dismissal of the original complaint because the common law afforded no remedy to a competitor where the wrong merely resulted in a diversion of customers without confusion or palming off is of no significance." 19 A.D.2d 600, 240 N.Y.S.2d 624 (1st Dept. 1963), aff'd 14 N.Y.2d 498, 197 N.E.2d 621 (1964).

d. Actionable—at least in an action brought by the Federal Trade Commission. Chamber of Commerce of Missoula, 5 F.T.C.D. 451 (1923). Professor Chafee, from whose lecture, Unfair Competition, 53 Harv.L.Rev. 1289 (1940), this situation is excerpted, concluded that "If Sears, Roebuck had gone to court, it would probably have failed to get an injunction." Id. at 1307.

e. Actionable. "I think a court of equity has a duty when presented with a novel situation to fashion remedies to protect parties and litigants against new harms where it appears that there is an inadequate remedy at law, to protect against what may be an irreparable harm. I think the court has the right to protect the artistic integrity of a product, whether it be a film or a play. . . ." Stevens v. National Broadcasting Co., 148 U.S.P.Q. 755, 758 (Cal.Super. Ct.1966).

B. LIMITS OF PROTECTION

1. PERSONAL INTERESTS: RIGHTS IN NAMES

DAVID B. FINDLAY, INC. v. FINDLAY

Court of Appeals of New York, 1966.
18 N.Y.2d 12, 271 N.Y.S.2d 652, 218 N.E.2d 531, 150 U.S.P.Q. 223,
modified 18 N.Y.2d 676, 219 N.E.2d 872, cert. denied 385 U.S. 930, 87
S.Ct. 289, 17 L.Ed.2d 212.

KEATING, J. When should a man's right to use his own name in his business be limited? This is the question before us.

The individual plaintiff David B. Findlay ("David") and the individual defendant Walstein C. Findlay ("Wally") are brothers. The Findlay art business was founded in 1870 by their grandfather in Kansas City. Their father continued and expanded the business with a Chicago branch managed by Wally and a New York branch established and managed by David on East 57th Street. In 1936 the Kansas City gallery was closed and in 1938, after a dispute, the brothers separated. By agreement David, as president of Findlay Galleries, Inc., and owner of nearly all of the stock of the original Missouri corporation, sold to Wally individually the Chicago gallery and allowed Wally to use the name "Findlay Galleries, Inc." in the conduct of his business in Chicago. Wally organized an Illinois corporation under the name "Findlay Galleries, Inc." in 1938 and has since operated his Chicago gallery. He also opened, in 1961, a Palm Beach, Florida, gallery.

David, since the separation, has operated his gallery on East 57th Street in Manhattan. For many years he has conducted his business on the second floor of 11–13 East 57th Street.

In October, 1963, Wally purchased the premises at 17 East 57th Street and informed David of his plans to open an art gallery. David objected to Wally's use of the name "Findlay" on 57th Street and by letter announced he would "resist any appropriation by you in New York of the name Findlay in connection with a gallery . . . any funds spent by you to establish a gallery at 17 East 57th Street under the name Findlay Galleries, Inc. (or any variation thereof using the name Findlay) are spent at your peril." David also, in self-defense and in an effort to survive, rented additional space at 15 East 57th Street so as to have a street level entrance.

David's objections and pleas seemed to have some effect on Wally. As renovation on the building was carried on from October, 1963 to September, 1964, a large sign proclaimed the coming opening of "W. C. F. Galleries, Inc." There was also a display and listing in the New York Telephone directory under the same name and similar advertisements in other publications. However, in September, 1964 the sign was suddenly changed to announce the imminent opening of

"Wally Findlay Galleries" affiliated with "Findlay Galleries, Inc." David immediately sought an injunction. Wally went ahead with his opening and erected a sidewalk canopy from the curb to the building displaying the name "Wally Findlay Galleries."

The trial court made very detailed findings and, based on them, enjoined defendant from using the names "Wally Findlay Galleries," "Findlay Galleries" and any other designation including the name "Findlay" in the conduct of an art gallery on East 57th Street. The Appellate Division has affirmed on the trial court's findings and we find evidence to sustain them.

The trial court concluded that if injunctive relief were not granted, plaintiff would continue to be damaged by confusion and diversion and would suffer great and irreparable loss in his business and in his name and reputation. In his quarter of a century on East 57th Street David has established a valuable good will and reputation as an art dealer. Through hard work, business ability and expenditure of large sums of money, David has reached the level where a significant portion of his business comes from people who have been referred to him by others and told to go to "Findlay's on 57th St."

The effect of Wally's new gallery, with its long canopy, can only be that those looking for "Findlay's on 57th St." will be easily confused and find their way into Wally's rather than David's gallery. Though Wally perhaps did not deliberately set out to exploit David's good will and reputation, the trial court found, and we agree, that such a result would follow if Wally were permitted to operate a gallery under the name "Wally Findlay Galleries" next door to David.

There were numerous instances of people telephoning or asking at David's for personnel of Wally's or for art work exhibited at Wally's. Many regular customers congratulated David on the opening of "his" new gallery next door. Moreover, advertisements frequently appeared on the same pages of the local press for "Findlay Galleries", "Findlay's", or "Wally Findlay Galleries" thus making it very difficult to tell whose advertisement it was. Even the art editors and reporters referred to Wally as "Findlay Galleries"—the name used for many years by David—or as "the new Findlay Gallery."

It is apparent that confusion has and must result from Wally's opening next to David. This is compounded by the fact that both brothers have for years specialized in French impressionist and post-impressionist painters. Therefore, quite naturally, both brothers have in the past dealt in the works of such famous deceased painters as Modigliani, Degas, Renoir, Gauguin, Bonnard, Braque, Monet and many others.

Although someone seeking a Renoir from David is unlikely to purchase a Degas from Wally, it *is* likely that with respect to some of the lesser-known impressionists such diversion might happen. More important, someone wishing to own a nude by Modigliani, a dancer by Degas or a portrait of a girl by Renoir would not necessarily have a particular painting in mind and would likely purchase any of these species, whether it be in Wally's or David's. The items sold by the two brothers are not unique, nonsubstitutional works.

Moreover, art, particularly modern art, is sold only to those who see it. Works of art are sold to those who cross the threshold of the art gallery and the more people you get into your gallery, the more art you will sell. To this end David has worked hard to develop the name "Findlay's on 57th St." and bring in customers. Many people who have the finances to purchase art do not necessarily have the knowledge to distinguish between the works of all the various painters represented by galleries such as Wally's or David's. For this reason they rely on the reputation of the gallery. David has spent over 25 years in developing satisfied customers who will tell others to go to "Findlay's on 57th St." This good will brings in customers who look for a work of art that suits their fancy and if Wally were to continue to use the name Findlay, it is inevitable that some would walk into Wally's by mistake and would have their tastes satisfied there, to David's great harm.

The so-called "sacred right" theory that every man may employ his own name in his business is not unlimited. Moreover, fraud or deliberate intention to deceive or mislead the public are not necessary ingredients to a cause of action.

The present trend of the law is to enjoin the use even of a family name when such use tends or threatens to produce confusion in the public mind. Whether this confusion should be satisfied by misplaced phone calls or confusing advertisements alone we do not decide because there has been a finding that diversion, as well as confusion, will exist if Wally is not enjoined. Thus it is clear that the "confusion" with which we are dealing includes impairment of good will of a business.

In Meneely v. Meneely (62 N.Y. 427) this court noted that one can use his own name provided he does not resort to any artifice or contrivance for the purpose of producing the impression that the establishments are identical, or do anything calculated to mislead the public.

Thirty-five years later, we noted that, as a general principle of law, one's name is his property and he is entitled to its use. However, it was equally a principle of law that no man can sell his goods as those of another. "He may not through unfairness, artifice, misrepresentation or fraud injure the business of another or induce the public to believe his product is the product of that other." (World's Dispensary Medical Ass'n v. Pierce, 203 N.Y. 419, 424, 96 N.E. 738, 740.)

Ryan & Son v. Lancaster Homes (15 N.Y.2d 812, 257 N.Y.S.2d 934, 205 N.E.2d 859, aff'g 22 A.D.2d 186, 254 N.Y.S.2d 473) is distinguishable from the present case because there was lacking in *Ryan* the crucial finding that in the absence of relief plaintiff would be damaged by confusion and diversion. There was no real competition between the two businesses. Again, unlike the instant case where

"Findlay's on 57th St." is synonymous in New York City with quality art galleries, "Homes by Ryan" had not become a trade name with a secondary meaning. The court reviewed the law and cited the rule in *Meneely*. "This rule has been qualified, as we have said, only to the extent that use of a family name will be restricted where such use tends or threatens to induce confusion in the public mind". (22 A.D. 2d, p. 190, 254 N.Y.S.2d, p. 477.)

In the present case Wally knew that David had conducted his business and built a reputation under the names "Findlay Galleries" and "Findlay's on 57th St." and that many years of effort and expenses had gone into promoting the name of "Findlay" in the art business on 57th Street. He also knew that people would come into his gallery looking for "Findlay Galleries" and even instructed his employees on this matter before he opened. Nonetheless he opened his gallery next door to David dealing in substantially similar works and using the name Findlay. The bona fides of Wally's intentions do not change the applicable principles. The objective facts of this unfair competition and injury to plaintiff's business are determinative, not the defendant's subjective state of mind. Wally's conduct constituted unfair competition and an unfair trade practice, and it is most inequitable to permit Wally to profit from his brother's many years of effort in promoting the name of "Findlay" on 57th Street. Wally should use any name other than "Findlay" in the operation of his business next door to his brother.

In framing its injunction the trial court went no farther than was necessary to avoid the harm threatened. It prevented the use of the name Findlay but limited this to the particular area in which its use would cause confusion and diversion—East 57th Street. It resolved the conflict with as little injury as possible to Wally. The proof showed and the trial court found that many, if not most of the leading art galleries, are now located on Madison Avenue and in the area of the 60's, 70's and 80's in New York City. Wally could probably have found an appropriate place for his New York gallery other than at 17 East 57th Street and can now either find such another location or remain where he is under some name such as "W. C. F. Galleries."

The decision in this case is in accord with the directions of our court: "The defendant has the right to use his name. The plaintiff has the right to have the defendant use it in such a way as will not injure his business or mislead the public. Where there is such a conflict of rights, it is the duty of the court so to regulate the use of his name by the defendant that, due protection to the plaintiff being afforded, there will be as little injury to him as possible." (World's Dispensary Med. Ass'n v. Pierce, supra, 203 N.Y. p. 425, 96 N.E. p. 740.)

The order of the Appellate Division should be affirmed, with costs.

BURKE, J. (dissenting). This court decided in Meneely v. Meneely (62 N.Y. 427, 431–432) more than 90 years ago—and the rule, well settled then, has been consistently followed ever since—that "every man has the absolute right to use his own name in his own business, even though he may thereby interfere with or injure the business of another person bearing the same name, provided he does not resort to any artifice or contrivance for the purpose of producing the impression that the establishments are identical, or do anything calculated to mislead. Where the only confusion created is that which results from the similarity of the names the courts will not interfere. A person cannot make a trade mark of his own name, and thus obtain a monopoly of it which will debar all other persons of the same name from using their own names in their own business." . . .

In the case before us, there is not the slightest support for any claim of dishonesty or deceit, not the slightest suggestion of a design on the part of the defendant to defraud or mislead the public or to palm off his business as that of his brother. And this was the view of the Trial Judge below who granted the injunction solely on the strength of the possible confusion which would result from the defendant's use of his own name. Thus, declaring that he did "not believe that Wally set out to deliberately exploit this good will and business reputation of the plaintiffs" (47 Misc.2d 649, 652, 262 N.Y.S.2d 1011), the Judge specifically ruled that it was immaterial "whether defendant *intended* to confuse and mislead, if in fact, his conduct tends or threatens to produce confusion." (47 Misc.2d, p. 656, 262 N.Y.S.2d 1015, italics supplied.)

As the decisions cited above establish, proof of confusion—understandably inevitable when there is a similarity of name—is irrelevant since confusion resulting from the honest use of one's own name is not actionable. This is especially appropriate in a case such as this, where the patrons or customers of the plaintiff and the defendant are discriminating and knowledgeable people usually intent on acquiring a particular work of art, people ordinarily fully aware that a desired painting or other work of art can be purchased only at a particular gallery and not apt to be misled into buying by a similarity of dealers' names. Too, the evidence of confusion which, as stated, is the predicate for the injunction in this case—telephone calls to the wrong gallery, misdeliveries, visitors seeking paintings in one gallery exhibited at the other—is not unlike that presented in Wholesale Serv. Supply Corp. v. Wholesale Bldg. Materials Corp. (304 N.Y. 834, 109 N.E.2d 718, aff'g 280 App.Div. 189, 190, 112 N.Y.S.2d 622, 623) and there held to be insufficient to justify the issuance of an injunction.

Moreover, there is no proof in this case of any actual damage suffered by plaintiff and in this respect it is similar to the Ryan case (15 N.Y.2d 812, 257 N.Y.S.2d 934, 205 N.E.2d 859, supra) in which this court decided that there must be shown, if not deception or palming off, at least real and substantial confusion *plus* damage resulting therefrom. No such damage appears here although plaintiff seems mostly to fear that its reputation may in the end be somewhat diminished. The Ryan rationale is thus directly in point. Plaintiff seems to fear not present damage but damage in the future. It has proved no financial loss at all, shown no injury whatsoever; it has produced no customer or anyone else to testify that he was confused between the two galleries.

Despite the finding of no deceit and in the face of a claim of confusion far weaker than that proven in the cases to which we have referred, the court now refuses to apply the rule of law observed for over a century. The exception rests apparently on the singular circumstance that this competition is between siblings. We are unable to see why that should prompt the court to grant one brother the exclusive right to use the family name in connection with what was originally the family art business. We, therefore, perceive no valid basis for prohibiting the defendant from using his own name in the conduct of his business at 17 East 57th Street in New York City.

We would reverse the order appealed from and dismiss the complaint.

Chief Judge DESMOND and Judges VAN VOORHIS and BERGAN concur with Judge KEATING; Judge BURKE dissents and votes to reverse in an opinion in which Judges FULD and SCILEPPI concur.

Order affirmed.

SULLIVAN v. ED SULLIVAN RADIO & T. V., INC.

Supreme Court of New York, Appellate Division, First Department, 1956.
1 A.D.2d 609, 152 N.Y.S.2d 227, 110 U.S.P.Q. 106.

COX, Justice.

In this proceeding, in which plaintiff moved for an injunction pendente lite, the facts are not in dispute. Appellant Ed Sullivan, who has been nationally known for over twenty years through his widely syndicated newspaper column, appearing in thirty-five newspapers throughout the country, including the Buffalo Courier-Express, is likewise known nationally in a much wider field as a radio and television personality presented weekly before an audience estimated at over 50 million people on the TV program, "The Ed Sullivan Show." This program is presented regularly in Buffalo through the facilities of Station WBEN–TV. Appellant also has been the subject of many articles and comments in magazines and newspapers, on radio and television. He has, in the past, endorsed particular brands of television sets and, in the future, expects to continue making such endorsements.

Respondent Ed Sullivan Radio & TV, Inc., engaged in the business of selling and repairing radio and television sets in Buffalo, N. Y., was incorporated in the state of New York on March 3, 1955, its three incorporators being Edward J. Sullivan, Robert J. Bender and Brunon V. Boroszewski. Edward J. Sullivan is the president and principal stockholder. This corporation took over the business formerly owned by this same Edward J. Sullivan individually and which was operated by him for some time prior to March 3, 1955, as a side line and on a part-time basis under the name "Ed Sullivan Radio & TV."

The question before us is whether or not a corporation of which the individual named Edward J. Sullivan is an incorporator, engaged in one phase of the radio and television field, may select the diminutive "Ed" for use in connection with the surname "Sullivan" of one of its incorporators as a part of its corporate title, when it is undisputed that the name "Ed Sullivan" is automatically identified by the general public with appellant *alone*, insofar as radio and television are concerned.

It is quite clear that, at the present time at least, there is no direct competition between appellant and respondent. However, both operate in the same general field and this court has consistently held that it is not essential for parties to be in competition with each other in order to sustain an injunction, .   .   . and injunctions have issued against the use of similar names in business even in the absence of a threat of confusion as to the source or sponsorship of the goods or services.

Although the courts usually will not interfere with the right of a person to use his own name in business, the present trend of the law is to enjoin the use even of a family name where such use tends or threatens to induce confusion in the public mind. .   .   .

Respondent herein makes use of no words in its corporate name which would indicate that it is engaged solely or exclusively in the business of selling and repairing radio and television sets. Since, therefore, it participates in the field in which appellant Ed Sullivan is broadly and generally known, to the degree of national prominence, respondent's use of its present title tends to identify appellant with the business of respondent. Moreover, appellant voices no objection to use of the name "Sullivan" as such nor even "E. J. Sullivan," nor the full name "Edward J. Sullivan," since he feels that such forms of the name would not induce or result in any confusion in the public mind. The objection here stems from the use of the diminutive form "Ed" in conjunction with the surname "Sullivan" in the combined name "Ed Sullivan" which appellant has continuously used throughout his entire career. In this regard it is to be noted that our courts have, on a number of occasions, enjoined the use even of variants of a name where such use threatened confusion in the public mind.

Although, in fact, but one isolated store in Buffalo is involved at the present time, nevertheless the state of facts may so change as to encompass a situation wherein there may be a series or a chain of similar stores throughout the country, in which case indeed, unless appellant had taken this present, prompt action, he might at a later date encounter great difficulty in obtaining an injunction because of his own laches. Also, at this stage the corporate enterprise would suffer minimal inconvenience in dropping the diminutive prefix, a situation which might not hold true at some future time.

Moreover, the significance of corporate identity is not to be lightly disregarded. Even on casual analysis there appears to be no present obstacle to interfere with or prevent the future sale or disposition by defendant's president, Edward J. Sullivan, of his interest in the business, thereby opening the door to others either to continue the business or by corporate amendment to extend the purposes and activities to more direct and active competition with the plaintiff.

The order appealed from should be reversed and a temporary injunction granted. Settle order.

Order unanimously reversed with $20 costs and disbursements to the appellant and the motion for a temporary injunction granted. Settle order on notice. All concur.

NOTES

1. In principle, unfair competition cases involving personal names are no different from those involving other sorts of commercial insignia. If his name is common and has no secondary meaning, plaintiff, to recover, must show that defendant's use of the name is part of an active scheme of passing off and that consumers have actually been confused. If plaintiff's name has attracted some secondary meaning, he need show only likelihood of confusion. And if the name is particularly distinctive, and secondary meaning particularly strong, consumer deception will be presumed and relief granted even absent proof that confusion is likely.

The often asserted difference between personal name and other unfair competition cases stems from the view that "A man's name is his own property, and he has the same right to its use and enjoyment as he has to that of any other species of property." The view was hardly more than dicta in the case that introduced it into the United States, Brown Chem. Co. v. Meyer, 139 U.S. 540, 544, 11 S.Ct. 625, 627, 35 L.Ed. 247 (1891). The name involved there, "Brown," was common—as indicated by the name of the opinion's author, Mr. Justice Brown. Since the name had captured scant secondary meaning and no confusion or fraud had been proved, the decision permitting defendant's use of the name can be easily rationalized in terms of general unfair competition doctrine. Compare Brown Sheet Iron & Steel Co. v. Brown Steel Tank Co., 198 Minn. 276, 269 N.W. 633 (1936), which recognized that free use of even a common name like Brown may be curtailed if, as to one user, it has gained secondary meaning.

Should the fact that the personal name employed by defendant is not his name—or, in the case of a corporation, is not the name of a founder—bar him from its use, or should it only constitute some evidence of his intent to palm off his goods or services as those of plaintiff whose name it is? Of plaintiff whose name also it is not?

2. Many personal name cases are, like *Findlay*, precipitated by a family dispute. In Edison v. Thomas A. Edison, Jr. Chem. Co., 128 F. 957 (D.Del.1904), Thomas A. Edison filed a complaint that sound-

ed more in parental dismay than in unfair competition, seeking to restrain his son, Thomas A. Edison, Jr., from using his name in competing fields of invention:

> That your orator has a son named Thomas A. Edison, Jr.,
> who is now about thirty years of age; that your orator's said
> son was employed by your orator in your orator's various inter-
> ests for a short time; that since that time your orator's said son
> has had no regular occupation, but as your orator is informed
> and believes, partially supports himself by trading on his name
> and by selling the use of his name to various unprincipled per-
> sons, who use the said name for the purpose of defrauding the
> public; that your orator's said son while he was in your orator's
> employ made no practical inventions, and your orator is satisfied
> that he has made no invention since that time.

An injunction was refused. Since defendant's advertisements referred to plaintiff only for the purpose of identifying its founder as
his son, the court concluded that "There is nothing in any of them to
confuse or confound, in the mind of any such [ordinarily intelligent
and prudent] person, the complainant either with his son, Thomas A.
Edison, Jr., or the defendant [corporation] with respect to the production and sale of the device." Id. at 961.

Greater success for plaintiff in actions between feuding relatives
was attained in Friend v. H. A. Friend & Co., Inc., 416 F.2d 526, 163
U.S.P.Q. 159 (9th Cir.), cert. denied 397 U.S. 914 (1969), and Lyon v.
Lyon, 246 Cal.App.2d 519, 152 U.S.P.Q. 719 (Cal.App.1966). Should
family cases, like *Findlay* and *Edison*, be decided on principles different from those governing nonfamily cases, like *Brown* and *Sullivan?*

3. When a founder leaves the company that bears his name, can
he, in competing with his former firm, publicize himself and his earlier track record? In Levitt Corp. v. Levitt, 593 F.2d 463, 201 U.S.P.
Q. 513 (2d Cir. 1979), the Second Circuit Court of Appeals concluded
that cases of this sort should be treated differently from garden variety cases like *Sullivan.* "Where, as here, however, the infringing
party has previously sold his business, including use of his name and
its goodwill to the plaintiff, sweeping injunctive relief is more tolerable." 593 F.2d 463, 468.

Defendant was the founder of Levitt & Sons, a major builder of
residential communities best known for its "Levittown" tract developments in New York and Pennsylvania. After fifty years at the helm
of Levitt & Sons, defendant merged the business into a wholly-owned
subsidiary of ITT Corporation, the predecessor in interest to plaintiff.
The new company succeeded to and continued to exploit Levitt &
Sons' goodwill, trademarks and trade names, including "Levitt" and
"Levittown." In November, 1975, as part of his arrangement with
ITT and the successor owners of Levitt & Sons, defendant covenanted
not to compete with Levitt & Sons until June, 1977. The agreement
provided that although defendant could enter the industry after that
time, he did not "have any right to use the name 'Levitt' as a corpo-

rate title, trademark or trade name in the construction business. He did retain the right to use his own name publicly as a corporate officer or director of a business enterprise, but only to the extent that such use would not be likely to create confusion with the corporate title, trademarks, or trade names of Levitt & Sons, Inc." 593 F.2d 463, 466.

In February, 1978, after the covenant not to compete had expired, defendant issued a press release stating that plaintiff's acquisition of Levitt Corporation was "totally confusing the general public and the business community," and that the question being posed by all is "who and what is the real Levitt." The press release announced that Mr. Levitt would soon reveal plans to build "a new Levittown in the United States." Subsequently, defendant placed advertisements in the *Washington Post* and the *New York Times* for "Levittown Florida," and referring to "Levitt and Sons" and to "Levitt's Engineering and Planning Department." "Most significantly, William Levitt identified himself as the founder of the company that had built the Levittowns of New York, New Jersey, and elsewhere." 593 F.2d 463, 466.

Agreeing with the district court that defendant Levitt had infringed the trademarks of the Levitt Corporation, and that his use of his name in conjunction with the marks had caused substantial confusion between the two enterprises, the court of appeals affirmed the district court's order enjoining defendant from using the term "Levittown" in connection with his Florida project and requiring defendant not only to remove the "Levittown" name from all advertising, maps, streets, government application forms and other documents, but also, upon plaintiff's request, to issue corrective advertising explaining the lawsuit in order to restore the plaintiffs to the position they held before Mr. Levitt invaded the Florida market.

Since defendant Levitt's skill in planning, site selection and construction doubtless played an important role in the success of his former company, should he, at the least, have been allowed to identify himself with its past ventures? The court also affirmed a part of the district court decree that permanently enjoined Levitt from publicizing his prior connection with Levitt & Sons "to avoid the likelihood of confusion that would arise if the defendants should invoke the names of earlier Levitt projects in reciting the highlights of his career." 593 F.2d 463, 467. The circuit court concluded that "under these circumstances, a disclaimer of any *current* relationship between Mr. Levitt and the corporation will not protect the plaintiff's rights, for the effect of such a statement would be to inform the public that the achievements to which Levitt Corporation justly lays claim really are attributable to the efforts of someone else, now in business for himself." 593 F.2d 463, 470 n. 12.

What does a company acquire when it buys goodwill? If defendant had labelled his original company with a coined name, like "Strathmore," rather than with his own name, do you think that the court would have allowed him to refer to his former association with the company by that name? Was the decision in *Levitt* properly sensitive to the expectations and interests of housing consumers?

2. ECONOMIC INTERESTS: THE PLACE OF UNFAIR COMPETITION IN THE COMPETITIVE PLAN

CRESCENT TOOL CO. v. KILBORN & BISHOP CO.

Circuit Court of Appeals, Second Circuit, 1917.
247 F. 299.

LEARNED HAND, District Judge. The cases of so-called "nonfunctional" unfair competition, starting with the "coffee mill case," Enterprise Mfg. Co. v. Landers, Frary & Clark, 131 Fed. 240, 65 C.C. A. 587, are only instances of the doctrine of "secondary" meaning. All of them presuppose that the appearance of the article, like its descriptive title in true cases of "secondary" meaning, has become associated in the public mind with the first comer as manufacturer or source, and, if a second comer imitates the article exactly, that the public will believe his goods have come from the first, and will buy, in part, at least, because of that deception. Therefore it is apparent that it is an absolute condition to any relief whatever that the plaintiff in such cases show that the appearance of his wares has in fact come to mean that some particular person—the plaintiff may not be individually known—makes them, and that the public cares who does make them, and not merely for their appearance and structure. It will not be enough only to show how pleasing they are, because all the features of beauty or utility which commend them to the public are by hypothesis already in the public domain. The defendant has as much right to copy the "nonfunctional" features of the article as any others, so long as they have not become associated with the plaintiff as manufacturer or source. The critical question of fact at the outset always is whether the public is moved in any degree to buy the article because of its source and what are the features by which it distinguishes that source. Unless the plaintiff can answer this question he can take no step forward; no degree of imitation of details is actionable in its absence.

In the case at bar [e] it nowhere appears that before 1910, when the defendant began to make its wrenches, the general appearance of

e. "This is an appeal from a temporary injunction granted by the District Court for Connecticut on the 25th day of January, 1917, restraining the defendant pendente lite from manufacturing and selling its adjustable wrenches. The facts as set forth in the affidavits are substantially as follows:

"The plaintiff is a New York corporation, organized in 1907 for the purpose of manufacturing tools, and has since that time been engaged in the manufacture among other things of pliers and wrenches. In December, 1908, it put upon the market an adjustable wrench, and has widely advertised the same from that time to the present. The wrench, on account of its appearance and new and original shape, pleased the public, and its sales grew rapidly from year to year, the plaintiff's wrench had come to indicate to the public any one maker as its source, or that the wrench had been sold in any part because of its source, as distinct from its utility or neat appearance. It is not enough to show that the wrench became popular under the name "Crescent"; the plaintiff must prove that before 1910 the public had already established the habit of buying it, not solely because they wanted that kind of wrench, but because they also wanted a Crescent, and thought all such wrenches were Crescents.

Upon the trial the plaintiff may, however, be able to establish this, and it is only fair to indicate broadly the considerations which will then determine the scope of his relief. In such cases neither side has an absolute right, because their mutual rights conflict. Thus the plaintiff has the right not to lose his customers through false representations that those are his wares which in fact are not, but he may not monopolize any design or pattern, however trifling. The defendant, on the other hand, may copy the plaintiff's goods slavishly down to the minutest detail; but he may not represent himself as the plaintiff in their sale. When the appearance of the goods has in fact come to represent a given person as their source, and that person is in fact the plaintiff, it is impossible to make these rights absolute; compromise is essential, exactly as it is with the right to use the common language in cases of "secondary" meaning. We can only say that the court must require such changes in appearance as will effectively distinguish the defendant's wares with the least expense to him; in no event may the plaintiff suppress the defendant's sale altogether. The proper meaning of the phrase "nonfunctional," is only this: That in

so that it became known to the jobbing trade and retailers and consumers as the 'Crescent' type of wrench. Its main structural features were all old in detail. It was adjustable to bolts and nuts of different sizes somewhat after the manner of a monkey wrench, but it was nevertheless quite different mechanically from a monkey wrench. It had a straight handle of web and rib construction, spreading slightly from the neck to the end, with a hole in the end of the web by which it could be hung up. No adjustable wrench of precisely the same character had ever appeared upon the market. There had, however, been adjustable wrenches, some with straight handles, some with web and rib curved handles, and there had been other tools with straight web and rib handles, somewhat broader at the end than at the neck. Plaintiff's name is plainly printed upon the web of the handle in raised letters. "The defendant is a Connecticut corporation, organized in 1896 and engaged in the manufacture of wrenches and other hardware for some 18 years past. Some time in 1910 it began the manufacture of an adjustable wrench, which it called its 'K & B 22½° adjustable.' This is substantially a direct facsimile of the plaintiff's wrench, with the exception that the defendant's name appears upon the web in place of the plaintiff's as follows: 'The Kilborn & Bishop Company, New Haven, Connecticut, U. S. A.,' in distinct raised letters. The defendant made no effort to imitate the boxes or packages of the plaintiff's wrench, nor did it use the word 'Crescent' in any way in its sale; but it did begin selling the goods in general competition with the plaintiff's wrenches until the order issued herein.

"There is evidence in the correspondence between the plaintiff and its customers that confusion has arisen between the plaintiff's wrenches and the defendant's, customers having supposed that the Kilborn & Bishop wrench was a Crescent, but there was no evidence that the defendant in any way facilitated this confusion." 247 F. 299–300.

such cases the injunction is usually confined to nonessential elements, since these are usually enough to distinguish the goods, and are the least burdensome for the defendant to change. Whether changes in them are in all conceivable cases the limit of the plaintiff's right is a matter not before us. If a case should arise in which no effective distinction was possible without change in functional elements, it would demand consideration; but the District Court may well find an escape here from that predicament. Certainly the precise extent and kind of relief must in the first instance be a matter for the discretion of that court.

Order reversed, and motion denied.

SEARS, ROEBUCK & CO. v. STIFFEL CO.

Supreme Court of the United States, 1964.
376 U.S. 225, 84 S.Ct. 784, 11 L.Ed.2d 661, 140 U.S.P.Q. 524.

Mr. Justice BLACK delivered the opinion of the Court.

The question in this case is whether a State's unfair competition law can, consistently with the federal patent laws, impose liability for or prohibit the copying of an article which is protected by neither a federal patent nor a copyright. The respondent, Stiffel Company, secured design and mechanical patents on a "pole lamp"—a vertical tube having lamp fixtures along the outside, the tube being made so that it will stand upright between the floor and ceiling of a room. Pole lamps proved a decided commercial success, and soon after Stiffel brought them on the market Sears, Roebuck & Company put on the market a substantially identical lamp, which it sold more cheaply, Sears' retail price being about the same as Stiffel's wholesale price. Stiffel then brought this action against Sears in the United States District Court for the Northern District of Illinois, claiming in its first count that by copying its design Sears had infringed Stiffel's patents and in its second count that by selling copies of Stiffel's lamp Sears had caused confusion in the trade as to the source of the lamps and had thereby engaged in unfair competition under Illinois law. There was evidence that identifying tags were not attached to the Sears lamps although labels appeared on the cartons in which they were delivered to customers, that customers had asked Stiffel whether its lamps differed from Sears', and that in two cases customers who had bought Stiffel lamps had complained to Stiffel on learning that Sears was selling substantially identical lamps at a much lower price.

The District Court, after holding the patents invalid for want of invention, went on to find as a fact that Sears' lamp was "a substantially exact copy" of Stiffel's and that the two lamps were so much alike, both in appearance and in functional details, "that confusion between them is likely, and some confusion has already occurred." On these findings the court held Sears guilty of unfair competition, enjoined Sears "from unfairly competing with [Stiffel] by selling or attempting to sell pole lamps identical to or confusingly similar to" Stiffel's lamp, and ordered an accounting to fix profits and damages resulting from Sears' "unfair competition."

The Court of Appeals affirmed. 313 F.2d 115. That court held that, to make out a case of unfair competition under Illinois law, there was no need to show that Sears had been "palming off" its lamps as Stiffel lamps; Stiffel had only to prove that there was a "likelihood of confusion as to the source of the products"—that the two articles were sufficiently identical that customers could not tell who had made a particular one. Impressed by the "remarkable sameness of appearance" of the lamps, the Court of Appeals upheld the trial court's findings of likelihood of confusion and some actual confusion, findings which the appellate court construed to mean confusion "as to the source of the lamps." The Court of Appeals thought this enough under Illinois law to sustain the trial court's holding of unfair competition, and thus held Sears liable under Illinois law for doing no more than copying and marketing an unpatented article. We granted certiorari to consider whether this use of a State's law of unfair competition is compatible with the federal patent law.

Before the Constitution was adopted, some States had granted patents either by special act or by general statute, but when the Constitution was adopted provision for a federal patent law was made one of the enumerated powers of Congress because, as Madison put it in The Federalist No. 43, the States "cannot separately make effectual provision" for either patents or copyrights. That constitutional provision is Art. I, § 8, cl. 8, which empowers Congress "To promote the Progress of Science and useful Arts, by securing for limited Times to Authors and Inventors the exclusive Right to their respective Writings and Discoveries." Pursuant to this constitutional authority, Congress in 1790 enacted the first federal patent and copyright law, and ever since that time has fixed the conditions upon which patents and copyright shall be granted. These laws, like other laws of the United States enacted pursuant to constitutional authority, are the supreme law of the land. When state law touches upon the area of these federal statutes, it is "familiar doctrine" that the federal policy "may not be set at naught, or its benefits denied" by the state law. Sola Elec. Co. v. Jefferson Elec. Co., 317 U.S. 172, 173, 176, 63 S.Ct. 172, 173, 87 L.Ed. 165 (1942). This is true, of course, even if the state law is enacted in the exercise of otherwise undoubted state power.

The grant of a patent is the grant of a statutory monopoly; indeed, the grant of patents in England was an explicit exception to the statute of James I prohibiting monopolies. Patents are not given as favors, as was the case of monopolies given by the Tudor monarchs, but are meant to encourage invention by rewarding the inventor with the right, limited to a term of years fixed by the patent, to exclude others from the use of his invention. During that period of time no one may make, use, or sell the patented product without the patentee's

authority. But in rewarding useful invention, the "rights and welfare of the community must be fairly dealt with and effectually
guarded." Kendall v. Winsor, 21 How. 322, 329, 16 L.Ed. 165 (1859).
To that end the prerequisites to obtaining a patent are strictly observed, and when the patent has issued the limitations on its exercise
are equally strictly enforced. To begin with, a genuine "invention"
or "discovery" must be demonstrated "lest in the constant demand
for new appliances the heavy hand of tribute be laid on each slight
technological advance in an art." Cuno Engineering Corp. v. Automatic Devices Corp., 314 U.S. 84, 92, 62 S.Ct. 37, 41, 86 L.Ed. 58
(1941). Once the patent issues, it is strictly construed, it cannot be
used to secure any monopoly beyond that contained in the patent, the
patentee's control over the product when it leaves his hands is sharply limited, and the patent monopoly may not be used in disregard of
the antitrust laws. Finally, and especially relevant here, when the
patent expires the monopoly created by it expires, too, and the right
to make the article—including the right to make it in precisely the
shape it carried when patented—passes to the public.

Thus the patent system is one in which uniform federal standards are carefully used to promote invention while at the same time
preserving free competition. Obviously a State could not, consistently with the Supremacy Clause of the Constitution, extend the life of
a patent beyond its expiration date or give a patent on an article
which lacked the level of invention required for federal patents. To
do either would run counter to the policy of Congress of granting
patents only to true inventions, and then only for a limited time.
Just as a State cannot encroach upon the federal patent laws directly,
it cannot, under some other law, such as that forbidding unfair competition, give protection of a kind that clashes with the objectives of
the federal patent laws.

In the present case the "pole lamp" sold by Stiffel has been held
not to be entitled to the protection of either a mechanical or a design
patent. An unpatentable article, like an article on which the patent
has expired, is in the public domain and may be made and sold by
whoever chooses to do so. What Sears did was to copy Stiffel's design and to sell lamps almost identical to those sold by Stiffel. This
it had every right to do under the federal patent laws. That Stiffel
originated the pole lamp and made it popular is immaterial. "Sharing in the goodwill of an article unprotected by patent or trade-mark
is the exercise of a right possessed by all—and in the free exercise of
which the consuming public is deeply interested." Kellogg Co. v. National Biscuit Co., 305 U.S., at 122, 59 S.Ct. at 115. To allow a State
by use of its law of unfair competition to prevent the copying of an
article which represents too slight an advance to be patented would
be to permit the State to block off from the public something which
federal law has said belongs to the public. The result would be that
while federal law grants only 14 or 17 years' protection to genuine inventions, States could allow perpetual protection to articles too lacking in novelty to merit any patent at all under federal constitutional

standards. This would be too great an encroachment on the federal patent system to be tolerated.

Sears has been held liable here for unfair competition because of a finding of likelihood of confusion based only on the fact that Sears' lamp was copied from Stiffel's unpatented lamp and that consequently the two looked exactly alike. Of course there could be "confusion" as to who had manufactured these nearly identical articles. But mere inability of the public to tell two identical articles apart is not enough to support an injunction against copying or an award of damages for copying that which the federal patent laws permit to be copied. Doubtless a State may, in appropriate circumstances, require that goods, whether patented or unpatented, be labeled or that other precautionary steps be taken to prevent customers from being misled as to the source, just as it may protect businesses in the use of their trademarks, labels, or distinctive dress in the packaging of goods so as to prevent others, by imitating such markings, from misleading purchasers as to the source of the goods. But because of the federal patent laws a State may not, when the article is unpatented and uncopyrighted, prohibit the copying of the article itself or award damages for such copying. The judgment below did both and in so doing gave Stiffel the equivalent of a patent monopoly on its unpatented lamp. That was error, and Sears is entitled to a judgment in its favor.

Reversed.

COMPCO CORP. v. DAY–BRITE LIGHTING, INC.

Supreme Court of the United States, 1964.
376 U.S. 234, 84 S.Ct. 779, 11 L.Ed.2d 669, 140 U.S.P.Q. 531.

Mr. Justice BLACK delivered the opinion of the Court.

As in Sears, Roebuck & Co. v. Stiffel Co., ante, . . . the question here is whether the use of a state unfair competition law to give relief against the copying of an unpatented industrial design conflicts with the federal patent laws. Both Compco and Day-Brite are manufacturers of fluorescent lighting fixtures of a kind widely used in offices and stores. Day-Brite in 1955 secured from the Patent Office a design patent on a reflector having cross-ribs claimed to give both strength and attractiveness to the fixture. Day-Brite also sought, but was refused, a mechanical patent on the same device. After Day-Brite had begun selling its fixture, Compco's predecessor began making and selling fixtures very similar to Day-Brite's. This action was then brought by Day-Brite. One count alleged that Compco had infringed Day-Brite's design patent; a second count charged that the public and the trade had come to associate this particular design with Day-Brite, that Compco had copied Day-Brite's distinctive design so as to confuse and deceive purchasers into thinking Compco's fixtures were actually Day-Brite's, and that by doing this Compco had unfairly competed with Day-Brite. The complaint prayed for both an accounting and an injunction.

The District Court held the design patent invalid; but as to the second count, while the court did not find that Compco had engaged in any deceptive or fraudulent practices, it did hold that Compco had been guilty of unfair competition under Illinois law. The court found that the overall appearance of Compco's fixture was "the same, to the eye of the ordinary observer, as the overall appearance" of Day-Brite's reflector, which embodied the design of the invalidated patent; that the appearance of Day-Brite's design had "the capacity to identify [Day-Brite] in the trade and does in fact so identify [it] to the trade"; that the concurrent sale of the two products was "likely to cause confusion in the trade"; and that "[a]ctual confusion has occurred." On these findings the court adjudged Compco guilty of unfair competition in the sale of its fixtures, ordered Compco to account to Day-Brite for damages, and enjoined Compco "from unfairly competing with plaintiff by the sale or attempted sale of reflectors identical to, or confusingly similar to" those made by Day-Brite. The Court of Appeals held there was substantial evidence in the record to support the District Court's finding of likely confusion and that this finding was sufficient to support a holding of unfair competition under Illinois law. 311 F.2d 26. Although the District Court had not made such a finding, the appellate court observed that "several choices of ribbing were apparently available to meet the functional needs of the product," yet Compco "chose precisely the same design used by the plaintiff and followed it so closely as to make confusion likely." 311 F.2d, at 30. A design which identifies its maker to the trade, the Court of Appeals held, is a "protectable" right under Illinois law, even though the design is unpatentable. We granted certiorari.

To support its findings of likelihood of confusion and actual confusion, the trial court was able to refer to only one circumstance in the record. A plant manager who had installed some of Compco's fixtures later asked Day-Brite to service the fixtures, thinking they had been made by Day-Brite. There was no testimony given by a purchaser or by anyone else that any customer had ever been misled, deceived, or "confused," that is, that anyone had ever bought a Compco fixture thinking it was a Day-Brite fixture. All the record shows, as to the one instance cited by the trial court, is that both Compco and Day-Brite fixtures had been installed in the same plant, that three years later some repairs were needed, and that the manager viewing the Compco fixtures—hung at least 15 feet above the floor and arranged end to end in a continuous line so that identifying marks were hidden—thought they were Day-Brite fixtures and asked Day-Brite to service them. Not only is this incident suggestive only of confusion *after* a purchase had been made, but also there is considerable evidence of the care taken by Compco to prevent customer confusion, including clearly labeling both the fixtures and the containers in which they were shipped and not selling through manufacturers' representatives who handled competing lines.

Notwithstanding the thinness of the evidence to support findings of likely and actual confusion among purchasers, we do not find it necessary in this case to determine whether there is "clear error" in these findings. They, like those in Sears, Roebuck & Co. v. Stiffel Co., supra, were based wholly on the fact that selling an article which is an exact copy of another unpatented article is likely to produce and did in this case produce confusion as to the source of the article. Even accepting the findings, we hold that the order for an accounting for damages and the injunction are in conflict with the federal patent laws. Today we have held in Sears, Roebuck & Co. v. Stiffel Co., supra, that when an article is unprotected by a patent or a copyright, state law may not forbid others to copy that article. To forbid copying would interfere with the federal policy, found in Art. I, § 8, cl. 8, of the Constitution and in the implementing federal statutes, of allowing free access to copy whatever the federal patent and copyright laws leave in the public domain. Here Day-Brite's fixture has been held not to be entitled to a design or mechanical patent. Under the federal patent laws it is, therefore, in the public domain and can be copied in every detail by whoever pleases. It is true that the trial court found that the configuration of Day-Brite's fixture identified Day-Brite to the trade because the arrangement of the ribbing had, like a trademark, acquired a "secondary meaning" by which that particular design was associated with Day-Brite. But if the design is not entitled to a design patent or other federal statutory protection, then it can be copied at will.

As we have said in Sears, while the federal patent laws prevent a State from prohibiting the copying and selling of unpatented articles, they do not stand in the way of state law, statutory or decisional, which requires those who make and sell copies to take precautions to identify their products as their own. A State of course has power to impose liability upon those who, knowing that the public is relying upon an original manufacturer's reputation for quality and integrity, deceive the public by palming off their copies as the original. That an article copied from an unpatented article could be made in some other way, that the design is "nonfunctional" and not essential to the use of either article, that the configuration of the article copied may have a "secondary meaning" which identifies the maker to the trade, or that there may be "confusion" among purchasers as to which article is which or as to who is the maker, may be relevant evidence in applying a State's law requiring such precautions as labeling; however, and regardless of the copier's motives, neither these facts nor any others can furnish a basis for imposing liability for or prohibiting the actual acts of copying and selling. And of course a State cannot hold a copier accountable in damages for failure to label or otherwise to identify his goods unless his failure is in violation of valid state statutory or decisional law requiring the copier to label or take other precautions to prevent confusion of customers as to the source of the goods.

Since the judgment below forbids the sale of a copy of an unpatented article and orders an accounting for damages for such copying, it cannot stand.

Reversed.

Mr. Justice HARLAN, concurring in the result.

In one respect I would give the States more leeway in unfair competition "copying" cases than the Court's opinions would allow. If copying is found, other than by an inference arising from the mere act of copying, to have been undertaken with the dominant purpose and effect of palming off one's goods as those of another or of confusing customers as to the source of such goods, I see no reason why the State may not impose reasonable restrictions on the future "copying" itself. Vindication of the paramount federal interest at stake does not require a State to tolerate such specifically oriented predatory business practices. Apart from this, I am in accord with the opinions of the Court, and concur in both judgments since neither case presents the point on which I find myself in disagreement.

NOTES

1. How wide a preemptive swath did *Sears* and *Compco* intend to cut? Although the decisions recognized that states might prohibit the imitation of trademarks in order to prevent consumer deception as to source of goods, would the Court require a showing of actual confusion before enjoining the infringement? Would likelihood of confusion suffice? What if the trademark action was brought on a dilution or zone of expansion theory, and plaintiff could show no consumer confusion?

How could the Court logically distinguish between goods or articles on the one hand, and packages and marks on the other? Can you think of situations in which the trademark *is* the article? In National Football League Properties, Inc. v. Consumer Enterprises, Inc., 26 Ill.App.3d 814, 327 N.E.2d 242, 185 U.S.P.Q. 550 (Ill.App.Ct., 1st Dist. 1975), cert. denied 423 U.S. 1018, 96 S.Ct. 454, 46 L.Ed.2d 390, 188 U.S.P.Q. 96, plaintiff, the exclusive licensing agent for the name and symbol of each club in the National Football League, obtained an injunction against defendant's unauthorized manufacture and sale of emblems duplicating club marks. Defendant unsuccessfully argued that it was "selling the emblem designs as merely decorative products," that the emblems were not "performing the trademark function of source identification," and that, under *Sears* and *Compco*, states cannot "prohibit the copying of unpatented and uncopyrighted" articles. 327 N.E.2d 242, 246. While the court could have rested its decision on *Sears'* exemption of trademarks, it chose instead to hold that a trademark could not be considered an "article" within the terms of *Sears* and *Compco*.

What force, if any, is left to *Sears* and *Compco* after the Court's decisions in *Aronson,* page 64, above, Kewanee v. Bicron, page 178, below, and Goldstein v. California, discussed at page 228? Does section 301 of the Copyright Act, considered at pages 223 to 232, effectively preempt state jurisdiction over any of the areas covered by *Sears* and *Compco?*

2. The sweep of Justice Black's language may have engulfed the Court's holdings in the principal cases. Consider, for example, a variety of conjecture as to what the Court held, excerpted from the symposium, Product Simulation: A Right or a Wrong?, 64 Colum.L. Rev. 1178 (1964):

> The effect of the Supreme Court decisions in the *Sears* and *Compco* cases is neither as disastrous as many who espouse greater design protection fear nor as comforting as many who eschew such protection hope. Daphne R. Leeds, p. 1178.

> In two companion rulings during its last term the Supreme Court appears to have placed product simulation on a constitutional pedestal and accorded it a privileged status. These rulings, couched in the absolute and unqualified language that is the hallmark of Justice Black's juristic art, may portend revolutional changes in the law of unfair competition. Milton Handler, p. 1184.

> When the Supreme Court released the *Sears* and *Compco* decisions it seemed, at first glance, that the law of unfair competition and related fields had become "disaster areas." The roof had seemingly fallen in on a vast structure of federal and state precedents laboriously built up since the days of the Court's famous decision in the *International News* case. Walter J. Derenberg, p. 1192.

> Unless one chooses to assail the whole concept of freedom of imitative competition the Court's general conclusion, as stated in the *Sears* opinion, seems to be unassailable. Ralph S. Brown, Jr., p. 1219.

> It is crucial to observe, however, that while broad opinions generally pre-empting state monopolies may well be handed down, *Sears* and *Compco* are certainly not such opinions. They are the easy cases where the state protection was substantially inconsistent with the federal statute. Paul Bender, p. 1237.

Although the obscurity of the *Sears* and *Compco* opinions has provided good sport for academics, it has troubled state and lower federal courts. There has been a discernible trend to distinguish, dismiss, or simply ignore the two decisions. The Second Circuit Court of Appeals at first treated the decisions lightly, Flexitized, Inc. v. National Flexitized Corp., 335 F.2d 774, 781 n. 4, 142 U.S.P.Q. 334 (1964), cert. denied, 380 U.S. 913, 85 S.Ct. 899, 13 L.Ed.2d 799, 144 U.S.P.Q. 780, but later had second thoughts, Ives Laboratories, Inc. v. Darby Drug Co., 601 F.2d 631, 644, 202 U.S.P.Q. 548 (2d Cir. 1979), (questioning "whether the *Flexitized* footnote adequately recognized the blow dealt by *Sears* and *Compco* to state unfair competition laws").

3. How would you have counselled plaintiff in *Crescent Tool* to market its wrench so that it would have been able to capture the goodwill that accrued to it? How would you have counselled plaintiff in *Sears*? In *Compco*?

What, if anything, did *Sears* and *Compco* add to *Crescent*? Implicit in the rule allowing simulation of an article's functional features, but not its distinctive nonfunctional features, is a longstanding accommodation of state law to federal competitive interests. "If any portion of the goods or their packages are functional, then, in determining whether protection should be extended, the functional features are properly judged only by Federal patent law standards, such as novelty and nonobviousness, and not by a State's law of unfair competition. If protection is given to such functional aspects under a State's unfair competition law the State, in effect, would be granting a perpetual monopoly, whereas the protection available under the federal patent laws is only a limited monopoly. But where the feature, or more aptly design, is a mere arbitrary embellishment, imitation may be forbidden where the requisite showing of secondary meaning is made." Duo-Tint Bulb & Battery Co., Inc. v. Moline Supply Co., 46 Ill.App.3d 145, 151, 4 Ill.Dec. 685, 360 N.E.2d 798 (3d Dist. 1977).

Courts occasionally deviate from the functionality principle. Some jurisdictions generally allow simulation of nonfunctional features while others prohibit simulation of functional features even absent proof of consumer confusion. "Most courts refuse to enjoin imitation of functional features, even when accompanied by fraudulent activities, but a substantial minority consider functionality irrelevant when deliberate fraud is involved." Note, Unfair Competition and the Doctrine of Functionality, 64 Colum.L.Rev. 544, 569 (1964).

Other courts differ not on principle, but application. Some equate functionality with strictly utilitarian aspects, following the Restatement definition that a feature of goods is functional if "it affects their purpose, action or performance, or the facility or economy of processing, handling or using them." Restatement of Torts § 742 (1938). Others expand functionality to include any feature, including esthetic appeal, affecting consumer choice. See Zippo Mfg. Co. v. Rogers Imports, Inc., 216 F.Supp. 670, 137 U.S.P.Q. 413 (S.D.N.Y. 1963). What effect do these rules have on adherence to design principles such as "form follows function"?

Careful readers of *Sears* and *Compco* thought that the Court had obliterated the functional-nonfunctional distinction by banning all state prohibitions of product simulation. See, for example, the essay by Brown, in Symposium, Product Simulation: A Right or a Wrong? 64 Colum.L.Rev. 1178, 1220–1221 (1964). Reread the next-to-last paragraph in Justice Black's *Compco* opinion to see if you agree. The Eighth Circuit Court of Appeals has characterized this crucial passage as dictum. "The law of trademark and the issues of functionality and secondary meaning were not before the Court. The issue before the Court was whether state law could extend the effective term of patent protection granted by the federal statutes." Truck Equipment Serv. Co. v. Fruehauf Corp., 536 F.2d 1210, 1214, 191 U. S.P.Q. 79 (8th Cir. 1976), cert. denied, 429 U.S. 861, 97 S.Ct. 164, 50 L.Ed.2d 139, 191 U.S.P.Q. 588. *Fruehauf's* revival of the functional-nonfunctional distinction has gained a following in state and federal courts. See, for example, Duo-Tint Bulb & Battery Co., Inc. v. Moline Supply Co., 46 Ill.App.3d 145, 4 Ill.Dec. 685, 360 N.E.2d 798 (3d Dist. 1977).

4. If any one thing was made clear in the *Sears* opinion, it is that states are free to regulate unfair competition when it takes the form of copying distinctive trade dress—"Doubtless a State may . . . protect businesses in the use of their trademarks, labels, or distinctive dress in the packaging of goods so as to prevent others, by imitating such markings, from misleading purchasers as to the source of goods." In many cases, however, the difference between a product's distinctive dress and its distinctive, nonfunctional features may be neither apparent nor real, and several courts have relied on this abstract distinction to avoid the preemptive effect of *Sears* and *Compco*.

In Samson Cordage Works v. Puritan Cordage Mills, 243 F.Supp. 1, 145 U.S.P.Q. 602 (W.D.Ky.1964), the court ruled on defendant's post-*Sears* motion to set aside a contempt judgment which had been entered two months before *Sears:* "The injunction involved here was not directed against defendant's copying of complainant's product itself. As this Court noted in its conclusions of law, relief would have been denied if complainant had merely sought to prevent defendant from copying its sash cord. Injunctive relief was granted originally because it was shown that the spiral pattern of spots embedded in the surface of the sash cord had been adopted by the complainant as a distinctive trade dress to indicate source, and that such spot pattern had acquired a second meaning. Having established the fact that a secondary meaning attached to the spiral spot pattern when it appeared on the sash cord, the complainant was entitled to protection in the exclusive use of its trade dress.

"The fact that the spot pattern of necessity becomes an integral part of the product itself makes this a borderline case between copying of a product's design and the copying of a product's trade dress. After a full adjudication of that issue between the parties here, it is not for this Court to say now that the injunction prohibits the copying of an unpatented article. The product involved is sash cord, and the defendant can make sash cord which is identical in physical qualities and has the same configuration as that produced by complainant. What defendant may not do under the injunction is decorate its cord with a spiral spot pattern in imitation of the markings on complainant's product." 243 F.Supp. 7–8.

For a pre-*Sears* argument that competitive principles require that trade dress simulation not be actionable, see Treece, Copying Methods of Product Differentiation: Fair or Unfair Competition? 38

Notre Dame Law. 244 (1963). See also Schultz, Trade Dress and Unfair Competition in Publishing and Packaging: When Imitation is *Not* the Sincerest Form of Flattery, 43 Brooklyn L.Rev. 654 (1977).

5. Ironically, the misappropriation doctrine announced in *International News Service* appears to have survived *Sears* and *Compco*. Of all of unfair competition's tenets, misappropriation was the most likely candidate for preemption. Its extensive monopoly is often used as a surrogate for copyright or patent protection in situations in which, for one reason or another, the federal laws withhold protection. Failing to reject *I.N.S.* explicitly, *Sears* and *Compco* invited state and lower federal courts to indulge such nice distinctions as the one made in Columbia Broadcasting System, Inc. v. Documentaries Unlimited, Inc., 42 Misc.2d 723, 248 N.Y.S.2d 809 (Sup.Ct.1964), where defendant was enjoined from incorporating in its phonograph record plaintiff's newscast of the assassination of President John Kennedy. *Sears* and *Compco* were inapplicable, the court held, because "copying" was not involved under the facts, only "appropriation."

Later decisions, guided by the careful methodology of the *Goldstein* and *Kewanee* cases, have tested misappropriation doctrine more sensitively and sensibly. See, for example, Synercom Technology, Inc. v. University Computing Co., 474 F.Supp. 37, 204 U.S.P.Q. 29 (N.D.Tex.1979).

See generally Dannay, The Sears-Compco Doctrine Today: Trademarks and Unfair Competition, 67 Trademark Rep. 132 (1976); Goldstein, Federal System Ordering of the Copyright Interest, 69 Colum.L.Rev. 49, 71–73 (1969); Note, The "Copying-Misappropriation" Distinction: A False Step in the Development of the Sears-Compco Pre-Emption Doctrine, 71 Colum.L.Rev. 1444 (1971).

III. TRADE SECRETS

A. THEORY OF PROTECTION

FOREST LABORATORIES, INC. v. FORMULATIONS, INC.

United States District Court of Wisconsin, 1969.
299 F.Supp. 202, 161 U.S.P.Q. 622, rev'd in part 452 F.2d 621,
171 U.S.P.Q. 731 (7th Cir.).

GORDON, District Judge.

This is an action for improper use and disclosure of what are alleged to be the plaintiff's trade secrets. Jurisdiction is based on diversity of citizenship, and state law is to be used to determine the substantive issues. In addition, the defendant, Pillsbury, has counterclaimed for a declaratory judgment of invalidity of the plaintiff's patent. . . .

I. The Trade Secret Cause of Action

It is alleged that Pillsbury has illegally used and divulged the plaintiff's trade secrets for packaging effervescent sweetener tablets. Originally the allegations included a claim that Pillsbury had also violated trade secrets for the manufacture of such sweeteners, but the plaintiff abandoned that attack and proceeded at trial only with respect to the packaging techniques.

The plaintiff is a manufacturer and packager of food and drug items. It claims to have developed a successful process for packaging effervescent sweetener tablets so that their shelf life is lengthy. The production and sale of effervescent sweetener tablets is limited to a small group of companies; of the approximately 1000 tablet manufacturers in the United States, only a few produce this type of tablet.

Tidy House Corporation, the defendant's predecessor, had been interested in marketing an effervescent sweetener tablet. Prior to 1957, Tidy House had engaged several firms to manufacture tablets for this purpose. However, Tidy House experienced difficulties with each of these sources of supply, and in 1958 Tidy House learned that the plaintiff manufactured such tablets. In December, 1958, Tidy House sent its technical director, Mr. Egan, and his co-employee, Mr. Steinhauser, to observe the plaintiff's operation in New York. During that visit Mr. Lowey, the president of the plaintiff, claims to have disclosed to Mr. Egan what are alleged to be Forest Laboratories' trade secrets for packaging. Shortly thereafter, the plaintiff began to supply Tidy House with tablets in bulk; Tidy House packaged the tablets for the consumer.

In 1960, the Tidy House assets were purchased by the Pillsbury Company, and the plaintiff continued to supply the tablets to what

141

became known as the Tidy House division of Pillsbury. This relationship continued until January, 1964, when Pillsbury engaged Formulations, Inc. as a new source of supply. Subsequently, the plaintiff brought this action, alleging that Pillsbury was using its confidential packaging secrets. In addition, the plaintiff charges that the defendant improperly disclosed such secrets to Mankato, Inc., a contract packager hired by Pillsbury in 1965.

The applicable law on trade secrets was set down in Abbott Laboratories v. Norse Chemical Corp., 33 Wis.2d 445, 147 N.W.2d 529, 152 U.S.P.Q. 640 (1967). The court determined that the Restatement of Torts correctly states the Wisconsin law. In particular, the Abbott court ruled that there were two essential elements to a cause of action for misappropriation of trade secrets: there must be an actual trade secret and there must likewise be a breach of confidence. Each factor will be discussed in turn.

A. Are These "Trade Secrets?"

A trade secret is defined by the Restatement as

"Any formula, pattern, device or compilation of information which is used in one's business, and which gives him an opportunity to obtain an advantage over competitors who do not know or use it. It may be a .   .   . process of .   .   . treating or preserving materials .   .   ." Restatement of Torts, § 757, comment (b).

The Restatement and Abbott set forth six factors to be considered in determining whether given information qualifies as a trade secret. These six factors are: (1) the extent to which the information is known outside of his business; (2) the extent to which it is known by employees and others involved in his business; (3) the extent of measures taken by him to guard the secrecy of the information; (4) the value of the information to him and to his competitors; (5) the amount of effort or money expended by him in developing the information; (6) the ease or difficulty with which the information could be properly acquired or duplicated by others.

The plaintiff contended at the trial that its packaging procedure consists of the following steps: (a) the entire packaging operation must take place in a room in which the relative humidity is maintained at 40% or less; (b) before packaging, the tablets are to be tempered in a room having 40% or less relative humidity for a period of between 24 to 48 hours; (c) before packaging, the bottles into which the tablets are to be packaged are to be tempered in a room having 40% or less relative humidity for a period of between 24 to 48 hours; (d) before packaging, the bottle caps are to be tempered in a room having 40% or less relative humidity for a period of between 24 to 48 hours; (e) before packaging, the cotton used to stuff the bottles is to be tempered in a room having 40% or less relative humidity for between 24 to 48 hours; (f) the bottles should not be washed; (g) an air space should remain in the bottles after the caps are applied.

The purpose of the foregoing procedure is to make certain that the tablets and the materials are dry and that they are in a state of equilibrium with each other. By using these techniques, the plaintiff asserts that it was able to produce and package a tablet with a high degree of stability. In contrast, the testimony shows that prior to the plaintiff's association with Tidy House, the latter had had difficulties with its prior suppliers whose products on occasion exploded on store shelves or otherwise proved unstable.

Pillsbury denies that the recited techniques constitute trade secrets. To determine that issue, we will consider seriatim, the six Abbott factors listed above.

(1) Pillsbury asserts that each step in the packaging procedure was well known in the trade, and that it cannot, therefore, qualify as secret material.

Pillsbury's expert witness, Dr. Wurster, a professor of pharmacy at the University of Wisconsin, testified that in his opinion these procedures were "just common knowledge." Professor Wurster prepared a compilation of textbook materials that he claimed set forth the procedures claimed by the plaintiff as trade secrets. (Def. exh. 1) This compilation makes references to the fact that effervescent tablets must be handled and packaged under controlled humidity conditions. Several of the articles refer to specific humidity levels; the references vary between 25% and 50%. The literature in evidence also contains admonitions that moisture must be kept out of the entire procedure. In addition, there was testimony that when Tidy House first became interested in effervescent tablets, it had been advised by The DuPont Corporation that operations would have to be conducted under low (40%) humidity conditions to eliminate moisture.

The foregoing supports my conclusion that the industry was quite well aware of point (a) listed in the plaintiff's procedure: that packaging operations must be conducted under controlled humidity (40%) conditions. I am also convinced that steps (f) and (g), which relate to washing of the bottles and an air space above the cotton, likewise cannot be claimed to be trade secrets. There was testimony that others in the industry refrained from the practice of washing the bottles. Competitive products introduced into evidence clearly show that other producers utilize an air space above the cotton.

While Dr. Wurster thought that all of the plaintiff's procedures were well known, nothing that he said or compiled persuades me that the tempering steps, numbered (b), (c), (d) and (e) were known in the industry. On the contrary, the plaintiff's witness, Mr. Reamer, a fully qualified expert in the field, testified that the tempering steps were "new, intriguing. I think it's a break-through . . ." It was also his opinion that the defendant's compilation of literature did not set forth these procedures.

Mr. Lowey testified that when he first became interested in effervescent tablets, he found that the literature on the subject did not teach him enough to package a stable tablet. It was only through trial and error, he averred, that he arrived at this process. As already noted, few firms engaged in packaging effervescent tablets, and those that did so often produced an inferior tablet. If proper techniques for packaging were broadly known, there would be little reason for this difficulty, unless the flaws stemmed from defective manufacturing practices.

The defendant asserts, however, that the tablet tempering stage [step (b)] is in the public domain because it is disclosed in the plaintiff's patent in suit. The argument is that under such circumstances plaintiff cannot claim this step as a secret. The patent discloses the tablet tempering step. The general rule is that the issuance of a patent which clearly discloses all essentials of a process destroys any secrecy that previously attached to that process. However, if there is a wrongful use or disclosure prior to the issuance of the patent, the wrongdoer will not be absolved from liability for his wrong committed during that prior period.

There is a decision in this circuit which holds that the wrongdoer may be permanently enjoined from use or disclosure even though the subsequently issued patent has made the information public. Shellmar Products Co. v. Allen-Qualley Co., 87 F.2d 104, 32 U.S. P.Q. 24 (7th Cir. 1936). That rule has been severely criticized in other circuits. See, e. g., Conmar Products Corp. v. Universal Slide Fastener Co., Inc., 172 F.2d 150, 80 U.S.P.Q. 108 (2d Cir. 1949). On the other hand, once the plaintiff has [been] issued a patent setting out the process, some courts hold that the disclosure in the patent precludes liability for use of the information subsequent to issue. Schreyer v. Casco Products Corp., 190 F.2d 921, 90 U.S.P.Q. 271 (2d Cir. 1951); Tempo Instrument, Inc. v. Logitek, Inc., 229 F.Supp. 1, 142 U.S.P.Q. 76 (N.Y.1964). The Shellmar case is often cited for the opposite conclusion.

In our case the confidential disclosure allegedly occurred in 1958; the improper use occurred in 1964 after Pillsbury discontinued purchases from Forest Laboratories. The patent was issued in March, 1965. There was an allegedly improper disclosure to Mankato, Inc. in May, 1965.

Since jurisdiction in this case is based upon diversity, Wisconsin law controls. However, the Wisconsin supreme court has not decided the instant question. In my opinion, the better rule is that which holds an improper use of a trade secret prior to the issuance of the patent to be an actionable wrong. This rule is in accord with the Restatement, which makes breach of faith an essence of the wrong. The plaintiff is not in a position to complain of a disclosure of the information occurring after his patent has issued. When the patent was issued, he dedicated his information to the public in return for a monopoly. To permit him to have both a monopoly and a cause of action for subsequent disclosure is inequitable. The plaintiff, in effect, has changed his position. Whereas he had previously kept this information secret (the sine qua non of a trade secret), he has now decided that it shall no longer be his knowledge alone. The key element of secrecy is gone. Therefore, Pillsbury cannot be held liable for any disclosure after March, 1965.

The improper adoption of steps (b) through (e), which were not well known in the industry, are actionable; on the other hand, steps (a), (f) and (g) were sufficiently well-known so that they cannot be called trade secrets.

(2) With reference to the second Abbott factor, the evidence discloses that only a handful of the plaintiff's employees knew of his packaging operations, and they were all bound by secrecy agreements.

(3) Mr. Lowey testified that all of his employees who deal with packaging were bound by secrecy agreements. There was also testimony that packaging information was closely guarded in the trade. (Tr. 46–47).

(4) The information would be of significant value to the plaintiff. Since technical problems prevent more than a few companies from packaging effervescent tablets, one who has the ability to do so is in an advantageous position.

(5) Mr. Lowey testified that he spent a long time developing and testing the process before he was able to devise a packaging procedure that insured stability. No exact time period was mentioned, however. There is no evidence as to the amount of money expended to develop the process. There is evidence that other firms in the industry hesitated to enter this particular field unless they had two years to test the stability of the product.

(6) This process is not so ingenious that it could not be duplicated by others; but invention is not the keynote of a trade secret under the liberal test of the Restatement. All that is needed is some procedure which gives an advantage over a competitor who does not have it. Restatement of Torts, § 757, comment (b).

My conclusion is that the tempering portions of the packaging process must be classified as a trade secret. The Restatement test is not overly stringent. Even though a given procedure seems simple by hindsight, that is not conclusive. A trade secret requires some process or method which is not obvious or generally known in the trade, and which gives the innovator a substantial advantage over a competitor. I find that the plaintiff has established the tempering process in connection with packaging as a trade secret.

B. *Was There a Confidential Relationship?*

The second issue presented is whether *these* trade secrets were given by Mr. Lowey to the defendant under circumstances which reveal that a confidential relationship existed between them.

At the outset, Pillsbury argues that even if a confidential relationship as to these secrets was established with Tidy House, Pillsbury would not be bound unless it had actual notice of these facts. It bases its argument on § 758, Restatement of Torts. That section deals with situations in which a distinct third party receives confidential information without being aware of its secret nature; but that section does not apply to the situation at hand. In this case, Pillsbury purchased all the assets of Tidy House, which thereafter became known as the Tidy House division of the Pillsbury Company. Most employees remained the same. In my opinion, Pillsbury, as successor, was bound by any confidential disclosure made to Tidy House. If Tidy House had notice that these secrets were confidentially disclosed, that knowledge does not end when the Tidy House personnel become Pillsbury employees. It does not matter, therefore, whether any member of the Pillsbury management actually received notice that the packaging information was a confidential trade secret.

The testimony on whether this information was given to Tidy House in confidence is contradictory. It is my conclusion, however, that the plaintiff has established that there was a confidential disclosure to Tidy House employees in 1958.

When early arrangements were made with Tidy House, which was looking for a new supplier of effervescent sweetener tablets, Mr. Lowey sent the plaintiff's manufacturing formula to Mr. Sherrard, Tidy House's purchasing agent. The letter which conveyed this information said that the formula was to be kept confidential. The letter also stated that "we agree with you that details on packaging, etc. should be taken up later." In December, 1956, Mr. Egan, the Tidy House technical director, and Mr. Steinhauser, Mr. Egan's associate, were authorized by Mr. Tieszin, the Tidy House Executive Vice President, to visit the plaintiff's facilities in New York. During that meeting, Mr. Lowey told Mr. Egan that Forest Laboratories did not want to package the tablets for the consumer because of a lack of space. Mr. Egan testified that he asked Mr. Lowey to give him "some advice as to the conditions under which this packaging should be carried on" because Tidy House had not previously packaged tablets. Both Mr. Lowey and Mr. Egan testified that Mr. Lowey agreed to furnish the packaging techniques in confidence; both men also testified that all of the trade secrets were communicated orally to Mr. Egan, who took notes at such meeting.

Mr. Egan testified that he then returned to Tidy House and both orally and in writing informed Mr. Sherrard, Mr. Tieszin, Mr. Williams, and "maybe" Mr. Rapp, the Tidy House President, that what he had learned at the meeting had been received in confidence.

Mr. Egan's written memo was never introduced into evidence, but Mr. Sherrard corroborated Mr. Egan's testimony by stating that although he did not remember seeing any memorandum, he did learn that the disclosure of packaging techniques to Mr. Egan had been made in confidence. Further, Mr. Egan's statement that he also informed Mr. Tieszin is uncontradicted.

Mr. Steinhauser, who accompanied Mr. Egan on the trip, testified that Mr. Lowey never cautioned Mr. Egan or himself that they were hearing confidential information. However, Mr. Steinhauser stated that the information disclosed was confidential on a "moral" basis. Mr. Rapp testified that neither Mr. Egan nor Mr. Steinhauser told him that any information given to them was to be kept in confidence, however, he also testified that he was never aware that *any* confidential relationship existed with the plaintiff and it is quite clear that a confidential relationship existed at least as to certain manufacturing information. Mr. Williams and Mr. McCarron also did not remember any statement that a confidential relationship existed.

Although the foregoing proof is conflicting, I believe that the record establishes that a confidential relationship as to packaging information arose in 1958 between the plaintiff and Tidy House. Mr. Sherrard's testimony corroborates the testimony of the participants —Mr. Lowey and Mr. Egan. It is uncontradicted that Mr. Egan also reported this information to Mr. Tieszin. The contrary negative assertions of Messrs. Rapp, Williams, and McCarron do not convince me otherwise.

I have concluded that a confidential relationship as to "packaging information" was established in 1958, but Pillsbury argues that *tempering* secrets were not disclosed at that time. Both Mr. Egan and Mr. Lowey testified that such data was supplied, and they both detailed what those secrets were. I believe that tempering information was discussed at the meeting between Mr. Lowey and Mr. Egan; such conclusion is not reversed by Mr. Steinhauser's statement that he only remembers a discussion of manufacturing techniques. Pillsbury points out that Mr. Egan had testified at a deposition taken some months before the trial that the tablet tempering secrets were disclosed by Mr. Lowey during 1960 when Pillsbury's packaging facilities were being conducted at its Omaha facility and not at the 1958 meeting. Mr. Egan explained this discrepancy by saying that his recollection had been refreshed. I find that the disclosure of the tablet tempering secrets was made in 1958, and thereafter Tidy House was under an agreement of confidence.

The defendant asserts that Mr. Lowey never formally reasserted after the 1958 meeting that the packaging techniques were trade secrets. While this may be true, the parties appear to have clearly *understood* that this was the case. Mr. Steinhauser, who met with Mr. Lowey in 1961, stated that while no specific admonition of secrecy was made at that time, "We had confidence in Mr. Lowey and I thought he had confidence in us and that is pretty much the way I recall it being handled." Mr. Boand, a Tidy House employee, also made a similar statement. Mr. Lowey testified that since a confidential relationship had been established in 1958, and since he was dealing with Tidy House employees or people who were under contract with them, he felt no need to reiterate what was already an established fact. I do not believe that Mr. Lowey was careless in his dealings with the defendant.

The Restatement provides as follows:

"The question is simply whether in the circumstances B knows or should know that the information is [the plaintiff's] trade secret and that its disclosure is made in confidence." Restatement of Torts, § 757, comment on cl. (b) at 14.

In regard to the tempering of materials, both Mr. Lowey and Mr. Egan stated that these steps were also disclosed in the meeting held in 1958. The defendant challenges this position and urges that the steps relating to the tempering of materials did not arise from Mr. Lowey but, instead, were the result of suggestions made by Mr. Pasternak of Magna, Inc. The latter company was hired in 1962 by Pillsbury to handle packaging.

The practice of tempering materials was utilized in 1962, but there was no reference to such procedures in the set of specifications which were composed when Pillsbury resumed its own packaging.

I conclude that the plaintiff has failed to satisfy its burden of proving that the tempering techniques as to materials (as distinguished from tablets) were its confidential trade secrets. While there are inconsistencies on both sides of the question, it is the plaintiff's burden to establish its case; in my opinion, it has failed on this point.

To entitle the plaintiff to recovery, it is only necessary that "some secret information relating to one or more essentials" belonging to the plaintiff has been misappropriated. Engelhard Industries, Inc. v. Research Instrumental Corp., 324 F.2d 347, 139 U.S.P.Q. 179 (9th Cir. 1963). In my opinion, the information regarding the *tablet* tempering step constitutes essential and confidential information belonging to the plaintiff. Therefore, if it was misappropriated, the defendant will be liable to the plaintiff.

As already noted, however, since the plaintiff's patent was issued in March, 1965, that is the cut-off date for any wrongdoing by the defendant. This court need not, therefore, examine the alleged improper disclosure to Mankato in May, 1965.

C. *Was There a Breach of Confidence by the Defendant?*

The plaintiff has alleged a wrongful use of the tablet tempering information by the defendant subsequent to the time that Pillsbury dropped Forest Laboratories as its supplier in January, 1964. Pillsbury, on the other hand, insists that it made no use of this information after that time. I think the record fairly establishes that Pillsbury made use of the tablet tempering procedure after the plaintiff was dismissed as supplier of the tablets.

Pillsbury's confidential manufacturing specifications for these tablets, dated March 19, 1964, disclosed the following notation:

> "Temper tablets 11805 in unopened supplier's containers for a minimum period of 48 hours. During tempering, handling and packaging of tablets maintain environmental:
>
> a. R. H. at 40%
>
> b. Temperature of 70° F."

Dr. Stein of Pillsbury testified that the purpose of this type of requirement was "to allow the temperature of the tablets to equilibrate with the temperature of the room."

The defendant argues that this specification is different from the plaintiff's trade secret because the former specifies tempering in an "unopened" container. Mr. Dienat, the defendant's witness, testified that experiments showed that it would take much longer for tablets to equilibrate in a closed container than in a container open to the air. Other witnesses testified that the tablets would still equilibrate.

In my opinion, the question of how long it would take the tablets to equilibrate is not controlling. An improper use need not be in exactly the same form as that contemplated by the plaintiff. Restatement of Torts, § 767, comment (b), p. 9. The only purpose of the tablet tempering procedure was to place the tablets in an ambient condition; that the defendant's method of utilizing this information may have been somewhat inefficient does not detract from the fact that the tablet tempering procedure was the plaintiff's secret and that it was improperly used by Pillsbury.

While the plaintiff has requested an injunction to prevent further use of the trade secret by the defendant, it is my opinion that such an injunction should not issue where, as here, the trade secret process has now been made public by the declarations made in the plaintiff's patent. Damages will suffice to compensate the plaintiff for its injury.

III. Conclusion

The plaintiff has established that the tablet tempering process was its trade secret; that it was given to the defendant in confidence, and that the defendant violated that confidence by using that process after Forest Laboratories was discharged as the tablet supplier. The other elements of the trade secret cause of action have not been established. The plaintiff is entitled to damages, but not to injunctive relief.

In addition, the court declines to exercise its jurisdiction to declare the rights of the parties in regard to the plaintiff's patent.

E. I. DUPONT deNEMOURS & CO. v. CHRISTOPHER

United States Court of Appeals, Fifth Circuit, 1970.
431 F.2d 1012, 166 U.S.P.Q. 421, cert. denied 400 U.S. 1024, 91 S.Ct. 581,
27 L.Ed.2d 637, reh. denied 401 U.S. 967, 91 S.Ct. 968, 28 L.Ed.2d 250.

Before WISDOM, GOLDBERG and INGRAHAM, Circuit Judges.

GOLDBERG, Circuit Judge:

This is a case of industrial espionage in which an airplane is the cloak and a camera the dagger. The defendants-appellants, Rolfe and Gary Christopher, are photographers in Beaumont, Texas. The Christophers were hired by an unknown third party to take aerial photographs of new construction at the Beaumont plant of E. I. Du-Pont deNemours & Company, Inc. Sixteen photographs of the Du-Pont facility were taken from the air on March 19, 1969, and these photographs were later developed and delivered to the third party.

DuPont employees apparently noticed the airplane on March 19 and immediately began an investigation to determine why the craft was circling over the plant. By that afternoon the investigation had disclosed that the craft was involved in a photographic expedition and that the Christophers were the photographers. DuPont contacted the Christophers that same afternoon and asked them to reveal the name of the person or corporation requesting the photographs. The Christophers refused to disclose this information, giving as their reason the client's desire to remain anonymous.

Having reached a dead end in the investigation, DuPont subsequently filed suit against the Christophers, alleging that the Christophers had wrongfully obtained photographs revealing DuPont's trade secrets which they then sold to the undisclosed third party. DuPont contended that it had developed a highly secret but unpatented process for producing methanol, a process which gave DuPont a competitive advantage over other producers. This process, DuPont alleged, was a trade secret developed after much expensive and time-consuming research, and a secret which the company had taken special precautions to safeguard. The area photographed by the Christophers was the plant designed to produce methanol by this secret process, and because the plant was still under construction parts of the process were exposed to view from directly above the construction area. Photographs of that area, DuPont alleged, would enable a skilled person to deduce the secret process for making methanol. DuPont thus contended that the Christophers had wrongfully appropriated DuPont trade secrets by taking the photographs and delivering them to the undisclosed third party. In its suit DuPont asked for damages to cover the loss it had already sustained as a result of the wrongful disclosure of the trade secret and sought temporary and permanent injunctions prohibiting any further circulation of the photographs already taken and prohibiting any additional photographing of the methanol plant.

The Christophers answered with motions to dismiss for lack of jurisdiction and failure to state a claim upon which relief could be granted. Depositions were taken during which the Christophers again refused to disclose the name of the person to whom they had delivered the photographs. DuPont then filed a motion to compel an answer to this question and all related questions.

On June 5, 1969, the trial court held a hearing on all pending motions and an additional motion by the Christophers for summary judgment. The court denied the Christophers' motions to dismiss for want of jurisdiction and failure to state a claim and also denied their motion for summary judgment. The court granted DuPont's motion to compel the Christophers to divulge the name of their client. Having made these rulings, the court then granted the Christophers' motion for an interlocutory appeal under 28 U.S.C.A. § 1292(b) to allow the Christophers to obtain immediate appellate review of the court's finding that DuPont had stated a claim upon which relief could be granted. Agreeing with the trial court's determination that DuPont had stated a valid claim, we affirm the decision of that court.

This is a case of first impression, for the Texas courts have not faced this precise factual issue, and sitting as a diversity court we must sensitize our *Erie* antennae to divine what the Texas courts would do if such a situation were presented to them. The only question involved in this interlocutory appeal is whether DuPont has asserted a claim upon which relief can be granted. The Christophers argued both at trial and before this court that they committed no "actionable wrong" in photographing the DuPont facility and passing these photographs on to their client because they conducted all of their activities in public airspace, violated no government aviation standard, did not breach any confidential relation, and did not engage in any fraudulent or illegal conduct. In short, the Christophers argue that for an appropriation of trade secrets to be wrongful there must be a trespass, other illegal conduct, or breach of a confidential relationship. We disagree.

It is true, as the Christophers assert, that the previous trade secret cases have contained one or more of these elements. However, we do not think that the Texas courts would limit the trade secret protection exclusively to these elements. On the contrary, in Hyde Corporation v. Huffines, 1958, 158 Tex. 566, 314 S.W.2d 763, the Texas Supreme Court specifically adopted the rule found in the Restatement of Torts which provides:

"One who discloses or uses another's trade secret, without a privilege to do so, is liable to the other if

(a) he discovered the secret by improper means, or

(b) his disclosure or use constitutes a breach of confidence reposed in him by the other in disclosing the secret to him. . . ."

Restatement of Torts § 757 (1939).

Thus, although the previous cases have dealt with a breach of a confidential relationship, a trespass, or other illegal conduct, the rule is much broader than the cases heretofore encountered. Not limiting itself to specific wrongs, Texas adopted subsection (a) of the Restatement which recognizes a cause of action for the discovery of a trade secret by any "improper" means.

The defendants, however, read Furr's Inc. v. United Specialty Advertising Co., Tex.Civ.App.1960, 338 S.W.2d 762, writ ref'd n. r. e., as limiting the Texas rule to breach of a confidential relationship. The court in Furr's did make the statement that

> The use of someone else's idea is not automatically a violation of the law. It must be something that meets the requirements of a 'trade secret' *and has been obtained through a breach of confidence* in order to entitle the injured party to damages and/or injunction. 338 S.W.2d at 766 (emphasis added).

We think, however, that the exclusive rule which defendants have extracted from this statement is unwarranted. In the first place, in Furr's the court specifically found that there was no trade secret involved because the entire advertising scheme claimed to be the trade secret had been completely divulged to the public. Secondly, the court found that the plaintiff in the course of selling the scheme to the defendant had voluntarily divulged the entire scheme. Thus the court was dealing only with a possible breach of confidence concerning a properly discovered secret; there was never a question of any impropriety in the discovery or any other improper conduct on the part of the defendant. The court merely held that under those circumstances the defendant had not acted improperly if no breach of confidence occurred. We do not read Furr's as limiting the trade secret protection to a breach of confidential relationship when the facts of the case do raise the issue of some other wrongful conduct on the part of one discovering the trade secrets of another. If breach of confidence were meant to encompass the entire panoply of commercial improprieties, subsection (a) of the Restatement would be either surplusage or persiflage, an interpretation abhorrent to the traditional precision of the Restatement. We therefore find meaning in subsection (a) and think that the Texas Supreme Court clearly indicated by its adoption that there is a cause of action for the discovery of a trade secret by any "improper means." Hyde Corporation v. Huffines, supra.

The question remaining, therefore, is whether aerial photography of plant construction is an improper means of obtaining another's trade secret. We conclude that it is and that the Texas courts would so hold. The Supreme Court of that state has declared that "the undoubted tendency of the law has been to recognize and enforce higher standards of commercial morality in the business world." Hyde Corporation v. Huffines, supra, 314 S.W.2d at 773. That court has quoted with approval articles indicating that the *proper* means of gaining possession of a competitor's secret process is "through inspection and analysis" of the product in order to create a duplicate. K & G Tool & Service Co. v. G & G Fishing Tool Service, 1958, 158 Tex. 594, 314 S. W.2d 782, 783, 788. Later another Texas court explained:

> "The means by which the discovery is made may be obvious, and the experimentation leading from known factors to presently unknown results may be simple and lying in the public domain. But these facts do not destroy the value of the discovery and will not advantage a competitor who by unfair means obtains the knowledge *without paying the price expended by the discoverer.*" Brown v. Fowler, Tex.Civ.App.1958, 316 S.W.2d 111, 114, writ ref'd n. r. e. (emphasis added).

We think, therefore, that the Texas rule is clear. One may use his competitor's secret process if he discovers the process by reverse engineering applied to the finished product; one may use a competitor's process if he discovers it by his own independent research; but one may not avoid these labors by taking the process from the discoverer without his permission at a time when he is taking reasonable precautions to maintain its secrecy. To obtain knowledge of a process without spending the time and money to discover it independently is *improper* unless the holder voluntarily discloses it or fails to take reasonable precautions to ensure its secrecy.

In the instant case the Christophers deliberately flew over the DuPont plant to get pictures of a process which DuPont had attempted to keep secret. The Christophers delivered their pictures to a third party who was certainly aware of the means by which they had been acquired and who may be planning to use the information contained therein to manufacture methanol by the DuPont process. The third party has a right to use this process only if he obtains this knowledge through his own research efforts, but thus far all information indicates that the third party has gained this knowledge solely by taking it from DuPont at a time when DuPont was making reasonable efforts to preserve its secrecy. In such a situation DuPont has a valid cause of action to prohibit the Christophers from improperly discovering its trade secret and to prohibit the undisclosed third party from using the improperly obtained information.

We note that this view is in perfect accord with the position taken by the authors of the Restatement. In commenting on improper means of discovery the savants of the Restatement said:

> "f. *Improper means of discovery.* The discovery of another's trade secret by improper means subjects the actor to liability independently of the harm to the interest in the secret. Thus, if one uses physical force to take a secret formula from another's pocket, or breaks into another's office to steal the formula, his conduct is wrongful and subjects him to liability apart from the rule stated in this Section. Such conduct is also an improper means of procuring the secret under this rule. But means may be improper under this rule even though they do not cause any

other harm than that to the interest in the trade secret. Examples of such means are fraudulent misrepresentations to induce disclosure, tapping of telephone wires, eavesdropping or other espionage. A complete catalogue of improper means is not possible. In general they are means which fall below the generally accepted standards of commercial morality and reasonable conduct." Restatement of Torts § 757, comment f at 10 (1939).

In taking this position we realize that industrial espionage of the sort here perpetrated has become a popular sport in some segments of our industrial community. However, our devotion to free wheeling industrial competition must not force us into accepting the law of the jungle as the standard of morality expected in our commercial relations. Our tolerance of the espionage game must cease when the protections required to prevent another's spying cost so much that the spirit of inventiveness is dampened. Commercial privacy must be protected from espionage which could not have been reasonably anticipated or prevented. We do not mean to imply, however, that everything not in plain view is within the protected vale, nor that all information obtained through every extra optical extension is forbidden. Indeed, for our industrial competition to remain healthy there must be breathing room for observing a competing industrialist. A competitor can and must shop his competition for pricing and examine his products for quality, components, and methods of manufacture. Perhaps ordinary fences and roofs must be built to shut out incursive eyes, but we need not require the discoverer of a trade secret to guard against the unanticipated, the undetectable, or the unpreventable methods of espionage now available.

In the instant case DuPont was in the midst of constructing a plant. Although after construction the finished plant would have protected much of the process from view, during the period of construction the trade secret was exposed to view from the air. To require DuPont to put a roof over the unfinished plant to guard its secret would impose an enormous expense to prevent nothing more than a school boy's trick. We introduce here no new or radical ethic since our ethos has never given moral sanction to piracy. The market place must not deviate far from our mores. We should not require a person or corporation to take unreasonable precautions to prevent another from doing that which he ought not do in the first place. Reasonable precautions against predatory eyes we may require, but an impenetrable fortress is an unreasonable requirement, and we are not disposed to burden industrial inventors with such a duty in order to protect the fruits of their efforts. "Improper" will always be a word of many nuances, determined by time, place, and circumstances. We therefore need not proclaim a catalogue of commercial improprieties. Clearly, however, one of its commandments does say "thou shall not appropriate a trade secret through deviousness under circumstances in which countervailing defenses are not reasonably available."

Having concluded that aerial photography, from whatever altitude, is an improper method of discovering the trade secrets exposed during construction of the DuPont plant, we need not worry about whether the flight pattern chosen by the Christophers violated any federal aviation regulations. Regardless of whether the flight was legal or illegal in that sense, the espionage was an improper means of discovering DuPont's trade secret.

The decision of the trial court is affirmed and the case remanded to that court for proceedings on the merits.

NOTES

1. On appeal, the district court's decisions in Forest Laboratories, Inc. v. Formulations, Inc. and in a subsequent phase of the litigation, 320 F.Supp. 211, 168 U.S.P.Q. 97 (E.D.Wis.1970), were affirmed in part and reversed in part. Forest Laboratories, Inc. v. Pillsbury Co., 452 F.2d 621, 171 U.S.P.Q. 731 (7th Cir. 1971). The part reversed is considered in note 7.

Although the circuit court agreed with the district court's result —imposing liability on Pillsbury—it disagreed with the lower court's reasoning. Adverting to the "well settled rule" that "a corporation which purchases the assets of another corporation does not, by reason of succeeding to the ownership of property, assume the obligations of the transferor corporation," the court reproved the district court's conclusion that "as Tidy House's successor, Pillsbury was bound by the confidential disclosure to Tidy House." "Moreover," the circuit court reasoned, "the knowledge of Tidy House's employees cannot properly be imputed to Pillsbury just because they went to work for Pillsbury."

The court then turned to Restatement, Torts, § 758, upon which Pillsbury had based its argument below:

Section 758(b) of the Restatement states:

'One who learns another's trade secret from a third person without notice that it is secret and that the third person's disclosure is a breach of his duty to the other, or who learns the secret through a mistake without notice of the secrecy and the mistake,

. . .

'(b) is liable to the other for a disclosure or use of the secret after the receipt of such notice unless prior thereto he has in good faith paid value for the secret or has so changed his position that to subject him to liability would be inequitable.'

"Thus under Sec. 758(b) of the Restatement of Torts, Pillsbury would be liable for its use of the secret after receipt of the notice unless prior thereto it had in good faith paid value for the secret. To satisfy this exception, Pillsbury argues that it purchased the trade secret when it acquired Tidy House's assets, and that Mr. Egan's communications did not occur until well after the acquisition. However, the record does not show that Pillsbury paid anything specifically for the trade secret. For all that appears on the record, Pillsbury's purchase

of Tidy House assets at most involved only the purchase of its packaging facilities as part of the existing marketing structure, which included plaintiff as supplier. Nothing has been brought to our attention which would show that Pillsbury actually gave value for Tidy
House's tempering expertise with a view toward independently exploiting that know-how for its intrinsic value." 452 F.2d 627–27.

2. Sections 757 and 758, dealing with trade secrets, were
dropped from the Restatement of Torts, Second, 1979 along with several other sections on interference with business relations. The first
Restatement had included these topics "despite the fact that the
fields of Unfair Competition and Trade Regulation were rapidly developing into independent bodies of law with diminishing reliance
upon the traditional principles of Tort law. In the more than 40
years since that decision was initially made, the influence of Tort law
has continued to decrease, so that it is now largely of historical interest." For this reason, "the Council formally reached the decision
that these chapters no longer belong in the Restatement of Torts, and
they are omitted from this Second Restatement." Restatement of
Torts, Second, Division 9, Introductory Note, at 1–2.

The decision will probably have little effect on the administration of trade secret law in the courts. *Forest Laboratories* and du-
Pont v. Christopher typify the many decisions that explicitly rely on
the Restatement rules. Because the rules have become so deeply
embedded in judicial decisions, the force of *stare decisis* will doubtless
ensure their long life.

3. Courts divide on whether to require that a trade secret possess some degree of novelty. *Forest Laboratories* takes the Restatement position that novelty is unnecessary: "All that is needed is
some procedure which gives an advantage over a competitor who
does not have it." 299 F.Supp. 202, 208. The contrary view, requiring a degree of novelty, is represented by Sarkes Tarzian, Inc. v. Audio Devices, Inc., 166 F.Supp. 250, 119 U.S.P.Q. 20 (S.D.Cal.1958),
aff'd 283 F.2d 695, 127 U.S.P.Q. 410 (9th Cir.), cert. denied 365 U.S.
869, 81 S.Ct. 903, 5 L.Ed.2d 859, 129 U.S.P.Q. 410: "While they need
not amount to invention, in the patent law sense, they must, at least,
amount to discovery." 166 F.Supp. 250, 265.

The division is in fact only nominal. Novelty is a function of secrecy, and all courts require that the subject information be secret.
Thus, in *Sarkes* jurisdictions the evidence typically adduced to defeat
novelty is widespread knowledge in the trade of the claimed or closely similar information—precisely the evidence used in both *Sarkes*
and *Forest* jurisdictions to disprove the secrecy claim.

4. How heavy must the cloak of secrecy be for subject matter
to qualify as a trade secret? Clearly, absolute secrecy is not required
for if the information were kept completely secret no one other than
its creator would know about it and there would rarely be need for
the law to intervene. Rather, the test is one of reasonableness in the
steps required to assure the information's secrecy. The answer to

the "question whether a plaintiff has taken 'all proper and reasonable steps' depends on the circumstances of each case considering the nature of the information sought to be protected as well *as the conduct of the parties*." USM Corp. v. Marson Fastener Corp., Mass.Adv.Sh. (1979) 2315, 393 N.E.2d 895, 902, 204 U.S.P.Q. 233 (1979) (emphasis the court's).

The Massachusetts Supreme Court ruled in *Marson* that plaintiff's safeguards, though by no means foolproof, were adequate. Plaintiff, "USM required supervisory, technical, and research personnel, including the defendant Lahnston, to sign nondisclosure agreements." While these agreements did not itemize the information that USM considered secret, "such specificity is not required to put employees on notice that their work involves access to trade secrets and confidential information." Nor was it fatal "that the blueprints and parts drawings were not labeled 'confidential' or 'secret' or that USM had not expressly informed its employees that these parts drawings were considered secret by USM." Finally, although USM conducted escorted tours for employees' families and its distributors, the company's plant security precautions "were sufficient to exclude the general public from the production areas of USM's plants, thereby denying access to USM's factory equipment." 393 N.E.2d 895, 901.

The *Marson* court contrasted the facts before it with those it had faced several years earlier in J. T. Healy & Son, Inc. v. James A. Murphy & Son, Inc., 357 Mass. 728, 260 N.E.2d 723, 166 U.S.P.Q. 443 (1970): "Applying this standard, we denied trade secret protection in *Healy* because the plaintiff had made a conscious policy decision to do nothing to safeguard the confidentiality of its manufacturing processes. In *Healy*, the employees were never informed that any of the manufacturing processes were considered secret; employees were not required to sign nondisclosure agreements; the plant was not partitioned into sections; and employees engaged in other work could plainly see the two 'secret processes' in operation. The plaintiff in *Healy*, other than excluding the general public from the manufacturing plant, took no security precautions whatever." 393 N.E.2d 902.

For an overview of the practical security measures that a firm can employ, together with a program of legal protection, see Arnold & McGuire, Law and Practice of Corporate Information Security, 57 J.P.O.S. (pts. 1 & 2) 169, 237 (1975).

5. Persons who neither are in a confidential relationship with the trade secret holder, nor have appropriated the secret improperly, are free to replicate and use the secret subject matter. This freedom extends to "reverse engineering," a technique by which the product of a secret formula or process is analyzed, first to retrace the steps essential to its creation and then to recreate the formula or process itself. See, for example, Kamin v. Kuhnau, 232 Or. 139, 374 P.2d 912 (1962).

This freedom to create or recreate independently means that any number of unrelated firms within a particular industry may eventually come to possess a single trade secret.   Once this possession becomes general, and the information becomes widely known in the industry, the secrecy requisite is no longer met and, under the rule usually followed, even those to whom the secret was imparted in confidence may use the information freely.

6.   Trade secret injunctions are problematic in both their length and breadth.   The conflict between the *Shellmar* and *Conmar* rules, reviewed in *Forest Laboratories*, concerns the appropriate length of the injunctive decree.   The *Shellmar* injunction was perpetual, permanently restraining defendant from using the trade secret, even after secrecy was lost through the issuance of a patent on its subject matter.   For a particularly extended application of the *Shellmar* approach see K & G Oil Tool & Service Co. v. G & G Fishing Tool Service, 158 Tex. 594, 314 S.W.2d 782, cert. denied 358 U.S. 898, 79 S.Ct. 223, 3 L.Ed.2d 149 (1958).

Conmar took as its premise the requirement that a trade secret may be protected only so long as it remains secret.   Under this rule, the injunction will not be permitted to exceed the duration of the trade secret itself and will be dissolved when the protected information enters public knowledge, as through widespread reverse engineering or the issuance of a patent.   Alternatively the injunction's length can be pre-set by judicial estimation of the time that it would take a competitor to reverse engineer the product or process.   See Schulenburg v. Signatrol, Inc., 33 Ill.2d 379, 212 N.E.2d 865, cert. denied 383 U.S. 959, 86 S.Ct. 1225, 16 L.Ed.2d 302 (1965).

The proper breadth of the injunctive decree raises distinct questions.   As an abstract proposition, the appropriator should be enjoined from using or disclosing only information that he obtained improperly.   While this goal is sometimes reached, it is more often found that to frame so discerning a decree is impractical or ineffectual.   In Head Ski Co. v. Kam Ski Co., 158 F.Supp. 919, 116 U.S.P.Q. 242 (D.Md.1958), defendants had been employed by plaintiff to assist it in the development of an improved type of ski.   At about the time that plaintiff's skis began to enjoy commercial success, defendants left plaintiff's employ to start their own ski manufacturing enterprise.   Although "the defendants could not have produced their ski at all, but for the knowledge gleaned from their employment by plaintiff," it was also found that defendants' product incorporated their own "innovation of importance" and "an important independent contribution."   Regardless, the court held that "A broad injunction appears to be necessary to protect plaintiff from unlawful use of its trade secrets by defendants   .   .   .   (whose) entire operation has been built upon plaintiff's techniques, methods, materials and design. In such a case injunction against manufacture of the product is appropriate."   158 F.Supp. 923–24.

Although expedient, *Head Ski* skirted a difficult problem.   It is difficult to determine in any case how much of the secret came from the claimant and how much from the appropriator's own, or independent resources.   Particularly in the employment context, to separate the employee's contributions from the secret itself is usually an impracticable task. The problem is deepened by the fact that an undiscriminating decree can effectively bar the appropriator from competing with the claimant at all. See Note, Injunctions to Protect Trade Secrets—The Goodrich and DuPont Cases, 51 Va.L.Rev. 917 (1965).

In the circumstances, would it be appropriate for a court to award damages or an accounting but withhold injunctive relief on the ground of undue hardship to the appropriator? Courts in patent cases sometimes refuse injunctions on the basis of disproportionate harm to the infringer. See page 628.

Questions of both duration and breadth are carefully examined in Winston Research Corp. v. Minnesota Mining & Mfg. Co., 350 F.2d 134, 146 U.S.P.Q. 422 (9th Cir. 1965). See also, Note, Trade Secrets: How Long Should an Injunction Last?, 26 U.C.L.A.Rev. 203 (1978); Berryhill, Trade Secret Litigation: Injunctions and Other Equitable Remedies, 48 Colo.L.Rev. 189 (1977). Trade secrets and the employment relationship are considered further beginning at p. 162, below.

7. In assessing monetary awards, courts draw selectively on such patent law approaches as accounting for profits, lost profits, reasonable royalty and attorneys' fees. In Forest Laboratories, Inc. v. Pillsbury Co., 452 F.2d 621, 171 U.S.P.Q. 731 (7th Cir. 1971), the court of appeals approved the lower court's award of $75,000 damages assessed on a reasonable royalty basis—"What the parties would have agreed upon, if both were reasonably trying to reach an agreement." 452 F.2d 621, 627. At the same time, the court overturned the district court's award of $15,000 attorneys' fees. "Just as the Ninth Circuit found no general federal rule or policy favoring an award of attorneys' fees to prevailing defendants in trade secret cases, Monolith Portland Midwest Co. v. Kaiser Aluminum & Chem. Corp., 407 F.2d 288, 298, 160 U.S.P.Q. 577, 584 (9th Cir. 1969), we find none favoring an award to prevailing plaintiffs. Wisconsin law is to the same effect. . . . In the absence of any overriding federal policy to the contrary, Wisconsin law should be followed." 452 F.2d 621, 628.

Recovery is frequently measured by the claimant's lost profits or the infringer's unlawfully gained profits. While the claimant is not entitled to a double recovery, he is " 'entitled to the profit he would have made had his secret not been unlawfully used, but not less than the monetary gain which the defendant reaped from his improper acts.' 2 R. Callmann, Unfair Competition, Trademarks and Monopolies § 59.3 at 496 (3d ed. 1968). Once the plaintiffs demonstrate that the defendants have made profits from sales of products incorporating the misappropriated rade secrets, the burden shifts to the defendants to demonstrate the portion of their profits which is not attributable to the trade secrets." Jet Spray Cooler, Inc. v. Crampton, Mass.Adv.Sh. 201, 385 N.E.2d 1349, 1358–1359 n. 14, 203 U.S.P.Q. 363

(1979). *Jet Spray* recognized that defendants had not sustained this burden, but did allow the corporate defendant to deduct from gross profits the bad debts it had incurred on sales of the infringing products and reasonable salaries and consultant fees it had paid to the individual defendants.

Should monetary awards, like injunctive decrees, be measured by the trade secret's probable life? Justice Kaplan, concurring in *Jet Spray*, noted "the feeling that the damages allowed are excessive. They are made so by being cast over a period of eleven years. The court indicates at note 13 that the 'secret' was a simple one, a result of ordinary mechanical skill, and intimates some doubt that it could survive as a protectible entity on October 1, 1975. I suspect that it had perished in that sense sometime before; that is to say, in the ordinary course of events the secret in substance would have become known and available at an earlier date, even if the defendants had not appropriated it and the plaintiffs had tried to keep it to themselves. This, however, was a matter of proof, and the trouble was, and is, that the record is virtually barren of the relevant facts and inferences." 385 N.E.2d 1349, 1364.

Can a trade secret claimant recover the cost of security measures taken to rebuff defendant's forays? Observing that such damages "might well, under different circumstances be proper," the court of appeals in Telex Corp. v. International Business Machines Corp., 510 F.2d 894, 184 U.S.P.Q. 521 (10th Cir. 1975), overturned the trial court's $3,000,000 award to IBM for "increased extraordinary security costs—additional guards, television cameras, sensors, locks, safes, computer-controlled access system and the like." The court of appeals failed to perceive "how the increased security costs were the proximate result of Telex's hiring of IBM employees. Telex was not climbing fences or breaking down doors in its appropriation of IBM trade secrets. Telex's methods were more subtle, involving the luring of IBM employees who brought with them the trade secrets in question." 510 F.2d 894, 933.

8. It is the wise trade secret claimant who does not rush into suit. "In such cases the greatest disadvantage of bringing suit is that plaintiff will have to disclose his trade secrets to defendant in the process of attempting to prove that defendant is using them. Although protective orders would be available to plaintiff to protect his disclosures in the course of litigation, they may not offer the degree of assurance plaintiff would like.

"A court, in entering a protective order, is faced with a seemingly unavoidable dilemma. If the order limits disclosure to the parties' counsel, it may well be impossible for the lawyers properly to prepare their cases, since they lack the technical background in the industry necessary to compare the processes involved. On the other hand, if a party's trade secrets are revealed to his opponent's technical staff, it may be virtually impossible to prevent their later use.

"Disclosures made in the course of litigation will have independent significance only in the event that plaintiff loses on his basic claim. In that event, plaintiff begins with one strike against him if he later tries to hold defendant liable for violation of the protective order. If defendant imposes a normal degree of industrial security, he may be able to use plaintiff's secrets without plaintiff ever becoming aware of it. Even assuming that plaintiff finds out about defendant's subsequent use, he will have difficulty proving that such use is due only to the disclosure under the protective order; a court, moreover, is less likely to foreclose defendant from use of a process because he may have learned it in the course of being unsuccessfully sued than if defendant's use is traceable to the wrongdoing of an ex-employee of plaintiff. In addition, defendant may, in the course of defending himself, discover a number of references in the literature or patents from which plaintiff's process can be put together, and it may be difficult to prove that the later use is necessarily due to plaintiff's disclosure rather than to defendant's search of sources in the public domain." Doyle & Joslyn, The Role of Counsel in Litigation Involving Technologically Complex Trade Secrets, 6 B.C.Ind. & Com.L.Rev. 743, 744 (1965).*

9. Trade secrets are routinely marked for safe handling in administrative practice. Local, state and federal agencies often waive their disclosure requirements or provide that trade secrets submitted to them will be maintained in confidence. The Freedom of Information Act, 5 U.S.C.A. § 552, which generally requires that, on public request, federal agencies disclose information that they have gathered, specifically exempts "trade secrets and commercial or financial information obtained from a person and privileged or confidential." 5 U.S.C.A. § 552(b)(4). An agency's view on the secrecy or confidentiality of submitted information will not always coincide with the submitter's and, given the Freedom of Information Act's mandate for openness, agencies will incline toward disclosing information that is only arguably confidential. A President's Biomedical Research Panel found, for example, that the Act enabled researchers to cull proprietary subject matter from grant applications made to agencies of the Department of Health, Education and Welfare. See Boffey, Grant Applications: Panel Finds New Laws Enable Stealing of Ideas, 193 Science 301 (July 23, 1976).

Having supplied information to a federal agency, how can the submitter control its disclosure by the agency? One approach is to charge that, by disclosing proprietary information, the agency has destroyed its value—effectively a taking of property without just compensation prohibited by the Fifth Amendment to the U.S. Constitution. See Wearly v. FTC, 462 F.Supp. 589 (D.N.J.1978), vacated on other grounds 616 F.2d 662 (3d Cir.). Alternatively, if the submitter was given no opportunity to contest the agency disclosure, it may allege that its right to procedural due process has been violated. See

Zotos International, Inc. v. Kennedy, 460 F.Supp. 268 (D.D.C.1978).
But see Carson Products Co. v. Califano, 594 F.2d 453 (5th Cir.
1979). Or, if the disclosure would violate the Trade Secrets Act, 18
U.S.C.A. § 1905, which makes it a crime for a federal official to disclose confidential information, the submitter can argue that the disclosure should be enjoined under the Administrative Procedure Act, 5
U.S.C.A. § 706(2)(A), because it is agency action that is not "in accordance with law." Chrysler Corp. v. Brown, 441 U.S. 281, 99 S.Ct.
1705, 60 L.Ed.2d 208 (1979).

For an overview of issues in the area, see Note, Protecting Con-
fidential Business Information from Federal Agency Disclosure After
Chrysler Corp. v. Brown, 80 Colum.L.Rev. 109 (1980); Clement, The
Rights of Submitters to Prevent Agency Disclosure of Confidential
Business Information: The Reverse Freedom of Information Act
Lawsuit, 55 Tex.L.Rev. 587 (1977). See also McGarity & Shapiro,
The Trade Secret Status of Health and Safety Testing Information:

Reforming Agency Disclosure Policies, 93 Harv.L.Rev. 837 (1980).

10. The standard treatises on the law of trade secrets in the
United States are R. Milgrim, Trade Secrets (1979) and R. Ellis,
Trade Secrets (1953). A. Turner, The Law of Trade Secrets (1962),
describes United States law in a chapter-by-chapter comparison with
English law. An introduction to relevant continental law considerations appears in Ladas, Legal Protection of Know-How, 54 Trademark Rep. 160 (1964) and Comment, Misappropriation of Trade Secrets, 53 Tul.L.Rev. 215 (1978). For an international perspective, see
A. Wise, Trade Secrets and Know-How Throughout the World
(1974). W. Wade, Industrial Espionage and Misuse of Trade Secrets
(1964), provides general counsel to firms engaged in the development
of trade secrets.

B. LIMITS OF PROTECTION

---

1. PERSONAL INTERESTS: RESTRAINTS ON POSTEMPLOYMENT COMPETITION

WEXLER v. GREENBERG

Supreme Court of Pennsylvania, 1960.
399 Pa. 569, 160 A.2d 430, 125 U.S.P.Q. 471.

COHEN, Justice.

Appellees, trading as Buckingham Wax Company, filed a complaint in equity to enjoin Brite Products Co., Inc., and its officers,
Greenberg, Dickler and Ford, appellants, from disclosing and using
certain formulas and processes pertaining to the manufacture of certain sanitation and maintenance chemicals, allegedly trade secrets.
After holding lengthy hearings, the Chancellor concluded that the
four formulas involved are trade secrets which appellant Greenberg

disclosed in contravention of his duty of nondisclosure arising from his confidential relationship with Buckingham. He decreed that appellants, jointly and severally, be enjoined permanently from disclosing the formulas or processes or any substantially similar formulas and from making or selling the resulting products. He also ordered an accounting for losses. After the dismissal by the court en banc of appellants' exceptions to the Chancellor's findings of fact and conclusions of law, the Chancellor's decree was made final and this appeal followed.

Buckingham Wax Company is engaged in the manufacture, compounding and blending of sanitation and maintenance chemicals. In March, 1949, appellant Greenberg, a qualified chemist in the sanitation and maintenance field entered the employ of Buckingham as its chief chemist and continued there until April 28, 1957. In the performance of his duties, Greenberg consumed half of his working time in Buckingham's laboratory where he would analyze and duplicate competitors' products and then use the resulting information to develop various new formulas. He would change or modify these formulas for color, odor or viscosity in order that greater commercial use could be made of Buckingham's products. The remainder of his time was spent in ordering necessary materials and interviewing chemical salesmen concerning new, better or cheaper ingredients for the multitude of products produced by Buckingham so that costs could be lowered and quality increased. As a result of his activities Greenberg was not only familiar with Buckingham's formulas, he was also fully conversant with the costs of the products and the most efficient method of producing them.

Appellant Brite Products Co., Inc., is a Pennsylvania corporation organized on or about August 1, 1956, when it succeeded to the business, formerly operated by appellant Dickler, known as "Gem Shine Sales Co." From October, 1952, to August, 1956, Dickler and Brite, in unbroken succession, did most of their purchasing from Buckingham; and from August, 1956, until August 20, 1957, the date of Brite's last order, Brite exclusively purchased Buckingham's manufactured products. These products were in turn distributed by Brite to its customers, mostly industrial users, marked with labels which identified said products as products of Brite. Brite's purchases of sanitation and maintenance products from Buckingham amounted annually to approximately $35,000.00.

Dickler, president of Brite, met Greenberg in 1952 as a result of his business transactions with Buckingham, and had contact with Greenberg over the years in connection with the special products which were being made by Buckingham, first for Gem Shine Sales Co. and then for Brite. In June, 1957, Greenberg first approached Dickler in reference to employment; and negotiations began for Greenberg to associate himself with Brite. An agreement between them was reached whereby Greenberg became a director, the treasurer and chief chemist of Brite and, as a further consideration, received 25% of Brite's outstanding and issued capital stock. In August, 1957,

Greenberg left Buckingham and went to work for Brite. At no time during Greenberg's employment with Buckingham did there exist between them a written or oral contract of employment or any restrictive agreement.

Prior to Greenberg's association with Brite, the corporation's business consisted solely of selling a complete line of maintenance and sanitation chemicals, including liquid soap cleaners, wax base cleaners, disinfectants and floor finishes. Upon Greenberg's arrival, however, the corporation purchased equipment and machinery and, under the guidance and supervision of Greenberg, embarked on a full-scale program for the manufacture of a cleaner, floor finish and disinfectant, products previously purchased from Buckingham. The formulas in issue in this litigation are the formulas for each of these respective products. The appellants dispute the Chancellor's findings as to the identity of their formulas with those of Buckingham, but there was evidence that a spectrophometer examination of the respective products of the parties revealed that the formulas used in making these products are substantially identical. Appellants cannot deny that they thought the products sufficiently similar as to continue delivery of their own products to their customers in the same cans and drums and with the same labels attached which they had previously used in distributing the products manufactured by Buckingham, and to continue using the identical promotional advertising material. Appellees' formulas had been developed during the tenure of Greenberg as chief chemist and are unquestionably known to him.

The Chancellor found that Greenberg did not develop the formulas for Brite's products after he left Buckingham, but rather that he had appropriated them by carrying over the knowledge of them which he had acquired in Buckingham's employ. The Chancellor went on to find that the formulas constituted trade secrets and that their appropriation was in violation of the duty that Greenberg owed to Buckingham by virtue of his employment and the trust reposed in him. Accordingly, the relief outlined above was ordered.

We are initially concerned with the fact that the final formulations claimed to be trade secrets were not *disclosed to* Greenberg by the appellees during his service or because of his position. Rather, the fact is that these formulas had been developed by Greenberg himself, while in the pursuit of his duties as Buckingham's chief chemist, or under Greenberg's direct supervision. We are thus faced with the problem of determining the extent to which a former employer, *without the aid of any express covenant*, can restrict his ex-employee, a highly skilled chemist, in the uses to which this employee can put his knowledge of formulas and methods he himself developed during the course of his former employment because this employer claims these same formulas, as against the rest of the world, as his trade secrets. This problem becomes particularly significant when one recognizes that Greenberg's situation is not uncommon. In this era of electronic, chemical, missile and atomic development, many skilled technicians and expert employees are currently in the process of developing potential trade secrets. Competition for personnel of this caliber is exceptionally keen, and the interchange of employment is commonplace. One has but to reach for his daily newspaper to appreciate the current market for such skilled employees. We must therefore be particularly mindful of any effect our decision in this case might have in disrupting this pattern of employee mobility, both in view of possible restraints upon an individual in the pursuit of his livelihood and the harm to the public in general in forestalling, to any extent, widespread technological advances.

The principles outlining this area of the law are clear. A court of equity will protect an employer from the unlicensed disclosure or use of his trade secrets by an ex-employee provided the employee entered into an enforceable covenant so restricting his use or was bound to secrecy by virtue of a confidential relationship existing between the employer and employee, Pittsburgh Cut Wire Co. v. Sufrin, 1944, 350 Pa. 31, 38 A.2d 33. Where, however, an employer has no legally protectable trade secret, an employee's "aptitude, his skill, his dexterity, his manual and mental ability, and such other subjective knowledge as he obtains while in the course of his employment, are not the property of his employer and the right to use and expand these powers remains his property unless curtailed through some restrictive covenant entered into with the employer." Id., 350 Pa. at page 35, 38 A.2d at page 34. The employer thus has the burden of showing two things: (1) a legally protectable trade secret; and (2) a legal basis, either a covenant or a confidential relationship, upon which to predicate relief.

Since we are primarily concerned with the fact that Buckingham is seeking to enjoin Greenberg from using formulas he developed without the aid of an agreement, we shall assume for the purpose of this appeal that the appellees have met their burden of proving that the formulas in issue are trade secrets. The sole issue for us to decide, therefore, is whether or not a confidential relationship existed between Greenberg and Buckingham binding Greenberg to a duty of nondisclosure.

The usual situation involving misappropriation of trade secrets in violation of a confidential relationship is one in which an employer *discloses to his employee* a pre-existing trade secret (one already developed or formulated) so that the employee may duly perform his work. In such a case, the trust and confidence upon which legal relief is predicated stems from the instance of the employer's *turning over to the employee* the pre-existing trade secret. It is then that a pledge of secrecy is impliedly extracted from the employee, a pledge which he carries with him even beyond the ties of his employment relationship. Since it is conceptually impossible, however, to elicit an implied pledge of secrecy from the sole act of an employee turning over to his employer a trade secret which he, the employee, has developed, as occurred in the present case, the appellees must show a different manner in which the present circumstances support the permanent cloak of confidence cast upon Greenberg by the Chancellor. The only avenue open to the appellees is to show that the nature of the employment relationship itself gave rise to a duty of nondisclosure.

The burden the appellees must thus meet brings to the fore a problem of accommodating competing policies in our law: the right of a businessman to be protected against unfair competition stemming from the usurpation of his trade secrets and the right of an individual to the unhampered pursuit of the occupations and livelihoods for which he is best suited. There are cogent socio-economic arguments in favor of either position. Society as a whole greatly benefits from technological improvements. Without some means of post-employment protection to assure that valuable developments or improvements are exclusively those of the employer, the businessman could not afford to subsidize research or improve current methods. In addition, it must be recognized that modern economic growth and development has pushed the business venture beyond the size of the one-man firm, forcing the businessman to a much greater degree to entrust confidential business information relating to technological development to appropriate employees. While recognizing the utility in the dispersion of responsibilities in larger firms, the optimum amount of "entrusting" will not occur unless the risk of loss to the businessman through a breach of trust can be held to a minimum.

On the other hand, any form of post-employment restraint reduces the economic mobility of employees and limits their personal freedom to pursue a preferred course of livelihood. The employee's bargaining position is weakened because he is potentially shackled by the acquisition of alleged trade secrets; and thus, paradoxically, he is restrained, because of his increased expertise, from advancing further in the industry in which he is most productive. Moreover, as previously mentioned, society suffers because competition is diminished by slackening the dissemination of ideas, processes and methods.

Were we to measure the sentiment of the law by the weight of both English and American decisions in order to determine whether it favors protecting a businessman from certain forms of competition or protecting an individual in his unrestricted pursuit of a livelihood, the balance would heavily favor the latter. Indeed, even where the individual has to some extent assumed the risk of future restriction by express covenant, this Court will carefully scrutinize the covenant for reasonableness "in the light of the need of the employer for protection and the hardship of the restriction upon the employes." Morgan's Home Equipment Corp. v. Martucci, 1957, 390 Pa. 618, 631, 136 A.2d 838, 846. It follows that no less stringent an examination of the relationship should be necessary where the employer has *not* seen fit to protect himself by binding agreement.

Coming to the case before us, in support of their position appellees cite mostly decisions involving the disclosure of pre-existing secrets to establish that a binding confidential relationship existed between Greenberg and Buckingham. As we have previously noted, the pre-existence itself gives rise to the implied pledge of confidence; these cases are thus inapposite here. In Extrin Foods, Inc. v. Leighton, 1952, 202 Misc. 592, 115 N.Y.S.2d 429, also cited by appellees, the New York Court found sufficient circumstances to give rise to an implied agreement not to reveal the trade secrets that the defendant developed during his employment. The employee therein, a chemist, was assigned a specific task for which he was given valuable leading information, including pre-existing trade secrets, careful supervision and license to enter into research and experimentation so as to attain the theretofore unobtainable goal which Extrin had been seeking. A similar situation may be found in Wireless Specialty Apparatus Co. v. Mica Condenser Co., Ltd., 1921, 239 Mass. 158, 131 N.E. 307, 16 A.L. R. 1170, where defendant engineers were enjoined from disclosing trade secrets they had developed while employed by the Wireless company. There, the company, in order to remain in business after the close of the war, had assigned its six engineers, including the defendants, to the specific research project of developing a method of manufacturing magneto condensers (the trade secret in issue) and had committed them to six months of extensive research and experimentation solely towards this end under the general supervision of its chief engineer.

As decisions of sister jurisdictions, these two cases, of course, are not binding upon this Court. Nevertheless, they are good examples of the kind of employment relationships in which a Court will find that a confidential relationship exists. Upon our examination of the record here, however, we find that the instant circumstances fall far short of such a relationship. The Chancellor's finding that Greenberg, while in the employ of Buckingham, never engaged in research nor conducted any experiments nor created or invented any formula was undisputed. There is nothing in the record to indicate that the formulas in issue were specific projects of great concern and concentration by Buckingham; instead it appears they were merely the result of Greenberg's routine work of changing and modifying formulas derived from competitors. Since there was no experimentation or research, the developments by change and modification were fruits of Greenberg's own skill as a chemist without any appreciable assistance by way of information or great expense or supervision by Buckingham, outside of the normal expenses of his job. Nor can we find anything that would indicate to Greenberg that these particular results were the goal which Buckingham expected him to find for its exclusive use. The Chancellor's finding that Greenberg knew at all times that it would be prejudicial and harmful to Buckingham for the formulas to be disclosed merely shows that Greenberg knew the value of his finds and the harmful effects that competition by similar products could bring. His knowledge, by itself, however, cannot support a finding that he was never to compete.

Accordingly, we hold that appellant Greenberg has violated no trust or confidential relationship in disclosing or using formulas which he developed or were developed subject to his supervision. Rather, we hold that this information forms part of the technical knowledge and skill he has acquired by virtue of his employment with Buckingham and which he has an unqualified privilege to use.

Having found Greenberg was privileged to disclose and use the formulas in issue, the case against the other appellants must also fall. With regard to appellants Brite, Dickler and Ford, the formulas here may be said to be trade secrets. Ownership of a trade secret, however, does not give the owner a monopoly in its use, but merely a proprietary right which equity protects against usurpation by unfair means. Former customers are legally entitled to compete with their suppliers, even if they use identical goods, as long as they do so properly. From the legal standpoint these appellants have done nothing improper. Greenberg approached Dickler here with a proposition; Dickler did not entice him away. Even so, what appellants wanted and needed was a qualified chemist in the maintenance and sanitation field; and who was better than the chemist of their supplier if they could properly get him. They sought not Buckingham's trade secrets, but Greenberg's expertise. Since we have found that Greenberg divulged only information which he had a privilege to divulge, no legal wrong has been committed. To hold that Greenberg had a privilege to divulge this information but that the other appellants committed a wrong in receiving it would be to render the privilege illusory.

Decree reversed, at appellees' costs.

REED, ROBERTS ASSOCIATES, INC. v. STRAUMAN

Court of Appeals of New York, 1976.
40 N.Y.2d 303, 386 N.Y.S.2d 677, 353 N.E.2d 590.

WACHTLER, Judge.

These cross appeals involve the efficacy of an employment contract provision barring an employee from either directly or indirectly competing with, or soliciting clients of, his former employer. This restrictive covenant is not a proper subject for specific enforcement since the services of the employee were not unique or extraordinary and the employer failed to establish a studied copying of a customer list.

Reed, Roberts Associates, Inc., with over 6,000 customers being served through some 21 offices scattered throughout the nation and with gross sales of almost $4 million, is one of the top three companies in its field. The lion's share of its business involves supplying advice and guidance to employers with respect to their obligations under State unemployment laws. The object of this service is to minimize the tax liability and administrative expenses involved in complying with these laws. Other services performed by Reed, Roberts include consultation regarding workmen's compensation, disability benefits and pension plans. This action was commenced by Reed,

Roberts to prevent a former employee from competing against them and soliciting their customers.

When John Strauman was hired by Reed, Roberts in November, 1962 he signed a restrictive covenant which read in pertinent part: "I do therefore consent that at no time shall I either directly or indirectly solicit any of your clients, and I do further agree that for a period of three years from the date of termination of my employment that I will not either directly or indirectly be engaged in, nor in any manner whatsoever become interested directly or indirectly, either as employee, owner, partner, agent, stockholder, director or officer of a corporation or otherwise, in any business of the type and character engaged in by your company within the geographical limits of the City of New York and the counties of Nassau, Suffolk and Westchester."

Strauman's first position as an employee of Reed, Roberts was technical man-auditor. Since he had four years' experience in the field by virtue of having previously worked for a major competitor, Strauman became a valuable employee and over the next 10 years received three important promotions rising to senior vice-president in charge of operations. Throughout his tenure with Reed, Roberts, Strauman was instrumental in devising most of the forms utilized by the company in rendering its service and in setting up its computer system. On becoming vice-president he was given increased responsibility with regard to internal affairs including the formulation of company policy. Importantly, however, he was not responsible for sales or obtaining new customers. The record indicates that while the business forms used by Reed, Roberts were unique to that service industry, they were not much different from those used by other companies.

After 11 years with Reed, Roberts, Strauman decided to strike off on his own and formed a company called Curator Associates, Inc. This company was in direct competition with his former employer and was even located in the same municipality. Although Reed, Roberts alleges that Curator has been soliciting its customers, Curator sustained losses of some $38,000 with gross sales of only $1,100 during its first year of operations. Nevertheless, fearful of competition from the former employee, Reed, Roberts commenced this action seeking to enforce the posttermination covenant not to compete signed by Strauman in 1962. Specifically Reed, Roberts seeks to enjoin Strauman and Curator from engaging in the business of unemployment tax control within the metropolitan area for a period of three years and to enjoin them from soliciting any of Reed, Roberts' customers permanently.

The trial court granted this relief in part. The court refused to prohibit defendants from engaging in a competitive enterprise finding that there were no trade secrets involved here and that although Strauman was a key employee his services were not so unique or extraordinary as to warrant restraining his attempt to compete with his former employer. Nevertheless the court believed that it would be unjust and unfair for Strauman to utilize his knowledge of Reed, Roberts' internal operations to solicit its clients and permanently enjoined defendants from doing so. The Appellate Division affirmed, without opinion. We believe the order of the Appellate Division should be modified to the extent of reversing so much thereof as grants a permanent injunction against the defendants.

Generally negative covenants restricting competition are enforceable only to the extent that they satisfy the overriding requirement of reasonableness. Yet the formulation of reasonableness may vary with the context and type of restriction imposed. For example, where a business is sold, anticompetition covenants will be enforceable, if reasonable in time, scope and extent. These covenants are designed to protect the goodwill integral to the business from usurpation by the former owner while at the same time allowing an owner to profit from the goodwill which he may have spent years creating. However, where an anticompetition covenant given by an employee to his employer is involved a stricter standard of reasonableness will be applied.

In this context a restrictive covenant will only be subject to specific enforcement to the extent that it is reasonable in time and area, necessary to protect the employer's legitimate interests, not harmful to the general public and not unreasonably burdensome to the employee. Undoubtedly judicial disfavor of these covenants is provoked by "powerful considerations of public policy which militate against sanctioning the loss of a man's livelihood" (Purchasing Assoc. v. Weitz, supra, 13 N.Y.2d p. 272, 246 N.Y.S.2d p. 604, 196 N.E.2d p. 247). Indeed, our economy is premised on the competition engendered by the uninhibited flow of services, talent and ideas. Therefore, no restrictions should fetter an employee's right to apply to his own best advantage the skills and knowledge acquired by the overall experience of his previous employment. This includes those techniques which are but "skillful variations of general processes known to the particular trade" (Restatement, Agency 2d, § 396, Comment b).

Of course, the courts must also recognize the legitimate interest an employer has in safeguarding that which has made his business successful and to protect himself against deliberate surreptitious commercial piracy. Thus restrictive covenants will be enforceable to the extent necessary to prevent the disclosure or use of trade secrets or confidential customer information. In addition injunctive relief may be available where an employee's services are unique or extraordinary and the covenant is reasonable. This latter principle has been interpreted to reach agreements between members of the learned professions.

With these principles in mind we consider first the issue of solicitation of customers in the case at bar. The courts below found, and Reed, Roberts does not dispute, that there were no trade secrets involved here. The thrust of Reed, Roberts' argument is that by virtue of Strauman's position in charge of internal administration he was privy to sensitive and confidential customer information which he should not be permitted to convert to his own use. The law enunciated in Leo Silfen, Inc. v. Cream, 29 N.Y.2d 387, 328 N.Y.S.2d 423, 278 N.E.2d 636 is dispositive. There, as here, the plaintiff failed to sustain its allegation that the defendant had pirated the actual customer list. Rather Silfen argued that in light of the funds expended to compile the list it would be unfair to allow the defendant to solicit the clients of his former employer. We held that where the employee engaged in no wrongful conduct and the names and addresses of potential customers were readily discoverable through public sources, an injunction would not lie. Similarly here there was no finding that Strauman acted wrongfully by either pilfering or memorizing the customer list. More important, by Reed, Roberts' own admission every company with employees is a prospective customer and the solicitation of customers was usually done through the use of nationally known publications such as Dun and Bradstreet's *Million Dollar Directory* where even the name of the person to contact regarding these services is readily available. It strains credulity to characterize this type of information as confidential. Consequently, the trial court's determination that Strauman and Curator should be permanently enjoined from soliciting Reed, Roberts' customers as of the date of his termination was erroneous.

Apparently, the employer is more concerned about Strauman's knowledge of the intricacies of their business operation. However, absent any wrongdoing, we cannot agree that Strauman should be prohibited from utilizing his knowledge and talents in this area. A contrary holding would make those in charge of operations or specialists in certain aspects of an enterprise virtual hostages of their employers. Where the knowledge does not qualify for protection as a trade secret and there has been no conspiracy or breach of trust resulting in commercial piracy we see no reason to inhibit the employee's ability to realize his potential both professionally and financially by availing himself of opportunity. Therefore, despite Strauman's excellence or value to Reed, Roberts the trial court's finding that his services were not extraordinary or unique is controlling and properly resulted in a denial of the injunction against operating a competing business.

Accordingly, the order of the Appellate Division should be modified in accordance with this opinion.

BREITEL, C. J., and JASEN, GABRIELLI, JONES, FUCHS-BERG and COOKE, JJ., concur.

Order modified, with costs to defendants, in accordance with the opinion herein and, as so modified, affirmed.

NOTES

1. In their attempts to restrain departing employees from using or disclosing information developed in the course of their employment, employers commonly take either or both of two precautions: (a) obtaining, at the outset of employment, the employee's covenant not to engage in postemployment competition, and (b) seeking to enjoin the employee's disclosure or use of trade secrets earlier imparted to him by the employer. While the covenant not to compete might appear to be a broader, far more effective precaution than trade secret protection, the two measures in fact have very similar effects.

(a) *Covenants Not to Compete.* Courts construe covenants not to compete narrowly. Presumptively invalid, these covenants are generally enforced only upon proof that they are reasonably necessary to the employer's business security. The covenant must reasonably delimit the breadth of its subject matter and the period and geographic area in which the former employee cannot compete. "Reasonable" breadth is roughly measured by the range of the employer's trade secrets along with some interstitial, otherwise unprotectable, technical information. In determining whether a covenant's duration is reasonable, courts generally employ the same measure that they use in determining how long a trade secret injunction may run: the time that it would take a competitor to arrive independently at the former employer's protected methods. See Allis Chalmers Mfg. Co. v. Continental Aviation & Engineering Corp., 225 F.Supp. 645, 655, 151 U.S.P.Q. 25 (E.D.Mich.1966).

(b) *Trade Secrets.* The effects of a trade secret injunction will characteristically exceed the bounds of the injunctive decree. Trade secrets commonly have value only in the industry in which the former employer is engaged so that an injunction against their use is in effect an injunction against their use in competition. See, for example, Head Ski Co. v. Kam Ski Co., 158 F.Supp. 919, 116 U.S.P.Q. 242 (D.Md.1958), discussed at page 158. Since the departing employee carries a potential trade secret lawsuit with him, he may encounter difficulty getting a job with a competitor of his former employer—unless, of course, the competitor was responsible for luring him away in the first place.

In many respects, then, the scope of an enforceable covenant not to compete roughly approximates the scope of protection that trade secret law would offer in the same circumstances. There are, however, two important differences. For purposes of sustaining the covenant not to compete, the employer need only show that the employee is in a position to use its trade secrets. To receive a trade secret injunction the employer must prove that the employee is in fact using the trade secrets. Second, in the trade secret action the employer bears the heavy burden of demonstrating that the particular information being used by the employee constitutes a trade secret and is not just part of the employee's general knowledge and skills.

2.   Absent an express contract between employer and employee allocating rights to inventions made by the employee in the course of his employment, all rights to the inventions belong to the employee. This general rule has two important exceptions. First, if the employee was specifically hired to engage in research and development an agreement will be implied that rights to his inventions belong to the employer. Solomons v. United States, 137 U.S. 342, 11 S.Ct. 88, 34 L.Ed. 667 (1890) ("If one is employed to devise or perfect an instrument, or a means for accomplishing a prescribed result, he cannot, after successfully accomplishing the work for which he was employed, plead title thereto as against his employer. That which he has been employed and paid to accomplish becomes, when accomplished, the property of his employer." 137 U.S. 342, 346, 11 S.Ct. 88, 89).

Second, if the employee was not hired specifically for research and development but made the invention during working hours, or with the use of his employer's equipment or materials, the employer obtains a "shop right," essentially an irrevocable, nonexclusive license to practice the invention. See, for example, Kinkade v. New York Shipbuilding Corp., 21 N.J. 362, 122 A.2d 360 (1956); United States v. Dubilier Condenser Corp., 289 U.S. 178, 188–89, 53 S.Ct. 554, 557–558, 77 L.Ed. 1114 (1933) ("Since the servant uses his master's time, facilities and materials to attain a concrete result, the latter is in equity entitled to use that which embodies his own property and to duplicate it as often as he may find occasion to employ similar appliances in his business. But the employer in such a case has no equity to demand a conveyance of the invention, which is the original conception of the employee alone, in which the employer had no part.").

Judged against this background, is the decision in Wexler v. Greenberg correct? For a contrary result on similar facts, see Basic Chemicals, Inc. v. Benson, 251 N.W.2d 220, 195 U.S.P.Q. 197 (Iowa 1977). Would *Wexler* be more acceptable if the court had ruled that the formulas Greenberg devised while working for Buckingham did not qualify for protection as trade secrets? Does it follow from *Wexler* that, in a subsequent action, Greenberg would be entitled to an injunction against Buckingham's continued use of the formulas that Greenberg had developed while in its employ?

3.   Courts are less willing to protect customer lists and connected marketing information than they are to protect technological trade secrets. The original reason for this reluctance was probably the nontechnical nature of the information. Courts rationalize their reluctance today in more principled terms—lack of secrecy or confidentiality, or insufficient investment in development of the customer list. In Burroughs Corp. v. Cimakasky, 346 F.Supp. 1398, 175 U.S.P. Q. 699 (E.D.Pa.1972), the court acknowledged that customer lists were protectable as trade secrets under Pennsylvania law, but concluded that they would not be protected when the "names and addresses of customers are easily ascertainable by observation or refer-

ence to directories." Holding for defendant, a former employee, the court noted that "in the cases in which a former employee has been enjoined from soliciting former customers the information retained has included specific information concerning the customers' needs which has been collected over the course of business by company agents solely for the use of the company." 346 F.Supp. 1398, 1400.

Restatement of Agency, Second, § 396 (1958) takes another approach. After termination of an agency relationship, the agent has no duty not to compete with the principal, but does have a duty "not to use or to disclose to third persons, on his own account or on account of others, in competition with the principal or to his injury, trade secrets, written lists of names, or other similar confidential matters given to him only for the principal's use or acquired by the agent in violation of duty. The agent is entitled to use general information concerning the method of business of the principal and the names of the customers retained in his memory, if not acquired in violation of his duty as agent." What reasons are there for the "memory rule," prohibiting the former employee from taking copies of customer lists with him, but allowing him to use any customer information that he can remember? What is the status of information that the employee has deliberately committed to memory?

4. Why is there so little litigation over the use of trade secrets by departing employees? Against the vast number of defections that occur each year, the number of reported cases is very small, and there is no indication that this number would be significantly increased by the addition of settled cases. Compare, for example, the decision for a former employer in B. F. Goodrich Co. v. Wohlgemuth, 117 Ohio App. 493, 192 N.E.2d 99, 137 U.S.P.Q. (1963), with its follow-up coverage, Brooks, Annals of Business, The New Yorker, p. 37 (Jan. 11, 1964), suggesting that, litigation notwithstanding, the highly skilled employee in fact enjoys considerable freedom in competitive employ.

One reason, doubtless, is the difficulty of proving that the employer's information qualifies as trade secrets, that the trade secrets are his, and that the departing employee is in fact using them. Even if the former employer had extracted a covenant against postemployment competition from all of its technical employees, it may be reluctant to take its chances that a court reviewing the covenant will hold it invalid. Litigation also unavoidably exposes other information that the former employer may wish to keep secret, including information about the trade secrets that *it* may have pirated from its competitors.

For background on law and practices in the area, see S. Lieberstein, Who Owns What is in Your Head? (1979).

5. Rules governing trade secrets and related postemployment restraints originated in commercial settings different in important respects from those that prevail today. The modern action for employee appropriation of trade secrets has been traced to Roman law's

actio servi corrupti. Under the general action for corruption of a slave, the slave owner was awarded double damages against a third person who maliciously enticed his slave to commit a wrong. Applied at the instance of a master against a business competitor, the *actio* compensated for the loss of business secrets divulged by the slave to the competitor at the latter's instigation. Damages included the diminution in the value of the slave and all other provable direct and indirect harm. See Schiller, Trade Secrets and the Roman Law: The Actio Servi Corrupti, 30 Colum.L.Rev. 837 (1930).

The fifteenth- and sixteenth-century cases, often cited as marking the common law's early distaste for postemployment restraints as departures from principles of economic freedom, should be viewed against the background of the craft guilds that were economically predominant at the time. Because the cases involved restraints imposed by masters upon apprentices to prolong their period of noncompetitive, and often wageless service, it has been argued that the decisions striking down the restraints should be narrowly interpreted as endorsements of the guild customs which established a limited indenture period. "If the early cases represent, in fact, the courts' attempt to assist the guilds and legislative bodies in shoring up the crumbling values of the medieval economic system, they cannot fairly be described as indicative of an attitude of economic liberalism." Blake, Employee Agreements Not To Compete, 73 Harv.L.Rev. 625, 632 (1960).

2. ECONOMIC INTERESTS: THE PLACE OF TRADE SECRETS IN THE COMPETITIVE PLAN

TABOR v. HOFFMAN

Court of Appeals of New York, Second Division, 1889.
118 N.Y. 30, 23 N.E. 12.

Appeal from a judgment of the general term of the supreme court in the fifth judicial department, affirming a judgment in favor of the plaintiff entered upon the decision of a special term.

The object of this action was to restrain the defendant from using certain patterns alleged to have been surreptitiously copied from patterns belonging to the plaintiff that had not been made public. The trial court found that the plaintiff, having invented a pump known as "Tabor's Rotary Pump," made a complete set of patterns to manufacture the same; that he necessarily spent much time, labor, and money in making and perfecting such patterns, which were always in his exclusive possession; that from time to time he made improvements upon the pump, and incorporated the same in the patterns, which were never thrown on the market nor given to the public; that one Francis Walz surreptitiously made for the defendant a duplicate set of said patterns from measurements taken from the patterns of the plaintiff, without his knowledge or consent, while they were in possession of said Walz to be repaired; that before the commencement of this action the defendant, with knowledge of all these facts and without the consent of the plaintiff, had commenced to make, and since then has made, pumps from said patterns, thus obtained; that plaintiff has established a large and profitable trade in said pumps, which "will be injured, and the plaintiff damaged, if the defendant is permitted" to continue to manufacture from said patterns. The trial court further found, upon the request of the defendant, "that a competent pattern-maker can make a set of patterns from measurements taken from the pump itself, without the aid of plaintiff's patterns," but refused to find, upon the like request, that this could be done "with little more expense and trouble than from measurements taken from plaintiff's said patterns." It appeared from the evidence that the finished pump "does not comply with the patterns," because it is made of brass and iron, which expand unequally in the finished casting, and also contract unequally when cooling during the process of casting; that some of the patterns are subdivided into sections, which greatly facilitates measurements and drawings, as each section can be laid flat upon the wood or paper; and that it would take longer to make a set of patterns from the pump than it would to copy the perfected patterns themselves. The special term, by its final decree, restrained the defendant "from manufacturing any more pumps from the set of patterns made by Francis Walz from measurements taken from the plaintiff's patterns, .   .   . and from selling, disposing of, or using in any manner said patterns."

VANN, J., (after stating the facts as above.)   It is conceded by the appellant that, independent of copyright or letters patent, an inventor or author has, by the common law, an exclusive property in his invention or composition, until by publication it becomes the property of the general public.   This concession seems to be well founded, and to be sustained by authority.   As the plaintiff had placed the perfected pump upon the market, without obtaining the protection of the patent laws, he thereby published that invention to the world, and no longer had any exclusive property therein.   But the completed pump was not his only invention, for he had also discovered means, or machines in the form of patterns, which greatly aided, if they were not indispensable, in the manufacture of the pumps.   This discovery he had not intentionally published, but had kept it secret, unless, by disclosing the invention of the pump, he had also disclosed the invention of the patterns by which the pump was made.   The precise question, therefore, presented by this appeal, as it appears to us, is whether there is a secret in the patterns that yet remains a secret, although the pump has been given to the world.   The pump consists of many different pieces, the most of which are made by running melted brass or iron in a mould.   The mould is formed by the use of patterns, which exceed in number the separate parts of the pump, as some of them are divided into several sections.   The different pieces out of which the pump is made are not of the same size as the corresponding patterns, owing to the shrinkage of the metal in cooling.   In constructing patterns it is necessary to make allowances, not only for the shrinkage, which is greater in brass than in iron, but also for the expansion of the completed casting under different conditions of heat and cold, so that the different parts of the pump will properly fit together and adapt themselves, by nicely balanced expansion and contraction, to pumping either hot or cold liquids. If the patterns were of the same size as the corresponding portions of the pump, the castings made therefrom would neither fit together, nor, if fitted, work properly when pumping fluids varying in temperature. The size of the patterns cannot be discovered by merely using the different sections of the pump, but various changes must be made, and those changes can only be ascertained by a series of experiments, involving the expenditure of both time and money. Are not the size and shape of the patterns, therefore, a secret which the plaintiff has not published, and in which he still has an exclusive property? Can it be truthfully said that this secret can be learned from the pump, when experiments must be added to what can be learned from the pump before a pattern of the proper size can be made? As more could be learned by measuring the patterns than could be learned by measuring the component parts of the pump, was there not a secret that belonged to the discoverer, until he abandoned it by publication, or it was fairly discovered by another? If a valuable medicine, not protected by patent, is put upon the market, any one may, if he can by chemical analysis and a series of experiments, or by any other use of the medicine itself, aided by his own resources only, discover the ingredients and their proportions. If he thus finds out the secret of the proprietor, he may use it to any extent that he desires without danger of interference by the courts. But, because this discovery may be possible by fair means, it would not justify a discovery by unfair means, such as the bribery of a clerk who, in the course of his employment, had aided in compounding the medicine, and had thus become familiar with the formula. The courts have frequently restrained persons who have learned a secret formula for compounding medicines, beverages, and the like, while in the employment of the proprietor, from using it themselves, or imparting it to others to his injury; thus, in effect, holding, as was said by the learned general term, "that the sale of the compounded article to the world was not a publication of the formula or device used in its manufacture." Hammer v. Barnes [26 How.Pr. 174].

The fact that one secret can be discovered more easily than another does not affect the principle. Even if resort to the patterns of the plaintiff was more of a convenience than a necessity, still, if there was a secret, it belonged to him, and the defendant had no right to obtain it by unfair means, or to use it after it was thus obtained. We think that the patterns were a secret device that was not disclosed by the publication of the pump, and that the plaintiff was entitled to the preventive remedies of the court. While the defendant could lawfully copy the pump, because it had been published to the world, he could not lawfully copy the patterns, because they had not been published, but were still, in every sense, the property of the plaintiff, who owned not only the material substance, but also the discovery which they embodied. The judgment should be affirmed, with costs. All concur, except Follett, C. J., dissenting, and Bradley and Haight, JJ., not sitting.

FOLLETT, C. J., (dissenting.) An inventor of a new and useful improvement has a right to its exclusive enjoyment, which right he may protect by a patent or by concealment. The plaintiff's patent had expired, and all of the parts of the pump represented by the patterns had been for a long time on sale in the form of a completed pump. The patent on the original invention having expired, and the plaintiff having voluntarily made the subsequent improvements public by selling the improved article, he lost his right to their exclusive use. The plaintiff's counsel concedes this, but says that while patterns could be made from the several parts of the pump, from which pumps like those made and sold by the plaintiff could be produced, it was more difficult to make patterns from sections of the pump than from the patterns. This was so found by the court, and cannot be gainsaid. The invention was not the patterns, but the idea represented by them, to which the plaintiff had lost his exclusive right. Neither the defendant nor the man who made the patterns sustained any relation by contract with the plaintiff. They were neither the servants nor partners of the plaintiff, and they owed him no duty not owed by the whole world. The act, at most, was a trespass, and the plaintiff made no case for equitable relief. It is neither asserted nor found that the defendant is unable to respond in damages. The cases cited to sustain the judgment arose out of the relation of master and servant, or between partners, and in all of them the idea had not been disclosed to the public, but had been kept secret by the inventor. The judgment should be reversed, and a new trial granted, with costs to abide the event.

KEWANEE OIL CO. v. BICRON CORP.

Supreme Court of the United States, 1974.
416 U.S. 470, 94 S.Ct. 1879, 40 L.Ed.2d 315, 181 U.S.P.Q. 673.

Mr. Chief Justice BURGER delivered the opinion of the Court.

We granted certiorari to resolve a question on which there is a conflict in the courts of appeals: whether state trade secret protection is pre-empted by operation of the federal patent law. In the instant case the Court of Appeals for the Sixth Circuit held that there was preemption. The Courts of Appeals for the Second, Fourth, Fifth, and Ninth Circuits have reached the opposite conclusion.

I

Harshaw Chemical Co., an unincorporated division of petitioner, is a leading manufacturer of a type of synthetic crystal which is useful in the detection of ionizing radiation. In 1949 Harshaw commenced research into the growth of this type crystal and was able to

produce one less than two inches in diameter. By 1966, as the result
of expenditures in excess of $1 million, Harshaw was able to grow a
17-inch crystal, something no one else had done previously. Harshaw
had developed many processes, procedures, and manufacturing techniques in the purification of raw materials and the growth and encap-
sulation of the crystals which enabled it to accomplish this feat.
Some of these processes Harshaw considers to be trade secrets.

The individual repondents are former employees of Harshaw who
formed or later joined respondent Bicron. While at Harshaw the individual respondents executed, as a condition of employment, at least
one agreement each, requiring them not to disclose confidential information or trade secrets obtained as employees of Harshaw. Bicron
was formed in August 1969 to compete with Harshaw in the production of the crystals and by April 1970, had grown a 17-inch crystal.

Petitioner brought this diversity action in United States District
Court for the Northern District of Ohio seeking injunctive relief and
damages for the misappropriation of trade secrets. The District
Court, applying Ohio trade secret law, granted a permanent injunction against the disclosure or use by respondents of 20 of the 40
claimed trade secrets until such time as the trade secrets had been released to the public, had otherwise generally become available to the
public, or had been obtained by respondents from sources having the
legal right to convey the information.

The Court of Appeals for the Sixth Circuit held that the findings
of fact by the District Court were not clearly erroneous, and that it
was evident from the record that the individual respondents appropriated to the benefit of Bicron secret information on processes obtained
while they were employees at Harshaw. Further, the Court of Appeals held that the District Court properly applied Ohio law relating
to trade secrets. Nevertheless, the Court of Appeals reversed the
District Court, finding Ohio's trade secret law to be in conflict with
the patent laws of the United States. The Court of Appeals reasoned
that Ohio could not grant monopoly protection to processes and manufacturing techniques that were appropriate subjects for consideration under 35 U.S.C.A. § 101 for a federal patent but which had been
in commercial use for over one year and so were no longer eligible for
patent protection under 35 U.S.C.A. § 102(b).

We hold that Ohio's law of trade secrets is not preempted by the
patent laws of the United States, and, accordingly, we reverse.

II

Ohio has adopted the widely relied-upon definition of a trade secret found at Restatement of Torts § 757, comment *b* (1939). According to the Restatement,

> "[a] trade secret may consist of any formula, pattern, device or
> compilation of information which is used in one's business, and
> which gives him an opportunity to obtain an advantage over

competitors who do not know or use it. It may be a formula for a chemical compound, a process of manufacturing, treating or preserving materials, a pattern for a machine or other device, or a list of customers."

The subject of a trade secret must be secret, and must not be of public knowledge or of a general knowledge in the trade or business. This necessary element of secrecy is not lost, however, if the holder of the trade secret reveals the trade secret to another "in confidence, and under an implied obligation not to use or disclose it." Cincinnati Bell Foundry Co. v. Dodds, 10 Ohio Dec. Reprint 154, 156, 19 Weekly L.Bull. 84 (Super.Ct.1887). These others may include those of the holder's "employees to whom it is necessary to confide it, in order to apply it to the uses for which it is intended." National Tube Co. v. Eastern Tube Co., [3 Ohio C.C.R. (n.s.) 459, (1902)] 462. Often the recipient of confidential knowledge of the subject of a trade secret is a licensee of its holder.

The protection accorded the trade secret holder is against the disclosure or unauthorized use of the trade secret by those to whom the secret has been confided under the express or implied restriction of nondisclosure or nonuse. The law also protects the holder of a trade secret against disclosure or use when the knowledge is gained, not by the owner's volition, but by some "improper means," Restatement of Torts § 757(a), which may include theft, wiretapping, or even aerial reconnaissance. A trade secret law, however, does not offer protection against discovery by fair and honest means, such as by independent invention, accidental disclosure, or by so-called reverse engineering, that is by starting with the known product and working backward to divine the process which aided in its development or manufacture.

Novelty, in the patent law sense, is not required for a trade secret. "Quite clearly discovery is something less than invention." A. O. Smith Corp. v. Petroleum Iron Works Co., 73 F.2d 531, 538 (C.A.6 1934); modified to increase scope of injunction, 74 F.2d 934 (1935). However, some novelty will be required if merely because that which does not possess novelty is usually known; secrecy, in the context of trade secrets, thus implies at least minimal novelty.

The subject matter of a patent is limited to a "process, machine, manufacture, or composition of matter, or . . . improvement thereof," 35 U.S.C.A. § 101, which fulfills the three conditions of novelty and utility as articulated and defined in 35 U.S.C.A. §§ 101 and 102, and nonobviousness, as set out in 35 U.S.C.A. § 103. If an invention meets the rigorous statutory tests for the issuance of a patent, the patent is granted, for a period of 17 years, giving what has been described as the "right of exclusion," R. Ellis, Patent Assignments and Licenses § 4, p. 7 (2d ed. 1943). This protection goes not only to copying the subject matter, which is forbidden under the Copyright Act, but also to independent creation.

III

The first issue we deal with is whether the States are forbidden to act at all in the area of protection of the kinds of intellectual property which may make up the subject matter of trade secrets.

Article I, § 8, cl. 8, of the Constitution grants to the Congress the power

"[t]o promote the Progress of Science and useful Arts, by securing for limited Times to Authors and Inventors the exclusive Right to their respective Writings and Discoveries. . . ."

In the 1972 Term, in Goldstein v. California, 412 U.S. 546, 93 S.Ct. 2303, 37 L.Ed.2d 163 (1973), we held that the cl. 8 grant of power to Congress was not exclusive and that, at least in the case of writings, the States were not prohibited from encouraging and protecting the efforts of those within their borders by appropriate legislation. The States could, therefore, protect against the unauthorized rerecording for sale of performances fixed on records or tapes, even though those performances qualified as "writings" in the constitutional sense and Congress was empowered to legislate regarding such performances and could pre-empt the area if it chose to do so. This determination was premised on the great diversity of interests in our Nation—the essentially nonuniform character of the appreciation of intellectual achievements in the various States. Evidence for this came from patents granted by the States in the 18th century.

Just as the States may exercise regulatory power over writings so may the States regulate with respect to discoveries. States may hold diverse viewpoints in protecting intellectual property relating to invention as they do in protecting the intellectual property relating to the subject matter of copyright. The only limitation on the States is that in regulating the area of patents and copyrights they do not conflict with the operation of the laws in this area passed by Congress, and it is to that more difficult question we now turn.

IV

The question of whether the trade secret law of Ohio is void under the Supremacy Clause involves a consideration of whether that law "stands as an obstacle to the accomplishment and execution of the full purposes and objectives of Congress." Hines v. Davidowitz, 312 U.S. 52, 67, 61 S.Ct. 399, 404, 85 L.Ed. 581 (1941). We stated in Sears, Roebuck & Co. v. Stiffel Co., 376 U.S. 225, 229, 84 S.Ct. 784, 11 L.Ed.2d 661 (1964), that when state law touches upon the area of federal statutes enacted pursuant to constitutional authority, "it is 'familiar doctrine' that the federal policy 'may not be set at naught, or its benefits denied' by the state law. Sola Elec. Co. v. Jefferson Elec. Co., 317 U.S. 173, 176, 63 S.Ct. 172, 173, 87 L.Ed. 165 (1942). This is true, of course, even if the state law is enacted in the exercise of otherwise undoubted state power."

The laws which the Court of Appeals in this case held to be in conflict with the Ohio law of trade secrets were the patent laws passed by the Congress in the unchallenged exercise of its clear power under Art. I, § 8, cl. 8, of the Constitution. The patent law does not explicitly endorse or forbid the operation of trade secret law. However, as we have noted, if the scheme of protection developed by Ohio respecting trade secrets "clashes with the objectives of the federal patent laws," Sears, Roebuck & Co. v. Stiffel Co., supra, 376 U.S., at 231, 84 S.Ct., at 789 then the state law must fall. To determine whether the Ohio law "clashes" with the federal law it is helpful to examine the objectives of both the patent and trade secret laws.

The stated objective of the Constitution in granting the power to Congress to legislate in the area of intellectual property is to "promote the Progress of Science and useful Arts." The patent laws promote this progress by offering a right of exclusion for a limited period as an incentive to inventors to risk the often enormous costs in terms of time, research, and development. The productive effort thereby fostered will have a positive effect on society through the introduction of new products and processes of manufacture into the economy, and the emanations by way of increased employment and better lives for our citizens. In return for the right of exclusion— this "reward for inventions," Universal Oil Co. v. Globe Co., 322 U.S. 471, 484, 64 S.Ct. 1110, 1116, 88 L.Ed. 1399 (1944)—the patent laws impose upon the inventor a requirement of disclosure. To insure adequate and full disclosure so that upon the expiration of the 17-year period "the knowledge of the invention enures to the people, who are thus enabled without restriction to practice it and profit by its use," United States v. Dubilier Condenser Corp., 289 U.S. 178, 187, 53 S.Ct. 554, 77 L.Ed. 1114 (1933), the patent laws require that the patent application shall include a full and clear description of the invention and "of the manner and process of making and using it" so that any person skilled in the art may make and use the invention. 35 U.S.C.A. § 112. When a patent is granted and the information contained in it is circulated to the general public and those especially skilled in the trade, such additions to the general store of knowledge are of such importance to the public weal that the Federal Government is willing to pay the high price of 17 years of exclusive use for its disclosure, which disclosure, it is assumed, will stimulate ideas and the eventual development of further significant advances in the art. The Court has also articulated another policy of the patent law: that which is in the public domain cannot be removed therefrom by action of the States.

> "[F]ederal law requires that all ideas in general circulation be dedicated to the common good unless they are protected by a valid patent." Lear, Inc. v. Adkins, 395 U.S., at 668, 89 S.Ct., at 1910.

The maintenance of standards of commercial ethics and the encouragement of invention are the broadly stated policies behind trade secret law. "The necessity of good faith and honest, fair dealing, is the very life and spirit of the commercial world." National Tube Co. v. Eastern Tube Co., 3 Ohio Cir.Ct.R. (n.s.), at 462. In A. O. Smith Corp. v. Petroleum Iron Works Co., 73 F.2d, at 539, the Court emphasized that even though a discovery may not be patentable, that does not

> "destroy the value of the discovery to one who makes it, or advantage the competitor who by unfair means, or as the beneficiary of a broken faith, obtains the desired knowledge without himself paying the price in labor, money, or machines expended by the discoverer."

In Wexler v. Greenberg, 399 Pa. 569, 578–579, 160 A.2d 430, 434–435 (1960), the Pennsylvania Supreme Court noted the importance of trade secret protection to the subsidization of research and development and to increased economic efficiency within large companies through the dispersion of responsibilities for creative developments.

Having now in mind the objectives of both the patent and trade secret law, we turn to an examination of the interaction of these systems of protection of intellectual property—one established by the Congress and the other by a State—to determine whether and under what circumstances the latter might constitute "too great an encroachment on the federal patent system to be tolerated." Sears, Roebuck & Co. v. Stiffel Co., 376 U.S., at 232, 84 S.Ct., at 789.

As we noted earlier, trade secret law protects items which would not be proper subjects for consideration for patent protection under 35 U.S.C.A. § 101. As in the case of the recordings in Goldstein v. California, Congress, with respect to nonpatentable subject matter, "has drawn no balance; rather, it has left the area unattended, and no reason exists why the State should not be free to act." Goldstein v. California, supra, 412 U.S., at 570, 93 S.Ct., at 2316 (footnote omitted).

Since no patent is available for a discovery, however useful, novel, and nonobvious, unless it falls within one of the express categories of patentable subject matter of 35 U.S.C.A. § 101, the holder of such a discovery would have no reason to apply for a patent whether trade secret protection existed or not. Abolition of trade secret protection would, therefore, not result in increased disclosure to the public of discoveries in the area of nonpatentable subject matter. Also, it is hard to see how the public would be benefited by disclosure of customer lists or advertising campaigns; in fact, keeping such items secret encourages businesses to initiate new and individualized plans of operation, and constructive competition results. This, in turn, leads to a greater variety of business methods than would otherwise be the case if privately developed marketing and other data were passed illicitly among firms involved in the same enterprise.

Congress has spoken in the area of those discoveries which fall within one of the categories of patentable subject matter of 35 U.S. C.A. § 101 and which are, therefore, of a nature that would be subject to consideration for a patent. Processes, machines, manufactures, compositions of matter, and improvements thereof, which meet the tests of utility, novelty, and nonobviousness are entitled to be patented, but those which do not, are not. The question remains whether those items which are proper subjects for consideration for a patent may also have available the alternative protection accorded by trade secret law.

Certainly the patent policy of encouraging invention is not disturbed by the existence of another form of incentive to invention. In this respect the two systems are not and never would be in conflict. Similarly, the policy that matter once in the public domain must remain in the public domain is not incompatible with the existence of trade secret protection. By definition a trade secret has not been placed in the public domain.

The more difficult objective of the patent law to reconcile with trade secret law is that of disclosure, the *quid pro quo* of the right to exclude. We are helped in this stage of the analysis by Judge Henry Friendly's opinion in Painton & Co. v. Bourns, Inc., 442 F.2d 216 (C. A.2 1971). There the Court of Appeals thought it useful, in determining whether inventors will refrain because of the existence of trade secret law from applying for patents, thereby depriving the public from learning of the invention, to distinguish between three categories of trade secrets:

> "(1) the trade secret believed by its owner to constitute a validly patentable invention; (2) the trade secret known to its owner not to be so patentable; and (3) the trade secret whose valid patentability is considered dubious." Id., at 224.

Trade secret protection in each of these categories would run against breaches of confidence—the employee and licensee situations—and theft and other forms of industrial espionage.

As to the trade secret known not to meet the standards of patentability, very little in the way of disclosure would be accomplished by abolishing trade secret protection. With trade secrets of nonpatentable subject matter, the patent alternative would not reasonably be available to the inventor. "There can be no public interest in stimulating developers of such [unpatentable] know-how to flood an overburdened Patent Office with applications [for] what they do not consider patentable." Ibid. The mere filing of applications doomed to be turned down by the Patent Office will bring forth no new public knowledge or enlightenment, since under federal statute and regulation patent applications and abandoned patent applications are held by the Patent Office in confidence and are not open to public inspection. 35 U.S.C.A. § 122; 37 C.F.R. § 1.14(b).

Even as the extension of trade secret protection to patentable subject matter that the owner knows will not meet the standards of patentability will not conflict with the patent policy of disclosure, it will have a decidedly beneficial effect on society. Trade secret law will encourage invention in areas where patent law does not reach, and will prompt the independent innovator to proceed with the discovery and exploitation of his invention. Competition is fostered and the public is not deprived of the use of valuable, if not quite patentable, invention.

Even if trade secret protection against the faithless employee were abolished, inventive and exploitive effort in the area of patentable subject matter that did not meet the standards of patentability would continue, although at a reduced level. Alternatively with the effort that remained, however, would come an increase in the amount of self-help that innovative companies would employ. Knowledge would be widely dispersed among the employees of those still active in research. Security precautions necessarily would be increased, and salaries and fringe benefits of those few officers or employees who had to know the whole of the secret invention would be fixed in an amount thought sufficient to assure their loyalty. Smaller companies would be placed at a distinct economic disadvantage, since the costs of this kind of self-help could be great, and the cost to the public of the use of this invention would be increased. The innovative entrepreneur with limited resources would tend to confine his research efforts to himself and those few he felt he could trust without the ultimate assurance of legal protection against breaches of confidence. As a result, organized scientific and technological research could become fragmented, and society, as a whole, would suffer.

Another problem that would arise if state trade secret protection were precluded is in the area of licensing others to exploit secret processes. The holder of a trade secret would not likely share his secret with a manufacturer who cannot be placed under binding legal obligation to pay a license fee or to protect the secret. The result would be to hoard rather than disseminate knowledge. Instead, then, of licensing others to use his invention and making the most efficient use of existing manufacturing and marketing structures within the industry, the trade secret holder would tend either to limit his utilization of the invention, thereby depriving the public of the maximum benefit of its use, or engage in the time-consuming and economically wasteful enterprise of constructing duplicative manufacturing and marketing mechanisms for the exploitation of the invention. The detrimental misallocation of resources and economic waste that would thus take place if trade secret protection were abolished with respect to employees or licensees cannot be justified by reference to any policy that the federal patent law seeks to advance.

Nothing in the patent law requires that States refrain from action to prevent industrial espionage. In addition to the increased costs for protection from burglary, wiretapping, bribery, and the other means used to misappropriate trade secrets, there is the inevitable cost to the basic decency of society when one firm steals from another. A most fundamental human right, that of privacy, is threatened when industrial espionage is condoned or is made profitable; the state interest in denying profit to such illegal ventures is unchallengeable.

The next category of patentable subject matter to deal with is the invention whose holder has a legitimate doubt as to its patentability. The risk of eventual patent invalidity by the courts and the costs associated with that risk may well impel some with a good-faith doubt as to patentability not to take the trouble to seek to obtain and defend patent protection for their discoveries, regardless of the existence of trade secret protection. Trade secret protection would assist those inventors in the more efficient exploitation of their discoveries and not conflict with the patent law. In most cases of genuine doubt as to patent validity the potential rewards of patent protection are so far superior to those accruing to holders of trade secrets, that the holders of such inventions will seek patent protection, ignoring the trade secret route. For those inventors "on the lin " as to whether to seek patent protection, the abolition of trade secret protection might encourage some to apply for a patent who otherwise would not have done so. For some of those so encouraged, no patent will be granted and the result

> "will have been an unnecessary postponement in the divulging of the trade secret to persons willing to pay for it. If [the patent does issue], it may well be invalid, yet many will prefer to pay a modest royalty than to contest it, even though *Lear* allows them to accept a license and pursue the contest without paying royalties while the fight goes on. The result in such a case would be unjustified royalty payments from many who would prefer not to pay them rather than agreed fees from one or a few who are entirely willing to do so." Painton & Co. v. Bourns, Inc., 442 F.2d, at 225.

The point is that those who might be encouraged to file for patents by the absence of trade secret law will include inventors possessing the chaff as well as the wheat. Some of the chaff—the nonpatentable discoveries—will be thrown out by the Patent Office, but in the meantime society will have been deprived of use of those discoveries through trade secret-protected licensing. Some of the chaff may not be thrown out. This Court has noted the difference between the standards used by the Patent Office and the courts to determine patentability. In Lear, Inc. v. Adkins, 395 U.S. 653, 89 S.Ct. 1902, 23 L.Ed.2d 610 (1969), the Court thought that an invalid patent was so serious a threat to the free use of ideas already in the public domain that the Court permitted licensees of the patent holder to challenge the validity of the patent. Better had the invalid patent never been issued. More of those patents would likely issue if trade secret law were abolished. Eliminating trade secret law for the doubtfully patentable invention is thus likely to have deleterious effects on society and patent policy which we cannot say are balanced out by the speculative gain which might result from the encouragement of some inventors with doubtfully patentable inventions which deserve patent protection to come forward and apply for patents. There is no conflict, then, between trade secret law and the patent law policy of disclosure, at least insofar as the first two categories of patentable subject matter are concerned.

The final category of patentable subject matter to deal with is the clearly patentable invention, i. e., that invention which the owner believes to meet the standards of patentability. It is here that the federal interest in disclosure is at its peak; these inventions, novel, useful and nonobvious, are " 'the things which are worth to the public the embarrassment of an exclusive patent.' " Graham v. John Deere Co., supra, at 9, 86 S.Ct., at 689 (quoting Thomas Jefferson). The interest of the public is that the bargain of 17 years of exclusive use in return for disclosure be accepted. If a State, through a system of protection, were to cause a substantial risk that holders of patentable inventions would not seek patents, but rather would rely on the state protection, we would be compelled to hold that such a system could not constitutionally continue to exist. In the case of trade secret law no reasonable risk of deterrence from patent application by those who can reasonably expect to be granted patents exists.

Trade secret law provides far weaker protection in many respects than the patent law. While trade secret law does not forbid the discovery of the trade secret by fair and honest means, e. g., independent creation or reverse engineering, patent law operates "against the world," forbidding any use of the invention for whatever purpose for a significant length of time. The holder of a trade secret also takes a substantial risk that the secret will be passed on to his competitors, by theft or by breach of a confidential relationship, in a manner not easily susceptible of discovery or proof. Where patent law acts as a barrier, trade secret law functions relatively as a sieve. The possibility that an inventor who believes his invention meets the standards of patentability will sit back, rely on trade secret law, and after one year of use forfeit any right to patent protection, 35 U.S. C.A. § 102(b), is remote indeed.

Nor does society face much risk that scientific or technological progress will be impeded by the rare inventor with a patentable invention who chooses trade secret protection over patent protection. The ripeness-of-time concept of invention, developed from the study of the many independent multiple discoveries in history, predicts that if a particular individual had not made a particular discovery others would have, and in probably a relatively short period of time. If something is to be discovered at all very likely it will be discovered by more than one person. Even were an inventor to keep his discovery completely to himself, something that neither the patent nor trade secret laws forbid, there is a high probability that it will be soon independently developed. If the invention, though still a trade secret, is put into public use, the competition is alerted to the existence of the inventor's solution to the problem and may be encouraged to make an extra effort to independently find the solution thus known to be possible. The inventor faces pressures not only from private industry, but from the skilled scientists who work in our universities and our other great publicly supported centers of learning and research.

We conclude that the extension of trade secret protection to clearly patentable inventions does not conflict with the patent policy of disclosure. Perhaps because trade secret law does not produce any positive effects in the area of clearly patentable inventions, as opposed to the beneficial effects resulting from trade secret protection in the areas of the doubtfully patentable and the clearly unpatentable inventions, it has been suggested that partial pre-emption may be appropriate, and that courts should refuse to apply trade secret protection to inventions which the holder should have patented, and which would have been, thereby, disclosed. However, since there is no real possibility that trade secret law will conflict with the federal policy favoring disclosure of clearly patentable inventions partial pre-emption is inappropriate. Partial pre-emption, furthermore, could well create serious problems for state courts in the administration of trade secret law. As a preliminary matter in trade secret actions, state courts would be obliged to distinguish between what a reasonable inventor would and would not correctly consider to be clearly patentable, with the holder of the trade secret arguing that the invention was not patentable and the misappropriator of the trade secret arguing its undoubted novelty, utility, and nonobviousness. Federal courts have a difficult enough time trying to determine whether an invention, narrowed by the patent application procedure and fixed in the specifications which describe the invention for which the patent has been granted, is patentable. Although state courts in some circumstances must join federal courts in judging whether an issued patent is valid, Lear, Inc. v. Adkins, supra, it would be undesirable to impose the almost impossible burden on state courts to determine the patentability —in fact and in the mind of a reasonable inventor—of a discovery which has not been patented and remains entirely uncircumscribed by expert analysis in the administrative process. Neither complete nor partial pre-emption of state trade secret law is justified.

Our conclusion that patent law does not pre-empt trade secret law is in accord with prior cases of this Court. Trade secret law and patent law have co-existed in this country for over one hundred years. Each has its particular role to play, and the operation of one does not take away from the need for the other. Trade secret law encourages the development and exploitation of those items of lesser or different invention than might be accorded protection under the patent laws, but which items still have an important part to play in the technological and scientific advancement of the Nation. Trade secret law promotes the sharing of knowledge, and the efficient operation of industry; it permits the individual inventor to reap the rewards of his labor by contracting with a company large enough to develop and exploit it. Congress, by its silence over these many years, has seen the wisdom of allowing the States to enforce trade secret protection. Until Congress takes affirmative action to the contrary, States should be free to grant protection to trade secrets.

Since we hold that Ohio trade secret law is not pre-empted by the federal patent law, the judgment of the Court of Appeals for the Sixth Circuit is reversed, and the case is remanded to the Court of Appeals with directions to reinstate the judgment of the District Court.

It is so ordered.

Mr. Justice POWELL took no part in the decision of this case.

Mr. Justice MARSHALL, concurring in the result.

Unlike the Court, I do not believe that the possibility that an inventor with a patentable invention will rely on state trade secret law rather than apply for a patent is "remote indeed." Ante, at 490. State trade secret law provides substantial protection to the inventor who intends to use or sell the invention himself rather than license it to others, protection which in its unlimited duration is clearly superior to the 17-year monopoly afforded by the patent laws. I have no doubt that the existence of trade secret protection provides in some instances a substantial disincentive to entrance into the patent system, and thus deprives society of the benefits of public disclosure of the invention which it is the policy of the patent laws to encourage. This case may well be such an instance.

But my view of sound policy in this area does not dispose of this case. Rather, the question presented in this case is whether Congress, in enacting the patent laws, intended merely to offer inventors a limited monopoly in exchange for disclosure of their invention, or instead to exert pressure on inventors to enter into this exchange by withdrawing any alternative possibility of legal protection for their inventions. I am persuaded that the former is the case. State trade secret laws and the federal patent laws have co-existed for many, many years. During this time, Congress has repeatedly demonstrated its full awareness of the existence of the trade secret system, without any indication of disapproval. Indeed, Congress has in a number of instances given explicit federal protection to trade secret information provided to federal agencies. See, e. g., 5 U.S.C.A. § 552(b)(4); 18 U.S.C.A. § 1905; see generally Appendix to Brief for Petitioner. Because of this, I conclude that there is "neither such actual conflict between the two schemes of regulation that both cannot stand in the same area, nor evidence of a congressional design to pre-empt the field." Florida Lime Avocado Growers v. Paul, 373 U.S. 132, 141, 83 S.Ct. 1210, 1217, 10 L.Ed.2d 248 (1963). I therefore concur in the result reached by the majority of the Court.

Mr. Justice DOUGLAS, with whom Mr. Justice BRENNAN concurs, dissenting.

Today's decision is at war with the philosophy of Sears, Roebuck & Co. v. Stiffel Co., 376 U.S. 225, 84 S.Ct. 784, 11 L.Ed.2d 661, and Compco Corp. v. Day-Brite Lighting, Inc., 376 U.S. 234, 84 S.Ct. 779, 11 L.Ed.2d 669. Those cases involved patents—one of a pole lamp and one of fluorescent lighting fixtures each of which was declared invalid. The lower courts held, however, that though the patents were invalid the sale of identical or confusingly similar products to the products of the patentees violated state unfair competition laws. We held that when an article is unprotected by a patent, state law may not forbid others to copy it, because every article not covered by a valid patent is in the public domain. Congress in the patent laws decided that where no patent existed, free competition should prevail; that where a patent is rightfully issued, the right to exclude others should obtain for no longer than 17 years, and that the States may not "under some other law, such as that forbidding unfair competition, give protection of a kind that clashes with the objectives of the federal patent laws," 376 U.S., at 231, 84 S.Ct., at 789.

The product involved in this suit, sodium iodide synthetic crystals, was a product that could be patented but was not. Harshaw the inventor apparently contributed greatly to the technology in that field by developing processes, procedures, and techniques that produced much larger crystals than any competitor. These processes, procedures, and techniques were also patentable; but no patent was sought. Rather Harshaw sought to protect its trade secrets by contracts with its employees. And the District Court found that, as a result of those secrecy precautions, "not sufficient disclosure occurred so as to place the claimed trade secrets in the public domain"; and those findings were sustained by the Court of Appeals.

The District Court issued a permanent injunction against respondents, ex-employees, restraining them from using the processes used by Harshaw. By a patent which would require full disclosure Harshaw could have obtained a 17-year monopoly against the world. By the District Court's injunction, which the Court approves and reinstates, Harshaw gets a permanent injunction running into perpetuity against respondents. In *Sears*, as in the present case, an injunction against the unfair competitor issued. We said: "To allow a State by use of its law of unfair competition to prevent the copying of an article which represents too slight an advance to be patented would be to permit the State to block off from the public something which federal law has said belongs to the public. The result would be that while federal law grants only 14 or 17 years' protection to genuine inventions, see 35 U.S.C.A. §§ 154, 173, States could allow perpetual protection to articles too lacking in novelty to merit any patent at all under federal constitutional standards. This would be too great an encroachment on the federal patent system to be tolerated." 376 U.S., at 231–232, 84 S.Ct., at 789.

The conflict with the patent laws is obvious. The decision of Congress to adopt a patent system was based on the idea that there will be much more innovation if discoveries are disclosed and patented than there will be when everyone works in secret. Society thus fosters a free exchange of technological information at the cost of a limited 17-year monopoly.

A trade secret, unlike a patent, has no property dimension. That was the view of the Court of Appeals, 478 F.2d 1074, 1081; and its

decision is supported by what Mr. Justice Holmes said in Du Pont de
Nemours Powder Co. v. Masland, 244 U.S. 100, 102, 37 S.Ct. 575, 576,
61 L.Ed. 1016:

> "The word property as applied to trade-marks and trade secrets
> is an unanalyzed expression of certain secondary consequences
> of the primary fact that the law makes some rudimentary re-
> quirements of good faith.   Whether the plaintiffs have any valu-
> able secret or not the defendant knows the facts, whatever they
> are, through a special confidence that he accepted.   The property
> may be denied but the confidence cannot be.   Therefore the
> starting point for the present matter is not property or due proc-
> ess of law, but that the defendant stood in confidential relations
> with the plaintiffs, or one of them.   These have given place to
> hostility, and the first thing to be made sure of is that the de-
> fendant shall not fraudulently abuse the trust reposed in him.   It
> is the usual incident of confidential relations.   If there is any
> disadvantage in the fact that he knew the plaintiffs' secrets he
> must take the burden with the good."

A suit to redress theft of a trade secret is grounded in tort damages for breach of a contract—a historic remedy.   Damages for
breach of a confidential relation are not pre-empted by this patent
law, but an injunction against use is pre-empted because the patent
law states the only monopoly over trade secrets that is enforceable
by specific performance;   and that monopoly exacts as a price full disclosure.   A trade secret can be protected only by being kept secret.
Damages for breach of a contract are one thing;   an injunction barring disclosure does service for the protection accorded valid patents
and is therefore pre-empted.

From the findings of fact of the lower courts, the process involved in this litigation was unique, such a great discovery as to
make its patentability a virtual certainty.   Yet the Court's opinion
reflects a vigorous activist antipatent philosophy.   My objection is
not because it is activist.   This is a problem that involves no neutral
principle.   The Constitution in Art. I, § 8, cl. 8, expresses the activist
policy which Congress has enforced by statutes.   It is that constitutional policy which we should enforce, not our individual notions of
the public good.

I would affirm the judgment below.

NOTES

1.   How extensively did *Kewanee* undermine *Sears* and *Compco*,
pages 130, 133 above?   Did *Kewanee* validate only trade secret rules
that rest on contract or confidence grounds?   Would the *Kewanee*
Court approve state law   decisions, like DuPont v. Christopher, page
150, that rest trade secret protection on a property rationale?   Or do
Sears and *Compco* continue to control cases of that sort?

This and other lines of inquiry are developed in Goldstein, Kewanee Oil Co. v. Bicron Corp.: Notes on a Closing Circle, 1974 Sup.Ct.

Rev. 81. For a different view, see Stern, A Reexamination of State Trade Secret Law after Kewanee, 42 Geo.Wash.L.Rev. 927 (1974). See also Wydick, Trade Secrets: Federal Preemption in Light of Goldstein and Kewanee, (pts. 1 & 2) 55 J.P.O.S. 736, 56 J.P.O.S. 4 (1973, 1974). Developments in the interim between *Sears* and *Kewanee* are surveyed in Adelman & Jaress, Inventions and the Law of Trade Secrets after Lear v. Adkins, 16 Wayne L.Rev. 77 (1969), and Milgrim, Sears to Lear to Painton: Of Whales and Other Matters, 46 N.Y.U.L.Rev. 17 (1971).

2. Compare Justice Douglas' dissenting observations in *Kewanee* that "the process involved in this litigation was unique, such a great discovery as to make its patentability a virtual certainty," and that "the Court's opinion reflects a vigorous activist anti-patent philosophy," with his position in cases in which patentability *was* an issue. See, for example, Note 2, at page 448.

3. *Kewanee* responded to a longstanding concern that trade secret protection takes business away from the patent system, diminishing the amount of technical information that the system would otherwise expose to public view. A survey aimed at comparing the extent to which firms depend on trade secret protection and on patent protection produced only inconclusive results. "In general the replies to the Institute's questionnaire suggest that smaller companies are increasing their reliance on trade secrets while medium and larger ones report no similar trend." Harris & Siegel, Protection of Trade Secrets: Initial Report, 8 Idea 360, 368 (1964).

4. A trade secret holder has some freedom to choose which aspects of his discovery to lodge in a patent and which to withhold as a trade secret. He cannot, however, withhold facts that are necessary to the public's understanding of the patented subject matter. Van Products Co. v. General Welding & Fabricating Co., 419 Pa. 248, 213 A.2d 769, 147 U.S.P.Q. 221 (1965), indicates the extent to which a patentee can maintain the veil of secrecy. Plaintiff there had received a patent on an air drier apparatus and had retained as a trade secret the formula for the chemical desiccant that was crucial to its operation. "Of course, the idea and the practical functioning of such a deliquescent desiccant could not be a secret, in itself, since the product was advertised, described, and sold on the open market. Its remarkable characteristics, vaunted in sales literature, were the exact factor which made the Van drier desirable (i. e., it was a desiccant which did not require regeneration). Therefore, it was only the composition which was secret, and remained so. . . ." 419 Pa. 248, 268–69, 213 A.2d 769, 780.

Does Tabor v. Hoffman follow or violate the general rule?

5. In Warner-Lambert Pharmaceutical Co., Inc. v. John J. Reynolds, Inc., 178 F.Supp. 655, 123 U.S.P.Q. 431 (S.D.N.Y.1959), aff'd 280 F.2d 197, 126 U.S.P.Q. 3 (2d Cir. 1960), plaintiff unsuccessfully sought a declaratory judgment relieving it of royalty obligations for the manufacture of Listerine, the formula of which had been sold to

plaintiff's predecessor by defendant's predecessor in 1881. The unpatented formula had since this time become public knowledge. Plaintiff argued that, for this reason, it should pay no tithe for what others were using free. Finding in the 1881, and subsequent, contracts no express or implied limitation on the royalty obligation, the court ruled that plaintiff must abide by the royalty schedule so long as it used the formula.

What flaws, if any, can you find in the court's reasoning on the policy ground: "In the patent and copyright cases the parties are dealing with a fixed statutory term and the monopoly granted by that term. This monopoly, created by Congress, is designed to preserve exclusivity in the grantee during the statutory term and to release the patented or copyrighted material to the general public for general use thereafter. This is the public policy of the statutes in reference to which such contracts are made and it is against this background that the parties to patent and copyright license agreements contract. Here, however, there is no such public policy. The parties are free to contract with respect to a secret formula or trade secret in any manner which they determine for their own best interests. A secret formula or trade secret may remain secret indefinitely. It may be discovered by someone else almost immediately after the agreement is entered into. Whoever discovers it for himself by legitimate means is entitled to its use. But that does not mean that one who acquires a secret formula or a trade secret through a valid and binding contract is then enabled to escape from an obligation to which he bound himself simply because the secret is discovered by a third party or by the general public." 178 F.Supp. 665.

Can *Warner-Lambert* be reconciled with cases that, like *Reed, Roberts*, page 168, trim down or void excessive covenants against post-employment competition? With cases that, like *Conmar*, page 158, confine injunctions to the time it would take to reverse engineer the trade secret in suit? What are *Kewanee's* implications for the continued vitality of *Warner-Lambert*? Note that the injunction approved in *Kewanee* was to last only "until such time as the trade secrets had been released to the public, had otherwise generally become available to the public or had been obtained by [defendants] from sources having the legal right to convey the information." Does *Aronson,* p. 64, above, offer a complete vindication of *Warner-Lambert*?

Recall that *Kewanee* and *Conmar* involved trade secret appropriations, while *Aronson* and *Warner-Lambert* involved negotiated licenses. Licensees can, between themselves, estimate the life and value of a secret and then settle on any mutually agreeable schedule for repaying its value—a continuing royalty, for example, or a lump sum representing the secret's continuing worth discounted to present value. Little reason exists for a court to intervene and rewrite the payment schedule. Where, however, a trade secret has been appropriated, and no voluntary bargain struck, courts do their best to approximate what the parties would have estimated as the secret's value. The natural starting point is for a court to estimate the secret's probable life, the same starting point as is used in fashioning trade secret injunctions.

Altman, A Quick Point Regarding Perpetual Trade Secret Royalty Liability, 13 J.Mar.L.Rev. 127 (1979), offers some penetrating insights into these and connected issues.

6.   The inventor who has doubts about the patentability of his invention faces a hard choice.   To rely on trade secret law means that protection will be limited by the realities of reverse engineering, faithless employees and the difficulties of enforcement.   To pursue a patent, however, entails not only the possibility of added expense without reward but, even if a patent issues, the risk that it may later be invalidated, by which point the secret information will have become public.   The Patent Act partially reduces the difficulty of this choice by requiring the Patent and Trademark Office to hold all patent applications in confidence so that trade secret protection is maintained even after the application is filed.   Rejection of the application will not destroy the inventor's interest.   35 U.S.C.A. § 122.

The Court of Customs and Patent Appeals has applied its rules of practice to maintain the secrecy on appeal of a patent application rejected by the Patent and Trademark Office.   In Application of Sarkar, 575 F.2d 870, 197 U.S.P.Q. 788 (C.C.P.A.1978), the court, recognizing the public's interest in access to court records and proceedings, nonetheless ordered that the record be sealed, and that the proceedings be conducted *in camera*.   "We are guided in our determination by the opinion of the Supreme Court in *Kewanee* . . . that, wherever possible, trade secret law and patent law should be administered in such manner that the former will not deter an inventor from seeking the benefit of the latter, because the public is *most* benefited by the early disclosure of the invention in consideration of the patent grant."   575 F.2d 870, 872 (emphasis in original).   See Note, Preservation of Trade Secret Protection During a Patent Application Appeal, 15 Wake Forest L.Rev. 559 (1979).

Although section 122 has secured applications against requests made under the Freedom of Information Act, it has not proved to be a complete guard against public prying.   See Irons & Sears v. Dann, 606 F.2d 1215, 202 U.S.P.Q. 798 (D.C.Cir. 1979), cert. denied 444 U.S. 1075, 100 S.Ct. 1021, 62 L.Ed.2d 757, 204 U.S.P.Q. 1060.

IV. COMMON LAW COPYRIGHT

See Statute Supplement 17 U.S.C.A. §§ 101, 102, 106, 301, 302.

The 1976 Copyright Act, which came into effect January 1, 1978, substantially preempts state common law copyright protection in favor of a single federal scheme. State law has not, however, been completely preempted. The 1976 Act protects only works fixed in a "tangible medium of expression," leaving protection of unfixed works to common law copyright. Also, significant pockets of state law may have survived for the protection even of fixed works. The Act's imprecision has forced one staunch advocate of preemption to acknowledge that "What we have hailed as a new unified system of copyright still turns out to have significant dual aspects, their extent depending on what is made of section 301. That vaunted assertion of federal preemption on examination begins to look like a paper tiger." Brown, Unification: A Cheerful Requiem for Common Law Copyright, 24 U.C.L.A.L.Rev. 1070, 1106 (1977).

From the first federal copyright act, passed in 1790, until the effective date of the present Act, copyright protection in the United States was divided between state and federal governments. State common law protection attached to a work from the moment of the work's creation. State law required no formalities such as copyright notice, registration or deposit; protection, which in theory could last forever, ended only on the work's publication. Upon publication, with copyright notice inscribed on all copies in the required form and place, the work came under the protection of the federal Copyright Act for a fixed term of twenty-eight years from the date of publication, renewable once.

"Publication" played a central role in the coordination of the state and federal copyright systems. Publication not only marked the end of a work's protection under state law and the beginning of protection under federal law. It also opened the abyss of public domain, for if a work was published without the statutorily required copyright notice on all authorized copies, federal protection would be forfeited and all rights to the work lost forever.

Friction between the state and federal systems grew over the years as the publication measure became increasingly artificial. An adequate mechanism for the eighteenth century, when works were typically distributed in printed copies, "publication" had to be twisted into new and different shapes to resolve the issues raised by emerging forms of dissemination. Did a work's broadcast over radio or television constitute publication, divesting common law copyright? Did the sale and distribution of phonograph records publish the recorded musical compositions? The answers given were intellectually unsatisfactory. Worse, they were unpredictable.

Courts tended to be lax in drawing the publication line so that rights would not be forfeited. As the line was increasingly stretched to satisfy the new proprietary interests, some courts and commentators expressed concern that, as a vehicle for perpetual protection, common law copyright was being applied in a way that seriously affronted the constitutional injunction of protection for "limited times." This growing dissatisfaction made common law copyright a natural target for statutory preemption in the discussions that surrounded the efforts to revise the 1909 Copyright Act.

The path to preemption was cleared by the revisors' proposal to alter the duration of copyright from a renewable term that ran for twenty-eight years from the date of publication, to a term measured by the life of the author plus fifty years. Since publication was no longer needed to begin counting the statutory term, it could also be ignored in determining when federal protection attached. Federal copyright could just as easily attach from the moment the work was first created, thus obviating the need for state common law protection. In the system that emerged, federal copyright attaches to a work when it is first fixed in tangible form. The House Report accompanying the bill that became the present Act gives some examples of unfixed works that remain subject to state protection: choreography that has never been filmed or notated, an extemporaneous speech, conversations, live broadcasts, "and a dramatic sketch or musical composition improvised or developed from memory and without being recorded or written down." H.R.Rep. No. 94–1476, 94th Cong. 2d Sess. 131 (1976).

"Publication," though displaced from its central role, is still important. A work published without copyright notice any time before January 1, 1978 remains in the public domain and is ineligible for protection under the present Act just as it was under the 1909 Act. Publication also has prospective importance. If a work is published on or after January 1, 1978, copyright notice must appear on all copies and the notice must specify the year of first publication. Publication starts the seventy-five year term of copyright for anonymous works, pseudonymous works and works made for hire since no natural life is available to measure the general statutory term of life plus fifty years. Finally, the new Act's definition of "publication" for these and other purposes closely tracks the definition that evolved at common law over the preceding two centuries. In giving shape to the new statutory formula, courts can be expected to draw on these earlier decisions. This chapter offers a sample of common law decisions before the Act and indicates some directions that preemption may take.

A. THEORY OF PROTECTION

LETTER EDGED IN BLACK PRESS, INC. v. PUBLIC BLDG. COMM'N OF CHICAGO

United States District Court of Illinois, 1970.
320 F.Supp. 1303, 168 U.S.P.Q. 559.

NAPOLI, District Judge.

Plaintiff seeks a declaratory judgment invalidating defendant's copyright to the Pablo Picasso sculpture entitled "The Chicago Picasso." The defendant is the Public Building Commission of Chicago (Commission) and the plaintiff is a publisher who desires to market a copy of the sculpture. Pursuant to Rule 56 of the Federal Rules of Civil Procedure both parties have moved for summary judgment. Succinctly, plaintiff maintains that defendant's copyright is invalid because the sculpture is in the public domain. Defendant asserts that the Chicago Picasso has never been in the public domain.

Statement of Facts

In 1963 certain of the Civic Center architects, representing the Commission, approached Picasso with a request to design a monumental sculpture for the plaza in front of the proposed Chicago Civic Center. By May, 1965, Picasso completed the maquette (model) of the sculpture. William E. Hartmann, the architect, who had been the chief liaison with Picasso, then had the maquette brought to the basement of the Art Institute of Chicago, without public notice. The design of the maquette was subjected to an engineering analysis to determine the feasibility of constructing the monumental sculpture and three Chicago charitable foundations undertook to finance the actual construction by contributing $300,000 toward the total cost of $351,959.17. An aluminum model of the design with some slight revisions was prepared as a guide to the construction of the sculpture, and Picasso approved a picture of this model on August 9, 1966.

The Commission, through its board, had been given a private viewing of the maquette. Subsequently, the Commission passed a resolution authorizing the payment of $100,000 to Picasso. This sum was intended as the purchase price for the entire right, title and interest in and to the maquette constituting Picasso's design for the monumental sculpture including the copyright, and copyright renewals. Hartmann proffered the $100,000 check to Picasso and asked the artist to sign a document referred to as the "formal Acknowledgment and Receipt." Picasso refused to accept the money or to sign the document. He stated that he wanted to make a gift of his work. In accordance with Picasso's wish, counsel for the Commission and William Hartmann prepared the following "Deed of Gift" which Picasso signed on August 21, 1966:

> The monumental sculpture portrayed by the maquette pictured above has been expressly created by me, Pablo Picasso, for in-

stallation on the plaza of the Civic Center in the City of Chicago, State of Illinois, United States of America. This sculpture was undertaken by me for the Public Building Commission of Chicago at the request of William E. Hartmann, acting on behalf of the Chicago Civic Center architects. I hereby give this work and the right to reproduce it to the Public Building Commission, and I give the maquette to the Art Institute of Chicago, desiring that these gifts shall, through them, belong to the people of Chicago.

In the fall of 1966 the Commission, the public relations department of the City of Chicago, the Art Institute of Chicago and the U. S. Steel Corporation, the latter being the prime contractor for the construction of the sculpture, began a campaign to publicize the Chicago Picasso. The campaign was directed by Hartmann, with help from Al Weisman, head of the public relations department of the advertising firm of Foote, Cone and Belding.

As part of the campaign at least two press showings were conducted. The first was held on September 20, 1966 when the maquette was placed on public exhibition at the Art Institute. No copyright notice was affixed to the maquette. The following notice was, however, posted in the Art Institute:

"The rights of reproduction are the property of the Public Building Commission of Chicago. © 1966. All Rights Reserved."

Press photographers attended the showing at the invitation of the Commission and the Art Institute and later published pictures of the maquette and aluminum model in Chicago newspapers and in magazines of national and international circulation. In addition the Commission supplied photographs of the maquette and the uncopyrighted architect's aluminum model to members of the public who requested them for publication. The second showing took place in December of 1966 when the U. S. Steel Corporation, with the knowledge of the Commission, had completed a twelve-foot six inch wooden model of the sculpture and invited the press to photograph the model. There was no copyright notice on the model and the pictures were published without copyright notice. U. S. Steel also hired a professional photographer to take pictures of the model and these pictures were used in the publicity drive.

The drive was seemingly successful for pictures of the Picasso design appeared in Business Week Magazine on May 6, 1967 and in Holiday Magazine in March, 1967. Fortune Magazine published three pages of color photographs about the Chicago Picasso including pictures of the U. S. Steel wooden model. The Chicago Sun Times, Midwest magazine published a cover story on the sculpture with a drawing of the maquette on the cover of the magazine. And a picture of the maquette was printed in U. S. Steel News, a house organ with a circulation of over 300,000. None of the photographs or drawings that were published in the above named publications bore any copyright notice whatever.

From June, 1967, through August 13, 1967, the maquette was displayed at the Tate Gallery in London, England. In conjunction with the exhibit at the Tate, a catalog was published wherein a picture of the maquette appeared. Neither on the maquette itself nor on the photograph in the catalog did copyright notice appear. The Commission had knowledge of these facts for on July 6, 1967, Hartmann had sent to the Chairman of the Commission the catalog which was placed in the Commission files.

On August 15, 1967, the monumental sculpture, "The Chicago Picasso" was dedicated in ceremonies on the Civic Center Plaza. The sculpture bore the following copyright:

© 1967 PUBLIC BUILDING COMMISSION OF CHICAGO ALL RIGHTS RESERVED

At the dedication, Mr. Hartmann, co-chairman of the event and master of ceremonies said:

" . . . Pablo Picasso . . . as you know gave the creation of the sculpture to the people of Chicago and his maquette to the Art Institute of Chicago."

The Chairman of the Public Building Commission, in his speech of dedication to the approximately 50,000 persons assembled for the ceremony, said:

"It's an occasion we've all been anticipating—the dedication of this great gift to our city by the world-renowned artist, Pablo Picasso," and

" . . . I dedicate this gift in the name of Chicago and wish it an abiding and happy stay in the City's heart."

In conjunction with the dedication a commemorative souvenir booklet of the Chicago Picasso dedication ceremonies was prepared by the Commission. The booklet which contained drawings and photographs of the maquette and the aluminum model were distributed to 96 distinguished men and women from all areas of Chicago life and to honored guests. Neither the booklet itself, nor any of the photographs shown therein, bore any copyright notice. Also, on the day of the dedication the United States Steel public relations office sent out a press release together with a photo of the monumental sculpture. The photograph bore no copyright notice.

Subsequent to the dedication, the Art Institute published its Annual Report which contained an uncopyrighted picture of the maquette. This publication had a circulation of 40,000 copies including museums and libraries. The Art Institute also continued selling a photograph of the maquette on a postcard. Between October 1966 and October 1967, 800 copies of this postcard were sold. In 1967, however, the Commission asked the Art Institute to stop selling the postcard and the Art Institute complied with this request.

In October 1967, the Commission caused to be engraved in the granite base of the sculpture the following legend:

"CHICAGO PICASSO

THE CREATION OF THE SCULPTURE WAS GIVEN TO THE PEOPLE OF CHICAGO BY THE ARTIST PABLO PICASSO

THE ERECTION OF THE SCULPTURE WAS MADE POSSIBLE THROUGH THE GENEROSITY OF

WOODS CHARITABLE FUND, INC.

CHAUNCEY AND MARION DEERING McCORMICK FOUNDATION

FIELD FOUNDATION OF ILLINOIS

DEDICATED AUGUST 15, 1967 RICHARD J. DALEY, MAYOR."

In November, 1967, the Commission stated its policy that no individuals shall be restricted from "full personal enjoyment of the sculpture, including the right to take photographs and make paintings, etchings and models of the same for personal, non-commerical purposes. " The Commission has also had a policy of granting licenses to copy the sculpture for commercial purposes. The Commission requires payment of a nominal fee and a royalty on copies sold. Several such licenses have been granted.

Finally on January 12, 1968, the Public Building Commission filed its application with the Register of Copyrights asking a copyright in the monumental sculpture entitled "The Chicago Picasso." In due course a certificate of copyright registration was issued to defendant.

Statement of Applicable Law

Defendant submits that the attaching of notice to the monumental sculpture on August 4, 1967, and the later registration of the copyright were acts sufficient to obtain a statutory copyright under 17 U.S.C.A. § 10 and 17 U.S.C.A. § 11. This attempt to establish a statutory copyright must fail, however, if the Chicago Picasso was in the public domain prior to August 4, 1967. Such a conclusion is inescapable given the statutory admonition of 17 U.S.C.A. § 8 that "[n]o copyright shall subsist in the original text of any work which is in the public domain . . ."

To determine how a work comes to be in the public domain it is necessary to explore the basis of the copyright protection. The common law copyright arises upon the creation of any work of art, be it a first sketch or the finished product. This common law right protects against unauthorized copying, publishing, vending, performing, and recording. The common law copyright is terminated by publication of the work by the proprietor of the copyright. Upon termination of the common law copyright, the work falls into the public domain if statutory protection is not obtained by the giving of the requisite notice.

In some of the early English decisions there was debate as to whether publication did indeed divest its owner of common law protection. Arguing that divestment should not occur upon publication, because of the seeming irrationality of such a rule, Lord Mansfield observed: " 'The copy is made common, because the law does not protect it: and the law can not protect it because it is made common.' "

In the United States, however, it has been clear, from the date the question first reached the Supreme Court, that the common law copyright is terminated upon the first publication. And as Judge Learned Hand noted in National Comics Publications v. Fawcett Publications, citing Donaldson v. Becket, "It is of course true that the publication of a copyrightable 'work' puts that 'work' into the public domain except so far as it may be protected by copyright. That has been unquestioned law since 1774."

One justification for the doctrine, that publication ipso facto divests an author of common law copyright protection, can be found in the copyright clause of the United States Constitution. Protection is granted, but only "for limited times." The inclusion of this caveat in the Constitution makes manifest the right of society to ultimately claim free access to materials which may prove essential to the growth of the society. The copyright clause, however, does not impinge on the right of privacy of a creator. An author who refrains from publication and uses his work for his own pleasure may enjoy the common law copyright protection in perpetuity. Once a work is published, however, the Constitution dictates that the time for which the statutory copyright protection is accorded starts to run. An author is not allowed to publish a work and then after a period of time has elapsed choose to invoke statutory copyright protection. If the statutory protection is not acquired at the time of publication by appropriate notice, the work is lost to the public domain. Any other rule would permit avoidance of the "limited times" provision of the Constitution.

An exception to this rule is that a limited publication does not divest the holder of his common law protection. A good definition of limited publication can be found in White v. Kimmell wherein the court found that a limited publication is a publication "which communicates the contents of a manuscript to a definitely selected group and for a limited purpose, without the right of diffusion, reproduction, distribution or sale." For example, if an artist shows a painting to a selected group of his friends, for the limited purpose of obtaining their criticism, the publication will be said to be limited and thus not divestive of the artist's common law copyright.

Applying these general principles of copyright law to the facts of the case at bar the court is persuaded that the copyright to the work of art known as the "Chicago Picasso" is invalid. General publication occurred without the requisite notice. Accordingly, the common law protection was lost upon publication and the work was thrust into the public domain.

While this suit could have been resolved on any one of several distinct theories the court has decided to base its opinion on the proposition that the Chicago Picasso was placed into the public domain prior to the attachment of copyright notice on the monumental sculpture. Accordingly, only cursory reference will be paid to the other issues presented in this action. Even limiting the opinion in this fashion, however, multiple and rather sophisticated arguments of the defendant must be met in order to sustain the court's opinion.

Defendant's Claim That the Models Did Not Need Copyright Notice

The defendant's basic contention is that the work of art is the properly copyrighted monumental sculpture not the models. In support of this thesis defendant correctly points out that what was always envisioned by the Civic Center architects and Picasso was a monumental sculpture for the Civic Center Plaza. There can only be one copyright in one work of art it is asserted, and that work allegedly is the sculpture in the Civic Center Plaza; not the various models used in its development. It is therefore concluded that copyright notice on the models was unnecessary before publication of the monumental sculpture.

The court takes a different view of the facts. When Picasso signed the deed of gift on August 21, 1966, there existed but a single copyright. Picasso had a common law copyright in the maquette. He gave the maquette itself to the Art Institute and the right to reproduce it to the defendant. The monumental sculpture did not exist at this point in time and accordingly there could be no copyright in the monumental sculpture, either common law or statutory. It is settled that a copyright can exist only in a perceptible, tangible work. It can not exist in a vision. When Picasso made his deed of gift the monumental sculpture was undeniably but a vision and thus not subject to copyright protection.

The maquette, however, was an original, tangible work of art which would have qualified for statutory copyright protection under 17 U.S.C.A. § 5(g). The court finds that when the maquette was published without statutory notice Picasso's work was forever lost to the public domain. When the monumental sculpture was finally completed it could not be copyrighted for it was a mere copy, albeit on a grand scale, of the maquette, a work already in the public domain.

Defendant's Claim That Display of the Maquette Did Not Constitute General Publication

Three arguments have been submitted to the effect that display of the maquette did not constitute general publication. First, defendant urges that display of the maquette at the Art Institute was a "limited" publication and thus did not place the Chicago Picasso in the public domain. In support of this position the defendant's prime authority is American Tobacco Co. v. Werckmeister. In the American Tobacco case an English artist painted a picture depicting a company of gentlemen with filled glasses, singing in chorus. The artist transferred the copyright in the picture to the Berlin Photographic Company, which company made copies of the painting bearing appropriate copyright notice. Immediately subsequent to transferring the copyright the artist, who retained ownership of the painting, placed the picture on exhibit at the Royal Academy. The picture as it hung in the gallery bore no notice of copyright. Several years later the Berlin Photographic Company brought an action claiming that the American Tobacco Company had infringed upon its copyright to the painting. As one of its defenses the American Tobacco Company argued that because the painting had been displayed in a public gallery without copyright notice it had been lost to the public domain and accordingly, the copyright was invalid. The court rejected this argument finding that the display in the gallery amounted to a limited publication and thus did not operate to divest the holder of the copyright of its rights. The basis for this decision was the finding that absolutely no copies were permitted to be made by anyone viewing the picture at the gallery. In fact, it was noted that guards were stationed in the gallery to rigidly enforce the rule of the Royal Academy that no copying take place. The court properly decided that the rational basis for the notice requirement would not be transgressed by showing a picture bearing no notice where that picture could not be copied. In closing dicta the Court in American Tobacco noted: "We do not mean to say that the public exhibition of a painting or statue, where all might see and freely copy it might not amount to publication within the statute, regardless of the artist's purpose or notice of reservation of rights which he takes no measure to protect."

It is this court's finding that the case at bar more closely resembles the situation postulated in the aforementioned dicta than it does the actual facts of the American Tobacco case. In the case at bar there were no restrictions on copying and no guards preventing copying. Rather every citizen was free to copy the maquette for his own pleasure and camera permits were available to members of the public. At its first public display the press was freely allowed to photograph the maquette and publish these photographs in major newspapers and magazines. Further, officials at this first public showing of the maquette made uncopyrighted pictures of the maquette available upon request. Were this activity classified as limited publication, there would no longer be any meaningful distinction between limited and general publication. The activity in question does not comport with any definition of limited publication. Rather, the display of the maquette constituted general publication.

Defendant's second assertion is that the display of the maquette was inconsequential since an unpublished work, model thereof, or copy thereof does not require a copyright notice. The court has no quarrel with this statement of law. The problem with this argument, however, is that it begs the question of whether or not there was general publication. Since there was general publication of the maquette, notice was required.

Finally, defendant argues that the Art Institute did not hold the copyright to the maquette and therefore could not have placed notice on the maquette. The answer to this assertion is that the Commission, the alleged holder of the copyright, was required to insure that proper notice was placed on the maquette. The Commission was able to place improper notice at the showing, i. e., notice in the room, but it did not comply with the statutory requirement that notice be placed on the work itself in order to be effective.

Defendant's Claim That Uncopyrighted Pictures Could be Used in the Publicity Campaign

The defendant's major defense to the use of uncopyrighted pictures of the models in the publicity drive is what appears to be an inverse application of the doctrine of "fair use." Generally it can be stated that certain acts of copying are defensible as "fair use." The doctrine of fair use, however, was meant to be used and has only been used, as a defense in infringement actions. The defendant can not cite a single authority to support its unique claim that the doctrine can be asserted to excuse a failure to put copyright notice on copies of a work of art intended for distribution to the press. The court after diligent research has also failed to find any support for the defendant's position. It seems appropriate to ask why defendant's desire for wide and favorable distribution of copies of the maquette and the other models could not have been fulfilled by distribution of pictures which had copyright notice printed on them.

Defendant has an additional defense to the uncopyrighted printing of pictures of the maquette, the wooden model, and the aluminum model. It is contended that the copies of the work of art that appeared in various newspapers and magazines without notice did not amount to divesting publication because these pictures were protected under the copyright secured by the media in their own publication. It is settled law that if a work is published in the press, without a separate notice in the name of the holder of the copyright of the work in question, that work has been published without valid notice. Defendant contends that the above statement of law has been overruled by Goodis v. United Artists, and that the Goodis case supports its position that the press copyright protects the interests of the work's owner. The issue in the Goodis case was "whether a magazine publisher who acquires only the right to serialize a novel before it is published in book form has such an interest in the work that notice of copyright in the publisher's name will protect the copyright of the author of the novel". The court in finding that the publisher's copyright did protect the author, based its opinion on the fact that the magazine had purchased a property interest in the novel, i. e., the right of first publication. Thus, the court found that the publisher's notice was sufficient since the magazine had obtained proprietorship of a portion of the copyright to the novel. The basic issue that the Goodis court decided was whether the doctrine of indivisibility of copyright was applicable to the situation presented in that case.

The case at bar is distinguishable from the Goodis decision for in the instant case the newspapers and magazines that published the pictures of the work of art did not have as the Goodis court said, "such an interest in the work that notice of copyright in the publisher's name will protect the copyright. . . ." The publishers in the case at bar had no interest whatever in the pictures of the work that they published. Accordingly, the court finds that the copyrights of the publishers in their own publications do not serve to rescue the defendant's copyright in this case.

Defendant's Claim That Publication of Pictures of the Models Constituted Infringement

The last major defense that the defendant advances in an attempt to excuse the uncopyrighted publication of the work of art is that the publications constituted unauthorized infringement, and therefore they did not place the work in the public domain. In a letter to Hartmann, before the deed of gift was signed, which letter the defendant characterizes as, "instructions to architects," the following directions were set out.

"In order for the PUBLIC BUILDING COMMISSION to preserve all rights in and to this work of art, it is essential that every publication of the work, whether of the maquette, photographs of the maquette, or the ultimate monumental sculpture, bear the following notice:

"© 1966 Public Building Commission of Chicago All Rights Reserved

"The notice must appear legibly on an exposed surface of the sculpture. Since notice is the essence of protection, we suggest consultation between us before publication of the work in any form.

"Would you, or someone at your office, see that the photographs, drawings, and all other reproductions of this work of art are marked with the foregoing copyright notice."

Also, in its contract with the builder of the sculpture the defendant included provisions requiring that notice be placed on the sculpture and on all reproductions and drawings of the design.

Given these instructions the defendant argues that many of the instances of publication were actually acts of infringement because they were unauthorized and accordingly did not defeat defendant's copyright. The court has found no evidence for the period before notice was attached to the monumental sculpture on August 4, 1967, that the Commission intended to have its orders carried out. Rather, the great bulk of the evidence before the court, shows that the Commission itself disregarded its own instructions. That instead of objecting to uncopyrighted publications, the Commission passively and in some cases actively engaged in the distribution of uncopyrighted pictures promoting the Chicago Picasso. The court on the facts before it could not find that any of the publications here in question constituted unauthorized infringing publications. Accordingly, this last defense submitted by the defendant must be rejected.

An analysis of the legal issues presented in this action compels the conclusion that the copyright to the Chicago Picasso is invalid due to the fact that the sculpture has entered the public domain. This decision comports with a strict adherence to copyright law and is also in consonance with the policy of enriching society which underlies our copyright system. The broadest and most uninhibited reproduction and copying of a provocative piece of public sculpture can only have the end result of benefiting society.

For all of the foregoing reasons this court hereby enters summary judgment in favor of the plaintiff and against the defendant.

KRAHMER v. LUING

Superior Court of New Jersey, Chancery Division, 1974.
127 N.J.Super. 270, 317 A.2d 96, 182 U.S.P.Q. 494.

FRANCIS, Justice.

This motion to dismiss the complaint by third-party defendants concerns the alleged pirating of certain residential architectural plans which plaintiffs assert are protected by common law copyright. A copy of the plans and specifications was filed by the property owner, Mrs. Betty Pease Krahmer, in the office of the borough building inspector, as required by borough ordinance. The residence was completed. Thereafter, John W. Hand, the contractor for the Krahmer home, built a second home for defendants Larry L. Luing and his wife from the drawings, plans, blueprints and specifications prepared by architect Richard David Chalfant for the Krahmer residence. Hand received these plans from defendant, A. Gregory Ogden, the local building inspector. Ogden, a licensed architect, made revisions in these plans, but these revisions were minor. Krahmer covenanted in her contract with Hand that the drawings and specifications were the property of her architect. Krahmer also asserts property rights in the drawings and specifications through her participation in the planning of the residence and her contract with Chalfant. Krahmer and Chalfant bring this action based on common law copyright for compensatory and punitive damages, claiming that defendants used their architectural plans without their consent. Defendants contend that plaintiffs lost their property rights in the architectural plans when, although in conformity with the dictates of a building ordinance, they filed these plans with the office of the borough building inspector.

New Jersey extends its common law copyright protection to "literary, dramatic or musical compositions, or designs for works of ornament or utility, planned by the mind of an artist .   .. ." Aronson v. Baker, 43 N.J.Eq. 365, 367, 12 A. 177, 178 (Ch. 1887). An architect's drawings and specifications clearly fall within the scope of common law copyright protection. Until publication, the common law copyright preserves the architect's work product from unauthorized interference, and he may maintain an action against anyone who uses it without his consent. See generally, Katz, "Copyright Protection of Architectural Plans, Drawings and Designs," 19 Law and Contemp.Probs. 224. There can also be no doubt that Krahmer has a protectable property interest in the Chalfant plans as a tenant in common. The issue thus narrows into the question of whether, under the circumstances here present, plaintiffs made a publication of their architectural plans.

A publication can be either general or limited in scope. If the publication is a limited publication, the restrictions limiting the use of the subject matter to some definite purpose preserve the architect's common law protection. The test is one of intention, i. e., did the act of the architect demonstrate an interest either to abandon his rights in the work or to dedicate it to the public?

> It is a fundamental rule that to constitute publication there must be such a dissemination of the work of art itself among the public as to justify that it took place with the intention of rendering such work common property. American Tobacco Co. v. Werckmeister, 207 U.S. 284, 299–300, 28 S.Ct. 72, 77, 52 L.Ed. 208 (1907).

The burden of proving that the publication is divestive is on the defendants.

The record does not support a finding that plaintiffs intended to render their plans common property by permitting them to be filed in the office of the borough building inspector. The purpose of the requirement of filing plans in a government office is to protect the public from unsafe construction. Such filing represents a limited publication because the mere filing of plans does "not result in the surrender of any rights inconsistent with such limited purpose." Shaw v. Williamsville Manor, Inc., 38 A.D.2d 442, 330 N.Y.S.2d 623, 625, 174 U.S.P.Q. 277 (App.Div.1972). "It is not the purpose of the filing requirement to facilitate and permit architectural plagiarism, or enable one to obtain free of charge the benefit of another's work". Edgar H. Wood Associates, Inc. v. Skene, 347 Mass. 351, 197 N.E.2d 886, 894, 141 U.S.P.Q. 454 (Sup.Jud.Ct.1964). "The architect derives no profit from the deposit of his plans with the building department. He does not thereby sell his work and has no intention of dedicating it to the public." Smith v. Paul, 174 Cal.App.2d 744, 750, 345 P.2d 546, 550, 123 U.S.P.Q. 463 (D.Ct.App.1959). No objective intention to make a general publication appears on the record. The few reported cases which favor the defendants' position simply do not represent the modern or the better view. The Shaw case, cited supra explicitly overrules Wright v. Eisle, 86 App.Div. 356, 83 N.Y.S. 887 (App.Div.1903). Moreover, it may be noted here that defendant Hand was under an affirmative contractual duty not to copy from these plans without the plaintiffs' consent.

The issue is also raised whether the erection of the residence described in the architectural plans constitutes such a general publication as will justify a copying of the *plans*. Performance is not a publication. "A structure is the result of plans, not a copy of them. It follows that building a structure and opening it to public gaze cannot be a publication of its plans." Katz, op. cit. at 236. "[T]he right fully to reproduce plans is a far more substantial aid to a builder unwilling to pay for architectural services than the right to make sketches or drawings of a completed structure." Edgar H. Wood Associates, Inc., supra. "Here the architect limited the use of his plans both as to the persons allowed to use the work [Mrs. Krahmer and her agent the builder] and to the use which such persons might make of the work [the construction of one house]." Smith, supra. These limitations as to persons and use meet the test of a limited publication. Of course, the interior or exterior is copyable by anyone with sufficient draftsmanship abilities. But construction of the residence is not a general publication of the architect's plans, drawings, blueprints and specifications; in short, his work product. See also, Tabor v. Hoffman, 118 N.Y. 30, 23 N.E. 12 (Ct.App.1889).

The cases and authorities cited by defendant are not persuasive. Commentators have sharply criticized the application of the performance rule to the field of architectural plans. But the fear that such application would result in "perpetual common law protection of unspecified scope to the work of the architect and to remove a majority of structures from the public domain," 73 Harv.L.Rev. at 1391, has proven to be unfounded. Moreover, federal copyright protection for published materials (17 U.S.C.A. § 1 et seq.) does not require the divestment of common law copyright protection for unpublished materials.

For the foregoing reasons, the motion to dismiss the complaint will be denied. Order accordingly.

NOTES

1. What are the purposes of common law copyright? One purpose is to facilitate a work's preparatory stages, assuring continued protection without the bother of formalities until the work is completed and ready for public dissemination. Was *Letter Edged in Black* true to this purpose? If it was the display of the maquette that divestitively published the work, how can the decision be reconciled with the long line of authority that performance does not publish a work? If it was the distribution of photographs of the maquette that was held to publish, how can the decision be reconciled with the long line of authority, reflected in *Krahmer*, that the construction and public exposure of a building does not divest rights in the underlying plans? Is a building a copy of its underlying plans or is it, as *Krahmer* suggests, more like a performance of the plans? Can *Letter Edged in Black* and *Krahmer* be reconciled on the ground that one involved the public distribution of two-dimensional copies of

a three-dimensional work, and the other involved a public display of a three-dimensional copy of a two-dimensional work?

If the Commission had required that copyright notice be affixed to all photographs of the maquette, as *Letter Edged in Black* suggests it should have done, what would the resulting notice have signified to reasonable viewers—that the Commission held the copyright to the maquette, or to the photograph of the maquette? If the Commission had affixed proper notice to the maquette, how likely is it that the notice would have been discernible in the photographs? Should *Letter Edged in Black* have held that the maquette was in the public domain, free for copying by all, but that the sculpture itself was protected and could be copied only with the Commission's consent? Would the distinction make a practical difference?

2. What are the intended boundaries of common law copyright? One boundary, frequently noted, is that the perpetual state right must give way to the durationally limited federal scheme once the work is completed and commercial rewards begin to accrue. Do the rules on architectural plans reflected in *Krahmer* honor this boundary? Is it appropriate to allow architects to reap commissions from a single set of plans indefinitely, and not require them to share the plans with the public at some statutorily defined point? Or can it be said that the architect is not in these cases benefiting from copyright protection in the sense that he would if he published copies of the plans for sale to other architects and builders? What of the answer given in DeSilva Constr. Corp. v. Herrald, 213 F.Supp. 184, 195, 137 U.S.P.Q. 96 (M.D.Fla.1962): "It is no hardship to require architects to comply with the notice requirements of the copyright statute, and there is no excuse for the failure to have a copyright notice on said plans."

The present Act, of course, resolves the issue of perpetual protection by preempting common law copyright and casting the plans—published or not—into the public domain fifty years after their author's demise.

3. What constitutes publication? The court in King v. Mister Maestro, Inc., 224 F.Supp. 101, 140 U.S.P.Q. 366 (S.D.N.Y.1963), ruled that common law rights in Dr. Martin Luther King's famous speech, "I Have a Dream," had not been lost even though the speech was delivered before a crowd of 200,000 people in the course of the August 28, 1963, civil rights march on Washington, was "broadcast by television and radio, recorded (sound and pictures) for newsreels, was later shown in movie houses, and of course was widely reported in the press." 224 F.Supp. 104. The court rested its decision in part on a rule formulated by Professor Nimmer: "A *sine qua non* of publication should be the acquisition by members of the public of a possessory interest in *tangible* copies of the work in question." Nimmer, Copyright Publication, 56 Colum.L.Rev. 185, 197 (1956) (emphasis in original). The court also drew on Ferris v. Frohman, 223 U.S. 424, 32 S.Ct. 263, 56 L.Ed. 492 (1912) and Nutt v. National Institute, Inc. for

the Improvement of Memory, 31 F.2d 236 (2d Cir. 1929), for the propositions, respectively, that the public performance of a play and the public delivery of a lecture are not divestitive publications. Judge Wyatt concluded, "it has never been suggested that the number of persons in the audience had any effect on the principle." 224 F.Supp. 101, 106.

Nor in the court's judgment did Dr. King's distribution of a mimeographed text to the press constitute publication. Though, to be sure, these were tangible copies, "it is clear that this was a *limited*, as proposed to a general, publication. There is nothing to suggest that copies of the speech were ever offered to the *public*; the fact is clear that the 'advance text' was given to the press only." 224 F. Supp. 101, 107 (emphasis the court's). Is the conclusion plausible in view of the purposes for which advance texts are ordinarily given to the press? Compare in this connection the distribution of photographs in *Letter Edged in Black*.

Professor Nimmer has since updated his restatement of the judicially evolved publication rule: "Publication occurs when by consent of the copyright owner, the original or tangible copies of a work are sold, leased, loaned, given away, or otherwise made available to the general public, or when an authorized offer is made to dispose of the work in any such manner even if the sale or other such disposition does not in fact occur." M. Nimmer, Copyright § 4.04 (1979). In Nimmer's view, the present statutory definition of publication, 17 U. S.C.A. § 101, "in general constitutes a codification of the definition evolved by case law prior to adoption of the present Act." Id. Do you agree?

Would the present Act require a finding of publication in King v. Mister Maestro? In Krahmer v. Luing? In *Letter Edged in Black*? Note that section 101 defines "copies" to include "the material object, other than a phonorecord, in which the work is first fixed."

The following sources are helpful: Strauss, Protection of Unpublished Works, Study No. 29, Studies Prepared for the Subcomm. on Patents, Trademarks, and Copyrights, Sen. Comm. on the Judiciary, 86th Cong. 2d Sess. (Comm.Print 1961); Selvin, Should Performance Dedicate? 42 Calif.L.Rev. 40 (1954); Kaplan, Publication in Copyright Law: The Question of Phonograph Records, 103 U.Pa.L.Rev. 469 (1955).

4. Although it is now well settled that common law rights in a work were lost upon its publication, it is not at all clear that, as often assumed, the Supreme Court fully endorsed this proposition in its first declaration on the subject, Wheaton v. Peters, 33 U.S. (8 Pet.) 591, 8 L.Ed. 1055 (1834). Wheaton, the Court's former official reporter, sought to enjoin the publication and distribution of his successor's series of "Condensed Reports," which included many opinions reported by Wheaton, on the ground that they infringed his statutory and common law rights.

Because it reversed the circuit court's summary dismissal of Wheaton's statutory claim and remanded for jury trial on the issues raised, the Court need not have broached the common law copyright question. Indeed, the independence of the statutory count aside, the common law question was not even squarely before the Court. All that the circuit court had decided was that the proposition asserted, that the common law right survived a work's publication, was sufficiently clouded by doubt to inhibit the court, sitting in equity, from issuing an injunction in aid of the right. The question, it concluded, should first be resolved on the law side. Yet, for Justice McLean, the prospect of harrowing the ground already plowed by the two noted English decisions, Millar v. Taylor, 4 Burr. 2302, 98 Eng.Rep. 201 (K.B.1769) and Donaldson v. Beckett, 2 Bro.P.C. 129, 1 Eng.Rep. 837 (H.L.1774), was too tantalizing to be lost for such small technical reasons.

The case might never have attained its subsequent celebrity had not the two dissenting justices, Thompson and Baldwin, also warmly taken up the common law issue. Justice Baldwin's opinion is of particular interest for its hint of the turn the litigation might have taken had Wheaton devoted his dwindling means to pursuit of the law action suggested by the circuit court rather than to the Supreme Court appeal. Agreeing that, because it was the forum state, Pennsylvania's law governed on the common law claim, and assuming what Justice McLean nowhere conclusively refuted, that prior to the first English copyright act, Statute of Anne, 8 Anne c. 19 (1710), the English Courts had recognized a common law right in published works, Baldwin faulted the majority's apparent conclusion that the English common law on the point had not been "brought into the wilds of Pennsylvania by its first adventurers." 33 U.S. 591, 660.

The question mooted in *Wheaton* and its English forebears is meticulously examined in Whicher, The Ghost of Donaldson v. Beckett: An Inquiry into the Constitutional Distribution of Powers Over the Law of Literary Property in the United States, 9 Bull.Cr.Soc. pts. I & II, 102, 194 (1961–1962) and briefly but adeptly in B. Kaplan, An Unhurried View of Copyright, 12–16, 25–27 (1967).

5.   Can a copyright proprietor obtain the best of both worlds by keeping an unpublished version of his work in common law copyright and publishing another version under statutory copyright? That was essentially the gambit that defendant tried in Classic Film Museum, Inc., v. Warner Bros., Inc., 597 F.2d 13, 202 U.S.P.Q. 467 (1st Cir. 1979). Defendant owned all rights in the unpublished screenplay and story for the film, "A Star is Born." It also owned the rights in the film itself until they expired in 1965. The circuit court affirmed the lower court's judgment against defendant's claim that plaintiff's unauthorized duplication of the film would infringe defendant's common law copyright in the underlying, unpublished screenplay and story. "The owner of a common law copyright in the underlying work cannot expand the statutorily created monopoly, the limitation of which is designed to place in the public domain not only

the copyrighted matter but also the good will generated throughout the period of the monopoly. This is the price to be paid by the copyright holder in exchange for the exclusive statutory monopoly he enjoyed." 597 F.2d 13, 14–15.

Defendant had relied on a series of cases stemming from G. Ricordi & Co. v. Paramount Pictures, Inc., 189 F.2d 469, 89 U.S.P.Q. 564 (2d Cir. 1951) cert. denied 342 U.S. 849, 72 S.Ct. 77, 96 L.Ed. 641, including Grove Press, Inc. v. Greenleaf Pub. Co., 247 F.Supp. 518, 147 U.S.P.Q. 99 (E.D.N.Y.1965). *Grove Press* involved a claim that copyright on the original, French language version of Jean Genet's *The Thief's Journal* was infringed by defendant's verbatim copying of an authorized English translation of the work. Statutory copyright on the English translation had been forfeited for failure to comply with one of the Copyright Act's formalities. The original French version, however, was still protected by a valid statutory copyright. Assuming that the English translation was in the public domain, the *Grove Press* court concluded that, by copying the translation, defendant had infringed the copyright in the underlying French work. *Grove Press* is reproduced at page 723 and *Ricordi* is discussed at page 733.

Do you agree with *Classic Films'* conclusion that defendant's "reliance upon the *Ricordi* line of cases is misplaced"? According to the court, "those cases solely concerned underlying works which were statutorily copyrighted; thus, any protection offered by the *Ricordi* doctrine was limited to the fixed life of the underlying copyright (28 years plus the renewal period). The *Ricordi* doctrine is not equally applicable where there is an underlying common-law copyright which might extend indefinitely." 597 F.2d 13, 14.

Can *Classic Films* be reconciled with *Krahmer?* In *Classic Films*, it was copying of the published derivative work that was directly in issue, while in *Krahmer* the defendant had directly copied the unpublished original work. In light of *Grove Press*, do these distinctions make a difference? Does Tabor v. Hoffman, a trade secret case cited in *Krahmer*, offer any insight into the question? (Tabor v. Hoffman appears at page 175.) Would Warner Bros. have had an action against plaintiff's direct copying of the screenplay? Against a verbatim transcription from the film and the reproduction and sale of these transcripts?

B. LIMITS OF PROTECTION

------

1. ECONOMIC INTERESTS: THE PREEMPTION OF COMMON LAW COPYRIGHT

GOLDSTEIN, PREEMPTED STATE DOCTRINES, INVOLUNTARY TRANSFERS AND COMPULSORY LICENSES: TESTING THE LIMITS OF COPYRIGHT *

24 U.C.L.A.L.Rev. 1107, 1110–1114, 1118–1120 (1977).

One of the new law's major changes is to provide federal copyright protection from the moment a work is first fixed in tangible form. This implies of course that state law is no longer needed to protect a work during its preparatory stages, traditionally the province of common law copyright. Section 301 makes this implication explicit by abolishing common law copyright for most purposes. With common law copyright gone, publication no longer determines whether and when federal copyright attaches. The new law puts to rest a question that has bedeviled generations of judges and lawyers: "What constitutes publication divesting common law copyright?"

Yet, section 301 solves the publication puzzle only to replace it with others, none of which offers any hope for certain resolution. The new difficulties stem from Congress' intent to abolish not only those doctrines denominated "common law copyright," but also "to preempt and abolish any rights under the common law or statutes of a State that are equivalent to copyright and that extend to works coming within the scope of the Federal copyright law."

Section 301(a) sets up two conditions, both of which must be met for a state law to be preempted. First, the state right must be "equivalent to any of the exclusive rights within the general scope of copyright as specified by section 106." Second, the right must be "in works of authorship that are fixed in a tangible medium of expression and come within the subject matter of copyright as specified by sections 102 and 103." Thus, where courts once grappled with the single question of publication, they must now answer two equally difficult questions: "Which state rights are equivalent to copyright, and which are not?" "What works come within the scope of the federal copyright law and what do not?"

The statutory formula is easily applied to the garden variety common law copyright case. If, for example, an author writes a novel, distributes it to a small circle of friends and later discovers that one friend has arranged for the novel's publication on his own, an action for common law copyright infringement would lie under the old law. Under the new law, no common law action will lie. The right sought to be vindicated is a right against copying, clearly equivalent

* Copyright © 1977 Paul Goldstein.

to the right established by section 106(1). And the novel is a work of authorship fixed in a tangible medium of expression coming within the subject matter of copyright under section 102(a)(1). Thus, the state law action is barred and the author must rely on the federal law for relief.

What happens, though, when state law is preempted and the federal law does not provide relief? Suppose that a bandleader records his band's rendition of a public domain melody and, in addition to the federal copyright notice, inscribes on each record the legend, "Not to Be Played in Discotheques." The bandleader will have a copyright in his sound recording. He will not, however, have a federal copyright action against unauthorized performance of the recording, for section 114 expressly excludes any right to perform from the rights attached to sound recordings. Deprived of federal protection, the bandleader turns to state law, pursuing an equitable servitude theory against the discotheque proprietor. Is the right secured by the equitable servitude equivalent to the right to perform secured by section 106(4)? And, if equivalent, does it matter that, as to this particular type of subject matter, the federal copyright law does not attach this particular type of right? Where the statute omits protection, may state law fill the gap? The House Committee Report suggests a negative answer, but the face of the statute does not require it.

Whether state law has been preempted will often be academic, for in most cases state protection will merely have been traded for federal protection under the new law. Yet, substantial areas remain in which federal copyright law extends no protection and for which, consequently, the question of preemption of state law becomes critical. It is in these areas, where precision is most needed, that section 301 will prove most ambiguous.

A. *"Rights That Are Equivalent"*

The first of the two conditions that must be met for a state right to be preempted under section 301 is that it be "equivalent to any of the exclusive rights within the general scope of copyright as specified by section 106." The immediate problem is to determine the intended meaning of "equivalent."

If Congress' intent was to preempt state doctrines whose *purpose* is equivalent to the purpose behind federal copyright, the section cuts too narrowly, for it is an easy matter to find an independent, non-copyright purpose for any state law. Common law copyright, for example, may seek to protect personal interests in privacy as well as strictly economic interests. If, however, the intent of Congress was to preempt state doctrines whose *effects* are equivalent to copyright, the section cuts too broadly, into state doctrines that Congress surely would have wanted to survive. Privacy, trade secrets and unfair competition are a few of the many state doctrines that, like section 106, prohibit the copying or distribution of protected subject matter and consequently produce effects equivalent to copyright.

For many years, the proposed legislation offered some insight into the rights that Congress intended to preempt. Until a last-minute amendment from the floor of the House, section 301 listed several examples of state doctrines that were not to be considered equivalent to copyright. Among them were "breaches of contract, breaches of trust, trespass, conversion, invasion of privacy, defamation, and deceptive trade practices such as passing off and false representation." Also exempted from preemption were rights against misappropriation "not equivalent to any such exclusive rights [within the general scope of copyright as specified by section 106]."[28]

It is not at all clear why these examples were stricken from the bill.[f] Whatever its motive, the amendment will complicate further the already tangled relationship between common law copyright and its surrounding state doctrines. The roots of common law copyright extend deep and wide into the jurisprudence of the states. Over the course of two centuries common law copyright has quite naturally served as a model for the development of other state doctrines. State doctrines equivalent in purpose or effect to common law copyright now abound. Any attempt to abolish common law copyright, either nominally or functionally, is bound to disrupt other traditional, well-developed and independently legitimate state doctrines because of their connection to common law copyright.   .   .   .

B.   *"The Subject Matter of Copyright"*

Section 301's second operative phrase, "works of authorship that are fixed in a tangible medium of expression and come within the subject matter of copyright specified by sections 102 and 103," is as ambiguous as the first. Section 102, entitled "Subject Matter of Copyright," in fact nowhere defines "the subject matter of copyright."[48] While sections 102 and 103 provide some examples of typical copyright subject matter, neither offers definitive guidelines to govern more difficult cases.

Section 102(a) approaches the definition of copyright subject matter obliquely. It states that copyright protection subsists "in original works of authorship fixed in any tangible medium of expression," and lists seven categories for "works of authorship." Among them are literary, musical, dramatic, choreographic, pictorial and audiovisual works, pantomimes and sound recordings. Section 102(b) provides that "copyright protection for an original work of authorship does not extend to any idea, procedure, process, system, method of operation, concept, principle, or discovery, regardless of the form in which it is described, explained, illustrated, or embodied in such work."

The main interpretational problem will probably be to determine the interplay between sections 102(b) and 301(a). Does section

28. S. 22, 94th Cong., 2d Sess. § 301(b)(3) (1976).

f. A transcript of the discussion on the House floor appears next, at page 217. (Ed.)

48. Nor does § 103, which deals with compilations and derivative works.

102(b) say that ideas, procedures and the like are not copyright subject matter and are consequently open to regulation by the states? Or does it say that they do constitute copyright subject matter as to which protection has been withheld?

The answers to these questions will prove particularly important to the continued administration of state trade secret law, for this branch of state intellectual property law protects interests in ideas, procedures, processes, systems, concepts or discoveries against conduct equivalent to copying. Where the secret in dispute is distant from the usual subject matter of copyright—a chemical formula, say, or a mechanical process—courts can be expected instinctively to hold against preemption if, indeed, any lawyer shows the creativity to make the argument. However, recipes, customer lists and business plans, all of which might look more like copyright subject matter, may pose greater difficulty.

The Act can be read to embody a congressional intent to include section 102(b)'s listed elements as part of copyright subject matter and thus, under section 301, removed from state regulation if the state right is equivalent to a right specified in section 106. The key to this analysis lies in section 102's use of the phrase "work of authorship" in both subsections, (a) and (b), to describe copyright subject matter. The phrase is the exclusive source of the subject matter categories listed as (1)–(7) in section 102(a), a list that, according to the House Report, "sets out the general area of copyrightable subject matter."[50] The use of the same phrase in section 102(b), where the statute precludes copyright protection, suggests that the listed items are original works of authorship—subject matter within the meaning of section 102(a)—and therefore subject to preemption although not protected under the statute.

An alternative, preferable interpretation of section 102(b) would leave the enumerated items open to protection by the states. This interpretation, which is connected to the first one, reads section 102(b) to specify that certain elements—ideas, procedures, and the like—contained in original works of authorship are not protected. Since these elements are not the "works of authorship" to which section 102(b) refers, they are not within the subject matter of copyright. There is support for this view in the House Committee Report which emphasizes that, as in the past, copyright extends only to the form of expression: "Section 102(b) in no way enlarges or contracts the scope of copyright protection under the present law. Its purpose is to restate, in the context of the new single Federal system of copyright, that the basic dichotomy between expression and idea remains unchanged."[52]

---

50. H.Rep. [No. 94–1476] at 53.

52. Id. But see id. at 131:

As long as a work fits within one of the general subject matter categories of sections 102 and 103, the bill prevents the States from protecting it even if it fails to achieve Federal statutory copyright because it is too minimal or lacking in originality to qualify, or because it has fallen into the public domain.

The fundamental problem with section 301's second condition for preemption is that the "subject matter of copyright" is also the subject matter of several independent and important state doctrines. Where, as often happens, these doctrines offer rights akin to copyright, preemption is threatened. As in the determination whether a right is "equivalent," courts will in applying this condition be forced to choose between artificial distinctions and improperly disruptive results. Artificial distinctions seem the lesser of the two evils.

CONGRESSIONAL RECORD, HOUSE, SEPTEMBER 22, 1976

122 Cong.Rec. 32015 (1976).

Mr. SEIBERLING, Mr. Chairman, my amendment is intended to save the "Federal preemption" of State law section, which is section 301 of the bill, from being inadvertently nullified because of the inclusion of certain examples in the exemptions from preemption.

This amendment would simply strike the examples listed in section 301(b)(3).[g]

The amendment is strongly supported by the Justice Department, which believes that it would be a serious mistake to cite as an exemption from preemption the doctrine of "misappropriation." The doctrine was created by the Supreme Court in 1922[h] and it has generally been ignored by the Supreme Court itself and by the lower courts ever since.

Inclusion of a reference to the misappropriation doctrine in this bill, however, could easily be construed by the courts as authorizing the States to pass misappropriation laws. We should not approve such enabling legislation, because a misappropriation law could be so broad as to render the preemption section meaningless.

Mr. RAILSBACK. Mr. Chairman, will the gentleman yield?

Mr. SEIBERLING. I yield to the gentleman from Illinois.

Mr. RAILSBACK. Mr. Chairman, may I ask the gentleman from Ohio, for the purpose of clarifying the amendment that by striking the word "misappropriation," the gentleman in no way is attempting to change the existing state of the law, that is as it may exist in certain States that have recognized the right of recovery relating to "misappropriation"; is that correct?

g. Before amendment, section 301(b)(3) read:

    (3) activities violating legal or equitable rights that are not equivalent to any of the exclusive rights within the general scope of copyright as specified by section 106, including rights against misappropriation not equivalent to any of such exclusive rights, breaches of contract, breaches of trust, trespass, conversion, invasion of privacy, defamation, and deceptive trade practices such as passing off and false representation. (Ed.)

h. *Sic*.: The reference was probably to the Court's 1918 decision in International News Serv. v. Associated Press, 248 U.S. 215, 39 S.Ct. 68, 63 L.Ed. 211 (1918). (Ed.)

Mr. SEIBERLING. That is correct. All I am trying to do is prevent the citing of them as examples in a statute. We are, in effect, adopting a rather amorphous body of State law and codifying it, in effect. Rather I am trying to have this bill leave the State law alone and make it clear we are merely dealing with copyright laws, laws applicable to copyrights.

Mr. RAILSBACK. Mr. Chairman, I personally have no objection to the gentleman's amendment in view of that clarification and I know of no objections from this side.

Mr. SEIBERLING. I thank the gentleman.

Mr. KASTENMEIER. Mr. Chairman, will the gentleman yield?

Mr. SEIBERLING. I will be glad to yield to the gentleman from Wisconsin.

Mr. KASTENMEIER. Mr. Chairman, I too have examined the gentleman's amendment and was familiar with the position of the Department of Justice. Unfortunately, the Justice Department did not make its position known to the committee until the last day of mark-up.

Mr. SEIBERLING. I understand.

Mr. KASTENMEIER. However, Mr. Chairman, I think that the amendment the gentleman is offering is consistent with the position of the Justice Department and accept it on this side as well.

Mr. SEIBERLING. I thank the gentleman.

The CHAIRMAN. The question is on the amendment offered by the gentleman from Ohio (MR. SEIBERLING).

The amendment was agreed to.

MITCHELL v. PENTON/INDUS. PUB. CO., INC.

United States District Court of Ohio, 1979.
486 F.Supp. 22, 205 U.S.P.Q. 242.

THOMAS, District Judge.

This action, originally filed in the United States District Court for the Southern District of Texas, was transferred to this court. It is currently before the court on defendant's motion to strike Count II of plaintiff's complaint, which charges defendant with the common law tort of "unfair competition."

Plaintiff's complaint contains two counts and is brought pursuant to 28 U.S.C.A. § 1338(a) and (b). Count I presents a claim for copyright infringement and alleges that plaintiff authored "an original" book entitled Records Retention which is "copyrightable subject matter under the laws of the United States." Plaintiff alleges that the book

provides a systematic and accurate guideline for the destruction and/or retention of business records which classified and simplified more than 1300 governmental regulations and statutes.

Plaintiff further alleges that he "spent many long hours" researching and preparing data which he compiled "by sending a questionnaire" to numerous federal and state agencies. Plaintiff then "followed up with additional correspondence and long distance telephone interviews" with the government agencies. Paragraph 3.9 of Count I states that:

> Defendant Penton has . . . infringed one or more of [plaintiff's] copyrights by publishing and placing upon the market an article entitled, "Records Maintenance: Prevent a Paper Pileup" . . . [which] was on information and belief copied largely from plaintiff's copyrighted book. . . .

Count II, as amended, presents several examples of recommended retention periods in plaintiff's copyrighted work and lists "similar titles and recommended retention periods in defendants' article 'Record Maintenance.' " It says that in defendants' article, numerous other portions are "coincidentally . . . identical or similar to the portions of plaintiff's book Records Retention." Plaintiff then alleges:

> Certain portions of the plaintiff's copyrighted work contains factual information compiled by Mitchell at great personal expense and effort. Defendant Penton has misappropriated many of the factual recitations contained within Records Retention. This misappropriation has saved Penton a tremendous amount of time, effort and money in preparation of their article, "Records Maintenance." Defendant Penton did little original research; instead they relied on the information previously gathered by Mr. Mitchell. As a result of this misappropriation, Penton has gained a headstart or commercial advantage which is unfair and unjust and which should not be countenanced by a court of equity.

Count II concludes that defendant has "willfully and deliberately misappropriated certain information contained [in plaintiff's book]" and "traded upon the good name and reputation of plaintiff, all to plaintiff's damage and detriment."

I.

Relying on Sears, Roebuck & Co. v. Stiffel Co., 376 U.S. 225, 84 S.Ct. 784, 11 L.Ed.2d 661, (1964) and Compco Corp. v. Day-Brite Lighting Inc., 376 U.S. 234, 84 S.Ct. 779, 11 L.Ed.2d 669, (1964), Penton argues:

> The U.S. Supreme Court in 1964 clearly enunciated the principle that, once Congress has enacted statutes for the protection of ideas, federal preemption comes into play. There is then no room for protection by the common law of the States, such as the law of unfair competition, for the mere copying of a publicly distributed item.

While recognizing that these cases dealt with federal protection under the patent laws, Penton notes that "the same principle applies when the protection is given by the federal copyright statutes."

In Sears, the Court set aside a district court injunction against Sears, affirmed by the Seventh Circuit. While invalidating a design patent of Stiffel's pole lamp, the district court enjoined Sears "from unfairly competing with [Stiffel] by selling or attempting to sell pole lamps identical to or confusingly similar to" Stiffel's lamp. In reversing and granting final judgment, the Court reasoned:

> What Sears did was to copy Stiffel's design and to sell lamps almost identical to those sold by Stiffel. This it had every right to do under the federal patent laws . . . To allow a State by use of its law of unfair competition to prevent the copying of an article which represents too slight an advance to be patented would be to permit the State to block off from the public something which federal law has said belongs to the public.

Sears, supra, at 231, 84 S.Ct. at 789.

The same ruling was reached in Compco. The district court invalidated Sun-Brite's[i] design patent of fluorescent lighting fixtures but enjoined Compco "from unfairly competing with [Sun-Brite] by the sale or attempted sale of reflectors identical to, or confusingly similar to" the fixtures made by Day-Brite. The Seventh Circuit affirmed. The Supreme Court reversed and granted judgment in favor of Compco.

Significantly, the Court noted:

> A State of course had power to impose liability upon those who, knowing that the public is relying upon an original manufacturer's reputation for quality and integrity, deceive the public by palming off their copies as the original.

Compco, supra, at 238, 84 S.Ct. at 782. Thus, the Court recognizes that 'a state common law unfair competition claim, based on one party's deceptive palming off of an article or work product and not merely upon the copying of another person's article or product, is not preempted by the federal patent laws. It remains to be considered whether the new copyright law has affected this exception to the preemptive application of the Supremacy Clause.

In Goldstein v. California, 412 U.S. 546, 93 S.Ct. 2303, 37 L.Ed.2d 163 (1973), the Court rejected the argument that "Congress so occupied the field of copyright protection as to preempt all comparable state action," noting that the Congress, the Copyright Office and the courts agreed that under the existing law, there was no preemption. That is no longer true. The new Copyright Act establishes preemption with respect to other laws. Section 301(a) provides:

> On and after January 1, 1978, all legal or equitable rights that are equivalent to any of the exclusive rights within the general scope of copyright as specified by section 106 in works of authorship that are fixed in a tangible medium of expression and come within the subject matter of copyright as specified by sec-

---

i. *Sic.* Presumably the court's reference is to Day-Brite. (Ed.)

tions 102 and 103, whether created before or after that date and whether published or unpublished, are governed exclusively by this title. Thereafter, no person is entitled to any such right or equivalent right in any such work under the common law or statutes of any State.

This language preempts and abrogates all legal and equitable rights arising under the common law or statutes of any state

(1) that are equivalent to any of the exclusive rights within the general scope of copyright as specified by Section 106 in works of authorship that are fixed in a tangible medium of expression, and

(2) come within the subject matter of copyright as specified by Section 102 and 103, whether created before or after that date and whether published or unpublished.

To sustain defendant's motion to dismiss, it must be found that plaintiff's second cause of action, asserting that "Defendant Penton has willfully and deliberately misappropriated certain information contained in the work, Records Retention, is a common law claim that is preempted by section 301(a). However, section 301(a) must be construed together with section 301(b) which reads:

(b) Nothing in this title annuls or limits any rights or remedies under the common law or statutes of any State with respect to—

(1) subject matter that does not come within the subject matter of copyright as specified by section 102 and 103, including works of authorship not fixed in any tangible medium of expression; or

. . .

(3) activities violating legal or equitable rights that are not equivalent to any of the exclusive rights within the general scope of copyright as specified by section 106.

By this language, Congress makes it clear that certain "rights or remedies under the common law or statutes of any State" are not annulled nor limited by the new copyright law. The legislative history discloses that the Conference substitute adopted the House amendment of section 301. This House amendment had "deleted the clause of section 301(b)(3) ". . . enumerating illustrative examples of causes of action, such as certain types of misappropriation, not preempted under section 301." House Conference Report No. 94–1733, 94th Cong., 2d Sess. 79 (1976). In clause (3), Congress thus generally categorizes causes of action that the new copyright law does not preempt.

By deleting the examples, Congress must have decided it was better to permit the states in the first instance through statutory or decisional law to specify or fashion "rights or remedies" that fall within clause (3), subject, of course, to court application of the copyright law limitations of clause (3). While deleted from clause (3), those causes of action remain illustrative of "certain types of misappropriation, not preempted under section 301." However, these exemplified causes of action could only be brought as a pendent state claim in conjunction with a copyright infringement action if indeed the pendent claim was recognized as a legally sufficient state action and provided the claim did not involve a legal or equitable right that is "equivalent to any of the exclusive rights within the general scope of copyright as specified by section 106."

If the plaintiff's second cause of action involved unfair competition by "passing off", it would constitute a cause of action which is available under Ohio law (were this the governing law). Under Fed. R.Civ.P. 8(e)(2), the plaintiff can plead inconsistent and alternative facts and claims. Moreover, a "passing off" claim would not concern the violation of legal or equitable rights that are "equivalent to any of the exclusive rights within the general scope of copyright as specified by section 106." However, plaintiff's second cause of action is not drafted as a "passing off" claim but rather as a broad "misappropriation" claim.

The undoubted right of the plaintiff to plead in the alternative may here be asserted only if the alternative pleading of "misappropriation" is legally sufficient. Plaintiff argues that "misappropriation" is an unpreempted state claim that can be joined with his copyright infringement claim in Count I. While the House Report says that " 'misappropriation' is not necessarily synonymous with copyright infringement," the court concludes that the plaintiff's attempt in the complaint, as amended, to plead a claim that is distinctive from copyright infringement and unpreempted by section 301(a) is unsuccessful.

Should the plaintiff prevail on its first cause of action demonstrating that its registered copyrights have been infringed, and the defendants fail in any defense and counterclaim of copyright invalidity, plaintiff's count of "misappropriation," an alternative claim by plaintiff's own characterization would become redundant. However, should plaintiff Mitchell fail to prove infringement or if infringed, defendant should show that the copyrights are invalid, then Sears and Compco come into play. These cases hold that once patent protection (similarly copyright protection) is denied, the alleged infringer has "every right to" copy the patented product or copyrighted work of authorship. Plaintiff alleges "misappropriation" by Penton of "many of the factual recitations contained within Records Retention." If proved, such a claim asserts in effect, if not in substance, what Stiffel and Sun-Brite unsuccessfully claimed in Sears and Compco.

Under this disposition, namely that "misappropriation" as claimed by the plaintiff does not circumvent Sears and Compco, it is unnecessary to reach the further question of whether plaintiff has or could frame a claim of "misappropriation" that is actionable under the law of the state where the alleged tort took place.

Defendant Penton's motion to dismiss the second count, as amended, is granted without prejudice to the plaintiff to assert a pendent state claim, consistent with this opinion and applicable state law.

It Is So Ordered.

NOTES

1. What state causes of action are "equivalent" to the rights secured by section 106? Each of the state rights discussed below may embrace copyright subject matter. If the state right is "equivalent," are there any reasons why it should *not* be preempted? If the state right is not "equivalent," are there any reasons why it *should* be preempted?

a. *Rights in Ideas.* Idea submissions in the form of script outlines and program formats are "literary works" and thus fall within the subject matter of copyright described in section 102(a)(1). Copyright law, because it protects expression, but not ideas, will not itself protect the submitter against the unauthorized use of his ideas. See pages 33 to 64, above. Will section 301 preempt a state law action on the ground that the action would give the submitter a right equivalent to copyright with respect to copyright subject matter? What if the action is rested on an express contract between submitter and recipient? On an implied contract? A quasi contract theory? A property theory? Might a court that is solicitous toward idea submitters, but that is also disposed to honor the language of section 301, avoid preemption by recasting a property claim as a contract implied in fact claim?

b. *Unfair Competition—Passing Off and Misappropriation.* Passing off doctrine was partially preempted by *Sears* and *Compco.* See page 130. How will it fare under section 301? Recall that the doctrine's requirements of deception and competition tightly confine its anticompetitive effects, making it a poor candidate for preemption. But what of the more expansive misappropriation doctrine? Rooted in traditional unfair competition doctrine, misappropriation has evolved into an independent rule against poaching on another's investment regardless of deception or competition, and is sometimes used to prevent copying where statutory or common law copyright will not. Does this potential use bring misappropriation within section 106(1)'s right to reproduce?

c. *State Trademark Law.* State trademark statutes sometimes protect emblems and insignia apart from any requirement of consumer deception. One distinction from copyright is that, for any rights to attach, the proprietor must commercially use the symbol. Does the distinction make a difference, or should state trademark rights be preempted? In a case arising under *Sears* and *Compco,* rather than section 301, the Pennsylvania Commonwealth Court held against preemption. Bicentennial Comm'n of Pennsylvania v. Olde Bradford Co., Inc., 26 Pa.Cmwlth. 636, 365 A.2d 172, 201 U.S.P.Q. 944 (1976).

In *Olde Bradford* the Commission charged that defendant had unlawfully manufactured decorative metalware bearing the Commission's official seal, for which a state trademark registration had been obtained. Defendant demurred that "the representation embodied in the seal is a work of art registrable under the federal copyright laws," and that "since the representation was published without the requisite notice, it is in the public domain and may be freely repro- duced by anyone in any manner." 26 Pa.Cmwlth. 636, 640, 365 A.2d 172, 175–176. Applying *Sears* and *Compco*, the court held that "if a count in plaintiffs' complaint alleges facts sufficient to make a claim cognizable under the state law of unfair competition, the demurrer should not be sustained." But, "if a count states a claim based on the mere copying of the unprotected design, a demurrer should be sustained." 26 Pa.Cmwlth. 636, 643, 365 A.2d 172, 177. Pointing to trademark law's connection to unfair competition, the court ruled against the demurrer to this count.

The court was less charitable in its treatment of the Commis- sion's claim based on a provision in the state's Bicentennial Act pro- hibiting both any reproduction of the Commission's marks and "use in a manner likely to cause confusion, to cause mistake or to deceive." In the court's view, the act contained elements both of unfair com- petition and copyright. Thus, the court concluded, "the dominant in- tent of the Act is to prohibit, as does federal copyright law, the mere unauthorized production of the Commission's marks. As such, the state law should be preempted." 26 Pa.Cmwlth. 636, 644, 365 A.2d 172, 177.

What result would the court have reached under section 301?

d. *Trade Secrets.* Will section 301 preempt a state law action against the misappropriation of secret drawings and specifications? An Alabama district court held that it would: "The essence of plain- tiff's complaint is that defendant has copied its drawings and specifi- cations and prepared derivative works based upon those drawings and specifications. Thus, the complaint fits squarely into § 106(1) and (2). It is undisputed that the drawings and specifications are "fixed in a tangible medium of expression". Finally, the drawings and spec- ifications in issue could certainly be characterized as pictorial or graphic works. Thus, this court is of the opinion that the require- ments of 17 U.S.C.A. § 301(a) are satisfied by the facts in this case." Avco Corp. v. Precision Air Parts, Inc., 496 P.T.C.J. A–1 (M.D.Ala. 1980).

According to the *Avco* court, Congress did not intend to preempt state trade secret law if the action involved elements "such as an in- vasion of personal rights or a breach of trust or confidentiality, that are different in kind from copyright infringement." But in this case plaintiff had not alleged that defendant "has committed any of the el- ements that allow the common law rights of 'trade secrets' to avoid preemption."

e. *Resale Royalty Acts.* California's Artist's Resale Royalties Act, Civil Code § 986 (West.Supp.1980), entitles artists to 5% of the sales price each time their works of art are resold. To qualify for the royalty, the sale must be made in California or by a California resident, must be at a profit to the seller, and the sales price must be $1,000 or more. The works covered—paintings, sculpture and drawings—clearly fall within the subject matter of copyright under section 102(a)(5). Is the artist's statutory right to recover a royalty on resale equivalent to section 106(3)'s right "to distribute copies . . . by sale or other transfer of ownership"?

Note that section 109(a) limits the copyright proprietor's control under 106(3) to the first sale of his work, presumably on the ground that to allow any further control would offend interests in free competition. By attaching conditions to resale, the California law exceeds the thrust of section 106(3) as modified by section 109(a). To hold that the new right is equivalent to copyright would appear to contradict the literal phrasing of the statute. But to hold that it is not equivalent to copyright would appear to contradict the policies of free alienability and federal supremacy underlying sections 109(a) and 301.

In an action arising before the present Act's effective date, a federal district court ruled that the California act was not preempted by the 1909 Copyright Act: "The right to vend applies to and terminates with the first sale of the copyrighted work. Since the California Resale Royalties Act only applies to resales, it does not conflict with the right to vend." Although the action arose too early for the present Act to apply, the court offered its opinion that the Resale Royalties Act would similarly not be preempted under section 301. The court rested its conclusion not on a close textual analysis of section 301 but on the recognition that "not only does the California law not significantly impair any federal interest, but it is the very type of innovative law-making that our federalist system is designed to encourage." Morseburg v. Balyon, 201 U.S.P.Q. 518, 520 (C.D.Cal. 1978), aff'd, 621 F.2d 972, 207 U.S.P.Q. 183 (9th Cir.), cert. denied, 49 U.S.L.W. 3350 (Nov. 10, 1980). See generally, Katz, Copyright Preemption Under the Copyright Act of 1976: The Case of *Droit de Suite*, 47 Geo.Wash.L.Rev. 200 (1978).

f. *Right of Privacy; Right of Publicity.* Both these rights will frequently embrace the subject matter of copyright. Are they equivalent to copyright? See page 240, note 4, and page 267, note 3.

2. Does the discussion between Congressmen Seiberling, Railsback and Kastenmeier provide any insight into the intent behind the removal of misappropriation and other state doctrines as examples of unpreempted state law? Did Seiberling's response to Railsback—"we are, in effect, adopting a rather amorphous body of State Law and codifying it"—accurately describe the effect of proposed section 301? Note that Railsback accepted the amendment as interpreted by Congressman Seiberling "to have this bill leave the State law alone and make it clear we are merely dealing with copyright laws". Is this interpretation consistent with the position of the Justice Department, reported by Seiberling at the outset of his remarks?

The status of the deleted state law examples is further confused by Congressman Kastenmeier's assent to the amendment as "consistent with the position of the Justice Department." In a July 27, 1976 letter to Kastenmeier describing its position, the Department stated: "While 'misappropriation' is almost certain to nullify preemption, any of the causes of action listed in paragraph (3) following the phrase 'as specified by section 106' may be construed to have the same effect. For example, a court could construe the copying of an uncopyrighted published book to be an invasion of the author's right to privacy, i. e., the right to keep the control of the publication of his book privately to himself. In order to more clearly delineate the [sic] courts the area to be preempted, we recommend striking the specific causes of action listed in paragraph (3) so as to amend that paragraph to preempt only: '(3) activities violating legal or equitable rights that are not equivalent to any of the exclusive rights within the general scope of copyright as specified by section 106.' "

The Seiberling amendment and the Justice Department letter were only the last steps in a prolonged scuffle over preemption in which misappropriation was the key concern. Section 301(b)(3), as first submitted to Congress in 1965, H.R. 4347, 89th Cong. 2d Sess. § 301(b)(3), exempted "Activities violating rights that are not equivalent to any of the exclusive rights within the general scope of copyright as specified by section 106, including breaches of contract, breaches of trust, invasion of privacy, defamation, and deceptive trade practices such as passing off and false representation." Where, however, "the cause of action involves the form of unfair competition commonly referred to as 'misappropriation,' which is nothing more than copyright protection under another name," then according to the 1966 House Report, "Section 301 is intended to have preemptive effect." H.R.Rep. No. 2237, 89th Cong., 2d Sess. 129.

The 1976 House Report was equally unequivocal—but to the opposite conclusion. " 'Misappropriation' is not necessarily synonymous with copyright infringement, and thus a cause of action labeled as 'misappropriation' is not preempted if it is in fact based neither on a right within the general scope of copyright as specified by section 106 nor on a right equivalent thereto." H.R.Rep. No. 94–1476, 94 Cong. 2d Sess. 132.

What is the status today of the doctrines other than misappropriation that had been mentioned in section 301(b)(3) before the Seiberling amendment? History suggests that they should continue to be used as examples of unpreempted state doctrines. In one form or another, the examples had been associated with section 301 from the beginning, forming the benchmark by which the section's thrust was understood and measured. It would offend the longer legislative history if courts now felt foreclosed from using these examples in applying the statutory phrase "equivalent to any of the exclusive rights within the general scope of copyright." As will soon enough become painfully clear, any attempt to apply the phrase without resort to the concrete examples will be an exercise in the absurd.

For an extensive analysis of the question, see Fetter, Copyright Revision and the Preemption of State "Misappropriation" Law: A Study in Judicial and Congressional Interaction, 25 Bull.Copyright Soc'y 367 (1978), which also reprints in Appendix IV, the Justice Department letter referred to above and, in Appendix III, the preemption provisions of the successive copyright bills beginning with section 19(a) of the Preliminary Draft Revision Bill of 1963.

3. Copyright preemption battles were fought in the courts for more than two decades before passage of the 1976 Act. As in Congress, misappropriation was the vexed doctrine. Recorded renditions —what the present Act calls "sound recordings"—were the principal objects of concern.

The beginnings of the dispute can be traced to the late 1940's when the introduction of the long playing record offered the means not only for rapid expansion of the record industry but also for the piracy of its products. In the middle 1960's tape cassettes brought expanded opportunities to the record industry. Their dividend for the pirates was even greater. Cassettes provided broader access to retail markets and required less costly equipment than disc piracy. An officer of the record industry's trade association, the Recording Industry Association of America, estimated that in 1969 one of every three prerecorded tapes sold in the United States was a pirated copy of a commercial release. See Livingstone, Piracy in the Record Industry, Stereo Review 60 (Feb.1970).

Because sound recordings were not protected under the 1909 Copyright Act, record producers turned to state law, particularly to misappropriation doctrine, for relief. New York had earlier applied misappropriation doctrine in the similar context of performance piracy. See Metropolitan Opera Ass'n, Inc. v. Wagner-Nichols Recorder Corp., page 107, above. In Capitol Records, Inc. v. Mercury Records Corp, 221 F.2d 657, 105 U.S.P.Q. 163 (2d Cir. 1955), the Second Circuit Court of Appeals applied the New York doctrine to outlaw defendant's duplication of plaintiff's recorded performances. Learned Hand dissented, arguing that the distribution and sale of records had published the performances, forfeiting state common law protection. The recordings were, in Hand's view, now in the public domain.

Neither Hand's well-wrought dissent, nor the Supreme Court's later decisions in *Sears* and *Compco*, curtailed the vigorous use of misappropriation doctrine in the fight against record pirates. Both state and federal courts made short work of *Sears* and *Compco*. Because the conduct condemned involved the "appropriation" of claimant's work, not its mere "copying," they reasoned, *Sears* and *Compco* did not apply. The purported distinction between "appropriation" and "copying," first made in Columbia Broadcasting System v. Documentaries Unlimited, 42 Misc.2d 723, 248 N.Y.S.2d 809, 140 U.S.P.Q. 686 (Sup.Ct.1964) has been relied on extensively since. State efforts were also bolstered by Goldstein v. California, 412 U.S. 546, 93 S.Ct. 2303, 37 L.Ed.2d 163 (1973), discussed in note 4 below, which rejected claims of preemption and validated a state criminal statute against record piracy. See, for example, A & M Records, Inc. v. M. V. C. Distributing Corp., 574 F.2d 312, 197 U.S.P.Q. 598 (6th Cir. 1978).

The 1971 Sound Recording Act, P.L. 92–140, 85 Stat. 391, and successor provisions in the present Act giving federal copyright protection to sound recordings, marked the end of state protection for recordings fixed on or after February 15, 1972, the effective date of the 1971 Act. Section 301(c) of the present Act exempts pre-February 15, 1972 recordings from preemption until February 15, 2047. Is there any limit to the state rights that can be created in works fixed before February 15, 1972? Sound recordings fixed on or after February 15, 1972 are, under the Act, protected only against dubbing, and enjoy no exclusive rights of simulation or performance. Are states free to extend rights against simulation and performance to pre-1972 works?

For more on these issues, see Brown, Publication and Preemption in Copyright Law: Elegiac Reflections on *Goldstein v. California*, 22 U.C.L.A.L.Rev. 1022 (1975); Goldstein, Federal System Ordering of the Copyright Interest, 69 Colum.L.Rev. 49 (1969); Kaplan, Performer's Right and Copyright: The Capitol Records Case, 69 Harv. L.Rev. 409 (1956); Kurlantzick, The Constitutionality of State Law Protection of Sound Recordings, 5 Conn.L.Rev. 204 (1972); Note, The "Copying-Misappropriation" Distinction: A False Step in the Development of the Sears-Compco Preemption Doctrine, 71 Colum.L. Rev. 1444 (1971).

4. The Supreme Court's evolving preemption jurisprudence, from *Sears* and *Compco* through Goldstein v. California and Kewanee v. Bicron, influenced section 301's evolution to its final form in the 1976 Act. The 1965 Supplementary Report of the Register of Copyrights, urging that misappropriation not be exempted from preemption, found support in the fact that, the year before in *Sears* and *Compco* the Supreme Court had "cut back" unfair competition "to the traditional concept of passing off." Supplementary Report of Register of Copyrights to House Judiciary Comm., 89th Cong. 2d Sess. 85 (Comm.Print 1965). A decade later the Copyright Office Draft Report reflected the changed judicial mood. "In view of the recent Supreme Court decisions in the *Goldstein* and *Kewanee* cases . . . Congress should reconsider the wording of section 301 and subsection (b) in particular. . . . Additions to the specific references in Clause (3) [to exempted state doctrines] appear justified by this judicial trend." Copyright Law Revision, Hearings on H.R. 2223 Before the Subcomm. on Courts, Civil Liberties and the Administration of Justice of the House Comm. on the Judiciary, 94th Cong. 1st Sess. 2081 (1975).

Goldstein v. California, the only one of these cases directly involving copyright subject matter, may also help to guide application of section 301 in the future. Petitioners in *Goldstein*, prosecuted under California Penal Code § 653 proscribing record piracy, had unsuccessfully moved to dismiss the complaint on the ground that section

653 contravened the 1909 Copyright Act which, for all relevant purposes at the time, refused protection to sound recordings. Petitioners' constitutional challenge was two-pronged. First, they argued, "Congress intended to allow individuals to copy any work which was not protected by a federal copyright." 412 U.S. 546, 551, 93 S.Ct. 2303, 2307. Since section 653 "prohibits the copying of works which are not entitled to federal protection . . . it conflicts directly with congressional policy and must fall under the Supremacy Clause of the Constitution." Second, petitioners contended that "the statute establishes a state copyright of unlimited duration and thus conflicts with Article I, § 8, cl. 8 of the Constitution" which restricts the congressional power to grants of copyright and patent protection for "limited times."

The Court's answer to the first argument reads like a primer on the federal system. The Court began with Federalist No. 32, defining those areas in which states are considered to have given up their reserved powers:

> . . . This alienation, of State sovereignty, would only exist in three cases: where the Constitution in express terms granted an exclusive authority to the Union; where it granted in one instance an authority to the Union, and in another prohibited the States from exercising the like authority; and where it granted an authority to the Union to which a similar authority in the States would be absolutely and totally contradictory and repugnant. 412 U.S. 546, 553, 93 S.Ct. 2303, 2308.

The "first two instances," the Court observed, "present no barrier to a State's enactment of copyright statutes": the grant to Congress of authority over copyright is nowhere termed exclusive, and the Constitution nowhere provides that the power is not to be exercised by the states.

The Court then turned to the formula's third component. Conceding that the "objective of the Copyright Clause was clearly to facilitate the granting of rights national in scope," the Court concluded that, although "the Copyright Clause thus recognizes the potential benefits of a national system, it does not indicate that all writings are of national interest or that state legislation is, in all cases, unnecessary or precluded." The Court went on, "since the subject matter to which the Copyright Clause is addressed may thus be of purely local importance and not worthy of national attention or protection, we cannot discern such an unyielding national interest as to require an inference that state power to grant copyrights has been relinquished to *exclusive* federal control." 412 U.S. 546, 555–558, 93 S.Ct. 2303, 2309–2311 (emphasis in original).

Since Congress had not expressly withdrawn power over sound recordings from the states, the Court ruled that the California statute was a permissible state exercise. Justice Marshall dissented, relying on the rule of statutory construction announced in *Sears* and *Compco*. "In view of the importance of not imposing unnecessary restraints on competition, the Court adopted in those cases a rule of construction that, unless the failure to provide patent or copyright protection for some class of works could clearly be shown to reflect a judgment that state regulation was permitted, the silence of Congress would be taken to reflect a judgment that free competition should prevail." 412 U.S. 546, 577–578, 93 S.Ct. 2303, 2320.

To petitioners' second argument, that the statute violated the Constitution's "limited times" restriction, the Court observed that "Section 8 enumerates those powers which have been granted *to Congress*; whatever limitations have been appended to such powers can only be understood as a limit on congressional, and not state, action." It added that, in any event, "it is not clear that the dangers to which this limitation was addressed apply with equal force to both the Federal Government and the States. When Congress grants an exclusive right or monopoly, its effects are pervasive; no citizen or State may escape its reach. As we have noted, however, the exclusive right granted by a State is confined to its borders. Consequently, even when the right is unlimited in duration, any tendency to inhibit further progress in science or the arts is narrowly circumscribed." 412 U.S. 546, 560–561, 93 S.Ct. 2303, 2312 (emphasis in original).

What guidance does *Goldstein* offer on the definition of "equivalent rights" for purposes of section 301? In close cases, will it be appropriate for courts to consider that a state right is never completely equivalent to copyright in that it never extends beyond the state's boundaries? What guidance does *Goldstein* give with respect to "the subject matter of copyright?" What does the Court's reliance on Federalist 32 say about states' continued competence to regulate ideas, procedures, systems and other subject matter mentioned in section 102(b)?

See generally, Goldstein, "Inconsistent Premises" and the "Acceptable Middle Ground": A Comment on Goldstein v. California, 21 Bull.Copyright Soc'y 25 (1973).

5. Federal statutory law, expressly exempted from preemption by section 301(d), will doubtless fill in some areas left unprotected by preempted state doctrines. Section 43(a) of the Lanham Act, discussed at page 418, is the prime candidate for active duty. Rolls-Royce Motors Ltd. v. Custom Cloud Motors, Inc., 190 U.S.P.Q. 80 (S. D.N.Y.1976), suggests the extent of section 43(a)'s possible reach into areas covered by now suspect state doctrines such as misappropriation. Plaintiff, the manufacturer of Rolls-Royce automobiles, successfully employed section 43(a) to obtain a preliminary injunction against defendant's copying of the distinctive Rolls-Royce grill. Defendant distributed a "Custom Cloud" kit, part of which contained a virtually exact replica of the Rolls-Royce grill, to be used in customizing Chevrolet Monte Carlo automobiles. Copyright protection was apparently out of the question, presumably because the grill had long been distributed by Rolls-Royce without copyright notice and because, in any event, it was unprotectable as an article of utility.

The court, relying on section 43(a), found "without hesitation," that the design of the Custom Cloud grill "is such as to falsely represent that its origin is Rolls-Royce. . . . This is an obvious case where the promoters of a new product are attempting to deceptively capitalize upon the well-established reputation of another party, built up over long years of dealings with the public, and based upon a large expenditure of money and effort both in the production of the product and in advertising. The violation of Section 43(a) of the Lanham Act is clear and should be enjoined." 190 U.S.P.Q. 81.

6. Section 301's pervasive ambiguity promises a difficult time for courts attempting to determine whether a state doctrine has been preempted under the Act. The preceding notes offer some guidelines, drawn from legislative history and Supreme Court jurisprudence, for administering section 301. Courts deciding hard preemption questions may also find it helpful to pursue some fundamental questions about the place of intellectual properties in the federal system.

In close cases, should courts strike the balance for or against the validity of the state doctrine in issue? As a practical matter, how seriously do state doctrines neighboring copyright intrude monopolistic elements into the marketplace of ideas, goods and services? Does the observation in Federalist Number 43, that "the states cannot separately make effectual provision" for copyright and patent protection necessarily imply, as many favoring preemption seem to think, that the states are barred from creating similar systems of intellectual property? Or does it mean only that the state systems will be relatively ineffectual?

Apart from these inherent limits on state exercises, what basis is there for assuming that states will seek to protect information any more aggressively than the federal government? In some cases, states may decide to curtail their monopolies to points far short of those chosen by Congress for the copyright system. Even in *I.N.S.*— that much maligned, pre-*Erie* avatar of misappropriation—the Court noted the possibility of confining the monopoly to "an extent consistent with the reasonable protection of complainant's newspapers, each in its own area and for a specified time after its publication, against the competitive use of pirated news by defendant's customers." 248 U.S. 215, 245–246, 39 S.Ct. 68, 75.

As a realistic matter, how likely is it that state courts and legislatures will take decisions against preemption as a license to curtail competition through extensive new intellectual property systems? Over the course of two centuries, state courts and legislatures have shown little inclination to erect intellectual property systems that even begin to approach the rigor of federal copyright, patent and trademark laws. Courts, bound by *stare decisis*, are unlikely to create any such extensive doctrines, and state legislatures are subject to the same kinds of lobbying pressures and political constraints as the Congress.

On balance, would it be better for courts to confine section 301's preemptive thrust to the literal borders of common law copyright, leaving the field open to all other state doctrines, including misappropriation?

2. PERSONAL INTERESTS: THE RIGHT OF PRIVACY

BRANDEIS & WARREN, THE RIGHT TO PRIVACY

4 Harv.L.Rev. 193, 197–202 (1890).

It is our purpose to consider whether the existing law affords a principle which can properly be invoked to protect the privacy of the individual; and, if it does, what the nature and extent of such protection is.

It is not however necessary, in order to sustain the view that the common law recognizes and upholds a principle applicable to cases of invasion of privacy, to invoke the analogy, which is but superficial, to injuries sustained, either by an attack upon reputation or by what the civilians called a violation of honor; for the legal doctrines relating to infractions of what is ordinarily termed the common-law right to intellectual and artistic property are, it is believed, but instances and applications of a general right to privacy, which properly understood afford a remedy for the evils under consideration.

The common law secures to each individual the right of determining, ordinarily, to what extent his thoughts, sentiments, and emotions shall be communicated to others. Under our system of government, he can never be compelled to express them (except when upon the witness-stand); and even if he has chosen to give them expression, he generally retains the power to fix the limits of the publicity which shall be given them. The existence of this right does not depend upon the particular method of expression adopted. It is immaterial whether it be by word or by signs, in painting, by sculpture, or in music. Neither does the existence of the right depend upon the nature or value of the thought or emotion, nor upon the excellence of the means of expression. The same protection is accorded to a casual letter or an entry in a diary and to the most valuable poem or essay, to a botch or daub and to a masterpiece. In every such case the individual is entitled to decide whether that which is his shall be given to the public. No other has the right to publish his productions in any form, without his consent. This right is wholly independent of the material on which, or the means by which, the thought, sentiment, or emotion is expressed. It may exist independently of any corporeal being, as in words spoken, a song sung, a drama acted. Or if expressed on any material, as a poem in writing, the author may have parted with the paper, without forfeiting any proprietary right in the composition itself. The right is lost only when the author himself communicates his production to the public,—in other words, publishes it. It is entirely independent of the copyright laws, and their extension into the domain of art. The aim of those statutes is to secure to the author, composer, or artist the entire profits arising from publication; but the common-law protection enables him to control absolutely the act of publication, and in the exercise of his own discretion, to decide whether there shall be any publication at all. The statutory right is of no value, *unless* there is a publication; the common-law right is lost *as soon as* there is a publication.

What is the nature, the basis of this right to prevent the publication of manuscripts or works of art? It is stated to be the enforcement of a right of property; and no difficulty arises in accepting this view, so long as we have only to deal with the reproduction of literary and artistic compositions. They certainly possess many of the attributes of ordinary property: they are transferable; they have a value; and publication or reproduction is a use by which that value is realized. But where the value of the production is found not in the right to take the profits arising from publication, but in the peace of mind or the relief afforded by the ability to prevent any publication at all, it is difficult to regard the right as one of property, in the common acceptation of that term. A man records in a letter to his son, or in his diary, that he did not dine with his wife on a certain day. No one into whose hands those papers fall could publish them to the world, even if possession of the documents had been obtained rightfully; and the prohibition would not be confined to the publication of a copy of the letter itself, or of the diary entry; the restraint extends also to a publication of the contents. What is the thing which is protected? Surely, not the intellectual act of recording the fact that the husband did not dine with his wife, but that fact itself. It is not the intellectual product, but the domestic occurrence. A man writes a dozen letters to different people. No person would be permitted to publish a list of the letters written. If the letters or the contents of the diary were protected as literary compositions, the scope of the protection afforded should be the same secured to a published writing under the copyright law. But the copyright law would not prevent an enumeration of the letters, or the publication of some of the facts contained therein. The copyright of a series of paintings or etchings would prevent a reproduction of the paintings as pictures; but it would not prevent a publication of a list or even a description of them. Yet in the famous case of Prince Albert v. Strange, the court held that the common-law rule prohibited not merely the reproduction of the etchings which the plaintiff and Queen Victoria had made for their own pleasure, but also "the publishing (at least by printing or writing), though not by copy or resemblance, a description of them, whether more or less limited or summary, whether in the form of a catalogue or otherwise." Likewise, an unpublished collection of news possessing no element of a literary nature is protected from piracy.

ESTATE OF HEMINGWAY v. RANDOM HOUSE, INC.

Court of Appeals of New York, 1968.
23 N.Y.2d 341, 296 N.Y.S.2d 771, 244 N.E.2d 250, 160 U.S.P.Q. 561.

FULD, Chief Judge.

On this appeal—involving an action brought by the estate of the late Ernest Hemingway and his widow against the publisher and author of a book, entitled "Papa Hemingway"—we are called upon to decide, primarily, whether conversations of a gifted and highly regarded writer may become the subject of common-law copyright, even though the speaker himself has not reduced his words to writing.

Hemingway died in 1961. During the last 13 years of his life, a close friendship existed between him and A. E. Hotchner, a younger and far less well-known writer. Hotchner, who met Hemingway in the course of writing articles about him, became a favored drinking and traveling companion of the famous author, a frequent visitor to his home and the adapter of some of his works for motion pictures and television. During these years, Hemingway's conversation with Hotchner, in which others sometimes took part, was filled with anecdote, reminiscence, literary opinion and revealing comment about actual persons on whom some of Hemingway's fictional characters were based. Hotchner made careful notes of these conversations soon after they occurred, occasionally recording them on a portable tape recorder.

During Hemingway's lifetime, Hotchner wrote and published several articles about his friend in which he quoted some of this talk at length. Hemingway, far from objecting to this practice, approved of it. Indeed, the record reveals that other writers also quoted Hemingway's conversation without any objection from him, even when he was displeased with the articles themselves.

After Hemingway's death, Hotchner wrote "Papa Hemingway," drawing upon his notes and his recollections, and in 1966 it was published by the defendant Random House. Subtitled "a personal memoir," it is a serious and revealing biographical portrait of the world-renowned writer. Woven through the narrative, and giving the book much of its interest and character, are lengthy quotations from Hemingway's talk, as noted or remembered by Hotchner. Included also are two chapters on Hemingway's final illness and suicide in which Hotchner, writing of his friend with obvious feeling and sympathy, refers to events, and even to medical information, to which he was privy as an intimate of the family. Hemingway's widow, Mary, is mentioned frequently in the book, and is sometimes quoted, but only incidentally.

The complaint, which seeks an injunction and damages, alleges four causes of action. The first three, in which the Estate of Hemingway and his widow join as plaintiffs, are, briefly stated, (1) that "Papa Hemingway" consists, in the main, of literary matter composed by Hemingway in which he had a common-law copyright; (2) that publication would constitute an unauthorized appropriation of Hemingway's work and would compete unfairly with his other literary creations; and (3) that Hotchner wrongfully used material which was imparted to him in the course of a confidential and fiduciary relationship with Hemingway. In the fourth cause of action, Mary Hemingway asserts that the book invades the right to privacy to which she herself is entitled under section 51 of the Civil Rights Law, Consol. Laws, c. 6.

The plaintiffs moved for a preliminary injunction. The motion was denied and the book was thereafter published. After its publication, the defendants sought and were granted summary judgment dismissing all four causes of action. The Appellate Division unanimously affirmed the resulting orders and granted the plaintiffs leave to appeal to this court.

Turning to the first cause of action, we agree with the disposition made below but on a ground more narrow than that articulated by the court at Special Term. It is the position of the plaintiffs (under this count) that Hemingway was entitled to a common-law copyright on the theory that his directly quoted comment, anecdote and opinion were his "literary creations," his "literary property," and that the defendant Hotchner's note-taking only performed the mechanics of recordation. And, in a somewhat different vein, the plaintiffs argue that "[w]hat for Hemingway was oral one day would be or could become his written manuscript the next day," that his speech, constituting not just a statement of his ideas but the very form in which he conceived and expressed them, was as much the subject of common-law copyright as what he might himself have committed to paper.

Common-law copyright is the term applied to an author's proprietary interest in his literary or artistic creations before they have been made generally available to the public. It enables the author to exercise control over the first publication of his work or to prevent publication entirely—hence, its other name, the "right of first publication." No cases deal directly with the question whether it extends to conversational speech and we begin, therefore, with a brief review of some relevant concepts in this area of law.

It must be acknowledged—as the defendants point out—that nearly a century ago our court stated that common-law copyright extended to " '[e]very new and innocent product of mental labor which has been *embodied in writing, or some other material form.*' " (Palmer v. DeWitt, 47 N.Y. 532, 537; emphasis supplied.) And, more recently, it has been said that "an author has no property right in his ideas unless . . . given embodiment in a tangible form." (O'Brien v. RKO Radio Pictures, D.C., 68 F.Supp. 13, 14). However, as a noted scholar in the field has observed "the underlying rationale for common law copyright (i. e., the recognition that a property status should attach to the fruits of intellectual labor) is applicable regardless of whether such labor assumes tangible form" (Nimmer, Copyright, § 11.1, p. 40). The principle that it is not the tangible embodiment of the author's work but the creation of the work itself which is protected finds recognition in a number of ways in copyright law.

One example, with some relevance to the problem before us, is the treatment which the law has accorded to personal letters—a kind of half-conversation in written form. Although the paper upon which the letter is written belongs to the recipient, it is the author who has the right to publish them or to prevent their publication. (See Baker v. Libbie, 210 Mass. 599, 605, 606, 97 N.E. 109, 37 L.R.A., N.S., 944.) In the words of the Massachusetts court in the Baker case (210 Mass., at pp. 605–606, 97 N.E. at p. 111), the author's right "is an interest in the intangible and impalpable thought and the particular verbal garments in which it has been clothed." Nor has speech itself been entirely without protection against reproduction for publication. The public delivery of an address or a lecture or the performance of a play is not deemed a "publication," and, accordingly, it does not deprive the author of his common-law copyright in its contents.

Letters, however—like plays and public addresses, written or not —have distinct, identifiable boundaries and they are, in most cases, only occasional products. Whatever difficulties attend the formulation of suitable rules for the enforcement of rights in such works, they are relatively manageable. However, conversational speech, the distinctive behavior of man, is quite another matter, and subjecting any part of it to the restraints of common-law copyright presents unique problems.

One such problem—and it was stressed by the court at Special Term (Schweitzer, J.)—is that of avoiding undue restraints on the freedoms of speech and press and, in particular, on the writers of history and of biographical works of the genre of Boswell's "Life of Johnson." The safeguarding of essential freedoms in this area is, though, not without its complications. The indispensable right of the press to report on what people have *done*, or on what has *happened* to them or on what they have *said in public* does not necessarily imply an unbounded freedom to publish whatever they may have *said in private conversation*, any more than it implies a freedom to copy and publish what people may have put down in *private writings*.

Copyright, both common-law and statutory, rests on the assumption that there are forms of expression, limited in kind, to be sure, which should not be divulged to the public without the consent of their author. The purpose, far from being restrictive, is to encourage and protect intellectual labor. The essential thrust of the First Amendment is to prohibit improper restraints on the *voluntary* public expression of ideas; it shields the man who wants to speak or publish when others wish him to be quiet. There is necessarily, and within suitably defined areas, a concomitant freedom *not* to speak publicly, one which serves the same ultimate end as freedom of speech in its affirmative aspect.

The rules of common-law copyright assure this freedom in the case of written material. However, speech is now easily captured by electronic devices and, consequently, we should be wary about excluding all possibility of protecting a speaker's right to decide when his words, uttered in private dialogue, may or may not be published at large. Conceivably, there may be limited and special situations in which an interlocutor brings forth oral statements from another party which both understand to be the unique intellectual product of the principal speaker, a product which would qualify for common-law copyright if such statements were in writing. Concerning such problems, we express no opinion; we do no more than raise the questions, leaving them open for future consideration in cases which may present them more sharply than this one does.

On the appeal before us, the plaintiffs' claim to common-law copyright may be disposed of more simply and on a more narrow ground.

The defendant Hotchner asserts—without contradiction in the papers before us—that Hemingway never suggested to him or to anyone else that he regarded his conversational remarks to be "literary creations" or that he was of a mind to restrict Hotchner's use of the notes and recordings which Hemingway knew him to be accumulating. On the contrary, as we have already observed, it had become a continuing practice, during Hemingway's lifetime, for Hotchner to write articles about Hemingway, consisting largely of quotations from the latter's conversation—and of all of this Hemingway approved. In these circumstances, authority to publish must be implied, thus negativing the reservation of any common-law copyright.

Assuming, without deciding, that in a proper case a common-law copyright in certain limited kinds of spoken dialogue might be recognized, it would, at the very least, be required that the speaker indicate that he intended to mark off the utterance in question from the ordinary stream of speech, that he meant to adopt it as a unique statement and that he wished to exercise control over its publication. In the conventional common-law copyright situation, this indication is afforded by the creation of the manuscript itself. It would have to be evidenced in some other way if protection were ever to be accorded to some forms of conversational dialogue.

Such an indication is, of course, possible in the case of speech. It might, for example, be found in prefatory words or inferred from the circumstances in which the dialogue takes place. Another way of formulating such a rule might be to say that, although, in the case of most intellectual products, the courts are reluctant to find that an author has "published," so as to lose his common-law copyright in the case of conversational speech—because of its unique nature—there should be a presumption that the speaker has not reserved any common-law rights unless the contrary strongly appears. However, we need not carry such speculation further in the present case since the requisite conditions are plainly absent here.

For present purposes, it is enough to observe that Hemingway's words and conduct, far from making any such reservation, left no doubt of his willingness to permit Hotchner to draw freely on their conversation in writing about him and to publish such material. What we have said disposes of the plaintiffs' claim both to exclusive and to joint copyright and we need not consider this aspect of the case any further. It follows, therefore, that the courts below were eminently correct in dismissing the first cause of action.

The second count does no more than put another label on the same allegations as those upon which the first was based. As Justice Schweitzer expressed the thought at Special Term, "[t]he reasoning which denies [the plaintiffs] protection or recovery on theories of common law copyright also operates to deny recovery on any theory of unfair competition." (53 Misc.2d 462, 472, 279 N.Y.S.2d 51, 62.) In point of fact, there is no competition of *any* kind, unfair or otherwise, shown by the plaintiffs' affidavits. Hotchner was not competing with Hemingway; the latter's acquiescence in Hotchner's practice of writing about him disposes of any such suggestion. There is not a word of proof, nor could there be, that, as alleged, the Hotchner book "unfairly compete[d] with other literary matter . . . created and written" by Hemingway. Moreover, the affidavits disclose nothing which resembles the "palming off" or other deceitful practice which must be present before an otherwise lawful use of literary material might be stamped as unfair competition. Since State law is sufficient to bar the plaintiffs' claim under the second cause of action, we have no need to consider the contention of the defendant Random House that the decisions in Sears, Roebuck & Co. v. Stiffel Co., 376 U.S. 225, 84 S.Ct. 784, 11 L.Ed.2d 661 and Compco Corp. v. Day-Brite Light., 376 U.S. 234, 84 S.Ct. 779, 11 L.Ed.2d 669 apply to preclude the plaintiffs' reliance on a State remedy for unfair competition. . . .

The orders appealed from should be affirmed, with costs.

BURKE, SCILEPPI, BERGAN, KEATING, BREITEL and JA-SEN, JJ., concur.

Orders affirmed.

NOTES

1. The general rule in New York and elsewhere is that rights against the invasion of privacy do not survive the victim. If Hotchner had sought to publish *Papa Hemingway* during the writer's lifetime, might Hemingway have received an injunction against publication on privacy grounds? On common law copyright grounds? By asserting a common law copyright claim in his lifetime, could Hemingway have effectively revoked his implied consent to Hotchner's publication?

How would Hemingway v. Random House have been decided under the present Copyright Act? Recall that, under the Act, federal copyright attaches when a work is first tangibly fixed; until the work is fixed, the author's common law copyright controls. Section 101's definition of "fixed" requires that the author consent to the fixation. Would Hemingway's failure to object to Hotchner's publication of his remarks be held to constitute the necessary consent? If Hemingway were alive, and an action was brought under the present Act, could he effectively revoke his authority to Hotchner's fixation by asserting the common law copyright claim? If not, would his privacy claim be preempted on the ground that it extended a right equivalent to copyright over copyright subject matter?

Hemingway's implications are explored in Thor, The Interview and the Problem of Common Law Copyright in Oral Statements, 17 Bull. Copyright Soc'y 88 (1969). The law of letters is considered in Cohn, Rights in Private Letters, 8 Bull. Copyright Soc'y 291 (1961) and in Note, 44 Iowa L.Rev. 705 (1959).

2. Common law copyright and the right of privacy differ in important ways not closely explored in the Brandeis and Warren essay. While the privacy action does not generally survive its subject, there is no bar to the survival of common law copyright. Also, Brandeis and Warren probably overstated the case for common law copyright's protection of ideas as distinct from the expression of ideas. Following the general rule that copyright protects expression, but not ideas, most courts would hold that the idea that the husband did not dine with the wife would not be protected but that the precise wording of the husband's entry in his diary—the expression of the idea—would be protected.

3. The correspondence of George Washington figured prominently in early American efforts to formulate rules respecting rights in letters. In Folsom v. Marsh, 9 Fed.Cas. 342, 345, 346 (C.C.D. Mass.1841), Justice Story rebuffed defendant's contention that Washington's correspondence, messages, addresses and the like "are not literary compositions, and, therefore, are not susceptible of being literary property." Finding plaintiff's rights to the papers—acquired under the President's bequest to his nephew, Mr. Justice Washington —to have been infringed, Story expressed his unwillingness to admit the "soundness or propriety" of "the supposed distinction between letters of business, or of a mere private or domestic character, and letters, which, from their character and contents, are to be treated as literary compositions. . . . It is highly probable, that neither Lord Chesterfield, nor Lord Oxford, nor the poet Gray nor Cowper, nor Lady Russell, nor Lady Montague, ever intended their letters for publication as literary compositions, although they abound with striking remarks, and elegant sketches, and sometimes with the most profound, as well as affecting, exhibitions of close reflection, and various knowledge and experience, mixed up with matters of business, personal anecdotes, and family gossip."

As to the apportionment of rights between a letter's author and its recipient, "In the first place, I hold that the author of any letter or letters; (and his representatives) whether they are literary compositions or familiar letters or letters of business, possess the sole and exclusive copyright therein; and that no persons, neither those to whom they are addressed, nor other persons, have any right or authority to publish the same upon their own account, or for their own benefit." In the second place, "the person to whom letters are addressed, has but a limited right, or special property, (if I may so call it), in such letters as a trustee, or bailee, for particular purposes, either of information or of protection, or of support of his own rights and character."

4. In a later case involving Washington's correspondence, it was suggested that to extend protection to letters on a perpetual basis would be neither necessary nor prudent. Concurring in the court's decision that letters from the general to his military secretary, Colonel Tobias Lear, could not, because the property in them rested in the author, be considered assets of Lear's estate, Justice Gould would have confined the perpetual common law copyright to a "reasonable length of time." "After such a period had elapsed, that there cease to be a probability that this right to publish was treated as a legal right, anyone might publish who could procure copies." Eyre v. Higbee, 35 Barb. 502 (N.Y.Sup.Ct. 1861).

Does the specific, statutory duration of author's life plus 50 years, embodied in the present Copyright Act, provide a better solution? Consider the reasoning of the Register of Copyrights: "Unpublished works, including letters, photographs, diaries, memoranda, home movies, tape recordings, and other personal material, would be protected by the statute under Section 301, and would go into the public domain when the statutory copyright expires at the end of the term provided in Sections 302 or 303. We believe the terms provided in those sections are long enough to avoid any questions of invasion of privacy." Copyright Law Revision, Part 6, 1965 Revision Bill 86, 89th Cong. 1st Sess. (1965).

What other prospects for privacy are lost under the present Act? Recall that common law copyright requires no compliance with any formalities. By contrast, the person who sues under the present Act to prohibit publication of his letters or memoirs must first register the work through the public acts of application and deposit of copies with the Copyright Office.

5. If the *Hemingway* court had not found an implied-in-fact authority for Hotchner to publish the conversations, could it have found an authority implied in law? The point, carefully shunted in Judge Fuld's opinion, was ventilated in Justice Schweitzer's opinion for the Supreme Court, below. "Were anyone to have common law copyright in his mere conversations (as opposed to prepared lectures or speeches), then the same right would have to extend to everyone. The effect on the freedom of speech and press would be revolutionary." Justice Schweitzer was troubled by the thought that "were we to limit reportage to non-verbatim accounts, the only result would be to detract from accuracy and encourage fictionalization. This would

serve no interest, public or private, whether applied to history, or biography, or both." 53 Misc.2d 462, 279 N.Y.S.2d 51, 60.

Can the problem be resolved through application of the fair use defense set out in section 107 of the Act? See pages 763 to 786 below. Should fair use be applied to unpublished materials with the same force as it is applied to published materials?

6. Another way to accommodate the public interest in access to unpublished subject matter would be to endorse the distinction, eschewed by Justice Story in Folsom v. Marsh, between literary and nonliterary subject matter, granting protection to the first but not the second. Although the distinction was also rejected in what may be the first case involving rights in letters, Pope v. Curl, 2 Atk. 342 (1741), a smattering of subsequent cases attempted to enforce it. See for example, Perceval v. Phipps, 2 V. & B. 19, 35 Eng.Rep. 225 (1813). Later cases, like *Folsom*, returned to the *Pope* view. Can you think of another, more pressing, danger to the public interest that might attend judicial attempts at this sort of qualitative distinction?

7. Who is the proprietor of a letter's contents—the writer or the recipient? Of the contents of a conversation—the speaker or the listener? Of the contents of an inquest transcript—the court reporter or the witnesses? Or the state? See Lipman v. Massachusetts, 475 F.2d 565, 176 U.S.P.Q. 449 (1st Cir. 1973). Of a series of lectures in Anthropology 1—the lecturer or the student who transcribes and presumably edits them? Or the university? See Williams v. Weisser, 273 Cal.App.2d 726, 78 Cal.Rptr. 542, 163 U.S.P.Q. 42 (1969).

For the trial court in *Hemingway*, the task of gauging the relative contributions of the parties to a conversation was sufficiently difficult to justify a holding that conversations should generate no rights at all. The Court of Appeals, on the other hand, suggested that "It may be, in the case of some kinds of dialogue or interview, that the difficulty would not be greater than in deciding other questions of degree, such as plagiarism." Can you think of other, more manageable ways to resolve the difficulty? Would characterization of the parties to the letter or conversation as "joint authors" be too easy a finesse?

V. RIGHT OF PUBLICITY

A. THEORY OF PROTECTION

HIRSCH v. S. C. JOHNSON & SON, INC.

Supreme Court of Wisconsin, 1979.
90 Wis.2d 379, 280 N.W.2d 129, 205 U.S.P.Q. 920.

HEFFERNAN, Justice.

This appeal involves only questions of law, for the judgment was granted upon the defendants' motion at the close of the plaintiff's evidence to dismiss for failure to prove the existence of a cause of action upon which relief can be granted.

Elroy Hirsch, the plaintiff, seeks damages for the unauthorized use of his nickname, "Crazylegs," on a shaving gel manufactured by the defendant, S. C. Johnson & Son, Inc. Johnson admitted in its answer that it knew that Hirsch is nicknamed "Crazylegs" and admitted that it marketed a product, a moisturizing shaving gel for women, under the name of "Crazylegs." It acknowledged that it had not received Hirsch's consent for the use of this nickname but also alleged that the name, "Crazylegs," was not exclusively used with reference to the plaintiff; and it denied any misappropriation or damage to the defendant. The case was tried for five days, and the motion to dismiss was brought at the close of the plaintiff's case.

Two legal issues surfaced as being controlling and were the subject matter of the motion to dismiss. The first is whether a cause of action for appropriation of a person's name for commercial use exists as a matter of Wisconsin common law. Johnson asserts that the cause of action for the appropriation of a person's name for trade purposes is part and parcel of the law of privacy and makes the further undisputed contention that the right of privacy has never been accepted in Wisconsin as a matter of common law and on numerous occasions has been rejected. The second issue is whether the plaintiff established a prima facie case of common law trademark or tradename infringement when he failed to allege or prove that his name had ever been used to identify a product or service.

We conclude that the plaintiff's pleadings and proof were sufficient to state a cause of action upon which relief can be granted under both theories. A cause of action for the appropriation of a person's name for trade purposes is different in nature from other privacy torts, and prior decisions of this court are not controlling. The appropriation cause of action protects not merely the right to be let alone but, rather, protects primarily the property rights in the publicity value of aspects of a person's identity.

242

In respect to the second issue, we base our conclusion upon the rationale that the trial court failed to consider the common law of tradename infringement (as distinguished from trademark infringement) and that, under tradename law, there need be no evidence of the prior marketing of a product or service under the plaintiff's nickname, "Crazylegs." It is sufficient to allege and prove the cause of action to show that "Crazylegs" designated the plaintiff's vocation or occupation as a sports figure and that the use of the name on a shaving gel for women created a likelihood of confusion as to sponsorship. We therefore reverse and remand the cause for a new trial.

. . .

It is undisputed that Elroy Hirsch is a sports figure of national prominence. The testimony showed that Hirsch was an outstanding athlete at the Wausau (Wisconsin) High School, and thereafter he entered the University of Wisconsin in 1942. From the outset he proved to be a superstar of the era. In the fourth game of his first season of play at Wisconsin, he acquired the name, "Crazylegs." In that game, Hirsch ran 62 yards for a touchdown, wobbling down the sideline looking as though he might step out of bounds at any moment. Hirsch's unique running style, which looked something like a whirling eggbeater, drew the attention of a sportswriter for the Chicago Daily News who tagged Hirsch with the nickname, "Crazylegs." It is undisputed that the name stuck, and Hirsch has been known as "Crazylegs" ever since. We take judicial notice of the fact that as recently as June 24, 1979, he was referred to as "Crazylegs" in the Madison newspaper, the "Wisconsin State Journal."

After the United States entered World War II, Hirsch left the University of Wisconsin and was assigned to Marine Corps Officer Training at the University of Michigan. He there participated in football, basketball, baseball, and track, and was the first person to earn four letters in one year at that school. His college and service athletic credits included 1942—All Big Ten, 1942—All American, Wisconsin, 1943—All American, Michigan, 1945—All Service El Toro Marines, and 1946—Most Valuable Player of the College All Star Game. He thereafter starred with the Chicago Rockets and the Los Angeles Rams, both professional teams. He also played professional basketball with the Racine, Wisconsin, Knights in 1948. He played football with the Los Angeles Rams from 1949 until 1957. During this period his professional achievements included 1951—All Pro NFL, 1952—Pro Ball Squad, 1953—All Pro NFL, and in 1970 he was named on the All Time All Pro Team for the first fifty years of football. He received numerous other athletic awards, and as recently as 1977 he received the Hickok Golden Link Award, one of the few recipients in history, on the basis of his outstanding traits of character, as well as for his athletic performance.

During his career as an athlete Hirsch did a number of advertisements, in all of which he was identified as "Crazylegs." After his active playing days, he was a general manager of the Rams football team and assistant to the president of the Rams organization. In 1969 he became athletic director of the University of Wisconsin.

In addition to there being evidence of numerous commercials which used the name, "Crazylegs," there was evidence introduced to show that a movie was made in the 1950s of his life called, "Crazy-legs All American." This movie is still being shown on television. Hirsch stated that he had been protective of his name and what type product it was connected with. He stated that he refused to do ciga-rette advertising and that he declined to do any advertising for liquor and that he had a beer commercial withdrawn after he became the athletic director at the University of Wisconsin. In each case his nickname, "Crazylegs," was used to identify him.

There was evidence to show that the usual minimum compensa-tion for the use of an athlete's name on an unrelated product was five percent of gross sales. Two expert witnesses testified, and it is un-disputed that these witnesses were experts in the business of repre-senting celebrities in the endorsement of products or in licensing the use of athletes' names for advertising purposes.

On the motion to dismiss, the defendants argued, and the court concluded, that a cause of action does not exist in Wisconsin for the unauthorized use of a person's name for the purposes of trade, even assuming, for the purpose of the motion, the factual finding that Johnson was using Hirsch's name without consent. The court also concluded, consistent with the defendants' argument, that an essential element of the cause of action for a common law trademark infringe-ment was the prior use of the name, "Crazylegs," to identify goods or services and that Hirsch had not produced such proof.

We consider these causes of action separately.

The defendants conceded that "Crazylegs" is the plaintiff's nick-name and that Johnson marketed a product under that name. It is clear from the record that the plaintiff presented sufficient credible evidence upon which a jury could find, as a matter of fact, that the name, "Crazylegs," identified Hirsch and that the use of that name had a commercial value to Johnson. The question dispositive of this appeal, although not of the case on retrial, is whether as a matter of law a cause of action exists for the unauthorized commercial use of the name, "Crazylegs." Subsequent to the operative facts in this case, the Wisconsin legislature in 1977 enacted sec. 895.50, Stats., un-der the general caption of the "Right of privacy." One of the defini-tions of "invasion of privacy" is included in the provisions of sec. 895.50 (2) (b):

> "The use, for advertising purposes or for purposes of trade, of the name, portrait or picture of any living person, without having first obtained the written consent of the person . . .."

Under the law enacted by the legislature in 1977, Hirsch would now have a cause of action. This statute, however, was enacted after Johnson's "Crazylegs" product was taken off the market, and the question here presented is whether plaintiff had a cause of action under the common law. We conclude that he did.

The defendants' basic argument is that the right of privacy was never recognized by this court as a part of the common law. The defendants fortify this argument by pointing out that the statute enacted in 1977 denominates the unconsented use of a person's name for advertising purposes as an "invasion of *privacy*." (Emphasis supplied.) We conclude that the right of a person to be compensated for the use of his name for advertising purposes or purposes of trade is distinct from other privacy torts which protect primarily the mental interest in being let alone. The appropriation tort is different because it protects primarily the property interest in the publicity value of one's name. Because the previous decisions of this court declining to recognize a right of privacy have not dealt with the appropriation tort, they are not controlling. From almost the very outset of the recognition of the right of privacy, there has been an intermingling or confusion of the right of privacy and the right of control of the commercial aspects of one's identity.

The right of privacy was first extensively discussed in a law review article by Samuel D. Warren and Louis D. Brandeis in The Right to Privacy, 4 Harv.L.Rev. 193 (1890). A reading of that article, which has been denominated as one of the most influential ever written, makes it clear that the authors were concerned not with the commercial exploitation of a celebrity's name, but were rather concerned with the right of a private individual to be left alone and not to have the private affairs of even public persons gossiped about in the press. It drew upon decisions based on principles of defamation and actions for breach of confidence.

The intermingling of the idea of the right of privacy and the right to control commercial exploitation of aspects of one's identity can be traced to one of the first cases to deal with the existence of a right of privacy. Roberson v. Rochester Folding Box Co., 171 N.Y. 538, 64 N.E. 442 (1902). In *Roberson*, the New York Court of Appeals held that no right existed to protect a young woman from the unauthorized use of her portrait, captioned, "Flour of the Family," to promote the sale of flour. The decision provoked a storm of public disapproval, and the following year the New York legislature enacted a statute making it both a misdemeanor and a tort to use a name or a picture without consent for the purposes of trade. N.Y.Sess.Laws 1903, ch. 132, secs. 1 and 2. See, Prosser, Privacy, 48 Cal.L.Rev. 383, 385 (1960). During the next fifty years, the right of privacy was recognized by decision in most states and by statute in several others, so that by 1961, only three states, including Wisconsin, had not recognized the right.

The defendants argue that this court's rejection of the right of privacy in other factual contexts constitutes a rejection of a cause of action for appropriation of the plaintiff's name for Johnson's commercial advantage. But Dean Prosser in his article has explained that the right of privacy as it has evolved is "not one tort but four," which are "distinct and only loosely related." Privacy, supra at 389, 422. He also states:

> "What has emerged from the decisions is no simple matter. It is not one tort, but a complex of four. The law of privacy comprises four distinct kinds of invasion of four different interests of the plaintiff, which are tied together by the common name, but otherwise have almost nothing in common . . .." (at 389)

The four torts Prosser lists are:

> "1. Intrusion upon the plaintiff's seclusion or solitude, or into his private affairs.

> "2. Public disclosure of embarrassing private facts about the plaintiff.

> "3. Publicity which places the plaintiff in a false light in the public eye.

> "4. Appropriation, for the defendant's advantage, of the plaintiff's name or likeness." (at 389)

The fourth tort—the tort of appropriation alleged by Hirsch in the present case—Prosser points out is "quite a different matter" (at 406) from the other three, because the interest is not so much a mental one as a proprietary one in the exclusive use of one's name and likeness. This distinction between the first three causes of action listed by Prosser and a cause of action for the appropriation of one's name was also made by Endejan, in The Tort of Misappropriation of Name or Likeness Under Wisconsin's New Privacy Law, 1978 Wisconsin Law Review 1029. Therein, in discussing the tort of appropriation, the author stated:

> "The interest to be protected here deals primarily with the individual's 'right of publicity' and not the right to be let alone in the classical sense of privacy. This concept of appropriation sought to prevent the use of a celebrity's personality without consent. Thus, the tort represents the protection of a property interest." (at 1030)

The term, "right of publicity," was apparently first used by Judge Jerome N. Frank in Haelan Laboratories, Inc. v. Topp's Chewing Gum, Inc., 202 F.2d 866 (2d Cir. 1953). Judge Frank wrote:

> "[I]t is common knowledge that many prominent persons (especially actors and ball-players), far from having their feelings bruised through public exposure of their likenesses, would feel sorely deprived if they no longer received money for authorizing advertisements, popularizing their countenances, displayed in newspapers, magazines, busses, trains and subways. This right of publicity would usually yield them no money unless it could be made the subject of an exclusive grant which barred any other advertiser from using their pictures." (at 868)

Building upon the rationale of *Haelan*, Melville B. Nimmer wrote in The Right of Publicity, 19 Law and Contemporary Problems 203 (1954):

"Well known personalities connected with these industries do not seek the 'solitude and privacy' which Brandeis and Warren sought to protect. Indeed, privacy is the one thing they do 'not want, or need.' Their concern is rather with publicity, which may be regarded as the reverse side of the coin of privacy. However, although the well known personality does not wish to hide his light under a bushel of privacy, neither does he wish to have his name, photograph, and likeness reproduced and publicized without his consent or without remuneration to him. With the tremendous strides in communications, advertising, and entertainment techniques, the public personality has found that the use of his name, photograph, and likeness has taken on a pecuniary value undreamed of at the turn of the century. [Footnotes omitted.]" (at 203–04)

Hence, Prosser, Frank, and Nimmer stress the significant distinction between the tort of appropriation and other torts involving invasion of privacy. The tort of appropriation protects a property right, not only the right of a person to be let alone or to live his life in seclusion without mention in the media. The incongruity of lumping a cause of action for appropriation or violation of the right of publicity with the other privacy torts is eloquently stated in the article by Treece, Commercial Exploitation of Names, Likenesses, and Personal Histories, 51 Tex.L.Rev. 637 (1973). Treece stated:

"An advertiser who appropriates an individual's personality either to attract attention to an advertisement or a product, to imply endorsement of a product or service, or to appeal to consumers' desires to associate with the individual depicted realizes an advertising benefit primarily because of the public image of the personality he has appropriated. The advertiser uses the audience appeal of the personality he has appropriated to sell goods. Audience appeal is a principal stock-in-trade of a celebrity. The celebrity creates audience appeal not only through the substantive achievements that bring him fame, but at the expense of the privacy that he must surrender in becoming a public personality. It would be ironic for a court to refuse to protect a celebrity's economic interest on the grounds that he had surrendered any interest in privacy.

"Since the primary advertising value of a celebrity's personality was created through the work and sacrifice of the celebrity, that value could constitute an interest that the law should protect." (at 646–47)

Because the right of publicity—the right to control the commercial exploitation of aspects of a person's identity—differs from other privacy rights, it is appropriate for this court to recognize a cause of action to protect this right, although other privacy rights were rejected in prior decisions of this court. Protection of the publicity value of one's name is supported by public-policy considerations, such as the interest in controlling the effect on one's reputation of commercial uses of one's personality and the prevention of unjust enrichment of those who appropriate the publicity value of another's identity. Moreover, where, as here, the record attempts to demonstrate that Hirsch over a period of years assiduously cultivated a reputation not only for skill as an athlete, but as an exemplary person whose identity was associated with sportsmanship and high qualities of character, and where the record demonstrates that much time and effort was devoted to that purpose, the rationale of Mercury Record Productions, Inc., v. Economic Consultants, Inc., 64 Wis.2d 163, 218 N.W.2d 705 (1974), is appropriate. It is a form of commercial immorality to "reap where another has sown." (at 176, 218 N.W.2d 705)

Despite the fact that it appears clearly appropriate that this court recognize a common law action to protect against the unconsented commercial appropriation of one's identity, we may be foreclosed from doing that if prior decisions of this court have expressly rejected that cause of action. We have examined all of the cases referred to us by the parties and conclude that this court has never before addressed the question of whether an individual has a cause of action for the appropriation by another of his identity for commercial purposes. . . .

The review of these cases demonstrates that the right of a person to control the commercial exploitation of the property right in the use of that person's name is not controlled by cases involving the right of privacy but no property interest. Rather, the asserted cause of action is dependent upon the cases that recognize the "right of publicity" and the limitations that the possessor of that property right may place upon the commercial and public use of the name.

The record is replete with evidence from which a jury could conclude that Elroy Hirsch's name indeed had commercial value. There was testimony that he had been paid for the use of the name in the past, and there was expert testimony by qualified persons who stated the reasonable compensation for the authorized use of his name or identity. That the tort is compensable is clear. As the commentator in The Tort of Misappropriation of Name or Likeness Under Wisconsin's New Privacy Law, 1978 Wis.L.Rev. 1029, 1046, supra, stated:

> "The rule is fairly well established that well known athletes have a property right in their identities and are allowed to recover for wrongful appropriation."

The fact that the name, "Crazylegs," used by Johnson, was a nickname rather than Hirsch's actual name does not preclude a cause of action. All that is required is that the name clearly identify the wronged person. In the instant case, it is not disputed at this juncture of the case that the nickname identified the plaintiff Hirsch. It is argued that there were others who were known by the same name. This, however, does not vitiate the existence of a cause of action. It may, however, if sufficient proof were adduced, affect the quantum of damages should the jury impose liability or it might preclude liability altogether. Prosser points out "that a stage or other fictitious name can be so identified with the plaintiff that he is entitled to protection against its use." 49 Cal.L.Rev., supra at 404. He writes that it would be absurd to say that Samuel L. Clemens would have a cause of action if that name had been used in advertising, but he would not have one for the use of "Mark Twain." If a fictitious name is used in a context which tends to indicate that the name is that of the plaintiff, the factual case for identity is strengthened.

The record shows that Johnson's first promotion of the product, "Crazylegs," was the sponsoring of a running event for women and the use of a television commercial similar to the "Crazylegs" cheer initiated at University of Wisconsin football games when Elroy Hirsch became athletic director. These facts may augment and further identify the sports context in which the name, "Crazylegs," has been particularly prominent. The question whether "Crazylegs" identifies Elroy Hirsch, however, is one of fact to be determined by the jury on remand, and full inquiry into that fact is not foreclosed by the defendants' concessions in the present procedural posture of the case.

Accordingly, we hold that a cause of action for appropriation of a person's name for trade purposes exists at common law in Wisconsin. The facts adduced in the plaintiff's case prima facie were sufficient for submission to the jury. The trial court erred when it concluded as a matter of law that Wisconsin cases which held that the right of privacy did not exist at common law in Wisconsin foreclosed the plaintiff from asserting a cause of action for the commercial misappropriation of his name and identity.

Additionally, Hirsch argued that the facts adduced established a prima facie case of common law tradename infringement. The trial court also ruled on this question as a matter of law. It concluded that the case did not involve trademarks or tradenames because there was no evidence showing Elroy Hirsch's name or the name, "Crazylegs," had ever been connected with a service or a product. The position of the trial court and the position urged by the defendant on this appeal is that no cause of action for tradename infringement will lie unless it is alleged and proved that the alleged tradename, "Crazylegs," was used by the plaintiff to identify goods or services and distinguish them from others. We conclude that this is an erroneous view of the law.

The misuse of a tradename is a portion of the law of unfair competition. We stated in J. I. Case Plow Works v. J. I. Case Threshing Machine Co., 162 Wis. 185, 155 N.W. 128 (1916), that the law of unfair competition is based on the maxim that, "One man may not reap where another has sown nor gather where another has strewn." (at 201, 155 N.W. at 134) Common law trademark and tradename infringement is a branch of the law of unfair competition, and the principles used in each are substantially similar. First Wisconsin National Bank of Milwaukee v. Wichman, 85 Wis.2d 54, 60, 270 N.W.2d 168 (1978). "Passing off," or misrepresenting one's goods or services as those of another, and direct competition are no longer considered to be essential elements of a cause of action for unfair competition. The modern approach to the law of unfair competition holds that:

"[P]roperty rights of commercial value are to be and will be protected from any form of unfair invasion or infringement or from any form of commercial immorality . . . ." Metropolitan Opera Ass'n, Inc. v. Wagner-Nichols Recorder Corp., 199 Misc. 786, 101 N.Y.S.2d 483, 492 (S.Ct.1950); see, also, Hogan v. A. S. Barnes & Co., Inc., 114 U.S.P.Q. 314, 316–19 (Pa.C.P., Philadelphia County, 1957).

As the discussion herein has demonstrated, the publicity value of a celebrity's name is built up by the investment of work, time, and money by the celebrity. The economic damage caused by unauthorized commercial use of a name may take many forms, including damage to reputation if the advertised product or service is shoddy and the dilution of the value of the name in authorized advertising. It was particularly the latter aspect of advertising with which the court concerned itself in Hogan, supra.

The court reached its conclusion that Hirsch proved no cause of action for common law trademark infringement because he proved only that the name, "Crazylegs," was used to identify himself and not to identify goods or services. In that conclusion the court was correct in stating that there was no proof that the name was used to identify goods or services.

The definition of "trademark" which was adopted by this court in First Wisconsin, supra, requires use in connection with goods and services. Such use, however, is not required where a name meets the definition of a tradename. The trial court failed to consider whether Hirsch's use of the name, "Crazylegs," met the definition of a tradename. Restatement 2d, Torts, sec. 716 (Tent.Draft No. 8, 1963), adopted as the common law of Wisconsin in First Wisconsin, supra, defined a tradename:

"A tradename is a designation which is used by a person to identify his business, vocation, or occupation, provided such use is not prohibited by legislative enactment or by an otherwise defined public policy."

Sec. 717 of the Restatement provided that one infringes a trademark or tradename if:

". . . without a privilege to do so, he uses on or in connection with his goods, services or business a designation which so resembles the other's previously used mark or tradename as to be likely to

"(a) cause confusion, mistake or deception, or

"(b) cause prospective purchasers to believe that

"(i) the actor's goods or services are those of the other, or

"(ii) the actor's goods or services emanate from the same source as the other's goods or services, or

"(iii) the actor's goods or services are approved or sponsored by the other, or

"(iv) the actor's business is the business of, or is in some manner associated or connected with, the other,

even though the actor does not use the designation with a purpose to deceive."

There was ample evidence for a jury to believe that "Crazylegs" designated Hirsch's vocation or occupation as a sports figure, first as a player and later in management and administration. There was also ample evidence to show the likelihood of confusion as to sponsorship of the product as the result of Johnson's use of the name, "Crazylegs."

Hirsch testified that there was actual confusion and that people told him that they assumed that he was sponsoring the product, and in fact he received orders for the product. For Hirsch to show that there was an infringement on the tradename, "Crazylegs," there was no necessity as a matter of law that the name had previously been identified with products and services. It was sufficient to show that the name was one used to identify Hirsch in his business or occupation and that the use of the name caused confusion or mistake in respect to the approval or sponsorship of the goods. The court erred in dismissing the cause of action for tradename infringement.

Various evidentiary problems have also been raised on this appeal by Hirsch. We agree with the position of the defendants on this appeal that only the questions of law heretofore discussed are before the court, and, accordingly, only those matters can be decided. These evidentiary problems may not, and probably will not, on retrial be presented to the court in the identical form posed in the first trial. We point out, however, that the objection to the introduction of evidence of the prior licensing by Hirsch of a restaurant bearing the name, "Crazylegs," on the grounds that it was not mentioned in pre-trial depositions and therefore constituted surprise, could hardly be appropriate on a retrial, because a full offer of proof has been made.

In addition, the plaintiff claims it was error for the trial court to refuse to permit a showing of the movie, "Crazylegs All American," to the jury. It is clear that the showing of that picture was highly relevant to the issues in the case. It therefore was admissible. The trial judge, however, excluded the full showing of the movie on the ground that it would be cumulative and prejudicial. We doubt that prejudice would result from the showing of the movie, but whether or not it was excluded from evidence because it was cumulative and time consuming was within the trial court's discretion. If the movie is again offered in evidence, the trial court will again be required to address itself to that point.

We conclude that Elroy Hirsch made out a prima facie case under two separate theories: The appropriation of his name for purposes of trade, and infringement of a tradename under the common law. Nevertheless, substantial problems of proof stand in the way of the plaintiff's eventual success in this lawsuit. As a result of the motion of the defendants in the nature of a demurrer to the evidence, crucial facts which must be proved are conceded but only for the purpose of this appeal. Upon retrial under the appropriation theory, Hirsch must prove that the name, "Crazylegs," identifies him and that he has suffered damages based either on his loss or Johnson's unjust enrichment. Under the common law tradename-infringement theory, he must prove that "Crazylegs" designates his vocation or occupation and that there is a likelihood of confusion tending to make the public believe that he sponsored the Johnson product. These are questions which must be determined by the jury. Because the plaintiff's complaint was dismissed prior to a jury determination of the factual issues, the cause must be remanded for a new trial.

Judgment reversed and cause remanded for a new trial consistent with directions herein.

DAY, Justice (dissenting).

I dissent. Up until the enactment of sec. 895.50, Stats., (1977), this Court has consistently refused to recognize a right of action in Wisconsin based on a common law right of privacy.

In Yoeckel v. Samonig, 272 Wis. 430, 434–435, 75 N.W.2d 925 (1956), this court declined to recognize a right of privacy and cited with approval the holding of Brunson v. Ranks Army Store, 161 Neb. 519, 73 N.W.2d 803, 806 (1955). The Nebraska court said:

> "Our research develops no Nebraska case holding that this court has in any form or manner adopted the doctrine of the right of privacy, and there is no precedent in this state establishing the doctrine. Nor has the legislature of this state conferred such a right of action by statute. We submit that if such a right is deemed necessary or desirable, such right should be provided for by action of our legislature and not by judicial legislation on the part of our courts. This is especially true in view of the nature of the right under discussion, under which right not even the truth of the allegations is a defense."

To avoid the effect of *Yoeckel,* Mr. Hirsch has characterized his cause of action as one based on the tort of appropriation of a person's name for commercial purposes, rather than the right of privacy. However, the "right of publicity" is but one facet of the right of privacy doctrine; both ideas are rooted in the theory that the individual has a right to control the use of his own name. In the absence of legislation, this court has refused to recognize such a right.

Concededly, the Wisconsin cases have not squarely dealt with the tort of appropriation of an individual's name or likeness. However, language in Meier v. Meurer, 8 Wis.2d 24, 98 N.W.2d 411 (1959), suggests that this court has conceptualized the rights of privacy and publicity as twin doctrines. *Meier* involved an action for libel, in which the plaintiffs brought an action to recover for the commercial use of their name in a sale by the defendants of assets formerly owned by the plaintiffs. The plaintiffs alleged that a valuable property right consisting of the name "Meier Bakery" had been irreparably damaged. This court reversed an order overruling a demurrer, stating:

> "Plaintiffs allege that defendants had no authority to use the Meier name. Unauthorized public use of another's name does not give rise to a cause of action for libel, and in several cases this court has decided that a cause of action for invasion of a right of privacy does not exist in this state."

What was implicit in *Meier* was explicit in Carson v. National Bank Of Commerce Trust & Savings, 501 F.2d 1082 (8th Cir. 1974). In that case a well known entertainer sought damages for a travel agency's unauthorized use of his name and picture to promote a tour known as "Nebraskan's Johnny Carson Tour of Las Vegas." Applying Nebraska law, the 8th Circuit held that there was no right to control the use of one's own name and image, whether characterized as an action for "misappropriation," or invasion of privacy. Relying on the same *Brunson* case cited in *Yoeckel*, the court said:

> "Brunson, argues plaintiff here, sought damages not for his loss of the opportunity to sell his name for commercial purposes, but for the mental suffering he underwent as a result of the revelation of an embarrassing incident, whereas Carson (mindful perhaps of the *Brunson* case) has carefully refrained from mentioning 'privacy' in his complaint and has argued that he seeks damages for the misappropriation of a 'valuable property right.' Nonetheless, the Court believes that whether the right for which plaintiff seeks protection is denominated his right to privacy or his 'right to publicity,' as plaintiff has characterized his first cause of action, it stems from Court recognition that an individual has the right to control the use of his own name and image and the publication of information about himself. If that right is conceded, several distinct causes of action may arise from it, depending upon the particular conditions; if one's pursuit of his own private activities is interfered with (the tort of 'intrusion'); if intimate details of one's personal life are made public; if publicity places one in a false light in the public eye; and, finally, if commercial use is made of one's name and image without consent. All these actions stem from the initial recognition of a right to control the use of one's own name and image, which the Nebraska Supreme Court explicitly rejected in *Brunson*. Plaintiff's characterization of his action as one seeking damages for 'misappropriation' cannot serve as a means to escape the rule of the *Brunson* case." Id. at 1084–85.

To similar effect is Maritote v. Desilu Productions, Inc., 230 F. Supp. 721 (W.D.Ill.1964), aff'd 345 F.2d 418 (7th Cir. 1965). In

Maritote, the administratrix of the estate of Al Capone sued Desilu Productions, Columbia Broadcasting System, Inc., and Westinghouse Electric Corporation, asserting that the defendants had been unjustly enriched through an alleged appropriation of the name, likeness and personality of Al Capone for use in television broadcasts of "The Untouchables."

Under Illinois law, the right of privacy did not survive the death of the individual, and as a result, the lawsuit was characterized as an appropriation of the deceased's property right in his name. The court commented, however:

> "Plaintiffs have attempted to evade the personal nature of an invasion of privacy suit, by attaching to it a new label, that of appropriation of a property right. Yet, despite the label, such an action remains one for invasion of privacy, under Illinois law, and must be subject to the restrictions imposed thereon.
>
> ". . .
>
> "The right sought to be asserted here falls squarely within the right of privacy concepts." Id. at 723.

In view of the fact that the legislature has now acted in this area, under principles of *stare decisis,* I would hold that Mr. Hirsch is foreclosed by Yoeckel v. Samonig from maintaining this action.

I would also hold that two simple words like "crazy" and "legs" whether spelled separately or as one word cannot as a matter of law under the facts here be regarded as the commercial "trade name" property of Mr. Hirsch. The record shows that other athletes have been so designated. If the name Elroy or Hirsch had been used with crazy and legs, a different case would present itself because it would show that Elroy Hirsch was the person whose name was being used for commercial purposes. A gel for the shaving of women's legs has no association with football or any of the other athletic activities of Mr. Hirsch. Here again a closer case might be presented if the subject of advertising was football helmets or football shoes but hardly women's leg shaving cream.

One can recall "Crazy" Guggenheim on television a few years ago or the famous "Legs" Diamond. It would be reaching beyond reason to say either had a monopoly on the words "crazy" or "legs." This writer finds it hard to see how combining the two words in this context gives Mr. Hirsch a proprietary interest in the words.

Counsel for Mr. Hirsch referred to an athlete called "Bulldog" Turner, but one could hardly claim the word "Bulldog" has become one person's property. There have been athletes known as "the horse," others known as "dizzy" and "daffy" but any of those names attached to a shaving cream for women's legs should not give rise to a cause of action for commercial exploitation of one's "name."

I would affirm. I am authorized to state that Mr. Justice Connor T. Hansen joins in this dissent.

NOTES

1. As used by courts today, the term "right of publicity" represents a result, not a doctrine or theory. The result, that celebrities can control the use of their name, likeness and reputation, rests on any one of three different theories—privacy, unfair competition and misappropriation—and there is little evidence today that the right of publicity has a life apart from these traditional common law doctrines. Haelan Laboratories, Inc. v. Topps Chewing Gum, Inc., 202 F.2d 866 (2d Cir. 1953), cert. denied 346 U.S. 816, 74 S.Ct. 26, 98 L. Ed. 343, said by some to have created an independent right of publicity, in fact made only a cursory effort to define the right and relied almost exclusively for precedent on New York misappropriation cases.

Publicity's underlying doctrines vary from state to state. For example, common law privacy doctrine proscribes a broader range of appropriative conduct than do privacy statutes such as New York Civil Rights Law §§ 50–51. The New York statute and its counterparts in other states require a use for "advertising purposes or for the purposes of trade," and cover only a "name, portrait or picture." By contrast, common law privacy doctrine is not limited to commercial appropriations and may embrace style of performance or other elements of an individual's reputation. See, for example, Lombardo v. Doyle, Dane & Bernbach, Inc., 58 A.D.2d 620, 396 N.Y.S.2d 661 (2d Dept.1977); Restatement, Second, Torts § 652C (1977).

Unfair competition as a vehicle for the right of publicity also varies from state to state. The Wisconsin Supreme Court's willingness to recognize Hirsch's unfair competition claim suggests that it holds a relatively generous view of rights against dilution. Jurisdictions less expansively inclined might have withheld relief on the ground that shaving products and athletic services are too far removed to have competitive consequence. See page 101, above. Misappropriation, probably the most commodious doctrine for securing publicity values, is less generally available than either privacy or unfair competition.

Gordon, Right of Property in Name, Likeness, Personality and History, 55 Nw.L.Rev. 553 (1960), is an early and instructive essay. See also, Felcher & Rubin, Privacy, Publicity, and the Portrayal of Real People by the Media, 88 Yale L.J. 1577 (1979); Pilpel, The Right of Publicity, 27 Bull. Copyright Soc'y 249 (1980); Rader, The "Right of Publicity": A New Dimension, 61 J.P.O.S. 228 (1979); Treece, Commercial Exploitation of Names, Likenesses and Personal Histories, 51 Tex.L.Rev. 637 (1973).

2. Courts divide on whether the right of publicity survives the celebrity's death. Some courts, following publicity's connections to privacy, hold that the right does not survive. See, for example, Lugosi v. Universal Pictures, 25 Cal.3d 813, 160 Cal.Rptr. 323, 603 P.2d 425 (1979). Other courts have detached publicity from its privacy

moorings to hold that it does survive. In Factors Etc., Inc. v. Pro
Arts, Inc., 579 F.2d 215, 205 U.S.P.Q. 751 (1978), cert. denied 440 U.
S. 908, 99 S.Ct. 1215, 59 L.Ed.2d 455, the Second Circuit Court of Ap-
peals invoked *Haelan Laboratories* to hold that the right of publicity
exists independent of New York's statutory right of privacy and that
Elvis Presley's successors were entitled to an injunction against de-
fendant's sale of posters of the late singer. See also Price v. Hal
Roach Studios, Inc., 400 F.Supp. 836, 844 (S.D.N.Y.1975).

An unfair competition rationale also seems to be at work in some
of these decisions. For example, the *Lugosi* court noted that there
was no evidence that the actor, Bela Lugosi, had in his lifetime used
his name or likeness in connection with any business, product or service. The court suggested that if he had thus commercially exploited
his name and likeness he might have created "a general acceptance
and good will for such business, product or service among the public,
the effect of which would have been to impress such business, product
or service with a secondary meaning, protectable under the law of unfair competition." 25 Cal.3d 813, 818, 160 Cal.Rptr. 323, 326. And
in Factors v. Pro Arts the court observed in a footnote that because
"the right was exploited during Presley's life, we need not, and therefore do not, decide whether the right would survive the death of the
celebrity if not exploited during the celebrity's life." 579 F.2d 215,
222 n. 11.

Courts generally give no reason for their insistence that, for the
right of publicity to survive, the celebrity must have exploited it during his life. Unfair competition provides the most fitting rationale:
the celebrity's exploitation of his name and likeness in connection
with goods and services should be treated no differently than the use
by ordinary folks of their names in connection with their goods and
services. If secondary meaning attaches, and if the business is transferred with the name, the exclusive right to use the name with the
business can last in perpetuity.

This rationale suggests that the privacy and unfair competition
sources of the right of publicity may be consecutive rather than alternative. Privacy doctrine, which is analogous to the common law right
of first publication, pages 195 to 241 above, gives the celebrity exclusive control over the timing of the first commercial use of his name or
likeness. Once having made that use, the law of unfair competition
comes into play, giving the celebrity protection commensurate with
the amount of secondary meaning that accrues.

This analysis only clarifies, but does not resolve, the issue whether the right of publicity should survive the celebrity. At common
law, the right of first publication survives the author. Is there any
reason why it should not do so here? At common law, a trade name,
unless used in business, is deemed abandoned. Is there any reason
why death should be identified as the point of abandonment? See generally, Felcher & Rubin, The Descendibility of the Right of Publicity:
Is There Commercial Life after Death? 89 Yale L.J. 1125 (1980).

3.   At least one court has looked to first principles rather than common law analogies for answers.   In Memphis Development Foundation v. Factors Etc., Inc., 616 F.2d 956, 205 U.S.P.Q. 784 (6th Cir. 1980), involving the right to reproduce Elvis Presley memorabilia, the court held that under Tennessee law the right to publicity does not survive the celebrity's death and that "after death the opportunity for gain shifts to the public domain, where it is equally open to all."   616 F.2d 956, 957.

The court began its analysis with the proposition that "although fame and stardom may be ends in themselves, they are normally by-products of one's activities and personal attributes, as well as luck and promotion."   From this it concluded that there "is no indication that changing the traditional common law rule against allowing heirs the exclusive control of the commercial use of their ancestor's name will increase the efficiency or productivity of our economic system. It does not seem reasonable to expect that such a change would enlarge the stock or quality of the goods, services, artistic creativity, information, invention or entertainment available."   Against these dubious benefits, the court saw reason for "serious reservations about making fame the permanent right of a few individuals to the exclusion of the general public"—"the intangible and shifting nature of fame and celebrity status, the presence of widespread public and press participation in its creation, the unusual psychic rewards and income that often flow from it during life and the fact that it may be created by bad as well as good conduct."   616 F.2d 956, 958, 959.

In the court's view, another drawback to allowing the right of publicity to pass on the celebrity's death is the practical problem of determining how long the right should last.   In Lugosi v. Universal Pictures, Justice Mosk, concurring, asked, "may the descendants of George Washington sue the Secretary of the Treasury for placing his likeness on the dollar bill?   May the descendants of Abraham Lincoln obtain damages for the commercial exploitation of his name and likeness by the Lincoln National Life Insurance Company or the Lincoln division of the Ford Motor Company?"   25 Cal.3d 813, 827, 160 Cal. Rptr. 323, 331.   Chief Justice Bird, dissenting in *Lugosi*, answered that, "since the right of publicity recognizes an interest in intangible property similar in many respects to creations protected by copyright law, that body of law is instructive."   The copyright term measured by the author's life plus fifty years "represents a reasonable evaluation of the period necessary to effect the policies underlying the right of publicity."   25 Cal.3d 813, 847, 160 Cal.Rptr. 323, 344.

Why not have the right of publicity last as long as its associated secondary meaning—the measure employed in unfair competition law?

4.   The right to publicity, where recognized, will protect a celebrity's name and likeness.   But what of his "creative talent, voice, vocal sounds and vocal comic delivery?"   In Lahr v. Adell Chem. Co., Inc., 300 F.2d 256, 132 U.S.P.Q. 662 (1st Cir. 1962), plaintiff Bert

Lahr complained that "defendant Adell Chemical Company, in advertising its product 'Lestoil' on television, used as a commercial a cartoon film of a duck and, without the plaintiff's consent 'as the voice of the aforesaid duck, an actor who specialized in imitating the vocal sounds of the plaintiff.' " Reading New York's privacy statute literally, to cover only a "name, portrait or picture," the court concluded that plaintiff might instead recover on his unfair competition count. "Plaintiff's complaint is that defendant is 'stealing his thunder' in the direct sense; that defendant's commercial had greater value because his audience believed it was listening to him . . . . It could well be found that defendant's conduct saturated plaintiff's audience to the point of curtailing his market." 300 F.2d 256, 259.

It is clear from the decisions that, to be protected, the claimant's voice and style of delivery must be at least as distinctive as his name or likeness. In Sinatra v. Goodyear Tire and Rubber Co., 435 F.2d 711, 168 U.S.P.Q. 12 (9th Cir. 1970), cert. denied 402 U.S. 906, 91 S. Ct. 1376, 28 L.Ed.2d 646, 169 U.S.P.Q. 321, Nancy Sinatra sought to enjoin defendant's broadcast of another performer's recording, in a closely similar style, of a song that Sinatra had popularized, "These Boots are Made for Walkin'." The Ninth Circuit Court of Appeals affirmed the dismissal of the complaint. Distinguishing *Lahr* as involving a claim of " 'secondary meaning' in pure sound," the court noted that Sinatra's complaint was "that the sound in connection with the music, lyrics and arrangement, which made her the subject of popular identification, ought to be protected. . . . One wonders whether her voice, and theatrical style, would have been identifiable if another song had been presented, and not 'her song,' which unfortunately for her was owned by others and licensed to the defendants." 435 F.2d 711, 716. See also, Booth v. Colgate-Palmolive Co., 362 F.Supp. 343, 179 U.S.P.Q. 819 (S.D.N.Y.1973).

The emphasis on distinctiveness that separates *Lahr* from *Sinatra* stems in part from the judicial concern that because many individuals have similar voices—and faces and names, for that matter—to protect other than the most unique attributes will expose advertisers to a torrent of claims. Does unfair competition's doctrine of secondary meaning offer a more fair, though possibly less efficient, vehicle for limiting claims? Under this approach, the concern expressed in Justice Day's *Hirsch* dissent might have been met on the remand if plaintiff were allowed to recover for the use of his nickname in those places where the term "Crazylegs" identified him, but not in those places where it identified someone else, or no one at all.

5. Will the right of publicity extend to an accessory associated with the celebrity, such as a professional race driver's distinctively colored racing car? See Motschenbacher v. R. J. Reynolds Tobacco Co., 498 F.2d 821, 827 (9th Cir. 1974) ("Having viewed a film of the [defendant's] commercial, we agree with the district court that the 'likeness' of plaintiff is itself unrecognizable; however, the court's further conclusion of law to the effect that the driver is not identifiable as plaintiff, is erroneous in that it wholly fails to attribute proper

significance to the distinctive decorations appearing on the car. As pointed out earlier, these markings were not only peculiar to the plaintiff's cars, but they caused some persons to think the car in question was plaintiff's and to infer that the person driving the car was the plaintiff.").

B. LIMITS OF PROTECTION

ZACCHINI v. SCRIPPS–HOWARD BROADCASTING CO.

Supreme Court of the United States, 1977.
433 U.S. 562, 97 S.Ct. 2849, 53 L.Ed.2d 965.

Mr. Justice WHITE delivered the opinion of the Court.

Petitioner, Hugo Zacchini, is an entertainer. He performs a "human cannonball" act in which he is shot from a cannon into a net some 200 feet away. Each performance occupies some 15 seconds. In August and September 1972, petitioner was engaged to perform his act on a regular basis at the Geauga County Fair in Burton, Ohio. He performed in a fenced area, surrounded by grandstands, at the fair grounds. Members of the public attending the fair were not charged a separate admission fee to observe his act.

On August 30, a freelance reporter for Scripps-Howard Broadcasting Co., the operator of a television broadcasting station and respondent in this case, attended the fair. He carried a small movie camera. Petitioner noticed the reporter and asked him not to film the performance. The reporter did not do so on that day; but on the instructions of the producer of respondent's daily newscast, he returned the following day and videotaped the entire act. This film clip, approximately 15 seconds in length, was shown on the 11 o'clock news program that night, together with favorable commentary.

Petitioner then brought this action for damages, alleging that he is "engaged in the entertainment business," that the act he performs is one "invented by his father and . . . performed only by his family for the last fifty years," that respondent "showed and commercialized the film of his act without his consent," and that such conduct was an "unlawful appropriation of plaintiff's professional property." Respondent answered and moved for summary judgment, which was granted by the trial court.

The Court of Appeals of Ohio reversed. The majority held that petitioner's complaint stated a cause of action for conversion and for infringement of a common-law copyright, and one judge concurred in the judgment on the ground that the complaint stated a cause of action for appropriation of petitioner's "right of publicity" in the film of his act. All three judges agreed that the First Amendment did not privilege the press to show the entire performance on a news program without compensating petitioner for any financial injury he could prove at trial.

Like the concurring judge in the Court of Appeals, the Supreme Court of Ohio rested petitioner's cause of action under state law on his "right to publicity value of his performance." 47 Ohio St.2d 224, 351 N.E.2d 454, 455 (1976). The opinion syllabus, to which we are to look for the rule of law used to decide the case, declared first that one may not use for his own benefit the name or likeness of another, whether or not the use or benefit is a commercial one, and second that respondent would be liable for the appropriation, over petitioner's objection and in the absence of license or privilege, of petitioner's right to the publicity value of his performance. The court nevertheless gave judgment for respondent because, in the words of the syllabus:

"A TV station has a privilege to report in its newscasts matters of legitimate public interest which would otherwise be protected by an individual's right of publicity, unless the actual intent of the TV station was to appropriate the benefit of the publicity for some non-privileged private use, or unless the actual intent was to injure the individual." Ibid.

We granted certiorari, to consider an issue unresolved by this Court: whether the First and Fourteenth Amendments immunized respondent from damages for its alleged infringement of petitioner's state-law "right of publicity." Insofar as the Ohio Supreme Court held that the First and Fourteenth Amendments of the United States Constitution required judgment for respondent, we reverse the judgment of that court.

I

If the judgment below rested on an independent and adequate state ground, the writ of certiorari should be dismissed as improvidently granted, Wilson v. Loew's Inc., 355 U.S. 597, 78 S.Ct. 526, 2 L. Ed.2d 519 (1958), for "[o]ur only power over state judgments is to correct them to the extent that they incorrectly adjudge federal rights. And our power is to correct wrong judgments, not to revise opinions. We are not permitted to render an advisory opinion, and if the same judgment would be rendered by the state court after we corrected its views of federal laws, our review could amount to nothing more than an advisory opinion." Herb v. Pitcairn, 324 U.S. 117, 125–126, 65 S.Ct. 459, 463, 89 L.Ed. 789 (1945). We are confident, however, that the judgment below did not rest on an adequate and independent state ground and that we have jurisdiction to decide the federal issue presented in this case.

There is no doubt that petitioner's complaint was grounded in state law and that the right of publicity which petitioner was held to possess was a right arising under Ohio law. It is also clear that respondent's claim of constitutional privilege was sustained. The source of this privilege was not identified in the syllabus. It is clear enough from the opinion of the Ohio Supreme Court, which we are permitted to consult for understanding of the syllabus, that in adjudicating the crucial question of whether respondent had a privilege to film and televise petitioner's performance, the court placed principal reliance on Time, Inc. v. Hill, 385 U.S. 374, 87 S.Ct. 534, 17 L.Ed.2d 456 (1967), a case involving First Amendment limitations on state tort actions. It construed the principle of that case, along with that of New York Times Co. v. Sullivan, 376 U.S. 254, 84 S.Ct. 710, 11 L. Ed.2d 686 (1964), to be that "the press has a privilege to report matters of legitimate public interest even though such reports might intrude on matters otherwise private," and concluded, therefore, that the press is also "privileged when an individual seeks to publicly exploit his talents while keeping the benefits private." 47 Ohio St.2d, at 234, 351 N.E.2d, at 461. The privilege thus exists in cases "where appropriation of a right of publicity is claimed." The court's opinion also referred to Draft 21 of the relevant portion of Restatement (Second) of Torts (1975), which was understood to make room for reasonable press appropriations by limiting the reach of the right of privacy rather than by creating a privileged invasion. The court preferred the notion of privilege over the Restatement's formulation, however, reasoning that "since the gravamen of the issue in this case is not whether the degree of intrusion is reasonable, but whether *First Amendment principles* require that the right of privacy give way to the public right to be informed of matters of public interest and concern, the concept of privilege seems the more useful and appropriate one." 47 Ohio St.2d, at 234 n. 5, 351 N.E.2d, at 461 n. 5. (Emphasis added.)   .   .   .

II

The Ohio Supreme Court held that respondent is constitutionally privileged to include in its newscasts matters of public interest that would otherwise be protected by the right of publicity, absent an intent to injure or to appropriate for some nonprivileged purpose. If under this standard respondent had merely reported that petitioner was performing at the fair and described or commented on his act, with or without showing his picture on television, we would have a very different case. But petitioner is not contending that his appearance at the fair and his performance could not be reported by the press as newsworthy items. His complaint is that respondent filmed his entire act and displayed that film on television for the public to see and enjoy. This, he claimed, was an appropriation of his professional property. The Ohio Supreme Court agreed that petitioner had "a right of publicity" that gave him "personal control over commercial display and exploitation of his personality and the exercise of his talents." [4] This right of "exclusive control over the publicity given to

---

4. The court relied on Housh v. Peth, 165 Ohio St. 35, 133 N.E.2d 340, 341 (1956), the syllabus of which held: "An actionable invasion of the right of privacy is the unwarranted appropriation or exploitation of one's personality, the publicizing of one's private affairs with which the public has no legitimate concern, or the wrongful intrusion into one's private activities in such a manner as to outrage or cause mental suffering, shame or humiliation to a person of ordinary sensibilities."

his performances" was said to be such a "valuable part of the benefit which may be attained by his talents and efforts" that it was entitled to legal protection. It was also observed, or at least expressly assumed, that petitioner had not abandoned his rights by performing under the circumstances present at the Geauga County Fair Grounds.

The Ohio Supreme Court nevertheless held that the challenged invasion was privileged, saying that the press "must be accorded broad latitude in its choice of how much it presents of each story or incident, and of the emphasis to be given to such presentation. No fixed standard which would bar the press from reporting or depicting either an entire occurrence or an entire discrete part of a public performance can be formulated which would not unduly restrict the 'breathing room' in reporting which freedom of the press requires." 47 Ohio St.2d, at 235, 351 N.E.2d, at 461. Under this view, respondent was thus constitutionally free to film and display petitioner's entire act.

The Ohio Supreme Court relied heavily on Time, Inc. v. Hill, 385 U.S. 374, 87 S.Ct. 534, 17 L.Ed.2d 456 (1967), but that case does not mandate a media privilege to televise a performer's entire act without his consent. Involved in Time, Inc. v. Hill was a claim under the New York "Right to Privacy" statute [6] that Life Magazine, in the course of reviewing a new play, had connected the play with a long-past incident involving petitioner and his family and had falsely described their experience and conduct at that time. The complaint sought damages for humiliation and suffering flowing from these nondefamatory falsehoods that allegedly invaded Hill's privacy. The Court held, however, that the opening of a new play linked to an actual incident was a matter of public interest and that Hill could not recover without showing that the Life report was knowingly false or was published with reckless disregard for the truth—the same rigorous standard that had been applied in New York Times Co. v. Sullivan, 376 U.S. 254, 84 S.Ct. 710, 11 L.Ed.2d 686 (1964).

Time, Inc. v. Hill, which was hotly contested and decided by a divided Court, involved an entirely different tort from the "right of publicity" recognized by the Ohio Supreme Court. As the opinion reveals in Time, Inc. v. Hill, the Court was steeped in the literature of privacy law and was aware of the developing distinctions and nuances in this branch of the law. The Court, for example, cited W. Prosser,

The court also indicated that the applicable principles of Ohio law were those set out in Restatement (Second) § 652C of Torts (Tent. Draft No. 13, 1967), and the comments thereto, portions of which were stated in the footnotes of the opinion. Also, referring to the right as the "right of publicity," the court quoted approvingly from Haelan Laboratories, Inc. v. Topps Chewing Gum, Inc., 202 F.2d 866, 868 (CA2 1953).

6. Section 51 of the New York Civil Rights Law (McKinney 1976) provides an action for injunction and damages for invasion of the "right of privacy" granted by § 50:

"A person, firm or corporation that uses for advertising purposes, or for the purposes of trade, the name, portrait or picture of any living person without having first obtained such person, or if a minor of his or her parent or guardian, is guilty of a misdemeanor."

Law of Torts 831–832 (3d ed. 1964), and the same author's well-known article, Privacy, 48 Calif.L.Rev. 383 (1960), both of which divided privacy into four distinct branches. The Court was aware that it was adjudicating a "false light" privacy case involving a matter of public interest, not a case involving "intrusion," 385 U.S., at 384–385, n. 9, 87 S.Ct., at 539, "appropriation" of a name or likeness for the purposes of trade, id., at 381, 87 S.Ct., at 538, or "private details" about a non-newsworthy person or event, id., at 383 n. 7, 87 S.Ct. at 539. It is also abundantly clear that Time, Inc. v. Hill did not involve a performer, a person with a name having commercial value, or any claim to a "right of publicity." This discrete kind of "appropriation" case was plainly identified in the literature cited by the Court and had been adjudicated in the reported cases.

The differences between these two torts are important. First, the State's interests in providing a cause of action in each instance are different. "The interest protected" in permitting recovery for placing the plaintiff in a false light "is clearly that of reputation, with the same overtones of mental distress as in defamation." Prosser, supra, 48 Calif.L.Rev., at 400. By contrast, the State's interest in permitting a "right of publicity" is in protecting the proprietary interest of the individual in his act in part to encourage such entertainment. As we later note, the State's interest is closely analogous to the goals of patent and copyright law, focusing on the right of the individual to reap the reward of his endeavors and having little to do with protecting feelings or reputation. Second, the two torts differ in the degree to which they intrude on dissemination of information to the public. In "false light" cases the only way to protect the interests involved is to attempt to minimize publication of the damaging matter, while in "right of publicity" cases the only question is who gets to do the publishing. An entertainer such as petitioner usually has no objection to the widespread publication of his act as long as he gets the commercial benefit of such publication. Indeed, in the present case petitioner did not seek to enjoin the broadcast of his act; he simply sought compensation for the broadcast in the form of damages.

Nor does it appear that our later cases, such as Rosenbloom v. Metromedia, Inc., 403 U.S. 29, 91 S.Ct. 1811, 29 L.Ed.2d 296 (1971); Gertz v. Robert Welch, Inc., 418 U.S. 323, 94 S.Ct. 2997, 41 L.Ed.2d 789 (1974); and Time, Inc. v. Firestone, 424 U.S. 448, 96 S.Ct. 958, 47 L.Ed.2d 154 (1976), require or furnish substantial support for the Ohio court's privilege ruling. These cases, like *New York Times*, emphasize the protection extended to the press by the First Amendment in defamation cases, particularly when suit is brought by a public official or a public figure. None of them involve an alleged appropriation by the press of a right of publicity existing under state law.

Moreover, Time, Inc. v. Hill, *New York Times, Metromedia, Gertz,* and *Firestone* all involved the reporting of events; in none of them was there an attempt to broadcast or publish an entire act for which the performer ordinarily gets paid. It is evident, and there is no claim here to the contrary, that petitioner's state-law right of publicity would not serve to prevent respondent from reporting the newsworthy facts about petitioner's act. Wherever the line in particular situations is to be drawn between media reports that are protected and those that are not, we are quite sure that the First and Fourteenth Amendments do not immunize the media when they broadcast a performer's entire act without his consent. The Constitution no more prevents a State from requiring respondent to compensate petitioner for broadcasting his act on television than it would privilege respondent to film and broadcast a copyrighted dramatic work without liability to the copyright owner, or to film and broadcast a prize fight, or a baseball game, where the promoters or the participants had other plans for publicizing the event. There are ample reasons for reaching this conclusion.

The broadcast of a film of petitioner's entire act poses a substantial threat to the economic value of that performance. As the Ohio court recognized, this act is the product of petitioner's own talents and energy, the end result of much time, effort, and expense. Much of its economic value lies in the "right of exclusive control over the publicity given to his performance"; if the public can see the act free on television, it will be less willing to pay to see it at the fair. The effect of a public broadcast of the performance is similar to preventing petitioner from charging an admission fee. "The rationale for [protecting the right of publicity] is the straightforward one of preventing unjust enrichment by the theft of good will. No social purpose is served by having the defendant get free some aspect of the plaintiff that would have market value and for which he would normally pay." Kalven, Privacy in Tort Law—Were Warren and Brandeis Wrong?, 31 Law & Contemp.Prob. 326, 331 (1966). Moreover, the broadcast of petitioner's entire performance, unlike the unauthorized use of another's name for purposes of trade or the incidental use of a name or picture by the press, goes to the heart of petitioner's ability to earn a living as an entertainer. Thus, in this case, Ohio has recognized what may be the strongest case for a "right of publicity"—involving, not the appropriation of an entertainer's reputation to enhance the attractiveness of a commercial product, but the appropriation of the very activity by which the entertainer acquired his reputation in the first place.

Of course, Ohio's decision to protect petitioner's right of publicity here rests on more than a desire to compensate the performer for the time and effort invested in his act; the protection provides an economic incentive for him to make the investment required to produce a performance of interest to the public. This same consideration underlies the patent and copyright laws long enforced by this Court. As the Court stated in Mazer v. Stein, 347 U.S. 201, 219, 74 S.Ct. 460, 471, 98 L.Ed. 630 (1954):

> "The economic philosophy behind the clause empowering Congress to grant patents and copyrights is the conviction that encouragement of individual effort by personal gain is the best

way to advance public welfare through the talents of authors and inventors in 'Science and useful Arts.' Sacrificial days devoted to such creative activities deserve rewards commensurate with the services rendered."

These laws perhaps regard the "reward to the owner [as] a secondary consideration," United States v. Paramount Pictures, 334 U.S. 131, 158, 68 S.Ct. 915, 929, 92 L.Ed. 1260 (1948), but they were "intended definitely to grant valuable, enforceable rights" in order to afford greater encouragement to the production of works of benefit to the public. Washingtonian Publishing Co. v. Pearson, 306 U.S. 30, 36, 59 S.Ct. 397, 400, 83 L.Ed. 470 (1939). The Constitution does not prevent Ohio from making a similar choice here in deciding to protect the entertainer's incentive in order to encourage the production of this type of work. Cf. Goldstein v. California, 412 U.S. 546, 93 S. Ct. 2303, 37 L.Ed.2d 163 (1973); Kewanee Oil Co. v. Bicron Corp., 416 U.S. 470, 94 S.Ct. 1879, 40 L.Ed.2d 315 (1974).

There is no doubt that entertainment, as well as news, enjoys First Amendment protection. It is also true that entertainment itself can be important news. But it is important to note that neither the public nor respondent will be deprived of the benefit of petitioner's performance as long as his commercial stake in his act is appropriately recognized. Petitioner does not seek to enjoin the broadcast of his performance; he simply wants to be paid for it. Nor do we think that a state-law damages remedy against respondent would represent a species of liability without fault contrary to the letter or spirit of Gertz v. Robert Welch, Inc., 418 U.S. 323, 94 S.Ct. 2997, 41 L.Ed.2d 789 (1974). Respondent knew that petitioner objected to televising his act but nevertheless displayed the entire film.

We conclude that although the State of Ohio may as a matter of its own law privilege the press in the circumstances of this case, the First and Fourteenth Amendments do not require it to do so.

Reversed.

Mr. Justice POWELL, with whom Mr. Justice BRENNAN and Mr. Justice MARSHALL join, dissenting.

Disclaiming any attempt to do more than decide the narrow case before us, the Court reverses the decision of the Supreme Court of Ohio based on repeated incantation of a single formula: "a performer's entire act." The holding today is summed up in one sentence:

"Wherever the line in particular situations is to be drawn between media reports that are protected and those that are not, we are quite sure that the First and Fourteenth Amendments do not immunize the media when they broadcast a performer's entire act without his consent."

I doubt that this formula provides a standard clear enough even for resolution of this case. In any event, I am not persuaded that the Court's opinion is appropriately sensitive to the First Amendment values at stake, and I therefore dissent.

Although the Court would draw no distinction, I do not view respondent's action as comparable to unauthorized commercial broadcasts of sporting events, theatrical performances, and the like where the broadcaster keeps the profits. There is no suggestion here that respondent made any such use of the film. Instead, it simply reported on what petitioner concedes to be a newsworthy event, in a way hardly surprising for a television station—by means of film coverage. The report was part of an ordinary daily news program, consuming a total of 15 seconds. It is a routine example of the press' fulfilling the informing function so vital to our system.

The Court's holding that the station's ordinary news report may give rise to substantial liability has disturbing implications, for the decision could lead to a degree of media self-censorship. Hereafter, whenever a television news editor is unsure whether certain film footage received from a camera crew might be held to portray an "entire act," he may decline coverage—even of clearly newsworthy events—or confine the broadcast to watered-down verbal reporting, perhaps with an occasional still picture. The public is then the loser. This is hardly the kind of news reportage that the First Amendment is meant to foster.

In my view the First Amendment commands a different analytical starting point from the one selected by the Court. Rather than begin with a quantitative analysis of the performer's behavior—is this or is this not his entire act?—we should direct initial attention to the actions of the news media: what use did the station make of the film footage? When a film is used, as here, for a routine portion of a regular news program, I would hold that the First Amendment protects the station from a "right of publicity" or "appropriation" suit, absent a strong showing by the plaintiff that the news broadcast was a subterfuge or cover for private or commercial exploitation.

I emphasize that this is a "reappropriation" suit, rather than one of the other varieties of "right of privacy" tort suits identified by Dean Prosser in his classic article. Prosser, Privacy, 48 Calif.L.Rev. 383 (1960). In those other causes of action the competing interests are considerably different. The plaintiff generally seeks to avoid any sort of public exposure, and the existence of constitutional privilege is therefore less likely to turn on whether the publication occurred in a news broadcast or in some other fashion. In a suit like the one before us, however, the plaintiff does not complain about the fact of exposure to the public, but rather about its timing or manner. He welcomes some publicity, but seeks to retain control over means and manner as a way to maximize for himself the monetary benefits that flow from such publication. But having made the matter public—having chosen, in essence, to make it newsworthy—he cannot, consistent with the First Amendment, complain of routine news reportage.

Since the film clip here was undeniably treated as news and since there is no claim that the use was subterfuge, respondent's actions were constitutionally privileged. I would affirm.

Mr. Justice STEVENS, dissenting.

The Ohio Supreme Court held that respondent's telecast of the "human cannonball" was a privileged invasion of petitioner's common-law "right of publicity" because respondent's actual intent was neither (a) to appropriate the benefit of the publicity for a private use, nor (b) to injure petitioner.

As I read the state court's explanation of the limits on the concept of privilege, they define the substantive reach of a common-law tort rather than anything I recognize as a limit on a federal constitutional right. The decision was unquestionably influenced by the Ohio court's proper sensitivity to First Amendment principles, and to this Court's cases construing the First Amendment; indeed, I must confess that the opinion can be read as resting entirely on federal constitutional grounds. Nevertheless, the basis of the state court's action is sufficiently doubtful that I would remand the case to that court for clarification of its holding before deciding the federal constitutional issue.

NOTES

1. Is the right of publicity subject to preemption under federal law? *Zacchini* characterized the state interest involved as "closely analogous to the goals of patent and copyright law, focusing on the right of the individual to reap the reward of his endeavors." 433 U. S. 562, 573, 97 S.Ct. 2849, 2856. Does this mean that the state doctrine should be preempted under the principles announced in *Sears* and *Compco*, pages 130, 133? Or is it likely that the Court did not raise the preemption issue because, after reflecting on *Goldstein* and *Kewanee*, pages 178, 228, it determined that the right of publicity should not be preempted?

2. What impact, if any, does section 301 of the Copyright Act have on the right of publicity? See Factors, Etc., Inc. v. Pro Arts, Inc., 496 F.Supp. 1090 (S.D.N.Y.1980). Did *Zacchini* involve a right "equivalent" to copyright within the terms of the Copyright Act? Was the protected performance the "subject matter" of copyright? The intermediate state court in *Zacchini* had rested its decision for plaintiff on a common law copyright theory. 47 Ohio St.2d 224, 351 N.E.2d 454, 193 U.S.P.Q. 734 (1976). Was Zacchini's performance the kind of subject matter that was protectable under common law copyright before January 1, 1978, the effective date of the present Copyright Act? Did the act of performance divestitively publish the subject matter? Is Zacchini's performance the kind of subject matter that continues to be protectable under common law copyright after January 1, 1978? Under the facts of the case, was the work ever "fixed" with Zacchini's authority? See page 213, above.

3. Because it involved a discrete performance rather than specific attributes of personality and reputation, *Zacchini* was not the garden variety publicity case. How will standard publicity decisions fare under *Sears, Compco* and section 301 of the Copyright Act?

Should the answer differ depending on the common law source to which the right is connected—privacy, unfair competition, or misappropriation?

4. *Zacchini* is explicated in Note, Copyright Infringement and the First Amendment, 79 Colum.L.Rev. 320 (1979); Note, State 'Copyright' Protection for Performers: The First Amendment Question, 1978 Duke L.J. 1198; and Note, Human Cannonballs and the First Amendment: Zacchini v. Scripps Howard Broadcasting Co., 30 Stan. L.Rev. 1185 (1978).

Part Three

FEDERAL LAW OF INTELLECTUAL PROPERTY

NOTE: JURISDICTIONAL COORDINATION OF STATE AND
FEDERAL CLAIMS

See Statute Supplement 28 U.S.C.A. § 1338.

The general aim of 28 U.S.C.A. § 1338(a) is to align the jurisdictional divisions between state and federal courts with the existing divisions between state and federal substantive law. Patent and copyright cases stem exclusively from federal statutes, and section 1338(a) lodges their exclusive jurisdiction in federal courts. Shared federal and state jurisdiction over trademark cases reflects the mixed federal and state content of these controversies. It is on the finer questions that the subsection falters. Sharp distinctions, often illusory in the substantive law, have been no more successfully sustained by the jurisdictional statute.

From the start, section 1338 could not withstand pressures for the assertion of federal nondiversity jurisdiction over causes that, though resting primarily on state law, touched some federal interest. Courts made inroads into section 1338's design well before the statute was overhauled by the addition of subsection (b) providing pendent jurisdiction. Administration of section 1338(b)'s exception has proved to be no less problematic than administration of section 1338(a)'s rule.

A. Section 1338(a): The Exclusive Jurisdiction
of State and Federal Courts

What makes a case a patent or copyright case, so that federal courts have exclusive jurisdiction? In a much-cited passage, Judge Friendly suggested that "an action 'arises under' the Copyright Act if and only if the complaint is for a remedy expressly granted by the Act, e. g., a suit for infringement or for the statutory royalties for record reproduction, or asserts a claim requiring construction of the Act . . . or, at the very least and perhaps more doubtfully, presents a case where a distinctive policy of the Act requires that federal principles control the disposition of the claim. The general interest that copyrights, like all other forms of property, should be enjoyed by their true owner is not enough to meet this last test." T. B. Harms Co. v. Eliscu, 339 F.2d 823, 828, 144 U.S.P.Q. 46 (2d Cir. 1964), cert. denied 381 U.S. 915, 85 S.Ct. 1534, 14 L.Ed.2d 435, 145 U.S.P.Q. 743. Do these indicia exclude any actions that should be included? Include any actions that should be excluded?

1. "The foreclosure of a mortgage is, no doubt, a civil action. Does it arise under any act of Congress 'relating to patents, copy-

rights and trade-marks' simply because . . . [17 U.S.C.A. § 28] provides that a copyright may be mortgaged?". Republic Pictures Corp. v. Security-First Nat'l Bank of Los Angeles, 197 F.2d 767, 94 U.S.P.Q. 291 (9th Cir. 1952). Finding little help in the dictionary definition of "relate" and in the legislative history of section 28, Judge Goodrich considered the question from "a wider aspect": "It is not just because a right has its origin in federal law that a federal court has jurisdiction over matters which grow from that right. A large number of land titles in this country originate with a grant from the United States of America. Yet no one would now seriously claim that federal courts had authority to hear and decide litigation involving disputes among persons claiming the land because of the original grant by the United States." 197 F.2d 767, 769.

Judge Goodrich found other "analogies pointing to a lack of jurisdiction which we think are very strong. It is to be noted that patents, copyrights and trade-marks are all mentioned in the same statute and string along together. The law is perfectly clear that matters having to do with assignment of patents and the like do not fall into the jurisdiction of federal courts because patents are granted under federal and not state law." 197 F.2d 767, 770.

2. Do cases involving allegations of coauthorship—and thus coownership—of a copyrighted work fall within federal jurisdiction? The court in Harrington v. Mure, 186 F.Supp. 655, 126 U.S.P.Q. 506 (S.D.N.Y.1960), answered no, at least where no claim of third-party infringement is made. "The sources of the obligations to assign and to account," the court reasoned, "are equitable doctrines relating to unjust enrichment and general principles of law governing the rights of co-owners, not remedial provisions of the Copyright Law." In contrast, an "equitable owner who sues for infringement sets forth facts in his complaint showing the validity of the copyright, the basis of his ownership interest, and the infringement by the defendant. Allegations as to equitable title are included to establish the plaintiff's standing as a 'copyright proprietor' to sue for infringement, but the foundation of the suit is the alleged infringement itself. . . . In other words, in order to determine the federal claim for infringement, the district court, as a preliminary matter, permits the plaintiff to establish the facts which underlie his claim of ownership. . . . Incidental power to hear and decide the title claim—a claim as to which the court lacks original jurisdiction—must, and does depend upon the specifically conferred power to adjudicate the infringement claim.

"Plaintiff has urged that to deprive him of a federal forum, the court must rely upon an untenable distinction between wrongful acts of a co-author and wrongful acts of a stranger to the creation of the copyrighted work. If a stranger exploits the composition and deprives the creator of his right to exclusive enjoyment of the fruits of his efforts, an infringement action will lie. But if a co-author, one who cannot be charged with infringement, authorizes the exploitation of the work and the exclusion of his collaborator, a technicality bars access to the federal court. The alleged technicality, however, is a direct result of the congressional plan with respect to copyright litigation. A federal court must find its jurisdiction in express provisions of federal statutes; it cannot assume constitutionally possible jurisdiction which has not been conferred by Congress." 186 F.Supp. 655, 657–658.

What if plaintiff sues for a declaration of rights in a work that he helped create, but that defendant claims is a work made "for hire" under section 201(b) of the Copyright Act? Although the action is not one for infringement, does it come within the Harms v. Eliscu indicia as "a claim requiring construction of the act" or a case where "a distinctive policy of the Act requires that federal principles control the disposition of the claim"? See Royalty Control Corp. v. Sanco, Inc., 175 U.S.P.Q. 641 (N.D.Cal.1972).

3. If, as *Harrington* asserted, a properly stated claim of third-party infringement will confer federal jurisdiction, can a claimant elect state jurisdiction by showing that the infringing third party is also a breaching licensee?

The United States Supreme Court has repeatedly endorsed the claimant's freedom to elect. Luckett v. Delpark, Inc., 270 U.S. 496, 46 S.Ct. 397, 70 L.Ed. 703 (1926), reviewed and synthesized the guidelines that govern the pleading of federal and state claims. With respect to federal claims, *Luckett* concluded that "a federal district court is held to have jurisdiction of a suit by a patentee for an injunction against infringement and for profits and damages, even though, in anticipation of a defense of a license or authority to use the patent, the complainant includes in his bill averments intended to defeat such a defense. If these averments do not defeat such defense, the patentee will lose his case on the merits, but the court's jurisdiction under the patent laws is not ousted." 270 U.S. 496, 510, 46 S.Ct. 397, 401.

As to state claims, *Luckett* ruled that "where a patentee complainant makes his suit one for recovery of royalties under a contract of license or assignment, or for damages for a breach of its covenants, or for a specific performance thereof, or asks the aid of the Court in declaring a forfeiture of the license or in restoring an unclouded title to the patent, he does not give the federal district court jurisdiction of the cause as one arising under the patent laws. Nor may he confer it in such a case by adding to his bill an averment that after the forfeiture shall be declared, or the title to the patent shall be restored, he fears the defendant will infringe and therefore asks an injunction to prevent it." 270 U.S. 496, 510–511, 46 S.Ct. 397, 402.

Consider whether it follows from *Luckett* that "a patent licensor whose licensee has broken the agreement is not without choice between a state and a federal forum. It can, for example, declare the license forfeited for breach of a condition subsequent and sue for infringement. If it is correct as to its right to declare such a forfeiture unilaterally (a question of state law) federal jurisdiction of the infringement suit exists." Milprint, Inc. v. Curwood, Inc., 562 F.2d 418, 420, 196 U.S.P.Q. 147 (7th Cir. 1977).

B.   Section 1338(b): Pendent Jurisdiction

Many of the claims that section 1338(a) splits between federal and state fora can be more conveniently disposed of in a single case in a single forum. Section 1338(b), intended to serve this convenience, imposes three jurisdictional requirements. For an attached nonfederal claim to be resolved by a federal court, (1) it must be for "unfair competition," and the federal claim to which it is attached must be both (2) "substantial" and (3) "related." Although all three terms are fuzzy, the first and second have caused the least trouble.

1.   Courts construe "unfair competition" broadly to embrace not only common law passing off and misappropriation, but also a wide variety of commercial misconduct such as appropriation of trade secrets and bad faith attempts to convince a competitor's customers that the competitor's product infringes a valid patent. See General Foods Corp. v. Struthers Scientific & Int'l Corp., 297 F.Supp. 271, 161 U.S.P.Q. 250 (D.Del.1969); Denys Fisher (Spirograph) Ltd. v. Louis Marx & Co. of West Virginia, 306 F.Supp. 956, 164 U.S.P.Q. 314 (N. D.W.Va.1969).

2.   Courts also read the term "substantial" liberally. In Walters v. Shari Music Publishing Corp., 193 F.Supp. 307, 129 U.S.P.Q. 145 (S.D.N.Y.1961), the court ruled that "it is entirely proper for a federal court to proceed with the determination of the state claim when, in the course of trial, and after the expenditure of considerable judicial effort, the supporting federal claim is found to be wanting in merit. However, there is a considerable difference between a federal claim which fails during trial and one which has been dismissed on pretrial motion. In the latter situation—the one presented in this case— there has been no substantial commitment of federal judicial resources to the state claim at the time the federal claim is rejected. Since a federal court should not be eager to offer its facilities for the trial of a case which has lost its federal character, the appropriate course, as indicated by Judge Magruder in Strachman v. Palmer, 1 Cir. 1949, 177 F.2d 427, 433, 12 A.L.R.2d 687, is to dismiss the action without prejudice." 193 F.Supp. 307, 308.

3.   The requirement that the attached federal claim be "related" is more obscure. The Reviser's Notes on section 1338(b) shed some light. "Subsection (b) is added and is intended to avoid 'piecemeal' litigation to enforce common-law and statutory copyright, patent, and trade-mark rights by specifically permitting such enforcement in a single civil action in the district court. While this is the rule under Federal decisions, this section would enact it as statutory authority. The problem is discussed at length in Hurn v. Oursler, 289 U.S. 238, 53 S.Ct. 586, 77 L.Ed. 1148 (1933), and in Musher Foundation v. Alba Trading Co., 127 F.2d 9 (2d Cir. 1942) (Majority and dissenting opinions)."

Hurn had put the proposition on a nice, conceptual basis. "The distinction to be observed is between a case where two distinct grounds in support of a single cause of action are alleged, one only of which presents a federal question, and a case where two separate and distinct causes of action are alleged, one only of which is federal in character. In the former, where the federal question averred is not plainly wanting in substance, the federal court, even though the federal ground be not established, may nevertheless retain and dispose of the case upon the non-federal *ground*; in the latter it may not do so upon the non-federal *cause of action*." 289 U.S. 238, 246, 53 S.Ct. 586, 589–590 (emphasis the Court's).

Musher read *Hurn* to hold that "a non-federal claim, over which the United States Court had no jurisdiction because of an absence of diverse citizenship, might be joined with a federal claim if the non-federal count differed from the federal count only because it asserted a different ground for recovery upon substantially the same state of facts," and ruled that the two claims before the court—one for patent infringement, the other for passing off—were insufficiently related to warrant the exercise of federal jurisdiction over the second. 127 F. 2d 9, 10. To Judge Clark, dissenting, it seemed clear that "the rule is wholly illusory unless we grant a reasonable and practical content to the yardstick and require for our unitary cause only a substantial amount of overlapping testimony, rather than complete identity of the facts." 127 F.2d 9, 11.

It was left for Judge Clark, dissenting in Kleinman v. Betty Dain Creations, Inc., 189 F.2d 546, 549, 89 U.S.P.Q. 404 (2d Cir. 1951), to uncover a more telling piece of legislative history. "The suggestion for the statute came from Professor Moore in a letter of March 7, ·1945, to Chief Code Reviser W. W. Barron and was that there be added to the grant of federal jurisdiction in cases under the patent, copyright, and trademark laws the following: 'and of all claims for unfair competition related thereto.' He supported this as constitutionally justified and 'needed to promote a uniform federal law on unfair competition; and to avoid the piecemeal litigation that is now compelled by some decisions, notably those in the Second Circuit,' citing particularly the dissent in Musher Foundation v. Alba Trading Co., 2 Cir., 127 F.2d 9, as stating 'the practical need for a different approach.' The reviser first tried out the idea in terms of joinder 'as a single cause of action,' Revision of Jud.Code, Prelim.Draft, Oct. 30, 1945, § 1360; but upon objection this was rejected as too limited and the present form substituted. That preliminary draft did carry as a 'Reviser's Note' the material which, without change of substance, now appears as the 'Reviser's Note' to the present § 1338(b) and which was erroneously relied on in this case below, D.C.S.D.N.Y., 88 F.Supp. 637, 639, as stating that the statute was 'no more than a restatement' of the former rule. While the note would doubtless have been more clearly expressed had it been written for the final form of the statute, yet it shows in several ways, including its reference to the Musher Foundation dissent, that it was written in the light of

Professor Moore's criticism, loc. cit. supra note 3, of our refusal to accept the repudiation of the 'Second Circuit rule' in Hurn v. Oursler, supra." 189 F.2d 546, 551 n. 6.

The facts of *Betty Dain* reveal how treacherous section 1338(b) can be when read in the combined light of its legislative history and Hurn v. Oursler. The complaint had stated two causes of action, "one for infringement of Patent No. 2,422,834 issued to the plaintiff on an application filed in January 1947, and one for breach of a contract to pay the plaintiff for use of the patented article." The court rejected jurisdiction over the second cause because it "sounds primarily in contract". The "complaint by the facts alleged and the relief sought sets forth the essentials of a license agreement and the failure to make payments thereunder. . . . A failure to make payments under a licensing agreement does not constitute the tort of unfair competition and is actionable only in contract." 189 F.2d 546, 548–549.

Judge Clark, however, restated the *Dain* facts in a way that supported the claim of federal jurisdiction—colorably under section 1338(b) and clearly under even a restrictive reading of *Hurn*. Stressing the allegation that the contract was rooted in plaintiff's confidential disclosure of his invention to defendant, and pointing to the contemporaneously broadening contours of unfair competition, Clark asked rhetorically: "And what could be more unfair or illegal than misappropriation of a confidential disclosure of an invention— all the more when backed up by a specific agreement to act in a fair and businesslike way by paying a reasonable compensation?" 189 F. 2d 546, 553.

4. Having afforded pendent jurisdiction, what substantive law should the federal court apply in its resolution of the state claim? State law—the obvious answer since Erie v. Tompkins—is also the generally accepted answer. In an extensive footnote to his opinion for the court in Maternally Yours, Inc. v. Your Maternity Shop, Inc., 234 F.2d 538, 540–41 n. 1, 110 U.S.P.Q. 462 (2d Cir. 1956), Judge Waterman reasoned that "despite repeated statements implying the contrary, it is the *source* of the right sued upon, and not the ground on which federal jurisdiction over the case is founded, which determines the governing law. . . . Thus, the *Erie* doctrine applies, whatever the ground for federal jurisdiction, to any issue or claim which has its source in state law." (emphasis the court's).

Reference to state law has been opposed on two grounds. Writing shortly after *Erie*, Professor Chafee noted that "before the *Tompkins* case, the United States judges were free to work out their own solutions in the light of cases in the United States Supreme Court and lower United States courts all over the country. They did not have to follow the decisions of a particular state court, but could apply a general federal law of Unfair Competition." Chafee objected that "this valuable body of law is now likely to be torn into pieces because of the *Tompkins* case. . . ." Chafee, Unfair Competition, 53 Harv.L.Rev. 1289, 1299 (1940).

Also, some observers claim that section 1338(b)'s requisite of relatedness not only justifies a single hearing for the state and federal claims but also requires application of a single, federal law. "Where jurisdiction of the federal courts is based on grounds other than diversity, there are apt to be presented federal as well as non-federal questions interwoven in various degrees. The application of different sources of governing law to various issues in the same lawsuit will create endless complications and result in fine-spun distinctions that will make those generated by Swift v. Tyson look like child's play. Nor do there seem to be any reasons of policy either necessitating or justifying the creation of such a maze of uncertainties." Zlinkoff, Erie v. Tompkins: In Relation to the Law of Trademarks and Unfair Competition, 42 Colum.L.Rev. 955, 988 (1942).

The shared premise of these arguments, that state unfair competition law differs in important ways from federal unfair competition law, is at least questionable. Since *Erie*, as before it, state courts continue to draw heavily on the unfair competition principles evolved by federal courts, with the result that there is in fact little difference between the two bodies of law. Thus, for Judge Clark concurring in *Maternally Yours,* "a more academic issue can hardly be conceived. Since problems of unfair competition in trade and trade names almost invariably concern also trade-marks and transcend state lines, it is not surprising that the governing law developed in the federal courts and much of its doctrine is connected with the names of great federal judges. So the issue is really whether we shall apply our regurgitation of the state redistillation of federal precedents or go more directly and realistically to the sources themselves. Actually, so far as I can discover, we have never found any difference in ultimate result, and so quite often lump federal and New York law together.
.   .   ." 248 F.2d 545.

I. TRADEMARK LAW

Marks have been used for centuries to indicate the ownership or source of goods. Some Greek vases of the fifth and sixth centuries B.C. have been found which bear their potter's mark. In the Middle Ages, merchants affixed distinctive marks to their goods before shipment to identify them in the event of shipwreck or piracy. Although such early practices may represent the beginnings of a tradition, these marks were essentially proprietary marks, intended to indicate ownership, and differed from modern trademarks which are intended to indicate the source or quality of goods.

Guild practices requiring craftsmen to affix production marks to their goods lie closer to the source of modern trademarks. "Every craft, of course, either had its own ordinances concerning such marks or administered statutory or municipal regulations of a similar nature. All of these regulations, whatever their source, made use of the production mark compulsory. Their expressed purpose was to facilitate the tracing of 'false' or defective wares and the punishment of the offending craftsman. The compulsory production mark likewise assisted the gild authorities in preventing those outside the gild from selling their products within the area of the gild monopoly." Over time, in certain trades, these marks became "asset marks—that is to say they became valuable symbols of individual good-will." This was particularly so in the case of durable goods, and goods transported great distances, "especially in the clothing and cutlery trades." F. Schechter, The Historical Foundations of the Law Relating to Trade-Marks 47 (1925).

Systematic legal protection of trademarks began to take shape in the early years of the nineteenth century. The starting point was the common law of deceit, from which courts in both England and the United States gradually evolved a distinct tort of passing off. An action for passing off would lie if plaintiff could prove that defendant had used plaintiff's mark to deceive consumers into thinking that plaintiff was the source of defendant's goods.

Intent to deceive was the gravamen of the action for passing off and remains so today in unfair competition cases in which plaintiff's symbol is descriptive or otherwise weak. In cases where plaintiff's symbol was arbitrary or otherwise highly distinctive, however, courts came to insist less on proof of fraudulent intent; the fact that defendant had copied a distinctive mark was itself evidence of intent to deceive. Courts eventually categorized the disputes over distinctive symbols as involving trademark infringement rather than unfair competition and conclusively removed any requirement that fraudulent intent be proved.

The first United States trademark statute, Act of July 8, 1870, ch. 230, 16 Stat. 198, preceded the first English trademark statute by five years. Like its English counterpart, the 1870 Act created few substantive rights of its own, providing instead for the registration of marks protected under common law. In 1876 the Act was amended to add criminal penalties for infringing or counterfeiting registered marks. Act of August 14, 1876, ch. 274, 19 Stat. 141.

In 1879 the United States Supreme Court ruled that the Act of 1870, as amended, was unconstitutional. Trade-Mark Cases, 100 U.S. 82, 25 L.Ed. 550 (1879). Justice Miller, writing for the Court, began by rejecting the claim that Art. I, § 8, cl. 8, the copyright-patent clause, gave Congress the necessary authority. "The ordinary trademark has no necessary relation to invention or discovery. The trademark recognized by the common law is generally the growth of a considerable period of use, rather than a sudden invention. It is often the result of accident rather than design, and when under the act of Congress it is sought to establish it by registration, neither originality, invention, discovery, science, nor art is in any way essential to the right conferred by that act. If we should endeavor to classify it under the head of writings of authors, the objections are equally strong. . . . The writings which are to be protected are the *fruits of intellectual labor*, embodied in the form of books, prints, engravings and the like. The trade-mark may be, and generally is, the adoption of something already in existence as the distinctive symbol of the party using it." 100 U.S. 82, at page 94 (emphasis in original).

Justice Miller also rejected the argument that the Act could be rested on the commerce clause. When "Congress undertakes to enact a law, which can only be valid as a regulation of commerce, it is reasonable to expect to find on the face of the law, or from its essential nature, that it is a regulation of commerce with foreign nations, or among the several States, or with the Indian tribes. If not so limited, it is in excess of the power of Congress. If its main purpose be to establish a regulation applicable to all trade, to commerce at all points, especially if it be that it is designed to govern the commerce wholly between the citizens of the same State, it is obviously the exercise of a power not confided to Congress." Because the Act stated no such jurisdictional limits, it could not be sustained under the commerce power. 100 U.S. 82, at pages 96–97.

Despite the care that Justice Miller took to narrow his holding, and to signal to Congress that it could repair the constitutional flaw by expressly limiting the Act to objects covered by the commerce clause, it soon became obvious that, with the Trademark Cases, federal trademark protection had started off on the wrong foot. Until passage of the Lanham Act, nearly three-quarters of a century later, Congress and the courts took few steps toward an enlarged federal role. Congress' first response to the Court's decision, the Act of March 3, 1881, 21 Stat. 502, expressly conditioned federal registration on the mark's use in foreign commerce or in commerce with the Indian tribes. Registration of marks used in interstate commerce came only with passage of the comprehensive Act of Feb. 20, 1905, c. 592, 33 Stat. 724. Influenced in part by the Trademark Cases, and in part by dicta in American Steel Foundries v. Robertson, 269 U.S. 372, 46 S.Ct. 160, 70 L.Ed. 317 (1926) and American Trading Co. v. Heacock Co., 285 U.S. 247, 52 S.Ct. 387, 76 L.Ed. 740, 12 U.S.P.Q. 453 (1932), courts, as late as 1932, assumed that "Congress has been given no power to legislate on the substantive law of trademarks," and that congressional authority is limited to providing "a federally controlled place of registration and to deny registration therein, where confusion would likely result to the trade from the trademark use of such registered marks." A. Leschen & Sons Rope Co. v. American Steel und Wire Co., 55 F.2d 455, 459, 12 U.S.P.Q. 272 (C.C.P.A.1932)

The Lanham Act, signed into law on July 5, 1946, represents the first major step toward substantive federal trademark legislation in the United States. The efforts at revision began in 1924, with the introduction of S. 2679. First spearheaded by Representative Albert Vestal, the revision effort was later taken over by Representative Fritz Lanham. Since 1946, the Lanham Act, which is the trademark statute now in force, has been amended several times. The 1962 "housekeeping" amendments, Act of October 9, 1962, P.L. 87–772, 76 Stat. 769, also contain some substance. See page 416, below. The 1975 amendments, Act of January 2, 1975, P.L. 93–600, § 3, 88 Stat. 1955, provided, among other things, for the award of attorneys' fees in exceptional cases.

Several historical and interpretative studies were published on the heels of the Lanham Act's passage. Among the more helpful are D. Robert, The New Trade-Mark Manual (1947); Callmann, The New Trade-Mark Act of July 5, 1946, 46 Colum.L.Rev. 929 (1946); Carter, Legislative History of the New Trade-Mark Act, 36 Trademark Rep. 121 (1946); Derenberg, At the Threshold of the Lanham Trade-Mark Act, 37 Trademark Rep. 297 (1947); Rogers, The Lanham Act and the Social Function of Trade-Marks, 14 L. & Contemp.Prob. 173 (1949).

For a superb study of the evolution of trademark law from its earliest origins, see F. Schechter, The Historical Foundations of the Law Relating to Trade-Marks (1925). See also, Burrell, Two Hundred Years of English Trademark Law, and Pattishall, Two Hundred Years of American Trademark Law, in American Bar Association, Two Hundred Years of English and American Patent, Trademark and Copyright Law, 35, 51 (1977); Diamond, The Historical Development of Trademarks, 65 Trademark Rep. 265 (1975); McClure, Trademarks and Unfair Competition: A Critical History of Legal Thought, 69 Trademark Rep. 305 (1979); Paster, Trademarks—Their Early History, 59 Trademark Rep. 551 (1969).

General reference works on trademark law and practice abound. Among them are J. T. McCarthy, Trademarks and Unfair Competition (1973); J. Gilson, Trademark Protection and Practice (1974); R. Callmann, The Law of Unfair Competition, Trademarks, and Monopolies (3d ed. 1967); E. Vandenburgh, Trademark Law and Procedure (2d ed. 1968); M. Beran, An Introduction to Trademark Practice (1970); and J. Calimafde, Trademarks and Unfair Competition (1970).

The Trademark Reporter, published bimonthly by the United States Trademark Association, is an excellent source of articles and items on topics of current importance.

A. REQUIREMENTS FOR PROTECTION

1. USE AND USE IN COMMERCE

See Statute Supplement 15 U.S.C.A. §§ 1051, 1055, 1127.

BLUE BELL, INC. v. FARAH MFG. CO.

United States Court of Appeals, Fifth Circuit, 1975.
508 F.2d 1260, 185 U.S.P.Q. 1.

GEWIN, Circuit Judge.

In the spring and summer of 1973 two prominent manufacturers of men's clothing created identical trademarks for goods substantially identical in appearance. Though the record offers no indication of bad faith in the design and adoption of the labels, both Farah Manufacturing Company (Farah) and Blue Bell, Inc. (Blue Bell) devised the mark "Time Out" for new lines of men's slacks and shirts. Both parties market their goods on a national scale, so they agree that joint utilization of the same trademark would confuse the buying public. Thus, the only question presented for our review is which [*ISSUE: PRIOR USE*] party established prior use of the mark in trade. A response to that seemingly innocuous inquiry, however, requires us to define the chameleonic term "use" as it has developed in trademark law.

After a full development of the facts in the district court both parties moved for summary judgment. The motion of Farah was granted and that of Blue Bell denied. It is not claimed that summary judgment procedure was inappropriate; the controversy presented relates to the application of the proper legal principles to undisputed facts. A permanent injunction was granted in favor of Farah but no damages were awarded, and Blue Bell was allowed to fill all orders for garments bearing the Time Out label received by it as of the close of business on December 5, 1973. For the reasons hereinafter stated we affirm.

Farah conceived of the Time Out mark on May 16, after screening several possible titles for its new stretch menswear. Two days later the firm adopted an hourglass logo and authorized an extensive advertising campaign bearing the new insignia. Farah presented its fall line of clothing, including Time Out slacks, to sales personnel on June 5. In the meantime, patent counsel had given clearance for use of the mark after scrutiny of current federal registrations then on file. One of Farah's top executives demonstrated samples of the Time Out garments to large customers in Washington, D.C. and New York, though labels were not attached to the slacks at that time. Tags containing the new design were completed June 27. With favorable evaluations of marketing potential from all sides, Farah sent one pair of slacks bearing the Time Out mark to each of its twelve regional sales managers on July 3. Sales personnel paid for the pants, and the garments became their property in case of loss.

Following the July 3 shipment, regional managers showed the goods to customers the following week. Farah received several orders and production began. Further shipments of sample garments were mailed to the rest of the sales force on July 11 and 14. Merchandising efforts were fully operative by the end of the month. The first shipments to customers, however, occurred in September.

Blue Bell, on the other hand, was concerned with creating an entire new division of men's clothing, as an avenue to reaching the "upstairs" market. Though initially to be housed at the Hicks-Ponder plant in El Paso, the new division would eventually enjoy separate headquarters. On June 18 Blue Bell management arrived at the name Time Out to identify both its new division and its new line of men's sportswear. Like Farah, it received clearance for use of the mark from counsel. Like Farah, it inaugurated an advertising campaign. Unlike Farah, however, Blue Bell did not ship a dozen marked articles of the new line to its sales personnel. Instead, Blue Bell authorized the manufacture of several hundred labels bearing the words Time Out and its logo shaped like a referee's hands forming a T. When the labels were completed on June 29, the head of the embryonic division flew them to El Paso. He instructed shipping personnel to affix the new Time Out labels to slacks that already bore the "Mr. Hicks" trademark. The new tags, of varying sizes and colors, were randomly attached to the left hip pocket button of slacks and the left hip pocket of jeans. Thus, although no change occurred in the design or manufacture of the pants, on July 5 several hundred pair left El Paso with two tags.

Blue Bell made intermittent shipments of the doubly-labeled slacks thereafter, though the out-of-state customers who received the goods had ordered clothing of the Mr. Hicks variety. Production of the new Time Out merchandise began in the latter part of August, and Blue Bell held a sales meeting to present its fall designs from September 4–6. Sales personnel solicited numerous orders, though shipments of the garments were not scheduled until October.

By the end of October Farah had received orders for 204,403 items of Time Out sportswear, representing a retail sales value of over $2,750,000. Blue Bell had received orders for 154,200 garments valued at over $900,000. Both parties had commenced extensive advertising campaigns for their respective Time Out sportswear.

Soon after discovering the similarity of their marks, Blue Bell sued Farah for common law trademark infringement and unfair competition, seeking to enjoin use of the Time Out trademark on men's clothing. Farah counterclaimed for similar injunctive relief. The district court found that Farah's July 3 shipment and sale constituted a valid use in trade, while Blue Bell's July 5 shipment was a mere "token" use insufficient at law to create trademark rights. While we affirm the result reached by the trial court as to Farah's priority of use, the legal grounds upon which we base our decision are somewhat different from those undergirding the district court's judgment.

Federal jurisdiction is predicated upon diversity of citizenship, since neither party has registered the mark pursuant to the Lanham Act. Given the operative facts surrounding manufacture and shipment from El Paso, the parties agree the Texas law of trademarks controls. In 1967 the state legislature enacted a Trademark Statute.[5] Section 16.02 of the Act explains that a mark is "used" when it is affixed to the goods and "the goods are sold, displayed for sale, or otherwise publicly distributed." Thus the question whether Blue Bell or Farah established priority of trademark use depends upon interpretation of the cited provision. Unfortunately, there are no Texas cases construing § 16.02. This court must therefore determine what principles the highest state court would utilize in deciding such a question. In view of the statute's stated purpose to preserve common law rights, we conclude the Texas Supreme Court would apply the statutory provision in light of general principles of trademark law.

A trademark is a symbol (word, name, device or combination thereof) adopted and used by a merchant to identify his goods and distinguish them from articles produced by others. Ownership of a mark requires a combination of both appropriation and use in trade. Thus, neither conception of the mark, nor advertising alone establishes trademark rights at common law. Rather, ownership of a trademark accrues when goods bearing the mark are placed on the market.

The exclusive right to a trademark belongs to one who first uses it in connection with specified goods. Such use need not have gained wide public recognition, and even a single use in trade may sustain trademark rights if followed by continuous commercial utilization.

The initial question presented for review is whether Farah's sale and shipment of slacks to twelve regional managers constitutes a valid first use of the Time Out mark. Blue Bell claims the July 3 sale was merely an internal transaction insufficiently public to secure trademark ownership. After consideration of pertinent authorities, we agree.

Secret, undisclosed internal shipments are generally inadequate to support the denomination "use." Trademark claims based upon shipments from a producer's plant to its sales office, and vice versa, have often been disallowed. Though none of the cited cases dealt with *sales* to intra-corporate personnel, we perceive that fact to be a distinction without a difference. The sales were not made to customers, but served as an accounting device to charge the salesmen with their cost in case of loss. The fact that some sales managers actively solicited accounts bolsters the good faith of Farah's intended use, but does not meet our essential objection: that the "sales" were not made to the public.

The primary, perhaps singular purpose of a trademark is to provide a means for the consumer to separate or distinguish one manu-

5. Vernon's Tex.Code, Ann., Bus. & Comm. §§ 16.01–16.28 (1968).

facturer's goods from those of another. Personnel within a corporation can identify an item by style number or other unique code. A trademark aids the public in selecting particular goods. As stated by the First Circuit:

> But to hold that a sale or sales are the sine qua non of a use sufficient to amount to an appropriation would be to read an unwarranted limitation into the statute, for so construed registration would have to be denied to any manufacturer who adopted a mark to distinguish or identify his product, and perhaps applied it thereon for years, if he should in practice lease his goods rather than sell them, as many manufacturers of machinery do. It seems to us that although evidence of sales is highly persuasive, the question of use adequate to establish appropriation remains one to be decided on the facts of each case, and that evidence showing, first, adoption, and, second, *use in a way sufficiently public to identify or distinguish the marked goods in an appropriate segment of the public mind as those of the adopter of the mark*, is competent to establish ownership . . ..

New England Duplicating Co. v. Mendes, 190 F.2d 415, 418, 90 U.S.P. Q. 151, 153 (1st Cir. 1951) (Emphasis added). Similarly, the Trademark Trial and Appeal Board has reasoned:

> To acquire trademark rights there has to be an "open" use, that is to say, a use has to be made to the relevant class of purchasers or prospective purchasers since a trademark is intended to identify goods and distinguish those goods from those manufactured or sold by others. There was no such "open" use, rather the use can be said to be an "internal" use, which cannot give rise to trademark rights.

Sterling Drug, Inc. v. Knoll A. G. Chemische Fabriken, supra at 631.

Farah nonetheless contends that a recent decision of the Board so undermines all prior cases relating to internal use that they should be ignored. In Standard Pressed Steel Co. v. Midwest Chrome Process Co., 183 U.S.P.Q. 758 (T.T.A.B.1974), the agency held that internal shipment of marked goods from a producer's manufacturing plant to its sales office constitutes a valid "use in commerce" for registration purposes.

An axiom of trademark law has been that the right to register a mark is conditioned upon its actual use in trade. Theoretically, then, common law use in trade should precede the use in commerce upon which Lanham Act registration is predicated. Arguably, since only a trademark owner can apply for registration, any activity adequate to create registrable rights must perforce also create trademark rights. A close examination of the Board's decision, however, dispels so mechanical a view. The tribunal took meticulous care to point out that its conclusion related solely to registration use rather than ownership use.

It has been recognized and especially so in the last few years that, in view of the expenditures involved in introducing a new product on the market generally and the attendant risk involved therein prior to the screening process involved in resorting to the federal registration system and in the absence of an "intent to use" statute, a token sale or a single shipment in commerce *may be sufficient to support an application to register a trademark* in the Patent Office notwithstanding that the evidence may not show what disposition was made of the product so shipped. That is, the fact that a sale or a shipment of goods bearing a trademark was *designed primarily to lay a foundation for the filing of an application for registration* does not, per se, invalidate any such application or subsequent registration issued thereon.

. . .

Inasmuch as it is our belief that a most liberal policy should be followed in a situation of this kind [*in which dispute as to priority of use and ownership of a mark is not involved*], applicant's initial shipment of fasteners, although an intra-company transaction in that it was to a company sales representative, was a bona fide shipment . . . .

Standard Pressed Steel Co. v. Midwest Chrome Process Co., supra at 764–65 (Emphasis added).

Priority of use and ownership of the Time Out mark are the only issues before this court. The language fashioned by the Board clearly indicates a desire to leave the common law of trademark ownership intact. The decision may demonstrate a reversal of the presumption that ownership rights precede registration rights, but it does not affect our analysis of common law use in trade. Farah had undertaken substantial preliminary steps toward marketing the Time Out garments, but it did not establish ownership of the mark by means of the July 3 shipment to its sales managers. The gist of trademark rights is actual use in trade. Though technically a "sale", the July 3 shipment was not "publicly distributed" within the purview of the Texas statute.

Blue Bell's July 5 shipment similarly failed to satisfy the prerequisites of a bona fide use in trade. Elementary tenets of trademark law require that labels or designs be affixed to the merchandise actually intended to bear the mark in commercial transactions. Furthermore, courts have recognized that the usefulness of a mark derives not only from its capacity to identify a certain manufacturer, but also from its ability to differentiate between different classes of goods produced by a single manufacturer. Here customers had ordered slacks of the Mr. Hicks species, and Mr. Hicks was the fanciful mark distinguishing these slacks from all others. Blue Bell intended to use the Time Out mark on an entirely new line of men's sportswear, unique in style and cut, though none of the garments had yet been produced.

While goods may be identified by more than one trademark, the use of each mark must be bona fide. Mere adoption of a mark without bona fide use, in an attempt to reserve it for the future, will not create trademark rights. In the instant case Blue Bell's attachment of a secondary label to an older line of goods manifests a bad faith attempt to reserve a mark. We cannot countenance such activities as a valid use in trade. Blue Bell therefore did not acquire trademark rights by virtue of its July 5 shipment.

We thus hold that neither Farah's July 3 shipment nor Blue Bell's July 5 shipment sufficed to create rights in the Time Out mark. Based on a desire to secure ownership of the mark and superiority over a competitor, both claims of alleged use were chronologically premature. Essentially, they took a time out to litigate their differences too early in the game. The question thus becomes whether we should continue to stop the clock for a remand or make a final call from the appellate bench. While a remand to the district court for further factual development would not be improper in these circumstances, we believe the interests of judicial economy and the parties' desire to terminate the litigation demand that we decide, if possible, which manufacturer first used the mark in trade.

Careful examination of the record discloses that Farah shipped its first order of Time Out clothing to customers in September of 1973. Blue Bell, approximately one month behind its competitor at other relevant stages of development, did not mail its Time Out garments until at least October. Though sales to customers are not the sine qua non of trademark use, they are determinative in the instant case. These sales constituted the first point at which the public had a chance to associate Time Out with a particular line of sportswear. Therefore, Farah established priority of trademark use; it is entitled to a decree permanently enjoining Blue Bell from utilization of the Time Out trademark on men's garments.

The judgment of the trial court is affirmed.

IN RE CASTLETON CHINA, INC.

156 U.S.P.Q. 691 (T.T.A.B.1968).

LEFKOWITZ, Member.

An application has been filed by Castleton China, Inc., to register "The Symphony Collection" on the Principal Register as a trademark for china dinnerware, use of the mark since January 4, 1965 being alleged.

It is alleged in the application that the mark is used in point-of-sale displays. Specimens filed with the application comprise brochures or booklets describing applicant's "The Symphony Collection" china dinnerware which applicant contends are "point-of-sale displays".

Registration has been refused on the ground (a) that the specimens submitted show the mark "The Symphony Collection" used merely as the name of a collection of various patterns for applicant's china dinnerware, and not as a trademark to distinguish applicant's goods in commerce and (b) that the specimens of record are advertising leaflets and, as such, do not evidence trademark use of the mark in connection with the goods as required by Rules 2.56 and 2.57.

Applicant has appealed.

The record discloses that the mark "The Symphony Collection" is used by applicant to identify a line of china dinnerware. The line is furnished in several patterns which differ in surface ornamentation, but the various corresponding pieces in each pattern are otherwise identical in shape, body, and glaze. Consistent with the theme of "The Symphony Collection", each pattern in it is identified to distinguish it from applicant's other patterns and assertedly from ware produced by competitors by a mark having a musical connotation such as "Musicalle," "Golden Melody," "Capella," "Andante," and the like. The designation "The Symphony Collection" does not appear on the goods, labels affixed to the goods, or on the containers for the goods. The only evidence of use of the mark is on the specimen brochures which according to an affidavit by applicant's Executive Vice-President, "were, and still are being, supplied throughout the country to the dealers in Castleton's Symphony Collection for use in displays on the counters and tables where specimen pieces, and not all pieces in all patterns in the line, are displayed for retail sale."

With regard to (a), the examiner has taken the position that because the mark in question identifies a line or a group of named patterns for applicant's china dinnerware and does not appear to be applied directly to the goods, it cannot function as a trademark for such dinnerware. This contention is obviously contrary to the facts of life in the marketplace which show numerous marks used to identify a variety of products including marks used to identify a line of individually named or trademarked merchandise without ever being physically applied to the goods as in the automobile industry where a mark such as "GM" does not appear on automobiles, per se, but nevertheless serves to identify a well-known line of automobiles and such designations as "Buick," "Chevrolet," "Pontiac," "Oldsmobile," etc. serve as product, or model marks within said line of cars. That is, the statute does not require affixation of a mark to the goods for establishing trademark use of a designation. Section 45 provides that, "For the purpose of this Act a mark shall be deemed to be used in commerce (a) on goods when it is placed in any manner on the goods or *their containers or the displays associated therewith or on tags or labels affixed thereto and the goods are sold* or transported in commerce (Italics added). It might well be that the examiner's rejection is premised on the belief that a pattern name and hence a designation for a line or group of pattern names cannot function as a trademark. But, it has long been held that a pattern or style designation may also function as a trademark. In the instant case, "The Symphony Collection" does not in any way describe applicant's china dinnerware and considering the manner in which it is used in the specimens filed with the application, we are of the opinion that "The Symphony Collection" could serve to identify and distinguish a particular line of applicant's dinnerware.

This case turns therefore on the resolution of (b) namely, whether or not the use of the mark "The Symphony Collection" on the brochure specimens constitutes trademark use of the mark within the meaning of the Statute. In other words, do these brochures constitute "displays associated with the goods" within the meaning thereof in the statute?

The examiner urges that the brochures do not constitute "displays associated with the goods" because they constitute promotional literature which, insofar as the record shows, do not accompany the dinnerware in shipment. Applicant, on the other hand, argues that:

> "Concededly, there is no evidence to show that the point-of-sale displays 'accompany the goods in shipment', but this is not a prerequisite under Sec. 45, provided the goods are sold in commerce. In other words, use on a display at the point of sale is no less a use of the mark in commerce because the display and goods may be shipped separately in interstate commerce for assembly and association at the point of sale."

Applicant then goes on to assert that since these brochures are placed on counters displaying its dinnerware, they constitute "displays associated with the goods" within the meaning of the statute.

Applicant is correct in its assertion that the statute does not require that the displays accompany the goods in commerce. As indicated above, Section 45 provides that a mark shall be deemed in use in commerce when the mark "is placed in any manner on the goods or the containers or the displays associated therewith or on the tags or labels affixed thereto *and* the goods are sold or transported in commerce" (Emphasis added). It is clear from the foregoing that the displays need not accompany the goods in commerce.

The record here shows that the mark appears on the brochures, the brochures are used on counters where specimens of applicant's dinnerware are displayed for retail sale, and applicant's dinnerware has been sold and transported through its various dealers in commerce. But, we nevertheless are not persuaded that brochures of this type, as used by applicant, constitute "displays associated with the goods" as contemplated by the statute.

A "display" is defined in Webster's Third New International Dictionary (1965), inter alia, as "(a) an exhibiting or showing of something: an unfolding or opening out to view", "(b) ostentatious shows: exhibition for effect", and "(d) an often artistic composition, conspicuous eye-catching construction or assemblage by which something (as merchandise or collector's items) is exhibited or advertised (his pictures are on—at the art gallery) also: the use of such constructions or assemblage (is the key of self service sales—Printer's Ink)". Thus, by its literal meaning, a "display associated with the goods" is a conspicuous, eye-catching assemblage of goods which leads to or induces sales of the merchandise so displayed. And, insofar as a mark is used in connection therewith, it must appear on the display itself in such a close physical association with the goods that a prospective purchaser viewing the display would immediately associate the mark with the goods. Applicant's brochures manifestly cannot be considered a "display associated with the goods" within the contemplation of the statute—they are essentially nothing more than conventional pamphlets used by producers of dinnerware to advertise their particular products. Use of a designation in advertising does not constitute use as a trademark. Moreover, while applicant's dinnerware may be displayed on tables by its retailers, the mark "The Symphony Collection" does not appear on such displays; and since the mark appears only in these brochures, it is obviously not used in such a manner as to immediately create an association of the mark with the goods so displayed.

It is therefore concluded that the brochures do not evidence use of "The Symphony Collection" as a trademark for china dinnerware within the meaning of the statute.

Decision

The refusal of registration is reversed as to (a) and affirmed as to (b).

NOTES

1. Does *Blue Bell* say that the test for trademark use will depend on whether priority or registration is the issue? Note that the opinion did not distinguish between precedents involving priority and precedents involving registration.

As a practical matter, what would be the effect of applying two different measures of use—one for determining registration, the other for priority? If, for example, Blue Bell had made sufficient use to obtain registration, followed several months later by a *bona fide* commercial use establishing priority, what would it have gained from the earlier registration? Would the registration have withstood a cancellation proceeding brought by Farah under Lanham Act § 14, 15 U.S. C.A. § 1064? How would Blue Bell have fared in an infringement action against Farah? By applying for early registration might Blue Bell have exposed itself to statutory liability? Lanham Act § 38, 15 U.S.C.A. § 1120 provides that "Any person who shall procure registration in the Patent and Trademark Office of a mark by false or fraudulent declaration or representation, oral or in writing, or by any false means, shall be liable in a civil action by any person injured thereby for any damages sustained in consequence thereof." See Blue Bell, Inc. v. Jaymar-Ruby, Inc., 497 F.2d 433, 182 U.S.P.Q. 65 (2d Cir. 1974).

2. The requirement that a mark be used before it can be registered poses a significant problem for mass marketing. By the time the producer has spent hundreds of thousands of dollars designing a new mark and testing its acceptance by consumers, a competitor may have beaten it to the market, acquiring rights through prior commercial use of an identical or confusingly similar mark. Consumer products companies try to avoid this problem through programs ranging

from early token sales of new products to systematic and substantial test marketing in major markets.

Judicial and administrative decisions offer few clear guidelines for identifying the necessary quantum for trademark use. Anthony L. Fletcher has identified several factors that courts weigh in favor of finding a genuine commercial use. In order of importance they are: (1) quantity and continuity of sale ("the question, of course, is how much is enough? Perhaps the answer is that he who needs to ask the question has not enough."); (2) consumer purchases ("such sales would seem to be a *sine qua non* of real use"); (3) business of mark owner; (4) quality control; (5) a distinguishing mark ("Blue Bell's trouble was that it slapped Time Out labels at random on slacks known, listed, ordered and sold as Mr. Hicks slacks."); (6) intent; (7) profit or loss ("plainly, this consideration is little more than a makeweight; there are plenty of *bona fide* marks whose products are sold at a loss"); (8) advertising; and (9) test market. Fletcher, "Time Out," "Snob," "Wipeout," and "Chicken of the Sea": The Death Knell of "Token Use"?   65 Trademark Rep. 336, 346–348 (1975).

Is it impossible to warehouse unused marks for future use? Fletcher answers, "Probably not. It is more difficult and considerably more expensive than the procedures currently practiced, but it still seems possible at least in the area of mass market goods where it has been most widely practiced. What should suffice in such situations . . . is a marketing effort which will permit a reasonable number of consumers to develop or practice brand loyalty to the product sold under the mark. If there are a few dozen or hundred regular purchasers and users of the product, then the trade in it would seem unquestionably to be *bona fide*, albeit perhaps modest." 65 Trademark Rep. 349.*

3.   The United States is one of the few countries to require that a mark be used before it can be registered. Other countries allow registration upon the applicant's statement of intent to use a mark. By treaty, and under Lanham Act § 44, 15 U.S.C.A. § 1126, the United States is committed to honor these foreign registrations. As a result, first users in the United States sometimes lose out to later users elsewhere.

S. C. M. v. Langis Foods Ltd., 539 F.2d 196, 190 U.S.P.Q. 288 (D.C.Cir.1976) illustrates the problem. On March 28, 1969 defendant, a Canadian corporation, filed applications to register three trademarks in Canada. On May 15, 1969 defendant began to use these marks in Canada. On the same day, doubtless by coincidence, plaintiff's predecessor in interest, a United States corporation, began to use the identical mark in the United States. On June 18, 1969, plaintiff applied for registration in the United States. On September 19, 1969, defendant applied for registration in the United States, claiming

priority on the basis of its Canadian applications. Registration issued to defendant and plaintiff petitioned for cancellation on the
ground that it, not defendant, was the mark's first user in the United
States. The Trademark Trial and Appeal Board held for defendant.
The District Court for the District of Columbia held for plaintiff.

The Court of Appeals reversed. "Our holding in this case is that
section 44(d) of the Trademark Act of 1946, which implements article 4 of the Paris Union Treaty, accorded to appellant Langis a 'right
to priority' for the six months following the filing of its Canadian application for registration, that is to say, from March 28, 1969 to September 27, 1969; and that an intervening use in the United States
during that period cannot invalidate Langis's right to registration in
this country pursuant to an application filed on September 19, 1969."
539 F.2d 196, 201.

The court left open the question whether defendant, Langis,
would have prevailed if it had made *no* use of the mark anywhere
prior to its United States application. "There are three possible positions that can be argued with respect to the use requirements applicable to section 44 filings by foreign nationals: (1) foreign nationals
must allege use in commerce; (2) though use in commerce is not required, foreign nationals must nevertheless allege use somewhere; or
(3) foreign nationals are not required to allege use at all. Section
44(d)(2) of the 1946 Act clearly exempts section 44(d) applications
from the section 1 requirement that applications allege use in commerce. As to the other two possible positions, the official policy of
the Patent Office has shifted with some regularity. See British Insulated Callender's Cables, Ltd., 83 U.S.P.Q. 319 (Comm'r 1949) (there
must be an allegation of use somewhere), overruled in Societe From-
ageries Bel, 105 U.S.P.Q. 392 (Comm'r 1955) (the 'Merry Cow' case)
(there is no use requirement), overruled in Certain Incomplete
Trademark Applications, 137 U.S.P.Q. 69 (Comm'r 1963) (there must
be an allegation of use somewhere). And there has been considerable
disagreement among commentators on the issue.

"The Trademark Trial and Appeal Board opinion in the instant
case erroneously states appellant Langis 'had made no use of the
marks "Lemon Tree," "Orange Tree" or "Apple Tree" . . . prior
to the filing of its applications in this country.' Nevertheless, the
Board citing the *Merry Cow* case, supra, upheld Langis's registration,
thus overruling Certain Incomplete Trademark Applications, supra,
and reinstating the policy that there is no use requirement.

"In the de novo proceeding below, the District Court reviewed
the Paris Union Treaty and the Trademark Act of 1946 and concluded that, 'the decision of the Board . . . which reverts to the
"Merry Cow" doctrine . . . is . . . in error.' 376 F.Supp.
966, 182 U.S.P.Q. 134. In this respect, the opinion of the District
Court is dictum. The record in the District Court clearly indicates
that applications filed by Langis with the Patent Office alleged use of
the marks in Canada during the applicable six month period, and
there was thus no reason for the District Court to rule on the *Merry*

Cow issue. The fact that the Trademark Trial and Appeal Board found it necessary to reach that question given its misstatement of the facts does not mean that, despite a record indicating to the contrary, the question was presented to the District Court. Appellee SCM contends that the *Merry Cow* issue is not presented by this case and we agree." 539 F.2d n. 12 at 201–202.

See generally, Schwartz, Minimum Use Requirements for Foreign Trade-Mark Owners, 68 Trademark Rep. 148 (1978); Zelnick, Shaking the Lemon Tree: Use and the Paris Union Treaty, 67 Trademark Rep. 329 (1977).

4. Congress is occasionally asked to move from the present system of first to use, first in right, to a system of first to register, first in right. See, for example, S. 2595, 92nd Cong. 1st Sess. 117 Cong. Rec. 33581, 33592 (1971). See also pages 943 to 955 below. One argument in favor of these proposals is that they will relieve the disparity, noted in *Langis*, between foreign and domestic registrants. Are there any other reasons to support these proposals? For an early argument that the use requirement conflicts with modern commercial needs, see Giles, Pre-Use Applications, 43 Trademark Rep. 1121 (1953).

What are the arguments against a system in which priority is awarded to the first applicant who indicates an intent to use the mark, with registration conditioned on actual use within six months of the application? Is it likely that applicants will defensively fill the register with marks of small present value? Would the system favor large firms over small firms? Entrenched firms over newcomers? Would a move to such a system be likely to entail a tightening of the other requirements for registration, such as the distinctiveness requirements of Lanham Act § 2, 15 U.S.C.A. § 1052? If Congress made the move, what would become of state doctrines that continue to award trademark and unfair competition rights on a first user basis?

5. *Use in Commerce.* To be registered, a mark must not only be used. It must also be used in commerce. The two requirements are not redundant. Use of the first sort initiates substantive rights in the mark and may be entirely intrastate. As already noted, this sort of use occurs with the first *bona fide* commercial transaction involving goods on which the mark appears. By contrast, the requirement of use in commerce is a jurisdictional requisite and will be satisfied so long as the goods are transported in commerce. "After a mark has been used or established in trade, mere transportation in commerce is sufficient for registration purposes, but it must have been used in trade somewhere before any rights in the mark accrue." Procter & Gamble Co. v. Jacqueline Cochran, Inc., 102 U.S.P.Q. 449, 450 (Comm'r 1954).

Although the Lanham Act defines commerce to mean "all commerce which may lawfully be regulated by Congress," the tendency has been to give the term a narrower scope than contemporary constitutional doctrine would allow. As late as 1957, the Court of Customs and Patent Appeals ruled that a Philadelphia restaurant could not obtain service mark registration for its name because it "failed to establish that the services for which registration is sought are rendered in commerce which may lawfully be regulated by Congress within the meaning of the Trademark Act of 1946." Application of Bookbinder's Restaurant, Inc., 44 C.C.P.A. 731, 240 F.2d 365, 368, 112 U.S.P.Q. 326, 328 (1957). The argument that the applicant's customers traveled to the restaurant in interstate commerce was of no avail.

Judicial and administrative attitudes began to change in the mid-1960's. In Application of Gastown, Inc., 51 C.C.P.A. 876, 326 F. 2d 780, 140 U.S.P.Q. 216 (1964), the Court of Customs and Patent Appeals allowed registration of a service mark used in a filling station situated on an interstate highway. Although the applicant was situated in only one state, its services to interstate travelers were in commerce. The court's specified rationale was that use in commerce includes use in intrastate commerce that directly affects interstate commerce.

Gastown involved a service mark. It was thirteen years before trademarks received similarly liberal treatment. In Application of Silenus Wines, Inc., 557 F.2d 806, 194 U.S.P.Q. 261 (1977), the Court of Customs and Patent Appeals held that applicant, a wine importer, was entitled to register a mark affixed to wine that it imported from France and sold only in Massachusetts. Recognizing that the applicant's importation "is not itself a 'use in commerce'," the court drew on the *Gastown* rationale to conclude, "thus, we hold that intrastate sale of goods by the party who caused those goods to move in regulatable commerce, directly affects that commerce and is itself regulatable. Clearly, intrastate sale of imported wines by the importer sufficiently affects commerce with foreign nations to qualify those intrastate sales for the Trademark Act definition of 'commerce'." 557 F. 2d 809.

For a thoughtful review of *Silenus* and its background, see Calhoun, Use in Commerce After Silenus: What Does It Mean? 70 Trademark Rep. 47 (1980).

6. The origins of trademark law's affixation requirement can be traced to the early practice of attaching or embedding marks in the goods whose source they were intended to identify. The law that developed around these marks assumed that marks could be effective only in connection with the goods to which they were affixed.

But what of marks for services? Since trademark law made affixation to goods necessary to a mark's inception and continued validity, logic dictated that there could be no valid trademark if there are no goods to which it can be affixed. Since services characteristically do not involve goods, it followed that service marks could not be protected as trademarks and must be protected, if at all, under the rules of unfair competition. Congress finally eluded this logic by ignoring it. The Lanham Act provides that service marks will be protected on a par with trademarks and that, since there are no goods to which these marks can properly be affixed, other uses that serve the same purpose as affixation will suffice.   See generally, Treece, Developments in the Law of Trademarks and Service Marks—Contributions of the Common Law, The Federal Act, State Statutes and the Restatement of Torts, 58 Calif.L.Rev. 885 (1970).

Advertising is one of the uses that is allowed to substitute for affixation in the case of service marks.   If Castleton China had engaged in the service of handpainting a variety of designs on customers' unpatterned dinnerware, and if the designs were collectively referred to as "The Symphony Collection" in brochures distributed throughout the United States, would the brochure reference qualify "The Symphony Collection" for registration as a service mark? Since the new logic of the Lanham Act, evidenced by its service mark provisions, is that affixation is not the only way to qualify a mark for protection, should courts loosen the affixation requirement when dealing with trademarks?   Did *Castleton* err in relying so strongly on the affixation metaphor?   On at least four occasions before the Lanham Act passed, Congress rejected attempts to broaden effective trademark use to include use in advertising and, in the Act, confined the departure from prior federal and common law to accrediting the use of trademarks in associated displays.   See D. Robert, The New Trade-Mark Manual 15 (1947).

2. DISTINCTIVENESS

See Statute Supplement 15 U.S.C.A. § 1052.

a. COMMON LAW THEORY

CANAL CO. v. CLARK

Supreme Court of the United States, 1871.
80 U.S. 311, 20 L.Ed. 581.

Mr. Justice STRONG delivered the opinion of the court.

The first and leading question presented by this case is whether the complainants have an exclusive right to the use of the words "Lackawanna coal," as a distinctive name or trade-mark for the coal mined by them and transported over their railroad and canal to market.

The averments of the bill are supported by no inconsiderable evidence. The complainants were undoubtedly, if not the first, among the first producers of coal from the Lackawanna Valley, and the coal sent to market by them has been generally known and designated as Lackawanna coal. Whether the name "Lackawanna coal" was devised or adopted by them as a trade-mark before it came into common use is not so clearly established. On the contrary the evidence shows that long before the complainants commenced their operations, and long before they had any existence as a corporation, the region of country in which their mines were situated was called "The Lackawanna Valley"; that it is a region of large dimensions, extending along the Lackawanna River to its junction with the Susquehanna, embracing within its limits great bodies of coal lands, upon a portion of which are the mines of the complainants, and upon other portions of which are the mines of The Pennsylvania Coal Company, those of The Delaware, Lackawanna, and Western Railroad Company, and those of other smaller operators. The word "Lackawanna," then, was not devised by the complainants. They found it a settled and known appellative of the district in which their coal deposits and those of others were situated. At the time when they began to use it, it was a recognized description of the region, and of course of the earths and minerals in the region.

The bill alleges, however, not only that the complainants devised, adopted, and appropriated the word, as a name or trade-mark for their coal, but that it had never before been used, or applied in combination with the word "coal," as a name or trade-mark for any kind of coal, and it is the combination of the word Lackawanna with the word coal that constitutes the trade-mark to the exclusive use of which they assert a right.

It may be observed there is no averment that the other coal of the Lackawanna Valley differs at all in character or quality from that mined on the complainants' lands. On the contrary, the bill alleges that it cannot easily be distinguished therefrom by inspection. The bill is therefore an attempt to secure to the complainants the exclusive use of the name "Lackawanna coal," as applied, not to any manufacture of theirs, but to that portion of the coal of the Lackawanna Valley which they mine and send to market, differing neither in nature or quality from all other coal of the same region.

Undoubtedly words or devices may be adopted as trademarks which are not original inventions of him who adopts them, and courts of equity will protect him against any fraudulent appropriation or imitation of them by others. Property in a trade-mark, or rather in the use of a trade-mark or name, has very little analogy to that which exists in copyrights, or in patents for inventions. Words in common use, with some exceptions, may be adopted, if, at the time of their adoption, they were not employed to designate the same, or like articles of production. The office of a trade-mark is to point out distinctively the origin, or ownership of the article to which it is affixed; or, in other words, to give notice who was the producer. This may, in many cases, be done by a name, a mark, or a device well known, but not previously applied to the same article.

But though it is not necessary that the word adopted as a trade-name should be a new creation, never before known or used, there are some limits to the right of selection. This will be manifest when it is considered that in all cases where rights to the exclusive use of a trade-mark are invaded, it is invariably held that the essence of the wrong consists in the sale of the goods of one manufacturer or vendor as those of another; and that it is only when this false representation is directly or indirectly made that the party who appeals to a court of equity can have relief. This is the doctrine of all the authorities. Hence the trademark must either by itself, or by association, point distinctively to the origin or ownership of the article to which it is applied. The reason of this is that unless it does, neither can he who first adopted it be injured by any appropriation or imitation of it by others, nor can the public be deceived. The first appropriator of a name or device pointing to his ownership, or which, by being associated with articles of trade, has acquired an understood reference to the originator, or manufacturer of the articles, is injured whenever another adopts the same name or device for similar articles, because such adoption is in effect representing falsely that the productions of the latter are those of the former. Thus the custom and advantages to which the enterprise and skill of the first appropriator had given him a just right are abstracted for another's use, and this is done by deceiving the public, by inducing the public to purchase the goods and manufactures of one person supposing them to be those of another. The trademark must therefore be distinctive in its original signification, pointing to the origin of the article, or it must have become such by association. And there are two rules which are not to be overlooked. No one can claim protection for the exclusive use of a trade-mark or trade-name which would practically give him a monopoly in the sale of any goods other than those produced or made by

himself. If he could, the public would be injured rather than protected, for competition would be destroyed. Nor can a generic name, or
a name merely descriptive of an article of trade, of its qualities, ingredients, or characteristics, be employed as a trade-mark and the exclusive use of it be entitled to legal protection. As we said in the
well-considered case of The Amoskeag Manufacturing Company v.
Spear, "the owner of an original trade-mark has an undoubted right
to be protected in the exclusive use of all the marks, forms, or symbols, that were appropriated as designating the true origin or ownership of the article or fabric to which they are affixed; but he has no
right to the exclusive use of any words, letters, figures, or symbols,
which have no relation to the origin or ownership of the goods, but
are only meant to indicate their names or quality. He has no right
to appropriate a sign or a symbol, which, from the nature of the fact
it is used to signify, others may employ with equal truth, and therefore have an equal right to employ for the same purpose."

And it is obvious that the same reasons which forbid the exclusive appropriation of generic names or of those merely descriptive of
the article manufactured and which can be employed with truth by
other manufacturers, apply with equal force to the appropriation of
geographical names, designating districts of country. Their nature is
such that they cannot point to the origin (personal origin) or ownership of the articles of trade to which they may be applied. They
point only at the place of production, not to the producer, and could
they be appropriated exclusively, the appropriation would result in
mischievous monopolies. Could such phrases, as "Pennsylvania
wheat," "Kentucky hemp," "Virginia tobacco," or "Sea Island cotton," be protected as trade-marks; could any one prevent all others
from using them, or from selling articles produced in the districts
they describe under those appellations, it would greatly embarrass
trade, and secure exclusive rights to individuals in that which is the
common right of many. It can be permitted only when the reasons
that lie at the foundation of the protection given to trade-marks are
entirely overlooked. It cannot be said that there is any attempt to
deceive the public when one sells as Kentucky hemp, or as Lehigh
coal, that which in truth is such, or that there is any attempt to appropriate the enterprise or business reputation of another who may
have previously sold his goods with the same description. It is not
selling one man's goods as and for those of another. Nothing is more
common than that a manufacturer sends his products to market, designating them by the name of the place where they were made. But
we think no case can be found in which other producers of similar
products in the same place, have been restrained from the use of the
same name in describing their goods. . . .

McAndrews v. Bassett is another case cited by the complainants.
The plaintiffs in that case were manufacturers of liquorice made
from roots and juice imported from Anatolia and Spain, and they
sent their goods to market stamped "Anatolia." Soon afterwards the
defendants made to order from a sample of the plaintiff's liquorice,

other liquorice which they also stamped "Anatolia." It was a clear case of an attempt to imitate the mark previously existing, and to put upon the market the new manufacture as that of the first manufacturers. It does not appear, from the report of the case, that the juice or roots from which the defendants' article was made came from Anatolia. If not their mark was false. Of course the Lord Chancellor enjoined them. In answer to the argument that the word Anatolia was in fact the geographical designation of a whole country, a word common to all, and that therefore there could be no property in it, he said, "Property in the word for all purposes cannot exist; but property in that word as applied by way of stamp upon a stick of liquorice does exist the moment a stick of liquorice goes into the market so stamped and obtains acceptance and reputation in the market." It was not merely the use of the word, but its application by way of stamp upon each stick of liquorice that was protected. Nothing in this case determines that a right to use the name of a region of country as a trade-mark for an article may be acquired, to the exclusion of others who produce or sell a similar article coming from the same region. . . .

It must then be considered as sound doctrine that no one can apply the name of a district of country to a well-known article of commerce, and obtain thereby such an exclusive right to the application as to prevent others inhabiting the district or dealing in similar articles coming from the district, from truthfully using the same designation. It is only when the adoption or imitation of what is claimed to be a trade-mark amounts to a false representation, express or implied, designed or incidental, that there is any title to relief against it. True it may be that the use by a second producer, in describing truthfully his product, of a name or a combination of words already in use by another, may have the effect of causing the public to mistake as to the origin or ownership of the product, but if it is just as true in its application to his goods as it is to those of another who first applied it, and who therefore claims an exclusive right to use it, there is no legal or moral wrong done. Purchasers may be mistaken, but they are not deceived by false representations, and equity will not enjoin against telling the truth.

These principles, founded alike on reason and authority, are decisive of the present case, and they relieve us from the consideration of much that was pressed upon us in the argument. The defendant has advertised for sale and he is selling coal not obtained from the plaintiffs, not mined or brought to market by them, but coal which he purchased from the Pennsylvania Coal Company, or from the Delaware, Lackawanna, and Western Railroad Company. He has advertised and sold it as Lackawanna coal. It is in fact coal from the Lackawanna region. It is of the same quality and of the same general appearance as that mined by the complainants. It is taken from the same veins or strata. It is truly described by the term Lackawanna coal, as is the coal of plaintiffs. The description does not point to its origin or ownership, nor indicate in the slightest degree the person, natural or artificial, who mined the coal or brought it to market. All the coal taken from that region is known and has been known for years by the trade, and rated in public statistics as Lackawanna coal. True the Delaware, Lackawanna, and Western Railroad Company have sometimes called their coal Scranton coal, and sometimes Scranton coal from the Lackawanna, and the Pennsylvania Coal Company have called theirs Pittston coal, thus referring to the parts of the region in which they mine. But the generic name, the comprehensive name for it all is Lackawanna coal. In all the coal regions there are numerous collieries, owned and operated by different proprietors, yet the product is truly and rightfully described as Schuylkill, Lehigh, or Lackawanna coal, according to the region from which it comes. We are therefore of opinion that the defendant has invaded no right to which the plaintiffs can maintain a claim. By advertising and selling coal brought from the Lackawanna Valley as Lackawanna coal, he has made no false representation, and we see no evidence that he has attempted to sell his coal as and for the coal of the plaintiffs. If the public are led into mistake, it is by the truth, not by any false pretense. If the complainants' sales are diminished, it is because they are not the only producers of Lackawanna coal, and not because of any fraud of the defendant. The decree of the Circuit Court dismissing the bill must, therefore, be Affirmed.

KELLOGG CO. v. NATIONAL BISCUIT CO., 305 U.S. 111, 118–119, 83 L.Ed. 73, 39 U.S.P.Q. 296 (1938). Mr. Justice BRANDEIS: . . . It is contended that the plaintiff has the exclusive right to the name "Shredded Wheat," because those words acquired the "secondary meaning" of shredded wheat made at Niagara Falls by the plaintiff's predecessor. There is no basis here for applying the doctrine of secondary meaning. The evidence shows only that due to the long period in which the plaintiff or its predecessor was the only manufacturer of the product, many people have come to associate the product, and as a consequence the name by which the product is generally known, with the plaintiff's factory at Niagara Falls. But to establish a trade name in the term "shredded wheat" the plaintiff must show more than a subordinate meaning which applies to it. It must show that the primary significance of the term in the minds of the consuming public is not the product but the producer. This it has not done. The showing which it has made does not entitle it to the exclusive use of the term shredded wheat but merely entitles it to require that the defendant use reasonable care to inform the public of the source of its product.

FRANKLIN KNITTING MILLS, INC. v. FASHIONIT SWEATER MILLS, INC., 297 F. 247, 248 (S.D.N.Y.1923), aff'd 4 F.2d 1018 (2d Cir. 1925). L. HAND, J.: . . . I have always been at a loss to know why so many marks are adopted which have an aura, or more, of description about them. With the whole field of possible coinage before them, it is strange that merchants insist upon adopting marks that are so nearly descriptive. Probably they wish to interject into the name of their goods some intimation of excellence, and are willing to incur the risk. In the case at bar the plaintiff, in my judgment, has gone beyond the line, and has chosen a mark which, if not of description, at least designates quality or character.

The word "Fashionknit," being made up of two words of common use, necessarily carries over into their conjunction the meanings of each. Two such words might indeed be so incompatible that their juxtaposition would make nonsense, as, for example, "Hardsoft" or "Illwell;" but, if they are not, the resulting syllables will generally carry a very perceptible significance. Here the elements chosen seem to me to fit into what it is true is an awkward, but is yet altogether a comprehensible, word. As applied to neckties, "Fashionknit" certainly means "knit in fashion" or "fashionably knit"; it can mean nothing else, and the mind naturally attributes some meaning to the combination of such usual words. Whether the plaintiff's ties are in fact knit in fashion is irrelevant; at least they assert it. As applied to sweaters, the same thing is true. It may be true, though I profess no expertness in the matter, that the possible variations in knitting sweaters are not wide. That makes no difference; the word, when used of knitted goods, is equivalent to "Fashionmade," which is certainly descriptive, and only such. I have not the least doubt that it produces the effect intended; that the plaintiff expected its customers vaguely to understand that its clothes were knitted as fashionable clothes should be knitted.

It is quite impossible to get any rule out of the cases beyond this: That the validity of the mark ends where suggestion ends and description begins. The nearest case is perhaps Judge Hough's decision on "Porosknit," Chalmers Knitting Co. v. Columbia, etc., Co. (C.C.) 160 Fed. 1013, though that mark was more clearly descriptive.

GENERAL SHOE CORP. v. ROSEN, 111 F.2d 95, 98, 45 U.S.P. Q. 196 (4th Cir. 1940). SOPER, J.: Between these two extremes lies a middle ground wherein terms of mingled qualities are found. It cannot be said that they are primarily descriptive or that they are purely arbitrary or fanciful without any indication of the nature of the goods which they denominate. Such terms, indeed, shed some light upon the characteristics of the goods, but so applied they involve an element of incongruity, and in order to be understood as descriptive, they must be taken in a suggestive or figurative sense through an effort of the imagination on the part of the observer. Many such suggestive terms have been approved as valid trade marks by the courts, e. g., "Mouse Seed" as applied to poisoned grain for mice, W. G. Reardon Laboratories v. B. & B. Exterminators, 4 Cir., 71 F.2d 515; "Arch Builder" and "Heel Leveler" as applied to shoes, In re Irving Drew Co., 54 App.D.C. 310, 297 F. 889; "Chicken of the Sea", as applied to canned tuna, Van Camp Sea Food Co. v. Alexander B. Stewart Organizations, Cust. & Pat.App., 50 F.2d 976. See, also, Sierra Chemical Co. v. Berettini, 7 Cir., 33 F.2d 397. In our opinion, the word "Friendly," as applied to shoes, belongs in this classification. Primarily it is applied to animate objects in the sense of pertaining to a friend or befitting friendship. When used in a figurative sense in connection with an article of apparel it suggests one that is comfortable or suited to the needs of the wearer, as is indicated in the slogan "Friendly to the Feet;" but its appropriateness in this respect becomes apparent to the reader only after some mental effort on his part.

PEDERSEN, THE ADVERTISING AGENCY ROLE IN SELECTION AND USE OF TRADEMARKS

47 Trademark Rep. 791, 799–800 (1957).*

More and more trademarks owe their real meaning—what they mean in people's minds—to concepts created and maintained by advertising. And advertising's efforts are directed at getting people to do something about brands—brands of ideas—as well as brands of goods and services.

So at J. Walter Thompson Company and other advertising agencies, we find ourselves concerned with many phases of trademarks. We work with our clients to create them. We try to keep them up to date with changing market conditions. We look for ways to increase their usefulness as working parts of the advertising—not just signatures. As new forms of presentations develop—like television—we adapt trademarks to them.

BAN. I suggest that BAN (upper case please) is a fine suggestive mark. It also suggests that if I had my way, I would ban (lower case, please) every abstract debate on arbitrary versus suggestive marks. The history of trademarks is replete with successes of both kinds—and even for goods of the same class. There's BOKAR and EIGHT O'CLOCK. IPANA and GLEEM. LUX and SWAN ad infinitum.

As the racetrack boys would say, a good trademark is not sired by law alone. The blood line must include ingenuity out of knowledge, and market conditions out of competition.

It seems that more and more smart money is going on suggestive entries. Why?

I suggest that it is because the dope sheets are showing up items like the following:

1. The initial cost of product development and mass production is high. The manufacturer needs to amortize quickly. This calls for building sales volume quickly. To be a winner, the new entry must be a fast starter.

2. Direct competition has never been so fast moving or hard hitting. There may be many other entries in the same race, including old favorites.

3. There has never been so much indirect competition—so many demands on the public's attention. There are lots of different races being run.

And so, from the merchant's viewpoint, a suggestive mark may be his best bet, if it has been carefully and imaginatively calculated to catch the public attention, if it carries a connotation that steps up the advertising message.

KING–SEELEY THERMOS CO. v. ALADDIN INDUSTRIES, INC.

United States Court of Appeals, Second Circuit, 1963.
321 F.2d 577, 138 U.S.P.Q. 349.

LEONARD P. MOORE, Circuit Judge.

This action by [sic] brought by appellant King-Seeley Thermos Co. (King-Seeley) to enjoin the defendant, Aladdin Industries, Incorporated from threatened infringement of eight trademark registrations for the word "Thermos" owned by appellant. Defendant answered, acknowledging its intention to sell its vacuum-insulated containers as "thermos bottles," asserted that the term "thermos" or "thermos bottle" is a generic term in the English language, asked that plaintiff's registrations of its trademark "Thermos" be cancelled and that it be adjudicated that plaintiff have no trademark rights in the word "thermos" on its vacuum bottles. The trial court held that plaintiff's registrations were valid but that the word "thermos" had become "a generic descriptive word in the English language . . . as a synonym for 'vacuum insulated' container." 207 F.Supp. 9.

The facts are set out at great length in the comprehensive and well-reasoned opinion of the district court and will not be detailed here. In that opinion, the court reviewed King-Seeley's corporate history and its use of the trademark "Thermos." He found that from 1907 to 1923, King-Seeley undertook advertising and educational campaigns that tended to make "thermos" a generic term descriptive of the product rather than of its origin. This consequence flowed from the corporation's attempt to popularize "Thermos bottle" as the name of that product without including any of the generic terms then used, such as "Thermos vacuum-insulated bottle." The court found that by 1923 the word "thermos" had acquired firm roots as a descriptive or generic word.

At about 1923, because of the suggestion in an opinion of a district court that "Thermos" might be a descriptive word, King-Seeley adopted the use of the word "vacuum" or "vacuum bottle" with the word "Thermos." Although "Thermos" was generally recognized in the trade as a trademark, the corporation did police the trade and notified those using "thermos" in a descriptive sense that it was a trademark. It failed, however, to take affirmative action to seek out generic uses by non-trade publications and protested only those which happened to come to its attention. Between 1923 and the early 1950's the generic use of "thermos" had grown to a marked extent in non-trade publications and by the end of this period there was widespread use by the unorganized public of "thermos" as a synonym for "vacuum insulated." The court concluded that King-Seeley had failed to use due diligence to rescue "Thermos" from becoming a descriptive or generic term.

Between 1954 and 1957, plaintiff showed awareness of the widespread generic use of "thermos" and of the need to educate the public to the word's trademark significance. It diversified its products to include those not directly related to containers designed to keep their contents hot or cold. It changed its name from the American Thermos Bottle Company to The American Thermos Products Company and intensified its policing activities of trade and non-trade publications. The court found, however, that the generic use of "thermos" had become so firmly impressed as a part of the everyday language of the American public that plaintiff's extraordinary efforts commencing in the mid-1950's came too late to keep "thermos" from falling into the public domain. The court also held that appellant's trademarks are valid and because there is an appreciable, though minority, segment of the consumer public which knows and recognizes plaintiff's trademarks, it imposed certain restrictions and limitations on the use of the word "thermos" by defendant.

We affirm the district court's decision that the major significance of the word "thermos" is generic. No useful purpose would be served by repeating here what is fully documented in the opinion of the court below.

Appellant's primary protest on appeal is directed at the district court's finding that

> "The word 'thermos' became a part of the public domain because of the plaintiff's wide dissemination of the word 'thermos' used as a synonym for 'vacuum-insulated' and as an adjectival-noun, 'thermos', through its educational and advertising campaigns and because of the plaintiff's lack of reasonable diligence in asserting and protecting its trademark rights in the word 'Thermos' among the members of the unorganized public, exclusive of those in the trade, from 1907 to the date of this action." 207 F.Supp. at 14.

We are not convinced that the trademark's loss of distinctiveness was the result of some failure on plaintiff's part. Substantial efforts to preserve the trademark significance of the word were made by plaintiff, especially with respect to members of the trade. However, there was little they could do to prevent the public from using "thermos" in a generic rather than a trademark sense. And whether the appropriation by the public was due to highly successful educational and advertising campaigns or to lack of diligence in policing or not is of no consequence; the fact is that the word "thermos" had entered the public domain beyond recall. Even as early as 1910 plaintiff itself asserted that "Thermos had become a household word."

Judge Anderson found that although a substantial majority of the public knows and used the word "thermos", only a small minority of the public knows that this word has trademark significance. He wrote at 207 F.Supp. 21–22:

"The results of the survey [conducted at the behest of the defendant] were that about 75% of adults in the United States who were familiar with containers that keep the contents hot or cold, call such a container a 'thermos'; about 12% of the adult American public know that 'thermos' has a trade-mark significance, and about 11% use the term 'vacuum bottle'. This is generally corroborative of the court's conclusions drawn from the other evidence, except that such other evidence indicated that a somewhat larger minority than 12% was aware of the trademark meaning of 'thermos'; and a somewhat larger minority than 11% used the descriptive term 'vacuum' bottle or other container."

The record amply supports these findings.

Appellant argues that the court below misapplied the doctrine of the Aspirin and Cellophane cases. Its primary contention is that in those cases, there was no generic name, such as vacuum bottle, that was suitable for use by the general public. As a result, to protect the use of the only word that identified the product in the mind of the public would give the owners of the trademark an unfair competitive advantage. The rule of those cases, however, does not rest on this factor. Judge Learned Hand stated the sole issue in Aspirin to be: "What do the buyers understand by the word for whose use the parties are contending? If they understand by it only the kind of goods sold, then, I take it, it makes no difference whatever what efforts the plaintiff has made to get them to understand more." 272 F. at 509. Of course, it is obvious that the fact that there was no suitable descriptive word for either aspirin or cellophane made it difficult, if not impossible, for the original manufacturers to prevent their trademark from becoming generic. But the test is not what is available as an alternative to the public, but what the public's understanding is of the word that it uses. What has happened here is that the public had become accustomed to calling vacuum bottles by the word "thermos." If a buyer walked into a retail store asking for a thermos bottle, meaning any vacuum bottle and not specifically plaintiff's product, the fact that the appellation "vacuum bottle" was available to him is of no significance. The two terms had become synonymous; in fact, defendant's survey showed that the public was far more inclined to use the word "thermos" to describe a container that keeps its contents hot or cold than the phrase "vacuum bottle."

Appellant asserts that the courts in a number of cases have upheld the continued exclusive use of a dual functioning trademark, which both identifies the class of product as well as its source. As this court recently indicated:

"a mark is not generic merely because it has *some* significance
to the public as an indication of the nature or class of an article.
. . . . In order to become generic the *principal* significance of
the word must be its indication of the nature or class of an article, rather than an indication of its origin."

Feathercombs, Inc. v. Solo Products Corp., 306 F.2d 251, 256 (2 Cir.),
cert. denied, 371 U.S. 910, 83 S.Ct. 253, 9 L.Ed.2d 170. But see
Marks v. Polaroid Corp., supra, 129 F.Supp. at 270 ("a defendant
alleging invalidity of a trademark for genericness must show that to
the consuming public as a whole the word has lost all its trademark
significance").

Since in this case, the primary significance to the public of the
word "thermos" is its indication of the nature and class of an article
rather than as an indication of its source, whatever duality of meaning the word still holds for a minority of the public is of little consequence except as a consideration in the framing of a decree. Since
the great majority of those members of the public who use the word
"thermos" are not aware of any trademark significance, there is not
enough dual use to support King-Seeley's claims to monopoly of the
word as a trademark.

No doubt, the Aspirin and Cellophane doctrine can be a harsh
one for it places a penalty on the manufacturer who has made skillful
use of advertising and has popularized his product. However, King-
Seeley has enjoyed a commercial monopoly of the word "thermos"
for over fifty years. During that period, despite its efforts to protect
the trademark, the public has virtually expropriated it as its own.
The word having become part of the public domain, it would be unfair to unduly restrict the right of a competitor of King-Seeley to use
the word.

The court below, mindful of the fact that some members of the
public and a substantial portion of the trade still recognize and use
the word "thermos" as a trademark, framed an eminently fair decree
designed to afford King-Seeley as much future protection as was possible. The decree provides that defendant must invariably precede
the use of the word "thermos" by the possessive of the name "Aladdin"; that the defendant must confine its use of "thermos" to the
lower-case "t"; and that it may never use the words "original" or
"genuine" in describing its product. In addition, plaintiff is entitled
to retain the exclusive right to all of its present forms of the trademark "Thermos" without change. These conditions provide a sound
and proper balancing of the competitive disadvantage to defendants
arising out of plaintiff's exclusive use of the word "thermos" and the
risk that those who recognize "Thermos" as a trademark will be deceived.

The courts should be ever alert, as the district court said, "to
eliminate confusion and the possibility of deceit." The purchasing
public is entitled to know the source of the article it desires to purchase. It is not within our province to speculate whether the dire

predictions made by appellant in forceful appellate argument will come to pass. Certain it is that the district court made every endeavor in its judgment to give as much protection to plaintiff as possible. The use by defendant of the now generic word "thermos" was substantially curtailed. Plaintiff's trademark "thermos" was protected in every style of printing except the lower case "thermos" and then the use of the word must be preceded by the possessive of defendant's name "Aladdin" or the possessive of "Aladdin" plus one of defendant's brand names. Any doubt about plaintiff's position in the field is removed by the prohibition against the use by defendant in labeling, advertising or publication of the words "genuine" or "original" in referring to the word "thermos". Furthermore, the district court has given both parties the opportunity to apply to it for such orders and directions as may be warranted in the light of changed circumstances and for the enforcement of compliance or for the punishment of violations. In our opinion the trial court has reached a most equitable solution which gives appropriate consideration to the law and the facts.

Affirmed.

NOTES

1.   Is distinctiveness a single requirement, or is it in fact a number of different requirements, each serving a different purpose? Does the disqualification of descriptive terms—"Fold-Shot" for a folding camera, for example—serve a purpose different from the disqualification of geographical terms—"Rochester," say, for the same item? Can the question whether a mark is distinctive be answered categorically, or is it more properly treated contextually and as a question of degree? For instance, can it be said that, as applied to folding cameras, the terms "Shur-Shot" and "Gold Medal" are or are not distinctive, or does correct analysis call for the consideration of other factors—the similarity between the terms used by plaintiff and defendant, and the similarity between the goods or services offered by each.

Does the distinctiveness requirement serve or disserve one of trademark law's professed objectives—protecting the consumer from deception respecting goods and services? Would the *Canal* Court have allowed plaintiff's action if defendant's coal had not been mined in the Lackawanna Valley? Compare American Washboard Co. v. Saginaw Mfg. Co., supra p. 71. If it had been mined there but its quality had been inferior to that of plaintiff's coal? Would the National Biscuit Company have had an action if Kellogg's product had not in fact been shredded wheat? If it had been shredded wheat, but of a quality inferior to plaintiff's product? Could defendant in *General Shoe* have successfully argued that plaintiff's "Friendly" shoes were, in fact, uncomfortable, poorly made and not at all friendly to the wearer's feet?

What do trademarks signify to consumers in today's marketplace? Should a term's distinctiveness turn on a showing "that the primary significance of the term in the minds of the consuming public is not the product but the producer"? How many consumers care to know the name of the company that produced the cereal they had for breakfast? How many even care to know that the same anonymous company that produced the last box of cereal is also responsible for the one they are about to buy—so long as the quality of the product is consistent? How much truth is there to the following truisms taken from Anti-Monopoly, Inc. v. General Mills Fun Group, Inc., 611 F.2d 296, 301, 204 U.S.P.Q. 978 (9th Cir. 1979): " 'The trademark can be a potent weapon in the competitive contest, for it guarantees, identifies, and sells the article to which it refers.' 3 R. Callman, Unfair Competition, Trademarks, and Monopolies, § 65 at 3 (1969). But all of these legitimate trademark purposes derive ultimately from the mark's representation of a single fact: the product's source."

Do trademarks do more, or less, than promise consistent quality of a single product? What motivates a consumer to purchase sunglasses or a wristwatch bearing the mark of Porsche, the German automobile manufacturer? Is there some point at which a mark takes on a life of its own, apart from any products to which it might be attached, and becomes itself an item for consumption?

For a challenging critique of orthodox distinctiveness theory, see Martin, The Meaning of Distinctiveness in Trademark Law, 45 Ill.L. Rev. 535 (1950).

2. The *Thermos* court was premature in its expression of optimism over the security to be afforded by the trial court decree. Judge Anderson's careful resolution, though it no doubt gave "appropriate consideration to the law and the facts," did not staunch the further erosion of plaintiff's rights in its mark. In 1968 the district court denied Aladdin's petition for a modification of the injunction, 289 F. Supp. 155, 159 U.S.P.Q. 604 (1968). On Aladdin's appeal, the court of appeals vacated the order of denial, 418 F.2d 31, 163 U.S.P.Q. 65 (2d Cir.).

Judge Anderson, who by now had ascended to the court of appeals, was designated to consider the petition on the remand to the district court. Recognizing that "it is unrealistic to assume that the situation has remained unchanged since 1962," and that "more than eight years of widespread use of the word 'thermos' as a generic term must, to a considerable degree, have brought home to the unorganized public, including the approximately 11% who in 1962 recognized and relied upon King-Seeley's trademarks, that there were both the trade name use and the generic use," he held that Aladdin was entitled to a modification of the decree, "which will, first, afford to it, in its advertising material, trade literature and press releases, the use of the word 'thermos' with an initial capital 'T' where such initial capitalization is required by the generally accepted and authoritatively approved rules of grammar, and second, eliminate the requirement that the use of lower case 'thermos,' in its advertising material, trade literature and press releases, be preceded by the possessive of 'Aladdin' or by the possessive of 'Aladdin' with one of Aladdin's brand names provided any such use makes clear that it emanates from Aladdin." 320 F.Supp. 1156, 1159, 166 U.S.P.Q. 381 (D.Conn.1970).

In Bayer v. United Drug Co., 272 F. 505 (S.D.N.Y.1921), Judge Learned Hand took a different approach to arresting the erosion of a mark possessing generic connotations. Finding that, for physicians, manufacturing chemists, and probably retail druggists, the term "Aspirin" had always functioned as a trademark and signified the plaintiff, but that for the general consuming public the term had become generic, describing acetylsalicylic acid, Hand entered a bifurcated decree enjoining defendant's use of the term in its sales to manufacturing chemists, physicians and retail druggists but permitting its unfettered use in direct sales to the general public. Given the typical ungainliness of names assigned on the basis of a product's chemical formula, could you, as counsel to a pharmaceutical concern, devise a program that would assure your client full trademark protection in both markets, professional and nonprofessional, identified by Judge Hand? See Weigel, Generic Names versus Trademarks, 52 Trademark Rep. 768 (1962) for one approach.

3.   Should a trademark used in connection with patented subject matter fall into the public domain upon expiration of the patent? In the *Shredded Wheat* case, excerpted above, the Court drew on broad dicta in Singer Mfg. Co. v. June Mfg. Co., 163 U.S. 169 (1896), for an affirmative answer: "Since during the life of the patent 'Shredded Wheat' was the general designation of the patented product, there passed to the public on the expiration of the patent, not only the right to make the article as it was made during the patent period, but also the right to apply thereto the name by which it had become known." 305 U.S. 118. That the term "Shredded Wheat" had a predominantly descriptive significance at the time the patents expired is clear. Is it clear, though, that as applied to plaintiff's product, the term was not fatally descriptive from the start? See Derenberg, "Shredded Wheat"—The Still-Born Trade-Mark, 16 N.Y.U.L.Q.Rev. 376 (1939).

The *Singer* Court did not, in fact, adopt a rule that trademarks used with patented subject matter are, as a matter of law, cast into the public domain upon the patent's expiration. It held only that previous patent protection is one of several facts to be considered in the determination whether a mark has become generic. The Court viewed the case as raising two essentially factual questions—"first, were the sewing machines made by the Singer Company so, in whole or in part, protected by patents as to cause the name 'Singer' to become, during the existence of the monopoly, the generic designation of such machines . . .   second, irrespective of the question of patent, was the name 'Singer' by the consent and acquiescence of Singer himself and that of the Singer Company, voluntarily used as a generic designation of the class and character of machines manufactured by I. M. Singer & Co. or the Singer Manufacturing Company so that in consequence of this voluntary action the name became the generic designation of the machines. . . . "

The Court's answer to the first question blended into its resolution of the second. Noting that, from "the beginning every machine had conspicuously marked on it the name of the manufacturer, 'I. M. Singer & Co.' or the 'Singer Mfg. Co.'; only occasionally was the word 'Singer' alone attached to any of the machines;" and that, at about the time the patents expired, "the trade-mark was affixed to the machines, and the name of the manufacturer, except as indicated by the trade-mark, disappeared, and was regularly supplanted by the word 'Singer' alone," the Court concluded: "This coincidence between the expiration of the patents and the appearance of the trade-mark on the machines and the use of the word 'Singer' alone tends to create a strong implication that the company, with the knowledge that the patents, which covered their machines, were about to expire substituted the trade-mark for the plain designation of the source of manufacture theretofore continuously used and added the word 'Singer' which had become the designation by which the public knew the machine, as a distinctive and separate mark, in order thereby to retain in the possession of the company the real fruits of the monopoly when that monopoly had passed away." 163 U.S. 181. After an extensive review of this and other facts, the Court decided that the mark "Singer" had become generic. It also ruled, however, that defendant was not at complete liberty and must accompany uses of the mark on its products with a clear indication that it, not Singer, was their source. For the suggestion that the "Singer" mark itself has been substantially resurrected, see Singer Mfg. Co. v. Redlich, 109 F. Supp. 623, 96 U.S.P.Q. 85 (S.D.Cal.1952).

4. In May, 1978 the Federal Trade Commission filed a petition under Lanham Act § 14, 15 U.S.C.A. § 1064, seeking cancellation of the trademark, "Formica," on the ground that the term had become generic as applied to "laminated sheets of wood, fabric, or paper impregnated with synthetic resin and consolidated under heat and pressure, for use on table tops, furniture and wall panelling." Petition for Cancellation, F. T. C. v. Formica Corp., Cancellation No. 11955, 200 U.S.P.Q. 182, 185 (T.T.A.B. May 31, 1978). The move produced a small furor among advertisers, the trademark bar and, eventually, in Congress. One result of the ensuing inquiry was that Congress cut off funds for the F.T.C. suit. On June 13, 1980, the Trademark Trial and Appeal Board dismissed the action with prejudice. 496 P.T.C.J. A–12 (Sept. 18, 1980).

For a superb review and analysis of the *Formica* petition and the ensuing judicial and legislative developments, see Comment, Section 14 of the Lanham Act—F.T.C. Authority to Challenge Generic Trademarks, 48 Fordham L.Rev. 437 (1980). The *Formica* petition and the economics of generic marks are considered in Folsom & Teply, Trademarked Generic Words, 89 Yale L.J. 1323 (1980).

5. What *practical* steps can a trademark owner take to prevent its mark from falling victim to genericide? What practical steps, in

addition to those already undertaken, could King-Seeley have taken to protect its mark, "Thermos"?

What *legal* steps can a trademark owner take to prevent its mark from becoming generic? Competitors' use of the mark on similar goods and services clearly falls within the ambit of trademark infringement actions. But what rights does the trademark owner have against individuals who use the term descriptively in conversation? What rights does it have against publishers of trade and popular journals and dictionaries that refer to the mark in its descriptive sense? In Selchow & Righter Co. v. McGraw-Hill Book Co., 580 F.2d 25, 198 U.S.P.Q. 577 (2d Cir. 1978), plaintiff, registrant of the mark "Scrabble" for use in connection with games, scoring devices, score pads and accessories, was allowed a preliminary injunction against defendant's distribution of "The Complete Scrabble Dictionary." The Court of Appeals agreed with the District Court that, because publication of defendant's book "might render the 'SCRABBLE' trademark generic," plaintiff had sufficiently demonstrated the possibility of irreparable injury. 580 F.2d 27.

See generally, Treece & Stephenson, Another Look at Descriptive and Generic Terms in American Trademark Law, 29 Sw.L.Rev. 547 (1975).

b. STATUTORY VARIATIONS ON THE COMMON LAW THEME

(i) "MERELY DESCRIPTIVE"

⋅IN RE SUN OIL CO.

United States Court of Customs and Patent Appeals, 1970.
426 F.2d 401, 165 U.S.P.Q. 718.

ALMOND, Judge.

Sun Oil Company brings this appeal from the decision of the Trademark Trial and Appeal Board, 155 U.S.P.Q. 600 (1967), affirming the examiner's refusal to allow appellant's application to register "Custom-Blended" for gasoline on the ground that the mark is merely descriptive of applicant's goods within the meaning of section 2(e)(1) of the Trademark Act of 1946 (15 U.S.C.A. § 1052(e)(1)) and because the evidence submitted has not clearly established a secondary meaning, denoting that the mark has become distinctive of appellant's goods, within section 2(f) of the Act (15 U.S.C.A. § 1052 (f).

The application seeking registration on the Principal Register alleges use since 1956. The mark is displayed on special pumps, called "blending pumps," at appellant's service stations. The application is designated a continuation of an earlier application filed July 13, 1961, in which registration on the Principal Register was sought for the same mark for gasoline and refused by the Trademark Trial and Appeal Board on the ground that the mark was merely a descriptive connotation to purchasers of applicant's goods.

In his Answer, the examiner predicated refusal of registration on the ground that Custom-Blended is merely descriptive of appellant's goods within the meaning of section 2(e)(1) because it is so highly descriptive of appellant's blended gasoline that it is incapable of becoming distinctive as claimed. It was the examiner's opinion that the term Custom-Blended merely informs purchasers that various grades of gasoline from appellant's blending pumps are custom blended for them; that the word "custom" is commonly used to indicate things made to order; that it has very little trademark significance when used in connection with blended gasoline; that appellant is not entitled to exclusive appropriation of this term, which so aptly describes custom-blended gasoline; and that the conclusion derived from surveys conducted by appellant is that purchasers who are acquainted with appellant's Blue Sunoco gasoline know that such gasoline is custom blended.

In affirming refusal of registration, the board stated that granted that the generic terms for appellant's blended gasolines are pump-blended and multiple-grade gasolines, there is no question that " 'Custom-Blended' has a merely descriptive significance in that it will immediately indicate to patrons of applicant's service stations that the various grades of gasoline dispensed thereat are custom blended to their needs and requirements;" that in view thereof and the decision on applicant's prior application, it was incumbent upon applicant to show that the facts and circumstances since that decision have changed in that " 'Custom-Blended' now serves as an indication of origin of applicant's gasoline to the general public;" that the case, therefore, turned upon the sufficiency of applicant's evidence in that regard; that "the only definite conclusion that can be drawn from the surveys is that purchasers who are acquainted with applicant's 'Sunoco' gasoline know that such gasoline is custom blended;" that this manifestly does not support applicant's assertion that Custom-Blended has acquired a secondary meaning as an indication of origin for gasoline, and that upon the record presented Custom-Blended does not possess anything "other than a descriptive significance to purchasers of gasoline."

We have given a synoptic analysis of the board's able, well-considered and exhaustive opinion without reiterating essential facts of record. These facts are detailed in their essence and relevancy and supportive of the board's conclusions so clearly and aptly enunciated in its decision. We, therefore, incorporate herein by reference the opinion of the board and affirm its refusal of registration. The decision of the Trademark Trial and Appeal Board is, accordingly, affirmed.

RICH, Acting Chief Judge, concurring.

I agree with the result reached by the majority which is supported by an opinion largely relying on and incorporating by reference the opinion of the board. While I do not disagree with anything said in the majority's opinion, I do not accord the survey evidence, by which it was attempted to show "secondary meaning," the significance apparently accorded it by the board. The examiner accorded it none. I do not agree with the board's statement that "This case turns upon the sufficiency of applicant's evidence" of "secondary meaning."

The examiner in this case was of the view, as the board reported, that Custom-Blended "is *so highly* descriptive of applicant's blended gasoline that it is *incapable* of becoming distinctive as claimed." (My emphasis.) If that is so, registration must be refused under 15 U.S.C.A. § 1052(e)(1) no matter what evidence of alleged "secondary meaning" is adduced; in other words, under the facts of this case the law proscribes the possibility of a de jure "secondary meaning," notwithstanding the existence of 15 U.S.C.A. § 1052(f) and a de facto "secondary meaning."

In my opinion, Custom-Blended is so highly descriptive that it cannot, under the law, be accorded trademark rights even though at some times, or to some people, or in some places, it has a de facto secondary meaning. My view was expressed by the examiner. I think that conclusively disposes of the matter. While I see no objection to pointing out to appellant that its evidence has not established "secondary meaning," I am unwilling to lead appellant or others to think that the fault was in the quantity or quality of its evidence rather than in the descriptiveness of the words sought to be registered. Appellant should not be encouraged to try again to prove "secondary meaning." The only particular in which I do not fully agree with the examiner is that he said the word "custom" in Custom-Blended "has very little trademark significance." I think it has none.

Appellant has argued that the descriptive term for its gasoline is "pump-blended." I do not question that that is a descriptive—or as appellant calls it "generic"—term; but a product may have more than one generically descriptive name. Because one merchandiser has latched onto one of the descriptive terms does not mean it can force its competitors to limit themselves to the use of the others, which appellant, it seems to me, is trying to do here. *All* of the generic names for a product belong in the public domain. The product itself, for example, is called gasoline in the United States but petrol in England. Clearly both of those names must remain free of proprietary claims, in either country. So it is, in my view, with respect to pump-blended and custom-blended. The examiner stated the factual basis for this view in pointing out that "custom," as in custom-built, custom-service, custom-cut, custom-made, custom-tailored, custom-work, etc., merely indicates that it is done according to the customer's desire. That is exactly how appellant's gasolines are pump-blended—to give the customer what he asks for. I can think of no descriptive term which is more apt.

FISHER, District Judge, dissenting.

Under the doctrine of "secondary meaning," a trademark, though originally descriptive of a type of product, is nonetheless entitled to registration if the mark has, by association with a business, come primarily to identify its user, rather than the product, to that part of the public interested in contracting with the trademark user. Whether a descriptive mark has acquired secondary meaning depends upon the particular facts of each case.

Briefly, it has been shown that appellant has used the mark in question for its gasoline exclusively and continuously over a period of some twelve years. There is evidence of extensive advertising of and sales of large volumes of gasoline under that mark during this period. Surveys of record suggest that in at least two areas where there are other marketers of multi-grade, pump-blended gasoline, the term Custom-Blended is associated in the public mind with this appellant in a preponderance which can only be accounted for by recognition of origin. There is no evidence which would imply that the mark is of such a descriptive nature that granting trademark rights therein to the user would deprive others of their right to normal use of the language.

In light of these facts, it is respectfully submitted that the decision of the Trademark Trial and Appeal Board should be reversed and registration granted on the basis that the mark Custom-Blended has acquired secondary meaning within Section 2(f) of the Act (15 U.S.C.A. § 1052(f)).

(ii.) "PRIMARILY GEOGRAPHICALLY DESCRIPTIVE"

›IN RE CHARLES S. LOEB PIPES, INC.

190 U.S.P.Q. 238 (T.T.A.B. 1976).

LEFKOWITZ, Member.

An application has been filed by Charles S. Loeb Pipes, Inc., doing business as 1776 Tobacco Company, to register the notation "OLD DOMINION" on the Principal Register as a trademark for pipe tobacco, use of the mark since August 20, 1968 being claimed.

Registration on the Principal Register has been refused on the ground that the mark "OLD DOMINION" is primarily geographically descriptive of applicant's goods within the meaning of Section 2(e)(2) of the statute.

Applicant has appealed.

The Examiner has made of record copies of pages from various dictionaries, almanacs, and the Encyclopedia Britannica which reveal that the designation "OLD DOMINION" is the nickname for the State of Virginia; that tobacco is the largest crop in Virginia; and that Virginia is one of the leading states in the manufacture of tobacco products. On the basis of these findings, the Examiner has taken the position that "OLD DOMINION" is a notation which is likely to be recognized by the purchasing public as the equivalent of Virginia and, as applied to applicant's tobacco products, would convey to them primarily a geographical significance.

Applicant, on the other hand, urges that many state names or nicknames are not known to people in other states, especially in other states far removed; that most Americans would not therefore recognize "OLD DOMINION" as being the nickname for the State of Virginia; that "OLD DOMINION" possesses nothing more than an archaic, nostalgic or romantic allusion to the early days in the south and that, as such, it would be completely fanciful to the great majority of Americans; and that, moreover, Virginia is known today not as a tobacco state, but rather as the principal state for the manufacture of synthetic fibers and is heavily engaged in the production of chemicals and chemical products. For all of these reasons plus the fact that the mark "OLD DOMINION" for grass seeds is the subject matter of an application filed by a Virginia concern that has recently been published for opposition purposes, applicant argues that the Examiner's holding that "OLD DOMINION" is primarily geographically descriptive of applicant's goods is incorrect and should be reversed.

.   .   .

The prohibition against the registration of geographic terms is based essentially upon the common law concept that geographic marks or names are descriptive designations to the extent that they may indicate the place from which a product comes or where it is manufactured or where the maker or dealer resides or where his place of business is located, and that therefore no one person can obtain an exclusive right to the use of a geographic name so as to preclude others who have businesses in the same area and deal in similar articles from truthfully representing to the public that their goods or services originate from the same place and from using the geographic term in connection with such goods or services. The Supreme Court in Elgin National Watch Co. v. Illinois Watch Case Co., 179 U.S. 665, 21 S.Ct. 270, 45 L.Ed. 365 (1901) stated this proposition as follows:

> "[T]he general rule is thoroughly established that words that do not in and of themselves indicate anything in the nature of origin, manufacture or ownership, but are merely descriptive of the place where an article is manufactured or produced cannot be monopolized as a trademark."

However, the Courts did provide protection against possible infringers in those cases where the parties plaintiffs established that the term in question had acquired a secondary meaning indicating not only the particular place of production but also that the article so marked emanates from a single or certain producer or manufacturer.

The trials and tribulations of those seeking to register geographic designations were often great and often insurmountable. Congress, by enacting the Act of 1905, intended to and did follow the common law principles relating to the appropriation of geographic terms as "trademarks" by precluding the registration of marks which were "merely a geographic name or term" [Sec. 5(b)]. Under this statute, geographic terms or names were defined to mean "nation, state, county, city, municipality, river, lake or the like" [Ex parte Tex-O-Kan Flour Mills Company, 37 U.S.P.Q. 416 (Comr., 1938)]; the fact that the term sought to be registered was little known in the United States was accorded no weight on the ground that the statute, in prohibiting registration of geographic terms, made no exception in favor of those terms which lack importance or of those which were not well known in the United States and even those geographic terms with alternative meanings, one of which may have been non-geographic, were held to be precluded from registration. In view of these decisions over the years, it was the practice of the Office to look a word up in an atlas or gazetteer or even a postal directory and then to refuse registration if there was any place in the world identified by that designation notwithstanding that the average consumer could not possibly have known of the existence of such a place.

While it would appear that the use of the notation "merely geographic" would suggest a recognition by the framers of the statute that a geographic term may in time come to have an additional meaning as an indication of origin for particular goods, and therefore should not be precluded from registration, the only provision of the statute possibly recognizing "distinctiveness" or "secondary meaning" was the "ten-year proviso" incorporated in Section 5; but this provision provided little assistance to those seeking registration under this statute.

This provision stated

"That nothing herein shall prevent the registration of any mark used by the applicant or his predecessor, or by those from whom title is claimed, in commerce with foreign nations or among the Indian tribes which was in actual and exclusive use as a trade mark of the applicant, or his predecessor from whom he derived title, *for ten years next preceding February twentieth, nineteen hundred and five* (Italics added).

The claim of distinctiveness, as indicated by the italic portion of the provision, must be for a ten-year period prior to February 20, 1905. Thus, any applicant who adopted and began to use his mark say in 1900 and continued to use it over an extensive period of time could not possibly have qualified under this provision. This was the effect of the decisions of the various tribunals during the period in which the Act of 1905 was in existence. In other situations involving composite marks, disclaimers of the geographic portions were required.

The Act of 1946, by the use of the words "primarily geographically descriptive" in Section 2(e)(2), intended "to change the former statute under which any term could be refused registration solely by reason of a geographical meaning, regardless of whether the geographical meaning of the word was minor or obscure or remote, or could not conceivably have any connection with the goods". See: Ex parte The London Gramophone Corporation, 98 U.S.P.Q. 362 (Comr., 1953). With the use of the words "primarily geographically descriptive," the Act of 1946 through the Section 2(f) provisions and the rules promulgated thereunder, as indicated above, did away with the "archaic" ten-year proviso, and brought the secondary meaning concept into a realistic and sensible approach consonant with the prevailing court decisions.

It is, however, readily apparent from the ensuing case law that it was not the purpose of the change to go to the other extreme and permit registration of all geographic terms as trademarks. The change from "merely a geographic name or term" to a "primarily geographically descriptive term" serves to permit registration of a geographic term so long as it is not primarily of that character. That is, it is not the intent of the present statute to refuse registration of a mark where the geographic meaning is minor or obscure and would not be known to the average purchaser of the goods. "There are certain words which, while containing the germ of geographic significance, cannot be identified with any specific geographic unit or are not used in a descriptive sense and hence do not fall within the ambit of proscribed trademarks." See: World Carpets, Inc. v. Dick Littrell's New World Carpets et al., 168 U.S.P.Q. 609 (C. A.5, 1971).

The underlying principle behind the liberalizing provisions of the Lanham Act has been asserted to be that the right to register should follow the right to use "as nearly as possible". See: In re E. I. du Pont de Nemours & Co., 177 U.S.P.Q. 563 (C.C.P.A., 1973). The concept of use over the years has been governed by the common law precepts relative to the right of appropriation by a prior user of different designations, including both descriptive and geographic terms, to the exclusion of such use by others, recognizing also the fact that, under certain conditions and circumstances, the doctrine of "secondary meaning" must be considered and applied if equity is to be done. These principles have to a large degree been found applicable in the provisions of Section 2 of the statute as well as in the interpretation thereof by this Office and the various appellate tribunals since the enactment of the statute.

It thus appears that the criteria for determining the registrability of a geographic designation under Section 2(e)(2) are (a) whether the term conveys to customers primarily or immediately a geographical connotation and then (b) whether the goods do in fact come from the place so named. If the notation in question does not convey an immediate or readily recognizable geographical significance to the average consumer, the mark is manifestly arbitrary, and the second question need not be pursued. However, if the response is in the affirmative, we proceed to the next question. If the goods actually come from the place named, the mark in question is primarily geographically descriptive of the goods and registrable on the Supplemental Register or on the Principal Register upon a showing under Section 2(f) of the statute that the mark has become distinctive of that party's goods in commerce. The rationale behind this is the common law concept that geographic terms should be free to be used by all business organizations within the geographical area to describe geographically the origin of their goods unless and until it can be shown by competent proof that the mark has acquired a secondary meaning and serves to identify and distinguish in commerce the goods of a single producer.

In the event that the goods do not come from the geographic area named, the mark is primarily geographically deceptively misdescriptive of such goods. As such, it is likewise registrable on the Supplemental Register or on the Principal Register with a persuasive showing that the mark has become distinctive of the applicant's goods in commerce within the contemplation of Section 2(f) of the statute. See: In re Application of Sweden Freezer Manufacturing Co., 159 U.S.P.Q. 246 (T.T.&A.Bd., 1968), wherein "SWEDEN" for goods not emanating from Sweden was deemed registrable on the Principal Register under the provisions of Section 2(f). On the other hand, See: The Singer Manufacturing Company et al. v. Birginal-Bigsby Corporation, 138 U.S.P.Q. 63 (C.C.P.A., 1963) wherein "AMERICAN BEAUTY" for sewing machines made in Japan was held to be primarily geographically deceptively misdescriptive. The theory behind this is that consumers have the right to be told the truth as to the origin of the goods that they purchase unless it can be shown that they have become conditioned over the years not to expect the goods to originate from the place identified by the mark and to associate goods bearing this term with a particular source.

As to Section 2(a) which provides for the refusal of registration of any mark which consists of or comprises deceptive matter, three factors must be present for a geographic term to fall within this proscribed category of marks. First, the term must convey primarily or immediately a geographical connotation. Second, the goods must not actually come from the area named by the mark. And three, the use of the term must be calculated, either planned, designed or implied, to deceive the public as to the geographical origin of the goods bearing the mark. As stated in In re Amerise, [160 U.S.P.Q. 687] at page 691:

> ". . . This contemplates situations where a party applies a geographical designation to a particular product knowing that it will bestow upon the product an appearance of greater quality or saleability not actually possessed by it with the intention thereby of inducing or misleading a particular class of consumers into purchasing this product. While such intent is often difficult to prove and especially in ex parte proceedings, intent can and has been inferred under those circumstances where a geographical area or place is well-known for the particular product as France for perfumes, Denmark for cheese, Switzerland for watches, and so forth. . . ."

If all three of these elements are present, the mark is deceptive within the contemplation of Section 2(a). Marks of this type have been refused registration and/or protection over the years. See: The Master, Wardens, Searchers, Assistants and Commonalty of the Company of Cutlers in Hallamshire in the County of York v. Cribben and Sexton Company, 97 U.S.P.Q. 153 (C.C.P.A.1953) ["SHEFFIELD" on stoves and ranges not made in Sheffield, England]; National Lead Company v. Michigan Bulb Company, 120 U.S.P.Q. 115 (Comr., 1959) ["DUTCH BOY" for flower bulbs not imported from Holland]; In re Richemond, 131 U.S.P.Q. 441 (T.T.&A.Bd., 1961) ["MAID IN PARIS" for perfume not made in Paris]; In re Danish Maid Cultured Products, Inc., 156 U.S.P.Q. 430 (T.T.&A.Bd., 1967) ["DANISH MAID CULTURED PRODUCTS" and a representation of the world famous statue of a little mermaid sitting on a rock which is located in Copenhagen, Denmark for activities relating to dairy products not produced in Denmark]; and In re The Salem China Company, 157 U.S.P.Q. 600 (T.T.&A.Bd., 1968) ["LIMOGES" for chinaware not made in Limoges, France or from clay indigenous to that area.]

The mark here in issue is "OLD DOMINION". It is clear from the documents made of record by the Examiner that this term is the accepted nickname for the State of Virginia. Obviously, not all people throughout the country are aware of this significance of "OLD DOMINION", and manifestly it is doubtful that many know the nicknames for all or even a portion of the fifty states. But, this is of no moment in a proceeding of this character for it is sufficient for our purposes that it is an accepted nickname for a state and would be recognized as such by a segment of the purchasing public.

Nicknames and even maps and geographical abbreviations used as trademarks, have, over the years, been treated under the common law and statutory interpretation in the same manner as ordinary geographical marks. See: Chappell et al. v. Goltsman et al., 91 U.S.P.Q. 30 (D.C.Ala.1951) ["BAMA" is geographically descriptive, being the nickname for Alabama, and, as such, is available for use as a trademark by all who, fairly and in good faith, choose to make use of it]; Dixie Oil Company of Alabama, Inc. v. Picayune "66" Oil Co., Inc., 170 U.S.P.Q. 236 (Miss.Sup.Ct.1971) and Hart Schaffner & Marx v. Empire Manufacturing Company, 94 U.S.P.Q. 171 (C.C.P.A.1952) ["DIXIE" is not susceptible of exclusive appropriation because it is a term generally understood and used to indicate the southern part of the United States and, as such, belongs in the public domain]; Quaker State Oil Refining Co. v. Steinberg, 325 Pa. 273, 189 A. 473 (Pa. Sup.Ct.1937) and Laughran v. Quaker City Chocolate & Confectionery Co., Inc., 296 F. 822 (C.A.3, 1924) ["QUAKER STATE" held to be the equivalent of Pennsylvania and prior user of "QUAKER STATE" was unable to enjoin use of "QUAKER CITY"]; Texas Farm Products Company v. Lone Star Producing Company, 144 U.S. P.Q. 312 (D.C.Tex.1964) ["LONE STAR" held to be indicative of Texas]; In re Canada Dry Ginger Ale, Incorporated, 32 U.S.P.Q. 49 (C.C.P.A.1936) [map of Canada held to be the equivalent of the word Canada]; Champion Spark Plug Company v. Globe-Union Manufacturing Company, 33 U.S.P.Q. 207 (C.C.P.A.1937) [a pictorial representation of a globe is "an alternative, or practical equivalent" of the word "GLOBE"; but it is not merely a geographical name or term under Section 5(b) of the Act of 1905 because "it identifies no particular geographical locations"]; and United States Blind Stitch Machine Corporation v. Union Special Machine Company, 159 U.S.P.Q. 637 (D.C.N.Y.1968) ["US" was held to be geographically descriptive as the equivalent of United States].

It is clear from the foregoing that nicknames and even abbreviations and maps of geographical areas and the name of the geographical area that they identify are, for purposes of registration, identical, and that the same criteria for registration must necessarily apply thereto.

"OLD DOMINION", as previously indicated, does identify the State of Virginia and this geographical significance would be readily apparent to a meaningful segment of the purchasing public especially within the State of Virginia and the surrounding area. Under these circumstances and the criteria detailed above, this term has a primarily geographical significance. However, in order to determine whether the term is primarily geographically descriptive or primarily geographically misdescriptive within the meaning of Section 2(e)(2), it is necessary to ascertain or answer the second question, namely, whether the goods actually come from the place identified by the mark. In this case, the goods are "pipe tobacco". While Virginia is a leading producer of tobacco, there is nothing of record to suggest that applicant's pipe tobacco comes from this state. If it does, "OLD DOMINION" is primarily geographically descriptive of the origin of the goods. And, if not, it is primarily geographically deceptively misdescriptive of the origin of the goods. In either event, under the theory of the registrability of geographical terms here expressed, "OLD DOMINION" comes within the proscription of Section 2(e)(2) and is registrable on the Principal Register only with a showing of distinctiveness under Section 2(f) of the statute.

The issuance of the registration of "OLD DOMINION" for grass seeds to a Virginia company on the Principal Register without resort to Section 2(f) referred to by applicant has been noted. However, the propriety of the issuance of said registration is not properly before us. There is no question but that it reflects an inconsistent practice in the Office concerning the registrability of geographical terms; but it is hoped that the utilization of the criteria for registration outlined herein will, for the most part, provide for a uniform practice within the Office and thereby avoid an inconsistent application of the statutory provisions relating to the registration of geographical terms.

Decision

The refusal of registration is affirmed.

(iii.) "PRIMARILY MERELY A SURNAME"

°IN RE STANDARD ELEKTRIK LORENZ AKTIENGESELLSCHAFT

United States Court of Customs and Patent Appeals, 1967.
371 F.2d 870, 152 U.S.P.Q. 563.

Appellant appeals from the decision of the Trademark Trial and Appeal Board affirming the examiner's refusal to register the mark "Schaub-Lorenz" on the Principal Register, 145 U.S.P.Q. 163.

Appellant, organized under the laws of the Federal Republic of Germany, alleged in its application prior registration of the mark in the Federal Republic of Germany. Registration is sought here under section 44(e), Trademark Act of 1946 (15 U.S.C.A. § 1126(e)), which provides, in part:

A mark duly registered in the country of origin of the foreign applicant may be registered on the principal register if eligible, otherwise on the supplemental register herein provided.

. . .

The board in its opinion set forth the position of the examiner and its reasoning as follows, 145 U.S.P.Q. at 163–164:

. . . This application is based upon applicant's ownership of a German registration rather than upon use of the mark in this country.

The Examiner of Trademarks has refused registration on the ground that applicant's mark is "merely a combination of two surnames and as such falls under the prohibition of Section 2(e)(3) of the Trademark Act of 1946."

Section 2 of the Trademark Act of 1946 [15 U.S.C.A. § 1052] provides that:

"No trademark by which the goods of the applicant may be distinguished from the goods of others shall be refused registration on the principal register on account of its nature unless it . . . (e) Consists of a mark which . . . (3) is primarily merely a surname."

In defense of its right of registration, applicant points out that the surname "Schaub" also means in the German language "a bundle of straw, sheaf," and that the surname "Lorenz" is also the name of a city in West Virginia and of a city in Brazil, in consequence of which, applicant strenuously argues that its mark cannot properly be considered as primarily merely a surname.

We are firmly of the opinion that, to the average member of the purchasing public, neither "Schaub" nor "Lorenz" would be likely to have any meaning other than as surnames. It is concluded, therefore, that applicant's mark is "primarily merely a surname" within the meaning of the Act, and hence that it is not

proper subject matter for registration on the Principal Register
in the absence of a showing that it has acquired in this country a
secondary meaning of indicating origin in applicant of the goods
to which it is applied. See Kimberly-Clark Corporation v. Marzall, Comr. Pats, [196 F.2d 772] 93 U.S.P.Q. 191 (C.A.D.C., 1952).

In addition to the evidence submitted by appellant as to the
meaning of Schaub and Lorenz, appellant argues that various city
telephone directories do not disclose any listing of Schaub-Lorenz.
The examiner cites the fact that various city telephone directories
disclose listings of Schaub and Lorenz individually.

Appellant also argues here that the mark has become known and
registered in many countries. The solicitor replies that no evidence
to this effect was submitted by appellant.

Appellant also cited Registration No. 386,174 of March 25, 1941,
for Lorenz, now expired, as evidence that the mark here is not primarily merely a surname. The examiner replied that registration
under the Trademark Act of 1920 does not support registrability on
the Principal Register.

Concerning legal precedents, the examiner and the board relied
on the decision in Kimberly-Clark, supra, wherein the court affirmed
the District Court's refusal to order registration on the Principal
Register of "Kimberly-Clark." The court in its opinion reasoned that
if neither Kimberly or Clark was registrable, as being primarily
merely surnames, then a combination of the two could not be registered. Appellant argues this decision is inapplicable here because,
unlike Kimberly-Clark, evidence has been submitted showing that
each term has meaning other than as a surname and appellant itself
does not use the combination as its corporate name.

Appellant argues the board failed to apply the correct test in resolving the issue of whether the mark is primarily merely a surname,
citing Ex parte Rivera Watch Corp., 106 U.S.P.Q. 145 (Com'r.Dec.
1955). This opinion states the proper test as being, "What is the primary significance of the mark to the purchasing public?" The mark
Rivera was held not to be primarily merely a surname. The opinion
also comments that an opposite conclusion in Kimberly-Clark might
have been reached if the above test had been applied. Appellant
argues in its brief:

> In addition to the Ex parte Rivera Watch Corp. case, supra,
> several subsequent cases held that marks which have different
> meanings in addition to meaning a surname are registrable. The
> discussed marks were initially rejected by the examiner on the
> ground that the respective marks were primarily merely sur-
> names.

> In Ex parte Omaha Cold Storage Co., 111 U.S.P.Q. 189
> (Com'r., 1956), the applicant's mark "Douglas" was held to be
> registrable and not primarily merely a surname. The Assistant
> Commissioner noted the various meanings of "Douglas" and how

it appeared from the record that "Douglas" was not the surname of any person connected with the applicant.

In Ex parte Gemex Co., 111 U.S.P.Q. 443 (Com'r., 1956), the applicant's mark "Wellington" was held to be registrable and not primarily merely a surname. The Assistant Commissioner noted the different meanings of the term and followed the rationale set forth in the Rivera case, supra stating:

". . . There is no way of knowing what the impact on the purchasing public is likely to be upon seeing 'Wellington' watch bracelets and straps, or with what, if anything, purchasers are likely to associate the mark."

"The rationale set forth in Ex parte Rivera Watch Corporation, 106 U.S.P.Q. 145 (Com'r., 1955), and in Ex parte Omaha Cold Storage Co., 111 U.S.P.Q. 189 (Com'r., 1956), leads to a conclusion here that 'Wellington' is not primarily merely a surname within the meaning of Section 2(e) of the statute when that section is read in the light of its legislative history."

The sole issue here is whether the mark sought to be registered, Schaub-Lorenz, was properly refused registration under section 2(e)(3) of the Trademark Act of 1946 as being primarily merely a surname. This provision of the act has been productive of diverse and not easily reconcilable decisions by the Trademark Trial and Appeal Board as well as by the courts. As stated by Assistant Commissioner Leeds in the Rivera case, 106 U.S.P.Q. at 146:

The decisions interpreting the phrase "primarily merely a surname" are not altogether consistent, nor do they establish clear guide lines for future determinations.

The examiner and the Trademark Trial and Appeal Board rely to a large extent on the Kimberly-Clark case, supra, which involved two cases consolidated on appeal. The first case concerned a mark whose dominant portion was "Kimberly Clark." It was refused registration under paragraph 5 of the Trademark Act of 1905 which denied registration of a mark which consisted merely of the name of a corporation. There is no similar issue present here as the mark sought to be registered is not the name of the appellant corporation. In an action brought by appellant in the U.S. District Court, DC, under RS 4915, the complaint was dismissed and the appeal to the Circuit Court of Appeals, DC, followed. On this aspect of the decision it would seem that there was no occasion for the Court of Appeals to express its opinion as to the import of section 2(e)(3) of the Trademark Act of 1946.

The second case involved the registrability of the mark "Kimberly-Clark" on the Principal Register under the 1946 Act. The Commissioner had offered registration on the Supplemental Register. The refusal to register the mark was made under section 2(e)(3) as a mark which was primarily merely a surname. The Court of Appeals affirmed "for the reasons given in our discussion" of the first case, 196 F.2d at 775, 93 U.S.P.Q. at 193.

It is not clear why the Court of Appeals in Kimberly-Clark refused registration on the Principal Register when, according to the court's opinion, "secondary significance" had been shown, 196 F.2d at 774, 93 U.S.P.Q. at 193. See section 2(f) of the Trademark Act of 1946 (15 U.S.C.A. § 1052(f)). As the board here commented, if appellant had shown "secondary meaning," section 2(f), then section 2(e)(3) expressly presents no bar to registration on the Principal Register. As to this aspect we agree with the board.

Nonetheless the board was of the view that as neither "Schaub" nor "Lorenz" would be likely to have any meaning other than as surnames, the combination Schaub-Lorenz was similarly defective. Apparently the board did not consider appellant's evidence to be persuasive.

We think the board's initial error arose from dissecting the marks. A mark must be considered in its entirety. In Ada Milling Co., 40 C.C.P.A. 1076, 205 F.2d 315, 98 U.S.P.Q. 267, this court had occasion to consider the mark "Startgrolay" for poultry feed. Registration was refused on the ground it was a combination of generically descriptive terms, starting, growing and laying. The court reversed the decision of the Patent Office on the ground that the mark, when viewed in its entirety, was capable of distinguishing the applicant's goods from those of others. The dissecting method employed in Kimberly-Clark and in In re Midy Laboratories, Inc., 26 C.C.P.A. 1294, 104 F.2d 617, 42 U.S.P.Q. 17, was properly rejected by the majority.

Section 2 states no trademark by which the goods of the applicant may be distinguished from the goods of others *shall be refused registration on the Principal Register* on account of its nature *unless it*—consists of a mark which is "primarily merely a surname." It is clear that the burden is on the Patent Office to prove that the trademark is primarily merely a surname. In Ex parte Gemex Co., 111 U.S.P.Q. 443, relied on by appellant, Assistant Commissioner Leeds stated:

> The Examiner of Trademarks expressed the opinion that the primary significance [see Ex parte Rivera, supra] of the mark [Wellington] presented is a surname significance, but he gave no rationale other than to cite its appearance in some telephone directories.   .   .   .

While there may be no hard and fast rule as to the amount of evidence necessary to demonstrate that a mark is or is not primarily merely a surname, we note here that the examiner cited only portions of the mark as being listed in telephone directories, relying on dissection of the mark which we find is error. No evidence was submitted that the *mark sought to be registered* was primarily merely a surname. Accordingly, we do not think the Patent Office has discharged its burden of proof and its decision must be reversed.

ALMOND, Judge, concurs in the result.

WORLEY, Chief Judge, dissents.

NOTES

1. A mark defective under Lanham Act § 2(e), 15 U.S.C.A. § 1052(e), may yet be registered on the Principal Register if it "has become distinctive of the applicant's goods in commerce." § 2(f). Acquisition of secondary meaning is the fact to be proved, and any evidence is admissible if it tends to show that the mark indicates a single source to consumers. In addition to direct evidence of consumer association, the statute and decisions approve a number of inferential bases. The Act allows proof of the applicant's substantially exclusive and continuous use of the mark for five years. Decisions have given weight to evidence of significant advertising expenditures and commercial success of the product or service in question.

Even abundant proof on these and other points has not always been conclusive. In Ex parte Hollywood Brands, Inc., 94 U.S.P.Q. 418 (Examiner-in-Chief 1952), the Patent Office refused to register "Butternut" for candies despite applicant's showing of almost exclusive use for more than thirty-six years, that one-third of its $1,135,000 advertising expenditures over the preceding six years had been devoted to the mark's promotion, and that the volume of "Butternut" candy sales for the preceding eight years had been $11,500,000. Applicant had also introduced supporting affidavits of forty-two individuals engaged in the candy trade.

The Court of Customs and Patent Appeals was more impressed than the Examiner-in-Chief. Noting "an increasing tendency to require more and still more proof from an applicant for registration under Section 2(f) than we think Congress fairly intended to impose," the court reversed, one member dissenting. Application of Hollywood Brands, Inc., 214 F.2d 139, 102 U.S.P.Q. 294 (C.C.P.A.1954). Although the standard of proof applied by the Patent Office has, since *Hollywood,* been observably lowered, it is at least arguable that the Court of Customs and Patent Appeals itself has on occasion departed from the spirit of its stricture. See, for example, In re Meyer & Wenthe, Inc., 46 C.C.P.A. 919, 267 F.2d 945, 122 U.S.P.Q. 372 (1959), and compare In re G. D. Searle & Co., 53 C.C.P.A. 1192, 360 F.2d 650, 145 U.S.P.Q. 619 (1966).

See generally, Lunsford, Mechanics of Proof of Secondary Meaning, 60 Trademark Rep. 263 (1970). For an interesting, contextual approach to the treatment of secondary meaning marks, see Garner, A Display Theory of Trademarks, 25 Geo.Wash.L.Rev. 53 (1956).

2. A mark that meets the requirements of neither § 2(e) nor § 2(f) may be registered on the Supplemental Register if, among other things, it is "capable of distinguishing applicant's goods or services." The Supplemental Register is open not only to nondistinctive marks but also to types of commercial insignia—labels, packages, configurations of goods, phrases and slogans, for example—that may be barred from the Principal Register. As might be expected, the rights accorded Supplemental Register marks are considerably narrower than those accorded Principal Register marks. See p. 354, below.

3. What policies account for the Act's restriction of rights in surnames? It may be helpful at this point to reconsider the materials at pp. 118–128 above. The first effective trademark act, Act of March 3, 1881, 21 Stat. 502, barred registration of any mark "which is merely the name of the applicant." Subsequent legislation varied the formula for denial. Given the law's traditional disinclination to protect personal names, what impulses might account for merchants' historic and widespread inclination to use personal names as the source designation for their goods and services? See Cassidy, Surnames as Trademarks, 41 Trademark Rep. 299 (1951).

4. "The discussions in the Congressional hearings make it clear beyond the shadow of a doubt that it is the intent of the section defining constructive abandonment that a registered mark which is so used by the owner as to cause it to lose its distinctiveness shall be deemed to be abandoned, and no rights to exclusive use on or in connection with goods or services may thereafter be claimed. It is equally clear from the hearings that rights in a mark may not be lost simply because it has achieved such popularity and celebrity that the public uses it to identify similar products made by others. In this latter event, the action on the part of the public must be coupled with acts of the registrant which have led the public to use it in a descriptive or generic sense. In other words, 'a company that has a good trade-mark and is making every effort to maintain its rights, should not lose the right because the public wants to use that name.' Failure of the owner and registrant to take every precaution to see to it that his mark is properly used, both by himself and others who may refer to it, may result in the abandonment of his rights." D. Robert, The New Trade-Mark Manual 34 (1947).*

Does this conclusion accurately represent the state of the law after *Thermos*? The state of the law as it should be? Compare Lanham Act § 14, 15 U.S.C.A. § 1064(c).

5. The merchant who designs his mark to perform an advertising function by suggesting the qualities of the goods or services with which it is used must chart a sometimes treacherous course between making the mark accurately suggestive, and thus descriptive, or inaccurately suggestive, and thus deceptive. Two Supreme Court cases provide common law guides to navigation. In Worden v. California Fig Syrup Co., 187 U.S. 516, 23 S.Ct. 161, 47 L.Ed. 282 (1903), the Court ruled that plaintiff, which marketed a laxative under the name, "Syrup of Figs," was not entitled to an injunction against defendant's use, in connection with its laxative, of the term, "Fig Syrup." Remarking that, "If this preparation is in fact a syrup of figs, the words are clearly descriptive, and not the proper subject of a trademark," the Court concluded that as plaintiff's compound in fact contained only minimal amounts of fig syrup and that, consequently, its use of

* Reprinted by permission from the New Trade-Mark Manual, by Daphne Robert, Copyright © 1947 by the Bureau of National Affairs, Inc., Washington, D.C. 20037.

the term tended to deceive consumers as to the nature of its product, it should be denied relief. In Coca-Cola Co. v. The Koke Co. of America, 254 U.S. 143, 41 S.Ct. 113, 65 L.Ed. 189 (1920), on the other hand, the Court ruled that, although plaintiff's product contained only trace amounts of coca leaf and cola nut derivative, "we are dealing here with a popular drink not with a medicine. . . . Coca-Cola probably means to most persons the plaintiff's familiar product to be had everywhere rather than a compound of particular substances." [j]

6. The consequences of disqualification on the "deceptive" and "deceptively misdescriptive" grounds differ sharply. Deceptively misdescriptive marks can be registered upon proof of secondary meaning under section 2(f). Deceptive marks can never be registered. Despite this difference in consequence, the statute nowhere defines the substance of the distinction between "deceptive" and "deceptively misdescriptive." The scant legislative history suggests only that both disqualifications were intended to serve the same purpose. Hearings on H.R. 5461 before the Subcomm. on Trademarks of the House Comm. on Patents, 77th Cong. 1st Sess. 84–87 (1941).

Consider the distinction essayed in Gold Seal Co. v. Weeks, 129 F.Supp. 928, 105 U.S.P.Q. 407 (D.D.C.1955) aff'd, 230 F.2d 832, 108 U.S.P.Q. 400 (D.C.Cir.), involving Gold Seal's action to compel registration on the Principal Register of "Glasswax," used in connection with a liquid for cleaning glass and metal. The Commissioner of Patents defended that if the product did contain wax the mark was descriptive and that if it did not contain wax it was deceptive or at least deceptively misdescriptive. The Court ruled first that the mark was not deceptive. "In analyzing the relationship of the mark to the product and its impact on the public, deception is found when an essential and material element is misrepresented, is distinctly false, and is the very element upon which the customer reasonably relies in purchasing one product over another. When, as here, the product contains an element which can only be known exactly by rigid scientific analysis, and such element does not appear as determinative in leading customers to buy the product, the mark is not deceptive."

The Court also ruled that the mark was not descriptive. "What it describes is a wax for glass. It does not describe a cleaner and polisher for metal as well as for glass, which is the true nature of the product." The Court did find, however, that the mark was deceptively misdescriptive. "The evidence establishes: that the product contains either no wax or wax in insufficient quantity to justify use of the word; that customers might justifiably believe it does contain the

j. "Before 1900 the beginning of the goodwill was more or less helped by the presence of cocaine, a drug that, like alcohol or caffein or opium, may be described as a deadly poison or as a valuable item of the pharmacopoeia according to the rhetorical purposes in view. The amount seems to have been very small, but it may have been enough to begin a bad habit and after the Food and Drug Act of June 30, 1906, c. 3915, 34 Stat. 768, if not earlier, long before this suit was brought, it was eliminated from the plaintiff's compound." 254 U.S. 143, 145–146.

element wax, whether or not it was significant to them in purchasing the product; that it is sold in association with other wax products; that other glass and metal cleaners do contain wax and have an appearance not basically dissimilar to plaintiff's product. We therefore find ourselves in accord with the holding of the Patent Office that the mark as employed in commerce is deceptively misdescriptive." 129 F.Supp. 928, 934–935.

On the deception grounds generally, see Germain, Trademark Registration Under Sections 2(a) and 2(e) of the Lanham Act: The Deception Decision, 44 Fordham L.Rev. 249 (1975); Merchant, Deceptive and Descriptive Marks, 56 Trademark Rep. 141 (1966).

3. STATUTORY SUBJECT MATTER

See Statute Supplement 15 U.S.C.A. §§ 1053, 1054, 1064(e), 1091–1096.

a. TYPES OF MARKS

(i.) *TRADEMARKS AND SERVICE MARKS*
IN RE CARSON

197 U.S.P.Q. 554 (T.T.A.B.1977).

RICE, Member.

An application has been filed by John W. Carson to register "JOHNNY CARSON" for entertainment services, namely, the rendering of entertainment to the general public by way of personal performances at shows such as by monologues, comedy routines and the hosting of guest appearances of others, use since 1952 being asserted.

Registration has been refused on the ground that the specimens filed show use of the designation "JOHNNY CARSON" only to identify the individual who performs or will perform the services claimed rather than as a mark used to identify and distinguish services rendered by applicant. That is, it is the Examiner's position that "JOHNNY CARSON" is not being used as a service mark. During the prosecution of the application, applicant submitted additional specimens showing, inter alia, use of the designation "THE JOHNNY CARSON SHOW" in a service mark manner. On the basis thereof, the Examiner advised applicant that its application would be allowed if applicant amended its mark to read "THE JOHNNY CARSON SHOW" and submitted a disclaimer of the word "Show", but applicant was unwilling to amend its mark in this fashion.

Applicant has appealed.

Applicant contends that his mark identifies both a service and an individual simultaneously, and hence is capable of registration as a service mark; that in the past marks which constitute the names of individuals have been passed to publication when use in the manner of a trademark or service mark has been demonstrated; that the fact that applicant is a well-known television and show business personality should not preclude him from registering the designation "JOHNNY CARSON" as a service mark; that the question presented herein is whether the specimens filed evidence service mark use of applicant's mark; that among the specimens of record are advertisements for one of applicant's concerts, which advertisements contain a picture of applicant as well as the name and address of the agency to which orders for tickets were to be mailed; that these specimens clearly meet the criteria set forth in In re Ames, 160 U.S.P.Q. 214 (T.T.&A.Bd., 1968); that other specimens submitted by applicant show use of the designation "THE JOHNNY CARSON SHOW" as a service mark; that the word "show" appearing therein is a generic description of the services rendered by applicant and thus, under the decision of In re Servel, Inc., 85 U.S.P.Q. 257 (C.C.P.A.1950), need not be included in the drawing of applicant's mark; that consumers would recognize the words "JOHNNY CARSON" as such; that no clarity of distinctiveness is gained by the addition of the word "show"; and that these specimens showing use of the mark "THE JOHNNY CARSON SHOW" are hence further evidence of applicant's use of "JOHNNY CARSON" as a service mark.

As indicated by the Board in In re Lee Trevino Enterprises, Inc., 182 U.S.P.Q. 253 (T.T.&A.Bd., 1974), the name of an individual may function not only to identify the individual but also as a trademark or service mark to identify goods sold or services rendered by the individual, or by an authorized corporation, in commerce. Accordingly, such a name may be registered provided that the specimens filed with the application evidence use of the name not just to identify the individual but rather to identify goods sold or services rendered by the applicant in commerce.

Thus the question to be determined herein is whether any of the various specimens of use made of record by applicant during the prosecution of its application show use of the designation "JOHNNY CARSON" to identify the entertainment services for which registration is sought.

The specimens which were originally filed with applicant's application consist of copies of a page from a newspaper whereon appears a picture of applicant together with the words: "JOHNNY CARSON is in the Congo Room at Del Webb's Hotel Sahara with Bette Midler." Inasmuch as these specimens contain no reference whatsoever to any services to be performed by applicant, they do not in our opinion show use of the name "JOHNNY CARSON" as a service mark.

However, applicant has also submitted a large number of additional specimens. The most pertinent of these are a group of advertisements characterized by use of the designation "JOHNNY CARSON" in connection with the words "IN CONCERT", such as an advertisement which appeared in the September 12, 1971 issue of The New York Times and which includes, inter alia, a picture of applicant and the words "IN CONCERT" to the left of and slightly above the designation "JOHNNY CARSON" in large letters, together with information as to place and times of performances and as to where and for how much tickets may be purchased; and another advertisement which appeared in the September 13, 1971 issue of Newsday and which similarly includes, inter alia, a picture of applicant and the words "IN CONCERT" directly below the designation "JOHNNY CARSON" in large letters, together with phone numbers for ticket purchases and information as to time and place of performance. These specimens, unlike those originally filed with applicant's application, demonstrate use of the name "JOHNNY CARSON" presented in a technical service mark manner in close association with a clear reference (i. e., "IN CONCERT") to entertainment services to be performed by him, together with information as to how members of the public may avail themselves of such services. In view thereof, we believe that these specimens are sufficient to establish that the designation "JOHNNY CARSON" is used by applicant not only as a name to identify himself but also as a service mark to identify services rendered by him in commerce. To hold otherwise would be to discriminate against applicant simply because he is an individual. Our conclusion is supported by certain supplemental specimens (which may or may not have been in use as of the filing date of this application) of record, such as the advertisements showing use of the phrase "THE JOHNNY CARSON SHOW" together with ticket information, which advertisements are illustrative of another way in which the mark "JOHNNY CARSON" is used; and advertisements showing use of the designation "JOHNNY CARSON" in close association with the phrase "3 BIG PERFORMANCES AT THE MUSIC HALL!", together with ticket information.

While it might appear at first blush that our conclusion herein is inconsistent with that reached in the case of In re Lee Trevino Enterprises, Inc., supra, each such case must, as indicated above, be decided on the basis of the specimens made of record therein. In the Trevino case, it was the opinion of the Board that those specimens which contained a reference to the services for which registration was sought did not show use of the designation "LEE TREVINO" set off in a service mark manner, but rather only as part of a textual reference to Lee Trevino as an individual; other specimens referred to services not listed in the identification of goods set forth in the application there involved; and the remainder neither referred to applicant's services nor had use of "LEE TREVINO" set off in a service mark manner.

Decision

The refusal to register is reversed.

*EX PARTE HANDMACHER–VOGEL, INC.

98 U.S.P.Q. 413 (Com'r. 1953).

LEEDS, Assistant Commissioner.

Application has been filed to register as a service mark on the principal register the word "Weathervane" superimposed upon a representation of a weathervane and enclosed within a circle formed of the words "Women's Open Golf Tournament," for the service of "conducting golf tournaments" in Class 107, Education and Entertainment. The words "Women's Open Golf Tournament" are disclaimed. Use is claimed since February, 1950. Registration was refused on the ground that the mark does not meet the statutory requirement of a service mark because the service claimed is a vehicle or medium employed by the applicant to advertise and promote the sale of its goods. Applicant has appealed from this refusal.

Handmacher-Vogel, Inc., the applicant herein, is a manufacturer and distributor of women's wearing apparel. It owns Registration No. 554,949, comprising the word "Weathervane," coupled with the representation of a weathervane, for women's suits; Registration No. 553,814, comprising the word "Weathervane," coupled with the word "Golfer" and a representation of a weathervane, for shirts, women's jackets and women's hats; and Registration No. 339,318, comprising the word "Weathervane" alone for piece goods made wholly or partially of cellulose derivatives. The word "Weathervane" has been used by applicant and its predecessor since 1936 in the piece goods field, and by applicant since 1941 in the women's apparel field.

The various papers, documents and exhibits filed in this case show that during the year 1950 Handmacher-Vogel, Inc., commenced conducting golf tournaments in four different places located in different States, and has, since that time, used the "Weathervane" mark involved here to identify such tournaments. In connection with the tournaments, the mark is used on entry blanks furnished by applicant to participants, on tickets sold, on information cards and score cards distributed by applicant, on advertising posters, and in newspaper advertising paid for by applicant. These papers, documents and exhibits are sufficient to support the claim of use of the mark in connection with services rendered in commerce which may lawfully be regulated by Congress.

Tickets to the tournaments are sold to the public, entry fees are charged the entrants, and prizes are awarded to both participating professional and amateur players.

Numerous press clippings have been filed, and these clippings show a widespread press coverage of the sporting events identified as "Weathervane Women's Open golf tournament," "Weathervane Cross Country golf tournament" and "Women's Weathervane golf tournament." They also indicate participation by some of the nation's outstanding golfers, namely, Babe D. Zaharias, Betsy Rawls, Patty Berg,

Louise Suggs, Betty Jameson, and Marlene and Alice Bauer. Prizes in the 1951 tournaments totalled $17,000. In other words, the tournaments conducted by applicant are of more than passing interest and importance as sporting events.

The original rejection states in part:

> "While the examiner does not take the position that a manufacturer or merchant may not also render services or that the same mark may not be used both as a trade mark and a service mark, it is his view that all services which constitute operations involved in the designing, production, sale, sales promotion, advertising or build-up of good-will of one's own goods do not constitute services within the purview of the Act."

As a broad and general statement this may be a substantially correct interpretation of the law.

The examiner has taken a narrow view of the statutory provisions dealing with registration of service marks, and has apparently given little or no weight to any evidence submitted other than the specimens filed with the application. These specimens are mailing pieces designed for distribution to retail outlets selling women's apparel manufactured by applicant. They contain such statements as: "This greatest of women's sporting events will make the immensely popular Weathervane line even more popular"; "Schedule tie-in ads now. Plan your Weathervane windows now. Plan to cash in on this event that means big volume for your store"; and "Each year you will benefit by the tremendous advertising and promotional value of this great event." After quoting from the specimens, he concluded:

> ". . . it is believed that the service claimed by the applicant is merely a means of advertising and promoting the sale of its goods; and as such is not considered a service within the meaning of the Statute."

This position was retained in final rejection. It is not clear just what the examiner's position would have been had the golf tournaments been instituted first in point of time and as a subsequent venture, the applicant decided to go into the manufacturing of women's apparel.

In the Examiner's Statement filed on appeal, the following appears:

> "While the applicant may be rendering a service in conducting these tournaments, this service *is rendered primarily as a means of promoting the sale of these goods* [women's apparel] and comes within the scope of the decisions cited. . . ."
> (Emphasis Added)

There is no evidence to support such a statement; but, on the contrary, the evidence indicates that in this case the services are entertainment services completely unrelated to the designing, production, sale, sales promotion or advertising of the applicant's goods sold under the "Weathervane" mark. None of such goods are designed, produced, advertised, promoted, sold or offered for sale at the tournaments. It cannot be said to be a sales promotion program directed to purchasers of such goods. The goods are nowhere mentioned in the press releases, on entry blanks, on tickets, on score cards, in advertising of the tournaments, or in announcements or information bulletins. If additional good-will attaches to the trade mark as a result of the services performed, it is not seen how this can have any bearing on the question of whether or not a bona fide service is being performed. Careful consideration of all the evidence submitted convinces me that the applicant here is performing a bona fide service unconnected with the manufacture and sale of its goods, and that any effect which the conducting of the golf tournaments under the "Weathervane" mark may have upon the sale of women's apparel under the same mark is remote and incidental.

A mark used by a person on or in connection with services normally expected of him and rendered merely as an accessory to and solely in furtherance of the sale, offering for sale, or distribution of his goods is not a service mark within the purview of the Act; but a manufacturer, seller or distributor of goods who supplies a bona fide service or services over and above those normally expected and only incidentally related to the furtherance of such manufacture, sale or distribution is entitled to have the registrability of his mark judged by the standards ordinarily applied in determining registrability—whether the mark used to identify the service is the same as or different from that used to identify the goods.

The examiner cited and relied on six cases, namely: Ex parte Pacific Coast Aggregates, Inc., 91 U.S.P.Q. 210; Ex parte Tampax, Inc., 91 U.S.P.Q. 215; Ex parte Radio Corporation of America, 92 U. S.P.Q. 247 (affirmed C.C.P.A. 98 U.S.P.Q. 157); Ex parte The El-well-Parker Electric Company, 93 U.S.P.Q. 229; Ex parte The Arco Company, 96 U.S.P.Q. 171; and Ex parte The Procter & Gamble Company, 97 U.S.P.Q. 78. The first five cases are readily distinguishable from the present case, and in view of the pendency of an appeal in the last mentioned case, comment is withheld. In each of the five cases the mark was used on or in connection with services rendered merely as an accessory to and solely in furtherance of the sale of the applicant's goods. In the first case, the claimed "service" consisted of preparing the applicant's concrete for sale. In the second the claimed "service" consisted of an advertisement containing a list of the physical characteristics of the applicant's goods and featuring some of those descriptions in the form of a slogan. In the third case the claimed "service" comprised the mere playing of the applicant's own phonograph records with an invitation to the public to purchase them. In the fourth the claimed "service" was the rendering of advice as to the use of applicant's industrial equipment. In the fifth case the claimed "service" was the mixing of applicant's paints and rendering advice as to color matching in using applicant's paints. None of these cases is controlling under the facts and circumstances of the present case.

The decision of the Examiner of Trade Marks is reversed.

(ii.) CERTIFICATION MARKS AND COLLECTIVE MARKS

IN RE FLORIDA CITRUS COMM'N

160 U.S.P.Q. 495 (T.T.A.B.1968).

LEFKOWITZ, Member.

An application has been filed by the Florida Citrus Commission to register the following as a certification mark for oranges and orally ingestible products which are made from oranges, use of the mark as a certification mark since on or before March 23, 1964 being alleged.

[C3047]

It is alleged in the application that:

"The certification mark is used by persons authorized by Applicant to certify that the goods bearing the mark are oranges grown within the State of Florida or are products which (1) are made from oranges grown within the State of Florida and (2) meet the Applicant's standards of identity."

Applicant is the owner of two subsisting registrations covering the designation "O.J.", per se, and the identical composite mark for which registration is sought herein as a service mark for services described as:

"Creation and promotion of standards for, and the promotion of consumer purchases of, orange juice, canned orange juice, chilled orange juice, and frozen concentrated orange juice, made from oranges grown within the State of Florida."

The application contains the statement that "Applicant is not engaged in the production or marketing of any goods to which the mark is applied as a certification mark."

Registration has been refused on the ground that it is the practice of the Patent Office not to register the same mark both as a service mark and as a certification mark in view of Section 14(e)(2) of the Act of 1946 which provides for the filing of a petition to cancel at any time in the case of a certification mark on the ground that the registrant engages in the production or marketing of any goods or services to which the certification mark is applied.

Applicant has appealed.

According to the record, applicant, The Florida Citrus Commission, is a corporate body organized under the Florida Statutes, as amended. It is an arm or branch of the State of Florida charged with taxing, and using the proceeds of such taxation to control, regulate, and promote the production of citrus products in Florida, and to administer various aspects of the Florida Citrus Code which relate to such things as the size of oranges and grapefruits, their solid to acid ratio, their juice content and color, the size of boxes in which they are shipped, and the markings, grading, and other indicia thereon. In like manner, it promulgates standards for the solid and acid contents, color, and taste of canned orange juice and canned grapefruit juice, canned blended juices, and frozen concentrates of orange juice. These activities are financed by a special tax on each box of citrus fruit grown in Florida. The enforcement of these standards is but one facet of the Florida Citrus Commission's activities. Part of the above-mentioned tax money is, pursuant to the Statutes, used to:

> "Conduct a campaign for commodity advertising, publicity, and sales promotion to increase the consumption of citrus fruits. . . ."

That same section of the Statute also directs the Commission to:

> "Decide upon some distinctive and suggestive trade name and to promote its use in all ways to advertise Florida citrus fruits."

Applicant, assertedly, pursuant to these statutory defined obligations, created the mark which is the subject of the instant application. The first use of the mark was on September 5, 1963 as a service mark to identify the Commission's regulating functions, and to identify certain advertising and promotion of Florida citrus fruit and citrus products. Applicant formally filed an application for registration thereof on September 10, 1963 submitting specimens reflecting usage of the mark on stationery employed by the Commission in the performance of its statutory duties and consumer advertising directed to promote the citrus products of Florida in general. This application matured in Registration No. 767,305 on March 24, 1964.

After the service mark had been used by the Commission for about six months, the Commission began to authorize, under its supervision and control, Florida citrus producers to use the identical trademark as a trademark on citrus fruit and fruit products produced by them to identify their Florida origin. The subject application was filed on November 13, 1964 accompanied by specimens showing use of the mark on a carton of orange juice distributed, in this instance, by Manhan Indian River Juices, Inc. There is no question but that the Florida Citrus Commission itself has, at no time, ever sold any citrus products of any sort under any mark much less the mark in question; and that the only use which the Commission itself has made of the mark is to employ it in connection with the services it renders to the Florida citrus industry and in the consumer advertising of the industry which it serves.

It is the examiner's position that the provisions of Section 14(e)(2) providing for the cancellation of a certification mark at any time on the ground that the registrant "engages in the production or marketing of any goods or services to which the certification mark is applied" prohibits the issuance of a registration for a certification mark to any applicant who engages in the production or marketing of any goods or any services under a mark identical to the certification mark.

The thrust of applicant's position is twofold, namely, that:

(A) The insertion of the language proscribing "the production or marketing of any goods or services to which the certification mark is applied" in Section 14(e)(2) of the Statute indicates a legislative intent that any question arising thereunder can and should only be considered in an inter partes case, and

(B) The language of Section 14(e)(2) was inserted in the Statute for the specific purpose of prohibiting the owner of a certification mark from actively engaging in the production or marketing of those same goods or same services to which the mark is applied as a certification mark.

It is applicant's argument that the language of Section 14(e)(2) was originally proposed in the form of a qualification of Section 4 and was intended to be considered by the Patent Office during the ex parte prosecution of an application for registration of a certification mark. The Congress, however, did not accept this proposal and instead inserted the language in Section 14 in such a way that the question of whether or not the owner of a registration "engages in the production or marketing of any goods or services to which the certification mark is applied" can only be decided in an inter partes proceeding.

The legislative history of the Lanham Act does reveal, as indicated by applicant, that there was an attempt to incorporate the language of Section 14(e)(2) as a subsection of Section 4, but the Congress chose to include it only as a part of Section 14(e)(2). . . .

While the language in Section 4 relating to the proscriptions concerning the use of a certification mark and a collective mark is somewhat vague and ambiguous and leaves much to be desired in the way of statutory language, it nevertheless appears therefrom that there is a prohibition against the registration of a certification mark where the use of the mark by the registrant or owner falsely suggests that he makes the goods or performs the services on or in connection with which the certification mark is used. This prohibition appears on its face not to be as broad in scope as the language in Section 14(e)(2) providing for the cancellation of a certification mark at any time where the registrant engages in the production or marketing of *any goods or services* to which the certification mark is applied. If applicant's theory, which concedes the broad character of Section 14(e)(2), is to be followed, the prohibition in Section 4 would be applied in ex parte proceedings and the prohibition set forth in Section

14(e)(2) in inter partes proceedings. The application of this "dual standard" is manifestly not feasible for it would give rise to situations where a registration of a certification mark would be subject to the filing of a petition to cancel under Section 14(e)(2) immediately after it is issued. Under these circumstances, it is of paramount interest to owners of certification marks that a single standard be used to determine both the right to register a certification mark and the right to maintain a certification mark registration. That is, the interpretation of Section 4 should be consonant with that of Section 14(e)(2) for to do otherwise would be to create a situation which the Congress and framers of the Statute surely did not intend.

We recognize that in view of the language in Section 4 referring *to the making or selling of the goods or services on or in connection with which such mark is used* and the language in Section 14(e)(2) precluding the production or marketing of *any goods or services to which the certification mark is applied,* a reasonable interpretation may be that the only proscription in both sections is against the owner of the mark from using the mark in connection with the production or marketing of the specific goods or services in connection with which the mark is being used by others as a certification mark. But, the language in these sections is likewise susceptible of the examiner's interpretation, namely, that in view of the specific function of a certification mark, the owner of a certification mark cannot apply the identical mark to any goods or services that it produces or sells.

.   .   .

Applicant's position on this point is that the legislative history of the Lanham Act indicates that the only purpose of the language incorporated in Sections 4 and 14(e)(2) was to prevent the registration of a certification mark for a specified product by a party who sells that product, and was in no way directed to barring such a registration by a party who actually uses the mark as a non-certification mark (service mark or trademark) on different products or services; that applicant is not engaged in the conduct sought to be precluded because it is not engaged in the production or marketing of any of the goods for which registration is sought as a certification mark; and that therefore applicant's ownership of a registration of the identical mark for services cannot preclude applicant from the registration sought herein. Applicant also urges that, in any event, the mere act of registration of the mark as a trademark or service mark as distinguished from proof of actual use of the certification mark in commerce in connection with the marketing or production of goods or services should not be deemed a bar under Section 4 or 14(e)(2) to the registration thereof as a certification mark.

A reading of the legislature hearings leading to the enactment of the Lanham Act reveals an intent to preclude the owner of a certification mark from producing or selling goods or services in connection with which the certification mark is to be used. That is, to prevent a party from certifying his own goods or services. It also appears therefrom that there was a continuing deep concern on the part of the framers of the Statute over the possible use of the certification mark as weapon to create a monopoly in a particular field and to perpetuate a fraud upon the purchasing public; and that they attempted through the proscriptive language in Sections 4 and 14(e)(2) to preclude the possibility of such fraudulent misuse occurring through the sanction of a Federal registration. These persons recognized, as we must do in determining which of the two possible constructions is to be applied, in a situation involving the registration of a certification mark, the particular or peculiar nature, character, and function of such a mark. A certification mark is a special creature created for a purpose uniquely different from that of an ordinary service mark or trademark as evidenced, inter alia, by the fact that Section 4 provides that a separate register be provided for such marks. It is a mark owned by one person and used by one or more parties on or in connection with their goods or services to certify quality, regional or other origin, and the like. As a consequence of the certification feature of the mark, it is a device which persons generally look for and many times are governed by in making their purchases. It is not unreasonable to assume that purchasers familiar with the use of a mark in connection with goods or services to certify quality, accuracy, or other characteristics of such goods or services will, upon encountering the identical mark on or in association with other goods or services, mistakenly attribute to it the same certification function as that to which they have been previously exposed. To permit the indiscriminate use of a certification mark with different goods or services will only lead to the dilution and impairment of the purpose and function of a certification mark as well as to practices wholly inconsistent with the public desirability of safeguarding the consuming public from confusion and damage not of its own making.

This is not intended to imply any devious intention on the part of applicant, the Florida Citrus Commission, in authorizing the use of its mark as a certification mark in the citrus fruit field and in using the identical mark itself as a service mark for services which it performs; but the standard to be applied in construing a portion of a Statute must necessarily have a general rather than a specific application. In order to effectuate the Congressional intent to maintain the true character of a certification mark and the unique function that it plays in the marketplace, it is our opinion that the owner of a certification mark cannot use the identical mark as a service mark or a trademark on or in connection with any goods or services that it markets or performs. A certification mark should be used only to certify. Any such other use is proscribed by both Section 4 and by Section 14(e)(2), the former as an ex parte bar to registration, and the latter as an inter partes ground for cancellation of an existing registration of a certification mark. . . .

Decision

The refusal of registration is affirmed.

LEACH, Member, dissenting.

The legislative hearings alluded to in the majority opinion do not in any way support the conclusion of my colleagues that a mark used as a certification mark for goods or services cannot be used by the owner thereof as a trademark or service mark for different goods or services.

Furthermore, I do not agree with my colleagues that there is any such ambiguity in the language of Sections 4 and 14 of the Act, insofar as it pertains to the issue hereof, as would necessitate resorting to the legislative hearings thereon to ascertain the intentions of the framers thereof. On the contrary, it is implicit therefrom that the only proscription against the registration of a mark as a certification mark is that the applicant not be engaged in the marketing of the specific goods or services in connection with which the mark is used as a certification mark.

In the present case, applicant is not engaged in the marketing of the goods for which it is seeking registration of its mark as a certification mark, and I would therefore reverse the examiner's refusal of registration.

BREITENFELD, COLLECTIVE MARKS—SHOULD THEY BE ABOLISHED?
47 Trademark Rep. 1, 3–6, 9, 14–15 (1957) *

Assistant Commissioner of Patents Leeds said in 1947: "Certification marks are now in our law and some administrative difficulties may have to be overcome before the distinction between collective marks and certification marks is clearly defined."

The Trademark Act of 1946 has been in effect for over nine years, and it seems that there is still confusion surrounding these marks. The fact is that the indistinction got off to a good start long before the Lanham Act, when collective marks first appeared in the law in 1938, by amendment to the 1905 Act. In commenting upon these 1938 collective marks, Dr. Derenberg said in 1948: "Most of the marks registered as collective marks under the (1938) amendment would appear to come within the definition of a certification mark rather than a collective mark under the new Act."

The lack of any clear distinction between collective and certification marks was apparent even while the Lanham Act was still in the process of being enacted. In an early form in which the House passed the Act, collective marks and certification marks were defined together in a single definition; and the later separation of the definitions did little to distinguish the marks clearly. Confusion has continued and, in addition, the separate definitions have given rise to other perplexing questions. . . .

In her book, Mrs. Leeds distinguished between collective and certification marks with an illustration of the use of the name INDIAN

RIVER for fruit. She pointed out that if the mark is used to indicate that the fruit comes from a certain region, it is a certification
mark, whereas, if it is used by members of an association "to distinguish the fruit of the members, and not to certify regional origin, it
is a 'collective mark'." This seems clear enough, but when organizations require that certain standards be met before membership is
granted, or that members can be drawn only from a certain region,
then membership itself may certify quality, regional origin, etc. In
such cases it is clear that if Mrs. Leeds' criterion is used, the mark
may be both a collective *and* a certification mark. . . .

To illustrate still more dramatically the lack of real distinction
between the marks appearing on the two registers, the reader is invited to check his collective-certification mark I.Q. by indicating in
the boxes on the left of the following list of marks, which, in his
opinion, are certification marks, and which are collective marks.

Cer-tifi-cation	Col-lec-tive	
1. ☐	☐	No. 568,413, granted to International Association of Clothing Designers, for Men's and Boys' clothing—namely, suits, overcoats, topcoats and sport coats; "The . . . mark is used upon the goods to indicate that the clothing is designed by a member of the association."
2. ☐	☐	No. 589,240, granted to Douglas Fir Plywood Association, for Plywood; "The . . . mark is used in connection with the goods to indicate that the plywood meets standards promulgated by the applicant."
3. ☐	☐	No. 567,487, granted to Prefinished Wallpanel Council, for Prefinished wall panels; "The . . . mark is used upon the goods to indicate the quality and commercial standard of the goods and that the manufacturer of the goods is a member of the Prefinished Wallpanel Council."
4. ☐	☐	No. 577,817, granted to The Irish Linen Guild, for Irish linen piece goods; "The . . . mark is used in connection with the goods to indicate membership in the association, source and origin, genuineness, and high quality of the goods."
5. ☐	☐	No. 529,630, granted to Paint Research Associates, Inc., for Ready-mixed paints, etc.; "The . . . mark is used upon the goods to indicate the quality of same."
6. ☐	☐	No. 589,483, granted to The Missouri Farmers Association, Inc., for Vegetable seeds, lawn seeds and field crop seeds; "The . . . mark is used in connection with the goods to indicate that they comply with certain requirements as to excellence and quality, which

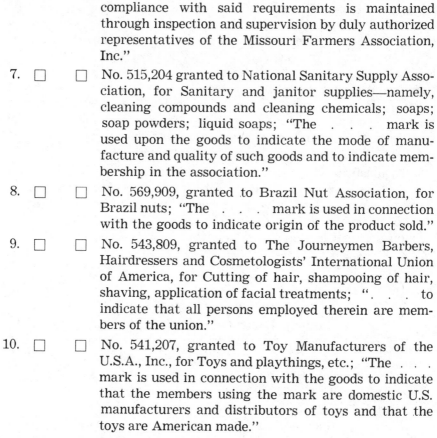

compliance with said requirements is maintained through inspection and supervision by duly authorized representatives of the Missouri Farmers Association, Inc."

7. ☐ ☐ No. 515,204 granted to National Sanitary Supply Association, for Sanitary and janitor supplies—namely, cleaning compounds and cleaning chemicals; soaps; soap powders; liquid soaps; "The . . . mark is used upon the goods to indicate the mode of manufacture and quality of such goods and to indicate membership in the association."

8. ☐ ☐ No. 569,909, granted to Brazil Nut Association, for Brazil nuts; "The . . . mark is used in connection with the goods to indicate origin of the product sold."

9. ☐ ☐ No. 543,809, granted to The Journeymen Barbers, Hairdressers and Cosmetologists' International Union of America, for Cutting of hair, shampooing of hair, shaving, application of facial treatments; ". . . to indicate that all persons employed therein are members of the union."

10. ☐ ☐ No. 541,207, granted to Toy Manufacturers of the U.S.A., Inc., for Toys and playthings, etc.; "The . . . mark is used in connection with the goods to indicate that the members using the mark are domestic U.S. manufacturers and distributors of toys and that the toys are American made."

If you studied the marks carefully and came to the conclusion that they are all certification marks except number 9, you are intelligent but mistaken. If you judged the even numbered registrations to be *collective* marks and the odd numbered registrations to be *certification* marks you were right; but the chances are that you peeked at this paragraph before making your choices.

It has been said that the essential difference between the two types of marks is that "collective marks indicate no more than mere association, while certification marks constitute a representation *with respect to the goods themselves* by someone other than the producer. The collective mark is a 'lodge button'; the certification mark is a 'guarantee'." . . .

The difference between a mark which "identifies" the goods or services of members of an organization and one which "certifies" that the labor on the goods or services was performed by the members of the organization is not only difficult to ascertain, but a distinction that seems wholly unnecessary. The elimination of one of these classifications seems advisable, therefore, and it is suggested that it be stricken from the definition of a *collective* mark. This would leave, in the section defining collective marks, only the reference to membership marks. Obviously, "membership" has reference to a "collection" of persons, and the obfuscating term "collective" is therefore redundant and could be eliminated entirely. A new definition is suggested for marks to be included on the newly-established "Collective Membership Register" (a more suitable name for which might well be the shorter, easier term: "Membership Register"):

"The term 'membership mark' means a mark used by the members of a cooperative, an association, or other collective group or organization to indicate membership in a union, an association or other organization."

This is believed to be a clean-cut statement of the membership "lodge-button" function of what is now known as a collective mark. It states what seems to have become Patent Office practice i. e., to classify *membership* registrations in one group (collective) and marks referring to *work done by members* in another (certification).

. . .

The fourth ground for cancellation of a certification mark refers to the discriminate refusal of a registrant to certify the goods or services of a person who establishes standards or conditions that the mark certifies, but whom the registrant doesn't wish to take into camp. Of course this is a real shortcoming of certification marks, not suffered by collective marks. In fact, it was cited by Derenberg in 1949, as being one of the causes for the limited number of applications to register marks as certification marks. Dr. Derenberg contended, at that time, that because of this restriction

". . . it would seem to be better business policy not to register such marks as certification marks, but wherever possible, as trademarks or service marks used by related companies."

As it happens, it appears that since then many registrants have registered such marks not only as trademarks or service marks but, in many instances, as collective marks.

However, is it sensible to maintain in existence a special register entitled "Collective Marks" merely to serve as a convenient alternative for those who own certification marks and are reluctant to register them as such? It would be preferable to amend the law to remove the cause of such reluctance; and if there is no legitimate need for collective marks they should be done away with.

b. CONTENT

IN RE BURGESS BATTERY CO.

United States Court of Customs and Patent Appeals, 1940.
112 F.2d 820, 46 U.S.P.Q. 39.

HATFIELD, Judge. This is an appeal from the decision of the Commissioner of Patents affirming the decision of the Examiner of Trade-Marks denying appellant's application for the registration of an alleged trade-mark under the Trade-Mark Act of February 20, 1905.

The mark in question, for use on "dry batteries" and "flash light cases," comprises, as stated in the decision of the Commissioner of

Patents, "alternating black and white stripes, unrestricted as to number or length or as to the shape or size of area covered by the striping. The specimens filed with the application show the stripes applied entirely about the goods and packages" by affixing thereto labels upon which the design is printed.

The tribunals of the Patent Office concurred in holding that appellant's alleged trade-mark, although in a general sense a design, is, in fact, merely a decorative or ornamental dress for appellant's goods, and that the distinctive feature of the alleged trade-mark is lost in repetition and in its ornamental relationship to the "dry batteries" and "flash light cases."

In his decision, the Examiner of Trademarks said:

The applicant submits affidavits to show that the mark was adopted for trade-mark purposes and that it functions as a trade-mark. That the mark may be recognized now as indicia of applicant's goods is saying no more than that the dress of goods is generally so recognized. If the mark is but a dress of goods, it seems immaterial that its adoption was inspired by a desire that it should function as an indication of origin.

. . . The symbol adopted by the applicant has a primary meaning of ornamentation and, in the absence of any copyright protection, is open to others for the purpose of ornamentation. Its eventual use as an indication of origin is, of course, protected by the law of unfair competition, but its registration as a trade-mark is believed forbidden by the above decision [Standard Paint Company v. Trinidad Asphalt Manufacturing Company, 220 U.S. 446, 31 S.Ct. 456, 55 L.Ed. 536]. . . .

It is contended by counsel for appellant that the "stripe design is physically susceptible of appropriation as a trademark," and that, although it may be ornamental and, in a sense, may function as a "dress" for appellant's goods, it has, through advertising and use, acquired a trade-mark significance.

In this connection, it is argued by counsel for appellant that certain affidavits of record clearly establish that appellant's "stripe design" indicates origin of appellant's goods.

We have given careful consideration to the affidavits of record, but are unable to concur in the views expressed by counsel for appellant. It appears from those affidavits that appellant's "batteries" are sometimes called for by "some of the customers" as "striped batteries," and that customers generally recognize appellant's batteries by the "striped labels."

It appears from the record, as stated by counsel for appellant, that appellant has instructed its salesmen to encourage the public "to recognize and call for the 'striped battery,' " and that one of the slogans in appellant's advertising is "Look for the black and white stripes."

It is unnecessary to cite authorities in support of the statement that the function of a trade-mark is to indicate the origin of the article to which such mark is applied. It is true that a trade-mark may consist of an emblem, a symbol, a figure, a device, a word or words, etc. However, we know of no authority which authorizes the registration of a purely ornamental or distinctive "dress" for an article.

That there is a distinction between a design for the external "dress" of an article and a mark to indicate origin in a trade-mark sense is not questioned here by counsel for appellant. A design may, as stated in the case of Ex parte Root Glass Company, 151 Ms.D. 623, lose its distinctive feature by repetition and become nothing more than an ornamentation or a distinctive design for the article to which it is attached. The primary object of such design or ornamentation not being for the exclusive purpose of indicating origin or ownership in a trade-mark sense, the design or ornamentation cannot be considered as a valid trade-mark.

We think it is apparent from the record that appellant's alleged trademark is a mere "dress" which gives a distinctive external appearance to appellant's goods; that it is such distinctive appearance which is recognized by "some" of the purchasing public as indicating appellant's goods; and that appellant's design is merely a colored label or dress of black and white alternating stripes, the office of which (design) is not to point out distinctly the origin or ownership of the articles to which the label is affixed. We are of opinion, therefore, as were the tribunals of the Patent Office that appellant's striped design is not registrable under the Trade-Mark Act of February 20, 1905.

The decision of the Commissioner of Patents is affirmed.

IN RE SWIFT & CO.

United States Court of Customs and Patent Appeals, 1955.
223 F.2d 950, 106 U.S.P.Q. 286.

COLE, Judge.

The Examiner-in-Chief of the United States Patent Office, acting for the Commissioner of Patents, has held that appellant's alleged trademark is not registrable on the Principal Register under the Trademark Act of 1946. In his opinion so ruling, Ex parte Swift & Company, 100 U.S.P.Q. 36, 37, the alleged mark is described as follows:

> "The product on which the mark is used is a household cleanser of the type sold in round cans the tops of which can be perforated to provide holes through which to shake the powdered material. The specimens submitted with the application consist of the labels which are placed around and cover the cylindrical sides of the cans. These labels, when viewed as on the cans, show a horizontal band of polka dot design in red background and white dots covering the lower third of the label and a similar but narrower band around the upper part of the label; the band

between these two is white, on which appears the words 'Swift's Cleanser,' repeated, and other printed matter. The polka dot design of the lower band is interrupted by the legend 'Pick the Polka-Dot package cleanser,' in two lines with the word 'cleanser' beneath the words 'polka dot.' The drawing which accompanies the application shows only the polka dot design of the label placed flat, namely the two rectangular polka dot bands separated by the white band, and omits all printed matter. There is no indication of color on the drawing."

The Examiner-in-Chief was of the opinion that appellant's polka dot banding was merely the background ornamentation of its label and, as such, could not function as a technical trademark, citing In re Burgess Battery Co., 27 C.C.P.A. (Patents) 1297, 112 F.2d 820, 46 U.S.P.Q. 39.

A specimen label (no colors shown) with the alleged mark thereon as actually used by appellant and the drawing accompanying the application for registration are reproduced herewith.

Our concern on appeal here from the decision of the Examiner-in-Chief being solely with appellant's right to register under the Trademark Act of 1946, the issue thus presented is whether appellant's polka dot banding is a trademark within the meaning of the statute and, if it is, whether it is entitled to be registered on the Principal Register.

Section 45 of the Act of 1946 [15 U.S.C.A.1952 Ed., 1127] provides:

> The term "trademark" includes any word, name, symbol, or device or any combination thereof adopted and used by a manufacturer or merchant to identify his goods and distinguish them from those manufactured or sold by others.

The above statutory concept of a trademark has long been recognized by the courts and is not unlike that given by the Supreme Court of the United States in Columbia Mill Company v. Alcorn, 150 U.S. 460, 14 S.Ct. 151, 152, 37 L.Ed. 1144, decided in 1893, wherein the court said "That to acquire the right to the exclusive use of a name, device, or symbol, as a trademark, it must appear that it was adopted for the purpose of identifying the origin or ownership of the article to which it is attached, or that such trademark must point distinctively, either by itself or by association, to the origin, manufacture, or ownership of the article on which it is stamped. It must be designed, as its primary object and purpose, to indicate the owner or producer of the commodity, and to distinguish it from like articles manufactured by others."

Appellant argued below, as it does here, that its mark is the symbol corresponding to the word "polka dot;" that it was adopted and has been used in trade in its present form since 1949 to identify and distinguish its product; that such trademark use is apparent from the fact that the labels carrying the design contain the phrase "Pick the Polka-Dot Package;" that this phrase has been used extensively in advertising its products; and that the public considers the polka dot design as the feature distinguishing such product from the goods of others.

We think that in a trademark sense appellant's polka dot banding is an artistic and unique design or pattern which may be constituted a trademark "device" within the meaning of Section 45, supra, if it is used primarily to perform the office of a trademark and is, in fact, by virtue of any distinctiveness it may possess, capable of so doing.

In the case of In re Burgess Battery Co., supra, the mark sought to be registered was for use on dry batteries and flash light cases and consisted of alternating black and white stripes, unrestricted as to number or length or as to the shape or size of area covered by the striping. The specimens accompanying the application showed the stripes applied entirely about the goods and packages by placing thereon labels upon which the striped design was printed. . . .
While in the cited case, [Burgess Battery,] the striped design was merely ornamental dress which was devoid of trademark significance, it does not thereby follow that a trademark device only incidentally ornamental, and in a sense decorative of the label upon which it ap-

pears, is not entitled to registration. Manifestly, if a distinctive trademark device or symbol is adopted and used primarily for the purpose of identifying and distinguishing a product, and it is capable of so doing, the mere fact that it renders the label to which it is applied more ornamental than it would otherwise be without that device thereon does not per se dictate a conclusion that it has no trademark function. In a limited sense, every device or symbol used as a trademark constitutes a part of the dress of the article to which it is applied but it is the conventional ornamentation or mere surface decoration as such that cannot be monopolized under a claim to trademark signification. The Burgess Battery case, supra, stands for the proposition that that which is only the attractive dress of an article, although it be distinctive in its appearance and sometimes recognized by purchasers as an indication of origin, does not have, as its primary function, an origin-authenticating purpose, and is hence not a trademark entitled to federal registration under the statute. Since the line distinguishing between mere ornamentation and ornamentation which is merely an incidental quality of a trademark is not always clearly ascertainable, the application of legal principles to fit one situation or the other requires proper reflection upon the impression likely to govern the ordinary purchaser in the market place. For that reason, the merits of each case of the character here presented must be individually and accordingly adjudged.

In its brief on appeal, appellant refers to the fact that a great deal of purchasing in retail outlets is of a casual nature (particularly in self-service types of stores) and, with regard thereto, it makes this observation:

> . . . Here the purchasers often engage in "impulse" buying. If their attention is caught by an item for which they have a need or have been induced to believe they have a need, as for example by advertising, they will pick up the item on this impulse even though the item was not one for which they entered the store to buy.
>
> In order for this to happen, however, it is imperative that their attention be focused on the item sufficiently for the "impulse" to occur. The focusing process often takes place at a time when the individual is too distant from the object to read any wording thereon. If the individual sees the item at a distance and is able to identify it by some symbol or device on the object that stands out at such a distance where the wording cannot, that symbol or device becomes the means by which the object is identified and the factor by which the impulse to purchase it is induced or occasioned.
>
> This identification at a distance can be one or a combination of two kinds of identification. In the first place, it can be an identification of the nature of the product. Naturally the trademark function of indicating origin does not become a part of this identification of the product. However, in addition to the identification of the product, the symbols or devices may be such as to

distinguish the product of a particular manufacturer from similar products of other manufacturers and thus serve as an indication of origin. When this is possible, and that was the intention in the adoption, that symbol or device clearly responds to the definition of a "trademark." It is not important that the purchaser think to himself "is this symbol or device a trademark." The significant question is was the symbol or device put on this object to enable the purchaser to pick it out and distinguish it from the goods of others, and is the purchaser able to so identify the object by means of this symbol or device.

It is axiomatic, of course, that a trademark must be distinctive in order to accomplish its function of indicating the producer of the article to which it is applied, and, with particular regard to symbols and devices, should be displayed with such prominence as will enable easy recognition. That appellant's design will instantaneously be recognized by the ordinary purchaser as a pattern of polka dot banding cannot admit of serious dispute. While to some extent it may thus be considered a commonplace design, we believe it is distinctive and does not retain its purely abstract significance as a common and merely ornamental design when applied in its particular form to the label of a can of household cleanser. We think a definite and lasting impression will be created by use of the design in association with the appellant's product whereby the average consumer will regard it as an unmistakable, certain, and primary means of identification pointing distinctly to the commercial origin of such product. The fact that the design may incidentally add to the attractiveness of appellant's label, and hence impart a certain distinctive appearance thereto, does not, in our opinion, vitiate its primary significance.

The Examiner-in-Chief also cited Campbell Soup Co. et al. v. Armour & Co., 175 F.2d 795, 81 U.S.P.Q. 430, 433, as authority for denying registration to appellant's trademark. In that case, the Circuit Court of Appeals for the Third Circuit was called upon to consider whether the plaintiff had exclusive trademark rights to a red and white label used on food products. One portion of the label (substantially half) was white and the remainder red, the colors appearing on the label in the form of an endless band running around the entire container. After stating the well settled rule that trademark rights cannot be acquired in color alone, the court said:

> Plaintiffs cite to us a number of cases, however, in which various color combinations as trademarks have been upheld. Here, too, the law is well settled. Color is a perfectly satisfactory element of a trademark if it is used in combination with a design in the form, for example, of a picture or a geometrical figure. The Barbasol case is typical [Barbasol Co. v. Jacobs, 7 Cir., 1947, 160 F.2d 336, 72 U.S.P.Q. 350]. Here was a package using several colors but in a distinct and arbitrary design. The mere division of a label into two background colors, as in this case, is not, however, distinct or arbitrary, and the District Court so found.

When we say that plaintiffs cannot have exclusive right to a trademark of a red and white label, we are by no means denying their right to acquire a trademark when the color is combined with other things in a distinctive design. . . .

We think it is apparent that the legal principles in the above case have no application to the factual situation here. While as actually used the banding of appellant's design appears in red and the polka dots thereon imposed are in white, these colors act only in association or combination with a design which is in itself distinctive and arbitrary as applied to household cleanser. As indicated, we think appellant's polka dot banding design is a trademark "device" distinguishing its product from articles of like kind sold by others, and that it is so recognized by the public as a primary means of identification. That it is entitled to registration on the Principal Register is clear from Section 2 of the Trademark Act of 1946 [15 U.S.C.A. § 1052] which provides:

No trademark by which the goods of the applicant may be distinguished from the goods of others shall be refused registration on the Principal Register on account of its nature unless it—.

. . .

Several subsections of Section 2 which there follow prohibit registration on the Principal Register of certain specified subject matter. None of these subsections are applicable here, and no issue has been raised with regard thereto.

For the reasons hereinbefore stated, the decision of the Examiner-in-Chief, acting for the Commissioner of Patents, is reversed.

JOHNSON and WORLEY, Judges, dissent.

NOTES

1. The evolution from *Burgess* to *Swift* reflects the modern trend in determining whether subject matter is registrable. *Burgess*, decided before passage of the Lanham Act, treated registration as a question of law—whether certain forms or types of subject matter, such as trade dress, are registrable. *Swift*, decided fifteen years later, treated the question as one of fact—whether, regardless of its type or form, the subject matter is capable of indicating source. Although, to be sure, the Act has not yet been construed to embrace some types of subject matter covered at unfair competition law's farthest reaches, there is no question about the direction in which decision is moving. Notes 2 to 7 below review several of the more common implements for distinguishing goods and indicate the extent to which the question of registrability has been converted from a question of law to a question of fact. Notes 8 to 10 explore two contexts in which registrability continues to be treated as a categorical question of law rather than as a factual question of distinctiveness.

2. *Color.* The use of color configurations as marks raises two questions. One arises when the color is integrated into the design of

the package or the goods themselves. In A. Leschen & Sons Rope Co. v. Broderick & Bascom Rope Co., 201 U.S. 166, 26 S.Ct. 425, 50 L.Ed. 710 (1906), the Court invalidated a mark described in its registration as consisting "of a red or other distinctively colored streak applied to or woven in a wire rope." Noting that the exhibit showed the distinctive strand to be red and that, "if the trade-mark were restricted to a strand thus colored, perhaps it might be sustained," the Court concluded that "the description of a colored streak, which would be answered by a streak of any color painted spirally with the strand, longitudinally *across* the strands, or by a circular streak around the rope was　.　.　.　too indefinite to be the subject of a valid trade-mark." 201 U.S. 166, 170, 26 S.Ct. 425, 426 (emphasis the Court's).

Second, color may be employed as background for a brand name or other insignia. In Marcalus Mfg. Co. v. Watson, 156 F.Supp. 161, 115 U.S.P.Q. 232 (D.D.C.1957), aff'd 258 F.2d 151, 118 U.S.P.Q. 7 (D.C.Cir.), registration was sought for a maroon-colored oval apart from any other insignia. As used on packages sold to the public, one of plaintiff's brand names always appeared superimposed on the oval. Stating that the test to be applied is whether the mark is in fact "a distinguishing mark and has been accepted by the public as such," the court agreed with the Patent Office fact finding that the oval did not on its own serve to distinguish plaintiff's goods. Conceding the point made in *Leschen*, that color may be a trademark "if it be impressed in a particular design, as a circle, square, triangle, a cross, or a star," 201 U.S. 166, 171, 26 S.Ct. 425, and that color used figuratively warranted broader and more immediate protection than color integrated into the design of package or goods, the court observed that marks used as background suffered their own special impediment. It referred to Application of Hillerich & Bradsby, 40 C.C.P.A. 990, 204 F.2d 287, 289, 97 U.S.P.Q. 451 (1953):

> .　.　.　buyers never see applicant's bats with only the oval thereon. Consequently, it is clear that usage of the oval per se has never been attempted as an origin-designating medium. The oval, not being inherently distinctive, must acquire that quality through such usage and association as will establish in the minds of the buying public that the oval on a bat clearly indicates a bat manufactured by the applicant. Proof indicative of the fact that the oval has enjoyed long and extensive usage in connection with other registered word trademarks does not fulfill that burden, but on the contrary would appear to make the applicant's task more difficult.

3. *Location on Goods.* In In re Kotzin, 47 C.C.P.A. 852, 276 F. 2d 411, 125 U.S.P.Q. 347 (1960), the Court of Customs and Patent Appeals affirmed a refusal to register a mark consisting of "a woven rectangular tag distinctively located by being vertically disposed and having one longitudinal edge inserted beneath and permanently attached by a seam or pleat across the waistband of the trousers. .　.　." The assistant commissioner had given as the ground for

refusal that the "distinctive location of a label is not a word, name, symbol or device adopted and used by one manufacturer or merchant to identify his goods and distinguish them from those of others. The location of a label is not and cannot be a trademark under the statutory definition." 118 U.S.P.Q. 465.

The C.C.P.A. affirmed on the facts, not the law. As a matter of law, the court believed "that anything recognized as a trademark prior to the 1946 Act would still be so considered, notwithstanding § 45," and "we do not see why the mark sought to be registered could not be considered to be either a symbol or device or a combination thereof." As a matter of fact, it found that because the tag "is, as the specimen shows, more accurately described as a label, bearing a word trademark, descriptive indications of origin, and descriptions of the goods, we do not believe that the purchasing public would regard the described location of this label as an indication of the origin of the goods," and that the evidence of secondary meaning was, on the record, insufficient to support registration under Section 2(f).

Kotzin set the stage for a case in which the primary purpose of the particularly positioned tag was not to bear a word mark and in which the tag had attracted considerable secondary meaning. The case was In re Levi Strauss & Co., 165 U.S.P.Q. 348 (T.T.A.B.1970), and the tag was the familiar rectangular bit of fabric affixed to applicant's garments at the hip pocket. The factual deficiencies of *Kotzin* were absent. Along with supporting letters, affidavits and results of reaction tests evidencing secondary meaning, "the advertisements illustrative of applicant's promotions of its goods show the garments displayed in such a fashion that the Tab is apparent to the reader and the Tab as so illustrated is without color and no mark or other indicia appears thereon, or if so, is illegible." To the examiner's argument "that applicant cannot obtain a registration (1) for a colorless tab or all tabs regardless of color (2) because of a particular location on its apparel," the Board answered, (1) that applicant had already obtained registration for red tabs, white tabs and black tabs similarly located and that "purchasers do recognize that applicant's Tab, notwithstanding differences in color, indicates origin with applicant," and (2) that "we do not see why a particular 'Tab' particularly located on particular goods cannot indicate origin."

4. *Ingredients.* Two apparently inconsistent lines of authority survived passage of the Lanham Act. One line of cases suggested that terms used only in connection with ingredients of compositions or components of articles are not registrable. The other line of cases indicated that they are. Assistant Commissioner Leeds set out to resolve the conflict in Winthrop-Stearns, Inc. v. Milner Products Co., 106 U.S.P.Q. 382 (Comm'r.1955), which involved a refusal to register "KoCal," for a brightening agent in applicant's "Pine-Sol" detergent, on the ground that it was "not a trademark use within the meaning of the statute."

After reviewing the cases, Assistant Commissioner Leeds determined that the second line of authority represented the correct view.

"The question is one of fact. If the mark is used to identify a component—e. g., an ingredient, an added substance, a finish, or a part—and distinguishes such component from those of others, and if it is properly used on or in connection with the goods, or on displays associated with the goods, and the goods are sold or transported in commerce, it is registrable even though it may have originally been an 'advertising gimmick' to aid the sales promotion. As stated, the question is a fact question, namely does the mark, as used, identify and distinguish the goods for which registration is sought?" 106 U. S.P.Q. 384–85.

The assistant commissioner concluded that, in the instant case, the record indicated "that applicant's mark was adopted and is used to identify and distinguish a whitening and brightening agent used as an ingredient in a detergent. If the application is amended so to identify the goods, the registration should issue."

5. *Corporate and Firm Names.* Questions of the registrability of firm names used in connection with goods are today generally treated as questions of fact. In In re Walker Process Equipment, Inc., 43 C.C.P.A. 913, 233 F.2d 329, 110 U.S.P.Q. 41 (1956), for example, the court affirmed the examiner's decision refusing registration on the Principal Register of the words, "Walker Process Equipment, Inc.," which applicant used on its goods in conjunction with the trademark, "Proquip," and the firm's address, "Aurora, Ill. U.S.A." From the fact that "Proquip," "which is unquestionably a trademark," constituted the most prominent feature of the label, the court drew the "natural inference . . . that the remaining words on the label are not to be considered a trademark." Further, the court concluded that the addition of the company's address indicated that the firm name was being used for the purpose of distinguishing the applicant from other producers rather than for the purpose of distinguishing applicant as the source of its goods.

In light of the distinction between the function of a firm name, to identify a producer, and the function of a trademark, to identify goods with a producer, should the governing principles differ when applicant seeks to register his firm name as a service mark rather than as a trademark? Compare Ex parte Great American Ins. Co., 111 U.S.P.Q. 163 (Comm'r.1956) with In re Amex Holding Corp., 163 U.S.P.Q. 558 (Comm'r.1969).

6. *Slogans.* Slogan trademarks gained entry to the Principal Register only after considerable rough going in the Patent Office in the early years of the Lanham Act's administration. The ground commonly given for refusing registration was that the slogan constituted "an advertising feature used in connection with the actual trademarks used by applicant upon the goods." Ex parte William Skinner & Sons, 82 U.S.P.Q. 315, 318 (Comm'r.1949).

The question of the registrability was eventually settled in the affirmative in American Enka Corp. v. Marzall, 92 U.S.P.Q. 111 (D. D.C.1952). The court there held plaintiff's slogan, "The Fate of a

Fabric Hangs by a Thread," to be registrable, reasoning that "certain combinations of words, albeit that they are also slogans, may properly function as trademarks." That this last terse statement represents the sum of the court's reasoning on the matter may, in retrospect, not appear surprising. Is it not self evident that a slogan is just "a combination" of "word[s]" within the terms of section 45? Or is this too simplistic a reading of section 45?

Because slogans are characteristically less concise than word or symbol marks, they inevitably invite the charge of descriptiveness, a charge frequently repelled on the general advertising ground that the slogan is only suggestive. In Lincoln Park Van Lines, 149 U.S.P.Q. 313 (1966), the Trademark Trial and Appeal Board reversed the examiner's refusal to register "From Maine's Cool Breeze to the Florida Keys" as a mark for applicant's moving and storage services conducted along the entire east coast. Alluding to applicant's assertion that "its mark is poetical or allegorical," the board concluded, "True the mark comprises bad poetry but nevertheless it is suggestive in connotation rather than descriptive."

If the slogan is overly suggestive it may be attacked as puffery —an objection apparently drawn from a pre-Lanham Act case, Burmel Handkerchief Corp. v. Cluett, Peabody & Co., 29 C.C.P.A. 1024, 127 F.2d 318, 53 U.S.P.Q. 369 (1942).

Slogan registration is comprehensively considered in Beran, Protection of Slogans in the Patent Office and the Courts, 57 Trademark Rep. 219 (1967).

7. *Packages; Buildings.* Color, location, names and slogans are clearly the stuff of which Principal Register marks are made—"any word, name symbol, or device or any combination thereof." The statutory case for registering packages and buildings is less clear. In Ex parte Minnesota Mining & Mfg. Co., 92 U.S.P.Q. 74 (1952), the Patent Office examiner-in-chief, affirming an examiner's refusal to register applicant's sleigh-shaped container for cellophane adhesive tape, noted that "the word 'device' appearing in the definition of a trademark cannot aid applicant. The word 'device,' which also appears in the older definitions, is not used as referring to a mechanical or structural device but is used in the sense of one of the definitions of the word: 'an artistic figure or design used as a heraldic bearing or as an emblem, badge, trademark, or the like,' rather than in one of the other meanings of the word." 92 U.S.P.Q. 76.

Ex parte Haig & Haig Ltd., 118 U.S.P.Q. 229 (Comm'r 1958) marked the first, faltering break from the position that packages are not registrable. Assistant Commissioner Leeds posed the issue obliquely: "The fundamental question, then, is not whether or not containers are registrable on the Principal Register, but it is whether or not what is presented" (applicant's well-known and distinctive pinch bottle for its Scotch whiskey) "is a trademark—a symbol or device—identifying applicant's goods and distinguishing them from those of others. This is really a question of fact and not of law.

. . . ." Observing that "customers of today order applicant's whiskey as 'Pinch' and 'Pinch bottle,'" and that applicant had registered the word, "Pinch," Leeds concluded that because "there is no way of identifying or asking for such brand of product other than by describing the contour or conformation of the container . . . the contour or conformation of the container may be a trademark—a symbol or device—which distinguishes the applicant's goods, and it may be registrable on the Principal Register." 118 U.S.P.Q. 230–231.

The assistant commissioner's decision was a *tour de force* that necessarily turned on the peculiar facts of the case. Taken literally, the decision offered little to encourage the use of package designs to designate source. It was, however, the spirit, not the holding, of *Haig & Haig* that prevailed. Two years later, the well-known Coca-Cola bottle configuration was registered on the Principal Register. See Lunsford, The Protection of Packages and Containers, 56 Trademark Rep. 567 (1966). The proposition that packages are registrable on the Principal Register is today unquestioned.

Having decided that a container's design can be registered as a trademark if it indicates the source of the goods that it contains, does it follow that the design of a structure can be registered as a service mark if it indicates the source of the services that it houses? The trend has been to allow the registration of buildings as marks so long as the applicant can overcome problems of distinctiveness and functionality. See Fotomat Corp. v. Cochran, 437 F.Supp. 1231, 194 U.S. P.Q. 128 (D.Kan.1977); Fotomat Corp. v. Photo Drive-Thru, Inc., 425 F.Supp. 693, 193 U.S.P.Q. 342 (D.N.J.1977). See generally, Fletcher, Buildings as Trademarks, 69 Trademark Rep. 229 (1979).

8. *Functional Features.* It has long been settled that "a configuration of an article cannot be registered as a trademark if the purpose of the configuration is to contribute functional advantages to the article in which it is embodied or if the configuration results from functional considerations." Best Lock Corp. v. Schlage Lock Co., 56 C.C.P.A. 1472, 413 F.2d 1195, 1199, 162 U.S.P.Q. 552 (1969). Applicant Best had sought registration on the Principal Register of its lock's figure 8 design, formed by the line of division between the lock core and housing. Holding for the opposer, Schlage, the court rested its decision exclusively on the fact that Best's lock had been the subject of a utility patent and that "the Best patent, explicitly disclosing the functional advantages to be derived from a figure 8 lock configuration, establishes the proposed mark as being primarily functional. . . . ." 413 F.2d 1195, 1200, citing In re Shenango Ceramics, Inc., 53 C.C.P.A. 1268, 362 F.2d 287, 150 U.S.P.Q. 115 (1966).

Dissenting, Judge Baldwin expressed concern with "the majority's acceptance of a single piece of evidence, the Best patent, as *conclusively* establishing functionality of such nature as to preclude registration. . . . *Shenango* is no precedent for holding that the evidentiary value of a patent is so great as to foreclose a party's efforts to introduce evidence contradictory to the specifications of the patent." 413 F.2d 1195, 1200 (emphasis the court's). In fact, *Shenango* had held that "a feature that is the subject of a utility patent goes into the public domain when the patent expires, Kellogg Co. v. National Biscuit Co., 305 U.S. 111, 119, 120–122, 59 S.Ct. 109, 83 L. Ed. 73 (1938); Singer Mfg. Co. v. June Mfg. Co., 163 U.S. 169, 185, 16 S.Ct. 1002, 41 L.Ed. 118 (1896). Such a feature, being free to be used by any person, thus cannot be a 'trademark [a 'symbol, or device' section 45] by which the goods of the applicant *may be distinguished.*'" 362 F.2d 287, 292. (Emphasis the court's.)

9. *Subject Matter of Expired Design Patents.* Application of Mogen David Wine Corp., 54 C.C.P.A. 1086, 372 F.2d 539, 152 U.S.P. Q. 593 (1967), raised the question whether *Sears* and *Compco,* the Supreme Court's seminal preemption decisions, pp. 130 and 133 above, require that registration be denied to subject matter that has once been covered by a design patent. On an earlier appeal, Application of Mogen David Wine Corp., 51 C.C.P.A. 1260, 328 F.2d 925, 140 U.S.P.Q. 575 (1964), decided before *Sears* and *Compco* were released, the court held that the design patent had no bearing on trademark registrability and remanded for decision on the factual issue, whether applicant's bottle for wines functioned distinctively as a trademark. On the second appeal, the court rebuffed the Commissioner's argument that *Sears* and *Compco* required the court to withdraw from the rule of law announced in the first appeal. The court did, however, affirm the Board's refusal to register on the ground that applicant had not shown that the bottle in fact served to indicate origin.

Because the "prior decision did not expressly consider *Sears* and *Compco,*" Judge Smith concurred for the purpose of more closely examining the implications of the two cases for federal trademark law. Smith started from the Supreme Court's affirmative answer to the question, "whether the use of a state unfair competition law to give relief against the copying of an unpatented industrial design conflicts with the federal patent laws," and concluded that "the Supreme Court did not purport to consider or to decide the boundaries between federal patent law and trademark law." Smith acknowledged that "the heart of the controversy here is the *duration* of these interests" —patent law providing for a limited term, trademark law for an indefinite term—but brushed aside the Commissioner's argument that applicant was seeking a "perpetual patent." Since the objectives of the two laws are discrete, Smith reasoned, each law is to be judged independently of the other. "The solicitor's brief portrays appellant as attempting to extract something from the 'public domain,' contrary to federal law. If the public recognizes and accepts appellant's container shape in a trademark sense, appellant seeks only federal recognition of that public interest. It is the public that is protected. . . . Perhaps the solicitor's argument is that the public has the 'right' to be confused, mistaken or deceived, or that recognizing the narrow interest of trademark owners in preventing confusion, mistake and deception is so great an 'evil' that sacrificing the public interest is a small price to pay. It seems to me that confusion in commerce would be an unnecessary and great price to pay." 372 F.2d 539, 542–545.

Seven years later, in Application of Honeywell, Inc., 497 F.2d 1344, 181 U.S.P.Q. 821 (C.C.P.A.1974) cert. denied, 419 U.S. 1080, 42 L.Ed.2d 674, 184 U.S.P.Q. 129, the court endorsed Judge Smith's rationale and rejected the argument that the subject matter of expired design patents should be treated on the same footing as the subject matter of expired utility patents. "We believe the solicitor has failed to draw a crucial distinction between functional subject matter disclosed in utility patents and subject matter disclosed in design patents, which may or may not be functional, in the context of their relationship with trademarks." 497 F.2d 1334, 1347.

Do you agree with *Honeywell's* implicit assumption that the public's interest in the free use of functional subject matter is more pressing than its interest in the free use of ornamental subject matter? Do you agree with *Mogen David's* assumption that the contemporary function of trademarks is to avoid consumer confusion, mistake or deception?

10. *Scandalous Subject Matter.* Like patent and copyright law, trademark law withholds protection from "immoral" subject matter. Because, however, trademark law evaluates proposed marks contextually, in connection with the goods or services with which they are used, the trademark prohibition operates somewhat differently.

In In re Riverbank Canning Co., 95 F.2d 327, 37 U.S.P.Q. 268 (C.C.P.A.1938), the Court applied the 1905 Act's counterpart to present section 2(a) to deny registration to applicant's mark, "Madonna," used in connection with wines. Conceding that the "word 'Madonna' is not per se scandalous" and that there already existed a number of registrations of the mark "applied to goods of various kinds, not containing alcohol, two of which registrations were granted to appellant," the court ruled that, used in connection with wine, the mark was bad. "We can readily understand that many who are accustomed to the use of wine as a beverage, remembering the Biblical times, would not be shocked at the use of the word 'Madonna' or a representation of the Virgin Mary as a trade-mark upon wine used for beverage purposes; but we also believe that there are many wine users who, knowing that the excessive use of wine is a great evil and not uncommon, would be shocked by such use of said mark upon wine, especially in view of the fact that such mark would probably be displayed, among other places, in barrooms."

What would happen if the legal bar to registration were dropped and the enforcement of sanctions left to the marketplace? Consider the suggestion made by Judge Jackson dissenting in *Riverbank Canning*: "If the use of the trade mark Madonna, as applied to the goods and articles mentioned, gave offense or scandal, it seems to me it would be noised about and probably these articles would have but scanty sale."

Should modern first amendment doctrine on commercial speech affect section 2(a)'s administration? How would you dispose of an application for "Acapulco Gold" as a trademark for suntan lotion? See In re Hepperle, 175 U.S.P.Q. 512 (T.T.A.B.1972). See generally, Note, Standing to Oppose Scandalous or Immoral Trademarks, 58 Neb.L.Rev. 249 (1978).

NOTE: THE SUPPLEMENTAL REGISTER

The Supplemental Register embraces a wider range of subject matter than the Principal Register and is far less insistent about the subject matter's distinctiveness. Section 23, 15 U.S.C.A. § 1091, allows any "trademark, symbol, label, package, configuration of goods, name, word, slogan, phrase, surname, geographical name, numeral or device or any combination of the foregoing" to be registered on the Supplemental Register and requires only that the mark be *"capable* of distinguishing applicant's goods or services." (Emphasis added.)

By design, the Supplemental Register encompasses virtually all subject matter protectable under state unfair competition law. The framers' intent in creating the Register was to continue the register established by the Trademark Act of 1920 and to "provide a quick and simple registration to protect American traders abroad." Hearings on S. 4811 before Senate Comm. on Patents, 69th Cong.2d Sess. 13 (1927) (statement of Edward S. Rogers). "In many foreign countries, the only way one can get trademark protection is by registration. That is generally so in Latin America. Moreover, in order to get protection there—and protection depends on registration—a foreigner must produce a certificate of registration from his home land, and one purpose of the supplemental register is to provide protection in foreign countries." Hearings on H.R. 4744 Before the Subcomm. on Trademarks of the House Comm. on Patents, 76th Cong.1st Sess. 127 (1939) (testimony of Edward S. Rogers).

As other nations drop the requirement that United States nationals seeking their protection show that they have a United States registration, the importance of the Supplemental Register's original objective has declined. Yet, domestically, the Supplemental Register has some continuing importance, offering an array of rights and remedies unavailable under state unfair competition law. Registration on the Supplemental Register assures access to federal courts without a showing of diversity jurisdiction, amount in controversy or pendent jurisdiction. Marks on the Supplemental Register are subject neither to opposition nor interferences; cancellation offers the only channel for attack.

Because the requirements for registration on the Supplemental Register are less exacting than those for registration on the Principal Register, it is no surprise that marks on the Supplemental Register enjoy a narrower range of rights. Among the advantages that do *not* attach to Supplemental Register registrations are the presumptions of validity, ownership, and exclusive right to use that attach to registrations on the Principal Register, and constructive notice of the registrant's claim of ownership of the mark. Registrations on the Supplemental Register cannot be deposited with the Secretary of the Treasury or otherwise employed to bar the importation of goods bearing infringing subject matter. Finally, the right to use the registered subject matter cannot become incontestable.

B. ADMINISTRATIVE PROCEDURES

See Statute Supplement 15 U.S.C.A. §§ 1051, 1056, 1057–1059, 1062–1064, 1066–1071, 1112, 1113, 1123.

Before investing heavily in a mark, a firm will typically arrange for a trademark search to determine whether the mark's use will infringe the trademark rights of anyone else and whether the mark will be entitled to federal registration. The search, often performed by a professional trademark search service, will be as wide and deep as the occasion warrants. At the least, the searcher will check the Patent and Trademark Office's application and registration files. If the firm intends a substantial merchandising program, it will probably also want the searcher to review the application and registration files in each of the states as well as trade journals and telephone directories. But even the most thorough search cannot assure that use of the mark will be free of infringement claims based on prior, undocumented common law uses, or that efforts at federal registration will not be stymied through any of the several avenues available for administrative challenge to Principal Register applications.

A. Examination

The first of the several administrative checkpoints confronting the hopeful Principal Register applicant is the trademark examiner's review of the application. After checking the application for compliance with the statutory formalities, the examiner reviews the application and any submitted evidence to determine whether registration is barred on any of the grounds specified in section 2 of the Lanham Act, 15 U.S.C.A. § 1052. The examiner will search prior registrations and pending applications to determine whether the mark is confusingly similar to any other mark previously used and not since abandoned. Trade periodicals are also consulted for any indications that the mark has a descriptive use in the industry in which it is used.

If the examiner rejects the application, the applicant can amend the application to meet the examiner's objections or, if he disagrees with the examiner, can file a response rebutting the grounds for rejection. If these efforts are unavailing and the mark is finally rejected, the applicant may take an appeal to the Trademark Trial and Appeal Board. 15 U.S.C.A. § 1070. If, on the other hand, the examiner determines that the mark is eligible for registration on the Principal Register, he will approve it for publication in the *Official Gazette*.

The initial *ex parte* proceeding before the trademark examiner is a relatively inexpensive vehicle for screening all applications for the most obvious, easily discovered objections. For the few applications that warrant more extensive scrutiny, the system relies on *inter partes* actions between the applicant and potentially injured competitors to weed out those that do not qualify for registration. The examiner's approval for publication in the *Official Gazette* sets the stage for the first three forms of *inter partes* proceeding—oppositions, concurrent use proceedings and interference proceedings.

B.   *Inter Partes* Proceedings

1.   *Oppositions*

Opposition proceedings, heard by the Trademark Trial and Appeal Board, give competitors a chance to oppose a mark before it is registered. To be heard, the opposer must file its opposition within thirty days of the mark's publication in the *Official Gazette*. To prevail, the opposer must demonstrate both that it is likely to be damaged by the mark's registration and that the mark is not entitled to registration under the terms of the Act. The opposer's claimed damage may be that applicant's mark is a descriptive term and that its registration will jeopardize the opposer's freedom to use the term descriptively in its own business. Or damage may be alleged because applicant's mark is confusingly similar to the opposer's registered or common law mark. Having established standing through proof of prospective damage, the opposer can then assert any of the available statutory grounds for denying registration. The grounds most typically asserted in opposition proceedings are the section 2 bars.

2.   *Concurrent Use Proceedings*

If the applicant's trademark search revealed an earlier, localized use of the same or similar mark by another, the applicant may initiate a concurrent use proceeding to limit its own registration to territories not yet occupied by the earlier user. Section 2(d) provides that the Commissioner may issue concurrent registrations when he determines that "confusion, mistake or deception is not likely to result from the continued use by more than one person of the same or similar marks under conditions and limitations as to the mode or place of use of the marks or the goods in connection with which such marks are used." The concurrent use application is first reviewed *ex parte* by a trademark examiner. 37 C.F.R. § 2.99(a) (1979). Then, after notice to interested parties named in the application, the application may become the subject of an *inter partes* proceeding before the Trademark Trial and Appeal Board. 15 U.S.C.A. § 1067.

3.   *Interferences*

Interference proceedings to determine priority of use may be pursued under section 16, 15 U.S.C.A. § 1066 any time that "application is made for the registration of a mark which so resembles a mark previously registered by another, or for the registration of which another has previously made application, as to be likely when applied to the goods or when used in connection with the services of the applicant to cause confusion or mistake or to deceive." The March 1, 1972 amendments to the Trademark Rules substantially confined interference proceedings "to rare cases in which a party might be able to prove that he would suffer irrevocable harm if his only recourse was to file an opposition or a petition for cancellation." These amendments were expected "virtually to eliminate interferences in trademark cases." 36 Fed.Reg. 18002–18003 (1971); 37 Fed.Reg. 2880 (1972).

4. Cancellation

Few trademark owners regularly read the *Official Gazette*, and many marks published for opposition will pass unnoticed by those most interested in resisting their registration. Fairness, and the public's interest in being free from confusion, require that these firms be given some later opportunity to object to registration. But fairness, and the public's interest in encouraging investment in marks, also require that the applicant be given some secure foundation upon which to rest its investment. Section 14, 15 U.S.C.A. § 1064, attempts to balance these interests by permitting cancellation of Principal Register registrations upon petition "by any person who believes that he is or will be damaged by the registration of a mark on the Principal Register." Registrations may be cancelled within five years of the date of registration on any ground that would have barred registration initially. After five years, the grounds for cancellation become more limited. See pages 385 to 386 below. Like opposition and concurrent use proceedings, cancellation petitions are heard by the Trademark Trial and Appeal Board.

C. Renewal

Because trademark rights turn on use, the duration of protection is necessarily indeterminate, lasting as long as the owner uses the mark commercially. To terminate the owner's exclusive rights at some fixed and arbitrary point, allowing competitors free use of the mark, would expose consumers to precisely the deception, confusion and mistake that the Act was intended to prevent. Unlike the Patent and Copyright Acts, which impose fixed terms, the Lanham Act provides that certificates of registration shall remain in force for twenty years, renewable indefinitely. 15 U.S.C.A. § 1058.

At the same time, the Act imposes two checkpoints to assure that marks no longer in use will drop from the register. The first checkpoint comes six years after the mark's registration. Under section 8, 15 U.S.C.A. § 1058, the registration of any mark "shall be canceled by the Commissioner at the end of six years following its date, unless within one year next preceding the expiration of such six years the registrant shall file in the Patent and Trademark Office an affidavit showing that said mark is still in use or showing that its nonuse is due to special circumstances which excuse such nonuse and is not due to any intention to abandon the mark." The next checkpoint is periodic, coming at the end of each twenty-year period. Under section 9, 15 U.S.C.A. § 1059, registrations may be renewed for twenty-year periods,

> from the end of the expiring period upon payment of the prescribed filing fee and the filing of a verified application therefor, setting forth those goods or services recited in the registration on or in connection with which the mark is still in use in commerce and having attached thereto a specimen or facsimile showing current use of the mark, or showing that any nonuse is due to special circumstances which excuse such nonuse and it is not due to any intention to abandon the mark. Such application may be made at any time within six months before the expiration of the period for which the registration was issued or renewed, or it may be made within three months after such expiration on payment of the additional fee herein prescribed.

If the examiner rejects the section 8 affidavit or the application for renewal, the registrant may petition the Patent and Trademark Commissioner for relief. 37 C.F.R. §§ 2.165(b); 2.184(b) (1979).

D.   Appeals

The Trademark Trial and Appeal Board hears appeals from *ex parte* decisions of the trademark examiner refusing registration. The Board is also the initial forum for *inter partes* proceedings—oppositions, concurrent use, interference and cancellations. The Patent and Trademark Commissioner will hear appeals from trademark examiner decisions rejecting a registrant's section 8 affidavit or application for renewal. A trademark owner who loses before the Board on an *ex parte* or *inter partes* matter, or before the Commissioner on a section 8 affidavit or registration renewal, may take an appeal either to the Court of Customs and Patent Appeals, under 15 U.S.C.A. § 1071 (a), or seek *de novo* review in a United States district court under 15 U.S.C.A. § 1071(b). Recourse from an adverse decision of the Court of Customs and Patent Appeals is directly to the Supreme Court under 28 U.S.C.A. § 1256, and from the District Court to the Circuit Court of Appeals, and then to the Supreme Court under 28 U.S.C.A. § 1254.

This fluent system of administrative checks and balances is not always realized in practice. An article in the August 7, 1980 *Wall Street Journal* reveals that, already short-handed, the Patent and Trademark Office had become mired in an unexpected surge of applications. "Three years ago, registering a name took about fourteen months. Today it's twenty-two months; by October it will be twenty-six. Often the gap is longer; Pepsi-Cola waited nearly thirty-four months before getting final approval in May for its On-Tap root beer." Abrams, Bottleneck in Trademark Office Disrupts Many Companies' Plans, Wall Street J., p. 19 August 7, 1980.

For details on administrative procedures under the Lanham Act, you may wish to consult, in addition to the standard treatises, a trio of articles by Stoughton, Registering on the Principal and Supplemental Register, 40 Trademark Rep. 893 (1950); *Inter Partes* Proceedings and Practice Under the New Trademark Rules, 46 Trademark Rep. 8 (1956); and Cancellation of Trademarks, 50 Trademark Rep. 890 (1960), and two by Lefkowitz, Trademarks and Attorneys in Action in Adversary Proceedings Before the Trademark Trial and Appeal Board, 56 Trademark Rep. 793 (1966) and Pleading and Practice in Adversary Proceedings Before the Trademark Trial and Appeal Board, 50 Trademark Rep. 1025 (1960).

See also, Leeds, Trademarks—The Rationale of Registrability, 26 Geo.Wash.L.Rev. 653 (1958); Derenberg, The Patent Office as Guardian of the Public Interest in Trade-Mark Registration Proceedings, 14 L. & Contemp.Prob. 288 (1949); Kaul, File Wrapper Estoppel in Trademark Cases, 59 Trademark Rep. 133 (1969), and Millstein, The Federal Trade Commission and the Excision of Trademarks, 55 Trademark Rep. 805 (1965).

C. RIGHTS AND REMEDIES

1. RIGHTS

See Statute Supplement 15 U.S.C.A. §§ 1057(b), 1060, 1065, 1072, 1115.

UNITED DRUG CO. v. THEODORE RECTANUS CO., 248 U.S. 90, 96–98, 100, 39 S.Ct. 48–50, 63 L.Ed. 141 (1918). Mr. Justice PITNEY: The entire argument for the petitioner is summed up in the contention that whenever the first user of a trade-mark has been reasonably diligent in extending the territory of his trade, and as a result of such extension has in good faith come into competition with a later user of the same mark who in equal good faith has extended his trade locally before invasion of his field by the first user, so that finally it comes to pass that the rival traders are offering competitive merchandise in a common market under the same trade-mark, the later user should be enjoined at the suit of the prior adopter, even though the latter be the last to enter the competitive field and the former have already established a trade there. Its application to the case is based upon the hypothesis that the record shows that Mrs. Regis and her firm, during the entire period of limited and local trade in her medicine under the Rex mark, were making efforts to extend their trade so far as they were able to do with the means at their disposal. There is little in the record to support this hypothesis; but, waiving this, we will pass upon the principal contention.

The asserted doctrine is based upon the fundamental error of supposing that a trade-mark right is a right in gross or at large, like a statutory copyright or a patent for an invention, to either of which, in truth, it has little or no analogy. There is no such thing as property in a trade-mark except as a right appurtenant to an established business or trade in connection with which the mark is employed. The law of trade-marks is but a part of the broader law of unfair competition; the right to a particular mark grows out of its use, not its mere adoption; its function is simply to designate the goods as the product of a particular trader and to protect his good will against the sale of another's product as his; and it is not the subject of property except in connection with an existing business.

The owner of a trade-mark may not, like the proprietor of a patented invention, make a negative and merely prohibitive use of it as a monopoly. . . .

Undoubtedly, the general rule is that, as between conflicting claimants to the right to use the same mark, priority of appropriation determines the question. But the reason is that purchasers have come to understand the mark as indicating the origin of the wares, so that its use by a second producer amounts to an attempt to sell his goods as those of his competitor. The reason for the rule does not extend to a case where the same trade-mark happens to be employed simultaneously by two manufacturers in different markets separate and remote from each other, so that the mark means one thing in one market, an entirely different thing in another. It would be a perversion of the rule of priority to give it such an application in our broadly extended country that an innocent party who had in good faith employed a trade-mark in one State, and by the use of it had built up a trade there, being the first appropriator in that jurisdiction, might afterwards be prevented from using it, with consequent injury to his trade and good-will, at the instance of one who theretofore had employed the same mark but only in other and remote jurisdictions, upon the ground that its first employment happened to antedate that of the first-mentioned trader.

a. GEOGRAPHIC BOUNDARIES

DAWN DONUT CO. v. HART'S FOOD STORES, INC.

United States Court of Appeals, Second Circuit, 1959.
267 F.2d 358, 121 U.S.P.Q. 430.

LUMBARD, Circuit Judge.

The principal question is whether the plaintiff, a wholesale distributor of doughnuts and other baked goods under its federally registered trademarks "Dawn" and "Dawn Donut," is entitled under the provisions of the Lanham Trademark Act to enjoin the defendant from using the mark "Dawn" in connection with the retail sale of doughnuts and baked goods entirely within a six county area of New

York State surrounding the city of Rochester. The primary difficulty arises from the fact that although plaintiff licenses purchasers of its mixes to use its trademarks in connection with the retail sales of food products made from the mixes, it has not licensed or otherwise exploited the mark at the retail level in defendant's market area for some thirty years.

We hold that because no likelihood of public confusion arises from the concurrent use of the mark in connection with retail sales of doughnuts and other baked goods in separate trading areas, and because there is no present likelihood that plaintiff will expand its retail use of the mark into defendant's market area, plaintiff is not now entitled to any relief under the Lanham Act, 15 U.S.C.A. § 1114. Accordingly, we affirm the district court's dismissal of plaintiff's complaint.

This is not to say that the defendant has acquired any permanent right to use the mark in its trading area. On the contrary, we hold that because of the effect of the constructive notice provision of the Lanham Act, should the plaintiff expand its retail activities into the six county area, upon a proper application and showing to the district court, it may enjoin defendant's use of the mark.

With respect to defendant's counterclaim to cancel plaintiff's registration on the ground that its method of licensing its trademarks violates the Lanham Act, a majority of the court holds that the district court's dismissal of defendant's counterclaim should be affirmed. They conclude that the district court's finding that the plaintiff exercised the degree of control over the nature and quality of the products sold by its licensees required by the Act was not clearly erroneous, particularly in view of the fact that the defendant had the burden of proving its claim for cancellation. I dissent from this conclusion because neither the finding of the trial judge nor the undisputed evidence in the record indicates the extent of supervision and control actually exercised by the plaintiff.

We are presented here with cross-appeals from a judgment entered by the District Court for the Western District of New York dismissing both plaintiff's complaint for infringement of its federally registered trademarks and defendant's counterclaim to cancel plaintiff's federal registrations.

Plaintiff, Dawn Donut Co., Inc., of Jackson, Michigan since June 1, 1922 has continuously used the trademark "Dawn" upon 25 to 100 pound bags of doughnut mix which it sells to bakers in various states, including New York, and since 1935 it has similarly marketed a line of sweet dough mixes for use in the baking of coffee cakes, cinnamon rolls and oven goods in general under that mark. In 1950 cake mixes were added to the company's line of products. Dawn's sales representatives call upon bakers to solicit orders for mixes and the orders obtained are filled by shipment to the purchaser either directly from plaintiff's Jackson, Michigan plant, where the mixes are manufactured, or from a local warehouse within the customer's state. For some years plaintiff maintained a warehouse in Jamestown, New York, from which shipments were made, but sometime prior to the commencement of this suit in 1954 it discontinued this warehouse and has since then shipped its mixes to its New York customers directly from Michigan.

Plaintiff furnishes certain buyers of its mixes, principally those who agree to become exclusive Dawn Donut Shops, with advertising and packaging material bearing the trademark "Dawn" and permits these bakers to sell goods made from the mixes to the consuming public under that trademark. These display materials are supplied either as a courtesy or at a moderate price apparently to stimulate and promote the sale of plaintiff's mixes.

The district court found that with the exception of one Dawn Donut Shop operated in the city of Rochester, New York during 1926–27, plaintiff's licensing of its mark in connection with the retail sale of doughnuts in the state of New York has been confined to areas not less than 60 miles from defendant's trading area. The court also found that for the past eighteen years plaintiff's present New York state representative has, without interruption, made regular calls upon bakers in the city of Rochester, N.Y., and in neighboring towns and cities, soliciting orders for plaintiff's mixes and that throughout this period orders have been filled and shipments made of plaintiff's mixes from Jackson, Michigan into the city of Rochester. But it does not appear that any of these purchasers of plaintiff's mixes employed the plaintiff's mark in connection with retail sales.

The defendant, Hart Food Stores, Inc., owns and operates a retail grocery chain within the New York counties of Monroe, Wayne, Livingston, Genesee, Ontario and Wyoming. The products of defendant's bakery, Starhart Bakeries, Inc., a New York corporation of which it is the sole stockholder, are distributed through these stores, thus confining the distribution of defendant's product to an area within a 45 mile radius of Rochester. Its advertising of doughnuts and other baked products over television and radio and in newspapers is also limited to this area. Defendant's bakery corporation was formed on April 13, 1951 and first used the imprint "Dawn" in packaging its products on August 30, 1951. The district court found that the defendant adopted the mark "Dawn" without any actual knowledge of plaintiff's use or federal registration of the mark, selecting it largely because of a slogan "Baked at midnight, delivered at Dawn" which was originated by defendant's president and used by defendant in its bakery operations from 1929 to 1935. Defendant's president testified, however, that no investigation was made prior to the adoption of the mark to see if anyone else was employing it. Plaintiff's marks were registered federally in 1927, and their registration was renewed in 1947. Therefore by virtue of the Lanham Act, 15 U.S.C.A. § 1072, the defendant had constructive notice of plaintiff's marks as of July 5, 1947, the effective date of the Act.

Defendant does not contest the similarity of the marks. Its principal contention is that because plaintiff has failed to exploit the

mark "Dawn" for some thirty years at the retail level in the Rochester trading area, plaintiff should not be accorded the exclusive right
to use the mark in this area. We reject this contention as inconsistent with the scope of protection afforded a federal registrant by the
Lanham Act.

Prior to the passage of the Lanham Act courts generally held
that the owner of a registered trademark could not sustain an action
for infringement against another who, without knowledge of the registration, used the mark in a different trading area from that exploited by the registrant so that public confusion was unlikely. By being
the first to adopt a mark in an area without knowledge of its prior
registration, a junior user of a mark could gain the right to exploit
the mark exclusively in that market.

But the Lanham Act, 15 U.S.C.A. § 1072, provides that registration of a trademark on the principal register is constructive notice of
the registrant's claim of ownership. Thus, by eliminating the defense
of good faith and lack of knowledge, § 1072 affords nationwide protection to registered marks, regardless of the areas in which the registrant actually uses the mark.

That such is the purpose of Congress is further evidenced by 15
U.S.C.A. § 1115(a) and (b) which make the certificate of registration
evidence of the registrant's "exclusive right to use the mark in commerce." "Commerce" is defined in 15 U.S.C.A. § 1127 to include all
the commerce which may lawfully be regulated by Congress. These
two provisions of the Lanham Act make it plain that the fact that
the defendant employed the mark "Dawn," without actual knowledge
of plaintiff's registration, at the retail level in a limited geographical
area of New York state before the plaintiff used the mark in that
market, does not entitle it either to exclude the plaintiff from using
the mark in that area or to use the mark concurrently once the plaintiff licenses the mark or otherwise exploits it in connection with retail sales in the area.

Plaintiff's failure to license its trademarks in defendant's trading
area during the thirty odd years that have elapsed since it licensed
them to a Rochester baker does not work an abandonment of the
rights in that area. We hold that 15 U.S.C.A. § 1127, which provides
for abandonment in certain cases of nonuse, applies only when the
registrant fails to use his mark within the meaning of § 1127, anywhere in the nation. Since the Lanham Act affords a registrant nationwide protection, a contrary holding would create an insoluble
problem of measuring the geographical extent of the abandonment.
Even prior to the passage of the Lanham Act, when trademark protection flowed from state law and therefore depended on use within
the state, no case, as far as we have been able to ascertain, held that
a trademark owner abandoned his rights within only part of a state
because of his failure to use the mark in that part of the state.

Accordingly, since plaintiff has used its trademark continuously
at the retail level, it has not abandoned its federal registration rights
even in defendant's trading area. . . .

Accordingly, we turn to the question of whether on this record plaintiff has made a sufficient showing to warrant the issuance of an injunction against the defendant's use of the mark "Dawn" in a trading area in which the plaintiff has for thirty years failed to employ its registered mark.

The Lanham Act, 15 U.S.C.A. § 1114, sets out the standard for awarding a registrant relief against the unauthorized use of his mark by another. It provides that the registrant may enjoin only that concurrent use which creates a likelihood of public confusion as to the origin of the products in connection with which the marks are used. Therefore if the use of the marks by the registrant and the unauthorized user are confined to two sufficiently distinct and geographically separate markets, with no likelihood that the registrant will expand his use into defendant's market, so that no public confusion is possible, then the registrant is not entitled to enjoin the junior user's use of the mark.

As long as plaintiff and defendant confine their use of the mark "Dawn" in connection with the retail sale of baked goods to their present separate trading areas it is clear that no public confusion is likely.

The district court took note of what it deemed common knowledge, that "retail purchasers of baked goods, because of the perishable nature of such goods, usually make such purchases reasonably close to their homes, say within about 25 miles, and retail purchases of such goods beyond that distance are for all practical considerations negligible." No objection is made to this finding and nothing appears in the record which contradicts it as applied to this case.

Moreover, we note that it took plaintiff three years to learn of defendant's use of the mark and bring this suit, even though the plaintiff was doing some wholesale business in the Rochester area. This is a strong indication that no confusion arose or is likely to arise either from concurrent use of the marks at the retail level in geographically separate trading areas or from its concurrent use at different market levels, viz. retail and wholesale in the same area.

The decisive question then is whether plaintiff's use of the mark "Dawn" at the retail level is likely to be confined to its current area of use or whether in the normal course of its business, it is likely to expand the retail use of the mark into defendant's trading area. If such expansion were probable, then the concurrent use of the marks would give rise to the conclusion that there was a likelihood of confusion.

The district court found that in view of the plaintiff's inactivity for about thirty years in exploiting its trademarks in defendant's trading area at the retail level either by advertising directed at retail purchasers or by retail sales through authorized licensed users, there was no reasonable expectation that plaintiff would extend its retail operations into defendant's trading area. There is ample evidence in the record to support this conclusion and we cannot say that it is clearly erroneous.

We note not only that plaintiff has failed to license its mark at the retail level in defendant's trading area for a substantial period of time, but also that the trend of plaintiff's business manifests a striking decrease in the number of licensees employing its mark at the retail level in New York state and throughout the country. In the 1922–1930 period plaintiff had 75 to 80 licensees across the country with 11 located in New York. At the time of the trial plaintiff listed only 16 active licensees not one of which was located in New York.

The normal likelihood that plaintiff's wholesale operations in the Rochester area would expand to the retail level is fully rebutted and overcome by the decisive fact that plaintiff has in fact not licensed or otherwise exploited its mark at retail in the area for some thirty years.

Accordingly, because plaintiff and defendant use the mark in connection with retail sales in distinct and separate markets and because there is no present prospect that plaintiff will expand its use of the mark at the retail level into defendant's trading area, we conclude that there is no likelihood of public confusion arising from the concurrent use of the marks and therefore the issuance of an injunction is not warranted. A fortiori plaintiff is not entitled to any accounting or damages. However, because of the effect we have attributed to the constructive notice provision of the Lanham Act, the plaintiff may later, upon a proper showing of an intent to use the mark at the retail level in defendant's market area, be entitled to enjoin defendant's use of the mark.

Since we have held that upon a proper subsequent showing the plaintiff may be entitled to injunctive relief, it is appropriate that we answer here the defendant's argument that such relief is beyond the constitutional reach of Congress because the defendant uses the mark only in intrastate commerce. Clearly Congress has the power under the commerce clause to afford protection to marks used in interstate commerce. That being so, the only relevant question is whether the intrastate activity forbidden by the Act is "sufficiently substantial and adverse to Congress' paramount policy declared in the Act. . . ." Mandeville Farms, Inc. v. American Crystal Sugar Co., 334 U.S. 219, 234, 68 S.Ct. 996, 1005, 92 L.Ed. 1328 (1948). The answer to such an inquiry seems plain in this case. If a registrant's right to employ its trademark were subject within every state's borders to preemption or concurrent use by local business, the protection afforded a registrant by the Lanham Act would be rendered virtually meaningless. Therefore we think it is within Congress' "necessary and proper" power to preclude a local intrastate user from acquiring any right to use the same mark. . . .

We are all agreed that the Lanham Act places an affirmative duty upon a licensor of a registered trademark to take reasonable measures to detect and prevent misleading uses of his mark by his licensees or suffer cancellation of his federal registration. The Act, 15 U.S.C.A. § 1064, provides that a trademark registration may be cancelled because the trademark has been "abandoned." And "abandoned" is defined in 15 U.S.C.A. § 1127 to include any act or omission by the registrant which causes the trademark to lose its significance as an indication of origin.

Prior to the passage of the Lanham Act many courts took the position that the licensing of a trademark separately from the business in connection with which it had been used worked an abandonment. The theory of these cases was that:

> "A trademark is intended to identify the goods of the owner and to safeguard his good will. The designation if employed by a person other than the one whose business it serves to identify would be misleading. Consequently a right to the use of a trademark or a trade name cannot be transferred in gross." American Broadcasting Co. v. Wahl Co., [121 F.2d 412, 413].

Other courts were somewhat more liberal and held that a trademark could be licensed separately from the business in connection with which it had been used provided that the licensor retained control over the quality of the goods produced by the licensee. But even in the duPont case the court was careful to point out that naked licensing, viz. the grant of licenses without the retention of control, was invalid. E. I. duPont de Nemours & Co. v. Celanese Corporation of America, [35 C.C.P.A. 1061, 167 F.2d 484, 489.]

The Lanham Act clearly carries forward the view of these latter cases that controlled licensing does not work an abandonment of the licensor's registration, while a system of naked licensing does. 15 U. S.C.A. § 1055 provides:

> "Where a registered mark or a mark sought to be registered is or may be used legitimately by related companies, such use shall inure to the benefit of the registrant or applicant for registration, and such use shall not affect the validity of such mark or of its registration, provided such mark is not used in such manner as to deceive the public."

And 15 U.S.C.A. § 1127 defines "related company" to mean "any person who legitimately controls or is controlled by the registrant or applicant for registration in respect to the nature and quality of the goods or services in connection with which the mark is used."

Without the requirement of control, the right of a trademark owner to license his mark separately from the business in connection with which it has been used would create the danger that products bearing the same trademark might be of diverse qualities. If the licensor is not compelled to take some reasonable steps to prevent misuses of his trademark in the hands of others the public will be deprived of its most effective protection against misleading uses of a trademark. The public is hardly in a position to uncover deceptive uses of a trademark before they occur and will be at best slow to detect them after they happen. Thus, unless the licensor exercises supervision and control over the operations of its licensees the risk that the public will be unwittingly deceived will be increased and this is precisely what the Act is in part designed to prevent. Clearly the only effective way to protect the public where a trademark is used by licensees is to place on the licensor the affirmative duty of policing in a reasonable manner the activities of his licensees.

The critical question on these facts therefore is whether the plaintiff sufficiently policed and inspected its licensees' operations to guarantee the quality of the products they sold under its trademarks to the public. The trial court found that: "By reason of its contacts with its licensees, plaintiff exercised legitimate control over the nature and quality of the food products on which plaintiff's licensees used the trademark 'Dawn.' Plaintiff and its licensees are related companies within the meaning of Section 45 of the Trademark Act of 1946." It is the position of the majority of this court that the trial judge has the same leeway in determining what constitutes a reasonable degree of supervision and control over licensees under the facts and circumstances of the particular case as he has on other questions of fact; and particularly because it is the defendant who has the burden of proof on this issue they hold the lower court's finding not clearly erroneous.

I dissent from the conclusion of the majority that the district court's findings are not clearly erroneous because (1) while it is true that the trial judge must be given some discretion in determining what constitutes reasonable supervision of licensees under the Lanham Act, it is also true that an appellate court ought not to accept the conclusions of the district court unless they are supported by findings of sufficient facts. It seems to me that the only findings of the district judge regarding supervision are in such general and conclusory terms as to be meaningless. In the absence of supporting findings or of undisputed evidence in the record indicating the kind of supervision and inspection the plaintiff actually made of its licensees, it is impossible for us to pass upon whether there was such supervision as to satisfy the statute. There was evidence before the district court in the matter of supervision, and more detailed findings thereon should have been made.

Plaintiff's licensees fall into two classes: (1) those bakers with whom it made written contracts providing that the baker purchase exclusively plaintiff's mixes and requiring him to adhere to plaintiff's directions in using the mixes; and (2) those bakers whom plaintiff permitted to sell at retail under the "Dawn" label doughnuts and other baked goods made from its mixes although there was no written agreement governing the quality of the foods sold under the Dawn mark.

The contracts that plaintiff did conclude, although they provided that the purchaser use the mix as directed and without adulteration, failed to provide for any system of inspection and control. Without such a system plaintiff could not know whether these bakers were adhering to its standards in using the mix or indeed whether they were selling only products made from Dawn mixes under the trademark "Dawn."

The absence, however, of an express contract right to inspect and supervise a licensee's operations does not mean that the plaintiff's method of licensing failed to comply with the requirements of the Lanham Act. Plaintiff may in fact have exercised control in spite of the absence of any express grant by licensees of the right to inspect and supervise.

The question then, with respect to both plaintiff's contract and non-contract licensees, is whether the plaintiff in fact exercised sufficient control.

Here the only evidence in the record relating to the actual supervision of licensees by plaintiff consists of the testimony of two of plaintiff's local sales representatives that they regularly visited their particular customers and the further testimony of one of them, Jesse Cohn, the plaintiff's New York representative, that "in many cases" he did have an opportunity to inspect and observe the operations of his customers. The record does not indicate whether plaintiff's other sales representatives made any similar efforts to observe the operations of licensees.

Moreover, Cohn's testimony fails to make clear the nature of the inspection he made or how often he made one. His testimony indicates that his opportunity to observe a licensee's operations was limited to "those cases where I am able to get into the shop" and even casts some doubt on whether he actually had sufficient technical knowledge in the use of plaintiff's mix to make an adequate inspection of a licensee's operations.

The fact that it was Cohn who failed to report the defendant's use of the mark "Dawn" to the plaintiff casts still further doubt about the extent of the supervision Cohn exercised over the operations of plaintiff's New York licensees.

Thus I do not believe that we can fairly determine on this record whether plaintiff subjected its licensees to periodic and thorough inspections by trained personnel or whether its policing consisted only of chance, cursory examinations of licensees' operations by technically untrained salesmen. The latter system of inspection hardly constitutes a sufficient program of supervision to satisfy the requirements of the Act.

Therefore it is appropriate to remand the counterclaim for more extensive findings on the relevant issues rather than hazard a determination on this incomplete and uncertain record. I would direct the district court to order the cancellation of plaintiff's registrations if it should find that the plaintiff did not adequately police the operations of its licensees.

But unless the district court finds some evidence of misuse of the mark by plaintiff in its sales of mixes to bakers at the wholesale level, the cancellation of plaintiff's registration should be limited to the use of the mark in connection with sale of the finished food products to the consuming public. Such a limited cancellation is within the power of the court. Section 1119 of 15 U.S.C.A. specifically provides that "In any action involving a registered mark the court may . . . order cancellation of registrations in whole or in part, . . ." Moreover, partial cancellation is consistent with § 1051(a)(1) of 15 U.S.C.A., governing the initial registration of trademarks which requires the applicant to specify "the goods in connection with which the mark is used and the manner in which the mark is used in connection with such goods. . . ."

The district court's denial of an injunction restraining defendant's use of the mark "Dawn" on baked and fried goods and its dismissal of defendant's counterclaim are affirmed.

b. PRODUCT BOUNDARIES: DILUTION

SCARVES BY VERA, INC. v. TODO IMPORTS LTD.

United States Court of Appeals, Second Circuit, 1976.
544 F.2d 1167, 192 U.S.P.Q. 289.

LUMBARD, Circuit Judge.

This appeal raises the familiar problem of determining under what circumstances a trademark owner may protect his trademark against use on products other than those to which the owner has applied it. Specifically, we must decide whether plaintiff, who uses the trademark "VERA" on a well-known line of women's scarves, apparel, and linens, is entitled to prevent defendant's use of the same mark on cosmetics and fragrances.

Appeal is from a judgment entered on August 28, 1975 after a two day bench trial in the Southern District of New York, Robert L. Carter, District Judge, dismissing plaintiff's action for trademark infringement and unfair competition. Plaintiff had been seeking injunctive relief, damages and an accounting.

For the reasons stated below we hold that the defendant infringed plaintiff's trademark, and that the plaintiff is entitled to injunctive relief. Accordingly, we reverse and remand.

Plaintiff Scarves by Vera, Inc. is a well known and highly successful fashion designer. Plaintiff designs and manufactures a line of women's signature scarves, medium-high fashion women's sportswear, and a variety of dining room, bedroom and bathroom linens. Defendant Todo Imports Ltd. is a New York corporation which, since 1970, has been the exclusive distributor in New York of certain cosmetics and toiletries manufactured by Vera Perfumeria y Cosmetica, S.A. of Barcelona, Spain (Vera S.A.).

On July 7, 1971, plaintiff commenced this action for trademark infringement and unfair competition under the Lanham Act of 1946, 15 U.S.C.A. § 1051 et seq., and under state law. Jurisdiction was based on 15 U.S.C.A. § 1121 and 28 U.S.C.A. § 1338.

In its complaint, plaintiff alleged its ownership of the registered trademark "VERA" on scarves, women's sportswear, and a large variety of linens. Plaintiff claimed that the defendant had infringed its trademark by using the mark "VERA" on cosmetics and toiletries manufactured in Spain by Vera, S.A. and distributed in the United States by the defendant. Plaintiff sought injunctive relief, damages and an accounting. Vera, S.A. was not named as a defendant and has not sought to intervene in this action.

The evidence adduced during the two day trial in October 1974 presented no substantial dispute as to the historical facts. In 1945 Mrs. Vera Neumann, her husband and a partner formed Scarves by Vera, a partnership which was plaintiff's predecessor. Plaintiff soon gained wide success as one of the first designers of high-fashion signature scarves. From the outset, plaintiff made scarves, women's blouses and some linen goods. Subsequently, plaintiff expanded into a wide variety of women's sportswear, including dresses, belts and sweaters, and a line of designer home accessory items, such as sheets, towels, table linens and place settings. The fabrics or facings of all these goods contained colorful patterns created by Mrs. Neumann, who is a well known artist.

Plaintiff's goods were sold under the trademark "VERA." Plaintiff is the owner of two registrations for the mark "VERA" in the United States Patent and Trademark Office. The first, covering scarves, neckties, blouses, shawls and kerchiefs, was filed on August 12, 1958 and issued on August 11, 1959. The second, covering the same items, plus a broad range of women's sportswear, apartment accessories and linens, was filed on September 2, 1969 and issued on August 11, 1970.

Plaintiff sells its goods in some 8,000 medium-to high-fashion department stores, boutiques and specialty shops across the nation. A representative sample of plaintiff's principal retail outlets includes Bergdorf Goodman, Bonwit Teller, Saks Fifth Avenue, Bloomingdale's, Macy's and Gimbel's.

Plaintiff introduced extensive evidence of its considerable success and wide recognition in the fashion-conscious consumer market. Plaintiff's sales rose from $10.5 million in 1966 to over $21 million in 1972, before falling to $18 million in 1973 due to the general economic downturn.

Plaintiff has spent more than $3 million since 1966 in advertising and promoting its products under the "VERA" trademark. Since 1970 plaintiff has spent $300 to $500 thousand dollars annually. In addition, the plaintiff's licensees and retailers have also contributed to the advertising pool pursuant to cooperative advertising arrangements.

The plaintiff also produced examples of its advertisements and an impressive volume of articles which had appeared in publications including the New York Times, The New Yorker, Vogue, Town & Country, Harper's Bazaar, and Mademoiselle. These articles, written by independent journalists about plaintiff's growth and products and discussing plaintiff along with such names as Blass, Cardin, Pucci, and St. Laurent, were evidence that plaintiff was recognized as a leader in the fashion industry. The plaintiff also called three experts on the fashion industry who testified that plaintiff was recognized among the top "name" designers, although plaintiff's apparel was slightly lower fashion than that of the other designers mentioned above.

Defendant is the exclusive distributor in New York State of products manufactured by Vera, S.A. in Spain pursuant to a written agreement dated June 1, 1970. Vera, S.A. was founded in the 1930s by its present owner, Abelardo Vera Martinez. Vera, S.A. obtained International Registration No. 134,216 in 1948 for the mark "VERA" for toiletries and cosmetics, and renewed that registration in 1968. However, the only registration which Vera, S.A. has in the United States is for the trademark "SIGLO DE ORO." Vera, S.A.'s United States trademark for "SIGLO DE ORO" was registered in 1967; the name "Vera (Espana)" appears on that registration in small type in the corner of the certificate to identify the manufacturer, rather than as part of the trademark. On May 6, 1971, Vera, S.A. filed a United States application for registration of the mark "VERA" for toiletries and cosmetics, including nail lacquer, lipstick, face powder, cologne, perfume, after-shave lotion, deodorants and soap. On May 29, 1973, Vera, S.A.'s application was published for opposition. Plaintiff filed an opposition, and proceedings have since been suspended pending termination of this action.

Vera, S.A. began exporting small amounts of perfumes and cosmetics from Spain into the United States in 1962. Soaps and other toiletries were later included. From 1962 to 1964 these items were handled by local distributors, and from 1964 to 1970 by Sara Feldschtein (now doing business as Vera Cosmetics, Ltd.).

Defendant introduced no evidence that Vera, S.A. ever sold its goods in the United States under the mark "VERA," with the exception of a single line of men's cologne sold after 1970. In its answer, defendant pleaded as an affirmative defense that "the notation 'Vera,' except in the case of cologne for men . . . was used to indicate the manufacturer and not the product" and that its products were "identified by such trademarks as 'SIGLO DE ORO,' 'ISABEL MARIA,' '74,' 'ISABELINA' " etc.

Although the defendant called one of Vera, S.A.'s officers from Spain to testify, defendant introduced no evidence regarding any labels used on its products before 1970 and no proof that the name "VERA" appeared prominently on those products, which were all sold under other trademarks. The only documentary evidence introduced by defendant—invoices, shipping records, and customs documents— indicated that "Vera" was used merely to identify the manufacturer, and was not used as a significant part of the marks under which Vera, S.A.'s items were sold. After mid or late 1970, defendant began to display the name "VERA" more prominently on its items, although all of these goods except for men's cologne were still sold under other trademarks.

Prior to 1971, Vera, S.A.'s sales in the United States were negligible. Its goods were sold primarily through Spanish language newspapers. Vera, S.A.'s records showed only seven sales to five customers between 1962 and 1964 amounting to $3,823.79. Between 1965 and 1970, Vera, S.A.'s sales in this country totalled no more than $25,000, ranging from $5,872.02 in 1965, to $1,211.98 in 1968 and $8,573.70 in 1970.

After 1970, when Vera, S.A. began distributing its products through defendant and began using the name "VERA" more prominently on its packaging, sales increased dramatically. Defendant's sales of Vera, S.A.'s products reached $100,000 annually by 1974. Defendant has greatly expanded the geographical market in which these items are sold. Defendant's products are now sold in New York through such stores as Gimbel's and Bloomingdale's—the very stores in which plaintiff's lines are sold—and advertised in prominent publications such as The New Yorker, The Daily News and The New York Post.

Plaintiff proved that most of the top designers also marketed their own lines of perfumes, cosmetics and toiletries, including such designers as Bill Blass, Cardin, Christian Dior, Lanvin, Norell, Patou, Pucci, Gucci, Hattie Carnegie, Chanel, Yves St. Laurent and Faberge.

In 1969 plaintiff considered selling its own line of cosmetics and fragrances. Columbia Broadcasting System first approached plaintiff to propose a joint venture, but plaintiff was advised to go into the field with a firm that had had experience. Plaintiff then approached Max Factor, but Max Factor had just come out with a new line of its own cosmetics and perfumes and was unwilling to make further investment at the time, even though it thought favorably of plaintiff's idea. Finally, plaintiff approached Estee Lauder, which did not want to put another line of cosmetics under a women's name on the market. Plaintiff took no further steps on the proposal.

Plaintiff noticed one of defendant's advertisements for sales representatives in the July 29, 1970 issue of Women's Wear Daily. The advertisement mentioned that defendant planned to introduce a line of toiletries from "VERA/BARCELONA SPAIN." By letter dated August 3, 1970, plaintiff warned defendant that it would bring suit if defendant began marketing its products under the name "VERA." Defendant did not respond, but instead began marketing its toiletries with prominent use of the name "VERA." On June 10, 1971 plaintiff again protested, and, after its second protest was ignored, commenced this action on July 7, 1971.

Judge Carter, in his opinion dated July 9, 1975, held that plaintiff was not entitled to injunctive relief against defendant's use of the name "VERA." He found the difference between plaintiff's mark "VERA" in script and defendant's use in block letters insignificant.

Despite plaintiff's success in the market, its large expenditures on advertising and the other evidence of plaintiff's wide recognition, the district court found plaintiff's mark to be weak because it was a common name and because a number of third parties had registrations which included the same name. The court noted that although plaintiff might argue that its mark has acquired secondary meaning with respect to scarves, the contention was "dubious" and, even if conceded, would "not establish plaintiff's right to bar use of the mark in other fields since there is . . . no right to a mark in gross." The court found no evidence that defendant intended to palm its products off as plaintiff's. The court also noted that although plaintiff "may not be barred by laches," the fact that Vera, S.A. had been importing its products into the United States since 1962 "with the mark Vera on them . . . does help underscore the fact that both parties have been operating in their respective fields for a long time without knowledge of each other . . . which further erodes any argument to the likelihood of confusion." The district court rejected plaintiff's claim that it was likely to enter the cosmetics and fragrance field "as other couturiers have done," and reasoned that the public would probably not identify defendant's products with plaintiff in view of the fact that plaintiff was not like the well-known and well-established figures in high fashion who use their names on cosmetics and fragrances.

The essential question here is whether plaintiff is entitled to protection of its trademark "VERA" against defendant's use of the name on cosmetics, perfumes and toiletries. We answer this question in the affirmative.

The trademark laws protect three interests which are present here: first, the senior user's interest in being able to enter a related field at some future time; second, his interest in protecting the good reputation associated with his mark from the possibility of being tarnished by inferior merchandise of the junior user; and third, the public's interest in not being misled by confusingly similar marks—a factor which may weigh in the senior user's favor where the defendant has not developed the mark himself.

We have heretofore protected the trademark owner's rights against use on related, non-competing products—a result in accord with the realities of mass media salesmanship and the purchasing behavior of consumers. See, e. g., Yale Electric Corp. v. Robertson, 26 F.2d 972 (2 Cir. 1928) (flashlights v. locks); L. E. Waterman Co. v. Gordon, 72 F.2d 272, (2 Cir. 1934) (mechanical pens and pencils v. razor blades); S. C. Johnson & Son, Inc. v. Johnson, 116 F.2d 427, (2 Cir. 1940) (waxes and floor cleaners v. fabric cleaners); Triangle Publications, Inc. v. Rohrlich, 167 F.2d 969, (2 Cir. 1948) (magazines v. girdles); Pure Foods, Inc. v. Minute Maid Corp., 214 F.2d 792, (5 Cir. 1954) (juices v. meats); Safeway Stores, Inc. v. Safeway Properties, Inc., 307 F.2d 495 (2 Cir. 1962) (groceries v. real estate); Communications Satellite Corp. v. Comcet, Inc., 429 F.2d 1245, (4

Cir. 1970) (communications services v. computers); Alfred Dunhill of London, Inc. v. Kasser Distillers Products Corp., 350 F.Supp. 1341, (E.D.Pa.1972), aff'd, 480 F.2d 917 (3 Cir. 1973) (pipes and tobacco v. Scotch whiskey). Even when we have rejected infringement claims with respect to non-competing goods, we have carefully limited our holdings.

Absent equities in the junior user's favor, he should be enjoined from using a similar trademark whenever the non-competitive products are sufficiently related that customers are likely to confuse the source of origin.

We turn now to the grounds for the district court's holding that defendant's use of the mark "VERA" did not infringe plaintiff's trademark.

As the district court pointed out, a trademark owner's right to relief where the products are non-competitive depends upon a number of variables including the strength of his mark; the degree of similarity between the two marks; the proximity of the products; the likelihood that the prior owner will bridge the gap; actual confusion; the defendant's good faith in adopting his mark; the quality of defendant's product and the sophistication of the buyers.

Plaintiff claims that the district court improperly concluded that "VERA" was a weak mark merely because it was a common name and because of third party registrations; that the district court erred in finding that Vera, S.A. had been importing its products into the United States under the "VERA" mark since 1962; that the district court erroneously concluded that plaintiff's and defendant's products were so unrelated that consumers were not likely to be misled; and that the district court erred in concluding that there was no reasonable probability that plaintiff would enter the cosmetics, fragrances and toiletries market. We agree with all of these claims except the last, as to which we need express no opinion.

Plaintiff's "VERA" trademark clearly is a strong mark. Plaintiff's sales figures, its advertising expenditures and the many articles written about plaintiff clearly established that plaintiff's "VERA" trademark was highly successful and widely recognized in the medium-high fashion market. Our conclusion that "VERA" is a strong mark is not affected by the fact that Vera is a common name. We need not decide whether such a name might provide a weaker mark in other circumstances, since we think plaintiff has clearly established secondary meaning entitling it to broad protection of the "VERA" mark. Moreover, even when the mark in question is the name of the junior user, his right to use the name on his products may be limited, and he may be compelled to add some distinguishing words to reduce the possibility of confusion.

In holding that plaintiff's trademark was weakened by third-party registrations, the district court relied upon the following registered marks: "Vera" for foods; "Vera Smart" for women's full fashion hosiery; "Vera Stewart" for cosmetics; "Vera Sharp" for cheeses;

"Medicamentie Vera" for a medical publication; "Vera Cruz" for textile products; and "Vera Horn" for women's apparel. We think the district court erred in giving such weight to these registrations.

The significance of third-party trademarks depends wholly upon their usage. Defendant introduced no evidence that these trademarks were actually used by third parties, that they were well promoted or that they were recognized by consumers. As the Court pointed out in Lilly Pulitzer, Inc. v. Lilli Ann Corp., 376 F.2d 324, 325, 153 U.S.P.Q. 406, 407 (C.C.P.A.1967), "the existence of these registrations is not evidence of what happens in the market place or that customers are familiar with their use." Compare Triumph Hosiery Mills, Inc. v. Triumph International Corp., supra, 308 F.2d at 199, 135 U.S.P.Q. at 48 n. 2 (207 registrations under same name). Moreover, all but one of the third-party registrations cited by the district court contained combinations of words, rather than the word "Vera" alone, and several were registered for entirely unrelated products, such as foods or a medical publication. The record does not contain any evidence to support the claim that plaintiff's trademark was weakened by uses of similar marks by third parties.

Likewise, we think the district court erred in attaching any significance to the fact that Vera, S.A. has been importing toiletries into the United States since 1962. There is no evidence in the record to support the district court's finding that Vera, S.A. had imported its products continuously since 1962 "under the mark Vera" or that "VERA" was part of Vera, S.A.'s trademark registered in the United States. Vera, S.A.'s only trademark registered in the United States is for "SIGLO DE ORO." On that registration the phrase "Vera (Espana)," rather than the name "Vera" alone, appears in small type, in the corner of the certificate merely to identify the manufacturer, not as part of the trademark.

Moreover, the significance of Vera, S.A.'s imports since 1962 depends upon its usage of the name "VERA." Defendant introduced no evidence that Vera, S.A. had ever sold its goods under the "VERA" trademark, with the exception of a single line of men's cologne sold after 1970. In its answer, defendant pleaded that the word Vera was merely used to identify the manufacturer and "not the product", and that its products were identified by other trademarks. Defendant introduced no copies of labels used on Vera, S.A.'s products prior to 1970, and no evidence that "Vera" was a prominent part of the name under which those products were sold before that date. Moreover, prior to 1970, Vera, S.A.'s sales in the United States were negligible, and it was not until 1970 or so that defendant began selling its products in some of the same stores in which plaintiff sold its goods.

On this record, we think the district court erred in concluding that Vera, S.A.'s sales in this country since 1962 negate any inference of confusion between plaintiff's and defendant's products. Moreover, the defendant has not introduced any evidence of longstanding sales under a similar mark that would in any way affect the equities of this case.

Finally, the district court found that the plaintiff was not likely to enter the cosmetics, perfume or toiletries market and that that market was unrelated to the apparel market in which plaintiff sold its goods. We have no need to decide whether there is a substantial likelihood that plaintiff will enter the cosmetics and fragrances market, although we cannot agree with defendant that this likelihood is small simply because the firms which plaintiff approached in 1969 were themselves unwilling to go through with the joint venture at that time.

Rather, we hold that defendant's products were by their nature so closely related to plaintiff's own products that plaintiff was entitled to protection against defendant's use of the mark "VERA" on its products. As Judge Learned Hand wrote in his frequently quoted opinion in Yale Electric Corp. v. Robertson, supra, 26 F.2d at 974, "it has come to be recognized that, unless the borrower's use is so foreign to the owner's as to insure against any identification of the two, it is unlawful."

We think the record clearly establishes that defendant's use of the name "VERA" on its products is likely to confuse customers. Plaintiff proved that many, if not most, of the leading designers sell perfumes and cosmetics under their own trademarks. The many newspaper articles which plaintiff introduced, as well as the testimony of plaintiff's expert witnesses, clearly established that plaintiff's recognition is equivalent to that of designers who had expanded into the cosmetics and fragrances fields. Like these other designers, plaintiff appeals to the name-conscious customer. Although plaintiff is not a couturier and sells medium fashion apparel, plaintiff's reputation as a "name" designer would, in all likelihood, lead many customers to think that cosmetics and fragrances sold under the "VERA" trademark were manufactured by plaintiff. Plaintiff's trademark is strong in the market in which it sells its goods. Moreover, defendant has recently expanded its marketing of cosmetics and fragrances, and is now selling those products in the very same stores in which plaintiff's lines are sold.

A trademark owner need not prove that a junior user's conduct will mislead all customers, but only that it is likely to mislead many customers. Moreover, as we have held on numerous occasions, "a showing of actual confusion is not necessary and in fact is very difficult to demonstrate" with reliable proof. W. E. Bassett Co. v. Revlon, Inc., 435 F.2d at 662.

We think that plaintiff, who has expended large sums in promoting its "VERA" trademark, and who has gained wide recognition in the market through its efforts is entitled to relief which will protect its good name against misassociation with defendant's products.

We direct the district court to enter appropriate injunctive relief protecting the plaintiff against any prominent display of the word

"VERA" on defendant's cosmetics, toiletries and fragrances. Since Vera is also the name of Vera, S.A.'s founder, defendant should be allowed to use that name in small type, but only in conjunction with other words which prevent any likelihood of confusion (e. g., "Vera y Cosmetica, S.A.").

An award of damages and an accounting "is not an automatic concomitant of the grant of injunctive relief," Grotrian, Helfferich, Schulz, Th. Steinweg Nachf. v. Steinway & Sons, 523 F.2d 1331, 1344, 186 U.S.P.Q. 436, 446–447 (2 Cir. 1975), and we do not think the plaintiff is entitled to such an award here. Although plaintiff promptly objected to defendant's first prominent use of the name "VERA", defendant's goods were non-competitive with plaintiffs, and so defendant's profits could not have come from diverting plaintiff's customers. Moreover, the district court's finding that defendant acted in good faith is not clearly erroneous, since Vera is also the surname of Vera, S.A.'s founder, since defendant might have believed that defendant's products were not sufficiently related to plaintiffs to infringe plaintiff's mark, and since Vera, S.A. sells its products in many countries other than the United States, thus reducing the likelihood that it adopted the "Vera" display solely to profit from plaintiff's good reputation.

Reversed and remanded with instructions to grant relief in accordance with this opinion.

NOTES

1. To what extent have constructive notice and dilution doctrines moved trademark rights away from their original dependence on trademark use? Can *Dawn Donut* and *Scarves by Vera* be reconciled with the common law rationale of *United Drug?* With the statutory insistence, noted at page 279 above, that a mark be used before it can be registered? With the rule that nonuse constitutes abandonment? See note 6, below. Would a statutory rule of partial abandonment be appropriate when a trademark owner has failed to enter a geographic, product or service market? Under the rule, the mark's first user would be given a specified period within which to exploit the mark in all markets. After that period, it would forfeit any possibility of exclusive rights in the unoccupied market. Would the rule be better or worse if it added that, after expiration of the specified period, the first user would also lose the right to *use* the mark in the unoccupied markets?

Can you reconcile Judge Lumbard's conclusions that an immediate injunction was improper in *Dawn Donut* but proper in *Scarves by Vera?* Are there any relevant differences between the business expectations that focus on future geographic markets and those that focus on future product or service markets? Is the difference between the two cases simply that the parties were more proximate, and the public more likely to be confused, in *Scarves by Vera* than in *Dawn Donut?*

What assumptions do *Dawn Donut* and *Scarves by Vera* make about the investment behavior of producers, their competitors, and their consumers? Since marketing plans can change overnight, and since small, specialized firms can be taken over by large diversified firms, is it anything more than a makeweight for courts even to attempt to consider the likelihood that a firm will enter an unoccupied market?

As a practical matter, *Dawn* converts the issue whether the competitor should cease using the senior user's mark from a legal question to a business question. In arriving at its business decision, the competitor will, of course, speculate as to whether and when the senior user will enter. What other factors should it weigh? If the competitor decides to risk the senior user's entry into its market, and immediately proceeds to invest heavily in the continued use and promotion of its mark, how will the public interest be safeguarded when the senior user does enter the competitor's market and obtains an injunction against the competitor's continued use of the mark?

See generally, Fletcher, The Chextra Case and Other Spawn of Dawn Donut, 66 Trademark Rep. 285 (1976); Alexander & Coil, Geographic Rights in Trademarks and Service Marks, 68 Trademark Rep. 101 (1978).

2. Say that *A* first used the mark, "Rex," in connection with its shampoo in 1961, limiting its distribution at the time to east coast states. In 1968, *A* applied, and was granted registration, for the mark on the Principal Register. In 1969, *B* first used the mark "Rex" in connection with its shampoo, limiting itself to retail sales in west coast states. In 1971, *A* began marketing its "Rex" shampoo on the west coast, strictly on a wholesale basis. Retail consumers on the west coast have never had contact with *A*'s mark. In an action, *A* v. *B* for an injunction, what result?

Say that *A* has not yet marketed its shampoo, on a wholesale or retail basis, on the west coast. In an action, *A* v. *B* for an injunction, what result? Sterling Brewing, Inc. v. Cold Spring Brewing Corp., 100 F.Supp. 412, 90 U.S.P.Q. 242 (D.Mass. 1951), the first case to apply section 22, 15 U.S.C.A. § 1072, to this sort of fact situation, held that the injunction should issue at once, even though "the plaintiff's zone of potential expansion of business cannot reasonably be expected to extend [into defendant's territory]." 100 F.Supp. 412, 415. Which decision, *Dawn* or *Sterling,* provides the better solution?

It is registration, not use or application, that provides constructive notice under section 22. The fact that use must precede application, and that a year or more may pass before a registration issues on the application, poses obvious timing problems for a mark's first user. Say that, in the example just given, *A* applied for registration in January, 1968. In April, 1968, *B* began its use on the west coast without actual notice of *A*'s prior use. *A*'s registration issued in December, 1968. According to two close students of the question, the rights of senior user, *A*, and junior user, *B*, "are not necessarily those which would have arisen at common law, but rather depend, in large part, on whether the junior user commenced in good faith prior to one of several significant dates in the federal registrant's file history: (1) date of registration, (2) date of publication of the applicant's mark, or (3) date of filing for federal registration." Alexander & Coil, Geographic Rights in Trademarks and Service Marks, 68 Trademark Rep. 101, 112 (1978).

3. There is probably no more intricate task in trademark law than coordinating the rights accruing to senior and junior users and senior and junior registrants under common law and under section 22's constructive notice provisions. It is clear that common law provides that, until a mark is registered, each user has rights in the territory it has occupied. But, to what extent will registration freeze the rights of one and expand the rights of the other? Say that *A* first used the mark, "Rex," in connection with its shampoo in 1951. It applied for registration on the Principal Register in 1954 and the registration issued in 1956. *A*'s distribution of the shampoo has at all times been restricted to three states, New York, New Jersey, and Connecticut. *B* first used the mark, "Rex," in connection with its shampoo in 1949 and applied for registration on the Principal Register in 1959. *B*'s distribution of its goods has at all times been restricted to three states, California, Oregon and Washington. Now, *B*'s 1959 application has become the basis for a concurrent use proceeding under section 2, 15 U.S.C.A. § 1052(d). What are the respective territorial rights of the parties?

Coastal Chemical Co., Inc. v. Dust-A-Way, Inc., 139 U.S.P.Q. 208, 210 (Com'r 1963), involved a similar factual pattern. The Commissioner noted that "while Coastal [*B*] is the prior user, Dust-A-Way [*A*] is the prior registrant" and that, under section 22, "when Registration 620,114 issued on January 24, 1956, notice was constructively served on the entire United States, including Coastal Chemical Company, Inc., that Dust-A-Way, Inc., claimed ownership of the trademark." Thus, the Commissioner concluded, Dust-A-Way's rights extended to the entire United States with the exception of those states actually occupied at the time by Coastal. The district court disagreed, ruling "that the parties should be granted concurrent use of their respective trademarks in the areas in which each has been the actual user." Ignoring the changes wrought by the Lanham Act, the court drew on *United Drug* for the proposition that "the ownership of a trademark is based upon its use not its registration." Coastal Chemical Co., Inc. v. Dust-A-Way, Inc., 263 F.Supp. 351, 353, 152 U.S.P.Q. 322 (W.D.Tenn.1967).

In 1970, the Court of Customs and Patent Appeals definitively outlined the substantive rules governing concurrent use. In re Beatrice Foods Co., 429 F.2d 466, 166 U.S.P.Q. 431. *Beatrice Foods* stated that, as a general rule, in concurrent use proceedings between two applicants, the senior user is entitled to a registration covering the entire United States, less the area in which the junior user has established territorial rights. But, the court noted, territorial rights need not be coextensive with territorial use. Among the other factors to be considered are the nature of the claimant's previous business and expansion activities, plans for expansion and the presence in the territory of claimant's products brought in from other areas. On the specific point raised in *Dust-A-Way,* the court observed, "where the prior user does not apply for registration before registration is granted to another, there may be valid grounds, based on a policy of rewarding those who first seek federal registration, and a consideration of the rights created by the existing registration, for limiting his registration to the area of actual use and permitting the prior registrant to retain the nationwide protection of the act restricted only by the territory of the prior user." 429 F.2d n. 13 at 474. *Beatrice Foods* was confirmed and elaborated upon in Weiner King, Inc. v. Wiener King Corp., 615 F.2d 512, 204 U.S.P.Q. 820 (C.C.P.A.1980).

See generally, Lefkowitz, A Concurrent Use Registration as a Reflection of Established Territorial Rights: Fact or Fiction, 65 Trademark Rep. 71 (1975); Kaul, Concurrent Use and Registration of Trademarks, 62 Trademark Rep. 581 (1972); Schwartz, Concurrent Registration Under the Lanham Trademark Act of 1946: What is the Impact on Section 2(d) of Section 22?, 55 Trademark Rep. 413 (1965).

4. Schechter, The Rational Basis for Trademark Protection, 40 Harv.L.Rev. 813 (1927) is the seminal article on trademark dilution. Its thesis has been criticized in Brown, Advertising and the Public Interest, 57 Yale L.J. 1165 (1948) and Middleton, Some Reflections on Dilution, 42 Trademark Rep. 175 (1952). The Middleton article also appraises the Lanham Act's impact upon dilution doctrine as do Deering, Trademarks on Noncompetitive Products, 36 Ore.L. Rev. 1 (1956) and Note, Dilution: Trademark Infringement or Will-O'-The Wisp? 77 Harv.L.Rev. 520 (1964). See also, Pattishall, The Dilution Rationale for Trademark—Trade Identity Protection, Its Progress and Prospects, 71 Nw.L.Rev. 618 (1976).

5. "If the owner of the trademark Servo seeks to prevent the registration of Servotorque, or Servospeed, for related products in the field of servomechanisms, is his position any stronger if he also owns Servoscope, Servosync, Servoflight, Servotherm, Servoflex and Servoboard? The Court of Customs and Patent Appeals said No. [Servo Corp. of America v. Electro-Devices, Inc., 289 F.2d 955, 129 U.S.P.Q. 352 (1961); Servo Corp. of America v. Kelsey-Hays Co., 289 F.2d 957, 129 U.S.P.Q. 354 (1961).]

"Can the owner of the trademarks Clean-Master, Sweep-Master, Dust-Master, and Dirt-Master for carpet sweepers prevail in an opposition against Squeez-Master for sponge mops? The Trademark Trial and Appeal Board said No. [Bissell, Inc. v. Easy Day Mfg. Co., 130 U.S.P.Q. 485 (1961).]

"On the other hand, the owner of the trademarks Fritos, Chilitos, Fritatos, Ta-Tos, Chee-Tos, Corntos, and Tos successfully opposed the registration of Prontos. [The Frito Co. v. Buckeye Foods, Inc., 130 U.S.P.Q. 347 (T.T.A.B.1961).]

"Each of these cases involved the problem of a 'family of trademarks.' This is a term applied to a group of trademarks, owned by one company, in which the same syllable or syllables recur. Eastman Kodak Company, for example, owns not only the well-known trademarks Kodak, Kodacraft, Kodafix, Kodaflat, Kodagraph, Kodaguide, Kodaline, Kodamatic, but numerous others starting with the characteristic prefix Koda, thus creating a 'family' of Koda trademarks." Breitenfeld, When Is a "Family of Trademarks" Effective? 52 Trademark Rep. 351 (1962).*

The Patent and Trademark Office has been reluctant to find rights in families of trademarks. The few cases in which it has sustained a family constellation reflect the view that, to be strong, the family should center around a widely traveled and acknowledged mark. A sprinkling of related uses of the mark, such as in slogans or in the firm name, may help. As to the recommended number of progeny, the more the better. For example, in Dan River Mills, Inc. v. Danfra Ltd., 120 U.S.P.Q. 126 (T.T.A.B.1959), Dan River Mills successfully deployed its family of marks, used in connection with textiles, in opposing the proposed registration of "Danfra" for men's clothes. At the time, Dan River owned about 30 marks—"Dan Master," "Dantwill," "Danshrunk" and "Dantone" among them—and used the parent mark in such other settings as the slogan, "It's a Dan River Fabric."

6. Rights in a trademark may be lost through abandonment. The rule usually stated is that "intention to abandon is the test, with non-use merely a mode of trying to prove intent." Poncy v. Johnson & Johnson, 460 F.Supp. 795, 803, 202 U.S.P.Q. 199, 206 (D.N.J.1978). In practice, nonuse is really the crucial fact for it lies at the heart of the general principle that trademark rights turn on trademark use. The stated concern for intent is probably little more than a bow in the direction of personal property law which has historically made intent the key to abandonment. A finding that a trademark owner has abandoned its rights by failing to pursue infringers can of course be rationalized on the ground that the owner's inaction reflects an intent to abandon the work. The better rationale is that since the mark is no longer being used exclusively by the owner it has lost its distinctiveness. Whatever rationale is given, the judicial bias is against finding abandonment. See, for example, Beech-Nut Packing Co. v. P. Lorillard Co., 273 U.S. 629, 47 S.Ct. 481, 71 L.Ed. 810 (1927).

The Lanham Act adds some objective standards to the common law definition of abandonment. In addition to defining "abandoned," section 45, 15 U.S.C.A. § 1127, provides that "nonuse for two consecutive years shall be *prima facie* abandonment." And section 8, 15 U. S.C.A. § 1058, although not directly concerned with abandonment, offers a surrogate in its provision that "the registration of any mark under the provisions of this chapter shall be canceled by the Commissioner at the end of six years following its date, unless within one year next preceding the expiration of such six years the registrant shall file in the Patent and Trademark Office an affidavit showing that said mark is still in use or showing that its nonuse is due to special circumstances which excuse such nonuse and is not due to any intention to abandon the mark."

The question of abandonment often arises in the context of trademark assignments and licenses. It is a hoary maxim that a trademark cannot be assigned in gross, that is, apart from the assignor's business, assets or goodwill. While transfers in gross are sometimes held to constitute abandonment, it is probably better on principle to treat the naked transfer as merely depriving the assignee of the priority created by its assignor's earlier use. A mark may also be held to have been abandoned if its owner licenses others to use the mark but fails to control the quality of goods or services that the licensees sell under the mark. As indicated by *Dawn Donut,* courts have been less than rigorous in requiring vigilant quality control programs.

Underlying the abandonment rules for both assignments and licenses is the assumption that trademarks signify consistent quality to consumers. To assign a mark without the underlying business, or to fail to police licensees, may lead to alterations in quality that will upset consumer expectations. Are there better sanctions than abandonment for prodding merchants toward consistency? Apart from legal rules, what private incentives do merchants have for assuring the consistent quality of wares and services marketed under their trade and service marks?

7. Second comers are free to use a registered mark's more common elements in a descriptive, non-trademark sense. For example, the owner of the trademark "Joy" for perfume was denied an injunction against the use on a bath oil label of the phrase, "JOY OF BATHING." In the court's opinion "the defendant's use of the word 'Joy' in JOY OF BATHING falls on the side closer to its primary meaning and hence does not invade any secondary meaning with which the plaintiff's use may have surrounded the word. . . . The use of the phrase JOY OF BATHING is designed to suggest the pleasure which will accompany the use of defendant's product in one's bath, and thus performs a descriptive function." Jean Patou, Inc. v. Jacqueline Cochran, Inc., 201 F.Supp. 861, 865, 133 U.S.P.Q. 242 (S. D.N.Y.1962), aff'd, 312 F.2d 125, 136 U.S.P.Q. 236 (2d Cir. 1963).

Called the "fair use" defense, this common law doctrine is also statutorily embodied in section 33(b)(4), 15 U.S.C.A. § 1115(b)(4), allowing as a defense to incontestability "that the use of the name, term, or device charged to be an infringement is a use, otherwise than as a trade or service mark . . . of a term or device which is descriptive of and used fairly and in good faith only to describe to users the goods or services of such party."

8.　What if the defendant uses a mark for satirical purposes? In Reddy Communications, Inc. v. Environmental Action Foundation, 477 F.Supp. 936, 203 U.S.P.Q. 144 (D.D.C.1979), the court dismissed an infringement action brought by the owner of the service mark, "Reddy Kilowatt"—a cartoon figure licensed for advertising use by investor-owned public utilities—against defendant's use of caricatures of Reddy Kilowatt in newsletters and magazines criticizing the electric power industry.　The gist of plaintiff's argument was that defendant, "by casting Reddy in a negative light as the 'villainous utility company' in its publications, has reduced Reddy's attractiveness to investor utilities as a public relations tool for promotion of the utility industry."　Recognizing that defendant had indeed imitated the "Reddy" mark, the court nonetheless concluded that "E.A.F.'s use of Reddy is merely incidental to the sale of its publications."　"Within the context of its publications　.　.　.　EAF's caricatures are dissimilar from Reddy in connotation and overall impression;　.　.　.　the EAF publications are obtained by careful, sophisticated purchasers who will view the EAF caricatures not in isolation but in conjunction with the surrounding text; and　.　.　.　the surrounding text and other identifying indicia adequately signal to the reader the critical use being made of Reddy by an opponent of the electric utility industry."　477 F.Supp. 936, 945–946, 948.

Most actions against satirical use have been allowed, probably because the actions have involved strong, well-advertised marks and defendants have typically lacked serious satirical purpose.　See, for example, Coca Cola Co. v. Gemini Rising, Inc., 346 F.Supp. 1183, 175 U.S.P.Q. 56 (E.D.N.Y.1972) (preliminary injunction granted against distributors of a "blown-up reproduction of the plaintiff's familiar 'Coca Cola' trademark and distinctive format except for the substitution of the script letters 'ine' for 'cola' so that the poster reads 'Enjoy Cocaine' ".).

Compare a decision noted by Professor Derenberg in which "the owner of the famous '4711' trademark for *eau de cologne* got an injunction in Cologne, Germany against a manure collector who used his telephone number, 4711, painted in 20-inch high numerals across both sides of his horse-drawn fertilizer wagon."　Derenberg, The Problem of Trademark Dilution and the Anti-dilution Statutes, 44 Calif.L. Rev. 439, 448 n. 49 (1956).

What consumers are likely to suffer what kind of confusion as a result of these satirical uses?　How, if at all, can the decisions for trademark owners in these cases be reconciled with traditional trademark rationales?　Might a trademark owner's failure to police these satirical uses lead to an eventual finding of abandonment?

These decisions can be contrasted with the "fair use" defense allowed by section 107 of the Copyright Act, pages 763 to 786 below. The wholesale introduction of copyright's fair use defense into trademark infringement actions has been rejected on the ground that "because the primary purpose of the trademark laws is to protect the public from confusion it would be somewhat anomalous to hold that the confusing use of another's trademark is 'fair use'." Dallas Cowboys Cheerleaders, Inc. v. Pussycat Cinema, Ltd., 604 F.2d 200, 206 n. 9, 203 U.S.P.Q. 161, 165 (2d Cir. 1979).

9. Congress and the courts sometimes compel copyright and patent owners to license their protected subject matter in order to forestall or dissipate monopoly effects. See pages 752 to 757 and 628 to 629 below. Should trademarks also be subjected to compulsory licensing in similar circumstances? What public interests weigh against the compulsory licensing of trademarks that do not weigh against the compulsory licensing of copyrights and patents?

A Federal Trade Commission administrative law judge thought that trademark compulsory licensing was an appropriate vehicle for correcting a market imbalance. Finding that Borden's trademark, "ReaLemon," used in connection with reconstituted lemon juice, was a significant barrier to the entry of new producers, Judge Hanscom ordered Borden to license the mark for ten years to any firm desiring to enter the reconstituted lemon juice market. Borden, Inc., 92 F.T. C. 669, 3 Trade Reg. Rep. (C.C.H. ¶ 21,194 Aug. 19, 1976). Acknowledging that the Commission had never before ordered the licensing of a trademark, Judge Hanscom rested his award of the remedy on the belief that it "is not essentially different from a requirement of compulsory licensing of a patent." 92 F.T.C. 775.

The decision drew considerable fire. The United States Trademark Association filed an *amicus* brief with the F.T.C. arguing that to require compulsory licensing "could have an adverse impact upon the interests of the public in the use of trademarks and upon the integrity of trademarks." According to the Association, compulsory trademark licensing disserves the public interest because "it permits more than one business to use a single trademark on goods, causing the trademark to fail in its essential purpose and producing public injury by impairing consumers' freedom of choice, whether or not all goods sold under the trademark are of equal quality." And the private value of the ReaLemon mark would be impaired to "the extent that its proprietor's right to the exclusive use thereof is abrogated for ten years. And, at the end of that term, it may be so diluted or sullied by the acts of competitor-licensees as to be worthless."

On November 7, 1978 the F.T.C. voted not to order compulsory licensing of the ReaLemon mark. Recognizing that "an order requiring licensing or suspension of a trademark may be ordered as a means of dissipating illegally used or acquired monopoly power," a majority of the Commission was "mindful that the remedy is a severe one, and should be imposed only where less drastic means appear unlikely to suffice." In the judgment of the majority "an order that simply prohibits Borden from pricing to exclude or minimize new entry should be sufficient to dissipate its unlawfully maintained monopoly position, which is the only permissible object of relief in this case." 92 F.T.C. 669, 807–808, 3 Trade Reg. Rep. C.C.H. ¶ 21,490 (1978).

See generally McCarthy, Compulsory Licensing of a Trademark: Remedy or Penalty? 67 Trademark Rep. 197 (1977); Palladino, Compulsory Licensing of a Trademark, 26 Buffalo L.Rev. 457 (1977); Ball, Government Versus Trademarks: Today—Pharmaceuticals, ReaLemon and Formica—Tomorrow? 68 Trademark Rep. 471 (1978). On the economics of compulsory licensing for trademarks, see Scherer, (Book Review), The Posnerian Harvest: Separating Wheat from Chaff, 86 Yale L.J. 974, 998–1000 (1977).

NOTE: INCONTESTABILITY AND IMMUNITY FROM CANCELLATION

The Lanham Act's incontestability provisions are far more limited and fragmented than their proponents had originally intended. The original hope was for a strong, unified standard that would govern both cancellation proceedings and infringement actions. Thus, an early bill had provided that, after five years on the Principal Register, a mark could not be cancelled and that, once this cancellation period had expired, the registrant's exclusive right to use its mark would be unassailable in infringement actions. H.R. 9041, 75th Cong. 3rd Sess., §§ 13, 14 (1938). The provisions that finally emerged from the push and tug of legislative compromise are the highly qualified incontestability provisions of sections 15 and 33(b), 15 U.S.C.A. §§ 1065, 1115(b) and section 14's cancellation provisions, 15 U.S.C.A. § 1064, which substantially parallel the incontestability provisions.

The principle that underlies sections 14, 15 and 33(b) is not too different from the underlying principle of common law adverse possession rules: if investment is to be encouraged, time and use must be allowed to heal many original defects. Each section focuses its curative power on a different context. Section 14 applies when the registrant is defending its mark against another's attempt to cancel it. Section 15 establishes the registrant's incontestable right to use the mark and applies when the registrant is defending an infringement action brought to enjoin it from using the mark. And section 33(b) applies when the registrant seeks to prevent another from using a confusingly similar mark. This last, offensive use of incontestability, though entirely consistent with the language and structure of section 33(b), was rejected in several early cases. See, for example, John Morell & Co. v. Reliable Packing Co., 295 F.2d 314, 131 U.S.P.Q. 155 (7th Cir. 1961); Tillamook County Creamery Ass'n v. Tillamook Cheese & Dairy Ass'n, 345 F.2d 158, 145 U.S.P.Q. 244 (9th Cir. 1965), cert. denied, 382 U.S. 903, 86 S.Ct. 239, 15 L.Ed.2d 157, 147 U. S.P.Q. 541. These early doubts have, however, been removed and the offensive use of incontestability is accepted today. See, for example, Union Carbide Corp. v. Ever-Ready, Inc., 531 F.2d 366, 188 U.S.P.Q. 623 (7th Cir. 1976), cert. denied, 429 U.S. 830, 97 S.Ct. 91, 50 L.Ed.2d 94, 191 U.S.P.Q. 416.

Section 14 approximates incontestability by providing that after five years on the Principal Register a mark will generally be immune from attack in a cancellation proceeding. Among the grounds left open for attack after the five-year period are fraudulent registration, abandonment, the mark's having become the "common descriptive name of an article or substance," and any of the grounds that would disqualify a mark from registration under section 2(a), (b) or (c). Thus, after five years a registered mark cannot be cancelled simply because it lacks distinctiveness or is confusingly similar to other marks.

Although section 14 is sometimes labeled an "incontestability" provision, it is in fact only sections 15 and 33(b) that expressly use and define that term. Section 15 provides that a registrant's right to use its mark in commerce "shall be incontestable" if the mark has been used for five consecutive years after its registration and the registrant files an affidavit to that effect. By the terms of section 15, incontestability can be defeated on the same grounds that, under section 14, would require cancellation after five years' registration. Additionally, section 15 provides that a registration will not become incontestable to the extent that use of the mark "infringes a valid right acquired under the law of any State or Territory by use of a mark or trade name continuing from a date prior to the date of the publication" of the registered mark. Also, "no incontestable right shall be acquired in a mark or trade name which is the common descriptive name of any article or substance, patented or otherwise."

Section 33(b) gives teeth to incontestability by providing that if the right to use a mark has become incontestable, the registration "shall be *conclusive evidence* of the registrant's exclusive right to use the registered mark in commerce on or in connection with the goods or services specified in the affidavit filed under the provisions of said section 1065 subject to any conditions or limitations stated therein." (Emphasis added). By contrast, certificates for contestable marks represent only *prima facie* evidence of the registrant's exclusive right to use. Section 33(a), U.S.C.A. § 1115(a). Section 33(b) also pulls some of these teeth, though, depriving the certificate of conclusive effect if, among other grounds, the registration or incontestable right was obtained fraudulently or the mark has been abandoned or has been or is being used to violate federal antitrust laws.

See generally, Fletcher, Incontestability and Constructive Notice: A Quarter Century of Adjudication, 63 Trademark Rep. 71 (1973); Ooms & Frost, Incontestability, 14 L. & Contemp. Prob. 220 (1949).

2: REMEDIES

See Statute Supplement 15 U.S.C.A. §§ 1111, 1114, 1116–1121, 1124.

MALTINA CORP. v. CAWY BOTTLING CO., INC.

United States Court of Appeals, Fifth Circuit, 1980.
613 F.2d 582, 205 U.S.P.Q. 489.

JOHNSON, Circuit Judge:

I. The Facts

Cawy Bottling Company (Cawy), defendant below, appeals from the judgment of the district court in favor of the plaintiffs Maltina Corporation and Julio Blanco-Herrera in their trademark infringement action. The district court enjoined Cawy from further infringement, awarded the plaintiffs $35,000 actual damages, and ordered the defendant to account for $55,050 of gross profit earned from the sale of infringing products.

Julio Blanco-Herrera fled to this country from Cuba in late 1960 after that country nationalized the company of which he was president and, along with his family, majority stockholder. Before that year, this company was one of the largest breweries and beverage distributors in Cuba. Among its products was malta, a dark, non-alcoholic carbonated beverage brewed similar to beer. The Cuban company distributed malta under the trademarks "Malta Cristal" and "Cristal" in Cuba and in the United States. The Cuban company had registered the marks both in Cuba and the United States. When Blanco-Herrera arrived in the United States, he formed the Maltina Corporation and assigned the "Cristal" trademark to it. He attempted to produce and distribute "Cristal" in this country, but despite his efforts Maltina Corporation was never able to obtain sufficient financial backing to produce more than $356 worth of "Cristal".

Cawy Bottling, however, had an altogether different experience in producing malta. At the outset, it attempted to register the "Cristal" trademark so that it might be utilized in marketing the product. This attempt was rejected by the Patent Office because of plaintiffs' prior registration. After this attempted registration and with the knowledge of the plaintiffs' ownership of the trademark, Cawy began producing and distributing malta under the "Cristal" label in February 1968.

In 1970 the plaintiffs sued Cawy under 15 U.S.C.A. § 1117 for trademark infringement and unfair competition. They sought an injunction against further use of their mark, damages, and an accounting. The district court dismissed the suit on the ground that Cuba's confiscation of the assets of Blanco-Herrera's Cuban corporation made Blanco-Herrera's assignment of the "Cristal" mark to the Maltina Corporation invalid. This Court reversed, holding Cuba's confiscation decree did not extend to the "Cristal" mark registered by the United States Patent Office, Maltina Corp. v. Cawy Bottling Co., 462 F.2d 1021, 174 U.S.P.Q. 74 (5th Cir.), cert. denied, 409 U.S. 1060, 176 U.S.P.Q. 33 (1972). On remand, the district court determined that the plaintiffs had a valid trademark. Cawy appealed, and we affirmed, Maltina Corp. v. Cawy Bottling Co., 491 F.2d 1391 (1974) (per curiam).

At trial on the merits, from which this appeal is taken, the district court determined that Cawy had infringed the plaintiffs' mark and assigned the case to a magistrate for determination of what recovery was appropriate under 15 U.S.C.A. Section 1117. Before holding a hearing the magistrate wrote a memorandum to the district court stating that he thought that the plaintiffs were entitled to an injunction but not to an accounting for defendant's profits.

After holding the hearing, however, the magistrate changed his recommendation. He noted that Cawy designed its "Cristal" label to resemble the label used by Maltina's predecessor in Cuba. He found that Cawy intended to exploit the reputation and good will of the "Cristal" mark and to deceive and mislead the Latin community into believing that the "Cristal" once sold in Cuba was now being sold in the United States. The magistrate further found that Cawy wilfully infringed the plaintiffs' mark and had been unjustly enriched to the detriment of plaintiffs' reputation and good will. He recommended that Cawy account to the plaintiffs for the profit it earned from the infringement, and he directed Cawy to report its sales of "Cristal" and associated costs to the plaintiffs for determination of its profits. The magistrate also found Cawy's infringement damaged the reputation and good will of the plaintiffs in the amount of $35,000. He recommended that Cawy compensate plaintiffs in that amount.

The district court, after a complete and independent review of the record, adopted the magistrate's recommendations as its order. As more fully discussed below, the district court eventually found Cawy liable to the plaintiffs for its gross profits from the sale of "Cristal", $55,050. The court entered judgment against Cawy for $55,050 gross profits plus $35,000 damages and enjoined Cawy from any further infringement of the plaintiffs' mark.

Cawy presents three arguments on appeal. First, it argues that an accounting was inappropriate. Second, that if an accounting was appropriate, the district court erred in awarding to the plaintiff Cawy's entire gross profits from the sales of "Cristal". Third, Cawy argues that the award of $35,000 actual damages cannot stand in the absence of any evidence to support it. We accept this final contention but reject the first two. Cawy does not complain on appeal of the district court's enjoining it from further infringement of the plaintiffs' mark.

II. Was an Accounting Appropriate?

Section 1117, 15 U.S.C.A. entitles a markholder to recover, subject to the principles of equity, the profits earned by a defendant from infringement of the mark. The courts have expressed two views of the circumstances in which an accounting is proper under 15 U.S.C.A. Section 1117. Some courts view the award of an accounting as simply a means of compensating a markholder for lost or diverted sales. Other courts view an accounting not as compensation for lost or diverted sales, but as redress for the defendant's unjust enrichment and as a deterrent to further infringement. See Maier Brewing Co. v. Fleischmann Distilling Corp., 390 F.2d 117, 121, 157 U.S.P.Q. 76, 78–79 (9th Cir.) cert. denied, 391 U.S. 966, 157 U.S.P.Q. 720 (1968). In this case, the plaintiffs never sold any appreciable amount of "Cristal" in the United States so they cannot claim that Cawy diverted any of their sales. Accordingly, we must decide whether diversion of sales is a prerequisite to an award of an accounting. We hold that it is not.

In Maier Brewing the Ninth Circuit awarded an accounting to a plaintiff who was not in direct competition with a defendant and who, accordingly, had not suffered any diversion of sales from the defendant's infringement. The court noted that the defendant had wilfully and deliberately infringed. It reasoned that awarding an accounting would further Congress' purpose in enacting 15 U.S.C.A. Section 1117 of making infringement unprofitable. This Court is in accord with this reasoning. See also Monsanto Chemical Co. v. Perfect Fit Products Manufacturing Co., 349 F.2d 389, 146 U.S.P.Q. 512 (2nd Cir. 1965) (holding that a trademark holder was entitled to an accounting to protect the public from infringement). The Fifth Circuit has not addressed the issue whether an accounting only compensates for diverted sales or whether an accounting serves the broader functions of remedying an infringer's unjust enrichment and deterring future infringement. A recent opinion by this Court, however, recognizes that a trademark is a protected property right. Boston Professional Hockey Association v. Dallas Cap and Emblem Manufacturing, Inc., 597 F.2d 71, 75, 202 U.S.P.Q. 536, 539 (5th Cir. 1979). This recognition of a trademark as property is consistent with the view that an accounting is proper even if the defendant and plaintiff are not in direct competition, and the defendants' infringement has not diverted sales from the plaintiff. The Ninth Circuit in Maier Brewing noted that the infringer had used the mark-holder's property to make a profit and that an accounting would force the infringer to disgorge its unjust enrichment. 390 F.2d at 121, 157 U.S.P.Q. at 78–79. Here, the only valuable property Blanco-Herrera had when he arrived in this country was his right to the "Cristal" mark. Cawy used this property, and an accounting is necessary to partially remedy its unjust enrichment.

The district court relied, in part, on W. E. Bassett Co. v. Revlon, Inc., 435 F.2d 656, 168 U.S.P.Q. 1 (2nd Cir. 1970), in ordering an accounting. That case held that an accounting should be granted "if the defendant is unjustly enriched, if the plaintiff sustained damages from the infringement, or if an accounting is necessary to deter a willful infringer from doing so again." Id. at 664, 168 U.S.P.Q. at 7.

Revlon sold a cuticle trimmer embossed with a "Cuti-Trim" mark "in the teeth of the Patent Office's refusal to register" that mark. Id. at 662, 168 U.S.P.Q. at 5. This was willful infringement that an accounting would deter in the future. In the instant case, the district court found that Cawy's "infringement was willful and that such infringement resulted in [Cawy] being unjustly enriched . . . ." Cawy used the "Cristal" mark after the Patent Office refused to register it. This clearly and explicitly supports the finding of willful infringement. An injunction alone will not adequately deter future infringement. In short, we find the district court properly ordered Cawy to account to the plaintiffs for the profits it earned from its willful infringement. This accounting serves two purposes: remedying unjust enrichment and deterring future infringement.

III. Did the District Court Err in Requiring Cawy to Account for Its Entire Gross Profit from the Sale of "Cristal"?

The district court ordered Cawy to account to the plaintiffs for $55,050, the entire gross profit (total revenue less cost of goods sold) from the sale of "Cristal". The district court did not allow Cawy to deduct overhead and other expenses. These expenses would have produced a net loss from the sale of "Cristal" and, if allowed, would have enabled Cawy to escape liability to the plaintiffs for its infringement.

Under 15 U.S.C.A. Section 1117, the plaintiff has the burden of showing the amount of the defendant's sales of the infringing product. The defendant has the burden of showing all elements of cost and other deductions. In this case, the court ordered Cawy to report its total sales of "Cristal" and associated costs to the plaintiffs. If the plaintiffs objected to Cawy's estimate of its net profits from "Cristal", they were to file their objection with the court. The record on appeal reflects that Cawy submitted three exhibits showing its net loss on "Cristal" sales. These exhibits are set out in the appendix. The plaintiffs filed their objections to Cawy's figures with the court. They accepted Cawy's estimate of gross revenues from the sale of "Cristal" and the cost of goods sold. Thus, they met the burden of proving the amount of sales of the infringing product. The plaintiffs, however, did not accept other deductions claimed by Cawy. Cawy claimed deductions for *"Expenses Specifically Identified with Malta Cristal"*, as set out in Exhibit 2. Plaintiffs objected to these claimed deductions because Cawy did not show they were actually spent on "Cristal". Cawy also claimed deductions for general overhead, apportioned to "Cristal" on the basis of the ratio of "Cristal" sales to Cawy's total sales. Exhibit 3 displays these claimed overhead deductions. The plaintiffs objected to the overhead deductions because the infringing product constituted only a small percentage of the defendant's business.

Cawy responded to the plaintiffs' objections by asserting that it did have "specific and detailed figures and corroborating sales slips, invoices and the like to support" its claims of expenses attributable to

[handwritten marginal note: BURDEN OF PROOF OF DEFENDANT AND PLAINTIFF]

"Cristal". Cawy failed, however, to submit any of this corroboration to the district court.

The district court, after noting that Cawy had the burden of establishing deductions from gross profits, disallowed Cawy's claims of expenses specifically attributable to "Cristal" as set forth in Exhibit 2. The court stated that it could not determine whether the advertising, sales commissions, legal fees, telephone, and other expenses claimed by Cawy related to "Cristal" sales or to the sales of other products. It then held that Cawy failed to sustain its burden of proof with respect to those claimed expenses. We cannot say that the district court erred in its holding. The record on appeal, like the record before the district court, simply affords no support for the contention that the claimed *"Expenses Specifically Identified with Malta Cristal"* actually related to "Cristal" sales. Furthermore, Cawy's claims of deductions of legal fees, as the district court noted, would not be allowable in any case. While we cannot tell whether these fees related to this suit, if they did, they would not be deductible.

The district court also disallowed Cawy's deductions of a proportionate part of its overhead expenses as set forth in Exhibit 3. Quoting from Société Anonyme v. Western Distilling Co., 46 F. 921 (C.C. E.D.Mo. 1891), the district court noted: "It appears that 'the unlawful venture increased the gross profits without swelling the gross expenses'." It then held that Cawy failed to sustain its burden of showing the propriety of allowing deductions for overhead. Again, we must agree with the district court that Cawy failed to meet its burden of showing its expenses in the absence from the record on appeal of any evidence that Cawy's production of "Cristal" actually increased its overhead expenses. Furthermore, we note that a proportionate share of overhead is not deductible when the sales of an infringing product constitute only a small percentage of total sales. See S. C. Johnson & Son, Inc. v. Drop Dead Co., 144 U.S.P.Q. 257 (S. D.Cal.1965) (disallowing overhead deduction when infringing sales were only 6% of total sales). Here, on the average, infringing sales constituted just over 6% of total sales. Accordingly, we think it unlikely, especially in the absence of any evidence to the contrary, that Cawy's production of "Cristal" increased its overhead expenses.

The district court properly ordered Cawy to account for its entire gross profit from the sale of "Cristal". Cawy failed to meet its burden of showing that the overhead and other expenses that it claimed in Exhibits 2 and 3 actually related to the production of "Cristal".

IV.　Did the District Court Err in Awarding the Plaintiffs $35,000 as Actual Damages for Cawy's Infringement?

The district court awarded the plaintiffs $35,000 as actual damages from Dawy's infringement. The record, however, is wholly devoid of support for this figure. Accordingly, we must reverse as to this element.

The plaintiffs have never been able to get sufficient financial backing to produce more than a very small amount of "Cristal" in the United States. That inability makes proof of actual damages from Cawy's infringement unlikely. In any event, the plaintiffs have had an opportunity to show their damages and have failed to do so. This Court concludes that plaintiffs should not have another opportunity to show their damages just as Cawy should not have another apportunity to prove its expenses.

In the ten years since the plaintiffs filed their original petition, this case has been before us three times. All litigation must end. We remand only for entry of judgment in accordance with this opinion.

Affirmed in part, reversed in part, and remanded for entry of judgment.

APPENDIX

DEFENDANT'S EXHIBIT 1

NET LOSS ON SALES OF MALTA CRISTAL

	1969	1970	1971	1972	1973	1974	1975	TOTAL
Revenues from sales of Malta Cristal	$40,032	$41,708	$83,861	$60,119	$31,099	$14,666	—	$271,482
Less cost of goods sold—Malta	31,883	34,059	67,285	46,438	25,209	11,558	—	216,432
GROSS PROFIT	8,149	7,646	16,576	13,681	5,890	3,108	—	55,050
Less expenses:								
per exhibit 2	8,165	6,479	10,175	17,870	17,007	9,353	500	69,549
per exhibit 3	6,683	4,250	7,859	6,448	3,199	1,762	—	30,201
TOTAL EXPENSES	14,848	10,729	18,034	24,318	20,206	11,115	500	99,750
NET LOSS ( )	$(6,699)	$(3,083)	$(1,458)	$(10,637)	$(14,316)	$(8,007)	$(500)	$(44,700)

CAWY BOTTLING CO., INC.

(s) Vincent Cossio

DEFENDANT'S EXHIBIT 2

EXPENSES SPECIFICALLY IDENTIFIED WITH
MALTA CRISTAL

	1969	1970	1971	1972	1973	1974	1975	TOTAL
Advertising	$ 2,277	$ 1,723	$ 4,299	$13,080	$13,124	$ 6,510	—	$ 41,013
Sales commissions	3,137	3,172	5,505	4,116	1,732	752	—	18,414
Legal fees	2,130	1,500	200	483	1,988	709	—	7,010
Telephone and Telegraph	43	84	171	191	163	13	—	665
Other	578	—	—	—	—	1,369	500	2,447
	$ 8,165	$ 6,479	$10,175	$17,870	$17,007	$ 9,353	$500	$ 69,549

DEFENDANT'S EXHIBIT 3

EXPENSES RELATED TO MALTA CRISTAL
ALLOCATED BASED ON SALES RATIO

	1969	1970	1971	1972	1973	1974	1975	TOTAL
Malta Cristal cases sold	15,139	15,439	30,451	21,471	10,849	5,238	-0-	98,287
Total number of cases sold	176,458	228,000	276,424	288,500	296,590	314,485	-0-	1,580,457
Ratio of Malta's cases to total cases sold	8.58%	6.77%	10.91%	7.44%	3.66%	1.67%	—	6.22%

EXPENSES RELATED TO MALTA:

1.	Repairs and maintenance	$ 1,323	$ 524	$ 762	$ 1,256	$ 663	$ 1,091	$ 5,619
2.	Rent	6,864	6,864	7,938	—	—	—	21,666
3.	Building depreciation	—	—	—	3,073	3,073	3,073	9,219
3.	Interest—mostly building	—	—	—	11,958	14,408	13,758	40,124
4.	Taxes other than payroll	4,932	8,065	5,645	12,456	11,964	10,791	53,853
5.	Payroll taxes	7,718	6,282	8,582	6,624	6,859	6,787	42,852
6.	Trucks' expenses	7,238	6,301	12,502	13,083	9,482	8,668	57,274
7.	Utilities	1,620	—	509	—	—	—	2,129
5.	Indirect labor	23,156	9,360	9,360	11,305	12,480	12,450	78,111
5.	Officers salaries	17,500	13,000	13,000	13,000	13,000	31,750	101,250
8.	Office expenses	403	665		1,046	767	1,503	4,384
9.	Sales promotion	808	95	275	1,513		82	2,773
10.	Insurance	3,536	5,031	6,967	6,566	8,722	8,265	39,087
11.	Uniforms	916	926	1,119	1,129	1,180	1,483	6,753
11.	Traveling	—	2,613	2,255	324	820	2,938	8,950
11.	Accounting fees	165	970	800	1,485	—	2,875	6,295
11.	Miscellaneous	1,714	2,088	2,320	1,843	3,980	—	11,945
	TOTAL EXPENSES	77,893	62,784	72,034	86,661	87,398	105,514	492,281
	MALTA TO TOTAL RATIO	8.58%	6.77%	10.91%	7.44%	3.66%	1.67%	
		$ 6,683	$ 4,250	$ 7,859	$ 6,448	$ 3,199	$ 1,762	$ 30,201

NOTES

1. Characterizing trademark rights as property rights may, as noted in *Maltina,* be "consistent with the view that an accounting is proper even if the defendant and plaintiff are not in direct competition." But does the property characterization compel the accounting remedy? *Maltina's* approach may obscure the real question—whether the trademark owner should be given profits earned in markets it has not yet entered. Should the answer to this question differ depending on whether the market not yet entered is a geographic market, as in *Maltina,* or a product or service market, as in dilution cases? Should the answer to the question be affected by the relative availability of injunctive relief? Reconsider the discussion of *Dawn Donut,* p. 360 above.

2. Because the remedies of damages and profits are intertwined, and because each alone serves at least two functions, the array of monetary awards available to the successful trademark owner is far richer than might appear from the face of section 35. Damages can be measured by

(1) loss of sales and profits caused by the infringer's use of the owner's mark; or

(2) consequent economic injury to the trademark owner's reputation and goodwill.

Profits earned by the infringer through its use of the mark can be treated

(1) as presumptively equivalent to the profits lost by the trademark owner and, thus, awarded on a compensatory basis; or,

(2) under the approach taken in *Maltina,* as unjust enrichment.

Type (1) profit awards are thus the intended equivalent of type (1) damage awards, the difference lying in the critical shift from owner to infringer of the burden of proof. The assumption implicit in this shift, that the owner's sales have been diverted by the infringer's, is warranted only when the parties are in competition. Type (2) profit awards, because they rest on an unjust enrichment rationale, do not require competition between the parties. To bar double recovery, an award of type (1) profits will preclude an award of type (1) damages but will not preclude an award of type (2) damages. Is an award of type (1) damages inconsistent with an award of type (2) profits? Restatement, Restitution § 136, Comment a (1937), explores the general principles that underlie these distinctions.

Monetary awards generally are considered in Price, Financial Recovery in an Action of Trademark Infringement, 47 Trademark Rep. 1297 (1957) and Note, An Accounting of Profits for Trade Symbol Infringement Based Upon a Theory of Restitution, 1963 Wash.U. L.Q. 243.

3. Under section 29, 15 U.S.C.A. § 1111, the owner of a registered mark can recover damages and profits only if it can show that the infringer knew of the registration or that notice of the registration, such as the familiar ®, accompanied displays of the mark.

If the registrant intentionally employs a false or misleading notice, its unclean hands will bar injunctive relief. See, for example, Fox-Stanley Photo Products, Inc. v. Otaguro, 339 F.Supp. 1293, 174 U.S.P.Q. 257 (D.Mass. 1972), Is it false marking if the notice of registration is located under a composite mark, one part of which is registered and one part of which is not? Compare Straus v. Notaseme Hosiery Co., 240 U.S. 179, 36 S.Ct. 288, 60 L.Ed. 590 (1916) with Coca-Cola Co. v. Victor Syrup Corp., 42 C.C.P.A. 751, 218 F.2d 596, 104 U.S.P.Q. 275 (1954).

4. In Fleischmann Distilling Corp. v. Maier Brewing Co., 386 U.S. 714, 87 S.Ct. 1404, 18 L.Ed.2d 475, 153 U.S.P.Q. 432 (1967), the Supreme Court ruled that a prevailing trademark owner is not entitled to recover attorney's fees, even from a deliberate infringer. Justice Stewart dissented. "Until this case, every federal court that has faced the issue has upheld judicial power to award counsel fees in trademark infringement cases. In order to overrule that unbroken line of authority, I would have to be satisfied that Congress has made any such declaration."

Congress soon made its intentions clear. P.L. 93–600, 88 Stat. 1955 (1975), provides in part that "the court in exceptional cases may award reasonable attorney fees to the prevailing party." 15 U. S.C.A. § 1117. The rationale for the remedy was that "effective enforcement of trademark rights is left to the trademark owners and they should, in the interest of preventing purchaser confusion, be encouraged to enforce trademark rights." The revisors recognized that "section 35 of the present Trademark Act provides for awarding treble damages in appropriate circumstances in order to encourage the enforcement of trademark rights. The availability of treble damages, however, cannot be regarded as a substitute for the recovery of attorney fees. In suits brought primarily to obtain an injunction, attorney fees may be more important than treble damages. Frequently, in a flagrant infringement where the infringement action is brought promptly, the measurable damages are nominal." Sen.Rep. No. 93–1400, (93d Cong. 2d Sess.)

5. Injunctions granted in unfair competition actions are typically shaped to meet the particular circumstances of the case. See page 91 above. Trademark injunctions, by contrast, are characteristically granted absolutely or not at all, with scant attention given to the possibilities in between. The reason for the difference lies in trademark's exclusive focus on marks and its disregard for contextual factors such as format, usage, typographic style and other overt elements of passing off.

For an adjudged infringer, the effects of an absolute injunction may be excessive. The infringer may have adopted the mark, and won considerable good will, all in good faith. An intermediate decree may be all that is needed to avoid consumer confusion. On the other hand, hazard to the public may attend outright refusal to grant an injunction. If an injunction is denied because plaintiff cannot show that defendant's use of the mark is likely to cause sufficient consumer confusion to warrant the decree, or because plaintiff has unclean hands or is guilty of laches, defendant's permitted use will continue to confuse at least some members of the public.

See generally, Latman, Preliminary Injunctions in Patent, Trademark and Copyright Cases, 60 Trademark Rep. 506 (1970); Dorr & Duft, Trademark Preliminary Injunctive Relief, 62 J.P.O.S. 3 (1980).

D. INFRINGEMENT

See Statute Supplement 15 U.S.C.A. §§ 1114, 1119, 1121.

PIKLE–RITE CO. v. CHICAGO PICKLE CO.

United States Dist. Court, Northern Dist. Illinois, 1959.
171 F.Supp. 671, 121 U.S.P.Q. 128.

JULIUS J. HOFFMAN, District Judge.

This is an action for trade-mark infringement and unfair competition in which the plaintiff seeks an injunction, an accounting and treble damages.

The plaintiff is an Illinois corporation having its principal office and place of business in Pulaski, Wisconsin. The defendant is an Illinois corporation having its principal office and place of business in Chicago. In 1932, plaintiff's predecessor, John A. Wood, established the business of preparing and selling bottled pickles and related products. In 1942, this business was taken over by Pikle-Rite Company, an unincorporated business entity which was incorporated in 1948. Since 1932, plaintiff and its predecessors have owned and used the trade-mark "Polka" to designate different varieties of pickles which are sold primarily in self-service grocery stores in Illinois, Wisconsin, Iowa, Michigan, Minnesota, Indiana and Ohio.   Since 1934, the name "Polka" has been registered as a trade-mark under the laws of Illinois.   On August 7, 1956, plaintiff was granted a federal trade-mark registration on the name "Polka."   As registered, the name is preceded and followed by a pair of musical notes.   The name "Polka," as applied to pickle products, is fanciful, arbitrary, non-descriptive and non-generic, and is a valid trade-mark.

Representative labels under which plaintiff markets some of its "Polka"-brand pickle products are as follows:

Although the plaintiff prepares and bottles other vegetables, its "Polka"-brand pickle products are its principal items of business. The plaintiff has advertised its "Polka"-brand products through the media of television, radio, newspapers, window posters, shelf posters and gifts such as pencils, lazy susans and plastic aprons. However, the evidence discloses no comprehensive advertising expenditures.

For the period January 1953 through June 1957, the total amount of sales of "Polka"-brand products was $311,184.11. The yearly amount of sales of these products was as follows:

1953	$ 49,014.75
1954	45,230.58
1955	68,461.56
1956	100,037.32
1957	48,439.90

(through June)

There is no evidence on the question whether the pickle business as a whole was substantially better in 1956 than it was in 1955. Nor is there any evidence on the question whether the plaintiff expanded its business or its advertising in 1956.

In December 1956, defendant began to distribute pickles in bottles which bore the brand-name "Pol-Pak." Defendant's label is as follows:

The defendant markets its products through self-service grocery stores. However, the evidence does not disclose whether the defendant utilizes this method exclusively or even primarily.

With reference to infringement, the basic issue in this case is *Issue* whether the defendant's use of the name "Pol-Pak" on its products ".   .   . is likely to cause confusion or mistake or to deceive purchasers as to the source of origin of such goods." 15 U.S.C.A. § 1114 (1) (a). For the reasons which follow, I am of the opinion that the defendant's brand-name "Pol-Pak" is confusingly similar to the plaintiff's trade-mark "Polka," and the plaintiff is entitled to injunctive relief. However, I am also of the opinion that the plaintiff is not entitled to an accounting and damages.

There is no dispute between the parties as to the law which is applicable to the instant case. In Northam Warren Corp. v. Universal Cosmetic Co., 7 Cir., 1927, 18 F.2d 774, at page 775, the law of infringement was stated as follows:

> Whether there is an infringement of a trade-mark does not depend upon the use of identical words, nor on the question as to whether they are so similar that a person looking at one would

be deceived into the belief that it was the other; but it is sufficient if one adopts a trade-name or a trade-mark so like another in form, spelling, or sound that one, *with a not very definite or clear recollection as to the real trade-mark, is likely to become confused or misled.* . . . (Emphasis added.) . . .

In determining whether the likelihood of confusion exists, it should be noted that:

The ascertainment of probability of confusion because of similarity of trade names presents a problem not solvable by a precise rule or measure. Rather is it a matter of varying human reactions to situations incapable of exact appraisement. We are to determine, as was the District Judge, the purchasing public's state of mind when confronted by somewhat similar trade names singly presented. Is the similarity of name or dress such as to delude the public or will the prospective buyer readily differentiate between the two names? We can only contemplate, speculate, and weigh the probabilities of deception arising from the similarities and conclude as our, and the District Judge's, reactions persuade us. Colburn v. Puritan Mills, 7 Cir., 1939, 108 F.2d 377, at page 378.

Although the question presented by the instant case cannot be solved by precise rule or measure, certain factors are relevant. Whether infringement exists is not to be determined solely by a side-by-side comparison of the names in question. Although it is proper to consider the names as a whole, the names should not be examined with a microscope to detect minute differences. To constitute infringement, it is not necessary that the defendant appropriate the whole of plaintiff's mark, and the imitation need only be slight if it attaches to the salient feature of plaintiff's mark. The court should also consider the form, spelling and sound of the marks in question; whether the products involved are the same or similar, whether the products are sold to the same prospective customers, and whether the conditions under which the products are purchased are the same or similar.

In the instant case, there is no evidence that any purchaser was, in fact, confused or misled by the defendant's use of the name of "Pol-Pak." However, it was not necessary for the plaintiff to prove actual confusion. The statutory test is likelihood of confusion.

I am of the opinion that the defendant's use of the name "Pol-Pak" gives rise to the likelihood of confusing similarity. The salient part of defendant's brand-name, i. e., "Pol," constitutes three-fifths of plaintiff's trade-mark. Common experience teaches that an individual will more readily remember the first part of a name than some other part. Further, to the extent that the defendant's pickles are sold in self-service grocery stores, the parties utilize the same or similar commercial channels, the prospective purchaser is the same, and the conditions under which the products are purchased are the same or similar. The names "Polka" and "Pol-Pak" are not more dissimilar than the names "Cutex" and "Cuticlean" which were held to be confusingly similar in Northam Warren Corp. v. Universal Cosmetic Co., 7 Cir., 1927, 18 F.2d 774. The Northam case also refutes defendant's contention that the name "Pol" is but an abbreviation for the descriptive word, "Polish," and is, therefore, not infringing. In the Northam case, the designation "Cuti" was an abbreviation for the descriptive or generic word, "cuticle," but the court held that "Cuticlean" infringed "Cutex."

The defendant contends that a side-by-side comparison of the *labels* in question discloses no confusing similarity. However, as noted above, infringement is not to be determined solely by such comparison. The reason for this rule is that the ultimate purchaser is seldom presented with the opportunity of making such comparison. Further, it is to be doubted that the labels, apart from the marks in question, should be considered. It has been asserted as a general rule that differences in labels should not be considered in determining whether defendant's brand-name infringes plaintiff's trade-mark. 1 Nims, Unfair Competition and Trade Marks, § 221k, p. 716 et seq. However, Nims cites, as a case contrary to the general rule, John Morrell & Co. v. Doyle, 7 Cir., 1938, 97 F.2d 232, certiorari denied 1938, 305 U.S. 643, 59 S.Ct. 146, 83 L.Ed. 415. In the Morrell case, the plaintiff sold dog food under the trade-mark "Red Heart" which comprised those words superimposed upon a red heart. The defendant sold dog and cat food under the brand-name "Strong Heart" which name was accompanied by the picture of a famous dog, Strongheart. In holding that the plaintiff's trade-mark was not infringed, the court considered and emphasized the picture of the dog, and the court expressly declined to consider the name "Strong Heart" in vacuo. In spite of this fact, I am of the opinion that the Morrell case does not derogate from the general rule. The rationale of that decision is that, with regard to the defendant's label,

> .   .   . the characteristic feature, the thing which appeals to the eye and which, no doubt, makes the lasting impression upon a person's memory, is not Strongheart or Heart, but the picture of a dog. Assuming that persons who are interested in dog foods are dog fanciers, what could make such an appeal or create such a lasting impression as an imposing picture of a dog and especially if it be the picture of a dog of fame such as the record here indicates to be the case?

Thus, the court merely held that the essence of defendant's brand-name was a picture and not a name. In the instant case, the salient part of defendant's label is the brand-name "Pol-Pak"; the picture of a pickle is without significance. Further, to the extent that the representation of Polish dancers is a salient part of plaintiff's label, the representation reinforces the trade-mark "Polka." It does not derogate from the mark as the picture of the dog derogated from the brand-name "Strong Heart." In addition, it should be noted that the plaintiff has advertised the name "Polka" apart from the representation of Polish dancers.

Even in an economy in which diverse methods of advertising are employed, the spoken word is of great importance. A prospective purchaser may learn of plaintiff's "Polka"-brand products from her neighbor; she may hear radio advertisements; she may hear and see television advertisements and the memory of the spoken word may exist long after the memory of the image has faded. Further, the law does not presume that the prospective purchaser will have the opportunity to make a side-by-side comparison of different products and brand-names. As stated in Colburn v. Puritan Mills, 7 Cir., 1939, 108 F.2d 377, at page 378:

> We are to determine, as was the District Judge, the purchasing public's state of mind when confronted by somewhat similar trade names *singly presented.* (Emphasis added.)

Also, it must be borne in mind that we are dealing neither with an unusual product which requires discriminating purchase nor with a purchasing public which is discriminating. To the contrary, it has been asserted that the average purchaser undergoes, while in a supermarket, an experience not unlike that of hypnosis. Packard, The Hidden Persuaders, pp. 91–2 (Cardinal Edition, 1958). Under such circumstances, it is not unduly harsh to restrain the defendant's use of the name "Pol-Pak." The defendant, in selecting a name for its product, could have drawn upon the entire range of its imagination. It chose not to do so and, instead, selected a name which is likely to confuse prospective purchasers of plaintiff's products. I conclude that the defendant's use of the name "Pol-Pak" should be enjoined.

Consideration will next be given to the territorial scope of the injunction. On this issue, a division of authority exists. In 87 C.J.S. Trade-Marks, etc. § 211d, p. 597, it is stated:

> The wrongful appropriation of plaintiff's trade-mark will be enjoined wherever it is used by him, including those places where he might do so in the course of normal business expansion. On the other hand, it has been held that injunctive relief should be limited to states in which plaintiff has established a market for the articles bearing his trade-mark. . . .

On the facts of the instant case, it is impossible to determine whether it may reasonably be anticipated that the plaintiff will expand its business. Accordingly, I am of the opinion that the injunction should be limited to those states in which plaintiff has established a market for its "Polka"-brand products.

The above discussion, although limited to the claim of trade-mark infringement, applies with equal vigor to plaintiff's claim of unfair competition, and as to both of these claims, I am of the opinion that plaintiff is entitled to no relief other than an injunction. In Square D. Co. v. Sorenson, 7 Cir., 1955, 224 F.2d 61, at pages 65–66, it was stated:

> Plaintiffs failed to prove fraud or a palming off by defendants of any article to persons who believed they were buying

plaintiff's product. While the absence of fraud or palming off does not undermine a finding of unfair competition (citing cases), the character of the conduct giving rise to the unfair competition is relevant to the remedy which should be afforded. An accounting will not be ordered merely because there has been an infringement (citing case). As under the trade mark act of 1905, under the present act an accounting has been denied where an injunction will satisfy the equities of the case.

In the instant case, the evidence is insufficient to warrant the conclusion that the defendant was guilty of fraud, palming off or intentional infringement, and I conclude that an injunction will satisfy the equities of the case. The defendant will bear the costs of this action. The plaintiff is directed to submit a judgment order in conformity with the views herein expressed on or before January 21, 1959.

McGREGOR–DONIGER, INC. v. DRIZZLE, INC.

United States Court of Appeals, Second Circuit, 1979.
599 F.2d 1126, 202 U.S.P.Q. 81.

MESKILL, Circuit Judge.

McGregor-Doniger Inc. ("McGregor"), a New York corporation founded in 1921, is a manufacturer of apparel for both men and women. Since 1947 McGregor has sold golf jackets under the trademark Drizzler, and in 1965 the company registered this mark for use in connection with golf jackets. Although McGregor had in the past used the word Drizzler in connection with other types of apparel, by 1965 the company had ceased using the mark in connection with any goods other than golf jackets. McGregor owns a variety of other trademarks, such as Brolly Dolly and Bernhard Altmann, which have been used in connection with goods other than golf jackets. Drizzler jackets sell for about $25 to $50.

Drizzle Inc. ("Drizzle"), a New York corporation established in 1969, sells only women's coats. Drizzle's coats, which are manufactured for Drizzle by various contractors, have been sold under the unregistered trademark Drizzle since the founding of the company. It appears from the record that Drizzle has to date employed no other trademark. Drizzle coats range in price from about $100 to $900.

In 1974 McGregor's management first became aware of the Drizzle company and of its use of the Drizzle mark in connection with the sale of women's coats. In January of 1975 McGregor notified Drizzle that if use of the Drizzle trademark on Drizzle's goods continued, legal proceedings would be instituted. The warning went unheeded and in March of 1975 McGregor brought suit against Drizzle in the United States District Court for the Southern District of New York, alleging trademark infringement, 15 U.S.C.A. § 1114, false designation of origin, 15 U.S.C.A. § 1125(a), and, in a pendent claim, common law unfair competition. McGregor sought an injunction barring Drizzle's further use of Drizzle as a trademark, an accounting for profits, damages, and other relief.

After a two-day bench trial, Judge Morris E. Lasker dismissed McGregor's complaint. 446 F.Supp. 160, 199 U.S.P.Q. 466 (S.D.N.Y. 1978). On appeal, McGregor challenges both the factual findings of the trial court and the trial court's interpretation of the legal significance of the facts found. Although the trial court's statement of the applicable principles needs modification, we conclude that reversal is not warranted.

Discussion

We are once again called upon to decide when a trademark owner will be protected against the use of its mark, or one very similar, on products other than those to which the owner has applied it. As we have observed before, the question "does not become easier of solution with the years." Polaroid Corp. v. Polarad Electronics Corp., 287 F.2d 492, 495, 128 U.S.P.Q. 411, 412–413 (2d Cir.), cert. denied, 368 U.S. 820, 82 S.Ct. 36, 7 L.Ed.2d 25, 131 U.S.P.Q. 499 (1961).

The crucial issue in these cases is "whether there is any likelihood that an appreciable number of ordinarily prudent purchasers are likely to be misled, or indeed simply confused, as to the source of the goods in question." Mushroom Makers, Inc. v. R. G. Barry Corp., 580 F.2d 44, 47, 199 U.S.P.Q. 65, 66–67 (2d Cir. 1978), cert. denied, 439 U.S. 1116, 99 S.Ct. 1022, 59 L.Ed.2d 75, 200 U.S.P.Q. 832 (U.S. Jan. 15, 1979), 3 R. Callmann, The Law of Unfair Competition, Trademarks and Monopolies § 84, at 929 (3d ed. 1969) (hereinafter Callmann). In assessing the likelihood of such confusion we consider the factors laid out in the now classic Polaroid formula:

> Where the products are different, the prior owner's chance of success is a function of many variables: the strength of his mark, the degree of similarity between the two marks, the proximity of the products, the likelihood that the prior owner will bridge the gap, actual confusion, and the reciprocal of defendant's good faith in adopting its own mark, the quality of defendant's product, and the sophistication of the buyers. Even this extensive catalogue does not exhaust the possibilities—the court may have to take still other variables into account.

Polaroid Corp. v. Polarad Electronics Corp., supra, 287 F.2d at 495, 128 U.S.P.Q. at 412–413, citing Restatement of Torts §§ 729, 730, 731. The parties agree that Judge Lasker was correct in giving consideration to each of the factors mentioned in Polaroid before reaching a decision on the ultimate question of likelihood of confusion.

1.   Strength of the Mark

The most complex issue raised by McGregor concerns the trial court's attempt to gauge the strength of the Drizzler mark. Our prior opinions and those of the district courts of this Circuit have left litigants and judges uncertain as to the appropriate way to demonstrate and determine the strength of a mark. In the hope of providing some guidance to bench and bar, we set out in some detail our view of this issue.

The term "strength" as applied to trademarks refers to the distinctiveness of the mark, or more precisely, its tendency to identify the goods sold under the mark as emanating from a particular, although possibly anonymous, source. The Restatement of Torts uses the term "distinctiveness" in place of the term "strength." § 731(f) and Comment e at 602. The strength or distinctiveness of a mark determines both the ease with which it may be established as a valid trademark and the degree of protection it will be accorded.

In an effort to liberate this aspect of trademark law from the "welter of adjectives" which had tended to obscure its contours, we recently reviewed the four categories into which terms are classified for trademark purposes. Abercrombie & Fitch Co. v. Hunting World, Inc., 537 F.2d 4, 9, 189 U.S.P.Q. 759, 764 (2d Cir. 1976). Arranged in ascending order of strength, these categories are: (1) generic, (2) descriptive, (3) suggestive, and (4) arbitrary or fanciful. A generic term can never become a valid trademark and cannot be registered. A descriptive term can be registered as a mark only if it has "become distinctive of the applicant's goods in commerce," 15 U.S.C.A. § 1052(f), that is, in the unfortunate parlance of the cases, only if it has acquired "secondary meaning." Suggestive marks, falling between the merely descriptive and the arbitrary or fanciful, are entitled to registration without proof of secondary meaning, as are fully arbitrary or fanciful terms. 537 F.2d at 9–11, 189 U.S.P.Q. at 764–765. The boundaries between these categories are not fixed.

> [A] term that is in one category for a particular product may be in quite a different one for another, because a term may shift from one category to another in light of differences in usage through time, because a term may have one meaning to one group of users and a different one to others, and because the same term may be put to different uses with respect to a single product.

Abercrombie & Fitch Co. v. Hunting World, Inc., supra, 537 F.2d at 9, 189 U.S.P.Q. at 764.

Thus, while these categories can be useful for analytical purposes, the strength of a mark depends ultimately on its distinctiveness, or its "origin-indicating" quality, in the eyes of the purchasing public. Two familiar examples suffice to illustrate this principle. A coined term, initially suggestive or even fanciful, can lose its full trademark status if it comes to signify to the public the generic name of an article rather than the source of a particular brand of that article. In contrast, a descriptive mark that is not distinctive on its face may acquire secondary meaning so as to identify the source of the goods and thus claim status as a valid mark deserving of registration and protection against infringement. In Judge Lasker's words, "strength may derive from the intrinsic quality of a mark or from its public history." 446 F.Supp. at 162, 199 U.S.P.Q. at 467.

The many cases announcing that a mark found to be suggestive, arbitrary or fanciful (i. e., more than merely descriptive) is entitled to protection without proof of secondary meaning are correct as far as they go, for any term that is more than descriptive can be established as a valid mark which others may not infringe. Where the products involved are competitive and the marks quite similar, for example, the senior user of a more-than-descriptive mark need not prove secondary meaning. And where the marks involved are virtually identical, even if the products are non-competitive, a senior user of a more-than-descriptive mark can carry its burden on the "strength of the mark" component of the Polaroid formula without proving secondary meaning. But these cases do not require us to hold that Judge Lasker erred in considering evidence of secondary meaning in determining whether McGregor is entitled to protection against the use, on non-competitive goods, of a mark similar to its own. The cases agree that it is appropriate to consider all factors bearing on the likelihood of confusion. We view evidence concerning the origin-indicating significance of a mark in the marketplace as relevant to and probative of the strength of a mark and hence useful in assessing the likelihood of confusion.

Consideration of evidence of secondary meaning will almost always work in favor of the senior user. Its mark, if registered, is presumptively distinctive. Proof of secondary meaning, acquired perhaps through successful advertising, can only enhance the strength of its mark and thus enlarge the scope of the protection to which it is entitled. On the other hand, the owner of a distinctive mark need not introduce·evidence of secondary meaning in order to gain protection for its mark against the confusing similarity of others. Thus, for example, the relatively small size of a senior user's advertising budget or sales volume will not diminish the strength of its valid mark, and the scope of protection accorded to that mark will not be narrowed because of such evidence. Only if the junior user carries the burden of affirmatively demonstrating that a term is generic is the senior user stripped of protection.

McGregor claims that the district court erred in requiring proof of secondary meaning. We agree with McGregor's contention that the decision of the Patent and Trademark Office to register a mark without requiring proof of secondary meaning affords a rebuttable presumption that the mark is more than merely descriptive. The trial court did in fact find the term Drizzler more than merely descriptive, although apparently only barely over the "suggestive" line. As a suggestive term, the Drizzler mark would be entitled to protection, regardless of proof of secondary meaning, *if* McGregor could prove that confusion of origin was likely to result from the use of a similar mark on non-competing goods. To the extent the district court held proof of secondary meaning *necessary*, it was in error. However, it was *not* error for the court to consider evidence bearing on the strength of the mark in determining the likelihood of consumer confusion and thus the scope of protection to which the Drizzler mark was entitled. Trademark strength is "an amorphous concept with little shape or substance when divorced from the mark's commercial context," E. I. DuPont de Nemours & Co. v. Yoshida Internat'l, Inc., supra, 393 F.Supp. at 512, 185 U.S.P.Q. at 604–605. We see no advantage to be derived from barring judicial consideration of the realities that give content to the concept of trademark strength.

2. Similarity of the Marks

"To the degree that the determination of 'likelihood of confusion' rests upon a comparison of the marks themselves, the appellate court is in as good a position as the trial judge to decide the issue." Miss Universe, Inc. v. Patricelli, 408 F.2d 506, 509, 161 U.S.P.Q. 129, 130–131 (2d Cir. 1969). There are two principles especially important to performing this task.

First, even close similarity between two marks is not dispositive of the issue of likelihood of confusion. "Similarity in and of itself is not the acid test. Whether the similarity is likely to provoke confusion is the crucial question." Callmann § 82.1(a), at 601–02 (footnote omitted). For this reason cases involving the alteration, addition or elimination of only a single letter from the old mark to the new reach divergent results. Second, in assessing the similarity of two marks, it is the effect upon prospective purchasers that is important. Restatement of Torts § 728, Comment b at 591.

The district court quite correctly took into consideration all the factors that could reasonably be expected to be perceived by and remembered by potential purchasers. "[T]he setting in which a designation is used affects its appearance and colors the impression conveyed by it." Id. § 729, Comment b at 593. Thus while observing that the typewritten and aural similarity of the two marks "approaches identity," the district judge noted that the contexts in which the respective marks are generally presented reduces the impact of this similarity. The court observed that the label in each Drizzler jacket prominently features the McGregor name, which is printed in striking plaid letters. In addition, although there was testimony that retail stores on occasion in independent advertisements omit the McGregor logo, the evidence showed that McGregor always emphasizes the company name in its own advertising of Drizzler jackets. The fact that a trademark is always used in conjunction with a company name may be considered by the trial court as bearing on the likelihood of confusion.

The law does not require that trademarks be carefully analyzed and dissected by the purchasing public. "[I]t is sufficient if the *impression* which the infringing product makes upon the consumer is such that he is likely to believe the product is from the same source as the one he knows under the trade-mark." Stix Products, Inc. v. United Merchants & Mfrs., Inc., 295 F.Supp. 479, 494, 160 U.S.P.Q. 777, 789–790 (S.D.N.Y.1968) (footnote omitted; emphasis added).

The court below properly focused on the general impression conveyed by the two marks. If Drizzle had chosen consistently to present its mark in red plaid lettering or to advertise its coats as the McGregor Drizzle line, we would be compelled to conclude that the similarity between the Drizzler mark and the Drizzle mark, *as generally presented to the public,* had been heightened and that the likelihood of confusion had been enhanced. Conversely, the fact that only one mark generally appears in close conjunction with the red plaid McGregor name increases the likelihood that the public, even when viewing the marks individually, will not confuse the two. The likelihood of confusion is further reduced by Drizzle's use of its mark to identify itself as the producer of the products advertised by it rather than as the name of a particular jacket or line of jackets, in contrast to McGregor's practice.

The district court's reasoning is sound. The differing methods of presentation of the two marks were properly examined. We agree with Judge Lasker's appraisal that they reduce to some degree the potential for confusion inherent in the close similarity between the two marks.

3. and 4. Product Proximity and Quality of Defendant's Product

The district court concluded on the basis of differences in appearance, style, function, fashion appeal, advertising orientation, and price that the competitive distance between Drizzler jackets and Drizzle coats is "significant." This conclusion is too amply supported by the evidence to be characterized as clearly erroneous.

McGregor does not claim that Drizzler jackets and Drizzle coats are directly competitive. Customers shopping for an inexpensive golf jacket are not likely to become confused by the similarity of the marks and mistakenly purchase a fashionable and expensive woman's coat. Thus the degree of proximity between the two products is relevant here primarily insofar as it bears on the likelihood that customers may be confused as to the *source* of the products, rather than as to the products themselves, and the concern is not direct diversion of purchasers but indirect harm through loss of goodwill or tarnishment of reputation. It is evident that customers would be more likely to assume that Drizzler golf jackets and Drizzle golf jackets come from the same source than they would be likely to assume that Drizzler golf jackets and Drizzle steam shovels come from the same source. Drizzle coats for women fall between the two extremes. In locating the appropriate place for Drizzle coats on this continuum, the district court considered many of the factors that are generally viewed as relevant.

The impression that noncompeting goods are from the same origin may be conveyed by such differing considerations as the physical attributes or essential characteristics of the goods, with specific reference to their form, composition, texture or quality, the service or function for which they are intended, the manner in which they are advertised, displayed or sold, the place where they are sold, or the class of customers for whom they are designed and to whom they are sold.

Callmann § 82.2(c), at 807.

Looking at these very factors, the district judge found:

> Beyond the fact that they might both be crudely classified as outerwear, the "Drizzler" and defendant's products have nothing in common. McGregor's garment is a relatively inexpensive, lightweight, waistlength jacket—a windbreaker . . .. As is apparent from advertisements for the jacket, it is intended for casual wear, particularly in connection with sports activities. Moreover, although the Drizzler can be worn by either men or women, sales are pitched primarily to the former . . .. Furthermore, a Drizzler is ordinarily sold in the men's department of stores which carry both men's and women's garments . . ..

> Unlike McGregor's products, the coats manufactured by Drizzle are distinctly and exclusively tailored for women. They are generally full length raincoats and capes. Although it is true that Drizzle manufactures a style that might be called a jacket . . . it is longer than the Drizzler and entirely different in appearance. Drizzle's garments are within the medium to high fashion range . . .. The price range of Drizzle's line, running from approximately $100 to $900 . . . reflects the coats' position in the fashion hierarchy.

446 F.Supp. at 164, 199 U.S.P.Q. at 469 (footnotes and citations to record omitted).

In Blue Bell, Inc. v. Jaymar-Ruby, Inc., 497 F.2d 433, 182 U.S.P. Q. 65 (2d Cir. 1974), we recognized that due to diversification in the garment business, men's apparel and women's apparel had in certain cases been regarded as sufficiently related to justify the denial of registration to similar marks. However, in Blue Bell we characterized the proximity between men's sportswear and women's sportswear as only "moderate" and held that the likelihood of confusion was reduced by the rather "detailed purchasing process" appropriate to the goods in question. 497 F.2d at 435–36, 182 U.S.P.Q. 66–67. We know of no case holding that, as a matter of law, the competitive distance between men's apparel and women's apparel cannot be demonstrated to be significant on the basis of the many factors relevant to such a determination. The district court's finding on this issue, based on the proper indicia and supported by the evidence, should not be disturbed.

The high quality of Drizzle's coats is not contested by McGregor.

5. Bridging the Gap

In assessing the likelihood of confusion, the district court was required to consider the likelihood that Drizzler would "bridge the gap," that is, the likelihood that McGregor would enter the women's coat market under the Drizzler banner. McGregor presented no evidence that such a step was being considered. Clearly the absence of any present intention or plan indicates that such expansion is less, rather than more, probable. Also of probative value is the fact that McGregor has for many years marketed its women's apparel undei names bearing no similarity to Drizzler—such as Brolly Dolly. On the other hand, the absence of a present intent to bridge the gap is not determinative. In a given case, sufficient likelihood of confusion may be established although likelihood of bridging the gap is not demonstrated. Because consumer confusion is the key, the assumptions of the typical consumer, whether or not they match reality, must be taken into account.

The district court's finding that it is unlikely that Drizzler will bridge the gap is not clearly erroneous. Nor does the evidence presented below regarding McGregor's own history of trademark use, as well as industry custom, compel the conclusion that, despite the improbability that McGregor will move into the women's coat market under the Drizzler trademark, consumers will assume otherwise.

6. Actual Confusion

McGregor's claim that the district court erred in considering the absence of proof of *actual* consumer confusion in assessing the *likelihood* of confusion is without merit. Actual confusion is one of several factors to be considered in making such a determination. Although we have recognized the difficulty of establishing confusion on the part of retail customers, the district judge quite properly noted that not a single instance of consumer confusion had actually been demonstrated. While a plaintiff need not prove actual confusion in order to prevail, "it is certainly proper for the trial judge to infer from the absence of actual confusion that there was also no likelihood of confusion." Affiliated Hosp. Prod., Inc. v. Merdel Game Mfg. Co., 513 F.2d 1183, 1188, 185 U.S.P.Q. 321, 324 (2d Cir. 1975).

Finally, the district court was not required, as McGregor urges, to find actual *consumer* confusion on the basis of the testimony of one McGregor employee that she had been momentarily confused by a Drizzle advertisement. The weighing of evidence, particularly where credibility judgments must be made, is for the trial judge. His determination regarding actual confusion is not clearly erroneous.

7. Good Faith

McGregor contends that the district court improperly placed the burden of proof on the good faith issue on McGregor rather than on Drizzle. However, assuming without deciding that McGregor is correct in its view of the proper placement of the burden of proof, there is simply no indication in Judge Lasker's opinion that this burden was in fact placed on McGregor.

We recently held that adoption of the mark Mushroom for women's sportswear despite actual and constructive notice of another company's prior registration of the mark Mushrooms for women's shoes was not necessarily indicative of bad faith, because the presumption of an exclusive right to use a registered mark extends only so far as the goods or services noted in the registration certificate. Mushroom Makers, Inc. v. R. G. Barry Corp., supra, 580 F.2d at 48, 199 U.S.P.Q. at 67–68. Here, as in Mushroom Makers, the district court was entitled to consider and to credit the uncontradicted testimony of Drizzle's witnesses that the Drizzle mark was selected without knowledge of McGregor's prior use of the Drizzler mark. "Normally, the alleged infringer's intent is an issue for district court determination," Grotrian, Helfferich, Schulz, Etc. v. Steinway & Sons, supra, 523 F.2d at 1338 n. 14, 186 U.S.P.Q. at 441–442 n. 14, and findings as to such intent will be upset only if clearly erroneous.

8. Sophistication of Buyers

McGregor asserts that the trial court erroneously considered only the typical "sophisticated" purchaser of Drizzle's coats, to the exclusion of the casual or unsophisticated purchaser. We do not read the decision below in this manner.

The relevant cases not only authorize but instruct the trial courts, in making a determination as to likelihood of confusion, to consider the level of sophistication of the relevant purchasers. "The general impression of the ordinary purchaser, buying under the normally prevalent conditions of the market and giving the attention such purchasers usually give in buying that class of goods, is the touchstone." Callmann § 81.2, at 577 (footnote omitted). As we observed recently in Taylor Wine Co. v. Bully Hill Vineyards, Inc., 569 F.2d 731, 733, 196 U.S.P.Q. 593, 593–594 (2d Cir. 1978), "every product has its own separate threshold for confusion of origin." The greater the value of an article the more careful the typical consumer can be expected to be; the average purchaser of an automobile will no doubt devote more attention to examining different products and determining their manufacturer or source than will the average purchaser of a ball of twine. The degree of reliance by consumers on labels and trademarks will also vary from product to product. It is easy to see that such differences in purchasing patterns affect the likelihood that confusion will result from the use of similar marks on noncompeting goods from different sources.

In some cases, of course, as where the products are identical and the marks are identical, the sophistication of buyers cannot be relied on to prevent confusion. For example, in Omega Importing Corp. v. Petri-Kine Camera Co., 451 F.2d 1190, 1195, 171 U.S.P.Q. 769, 772–773 (2d Cir. 1971), we held that even though the ordinary purchaser would be expected to make "more than a casual inspection" before buying an expensive camera, such inspection would be of doubtful value because the cameras from each of two different sources were both labelled "Exakta." In the instant case, however, where both the products involved and the marks involved are distinguishable, the care exercised by typical consumers is likely to reduce confusion.

In Omega we noted that where a buyer market was composed of both discriminating and relatively unknowledgeable buyers, a court must consider the probability of confusion on the part of the latter as well as the former. However, it is also true that the crucial issue is confusion on the part of an "appreciable number" of consumers. Mushroom Makers, Inc. v. R. G. Barry Corp., supra, 580 F.2d at 47, 199 U.S.P.Q. at 66–67. At a certain point, confusion "will be too slight to bring the case above the rule of de minimis." Triumph Hosiery Mills v. Triumph Internat'l Corp., supra, 308 F.2d at 199, 135 U.S.P.Q. at 47–48. "The remote possibility of occasional confusion in those who observe less than ordinary care under the circumstances does not concern us." Modular Cinemas of America, Inc. v. Mini Cinemas Corp., supra, 348 F.Supp. at 582, 175 U.S.P.Q. at 358–359. " 'The purchasing public must be credited with at least a modicum of intelligence .   . ..' " Carnation Co. v. California Growers Wineries, 97 F.2d 80, 81, 37 U.S.P.Q. 735, 735–736 (C.C.P.A.1938).

McGregor offered no evidence establishing that any significant number of Drizzle purchasers are casual or unsophisticated. The district court was entitled to rely on the evidence indicating that the relevant purchasing group in fact tends to be sophisticated and knowledgeable about women's apparel. We cannot classify his findings in this regard as clearly erroneous.

Conclusion

In trademark infringement cases involving non-competing goods, it is rare that we are "overwhelmed by the sudden blinding light of the justness of one party's cause." King Research, Inc. v. Shulton, Inc., supra, 454 F.2d at 69, 172 U.S.P.Q. at 323. Most often our affirmances in such cases rest on the more modest conclusion that the trial judge was not wrong in reaching the result appealed from. It is on this basis that we affirm the district judge's decision. Judge Lasker applied the correct legal standard (likelihood of confusion) and the correct criteria (those enumerated in Polaroid) in reaching his result. Moreover, he quite properly regarded no single factor as determinative. Although the two marks at issue are concededly quite similar, the court below found that the Drizzler mark is only moderately strong, that the competitive distance between the products is significant, that there was no intention to bridge the gap, that no actual confusion has occurred, and that Drizzle adopted its mark in good faith. Thus the court's conclusion that likelihood of confusion had not been proved by McGregor is amply supported by its findings, none of which is clearly erroneous. And we do not believe that the error in analysis discussed in our opinion today compels reversal of the result reached by the district court.

Because McGregor has failed to establish a likelihood of confusion, the balance of interests of necessity tips in Drizzle's favor. Because the goods are concededly not competitive, McGregor's sales of Drizzler jackets cannot be expected to suffer. Where non-competitive goods are involved the trademark laws protect the senior user's interest in an untarnished reputation and his interest in being able to enter a related field at some future time. Because consumer confusion as to source is unlikely, McGregor's reputation cannot be expected to be harmed. Because of the improbability that McGregor will enter the women's coat field under the Drizzler name, its right to expand into other fields has not been unduly restricted. Thus we see no injury to McGregor resulting from denial of the relief requested. On the other hand, if forced to give up its mark Drizzle could be expected to be harmed by loss of the goodwill that has been associated with the Drizzle name since 1969.

As we noted in Chandon Champagne Corp. v. San Marino Wine Corp., 335 F.2d 531, 536, 142 U.S.P.Q. 239, 243 (2d Cir. 1964):

> Although this court was the leader in granting relief to a trademark owner when there had been and was no likelihood of actual diversion [i. e., in cases involving non-competitive products], we have likewise emphasized that, in such cases, "against these legitimate interests of the senior user are to be weighed the legitimate interests of the innocent second user" and that we must balance "the *conflicting interests* both parties have in the unimpaired continuation of their trade mark use." Avon Shoe Co. v. David Crystal, Inc. [supra, 279 F.2d at 613, 125 U.S.P.Q. at 612–613].

Following this approach, this Court has frequently supplemented its consideration of the Polaroid factors by balancing the conflicting interests of the parties involved. Particularly when viewed in light of a balancing of the interests involved, the decision below warrants affirmance.

SEARS, ROEBUCK & CO. v. ALLSTATE DRIVING SCHOOL, 301 F.Supp. 4, 163 U.S.P.Q. 335 (E.D.N.Y.1969). ZAVATT, J.: . . . Prior to the trial of this case, and in preparation for it, plaintiffs engaged a market analyst to conduct a telephone survey in order to try to establish that the public is likely to be confused as to the origin of defendant's services. They had hoped that the survey would indicate that a large number of persons responding to it were actually confused, and that therefore, the court would draw the inference that there was a strong likelihood of confusion as to the origin of defendant's services. The results of the survey were offered through the testimony of Albert Sindlinger, President of Sindlinger & Co., located in Philadelphia, Pennsylvania. Mr. Sindlinger supervised the preparation of the survey questionnaire, and the tabulation of the results. Two interviewers and one supervisor testified. All but three of the remaining interviewers were available in court to testify. The parties stipulated that these people would give the same answers to the questions posed as those who did testify.

999 telephone interviews were tabulated over a two week period by 24 women who were part-time employees of Sindlinger & Co. Every telephone call was placed from Philadelphia to a Suffolk County residential subscriber chosen by a random selection procedure devised by Sindlinger. These employees, all but two of whom were high school graduates, worked approximately 20 hours per week at the rate of $1.60 per hour (the minimum wage). They were not skilled or experienced public opinion researchers. They had received preliminary "training" for a three day period. It consisted of listening to telephone calls made by other Sindlinger employees for other surveys. They were able to listen only to the questions posed by the interviewers; they could not overhear the responses to those questions. They received no special instructions regarding the manner of asking questions, or of recording responses. The nature of the tabulating process required that short responses be recorded. Therefore, summaries of actual answers were recorded where the answers were too long to record verbatim. Supervisors could have monitored any interview they chose to, but they generally did so only when a particular interviewer requested assistance. Since many other surveys were being conducted by Sindlinger & Co. during this period, the supervisors could not be sure that any interviews were monitored in this particular survey.

The answers which were recorded by the interviewers were coded and tabulated according to Sindlinger's instructions. The report containing the computer tabulation of the responses was received in evidence. The defendant, after initially objecting to its admissibility at the trial, now concedes that it was properly admitted, but argues that very little weight ought to be attributed to the findings. The report indicates that 37.6% of the respondents were of the opinion that Sears owns or operates the Allstate Driving School, and that an additional 12.2% thought that Allstate Insurance owns or operates the Allstate Driving School. Other responses such as "Allstate Company" and "Allstate" are inconclusive as far as plaintiffs seek to interpret them as further evidence of confusion. Finally, 39.1% responded that they did not have an opinion as to the ownership or operation of the Allstate Driving School. The results are much more impressive when restricted to those respondents who had an opinion (60.1% of the total sample). Of these 61.8% indicated that in their opinion Sears owns or operates the Allstate Driving School, and 20.1% indicated Allstate Insurance. Thus, 49.8% of the total sample (which includes those who "didn't know") were of the opinion that one of the plaintiffs owns or operates the Allstate Driving School, while 81.9% of those who had an opinion indicated that one of the plaintiffs owns or operates the Allstate Driving School. This survey is not of sufficient weight to persuade the court, in the light of all the other evidence in the case, that the ordinary prospective purchaser is likely to be confused as to the origin of defendant's services. There are several inadequacies in the design and execution of the survey which lead the court to give it little weight. Only some of the more serious are analyzed here.

The women who conducted the telephone interviews were low paid, part time employees of Sindlinger & Co. rather than professional public opinion researchers. Their brief training period did not even include their observation of a single complete interview. That is, they heard only the questions asked and they observed the recording of the responses, but they never heard the responses personally. Since the accuracy of a survey such as this depends heavily on the good judgment of the interviewers, this training deficiency is particularly relevant when weighing the results. Unforeseen circumstances may arise which must be solved quickly by the interviewer without the assistance of a supervisor. Recording errors may occur not only through inadvertent error, but also when an interviewer exercises poor judgment in interpreting a response. See H. C. Barksdale, The Use of Survey Research Findings as Legal Evidence 28, 33 (1957). The evidence in this case indicates that the interviewers were indeed often called upon to interpret and summarize responses so that they could later be coded for computer tabulation.

For example, in answer to the question "In your opinion—who owns or operates the Allstate Driving School?" 3.5% responded with "Allstate Company" and 4.4% with "Allstate." While these responses were accurately recorded, there is certainly a danger that many of the other responses which should have been tabulated in these categories (and thus less helpful to plaintiffs) were coded as "Allstate Insurance Co." The danger is amplified by the fact that the term "Allstate" has a secondary meaning widely known to the general public and hence probably to the interviewers and, therefore, interviewers exercising poor judgment might have improperly recorded the response "Allstate Company" or "Allstate" as "Allstate Insurance Co." It would appear obvious that if professionals were not to be used then at the very least it would have been wiser to provide interviewer trainees with the opportunity to overhear a sampling of responses so that they might have gained useful experience in interpretation and recording.

The questionnaire itself raises serious problems. Question 19 is the key to the study ("In your opinion—who owns or operates the Allstate Driving School?"). However, the sequence in which the questions were asked, and the content of the other questions, necessarily had an impact on the nature of the responses. One of the dangers inherent in an ex parte solicitation of public opinion was noted in National Biscuit Co. v. Princeton Mining Co., 137 U.S.P.Q. 250:

> "It is of course recognized that proof of a substantial amount of actual confusion of marks as an incident to bona fide purchases of goods under the normal circumstances and conditions surrounding the sale thereof constitutes the best evidence of

continued confusion of the marks. On the other hand, a survey, such as that of opposer, intended to demonstrate the same thing, and not conducted in the presence of other persons who might be vitally concerned therewith, might frequently be carried out in such a manner, whether designedly or not, as practically to insure the desired results, and it ordinarily would be impossible to ascertain from the recollections of the persons participating therein what factors of conversation, expression or the like may have been responsible for the results obtained." 137 U.S.P.Q. at 253.

The Fifth Circuit in Sears, Roebuck & Co. v. All States Life Insurance Co., supra, went so far as to say that:

> "[I]t is not truly illustrative of what the public thinks to permit one party to propound questions [in a survey] chosen on its behalf, however fairly attempted, with no opportunity given to the other party to test the answers given by the persons interviewed." 246 F.2d at 172, 114 U.S.P.Q. at 26.

Two examples of suggestion readily come to mind. There are several introductory questions (4 through 10) included in the survey ostensibly for "interest value," that is, to maintain the interviewee's interest so that he or she will respond later to the key question. Question 6 asks "What does the name Coldspot mean to you?" Those who respond to this question without naming Sears (the manufacturer and retailer for Coldspot appliances) are then asked specifically "Where would you go to buy a Coldspot product?" The only correct answer to this inquiry would be Sears. At this very early stage of the questioning, therefore, the name Sears was brought to the attention of a large number of the respondents. In fact, almost 45% of those who completed interviews identified the trade name "Coldspot" with Sears.

The second example of suggestion appears by way of a series of questions which, when considered together, might be characterized as leading. Before any mention is made of the Allstate Driving School interviewers asked, "What does the name Allstate mean to you?"; "Have you ever bought any Allstate products?"; "What . . . and where did you buy it?"; "Do you recall seeing the name Allstate mentioned recently in any advertisement anywhere?"; "What do you recall being advertised?". As this court has found, "Allstate" has developed a secondary meaning, and is widely known by consumers in the automotive related field to be a brand name for automobile accessories and insurance. Suffice to say, as might be expected, a large number of respondents associated "Allstate" with either or both plaintiffs, and had themselves purchased various "Allstate" products. Of course, that plaintiff's trademark is widely known does not by itself indicate a likelihood of confusion. With this preliminary build-up accomplished, however, the questions begin to probe in the area of driving schools. Question 14(a) asks, "Can you name any driving schools that are located within the Suffolk County area?" If the response to this question did not include the Allstate Driving School, the respondent was asked, "Have you ever heard of the Allstate Driving School?" (only 9.3% said that they had heard of the school and only 1.4% [fourteen persons] knew its correct location). Eventually the clincher is asked: "In your opinion—who owns or operates the Allstate Driving School?" It is not surprising that after Sears and its "Allstate" products were repeatedly brought to the attention of the respondents, who by this time were thinking of the plaintiffs, a large number were of the opinion that one or both of the plaintiffs owns or operates the Allstate Driving School.

One of the dangers inherent in a consumer reaction test is that it is not administered in the context of the market place. Respondents to such a test do not consider those factors which are relevant to the particular purchasing decision at hand. They must give their opinion in a vacuum without regard to the type of advertising or manner of marketing used in connection with the goods and services involved. For example, the respondents to the survey in this case were unaware that the defendant advertised only in the Suffolk County classified telephone directory; that the school was operated from the owner's home, which was located in a residential area; that only one automobile was used for instruction. This danger is emphasized when they have been indoctrinated to think in terms of famous brand names in general (see questions 4 to 9) and "Allstate" in particular, before being asked the $64 question, and where the survey is the only evidence of confusion. In no case which has come to the attention of the court, in which surveys were used to support a finding of a substantial likelihood of confusion, was the particular survey the only evidence relating to that issue. Concrete instances of actual confusion by purchasers were introduced to buttress the findings of the survey.　　　　　.

It is important to bear in mind that the relevant group with which we are concerned is the prospective purchaser of plaintiffs' or defendant's products and services. It is their confusion that would be noteworthy. In face of this legal imperative, the survey questionnaire does not inquire whether or not those interviewed had driver's licenses, or owned automobiles, or were considering taking lessons, etc. [They were asked whether they had already taken lessons.] In addition, it is arguable that the universe selected by Sindlinger for this survey, the entire County of Suffolk, was too large. Since 80% of defendant's business comes from within the 8 to 10 mile radius of the school, a more accurate sampling of prospective purchasers would have confined itself to this geographic area.

NOTES

1. Despite frequent exhortations that marks should be viewed in their entirety, courts in infringement cases will usually first dissect the mark to separate its distinctive and protectable components from those that are nondistinctive. Against this background, the court will then evaluate plaintiff's and defendant's marks in their entirety to determine the likelihood of confusion.

Flintkote Co. v. Tizer, 158 F.Supp. 699, 701, 115 U.S.P.Q. 3, 4 (E.D.Pa.1957), aff'd 266 F.2d 849, 121 U.S.P.Q. 284 (3rd Cir.) is typical. "As to the alleged infringement of Tile-Tex by Tile-Tone, we start with the fact that the word 'tile' is wholly descriptive, could not by itself qualify as a trademark, and can be freely used by anyone. When it is used as one part of a trademark, the combination may be registrable, but when it comes to the question of infringement, while the entire mark must be considered as a whole, the descriptive word cannot constitute the dominant part of it. Whatever confusion may be caused by the fact that the same descriptive word appears in the two marks must be discounted. Conversely, infringement cannot be found if the nondescriptive parts of the two marks are distinctive enough to prevent confusion." Would a similarly careful dissection of the two marks in *Pikle-Rite* have produced a different result in that case? Might Chicago Pickle have availed itself of the fair use defense, discussed at page 382 above?

2. Trademark's common law design, transformed in many respects by the Lanham Act, was further altered by "housekeeping" amendments to the Act, P.L. 87–772, 76 Stat. 769, passed in 1962. One amendment went beyond housekeeping to strike the last twelve words from section 32's prescription, "is likely to cause confusion, or to cause mistake, or deceive purchasers as to the source of origin of such goods or services."

The amendment's implications were briefly explored in Syntex Laboratories, Inc. v. Norwich Pharmacal Co., 437 F.2d 566, 169 U.S. P.Q. 1 (2d Cir. 1971). Defendant there argued that, in finding that its unregistered mark "Vagestrol" for a vaginal suppository product, infringed plaintiff's registered mark, "Vagitrol" for a vaginal cream product, the trial court erred in choosing a test for infringement that looked to confusion of the products themselves by physicians and pharmacists instead of to confusion among ordinary prudent purchasers as to the "source of origin." Noting that the amendment of section 32 evidenced Congress's "clear purpose to outlaw the use of trademarks which are likely to cause confusion, mistake or deception of any kind, not merely of purchasers nor simply as to source of origin," Judge Lumbard concluded that, "in a case such as the one at Bar where *product* confusion could have dire effects upon public health, looking to such confusion, in addition to source-of-origin confusion, in determining whether there has been trademark infringement is entirely in accord with public policy, as well as with the Lanham Act." 437 F.2d 566, 568–569 (emphasis in original).

Although the special facts of *Syntex* doubtless justified the decision reached, are "purchasers" and "source of origin" to be disregarded in garden variety infringement cases?

3. What is meant by the word, "likely," in the statutory phrase, "likely to cause confusion . . ."? Does it refer to a statistical likelihood that some segment of the relevant public will actually be confused, or does it refer to a situation in which each and every

member of the relevant public is likely to be confused? Some courts
have inclined to the first measure and some to the second. Few, if
any, have acknowledged the division. The second circuit apparently
adheres to the first gloss—"the test is the likelihood that an appreciable number of ordinarily prudent prospective purchasers will be
confused," Sears Roebuck & Co. v. Allstate Driving Sch., 163 U.S.P.Q.
342, p. 411 above. The passage from *Northam Warren* excerpted in
Pikle-Rite, above, suggests that the seventh circuit adopts the second
gloss.

The distinction between the first and second meanings of "likely"
had little practical import ·in the simpler, not distant past when the
case for likelihood of confusion was made out if the trier of fact felt
that *it* would likely be confused by the accused infringing use. Yet,
with the widespread acceptance and use of survey results, the distinction assumes real importance. If the appropriate likelihood is of the
first sort, then the survey should be structured to identify that fraction of the public that is actually confused by the accused use. If the
appropriate likelihood is of the second sort, then it would appear that
the survey should be designed to measure the extent to which each
person canvassed is likely to be confused by the challenged use.

Techniques for the design and conduct of surveys are considered
in Symposium, The Structure and Uses of Survey Evidence in Trademark Cases, 67 Trademark Rep. 97 (1977); Licht, Christophersen &
Sammis, Public Opinion Polls as Evidence in Unfair Competition Cases, 2 Prac.Law. 15 (1956); Pattishall, Reaction Test Evidence in
Trade Identity Cases, 49 Trademark Rep. 145 (1959); Lunsford, Private Investigators as Amici Curiae in Trade Identity Cases, 57 Trademark Rep. 32 (1967); Shryock, Survey Evidence in Contested Trademark Cases, 57 Trademark Rep. 377 (1967).

4. "Equity judges certainly are better equipped mentally than
the average run of people and their training tends to make them
more inclined to analyze and discriminate. Unconsciously the judge
projects his mentality on to that of the 'unwary purchaser' so that
this mythical person becomes judicially quite a different individual
from the one which he is in fact and is transformed into what the
court thinks he ought to be, and more frequently still what the court
himself is. This metamorphosis of the unwary purchaser is all in the
direction of greater care and greater ability to discriminate. The il-
literate consumer of plug tobacco, as he is in fact, would in all probability not recognize himself if he were suddenly confronted with the
person whom the court strives to protect from imposition in a trademark case involving tin tags. His judicially injected intelligence and
perception would doubtless astonish him. Courts cannot help endow-
ing the unwary purchaser with a part of their own intellectuality and
regard with impatience evidence which seeks to credit him with less."
Rogers, The Unwary Purchaser, 8 Mich.L.Rev. 613 (1910).

Consider whether projection of the judicial mentality may make
the unwary purchaser less, not more, discriminating than he or she in

fact is. Judge Frank's dissent from the decision in Triangle Publications, Inc. v. Rohrlich, 167 F.2d 969, 77 U.S.P.Q. 294 (2d Cir. 1948)
—that defendant's use of the term, "Miss Seventeen," would confuse
purchasers into thinking that defendant's girdles were sponsored by,
or somehow associated with, plaintiff's "Seventeen" magazine—amply
evidences the comparative shrewdness of male judges and female
shoppers: "As neither the trial judge nor any member of this court is
(or resembles) a teen-age girl or the mother or sister of such a girl,
our judicial notice apparatus will not work well unless we feed it with
information directly obtained from 'teen-agers' or from their female
relatives accustomed to shop for them. Competently to inform ourselves, we should have a staff of investigators like those supplied to
administrative agencies. As we have no such staff, I have questioned
some adolescent girls and their mothers and sisters, persons I have
chosen at random. I have been told uniformly by my questionees
that no one could reasonably believe that any relation existed between plaintiff's magazine and defendant's girdles."   167 F.2d 969,
976.

E. RIGHTS BEYOND TRADEMARK: LANHAM ACT § 43(a)

See Statute Supplement 15 U.S.C.A. §§ 1125, 1126.

L'AIGLON APPAREL, INC. v. LANA LOBELL, INC.

United States Court of Appeals, Third Circuit, 1954.
214 F.2d 649, 102 U.S.P.Q. 94.

HASTIE, Circuit Judge.

Plaintiff, a manufacturer, and defendant, a retailer, are both
members of the dress industry, selling dresses in commerce. Each is
incorporated in Pennsylvania. Alleging a fraudulent and injurious
use of a picture of plaintiff's dress in defendant's advertising, the
plaintiff brought this action under the Lanham Trade-Mark Act of
1946 for damages and injunctive relief. Defendant moved to dismiss
the complaint on the ground that it failed to state a cause of action.
The court granted defendant's motion on that ground and also because, in the absence of diversity of citizenship, the court believed
there was no federal jurisdiction. D.C., 118 F.Supp. 251. Plaintiff
appealed.

The complaint explicitly undertakes to state a cause of action
"under §§ 39, 43(a) and 44(b), (h) and (i) of the Lanham Act
. . . ." The district court concluded that Section 44 was inapplicable but did not comment on Section 43(a) as implemented by Section 39. We think Section 43(a) is applicable.

On its face Section 43(a) seems rather clearly to cover the
present claim. It provides in relevant part that "Any person who
shall . . . use in connection with any goods . . . any false
description or representation, including words or other symbols tending falsely to describe or represent the same, and shall cause such
goods . . . to enter into commerce, . . . shall be liable to

a civil action by any person . . . who believes that he is or is likely to be damaged by the use of any such false description or representation." Section 39 gives federal district courts jurisdiction of causes arising under this statute regardless of the amount in controversy or the citizenship of the litigants.

The present complaint alleges that plaintiff created and alone sold to the retail trade throughout the country a certain distinctively styled dress. To advertise this dress plaintiff published pictures of it, together with its price, $17.95, in advertisements in leading newspapers and in some two million individual mailing pieces distributed through retailers. In this way the picture and price of this dress became associated in the minds of many readers and identified as plaintiff's $17.95 dress.

It is further alleged that, at about the same time, defendant was offering for sale through mail order and otherwise in interstate commerce a dress which in fact was much inferior to plaintiff's in quality and notably different in appearance. In this connection defendant published under its name in a magazine of national circulation a display advertisement worded and designed to promote the mail order sale of its dress at a stated price of $6.95, but showing as the most prominent feature of the advertisement an actual photographic reproduction of plaintiff's dress, thus fraudulently represented as the article defendant was selling for $6.95. Plaintiff alleges that this misrepresentation caused some trade to be diverted from plaintiff to defendant and caused other trade to be lost by plaintiff as a result of the mistaken impression conveyed to those familiar with the advertising of both parties that plaintiff was offering for $17.95 a dress worth only $6.95.

In relation to the language of Section 43(a) this complaint states about as plain a use of a false representation in the description of goods sold in commerce as could be imagined. And plaintiff's alleged damage as a result of defendant's misrepresentation may well be demonstrable within the normal requirements of legal proof and in such way as to entitle plaintiff to relief authorized by the statute. Thus, Section 43(a) seems to cover this case clearly and without ambiguity.

What then is the difficulty? It is, if we rightly understand defendant's position, that before the 1946 enactment of this statute, federal courts had imposed such restrictions on liability for unfair competition that one in plaintiff's position could not recover for the kind of conduct here charged. Therefore, it is argued, federal courts should so construe the statute as to preserve these judge-made limitations on liability.

We quickly dispose of a claim that relevant limitations on liability are to be derived from Mosler Safe Co. v. Ely-Norris Safe Co., 1927, 273 U.S. 132, 47 S.Ct. 314, 71 L.Ed. 578. For that case expresses no more than the Court's judgment as to the inadequacy at common law of a particular pleading of injury as the result of a defendant's misrepresentation that his product contained an important fea-

ture of another's product.   Here we see no inadequacy in the present
plaintiff's statement of such an injury as Section 43(a) explicitly
makes the proper subject of redress.

It is also urged that before 1946 a line of cases beginning with
American Washboard Co. v. Saginaw Mfg. Co., 6 Cir., 1900, 103 F.
281, established the doctrine that in the area of present concern misrepresentations about goods were actionable only if they had led or
were likely to lead customers, through confusion of defendant's and
plaintiff's goods, to buy the former under the misapprehension that
they were the latter.   "Palming off", narrowly conceived, was said to
be essential to any recovery.   And the view has been expressed judicially that some such limitation is to be read into Section 43(a) of
the Lanham Act.   Chamberlain v. Columbia Pictures Corp., 9 Cir.,
1951, 186 F.2d 923; Samson Crane Co. v. Union National Sales, Inc.,
D.C.Mass.1949, 89 F.Supp. 218, 222.   But we think it could as plausi-
bly be argued that Section 43(a) reflects the more modern viewpoint
of Section 761 of the Restatement of Torts, which provides:

> "One who diverts trade from a competitor by fraudulently
> representing that the goods which he markets have ingredients
> or qualities which in fact they do not have but which the goods
> of the competitor do have, is liable to the competitor for the
> harm so caused, if,
>
> " '(a) when making the representation he intends that it
> should, or knows or should know that it is likely to, divert trade
> from the competitor, ...' "

However, we reject this entire approach to the statute.   We find
nothing in the legislative history of the Lanham Act to justify the
view that this section is merely declarative of existing law.   Indeed,
because we find no ambiguity in the relevant language in the statute
we would doubt the propriety of resort to legislative history even if
that history suggested that Congress intended less than it said.   It
seems to us that Congress has defined a statutory civil wrong of false
representation of goods in commerce and has given a broad class of
suitors injured or likely to be injured by such wrong the right to relief in the federal courts.   This statutory tort is defined in language
which differentiates it in some particulars from similar wrongs which
have developed and have become defined in the judge made law of
unfair competition.   Perhaps this statutory tort bears closest resemblance to the already noted tort of false advertising to the detriment
of a competitor, as formulated by the American Law Institute out of
materials of the evolving common law of unfair competition.   See
Torts Restatement, Section 761, supra.   But however similar to or
different from pre-existing law, here is a provision of a federal statute which, with clarity and precision adequate for judicial administration, creates and defines rights and duties and provides for their
vindication in the federal courts.

We are satisfied that no limitation appears on the face of Section
43(a) and none can properly be imposed which would make the

present complaint an insufficient statement of a cause of action under that section. Of course, Section 39 makes it unnecessary to show diversity of citizenship or any jurisdictional amount. It follows that the dismissal of the complaint was error.

While we reverse the judgment of the district court on the ground that a cause of action has been stated under Section 43(a) of the Lanham Act, the complaint also predicated jurisdiction on Section 44(b), (h), and (i). The district court ruled that this section was not applicable to this type of case. The matter is important and it is clearly in issue. Therefore, although we could dispose of the present appeal without passing on this issue, thus leaving the district courts which look to us for guidance to speculate on the significance of our silence, we think it better to say now that we agree with the district court in its construction of Section 44. [The court's discussion of section 44, omitted here, is discussed in Note 6, below.]

.   .   .   The judgment will be reversed and the cause remanded for further proceedings in conformity with this opinion.

FEDERAL-MOGUL-BOWER BEARINGS, INC. v. AZOFF

United States Court of Appeals, Sixth Circuit, 1963.
313 F.2d 405, 136 U.S.P.Q. 500.

McALLISTER, Circuit Judge.

Appellant seeks review of an order dismissing its complaint on the ground that it did not state a cause of action. It is the contention of appellant that it alleged in its complaint sufficient facts to maintain its claim against appellees, for false description and representation, under the Lanham Act, 15 U.S.C.A. § 1125(a).

The above section of the Lanham Act provides:

"False designations of origin and false descriptions forbidden. Any person who shall affix, apply, or annex, or use in connection with any goods or services, or any container or containers for goods, a false designation of origin, or any false description or representation, including words or other symbols tending falsely to describe or represent the same, and shall cause such goods or services to enter into commerce, and any person who shall with knowledge of the falsity of such designation of origin or description or representation cause or procure the same to be transported or used in commerce or deliver the same to any carrier to be transported or used, shall be liable to a civil action by any person doing business in the locality falsely indicated as that of origin or in the region in which said locality is situated, or by any person who believes that he is or is likely to be damaged by the use of any such false description or representation."

The following allegations appear in the complaint:

Appellant is a corporation organized under the laws of Michigan, having its principal office in Detroit. Appellees are copartners, having their principal place of business in Cleveland, Ohio. Appellant company has, for many years, been engaged in manufacturing, transporting, distributing, marketing, and selling, both in interstate commerce and foreign commerce, engine bearings and connecting rods for internal combustion engines, which have been sold and distributed in packages and containers, which are distinguished by features, including the size of the container, the symbol, printing, background, general arrangements, form, and the coloration thereof. These packages and containers of appellant, according to the complaint, have long been known, and are presently recognized by the trade and by the public in interstate and foreign commerce as identifying and distinguishing the engine bearings and connecting rods contained in these packages and containers, as being the product of appellant, and, further, as identifying the appellant as the source of these bearings and connecting rods. Thereby appellant has acquired and enjoys a large and valuable reputation of good will with the trade and with the public, both domestic and foreign, for its engine bearings and connecting rods which are contained and marketed in these distinctive packages and containers.

The complaint further alleged:

Appellees, within several months prior to the initiation of this action, and during its pendency, transported and continued to transport, distribute, market, sell, and cause to be entered into and used in commerce, both interstate and foreign, and particularly in foreign commerce, engine bearings and connecting rods which compete with the engine bearings and connecting rods of appellant, and these engine bearings and connecting rods of appellees were being so transported, sold, or otherwise placed in interstate and foreign commerce in packages and containers, which imitate and so nearly resemble the packages and containers of appellant in the collocation of distinctive features, as to falsely represent the engine bearings and connecting rods packaged in appellees' containers as being the goods of appellant, and also as being goods originating from appellant.

The complaint further declared that the false representations of appellees are such as to be likely to cause confusion in trade and commerce, and particularly in foreign commerce, of appellees' bearings and connecting rods with those of appellant; that appellees had knowledge of appellant's trade and commerce, particularly foreign commerce in its engine bearings and connecting rods, and deliberately adopted and used the imitative packages and containers with an intent to deceive the trade and public, and particularly those who do not readily read or understand the English language, into mistaking and confusing the engine bearings and connecting rods of appellees for, and with, those of appellant; that the acts of appellees were done with, and for the purpose of, unlawfully appropriating and trading upon the good will and reputation of appellant; and that appellees, in so using the imitative packages and containers not only falsely represent that their bearings and connecting rods are the product of appellant, but also falsely represent that these products originate with appellant.

The acts of appellees, it was claimed by appellant, had caused, and were causing great and irreparable damage to appellant's business, reputation, and good will in the manufacture, distribution and sale of its products in interstate and foreign commerce.

Under the Lanham Act, above quoted, any person who shall use, in connection with any containers for goods, a false designation of origin, or any false description or *representation,* including symbols tending falsely to represent the same, and shall with knowledge of the falsity of such designation of origin, or description, procure the same to be transported or used in commerce, is liable to a civil action by any person doing business in the locality falsely indicated as that of origin or in the region in which said origin is located, or by any person who believes he is, or is likely to be damaged by the use of any such false description or representation.

The trial court was of the view that any attempt to characterize the complaint as charging a "false description or representation" was without merit. Moreover, the trial court held that the word, "origin," in the Act, referred to geographical origin rather than to "origin by manufacturer." Observing that a question of jurisdiction should be construed most strictly against jurisdiction, the trial court remarked that there were adequate remedies in the state courts and that if the Lanham Act were applied to the facts in this case, not only might the plaintiff bring this action, but any person doing business near one of the plaintiff's plants might also bring suit; and such a construction would open nearly all the field of unfair competition to federal jurisdiction.

The allegations that appellees sold, transported, or placed in interstate commerce, bearings and connecting rods in packages or containers which imitate and so nearly resemble the packages and containers of appellant in collocation of distinctive features as to falsely represent them to be the goods of appellant, and that appellees deliberately adopted and used the imitative packages and containers with an intent to deceive the trade and public into confusing the bearings and rods of appellees with those of appellant, and that they falsely represented that their bearings and connecting rods were the product of appellant are allegations, which in our opinion charge a false description or misrepresentation, as those terms are used in the statute.

We are further of the opinion that the word, "origin," in the Act does not merely refer to geographical origin, but also to origin of source or manufacture. In Eastman Kodak Co. v. Royal-Pioneer Paper Box Mfg. Co., 197 F.Supp. 132, 135 (D.C.Pa.), the court, in discussing the applicability of the Lanham Act to the case before it, said:

> "Defendant has caused its deceptively similar photographic film return boxes to enter into, be transported and used in commerce throughout the United States and in the Commonwealth

of Pennsylvaina and has thereby enabled the false designation by others that the service in connection with which such boxes are employed originated with plaintiff. Such false designation constitutes a violation of Section 43(a) of the Lanham Act, 15 U.S. C.A., Section 1125(a)."

We come, then, to the question of what area of unfair competition is subject to federal jurisdiction under the provisions of the Lanham Act.

Section 45 of the Lanham Act, (15 U.S.C.A. § 1127), in its last paragraph, provides:

"The intent of this chapter is to regulate commerce within the control of Congress by making actionable the deceptive and misleading use of marks in such commerce; to protect registered marks used in such commence (sic) from interference by State, or territorial legislation; to protect persons engaged in such commerce against unfair competition; to prevent fraud and deception in such commerce by the use of reproductions, copies, counterfeits, or colorable imitations of registered marks; and to provide rights and remedies stipulated by treaties and conventions respecting trade-marks, trade names, and unfair competition entered into between the United States and foreign nations."

The terms "mark," and "trade-mark," are defined by the foregoing section as follows:

"The term 'mark' includes any trade-mark, service mark, collective mark, or certification mark entitled to registration under this chapter whether registered or not."

"The term 'trade-mark' includes any word, name, symbol, or device or any combination thereof adopted and used by a manufacturer or merchant to identify his goods and distinguish them from those manufactured or sold by others."

As observed by appellant, the Lanham Act does not provide a right of action for trade-mark infringement generally; it leaves to the state courts, administering the state laws, and to the diversity cases, those cases for common law trade-mark infringement that do *not* arise out of deceptive and misleading use of such marks in interstate and foreign commerce. But it does provide a right of action to persons engaged in interstate and foreign commerce, against deceptive and misleading use of common law trademarks, and against deceptive and misleading use of words, names, symbols, or devices, or any combination thereof, which have been adopted by a manufacturer or merchant to identify his goods and distinguish them from those manufactured by others, where such misleading use is carried on, in the channels of interstate and foreign commerce, which is subject to regulation by Congress.

In Samson Crane Co. v. Union Nat'l Sales, Inc. et al., 87 F.Supp. 218, 222 (D.C.Mass.), affirmed by per curiam opinion in 180 F.2d 896 (C.A.1), the court, in considering the intent of the Lanham Act, and in denying the complaint therein filed for failure to allege misrepresentation *in interstate commerce*, stated:

> "The intent of Congress in passing the Act is set forth in the final paragraph of Section 1127. Only one phrase of that paragraph fails to use the word 'mark'. And that phrase ('to protect persons engaged in such commerce against unfair competition') must in such a context be construed to refer not to any competitive practice which in the broad meaning of the words might be called unfair, but to that 'unfair competition' which has been closely associated with the misuse of trademarks, i. e., the passing off of one's goods as those of a competitor. It is clear, both from this statement of the intent and from a reading of the Act as a whole, that the primary purpose of the Act was to eliminate deceitful practices in interstate commerce involving the misuse of trademarks, but along with this it sought to eliminate other forms of misrepresentations which are of the same general character even though they do not involve any use of what can technically be called a trade-mark. The language of Section 43(a) is broad enough to include practices of this latter class. But the section should be construed to include only such false descriptions or representations as are of substantially the same economic nature as those which involve infringement or other improper use of trade-marks. It should not be interpreted so as to bring within its scope any kind of undesirable business practice which involves deception, when such practices are outside the field of the trade-mark laws, .　.　. ."

The legislative history of the Lanham Act indicates that Congress intended to fashion a new federal remedy against a particular kind of unfair competition that the common law had effectively protected.

In accordance with the foregoing, it is our view that the complaint stated a cause of action under the Lanham Act. The order dismissing the complaint is, therefore, set aside, and the case is remanded to the District Court for further proceedings.

NOTES

1. For several years after its enactment, section 43(a) was applied sparingly. *L'Aiglon*, decided in 1954, was the first decision to declare authoritatively that section 43(a) created a federal cause of action against misrepresentation, unencumbered by limitations like those imposed in *American Washboard* and *Ely-Norris*, pages 71, 76 above.

The Lanham Act had been law for a decade before a circuit court suggested that section 43(a) also proscribed common law trademark violations. *Joshua Meier Co. v. Albany Novelty Mfg. Co.*, 236 F.2d 144, 111 U.S.P.Q. 197 (2d Cir. 1956). *Federal-Mogul*, decided seven years later, was the first definitive decision on section 43(a)'s coverage of common law passing off. For the view that section 43(a) was not intended to cover common law trademark infringement and passing off, see Germain, Unfair Trade Practices Under Section 43(a) of the Lanham Act: You've Come A Long Way, Baby—Too Far Maybe? 49 Indiana L.J. 84, 109–112 (1973).

2. Can section 43(a) be used to regulate fields in which state doctrines have been preempted under section 301 of the Copyright Act page 213, above, and *Sears* and *Compco*, page 130 above? Section 301(d) expressly excludes federal laws from that section's general preemptive thrust. And courts have generally held that *Sears* and *Compco* were concerned with state, not federal, law and thus do not apply to section 43(a) actions. See, for example, Ives Laboratories, Inc. v. Darby Drug Co., Inc., 601 F.2d 631, 202 U.S.P.Q. 548 (2d Cir. 1979). One decision, Truck Equipment Serv. Co. v. Fruehauf Corp., 536 F.2d 1210, 191 U.S.P.Q. 79 (8th Cir.) cert. denied, 429 U.S. 861, 97 S.Ct. 164, 50 L.Ed.2d 139, 191 U.S.P.Q. 588, allowed an action against product simulation under section 43(a) that, had it been brought as a state action, probably would have been preempted under *Sears* and *Compco*.

For a helpful overview of section 43(a)'s contemporary coverage, see Comment, The Present Scope of Recovery for Unfair Competition Violations Under Section 43(a) of the Lanham Act, 58 Neb.L.Rev. 159 (1978).

3. The main task of section 43(a) decisions today is defining the range of actionable conduct. Closest to *L'Aiglon* are cases in which defendant removes plaintiff's trademark and other identifying insignia from plaintiff's product, replaces them with its own, and then uses the mislabeled product as a demonstration model for its own inferior imitation. See, for example, Crossbow, Inc. v. Dan-Dee Imports, Inc., 266 F.Supp. 335, 153 U.S.P.Q. 163 (S.D.N.Y.1967). Typical of section 43(a) actions somewhat farther afield are Mutation Mink Breeders Ass'n v. Lou Nierenberg Corp., 23 F.R.D. 155, 120 U.S.P.Q. 270 (S.D.N.Y.1959) (plaintiff, trade association, prevails against defendant's use of the word "mink" on its "fake-fur" fabrics) and Consumer's Union of U.S., Inc. v. Theodore Hamm Brewing Co., 314 F.Supp. 697, 166 U.S.P.Q. 48 (D.C.Conn.1970) (defendant's advertisements misrepresented the ratings its product had received from the Consumer's Union).

Disparagement, because it misrepresents the quality of plaintiff's product, not defendant's, is not actionable under section 43(a). See, for example, Bernard Food Industries v. Dietene Co., 415 F.2d 1279, 163 U.S.P.Q. 264 (7th Cir. 1969) cert. denied, 397 U.S. 912, 90 S.Ct. 911, 25 L.Ed.2d 92, 164 U.S.P.Q. 481. But if the attack on plaintiff's product falsely implies that defendant's is more worthy, an action might lie. Thus, in American Home Products Corp. v. Johnson & Johnson, 577 F.2d 160, 198 U.S.P.Q. 132 (2d Cir. 1978), the producers of Anacin were held to have violated section 43(a) by advertising on television and in magazines that Anacin was more effective than opponent's Tylenol. ("That section 43(a) of the Lanham Act encompasses more than literal falsehoods cannot be questioned. Were it otherwise, clever use of innuendo, indirect intimations, and ambiguous suggestions could shield the advertisement from scrutiny precisely when protection against such sophisticated deception is most needed. It is equally well established that the truth or falsity of the advertisement usually should be tested by the reactions of the public.") 577 F.2d 160, 165.

4. Courts will not find in section 43(a) a salve for every conceivable competitive injury. For example, in Societe Comptoir De L'Industrie Cotonniere Etablissements Boussac v. Alexander's Dept. Stores, 299 F.2d 33, 132 U.S.P.Q. 475 (2d Cir. 1962), the Second Circuit Court of Appeals refused to enjoin defendant from truthfully advertising that its inexpensive dresses were copies of original Dior designs. "The Lanham Act does not prohibit a commercial rival's truthfully denominating his goods a copy of a design in the public domain, though he uses the name of the designer to do so." 299 F.2d 33, 36.

Section 43(a) also gave no aid to the Girl Scouts of America in its attempt to secure a preliminary injunction against Personality Posters' distribution of a poster that depicted "a smiling girl dressed in the well-known green uniform of the Junior Girl Scouts, with her hands clasped above her protruding, clearly pregnant abdomen. The caveat 'be prepared' appears next to her hands." With the terse observation that "plaintiff has failed utterly to establish the requisite element of customer confusion," the court dismissed the claim that defendant had violated section 43(a) by using plaintiff's marks and insignia to designate falsely the paternity of its poster. Girl Scouts of the United States of America v. Personality Posters Mfg. Co., 304 F.Supp. 1228, 1230–1231, 163 U.S.P.Q. 505 (S.D.N.Y.1969).

Alfred Dunhill, Ltd. v. Interstate Cigar Co., Inc., 364 F.Supp. 366, 177 U.S.P.Q. 346 (S.D.N.Y.1973), rev'd 499 F.2d 232, 183 U.S. P.Q. 193 (2d Cir.) raised a more subtle question about section 43(a)'s scope. Does the language "affix, apply, or annex or use" cover acts of omission as well as commission? The lower court answered that it does, and enjoined defendant from distributing damaged tobacco, bearing plaintiff's trademark, purchased from plaintiff's agent at salvage prices. In the court's judgment, "sales of damaged tobacco in tins bearing trademarks associated with high quality tobacco without adequate warnings to customers that the goods are damaged, involve false representations of their quality." 364 F.Supp. 366, 372. The court of appeals reversed, finding that the district court's decision "cannot be reached through an interpretation of the statutory language or legislative or judicial history of the Lanham Act." The court also noted that Dunhill's problem was in part of its own making. "If Dunhill had wished to distinguish the salvaged tobacco from that sold through its normal channels of distribution, it should have done so while the allegedly damaged tobacco was still under its control and before it was released into the salvage markets. From the

beginning Dunhill was in the best position to effect the relabeling."
499 F.2d 232, 237–238.

5. Do consumers have standing to sue under section 43(a)'s
broad invitation to "any person who believes that he is or is likely to
be damaged"? In Colligan v. Activities Club of New York, Ltd., 422
F.2d 686, 170 U.S.P.Q. 113 (2d Cir. 1971), cert. denied, 404 U.S. 1004,
92 S.Ct. 559, 30 L.Ed.2d 557, 172 U.S.P.Q. 97, plaintiffs, disappointed
ski weekenders, sought monetary and injunctive relief—the latter on
behalf of "all high school students within the New York metropolitan
area who are likely to be deceived and thereby injured by defendants'
similarly deceptive practices in the future"—against defendant which,
they alleged, had deceived and damaged them by "use of false descriptions and representations of the nature, sponsorship, and licensing of their interstate ski tour service." 442 F.2d 686, 687. The
court of appeals affirmed the district court's dismissal of the complaint. "Congress' purpose in enacting section 43(a) was to create a
special and limited unfair competition remedy, virtually without regard for the interests of consumers generally and almost certainly
without any consideration of consumer rights of action in particular.
The Act's purpose, as defined in section 45 is exclusively to protect
the interests of a purely commercial class against unscrupulous commercial conduct." 442 F.2d 686, 692.

The district court in Arnesen v. Raymond Lee Organization, Inc.,
333 F.Supp. 116, 172 U.S.P.Q. 1 (C.D.Cal.1971), looked to another
part of section 45's statement of purpose to support its conclusion
that section 43(a) does give standing to consumers. "The liability
clause of section 43(a) is clear on its face; it applies to any person
who is or is likely to be damaged. Defendant would have us construe
against the plain language of the statute. Since the liability clause
also mentions 'any person doing business' it would be plausible to apply the *ejusdem generis* rules and thus construe the subsequent use of
the words 'any person' to mean any person doing business or any
competitor. If the purpose of the Lanham Act were solely to protect
competitors this construction would be sound. However, the plain
language of the intent section, 15 U.S.C.A. § 1127 makes actionable,
inter alia, the deceptive and misleading use of marks and descriptions. Since that same section defines 'persons' as both natural and
juristic persons, this Court cannot conclude that competitors were the
only persons protected by the Act." 333 F.Supp. 116, 120. Class action status was later denied. 59 F.R.D. 145, 179 U.S.P.Q. 210 (C.D.
Cal.).

6. While accrediting section 43(a) as the basis for plaintiff's
unfair competition claim, *L'Aiglon* rejected section 44, 15 U.S.C.A. §
1126, as an alternative ground for recovery. The gist of plaintiff's
argument was that section 44(b), (h) and (i), which grants United
States citizens or residents protection against unfair competition
identical to the protection afforded nationals of countries with which
the United States has trademark treaty relations, effectively created

a federal law of unfair competition, enforceable in federal courts apart from pendent or diversity jurisdiction. The *L'Aiglon* court was "impressed" that section 44, unlike section 43, "is found under Title 9 of the Act which is entitled 'International Conventions.' Was it the intent of Congress, when it used the foregoing language in a title implementing international conventions, to establish a federal law of unfair competition in commerce unrelated to any matter arising out of some international convention or treaty? The legislative history of the Act suggests a negative answer." 214 F.2d 653.

The position that section 44 created a federal law of unfair competition governing conduct affecting interstate commerce was first judicially accepted in Stauffer v. Exley, 184 F.2d 962, 87 U.S.P.Q. 40 (9th Cir. 1950). The view has enjoyed limited currency in the other circuits which, like *L'Aiglon*, have taken the position that the only effect of section 44 is to give United States citizens and nationals reciprocal rights against foreign nationals who compete unfairly with them.

II. PATENT LAW

The first known system for awarding patents for inventions in the useful arts dates to Venice in the mid-fifteenth century. The Venetian system, codified into a general patent statute in 1474, sought to spur the introduction of new technologies and industries by awarding patentees the exclusive right to practice their art for a specified period, generally ranging from ten to fifty years. Some patents issued to technologies that had been imported into Venice from other regions and that doubtless had been invented by someone other than the individual seeking the patent. Other patented inventions clearly originated with the patentee. Bruce Bugbee writes of a 1460 patent "issued to one Jacobus 'in reward of his pertinent thoughts and labors' as the 'first inventor and builder' of a water-raising mechanism. Evidently a true patent of invention, it carried a term of protection extending for the life of the grantee. Each imitator constructing such a device in Venetian territory without the 'express license' of Jacobus was to be fined 1,000 gold ducats and the infringing machines were to be 'thoroughly destroyed.' " B. Bugbee, Genesis of American Patent and Copyright Law 21 (1967).

Early English patent practice followed the Venetian model, awarding durationally limited monopolies to originators of new devices and to importers of already established crafts and industries. The system was generally ratified by the Statute of Monopolies, 21 Jac. 1 c. 3 (1624), probably the major document in the history of English patent law. The Statute, which prohibited monopolies "for the sole buying, selling, making, working, or using of anything within this Realm," was enacted in response to the Crown's overly generous grants of monopolies to court favorites to manufacture such common items as vinegar and starch. The Statute did, however, allow the Crown to grant patents for fourteen years or less "to the true and first inventor or inventors" for "the sole working or making of any manner of new manufactures within this realm" provided "they be not contrary to the law nor mischievous to the state, by raising prices of commodities at home, or hurt of trade, or generally inconvenient."

The American colonies and, after the Revolution, the state legislatures, generally followed England's ad hoc system, awarding patents through private acts passed in response to individual petitions. The first federal patent law, Act of April 10, 1790, ch. 7, 1 Stat. 109–110, was a general, rather than a private act, authorizing patents for "any useful art, manufacture, engine, machine, or device, or any improvement therein not before known or used." Upon a showing that the claimed invention was "sufficiently useful and important," a patent board composed of the Secretary of State, the Secretary of War and the Attorney General was to grant a patent for a term of up to fourteen years. However, the burden of examining patent applications soon proved too heavy for these busy civil servants, and a new patent law, Act of February 21, 1793, ch. 11, 1 Stat. 318, substituted the simple act of registration for the previous examination system. The new act also eliminated the requirement that the invention be "sufficiently useful and important." The examination system and inventiveness requirement were reinstated by the Act of July 4, 1836, ch. 357, 5 Stat. 117, which also fixed the patent term at fourteen years with a seven year renewal period.

To the chagrin of many observers today, the 1836 Act continues to provide the basic structure and principles of United States patent law. The Act's last major revision, in the Act of July 19, 1952, 66 Stat. 792, left the basic system virtually unchanged. It did, however, codify the law as Title 35 of the United States Code.

Almost immediately on the heels of the 1952 Act, bills aimed at substantial patent reform were introduced into Congress. These efforts gained impetus from the publication in 1966 of the Report of the President's Commission on the Patent System recommending, among other objects, that the patent law be reformed to accelerate the disclosure of technological advances, increase the reliability of patents and lower the costs of obtaining and litigating them. The Report was followed by the proposal of a Patent Reform Act in 1967, S. 1042, 89th Cong., 1st Sess. (1967), and then by successive reform bills initiated inside the administration and out. The reform effort intensified in the 93rd and 94th Congresses; three major, quite different, Senate bills were introduced and heatedly discussed in the 93rd Congress. These efforts came to naught, however, and legislative interest in sweeping patent reform has for the moment abated.

B. Bugbee, Genesis of American Patent and Copyright Law (1967) thoughtfully chronicles the history of United States patent, as well as copyright, law from its early European roots. Summary reviews of the English and American history appear in a special number of the Journal of the Patent Office Society celebrating the centennial of the 1836 Act, 18 J.P.O.S. No. 7 (1936), and in American Bar Association, Two-Hundred Years of English and American Patent, Trademark and Copyright Law, 3, 21 (1976). Developments since 1952 are closely reviewed in Scott & Unkovic, Patent Law Reform: A Legislative Perspective of an Extended Gestation, 16 Wm. & Mary L.Rev. 937 (1975).

Professor Donald Chisum's fine work, Patents (1980), is the leading treatise. Peter D. Rosenberg's considerably shorter work, Patent Law Fundamentals (1981), provides an excellent introduction to the field. The American Patent Law Association Quarterly Journal and the Journal of the Patent Office Society regularly publish topical papers.

A. REQUIREMENTS FOR PROTECTION

1. STATUTORY STANDARDS

See Statute Supplement 35 U.S.C.A. §§ 100–104, 111, 116–118; 256.

a. SECTION 103: NONOBVIOUSNESS

GRAHAM v. JOHN DEERE CO.

Supreme Court of the United States, 1965.
383 U.S. 1, 86 S.Ct. 684, 15 L.Ed.2d 545, 148 U.S.P.Q. 459.

Mr. Justice CLARK delivered the opinion of the Court.

After a lapse of 15 years, the Court again focuses its attention on the patentability of inventions under the standard of Art. I, § 8, cl. 8, of the Constitution and under the conditions prescribed by the laws of the United States. Since our last expression on patent validity, A. & P. Tea Co. v. Supermarket Corp., 340 U.S. 147, 71 S.Ct. 127, 95 L. Ed. 162 (1950), the Congress has for the first time expressly added a third statutory dimension to the two requirements of novelty and utility that had been the sole statutory test since the Patent Act of 1793. This is the test of obviousness, i. e., whether "the subject matter sought to be patented and the prior art are such that the subject matter as a whole would have been obvious at the time the invention was made to a person having ordinary skill in the art to which said subject matter pertains. Patentability shall not be negatived by the manner in which the invention was made." § 103 of the Patent Act of 1952, 35 U.S.C.A. § 103.

The questions, involved in each of the companion cases before us, are what effect the 1952 Act had upon traditional statutory and judicial tests of patentability and what definitive tests are now required. We have concluded that the 1952 Act was intended to codify judicial precedents embracing the principle long ago announced by this Court in Hotchkiss v. Greenwood, 52 U.S. (11 How.) 248, 13 L.Ed. 683 (1851), and that, while the clear language of § 103 places emphasis on an inquiry into obviousness, the general level of innovation necessary to sustain patentability remains the same. .   .   .

II.

At the outset it must be remembered that the federal patent power stems from a specific constitutional provision which authorizes the Congress "To promote the Progress of .   .   . useful Arts, by securing for limited Times to .   .   . Inventors the exclusive Right to their .   .   . Discoveries." Art. I, § 8, cl. 8. The clause is both a grant of power and a limitation. This qualified authority, unlike the power often exercised in the sixteenth and seventeenth centuries by the English Crown, is limited to the promotion of advances in the "useful arts." It was written against the backdrop of the practices—eventually curtailed by the Statute of Monopolies— of the Crown in granting monopolies to court favorites in goods or businesses which had long before been enjoyed by the public. The Congress in the exercise of the patent power may not overreach the restraints imposed by the stated constitutional purpose. Nor may it enlarge the patent monopoly without regard to the innovation, advancement or social benefit gained thereby. Moreover, Congress may not authorize the issuance of patents whose effects are to remove existent knowledge from the public domain, or to restrict free access to materials already available. Innovation, advancement, and things which add to the sum of useful knowledge are inherent requisites in a patent system which by constitutional command must "promote the Progress of . . . useful Arts." This is the *standard* expressed in the Constitution and it may not be ignored. And it is in this light that patent validity "requires reference to a standard written into the Constitution." A. & P. Tea Co. v. Supermarket Corp., supra, at 154 (concurring opinion).

Within the limits of the constitutional grant, the Congress may, of course, implement the stated purpose of the Framers by selecting the policy which in its judgment best effectuates the constitutional aim. This is but a corollary to the grant to Congress of any Article I power. Within the scope established by the Constitution, Congress may set out conditions and tests for patentability. It is the duty of the Commissioner of Patents and of the courts in the administration of the patent system to give effect to the constitutional standard by appropriate application, in each case, of the statutory scheme of the Congress.

Congress quickly responded to the bidding of the Constitution by enacting the Patent Act of 1790 during the second session of the First Congress. It created an agency in the Department of State headed by the Secretary of State, the Secretary of the Department of War and the Attorney General, any two of whom could issue a patent for a period not exceeding 14 years to any petitioner that "hath . . . invented or discovered any useful art, manufacture, . . . or device, or any improvement therein not before known or used" if the board found that "the invention or discovery [was] sufficiently useful and important. . . ." 1 Stat. 110. This group, whose members administered the patent system along with their other public duties, was known by its own designation as "Commissioners for the Promotion of Useful Arts."

Thomas Jefferson, who as Secretary of State was a member of the group, was its moving spirit and might well be called the "first administrator of our patent system." See Federico, Operation of the Patent Act of 1790, 18 J.Pat.Off.Soc. 237, 238 (1936). He was not only an administrator of the patent system under the 1790 Act, but was also the author of the 1793 Patent Act. In addition, Jefferson was himself an inventor of great note. His unpatented improvements on plows, to mention but one line of his inventions, won acclaim and recognition on both sides of the Atlantic. Because of his active interest and influence in the early development of the patent system, Jefferson's views on the general nature of the limited patent monopoly under the Constitution, as well as his conclusions as to conditions for patentability under the statutory scheme, are worthy of note.

Jefferson, like other Americans, had an instinctive aversion to monopolies. It was a monopoly on tea that sparked the Revolution and Jefferson certainly did not favor an equivalent form of monopoly under the new government. His abhorrence of monopoly extended initially to patents as well. From France, he wrote to Madison (July 1788) urging a Bill of Rights provision restricting monopoly, and as against the argument that limited monopoly might serve to incite "ingenuity," he argued forcefully that "the benefit even of limited monopolies is too doubtful to be opposed to that of their general suppression," V Writings of Thomas Jefferson, at 47 (Ford ed., 1895).

His views ripened, however, and in another letter to Madison (Aug. 1789) after the drafting of the Bill of Rights, Jefferson stated that he would have been pleased by an express provision in this form:

> "Art 9. Monopolies may be allowed to persons for their own productions in literature & their own inventions in the arts, for a term not exceeding _____ years but for no longer term & no other purpose." Id., at 113.

.   .   . He rejected a natural-rights theory in intellectual property rights and clearly recognized the social and economic rationale of the patent system. The patent monopoly was not designed to secure to the inventor his natural right in his discoveries. Rather, it was a reward, an inducement, to bring forth new knowledge. The grant of an exclusive right to an invention was the creation of society —at odds with the inherent free nature of disclosed ideas—and was not to be freely given. Only inventions and discoveries which furthered human knowledge, and were new and useful, justified the special inducement of a limited private monopoly. Jefferson did not believe in granting patents for small details, obvious improvements, or frivolous devices. His writings evidence his insistence upon a high level of patentability.

As a member of the patent board for several years, Jefferson saw clearly the difficulty in "drawing a line between the things which are worth to the public the embarrassment of an exclusive patent, and those which are not." The board on which he served sought to draw such a line and formulated several rules which are preserved in Jefferson's correspondence. Despite the board's efforts, Jefferson saw "with what slow progress a system of general rules could be matured." Because of the "abundance" of cases and the fact that the investigations occupied "more time of the members of the board than they could spare from higher duties, the whole was turned over to the judiciary, to be matured into a system, under which every one might know when his actions were safe and lawful." .   .   . Apparently Congress agreed with Jefferson and the board that the courts should develop additional conditions for patentability. Although the Patent Act was amended, revised or codified some 50 times between 1790 and 1950, Congress steered clear of a statutory set of requirements other than the bare novelty and utility tests reformulated in Jefferson's draft of the 1793 Patent Act.

III.

The difficulty of formulating conditions for patentability was heightened by the generality of the constitutional grant and the statutes implementing it, together with the underlying policy of the patent system that "the things which are worth to the public the embarrassment of an exclusive patent," as Jefferson put it, must outweigh the restrictive effect of the limited patent monopoly. The inherent problem was to develop some means of weeding out those inventions which would not be disclosed or devised but for the inducement of a patent.

This Court formulated a general condition of patentability in 1851 in Hotchkiss v. Greenwood, 11 How. 248. The patent involved a mere substitution of materials—porcelain or clay for wood or metal in doorknobs—and the Court condemned it, holding:

> "[U]nless more ingenuity and skill . . . were required . . . than were possessed by an ordinary mechanic acquainted with the business, there was an absence of that degree of skill and ingenuity which constitute essential elements of every invention. In other words, the improvement is the work of the skilful mechanic, not that of the inventor." At p. 267.

Hotchkiss, by positing the condition that a patentable invention evidence more ingenuity and skill than that possessed by an ordinary mechanic acquainted with the business, merely distinguished between new and useful innovations that were capable of sustaining a patent and those that were not. The Hotchkiss test laid the cornerstone of the judicial evolution suggested by Jefferson and left to the courts by Congress. The language in the case, and in those which followed, gave birth to "invention" as a word of legal art signifying patentable inventions. Yet, as this Court has observed, "[t]he truth is the word ['invention'] cannot be defined in such manner as to afford any substantial aid in determining whether a particular device involves an exercise of the inventive faculty or not." McClain v. Ortmayer, 141 U.S. 419, 427, 12 S.Ct. 76, 78, 35 L.Ed. 800 (1891); A. & P. Tea Co. v. Supermarket Corp., supra, at 151. Its use as a label brought about a large variety of opinions as to its meaning both in the Patent Office, in the courts, and at the bar. The Hotchkiss formulation, however, lies not in any label, but in its functional approach to questions of patentability. In practice, Hotchkiss has required a comparison between the subject matter of the patent, or patent application, and the background skill of the calling. It has been from this comparison that patentability was in each case determined.

IV.

The 1952 Patent Act

The Act sets out the conditions of patentability in three sections. An analysis of the structure of these three sections indicates that patentability is dependent upon three explicit conditions: novelty and utility as articulated and defined in § 101 and § 102, and nonobviousness, the new statutory formulation, as set out in § 103. The first two sections, which trace closely the 1874 codification, express the "new and useful" tests which have always existed in the statutory scheme and, for our purposes here, need no clarification. The pivotal section around which the present controversy centers is § 103. It provides:

"§ 103. *Conditions for patentability; non-obvious subject matter*

"A patent may not be obtained though the invention is not identically disclosed or described as set forth in section 102 of this title, if the differences between the subject matter sought to be patented and the prior art are such that the subject matter as a whole would have been obvious at the time the invention was made to a person having ordinary skill in the art to which said subject matter pertains. Patentability shall not be negatived by the manner in which the invention was made."

The section is cast in relatively unambiguous terms. Patentability is to depend, in addition to novelty and utility, upon the "non-obvious" nature of the "subject matter sought to be patented" to a person having ordinary skill in the pertinent art.

The first sentence of this section is strongly reminiscent of the language in Hotchkiss. Both formulations place emphasis on the pertinent art existing at the time the invention was made and both are implicitly tied to advances in that art. The major distinction is that Congress has emphasized "nonobviousness" as the operative test of the section, rather than the less definite "invention" language of Hotchkiss that Congress thought had led to "a large variety" of expressions in decisions and writings. . . .

It is undisputed that this section was, for the first time, a statutory expression of an additional requirement for patentability, originally expressed in Hotchkiss. It also seems apparent that Congress intended by the last sentence of § 103 to abolish the test it believed this Court announced in the controversial phrase "flash of creative genius," used in Cuno Corp. v. Automatic Devices Corp., 314 U.S. 84, 62 S.Ct. 37, 86 L.Ed. 58 (1941).

It is contended, however, by some of the parties and by several of the *amici* that the first sentence of § 103 was intended to sweep away judicial precedents and to lower the level of patentability. Others contend that the Congress intended to codify the essential purpose reflected in existing judicial precedents—the rejection of insignificant variations and innovations of a commonplace sort—and also to focus inquiries under § 103 upon nonobviousness, rather than upon "invention," as a means of achieving more stability and predictability in determining patentability and validity.

The Reviser's Note to this section, with apparent reference to Hotchkiss, recognizes that judicial requirements as to "lack of patentable novelty [have] been followed since at least as early as 1850." The note indicates that the section was inserted because it "may have some stablizing effect, and also to serve as a basis for the addition at a later time of some criteria which may be worked out." To this same effect are the reports of both Houses, supra, which state that the first sentence of the section "paraphrases language which has often been used in decisions of the courts, and the section is added to the statute for uniformity and definiteness."

We believe that this legislative history, as well as other sources, shows that the revision was not intended by Congress to change the general level of patentable invention. We conclude that the section was intended merely as a codification of judicial precedents embracing the Hotchkiss condition, with congressional directions that inquiries into the obviousness of the subject matter sought to be patented are a prerequisite to patentability.

V.

Approached in this light, the § 103 additional condition, when followed realistically, will permit a more practical test of patentability. The emphasis on nonobviousness is one of inquiry, not quality, and, as such, comports with the constitutional strictures.

While the ultimate question of patent validity is one of law, the § 103 condition, which is but one of three conditions, each of which must be satisfied, lends itself to several basic factual inquiries. Under § 103, the scope and content of the prior art are to be determined; differences between the prior art and the claims at issue are to be ascertained; and the level of ordinary skill in the pertinent art resolved. Against this background, the obviousness or nonobviousness of the subject matter is determined. Such secondary considerations as commercial success, long felt but unsolved needs, failure of others, etc., might be utilized to give light to the circumstances surrounding the origin of the subject matter sought to be patented. As indicia of obviousness or nonobviousness, these inquiries may have relevancy.

This is not to say, however, that there will not be difficulties in applying the nonobviousness test. What is obvious is not a question upon which there is likely to be uniformity of thought in every given factual context. The difficulties, however, are comparable to those encountered daily by the courts in such frames of reference as negligence and scienter, and should be amenable to a case-by-case development. We believe that strict observance of the requirements laid down here will result in that uniformity and definiteness which Congress called for in the 1952 Act.

While we have focused attention on the appropriate standard to be applied by the courts, it must be remembered that the primary responsibility for sifting out unpatentable material lies in the Patent Office.   To await litigation is—for all practical purposes—to debilitate the patent system.   We have observed a notorious difference between the standards applied by the Patent Office and by the courts. While many reasons can be adduced to explain the discrepancy, one may well be the free rein often exercised by Examiners in their use of the concept of "invention."   In this connection we note that the Patent Office is confronted with a most difficult task.   Almost 100,000 applications for patents are filed each year.   Of these, about 50,000 are granted and the backlog now runs well over 200,000.   1965 Annual Report of the Commissioner of Patents 13–14.   This is itself a compelling reason for the Commissioner to strictly adhere to the 1952 Act as interpreted here.   This would, we believe, not only expedite disposition but bring about a closer concurrence between administrative and judicial precedent.

Although we conclude here that the inquiry which the Patent Office and the courts must make as to patentability must be beamed with greater intensity on the requirements of § 103, it bears repeating that we find no change in the general strictness with which the overall test is to be applied.   We have been urged to find in § 103 a relaxed standard, supposedly a congressional reaction to the "increased standard" applied by this Court in its decisions over the last 20 or 30 years.   The standard has remained invariable in this Court. Technology, however, has advanced—and with remarkable rapidity in the last 50 years.   Moreover, the ambit of applicable art in given fields of science has widened by disciplines unheard of a half century ago.   It is but an evenhanded application to require that those persons granted the benefit of a patent monopoly be charged with an awareness of these changed conditions.   The same is true of the less technical, but still useful arts.   He who seeks to build a better mousetrap today has a long path to tread before reaching the Patent Office.

We now turn to the application of the conditions found necessary for patentability to the cases involved here:

A.   The Patent in Issue in No. 11, Graham v. John Deere Co.

This patent, No. 2,627,798 (hereinafter called the '798 patent) relates to a spring clamp which permits plow shanks to be pushed upward when they hit obstructions in the soil, and then springs the shanks back into normal position when the obstruction is passed over. The device, which we show diagrammatically in the accompanying sketches (Appendix, Fig. 1), is fixed to the plow frame as a unit. The mechanism around which the controversy centers is basically a hinge.   The top half of it, known as the upper plate (marked 1 in the sketches), is a heavy metal piece clamped to the plow frame (2) and is stationary relative to the plow frame.   The lower half of the hinge, known as the hinge plate (3), is connected to the rear of the upper plate by a hinge pin (4) and rotates downward with respect to it. The shank (5), which is bolted to the forward end of the hinge plate (at 6), runs beneath the plate and parallel to it for about nine inches, passes through a stirrup (7), and then continues backward for several feet curving down toward the ground. The chisel (8), which does the actual plowing, is attached to the rear end of the shank. As the plow frame is pulled forward, the chisel rips through the soil, thereby plowing it. In the normal position, the hinge plate and the shank are kept tight against the upper plate by a spring (9), which is atop the upper plate. A rod (10) runs through the center of the spring, extending down through holes in both plates and the shank. Its upper end is bolted to the top of the spring while its lower end is hooked against the underside of the shank.

When the chisel hits a rock or other obstruction in the soil, the obstruction forces the chisel and the rear portion of the shank to move upward. The shank is pivoted (at 11) against the rear of the hinge plate and pries open the hinge against the closing tendency of the spring. (See sketch labeled "Open Position," Appendix, Fig. 1.) This closing tendency is caused by the fact that, as the hinge is opened, the connecting rod is pulled downward and the spring is compressed. When the obstruction is passed over, the upward force on the chisel disappears and the spring pulls the shank and hinge plate back into their original position. The lower, rear portion of the hinge plate is constructed in the form of a stirrup (7) which brackets the shank, passing around and beneath it. The shank fits loosely into the stirrup (permitting a slight up and down play). The stirrup is designed to prevent the shank from recoiling away from the hinge plate, and thus prevents excessive strain on the shank near its bolted connection. The stirrup also girds the shank, preventing it from fishtailing from side to side.

In practical use, a number of spring-hinge-shank combinations are clamped to a plow frame, forming a set of ground-working chisels capable of withstanding the shock of rocks and other obstructions in the soil without breaking the shanks.

Background of the Patent.

Chisel plows, as they are called, were developed for plowing in areas where the ground is relatively free from rocks or stones. Originally, the shanks were rigidly attached to the plow frames. When such plows were used in the rocky, glacial soils of some of the Northern States, they were found to have serious defects. As the chisels hit buried rocks, a vibratory motion was set up and tremendous forces were transmitted to the shank near its connection to the frame. The shanks would break. Graham, one of the petitioners, sought to meet that problem, and in 1950 obtained a patent, U.S. No. 2,493,811 (hereinafter '811), on a spring clamp which solved some of the difficulties. Graham and his companies manufactured and sold the '811 clamps. In 1950, Graham modified the '811 structure and filed for a patent. That patent, the one in issue, was granted in 1953. This suit against competing plow manufacturers resulted from charges by petitioners that several of respondents' devices infringed the '798 patent.

The Prior Art.

Five prior patents indicating the state of the art were cited by the Patent Office in the prosecution of the '798 application. Four of these patents, 10 other United States patents and two prior-use spring-clamp arrangements not of record in the '798 file wrapper were relied upon by respondents as revealing the prior art. The District Court and the Court of Appeals found that the prior art "as a whole in one form or another contains all of the mechanical elements of the '798 Patent." One of the prior-use clamp devices not before the Patent Examiner—Glencoe—was found to have "all of the elements."

We confine our discussion to the prior patent of Graham, '811, and to the Glencoe clamp device, both among the references asserted by respondents. The Graham '811 and '798 patent devices are similar in all elements, save two: (1) the stirrup and the bolted connection of the shank to the hinge plate do not appear in '811; and (2) the position of the shank is reversed, being placed in patent '811 above the hinge plate, sandwiched between it and the upper plate. The shank is held in place by the spring rod which is hooked against the bottom of the hinge plate passing through a slot in the shank. Other differences are of no consequence to our examination. In practice the '811 patent arrangement permitted the shank to wobble or fishtail because it was not rigidly fixed to the hinge plate; moreover, as the hinge plate was below the shank, the latter caused wear on the upper plate, a member difficult to repair or replace.

Graham's '798 patent application contained 12 claims. All were rejected as not distinguished from the Graham '811 patent. The inverted position of the shank was specifically rejected as was the bolting of the shank to the hinge plate. The Patent Office examiner found these to be "matters of design well within the expected skill of the art and devoid of invention." Graham withdrew the original claims and substituted the two new ones which are substantially those in issue here. His contention was that wear was reduced in patent '798 between the shank and the heel or rear of the upper plate. He also emphasized several new features, the relevant one here being that the bolt used to connect the hinge plate and shank maintained the upper face of the shank in continuing and constant contact with the underface of the hinge plate.

Graham did not urge before the Patent Office the greater "flexing" qualities of the '798 patent arrangement which he so heavily relied on in the courts. The sole element in patent '798 which petitioners argue before us is the interchanging of the shank and hinge plate and the consequences flowing from this arrangement. The contention is that this arrangement—which petitioners claim is not disclosed in the prior art—permits the shank to flex under stress for its *entire* length. As we have sketched (see sketch, "Graham '798 Patent" in Appendix, Fig. 2), when the chisel hits an obstruction the resultant force (A) pushes the rear of the shank upward and the shank pivots against the rear of the hinge plate at (C). The natural tendency is for that portion of the shank between the pivot point and the bolted connection (i. e., between C and D) to bow downward and away from the hinge plate. The maximum distance (B) that the shank moves away from the plate is slight—for emphasis, greatly exaggerated in the sketches. This is so because of the strength of the shank and the short—nine inches or so—length of that portion of the shank between (C) and (D). On the contrary, in patent '811 (see sketch, "Graham '811 Patent" in Appendix, Fig. 2), the pivot point is the upper plate at point (c); and while the tendency for the shank to bow between points (c) and (d) is the same as in '798, the shank is restricted because of the underlying hinge plate and cannot flex as freely. In practical effect, the shank flexes only between points (a) and (c), and not along the entire length of the shank, as in '798. Petitioners say that this difference in flex, though small, effectively absorbs the tremendous forces of the shock of obstructions whereas prior art arrangements failed.

The Obviousness of the Differences.

We cannot agree with petitioners. We assume that the prior art does not disclose such an arrangement as petitioners claim in patent '798. Still we do not believe that the argument on which petitioners' contention is bottomed supports the validity of the patent. The tendency of the shank to flex is the same in all cases. If free-flexing, as petitioners now argue, is the crucial difference above the prior art, then it appears evident that the desired result would be obtainable by not boxing the shank within the confines of the hinge. The only other effective place available in the arrangement was to attach it below the hinge plate and run it through a stirrup or bracket that would not disturb its flexing qualities. Certainly a person having ordinary skill in the prior art, given the fact that the flex in the shank could be utilized more effectively if allowed to run the entire length of the shank, would immediately see that the thing to do was what Graham did, i. e., invert the shank and the hinge plate.

Petitioners' argument basing validity on the free-flex theory raised for the first time on appeal is reminiscent of Lincoln Engineering Co., v. Stewart-Warner Corp., 303 U.S. 545, 58 S.Ct. 662, 82 L.Ed. 1008 (1938), where the Court called such an effort "an afterthought. No such function . . . is hinted at in the specifications of the patent. If this were so vital an element in the functioning of the apparatus it is strange that all mention of it was omitted." At p. 550. No "flexing" argument was raised in the Patent Office. Indeed, the trial judge specifically found that "flexing is not a claim of the patent in suit . . ." and would not permit interrogation as to flexing in the accused devices. Moreover, the clear testimony of petitioners' experts shows that the flexing advantages flowing from the '798 arrangement are not, in fact, a significant feature in the patent.

We find no nonobvious facets in the '798 arrangement. The wear and repair claims were sufficient to overcome the patent examiner's original conclusions as to the validity of the patent. However, some of the prior art, notably Glencoe, was not before him. There the hinge plate is below the shank but, as the courts below found, all of the elements in the '798 patent are present in the Glencoe structure. Furthermore, even though the position of the shank and hinge plate appears reversed in Glencoe, the mechanical operation is identical. The shank there pivots about the underside of the stirrup, which in Glencoe is *above* the shank. In other words, the stirrup in Glencoe serves exactly the same function as the heel of the hinge plate in '798. The mere shifting of the wear point to the heel of the '798 hinge plate from the stirrup of Glencoe—itself a part of the hinge plate—presents no operative mechanical distinctions, much less nonobvious differences.

The judgment of the Court of Appeals in No. 11 is affirmed.

APPENDIX TO OPINION OF THE COURT.

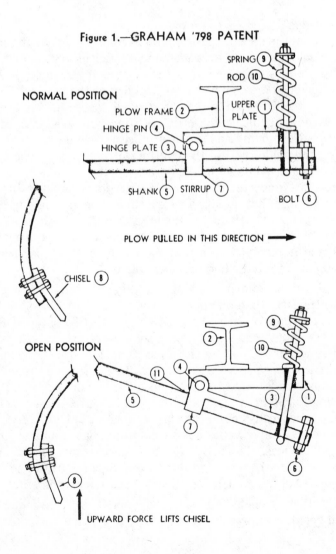

Figure 1.—GRAHAM '798 PATENT

Figure 2.—FLEX COMPARISON

GRAHAM '798 PATENT

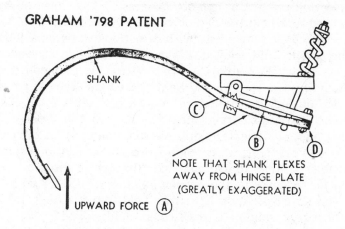

SHANK

Ⓒ   Ⓑ   Ⓓ

NOTE THAT SHANK FLEXES
AWAY FROM HINGE PLATE
(GREATLY EXAGGERATED)

UPWARD FORCE Ⓐ

GRAHAM '811 PATENT

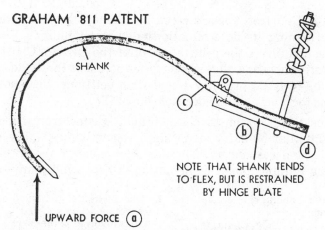

SHANK

ⓒ   ⓑ   ⓓ

NOTE THAT SHANK TENDS
TO FLEX, BUT IS RESTRAINED
BY HINGE PLATE

UPWARD FORCE ⓐ

SAKRAIDA v. AG PRO, INC.

Supreme Court of the United States, 1976.
425 U.S. 273, 96 S.Ct. 1532, 47 L.Ed.2d 784, 189 U.S.P.Q. 449.

Mr. Justice BRENNAN delivered the opinion of the Court.

Respondent Ag Pro, Inc., filed this action against petitioner Sakraida on October 8, 1968, in the District Court for the Western District of Texas for infringement of United States Letters Patent 3,223,070, entitled "Dairy Establishment," covering a water flush system to remove cow manure from the floor of a dairy barn. The patent was issued December 14, 1965, to Gribble and Bennett, who later assigned it to respondent.

The District Court's initial grant of summary judgment for petitioner was reversed by the Court of Appeals for the Fifth Circuit. 437 F.2d 99 (1971). After a trial on remand, the District Court again entered a judgment for petitioner. The District Court held that the patent "does not constitute invention, is not patentable, and is not a valid patent, it being a combination patent, all of the elements of which are old in the dairy business, long prior to 1963, and the combination of them as described in the said patent being neither new nor meeting the test of non-obviousness." The Court of Appeals again reversed and held the patent valid. 474 F.2d 167 (1973). On rehearing, the court remanded "with directions to enter a judgment holding the patent valid, subject, however, to . . . consideration of a motion under Fed.Rule Civ.Proc. 60(b)(2), to be filed in the District Court by the [petitioner] Sakraida on the issue of patent validity based on newly discovered evidence." 481 F.2d 668, 669 (1973). The District Court granted the motion and ordered a new trial. The Court of Appeals again reversed, holding that the grant of the motion was error, because "the record on the motion establishes that [petitioner] failed to exercise due diligence to discover the new evidence prior to entry of the former judgment." 512 F.2d 141, 142 (1975). The Court of Appeals further held that "[o]ur prior determination of patent validity is reaffirmed." Id., at 144. We granted certiorari. 423 U.S. 891, 96 S.Ct. 186, 46 L.Ed.2d 121 (1975). We hold that the Court of Appeals erred in holding the patent valid and also in reaffirming its determination of patent validity. We therefore reverse and direct the reinstatement of the District Court's judgment for petitioner, and thus we have no occasion to decide whether the Court of Appeals properly found that petitioner had not established a case for a new trial under Rule 60(b)(2).

Systems using water to clean animal wastes from barn floors have been familiar on dairy farms since ancient times.[1] The District Court found, and respondent concedes, that none of the 13 elements of the Dairy Establishment combination is new,[2] and many of those

---

1. Among the Labors of Hercules is the following:

"Hercules was next sent to Augeas King of Elis, who had immense droves of cattle. The stables usually occupied by these animals were in an incredibly filthy state, as they had not been cleaned in years; and now Hercules was given the task to remove the accumulated filth, and make a complete purification of the premises.

"Close by these stables rushed a torrent, or rather a river, the Alpheus. Hercules, with one glance, saw the use he could make of this rushing stream, which he dammed and turned aside from its course, so that the waters passed directly through the stables, carrying away all impurities, and finally washing them perfectly clean." Guerber, Myths of Greece and Rome 221 (1893).

2. The District Court found as follows respecting Claims 1 and 3, the only claims involved in the case:

"1. I find that the 'dairy establishment' as described in United States Letters Patent 3,233,070 is composed of 13 separate items, as follows:

"(a) '. . . a smooth, evenly contoured, paved surface forming a floor providing a walking surface . . . .'

"(b) '. . . drain means for draining wash water from such floor opening to the top of the floor.'

"(c) '. . . said smooth, evenly contoured surface which forms such floor sloping toward said drain . . . .'

"(d) '. . . multiple rest areas with individual stalls for each cow and with each of said stalls having a bottom which is also a smooth pavement . . . .'

"(e) '. . . which is disposed at an elevation above the paved surface forming the floor . . . .'

elements, including storage of the water in tanks or pools, appear in at least six prior patented systems.[3] The prior art involved spot delivery of water from tanks or pools to the barn floor by means of high pressure hoses or pipes. That system required supplemental hand labor, using tractor blades, shovels, and brooms, and cleaning by these methods took several hours. The only claimed inventive feature of the Dairy Establishment combination of old elements is the provision for abrupt release of the water from the tanks or pools directly onto the barn floor, which causes the flow of a sheet of water that washes all animal waste into drains within minutes and requires no supplemental hand labor. As an expert witness for respondent testified concerning the effect of Dairy Establishment's combination, "water at the bottom has more friction than this water at the top and it keeps moving ahead and as this water keeps moving ahead we get a rolling action of this water which produced the cleaning action . . . You do not get this in a hose . . . [U]nless that water is continuously directed toward the cleaning area the cleaning action almost ceases instantaneously . . ."[4]

"(f) '. . . said stalls being dimensioned so that a cow can comfortably stand or lie in the stall, but offal from the cow falls outside the stall bottom and onto the floor providing the walking surface in the barn . . .'

"(g) '. . . said barn further including defined feeding areas having feeding troughs . . .'

"(h) '. . . a cow-holding area.'

"(i) '. . . a milking area.'

"(j) '. . . a transfer area all bottomed with the walking surface forming said floor in the barn . . .'

"(k) '. . . and floor washing means for washing the floor providing the walking surface in the barn where said floor bottom, said feeding, holding, milking and transfer areas operable to send wash water flowing over the floor with such water washing any cow offal thereon into the said drain means, said floor washing means including means located over a region of said floor which is uphill from said drain means constructed to collect water as a pool above said floor and operable after such collection of water as a pool to dispense the water as a sheet of water over said floor.'

"(l) A tank on a mounting, so that it can be tilted, and the water poured out to cascade on the floor to form a sheet.

"(m) A floor-washing means comprising a dam for damming or collecting water as a pool directly on the floor, which such dam abruptly openable to send water cascading as a sheet over the floor towards the drain.

"2. I further find that each of the items above-described were not new, but had been used in the dairy business prior to the time the application for the said Gribble patent, made the subject of this action, had been filed in the Patent Office of the United States on November 5, 1963."

3. The District Court found
"that many of the items going to make up Plaintiff's claim for a patent were disclosed in prior patents, known respectively as the McCormack patent, the Holz patent, the Ingraham patent, the Kreutzer patent, the Bogert patent, and the Luks patent; and that the statements of the Examiner's opinions refusing to issue a patent are true as to all items there stated to be covered in prior patents or publications."

4. This witness testified that
"water has energy and it can be used in many different ways. In a hose the energy is used by impact, under pressure, external force that is applied to this pressure—to this water, whereas the water that comes down as a sheet or wall of

The District Court found that "[n]either the tank which holds the water, nor the means of releasing the water quickly is new, but embrace tanks and doors which have long been known," and further that "their use in this connection is one that is obvious, and the patent in that respect is lacking in novelty. The patent does not meet the non-obvious requirements of the law." The District Court therefore held that Dairy Establishment "may be relevant to commercial success, but not to invention," because the combination "was reasonably obvious to one with ordinary skill in the art." Moreover, even if the combination filled a 'long-felt want and . . . has enjoyed commercial success, those matters, without invention, will not make patentability." Finally, the District Court concluded "that to those skilled in the art, the use of the old elements in combination was not an invention by the obvious-nonobvious standard. Even though the dairy barn in question attains the posture of a successful venture, more than that is needed for invention."[5] The Court of Appeals disagreed with the District Court's conclusion on the crucial issue of obviousness.

It has long been clear that the Constitution requires that there be some "invention" to be entitled to patent protection. As we explained in Hotchkiss v. Greenwood, 11 How. 248, 267, 13 L.Ed. 683, 691 (1851): '[U]nless more ingenuity and skill . . . were required . . . than were possessed by an ordinary mechanic acquainted with the business, there was an absence of that degree of skill and ingenuity which constitute essential elements of every invention. In other words, the improvement is the work of the skillful mechanic, not that of the inventor." This standard was enacted in 1952 by Congress in 35 U.S.C.A. § 103 "as a codification of judicial precedents . . . with Congressional directions that inquiries into the obviousness of the subject matter sought to be patented are a

water has built in energy because of its elevation and as this water is released it does the same thing water does in a flooded stream. As this water—I will try to make this clear, and I hope I can, on the surface of this pavement there are these piles of manure droppings. This pavement is smooth and this water moves down over this manure. The water at the bottom has more friction than this water on the top and it keeps moving ahead and as this water keeps moving ahead we get a rolling action of this water which produced the cleaning action. That is the key to this method of cleaning. You do not get this in a hose. You do not get it in a gutter as has been used in the past, I might just mention a little bit about the hose. This squirting water on a floor—proba-

bly have done it on our own sidewalks or walkways, and I just mention that, that unless that water is continuously directed towards the cleaning area the cleaning action almost ceases instantaneously. Now the movie that was shown earlier very dramatically illustrated that point. The cleaning action—as soon as the hoses moved to one side the cleaning action ceased here and that is why this hose was moved back and forth, to drive this stuff on down to where we want it."

5. The court also "conclude[d] that while the combination of old elements may have performed a useful function, it added nothing to the nature and quality of dairy barns theretofore used."

prerequisite to patentability." Graham v. John Deere Co., 383 U.S. 1, 17, 86 S.Ct. 684, 693, 15 L.Ed.2d 545, 556 (1966). . . . .

The ultimate test of patent validity is one of law, A & P Tea Co. v. Supermarket Corp., 340 U.S. 147, 155, 71 S.Ct. 127, 131, 95 L.Ed. 162, 168 (1950), but resolution of the obviousness issue necessarily entails several basic factual inquiries, Graham v. John Deere Co., supra, at 17.

"Under § 103, the scope and content of the prior art are to be determined; differences between the prior art and the claims at issue are to be ascertained; and the level of ordinary skill in the pertinent art resolved." Ibid.

3
CRITERIA

The Court of Appeals concluded that "the facts presented at trial clearly do not support [the District Court's] finding of obviousness under the three-pronged Graham test . . . ." 474 F.2d, at 172. We disagree and hold that the Court of Appeals erroneously set aside the District Court's findings.

The scope of the prior art was shown by prior patents, prior art publications, affidavits of people having knowledge of prior flush systems analogous to respondent's, and the testimony of a dairy operator with 22 years experience who described flush systems he had seen on visits to dairy farms throughout the country. Our independent examination of that evidence persuades us of its sufficiency to support the District Court's finding "as a fact that each and all of the component parts of this patent . . . were old and well-known throughout the dairy industry long prior to the date of the filing of the application for the Gribble patent . . . [w]hat Mr. Gribble referred to . . . as the essence of the patent, to-wit, the manure flush system, was old, various means for flushing manure from dairy barns having been used long before the filing of the application . . . ." Indeed, respondent admitted at trial "that the patent is made up of a combination of old elements" and "that all elements are individually old . . . ." Accordingly, the District Court properly followed our admonition in A & P Tea Co. v. Supermarket Corp., supra, at 152: "Courts should scrutinize combination patent claims with a care proportioned to the difficulty and improbability of finding invention in an assembly of old elements . . . . A patent for a combination which only unites old elements with no change in their respective functions . . . obviously withdraws what already is known into the field of its monopoly and diminishes the resources available to skillful men . . . ."

The Court of Appeals recognized that the patent combined old elements for applying water to a conventional sloped floor in a dairy barn equipped with drains at the bottom of the slope and that the purpose of the storage tank—to accumulate a large volume of water capable of being released in a cascade or surge—was equally conventional. 474 F.2d, at 169. It concluded, however, that the element lacking in the prior art was any evidence of an arrangement of the old elements to effect the abrupt release of a flow of water to wash animal wastes from the floor of a dairy barn. Ibid. Therefore, "although the [respondent's] flush system does not embrace a complicated technical improvement, it does achieve a synergistic result through a novel combination." Id., at 173.

We cannot agree that the combination of these old elements to produce an abrupt release of water directly on the barn floor from storage tanks or pools can properly be characterized as synergistic, that is, "result[ing] in an effect greater than the sum of the several effects taken separately." Anderson's-Black Rock v. Pavement Co., 396 U.S. 57, 61 (1960). Rather, this patent simply arranges old elements with each performing the same function it had been known to perform, although perhaps producing a more striking result than in previous combinations. Such combinations are not patentable under standards appropriate for a combination patent. Under those authorities this assembly of old elements that delivers water directly rather than through pipes or hoses to the barn floor falls under the head of "the work of the skillful mechanic, not that of the inventor." Hotchkiss v. Greenwood, supra, at 267. Exploitation of the principle of gravity adds nothing to the sum of useful knowledge where there is no change in the respective functions of the elements of the combination; this particular use of the assembly of old elements would be obvious to any person skilled in the art of mechanical application.

Though doubtless a matter of great convenience, producing a desired result in a cheaper and faster way, and enjoying commercial success, Dairy Establishment "did not produce a 'new or different function' . . . within the test of validity of combination patents." Anderson's-Black Rock v. Pavement Co., supra, at 60. These desirable benefits "without invention will not make patentability." A & P Tea Co. v. Supermarket, etc. Co., supra, at 153.

Reversed.

NOTES

1.   Section 103's silver anniversary was celebrated in a wide-ranging anthology, Nonobviousness—The Ultimate Condition of Patentability (J. Witherspoon, Ed. 1980). See also Schneider, Non-Obviousness, The Supreme Court, and the Prospects for Stability, 60 J. P.O.S. 304 (1978). For an historical and economic analysis, see Kitch, Graham v. John Deere Co.: New Standards for Patents, 1966 Sup.Ct.Rev. 293. For a comparative view, see Pagenberg, The Evaluation of the "Inventive Step" in the European Patent System—More Objective Standards Needed, 9 Int'l.Rev.Indus.Prop. & Copyright L. 1, 121 (Pts. 1 & 2) (1978).

2.   Congress in section 103, and the Supreme Court in *John Deere* and its two companion cases,[k] sought to stabilize what had

k. Calmar, Inc. v. Cook Chemical Co.; Colgate-Palmolive Co. v. Cook Chemical Co., 383 U.S. 1, 26, 86 S.Ct. 684, 15 L.Ed.2d 545, 148 U.S.P.Q. 459 (1966); United States v. Adams, 383 U.S. 39, 86 S.Ct. 708, 15 L.Ed.2d 572, 148 U.S.P.Q. 479 (1966).

long been perceived as a fugitive standard of invention. The standard's drastic fluctuations—from high to low, subjective to objective, positive to negative—seriously complicated private decisions whether, and how heavily, to invest in developing new products and in copying or inventing around a competitor's patented subject matter.

The Supreme Court had not in the past lent a particularly steady hand to guide lower court decisions. It continually found new ways to phrase the invention standard, and even its most nominal deviation from a previously expressed standard would trigger strong reactions in the lower courts. One survey of circuit court decisions of that era observed:

> Back in the late twenties you can see the courts were holding from 35% to 40% of all the litigated patents valid and infringed. Following this period, the trend is downward, and in 1937 and 1938 came the TNEC hearings which had a definitely anti-patent flavor. In 1941 the *Cuno* case was decided, with its "flash of genius" test, and in the following year, 1942, only 10% of the litigated patents were upheld. Then things tended to improve a little bit up to the point where the *Graver v. Linde* case was decided . . . that was the only case in which either Mr. Justice Douglas or Mr. Justice Black ever voted to uphold a patent. Right after that the curve climbs back almost to 30%, but the gain was short-lived. In the following year came the *A & P* case and *Crest v. Trager* (the infant feeding device). The curve then drops back down to 7%, the lowest point at any time during the thirty year period. The new Patent Act was passed in 1952, and presumably as a result the curve has shot up, wavering at first, but in 1956 it reached 33%, and in 1957 through September 9th, 30%, which seems to me quite encouraging.

[Discussion following presentation of paper by Cooch, The Standard of Invention in the Courts, in Dynamics of the Patent System, 34, 56 (W.Ball., Ed. 1960).]

Four years after *Deere*, the Court wavered on its newly announced standard. Anderson's-Black Rock, Inc. v. Pavement Salvage Co., Inc., 396 U.S. 57, 90 S.Ct. 305, 24 L.Ed.2d 258, 163 U.S.P.Q. 673 (1969). *Sakraida* only confirmed that the prospects are not good for a certain, uniform and objective standard of invention.

3. The circuits divide sharply over how, and how high, to set the invention standard. As a result, the adroit forum-shopping patent owner can, by choosing the right circuit for suit, save a patent that might fall in another circuit, and the alert infringer can pick a less hospitable circuit to pursue its action for a declaratory judgment declaring the patent invalid. One study of patentability decisions revealed that "the Fourth and Fifth Circuits have been the places to sue on a borderline patent. They held approximately 40% valid and infringed in that period [1945–1957]. The First, Third, Sixth, Seventh, Ninth and Tenth Circuits are fairly close together at 19% plus or minus 2.4%. And finally, the Second and Eighth Circuits held ap-

proximately 6% of the patents coming before them valid, the Second Circuit being the lowest with 4.8%" Cooch, note 2 above, at pages 56, 59.

John Deere had little success in bringing the circuits into line. The Second, Fourth, and Sixth Circuits continued to apply the statutory standard of section 103. The Third, Fifth, Eighth, and Ninth Circuits applied nonstatutory standards, often purported to rest on nonobviousness but, really, unfathomable tests such as "the whole must exceed the sum of its parts" or "elements must function differently when in combination than outside of it." The First, Seventh and Tenth Circuits applied no consistent standard at all. See Note, Impact of the Supreme Court Section 103 Cases on the Standard of Patentability in the Lower Federal Courts, 35 Geo.Wash.L.Rev. 818, 826 (1967). See also, Note, the Standard of Patentability—Judicial Interpretation of Section 103 of the Patent Act, 63 Colum.L.Rev. 306 (1963); Note, 34 Geo.Wash.L.Rev. 802, 803–805 (1966).

Even *Sakraida*, widely excoriated by the commentators, has not been treated uniformly in the Circuits. The Seventh Circuit has vigorously repudiated the test. Republic Industries, Inc. v. Schlage Lock Co., 592 F.2d 963, 200 U.S.P.Q. 769 (1979). The Ninth Circuit, which at first accepted the test, later moderated its view. Compare Herschensohn v. Hoffman, 593 F.2d 893, 201 U.S.P.Q. 721 (1979) cert. denied, 444 U.S. 842, 100 S.Ct. 84, 62 L.Ed.2d 55, 203 U.S.P.Q. 720 with Palmer v. Orthokinetics, Inc., 611 F.2d 316, 204 U.S.P.Q. 893 (1980). The Second and Third Circuits have steered an essentially noncommittal course around the test, while the Tenth Circuit has apparently rejected, and the Sixth Circuit accepted, it. See Champion Spark Plug Co. v. Gyromat Corp., 603 F.2d 361, 202 U.S.P.Q. 785 (2d Cir. 1979), cert. denied, 445 U.S. 916, 100 S.Ct. 1276, 63 L.Ed.2d 600; Sims v. Mack Truck Corp., 608 F.2d 87, 203 U.S.P.Q. 961 (3d Cir. 1979), cert. denied, 445 U.S. 930, 100 S.Ct. 1319, 63 L.Ed.2d 764, 205 U.S.P.Q. 488; Plastic Container Corp. v. Continental Plastics of Oklahoma, Inc., 607 F.2d 885, 203 U.S.P.Q. 27 (10th Cir. 1979), cert. denied, 444 U.S. 1018, 100 S.Ct. 672, 62 L.Ed.2d 648, 204 U.S.P.Q. 696; Hanson v. Alpine Val. Ski Area, Inc., 611 F.2d 156, 204 U.S.P.Q. 803 (6th Cir. 1979).

4. *Sakraida* clearly intended that a special test of invention be applied to combination patents. The decision was far less clear in defining the relationship between this special test and section 103's general test of nonobviousness. Does *Sakraida* hold that the special test will, in the case of combinations, substitute for the general test, or does it hold that the special and general tests are to operate together? If the latter, are the two tests distinct, one requiring a showing that the combination is "synergistic," the other that it was nonobvious? Or, are the tests more closely tied, with the absence of synergy being strong, if not conclusive, evidence that the combination would have been obvious to one ordinarily skilled in the art?

All of this assumes that combination patents can easily be separated from other patents. What limits are there to the Court's conception of "combination patents"? What patent subject matter is not, at bottom, a combination of old elements or old steps? Is it possible that the intended distinction is really between *mechanical* combinations and other subject matter? Between subject matter whose elemental attributes are readily grasped by courts and subject matter whose attributes are not? See generally, Note, 45 Geo.Wash.L.Rev. 546 (1977).

5. Obviousness may be proved inferentially. The three main inferential bases, sometimes called "subtests of nonobviousness," are long-felt demand for the subject matter, commercial acquiescence in its patentability, and commercial success. The subtest of long-felt demand assumes that all firms characteristically seek to correct defects that increase production costs or decrease product quality so that, if a corrective method or apparatus had been obvious to workers ordinarily skilled in the industry, the invention would have been adopted prior to its creation by the patentee. This conclusion will of course be undercut by evidence that the patentee's solution would have been impossible but for a recent and related advance in the art. See, for example, Otto v. Koppers Co., 246 F.2d 789, 114 U.S.P.Q. 188 (4th Cir. 1957), cert. denied, 355 U.S. 939, 78 S.Ct. 427, 2 L.Ed.2d 420, 116 U.S.P.Q. 602; Allen v. Standard Crankshaft and Hydraulic Co., 323 F.2d 29, 139 U.S.P.Q. 20 (4th Cir. 1963).

The reason for admitting proof of commercial acquiescence is that when competitors, who have the greatest interest in attacking a patent, secure licenses under the patent or engage in research to duplicate the advantages of the patented subject matter without infringing the patent, it is a good indication that they view the subject matter as patentable. Since they are at least ordinarily skilled in the art, this is, in turn, good evidence of patentability under Section 103. See, for example, Eibel Process Co. v. Minnesota & Ontario Paper Co., 261 U.S. 45, 43 S.Ct. 322, 67 L.Ed. 523 (1923); Georgia Pacific Corp. v. United States Plywood Corp., 258 F.2d 124, 118 U.S.P.Q. 122 (2d Cir. 1958), cert. denied, 358 U.S. 844, 79 S.Ct. 124, 3 L.Ed.2d 112. But see, Kleinman v. Kobler, 230 F.2d 913, 914, 108 U.S.P.Q. 301 (2d Cir. 1956), cert denied, 352 U.S. 830, 77 S.Ct. 44, 1 L.Ed.2d 124. ("to take a license calling for small royalty payments, frequently involves less expense than prolonged litigation. . . .") What are the implications for this "subtest" of the Supreme Court's decision in Lear, Inc. v. Adkins, infra p. 617? See generally, Note, Subtests of Nonobviousness: A Nontechnical Approach to Patent Validity, 112 U.Pa.L. Rev. 1169 (1964).

Although commercial success is the evidence most frequently used to prove patentability, the rationale for its admission is clouded. Under one view, it is the positive consumer judgment denoted by commercial success that indicates the presence of patentable invention. Minerals Separation, Ltd. v. Hyde, 242 U.S. 261, 37 S.Ct. 82, 61 L.Ed. 286 (1916). Under another view, commercial success is assumed to be the goal of all competitors in an industry. Had the successful subject matter been obvious to others at the time of its creation, they naturally would have preceded the patentee in its development. See The Barbed Wire Patent, 143 U.S. 275, 12 S.Ct. 443, 36 L. Ed. 154 (1892); S.H. Kress Co. v. Aghnides, 246 F.2d 718, 114 U.S. P.Q. 187 (4th Cir. 1957), cert. denied, 355 U.S. 899, 78 S.Ct. 261, 2 L. Ed.2d 189.

The second rationale is more accurately attuned to section 103. Under either rationale, it must be shown that the commercial success stems from the nature of the patented subject matter and not from such extrinsic factors as its unreasonably low price or the patent proprietor's elaborate advertising efforts, Ling-Tempco-Vought, Inc. v. Kollsman Instrument Corp., 372 F.2d 263, 152 U.S.P.Q. 446 (2d Cir. 1967); increases in demand brought on by wartime conditions, Goodyear Tire and Rubber Co., Inc. v. Ray-O-Vac Co., 321 U.S. 275, 281, 64 S.Ct. 593, 88 L.Ed. 721, 60 U.S.P.Q. 386 (1944) (Jackson, J. dissenting); or a government agency's promotion of the patented product, Brooks v. Stoffel Seals Corp., 266 F.2d 841, 121 U.S.P.Q. 333 (2d Cir. 1959), cert. denied, 361 U.S. 833, 80 S.Ct. 154, 4 L.Ed.2d 119.

To characterize these points as "subtests" tends to obscure the fact that they are not tests at all, only inferential bases, and that any evidence should be admissible if it can support the inference of nonobviousness. For example, it has been considered good evidence of nonobviousness that the patentee's ordinarily skilled researchers spent several months in developing a workable method for pressurizing shaving cream; that defendant had engaged in research with the same objective but with no success; and that, even after analyzing patentee's product, defendant was unable to replicate it. Colgate Palmolive Co. v. Carter Products Co., 230 F.2d 855, 108 U.S.P.Q. 383 (4th Cir. 1956).

6. Increasingly, courts rely upon expert testimony for the determination of patentability. If the court is unconvinced by both parties' witnesses it may, usually with the parties' consent, appoint an independent expert. See, for example, Reeves Bros. Inc. v. United States Laminating Corp., 282 F.Supp. 118, 157 U.S.P.Q. 235 (E.D.N. Y. 1968), aff'd, 417 F.2d 869 (2d Cir.).

There is good reason for courts to rely on expert testimony when the relevant art is technical and complex. Is there even greater reason to defer to expertise in cases involving subject matter easily comprehensible to the layman, where the common judicial tendency is to equate an advance's apparent simplicity with its obviousness—to conclude, "I could have done that"?

7. Was the Supreme Court in *Deere* correct to criticize the Patent Office for applying an invention standard more liberal than the one announced by the Court? Very few issued patents will ever enjoy commercial success. Fewer still will have their validity tested in litigation. Can you think of a more efficient system than one which has the Patent and Trademark Office make a comparatively quick pass at investigating the prior art behind all the patent applications presented to it and postpones closer, more costly inquiry to infringe-

ment actions involving the relatively few patents that turn out to have commercial significance?

Different standards may also stem from the different proofs available to the Patent and Trademark Office and to the courts. In Patent and Trademark Office proceedings nonobviousness is measured directly. The examiner compares the subject matter in question with the relevant prior art and determines whether the subject mater would have been obvious to a worker ordinarily skilled in the art. By the time the patent reaches the courts in the context of an infringement or declaratory judgment action, evidence bearing on commercial success and acquiescence will typically have become available. Although these subtests are supposed to exert only a secondary influence, failure to meet them will certainly contribute to a court's decision to invalidate the patent.

Does the invalidation of a large portion of the patents coming into the courts indicate a flaw in the patent system, or does it suggest that the two tribunals are effectively serving different functions—the Patent and Trademark Office to grant patents on the basis of prior art appraisals, and the courts to weed out subject matter that subsequently-occurring events show to have been obvious.

8. Judicial style and taste play an important but largely ignored role in decisions on patentability. *Sakraida's* amorphous "synergy" test has a lineage that traces back to *Cuno's* "flash of creative genius" and to that term's origins in Hollister v. Benedict & Burnham Mfg. Co., 113 U.S. 59, 5 S.Ct. 717, 28 L.Ed. 901 (1885). Although some courts and commentators may characterize these as aberrant tests of invention, it is unlikely that any judicial or even legislative proscription will ever curtail their use.

What is synergy's role in patentability decisions? While the term is certainly more than a rhetorical flourish, it is also clearly less than a test for invention. Nonobviousness, and its precedents going back to Hotchkiss v. Greenwood, form the true test for invention, establishing the objective benchmarks needed to rationalize private investment in research and development aimed at producing patentable products and processes. Synergy, by contrast, is an escape valve, an ad hoc regulatory device used by courts to say "no" to patent subject matter that, though it has passed the nonobviousness test, somehow seems too common to warrant the social costs of a patent.

One proper question to ask about synergy and its precursors and successors is whether, and how substantially, they disrupt investment expectations. If these measures reduce the incentive to invest in and disclose desired research and development, it is appropriate to consider whether they are in fact needed to guard against monopolies over common subject matter. Undesired monopolies may, for example, be more effectively controlled through the rigorous enforcement of infringement rules. Courts are less inclined to find that patents covering small, incremental advances have been infringed than they are to find that patents on pioneer inventions have been infringed. See pages 633 to 651 below. Would reliance on infringement determinations rather than patentability standards necessarily give weak and untested patents an unwarranted power in the marketplace?

b. SECTION 102: NOVELTY AND THE STATUTORY BARS

APPLICATION OF BORST

United States Court of Customs and Patent Appeals, 1965.
52 C.C.P.A. 1398, 345 F.2d 851, 145 U.S.P.Q. 554, cert. denied 382 U.S. 973,
86 S.Ct. 537, 15 L.Ed.2d 465, 148 U.S.P.Q. 771.

SMITH, Judge.

The invention for which appellant seeks a patent comprises means for safely and effectively controlling a relatively large neutron output by varying a small and easily controlled neutron input source.

. . .

Appellant asserts that the claimed invention affords a revolutionary approach to the safety problem in the nuclear reactor art. As the amplifier is said to be inherently safe from divergent nuclear chain reaction, the intricate systems needed to monitor and control the operation of conventional neutron amplifiers to prevent an explosion are unnecessary.

The single reference relied upon by the Patent Office in rejecting the appealed claims is an Atomic Energy Commission document entitled "KAPL–M–RWS–1, A Stable Fission Pile with High Speed Control." The document is in the form of an unpublished memorandum authored by one Samsel, and will hereinafter be referred to as "Samsel." Samsel is dated February 14, 1947 and was classified as a secret document by the Commission until March 9, 1957, when it was declassified. In essence, Samsel sets forth and discusses the problems present in the control of a nuclear reactor, the concept of use of successive fuel stages to effect such control, and a description of the arrangement, composition and relative proportions of materials required to obtain the sought-for results. Samsel is prefaced by a statement that it was made to record an idea, and it nowhere indicates that the idea had been tested in an operating reactor.

The Patent Office does not invoke Samsel as a publication (which it apparently was not, at any pertinent date). Rather, the contention is that Samsel constitutes evidence of prior knowledge within the meaning of 35 U.S.C.A. § 102(a).

While there seems to be some disagreement on the part of the solicitor, we think the most reasonable interpretation of the examiner's rejection, and one which is concurred in by the board and by appellant, is that claims 27, 30, 31 and 32 are fully met by Samsel and thus the subject matter defined therein is unpatentable because it was known by another in this country prior to appellant's invention thereof. As to claims 28, 29 and 33, even though not fully met by Samsel, they are said to be obvious within the meaning of 35 U.S.C.A. § 103 in view of the prior knowledge evidenced by Samsel.

Our own independent consideration of Samsel has convinced us that it contains adequate enabling disclosure of the invention of claims 27 and 30–32, and appellant does not appear to contend otherwise. Rather, appellant contends that Samsel is not available as evidence of prior knowledge under sections 102(a) and 103. Appellant also argues that, even if Samsel is available, the subject matter of claims 28, 29 and 33 is not obvious in view thereof. We agree with this characterization of the essential issues presented on this appeal, and will treat them in the order stated above.

In the case of In re Schlittler, 234 F.2d 882, 43 C.C.P.A. 986, this court was presented with the following situation: A manuscript containing an anticipatory disclosure of the appellants' claimed invention had been submitted to The Journal of the American Chemical Society and was later published. The date to which the appellants' application was entitled for purposes of constructive reduction to practice was earlier than the publication date of the Journal article, and therefore the Patent Office did not contend that the "printed publication" portion of section 102(a) was applicable. However, the manuscript bore a notation that it had been received by the publisher on a date prior to the effective filing date of the appellants' application. On the basis of this notation the Patent Office argued that the article constituted sufficient evidence of prior knowledge under section 102(a).

After an exhaustive review of the authorities, and of the legislative history of the Patent Act of 1952, this court rejected the contention of the Patent Office, and concluded that such a document was not proper evidence of prior knowledge. In reversing, the court stated (234 F.2d at 886, 433 C.C.P.A. at 992):

> "In our opinion, one of the essential elements of the word 'known' as used in 35 U.S.C.A. § 102(a) is knowledge of an invention which has been completed by reduction to practice, actual or constructive, and is not satisfied by disclosure of a conception only."

And therefore, since the Journal article, "at best, could be evidence of nothing more than conception and disclosure of the invention," the

> ". . . placing of the Nystrom article in the hands of the publishers did not constitute either prima facie or conclusive evidence of knowledge or use by others in this country of the invention disclosed by the article, within the meaning of Title 35, § 102(a) of the United States Code, since the knowledge was of a conception only and not of a reduction to practice."

Another aspect of the court's discussion in Schlittler involved the well-established principle that "prior knowledge of a patented invention would not invalidate a claim of the patent unless such knowledge was available to the public." After reaffirming that principle, the court went on to state:

> "Obviously, in view of the above authorities, the mere placing of a manuscript in the hands of a publisher does not neces-

sarily make it available to the public within the meaning of said authorities."

However, the court did not go on to determine whether the Journal article was in fact available to the public, since such determination was deemed unnecessary for disposition of the case, under the court's theory.

We shall consider first the public availability aspect of the Schlittler case. Although that portion of the Schlittler opinion is clearly dictum, we think it just as clearly represents the settled law. [The knowledge contemplated by section 102(a) must be accessible to the public.] In addition to Schlittler and cases cited therein, see, e. g., Minneapolis-Honeywell Regulator Co. v. Midwestern Instruments, Inc., 7 Cir., 298 F.2d 36 (7th Cir. 1961); Rem-Cru Titanium, Inc. v. Watson, 152 F.Supp. 282 (D.D.C.1957).

In the instant case, Samsel was clearly not publicly available during the period it was under secrecy classification by the Atomic Energy Commission. We note that the date of declassification, however, was prior to appellant's filing date, and it is perhaps arguable that Samsel became accessible to the public upon declassification. But we do not find it necessary to decide that difficult question, for there is a statutory provision which is, we think, dispositive of the question of publicity. Section 155 of the Atomic Energy Act of 1954 (42 U.S.C. A. § 2185) provides:

> "In connection with applications for patents covered by this subchapter, the fact that the invention or discovery was known or used before shall be a bar to the patenting of such invention or discovery even though such prior knowledge or use was under secrecy within the atomic energy program of the United States."

We think the meaning and intent of this provision is so clear as to admit of no dispute: With respect to subject matter covered by the patent provisions of the Atomic Energy Act, prior knowledge or use under section 102(a) *need not* be accessible to the public. Therefore, Samsel is available as evidence of prior knowledge insofar as the requirement for publicity is concerned.

The remaining consideration regarding the status of Samsel as evidence of prior knowledge directly calls into question the correctness of the unequivocal holding in Schlittler that the knowledge must be of a reduction to practice, either actual or constructive. After much deliberation, we have concluded that such a requirement is illogical and anomalous, and to the extent Schlittler is inconsistent with the decision in this case, it is hereby expressly overruled.

The mere fact that a disclosure is contained in a patent or application and thus "constructively" reduced to practice, or that it is found in a printed publication, does not make the disclosure itself any more meaningful to those skilled in the art (and thus, ultimately, to the public). Rather, the criterion should be whether the disclosure is *sufficient to enable one skilled in the art to reduce the disclosed in-*

vention to practice. In other words, the disclosure must be such as will give possession of the invention to the person of ordinary skill. Even the act of publication or the fiction of constructive reduction to practice will not suffice if the disclosure does not meet this standard.

Where, as is true of Samsel, the disclosure constituting evidence of prior knowledge contains, in the words of the Board of Appeals, "a description of the invention fully commensurate with the present patent application," we hold that the disclosure need not be of an invention reduced to practice, either actually or constructively. We therefore affirm the rejection of claims 27, 30, 31 and 32. . . . Modified.

NOTE, NOVELTY AND REDUCTION TO PRACTICE: PATENT CONFUSION

75 Yale L.J. 1194–96, 1198–1201 (1966).*

The rewards of a patent monopoly are reserved for contributions which may significantly increase existing knowledge. Under the present law an applicant must show not only that his device was an "invention" and had "utility," but also that it meets the requirement of "novelty." The prerequisite of novelty reflects a basic policy of the law to reward only those inventors who first place the device in the public domain. If knowledge of the subject sought to be patented has already been made available to the public, then a patent grant would not only serve no useful purpose, but would injure the public by removing existing knowledge from the public domain.

The novelty requirement is spelled out in Section 102(a) of the Patent Act of 1952: a patent will be barred for lack of novelty if the invention had previously been described in a prior patent or printed publication, or if it had been "known or used by others." While prior patents and printed publications are relatively clear categories, the "known or used by others" obstacle is ill-defined; read expansively, it would bar *any* invention which had previously been thought of—however vaguely—by someone else. To prevent yesterday's science-fiction from becoming today's patent bar, courts have long read the statutory language restrictively. An invention was not "known or used" unless it had been *actually reduced to practice,* by building a working and tested embodiment, *or constructively reduced to practice,* by filing a detailed patent application, which later ripened into a patent. And it was not known or used "by others" unless the inventor had made knowledge of his device available to the public.

This interpretation has been upset by a recent decision of the Court of Customs and Patent Appeals, In re Borst, which may severely tighten the requirement of novelty. . . .

* Copyright 1966 by the Yale Law Journal Co., Inc. Reprinted by permission of the Yale Law Journal Company and Fred B. Rothman & Company from *The Yale Law Journal,* Vol. 75, pp. 1194–1196, 1198–1201.

The potential impact of *Borst* is its effect on the old rules for determining when a prior description would bar a patent. Before *Borst*, a mere description of an idea or conception could defeat a claim of novelty only if it were included in a "printed publication" or a patent. These descriptions, and no others, were thought likely to bring knowledge of the invention to the public. And unless the public knew of the earlier discovery, the subsequent invention would be considered novel.

The "printed publication" clause has consistently been interpreted in light of this purpose—to bar a patent only if the earlier invention were known to society. At the time the statute was enacted, the printing press was the only device for inexpensive reproduction of documents. As techniques have grown, courts have broadened the definition of "printing" to include typewritten and mimeographed documents deposited in public libraries. Provision for dissemination of the knowledge is supplied by the "publication" requirement, under which a printed document will not bar a patent unless it has been made available to the public. In Badowski v. United States [164 F. Supp. 252 (1958)], for example, the government challenged a patent by unearthing a Russian document describing the device. The court found that the document had been obtained in 1958 only after "months of diplomatic endeavor by defendant's embassy in Moscow." There was no evidence that it had ever been accessible to the public in any country prior to the 1942 patent application; nor had the document been contained in any library anywhere, even at the time of litigation. Consequently, the document was held not to be a prior publication, and the patent was granted. Similarly, private reports, confidential papers, and documents intended for distribution solely within an organization have all failed the publication test. On the other hand, even a single copy of a typed thesis meets the publication test if it has been deposited in a public library.

What *Borst* may do is to add another bar to novelty: a memorandum describing an idea but which falls short of the requirements for printed publication. Unless construed with care, the new bar to novelty may prove a troublesome category.

First, *Borst* weakens the dissemination requirement for written descriptions. Unpublished memoranda necessarily fall short of the level of distribution demanded of publications, and yet the court left unclear exactly what lesser requirement *Borst*-type disclosures must meet. If no significant dissemination is required, severe damage may be done to patent policy. Inventors may be discouraged from investing in an idea if an obscure prior disclosure may lurk as a threat to patentability. Moreover, there is no reasonable basis for denying the second inventor a patent where the first invention was effectively kept from public knowledge.

Second, *Borst*-type disclosures may be used to avoid the goals of the printed publication rule. Publishing involves effort; costs are high, access to scientific journals limited, and libraries restrictive in what they will allow deposited. *Borst* may tempt inventors to use the easier method of protecting their discoveries from being patented by a later inventor at the expense of the greater exchange of information provided by publications.

A more serious defect is that the *Borst*-type disclosure avoids the time limit which patent law imposes on printed publications. Under § 102(b), an inventor loses his patent rights if he does not file an application within one year of publication, public use or sale or patenting of the device. *Borst*-type disclosures, being none of these, do not fall within the one year rule. The decision may thus defeat the policy of this section by enabling inventors to enjoy the pre-patent fruits of discovery with the security that a later inventor cannot gain a patent, but without effectively bringing their ideas before the public.

Finally, *Borst*-type disclosures contain no assurances that the device is of any worth—assurances which other methods of barring patents all possess. An actual reduction to practice proves an invention works. Constructive reductions—the filing of patent applications—are not likely to be based on mere conjecture. Not only do filing and attorney fees exert a sobering effect, but the Commissioner of Patents may require a working model of an invention whose operativeness appears doubtful. Printing expenses, or the scrutiny of publishers and editors, help assure that purely frivolous claims are not likely to be found in printed publications. Moreover, the scientific community is likely to judge irresponsible representations harshly; the risk of reputation helps insure that discoveries revealed in publication are of practical benefit. . . .

METALLIZING ENGINEERING CO., INC. v. KENYON BEARING & AUTO PARTS CO., INC.

United States Circuit Court of Appeals, Second Circuit, 1946.
153 F.2d 516, 68 U.S.P.Q. 54, cert. denied 328 U.S. 840, 66 S.Ct. 1016,
90 L.Ed. 1615, 69 U.S.P.Q. 631.

L. HAND, Circuit Judge.

The defendants appeal from the usual decree holding valid and infringed all but three of the claims of a reissued patent, issued to the plaintiff's assignor, Meduna; the original patent issued on May 25, 1943, upon an application filed on August 6, 1942. . . . The only question which we find necessary to decide is as to Meduna's public use of the patented process more than one year before August 6, 1942. The district judge made findings about this, which are supported by the testimony and which we accept. They appear as findings 8, 9, 10, 11, 12 and 13 on pages 46 and 47 of volume 62 of the Federal Supplement; and we cannot improve upon his statement. The kernel of them is the following: "the inventor's main purpose in his use of the process prior to August 6, 1941, and especially in respect to all jobs for owners not known to him, was commercial, and . . . an experimental purpose in connection with such use was subordinate only." Upon this finding he concluded as matter of law that, since the use before the critical date—August 6, 1941—was not primarily for the purposes of experiment, the use was not excused for that reason. Moreover, he also concluded that the use was not public but secret, and for that reason that its predominantly commercial character did prevent it from invalidating the patent. For the last he relied upon our decisions in Peerless Roll Leaf Co. v. Griffin & Sons, 29 F.2d 646, and Gillman v. Stern, 114 F.2d 28. We think that his analysis of Peerless Roll Leaf Co. v. Griffin & Sons, was altogether correct, and that he had no alternative but to follow that decision; on the other hand, we now think that we were then wrong and that the decision must be overruled for reasons we shall state. Gillman v. Stern, supra, was, however, rightly decided.

Section one of the first and second Patent Acts, 1 Stat. 109 and 318, declared that the petition for a patent must state that the subject matter had not been "before known or used." Section six of the Act of 1836, 5 Stat. 117, changed this by providing in addition that the invention must not at the time of the application for a patent have been "in public use or on sale" with the inventor's "consent or allowance"; and § 7 of the Act of 1839, 5 Stat. 353, provided that "no patent shall be held to be invalid by reason of such purchase, sale, or use prior to the application for a patent . . . except on proof of abandonment of such invention to the public; or that such purchase, sale, or prior use has been for more than two years prior to such application. . . ." Section 4886 of the Revised Statutes made it a condition upon patentability that the invention shall not have been "in public use or on sale for more than two years prior to his application," and that it shall not have been "proved to have been abandoned." This is in substance the same as the Act of 1839, and is precisely the same as § 31 of Title 35, U.S.C.A. except that the prior use is now limited to the United States, and to one year before the application. § 1, Chap. 391, 29 Stat. 692; § 1, Chap. 450, 53 Stat. 1212, 35 U.S.C.A. § 31. So far as we can find, the first case which dealt with the effect of prior use by the patentee was Pennock v. Dialogue, 2 Pet. 1, 4, 7 L.Ed. 327, in which the invention had been completed in 1811, and the patent granted in 1818 for a process of making hose by which the sections were joined together in such a way that the joints resisted pressure as well as the other parts. It did not appear that the joints in any way disclosed the process; but the patentee, between the discovery of the invention and the grant of the patent, had sold 13,000 feet of hose; and as to this the judge charged: "If the public, with the knowledge and tacit consent of the inventor, be permitted to use the invention, without opposition, it is a fraud on the public afterwards to take out a patent." The Supreme Court affirmed a judgment for the defendant, on the ground that the invention had been "known or used before the application." "If an inventor should be permitted to hold back from the knowledge of the public the secrets of his invention; if he should . . . make and sell his invention publicly, and thus gather the whole profits, . . . it would materially retard the progress of science and the useful arts" to allow him fourteen years of legal monopoly "when the danger of competition should force him to secure the exclusive right" 2 Pet. at page 19, 7 L.Ed. 327. In Shaw v. Cooper, 7 Pet. 292, 8 L.Ed. 689, the public use was not by the inventor, but he had neglected to prevent it after he had learned of it, and this defeated the patent. "Whatever may be the intention of the inventor, if he suffers his invention to go into public use, through any means whatsoever, without an immediate assertion of his right, he is not entitled to a patent" 7 Pet. at page 323, 8 L.Ed. 689. In Kendall v. Winsor, 21 How. 322, 16 L.Ed. 165, the inventor had kept the machine secret, but had sold the harness which it produced, so that the facts presented the same situation as here. Since the jury brought in a verdict for the defendant on the issue of abandonment, the case adds nothing except for the dicta on page 328 of 21 How., 16 L.Ed. 165: "the inventor who designedly, and with the view of applying it indefinitely and exclusively for his own profit, withholds his invention from the public, comes not within the policy or objects of the Constitution or acts of Congress." In Egbert v. Lippmann, 104 U.S. 333, 26 L.Ed. 755, although the patent was for the product which was sold, nothing could be learned about it without taking it apart, yet it was a public use within the statute. In Hall v. Macneale, 107 U.S. 90, 2 S.Ct. 73, 27 L.Ed. 367, the situation was the same.

Coming now to our own decisions (the opinions in all of which I wrote), the first was Grasselli Chemical Co. v. National Aniline & Chemical Co., 2 Cir., 26 F.2d 305, in which the patent was for a process which had been kept secret, but the product had been sold upon the market for more than two years. We held that, although the process could not have been discovered from the product, the sales constituted a "prior use," relying upon Egbert v. Lippmann, supra, 104 U.S. 333, 26 L.Ed. 755, and Hall v. Macneale, supra, 107 U.S. 90, 2 S.Ct. 73, 27 L.Ed. 367. There was nothing in this inconsistent with what we are now holding. But in Peerless Roll Leaf Co. v. Griffin & Sons, supra, 2 Cir., 29 F.2d 646, where the patent was for a machine, which had been kept secret, but whose output had been freely sold on the market, we sustained the patent on the ground that "the sale of the product was irrelevant, since no knowledge could possibly be acquired of the machine in that way. In this respect the machine differs from a process   .   .   .   or from any other invention necessarily contained in a product" 29 F.2d at page 649. So far as we can now find, there is nothing to support this distinction in the authorities, and we shall try to show that we misapprehended the theory on which the prior use by an inventor forfeits his right to a patent. In Aerovox Corp. v. Polymet Manufacturing Corp., supra, 2 Cir., 67 F.2d 860, the patent was also for a process, the use of which we held not to have been experimental, though not secret. Thus our decision sustaining the patent was right; but apparently we were by implication reverting to the doctrine of the Peerless case when we added that it was doubtful whether the process could be detected from the product, although we cited only Hall v. Macneale, supra, 107 U.S. 90, 2 S.Ct. 73, 27 L.Ed. 367, and Grasselli Chemical Co. v. National Aniline Co., supra (2 Cir., 26 F.2d 305). In Gillman v. Stern, supra, 2 Cir., 114 F.2d 28, it was not the inventor, but a third person who used the machine secretly and sold the product openly, and there was therefore no question either of abandonment or forfeiture by the inventor. The only issue was whether a prior use which did not disclose the invention to the art was within the statute; and it is well settled that it is not. As in the case of any other anticipation, the issue of invention must then be determined by how much the inventor has contributed any new information to the art.

From the foregoing it appears that in Peerless Roll Leaf Co. v. Griffin & Sons, supra, 2 Cir., 29 F.2d 646, we confused two separate doctrines: (1) The effect upon his right to a patent of the inventor's competitive exploitation of his machine or of his process; (2) the contribution which a prior use by another person makes to the art. Both do indeed come within the phrase, "prior use"; but the first is a defence for quite different reasons from the second. It had its origin —at least in this country—in the passage we have quoted from Pennock v. Dialogue, supra, 2 Pet. 1, 7 L.Ed. 327; i. e., that it is a condition upon an inventor's right to a patent that he shall not exploit his discovery competitively after it is ready for patenting; he must content himself with either secrecy, or legal monopoly. It is true that for the limited period of two years he was allowed to do so, possibly in order to give him time to prepare an application; and even that has been recently cut down by half. But if he goes beyond that period of probation, he forfeits his right regardless of how little the public may have learned about the invention; just as he can forfeit it by too long concealment, even without exploiting the invention at all. Such a forfeiture has nothing to do with abandonment, which presupposes a deliberate, though not necessarily an express, surrender of any right to a patent. Although the evidence of both may at times overlap, each comes from a quite different legal source: one, from the fact that by renouncing the right the inventor irrevocably surrenders it; the other, from the fiat of Congress that it is part of the consideration for a patent that the public shall as soon as possible begin to enjoy the disclosure.

It is indeed true that an inventor may continue for more than a year to practice his invention for his private purposes or his own enjoyment and later patent it. But that is, properly considered, not an exception to the doctrine, for he is not then making use of his secret to gain a competitive advantage over others; he does not thereby extend the period of his monopoly. Besides, as we have seen, even that privilege has its limits, for he may conceal it so long that he will lose his right to a patent even though he does not use it at all. With that question we have not however any concern here.

Judgment reversed; complaint dismissed.

NOTE, 69 HARV.L.REV. 388–389 (1955) *: Plaintiff had patented a process for coating optical glass in which heat was applied to the glass while it was being coated with a metallic salt. The identical method had been conceived earlier by another scientist who, after utilizing it briefly in the manufacture and sale of lenses, had abandoned it. Although sale of the lenses could not inform the public as to the method used, the scientist had revealed the details of this process to some associates, only one of whom was pledged to secrecy. In a suit for patent infringement, the defendant contended that the patent was invalid because of anticipation by others and lack of inventiveness. Held, judgment for plaintiff affirmed. (1) There had been no prior public use of the invention by another person so as to invalidate the patent. (2) The Patent Act of 1952, 35 U.S.C.A. § 103, repudiates recent Supreme Court standards of inventiveness which this patent would not satisfy, and restores earlier criteria, under which the patent is valid. Lyon v. Bausch & Lomb Optical Co., 224 F.2d 530 (2d Cir. 1955), petition for cert. filed, 24 U.S.Law Week 3059 (U.S. Sept. 9, 1955) (No. 379).

A patent may be invalidated by a prior public use or sale by the patentee or by another person, 35 U.S.C.A. § 102(b), or by a prior invention which has not been "abandoned, suppressed or concealed," 35 U.S.C.A. § 102(g). Judge Hand, writing for the court in the instant case, stated that the impossibility of deducing the process from the lenses sold by the prior inventor would not necessarily prevent their sale from being a public use. In taking this view, he apparently disregarded a distinction which he had earlier attempted to introduce in Metallizing Engineering Co. v. Kenyon Bearing & Auto Parts Co., 153 F.2d 516 (2d Cir.), cert. denied, 328 U.S. 840, 66 S.Ct. 1016, 90 L.Ed. 1615 (1946), between public use by the patentee and by another inventor. Judge Hand, holding in that case that a patentee's commercial sale was a public use despite the concealment of the invented process, had emphasized that the statutory purpose was to prevent a patentee from exploiting his own invention before obtaining a government monopoly for a limited period. He then pointed out that sales by other inventors were significant only insofar as they might furnish sufficient information to the industry to prevent a meaningful contribution by a later invention. However, in the instant case, where the sales in question were made by a person other than the patentee, the court stated that the law does not require an inquiry as to whether any information was furnished by the product sold. But it seemed to view § 102(b), in its application to persons other than the patentee as qualified by § 102(g), and thus concluded that the prior inventor's abandonment of the process when it had just emerged from the experimental stage prevented a finding of public use. This factor of early abandonment, however, seems relevant to the issue of public use only insofar as it might indicate a lack of disclosure to the industry of significant technical progress.

IN RE THEIS

United States Court of Customs and Patent Appeals, 1979.
610 F.2d 786, 204 U.S.P.Q. 188.

RICH, Judge.

This appeal is from the decision of the Patent and Trademark Office (PTO) Board of Appeals (board) affirming the rejection of claims 11–23, all claims in application serial No. 604,930, filed August 15, 1975 entitled "Programmed Conversation Recording System." The claims were rejected under 35 U.S.C.A. § 102(b) as drawn to subject matter which had been on sale for more than one year prior to the filing date of the parent application. We affirm.

The Invention

Appellant's invention is a system capable of simulating a conversation with a respondent. The system is programmed with a series of prerecorded statements or questions which are played to the respondent. After hearing each statement, the respondent has an indefinite time in which to give a response which is recorded by the system. The system then responds to the voice or vocal pauses made by the respondent by playing the next statement or question to the respondent and recording the corresponding response until the needed information has been obtained.

Claim 11 is illustrative:

11. Apparatus for simulating a conversation with a respondent including a plurality of prerecorded messages which are playable in sequence in response to a corresponding response from the respondent comprising:

> means for detecting a pause in the respondent's communication;

> means responsive to said pause for playing the next prerecorded message;

> means for detecting a lack of response from the respondent to a prerecorded message; and

> means responsive to said lack of a response for altering said sequence.

Although one of the principal uses contemplated by appellant for his system is in conjunction with a telephone system wherein the respondent is a telephone caller, the claims are not limited to include telephone apparatus. Appellant's specification states that "the system has a number of applications that do not utilize the telephone system," and cites several examples of non-telephone related applications.

Background

In order to overcome a 35 U.S.C.A. § 102(a) rejection based upon a patent issued to Winterhalter, cited by appellant in a prior art statement to the PTO, appellant submitted an affidavit under Rule 131 to swear back of that reference.[2]   Included in the affidavit, dated June 22, 1976, were exhibits I, J, and K, all invoices evidencing delivery to customers of systems embodying the claimed invention.   The affidavit stated that the systems were delivered prior to June 4, 1973, the filing date of the reference.

In response, the examiner entered a rejection under § 102(b), stating:

> Applicant's exhibits I through J [sic K] suggest that the device was "on sale" more [than] one year prior to the filing date of the original application.   In order to overcome this rejection applicant should research the criteria for "experimental use" and then set forth facts which show applicant meets the criteria.

The critical date, one year prior to the date on which appellant's parent application was filed, is February 4, 1973.

In an attempt to overcome the § 102(b) rejection, appellant submitted three additional affidavits of his own, two affidavits by Buchberger, his engineering assistant, and one affidavit by Mitchel, vice president of Market Facts, Inc. (Market Facts), a recipient of two of the systems.

Appellant's additional affidavits stated that six systems had been offered to customers including Montgomery Ward, J. C. Penney, Market Facts, and Household Finance Corporation, prior to the critical date.   In addition, appellant's affidavits, and those of Buchberger, detailed the nature of the problems encountered with the systems, concluded that the systems were incapable of functioning in their intended manner until after the critical date, and set forth the various procedures undertaken to cure the defects.

The Mitchel affidavit corroborated that the systems were delivered to Market Facts and installed prior to the critical date.   The affidavit further stated that the systems did not function, that appellant expended considerable effort in attempts to get them to work, and that the systems never did function as intended and were disconnected.   Accompanying the affidavit were exhibits A, B, and C, copies of correspondence between applicant and Market Facts concerning the acquisition by Market Facts of the systems in question.

The examiner was of the opinion that Exhibits A thru C, submitted with the Mitchel affidavit, evidenced a contract of sale between appellant and Market Facts.   In exhibit A, Mitchel states: "The units when installed will not be considered purchased until both are working to the complete satisfaction of Market Facts."   In exhibit B, Mitchell states, in toto, *"This letter serves as purchase authorization for two Con-Mode [system trademark] units. This purchase is made* under the conditions of our letter to you dated December 6, 1972, and your letter to Market Facts dated December 20, 1972."   (Emphasis ours.)

<hr>

2. The examiner's § 102(a) rejection was reversed by the board.

Appellant contended that the deliveries made prior to the critical date were for experimental purposes and thus fell under the exception to the statutory loss of right to patent provision, § 102(b), which exception has existed at least since Elizabeth v. Pavement Co., 97 U.S. 126, 24 L.Ed. 1000 (1877). For this argument, he relies on the fact that the systems did not work as delivered, the fact that several of the invoices for systems delivered prior to the critical date contained the legend "6 month evaluation," and the fact that the systems, after installation, were constantly modified and repaired by appellant and Buchberger in an attempt to get them to function properly.

Before the board, appellant argued that although the equipment was delivered to various recipients, title to the equipment remained with appellant, and so no "sales" were consummated. He further denied the systems were on sale because they were used by the recipients for evaluation purposes.

Appellant continued to press his argument that the use of the systems prior to the critical date was experimental in nature. In addition, appellant argued that since the systems were inoperative for their intended purposes, they did not embody the claimed invention. Thus, according to appellant, that which was in use prior to the critical date was not the claimed invention, making the loss of right provision of § 102(b) inapplicable.

The Board

The board found that the systems bearing serial Nos. 001–004 were delivered prior to the critical date. The board noted that, of the systems delivered prior to the critical date, only serial No. 001 was, according to the invoice, delivered for a "6 month evaluation." Although Mitchel averred in his affidavit that the systems delivered to Market Facts were for a six-month evaluation period, the board found that this was contradicted by exhibits A, B, and C accompanying the affidavit. The board observed that these letters (portions of which we have quoted supra) were silent regarding any evaluation, experimentation, or control of the systems by appellant.

Appellant had urged that the statement in exhibit A (Mitchel's letter of December 6, 1972), viz: "The units when installed will not be considered purchased until both are working to the complete satisfaction of Market Facts," corroborated the statement in the Mitchel affidavit that the systems were delivered for a six-month evaluation period. However, the board viewed this statement as "no more than a demand for a money back guarantee; a warranty, a right of recission or a right to a refund." The board viewed the exhibits as evidence of a contract of sale:

> The correspondence manifestly constitutes an offer to buy under certain conditions, a counter offer to sell on modified conditions and a purchase authorization. In our opinion, this correspondence between appellant and Mitchel is clear evidence that the equipment was "on sale" prior to the critical date. Whether or

not a sale was, in fact, consummated is not controlling, although, as we view the evidence, a sale to Market Facts was made prior to the critical date.

The board held that other evidence of record tended to bolster its conclusion that the system was on sale prior to the critical date. A letter from appellant responding to questions from Lee Weber, Marketing Manager of Sears Roebuck, dated December 21, 1971, about appellant's "ability to produce adequately for Sears' requirements," purported to "clarify our production abilities" and proposed "a special production line for your requirements." Status reports regarding appellant's attempts to sell to Sears and Wards, both dated February 2, 1972, detailed appellant's plans to have those two giant retailers test the systems against competing systems with the ultimate objective of making a sale. A letter to Charles Brown of Associated Merchandising, dated June 14, 1972, described the system and advised that within a week appellant would be in touch to give Brown a phone number to call for a demonstration of the system. A letter from appellant to John H. Rosenhein of Universal Training Systems Company, dated July 10, 1972, offered to show Rosenhein what Wards and Sears were doing with the system, referring to them as "customers."

Finally, the board relied on a press release, dated January 7, 1973, announcing the system at the National Retail Merchant's Association Annual Retailer's Business and Equipment Exposition, as "strong evidence of an 'on sale' status." At this retailer's trade show, appellant had placed a demonstration model on display. The press release concluded:

> The CON–MODE [trademark used to identify appellant's system] has been developed by Morgan Industries, Inc. and patents are being applied for according to the Company. Conversational Voice Terminal Corporation will act as the national sales and service organization for this important product. *First deliveries are being made this month. If you want to try a CON–MODE call our demonstration system at 312–463–2870!* [Emphasis ours.]

The board rejected appellant's contention that the activity prior to the critical date was, in the eyes of the law, for test and evaluation purposes. It noted that the Sears and Wards status reports indicated that the field tests in which appellant wanted the system included were for the benefit of the retailers, not appellant, and would not have been under appellant's control. As for the "6 month evaluation" notation on invoices for system serial Nos. 001, 002, 005, and 006, the board found the notation ambiguous, since there was "no indication as to evaluation by whom, for what purpose or for whose benefit [the evaluations were to be conducted] and there is certainly no indication that the equipments were subject to appellant's supervision and control." The board concluded that any evaluation was for the purposes of the recipients of the systems, not appellant.

Regarding the averments in the affidavits of Theis and Buchberger that the systems had been modified and tested virtually every day, the board stated that there was no evidence that this was done for the benefit of appellant. It also pointed out that, according to the affidavits, not all of the systems were subjected to such rigorous procedures.

The board further observed that nowhere in the invoices or correspondence had appellant indicated that any limitations or restrictions or injunctions of secrecy had been imposed upon the users of the systems during the six-month evaluation period, citing In re Blaisdell, 44 C.C.P.A. 846, 242 F.2d 779, 113 U.S.P.Q. 289 (1957). Also, the board found no evidence that the recipients of the systems undertook to supply test or operational data to appellant.

Finally, the board rejected appellant's argument that the systems delivered prior to the critical date did not function for their intended purpose and thus could not have embodied the claimed invention, since the claims required that the system function properly in "conversing" with a respondent. Appellant had relied for this proposition on Kayton, Patent Law Perspectives § A.3[5] at A449–A451 (1967–68 Annual Review). The board found that many of the problems encountered by appellant with the systems were caused by the interface with telephone equipment when the system was used in conjunction with a telephone system.

While the board acknowledged that the problems were real in the environments in which the systems were used, it felt that the problems were not germane to the claimed subject matter. The claims are silent with respect to the environment in which the system is to operate, not being limited to use of the system in conjunction with a telephone, although the specification states that the system is chiefly used with telephone equipment. The board held that experimentation to perfect such nonclaimed features does not fall within the experimental exception to the loss of right under § 102(b) on the authority of Minnesota Mining and Manufacturing Co. v. Kent Industries, Inc., 409 F.2d 99, 161 U.S.P.Q. 321 (6th Cir. 1969).

Appellant's Arguments

Before this court, appellant continues to urge that the loss of right provision of § 102(b) cannot apply since the devices delivered prior to the critical date were "inoperative" until long after the critical date. He cites Illinois Tool Works, Inc. v. Solo Cup Co., 179 U.S. P.Q. 322 (N.D.Ill.1973), and other cases for the proposition "that a device which is inoperative for its normal and intended purpose has 'absolutely no prior art status' even if it is 'on sale or in public use' more than one year prior to the effective filing date of a patent application."

Also, appellant continues to argue that the devices delivered prior to the critical date were the subject of bona fide experimentation and thus exempt from § 102(b). He relies on the notation "6 month evaluation" on several of the invoices, and further on the fact that the systems did undergo major modifications while in use at their respective locations before they were usable for their intended purpose.

Finally, appellant argues that public policy considerations demand that he be allowed to properly perfect his invention before being required to apply for a patent. He states that the actions of the PTO in this case work an unnecessary hardship on inventors by forcing them to file their applications before they can make a reasonable determination that their inventions are worth the time and expense of seeking patent protection.

Opinion

An inventor loses his right to a patent if he has placed his invention "on sale in this country, more than one year prior to the date of the application for patent in the United States." 35 U.S.C.A. § 102(b). RULE Even a single, unrestricted sale brings into operation this bar to patentability. Consolidated Fruit-Jar Co. v. Wright, 94 U.S. 92, 94, 24 L.Ed. 68 (1876).

Appellant makes three main contentions. He disputes the finding that the systems were "on sale" prior to the critical date, although he admits that as many as six systems may have been delivered prior to that date. He asserts that § 102(b) cannot apply because his devices were inoperative and thus did not embody the claimed invention, and that any activity prior to the critical date was bona fide experimentation, exempting him from the effect of § 102(b) on the authority of cases such as Elizabeth v. Pavement Co., supra. We shall deal with these contentions in order.

a. The "On Sale" Issue

We think the board had ample evidence by which it could properly conclude that at least one sale took place prior to the critical date. In the absence of an exception to the statutory bar, this would suffice to bar appellant from a patent. Consolidated Fruit-Jar v. Wright, supra. Although it is not clear from the record that delivery of the systems to Market Facts actually took place prior to the critical date, delivery is not the crucial event.

For § 102(b) to apply, it is not necessary that a sale be consummated. It suffices that the claimed invention, reduced to practice, was placed on sale, i. e., offered to potential customers, prior to the critical date. Even if no delivery is made prior to the critical date, the existence of a sales contract prior to that date has been held to constitute an "on sale" status for the invention if it has been reduced "to a reality." Hobbs v. United States, Atomic Energy Commission, 451 F.2d 849, 859, 171 U.S.P.Q. 713, 720 (5th Cir. 1971) and cases cited. As the court there said, "an invention passes out of the experimental stage and becomes a reality for purpose of the statutory bar even though it may later be refined or improved." The fact that delivery may have occurred after the critical date is of no moment.

The record shows that, as early as December 6, 1972, almost two months prior to the critical date, appellant was negotiating with Market Facts in an attempt to sell his systems. We agree with the board that the correspondence between appellant and Mitchel (exhibits A–C accompanying the Mitchel affidavit) appears to constitute a contract of sale for a presently available system.

The Market Facts invoice does not indicate that the delivery was for an evaluation period. Neither the board nor this court consider that the Mitchel exhibits provide any support for the contention that Market Facts was to evaluate the system for appellant's benefit. Thus the board was correct in refusing to give weight to the statement in the Mitchel affidavit that the transaction was for experimental purposes.

There was other independent evidence before the board which justifies the conclusion that the system was "on sale" prior to the critical date. Appellant's correspondence with Sears, and the status reports concerning Sears and Wards, as well as the press release for the National Retail Merchant's Association trade show were considered by the board to be "strong evidence" on this point.[6] "On sale" status may be found from activity by the inventor or his company in attempting to market the invention. This is because the inventor's loss of right to a patent flows from the attempt to profit from the invention by commercial exploitation beyond the grace period allowed by Congress.

b. *The Experimental Exception Issue*

Appellant argues that loss of right under § 102(b) should not apply here because the system was the subject of bona fide experimentation prior to the critical date. Since we have agreed with the board that appellant's system was "on sale" prior to the critical date, appellant must show that he comes under the Elizabeth v. Pavement Co. experimental use or sale exception by proof which is "full, unequivocal, and convincing." Smith & Griggs Manufacturing Co. v. Sprague, 123 U.S. 249, 264, 8 S.Ct. 122, 3 L.Ed. 141 (1887).

Appellant's argument must fail. We agree with the analysis made by the board. The notation "6 month evaluation" on several of the invoices is equivocal. It is not clear on the face of the invoices who is to benefit from the evaluation. It is as likely that the evaluation was for the benefit of the customer, who would want to know if the system suited his purposes, as for the benefit of appellant. Such "market testing" does not fall within the experimental use exception, because it is "a trader's, and not an inventor's experiment." Smith & Davis Manufacturing Co. v. Mellon, 58 F. 705, 707 (8th Cir. 1893). In addition, the notation does not appear on all of the invoices. As

---

6. We find the activities of appellant at the trade show to be particularly probative. Appellant was unquestionably seeking to penetrate the market at the time of the show. The statement in appellant's press release, "First deliveries are being made this month," is a fairly strong indication that the system was "on sale" at that time, and is inconsistent with the assertion that the system was still in the development stage.

we have already discussed, with respect to the systems delivered to Market Facts, there were no restrictions or qualifications for the benefit of appellant. The full price was charged. Like the board, we view that transaction as an outright sale.

It is settled law that the experimental sale exception does not apply to experiments performed with respect to non-claimed features of an invention. It appears from the record that most of the "experimenting" done on the systems was done for the purpose of correcting problems with the telephone interface. The claims do not require that the system be used with a telephone system. Thus, any work done to improve the operation of the system as it is used with telephone equipment does not aid appellant's experimental use argument.

Although appellant has alleged that other problems, not related to the telephone system, were encountered with his system, we do not believe that his efforts to correct those problems, in the context of all of the facts developed in the record, warrant a reversal of the board's decision. We agree with the board that the problems associated with the pause timing, spurious noise from radio interference and other nearby equipment, drifting filters, and arcing relay contacts were solvable by routine debugging, setup, and installation adjustments.[8]

The context in which all of appellant's activities in the period immediately preceding the critical date exist is clearly that of an attempt at market penetration. Even if there is a bona fide experimental purpose, an inventor may not commercially exploit his invention for more than one year prior to the filing of his patent application. The experimental exception applies only if the commercial exploitation is merely incidental to the primary purpose of experimentation to perfect the invention. On the strength of the evidence of record, the board was correct in holding that the primary motivation behind appellant's activities was commercial, and that the experimental use or sale exception should not apply in this case.[9]

c. The Inoperativeness Issue

Appellant also relies on the theory that the bar of § 102(b) should not apply because, at the time prior to the critical date when Market Facts and others were using the systems, the systems were "inoperative." It appears that appellant argues the views appearing in the treatise, Patent Law Perspectives (PLP). The theory is that

---

8. It appears that all these problems were solved without the need to change any of the major functional blocks of the system. Flattening filter response, supplying arc suppression and radio frequency interference suppression capacitors, and adjusting pause intervals are minor "tune up" procedures not requiring an inventor's skills, but rather the skills of a competent technician, such as appellant's assistant Buchberger.

9. Like the PTO, we find it difficult to believe that major retailers, such as Sears and Wards, would permit appellant to experiment with his system on their telephone lines at the expense of their high volume mail-order business. Appellant's status reports, previously referred to, indicate that what Sears and Wards had in mind was comparative testing between appellant's system and competing systems to determine which was more suitable for their needs.

during the period when the invention is not yet operative it does not exist since it has not yet been reduced to practice, and therefore cannot be used, sold, or placed on sale.

We find this argument wanting because appellant has failed to show that the *claimed invention* was inoperative. As pointed out by the board, the chief cause of the alleged inoperativeness of appellant's systems in the hands of users was telephone line interface problems. In view of the fact that the claims do not require the use of telephones, these problems could not have prevented a reduction to practice under the PLP analysis because the invention claimed is independent of telephones and can be reduced to practice without them.

Furthermore, with respect to the other problems referred to in the affidavits, we view them as minor and not precluding actual reduction to practice in the eyes of one of ordinary skill in the art.[11] In any event, there is no evidence that the demonstration model was in any way defective. We find it difficult to imagine that appellant would demonstrate an inoperative system at a trade show and elsewhere in an attempt to drum up business.

One further argument pressed by appellant with regard to this issue deserves comment. In his brief here, appellant states that it is the law "that a device which is inoperative for its normal and intended purpose has 'absolutely no prior art status' even if it is 'on sale or in public use' more than one year prior to the effective filing date of a patent application." For this proposition, he cites, inter alia, Illinois Tool Works, Inc. v. Solo Cup Co., supra.

Appellant's reliance on this case is misplaced. *Prior art* is not involved in this case. Here appellant has *lost his right to a patent* by attempting to commercially exploit his invention for a period longer than Congress allows. This is not the same as refusing to treat a defective reference as prior art, which is what was involved in the Illinois Tool Works case. In the former situation, an inventor, by delay, *forfeits* a right he would otherwise enjoy; in the latter situation a defective reference is disregarded because it does not work.

Appellant argues that public policy demands that he be given time to adequately develop his invention before being forced to file a patent application. All we have to say is that the law gives him a year. He cannot expand it.

The decision of the board is affirmed.

Affirmed.

NOTES

1. The path through section 102 is tortuous and strewn with snares. Patent law's refusal to protect subject matter that will not

---

11. There is no requirement that an invention function perfectly in order to be reduced to practice or considered as on sale or in public use. All that is necessary is that the invention be commercially operable; it may have problems which are not due to "fundamental defects." National Biscuit Co. v. Crown Baking Co., 105 F. 2d 422, 424, 42 U.S.P.Q. 214, 215 (1st Cir. 1939).

increase the present store of information does at least offer a rough-and-ready guide through the thicket: if the subject matter sought to be patented is disclosed by any other source, the patent, because it will serve no socially useful purpose, will be denied.

Section 102's complexity lies not so much in its deviation from this principle as in its reliance upon several distinctions for the principle's enforcement. Consider, for example, the distinctions that underlie this synthesis of the novelty requirements: An inventor cannot obtain a patent for his subject matter if it has been known or used in this country by others before he invented it, or if it has been patented or described in a printed publication in this or a foreign country more than one year before he applied for a patent, or if it has been in public use or on sale in this country for more than one year before the date of his application.

These distinctions, explored in the notes that follow, interrelate in permutations of two and three, a fact that stirs no little confusion in courts and law offices.

2. There is some overlap between the terms that subsections 102(a) and (b) employ to itemize and distinguish among the various anticipating sources—"known," "used," "patented," "described in a printed publication," "public use," and "sale." For example, although a patent can anticipate even if it is not printed, a patent once printed also constitutes a printed publication. When, as in some countries, an invention's complete specifications are published before the patent is granted, it is the printed publication rather than the patent that poses the earlier bar. And since for a sale to anticipate under section 102(b) it can be neither secret nor conditional, some "knowledge" or "use" of the invention will be implicit in the transaction. See generally, Note, New Guidelines for Applying the On Sale Bar to Patentability, 24 Stan.L.Rev. 730 (1972).

Two requirements are common to all these sources of prior art. First, the anticipating source must place the claimed subject matter within public reach. Second, the source must disclose the subject matter for which patent protection is sought with sufficient clarity to instruct those skilled in the relevant art to recreate it. This second requirement, explicated in *Borst*, has received more liberal treatment in some circuits than in others. Compare, for example, Bros, Inc. v. W. E. Grace Mfg. Co., 351 F.2d 208, 147 U.S.P.Q. 1 (5th Cir. 1965), cert. denied, 383 U.S. 936, 86 S.Ct. 1065, 15 L.Ed.2d 852, 148 U.S.P.Q. 772 with Bros Inc. v. Browning Mfg. Co., 317 F.2d 413, 137 U.S.P.Q. 624 (8th Cir. 1963), cert. denied, 375 U.S. 825, 84 S.Ct. 67, 11 L.Ed.2d 25, 139 U.S.P.Q. 565, and with Gibson-Stewart Co. v. William Bros. Boiler & Mfg. Co., 264 F.2d 776, 120 U.S.P.Q. 352 (6th Cir. 1959), cert. denied, 360 U.S. 929, 79 S.Ct. 1448, 3 L.Ed.2d 1544, 121 U.S.P.Q. 654.

3. What is a "printed publication"? In a long and thoughtful essay, Gerald Rose concludes that the law on the subject is "a mud-

dled mess." Rose samples some holdings on what is and is not a printed publication:

"(a) a handwritten manuscript in a public library is *not*.

(b) A single typewritten thesis in a college library *is*.

(c) a scientific paper delivered orally to an audience is *not*.

(d) a scientific paper submitted for refereeing before publication *is*.

(e) an article in a Russian library was *not*.

(f) an instruction sheet distributed on one island in Japan *is*.

(g) a microfilm in the Library of Congress *is* or *is not*, depending on whether it is properly indexed.

. (h) a trade circular that is thrown away *is*."

Rose, Do You Have a "Printed Publication?" If Not, Do You Have Evidence of Prior "Knowledge or Use?" 61 J.P.O.S. 643, 644 (1979).

One way to clear the "printed publication" muddle is to consult the term's intended function within the context of section 102. The term printed publication embodies section 102's requirement that prior art be publicly accessible. The fact that a reference is both printed and published offers strong evidence of its public availability. Indeed, the leading case on the point concluded that "once it has been established that the item has been both printed and published, it is not necessary to further show that any given number of people actually saw it or that any specific number of copies have been circulated. The law sets up a *conclusive presumption* to the effect that the public has knowledge of the publication when a single printed copy is proved to have been so published." In re Tenney, 45 C.C.P.A. 894, 254 F.2d 619, 626–627, 117 U.S.P.Q. 348 (1958) (emphasis the court's). See also, In re Bayer, 568 F.2d 1357, 196 U.S.P.Q. 670 (C. C.P.A.1978).

When, if at all, did publication occur under the following facts: On April 30, 1959, a printer delivered a report disclosing the claimed subject matter to *J*, a research laboratory's technical editor. On May 5, 1959, *J* mailed these copies to individuals on a distribution list. *J*, testifies "that if counsel had come to her office on April 30, and requested a copy of the report, he would 'very likely' have been given one." Both parties concede that if the report was published more than one year before May 3, 1960, the patent would be invalid under section 102(b). See University of Illinois Foundation v. Blonder-Tongue Laboratories, Inc., 422 F.2d 769, 164 U.S.P.Q. 545 (7th Cir. 1970), vacated, 402 U.S. 313, 91 S.Ct. 1434, 28 L.Ed.2d 788, 167 U.S.P.Q. 321. Would the invention have been "known" under section 102(a)?

4. Section 102 distinguishes between anticipating events that occur in the United States and those that occur abroad. Two questions frequently arise in determining whether a foreign patent or printed publication anticipates: Does the foreign document, regardless of its characterization under local law, in fact constitute a patent

or printed publication? If so, to what extent does the patent or publication disclose the subject matter in question?

Both questions were raised and answered in Carter Products Inc. v. Colgate-Palmolive Co., 130 F.Supp. 557, 104 U.S.P.Q. 314 (D.Md. 1955), aff'd, 230 F.2d 855, 108 U.S.P.Q. 383 (4th Cir.). Defendant argued that, over a year before the patent in suit was applied for, an Argentine patent had been granted on identical subject matter. The Argentine patent, defendant contended, also constituted a printed publication so that patentability was barred on not one, but two section 102(b) grounds.

Reasoning from the undisputed premise "that what was publicly known or used in the foreign country is not a bar to a United States patent unless such was either patented or described in a printed publication in the foreign country," the court rebutted both contentions. First, "since the Argentine patent is a typewritten document, it could not qualify as printed." Second, the court found it "necessary to determine what was in fact 'patented' by the Argentine patent." Resting its conclusion upon the testimony of two experts in Argentine law and upon a statement in the patent itself, the court ruled that the scope of the patent was limited to its claim, which in no way taught the subject matter in question: "the three composition examples set forth in the Argentine patent, upon which defendants rely .   .   . bear no relationship to the claimed subject matter of the Argentine patent, and also are unrelated to anything else in the patent specification." The court was alternatively disposed to ignore Argentine law entirely and impose the United States domestic rule of patent construction: "That nothing is to be treated as patented except what is actually claimed therein is well settled under our decisions."

Goldman, Anticipatory Value of Foreign Patents, 37 J.P.O.S. 405 (1955), surveys the functions of foreign prior art. Coordination of the timing of domestic and foreign applications under sections 102(d), 119, and 185 is discussed in the Goldman article and in Note, Foreign Priority Rights Under Section 119 of the Patent Act of 1952, 25 Geo.Wash.L.Rev. 75 (1956), and Fishman, An Analysis of the Combined Effect of 35 U.S.C.A. § 119 and 35 U.S.C.A. § 102(e), 46 J.P.O.S. 181 (1964). See generally, Chisum, Foreign Activity: Its Effect on Patentability Under United States Law, 11 Int'l.Rev.Indus.Prop. & Copyright L. 26 (1980).

5. Section 102 also distinguishes between the acts of an inventor seeking patent protection and the acts of others. Comparison of subsections (a) and (b) reveals a difference not only in operative point of time, but a difference in the range of persons whose conduct is relevant. Knowledge or use under subsection (a) must be "by others," while public use or sale in (b) is not so limited. Simply, under section 102(b), the incautious inventor may discover that he has barred his own claim. Although this bar looks exactly like the novelty bar, its motive is clearly different. "It is well settled that the policy consideration behind the 'public use' rule is to stimulate a seasona-

ble disclosure of new inventions within the framework of the patent laws." Atlas v. Eastern Airlines, Inc., 311 F.2d 156, 136 U.S.P.Q. 4 (1st Cir. 1962). An analogous motive underlies subsections (d), (e) and, in part, (g).

See generally, Zieg, Developments in the Law of "On Sale," 58 J.P.O.S. 470 (1976).

6. Was section 102(b) applied too strictly in Egbert v. Lippmann, 104 U.S. 333, 26 L.Ed. 755 (1881)? Defendant, charged with infringement, argued that the subject matter in suit—corset springs—had been publicly used by its inventor more than two years (the grace period then in effect) before he filed his patent application. Evidently, eleven years before filing, the inventor had presented his fiancee with a pair of the corset springs. During this period she was the only person to use them and, by their nature, they were not exposed to public view.

The Court, concerned that the inventor had "slept on his rights for eleven years," decided that the facts supported a finding of public use. To be public, the Court declared, a use need not be of more than one device, nor by more than one person. The decisive fact was that the inventor had given the device to his fiancee without at the same time restricting its use. Justice Miller indulged some refreshing realism in his dissent: "It may well be imagined that a prohibition to the party so permitted against exposing her use of the steel spring to public observation would have been supposed to be a piece of irony."

Even the *Egbert* Court recognized that experimental use should not constitute public use and that any block of time devoted to the invention's development and refinement should be excluded from computation of the prior use period. As indicated in *Theis,* the experimental use exception is applied stringently and requires a careful distinction between tests of the invention's utility and practical value, which are excluded from the time computation, and tests of its marketability and commercial value, which are included. The experimental use exception is thoughtfully examined in Note, The Public Use Bar to Patentability: Two New Approaches to the Experimental Use Exception, 52 Minn.L.Rev. 851 (1968).

7. Several of section 102's distinctions are rehearsed in section 102(g). Subsection (g)'s bar is, for example, limited to prior inventions made in "this country" by "another". Also, the term, "abandoned," holds the same consequence for the prior inventor under section 102(g) as it does for the applicant inventor under section 102(c).

Unlike its companion subsections, however, section 102(g) does double service. It forms the basis for determining which of two or more applicants claiming priority for the same invention is to be awarded a patent. The role of these determinations, rendered in the first instance in the Patent and Trademark Office in the course of interference proceedings, is noted at p. 575, below.

See generally, Roberts, First to Invent—A Fading Concept?, 61 J.P.O.S. 350 (1979).

8. To qualify for protection, patent subject matter must have been "conceived" and "reduced to practice." The distinction between conception and reduction to practice is central to the operation of section 102's novelty provisions. Section 102(g) employs the distinction to determine priority of invention as between competing inventors. It assigns priority not to the first inventor who completed the invention—conceived and reduced it to practice—but rather to the first who conceived it. Reduction to practice comes into play only in the requirement that priority may be defeated if the first inventor to conceive was not reasonably diligent in reducing his conception to practice. The distinction is also implicit in subsections 102(a) and (b). For anticipating subject matter to have been patented, used or known, it must have been reduced to practice. Knowledge or use of a conception alone will not anticipate.

The measure of conception is simple enough. It requires that there exist at the threshold of the invention some idea of a useful result to be achieved and some specific method for achieving that result. Reduction to practice, which requires that the conception be embodied in some readily utilizable form, has received three different formulations. The first, original formula identifies reduction with that moment at which the invention is first made to work in the environment in which it is to be used rather than in some experimental setting. Under this rule, a voting machine intended for use in public elections is not reduced to practice by its use in the election of a corporate board of directors. Occumpaugh v. Norton, 25 App.D.C. 90 (D.C.Cir. 1905).

The Telephone Cases, 126 U.S. 1, 8 S.Ct. 778, 31 L.Ed. 863 (1888), involving two of Alexander Bell's patents, established the first broad exception to the orthodox formula. The Court there decided that it was inconsequential that, at the time the patent in dispute issued to him, Bell had not reduced his device to actual practice, nor even demonstrated that it could transmit intelligible sounds. Actual reduction was unnecessary, the Court held, since Bell had in the specifications of his patent application described the device with sufficient accuracy to instruct a workman ordinarily skilled in the art to construct a manifestly operative device. The Court viewed reduction to practice as a function of two statutory objectives—that patented subject matter be operative, and that it be placed in a form capable of teaching the public how to recreate it. The first objective could be met under the statutory test of utility, for which proof of operability short of reduction will suffice. The second could be met by the detailed and precise specifications required for the patent application. From this the Court concluded that the filing of a patent application should operate as a constructive reduction to practice of the underlying invention.

Borst, decided almost a century later, invoked the same statutory objectives to derive the third formulation of reduction to practice.

c.   SECTIONS 102 AND 103 IN CONCERT: WHAT IS PRIOR ART?

APPLICATION OF FOSTER, 343 F.2d 980, 987–990, 145 U.S.P.Q.
166 (C.C.P.A.), cert. denied, 383 U.S. 966, 86 S.Ct. 1270, 16 L.Ed.2d
307, 149 U.S.P.Q. 906 (1965).   ALMOND, J.: Sections 101, 102 and
103, generally speaking, deal with two different matters: (1) the
factors to be considered in determining whether a patentable invention
has been *made*, i. e., novelty, utility, unobviousness, and the categories
of patentable subject matter; and (2) "loss of right to patent" as stated
in the heading of section 102, even though an otherwise patentable invention has been made.   On the subject of loss of right, appellant's brief
contains a helpful review of the development of the statutory law since
1793.   It says:

> "In 1897 the patent laws were amended to make the
> .   .   . two-year bar period apply to all public uses, publica-
> tions and patents *regardless of the source* from which they ema-
> nated.   The change was a consequence, primarily, of greatly im-
> proved communications within the country which had rendered
> inventors easily able to acquire knowledge of the public acts of
> others within their own fields.   It was reasoned that any inven-
> tor who *delayed in filing* a patent application for more than two
> years after a public disclosure of the invention would obtain *an
> undeserved reward in derogation of the rights of the public* if he
> were granted a patent.

> "In 1939, in recognition of further improvements in commu-
> nications, Congress reduced the two-year bar period to one year.

> .   .   .

> "That 1939 Act was carried over unchanged in the 1952 re-
> codification of the patent laws as 35 U.S.C.A. § 102(b).   .   .   .

> "Manifestly, Section 102(b) from its earliest beginnings has
> been and was intended to be directed toward the encouragement
> of *diligence* in the filing of patent applications and the protection
> of the public from monopolies on subject matter which had al-
> ready been fully disclosed to it."

These statements are in accord with our understanding of the
history and purposes of section 102(b).   It presents a sort of statute
of limitations, formerly two years, now one year, within which an inventor, even though he has made a patentable invention, must act on
penalty of loss of his right to patent.   What starts the period running
is clearly the availability of the invention *to the public* through the
categories of disclosure enumerated in 102(b), which include "a
printed publication" anywhere describing the invention.   There appears to be no dispute about the operation of this statute in "complete anticipation" situations but *the contention seems to be that
102(b) has no applicability where the invention is not completely disclosed in a single patent or publication,* that is to say where the rejec-

tion involves the addition to the disclosure of the reference of the ordinary skill of the art or the disclosure of another reference which indicates what those of ordinary skill in the art are presumed to know, *and to have known for more than a year before the application was filed.* Upon a complete reexamination of this matter we are convinced that the contention is contrary to the policy consideration which motivated the enactment by Congress of a statutory bar. On logic and principle we think this contention is unsound, and we also believe it is contrary to the patent law as it has actually existed since at least 1898.

First, as to principle, since the purpose of the statute has always been to require filing of the application within the prescribed period after the time the public came into possession of the invention, we cannot see that it makes any difference *how* it came into such possession, whether by a public use, a sale, a single patent or publication, or by combinations of one or more of the foregoing. In considering this principle *we assume*, of course, that by these means *the invention has become obvious* to that segment of the "public" having ordinary skill in the art. Once this has happened, the purpose of the law is to give the inventor only a year within which to file and this would seem to be liberal treatment. Whenever an applicant undertakes, under Rule 131,[1] to swear back of a reference having an effective date more than a year before his filing date, he is automatically conceding that he made his invention more than a year before he filed. If the reference contains enough disclosure to make his invention obvious, the principle of the statute would seem to require denial of a patent to him. The same is true where a combination of two publications or patents makes the invention obvious and they both have dates more than a year before the filing date.

As to dealing with the express language of 102(b), for example, "described in a printed publication," technically, we see no reason to so read the words of the statute as to preclude the use of more than one reference; nor do we find in the context anything to show that "a printed publication" cannot include two or more printed publica-

---

1. *"131. Affidavit of prior invention to overcome cited patent or publication.* (a) When any claim of an application is rejected on reference to a domestic patent which substantially shows or describes but does not claim the rejected invention, or on reference to a foreign patent or to a printed publication, and the applicant shall make oath to facts showing a completion of the invention in this country before the filing date of the application on which the domestic patent issued, or before the date of the foreign patent, or before the date of the printed publication, then the patent or publication cited shall not bar the grant of a patent to the applicant, *unless the date of such pat-*

ent or printed publication be more than one year prior to the date on which the application was filed in this country." [Emphasis ours.]

The italicized clause at the end of the foregoing paragraph or its equivalent has been present in the rule and its predecessor Rule 75 since January 1, 1898, when the rule was amended to include:

". . . unless the date of such patent or printed publication is more than two years prior to the date on which application was filed in this country."

[Opinion of court, 343 F.2d 980, 987 n. 8.]

tions. We do not have two publications here, but we did in Palmquist [319 F.2d 547, 138 U.S.P.Q. 234 (1963)] and it is a common situation.

As to what the law has been, more particularly what it was prior to 1953, when the new patent act and its section 103 became effective, there is a paucity of direct precedents on the precise problem. We think there is a reason for this. Under the old law (R.S. § 4886, where 102(b) finds its origin) patents were refused or invalidated on references dated more than a year before the filing date because the invention was anticipated or, if they were not, then *because there was no "invention,"* the latter rejection being based either on (a) a single nonanticipatory reference plus the skill of the art *or (b) on a plurality of references.* There was no need to seek out the precise statutory basis because it was R.S. § 4886 in any event, read in the light of the Supreme Court's interpretation of the law that there must always be "invention." This issue was determined on the disclosures of the references relied on and if they had dates more than one year before the filing date, it was assumed they could be relied on to establish a "statutory bar." There was an express prohibition in Rule 131 and in its predecessor Rule 75 against antedating a reference having a date more than a year prior to the filing date and there was no basis on which to contest it. .   .   .

It would seem that the practical operation of the prior law was that references having effective dates more than a year before applicant's filing date were always considered to be effective as references, regardless of the applicant's date of invention, and that rejections were then predicated thereon for "lack of invention" without making the distinction which we now seem to see as implicit in sections 102 and 103, "anticipation" or no novelty situations under 102 and "obviousness" situations under 103. But on further reflection, we now feel bound to point out that of equal importance is the question of *loss of right* predicated on a one-year *time-bar* which, it seems clear to us, has never been limited to "anticipation" situations, involving only a single reference, but has included as well "no invention" (now "obviousness") situations. It follows that where the time-bar is involved, *the actual date of invention becomes irrelevant* and that it is not in accordance with either the letter or the principle of the law, or its past interpretation over a very long period, to permit an applicant to dispose of a reference having a date more than one year prior to his filing date by proving his actual date of invention.

Such a result was permitted by our decision in Palmquist and to the extent that it permitted a reference, having a publication date more than one year prior to the United States filing date to which the applicant was entitled, to be disposed of by proof of a date of invention earlier than the date of the reference, that decision is hereby overruled.

We wish to make it clear that this ruling is predicated on our construction of section 102(b) and has no effect on the statements in

Palmquist respecting the determination of obviousness under section 103 when a statutory time-bar is not involved. The existence of unobviousness under that section, as a necessary prerequisite to patentability, we reiterate, must be determined as of "the time the invention was made" without utilizing after-acquired knowledge.

HAZELTINE RESEARCH, INC. v. BRENNER

Supreme Court of the United States, 1965.
382 U.S. 252, 86 S.Ct. 335, 15 L.Ed.2d 304, 147 U.S.P.Q. 429.

Mr. Justice BLACK delivered the opinion of the Court.

The sole question presented here is whether an application for patent pending in the Patent Office at the time a second application is filed constitutes part of the "prior art" as that term is used in 35 U.S.C.A. § 103, which reads in part:

> "A patent may not be obtained .   .   . if the differences between the subject matter sought to be patented and the prior art are such that the subject matter as a whole would have been obvious at the time the invention was made to a person having ordinary skill in the art.   .   .   ."

The question arose in this way. On December 23, 1957, petitioner Robert Regis filed an application for a patent on a new and useful improvement on a microwave switch. On June 24, 1959, the Patent Examiner denied Regis' application on the ground that the invention was not one which was new or unobvious in light of the prior art and thus did not meet the standards set forth in § 103. The Examiner said that the invention was unpatentable because of the joint effect of the disclosures made by patents previously issued, one to Carlson (No. 2,491,644) and one to Wallace (No. 2,822,526). The Carlson patent had been issued on December 20, 1949, over eight years prior to Regis' application, and that patent is admittedly a part of the prior art insofar as Regis' invention is concerned. The Wallace patent, however, was pending in the Patent Office when the Regis application was filed. The Wallace application had been pending since March 24, 1954, nearly three years and nine months before Regis filed his application and the Wallace patent was issued on February 4, 1958, 43 days after Regis filed his application.[1]

After the Patent Examiner refused to issue the patent, Regis appealed to the Patent Office Board of Appeals on the ground that the Wallace patent could not be properly considered a part of the prior art because it had been a "co-pending patent" and its disclosures were secret and not known to the public. The Board of Appeals rejected this argument and affirmed the decision of the Patent Examiner. Regis and Hazeltine, which had an interest as assignee, then instituted the present action in the District Court pursuant to 35 U.S.C.A. §

---

1. It is not disputed that Regis' alleged invention, as well as his application, was made after Wallace's application was filed. There is, therefore, no question of priority of invention before us.

145 to compel the Commissioner to issue the patent. The District Court agreed with the Patent Office that the co-pending Wallace application was a part of the prior art and directed that the complaint be dismissed. 226 F.Supp. 459. On appeal the Court of Appeals affirmed per curiam. 119 U.S.App.D.C. 261, 340 F.2d 786. We granted certiorari to decide the question of whether a co-pending application is included in the prior art, as that term is used in 35 U.S.C.A. § 103. 380 U.S. 960.

Petitioners' primary contention is that the term "prior art," as used in § 103, really means only art previously publicly known. In support of this position they refer to a statement in the legislative history which indicates that prior art means "what was known before as described in section 102." [2] They contend that the use of the word "known" indicates that Congress intended prior art to include only inventions or discoveries which were already publicly known at the time an invention was made.

If petitioners are correct in their interpretation of "prior art," then the Wallace invention, which was not publicly known at the time the Regis application was filed, would not be prior art with regard to Regis' invention. This is true because at the time Regis filed his application the Wallace invention, although pending in the Patent Office, had never been made public and the Patent Office was forbidden by statute from disclosing to the public, except in special circumstances, anything contained in the application.

The Commissioner, relying chiefly on Alexander Milburn Co. v. Davis-Bournonville Co., 270 U.S. 390, 46 S.Ct. 324, 70 L.Ed. 651, contends that when a patent is issued, the disclosures contained in the patent become a part of the prior art as of the time the application was filed, not, as petitioners contend, at the time the patent is issued. In that case a patent was held invalid because, at the time it was applied for, there was already pending an application which completely and adequately described the invention. In holding that the issuance of a patent based on the first application barred the valid issuance of a patent based on the second application, Mr. Justice Holmes, speaking for the Court, said, "The delays of the patent office ought not to cut down the effect of what has been done. . . . [The first applicant] had taken steps that would make it public as soon as the Patent Office did its work, although, of course, amendments might be required of him before the end could be reached. We see no reason in the words or policy of the law for allowing [the second applicant] to profit by the delay. . . ." At p. 401, 46 S.Ct. at p. 325.

In its revision of the patent laws in 1952, Congress showed its approval of the holding in *Milburn* by adopting 35 U.S.C.A. § 102(e) which provides that a person shall be entitled to a patent unless "(e) the invention was described in a patent granted on an application for patent by another filed in the United States before the invention

2. H.R.Rep. No. 1923, 82d Cong., 2d
    Sess., p. 7 (1952).

thereof by the applicant for patent." Petitioners suggest, however, that the question in this case is not answered by mere reference to § 102(e), because in *Milburn*, which gave rise to that section, the co-pending applications described the same identical invention. But here the Regis invention is not precisely the same as that contained in the Wallace patent, but is only made obvious by the Wallace patent in light of the Carlson patent. We agree with the Commissioner that this distinction is without significance here. While we think petition-ers' argument with regard to § 102(e) is interesting, it provides no reason to depart from the plain holding and reasoning in the *Milburn* case. The basic reasoning upon which the Court decided the *Milburn* case applies equally well here. When Wallace filed his application, he had done what he could to add his disclosures to the prior art. The rest was up to the Patent Office. Had the Patent Office acted faster, had it issued Wallace's patent two months earlier, there would have been no question here. As Justice Holmes said in *Milburn*, "The de-lays of the patent office ought not to cut down the effect of what has been done." P. 401, 46 S.Ct. at p. 325.

To adopt the result contended for by petitioners would create an area where patents are awarded for unpatentable advances in the art. We see no reason to read into § 103 a restricted definition of "prior art" which would lower standards of patentability to such an extent that there might exist two patents where the Congress has plainly di-rected that there should be only one.

Affirmed.

NOTES

1. *Foster* has generally been followed in the circuits. See, for example, Frantz Mfg. Co. v. Phenix Mfg. Co., 457 F.2d 314, 173 U.S. P.Q. 266 (7th Cir. 1972); Package Devices, Inc. v. Sun Ray Drug Co., 432 F.2d 272, 167 U.S.P.Q. 193 (3d Cir. 1970), cert. denied, 401 U.S. 956, 91 S.Ct. 977, 28 L.Ed.2d 239, 168 U.S.P.Q. 737. But see Tee-Pak, Inc. v. St. Regis Paper, 491 F.2d 1193, 181 U.S.P.Q. 75 (6th Cir. 1974). *Hazeltine*, too, has been accepted.

Foster allows a wider range of references to bar patentability un-der section 102(b) than the "complete anticipation" measure of sec-tion 102(a). *Hazeltine* rolls the section 103 measure forward to in-clude references that first arise or become public after the date of in-vention. To what extent does the combined logic of the two decisions obliterate the distinctions between sections 102 and 103?

2. Judge Smith, who wrote for a unanimous court in *Palmquist*, dissented in *Foster* which overruled it. In Smith's view, neither sec-tion 102 nor 103 expressly addressed the issue raised by *Foster* and *Palmquist*, and the court reached too far to repair the legislative oversight. According to Smith, the majority decision "amounts to an interpretation of section 102(b) as though it contained the following italicized words:

A person shall be entitled to a patent unless—. . . (b) the invention was patented or described in a printed publication in

this or a foreign country or in public use or on sale in this country *or unless the invention became obvious* more than one year prior to the date of the application for patent in the United States
. . . .

Further, "the majority must also intend to rewrite section 103 so that the phrase 'at the time the invention was made' now is to be limited by a proviso which reduces this time to a period of one year prior to the filing of the application." 343 F.2d 980, 996–997.

In Smith's opinion the majority decision also contradicted good patent policy. "In overruling *Palmquist*, the majority gives lip service to the truism that 'section 103 per se has nothing whatever to do' with the issue of loss of right to patent, but then proceeds to decide the case as one of obviousness using Binder [the defeating reference] as *prior art* under section 103, which it most emphatically is not, since it did not exist 'at the time the invention was made'. . . . Today's decision destroys any meaningful differences that may have existed in the past between sections 102(a) and (b) and section 103. . . . Most disturbing of all is the fact that from this day forward obviousness under section 103 will be tested, *not as of the time the invention was made, but as of one year prior to the filing date of the application.*" 343 F.2d 980, 998–999 (Emphasis in original).

3. Does a prior invention under section 102(g) constitute prior art for purposes of section 103? In re Bass, 59 C.C.P.A. 1342, 474 F. 2d 1276, 177 U.S.P.Q. 178 (1973), answered that it does. Noting a "close parallel" to the situation in *Hazeltine*, which involved section 102(e), the court concluded that "the considerations expressed are equally applicable to prior inventions under section 102(g)," and held that "the use of the prior invention of another who had not abandoned, suppressed, or concealed it, under the circumstances of this case which include the disclosure of such invention in an issued patent, is available as 'prior art' within the meaning of that term in section 103 by virtue of section 102(g)." 474 F.2d 1276, 1286–1287, 177 U.S.P.Q. 178, 186. See also Sutter Products Co. v. Pettibone Mulliken Corp., 428 F.2d 639, 166 U.S.P.Q. 100 (7th Cir. 1970); In re Clemens, 622 F.2d 1029, 206 U.S.P.Q. 289 (C.C.P.A. 1980).

Writing for the majority, Judge Rich crystallized some underlying assumptions about the structure of section 102. "The anatomy of section 102 is fairly clear. As forecast in its heading, it deals with the two questions of 'novelty and loss of right.' It also deals with originality in subsection (f) which says that one who 'did not himself invent the subject matter' (i. e., he did not originate it) has no right to a patent on it. Subsections (c) on abandonment and (d) on first patenting the invention abroad, before the date of the U.S. application, on an application filed more than a year before filing in the U. S., are loss of right provisions and in no way relate to 'prior art'. Of course, (c), (d) and (f) have no relation to section 103 and no relevancy to what is 'prior art' under section 103. Only the remaining portions of section 102 deal with prior art. Three of them, (a), (e) and (g), deal with events prior to applicant's *invention* date and the other, (b), with events more than one year prior to the U.S. *application* date. These are the 'prior art' subsections." 474 F.2d 1276, 1290.

4. The issues pursued in *Foster, Hazeltine, Bass* and their progeny have attracted abundant commentary. See generally, Chisum, Sources of Prior Art in Patent Law, 52 Wash.L.Rev. 1 (1976). For a comprehensive pre-*Hazeltine* discussion of questions of length and breadth of prior art, see Sobel, Prior Art and Obviousness, 47 J.P.O.S. 79 (1965).

See also, Stiefel, Section 102(f) as a Basis for Section 103 Prior Art—Myth or Reality, 61 J.P.O.S. 734 (1979); Klitzman, 35 U.S.C. § 102(g) As Establishing Prior Art, 58 J.P.O.S. 505 (1976); Jorda, Section 102(g) Prior Invention as Section 103 Prior Art: Impact on Corporate Research, 58 J.P.O.S. 523 (1976) (also containing a bibliography).

d. UTILITY

LOWELL v. LEWIS, 15 Fed.Cas. 1018 (No. 8568) (C.C.D.Mass. 1817). STORY, Circuit Justice (charging jury): The present action is brought by the plaintiff for a supposed infringement of a patent-right, granted, in 1813, to Mr. Jacob Perkins (from whom the plaintiff claims by assignment) for a new and useful improvement in the construction of pumps. The defendant asserts, in the first place, that the invention is neither new nor useful; and, in the next place, that the pumps used by him are not of the same construction as those of Mr. Perkins, but are of a new invention of a Mr. Baker, under whom the defendant claims by assignment.   .   .   .

To entitle the plaintiff to a verdict, he must establish, that his machine is a new and useful invention; and of these facts his patent is to be considered merely prima facie evidence of a very slight nature. He must, in the first place, establish it to be a useful invention; for the law will not allow the plaintiff to recover, if the invention be of a mischievous or injurious tendency. The defendant, however, has asserted a much more broad and sweeping doctrine; and one, which I feel myself called upon to negative in the most explicit manner. He contends that it is necessary for the plaintiff to prove that his invention is of general utility; so that in fact, for the ordinary purposes of life, it must supersede the pumps in common use. In short, that it must be, for the public, a better pump than the common pump; and that unless the plaintiff can establish this position, the law will not give him the benefit of a patent, even though in some peculiar cases his invention might be applied with advantage. I do not so understand the law. The patent act (Act Feb. 21, 1793, c. 11 [1 Stat. 31]) uses the phrase "useful invention" mere incidentally; it occurs only in the first section, and there it seems merely descriptive of the subject matter of the application, or of the conviction of the applicant. The language is, "when any person or persons shall allege, that he or they have invented any new and useful art, machine," &c.,

he or they may, on pursuing the directions of the act, obtain a patent. Neither the oath required by the second section, nor the special matter of defence allowed to be given in evidence by the sixth section of the act, contains any such qualification or reference to general utility, to establish the validity of the patent. Nor is it alluded to in the tenth section as a cause, for which the patent may be vacated. To be sure, all the matters of defence or of objection to the patent are not enumerated in these sections. But if such an one as that now contended for had been intended, it is scarcely possible to account for its omission. In my judgement the argument is utterly without foundation. All that the law requires is, that the invention should not be frivolous or injurious to the well-being, good policy, or sound morals of society. The word "useful," therefore, is incorporated into the act in contradistinction to mischievous or immoral. For instance, a new invention to poison people, or to promote debauchery, or to facilitate private assassination, is not a patentable invention. But if the invention steers wide of these objections, whether it be more or less useful is a circumstance very material to the interests of the patentee, but of no importance to the public. If it be not extensively useful, it will silently sink into contempt and disregard. There is no pretence, that Mr. Perkins' pump is a mischievous invention; and if it has been used injuriously to the patentee by the defendant, it certainly does not lie in his mouth to contest its general utility. Indeed the defendant asserts, that Baker's pump is useful in a very eminent degree, and, if it be substantially the same as Perkins's, there is an end of the objection; if it be not substantially the same, then the plaintiff must fail in his action. So that, in either view, the abstract question seems hardly of any importance in this cause.

BRENNER v. MANSON

Supreme Court of the United States, 1966.
383 U.S. 519, 86 S.Ct. 1033, 16 L.Ed.2d 69, 148 U.S.P.Q. 689.

Mr. Justice FORTAS delivered the opinion of the Court.

.   .   .   Our starting point is the proposition, neither disputed nor disputable, that one may patent only that which is "useful." In Graham v. John Deere Co., 383 U.S. 1, at 5–10, 86 S.Ct. 684, at 687–690, 148 U.S.P.Q. 459, we have reviewed the history of the requisites of patentability, and it need not be repeated here. Suffice it to say that the concept of utility has maintained a central place in all of our patent legislation, beginning with the first patent law in 1790 and culminating in the present law's provision that

> "Whoever invents or discovers any new and useful process, machine, manufacture, or composition of matter, or any new and useful improvement thereof, may obtain a patent therefor, subject to the conditions and requirements of this title."

As is so often the case, however, a simple, everyday word can be pregnant with ambiguity when applied to the facts of life. That this is so is demonstrated by the present conflict between the Patent Office and the C.C.P.A. over how the test is to be applied to a chemical process which yields an already known product whose utility—other than as a possible object of scientific inquiry—has not yet been evidenced. It was not long ago that agency and court seemed of one mind on the question. In Application of Bremner, 182 F.2d 216, 217, 37 C.C.P.A. (Pat.) 1032, 1034, 86 U.S.P.Q. 74, 75, the court affirmed rejection by the Patent Office of both process and product claims. It noted that "no use for the products claimed to be developed by the processes had been shown in the specification." It held that "It was never intended that a patent be granted upon a product, or a process producing a product, unless such product be useful." Nor was this new doctrine in the court.

The Patent Office has remained steadfast in this view. The C. C.P.A. however, has moved sharply away from Bremner. The trend began in Application of Nelson, 280 F.2d 172, 47 C.C.P.A. (Pat.), 1031, 126 U.S.P.Q. 242. There, the court reversed the Patent Office's rejection of a claim on a process yielding chemical intermediates "useful to chemists doing research on steroids," despite the absence of evidence that any of the steroids thus ultimately produced were themselves "useful." The trend has accelerated, culminating in the present case where the court held it sufficient that a process produces the result intended and is not "detrimental to the public interest." 333 F.2d, at 238, 52 C.C.P.A., at 745, 142 U.S.P.Q. at 38.

It is not remarkable that differences arise as to how the test of usefulness is to be applied to chemical processes. Even if we knew precisely what Congress meant in 1790 when it devised the "new and useful" phraseology and in subsequent re-enactments of the test, we should have difficulty in applying it in the context of contemporary chemistry where research is as comprehensive as man's grasp and where little or nothing is wholly beyond the pale of "utility"—if that word is given its broadest reach.

Respondent does not—at least, in the first instance—rest upon the extreme proposition, advanced by the court below, that a novel chemical process is patentable so long as it yields the intended product and so long as the product is not itself "detrimental." Nor does he commit the outcome of his claim to the slightly more conventional proposition that any process is "useful" within the meaning of § 101 if it produces a compound whose potential usefulness is under investigation by serious scientific researchers, although he urges this position too as an alternative basis for affirming the decision of the C.C.P.A. Rather, he begins with the much more orthodox argument that his process has a specific utility which would entitle him to a declaration of interference even under the Patent Office's reading of § 101. The claim is that the supporting affidavits filed pursuant to Rule 204(b), by reference to Ringold's 1956 article, reveal that an adjacent homologue of the steroid yielded by his process has been demonstrated to have tumor-inhibiting effects in mice, and that this discloses the requisite utility. We do not accept any of these theories as an adequate basis for overriding the determination of the Patent Office that the "utility" requirement has not been met.

Even on the assumption that the process would be patentable were respondent to show that the steroid produced had a tumor-inhibiting effect in mice, we would not overrule the Patent Office finding that respondent has not made such a showing. The Patent Office held that, despite the reference to the adjacent homologue, respondent's papers did not disclose a sufficient likelihood that the steroid yielded by his process would have similar tumor-inhibiting characteristics. Indeed, respondent himself recognized that the presumption that adjacent homologues have the same utility has been challenged in the steroid field because of "a greater known unpredictability of compounds in that field." In these circumstances and in this technical area, we would not overturn the finding of the Primary Examiner, affirmed by the Board of Appeals and not challenged by the C.C. P.A.

The second and third points of respondent's argument present issues of much importance. Is a chemical process "useful" within the meaning of § 101 either (1) because it works—i. e., produces the intended product? or (2) because the compound yielded belongs to a class of compounds now the subject of serious scientific investigation? These contentions present the basic problem for our adjudication. Since we find no specific assistance in the legislative materials underlying § 101, we are remitted to an analysis of the problem in light of the general intent of Congress, the purposes of the patent system, and the implications of a decision one way or the other.

In support of his plea that we attenuate the requirement of "utility," respondent relies upon Justice Story's well-known statement that a "useful" invention is one "which may be applied to a beneficial use in society, in contradistinction to an invention injurious to the morals, health, or good order of society, or frivolous and insignificant"—and upon the assertion that to do so would encourage inventors of new processes to publicize the event for the benefit of the entire scientific community, thus widening the search for uses and increasing the fund of scientific knowledge. Justice Story's language sheds little light on our subject. Narrowly read, it does no more than compel us to decide whether the invention in question is "frivolous and insignificant"—a query no easier of application than the one built into the statute. Read more broadly, so as to allow the patenting of any invention not positively harmful to society, it places such a special meaning on the word "useful" that we cannot accept it in the absence of evidence that Congress so intended. There are, after all, many things in this world which may not be considered "useful" but which, nevertheless, are totally without a capacity for harm.

It is true, of course, that one of the purposes of the patent system is to encourage dissemination of information concerning discoveries and inventions. And it may be that inability to patent a process to some extent discourages disclosure and leads to greater secrecy than would otherwise be the case. The inventor of the process, or the corporate organization by which he is employed, has some incentive to keep the invention secret while uses for the product are searched out. However, in light of the highly developed art of drafting patent claims so that they disclose as little useful information as possible—while broadening the scope of the claim as widely as possible—the argument based upon the virtue of disclosure must be warily evaluated. Moreover, the pressure for secrecy is easily exaggerated, for if the inventor of a process cannot himself ascertain a "use" for that which his process yields, he has every incentive to make his invention known to those able to do so. Finally, how likely is disclosure of a patented process to spur research by others into the uses to which the product may be put? To the extent that the patentee has power to enforce his patent, there is little incentive for others to undertake a search for uses.

Whatever weight is attached to the value of encouraging disclosure and of inhibiting secrecy, we believe a more compelling consideration is that a process patent in the chemical field, which has not been developed and pointed to the degree of specific utility, creates a monopoly of knowledge which should be granted only if clearly commanded by the statute. Until the process claim has been reduced to production of a product shown to be useful, the metes and bounds of that monopoly are not capable of precise delineation. It may engross a vast, unknown, and perhaps unknowable area. Such a patent may confer power to block off whole areas of scientific development, without compensating benefit to the public. The basic quid pro quo contemplated by the Constitution and the Congress for granting a patent monopoly is the benefit derived by the public from an invention with substantial utility. Unless and until a process is refined and developed to this point—where specific benefit exists in currently available form—there is insufficient justification for permitting an applicant to engross what may prove to be a broad field.

These arguments for and against the patentability of a process which either has no known use or is useful only in the sense that it may be an object of scientific research would apply equally to the patenting of the product produced by the process. Respondent appears to concede that with respect to a product, as opposed to a process, Congress has struck the balance on the side of nonpatentability unless "utility" is shown. Indeed, the decisions of the C.C.P.A. are in accord with the view that a product may not be patented absent a showing of utility greater than any adduced in the present case. We find absolutely no warrant for the proposition that although Congress intended that no patent be granted on a chemical compound whose sole "utility" consists of its potential role as an object of use-testing, a different set of rules was meant to apply to the process which yielded the unpatentable product. That proposition seems to us little more than an attempt to evade the impact of the rules which concededly govern patentability of the product itself.

This is not to say that we mean to disparage the importance of contributions to the fund of scientific information short of the invention of something "useful," or that we are blind to the prospect that what now seems without "use" may tomorrow command the grateful attention of the public. But a patent is not a hunting license. It is not a reward for the search, but compensation for its successful conclusion. "[A] patent system must be related to the world of commerce rather than to the realm of philosophy. .   . ."

The judgment of the C.C.P.A. is reversed.

Mr. Justice DOUGLAS, while acquiescing in Part I of the Court's opinion, dissents on the merits of the controversy for substantially the reasons stated by Mr. Justice HARLAN.

Mr. Justice HARLAN, concurring in part and dissenting in part.

While I join the Court's opinion on the issue of certiorari jurisdiction, I cannot agree with its resolution of the important question of patentability.

Respondent has contended that a workable chemical process, which is both new and sufficiently nonobvious to satisfy the patent statute, is by its existence alone a contribution to chemistry and "useful" as the statute employs that term. Certainly this reading of "useful" in the statute is within the scope of the constitutional grant, which states only that "[t]o promote the Progress of Science and useful Arts," the exclusive right to "Writings and Discoveries" may be secured for limited times to those who produce them. Art. I, § 8. Yet the patent statute is somewhat differently worded and is on its face open both to respondent's construction and to the contrary reading given it by the Court. In the absence of legislative history on this issue, we are thrown back on policy and practice. Because I believe that the Court's policy arguments are not convincing and that past practice favors the respondent, I would reject the narrow definition of "useful" and uphold the judgment of the Court of Customs and Patent Appeals (hereafter C.C.P.A.).

The Court's opinion sets out about half a dozen reasons in support of its interpretation. Several of these arguments seem to me to have almost no force. For instance, it is suggested that "[u]ntil the process claim has been reduced to production of a product shown to be useful, the metes and bounds of that monopoly are not capable of precise delineation" and "[i]t may engross a vast, unknown, and perhaps unknowable area." I fail to see the relevance of these assertions; process claims are not disallowed because the products they produce may be of "vast" importance nor, in any event, does advance knowledge of a specific product use provide much safeguard on this score or fix "metes and bounds" precisely since a hundred more uses may be found after a patent is granted and greatly enhance its value.

The further argument that an established product use is part of "[t]he basic *quid pro quo*" for the patent or is the requisite "successful conclusion" of the inventor's search appears to beg the very question whether the process is "useful" simply because it facilitates further research into possible product uses. The same infirmity seems to inhere in the Court's argument that chemical products lacking immediate utility cannot be distinguished for present purposes from the processes which create them, that respondent appears to concede and the C.C.P.A. holds that the products are nonpatentable, and that therefore the processes are nonpatentable. Assuming that the two classes cannot be distinguished, a point not adequately considered in the briefs, and assuming further that the C.C.P.A. has firmly held such products nonpatentable this permits us to conclude only that the C.C.P.A. is wrong either as to the products or as to the processes and affords no basis for deciding whether both or neither should be patentable absent a specific product use.

More to the point, I think, are the Court's remaining, prudential arguments against patentability: namely that disclosure induced by allowing a patent is partly undercut by patent-application drafting techniques, that disclosure may occur without granting a patent, and that a patent will discourage others from inventing uses for the product. How far opaque drafting may lessen the public benefits resulting from the issuance of a patent is not shown by any evidence in this case but, more important, the argument operates against all patents and gives no reason for singling out the class involved here. The thought that these inventions may be more likely than most to be disclosed even if patents are not allowed may have more force; but while empirical study of the industry might reveal that chemical researchers would behave in this fashion, the abstractly logical choice for them seems to me to maintain secrecy until a product use can be discovered. As to discouraging the search by others for product uses, there is no doubt this risk exists but the price paid for any patent is that research on other uses or improvements may be hampered because the original patentee will reap much of the reward. From the standpoint of the public interest the Constitution seems to have resolved that choice in favor of patentability.

What I find most troubling about the result reached by the Court is the impact it may have on chemical research. Chemistry is a highly interrelated field and a tangible benefit for society may be the outcome of a number of different discoveries, one discovery building upon the next. To encourage one chemist or research facility to invent and disseminate new processes and products may be vital to progress, although the product or process be without "utility" as the Court defines the term, because that discovery permits someone else to take a further but perhaps less difficult step leading to a commercially useful item. In my view, our awareness in this age of the importance of achieving and publicizing basic research should lead this Court to resolve uncertainties in its favor and uphold the respondent's position in this case.

This position is strengthened, I think, by what appears to have been the practice of the Patent Office during most of this century. While available proof is not conclusive, the commentators seem to be in agreement that until Application of Bremner, 182 F.2d 216, 37 C. C.P.A. (Pat.) 1032, 86 U.S.P.Q. 74, in 1950, chemical patent applications were commonly granted although no resulting end use was stated or the statement was in extremely broad terms. Taking this to be true, Bremner represented a deviation from established practice which the C.C.P.A. has now sought to remedy in part only to find that the Patent Office does not want to return to the beaten track. If usefulness was typically regarded as inherent during a long and prolific period of chemical research and development in this country, surely this is added reason why the Court's result should not be adopted until Congress expressly mandates it, presumably on the basis of empirical data which this Court does not possess.

Fully recognizing that there is ample room for disagreement on this problem when, as here, it is reviewed in the abstract, I believe the decision below should be affirmed.

NOTES

1. Principles of early English patent law underlie the measure of utility adopted by Justice Story in Lowell v. Lewis. A year later, Story returned to these principles in the course of a more extensive commentary, 16 U.S. 302 (1818), to observe that, in sanctioning letters patent, the Statute of Monopolies, 21 Jac. I ch. III (1623), expressly required that "they be not contrary to the law, nor mischievous to the state, by raising prices of commodities at home, or hurt of trade, or generally inconvenient. . . ."

Whether or not Justice Story's inference was proper, his test of utility took hold in American patent jurisprudence. Rickard v. Du Bon, 103 F. 868 (2d Cir. 1900), is typical. Defendant, accused of infringing plaintiff's patented process for flecking the leaves of tobacco plants, countered that the patent was invalid for lack of utility. Conceding that the process effectively achieved its avowed purpose, defendant argued that the purpose itself was fraudulent. The many consumers who believed that cigars with spotted leaf wrappers are better than those with unspotted wrappers were deceived into thinking that the wrappers treated by plaintiff's process belonged to the better class.[m] Ruling for the defendant, the court agreed with the trial judge that, "the patent was void for want of utility, 'except to deceive.' "

Under the *Rickard* test, utility will be found if the subject matter in question can be put to some beneficial use. Thus, had plaintiff succeeded in proving his claim that his treatment also improved the burning quality of the leaf, the court probably would have validated

m. *Caveat* cigar smokers: "The notion has long prevailed with a numerous class of smokers that cigars having spotted wrappers are superior to those without them. This notion is a pure delusion. It originated and has been propagated by the coincidence that much choice tobacco is spotted, being raised in localities where this characteristic is imparted by natural causes, although without improving or impairing the quality of the leaf." 103 F. 868, 869.

the patent. Consider the utility, under this test, of narcotic compounds that are generally dangerous but also possess some therapeutic capacity, or of a safecracking device that can be applied to surgical advantage. Is it a proper function of patent law to discriminate among permitted and proscribed areas of conduct?

For a critical examination of decisions on the subject, see Meyer, Utility Requirement in the Statute, 49 J.P.O.S. 533 (1967).

2. "Operability," in the patent lexicon, is quite different from "utility." Operability's function is to assist in determinations of actual reduction to practice. Recall from the earlier discussion of novelty that invention consists of conception and reduction to practice, and that reduction to practice is demonstrated either actually, through completion of a working model of the invention, or constructively, through the filing of a patent application. Operability is the hallmark of actual reduction to practice.

Even if an invention is inoperative as disclosed, it will be considered operative if it can be made operative by procedures that would naturally occur to a worker ordinarily skilled in the relevant art. Bennett v. Halahan, Aronsen and Lyon, 285 F.2d 807, 128 U.S. P.Q. 398 (C.C.P.A.1961). Also, an invention is considered operative if it substantially achieves its avowed purpose. Hildreth v. Mastoras, 257 U.S. 27, 42 S.Ct. 20, 66 L.Ed.2d 112 (1921). Excluded from the benefits of both these rules is the invention that, unless it is perfect, is no good at all. In McKenzie v. Cummings, 24 App.D.C. 137 (D.C. Cir. 1904), for example, the court ruled that a vote-registering machine that failed to properly register one of every hundred votes cast was inoperative. Distinguishing Coffee v. Guerrant, 3 App.D.C. 497 (D.C.Cir. 1894), in which the operability of a tobacco-stemming device with 70% efficiency was sustained, the court held that, "In order to be operative at all, absolute accuracy is here required."

Although an invention's operability may be saved under either of these two meliorative rules, some positive evidence of operability may be required. Proof of commercial success, typically associated with section 103's nonobviousness requisite, is frequently adduced. If the invention obviously contradicts established physical laws, as in the case of a perpetual motion machine, or if absolute accuracy is critical, the Commissioner may avail himself of the authority provided by section 114 to require that the applicant furnish a working model of his subject matter. For affirmance of the Commissioner's request in the case of some particularly outlandish claims, see Upton v. Ladd, 227 F.Supp. 261, 140 U.S.P.Q. 646 (D.D.C.1964). See generally, Ederer, On Operability as an Aspect of Patent Law, 42 J.P.O. S. 398 (1960).

3. In a footnote, *Manson* raised but did not decide the question of the proper utility test to be applied to pharmaceuticals. 383 U.S. 519, 531 n. 17, 86 S.Ct. 1033, 1040. One line of decision, dating from the early 1900's, engrafted on the general utility requisite a specific requirement that a drug's fitness for human use be convincingly

proved. Proof of successful tests on laboratory animals was considered insufficient to establish utility. "While the granting of a patent does not legally constitute a certificate that the medicine to which it relates is a good medicine and will cure the disease or successfully make the test which it was intended to do, nevertheless, the granting of such a patent gives a kind of official imprimatur to the medicine in question on which as a moral matter some members of the public are likely to rely." Isenstead v. Watson, 157 F.Supp. 7, 115 U.S.P.Q. 408 (D.D.C.1957).

The modern trend, inaugurated by In re Krimmel, 292 F.2d 948, 130 U.S.P.Q. 215 (C.C.P.A.1961), has been to liberalize the utility test for pharmaceuticals. The applicant in *Krimmel* sought a patent for an eye medicine that he had successfully tested on rabbits. The examiner, affirmed by the Board of Appeals, ruled that absent a showing of successful tests on humans, utility had not been proved. The Court of Customs and Patent Appeals reversed, holding that applicant had proved some usefulness for his medicine—to cure eye disease in rabbits—and that this was sufficient to meet the statutory test. The court took another liberalizing step the following year when, in In re Hartop, 311 F.2d 249, 135 U.S.P.Q. 419 (C.C.P.A. 1962), it held that although the applicant specifically asserted that his medicine had utility for humans, but had only demonstrated its safety and effectiveness on animals, "appellants' claimed solutions have been shown to be useful within the meaning of U.S.C.A. § 101. .   .   .   We think that a sufficient probability of safety in human therapy has been demonstrated in the case at bar to set aside the requirements of 35 U.S.C.A. § 101 that appellants' invention be useful."

In re Anthony, 414 F.2d 1383, 162 U.S.P.Q. 594 (C.C.P.A.1969), expanded on the rationale underlying *Krimmel* and *Hartop*: "Congress has given the responsibility to the FDA, not to the Patent Office, to determine in the first instance whether drugs are sufficiently safe for use that they can be introduced in the commercial market, under the conditions prescribed, recommended, or suggested in the proposed labeling thereof. .   .   ." The court emphasized that although 21 U.S.C.A. § 372(d) authorizes the Secretary of Health, Education and Welfare to furnish the Commissioner of Patents with FDA data respecting drugs for which a patent is sought, this information has only persuasive, and not binding, effect on the issue of utility.

See also Application of Malachowski, 530 F.2d 1402, 189 U.S.P.Q. 432 (C.C.P.A.1976); Nelson v. Bowler, 626 F.2d 853, 206 U.S.P.Q. 881 (C.C.P.A.1980).

e. ORIGINALITY

For a valid patent to issue, the claimed invention must have originated with the applicant or applicants. See 35 U.S.C.A. § 102(f). The originality requirement is obviously not absolute. The inventor may draw his ideas from other sources and he may arrange for others to assemble his invention, all without losing his claim of originality. But, for the patent to be valid, the named inventor or inventors must themselves have conceived the specific invention claimed. In International Carrier-Call & Television Corp. v. Radio Corp. of America, 142 F.2d 493, 61 U.S.P.Q. 392 (2d Cir. 1944), the court ruled that a patentee, who had merely asked an engineer to build an intercom that would perform more efficiently than an already existing device, was too far removed from the resulting subject matter to be considered its inventor. As a consequence, his patent was invalid. "An employer who seeks to patent the fruits of his employees' labors must go further than merely to express a purpose to be realized. . . . It is one thing for an employer to suggest improvements of a device with sufficient elaboration to enable a person skilled in the art to make a machine embodying the employer's conception; it is another to suggest merely a desired result without any disclosure of the means by which it is to be attained." 142 F.2d 493, 496. Connected to the originality requirement is section 111's general requirement that application for a patent be made by the inventor.

Insistence that the patent application accurately identify the inventor or inventors becomes particularly problematic in modern research and development departments where joint, rather than individual, invention is the rule. An invention may be the product of many hands, from the research director, who first suggested and guided the idea, to product engineers and technicians who executed it. And what of the patent attorney who, in advising on prior art, may have suggested important, patentable alterations in the invention? Because some products and processes are developed over long periods, workers will be leaving and joining the research team at all stages of development. These and other realities of large scale research and development create a substantial risk that the patent application will be underinclusive, omitting some inventors, or overinclusive, naming some noninventors.

Judicial decisions offer only the broadest guidelines for determining when a contributor to an invention will be considered a co-inventor. Worden v. Fisher, 11 F. 505, (C.C.E.D.Mich.1882) made what has become the classic statement of criteria for joint inventorship:

> To constitute two persons joint inventors it is not necessary that exactly the same idea should have occurred to each at the same time, and that they should work out together the embodiment of this idea in a perfected machine. Such a coincidence of ideas would scarcely ever occur to two persons at the same time. If an idea is suggested to one, and he even goes so far as to construct a machine embodying this idea, but it is not a completed and working machine, and another person takes hold of it, and by their joint labors, one suggesting one thing and the other another, a perfect machine is made, a joint patent may properly issue to them. If, upon the other hand, one person invents a distinct part of a machine, and another person invents another distinct and independent part of the same machine, then each should obtain a patent for his own invention.

After reviewing *Worden* and many later decisions, John Tresansky arrived at the following restatement: "Joint inventorship exists where parties working in a cooperative effort to solve a problem make a mental contribution to the final conception of the solution. All of the parties need not have participated in each contribution nor need the contribution of each party have occurred simultaneously while working proximately with the others. The contributions of each need not be equal either qualitatively or quantitatively. The contributors need not personally have performed the actual reduction to practice of the inventive concept." Tresansky, Joint Inventorship, 7 A.P.L.A.Q.J. 96, 108–109 (1979).*

The hazards of misjoinder and nonjoinder are significantly reduced by the fact that courts generally are slow to invalidate patents on these essentially technical grounds and, further, attach a presumption of correctness to the patentee's identification of inventors. Also, sections 116 and 256 respectively create procedures for correcting the identification of inventors in applications and in patents. The provisions require a showing that the misjoinder or nonjoinder was the result of a mistake made without intent to deceive. "Sections 116 and 256 evidence realization on the part of Congress that because of the haziness of the boundaries of co-inventorship status and the realities of work in large research labs, misjoinder is bound to be common and should be easily correctable at any time with no loss of benefit under the law." Mueller Brass Co. v. Reading Indus., 352 F.Supp. 1357, 1379, 176 U.S.P.Q. 361 (E.D.Pa.1972), aff'd without opinion 487 F.2d 1395, 180 U.S.P.Q. 547.

What if the patent fails to name *any* of the true inventors? The Act contains no provisions comparable to sections 116 or 256 for correcting the misidentification of an invention's sole inventor—from *A* named as the inventor, to *B* who was in fact the inventor. In a much-discussed decision, the District of Columbia Court of Appeals read section 116 broadly and relied on section 251's reissue provisions to allow correction of a wrongly named sole inventor in a pending application and in an issued patent. A. F. Stoddard & Co., Ltd. v. Dann, 564 F.2d 556, 195 U.S.P.Q. 97 (1977). "Congress having provided [in section 116] for the correction of innocent error in stating the inventive entity when the application is filed, whether that entity be singular or plural, we see no rational reason to discriminate against the correction of the same innocent error involving sole inventors and their assignees, or to impute that intent to Congress." 564 F.2d 556, 566.

See Meiklejohn, Misjoinder, Non-Joinder and Whatever—Stoddard v. Dann, 60 J.P.O.S. 487 (1978); Welch, Stoddard v. Dann—Fundamental Principles from A to C, 61 J.P.O.S. 185 (1979). Articles on several joint inventorship topics are collected at 7 A.P.L.A.Q. J. No. 2 (1979).

* Reprinted with permission of A.P.L.A.
Quarterly Journal.

2. STATUTORY SUBJECT MATTER

See Statute Supplement 35 U.S.C.A. §§ 100, 101, 161–164, 171–173; 289.

a. UTILITY PATENTS

DIAMOND v. CHAKRABARTY

Supreme Court of the United States, 1980.
447 U.S. 303, 100 S.Ct. 2204, 65 L.Ed.2d 144, 206 U.S.P.Q. 193.

Mr. Chief Justice BURGER delivered the opinion of the Court.

We granted certiorari to determine whether a live, human-made micro-organism is patentable subject matter under 35 U.S.C.A. § 101.

I.

In 1972, respondent Chakrabarty, a microbiologist, filed a patent application, assigned to the General Electric Company. The application asserted 36 claims related to Chakrabarty's invention of "a bacterium from the genus Pseudomonas containing therein at least two stable energy-generating plasmids, each of said plasmids providing a separate hydrocarbon degradative pathway." [1] This human-made, genetically engineered bacterium is capable of breaking down multiple components of crude oil. Because of this property, which is possessed by no naturally occurring bacteria, Chakrabarty's invention is believed to have significant value for the treatment of oil spills. [2]

Chakrabarty's patent claims were of three types: first, process claims for the method of producing the bacteria; second, claims for an inoculum comprised of a carrier material floating on water, such as straw, and the new bacteria; and third, claims to the bacteria themselves. The patent examiner allowed the claims falling into the first two categories, but rejected claims for the bacteria. His decision rested on two grounds: (1) that micro-organisms are "products of nature," and (2) that as living things they are not patentable subject matter under 35 U.S.C.A. § 101.

[handwritten: PATENT DENIED]

1. Plasmids are hereditary units physically separate from the chromosomes of the cell. In prior research, Chakrabarty and an associate discovered that plasmids control the oil degradation abilities of certain bacteria. In particular, the two researchers discovered plasmids capable of degrading camphor and octane, two components of crude oil. In the work represented by the patent application at issue here, Chakrabarty discovered a process by which four different plasmids, capable of degrading four different oil components, could be transferred to and maintained stably in a single Pseudomonas bacteria, which

itself has no capacity for degrading oil.

2. At present, biological control of oil spills requires the use of a mixture of naturally occurring bacteria, each capable of degrading one component of the oil complex. In this way, oil is decomposed into simpler substances which can serve as food for acquatic life. However, for various reasons, only a portion of any such mixed culture survives to attack the oil spill. By breaking down multiple components of oil, Chakrabarty's micro-organism promises more efficient and rapid oil-spill control.

DENIAL AFFIRMED

Chakrabarty appealed the rejection of these claims to the Patent Office Board of Appeals, and the Board affirmed the Examiner on the second ground.[3] Relying on the legislative history of the 1930 Plant Patent Act, in which Congress extended patent protection to certain asexually reproduced plants, the Board concluded that § 101 was not intended to cover living things such as these laboratory created microorganisms.

DENIAL REVERSED

CERT. GRANTED REMAND

DENIAL REVERSAL AFFIRMED

The Court of Customs and Patent Appeals, by a divided vote, reversed on the authority of its prior decision in In re Bergy, 563 F.2d 1031, 195 U.S.P.Q. 344 (1978), which held that "the fact that microorganisms . . . are alive . . . [is] without legal significance" for purposes of the patent law. Subsequently, we granted the Government's petition for certiorari in Bergy, vacated the judgment, and remanded the case "for further consideration in light of Parker v. Flook, 437 U.S. 584 [98 S.Ct. 2522, 57 L.Ed.2d 451], 198 U.S.P.Q. 193." 438 U.S. 902, 98 S.Ct. 3119, 57 L.Ed.2d 1145, 198 U.S.P.Q. 257 (1978). The Court of Customs and Patent Appeals then vacated its judgment in Chakrabarty and consolidated the case with Bergy for reconsideration. After re-examining both cases in the light of our holding in Flook, that court, with one dissent, reaffirmed its earlier judgments. 596 F.2d 952, 201 U.S.P.Q. 352 (1979).

CERT. GRANTED

The Government again sought certiorari, and we granted the writ as to both Bergy and Chakrabarty. 444 U.S. 924, 100 S.Ct. 261, 62 L.Ed.2d 180, 204 U.S.P.Q. 608 (1979). Since then, Bergy has been dismissed as moot, 444 U.S. 1028, 100 S.Ct. 696, 62 L.Ed.2d 664 (1980), leaving only Chakrabarty for decision.

II.

The Constitution grants Congress broad power to legislate to "promote the Progress of Science and the useful Arts, by securing for limited times to authors and inventors the exclusive right to their respective writings and discoveries." Art. I, § 8. The patent laws promote this progress by offering inventors exclusive rights for a limited period as an incentive for their inventiveness and research efforts. Kewanee Oil Co. v. Bicron Corp., 416 U.S. 470, 480–481, 94 S.Ct. 1879, 1885–1886, 40 L.Ed.2d 315, 181 U.S.P.Q. 673, 678 (1974); Universal Oil Co. v. Globe Co., 322 U.S. 471, 484, 64 S.Ct. 1110, 1116, 88 L.Ed. 1399, 61 U.S.P.Q. 382, 388 (1944). The authority of Congress is exercised in the hope that "[t]he productive effort thereby fostered will have a positive effect on society through the introduction of new products and processes of manufacture into the economy, and the emanations by way of increased employment and better lives for our citizens." Kewanee, supra, at 480, 94 S.Ct., at 1885–86, 181 U.S. P.Q. at 678.

---

3. The Board concluded that the new bacteria were not "products of nature," because Pseudomonas bacteria containing two or more different energy-generating plasmids are not naturally occurring.

The question before us in this case is a narrow one of statutory interpretation requiring us to construe 35 U.S.C.A. § 101, which provides:

> "Whoever invents or discovers any new and useful process, machine, manufacture, or composition of matter, or any new and useful improvement thereof, may obtain a patent therefor, subject to the conditions and requirements of this title."

Specifically, we must determine whether respondent's microorganism constitutes a "manufacture" or "composition of matter" within the meaning of the statute.

III.

In cases of statutory construction we begin, of course, with the language of the statute. And "unless otherwise defined, words will be interpreted as taking their ordinary, contemporary, common meaning." Perrin v. United States, 444 U.S. 37, 100 S.Ct. 311, 314, 62 L.Ed.2d 199 (1979). We have also cautioned that courts "should not read into the patent laws limitations and conditions which the legislature has not expressed." United States v. Dubilier Condenser Corp., 289 U.S. 178, 199, 53 S.Ct. 554, 561, 77 L.Ed. 1114, 17 U.S.P.Q. 154, 162 (1933). *STATUTORY CONSTRUCTION*

Guided by these canons of construction, this Court has read the term "manufacture" in § 101 in accordance with its dictionary definition to mean "the production of articles for use from raw materials prepared by giving to these materials new forms, qualities, properties, or combinations whether by hand labor or by machinery." American Fruit Growers, Inc. v. Brogdex Co., 283 U.S. 1, 11, 51 S.Ct. 328, 330, 75 L.Ed. 801, 8 U.S.P.Q. 131, 133 (1931). Similarly, "composition of matter" has been construed consistent with its common usage to include "all compositions of two or more substances and .   .   . all composite articles, whether they be the results of chemical union, or of mechanical mixture, or whether they be gases, fluids, powders, or solids." Shell Dev. Co. v. Watson, 149 F.Supp. 279, 280, 113 U.S.P.Q. 265, 266 (D.C.1957) (citing 1 A. Deller, Walker on Patents § 14, p. 55 (1st ed. 1937)). In choosing such expansive terms as "manufacture" and "composition of matter," modified by the comprehensive "any," Congress plainly contemplated that the patent laws would be given wide scope. *MANUFACTURER* *COMPOSITION OF MATTER*

The relevant legislative history also supports a broad construction. The Patent Act of 1793, authored by Thomas Jefferson, defined statutory subject matter as "any new and useful art, machine, manufacture, or composition of matter, or any new or useful improvement [thereof]." Act of Feb. 21, 1793, ch. 11, § 1, 1 Stat. 318. The Act embodied Jefferson's philosophy that "ingenuity should receive a liberal encouragement." V Writings of Thomas Jefferson, at 75–76. See Graham v. John Deere Co., 383 U.S. 1, 7–10, 86 S.Ct. 684, 688–690, 15 L.Ed 2d 545, 148 U.S.P.Q. 459, 462–464 (1966). Subsequent patent statutes in 1836, 1870 and 1874 employed this same broad language. *LEGISLATIVE HISTORY*

In 1952, when the patent laws were recodified, Congress replaced the word "art" with "process," but otherwise left Jefferson's language intact. The Committee Reports accompanying the 1952 act inform us that Congress intended statutory subject matter to "include anything under the sun that is made by man." S.Rep.No.1979, 82d Cong., 2d Sess., 5 (1952); H.R.Rep.No.1923, 82d Cong., 2d Sess., 6 (1952).

LIMITATIONS ON §101

This is not to suggest that § 101 has no limits or that it embraces every discovery. The laws of nature, physical phenomena, and abstract ideas have been held not patentable. See Parker v. Flook, 437 U.S. 584, 98 S.Ct. 2522, 57 L.Ed.2d 451, 198 U.S.P.Q. 193 (1978); Gottschalk v. Benson, 409 U.S. 63, 67, 93 S.Ct. 253, 255, 34 L.Ed.2d 273, 175 U.S.P.Q. 673, 674–675 (1973); Funk Seed Co. v. Kalo Co., 333 U.S. 127, 130, 68 S.Ct. 440, 441, 92 L.Ed. 588, 76 U.S.P.Q. 280, 281 (1948); O'Reilly v. Morse, 15 How. 61, 112–121, 14 L.Ed. 601 (1853); Le Roy v. Tatham, 14 How. 155, 175, 14 L.Ed. 367 (1852). Thus, a new mineral discovered in the earth or a new plant found in the wild is not patentable subject matter. Likewise, Einstein could not patent his celebrated law that $E = mc^2$; nor could Newton have patented the law of gravity. Such discoveries are "manifestations of . . . nature, free to all men and reserved exclusively to none." Funk, supra, at 130, 76 U.S.P.Q. at 281.

Judged in this light, respondent's micro-organism plainly qualifies as patentable subject matter. His claim is not to a hitherto unknown natural phenomenon, but to a nonnaturally occurring manufacture or composition of matter—a product of human ingenuity "having a distinctive name, character [and] use." Hartranft v. Wiegmann, 121 U.S. 609, 615, 7 S.Ct. 1240, 1243, 30 L.Ed. 1012 (1887). The point is underscored dramatically by comparison of the invention here with that in Funk. There, the patentee had discovered that there existed in nature certain species of root-nodule bacteria which did not exert a mutually inhibitive effect on each other. He used that discovery to produce a mixed culture capable of inoculating the seeds of leguminous plants. Concluding that the patentee had discovered "only some of the handiwork of nature," the Court ruled the product nonpatentable:

"Each of the species of root-nodule bacteria contained in the package infects the same group of leguminous plants which it always infected. No species acquires a different use. The combination of the six species produces no new bacteria, no change in the six bacteria, and no enlargement of the range of their utility. Each species has the same effect it always had. The bacteria perform in their natural way. Their use in combination does not improve in any way their natural functioning. They serve the same ends nature originally provided and act quite independently of any effort by the patentee." 333 U.S., at 127, 68 S.Ct., at 442, 76 U.S.P.Q. at 280.

Here, by contrast, the patentee has produced a new bacterium with markedly different characteristics from any found in nature and one having the potential for significant utility. His discovery is not nature's handiwork, but his own; accordingly it is patentable subject matter under § 101.

IV.

Two contrary arguments are advanced, neither of which we find persuasive.

A.

The Government's first argument rests on the enactment of the 1930 Plant Patent Act, which afforded patent protection to certain asexually reproduced plants, and the 1970 Plant Variety Protection Act, which authorized patents for certain sexually reproduced plants but excluded bacteria from its protection. In the Government's view, the passage of these Acts evidences congressional understanding that the terms "manufacture" or "composition of matter" do not include living things; if they did, the Government argues, neither Act would have been necessary.

We reject this argument. Prior to 1930, two factors were thought to remove plants from patent protection. The first was the belief that plants, even those artificially bred, were products of nature for purposes of the patent law. This position appears to have derived from the decision of the Patent Office in Ex parte Latimer, 1889 C.D. 123, in which a patent claim for fiber found in the needle of the Pinus australis was rejected. The Commissioner reasoned that a contrary result would permit "patents [to] be obtained upon the trees of the forests and the plants of the earth, which of course would be unreasonable and impossible." Id., at 126. The Latimer case, it seems, came to "set[] forth the general stand taken in these matters" that plants were natural products not subject to patent protection. H. Thorne, Relation of Patent Law to Natural Products, 6 J.Pat.Off.Soc. 23, 24 (1923). The second obstacle to patent protection for plants was the fact that plants were thought not amenable to the "written description" requirement of the patent law. See 35 U.S.C.A. § 112. Because new plants may differ from old only in color or perfume, differentiation by written description was often impossible.

In enacting the Plant Patent Act, Congress addressed both of these concerns. It explained at length its belief that the work of the plant breeder "in aid of nature" was patentable invention. S.Rep. No.315, 71st Cong., 2d Sess., 6–8 (1930); H.R.Rep.No.1129, 71st Cong., 2d Sess., 7–9 (1930). And it relaxed the written description requirement in favor of "a description . . . as complete as is reasonably possible." 35 U.S.C.A. § 162. No Committee or Member of Congress, however, expressed the broader view, now urged by the Government, that the terms "manufacture" or "composition of matter" exclude living things. The sole support for that position in the legislative history of the 1930 Act is found in the conclusory statement of Secretary of Agriculture Hyde, in a letter to the Chairmen of the

House and Senate committees considering the 1930 Act, that "the patent laws . . . at the present time are understood to cover only inventions or discoveries in the field of inanimate nature." See S.Rep.No.315, supra, at Appendix A; H.R.Rep.No.1129, supra, at Appendix A. Secretary Hyde's opinion, however, is not entitled to controlling weight. His views were solicited on the administration of the new law and not on the scope of patentable subject matter—an area beyond his competence. Moreover, there is language in the House and Senate Committee reports suggesting that to the extent Congress considered the matter it found the Secretary's dichotomy unpersuasive. The reports observe:

> "There is a clear and logical distinction *between the discovery of a new variety of plant and of certain inanimate things*, such for example, as a new and useful natural mineral. The mineral is created wholly by nature unassisted by man. . . . On the other hand, a plant discovery resulting from cultivation is unique, isolated, and is not repeated by nature, nor can it be reproduced by nature unaided by man. . . ." S.Rep.No.315, supra, at 6; H.R.Rep.No.1129, supra, at 7 (emphasis added).

Congress thus recognized that the relevant distinction was not between living and inanimate things, but between products of nature, whether living or not, and human-made inventions. Here respondent's microorganism is the result of human ingenuity and research. Hence, the passage of the Plant Patent Act affords the Government no support.

Nor does the passage of the 1970 Plant Variety Protection Act support the Government's position. As the Government acknowledges, sexually reproduced plants were not included under the 1930 Act because new varieties could not be reproduced true-to-type through seedlings. Brief for United States 27, n. 31. By 1970, however, it was generally recognized that true-to-type reproduction was possible and that plant patent protection was therefore appropriate. The 1970 Act extended that protection. There is nothing in its language or history to suggest that it was enacted because § 101 did not include living things.

In particular, we find nothing in the exclusion of bacteria from plant variety protection to support the Government's position. The legislative history gives no reason for this exclusion. As the Court of Customs and Patent Appeals suggested, it may simply reflect congressional agreement with the result reached by that court in deciding In re Arzberger, 112 F.2d 834, 46 U.S.P.Q. 32 (1940), which held that bacteria were not plants for the purposes of the 1930 Act. Or it may reflect the fact that prior to 1970 the Patent Office had issued patents for bacteria under § 101.[9] In any event, absent some clear indi-

---

9. In 1873, the Patent Office granted Louis Pasteur a patent on "yeast, free from organic germs of disease, as an article of manufacture." And in 1967 and 1968, immediately prior to the passage of the Plant Variety Protection Act, that office granted two patents which, as the Government concedes, state claims for living microorganisms. The Reply Brief of United States, at 3, and n.2.

cation that Congress "focused on [the] issues . . . directly related to the one presently before the Court," SEC v. Sloan, 436 U.S. 103, 120–121, 98 S.Ct. 1702, 1713, 56 L.Ed.2d 148 (1978), there is no basis for reading into its actions an intent to modify the plain meaning of the words found in § 101.

B.

The Government's second argument is that microorganisms cannot qualify as patentable subject matter until Congress expressly authorizes such protection. Its position rests on the fact that genetic technology was unforeseen when Congress enacted § 101. From this it is argued that resolution of the patentability of inventions such as respondent's should be left to Congress. The legislative process, the Government argues, is best equipped to weigh the competing economic, social, and scientific considerations involved, and to determine whether living organisms produced by genetic engineering should receive patent protection. In support of this position, the Government relies on our recent holding in Parker v. Flook, 437 U.S. 584, 98 S. Ct. 2522, 57 L.Ed.2d 451, 198 U.S.P.Q. 193 (1978), and the statement that the judiciary "must proceed cautiously when . . . asked to extend patent rights into areas wholly unforeseen by Congress." Id., at 596.

It is, of course, correct that Congress, not the courts, must define the limits of patentability; but it is equally true that once Congress has spoken it is "the province and duty of the judicial department to say what the law is." Marbury v. Madison, 1 Cranch 137, 177, 2 L. Ed. 60 (1803). Congress has performed its constitutional role in defining patentable subject matter in § 101; we perform ours in construing the language Congress has employed. In so doing, our obligation is to take statutes as we find them, guided, if ambiguity appears, by the legislative history and statutory purpose. Here, we perceive no ambiguity. The subject matter provisions of the patent law have been cast in broad terms to fulfill the constitutional and statutory goal of promoting "the Progress of Science and the useful Arts" with all that means for the social and economic benefits envisioned by Jefferson. Broad general language is not necessarily ambiguous when congressional objectives require broad terms.

Nothing in Flook is to the contrary. That case applied our prior precedents to determine that a "claim for an improved method of calculation, even then tied to a specific end use, is unpatentable subject matter under § 101." 437 U.S., at 595, n. 18, 98 S.Ct., at 2528, n. 18, 198 U.S.P.Q. at 199, n. 18. The Court carefully scrutinized the claim at issue to determine whether it was precluded from patent protection under "the principles underlying the prohibition against patents for 'ideas' or phenomena of nature." Id., at 593, 98 S.Ct., at 2527, 198 U.S.P.Q. at 198–199. We have done that here. Flook did not announce a new principle that inventions in areas not contemplated by Congress when the patent laws were enacted are unpatentable per se.

To read that concept into Flook would frustrate the purposes of the patent law. This Court frequently has observed that a statute is not to be confined to the "particular application[s] . . . contemplated by the legislators." Barr v. United States, 324 U.S. 83, 90, 65 S.Ct. 522, 525, 89 L.Ed. 765 (1945). This is especially true in the field of patent law. A rule that unanticipated inventions are without protection would conflict with the core concept of the patent law that anticipation undermines patentability. Mr. Justice Douglas reminded that the inventions most benefiting mankind are those that "push back the frontiers of chemistry, physics, and the like." A. & P. Tea Co. v. Supermarket Corp., 340 U.S. 147, 154, 71 S.Ct. 127, 131, 95 L.Ed. 162, 87 U.S.P.Q. 303, 306–307 (1950) (concurring opinion). Congress employed broad general language in drafting § 101 precisely because such inventions are often unforeseeable.[10]

To buttress its argument, the Government, with the support of amicus, points to grave risks that may be generated by research endeavors such as respondent's. The briefs present a gruesome parade of horribles. Scientists, among them Nobel laureates, are quoted suggesting that genetic research may pose a serious threat to the human race, or, at the very least, that the dangers are far too substantial to permit such research to proceed apace at this time. We are told that genetic research and related technological developments may spread pollution and disease, that it may result in a loss of genetic diversity, and that its practice may tend to depreciate the value of human life. These arguments are forcefully, even passionately presented; they remind us that, at times, human ingenuity seems unable to control fully the forces it creates—that, with Hamlet, it is sometimes better "to bear those ills we have than fly to others that we know not of."

It is argued that this Court should weigh these potential hazards in considering whether respondent's invention is patentable subject matter under § 101. We disagree. The grant or denial of patents on micoorganisms is not likely to put an end to genetic research or to its attendant risks. The large amount of research that has already occurred when no researcher had sure knowledge that patent protection would be available suggests that legislative or judicial fiat as to patentability will not deter the scientific mind from probing into the unknown any more than Canute could command the tides. Whether respondent's claims are patent\.ble may determine whether research efforts are accelerated by the hope of reward or slowed by want of incentives, but that is all.

What is more important is that we are without competence to entertain these arguments—either to brush them aside as fantasies generated by fear of the unknown, or to act on them. The choice we

---

10. Even an abbreviated list of patented inventions underscores the point: telegraph (Morse No. 1647); telephone (Bell, No. 174,465); electric lamp (Edison, No. 223,898); airplane (the Wrights; No. 821,393); transistor (Bardeen & Brattain, No. 2,524,035); neutronic reactor (Fermi & Szilard, No. 2,708,656); laser (Schawlow & Townes, No. 2,929,922). See generally Revolutionary Ideas, Patents & Progress in America, Office of Patents (1976).

are urged to make is a matter of high policy for resolution within the legislative process after the kind of investigation, examination, and study that legislative bodies can provide and courts cannot. That process involves the balancing of competing values and interests, which in our democratic system is the business of elected representatives. Whatever their validity, the contentions now pressed on us should be addressed to the political branches of the government, the Congress and the Executive, and not to the courts.

We have emphasized in the recent past that "[o]ur individual appraisal of the wisdom or unwisdom of a particular [legislative] course . . . is to be put aside in the process of interpreting a statute." TVA v. Hill, 437 U.S. 153, 194, 98 S.Ct. 2279, 2302, 57 L. Ed.2d 117 (1978). Our task, rather, is the narrow one of determining what Congress meant by the words it used in the statute; once that is done our powers are exhausted. Congress is free to amend § 101 so as to exclude from patent protection organisms produced by genetic engineering. Compare 42 U.S.C.A. § 2181, exempting from patent protection inventions "useful solely in the utilization of special nuclear material or atomic energy in an atomic weapon." Or it may choose to craft a statute specifically designed for such living things. But, until Congress takes such action, this Court must construe the language of § 101 as it is. The language of that section fairly embraces respondent's invention.

Accordingly, the judgment of the Court of Customs and Patent Appeals is affirmed.

Affirmed.

Mr. Justice BRENNAN, with whom Mr. Justice WHITE, Mr. Justice MARSHALL, and Mr. Justice POWELL join, dissenting.

I agree with the Court that the question before us is a narrow one. Neither the future of scientific research, nor even the ability of respondent Chakrabarty to reap some monopoly profits from his pioneering work, is at stake. Patents on the processes by which he has produced and employed the new living organism are not contested. The only question we need decide is whether Congress, exercising its authority under Art. I, § 8, of the Constitution, intended that he be able to secure a monopoly on the living organism itself, no matter how produced or how used. Because I believe the Court has misread the applicable legislation, I dissent.

The patent laws attempt to reconcile this Nation's deepseated antipathy to monopolies with the need to encourage progress. Given the complexity and legislative nature of this delicate task, we must be careful to extend patent protection no further than Congress has provided. In particular, were there an absence of legislative direction, the courts should leave to Congress the decisions whether and how far to extend the patent privilege into areas where the common understanding has been that patents are not available.

In this case, however, we do not confront a complete legislative vacuum. The sweeping language of the Patent Act of 1793, as re-enacted in 1952, is not the last pronouncement Congress has made in this area. In 1930 Congress enacted the Plant Patent Act affording patent protection to developers of certain asexually reproduced plants. In 1970 Congress enacted the Plant Variety Protection Act to extend protection to certain new plant varieties capable of sexual reproduction. Thus, we are not dealing—as the Court would have it—with the routine problem of "unanticipated inventions." In these two Acts Congress has addressed the general problem of patenting animate inventions and has chosen carefully limited language granting protection to some kinds of discoveries, but specifically excluding others. These Acts strongly evidence a congressional limitation that excludes bacteria from patentability.

First, the Acts evidence Congress' understanding, at least since 1930, that § 101 does not include living organisms. If newly developed living organisms not naturally occurring had been patentable under § 101, the plants included in the scope of the 1930 and 1970 Acts could have been patented without new legislation. Those plants, like the bacteria involved in this case, were new varieties not naturally occurring. Although the Court rejects this line of argument, it does not explain why the Acts were necessary unless to correct a pre-existing situation. I cannot share the Court's implicit assumption that Congress was engaged in either idle exercises or mere correction of the public record when it enacted the 1930 and 1970 Acts. And Congress certainly thought it was doing something significant. The committee reports contain expansive prose about the previously unavailable benefits to be derived from extending patent protection to plants. Because Congress thought it had to legislate in order to make agricultural "human-made inventions" patentable and because the legislation Congress enacted is limited, it follows that Congress never meant to make patentable items outside the scope of the legislation.

Second, the 1970 Act clearly indicates that Congress has included bacteria within the focus of its legislative concern, but not within the scope of patent protection. Congress specifically excluded bacteria from the coverage of the 1970 Act. 7 U.S.C.A. § 2402(a). The Court's attempts to supply explanations for this explicit exclusion ring hollow. It is true that there is no mention in the legislative history of the exclusion, but that does not give us license to invent reasons. The fact is that Congress, assuming that animate objects as to which it had not specifically legislated could not be patented, excluded bacteria from the set of patentable organisms.

The Court protests that its holding today is dictated by the broad language of § 101, which "cannot be confined to the 'particular application[s] . . . contemplated by the legislators.'" But as I have shown, the Court's decision does not follow the unavoidable implications of the statute. Rather, it extends the patent system to cover living material even though Congress plainly has legislated in the belief that § 101 does not encompass living organisms. It is the role of Congress, not this Court, to broaden or narrow the reach of the patent laws. This is especially true where, as here, the composition sought to be patented uniquely implicates matters of public concern.

DIAMOND v. DIEHR

49 U.S. Law Week 4194 (March 3, 1981).

— U.S. —, — S.Ct. —, — L.Ed.2d —, — U.S.P.Q. —.

Mr. Justice REHNQUIST delivered the opinion of the Court.

We granted certiorari to determine whether a process for curing synthetic rubber which includes in several of its steps the use of a mathematical formula and a programmed digital computer is patentable subject matter under 35 U.S.C.A. § 101.

I

The patent application at issue was filed by the respondents on August 6, 1975. The claimed invention is a process for molding raw, uncured synthetic rubber into cured precision products. The process uses a mold for precisely shaping the uncured material under heat and pressure and then curing the synthetic rubber in the mold so that the product will retain its shape and be functionally operative after the molding is completed.[1]

Respondents claim that their process ensures the production of molded articles which are properly cured. Achieving the perfect cure depends upon several factors including the thickness of the article to be molded, the temperature of the molding process, and the amount of time that the article is allowed to remain in the press. It is possible using well-known time, temperature, and cure relationships to calculate by means of the Arrhenius equation [2] when to open the press and remove the cured product. Nonetheless, according to the respondents, the industry has not been able to obtain uniformly accurate cures because the temperature of the molding press could not

1. A "cure" is obtained by mixing curing agents into the uncured polymer in advance of molding, and then applying heat over a period of time. If the synthetic rubber is cured for the right length of time at the right temperature, it becomes a useable product.

2. The equation is named after its discoverer Svante Arrhenius and has long been used to calculate the cure time in rubber molding presses. The equation can be expressed as follows:

$$\ln v = CZ + x$$

wherein ln v is the natural logarithm of v, the total required cure time; C is the activation constant, a unique figure for each batch of each compound being molded, determined in accordance with rheometer measurements of each batch; Z is the temperature in the mold; and x is a constant dependent on the geometry of the particular mold in the press. A rheometer is an instrument to measure flow of viscous substances.

be precisely measured thus making it difficult to do the necessary computations to determine cure time.[3] Because the temperature *inside* the press has heretofore been viewed as an uncontrollable variable, the conventional industry practice has been to calculate the cure time as the shortest time in which all parts of the product will definitely be cured, assuming a reasonable amount of mold-opening time during loading and unloading. But the shortcoming of this practice is that operating with an uncontrollable variable inevitably led in some instances to overestimating the mold-opening time and over-curing the rubber, and in other instances to underestimating that time and undercuring the product.[4]

Respondents characterize their contribution to the art to reside in the process of constantly measuring the actual temperature inside the mold. These temperature measurements are then automatically fed into a computer which repeatedly recalculates the cure time by use of the Arrhenius equation. When the recalculated time equals the actual time that has elapsed since the press was closed, the computer signals a device to open the press. According to the respondents, the continuous measuring of the temperature inside the mold cavity, the feeding of this information to a digital computer which constantly recalculates the cure time, and the signaling by the computer to open the press, are all new in the art.

The patent examiner rejected the respondents' claims on the sole ground that they were drawn to nonstatutory subject matter under 35 U.S.C.A. § 101.[5] He determined that those steps in respondents'

3. During the time a press is open for loading, it will cool. The longer it is open, the cooler it becomes and the longer it takes to re-heat the press to the desired temperature range. Thus, the time necessary to raise the mold temperature to curing temperature is an unpredictable variable. The respondents claim to have overcome this problem by continuously measuring the actual temperature in the closed press through the use of a thermocouple.

4. We note that the Government does not seriously contest the respondents' assertions regarding the inability of the industry to obtain accurate cures on a uniform basis.

5. Respondents' application contained 11 different claims. Three examples are claims 1, 2, and 11 which provide:
"1. A method of operating a rubber-molding press for precision molded compounds with the aid of a digital computer, comprising:
"providing said computer with a data base for said press including at least,

"natural logarithm conversion data (ln),
"the activation energy constant (C) unique to each batch of said compound being molded, and
"a constant (x) dependent upon the geometry of the particular mold of the press,
"initiating an interval timer in said computer upon the closure of the press for monitoring the elapsed time of said closure,
"constantly determining the temperature (Z) of the mold at a location closely adjacent to the mold cavity in the press during molding,
"constantly providing the computer with the temperature (Z),
"repetitively calculating in the computer, at frequent intervals during each cure, the Arrhenius equation for reaction time during the cure, which is
"$\ln v = CZ + x$
"where v is the total required cure time,
"repetitively comparing in the computer at said frequent intervals during the cure each said calculation of the total required cure

claims that are carried out by a computer under control of a stored program constituted nonstatutory subject matter under this Court's decision in Gottschalk v. Benson, 409 U.S. 63 (1972). The remaining steps—installing rubber in the press and the subsequent closing of the press—were "conventional in nature and cannot be the basis of patentability." The examiner concluded that respondents' claims defined and sought protection of a computer program for operating a rubber molding press.

The Patent and Trademark Office Board of Appeals agreed with the examiner, but the Court of Customs and Patent Appeals reversed. The court noted that a claim drawn to subject matter otherwise statutory does not become nonstatutory because a computer is involved. The respondents' claims were not directed to a mathematical algorithm or an improved method of calculation but rather recited an improved process for molding rubber articles by solving a practical problem which had arisen in the molding of rubber products.

time calculated with the Arrhenius equation and said elapsed time, and

"opening the press automatically when a said comparison indicates equivalence.

"2. The method of claim 1 including measuring the activation energy constant for the compound being molded in the press with a rheometer and automatically updating said data base within the computer in the event of changes in the compound being molded in said press as measured by said rheometer.

"11. A method of manufacturing precision molded articles from selected synthetic rubber compounds in an openable rubber molding press having at least one heated precision mold, comprising:

"(a) heating said mold to a temperature range approximating a predetermined rubber curing temperature,

"(b) installing prepared unmolded synthetic rubber of a known compound in a molding cavity of a predetermined geometry as defined by said mold,

"(c) closing said press to mold said rubber to occupy said cavity in conformance with the contour of said mold and to cure said rubber by transfer of heat thereto from said mold,

"(d) initiating an interval timer upon the closure of said press for monitoring the elapsed time of said closure,

"(e) heating said mold during said closure to maintain the temperature thereof within said range approximating said rubber curing temperature,

"(f) constantly determining the temperature of said mold at a location closely adjacent said cavity thereof throughout closure of said press,

"(g) repetitively calculating at frequent periodic intervals throughout closure of said press the Arrhenius equation for reaction time of said rubber to determine total required cure time v as follows:

"$\ln v = cz + x$

"wherein c is an activation energy constant determined for said rubber being molded and cured in said press, z is the temperature of said mold at the time of each calculation of said Arrhenius equation, and x is a constant which is a function of said predetermined geometry of said mold,

"(h) for each repetition of calculation of said Arrehenius equation herein, comparing the resultant calculated total required cure time with the monitored elapsed time measured by said interval timer,

"(i) opening said press when a said comparison of calculated total required cure time and monitored elapsed time indicates equivalence, and

"(j) removing from said mold the resultant precision molded and cured rubber article."

The Government sought certiorari arguing that the decision of the Court of Customs and Patent Appeals was inconsistent with prior decisions of this Court. Because of the importance of the question presented, we granted the writ.

II

Last Term in Diamond v. Chakrabarty, —— U.S. —— (1980), this Court discussed the historical purposes of the patent laws and in particular 35 U.S.C.A. § 101. As in *Chakrabarty*, we must here construe 35 U.S.C.A. § 101 which provides:

"Whoever invents or discovers any new or useful process, machine, manufacture, or composition of matter, or any new and useful improvement thereof, may obtain a patent therefor, subject to the conditions and requirements of this Title."

In cases of statutory construction, we begin with the language of the statute. Unless otherwise defined, "words will be interpreted as taking their ordinary, contemporary, common meaning," Perrin v. United States, —— U.S. —— (1979), and, in dealing with the patent laws, we have more than once cautioned that "courts 'should not read into the patent laws limitations and conditions which a legislature has not expressed.'" Diamond v. Chakrabarty, —— U.S., at ——, quoting United States v. Dubilier Condenser Corp., 289 U.S. 178, 199 (1933).

The Patent Act of 1793 defined statutory subject matter as "any new and useful art, machine, manufacture or composition of matter, or any new or useful improvement [thereof]." Act of Feb. 21, 1793, ch. 11, § 1, 1 Stat. 318. Not until the patent laws were recodified in 1952 did Congress replace the word "art" with the word "process." It is that latter word which we confront today, and in order to determine its meaning we may not be unmindful of the Committee Reports accompanying the 1952 Act which inform us that Congress intended statutory subject matter to "include anything under the sun that is made by man." S.Rep.No.1979, 82d Cong., 2d Sess., 5 (1952) H.R. Rep.No.1923, 82d Cong., 2d Sess., 6 (1952).

Although the term "process" was not added to 35 U.S.C.A. § 101 until 1952, a process has historically enjoyed patent protection because it was considered a form of "art" as that term was used in the 1793 Act. In defining the nature of a patentable process, the Court stated:

"That a process may be patentable, irrespective of the particular form of the instrumentalities used, cannot be disputed. . . . A process is a mode of treatment of certain materials to produce a given result. It is an act, or a series of acts, performed upon the subject matter to be transformed and reduced to a different state or thing. If new and useful, it is just as patentable as is a piece of machinery. In the language of the patent law, it is an art. The machinery pointed out as suitable to perform the process may or may not be new or patentable; whilst the process

itself may be altogether new, and produce an entirely new result. The process requires that certain things should be done
with certain substances, and in a certain order; but the tools
to be used in doing this may be of secondary consequence." Cochrane v. Deener, 94 U.S. 780, 787–788 (1876).

Analysis of the eligibility of a claim of patent protection for a
"process" did not change with the addition of that term to § 101.
Recently, in Gottschalk v. Benson, 409 U.S. 663 (1972), we repeated
the above definition recited in Cochrane v. Deener, adding "Transformation and reduction of an article 'to a different state or thing'
is the clue to the patentability of a process claim that does not include
particular machines." Id., at 70.

Analyzing respondents' claims according to the above statements
from our cases, we think that a physical and chemical process for
molding precision synthetic rubber products falls within the § 101
categories of possibly patentable subject matter. That respondents'
claims involve the transformation of an article, in this case raw uncured synthetic rubber, into a different state or thing cannot be disputed. The respondents' claims describe in detail a step-by-step method for accomplishing such beginning with the loading of a mold with
raw uncured rubber and ending with the eventual opening of the press
at the conclusion of the cure. Industrial processes such as this are
the type which have historically been eligible to receive the protection of our patent laws.

III

Our conclusion regarding respondents' claims is not altered by
the fact that in several steps of the process a mathematical equation
and a programmed digital computer are used. This Court has undoubtedly recognized limits to § 101 and every discovery is not embraced within the statutory terms. Excluded from such patent protection are laws of nature, physical phenomena and abstract ideas.
See Parker v. Flook, 437 U.S. 584 (1978); Gottschalk v. Benson, 409
U.S. 63, 67 (1973); Funk Bros. Seed Co. v. Kalo Co., 333 U.S. 127,
130 (1948). "An idea of itself is not patentable," Rubber-Tip Pencil
Co. v. Howard, 20 Wall. 498, 507 (1874). "A principle, in the abstract,
is a fundamental truth; an original cause; a motive; these cannot
be patented, as no one can claim in either of them an exclusive right."
Le Roy v. Tatham, 14 How. 156, 175 (1852). Only last Term, we explained:

> "[A] new mineral discovered in the earth or a new plant found
> in the wild is not patentable subject matter. Likewise, Einstein
> could not patent his celebrated law that $E=mc^2$; nor could New-
> ton have patented the law of gravity. Such discoveries are 'mani-
> festations of . . , nature, free to all men and reserved ex-
> clusively to none.'" Diamond v. Chakrabarty, —— U.S. ——, ——,
> quoting Funk Bros. Seed Co. v. Kalo Co., 333 U.S. 127, 130 (1948).

Our recent holdings in Gottschalk v. Benson, supra, and Parker v. Flook, supra, both of which are computer-related, stand for no more than these long established principles. In *Benson,* we held unpatentable claims for an algorithm used to convert binary code decimal numbers to equivalent pure binary numbers. The sole practical application of the algorithm was in connection with the programming of a general purpose digital computer. We defined "algorithm" as a "procedure for solving a given type of mathematical problem," and we concluded that such an algorithm, or mathematical formula, is like a law of nature, which cannot be the subject of a patent.

Parker v. Flook, supra, presented a similar situation. The claims were drawn to a method for computing an "alarm limit." An "alarm limit" is simply a number and the Court concluded that the application sought to protect a formula for computing this number. Using this formula, the updated alarm limit could be calculated if several other variables were known. The application, however, did not purport to explain how these other variables were to be determined, nor did it purport "to contain any disclosure relating to the chemical processes at work, the monitoring of process variables, or the means of setting off an alarm system. All that is provided is a formula for computing an updated alarm limit." 437 U.S., at 586.

In contrast, the respondents here do not seek to patent a mathematical formula. Instead, they seek patent protection for a process of curing synthetic rubber. Their process admittedly employs a well known mathematical equation, but they do not seek to pre-empt the use of that equation. Rather, they seek only to foreclose from others the use of that equation in conjunction with all of the other steps in their claimed process. These include installing rubber in a press, closing the mold, constantly determining the temperature of the mold, constantly recalculating the appropriate cure time through the use of the formula and a digital computer and, automatically opening the press at the proper time. Obviously, one does not need a "computer" to cure natural or synthetic rubber, but if the computer use incorporated in the process patent significantly lessens the possibility of "overcuring" or "undercuring," the process as a whole does not thereby become unpatentable subject matter.

Our earlier opinions lend support to our present conclusion that a claim drawn to subject matter otherwise statutory does not become nonstatutory simply because it uses a mathematical formula, computer program or digital computer. In Gottschalk v. Benson, supra, we noted "It is said that the decision precludes a patent for any program servicing a computer. We do not so hold." 409 U.S., at 71. Similarly, in Parker v. Flook, supra, we stated, "A process is not unpatentable simply because it contains a law of nature or a mathematical algorithm." 437 U.S., at 590. It is now commonplace that an *application* of a law of nature or mathematical formula to a known structure or process may well be deserving of patent protection. As Mr. Justice Stone explained four decades ago:

"While a scientific truth, or the mathematical expression of it, is not a patentable invention, a novel and useful structure created with the aid of knowledge of scientific truth may be." Mackay Radio Corp. & Telegraph Co. v. Radio Corp. of America, 306 U.S. 86, 94 (1939).

We think this statement in *Mackay* takes us a long way toward the correct answer in this case. Arrhenius' equation is not patentable in isolation, but when a process for curing rubber is devised which incorporates in it a more efficient solution of the equation, that process is at the very least not barred at the threshold by § 101.

In determining the eligibility of respondents' claimed process for patent protection under § 101, their claims must be considered as a whole. It is inappropriate to dissect the claims into old and new elements and then to ignore the presence of the old elements in the analysis. This is particularly true in a process claim because a new combination of steps in a process may be patentable even though all the constituents of the combination were well known and in common use before the combination was made. The "novelty" of any element or steps in a process, or even of the process itself, is of no relevance in determining whether the subject matter of a claim falls within the § 101 categories of possibly patentable subject matter.[12]

It has been urged that novelty is an appropriate consideration under § 101. Presumably, this argument results from the language in § 101 referring to any "new and useful" process, machine, etc. Section 101, however, is a general statement of the type of subject matter that is eligible for patent protection "subject to the conditions and requirements of this title." Specific conditions for patentability follow and § 102 covers in detail the conditions relating to novelty. The question therefore of whether a particular invention is novel is "fully apart from whether the invention falls into a category of statutory subject matter." In re Bergy, 596 F.2d 952, 961 (CCPA 1979). The legislative history of the 1952 Patent Act is in accord with this reasoning. The Senate Report provided:

"Section 101 sets forth the subject matter that can be patented, 'subject to the conditions and requirement of this title.' The conditions under which a patent may be obtained follow, and *Sec-*

---

12. It is argued that the procedure of dissecting a claim into old and new elements is mandated by our decision in *Flook* which noted that a mathematical algorithm must be assumed to be within the "prior art." It is from this language that the Government premises its argument that if everything other than the algorithm is determined to be old in the art, then the claim cannot recite statutory subject matter. The fallacy in this argument is that we did not hold in *Flook* that the mathematical algorithm could not be considered at all when making the § 101 determination. To accept the analysis proffered by the Government would, if carried to its extreme, make all inventions unpatentable because all inventions can be reduced to underlying principles of nature which, once known, make their implementation obvious. The analysis suggested by the Government would also undermine our earlier decisions regarding the criteria to consider in determining the eligibility of a process for patent protection.

tion 102 covers the conditions relating to novelty." S.Rep.No. 1979, 82d Cong., 2d Sess., 5 (1952) (emphasis supplied).

It is later stated in the same report:

> "Section 102, in general, may be said to describe the statutory novelty required for patentability, and includes, in effect, the amplification and definition of 'new' in Section 101." Id., at 6.

Finally, it is stated in the "Revision Notes":

> "The corresponding section of [the] existing statute is split into two sections, Section 101 relating to the subject matter for which patents may be obtained, and Section 102 defining statutory novelty and stating other conditions for patentability." Id., at 17.

In this case, it may later be determined that the respondents' process is not deserving of patent protection because it fails to satisfy the statutory conditions of novelty under § 102 or nonobviousness under § 103. A rejection on either of these grounds does not affect the determination that respondents' claims recited subject matter which was eligible for patent protection under § 101.

IV

We have before us today only the question of whether respondents' claims fall within the § 101 categories of possibly patentable subject matter. We view respondents' claims as nothing more than a process for molding rubber products and not as an attempt to patent a mathematical formula. We recognize, of course, that when a claim recites a mathematical formula (or scientific principle or phenomenon of nature), an inquiry must be made into whether the claim is seeking patent protection for that formula in the abstract. A mathematical formula as such is not accorded the protection of our patent laws and this principle cannot be circumvented by attempting to limit the use of the formula to a particular technological environment. Similarly, insignificant post-solution activity will not transform an unpatentable principle into a patentable process.[14] To hold otherwise would

---

14. Arguably, the claims in *Flook* did more than present a mathematical formula. The claims also solved the calculation in order to produce a new number or "alarm limit" and then replaced the old number with the number newly produced. The claims covered all uses of the formula in processes "comprising the catalytic chemical conversion of hydrocarbons." There are numerous such processes in the petrochemical and oil refinery industries and the claims therefore covered a broad range of potential uses. The claims, however, did not cover every conceivable application of the formula. We rejected in *Flook* the argument that because all possible uses of the mathematical formula were not pre-empted, the claim should be eligible for patent protection. Our reasoning in *Flook* is in no way inconsistent with our reasoning here. A mathematical formula does not suddenly become patentable subject matter simply by having the applicant acquiesce to limiting the reach of the patent for the formula to a particular technological use. A mathematical formula in the abstract is nonstatutory subject matter regardless of whether the patent is intended to cover all uses of the formula or only limited uses. Similarly, a mathematical formula does not become patentable subject matter merely by including in the claim for the formula token post-solution activity such as

allow a competent draftsman to evade the recognized limitations on the type of subject matter eligible for patent protection. On the other hand, when a claim containing a mathematical formula implements or applies that formula in a structure or process which, when considered as a whole, is performing a function which the patent laws were designed to protect (e. g., transforming or reducing an article to a different state or thing), then the claim satisfies the requirements of § 101. Because we do not view respondents' claims as an attempt to patent a mathematical formula, but rather to be drawn to an industrial process for the molding of rubber products, we affirm the judgment of the Court of Customs and Patent Appeals.

Justice STEVENS, with whom Justice BRENNAN, Justice MARSHALL, and Justice BLACKMUN join, dissenting.

The starting point in the proper adjudication of patent litigation is an understanding of what the inventor claims to have discovered. The Court's decision in this case rests on a misreading of the Diehr and Lutton patent application. Moreover, the Court has compounded its error by ignoring the critical distinction between the character of the subject matter that the inventor claims to be novel—the § 101 issue—and the question whether that subject matter is in fact novel —the § 102 issue.

I

Before discussing the major flaws in the Court's opinion, a word of history may be helpful. As the Court recognized in Parker v. Flook, 437 U.S. 584, 595 (1978), the computer industry is relatively young. Although computer technology seems commonplace today, the first digital computer capable of utilizing stored programs was developed less than 30 years ago. Patent law developments in response to this new technology are of even more recent vintage. The subject of legal protection for computer programs did not begin to receive serious consideration until over a decade after completion of the first programmable digital computer. It was 1968 before the federal courts squarely addressed the subject, and 1972 before this Court announced its first decision in the area.

Prior to 1968, well-established principles of patent law probably would have prevented the issuance of a valid patent on almost any conceivable computer program. Under the "mental steps" doctrine, processes involving mental operations were considered unpatentable. The mental steps doctrine was based upon the familiar principle that a scientific concept or mere idea cannot be the subject of a valid patent. The doctrine was regularly invoked to deny patents to inventions consisting primarily of mathematical formulae or methods of

the type claimed in *Flook*. We were careful to note in *Flook* that the patent application did not purport to explain how the variables used in the formula were to be selected, nor did the application contain any disclosure relating to chemical processes at work or the means of setting off an alarm or adjusting the alarm limit. All the application provided was a "formula for computing an updated alarm limit."

computation. It was also applied against patent claims in which a mental operation or mathematical computation was the sole novel element or inventive contribution; it was clear that patentability could not be predicated upon a mental step. Under the "function of a machine" doctrine, a process which amounted to nothing more than a description of the function of a machine was unpatentable. This doctrine had its origin in several 19th-century decisions of this Court, and it had been consistently followed thereafter by the lower federal courts. Finally, the definition of "process" announced by this Court in Cochrane v. Deener, 94 U.S. 780, 787–788 (1876), seemed to indicate that a patentable process must cause a physical transformation in the materials to which the process is applied.

Concern with the patent system's ability to deal with rapidly changing technology in the computer and other fields led to the formation in 1965 of the President's Commission on the Patent System. After studying the question of computer program patentability, the Commission recommended that computer programs be expressly excluded from the coverage of the patent laws; this recommendation was based primarily upon the Patent Office's inability to deal with the administrative burden of examining program applications. At approximately the time that the Commission issued its report, the Patent Office published notice of its intention to prescribe guidelines for the examination of applications for patents on computer programs. Under the proposed guidelines, a computer program, whether claimed as an apparatus or as a process, was unpatentable. The Patent Office indicated, however, that a programmed computer could be a component of a patentable process if combined with unobvious elements to produce a physical result. The Patent Office formally adopted the guidelines in 1968.

The new guidelines were to have a short life. Beginning with two decisions in 1968, a dramatic change in the law as understood by the Court of Customs and Patent Appeals took place. By repudiating the well-settled "function of a machine" and "mental steps" doctrines, that court reinterpreted § 101 of the Patent Code to enlarge drastically the categories of patentable subject matter. This reinterpretation would lead to the conclusion that computer programs were within the categories of inventions to which Congress intended to extend patent protection.

In In re Tarczy-Hornoch, 397 F.2d 856 (CCPA 1968), a divided Court of Customs and Patent Appeals overruled the line of cases developing and applying the "function of a machine" doctrine. The majority acknowledged that the doctrine had originated with decisions of this Court and that the lower federal courts, including the Court of Customs and Patent Appeals, had consistently adhered to it during the preceding 70 years. Nonetheless, the court concluded that the doctrine rested on a misinterpretation of the precedents and that it was contrary to "the basic purposes of the patent system and productive of a range of undesirable results from the harshly inequitable to the silly." Id., at 867. Shortly thereafter, a similar fate befell the "mental steps" doctrine. In In re Prater, 415 F.2d 1378 (1968), modified on rehearing, 415 F.2d 1393 (CCPA 1969), the court found that the precedents on which that doctrine was based either were poorly reasoned or had been misinterpreted over the years. The court concluded that the fact that a process may be performed mentally should not foreclose patentability if the claims reveal that the process also may be performed without mental operations. This aspect of the original *Prater* opinion was substantially undisturbed by the opinion issued after rehearing. However, the second *Prater* opinion clearly indicated that patent claims broad enough to encompass the operation of a programmed computer would not be rejected for lack of patentable subject matter.

The Court of Customs and Patent Appeals soon replaced the overruled doctrines with more expansive principles formulated with computer technology in mind. In In re Bernhart, 417 F.2d 1395 (CCPA 1969), the court reaffirmed *Prater*, and indicated that all that remained of the mental steps doctrine was a prohibition on the granting of a patent that would confer a monoply on all uses of a scientific principle or mathematical equation. The court also announced that a computer programmed with a new and unobvious program was physically different from the same computer without that program; the programmed computer was a new machine or at least a new improvement over the unprogrammed computer. Therefore, patent protection could be obtained for new computer programs if the patent claims were drafted in apparatus form.

The Court of Customs and Patent Appeals turned its attention to process claims encompassing computer programs in In re Musgrave, 431 F.2d 882 (CCPA 1970). In that case, the court emphasized the fact that *Prater* had done away with the mental steps doctrine; in particular, the court rejected the Patent Office's continued reliance upon the "point of novelty" approach to claim analysis.[15] The court also announced a new standard for evaluating process claims under § 101: any sequence of operational steps was a patentable process under § 101 as long as it was within the "technological arts." This standard effectively disposed of any vestiges of the mental steps doctrine remaining after *Prater* and *Bernhart*. The "technological arts" standard was refined in In re Benson, 441 F.2d 682 (CCPA 1971), in which the court held that computers, regardless of the uses to which they are put, are within the technological arts for purposes of § 101.

In re Benson, of course, was reversed by this Court in Gottschalk v. Benson, 409 U.S. 63 (1972). Justice Douglas' opinion for a unanimous Court made no reference to the lower court's rejection of the mental steps doctrine or to the new technological arts standard. Rather, the Court clearly held that new mathematical procedures that

---

15. Under the "point of novelty" approach, if the novelty or advancement in the art claimed by the inventor resided solely in a step of the process embodying a mental operation or other unpatentable element, the claim was rejected under § 101 as being directed to nonstatutory subject matter.

can be conducted in old computers, like mental processes and abstract intellectual concepts, are not patentable processes within the meaning of § 101.

The Court of Customs and Patent Appeals had its first opportunity to interpret *Benson* in In re Christensen, 478 F.2d 1392 (CCPA 1973). In *Christensen*, the claimed invention was a method in which the only novel element was a mathematical formula. The court resurrected the point of novelty approach abandoned in *Musgrave* and held that a process claim in which the point of novelty was a mathematical equation to be solved as the final step of the process did not define patentable subject matter after *Benson*. Accordingly, the court affirmed the Board of Patent Appeals' rejection of the claims under § 101.

The Court of Customs and Patent Appeals in subsequent cases began to narrow its interpretation of *Benson*. In In re Johnston, 502 F.2d 765 (CCPA 1974), the court held that a record-keeping machine system which comprised a programmed digital computer was patentable subject matter under § 101. The majority dismissed *Benson* with the observation that *Benson* involved only process, not apparatus, claims. Judge Rich dissented, arguing that to limit *Benson* only to process claims would make patentability turn upon the form in which a program invention was claimed. The court again construed *Benson* as limited only to process claims in In re Noll, 545 F.2d 141 (CCPA 1976), cert. denied, 434 U.S. 875 (1977); apparatus claims were governed by the court's pre-*Benson* conclusion that a programmed computer was structurally different from the same computer without that particular program. In dissent, Judge Lane, joined by Judge Rich, argued that *Benson* should be read as a general proscription of the patenting of computer programs regardless of the form of the claims. Judge Lane's interpretation of *Benson* was rejected by the majority in In re Chatfield, 545 F.2d 152 (CCPA 1976), cert. denied, 434 U.S. 875 (1977), decided on the same day as *Noll*. In that case, the court construed *Benson* to preclude the patenting of program inventions claimed as processes only where the claims would pre-empt all uses of an algorithm or mathematical formula. The dissenting judges argued, as they had in *Noll*, that *Benson* held that programs for general-purpose digital computers are not patentable subject matter.

Following *Noll* and *Chatfield*, the Court of Customs and Patent Appeals consistently interpreted *Benson* to preclude the patenting of a program-related process invention only when the claims, if allowed, would wholly pre-empt the algorithm itself. One of the cases adopting this view was In re Flook, 559 F.2d 21 (CCPA 1977), which was reversed in Parker v. Flook, 437 U.S. 584 (1978). Before this Court decided *Flook*, however, the lower court developed a two-step procedure for analyzing program-related inventions in light of *Benson*. In In re Freeman, 573 F.2d 1237 (CCPA 1978), the court held that such inventions must first be examined to determine whether a mathematical algorithm is directly or indirectly claimed; if an algorithm is

recited, the court must then determine whether the claim would
wholly pre-empt that algorithm. Only if a claim satisfied both inquiries was *Benson* considered applicable.

In *Flook*, this Court clarified *Benson* in three significant respects.
First, *Flook* held that the *Benson* rule of unpatentable subject matter
was not limited, as the lower court believed, to claims which wholly
pre-empted an algorithm or amounted to a patent on the algorithm
itself. Second, the Court made it clear that an improved method of
calculation, even when employed as part of a physical process, is not
patentable subject matter under § 101. Finally, the Court explained
the correct procedure for analyzing a patent claim employing a
mathematical algorithm. Under this procedure, the algorithm is
treated for § 101 purposes as though it were a familiar part of the
prior art; the claim is then examined to determine whether it discloses "some other inventive concept."

Although the Court of Customs and Patent Appeals in several
post-*Flook* decisions held that program-related inventions were not
patentable subject matter under § 101, in general *Flook* was not en-
thusiastically received by that court. In In re Bergy, 596 F.2d 952
(CCPA 1979), the majority engaged in an extensive critique of *Flook*,
concluding that this Court had erroneously commingled "distinct statutory provisions which are conceptually unrelated." In subsequent
cases, the court construed *Flook* as resting on nothing more than the
way in which the patent claims had been drafted, and it expressly
declined to use the method of claim analysis spelled out in that decision. The Court of Customs and Patent Appeals has taken the position that, if an application is drafted in a way that discloses an entire process as novel, it defines patentable subject matter even if the
only novel element that the inventor claims to have discovered is a
new computer program. The court interpreted *Flook* in this manner
in its opinion in this case. In my judgment, this reading of *Flook*—
although entirely consistent with the lower court's expansive approach
to § 101 during the past 12 years—trivializes the holding in *Flook*,
the principle that underlies *Benson*, and the settled line of authority
reviewed in those opinions.

II

As I stated at the outset, the starting point in the proper adjudication of patent litigation is an understanding of what the inventor
claims to have discovered. Indeed, the outcome of such litigation is
often determined by the judge's understanding of the patent application. This is such a case.

In the first sentence of its opinion, the Court states the question
presented as "whether a process for curing synthetic rubber . . .
is patentable subject matter." Of course, that question was effectively answered many years ago when Charles Goodyear obtained his patent on the vulcanization process. The patent application filed by Diehr
and Lutton, however, teaches nothing about the chemistry of the synthetic rubber-curing process, nothing about the raw materials to be

used in curing synthetic rubber, nothing about the equipment to be used in the process, and nothing about the significance or effect of any process variable such as temperature, curing time, particular compositions of material, or mold configurations. In short, Diehr and Lutton do not claim to have discovered anything new about the process for curing synthetic rubber.

As the Court reads the claims in the Diehr and Lutton patent application, the inventors' discovery is a method of constantly measuring the actual temperature inside a rubber molding press. As I read the claims, their discovery is an improved method of calculating the time that the mold should remain closed during the curing process. If the Court's reading of the claims were correct, I would agree that they disclose patentable subject matter. On the other hand, if the Court accepted my reading, I feel confident that the case would be decided differently.

There are three reasons why I cannot accept the Court's conclusion that Diehr and Lutton claim to have discovered a new method of constantly measuring the temperature inside a mold. First, there is not a word in the patent application that suggests that there is anything unusual about the temperature-reading devices used in this process—or indeed that any particular species of temperature-reading device should be used in it. Second, since devices for constantly measuring actual temperatures—on a back porch, for example—have been familiar articles for quite some time, I find it difficult to believe that a patent application filed in 1975 was premised on the notion that a "process of constantly measuring the actual temperature" had just been discovered. Finally, the Board of Patent Appeals expressly found that "the only difference between the conventional methods of operating a molding press and that claimed in [the] application rests in those steps of the claims which relate to the calculation incident to the solution of the mathematical problem or formula used to control the mold heater and the automatic opening of the press." This finding was not disturbed by the Court of Customs and Patent Appeals and is clearly correct.

A fair reading of the entire patent application, as well as the specific claims, makes it perfectly clear that what Diehr and Lutton claim to have discovered is a method of using a digital computer to determine the amount of time that a rubber molding press should remain closed during the synthetic rubber curing process. There is no suggestion that there is anything novel in the instrumentation of the mold, in actuating a timer when the press is closed, or in automatically opening the press when the computed time expires. Nor does the application suggest that Diehr and Lutton have discovered anything about the temperatures in the mold or the amount of curing time that will produce the best cure. What they claim to have discovered, in essence, is a method of updating the original estimated curing time by repetitively recalculating that time pursuant to a well-known mathematical formula in response to variations in temperature within the mold. Their method of updating the curing time calculation is strikingly reminiscent of the method of updating alarm limits that Dale Flook sought to patent.

Parker v. Flook, 437 U.S. 584 (1978), involved the use of a digital computer in connection with a catalytic conversion process. During the conversion process, variables such as temperature, pressure, and flow rates were constantly monitored and fed into the computer; in this case, temperature in the mold is the variable that is monitored and fed into the computer. In *Flook*, the digital computer repetitively recalculated the "alarm limit"—a number that might signal the need to terminate or modify the catalytic conversion process; in this case, the digital computer repetitively recalculates the correct curing time—a number that signals the time when the synthetic rubber molding press should open.

The essence of the claimed discovery in both cases was an algorithm that could be programmed on a digital computer. In *Flook*, the algorithm made use of multiple process variables; in this case, it makes use of only one. In *Flook*, the algorithm was expressed in a newly-developed mathematical formula; in this case, the algorithm makes use of a well-known mathematical formula. Manifestly, neither of these differences can explain today's holding.[32] What I believe does explain today's holding is a misunderstanding of the applicants' claimed invention and a failure to recognize the critical difference between the "discovery" requirement in § 101 and the "novelty" requirement in § 102.

III

The Court misapplies Parker v. Flook because, like the Court of Customs and Patent Appeals, it fails to understand or completely disregards the distinction between the subject matter of what the in-

32. Indeed, the most significant distinction between the invention at issue in *Flook* and that at issue in this case lies not in the characteristics of the inventions themselves, but rather in the drafting of the claims. After noting that "[t]he Diehr claims are reminiscent of the claims in *Flook*," Blumenthal & Riter, 62 J.Pat. Off. Soc'y, at 502–503, the authors of a recent article on the subject observe that the Court of Customs and Patent Appeals' analysis in this case "lends itself to an interesting exercise in claim drafting." Id., at 505. To illustrate their point, the authors redrafted the Diehr and Lutton claims into the format employed in the *Flook* application:

"An improved method of calculating the cure time of a rubber molding process utilizing a digital computer comprising the steps of:
"a. . inputting into said computer input values including
"1. natural logarithm conversion data (ln),
"2. an activation energy constant (C) unique to each batch of rubber being molded,
"3. a constant (X) dependent upon the geometry of the particular mold of the press, and
"4. continuous temperature values (Z) of the mold during molding;
"b. operating said computer for
"1. counting the elapsed cure time,
"2. calculating the cure time from the input values using the Arrhenius equation ln $V=CZ+X$, where v is the total cure time, and
"c. providing output signals from said computer when said calculated cure time is equal to said elapsed cure time." Id., at 505.
The authors correctly conclude that even the lower court probably would have found that this claim was drawn to unpatentable subject matter under § 101.

ventor *claims* to have discovered—the § 101 issue—and the question whether that claimed discovery is in fact novel—the § 102 issue. If there is not even a claim that anything constituting patentable subject matter has been discovered, there is no occasion to address the novelty issue. Or, as was true in *Flook*, if the only concept that the inventor claims to have discovered is not patentable subject matter, § 101 requires that the application be rejected without reaching any issue under § 102; for it is irrelevant that unpatentable subject matter—in that case a formula for updating alarm limits—may in fact be novel.

Proper analysis, therefore, must start with an understanding of what the inventor claims to have discovered—or phrased somewhat differently—what he considers his inventive concept to be. It seems clear to me that Diehr and Lutton claim to have developed a new method of programming a digital computer in order to calculate—promptly and repeatedly—the correct curing time in a familiar process. In the § 101 analysis, we must assume that the sequence of steps in this programming method is novel, unobvious, and useful. The threshold question of whether such a method is patentable subject matter remains.

If that method is regarded as an "algorithm" as that term was used in Gottschalk v. Benson, supra, and in Parker v. Flook, supra, and if no other inventive concept is disclosed in the patent application, the question must be answered in the negative. In both *Benson* and *Flook*, the parties apparently agreed that the inventor's discovery was properly regarded as an algorithm; the holding that an algorithm was a "law of nature" that could not be patented therefore determined that those discoveries were not patentable processes within the meaning of § 101.

As the Court recognizes today, *Flook* also rejected the argument that patent protection was available if the inventor did not claim a monopoly on every conceivable use of the algorithm but instead limited his claims by describing a specific post-solution activity—in that case setting off an alarm in a catalytic conversion process. In its effort to distinguish *Flook* from the instant case, the Court characterizes that post-solution activity as "insignificant," or as merely "token" activity. As a practical matter, however, the post-solution activity described in the *Flook* application was no less significant than the automatic opening of the curing mold involved in this case. For setting off an alarm limit at the appropriate time is surely as important to the safe and efficient operation of a catalytic conversion process as is actuating the mold-opening device in a synthetic rubber curing process. In both cases, the post-solution activity is a significant part of the industrial process. But in neither case should that activity have any *legal* significance because it does not constitute a part of the inventive concept that the applicants claimed to have discovered.[39]

39. In *Flook*, the Court's analysis of the post-solution activity recited in the patent application turned, not on the relative significance of that activity in the catalytic conversion process, but rather on the fact that that activity

In Gottschalk v. Benson, we held that a program for the solution by a digital computer of a mathematical problem was not a patentable process within the meaning of § 101.   In Parker v. Flook, we further held that such a computer program could not be transformed into a patentable process by the addition of post-solution activity that was not claimed to be novel.   That holding plainly requires the rejection of Claims 1 and 2 of the Diehr and Lutton application quoted in the Court's opinion.   In my opinion, it equally requires rejection of Claim 11 because the presolution activity described in that claim is admittedly a familiar part of the prior art.

Even the Court does not suggest that the computer program developed by Diehr and Lutton is a patentable discovery.   Accordingly, if we treat the program as though it were a familiar part of the prior art—as well-established precedent requires—it is absolutely clear that their application contains no claim of patentable invention.   Their application was therefore properly rejected under § 101 by the Patent Office and the Board of Patent Appeals.

IV

The broad question whether computer programs should be given patent protection involves policy considerations that this Court is not authorized to address.   As the numerous briefs *amicus curiae* filed in Gottschalk v. Benson, supra, Dann v. Johnston, supra, Parker v. Flook, supra, and this case demonstrate, that question is not only difficult and important, but apparently also one that may be affected by institutional bias.   In each of those cases, the spokesmen for the organized patent bar have uniformly favored patentability and industry representatives have taken positions properly motivated by their economic self-interest.   Notwithstanding fervent argument that patent protection is essential for the growth of the software industry, commentators have noted that "this industry is growing by leaps and bounds without it." [43]   In addition, even some commentators who believe that legal protection for computer programs is desirable have expressed doubts that the present patent system can provide the needed protection.

Within the Federal Government, patterns of decision have also emerged.   Gottschalk, Dann, Parker, and Diamond were not ordinary

---

was not a part of the applicant's discovery:

"The notion that post-solution activity, no matter how conventional or obvious in itself, can transform an unpatentable principle into a patentable process exalts form over substance.   A competent draftsman could attach some form of post-solution activity to almost any mathematical formula: the Pythagorean theorem would not have been patentable, or partially patentable, because a patent applica-

tion contained a final step indicating that the formula, when solved, could be usefully applied to existing surveying techniques.   The concept of patentable subject matter under § 101 is not 'like a nose of wax which may be turned and twisted in any direction. . . .' White v. Dunbar, 119 U.S. 47, 51." 437 U.S., at 590 (footnote omitted).

43. Gemignani, supra, 7 Rut.J.Comp., Tech. & L., at 309.

litigants—each was serving as Commissioner of Patents and Trademarks when he opposed the availability of patent protection for a program-related invention. No doubt each may have been motivated by a concern about the ability of the Patent Office to process effectively the flood of applications that would inevitably flow from a decision that computer programs are patentable.[45] The consistent concern evidenced by the Commissioner of Patents and Trademarks and by the Board of Patent Appeals of the Patent and Trademark Office has not been shared by the Court of Customs and Patent Appeals, which reversed the Board in *Benson, Johnston*, and *Flook*, and was in turn reversed by this Court in each of those cases.

Scholars have been critical of the work of both tribunals. Some of that criticism may stem from a conviction about the merits of the broad underlying policy question; such criticism may be put to one side. Other criticism, however, identifies two concerns to which federal judges have a duty to respond. First, the cases considering the patentability of program-related inventions do not establish rules that enable a conscientious patent lawyer to determine with a fair degree of accuracy which, if any, program-related inventions will be patentable. Second, the inclusion of the ambiguous concept of an "algorithm" within the "law of nature" category of unpatentable subject matter has given rise to the concern that almost any process might be so described and therefore held unpatentable.

In my judgment, today's decision will aggravate the first concern and will not adequately allay the second. I believe both concerns would be better addressed by (1) an unequivocal holding that no program-related invention is a patentable process under § 101 unless it makes a contribution to the art that is not dependent entirely on the utilization of a computer, and (2) an unequivocal explanation that the term "algorithm" as used in this case, as in *Benson* and *Flook*, is synonymous with the term "computer program." Because the invention claimed in the patent application at issue in this case makes no contribution to the art that is not entirely dependent upon the utilization of a computer in a familiar process, I would reverse the decision of the Court of Customs and Patent Appeals.

NOTES

1. Why should patent law refuse protection to newly discovered natural principles? The reason commonly given is that, as techno-

---

45. This concern influenced the President's Commission on the Patent System when it recommended against patent protection for computer programs. In its report, the President's Commission stated:

"The Patent Office now cannot examine applications for programs because of the lack of a classification technique and the requisite search files. Even if these were available, reliable searches would not be feasible or economic because of the tremendous volume of prior art being generated. Without this search, the patenting of programs would be tantamount to mere registration and the presumption of validity would be all but nonexistent." Report of the President's Commission on the Patent System, "To Promote the Progress of . . . Useful Arts" in an Age of Exploding Technology 13 (1966).

logical building blocks, natural principles are too important to be subjected to private control. What dangers, if any, would in fact attend private control of basic principles? What effect, if any, does the absence of patent protection have on private incentive to invest in the research required to discover important and far-reaching principles? Can firm size, industry structure and public subsidies safely be relied upon to produce needed levels and directions of investment in basic research?

2. What is left of *Flook* after *Diehr*? Of *Benson*?

Does *Diehr* give applicants an incentive to claim inventions without disclosing the inventions' underlying mathematical principles, even if the principles are entirely new? Is such an incentive appropriate? What if the inventor arrived at the invention through serendipity, with no knowledge of the underlying principle?

For a superb review and analysis of the interplay of decisions between the Court of Customs and Patent Appeals and the Supreme Court in the years before *Diehr*, see Comment, Computer Program Patentability—The C.C.P.A. Refuses to Follow the Lead of the Supreme Court in Parker v. Flook, 58 N. Carolina L. Rev. 319 (1980).

3. Patent law has long refused to protect methods that implicate mental steps or processes in their operation. The main reason for the exclusion is the belief that the subjective element of human participation will rob patent disclosures of the precision needed to enable research and, after the patent expires, replication by others. As noted in the *Diehr* dissent, it was the mental steps doctrine that hobbled early efforts to obtain patents for computer programs which, it was thought, did no more than reproduce or rely on mental steps. See In re Prater, 415 F.2d 1393, 162 U.S.P.Q. 541 (C.C.P.A.1969).

The mental steps doctrine has been applied to disqualify a wide variety of claims on subject matter other than computer programs. In Johnson v. Duquesne Light Co., 29 F.2d 784 (W.D.Pa.1928), aff'd without opinion 34 F.2d 1020, a method of testing strings of suspension insulators in live transmission wires was rejected on the ground that the "lineman making the test must know from experience about what the normal voltage distribution is over the different insulators of the string." According to the court, the claims did not "prescribe a method which, if followed, will produce a certain result." To be patentable, "a method laid down to be followed must produce the desired result from the mere following of the method described." 29 F.2d 784, 785–786.

The fact of human participation has also barred patents for subject matter intended to affect human behavior. In Ex parte Mayne, 59 U.S.P.Q. 342 (Pat.Off.Bd.Apps.1943), the applicant's claims for a method of combating seasickness "and causing the person voluntarily to manifest his apprehension thereof" were rejected because the "term 'causing' here is deemed inapt for the manifestation of apprehension is purely a mental effect." 59 U.S.P.Q. 342, 344. These decisions have not been seriously challenged and have been accepted by even the most severe critics of the mental process doctrine. No principle has been offered, however, to distinguish these cases from cases accepting the patentability of medical technologies whose effects are similarly "mental."

4. *Chakrabarty* attracted considerable commentary even before the Supreme Court's decision. See, for example, the wide-ranging symposium in 7 A.P.L.A.Q.J. 175 et seq., (1979). See also Guttag, The Patentability of Microorganisms: Statutory Subject Matter and Other Living Things, 13 U.Rich.L.Rev. 247 (1979); Note, Patentability of Living Organisms Under 35 U.S.C.A. § 101, 91 Harv.L.Rev. 1357 (1978).

5. The 1952 amendments to the Patent Act replaced the term "art" with "process" and defined "process" to mean "process, art or method, and includes a new use of a known process, machine, manufacture, composition of matter, or material." 35 U.S.C.A. § 101(b). The definition confirmed a line of decisions that had allowed process patents for new uses of old products, such as the use of the old and well-known compound, DDT, in insects sprays. Ex parte Muller, 81 U.S.P.Q. 261 (Pat.Off.Bd.App.1947). The new definition also dispelled the lingering question left by a much earlier decision, Morton v. New York Eye Infirmary, 17 F.Cas. 879 (C.C.S.D.N.Y.1862) (No. 9865) which held that plaintiffs, who had discovered the anesthetic qualities of the old compound, ether, were not entitled to a patent on the process of using ether as an anesthetic in surgery.

The claimed invention in a "new use" patent will often combine an old process and an old product to produce a new result. Does this suggest that "new use" applicants face higher hurdles under sections 102 and 103 than applicants whose subject matter involves entirely new processes or products? What is the effect of *Sakraida's* synergy test on this class of invention?

As a practical matter, what range of protection do "new use" patents give? Since the patent owner has no rights in the old product, it can bring a direct infringement action only against those who use the old product according to the method described in the patent. How much success is the patent owner likely to enjoy in bringing a contributory infringement action against the manufacturer of the old product that is used to infringe the process patent? See pages 592 to 619 below.

b. DESIGN PATENTS

SCHWINN BICYCLE CO. v. GOODYEAR TIRE & RUBBER CO.

United States Court of Appeals, Ninth Circuit, 1970.
444 F.2d 295, 168 U.S.P.Q. 258.

Before BROWNING, WRIGHT and KILKENNY, Circuit Judges.

WRIGHT, Circuit Judge.

This is an appeal from a decision of the district court granting summary judgement to defendant-appellee Goodyear on the ground that plaintiff-appellant Schwinn's design patent for a bicycle seat is invalid and, if valid, is not infringed by a similar bicycle seat manufactured by Goodyear. We are in agreement with the district court's determination of invalidity and affirm.

I. The Patent in Suit and The Prior Art Advertisement

The patent in suit is a design patent, U.S. Patent No. D 204, 121. It issued on March 15, 1966, as a result of an application filed on January 15, 1965 by Frank P. Brilando, assigned to the appellant Schwinn. Three views of the patented design are shown in figure 1 hereof.

The sole reference relied upon in appellee's motion for summary judgment is a prior art bicycle seat, also manufactured by appellant Schwinn, which is illustrated in an advertisement from the June 1963 issue of American Bicyclist & Motorcyclist, page 9, reproduced herein as figure 2.

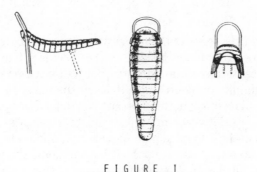

FIGURE 1

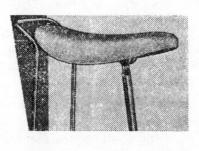

FIGURE 2

Appellant Schwinn concedes that this advertisement was published more than one year prior to the filing of the application which ultimately matured into the patent in suit. Schwinn also concedes that bicycle seats of the type advertised were sold in this country more than one year prior to the filing date. The advertisement and the seat illustrated are therefore prior art references under 35 U.S.C.A. §§ 102 (a)(b) and 103 which are made specifically applicable to design patents under 35 U.S.C.A. § 171. Both the advertisement and the bicycle seat were before the district court during its consideration of the motion for summary judgment.

The file history of the design patent in suit is relatively short and reveals the fact that the Brilando application was initially rejected by the Patent Office. As originally filed, there was some question whether the design included the half loop illustrated in figure 1 hereof. The Patent Examiner rejected the application as unpatentable over the advertisement of figure 2 (referred to in his remarks as the "Schwinn Item") on the ground that "(t)he Schwinn Item discloses a bicycle seat having an overall appearance of striking similarity to that claimed herein. . . ."

Following this rejection, the drawings were modified to include the half loop as part of the design. In his argument to the examiner in favor of patentability, the patentee pointed out certain "functional differences" which were said to be "felt by the observer." Particular emphasis was placed upon the "almost vertically disposed half-loop" of the proffered design as compared to the "horizontally disposed rearwardly extending half-loop" of the bicycle seat shown in the advertisement. This argument was supported by supplementary photographs of the prior art bicycle seat which form part of the file history.

The combination of this argument plus a personal interview with the examiner apparently persuaded him to change his mind because the application was then allowed without further comment.

II.   The Propriety of Summary Judgment

First, it is well established that summary judgment is proper only where the showing made is such that "there is no genuine issue as to any material fact and that the moving party is entitled to a judgment as a matter of law." Fed.R.Civ.Proc. 56(c). There is no serious contention here that there are factual issues which make summary judgment improper. In its motion, defendant relied upon the bicycle seat illustrated in figure 2, one of which was before the district court together with the advertisement and the supplementary photographs that appear in the file history.

It is true that summary judgment is seldom used in patent cases. This is largely a result of the technological problems which ordinarily arise in litigation involving a utility (as opposed to design) patent. In such cases, the trial court often needs the assistance of expert testimony to determine the nature of the patented device as well as the scope and content of the pertinent prior art. There is no such need for expert testimony in litigation involving a design patent of this type where no special technological problems are presented and the legal issues, as will be seen hereinafter, are particularly adapted to summary disposition.

We think it quite clear, therefore, that the controversy here was especially susceptible to adjudication on a motion for summary judgment.

III.   The Validity of The Patent

In granting Goodyear's motion for summary judgment, the district court ruled that the patent was invalid as fully anticipated by the prior art per 35 U.S.C.A. § 102 as well as, in the alternative, being obvious under 35 U.S.C.A. § 103.   Appellee does not now rely upon the finding of anticipation, arguing only that the district court was correct in concluding that the patent is obvious.   We do not reach the question of anticipation but instead treat only the district court's determination that the design is obvious in view of the bicycle seat illustrated in the prior art advertisement, a conclusion with which we are in full agreement.

In order for a design to be patentable, it must be (1) new, (2) original, (3) ornamental, (4) non-obvious, and (5) not primarily for functional or utilitarian purposes.   This controversy involves only one of these criteria, i. e., non-obviousness.

The statutory requirement of non-obviousness is found in 35 U.S.C.A. § 103 which prohibits the patenting of an invention, even though not identically shown in the prior art, if "the differences between the subject matter sought to be patented and the prior art are such that the subject matter as a whole would have been obvious at the time the invention was made to a person having ordinary skill in the art to which said subject matter pertains."

The most definitive statement of the requirement of non-obviousness and the approach to be taken by the federal courts in determining this question is found in Graham v. John Deere Co., 383 U.S. 1, 86 S.Ct. 684, 15 L.Ed.2d 545, 148 U.S.P.Q. 459 (1966).

> "Under § 103, the scope and content of the prior art are to be determined;   differences between the prior art and the claims at issue are to be ascertained;   and the level of ordinary skill in the pertinent art resolved.   Against this background, the obviousness or nonobviousness of the subject matter is to be determined.   Such secondary considerations as commercial success, long felt but unsolved needs, failure of others, etc. might be utilized to give light to the circumstances surrounding the origin of the subject matter sought to be patented."

Graham involved a mechanical (or utility) patent and some of the language therein does not fit design patent cases with precision.

Nonetheless, the statutory criteria of non-obviousness is specifically incorporated into design patent applications by the language of 35 U. S.C.A. § 171, and we are convinced that the approach of Graham is equally applicable where the question is the obviousness of a design patent.

A.   The Prior Art

Little needs to be said about the prior art involved here since the motion for summary judgment was predicated solely upon the bicycle seat as illustrated in figure 2. Because of the test for obviousness of design patents (see III, C, infra), a literal description of the visual image presented by the prior art involved here is unnecessary.

B.   Differences Between the Prior Art and The Claims at Issue

Since this is a design patent there is but a single statutory claim which provides that the invention claimed is "the ornamental design for a bicycle seat, as shown and described." By the same token, it seems inappropriate to discuss in detail the differences between the patented design and the prior art since those differences relate to individual elements and their specific functions. Undue reference to such differences in a design patent case seems to us to lead to improper emphasis on particular aspects of a design when the proper test is the impression created by the overall appearance.

Nevertheless we think it appropriate to point out some of the differences which are not apparent from the single view of figure 2. Borrowing the language which the patentee himself used in his negotiations with the Patent Office following the initial rejection, we note that the prior art bicycle seat is "relatively flat" and somewhat "broader than the [patented] design" with a "substantially horizontally disposed rearwardly extending half-loop." This is to be compared to the patented design which "curves upwardly toward the rear" and has "an almost vertically disposed half-loop."

C.   Level of Ordinary Skill in the Art

In design patent cases, there has been some confusion as to the appropriate method of determining the level of ordinary skill in the art. See In re Laverne, 356 F.2d 1003, 53 C.C.P.A. 1158, 148 U.S.P.Q. 674 (1966). In Laverne, the Court of Customs and Patent Appeals (which has the responsibility of deciding numerous cases from the Patent Office regarding the patentability of designs), rejected the suggestion that the pertinent inquiry was to be "expected skill of a competent designer" and re-affirmed its view that the determination must be "obviousness to the ordinary intelligent man."

We think this is the appropriate measure and one which has substantial historical backing. Over 70 years ago, the Supreme Court stated the test thus:

> "The test is the eye of an ordinary observer, the eyes of men generally, of observers of ordinary acuteness, bringing to the ex-

amination of the article upon which the design has been placed that degree of observation which men of ordinary intelligence give." Smith v. Whitman Saddle Co., 148 U.S. 674, 680, 13 S.Ct. 768, 770, 37 L.Ed. 606 (1893).

D. *Inquiry into Obviousness*

In light of the three foregoing criteria, we are now compelled to conclude that there is such a substantial similarity in overall appearance between the patented design and the prior art relied upon here as to make that design obvious within 35 U.S.C.A. § 103.

We are not unaware that this determination is largely subjective and susceptible of individual differences and interpretations. However, "the determination of patentability in design cases must finally rest on the subjective conclusion of each judge." Following the approach specified in Graham v. John Deere Co., supra, we think that this design is obvious in overall appearance when viewed through the eyes of the ordinary observer.

E. *Secondary Considerations*

Appellant has introduced substantial evidence of acceptance of its design as well as the commercial success thereof. We note, for example, that some 25 parties have been charged with infringement at varied times and the charges resulted in agreements not to infringe or, in about four or five instances, agreements to pay royalties under a license from Schwinn.

Reference need be made to such secondary considerations only when the question of obviousness is uncertain and inquiry into the "circumstances surrounding the origin of the subject matter" become of importance. We do not think there is such uncertainty here.

It is also relevant to mention other factors, in addition to alleged inventiveness, which might have contributed to the acceptance in the market place and commercial success relied upon by appellant Schwinn. We are not unmindful of the position of Schwinn as a national leader in the design and manufacture of bicycles. In a four-year period (1964–68), Schwinn sold over 1,200,000 of the patented bicycle seats, either as original or replacement equipment. Without undue inquiry into the field of consumer psychology, we think it evident that the sponsorship of this particular design by a company like Schwinn may be largely responsible for the success of the design.

We note also that Schwinn has apparently licensed its competitors to manufacture and sell the patented design for the relatively moderate royalty rate of five cents per unit. While we think it somewhat inappropriate to conjecture as to a reasonable rate for this product, we do not believe that the royalty was so significant as to offer any substantial economic reason to contest the validity of the patented design.

We are not suggesting, of course, that there is anything even remotely improper about good faith charges of infringement followed by patent licenses at a relatively moderate royalty. What we are saying is that the mere existence of these licenses does not, under these circumstances, add materially to establishing inventiveness on the ground of commercial success.

F. *Presumption of Validity*

Finally, we are referred to the fact that 35 U.S.C.A. § 282 provides that "a patent shall be presumed valid." We are also aware that the presumption of validity is said to be strengthened when, as here, the prior art relied upon to establish invalidity has been fully considered by the Patent Office.

The importance of having the prior art considered by the Patent Office is, of course, founded in large part upon the expertise of that office, particularly in complex utility patents where technical skill is necessary to evaluate fully the scope and content of the prior art. That expertise is not, however, of special weight in this setting since there is no substantial need for technical knowledge involved in the determination of the similarity of two designs in the "eyes of the ordinary observer." Our eyes view this matter as did the district court's and though strengthened by the considerations of the Patent Office, the presumption of § 282 is far from conclusive and does not permit the patentee to prevail here.

IV. Conclusions

We conclude that the design patent involved here is invalid for obviousness under 35 U.S.C.A. § 103. The district court's grant of summary judgment is affirmed on this ground alone.

Having determined that the patent is invalid, an appellate court need not make further inquiry into the question of infringement and none is made here.

Affirmed.

TRANSMATIC, INC. v. GULTON INDUS., INC.

United States Court of Appeals, Sixth Circuit, 1979.
601 F.2d 904, 202 U.S.P.Q. 559.

CELEBREZZE, Circuit Judge.

A utility patent, sometimes referred to as a mechanical patent, may be obtained by an inventor for "any new and useful process, machine, manufacture, or composition of matter, or any new and useful improvement thereof." A design patent may be procured for "any new, original and ornamental design for an article of manufacture."

It is also a general rule of patent law that one may obtain only one patent per invention—double patenting is not allowed and results in all but the first-issued patent on the invention being declared invalid. The instant case, one of first impression in this circuit, requires this court to analyze the inter-relationship of these principles.

Plaintiff-appellee, Transmatic, Inc., brought this action seeking a declaration that a utility patent held by defendants-appellants, Gulton Industries, Inc. and Patent License Corp., was invalid. The grounds asserted for such invalidity included that the utility patent constituted double patenting of a previously issued design patent held by Gulton and Patent License. The district court agreed that double patenting had occurred and granted summary judgment in Transmatic's favor. 442 F.Supp. 911, 196 U.S.P.Q. 788 (E.D.Mich.1977). We reverse.

I.

The patents involved in this lawsuit are both for interior lighting fixtures which are employed along the ceilings of buses, subway cars, and other mass transit coaches. Their general use is depicted in the following figure:

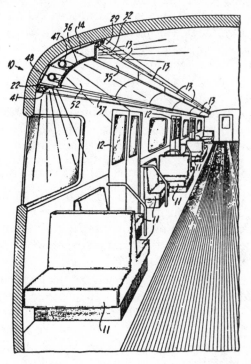

Appendix, at 26; Figure 1, Utility Patent.

The utility patent, No. 3,210,875 (hereinafter " '875 patent" or "utility patent"), was applied for on February 5, 1963, and issued on October 12, 1965, for a term of seventeen years. The named inventor was Norbert Schwenkler. The patent was assigned to Patent License, which is a wholly owned subsidiary of Gulton, the exclusive licensee. The lighting fixture is shown in the following cross-sectional figure:

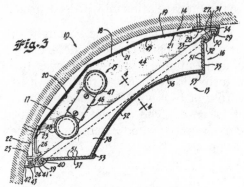

Appendix, at 27; Figure 3, Utility Patent.

The four claims of the '875 patent are:

1.   A cornice type lighting fixture comprising a light source housing, a light transmitting panel, and a light source in said housing, said panel including a pair of lens sections disposed in approximately right angular and spaced relation for controlled multiple directional concentrated light transmission, one of said lens sections being at least generally remote from said source, a translucent display section intermediate said lens sections for illumination of a display forming a part thereof, said display section being of an area which is substantially greater than the area of either of said lens sections, and means on said display section for detachably mounting a display thereover, said housing including light reflective inner surface portions arranged to direct light from said source at least to said display section and remote lens section.

2.   The fixture of claim 1 wherein said display section is of arcuate configuration with said display mounting means arranged along opposite margins thereof for retention of a display against the outer surface of said display section in arcuately conforming relation.

3.   The fixture of claim 1 wherein said panel is of generally U-shape longitudinally thereof and projects from said housing, said lens sections being provided with means attaching said panel to said housing.

4.   The fixture of claim 1 wherein said housing includes a specular inner surface portion and a light diffusing inner surface portion, said specular surface portion being arranged for the reflection of light toward said remote lens section and said diffusing surface portion being arranged for the reflection of light toward said display section.

Appendix, at 31; Claims of Utility Patent.

The design patent, Des. No. 201,380 (hereinafter " '380 patent" or "design patent"), was applied for on February 14, 1963, after the utility patent application, and issued on June 15, 1965, before issuance of the utility patent, for a term of fourteen years. Again, the named inventor was Norbert Schwenkler and Patent License was the assignee and Gulton the exclusive licensee. The fixture is shown in the following figures:

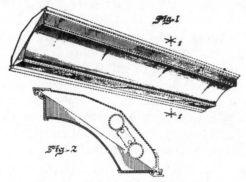

Appendix, at 32; Figures 1 & 2, Design Patent.

The sole claim of the '380 patent is:

The ornamental design for a lighting fixture, as shown and described.

Appendix, at 32; Claim of Design Patent.

In the mid-1970's Transmatic began to manufacture a lighting fixture similar to those covered by these patents. Gulton learned of this development and sought to persuade potential Transmatic customers that Transmatic's fixtures would infringe upon Gulton's patents. This led to Transmatic's filing of this lawsuit seeking a declaration that the '875 patent was invalid and not infringed by Transmatic's lighting fixtures.

After considerable discovery, Transmatic moved the district court to enter summary judgment in its favor declaring the '875 patent invalid. Transmatic argued that the '875 constituted double patenting of the later filed but earlier issued '380 patent. The district court agreed, entered summary judgment in Transmatic's favor and entered an order declaring the '875 patent invalid. The significance of invalidating the '875 patent stems from its longer term, as a utility patent, of seventeen years, which extends to October 1982. The term of the earlier issued and unchallenged '380 patent, as a design patent, is only fourteen years, which extends only to June 1979. Gulton and Patent License appeal, arguing that the '875 patent is not-invalid for double patenting.

II.

We initially address appellants' argument that the rule against double patenting has no application when comparing utility and design patents. Noting the separate statutory authorizations for the two types of patents (35 U.S.C.A. §§ 101 & 171), they argue that applying double patenting principles in this context would run afoul of the rule of statutory construction that separate statutory enactments should be given their full effect. They further note that Congress has created four devices to protect intellectual and industrial property—copyright, trademark, design patent and utility patent. They argue that just as copyright registration of an ornamental design has been held not to bar a design patent on the identical design, Application of Yardley, 493 F.2d 1389, 1393–94, 181 U.S.P.Q. 331, 334–335 (C.C.P.A.1974), and a design patent on the configuration of a bottle has been held not to bar trademark registration of the same bottle, Application of Mogen David Wine Corp., 328 F.2d 925, 51 C.C.P.A. 1260, 140 U.S.P.Q. 575 (1964), so should a design patent be held not to bar a utility patent on the identical invention. In sum, they contend the four Congressionally created protections are mutually exclusive so that double patenting would apply only when comparing two utility patents or two design patents.

This argument is not insubstantial. There is some support for this position in Gross v. Norris, 18 F.2d 418, 420 (D.Md.1927), aff'd in part, rev'd in part, on other grounds, 26 F.2d 898 (4th Cir. 1928). The argument has been expressly rejected, however, by the Court of Customs and Patent Appeals. Application of Thorington, 418 F.2d 528, 535–37, 57 C.C.P.A. 759, 163 U.S.P.Q. 644, 649–651 (1969), cert. den. 397 U.S. 1038, 90 S.Ct. 1356, 25 L.Ed.2d 649, 165 U.S.P.Q. 290 (1970), citing cases. We elect to follow the C.C.P.A.

The C.C.P.A. conceded in Thorington that there is no statutory basis for applying double patenting principles in the design vs. utility context, as there is when comparing utility patents or design patents.[11] Rather, the rule in this context is based upon a judicially recognized doctrine that a holder of a patent may not extend the term of his patent beyond that permitted by law. We accept this reasoning and hold that the rule against double patenting applies in the utility vs. design context.[12]

11. The statutory basis for the rule in the utility vs. utility or design vs. design context stems from a construction of 35 U.S.C.A. § 101 ("may obtain a [utility] patent") and § 171 ("may obtain a [design] patent"). 418 F.2d at 536, 163 U.S.P.Q. at 649–650.

12. If we wrote on a clean slate, we might not ultimately agree with appellants' position but we would give it more credence than did the C.C.P.A. in Thorington. We feel constrained, however, to follow the C.C.P.A.'s holding due to the unique position of that court in the overall scheme of patent law. Generally speaking, the C.C.P.A. reviews the decisions of the Patent Office's Board of Appeals relative to the issuance of patents. See 35 U.S.C.A. §§ 134 & 141. So long as the C.C.P.A. denies the issuance of a design patent based upon double patenting of a prior utility patent, and vice versa, the second patent should never issue if full disclosure is made to the Patent Office and C.C.P.A. and if the second patent is susceptible to a double patenting charge. Thus, if we were to hold that double patenting does not apply when comparing design and utility patents, we would encourage less than full disclosure before the Patent Office and C.C.P.A. This could yield the anomalous result of our sanctioning a patent issued only because of deception. We choose to avoid this unseemly confrontation with the C.

III.

Having decided that double patenting applies to this case, its application is no easy task. The judicially created rule against double patenting is of long standing. But the issue almost always arises in cases involving either two utility patents, or, less frequently, two design patents. One recent case involving utility and design patents is Ropat Corp. v. McGraw-Edison Co., 535 F.2d 378, 191 U.S.P.Q. 556 (7th Cir. 1976), wherein the court stated:

> The patent laws, of course, provide that a design patent and a utility patent may well be issued on the same construction. However, each such patent must claim a separate, distinct patentable invention.

In order to determine whether the "same invention" is claimed in two patents, their claims must be compared to determine whether they define the same subject matter. And when the double patenting situation involves a design patent and a utility patent, we recognize that it is "not easy to compare utility word claims with design picture claims in determining if the 'same invention' is being claimed." Application of Swett, 451 F.2d 631, 635, 59 C.C.P.A. 726, 172 U.S.P.Q. 72, 75 (1971). In comparing their claims, the mere use of the same design claimed in the design patent as the vehicle for describing the utility claimed in the utility patent is not dispositive.

> The law of double patenting in the precise situation where a design patent and a utility patent are involved is plagued by a dearth of case law. A review of the cases which do exist reveals various "tests" for determining whether a design patent and a utility patent claim the "same invention." We believe the best formulation of the applicable standard in this situation is that set forth in such decisions as In re Hargraves, 53 F.2d 900, [19 C.C.P.A. 784], 11 U.S.P.Q. 240 (Cust. & Pat.App.1931), and Application of DuBois, 262 F.2d 88, 46 C.C.P.A. 744, 120 U.S.P.Q. 198 (1958). Those cases state that double patenting exists if the feature in which the novel esthetic effect resides is the identical feature which produces the novel function so that a structure embodying the mechanical invention would of necessity embody the design, and vice versa.

535 F.2d at 381–82, 191 U.S.P.Q. at 558–559 (footnotes omitted).

While the court in Ropat reached a different result than we do today, we agree with the above principles and adopt them as governing in the instant case.

The '875 patent has no single feature but rather a combination of features which produce its novel function. The question for decision thus becomes: is the feature in which the novel aesthetic effect resides in the '380 patent identical to the features which produce the

C.P.A. We leave to the Supreme Court any eventual holding that double patenting does not apply in this context.

novel function in the '875 patent so that a structure embodying the mechanical invention would of necessity embody the design, and vice versa?   And since a patent is measured by its claims, the question could alternatively be phrased: would a device embodying the claims of the '875 patent necessarily embody the claim of the '380 patent, and vice versa?   We think the answer to both questions is "no."

The critical essence of the subject of a design patent is its distinctive appearance.   It is "the effect upon the eye" which controls. Gorham Co. v. White, 81 U.S. (14 Wall.) 511, 526, 20 L.Ed. 731 (1871); Thabet Mfg. Co. v. Kool Vent Metal Awning Corp., 226 F.2d 207, 212, 107 U.S.P.Q. 61, 65–66 (6th Cir. 1955).   A design patent can be based only upon visible characteristics; it cannot be based upon elements which are concealed during normal use.   The appearance of the '380 patent is best set forth in the figures reproduced above, but it can be verbally described as follows: two similarly sized rectangular lens panels at right angles to one another, the lower lens in a horizontal plane and the upper lens in a vertical plane, each lens connected by a concave display panel which is larger than either lens panel and which has slots in which advertising may be placed.

This same appearance would seem to necessarily result from a lighting fixture which embodied the claims of the '875 patent.   Claim 1 of the '875 patent provides, in part: "a cornice type lighting fixture comprising a light source housing, a light transmitting panel, .   .   . said panel including a pair of lens sections disposed in approximately right angular and spaced relation .   .   ., a .   .   . display section intermediate said lens sections .   .   ., said display section being of an area which is substantially greater than the area of either of said lens sections, and means on said display section for detachably mounting a display thereover .   .   . "   Claim 2 of the '875 patent reads: "The fixture of claim 1 wherein said display section is of arcuate configuration with said display mounting means arranged along opposite margins thereof for retention of a display against the outer surface of said display section in arcuately conforming relation."   We think *these portions* of the '875 patent claims define the same thing that is defined in the '380 patent claim, and vice versa.

But the '875 patent has additional claims, concerning the location of the light source, the reflective (specular) backing, the translucent display panel and the like, which are not claimed in the '380 patent and which would not necessarily be embodied in the device disclosed in the '380 patent.   In other words, a device embodying the claims of the '875 patent might necessarily embody the claim of the '380 patent, but *not* vice versa.   A lighting fixture which embodied the claims of the '875 patent would look like the lighting fixture claimed in the '380 patent, but a lighting fixture which looks like that claimed in the '380 patent would of necessity embody only some, not all, of the claims of the '875 patent.

Concededly, Figure 3 of the '875 patent, and Figure 2 of the '380 patent, but for the patent reference numerals in the former, are mirror images of each other. But, as stated earlier, "the mere use of the same design claimed in the design patent as the vehicle for describing the utility claimed in the utility patent is not dispositive." Ropat, supra, 535 F.2d at 381, 191 U.S.P.Q. at 558. Similarly, the mere use of the same figure depicted in the utility patent as the vehicle for depicting the design claimed in the design patent is not dispositive.

The principal error in the district court's analysis was attributing more to the design patent than it actually did, or could, claim. All that can be claimed in a design patent is appearance, so the '380 patent could only claim the outer shell of the fixture depicted in Figure 2—viz., the lens panels and display section. Indeed, the '380 patent specifications state: "The dominant features of my design reside in the portions shown in full lines." The interior portions of the fixture in Figure 2, including the lighting source (and its location), the backing, and the means for attaching the lens panels to the housing, are shown in dotted lines. They simply were not and could not be a part of the claim of the '380 patent. The district court erred in so considering them. See 442 F.Supp. at 914, 196 U.S.P.Q. at 790–791.

The district court reasoned in the alternative that even if all of Figure 2 were not claimed in the '380 patent it would be so treated if "the balance of the illustration aside from the lens panel is so obvious that it is implied in any event." Id. at 915, 196 U.S.P.Q. at 791–792. We agree that a design patent could be treated as claiming items necessarily implied even if not expressly claimed, but we disagree that such occurred here. We realize that since the '380 patent was titled "lighting fixture," "it readily appears that a lighting source was required." Id. at 916, 196 U.S.P.Q. at 792–793. But nothing is readily apparent about the *location* of the lighting source or the type of bulb to be used. And we disagree that "it readily appears . . . that the fixture would have a back which would be a reflective surface." Id. It might seem more likely that such a backing would be reflective but this can hardly be said to be necessarily implied from the mere design. It could well be the case that some might think a reflective backing produced a too harsh lighting effect. The means for attaching the lens panels to the housing are also not necessarily implied from the depiction of the lens panels alone. Nor is the peculiar shape of the backing noted in the '875 patent necessarily implied merely from the lens panels alone. Finally, it is not necessarily implied from the '380 patent that its display section would be translucent, as is expressly claimed in Claim 1 of the '875 patent; it could be transparent or opaque.

It is apparent that both patents at issue in this cause relate to the same general purpose, viz., illumination of mass transit coaches. It is equally apparent that it was contemplated that the lens panels and display section covered by the '380 patent would be used with the overall fixture covered by the '875 patent. But they are not for the "same invention." It is well settled that "a design patent and a utility patent may well be issued on the same construction." Ropat, supra, 535 F.2d at 381, 191 U.S.P.Q. at 558. The claims of the '875 patent and the '380 patent do not "cross-read," as this circuit requires to demonstrate double patenting.

There is a heavy burden of proof on one seeking to show double patenting, which burden Transmatic has not carried. Double patenting is rare in the context of utility vs. design patents. This is not such a case.

We hold that the '875 patent is not invalid for double patenting of the '380 patent.

The judgment of the district court is reversed and the cause remanded for further proceedings consistent with this opinion.

NOTES

1. The incorporation of the design patent provisions in the basic utility patent statute was dictated mainly by expedience. One reason the design provisions appear in the Patent Act, rather than in the Copyright Act or a tailor-made statute, is that it was the Commissioner of Patents who first communicated the need for their enactment to Congress. Congress gave little systematic attention to the substantial differences between utility and design subject matter, such as the fact that the Patent Office's lengthy examination procedures are entirely out of keeping with the needs of the many designs that enjoy only a short commercial season. Apart from the few specifically stated exceptions from the statute's general application, the Act leaves courts at large in determining the extent to which utility principles should govern design patent cases.

For an introduction to the role of the trademark and copyright laws in protecting designs, see page 350 above and page 709 below. Proposals to lodge design protection in a discrete federal design rights statute have been regularly introduced, but without success. See, for example, S. 644, 92d Cong., 1st Sess. Title 3 (1971). See generally, Note, Protection for the Artistic Aspects of Articles of Utility, 72 Harv.L.Rev. 1520 (1952); Note, Statutory Design-Rights: Solution to the Unfair Competition of Piracy, 34 Geo.Wash.L.Rev. 110 (1965); Comment, Trade Regulation: Legal Protection of Commercial Designs, 1959 Wis.L.Rev. 652; Pogue, Borderland—Where Copyright and Design Patent Meet, 52 Mich.L.Rev. 33 (1953).

On design patents generally, see Hudson, A Brief History of the Development of Design Patent Protection in the United States, 30 J. P.O.S. 380 (1948); Michaelson, The Nature of the Protection of Artistic and Industrial Design, 37 J.P.O.S. 543 (1955).

2. Is *Schwinn's* "ordinary intelligent man" approach to nonobviousness appropriate? What effect does it have on the level and direction of investment in the development of design subject matter?

Fields v. Schuyler, 472 F.2d 1304, 175 U.S.P.Q. 514 (D.C.Cir. 1972), cert. denied, 411 U.S. 987, 93 S.Ct. 2270, 36 L.Ed.2d 965, 177 U.S.P.Q. 673 (1973), rejected the *Schwinn* approach, seeing no reason to depart in design cases from section 103's "ordinary skill in the art" formula. "If the ultimate standard were to turn on originality from the point of view of the average observer, commercial success would become a virtually conclusive determinant, and not merely a secondary indicator, of patentability." 472 F.2d 1304, 1306.

The excerpted passage used in *Schwinn* to support the court's position on nonobviousness has a more interesting lineage than the terse attribution to Smith v. Whitman Saddle would suggest. To begin with, the passage originates not in *Whitman*, but in Jennings v. Kibbe, 10 F. 669 (C.C.S.D.N.Y.1882), and was only quoted in the *Whitman* opinion. *Jennings*, in turn, drew the stated formula from Gorham Mfg. Co. v. White, 81 U.S. (14 Wall.) 511, 20 L.Ed. 731 (1871), which applied it *not* to determine nonobviousness, but to determine whether infringement of admittedly patentable subject matter had occurred—whether, that is, the differences between the patented subject matter and the accused subject matter were sufficient for the defendant to escape the charge of infringement. Should the distinction make a difference?

3. Subjective elements pointing to invention have always played a larger role in design patent cases than in utility patent cases. A half-century after the design provisions were enacted, Smith v. Whitman Saddle Co., 148 U.S. 674, 679, 13 S.Ct. 768, 770, 37 L.Ed. 606 (1893), announced the first definitive design patent standard, requiring that "there must be something akin to genius—an effort of the brain as well as the hand. The adaptation of old devices or forms to new purposes, however convenient, useful or beautiful they may be in their new role, is not invention."

Whitman's concern for "something akin to genius" can be traced to the language of the design patent provisions then in force—"Any person who, by his own industry, genius, efforts, and expense, has invented and produced any new and original design. . . ." Yet, after the statute's amendment to eliminate all reference to "genius," courts continued to employ the term to define a relatively high standard of invention. Even after the enactment of section 103, eschewing use of a subjective standard, courts in design cases persist in requiring proof of subjective elements.

Blisscraft of Hollywood v. United Plastics Co., 294 F.2d 694, 696, 131 U.S.P.Q. 55 (2d Cir. 1961), typifies the contemporary approach. "To be patentable, a design, in addition to being new and inventive, must be ornamental. This means that it must be the product of aesthetic skill and artistic conception. Plaintiff's pitcher has no particularly aesthetic appeal in line, form, color, or otherwise. It contains no dominant artistic motif either in detail or in its overall conception. Its lid, body, handle and base retain merely their individual characteristics when used in conjunction with each other without producing any combined artistic effect. The reaction which the pitcher inspires is simply that of the usual, useful and not unattractive piece of kitchenware. The design fails to meet the ornamental prerequisite of the statute."

4. Another point at which design patent law diverges from utility patent law, and joins with trademark, unfair competition and copyright law, is in its requirement that, to be protected, the subject matter not serve a primarily functional purpose. Barofsky v. General Elec. Corp., 396 F.2d 340, 343, 158 U.S.P.Q. 178 (9th Cir. 1968), cert. denied, 393 U.S. 1031, 89 S.Ct. 644, 21 L.Ed.2d 575, 160 U.S.P.Q. 832 (1969) states the general rule: "The basic question here is whether the complete design for which a patent has been obtained primarily serves a utilitarian purpose. Consideration of that question necessarily involves an analysis of the design as a whole. The only way to make such an analysis is to note the individual features and functions of the design, evaluate their relative importance, and observe how they each contribute to the overall conception for which the patent has been issued. . . .

"Proceeding in this manner, it would not be proper to invalidate a design because one or more minor features primarily serve a utilitarian purpose. But invalidation is indicated if the individual features which are found to serve, primarily, a functional purpose may fairly be labeled as dominant, in the sense that they are chiefly relied upon as contributing to the over-all design the qualities of newness, originality, ornamentation and non-obviousness.

"This principle is demonstrated by our decision in Payne Metal Enterprises Ltd. v. McPhee, [382 F.2d 541 (9th Cir. 1967)] involving the design for a liquor pourer. In determining whether the design was non-obvious, the trial court gave primary consideration to two features of the design, a 'pinched-in' waistline at the point at which the so-called 'skirt' joins the body of the apparatus, and the fact that the 'skirt' flows freely away from the body. The trial court held that both of these features were non-obvious and that the patent was not invalid on any other ground. Reversing, we held that the skirt feature was obvious, and that the pinched-in waistline was dictated primarily by functional requirements."

c. PLANT PATENTS

YODER BROS., INC. v. CALIFORNIA-FLORIDA PLANT CORP.

United States Court of Appeals, Fifth Circuit, 1976.
537 F.2d 1347, 193 U.S.P.Q. 264, cert. denied, 429 U.S. 1094, 97 S.Ct.
1108, 51 L.Ed.2d 540, 200 U.S.P.Q. 128.

GOLDBERG, Circuit Judge:

In this clash between two giants of the chrysanthemum business, we confront a myriad of antitrust and plant patent issues. Yoder Brothers (Yoder), plaintiff in the district court, sued, alleging infringement of twenty-one chrysanthemum plant patents by California-Florida Plant Corp. (CFPC) and California-Florida Plant Corp. of Florida (CFPCF) (sometimes referred to collectively as Cal-Florida). CFPC and CFPCF denied the infringement and filed antitrust counterclaims under sections 1 and 2 of the Sherman Act. As to seven of the chrysanthemum plant patents, the lower court directed verdicts for Yoder that the patents were valid and infringed and awarded treble damages. The court also ruled for Yoder on Cal-Florida's section 2 claim. CFPC and CFPCF, however, prevailed in their antitrust counterclaim under section 1 and received treble damages for Yoder's derelictions.

Because many of the issues in this case turn on the particular nature of the ornamental plant industry and the specific characteristics of chrysanthemums, we shall describe the background facts in some detail before discussing the many complex legal issues presented on this appeal. Following our description of the facts, we shall briefly sketch the procedural history of the case. Finally, we shall consider the antitrust claims and the issues relating to the plant patent law.

I. General Background

A. *The Chrysanthemum Industry*

Chrysanthemums, in their natural state, blossom only during the fall. This is because they are photoperiodic in nature, meaning that their growth is affected by the relative lengths of lightness and darkness in the day. When the days are long, the chrysanthemum plant remains in a vegetative state. As the nights become longer, the initiation process of the chrysanthemum bud begins. Thus, in early August, when the nights achieve a duration of nine and one-half continuous dark hours, the chrysanthemum plant in its natural state will begin the process of developing a flower. During the fall and early winter months, the mature flower appears.

Yoder began doing business in the 1930's as a simple greenhouse operator, specializing in tomatoes. Soon thereafter, because the fall tomato crop was less profitable than the spring crop, it decided to replace the fall crop with chrysanthemums. In 1939 or 1940, Yoder employees began research into out-of-season flowering of chrysanthemums. By applying black cloth shades over the chrysanthemums when dark hours were needed and applying artificial light when light hours were needed, it became possible to flower chrysanthemums on a year-round basis. Yet this breakthrough was not without its problems. For example, the use of black cloth shades resulted in an abnormally high temperature build-up around the plants, which in turn retarded bud initiation. Similarly, when the finishing temperatures were too warm, the chrysanthemums would not hold their color. In an effort to adjust for these conditions and to improve the quality of the chrysanthemum generally, Yoder initiated a breeding program in the early 1940's. One of the most important goals of the breeding program was the development of new varieties for consumers.

Although the ornamental plant industry encompasses many different kinds of flowers, including azaleas, carnations, roses, african violets, geraniums, snapdragons, and others, chrysanthemums are one of the most popular of the genre. According to the United States Department of Agriculture, in 1971 approximately 2,134 growers in twenty-three states sold nearly 145 million blooms from about 129 million standard variety chrysanthemum plants, 34.5 million blooms from 136 million pompon chrysanthemum plants, and 17.5 million potted chrysanthemum plants. At the time of the trial there were over 475 different varieties of chrysanthemums available. The total wholesale value of growers' sales in the twenty-three states that year was approximately 83.5 million dollars.

Chrysanthemums have been subject to intensive breeding efforts over the past thirty years; each individual specimen is a genetically unique complex organism. Several definitions of the term "variety" of chrysanthemum were offered at trial. Mr. Duffett, Yoder's head breeder, defined a variety as a group of individual plants which, on the basis of observation by skilled floriculturists and according to reasonable commercial tolerances, display identical characteristics under similar environments. Cal-Florida defined variety in its complaint as "a subspecies or class of chrysanthemums distinguishable from other subspecies or classes of chrysanthemums by distinct characteristics, such as color, hue, shape and size of petal or blossom or any of them."

New varieties of chrysanthemums are developed in two major ways: by sexual reproduction and by mutagenic techniques. Sexual reproduction, the result of self or cross pollination, produces a genetically unique seedling, the characteristics of which are impossible to predict. Mutagenic techniques simply accelerate the natural rate of mutation in the chrysanthemum plant itself. A mutation was defined by Mr. Duffett as "a change in the number of chromosomes or a change in the chromosome position or a specific change in the genes within those chromosomes." Technically, only those mutations that first express themselves as bud variations are properly called "sports"; however, the word is used loosely in the industry as a general synonym for mutation, and we will so use it. Two types of sports can appear: spontaneous sports and radiation sports. The cells of all living things occasionally mutate, and spontaneous sports are simply the result of that process. Radiation sports, on the other hand, are induced artificially, through exposure to such things as gamma radiation from radioactive cobalt and X-rays. These techniques do nothing that could not occur in nature apart from speeding up the natural mutation process. Although most of the mutations induced by radiation are not commercially usable plants, a skilled breeder will select for further development those that display such desirable characteristics as fast response time, temperature tolerance, durability, size, and vigor.

After a breeder has successfully isolated a new variety, the only way he can preserve his creation is by means of asexual reproduction. In the case of chrysanthemums, the most common techique of asexual reproduction is the taking of cuttings from a stock plant. Cuttings, as defined in the Cal-Florida complaint, are "sections or parts of chrysanthemum plants which may be grown into mature plants for sale as cut flowers and/or potted plants or from which additional cuttings may be harvested." According to Yoder's suggested definition, cuttings are simply immature chrysanthemum plants. Since a cutting is genetically identical to the parent plant, it will develop into a plant whose characteristics match the parent's exactly, so long as the same environmental conditions obtain. A central fact of life in the chrysanthemum industry is the ease with which cuttings can be taken from parent plants: from one chrysanthemum, it is theoretically possible to develop an infinitely large stock, by taking cuttings, maturing some into flowered plants, taking more cuttings, and so on.

Over the years since Yoder first entered the chrysanthemum business, the industry has become internally specialized. At the first functional level are the breeders, who create new varieties of chrysanthemums. Breeding is an expensive, complex procedure. The breeder must possess the skill and discrimination to spot potential new varieties and recognize whether they possess desirable traits; facilities for elaborate testing and development must be available. Because chrysanthemums mutate rapidly, a breeder must always be on the lookout for new changes.

At the next level in the industry are the propagator-distributors. The propagator-distributors build up mother stock from sources such as breeders, retail florists, or their existing flowers, and reproduce cuttings from that mother stock. In a sense they are simply mass producers of cuttings. They do not develop cuttings to the mature flower stage (except for purposes of their own testing). Next are the growers, who develop cuttings purchased from propagator-distributors into mature plants either for cut flowers or potted plants. Combining the function of propagator-distributors and growers are the self-propagators. Cal-Florida defined a "self-propagator" as "a person who either buys or establishes stock and takes cuttings for the sole purpose of producing cut flowers and/or potted plants for resale or own use." In other words, the self-propagators are vertically integrated into one step. Finally, the growers (or self-propagators) sell their products to retail florists, who in turn sell to ultimate consumers.

[The court's description of the procedural history of the case, and its discussion and resolution of the antitrust issues are omitted.]

IV.   Plant Patents

A.   Introduction

With the antitrust issues decided, we return to the problem that initially gave rise to this lawsuit—Yoder's allegation that Cal-Florida was infringing its plant patents and its consequent demand for damages. Cal-Florida responded with the predictable assertions of patent invalidity and noninfringement, among others. As discussed above, the only issues before this Court concern the seven patents that the district court ruled valid and infringed as a matter of law:[30] Red Torch, Gold Marble, Morocco, Promenade, Southern Gold, Mountain Snow, and Mountain Sun. After considerable thought, we have decided that the district court correctly ruled that Cal-Florida failed to rebut the statutory presumption of validity with sufficient relevant evidence. Nevertheless, we hold that the court should not have trebled the damages found for the infringement, in light of the difficulty and novelty of the issues presented and the good faith defense of invalidity.

B.   Constitutional and Statutory Background

Article I, section 8, clause 8 of the Constitution provides that Congress shall have the power:

> To promote the Progress of Science and useful Arts, by securing for limited Times to Authors and Inventors the exclusive Right to their respective Writings and Discoveries; . . .

Although the first legislation implementing this provision for mechanical inventions was passed in 1790 by the first Congress, 1 Stat. 109, Congress did not include plants within the clause's protection until 1930. Act of May 23, 1930, 46 Stat. 376. In its present form, the principal statute allowing patents on plants reads:

> Whoever invents or discovers and asexually reproduces any distinct and new variety of plant, including cultivated sports, mutants, hybrids, and newly found seedlings, other than a tuberprop-

---

30. An eighth plant patent, Deep Conquest, was found valid and infringed by the jury. Cal-Florida's only point regarding that patent goes to the court's trebling of the damages for infringement. See Part IV. E., infra.

agated plant or a plant found in an uncultivated state, may obtain a patent therefor, subject to the conditions and requirements of this title.

The provisions of this title relating to patents for inventions shall apply to patents for plants, except as otherwise provided.

35 U.S.C.A. § 161. Since section 161 makes the general patent law applicable to plant patents except as otherwise provided, we take as our starting point the general requisites for patentability, and then apply them as well as we can to plants.

Normally, the three requirements for patentability are novelty, utility, and nonobviousness. For plant patents, the requirement of distinctness replaces that of utility, and the additional requirement of asexual reproduction is introduced.

The concept of novelty refers to novelty of conception, rather than novelty of use; no single prior art structure can exist in which all of the elements serve substantially the same function. In Beckman Instruments, Inc. v. Chemtronics, Inc., 5 Cir., 439 F.2d 1369, 1375, cert. denied, 1970, 400 U.S. 956, 91 S.Ct. 353–54, 27 L.Ed.2d 264, this Court said:

> [S]ection 102, which pertains to novelty, requires that the patentee be the original inventor of the object claimed in his patent, and also that the invention not have been known or used by others before his discovery of it. . . . Furthermore the prior art is to be considered as covering all uses to which it could have been put.

As applied to plants, the Patent Office Board of Appeals held that a "new" plant had to be one that literally had not existed before, rather than one that had existed in nature but was newly found, such as an exotic plant from a remote part of the earth.[34] Ex parte Foster, 90 U.S.P.Q. 16 (1951). In Application of Greer, Ct.Cust. & Pat.App. 1973, 484 F.2d 488, the court indicated that the Board believed that novelty was to be determined by a detailed comparison with other known varieties.

The legislative history of the Plant Patent Act is of considerable assistance in defining "distinctness." The Senate Report said:

> [I]n order for the new variety to be distinct it must have characteristics clearly distinguishable from those of existing varieties and it is immaterial whether in the judgment of the Patent Office the new characteristics are inferior or superior to those of existing varieties. Experience has shown the absurdity of many

---

34. In order for a plant to have "existed" before in nature, we think that it must have been capable of reproducing itself. Thus, we have concluded that the mere fact that a sport of a plant had appeared in the past would not be sufficient to preclude the patentability of the plant on novelty grounds, since each sport is a one-time phenomenon absent human intervention. See in this connection the discussion on validity, at IV. C., infra.

views held as to the value of new varieties at the time of their creation.

> The characteristics that may distinguish a new variety would include, among others, those of habit; immunity from disease; or soil conditions; color of flower, leaf, fruit or stems; flavor; productivity, including ever-bearing qualities in case of fruits; storage qualities; perfume; form; and ease of asexual reproduction. Within any one of the above or other classes of characteristics the differences which would suffice to make the variety a distinct variety, will necessarily be differences of degree.

S.Rep. 315, 71st Cong., 2d Sess. (1930). (Emphasis omitted.) A definition of "distinctness" as the aggregate of the plant's distinguishing characteristics seems to us a sensible and workable one.

The third requirement, nonobviousness, is the hardest to apply to plants, though we are bound to do so to the best of our ability. The traditional three part test for obviousness, as set out in *John Deere*, inquires as to (1) the scope and content of the prior art, (2) the differences between the prior art and the claims at issue, and (3) the level of ordinary skill in the prior art. 383 U.S. at 17, 86 S.Ct. at 694, 15 L.Ed.2d at 556. Secondary characteristics such as commercial success, long felt but unsolved needs, and failure of others can be used to illuminate the circumstances surrounding the subject matter sought to be patented.

The Supreme Court has viewed the obviousness requirement of section 103 as Congress's articulation of the constitutional standard of invention. Dann v. Johnston, 425 U.S. at 225, 96 S.Ct. at 1397, 47 L.Ed.2d at 698. In *Dann*, the Court commented that

> [a]s a judicial test, "invention"—i. e., "an exercise of the inventive faculty,"   .   .   .—has long been regarded as an absolute prerequisite to patentability.

425 U.S. at 225, 96 S.Ct. at 1397, 47 L.Ed.2d at 697–98 (citation omitted). An "invention" is characterized by a degree of skill and ingenuity greater than that possessed by an ordinary mechanic acquainted with the business. The obviousness requirement appears to presume that if the gap between the prior art and the claimed improvement is small, then an ordinary mechanic skilled in the art would have been able to create the improvement, thus leading to the conclusion that the improvement was obvious and a patentable invention not present. Section 103 requires the determination of obviousness *vel non* to be made with reference to the time the invention was made. Obviousness, like the general question of patent validity, is ultimately a question of law, though factual inquiries are often necessary to its resolution.

Rephrasing the *John Deere* tests for the plant world, we might ask about (1) the characteristics of prior plants of the same general type, both patented and nonpatented, and (2) the differences between the prior plants and the claims at issue. We see no meaningful way to apply the third criterion to plants—i. e. the level of ordinary skill in the prior art. Criteria one and two are reminiscent of the "distinctness" requirement already in the Plant Patent Act. Thus, if we are to give obviousness an independent meaning, it must refer to something other than observable characteristics.

We think that the most promising approach toward the obviousness requirement for plant patents is reference to the underlying constitutional standard that it codifies—namely, invention.

The general thrust of the "invention" requirement is to ensure that minor improvements will not be granted the protection of a seventeen year monopoly by the state. In the case of plants, to develop or discover a new variety that retains the desirable qualities of the parent stock and adds significant improvements, and to preserve the new specimen by asexually reproducing it constitutes no small feat.

This Court's case dealing with the patent on the chemical compound commonly known as the drug "Darvon," Eli Lilly & Co. v. Generix Drug Sales, Inc., 5 Cir. 1972, 460 F.2d 1096, provides some insight into the problem of how to apply the "invention" requirement to a new and esoteric subject matter. The court first noted that

[a]nalogical reasoning is necessarily restricted in many chemical patent cases because of the necessity for physiological experimentation before any use can be determined.

. . .

In fact, such lack of predictability of useful result from the making of even the slightest variation in the atomic structure or spatial arrangement of a complex molecule . . . deprives the instant claims of obviousness and anticipation of most of their vitality . . ..

460 F.2d at 1101. The court resolved the apparent dilemma by looking to the therapeutic value of the new drug instead of to its chemical composition:

[R]eason compels us to agree that novelty, usefulness and non-obviousness inhere in the true discovery that a chemical compound exhibits a new needed medicinal capability, even though it be closely related in structure to a known or patented drug.

460 F.2d at 1103.

The same kind of shift in focus would lead us to a more productive inquiry for plant patents. If the plant is a source of food, the ultimate question might be its nutritive content or its prolificacy. A medicinal plant might be judged by its increased or changed therapeutic value. Similarly, an ornamental plant would be judged by its increased beauty and desirability in relation to the other plants of its type, its usefulness in the industry, and how much of an improvement it represents over prior ornamental plants, taking all of its characteristics together.

Before reaching the issues on appeal, we make a final comment about the requirement of asexual reproduction. It has been described as the "very essence" of the patent. Langrock, Plant Patents—Biological Necessities in Infringement Suits, 41 J.Pat.Off.Soc. 787 (1959). Asexual reproduction is literally the only way that a breeder can be sure he has reproduced a plant identical in every respect to the parent. It is quite possible that infringement of a plant patent would occur only if stock obtained from one of the patented plants is used, given the extreme unlikelihood that any other plant could actually infringe. If the alleged infringer could somehow prove that he had developed the plant in question independently, then he would not be liable in damages or subject to an injunction for infringement. This example illustrates the extreme extent to which asexual reproduction is the heart of the present plant patent system: the whole key to the "invention" of a new plant is the discovery of new traits *plus* the foresight and appreciation to take the step of asexual reproduction.

C.   *Yoder's Plant Patents—Validity*

During the trial, Cal-Florida offered as evidence certain documents showing that growers had found mutations on the Mandalay variety that were the same as the patented variety Glowing Mandalay —i. e. evidence that the sport Glowing Mandalay had recurred. Although Glowing Mandalay is no longer in the case, Cal-Florida later proffered similar evidence with respect to Gold Marble, Promenade, and Red Torch, which are three of the patents whose validity is challenged on appeal. Gold Marble, Promenade, and Red Torch are all sport patents, meaning that they first appeared as a sport of another plant, in contrast to seedling patents, which develop from seeds. Of the remaining four challenged patents, two were sport patents and two were seedling patents. Cal-Florida never proffered any sport recurrence evidence as to the other two sport patents, Mountain Sun and Southern Gold, nor did it offer any specific evidence attacking the seedling patents, Morocco and Mountain Snow. Since we find that the district court's ruling on the sport recurrence evidence did not preclude Cal-Florida from introducing other types of evidence to attack the validity of the patents, and since no sport recurrence evidence was introduced as to Mountain Sun and Southern Gold, we find no warrant on appeal to disturb the ruling that Mountain Sun, Southern Gold, Morocco, and Mountain Snow were valid and infringed. Plant patents, like others, enjoy a statutory presumption of validity that was not rebutted as to those four.

At the time the court rejected the sport return evidence for Glowing Mandalay, it made a ruling designed to apply to the rest of the trial with respect to that kind of evidence. That ruling is the focus of Cal-Florida's cross appeal on the plant patent validity point. Because of its importance, we set out the pertinent parts in some detail here:

> [I]t seems clear that it was the Congressional intent that a person who discovered an asexually reproduced variety of a new and distinct plant was entitled to a patent.

It was not contemplated, apparently, that he invent, in the term that is used, or in the significance of that term, as we understand it, traditional concept of inventing a machine. . . .

. . .

In any event, the issue presented here is a rather narrow one and it has some practical overtones.

I am frank to confess that I think Mr. Foster's [Yoder's counsel] presentation here . . . is very persuasive. In all probability, this will be, or may be, the ultimate result of this trial. It may not be, after we have listened to the testimony, of course, of Mr. Boone's [Cal–Florida's counsel] other witnesses who are coming in to testify on the genetics of this thing, but on this one narrow limited issue, it would seem that the plaintiffs [Yoder] were entitled to prevail.

. . .

Therefore, the objection to the introduction of the various letters and documents from . . . the growers and plant propagators around the country, which were forwarded to Yoder Brothers over the years, is sustained.

Cal-Florida construes the above-quoted ruling as an all-encompassing holding that the constitutional standard of invention does not apply to plant patents. It further claims that since the ruling was admittedly intended to apply to the entire trial, it was precluded from offering evidence on the issues of newness, distinctness, and obviousness by the court's action. In fact, it never even tried to introduce the expected expert genetics testimony, although it did make a formal offer of more sport return evidence at a later time in the trial.

Yoder disputes the breadth of the ruling and its effect on any other evidence Cal-Florida might have offered, and notes that the court's actual ruling on the issues of newness and distinctness did not come until some two weeks later. With regard to the ruling on the admissibility of the evidence, Yoder argues that the documents would not have shown lack of distinctness, since the fact that a sport with particular traits recurs says nothing about what those traits are and how they differ from other plants. Furthermore, Yoder argues that the documents would not have shown obviousness, because if sport recurrence were evidence of obviousness, then almost no mutations would be patentable, and that would be contrary to Congress' intent.

We do not construe the district court's evidentiary ruling as anything more than that; in our opinion, it simply held that the sport recurrence evidence was not relevant to any of the patent validity issues. We therefore confine our remarks accordingly.

The only possible probative value of the sport recurrence evidence would be to show that a sport of that particular size, shape, color, or other trait is predictable from a given variety of parent plant. Thus, we must first determine whether Congress intended predictability to negate the possibility of "invention." Next, if Congress considered that factor irrelevant, we must decide if the Constitution is offended by permitting patents on the kinds of sports that recur.

Both the language of the statute and its legislative history persuade us that Congress did not intend to exclude the kind of mutation that might recur from the Act's protection. Instead, both Senate Report 315, 71st Cong., 2d Sess. (1930), on the original bill, and Senate Report 1937, 83d Cong., 2d Sess. (1954), on the 1954 amendment, speak generally about sports and mutations. The 1954 amendment was added to clarify Congress' intention that seedlings should be patentable, but in the process of describing the bill, the report states:

> The enactment of this legislation will remove any doubt that the legislative intent of the Congress clearly means that sports, mutants, hybrids, and seedlings, discovered by persons engaged in agriculture or horticulture, should be patentable. .   .   .

S.Rep. 1937, supra.

Although we are willing to assume for purposes of this argument that some mutations may appear that would have been genetically impossible before—i. e. that a fundamental change in the biochemical structure of the chromosome may take place—by far the majority of mutations and sports of chrysanthemums are predictable to some extent for those skilled in the field. For example, the testimony at trial indicated that a yellow sport could be expected from a white chrysanthemum. Indeed, part of the skill required of a chrysanthemum breeder is to know what to look for and to take steps immediately to preserve it by asexual reproduction if the desired trait appears. Given that fact, we think that the purpose of the Plant Patent Act would be frustrated by a requirement that only those rare, never-before-seen, if not genetically impossible sports or mutations would be patentable. That purpose was "to afford agriculture, so far as practicable, the same opportunity to participate in the benefits of the patent system as has been given industry, and thus assist in placing agriculture on a basis of economic equality with industry." S.Rep. 315, supra. To make it significantly more difficult to obtain a plant patent than another type of patent would frustrate that purpose.

We therefore find that Congress did not intend to exclude the kind of sport that recurs frequently from the Plant Patent Act. That being the case, the district court correctly ruled that the evidence proffered by Cal-Florida was irrelevant, as a matter of statutory law.

The only way that the Constitution would be offended by permitting patents on recurring sports would be if such leniency indicated that no "invention" was present. We do not think that sport recurrence would negate invention, however. An infinite number of a certain sized sport could appear on a plant, but until someone recognized its uniqueness and difference and found that the traits could be preserved by asexual reproduction in commercial quantities, no patentable plant would exist. An objective judgment of the value of the sport's new and different characteristics—i. e. nutritive value, ornamental value, hardiness, longevity, etc.—would not depend in any way on whether a similar sport had appeared in the past, or whether that particular sport was predictable. We therefore find no reason to disturb our approval of the district court's evidentiary ruling based on the constitutional standard of invention. As that standard applies to plant patents, the proffered evidence was irrelevant.

Viewing the evidence offered on the patent validity question as a whole, we find that Cal-Florida failed to rebut the statutory presumption of validity as to Gold Marble, Promenade, and Red Torch, as well as the other four discussed above. Thus, the lower court's finding of validity must be affirmed on this record.

D. Patent Infringement

On cross appeal, Cal-Florida asserts that the absence of flowering plants grown from the cuttings it had admittedly taken from Yoder's patented plants was fatal to Yoder's infringement counts. This is because the patent claim in each instance describes a mature flowering plant, and it is Cal-Florida's position that only another mature flowering plant could directly infringe. Yoder retorts that the Plant Patent Act provides that

> [i]n the case of a plant patent the grant shall be of the right to exclude others from asexually reproducing the plant or selling or using the plant so reproduced.

35 U.S.C.A. § 163. The district court ruled that the act of asexual reproduction was complete at the time the cutting was taken. Finally, the pretrial stipulations established that Cal-Florida had taken plant material, or cuttings, from Yoder's patented plants.

We agree with Yoder that it was not necessary to prove that the cuttings actually matured into flowered plants to show infringement. Under such a rule, it would be virtually impossible for a propagator-distributor directly to infringe a patent, despite the vital role he plays in dissemination of plant material. Furthermore, we think section 163 is plain in its statement that a patentee may exclude others from asexually reproducing, selling or using the plant. The negative inference to be drawn from this is that commission of one of those acts would constitute infringement. We therefore affirm the finding of infringement.

E. Treble Damages for Infringement

Section 284 of Title 35, U.S. Code, provides that the court shall award damages to the claimant upon a finding for him, and further provides that

> [w]hen the damages are not found by a jury, the court shall assess them. In either event the court may increase the damages up to three times the amount found or assessed.

Although a trial court has considerable discretion in assessing damages under this section, an appellate court can reverse the trebling of damages if an abuse of discretion is shown. Where the issue of patentability is close and litigated in good faith, the court should be more reluctant to impose punitive damages. In this case, the jury was instructed that the seven patents now on appeal were valid and infringed. In response to a special interrogatory inquiring about the amount of damages for each patent found valid and infringed by either the court or the jury, the jury entered figures as to those seven, and in addition, as to Deep Conquest. It then found that the infringement was willful as to the seven valid and infringed patents. It left blank, however, the space wherein it was to indicate by what factor the damage figure should be multiplied. The district court then trebled the damage amounts found by the jury, from which action Cal-Florida appeals.

Cal-Florida's principal effort to avoid the district court's trebling of the damages rests on a recital of its conduct and on protestations of its good faith both before and after suit was filed. It correctly points out that this case presented difficult issues of first impression on the Plant Patent Act and that it therefore had a good faith belief that the patents were invalid. The parties had extensive negotiations concerning the patents prior to the filing of the suit. Finally, Cal-Florida asserts that it did discontinue handling patented varieties after suit was filed.

In light of the above factors, we believe the district court abused its discretion in trebling the damages here. The primary reason that impels us to reverse on this point is the novelty of the issues presented. Cal-Florida has argued its case against the validity of these patents forcefully, and it is no small task to decide how to fit plants into the niches normally used by mechanical, design, or process inventions. The jury's finding that the infringement was willful was advisory only. Although we have affirmed the district court's findings of validity and infringement, we direct that only actual damages should be awarded to Yoder, the successful claimant.

The subtleties of the chrysanthemum business have given rise to a welter of legal issues in this case, both patent and antitrust. To summarize our holdings on the patent claims briefly, we have agreed with the lower court that evidence of sport recurrence is irrelevant to the patentability of plants, and that insufficient evidence was introduced to rebut the statutory presumption of patent validity. We have thus affirmed the court's holding that the seven plant patents were valid and infringed. Finally, we have held that the novelty and difficulty of the plant patent issues in this case rendered the lower court's trebling of the jury's award an abuse of discretion.

V.   Conclusion

In light of our ruling on the price differential theory of damages we reverse and remand the antitrust claims for retrial of damages. We affirm the district court's ruling of patent validity and infringement; and finally, we direct that the patent damage award be reduced to actual damages.

Affirmed in part, reversed and remanded in part.

NOTES

1.   *Yoder* is discussed in Jeffery, The Patentability and Infringement of Sport Varieties: Chaos or Clarity, 59 J.P.O.S. 645 (1977). See generally, Magnuson, A Short Discussion of Various Aspects of Plant Patents, 30 J.P.O.S. 493 (1948); Note, 61 Mich.L.Rev. 997 (1963).

2.   The scope and thrust of the plant patent provisions have been defined in a bare handful of judicial decisions.   Legislative history has been particularly influential.   Thus, in answering the questions, "what is meant by 'invented or discovered' and by 'new variety of plant' in the statute," The Board of Appeals in Ex parte Foster, 90 U.S.P.Q. 16 (1951), turned to the legislative history to determine whether "these words mean that the plant must be new in fact in the sense that the plant did not exist before," or whether "they include what is old and has existed before but what has been merely newly found."   "The bill which resulted in the Act was Senate Bill 4015 introduced March 24, 1930, by Senator Townsend, superseding a previous bill, S. 3530 February 11, 1930.   This bill defined the added class of patentable subject matter in the words in italics in the following quotation from the bill: 'Any person   .   .   .   *who has invented or discovered and asexually reproduced (1) any distinct and new variety of plant or (2) any distinct and newly found variety of plant, other than a tuberpropagated plant,*   .   .   .   *may*   .   .   .   obtain a patent therefore.'   Two classes of plants were thus specified in the bill, one, distinct and new varieties of plants, and two, distinct and newly found varieties of plants, and a clear distinction made between new plants and newly found plants.

"The Senate Committee on Patents reported the bill favorably, with amendments, Senate Report No. 315, 71st Congress, April 3, 1930.   One of the amendments consisted in striking out from the bill the words 'or (2) any distinct and newly found variety of plant,' thus eliminating newly found plants from the scope of the bill.   In explanation of this amendment the Senate Committee Report (page 1) states that it 'eliminates from the scope of the bill patents for varieties of plants which exist in an uncultivated or wild state, but are newly found by plant explorers or others.' "   90 U.S.P.Q. 17–18.

3.   Will the depiction of an applicant's roses in a printed publication more than one year before he files patent applications on them defeat patentability under section 102(b)?   Judge Smith, writing for the Court of Customs and Patent Appeals in Application of LeGrice, 301 F.2d 929, 133 U.S.P.Q. 365 (1962), concluded that it would not.

Smith conceded that "Congress, by enacting no exception to 35 U.S.C.A. § 102(b) with respect to patents for plants, intended that it be interpreted the same for plant patents as it has been interpreted in relation to patents for other inventions." 301 F.2d 929, 933. Yet, because of the special nature of plant subject matter, application of section 102 required special consideration. "Appellant in his brief points out 'The description of a plant in a plant patent or in a printed publication at best can only recite, as historical facts, that at one time a certain plant existed, was discovered in a certain manner, and was asexually reproduced. This information may be interesting history, but cannot enable others to reproduce the plant.   . . . Prior public use and sale of a plant are the avenues by which a plant enters the public domain.' " 301 F.2d 929, 935.

According to Smith, "In the case of manufactured articles, processes and chemical compositions, a different situation prevails. Written descriptions and drawings and publications can often enable others to manufacture the article, practice the process or produce the chemical composition. Thus, with respect to publications in these fields, there is a valid basis in public policy for 35 U.S.C.A. § 102(b) which bars the granting of patents on inventions 'described in a printed publication in this or a foreign country   .   .   .   more than one year prior to the date of the application for patent in the United States.' " Id.

.   .   .   "The Board of Appeals stated in its decision below that 'it is no more absurd to use a disclosure which is not enabling as a bar than it is to grant a patent on such a disclosure; the disclosure in the specifications of these applications are admittedly just as unenabling as the disclosures of the publications.' The answer to this apparent anomaly lies in 35 U.S.C.A. § 162 in which Congress 'otherwise provided' by specifically allowing for such a description in plant patent applications. *No such allowance has been made in 35 U.S.C.A. § 102(b) with reference to the sufficiency of the description of new plant varieties in printed publications.*

"Another answer to this apparent 'anomaly' is implicit in 35 U.S.C.A. § 163. The plant patent grant differs from that given with respect to other inventions. Infringers must be shown to have asexually reproduced or sold or used the plant on which the patent was granted. This section implicitly recognizes there is no possibility of producing the plant *from a disclosure* as 35 U.S.C.A. § 112 contemplates. Therefore, there is no requirement for any how-to-make disclosure in the application for a plant patent." 301 F.2d 929, 944.

4. The plant patent provisions authorize protection only for asexually reproduced plant varieties. The Plant Variety Protection Act, enacted December 24, 1970, Pub.L. No. 91–577, 84 Stat. 1542, and amended on December 22, 1980, Pub.L. No. 96–574, 94 Stat. 3350, offers protection for new varieties of plants that reproduce sexually, through seeds. A certificate of plant variety protection will issue if the applicant's variety meets the statutory requirements of distinctness, uniformity and stability, and passes several novelty and other statutory bars comparable to those imposed by section 102 of the Patent Act. §§ 41, 42. Protection, which may be effected through the award of damages, attorney's fees and injunctive relief, lasts for a period of eighteen years from the date the certificate is issued. §§ 83, 123–125. The Act is administered by the Plant Variety Protection Office in the United States Department of Agriculture.

Among the reasons given for enacting the law were that "it will allow our Government Agricultural experiment stations to increase their efforts on needed basic research." Also, according to the House Report, "the new law will definitely stimulate plant breeding. Experience in England provides a good case history. Prior to the enactment of its Plant Varieties and Seeds Act 1964, little plant breeding was done in England by private companies, and not much was done by government agencies. Since the new law came into effect, there has been a great upsurge of plant breeding, and a once moribund seed industry is now showing signs of great new vitality." H.R.Rep.No. 91–1605, 91st Cong., 2d Sess. (1970).

B. ADMINISTRATIVE PROCEDURES

See Statute Supplement 35 U.S.C.A. §§ 1–14, 21–26, 31–33, 41–42, 111–122, 131–135, 141–146, 151–154, 251–256.

This section narrates the application, prosecution and grant to Baxter I. Scoggin, Jr., of Patent No. 2,870,943 for a pump-type liquid sprayer with hold-down cap. The section also introduces the litigation, culminating in Calmar, Inc. v. Cook Chem. Co., 383 U.S. 1, 26, 86 S.Ct. 684, 698, 15 L.Ed.2d 545, 148 U.S.P.Q. 459 (1966), that subsequently enmeshed the Scoggin patent.

For introductory reading, see Roberts, A Reappraisal of the American System of Patent Examining, 48 J.P.O.S. 156 (1966); Frost, Patent Office Performance in Perspective, 54 Mich.L.Rev. 591 (1956); Woodward, A Reconsideration of the Patent System as a Problem of Administrative Law, 55 Harv.L.Rev. 950 (1942); The European Patent Convention as a Guide to Modernizing Our Patent Examination System, 8 IDEA 405 (1964).

1. APPLICATION

Once a preliminary search of the art has been completed, and a decision reached to file a patent application, the application is assembled for submission to the Patent Office. Typically, the application consists of a signed oath or declaration, power of attorney and petition form, an executed assignment if one has been made, filing fee, receipt postcard, transmittal letter, and the claims, specifications and drawings. Substantively, it is the last three items that are the most important.

a. CLAIMS

"Having thus described the invention what is claimed as new and desired to be secured by Letters Patent is:

"1. In a closure assembly for an open-top container having a perforated cap over said open top thereof mounting a spray unit including a barrel provided with a tubular extension passing coaxially upwardly through the perforation in said cap, a plunger reciprocally carried by the barrel and normally extending therebeyond and a spray head on the upper end of the plunger above said extension, the combination with said spray unit of an annular retainer telescoped over and secured to the extension above said cap and provided with external, circumferentially disposed screw threads and an annular, continuous segment at the upper part of the retainer above said screw threads, and a cup-shaped hold-down member housing the head and holding the plunger depressed at substantially the innermost path of travel thereof within the barrel, said member being provided with internal screw threads complementally engaging said screw threads on the retainer and having an internal, circumferentially extending, continuous shoulder disposed to engage said segment around the entire periphery thereof and thereby present a liquid-tight seal located between the spray head and said threads on the retainer and said member respectively, said shoulder being spaced from the lower annular peripheral edge of the member a distance at least slightly less than the distance from that portion of said segment normally engaged by said shoulder, to the proximal upper surface of the cap whereby said lower edge of the member is maintained out of contacting relationship with the cap when the member is on the retainer in a position with said shoulder in tight sealing engagement with the segment.

"2. A closure assembly as set forth in claim 1 wherein one of the normally interengaged surfaces of the shoulder and segment respectively is substantially conical to present an inclined annular face coaxial with the member and said retainer and of sufficient diameter at the largest end thereof to cause the seal effected between the shoulder and said segment to become tighter as the shoulder slides on said segment during shifting of the member toward the cap.

"3. A closure assembly as set forth in claim 2 wherein said retainer is provided with a continuous, annular rib integral with the normally upper edge thereof and defining said segment, said rib having an outwardly facing, inclined surface presenting said conical face of greatest external diameter at the zone of juncture of the rib with the retainer, said member having a pair of inner, coaxial, longitudinally spaced, cylindrical surfaces, the innermost cylindrical surface having a smaller diameter than the outermost cylindrical surface and presenting said shoulder therebetween lying in a plane perpendicular to the axes of said cylindrical surfaces, the diameter of said innermost cylindrical surface of the member being intermediate the diameters of opposed external end margins of said rib.

"4. A closure assembly as set forth in claim 3 wherein the member and retainer are constructed of materials having different coefficients of hardness whereby one of the interengaged faces of the rib and said shoulder respectively is deformed as the member is shifted toward the cap to thereby produce a more effective seal therebetween."

Like a land survey map, each claim of a patent describes the boundaries of the patent owner's property. Note, for example, that in claim 1, which is presented as a one-sentence paragraph, each of the comma-separated clauses following the words, "the combination with said spray unit of" cooperatively defines an essential structural element of the invention—a "retainer." By use of more specific language and additional structural elements, each of the four claims successively confines the invention's boundaries. Thus if, because of its breadth, claim 1 is declared invalid as anticipated by the prior art, claim 2 may be saved by reason of its narrower construction. Note that claim 1 is complete in itself and, for this reason, is characterized as an "independent claim." Claims 2–4, on the other hand, are written in "dependent" form, with claim 2 including the elements of claim 1, claim 3 including the elements of claims 2 and 1, and claim 4 including the elements of claims 1, 2, and 3.

b. SPECIFICATION

The language of the specification is the dictionary, or exegesis, for the claims. Both drawings and specification must clearly support the claims.

The format followed in the Scoggin specification was: title; statement of the field of invention [col. 1, lines 15–18]; background description of the prior art, setting forth the problem to be solved [col. 1, lines 19–35]; series of objects to which the claims should respond [col. 1, lines 36–57]; brief description of the drawings [col. 1, lines 58–72]; and, using reference numerals for the correspondingly labelled drawing elements, a detailed description of a preferred embodiment of the invention's construction and operation. Under the practice preferred by the Patent and Trademark Office, the format employs subtitle headings to identify title, abstract of the disclosure, cross-references, background of the invention (field and prior art), summary of the invention, brief description of the invention (field and prior art), summary of the invention, brief description of the drawings, and a detailed description of the invention:

2,870,943

PUMP-TYPE LIQUID SPRAYER HAVING
HOLD-DOWN CAP

Baxter I. Scoggin, Jr., Kansas City, Mo., assignor, by mesne assignments, to Cook Chemical Company, Kansas City, Mo., a corporation of Missouri

Application March 4, 1957, Serial No. 643,711

4 Claims. (Cl 222-182)

This invention relates to improvements in structures for dispensing liquids wherein is provided a spray-type hand pump mounted within a container for the liquid through use of the closure cap of such container.

It is common practice, as exemplified for example by Patent No. 2,362,080, issued November 7, 1944, to dispense various types of liquids such as insecticides, through use of a finger-manipulated spray pump normally sold as a component part of the container itself. The pump includes a vertically reciprocable plunger extending upwardly beyond the top of the cap within which the pump is mounted and provided with a spray head or nozzle structure capable of emitting a fine mist-like spray when the plunger is depressed by engagement with a finger-receiving saddle forming a part of the spray head.

Difficulties have been experienced in the field by virtue of the inherent nature of such structure since accidental actuation of the plunger causes dispensing of the fluid and oftentimes the material is used in part by store employees prior to sale because of the ready accessibility to the pump itself.

It is the most important object of the present invention, therefore, to provide structure for rendering the pump inoperable during shipment and while in storage, as well as on the shelves of the retail dealer.

Another important object of the present invention is to provide structure capable of carrying out the functions above set forth which is also adapted to enclose the head of the plunger and thereby protect the same, as well as handlers of the merchandise by virtue of the fact that the said plunger is completely enclosed and held at the innermost end of its reciprocable path of travel.

A further object of the instant invention is to provide a hold-down cap that may be quickly and easily applied and removed by virtue of a releasable attachment to a part of the entire unit such as by use of screw-threaded interengagement therewith.

A further object of this invention is to provide improvements of the aforementioned character that advantageously employs a part of the unit which has a secondary function of attaching the barrel of the spray pump to the closure cap of the container.

Other objects include important details of construction to be made clear or become apparent as the following specification progresses, reference being had to the accompanying drawing, wherein:

Figure 1 is a fragmentary, elevational view of a liquid container showing a pump-type sprayer as a part thereof and including the novel hold-down cap of the instant invention, parts being in section for clearness.

Figure 2 is a fragmentary, vertical, cross-sectional view through the container and its cap showing the pump assembly in its operable position with the hold-down cap removed; and

Figure 3 is an exploded perspective view showing the hold-down cap and certain parts of the sprayer with which the same is operably associated.

Pump-type sprayer 10 for liquid container 12 is attached to cap 14 for retention thereby when cap 14 is removed from threaded neck 16 of container 12, and if desired, there may be provided sufficient clearance between cup-shaped retainer 18 and annular outturned flange 20 to permit rotation of cap 14 relative to sprayer 10.

Both cap or closure 14 and retainer 18 are received by a cylindrical extension 22 of frusto-conical barrel 24, forming a part of the sprayer 10, extension 22 being integral with flange 20 at the innermost edge of the latter. Flange 20 is integral with barrel 24 near the larger, uppermost edge of the latter and is held against the under side of gasket 38 in the cap 14 when the sprayer 10 is operably associated with container 12.

Retainer 18 is provided with a central opening 25 which receives tubular plunger 26 and has a cavity 27 that accommodates the enlarged extension 22 as is clear in Fig. 2. Retainer 18 is fitted tightly over the extension 22 and maintains the retainer in place with flange 20 against gasket 38 as above set forth.

Reduced end 28 of barrel 24 receives a tube 30 that extends to the bottom of container 12, it being understood that the sprayer 10 is internally constructed in a suitable manner as, for example, in accordance with teachings of the aforementioned patent to pump liquid from the container 12 into the tube 30 and thence through nozzle 32 forming a part of a spray head 34 secured to the uppermost end of plunger 26. The enlarged head 34 is normally depressed by one finger as the operator grasps the container 12 as is well understood in this art.

Cap 14 has a clearance opening therein, as best shown in Fig. 2, for the extension 22 of barrel 24 and when the cap 14 is in screw-threaded engagement with neck 16, the gasket 38 which surrounds barrel 24, is clamped tightly between flange 20 and the under side of the top of cap 14.

A hold-down member broadly designated by the numeral 40, is provided to hold the plunger 26 at the lowermost end of its path of travel within the barrel 24 in the manner illustrated by Fig. 1, it being understood as by reference to said patent, that a spring (not shown) within the barrel 24, yieldably biases the plunger 26 upwardly to the position shown in Fig. 2. The hold-down member 40 is preferably in the nature of a hollow cap so that the same not only encloses or houses the upper end of plunger 26, i. e. spray head 34, but releasably attaches to the retainer 18 and also houses the latter.

A cylindrical bore 42 within the hold-down cap 40 receives the head 34 as seen in Fig. 1, and enlargement of the bore 42 adjacent the lowermost open end of the cap 40 is provided with internal screw threads 44 that mesh with external screw threads 46 on the retainer 18, thereby releasably attaching the cap 40 to the retainer 18.

An enlarged, annular boss 48 on the cap 40 is provided with a ribbed, outermost surface to facilitate mounting and removal of the cap 40 relative to retainer 18. A downwardly-facing shoulder 50 within the cap 40 engages the upper surface of retainer 18, thereby preventing engagement between cap 40 and closure 14 to prevent forcing of the retainer 18 from its tight press-fit engagement with extension 22. As illustrated, the screw threads 46 on the retainer 18 are in the nature of a pair of substantially semi-circular, spirally arranged sections 52 and 54, permitting molding of the retainer 18 with its screw threads 46 as a single unitary part.

In addition to the seal provided between shoulder 50 and the top surface of retainer 18, there is established an additional annular seal between annular rib 56 and the annular surface of cap 40 immediately adjacent to shoulder 50. This seal is clearly illustrated in Figure 1. The cross-sectional contour of rib 56 is as shown in Fig. 2 to present an upwardly and inwardly inclined annular face which snugly fits against the "corner," or line of juncture between shoulder 50 and the adjacent annular inner face of cap 40.

The interfitting surfaces between extension 22 and retainer 18 are as illustrated in Fig. 2. There is an annular notch formed in extension 22 at the outer extremity thereof and this notch 58 receives a similarly formed, continuous annular projection 60 formed integrally with retainer 18 and at a point where elements 58 and 60 will interlock when the parts are in assembled condition.

Thus, any accidental leakage or seepage from container 12 through the parts after they are assembled is obviated.

The material from which retainer 18 is produced is soft enough to be slightly compressed when shoulder 50 and the corner adjacent thereto, rides along the upwardly and inwardly inclined outer face of rib 56 when cap 40 is moved to position.

c. DRAWINGS

Anything that is claimed must be shown in the drawings.

Jan. 27, 1959   B. I. SCOGGIN, JR   **2,870,943**

PUMP-TYPE LIQUID SPRAYER HAVING HOLD-DOWN CAP

Filed March 4, 1957

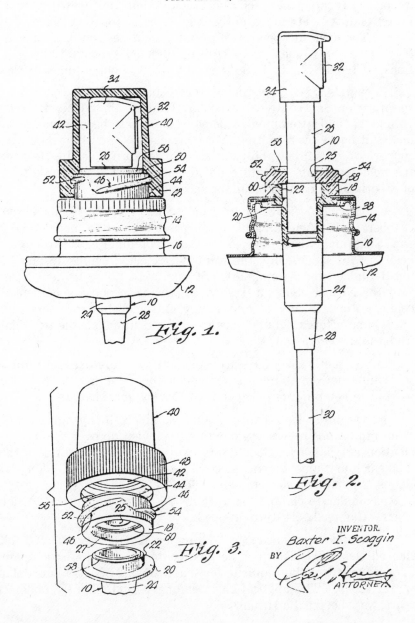

Fig. 1.

Fig. 2.

Fig. 3.

INVENTOR.
Baxter I. Scoggin
BY
ATTORNEY

2. PROSECUTION

The claims, specification and drawings set out above are taken not from Scoggin's original application, filed March 4, 1957, but from a strikingly different document—the patent finally issued. The Patent Office positions and the argument and negotiation that produced the differences—a small change in the specification and a complete revision of the claims—typify the basic format of the patent prosecution.

a. *First Office Action.* Scoggin received the first Office Action November 5, 1957. In this first action, the examiner pointed out a minor discrepancy between the specification and drawings and rejected claims 1–11; apparently inadvertently, he overlooked claims 12–15. The examiner gave two grounds for rejection of claims 1–11: they were (1) vague and indefinite; and (2) "substantially met by Lohse"—Patent No. 2,119,884 issued to F. W. Lohse, June 7, 1938.

Scoggin's first amendment, filed April 30, 1958, corrected the specification as required, cancelled claims 1–15, added new claims 16 and 17, and attempted to demonstrate that the new claims were distinguishable over Lohse. The new claims and the arguments in support of their allowability stressed a leakproof sealing feature of the hold-down cap, a feature not defined in the original claims and only peripherally alluded to in the specification.

b. *Second Office Action.* The examiner initiated this action on October 1, 1958, widening his prior art references to include two patents, Slade and Nilson, covering threaded container caps without spray head. More specifically, the examiner rejected claims 16 and 17 as unpatentable over a combination of prior art—Lohse in view of either Slade or Nilson. Scoggin responded with a second amendment cancelling claims 16 and 17 and adding extremely narrow new claims, 18–24, and offered detailed arguments to distinguish the new claims from the cited art.

Subsequently, Scoggin's attorney and the examiner met for a personal interview in the course of which the examiner cited two new patents in combination with Lohse—Darley and Mellon.

At the interview, attorney and examiner finally agreed on the claim limitations necessary to define the invention over the new combination of prior art. Shortly afterward, Scoggin submitted a third, supplementary amendment cancelling claims 18–24 and adding new claims, 25–28. Apart from being more definite in three areas, claim 25 was similar to claim 18 and claims 26–28 were identical to claims 19–21. Claims 22–24 were dropped.

c. *Notice of Allowance.* The notice, dated November 20, 1958, allowed claims 25–28, which became claims 1–4 of the issued patent. Upon payment of the requisite fee, Patent No. 2,870,943 issued January 27, 1959. The application's pending period, slightly under two years, was shorter than usual.

LOHSE PATENT 2,119,884
(Prior art 1938)

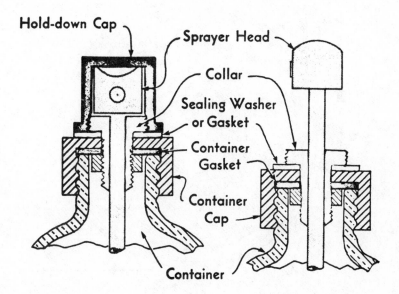

Hold-down Cap

Sprayer Head

Collar

Sealing Washer
or Gasket

Container
Gasket

Container
Cap

Container

July 22, 1958

W. J. SLADE

2,844,290

DETERGENT CAN

Filed July 27, 1955

FIG.1.

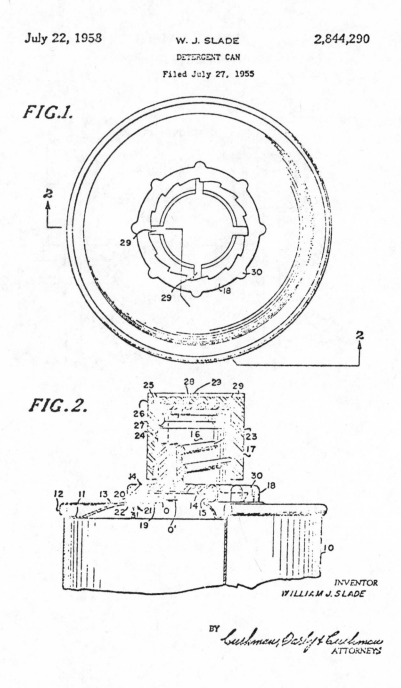

FIG.2.

INVENTOR

WILLIAM J. SLADE

BY

ATTORNEYS

May 24, 1938.

O. G. NILSON

2,118,222

COMBINED CAP AND SPOUT FOR LIQUID-DISPENSING CONTAINERS

Filed Feb. 17, 1936

2 Sheets—Sheet 1

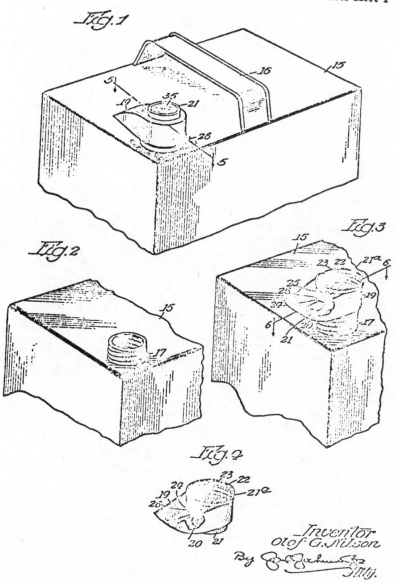

Inventor
Olof G. Nilson
By
Atty.

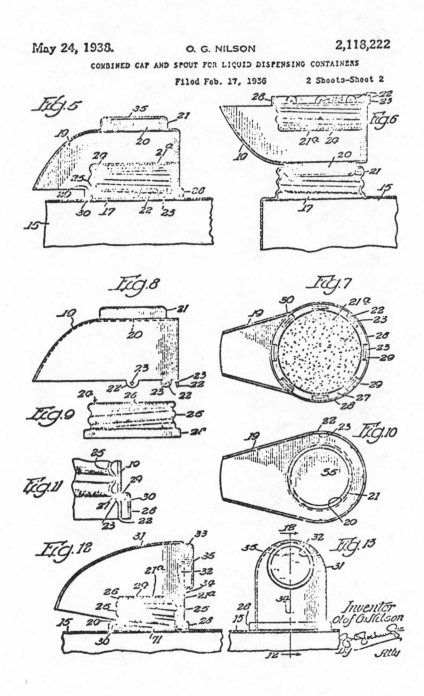

May 24, 1938.   O. G. NILSON   2,118,222

COMBINED CAP AND SPOUT FOR LIQUID DISPENSING CONTAINERS

Filed Feb. 17, 1936   2 Sheets-Sheet 2

Inventor
Olof O. Nilson
By
Attys

Mar. 6, 1923.

J. W. DARLEY, JR

CONTAINER

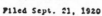

Filed Sept. 21, 1920

1,447,712

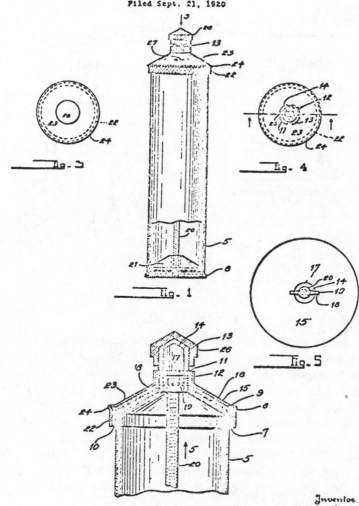

Inventor.

John W. Darley Jr.

FIG. 5. MELLON PATENT 2,586,687
(Prior art 1952)

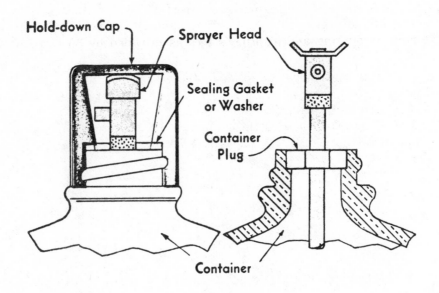

Hold-down Cap

Sprayer Head

Sealing Gasket
or Washer

Container
Plug

Container

3. JUDICIAL REVIEW

"By 1956 Scoggin had perfected the shipper-sprayer in suit and a patent was granted in 1959 to Cook Chemical as his assignee. In the interim Cook Chemical began to use Scoggin's device and also marketed it to the trade. The device was well received and soon became widely used. In the meanwhile, Calmar employed two engineers, Corsette and Cooprider, to perfect a shipper-sprayer and by 1958 it began to market its SS–40, a device very much similar to Scoggin's. When the Scoggin patent issued, Cook Chemical charged Calmar's SS–40 with infringement and this suit followed." Calmar, Inc. v. Cook Chem. Co., 383 U.S. 1, 28–29, 86 S.Ct. 684, 699, 700, 15 L.Ed.2d 545 (1966).

Upon being charged with infringement, Calmar, on April 27, 1959, instituted a declaratory judgment action against Cook Chemical in Cook's home district, the Western District of Missouri. The complaint asked the court to declare Scoggin's patent invalid and not infringed by Calmar. On October 5, 1960, the Colgate-Palmolive Company, a customer of Calmar, and user-seller of the Calmar device, brought a similar action in the same court. In its answers to both complaints, Cook admitted jurisdiction and the existence of a justiciable controversy, and counterclaimed for a declaration of the validity of the patent and a finding that it was infringed by Calmar's device.

The actions were consolidated for trial on the issues of validity and infringement only.

The court's judgment, rendered July 31, 1963, decreed that (1) Cook was owner of the patent; (2) claims 1 and 2 were valid; (3) Calmar infringed claims 1 and 2 by manufacture and sale, and Colgate infringed claims 1 and 2 by use and sale; (4) plaintiffs' request for relief was dismissed; (5) plaintiffs were permanently enjoined from making, using or selling the accused device; (6) defendant was entitled to damages and an accounting and (7) defendant could move for an accounting and attorney's fees as provided by 35 U.S.C.A. § 285.

Calmar and Colgate appealed to the Court of Appeals for the Eighth Circuit, which affirmed the judgment below, holding claims 1 and 2 valid and infringed. On certiorari to the court of appeals, the Supreme Court considered the *Calmar* and *Colgate* cases along with Graham v. John Deere Co., page 432, above, and rendered its decision on February 21, 1966.

CALMAR, INC. v. COOK CHEM. CO.

Supreme Court of the United States, 1966.
383 U.S. 1, 26, 86 S.Ct. 684, 698, 15 L.Ed.2d 545, 148 U.S.P.Q. 459.

CLARK, J.

The Opinions of the District Court and the Court of Appeals

At the outset it is well to point up that the parties have always disagreed as to the scope and definition of the invention claimed in the patent in suit. Cook Chemical contends that the invention encompasses a unique combination of admittedly old elements and that patentability is found in the result produced. Its expert testified that the invention was "the first commercially successful, inexpensive integrated shipping closure pump unit which permitted automated assembly with a container of household insecticide or similar liquids to produce a practical, ready-to-use package which could be shipped without external leakage and which was so organized that the pump unit with its hold-down cap could be itself assembled and sealed and then later assembled and sealed on the container without breaking the first seal." Cook Chemical stresses the long-felt need in the industry for such a device; the inability of others to produce it; and its commercial success—all of which, contends Cook, evidences the nonobvious nature of the device at the time it was developed. On the other hand, Calmar says that the differences between Scoggin's shipper-sprayer and the prior art relate only to the design of the overcap and that the differences are so inconsequential that the device as a whole would have been obvious at the time of its invention to a person having ordinary skill in the art.

Both courts accepted Cook Chemical's contentions. While the exact basis of the District Court's holding is uncertain, the court did find the subject matter of the patent new, useful and nonobvious. It concluded that Scoggin "had produced a sealed and protected sprayer unit which the manufacturer need only screw onto the top of its container in much the same fashion as a simple metal cap." 220 F. Supp., at 418. Its decision seems to be bottomed on the finding that the Scoggin sprayer solved the long-standing problem that had confronted the industry. The Court of Appeals also found validity in the "novel 'marriage' of the sprayer with the insecticide container" which took years in discovery and in "the immediate commercial success" which it enjoyed. While finding that the individual elements of the invention were "not novel per se" the court found "nothing in the prior art suggesting Scoggin's unique combination of these old features   .   .   .   as would solve the   .   .   .   problems which for years beset the insecticide industry." It concluded that "the .   .   .   [device] meets the exacting standard required for a combination of old elements to rise to the level of patentable invention by fulfilling the long-felt need with an economical, efficient, utilitarian apparatus which achieved novel results and immediate commercial success." 336 F.2d, at 114.

The Prior Art

Only two of the five prior art patents cited by the Patent Office Examiner in the prosecution of Scoggin's application are necessary to our discussion, i. e., Lohse U. S. Patent No. 2,119,884 (1938) and Mellon U. S. Patent No. 2,586,687 (1952). Others are cited by Calmar that were not before the Examiner, but of these our purposes require discussion of only the Livingstone U. S. Patent No. 2,715,480 (1953). Simplified drawings of each of these patents are reproduced in the Appendix, Figs. 4–6, for comparison and description.

The Lohse patent (Fig. 4) is a shipper-sprayer designed to perform the same function as Scoggin's device. The differences, recognized by the District Court, are found in the overcap seal which in Lohse is formed by the skirt of the overcap engaging a washer or gasket which rests upon the upper surface of the container cap. The court emphasized that in Lohse "[t]here are no seals above the threads and below the sprayer head." 220 F.Supp., at 419.

The Mellon patent (Fig. 5), however, discloses the idea of effecting a seal above the threads of the overcap. Mellon's device, likewise a shipper-sprayer, differs from Scoggin's in that its overcap screws directly on the container, and a gasket, rather than a rib, is used to effect the seal.

Finally, Livingstone (Fig. 6) shows a seal above the threads accomplished without the use of a gasket or washer. Although Livingstone's arrangement was designed to cover and protect pouring spouts, his sealing feature is strikingly similar to Scoggin's. Livingstone uses a tongue and groove technique in which the tongue, located on the upper surface of the collar, fits into a groove on the inside of the overcap. Scoggin employed the rib and shoulder seal in the identical position and with less efficiency because the Livingstone technique is inherently a more stable structure, forming an interlock that withstands distortion of the overcap when subjected to rough handling. Indeed, Cook Chemical has now incorporated the Livingstone closure into its own shipper-sprayers as had Calmar in its SS–40.

The Invalidity of the Patent

Let us first return to the fundamental disagreement between the parties. Cook Chemical, as we noted at the outset, urges that the invention must be viewed as the overall combination, or—putting it in the language of the statute—that we must consider the subject matter sought to be patented taken as a whole. With this position, taken in the abstract, there is, of course, no quibble. But the history of the prosecution of the Scoggin application in the Patent Office reveals a substantial divergence in respondent's present position.

As originally submitted, the Scoggin application contained 15 claims which in very broad terms claimed the entire combination of spray pump and overcap. No mention of, or claim for, the sealing features was made. All 15 claims were rejected by the Examiner because (1) the applicant was vague and indefinite as to what the invention was, and (2) the claims were met by Lohse. Scoggin canceled these claims and submitted new ones. Upon a further series of rejections and new submissions, the Patent Office Examiner, after an office interview, at last relented. It is crystal clear that after the first rejection, Scoggin relied entirely upon the sealing arrangement as the exclusive patentable difference in his combination. It is likewise clear that it was on that feature that the Examiner allowed the claims. In fact, in a letter accompanying the final submission of claims, Scoggin, through his attorney, stated that "agreement was reached between the Honorable Examiner and applicant's attorney relative to *limitations* which must be in the claims in order to define novelty over the previously applied disclosure of Lohse when considered in view of the newly cited patents of Mellon and Darley, Jr." (Italics added.)

Moreover, those limitations were specifically spelled out as (1) the use of a rib seal and (2) an overcap whose lower edge did not contact the container cap. Mellon was distinguished, as was the Darley patent, infra, n. 18, on the basis that although it disclosed a hold-down cap with a seal located above the threads, it did not disclose a rib seal disposed in such position as to cause the lower peripheral edge of the overcap "to be maintained out of contacting relationship with [the container] cap . . . when . . . [the overcap] was screwed [on] tightly. . . ." Scoggin maintained that the "obvious modification" of Lohse in view of Mellon would be merely to place the Lohse gasket above the threads with the lower edge of the overcap remaining in tight contact with the container cap or neck of the container itself. In other words, the Scoggin invention was limited to the use of a rib—rather than a washer or gasket—and the existence of a slight space between the overcap and the container cap.

It is, of course, well settled that an invention is construed not only in the light of the claims, but also with reference to the file wrapper or prosecution history in the Patent Office. Claims as allowed must be read and interpreted with reference to rejected ones and to the state of the prior art; and claims that have been narrowed in order to obtain the issuance of a patent by distinguishing the prior art cannot be sustained to cover that which was previously by limitation eliminated from the patent.

Here, the patentee obtained his patent only by accepting the limitations imposed by the Examiner. The claims were carefully drafted to reflect these limitations and Cook Chemical is not now free to assert a broader view of Scoggin's invention. The subject matter as a whole reduces, then, to the distinguishing features clearly incorporated into the claims. We now turn to those features.

As to the space between the skirt of the overcap and the container cap, the District Court found:

"Certainly without a space so described, there could be no inner seal within the cap, but such a space is not new or novel, but it is necessary to the formation of the seal within the hold-down cap.

"To me this language is descriptive of an element of the patent but not a part of the invention. It is too simple, really, to require much discussion. In this device the hold-down cap was intended to perform two functions—to hold down the sprayer head and to form a solid tight seal between the shoulder and the collar below. In assembling the element it is necessary to provide this space in order to form the seal." 220 F.Supp. at 420. (Italics added.)

The court correctly viewed the significance of that feature. We are at a loss to explain the Examiner's allowance on the basis of such a distinction. Scoggin was able to convince the Examiner that Mellon's cap contacted the bottle neck while his did not. Although the drawings included in the Mellon application show that the cap might touch the neck of the bottle when fully screwed down, there is nothing—absolutely nothing—which indicates that the cap was designed at any time to *engage* the bottle neck. It is palpably evident that Mellon embodies a seal formed by a gasket compressed between the cap and the bottle neck. It follows that the cap in Mellon will not seal if it does not bear down on the gasket and this would be impractical, if not impossible, under the construction urged by Scoggin before the Examiner. Moreover, the space so strongly asserted by Cook Chemical appears quite plainly on the Livingstone device, a reference not cited by the Examiner.

The substitution of a rib built into a collar likewise presents no patentable difference above the prior art. It was fully disclosed and dedicated to the public in the Livingstone patent. Cook Chemical argues, however, that Livingstone is not in the *pertinent* prior art because it relates to liquid containers having pouring spouts rather than pump sprayers. Apart from the fact that respondent made no such objection to similar references cited by the Examiner, so restricted a view of the applicable prior art is not justified. The problems confronting Scoggin and the insecticide industry were not insecticide problems; they were mechanical closure problems. Closure devices in such a closely related art as pouring spouts for liquid containers are at the very least pertinent references.

Cook Chemical insists, however, that the development of a workable shipper-sprayer eluded Calmar, who had long and unsuccessfully sought to solve the problem. And, further, that the long-felt need in the industry for a device such as Scoggin's together with its wide commercial success supports its patentability. These legal inferences or subtests do focus attention on economic and motivational rather than technical issues and are, therefore, more susceptible of judicial treatment than are the highly technical facts often present in patent litigation. Such inquiries may lend a helping hand to the judiciary which, as Mr. Justice Frankfurter observed, is most ill-fitted to discharge the technological duties cast upon it by patent legislation. Marconi Wireless Co. v. United States, 320 U.S. 1, 60, 63 S.Ct. 1393, 87 L.Ed. 1731 (1943). They may also serve to "guard against slipping into use of hindsight," Monroe Auto Equipment Co. v. Heckethorn Mfg. & Supply Co., 332 F.2d 406, 412 (1964), and to resist the temptation to read into the prior art the teachings of the invention in issue.

However, these factors do not, in the circumstances of this case, tip the scales of patentability. The Scoggin invention, as limited by the Patent Office and accepted by Scoggin, rests upon exceedingly small and quite nontechnical mechanical differences in a device which was old in the art. At the latest, those differences were rendered apparent in 1953 by the appearance of the Livingstone patent, and unsuccessful attempts to reach a solution to the problems confronting Scoggin made before that time became wholly irrelevant. It is also irrelevant that no one apparently chose to avail himself of knowledge stored in the Patent Office and readily available by the simple expedient of conducting a patent search—a prudent and nowadays common preliminary to well organized research. To us, the limited claims of the Scoggin patent are clearly evident from the prior art as it stood at the time of the invention.

We conclude that the claims in issue in the Scoggin patent must fall as not meeting the test of § 103, since the differences between them and the pertinent prior art would have been obvious to a person reasonably skilled in that art.

The judgment of the Court of Appeals in No. 11 is affirmed. The judgment of the Court of Appeals in Nos. 37 and 43 is reversed and the cases remanded to the District Court for disposition not inconsistent with this opinion.

It is so ordered.

NOTES

1. Infringement actions and declaratory judgment actions are only two of the contexts in which a patent's validity and the actions of the Patent and Trademark Office can be tested. In investigating the importation of infringing products under section 337 of the Tariff Act of 1930, the International Trade Commission has the incidental power to determine whether the patent in issue is valid. See for example In re Certain Steel Toy Vehicles, 197 U.S.P.Q. 873 (U.S.Int'l Trade Comm.1978). Even state courts are occasionally called upon to determine patentability. In Lear v. Adkins, discussed at page 617, below, the United States Supreme Court remanded a patent license action to the California Supreme Court to determine the validity of the underlying patent.

2. Patent applicants can appeal an examiner's rejection of their claims to the Patent and Trademark Office's Board of Appeals. Two mutually exclusive avenues exist for review of an adverse Board of Appeals decision. By one route, the dissatisfied applicant may take an appeal on the record to the Court of Customs and Patent Appeals, an Article 3 court whose decisions are directly reviewable, on certiorari, by the Supreme Court. Alternatively, the applicant can seek review and reversal of the Board of Appeal's decision through a de novo civil action against the Commissioner of Patents and Trademarks in the District Court for the District of Columbia. The District Court's decision is reviewable on appeal to the District of Columbia Court of Appeals and from there, on certiorari, to the Supreme Court.

See generally, Lipscomb, Appeals from Patent Office Decisions, 50 J.P.O.S. 178 (1968).

3. Historically, the Patent and Trademark Office could not reconsider the scope or validity of issued patents. The main exception to the rule was the Office's reissue practice under which, when "any patent is, through error without any deceptive intention, deemed wholly or partly inoperative or invalid, by reason of a defective specification or drawing, or by reason of the patentee claiming more or less than he had a right to claim in the patent, the Commissioner shall, on the surrender of such patent and the payment of the fee required by law, reissue the patent for the invention disclosed in the original patent, and in accordance with a new amended application for the unexpired part of the term of the original patent. No new matter shall be introduced into the application for reissue." 35 U.S.C.A. § 251.

On March 1, 1977, the Patent and Trademark Office dramatically altered its reissue practice to effectively allow a limited reexamination of a patent's claims in light of newly disclosed prior art. 37 C. F.R. § 1.175(a)(4)(1979). The purpose of the new rule was "to improve the quality and reliability of issued patents by strengthening patent examining and appeal procedures. . . . The rules afford patent owners an opportunity, through the filing of a reissue application, to obtain a ruling from an examiner on the pertinence of additional prior art after a patent has been issued. . . . Thus, a patentee may file a reissue if he believes his patent is valid over prior art not previously considered by the Office, but would like to have a reexamination. The procedure may be used at any time during the life of a patent. During litigation, a federal court may, if it chooses, stay proceedings to permit new art to be considered by the Office." 42 Fed.Reg. 5588 (1977).

Several courts have accepted the invitation to stay patent validity litigation while reissue is pursued. See for example, Fisher Controls Co. v. Control Components, Inc., 443 F.Supp. 581, 582, 196 U.S. P.Q. 817 (S.D.Iowa 1977) ("[S]everal distinct advantages can be observed in allowing examination of a reissue application before continuing with patent litigation: (1) All prior art presented to the Court will have been first considered by the P.T.O., with its particular expertise. (2) Many discovery problems relating to prior art can be alleviated by the P.T.O. examination. (3) In those cases resulting in effective invalidity of the patent, the suit will likely be dismissed. (4) The outcome of the reexamination may encourage a settlement without the further use of the Court. (5) The record of reexamination would likely be entered at trial, thereby reducing the complexity and length of the litigation. (6) Issues, defenses, and evidence will be more easily limited in pre-trial conferences after reexamination. (7) The cost will likely be reduced both for the parties and the court.")

On December 12, 1980, President Carter signed into law Public Law 96–517, 94 Stat. 3015, providing, among other things, that "Any person at any time may file a request for reexamination by the Office of any claim of a patent on the basis of any prior art . . . . " See Statute Supp. Pub.Law No. 96–517 § 302.

On reissue generally, see Dunner & Lipsey, The New Reissue Practice, 61 J.P.O.S. 68 (1979), and Silverman, To Err is Human— Patent Reissues and the Doctrine of Intervening Rights, 48 J.P.O.S. 696, 727 (1966). For a critical view of the 1977 amendments see Irons & Sears, Patent "Reexamination": A Case of Administrative Arrogation, 1980 Utah L.Rev. 287.

What interests would be served by a system that postponed *all* examination to a point sometime after the patent issues? See McKie, Is Deferred Examination of Patent Applications Desirable in the United States? 55 J.P.O.S. 691 (1973).

4. Interferences, often lengthy and complex, begin with the Commissioner's finding that a patent application's subject matter is claimed in—interferes with—an unexpired patent or another pending application. The Board of Patent Interferences, an administrative unit of the Patent and Trademark Office, then determines priority of invention as between the two or more parties claiming substantially the same invention.

Interference practice is examined in Wikstrom, Patent Interference Practice (1965) and Baker, Outline of Patent Office Interference Practice (19th ed. 1977). See also, Calvert, An Overview of Interference Practice, 62 J.P.O.S. 290 (1980). An intriguing approach to problems encountered in interference proceedings appears in Stern, Priority Paradoxes in Patent Law, 16 Vand.L.Rev. 131 (1962).

C. RIGHTS AND REMEDIES

See Statute Supplement 35 U.S.C.A. §§ 154, 261–262, 271–272, 283–287, 292.

1. STATUTORY RIGHTS

DEEPSOUTH PACKING CO., INC. v. LAITRAM CORP.

Supreme Court of the United States, 1972.
406 U.S. 518, 92 S.Ct. 1700, 32 L.Ed.2d 273, 173 U.S.P.Q. 769.

Mr. Justice WHITE delivered the opinion of the Court.

The United States District Court for the Eastern District of Louisiana has written:

> "Shrimp, whether boiled, broiled, barbecued or fried, are a gustatory delight, but they did not evolve to satisfy man's palate. Like other crustaceans, they wear their skeletons outside their bodies in order to shield their savory pink and white flesh against predators, including man. They also carry their intestines, commonly called veins, in bags (or sand bags) that run the length of their bodies. For shrimp to be edible, it is necessary to remove their shells. In addition, if the vein is removed, shrimp become more pleasing to the fastidious as well as more palatable." [1]

Such "gustatory" observations are rare even in those piscatorily favored federal courts blissfully situated on the Nation's Gulf Coast, but they are properly recited in this case. Petitioner and respondent both hold patents on machines that devein shrimp more cheaply and efficiently than competing machinery or hand labor can do the job. Extensive litigation below has established that respondent, the Laitram Corp., has the superior claim and that the distribution and use of petitioner Deepsouth's machinery in this country should be enjoined to prevent infringement of Laitram's patents. Laitram Corp. v. Deepsouth Packing Co., 443 F.2d 928 (CA5 1971). We granted certiorari, 404 U.S. 1037, 92 S.Ct. 702, 30 L.Ed.2d 728 (1972), to consider a related question: Is Deepsouth, barred from the American market by Laitram's patents, also foreclosed by the patent laws from exporting its deveiners, in less than fully assembled form, for use abroad?

1. Laitram Corp. v. Deepsouth Packing
Co., 301 F.Supp. 1037, 1040 (1969).

I

A rudimentary understanding of the patents in dispute is a prerequisite to comprehending the legal issue presented. The District
Court determined that the Laitram Corp. held two valid patents for
machinery used in the process of deveining shrimp. One, granted in
1954,[2] accorded Laitram rights over a "slitter" which exposed the
veins of shrimp by using water pressure and gravity to force the
shrimp down an inclined trough studded with razor blades. As the
shrimp descend through the trough their backs are slit by the blades
or other knife-like objects arranged in a zig-zag pattern. The second
patent, granted in 1958, covers a "tumbler," "a device to mechanically remove substantially all veins from shrimp whose backs have previously been slit" by the machines described in the 1954 patent. This
invention uses streams of water to carry slit shrimp into and then out
of a revolving drum fabricated from commercial sheet metal. As
shrimp pass through the drum the hooked "lips" of the punched metal, "projecting at an acute angle from the supporting member and
having a smooth rounded free edge for engaging beneath the vein of
a shrimp and for wedging the vein between the lip and the supporting
member," App. 131, engage the veins and remove them.

Both the slitter and the tumbler are combination patents; that
is, "[n]one of the parts referred to are new, and none are claimed as
new; nor is any portion of the combination less than the whole
claimed as new, or stated to produce any given result. The end in
view is proposed to be accomplished by the union of all, arranged and
combined together in the manner described. And this combination,
composed of all the parts mentioned in the specification, and arranged with reference to each other, and to other parts of the [ma-
chine] in the manner therein described, is stated to be the improvement, and is the thing patented." Prouty v. Ruggles, 16 Pet. 336,
341, 10 L.Ed. 985, 987 (1842).

The slitter's elements as recited in Laitram's patent claim were:
an inclined trough, a "knife" (actually, knives) positioned in the
trough, and a means (water sprayed from jets) to move the shrimp
down the trough. The tumbler's elements include a "lip," a "support
member," and a "means" (water thrust from jets). As is usual in
combination patents, none of the elements in either of these patents
were themselves patentable at the time of the patent, nor are they
now. The means in both inventions, moving water, was and is, of
course, commonplace. (It is not suggested that Deepsouth infringed
Laitram's patents by its use of water jets.) The cutting instruments
and inclined troughs used in slitters were and are commodities available for general use. The structure of the lip and support member in
the tumbler were hardly novel: Laitram concedes that the inventors

2. This patent expired shortly before
argument in this court and is therefore not relevant to Laitram's claim
for injunctive relief. It is described,
however, because Laitram claims
damages for Deepsouth's asserted
past exportation of the parts of this
machine.

merely adapted punched metal sheets ordered from a commercial catalog in order to perfect their invention. The patents were warranted not by the novelty of their elements but by the novelty of the combination they represented. Invention was recognized because Laitram's assignors combined ordinary elements in an extraordinary way—a novel union of old means was designed to achieve new ends. Thus, for both inventions "the whole in some way exceed[ed] the sum of its parts." Great A. & P. Tea Co. v. Supermarket Equipment Corp., 340 U.S. 147, 152, 71 S.Ct. 127, 95 L.Ed. 162, 166 (1950).

II

The lower court's decision that Laitram held valid combination patents entitled the corporation to the privileges bestowed by 35 U.S. C.A. § 154, the keystone provision of the patent code. "[F]or the term of seventeen years" from the date of the patent, Laitram had "the right to exclude others from making, using, or selling the invention throughout the United States. . . ." The § 154 right in turn provides the basis for affording the patentee an injunction against direct, induced, and contributory infringement, 35 U.S.C.A. § 283, or an award of damages when such infringement has already occurred, 35 U.S.C.A. § 284. Infringement is defined by 35 U.S.C.A. § 271 in terms that follow those of § 154:

"(a) Except as otherwise provided in this title, whoever without authority makes, uses or sells any patented invention, within the United States during the term of the patent therefor, [directly] infringes the patent.

"(b) Whoever actively induces infringement of a patent shall be liable as an infringer.

"(c) Whoever sells a component of a patented machine, manufacture, combination or composition, or a material or apparatus for use in practicing a patented process, constituting a material part of the invention, knowing the same to be especially made or especially adapted for use in an infringement of such patent, and not a staple article or commodity of commerce suitable for substantial noninfringing use, shall be liable as a contributory infringer."

As a result of these provisions the judgment of Laitram's patent superiority forecloses Deepsouth and its customers from any future use (other than a use approved by Laitram or occurring after the Laitram patent has expired) of its deveiners "throughout the United States." The patent provisions taken in conjunction with the judgment below also entitle Laitram to the injunction it has received prohibiting Deepsouth from continuing to "make" or, once made, to "sell" deveiners "throughout the United States." Further, Laitram may recover damages for any past unauthorized use, sale, or making "throughout the United States." This much is not disputed.

But Deepsouth argues that it is not liable for every type of past sale and that a portion of its future business is salvageable. Section

154 and related provisions obviously are intended to grant a patentee a monopoly only over the United States market; they are not intended to grant a patentee the bonus of a favored position as a flagship company free of American competition in international commerce. Deepsouth, itself barred from using its deveining machines, or from inducing others to use them "throughout the United States," barred also from making and selling the machines in the United States, seeks to make the parts of deveining machines, to sell them to foreign buyers, and to have the buyers assemble the parts and use the machines abroad.[5] Accordingly, Deepsouth seeks judicial approval, expressed through a modification or interpretation of the injunction against it, for continuing its practice of shipping deveining equipment to foreign customers in three separate boxes, each containing only parts of the 1¾-ton machines, yet the whole assemblable in less than one hour.[6] The company contends that by this means both the "making" and the "use" of the machines occur abroad and Laitram's lawful monopoly over the making and use of the machines throughout the United States is not infringed.

Laitram counters that this course of conduct is based upon a hyper technical reading of the patent code that, if tolerated, will deprive it of its right to the fruits of the inventive genius of its assignors. "The right to make can scarcely be made plainer by definition . . .," Bauer v. O'Donnell, 229 U.S. 1, 10, 33 S.Ct. 616, 57 L.Ed. 1041, 1043 (1913). Deepsouth in all respects save final assembly of the parts "makes" the invention. It does so with the intent of having the foreign user effect the combination without Laitram's permission. Deepsouth sells these components as though they were the machines themselves; the act of assembly is regarded, indeed advertised, as of no importance.

The District Court, faced with this dispute, noted that three prior circuit courts had considered the meaning of "making" in this context and that all three had resolved the question favorably to Deepsouth's position. See Hewitt-Robins, Inc. v. Link-Belt Co., 371 F.2d 225 (CA7 1966); Cold Metal Process Co. v. United Engineering & Foundry Co., 235 F.2d 224 (CA3 1956); and Radio Corp. of America v. Andrea, 79 F.2d 626 (CA2 1935). The District Court held that its injunction should not be read as prohibiting export of the ele-

---

5. Deepsouth is entirely straightforward in indicating that its course of conduct is motivated by a desire to avoid patent infringement. Its president wrote a Brazilian customer:

"We are handicapped by a decision against us in the United States. This was a very technical decision and we can manufacture the entire machine without any complication in the United States, with the exception that there are two parts that must not be assembled in the United States, but assembled after the machine arrives in Brazil."

Quoted in Laitram Corp. v. Deepsouth Packing Co., 443 F.2d 928, 938 (C.A.5 1971).

6. As shipped, Deepsouth's tumbler contains a deveining belt different from Laitram's support member and lip. But the Laitram elements are included in a separate box and the Deepsouth tumbler is made to accommodate the Laitram elements. The record shows that many customers will use the machine with the Laitram parts.

ments of a combination patent even when those elements could and predictably would be combined to form the whole.

> "It may be urged that .   .   . [this] result is not logical.
> .   .   . But it is founded on twin notions that underlie the patent laws. One is that a combination patent protects only the combination. The other is that monopolies—even those conferred by patents—are not viewed with favor. These are logic enough." 310 F.Supp. 926, 929 (1970).

The Court of Appeals for the Fifth Circuit reversed, thus departing from the established rules of the Second, Third, and Seventh Circuits. In the Fifth Circuit panel's opinion, those courts that previously considered the question "worked themselves into .   .   . a conceptual box" by adopting "an artificial, technical construction" of the patent laws, a construction, moreover, which in the opinion of the panel, "[subverted] the Constitutional scheme of promoting 'the Progress of Science and useful Arts'" by allowing an intrusion on a patentee's rights, 443 F.2d, at 938–939, citing U.S.Const., Art. I, § 8.

III

We disagree with the Court of Appeals for the Fifth Circuit.[7] Under the common law the inventor had no right to exclude others from making and using his invention. If Laitram has a right to suppress Deepsouth's export trade it must be derived from its patent grant, and thus from the patent statute. We find that 35 U.S.C.A. § 271, the provision of the patent laws on which Laitram relies, does not support its claim.

Certainly if Deepsouth's conduct were intended to lead to use of patented deveiners inside the United States, its production and sales activity would be subject to injunction as an induced or contributory infringement. But it is established that there can be no contributory infringement without the fact or intention of a direct infringement. "In a word, if there is no [direct] infringement of a patent there can be no contributory infringer." Mercoid Corp. v. Mid-Continent Co., 320 U.S. 661, 677, 64 S.Ct. 268, 88 L.Ed. 376, 387 (1944) (Frankfurter, J., dissenting on other grounds). Aro Mfg. Co. v. Convertible Top Replacement Co., 365 U.S. 336, 341–342, 81 S.Ct. 599, 5 L.Ed.2d 592, 596–597 (1961), succinctly articulates the law:

> "It is plain that § 271(c)—a part of the Patent Code enacted in 1952—made no change in the fundamental precept that there can be no contributory infringement in the absence of a direct infringement. That section defines contributory infringement in terms of direct infringement—namely the sale of a component of a patented combination or machine for use 'in an infringement of such patent.'"

7. For simplicity's sake, we, like the lower courts, will discuss only Deepsouth's claim as to permissible future conduct. It is obvious, however, that what we say as to the scope of the injunction in Laitram's favor applies also to the calculation of damages that Laitram may recover.

The statute makes it clear that it is not an infringement to make or use a patented product outside of the United States. Thus, in order to secure the injunction it seeks, Laitram must show a § 271(a) direct infringement by Deepsouth in the United States, that is, that Deepsouth "makes," "uses," or "sells" the patented product within the bounds of this country.

Laitram does not suggest that Deepsouth "uses" the machines. Its argument that Deepsouth sells the machines—based primarily on Deepsouth's sales rhetoric and related indicia such as price [9]—cannot carry the day unless it can be shown that Deepsouth is selling the "patented invention." The sales question thus resolves itself into the question of manufacture: did Deepsouth "make" (and then sell) something cognizable under the patent law as the patented invention, or did it "make" (and then sell) something that fell short of infringement?

The Court of Appeals, believing that the word "makes" should be accorded "a construction in keeping with the ordinary meaning of that term," 443 F.2d, at 938, held against Deepsouth on the theory that "makes" "means what it ordinarily connotes—the substantial manufacture of the constituent parts of the machine." Id., at 939. Passing the question of whether this definition more closely corresponds to the ordinary meaning of the term than that offered by Judge Swan in Andrea 35 years *earlier* (something is made when it reaches the state of final "operable" assembly), we find the Fifth Circuit's definition unacceptable because it collides head on with a line of decisions so firmly embedded in our patent law as to be unassailable absent a congressional recasting of the statute.

We cannot endorse the view that the "substantial manufacture of the constituent parts of [a] machine" constitutes direct infringement when we have so often held that a combination patent protects only against the operable assembly of the whole and not the manufacture of its parts. "For as we pointed out in Mercoid v. Mid-Continent Investment Co., [320 U.S. 661, 676, 64 S.Ct. 268, 88 L.Ed. 376] a patent on a combination is a patent on the assembled or functioning whole, not on the separate parts." Mercoid Corp. v. Minneapolis-Honeywell Regulator Co., 320 U.S. 680, 684, 64 S.Ct. 278, 88 L.Ed. 396, 399 (1944). . . .

It was this basic tenet of the patent system that led Judge Swan to hold in the leading case, Radio Corp. of America v. Andrea, 79 F. 2d 626 (1935), that unassembled export of the elements of an invention did not infringe the patent.

---

9. Deepsouth sold the less than completely assembled machine for the same price as it had sold fully assembled machines. Its advertisements, correspondence, and invoices frequently referred to a "machine," rather than to a kit or unassembled parts. See Brief for Respondent 8–11.

"[The] relationship is the essence of the patent.

". . . No wrong is done the patentee until the combination is formed. His monopoly does not cover the manufacture or sale of separate elements capable of being, but never actually, associated to form the invention. Only when such association is made is there a direct infringement of his monopoly, and not even then if it is done outside the territory for which the monopoly was granted." Id., at 628.

We reaffirm this conclusion today.

IV

It is said that this conclusion is derived from too narrow and technical an interpretation of the statute, and that this Court should focus on the constitutional mandate

"[t]o promote the Progress of Science and useful Arts, by securing for limited Times to Authors and Inventors the exclusive Right to their respective Writings and Discoveries . . .," Art. I, § 8,

and construe the statute in a manner that would, allegedly, better reflect the policy of the Framers.

We cannot accept this argument. The direction of Art. I is that *Congress* shall have the power to promote the progress of science and the useful arts. When, as here, the Constitution is permissive, the sign of how far Congress has chosen to go can come only from Congress. We are here construing the provisions of a statute passed in 1952. The prevailing law in this and other courts as to what is necessary to show a patentable invention when a combination of old elements is claimed was clearly evident from the cases when the Act was passed; and at that time Andrea, representing a specific application of the law of infringement with respect to the export of elements of a combination patent, was 17 years old. When Congress drafted § 271, it gave no indication that it desired to change either the law of combination patents as relevant here or the ruling of Andrea. Nor has it on any more recent occasion indicated that it wanted the patent privilege to run farther than it was understood to run for 35 years prior to the action of the Court of Appeals for the Fifth Circuit.

Moreover, we must consider petitioner's claim in light of this Nation's historical antipathy to monopoly and of repeated congressional efforts to preserve and foster competition. As this Court recently said without dissent:

"[I]n rewarding useful invention, the 'rights and welfare of the community must be fairly dealt with and effectually guarded.' Kendall v. Winsor, 21 How. 322, 329, 16 L.Ed. 165, 168 (1859). To that end the prerequisites to obtaining a patent are strictly observed, and when the patent has issued the limitations on its exercise are equally strictly enforced." Sears, Roebuck & Co. v.

Stiffel Co., 376 U.S. 225, 230, 84 S.Ct. 784, 11 L.Ed.2d 661, 666 (1964).

It follows that we should not expand patent rights by overruling or modifying our prior cases construing the patent statutes, unless the argument for expansion of privilege is based on more than mere inference from ambiguous statutory language. We would require a clear and certain signal from Congress before approving the position of a litigant who, as respondent here, argues that the beachhead of privilege is wider, and the area of public use narrower, than courts had previously thought. No such signal legitimizes respondent's position in this litigation.

In conclusion, we note that what is at stake here is the right of American companies to compete with an American patent holder in foreign markets. Our patent system makes no claim to extraterritorial effect; "these acts of Congress do not, and were not intended to, operate beyond the limits of the United States," Brown v. Duchesne, 19 How. at 195, 15 L.Ed. at 595; and we correspondingly reject the claims of others to such control over our markets. To the degree that the inventor needs protection in markets other than those of this country, the wording of 35 U.S.C.A. §§ 154 and 271 reveals a congressional intent to have him seek it abroad through patents secured in countries where his goods are being used. Respondent holds foreign patents; it does not adequately explain why it does not avail itself of them.

V

In sum: the case and statutory law resolves this case against the respondent. When so many courts have so often held what appears so evident—a combination patent can be infringed only by combination—we are not prepared to break the mold and begin anew. And were the matter not so resolved, we would still insist on a clear congressional indication of intent to extend the patent privilege before we could recognize the monopoly here claimed. Such an indication is lacking. Accordingly, the judgment of the Court of Appeals for the Fifth Circuit is reversed and the case is remanded for proceedings consistent with this opinion.

It is so ordered.

Mr. Justice BLACKMUN, with whom The Chief Justice, Mr. Justice POWELL, and Mr. Justice REHNQUIST join, dissenting.

Because our grant of certiorari was limited, 404 U.S. 1037, 92 S. Ct. 702, 30 L.Ed.2d 728 (1972), the customarily presented issues of patent validity and infringement are not before us in this case. I necessarily accept, therefore, the conclusion that the Laitram patents are valid and that the Deepsouth deveining machine, when manufactured and assembled in the United States, is an infringement. The Court so concedes. The Court, however, denies Laitram patent law protection against Deepsouth's manufacture and assembly when the mere assembly is effected abroad. It does so on the theory that there then is no "making" of the patented invention in the United States even though every part is made here and Deepsouth ships all the parts in response to an order from abroad.

With all respect, this seems to me to be too narrow a reading of 35 U.S.C.A. §§ 154 and 271(a). In addition, the result is unduly to reward the artful competitor who uses another's invention in its entirety and who seeks to profit thereby. Deepsouth may be admissive and candid or, as the Court describes it, "straightforward," in its "sales rhetoric," but for me that rhetoric reveals the very iniquitous and evasive nature of Deepsouth's operations. I do not see how one can escape the conclusion that the Deepsouth machine was *made* in the United States, within the meaning of the protective language of §§ 154 and 271(a). The situation, perhaps, would be different were parts, or even only one vital part, manufactured abroad. Here everything was accomplished in this country except putting the pieces together as directed (an operation that, as Deepsouth represented to its Brazilian prospect, would take "less than one hour"), all much as the fond father does with his little daughter's doll house on Christmas Eve. To say that such assembly, accomplished abroad, is not the prohibited combination and that it avoids the restrictions of our patent law, is a bit too much for me. The Court has opened the way to deny the holder of the United States combination patent the benefits of his invention with respect to sales to foreign purchasers.

I also suspect the Court substantially overstates when it describes Radio Corp. of America v. Andrea, 79 F.2d 626 (C.A.2 1935), as a "leading case," and when it imputes to Congress, in drafting the 1952 statute, an awareness of Andrea's "prevailing law." Andrea was seriously undermined only two years after its promulgation, when the Court of Appeals modified its decree on a second review. Radio Corp. of America v. Andrea, 90 F.2d 612 (C.A.2 1937). Its author, Judge Swan himself, dissenting in part from the 1937 decision, somewhat ruefully allowed that his court was overruling the earlier decision. I therefore would follow the Fifth Circuit's opinion in the present case, 443 F.2d 936 (1971), and would reject the reasoning in the older and weakened Andrea opinion and in the Third and Seventh Circuit opinions that merely follow it.

By a process of only the most rigid construction, the Court, by its decision today, fulfills what Judge Clark, in his able opinion for the Fifth Circuit, distressingly forecast:

"To hold otherwise [as the Court does today] would subvert the Constitutional scheme of promoting 'the Progress of Science and useful Arts, by securing for limited Times to Authors and Inventors the exclusive Right to their respective Writings and Discoveries.' U.S.Const., art. I § 8 Cl. 8. It would allow an infringer to set up shop next door to a patent-protected inventor whose product enjoys a substantial foreign market and deprive him of his valuable business. If this Constitutional protection is to be

fully effectuated, it must extend to an infringer who manufactures in the United States and then captures the foreign markets
from the patentee. The Constitutional mandate cannot be limited to just manufacturing and selling within the United States.
The infringer would then be allowed to reap the fruits of the
American economy—technology, labor, materials, etc.—but
would not be subject to the responsibilities of the American patent laws. We cannot permit an infringer to enjoy these benefits
and then be allowed to strip away a portion of the patentee's
protection." 443 F.2d, at 939.

I share the Fifth Circuit's concern and I therefore dissent.

WILBUR-ELLIS CO. v. KUTHER

Supreme Court of the United States, 1964.
377 U.S. 422, 84 S.Ct. 1561, 12 L.Ed.2d 419, 141 U.S.P.Q. 703.

Mr. Justice DOUGLAS delivered the opinion of the Court.

Respondent is the owner of a combination patent covering a
fish-canning machine. A number of machines covered by the patent
were manufactured and sold under his authorization. Among them
were the four machines in suit, petitioner Wilbur-Ellis Company
being the second-hand purchaser. Respondent received out of the
original purchase price a royalty of $1,500 per machine. As original-
ly constructed each of these machines packed fish into "1-pound"
cans: 3 inches in diameter and 4¹⁄₁₆ inches high. Three of the machines when acquired by Wilbur-Ellis were corroded, rusted, and inoperative; and all required cleaning and sandblasting to make them
usable. Wilbur-Ellis retained petitioner Leuschner to put the machines in condition so they would operate and to resize six of the 35
elements that made up the patented combination. The resizing was
for the purpose of enabling the machines to pack fish into "5-ounce"
cans: 2¹⁄₈ inches in diameter and 3½ inches long. One of the six elements was so corroded that it could be rendered operable only by
grinding it down to a size suitable for use with the smaller "5-ounce"
can.

This suit for infringement followed; and both the District Court,
200 F.Supp. 841, and the Court of Appeals, 314 F.2d 71, held for respondent. The case is here on certiorari. 373 U.S. 921, 83 S.Ct.
1525, 10 L.Ed.2d 41.

We put to one side the case where the discovery or invention resided in or embraced either the size or locational characteristics of
the replaced elements of a combination patent or the size of the commodity on which the machine operated. The claims of the patent before us do not reach that far. We also put to one side the case where
replacement was made of a patented component of a combination patent. We deal here with a patent that covered only a combination of
unpatented components.

The question in terms of patent law precedents is whether what was done to these machines, the original manufacture and sale of which had been licensed by the patentee, amounted to "repair," in which event there was no infringement, or "reconstruction," in which event there was. The idea of "reconstruction" in this context has the special connotation of those acts which would impinge on the patentee's right *"to exclude others from making,"* 35 U.S.C.A. § 154, the article. As stated in Wilson v. Simpson, 9 How. 109, 123, 13 L.Ed. 66, ". . . when the material of the combination ceases to exist, in whatever way that may occur, the right to renew it depends upon the right to make the invention. If the right to make does not exist, there is no right to rebuild the combination." On the other hand, "When the wearing or injury is partial, then repair is restoration, and not reconstruction." Ibid. Replacing worn-out cutting knives in a planing machine was held to be "repair," not "reconstruction," in Wilson v. Simpson, supra. Our latest case was Aro Mfg. Co. v. Convertible Top Replacement Co., 365 U.S. 336, 81 S.Ct. 599, 5 L.Ed.2d 592, which a majority of the Court construe as holding that it was not infringement to replace the worn-out fabric of a patented convertible automobile top, whose original manufacture and sale had been licensed by the patentee. See No. 75, Aro Mfg. Co. v. Convertible Top Replacement Co., 376 U.S. 476, 84 S.Ct. 1526, decided this day. . . .

Whatever view may be taken of the holding in the first Aro case, the majority believe that it governs the present one. These four machines were not spent; they had years of usefulness remaining though they needed cleaning and repair. Had they been renovated and put to use on the "1-pound" cans, there could be no question but that they were "repaired," not "reconstructed," within the meaning of the cases. When six of the 35 elements of the combination patent were resized or relocated, no invasion of the patent resulted, for as we have said the size of cans serviced by the machine was no part of the invention; nor were characteristics of size, location, shape and construction of the six elements in question patented. Petitioners in adapting the old machines to a related use were doing more than repair in the customary sense; but what they did was kin to repair for it bore on the useful capacity of the old combination, on which the royalty had been paid. We could not call it "reconstruction" without saying that the patentee's right "to exclude others from making" the patented machine, 35 U.S.C.A. § 154, had been infringed. Yet adaptation for use of the machine on a "5-ounce" can is within the patent rights purchased, since size was not an invention.

The adaptation made in the six nonpatented elements improved the usefulness of these machines. That does not, however, make the adaptation "reconstruction" within the meaning of the cases. We are asked in substance to treat the case as if petitioners had a license for use of the machines on "1-pound" cans only. But the sales here were outright, without restriction. Adams v. Burke, 17 Wall. 453, 456, 21 L.Ed. 700, therefore controls:

".   .   . when the patentee, or the person having his rights, sells a machine or instrument whose sole value is in its use, he receives the consideration for its use and he parts with the right to restrict that use."

Reversed.

Mr. Justice HARLAN would affirm the judgment substantially for the reasons given in the majority opinion in the Court of Appeals, 314 F.2d 71.

SPECIAL EQUIPMENT CO. v. COE, 324 U.S. 370, 380, 65 S.Ct. 741, 89 L.Ed. 1006, 64 U.S.P.Q. 525 (1945). DOUGLAS, J., dissenting: The right of suppression of a patent came into the law over a century after the first patent act was passed. In 1886 Judge Blodgett had ruled that a patentee "is bound either to use the patent himself or allow others to use it on reasonable or equitable terms." Hoe v. Knap, 27 F. 204, 212. In 1896 that rule was repudiated by the Circuit Court of Appeals for the Sixth Circuit in Heaton-Peninsular Button-Fastener Co. v. Eureka Specialty Co., 77 F. 288, 295, where the court stated that a patentee's "title is exclusive, and so clearly within the constitutional provisions in respect of private property that he is neither bound to use his discovery himself, nor permit others to use it." That theory was adopted by this Court in Continental Paper Bag Co. v. Eastern Paper Bag Co., 210 U.S. 405, 28 S.Ct. 748, 52 L. Ed. 1122, decided in 1908. That was an infringement suit. One defense was that the patentee had suppressed the patent. The Court held, Mr. Justice Harlan dissenting, that suppression of the patent was no defense; that the patentee's "right can only retain its attribute of exclusiveness by a prevention of its violation." Id., p. 430.

I think it is time to be rid of that rule. It is inconsistent with the Constitution and the patent legislation which Congress has enacted.   .   .   .

It is a mistake therefore to conceive of a patent as but another form of private property. The patent is a privilege "conditioned by a public purpose." Mercoid Corp. v. Mid-Continent Co., 320 U.S. 661, 666, 64 S.Ct. 268, 88 L.Ed. 376. The public purpose is "to promote the progress of science and useful arts." The exclusive right of the inventor is but the means to that end. That was early recognized by this Court. But the Paper Bag case marked a radical departure from that theory. It treated the "exclusive" right of the inventor as something akin to an "absolute" right. It subordinated the public purpose of the grant to the self-interest of the patentee.   .   .   .

It is difficult to see how that use of patents can be reconciled with the purpose of the Constitution "to promote the progress of science and the useful arts." Can the suppression of patents which arrests the progress of technology be said to promote that progress? It is likewise difficult to see how suppression of patents can be reconciled with the provision of the statute which authorizes a grant of the "exclusive right to make, use, and vend the invention or discovery." Rev.Stat. § 4884, 35 U.S.C.A. § 40. How may the words "to make, use, and vend" be read to mean "not to make, not to use, and not to vend"? Take the case of an invention or discovery which unlocks the doors of science and reveals the secrets of a dread disease. Is it possible that a patentee could be permitted to suppress that invention for seventeen years (the term of the letters patent) and withhold from humanity the benefits of the cure? But there is no difference in principle between that case and any case where a patent is suppressed because of some immediate advantage to the patentee.

NOTES

1. Would the Court have reached a different result in *Laitram* and in *Wilbur-Ellis* if the patented combinations in suit had revealed a "synergistic" result? Apart from a shared antipathy to mechanical combinations, is there any functional connection between cases like *Sakraida,* p. 443 above, dealing with patentability, and cases like *Laitram* and *Wilbur-Ellis* dealing with infringement?

Would the patent owner in *Laitram* have strengthened its case by adopting the practice of shipping all of *its* machines unassembled? What, if anything, could the patent owner in *Wilbur-Ellis* have done to strengthen its case?

See generally, Note, Operable Versus Substantial Assembly of Patented Combinations: A Critique of Deepsouth v. Laitram, 26 Stan.L.Rev. 893 (1974).

2. Aro Mfg. Co., Inc. v. Convertible Top Replacement Co., Inc., 365 U.S. 336, 81 S.Ct. 599, 5 L.Ed.2d 592, 128 U.S.P.Q. 354 (1961), mentioned in *Wilbur-Ellis*, held that replacement of the fabric in a convertible automobile top constituted a repair, rather than a reconstruction, of the entire top assembly so that the unauthorized manufacture and sale of these replacement fabrics did not directly or contributorily infringe the combination patent covering the top assembly. Writing for the Court, Justice Whittaker stated the question for decision to be "whether the owner of a combination patent, comprised entirely of unpatented elements, has a patent monopoly on the manufacture, sale or use of the several unpatented components of the patented combination." By framing the issue in terms of the distinction between unpatented and patented components, rather than between repair and reconstruction, Justice Whittaker necessarily anticipated the decision in the case; replacement of any part of a combination, no matter how significant, can never be reconstruction. "The decisions of this Court require the conclusion that reconstruction of a patented entity, comprised of unpatented elements, is limited to such a true reconstruction of the entity as to 'in fact make a new article' . . . after the entity, viewed as a whole, has become spent."

Justice Brennan, concurring, and Justice Harlan, dissenting, disagreed with Justice Whittaker's test. According to Justice Harlan, "none of the past cases in this Court or in the lower federal courts remotely suggests that 'reconstruction' can be found only in a situation where the patented combination has been rebuilt de novo from the ground up." Because the two lower courts "adverted to all the relevant standards," Justice Harlan thought it prudent to defer to their decisions.

Justice Brennan perceived "circumstances in which the replacement of a singly unpatented component of a patented combination short of a second creation of the patent entity may constitute 'reconstruction.'" Brennan interpreted the precedents to require that the determination in any case "be based upon the consideration of a number of factors. . . . Appropriately to be considered are the life of the part replaced in relation to the useful life of the whole combination, the importance of the replaced element to the inventive concept, the cost of the component relative to the cost of the combination, the common sense understanding and intention of the patent owner and the buyer of the combination as to its perishable components, whether the purchased component replaces a worn-out part or is bought for some other purpose, and other pertinent factors." Although the district and circuit courts below had considered factors of this sort, Justice Brennan concurred in the reversal because, under his own application, the replacement of tops constituted repair.

3. What incentives do patent owners have to suppress their inventions? How likely is it that the owner of a patent on an invention that "unlocks the doors of science and reveals the secrets of a dread disease" will, in Justice Douglas's words, "suppress the invention" and "withhold from humanity the benefits of the cure," rather than cash in on the value of his discovery? Are situations in which patent owners are economically motivated to suppress their inventions also likely to implicate antitrust violations? Does compulsory licensing offer an effective and efficient antidote to suppression in areas perceived to have great social or economic significance? The federal Clean Air Act, 42 U.S.C.A. 1857 H-6, provides for mandatory patent licensing under a narrowly defined set of circumstances. Is it preferable in these settings to rely on the government's condemnation power?

Many countries remedy patent suppression through compulsory licensing. Generally these systems provide that if a patent owner fails to exploit an invention within a specified period, anyone may, upon payment of a predetermined reasonable royalty, take a license under the patent. One observer notes that there are very few applications for these compulsory licenses. He concludes that this "does not mean, however, that the system has no effect, but rather that the prospective licensee and patentee usually try to reach an agreement directly rather than through official channels, with the patentee of course realizing that compulsory licensing is available if agreement is not reached." Goldsmith, Patent Protection for United States Inventions in the Principal European Countries—Existing Systems, 6 B.C. Comm. & Indus.L.Rev. 533, 535 (1965). See also, Tanabe, Compulsory Licensing in Japanese Patent Law, 8 Int'l Rev.Indus.Prop. & Copyright L. 42 (1977).

4.   Does the seventeen-year patent term represent a carefully set balance between the competing interests in adequate incentive and in free public participation in the protected subject matter?

The first patent act, Act of April 10, 1790, ch. 7, 1 Stat. 109, specified a fourteen-year term, copying the term employed in the English Statute of Monopolies of 1623, 21 Jac. 1, ch. 3. The English term had been based on the seven-year apprenticeship period universally practiced by the mid-sixteenth century. Underlying the fourteen-year term was the theory that an invention should come into general use only after the artisan-inventor had the opportunity to instruct two consecutive sets of apprentices in the subject matter.

Act of July 4, 1836, ch. 357, 5 Stat. 117, supplemented the fourteen-year term with a seven-year renewal period, and it was a Senate attempt to repeal this renewal period that, in 1861, precipitated enactment of the present seventeen-year term. The House favored retention of the seven-year renewal period. To accommodate the House position with the Senate's, the Conference Committee roughly split the difference and reported out a provision changing the term to seventeen years and dropping the renewal period.

How efficient is a single term, uniformly applicable to all sorts of subject matter? Consider one economist's view of the present system: "[A] moment's consideration suggests that patents of uniform duration unduly reward some inventions and inadequately compensate others. Surely, all inventions cannot be exploited in exactly the same length of time nor can the monetary profitability, if any, of patent monopolies of uniform length be equated to the social contribution of the inventions covered." White, Why a Seventeen Year Patent?, 38 J.P.O.S. 839, 842 (1956). Custom-tailored terms, varying in length from three to twenty years, were common under early colonial patent practice and are roughly approximated in 35 U.S.C.A. § 173's provision that "Patents for designs may be granted for the term of three years and six months, or for seven years, or for fourteen years, as the applicant, in his application, elects."

5.   Is it preferable for the Patent and Trademark Office to deny questionable patents on obviousness grounds or to allow the patent and rely on courts to sharply confine the rights that attach, as in *Laitram* and *Wilbur-Ellis*?

"Section 271 of the Patent Act provides that '. . . whoever without authority makes, uses or sells any patented invention, within the United States during the term therefore, infringes the patent.' And therein lies one of the principal mischiefs of the patent law. Ordinarily, a patent owner who believes his patent to be infringed by a product sues the offending manufacturer. If the patent owner prevails, he may have damages and an injunction, and he is thereby secured in his exclusive right to make, use, or sell the patent invention. But, as § 271 explicitly declares, he is not confined to a remedy against the manufacturer. He may, if he elects, sue the manufacturer's customers who 'use or sell.' And in so doing he may in effect by the very assertion of his claim of infringement, regardless of its merit, impair the salability of the accused goods. He thus can achieve for himself or his licensees a competitive advantage even though his patent may ultimately be declared to be invalid.

"Statistically, his patent probably will be declared invalid if a court ever passes on it. Nevertheless, there are profits to be derived even from those patents which do not survive litigation. There is evidence that some patent owners assert their patents not to vindicate their rights, but to harass competitors by burdensome patent infringement litigation or by the threat of such litigation. Courts and critics of the patent system have perceived this abuse. It is recognized that in many instances patents serve not to reward an inventor or his assignee for a signal contribution to technology, but as an instrument of unfair competition." Ladd, Business Aggression Under the Patent System, 26 U.Chi.L.Rev. 353–354 (1959).* The problems of, and limited remedies for, patent aggression are also considered in Stedman, Invention and Public Policy, 12 Law & Contemp.Prob. 649 (1947); Borkin, The Patent Infringement Suit—Ordeal by Trial, 17 U.Chi.L.Rev. 634 (1950); Final Report and Recommendations of the Temporary National Economic Committee, Sen.Doc.No. 35, 77th Cong. 1st Sess. 36 (1941).

6. Section 271(b) imposes liability on anyone who actively induces direct infringement. Among the acts that may be proscribed are distribution of brochures advertising the sale of infringing equipment or instructing in the use of a patented process, purchase of articles made by an infringing process, indemnification of an infringer, and encouragement of a licensee to breach his patent license agreement.

Consider the advantages that section 271(b) may give patentees in the following situations:

The direct infringer is judgment proof and the contributory infringer is solvent; the direct infringer's liability is limited by its corporate form and certain corporate officers can be treated as contributory infringers. See Timely Products Corp. v. Arron, 303 F.Supp. 713, 163 U.S.P.Q. 663 (D.C.Conn.1969).

A foreign national has committed all acts of direct infringement abroad but has distributed brochures for the accused subject matter to buyers in the United States. See Olin Mathieson Chem. Corp. v. The Molins Organisations, Ltd., 261 F.Supp. 436, 152 U.S.P.Q. 63 (E.D.Va.1966).

Acts of contributory, but not direct, infringement have occurred in the district most convenient for suit under the patent venue statute. See Watsco, Inc. v. Henry Valve Co., 232 F.Supp. 38, 142 U.S.P.Q. 219 (S.D.N.Y.1964).

A contributory infringer, but not a direct infringer, exhibits the animus necessary to recovery of treble or otherwise increased damages.

Miller, Some Views on the Law of Patent Infringement by Inducement, 53 J.P.O.S. 86, 139 (1971), is a comprehensive survey of the subject.

2. PATENTS IN THE MARKETPLACE

BAXTER, LEGAL RESTRICTIONS ON EXPLOITATION OF THE PATENT MONOPOLY: AN ECONOMIC ANALYSIS

76 Yale L.J. 267, 275–279; 312–314 (1966).*

II. The Patent Monopoly

The patentee's exclusive right to make, use and sell his invention is deceptive in its apparent simplicity. Very rarely would a patentee choose to invoke his right in accordance with the literal meaning of the statutory terms and deny to others all that he might deny. The holder of a process patent who was an integrated manufacturer-seller of an unpatented product yielded by the process might choose to license no one and extract his reward exclusively through monopoly profits in marketing the product. In such a case no one but the patentee would be making, using or selling the invention. But if the patent is on an endproduct, then, though no formal licenses are issued, those to whom the product is sold will use the invention and have an implied license to do so. In the vast majority of cases the patentee obtains his reward not by affirmatively asserting his exclusive right but by extracting a consideration for a total or partial waiver of that right.

As the reference to partial waiver underscores, the patentee is not limited to the alternatives of full assertion or total waiver but can, for a price, allow others to engage in some but less than all of the conduct that assertion of his exclusive right would preclude. Thus as T. R. Powell insisted with characteristic lucidity almost a half century ago, analysis is aided if the patentee is viewed as having not a single right but a whole bundle of rights to exclude, all, any one or none of which may be waived. The courts, in giving effect to the statutory phrase, have consistently arrived at results incompatible with any other view.

Just as the use of the word "right" in the statute quite properly did not preclude results consistent only with use of the word "rights," so also no dictate of grammar or metaphysics should be thought to allow waiver of one particular group of patentee rights but to preclude waiver of another, nor to allow waiver of a group of rights in exchange for one type of consideration but preclude it for another type. On these points, however, the courts have had more difficulty. A license to use a patented machine with, but only with, supplies furnished by the patentee was first upheld and later struck down. A license to resell a patented product purchased from the patentee at, but only at, a price set by the patentee was struck down; but a license to manufacture and sell a product at, but only at, a price set by the patentee was upheld. These results may be right or wrong, but sound answers to the problems the cases posed cannot be reached by parsing the highly general language of the statute, by metaphysical assertions that the right to exclude totally necessarily embraces the right to exclude partially or by framing question-begging generalities about what is "normally and reasonably adapted to secure pecuniary reward." By the first sale of a patented article, the Supreme Court has said, "the article . . . [is] thereby carried outside the monopoly of the patent law and rendered free of every restriction which the vendor may attempt to put upon it." But quite obviously the article is not carried outside the monopoly in the sense that a chair may be carried outside a room; no phenomenon susceptible to empirical validation is involved. The Court's statement was not made because it was true; it is "true" only because the statement was made and will be "true" only until the Court or Congress makes a contrary statement.

No one type of consideration more than any other extracted in exchange for a waiver of all or part of the patentee's rights is, for merely logical reasons, "normally and reasonably adapted to secure" the objectives of the patentee. The disadvantages which attend use of the monopoly-subsidy device are tolerable only because of the offsetting advantages of private bargaining—only because private bargaining simultaneously can yield to both the patentee and the licensee more of what each, given his unique situation, deems of value. A promise by the licensee to murder the patentee's mother-in-law is as much "within the patent monopoly" as is the sum $50.00; and it is not the patent laws which tell us that the former agreement is unenforceable and subjects the parties to criminal sanctions.

The last example, while silly in its extremity, nevertheless illustrates two important points. The value to the patentee of the licensee conduct sought by the patentee may exceed its cost to the licensee. Hence both parties may be better off as a consequence of their exchange. Therein, of course, lies the great value of private arrangements. But therein, too, lies their danger; for conduct of value to the patentee may be highly injurious to third persons. Indeed it may be of value to the patentee precisely because it is injurious to third persons. Courts should be alert to penalize such bargains by imposing on the immediate parties the sanction of nullity and other appropriate sanctions. Only rarely will the policies calling for protection of third persons be found in the patent laws; to search for them there is generally futile, to purport to find them there is generally duplicitous and confusing.

Effect of licensee conduct on third persons may or may not, depending on the circumstances, constitute adequate reason for striking down a license agreement. But only in most extraordinary circumstances will the effect on the licensee justify so doing. As a class patent licensees are unlikely candidates for "ward of the court" status, and cases that rest on the premise of overreaching are likely to be unsound, either in their reasoning or in both reasoning and result.

From this conclusion—that legality of a patent license properly turns on its impact on third persons and on whether the parties are privileged to impose this effect—it follows that too much significance has been accorded in the past to the distinction between condition and covenant. Any of the typical license limitations can be imposed through either device. A license can be broad in its waiver of patentee rights and contain a promise by the licensee that he will not sell the patented product for less than a specified price; or it may license only those sales which are made at prices equal to or exceeding a specified price. A license may authorize generally use of a patented machine and contain a promise by the licensee to buy all supplies used with the machine from the patentee; or it may license use of the machine only in conjunction with supplies purchased from the patentee. It may license manufacture and sale generally and contain a licensee covenant to confine his activities to Hecate County; or it may license the activities only in that county. If in each of these cases the conduct of the licensee will be the same, then the third person impact will be the same and there is no basis for upholding one form and invalidating the other.

In general the distinction between covenant and condition should be disregarded because there is no reason to suppose that licensee conduct will be affected by the form used. In either case he is liable to sanctions if he engages in unauthorized conduct—damages for breach and perhaps an injunction in the case of covenant; an infringement suit for damages and injunction in the case of condition. To the extent that the licensee is dependent upon good relations with the patentee, unauthorized operations are as much deterred by condition as by covenant: infringers no less than promise-breakers are pariahs in the business community.

That the distinction between covenant and condition is generally without substance is so clear that one seeks explanation of how it came to be accorded significance. Explanations of nonsense are necessarily somewhat speculative, but the probable origins of the foible are several. First, availability of a federal forum often turns on the distinction. Suit to enforce a condition usually takes the form of an infringement charge and hence "arises under" the patent laws; but suit for breach of covenant must be brought in the state courts unless diversity is present. Second, there is great confusion in the cases regarding the circumstances under which a defendant in a contract action may assert an anti-trust defense, but where the suit is for infringement a defense of "misuse" generally is allowed. Finally it is more difficult, apparently, for courts to perceive anticompetitive effects of conditions than of covenants. A promise not to sell at prices below the patentee's or outside a set territory falls neatly alongside the "contract in restraint of trade" phraseology of the Sherman Act. But when faced with a comparable condition, the courts tend to reason that *all* competition was forbidden before the license and hence no suppression of competition could be attributable to a license which made *some* competition possible. Even to the extent that this latter analysis is sound—and it sounds much better before careful scrutiny than afterward—the distinction between condition and covenant is not aided; for it is equally true that there would have been no occasion for the promise not to compete by certain acts but for the authorization found in the same document to compete in other ways. Maximum rational significance is accorded the distinction between covenant and condition when it is viewed, in conjunction with other circumstances, as probative of future licensee conduct.

.   .   .

VII.   Restrictions on Licensee Conduct

The basic thesis of this paper is that validity of patent license agreements is determined by the nature of the conduct the agreement is likely to induce. The patent law explicitly authorizes the extraction of monopoly profits by restricting utilization of and raising the price for using the invention. The antitrust laws explicitly forbid interference with the processes of competition to the end that prices will be reduced, output will be increased and resource allocation will be more nearly optimal. It is convenient to describe the patentee's freedom to monopolize as an "exception" to the antitrust laws' general mandate of competitive behavior; but I do not suggest that because the freedom is an "exception" to the general mandate it should be narrowly construed. It should be construed neither narrowly nor broadly but rather to achieve its obvious purpose—the subsidization of innovative activity. Yet, because the patentee's authority is an island of permission in a sea of prohibition, there is no area at the edge of permission toward which the law is indifferent: what is not authorized is forbidden. Every case which presents the issue of patentee freedom to monopolize necessarily presents a reciprocal issue of prohibited interference with competitive processes.

If the patentee has engaged in, or induced by agreement, conduct which restricts output of his invention, it would seem that he stands safely on his isle of permission. If he has engaged in or induced conduct that restricts output of any other good or service, it would seem that he has stepped into prohibited waters. But the metaphor is too simple, and fails. A restriction on use of the invention will in almost every case have the consequence of restricting output of other goods and services. If, for example, the invention has a physical embodiment, restriction on the invention will necessarily restrict the unpatented goods and services which are production inputs of the physical embodiment.

One is tempted, therefore, to fall back either to language of patentee "purpose" or to language of "direct" and "indirect" restraints. But in this context as in others those phrases tend more to obscure than to clarify. Articulated as tests, the concepts inevitably degenerate to inarticulate statements of legal conclusion. I suggest a formulation less crisp to the ear but better calculated to focus the mind on relevant differences: a patentee is entitled to extract monopoly income by restricting utilization of his invention, notwithstanding that utilization of other goods and services are consequently restricted, provided that in each case he confines the restriction to his invention as narrowly and specifically as the technology of his situation and the practicalities of administration permit. This formulation, I believe, gives appropriate scope to both antitrust and patent policy, is sufficiently specific to enable courts to reach reasonable results through reasoned applications, and, in the process of application, will be suggestive of even more specific subsidiary rules.

The standard must be read with emphasis on its first phrase: The patentee is entitled "*to extract monopoly income* by imposing restrictions." Generation of returns to patentees is the immediate objective of the patent laws and the only justification for tolerating the many baleful results of those laws. The only justification for using monopoly as opposed to direct government subsidy to induce innovation is to utilize the competitive processes of the private economy to assess and reward proportionately the value of each particular invention. This process of competitive assessment assumes that licensees will resist patentee demands and that out of the bargaining process between them will emerge a stream of benefits to the patentee and a stream of detriments to the licensee roughly comparable to the ultimate value of the invention to the licensee and to society. If the licensee conduct demanded by the patentee is only the payment of royalties, the hoped for comparability of monopoly income with invention utility will usually be achieved. But if other types of licensee conduct are demanded, no such comparability is necessarily to be expected. The value to the patentee of licensee conduct may far exceed its detriment to the licensee; indeed, the conduct may be as beneficial to the licensee as to the patentee, in which case the licensee has no incentive to resist the demands, and any expectation of comparability is foolish. In the absence of comparability, the social loss caused by restricting the use of the invention and otherwise permissible incidental restrictions on other goods and services may exceed, and often far exceed, the value of patentee contribution to knowledge.

There are then two critical points that underlie analysis of any particular situation: first, minimizing incidental restriction to the extent technologically and administratively feasible; and second, forbidding patentee demands for conduct of a nature that destroys assurance of comparability between restriction and invention utility.

DAWSON CHEM. CO. v. ROHM & HAAS CO.

Supreme Court of the United States, 1980.
— U.S. —, 100 S.Ct. 2601, 65 L.Ed.2d 696, 206 U.S.P.Q. 385.

Mr. Justice BLACKMUN delivered the opinion of the Court.

This case presents an important question of statutory interpretation arising under the patent laws. The issue before us is whether the owner of a patent on a chemical process is guilty of patent misuse, and therefore is barred from seeking relief against contributory infringement of its patent rights, if it exploits the patent only in conjunction with the sale of an unpatented article that constitutes a material part of the invention and is not suited for commercial use outside the scope of the patent claims. The answer will determine whether respondent, the owner of a process patent on a chemical herbicide, may maintain an action for contributory infringement against other manufacturers of the chemical used in the process. To resolve this issue, we must construe the various provisions of 35 U.S.C.A. § 271, which Congress enacted in 1952 to codify certain aspects of the doctrines of contributory infringement and patent misuse that previously had been developed by the judiciary.

I

The doctrines of contributory infringement and patent misuse have long and interrelated histories. The idea that a patentee should be able to obtain relief against those whose acts facilitate infringement by others has been part of our law since Wallace v. Holmes, 29 F.Cas. 74 (No. 17,100) (C.C.Conn.1871). The idea that a patentee should be denied relief against infringers if he has attempted illegally to extend the scope of his patent monopoly is of somewhat more recent origin, but it goes back at least as far as Motion Picture Patents Co. v. Universal Film Mfg. Co., 243 U.S. 502, 37 S.Ct. 416, 61 L.Ed. 871 (1917). The two concepts, contributory infringement and patent misuse, often are juxtaposed, because both concern the relationship between a patented invention and unpatented articles or elements that are needed for the invention to be practiced.

Both doctrines originally were developed by the courts. But in its 1952 codification of the patent laws Congress endeavored, at least in part, to substitute statutory precepts for the general judicial rules that had governed prior to that time. Its efforts find expression in 35 U.S.C.A. § 271:

"(a) Except as otherwise provided in this title, whoever without authority makes, uses or sells any patented invention, within the United States during the term of the patent therefor, infringes the patent.

"(b) Whoever actively induces infringement of a patent shall be liable as an infringer.

"(c) Whoever sells a component of a patented machine, manufacture, combination or composition, or a material or apparatus for use in practicing a patented process, constituting a material part of the invention, knowing the same to be especially made or especially adapted for use in an infringement of such patent, and not a staple article or commodity of commerce suitable for substantial noninfringing use, shall be liable as a contributory infringer.

"(d) No patent owner otherwise entitled to relief for infringement or contributory infringement of a patent shall be denied relief or deemed guilty of misuse or illegal extension of the patent right by reason of his having done one or more of the following: (1) derived revenue from acts which if performed by another without his consent would constitute contributory infringement of the patent; (2) licensed or authorized another to perform acts which if performed without his consent would constitute contributory infringement of the patent; (3) sought to enforce his patent rights against infringement or contributory infringement."

Of particular import to the present controversy are subsections (c) and (d). The former defines conduct that constitutes contributory infringement; the latter specifies conduct of the patentee that is *not* to be deemed misuse.

A

The catalyst for this litigation is a chemical compound known to scientists as "3, 4-dichloropropionanilide" and referred to in the chemical industry as "propanil." In the late 1950's, it was discovered that this compound had properties that made it useful as a selective, "post-emergence" herbicide particularly well suited for the cultivation of rice. If applied in the proper quantities, propanil kills weeds normally found in rice crops without adversely affecting the crops themselves. It thus permits spraying of general areas where the crops are already growing, and eliminates the necessity for hand weeding or flooding of the rice fields. Propanil is one of several herbicides that are commercially available for use in rice cultivation.

Efforts to obtain patent rights to propanil or its use as a herbicide have been continuous since the herbicidal qualities of the chemical first came to light. The initial contender for a patent monopoly for this chemical compound was the Monsanto Company. In 1957, Monsanto filed the first of three successive applications for a patent on propanil itself. After lengthy proceedings in the United States Patent Office, a patent, No. 3,382,280, finally was issued in 1968. It was declared invalid, however, when Monsanto sought to enforce it by suing Rohm and Haas Company (Rohm & Haas), a competing manufacturer, for direct infringement. Monsanto Co. v. Rohm & Haas Co., 312 F.Supp. 778 (E.D.Pa.1970), aff'd, 456 F.2d 592 (C.A. 3), cert. denied, 407 U.S. 934, 92 S.Ct. 2463, 32 L.Ed.2d 817 (1972). The District Court held that propanil had been implicitly revealed in prior art dating as far back as 1902, even though its use as a herbicide had been discovered only recently. 312 F.Supp., at 787–790. Monsanto subsequently dedicated the patent to the public, and it is not a party to the present suit.

Invalidation of the Monsanto patent cleared the way for Rohm & Haas, respondent here, to obtain a patent on the method or process for applying propanil. This is the patent on which the present lawsuit is founded. Rohm & Haas' efforts to obtain a propanil patent began in 1958. These efforts finally bore fruit when, on June 11, 1974, the United States Patent Office issued Patent No. 3,816,092 (the Wilson patent) to Harold F. Wilson and Dougal H. McRay. The patent contains several claims covering a method for applying propanil to inhibit the growth of undesirable plants in areas containing established crops.[2] Rohm & Haas has been the sole owner of the patent since its issuance.

Petitioners, too, are chemical manufacturers. They have manufactured and sold propanil for application to rice crops since before Rohm & Haas received its patent. They market the chemical in containers on which are printed directions for application in accordance with the method claimed in the Wilson patent. Petitioners did not cease manufacture and sale of propanil after that patent issued, despite knowledge that farmers purchasing their products would infringe on the patented method by applying the propanil to their crops. Accordingly, Rohm & Haas filed this suit, in the United States District Court for the Southern District of Texas, seeking injunctive relief against petitioners on the ground that their manufacture and sale of propanil interfered with its patent rights.

The complaint alleged not only that petitioners contributed to infringement by farmers who purchased and used petitioners' propanil, but that they actually induced such infringement by instructing farmers how to apply the herbicide. See 35 U.S.C.A. §§ 271(b) and (c). Petitioners responded to the suit by requesting licenses to practice the patented method. When Rohm & Haas refused to grant such licenses, however, petitioners raised a defense of patent misuse and counterclaimed for alleged antitrust violations by respondent. The parties entered into a stipulation of facts and petitioners moved for partial summary judgment. They argued that Rohm & Haas has misused its patent by conveying the right to practice the patented method only to purchasers of its own propanil.

2. The Wilson patent contains several claims relevant to this proceeding. Of these the following are illustrative:

  1. "A method for selectively inhibiting growth of undesirable plants in an area containing growing undesirable plants in an established crop, which comprises applying to said area, 3, 4-dichloropropionanilide at a rate of application which inhibits growth of said unde-

sirable plants and which does not adversely affect the growth of said established crop."

  2. "The method according to claim 1 wherein the 3, 4-dichloropropionanilide is applied in a composition comprising 3, 4-dichloropropionanilide and an inert diluent therefor at a rate of between 0.5 and 6 pounds of 3, 4-dichloropropionanilide per acre." App. 69–70.

The District Court granted summary judgment for petitioners. 191 U.S.P.Q. 691 (1976). It agreed that Rohm & Haas was barred from obtaining relief against infringers of its patent because it had attempted illegally to extend its patent monopoly. The District Court recognized that 35 U.S.C.A. § 271(d) specifies certain conduct which is not to be deemed patent misuse. The court ruled, however, that "[t]he language of § 271(d) simply does not encompass the totality of [Rohm & Haas'] conduct in this case." 191 U.S.P.Q. at 704. It held that respondent's refusal to grant licenses, other than the "implied" licenses conferred by operation of law upon purchasers of its propanil, constituted an attempt by means of a "tying" arrangement to effect a monopoly over an unpatented component of the process. The District Court concluded that this conduct would be deemed patent misuse under the judicial decisions that preceded § 271(d), and it held that "[n]either the legislative history nor the language of § 271 indicates that this rule has been modified." 191 U.S.P.Q. at 707.

The United States Court of Appeals for the Fifth Circuit reversed. 599 F.2d 685 (1979). It emphasized the fact that propanil, in the terminology of the patent law, is a "nonstaple" article, that is, one that has no commercial use except in connection with respondent's patented invention. After a thorough review of the judicial developments preceding enactment of § 271, and a detailed examination of the legislative history of that provision, the court concluded that the legislation restored to the patentee protection against contributory infringement that decisions of this Court theretofore had undermined. To secure that result, Congress found it necessary to cut back on the doctrine of patent misuse. The Court of Appeals determined that, by specifying in § 271(d) conduct that is not to be deemed misuse, "Congress *did* clearly provide for a patentee's right to exclude others and reserve to itself, if it chooses, the right to sell nonstaples used substantially only in its invention." 599 F.2d, at 704 (emphasis in original). Since Rohm & Haas' conduct was designed to accomplish only what the statute contemplated, the court ruled that petitioners' misuse defense was of no avail.

We granted certiorari, 444 U.S. 1012, 100 S.Ct. 659, 62 L.Ed.2d 640 (1980), to forestall a possible conflict in the lower courts and to resolve an issue of prime importance in the administration of the patent law.

B

For present purposes certain material facts are not in dispute. First, the validity of the Wilson patent is not in question at this stage in the litigation. We therefore must assume that respondent is the lawful owner of the sole and exclusive right to use, or to license others to use, propanil as a herbicide on rice fields in accordance with the methods claimed in the Wilson patent. Second, petitioners do not dispute that their manufacture and sale of propanil together with instructions for use as a herbicide constitute contributory infringement of the Rohm & Haas patent. Accordingly, they admit that propanil constitutes "a material part of [respondent's] invention," that it is "especially made or especially adapted for use in an infringement of [the] patent," and that it is "not a staple article or commodity of commerce suitable for substantial noninfringing use," all within the language of 35 U.S.C.A. § 271(c). They also concede that they have produced and sold propanil with knowledge that it would be used in a manner infringing on respondent's patent rights. To put the same matter in slightly different terms, as the litigation now stands, petitioners admit commission of a tort and raise as their only defense to liability the contention that respondent, by engaging in patent misuse, comes into court with unclean hands.

As a result of these concessions, our chief focus of inquiry must be the scope of the doctrine of patent misuse in light of the limitations placed upon that doctrine by § 271(d). On this subject, as well, our task is guided by certain stipulations and concessions. The parties agree that Rohm & Haas makes and sells propanil; that it has refused to license petitioners or any others to do the same; that it has not granted express licenses either to retailers or to end users of the product; and that farmers who buy propanil from Rohm & Haas may use it, without fear of being sued for direct infringement, by virtue of an "implied license" they obtain when Rohm & Haas relinquishes its monopoly by selling the propanil. The parties further agree that §§ 271(d)(1) and (3) permit respondent both to sell propanil itself and to sue others who sell the same product without a license, and that under § 271(d)(2) it would be free to demand royalties from others for the sale of propanil if it chose to do so.

The parties disagree over whether respondent has engaged in any additional conduct that amounts to patent misuse. Petitioners assert that there has been misuse because respondent has "tied" the sale of patent rights to the purchase of propanil, an unpatented and indeed unpatentable article, and because it has refused to grant licenses to other producers of the chemical compound. They argue that § 271(d) does not permit any sort of tying arrangement, and that resort to such a practice excludes respondent from the category of patentees "otherwise entitled to relief" within the meaning of § 271(d). Rohm & Haas, understandably, vigorously resists this characterization of its conduct. It argues that its acts have been only those that § 271(d), by express mandate, excepts from characterization as patent misuse. It further asserts that if this conduct results in an extension of the patent right to a control over an unpatented commodity, in this instance the extension has been given express statutory sanction.

II

Our mode of analysis follows closely the trail blazed by the District Court and the Court of Appeals. It is axiomatic, of course, that statutory construction must begin with the language of the statute itself. But the language of § 271 is generic and freighted with a meaning derived from the decisional history that preceded it. The Court

of Appeals appropriately observed that more than one interpretation
of the statutory language has a surface plausibility.   To place § 271
in proper perspective, therefore, we believe that it is helpful first to
review in detail the doctrines of contributory infringement and patent
misuse as they had developed prior to Congress' attempt to codify the
governing principles.

As we have noted, the doctrine of contributory infringement had
its genesis in an era of simpler and less subtle technology.   Its basic
elements are perhaps best explained with a classic example drawn
from that era.   In Wallace v. Holmes, supra, the patentee had invented a new burner for an oil lamp.   In compliance with the technical
rules of patent claiming, this invention was patented in a combination
that also included the standard fuel reservoir, wick tube, and chimney
necessary for a properly functioning lamp.   After the patent issued, a
competitor began to market a rival product including the novel burner but not the chimney.   Under the sometimes scholastic law of patents, this conduct did not amount to direct infringement, because the
competitor had not replicated every single element of the patentee's
claimed combination.   Yet the court held that there had been "palpa-
ble interference" with the patentee's legal rights, because purchasers
would be certain to complete the combination, and hence the infringement, by adding the glass chimney.   The court permitted the patentee to enforce his rights against the competitor who brought about
the infringement, rather than requiring the patentee to undertake the
almost insuperable task of finding and suing all the innocent purchasers who technically were responsible for completing the infringement.

The *Wallace* case demonstrates, in a readily comprehensible setting, the reason for the contributory infringement doctrine.   It exists
to protect patent rights from subversion by those who, without directly infringing the patent themselves, engage in acts designed to facilitate infringement by others.   This protection is of particular importance in situations, like the oil lamp case itself, where enforcement
against direct infringers would be difficult, and where the technicali-
ties of patent law make it relatively easy to profit from another's invention without risking a charge of direct infringement.

Although the propriety of the decision in Wallace v. Holmes seldom has been challenged, the contributory infringement doctrine it
spawned has not always enjoyed full adherence in other contexts.
The difficulty that the doctrine has encountered stems not so much
from rejection of its core concept as from a desire to delimit its outer
contours.   In time, concern for potential anticompetitive tendencies
inherent in actions for contributory infringement led to retrenchment
on the doctrine.   The judicial history of contributory infringement
thus may be said to be marked by a period of ascendancy, in which
the doctrine was expanded to the point where it became subject to
abuse, followed by a somewhat longer period of decline, in which the
concept of patent misuse was developed as an increasingly stringent
antidote to the perceived excesses of the earlier period.

The doctrine of contributory infringement was first addressed by this Court in Morgan Envelope Co. v. Albany Paper Co., 152 U.S. 425, 14 S.Ct. 627, 38 L.Ed. 500 (1894). That case was a suit by a manufacturer of a patented device for dispensing toilet paper against a supplier of paper rolls that fit the patented invention. The Court accepted the contributory infringement doctrine in theory but held that it could not be invoked against a supplier of perishable commodities used in a patented invention. The Court observed that a contrary outcome would give the patentee "the benefit of a patent" on ordinary articles of commerce, a result that it determined to be unjustified on the facts of that case. Id., at 433, 14 S.Ct., at 630.

Despite this wary reception, contributory infringement actions continued to flourish in the lower courts. Eventually the doctrine gained more wholehearted acceptance here. In Leeds & Catlin Co. v. Victor Talking Machine Co., 213 U.S. 325, 29 S.Ct. 503, 53 L.Ed. 816 (1909), the Court upheld an injunction against contributory infringement by a manufacturer of phonograph discs specially designed for use in a patented disc-and-stylus combination. Although the disc itself was not patented, the Court noted that it was essential to the functioning of the patented combination, and that its method of interaction with the stylus was what "mark[ed] the advance upon the prior art." Id., at 330, 29 S.Ct., at 504. It also stressed that the disc was capable of use only in the patented combination, there being no other commercially available stylus with which it would operate. The Court distinguished the result in *Morgan Envelope* on the broad grounds that "[n]ot one of the determining factors there stated exists in the case at bar," and it held that the attempt to link the two cases "is not only to confound essential distinctions made by the patent laws, but essential differences between entirely different things." 213 U.S., at 335, 29 S.Ct., at 506.

The contributory infringement doctrine achieved its high-water mark with the decision in Henry v. A. B. Dick Co., 224 U.S. 1, 32 S. Ct. 364, 56 L.Ed. 645 (1912). In that case a divided Court extended contributory infringement principles to permit a conditional licensing arrangement whereby a manufacturer of a patented printing machine could require purchasers to obtain all supplies used in connection with the invention, including such staple items as paper and ink, exclusively from the patentee. The Court reasoned that the market for these supplies was created by the invention, and that sale of a license to use the patented product, like sale of other species of property, could be limited by whatever conditions the property owner wished to impose. The *A. B. Dick* decision and its progeny in the lower courts led to a vast expansion in conditional licensing of patented goods and processes used to control markets for staple and nonstaple goods alike.

This was followed by what may be characterized through the lens of hindsight as an inevitable judicial reaction. In Motion Picture Patents Co. v. Universal Film Co., 243 U.S. 502, 37 S.Ct. 416, 61 L.Ed. 871 (1917), the Court signalled a new trend that was to continue for years thereafter. The owner of a patent on projection equipment attempted to prevent competitors from selling film for use in the patented equipment by attaching to the projectors it sold a notice purporting to condition use of the machine on exclusive use of its film. The film previously had been patented but that patent had expired. The Court addressed the broad issue whether a patentee possessed the right to condition sale of a patented machine on the purchase of articles "which are no part of the patent machine, and which are not patented." 243 U.S., at 508, 37 S.Ct., at 417. Relying upon the rule that the scope of a patent "must be limited to the invention described in the claims," id., at 511, 37 S.Ct., at 419, the Court held that the attempted restriction on use of unpatented supplies was improper:

> "Such a restriction is invalid because such a film is obviously not any part of the invention of the patent in suit; because it is an attempt, without statutory warrant, to continue the patent monopoly in this particular character of film after it has expired, and because to enforce it would be to create a monopoly in the manufacture and use of moving picture films, wholly outside of the patent in suit and of the patent law as we have interpreted it." Id., at 518, 37 S.Ct., at 421.

By this reasoning, the Court focused on the conduct of the patentee, not that of the alleged infringer. It noted that as a result of lower court decisions, conditional licensing arrangements had greatly increased, indeed, to the point where they threatened to become "perfect instrument[s] of favoritism and oppression." Id., at 515, 37 S. Ct., at 420. The Court warned that approval of the licensing scheme under consideration would enable the patentee to "ruin anyone unfortunate enough to be dependent upon its confessedly important improvements for the doing of business." Ibid. This ruling was directly in conflict with Henry v. A. B. Dick Co., supra, and the Court expressly observed that that decision "must be regarded as overruled." 243 U.S., at 518, 37 S.Ct., at 421.

The broad ramifications of the *Motion Picture* case apparently were not immediately comprehended, and in a series of decisions over the next three decades litigants tested its limits. In Carbice Corp. v. American Patents Co., 283 U.S. 27, 51 S.Ct. 334, 75 L.Ed. 819 (1931), the Court denied relief to a patentee who, through its sole licensee, authorized use of a patented design for a refrigeration package only to purchasers from the licensee of solid carbon dioxide ("dry ice"), a refrigerant that the licensee manufactured. The refrigerant was a well-known and widely used staple article of commerce, and the patent in question claimed neither a machine for making it nor a process for using it. Id., at 29, 51 S.Ct., at 334. The Court held that the patent holder and its licensee were attempting to exclude competitors in the refrigerant business from a portion of the market, and that this conduct constituted patent misuse. It reasoned:

> "Control over the supply of such unpatented material is beyond the scope of the patentee's monopoly; and this limitation, inher-

ent in the patent grant, is not dependent upon the peculiar function or character of the unpatented material or on the way in which it is used. Relief is denied because the [licensee] is attempting, without sanction of law, to employ the patent to secure a limited monopoly of unpatented material used in applying the invention." Id., at 33–34, 51 S.Ct., at 336.

The Court also rejected the patentee's reliance on the *Leeds & Catlin* decision. It found "no suggestion" in that case that the owner of the disc-stylus combination patent had attempted to derive profits from the sale of unpatented supplies as opposed to a patented invention. Id., at 34, 51 S.Ct., at 336.

Other decisions of a similar import followed. Leitch Mfg. Co. v. Barber Co., 302 U.S. 458, 58 S.Ct. 288, 82 L.Ed. 371 (1938), found patent misuse in an attempt to exploit a process patent for the curing of cement through the sale of bituminous emulsion, an unpatented staple article of commerce used in the process. The Court eschewed an attempt to limit the rule of *Carbice* and *Motion Picture* to cases involving explicit agreements extending the patent monopoly, and it stated the broad proposition that "every use of a patent as a means of obtaining a limited monopoly of unpatented material is prohibited." Id., at 463, 58 S.Ct., at 290. Morton Salt Co. v. G. S. Suppiger Co., 314 U.S. 488, 492–494, 62 S.Ct. 402, 405–406, 86 L.Ed. 363 (1942), which involved an attempt to control the market for salt tablets used in a patented dispenser, explicitly linked the doctrine of patent misuse to the "unclean hands" doctrine traditionally applied by courts of equity. Its companion case, B. B. Chemical Co. v. Ellis, 314 U.S. 495, 495–498, 62 S.Ct. 406, 406–408, 86 L.Ed. 367 (1942), held that patent misuse barred relief even where infringement had been actively induced, and that practical difficulties in marketing a patented invention could not justify patent misuse.

Although none of these decisions purported to cut back on the doctrine of contributory infringement itself, they were generally perceived as having that effect, and how far the developing doctrine of patent misuse might extend was a topic of some speculation among members of the patent bar. The Court's decisions had not yet addressed the status of contributory infringement or patent misuse with respect to nonstaple goods, and some courts and commentators apparently took the view that control of nonstaple items capable only of infringing use might not bar patent protection against contributory infringement. This view soon received a serious, if not fatal, blow from the Court's controversial decisions in Mercoid Corp. v. Mid-Continent Investment Co., 320 U.S. 661, 64 S.Ct. 268, 88 L.Ed. 376 (1944) (*Mercoid I*), and Mercoid Corp. v. Minneapolis-Honeywell Regulator Co., 320 U.S. 680, 64 S.Ct. 278, 88 L.Ed. 396 (1944) (*Mercoid II*). In these cases, the Court definitely held that any attempt to control the market for unpatented goods would constitute patent misuse, even if those goods had no use outside a patented invention. Because these cases served as the point of departure for congressional legislation, they merit more than passing citation.

Both cases involved a single patent that claimed a combination of elements for a furnace heating system. Mid-Continent was the owner of the patent, and Honeywell was its licensee. Although neither company made or installed the furnace system, Honeywell manufactured and sold stoker switches especially made for and essential to the system's operation. The right to build and use the system was granted to purchasers of the stoker switches, and royalties owed the patentee were calculated on the number of stoker switches sold. Mercoid manufactured and marketed a competing stoker switch that was designed to be used only in the patented combination. Mercoid had been offered a sublicense by the licensee but had refused to take one. It was sued for contributory infringement by both the patentee and the licensee, and it raised patent misuse as a defense.

In *Mercoid I* the Court barred the patentee from obtaining relief because it deemed the licensing arrangement with Honeywell to be an unlawful attempt to extend the patent monopoly. The opinion for the Court painted with a very broad brush. Prior patent misuse decisions had involved attempts "to secure a partial monopoly in supplies consumed . . . or unpatented materials employed" in connection with the practice of the invention. None, however, had involved an integral component necessary to the functioning of the patented system. 320 U.S., at 665, 64 S.Ct., at 271. The Court refused, however, to infer any "difference in principle" from this distinction in fact. Ibid. Instead, it stated an expansive rule that apparently admitted no exception:

> "The necessities or convenience of the patentee do not justify any use of the monopoly of the patent to create another monopoly. The fact that the patentee has the power to refuse a license does not enable him to enlarge the monopoly of the patent by the expedient of attaching conditions to its use. . . . The method by which the monopoly is sought to be extended is immaterial. . . . When the patentee ties something else to his invention, he acts only by virtue of his right as the owner of property to make contracts concerning it and not otherwise. He then is subject to all the limitations upon that right which the general law imposes upon such contracts. The contract is not saved by anything in the patent laws because it relates to the invention. If it were, the mere act of the patentee could make the distinctive claim of the patent attach to something which does not possess the quality of invention. Then the patent would be diverted from its statutory purpose and become a ready instrument for economic control in domains where the anti-trust acts or other laws not the patent statutes define the public policy." Id., at 666, 64 S.Ct., at 271.

The Court recognized that its reasoning directly conflicted with Leeds & Catlin Co. v. Victor Talking Machine Co., supra, and it registered disapproval, if not outright rejection, of that case. 320 U.S., at 668, 64 S.Ct., at 272. It also recognized that "[t]he result of this decision, together with those which have preceded it, is to limit substantially the doctrine of contributory infringement." Id., at 669, 64 S.Ct., at 273. The Court commented, rather cryptically, that it would not "stop to consider" what "residuum" of the contributory infringement doctrine "may be left." Ibid.

Mercoid II did not add much to the breathtaking sweep of its companion decision. The Court did reinforce, however, the conclusion that its ruling made no exception for elements essential to the inventive character of a patented combination. "However worthy it may be, however essential to the patent, an unpatented part of a combination patent is not more entitled to monopolistic protection than any other unpatented device." 320 U.S., at 684, 64 S.Ct., at 280.

What emerges from this review of judicial development is a fairly complicated picture, in which the rights and obligations of patentees as against contributory infringers have varied over time. We need not decide how respondent would have fared against a charge of patent misuse at any particular point prior to the enactment of 35 U.S.C.A. § 271. Nevertheless, certain inferences that are pertinent to the present inquiry may be drawn from these historical developments.

First, we agree with the Court of Appeals that the concepts of contributory infringement and patent misuse "rest on antithetical underpinnings." 599 F.2d, at 697. The traditional remedy against contributory infringement is the injunction. And an inevitable concomitant of the right to enjoin another from contributory infringement is the capacity to suppress competition in an unpatented article of commerce. Proponents of contributory infringement defend this result on the grounds that it is necessary for the protection of the patent right, and that the market for the unpatented article flows from the patentee's invention. They also observe that in many instances the article is "unpatented" only because of the technical rules of patent claiming, which require the placement of an invention in its context. Yet suppression of competition in unpatented goods is precisely what the opponents of patent misuse decry. If both the patent misuse and contributory infringement doctrines are to coexist, then, each must have some separate sphere of operation with which the other does not interfere.

Second, we find that the majority of cases in which the patent misuse doctrine was developed involved undoing the damage thought to have been done by *A. B. Dick*. The desire to extend patent protection to control of staple articles of commerce died slowly, and the ghost of the expansive contributory infringement era continued to haunt the courts. As a result, among the historical precedents in this Court, only the *Leeds & Catlin* and *Mercoid* cases bear significant factual similarity to the present controversy. Those cases involved questions of control over unpatented articles that were essential to the patented inventions, and that were unsuited for any commercial noninfringing use. In this case, we face similar questions in connection with a chemical, propanil, the herbicidal properties of which are essential to the advance on prior art disclosed by respondent's patented process. Like the record disc in *Leeds & Catlin* or the stoker switch in the *Mercoid* cases, and unlike the dry ice in *Carbice* or the bituminous emulsion in *Leitch,* propanil is a nonstaple commodity which has no use except through practice of the patented method. Accordingly, had the present case arisen prior to *Mercoid,* we believe it fair to say that it would have fallen close to the wavering line between legitimate protection against contributory infringement and illegitimate patent misuse.

III

The *Mercoid* decisions left in their wake some consternation among patent lawyers and a degree of confusion in the lower courts. Although some courts treated the *Mercoid* pronouncements as limited in effect to the specific kind of licensing arrangement at issue in those cases, others took a much more expansive view of the decision. Among the latter group, some courts held that even the filing of an action for contributory infringement, by threatening to deter competition in unpatented materials, could supply evidence of patent misuse. This state of affairs made it difficult for patent lawyers to advise their clients on questions of contributory infringement and to render secure opinions on the validity of proposed licensing arrangements. Certain segments of the patent bar eventually decided to ask Congress for corrective legislation that would restore some scope to the contributory infringement doctrine. With great perseverance, they advanced their proposal in three successive Congresses before it eventually was enacted in 1952 as 35 U.S.C.A. § 271.

A

The critical inquiry in this case is how the enactment of § 271 affected the doctrines of contributory infringement and patent misuse. Viewed against the backdrop of judicial precedent, we believe that the language and structure of the statute lend significant support to Rohm & Haas' contention that, because § 271(d) immunizes its conduct from the charge of patent misuse, it should not be barred from seeking relief. The approach that Congress took toward the codification of contributory infringement and patent misuse reveals a compromise between those two doctrines and their competing policies that permits patentees to exercise control over nonstaple articles used in their inventions.

Section 271(c) identifies the basic dividing line between contributory infringement and patent misuse. It adopts a restrictive definition of contributory infringement that distinguishes between staple and nonstaple articles of commerce. It also defines the class of nonstaple items narrowly. In essence, this provision places materials like the dry ice of the *Carbice* case outside the scope of the contributory infringement doctrine. As a result, it is no longer necessary to resort to the doctrine of patent misuse in order to deny patentees control over staple goods used in their inventions.

The limitations on contributory infringement written into § 271(c) are counterbalanced by limitations on patent misuse in § 271(d). Three species of conduct by patentees are expressly excluded from characterization as misuse. First, the patentee may "deriv[e] revenue" from acts that "would constitute contributory infringement" if "performed by another without his consent." This provision clearly signifies that a patentee may make and sell nonstaple goods used in connection with his invention. Second, the patentee may "licens[e] or authoriz[e] another to perform acts" which without such authorization would constitute contributory infringement. This provision's use in the disjunctive of the term "authoriz[e]" suggests that more than explicit licensing agreements is contemplated. Finally, the patentee may "enforce his patent rights against . . . contributory infringement." This provision plainly means that the patentee may bring suit without fear that his doing so will be regarded as an unlawful attempt to suppress competition. The statute explicitly states that a patentee may do "one or more" of these permitted acts, and it does not state that he must do any of them.

In our view, the provisions of § 271(d) effectively confer upon the patentee, as a lawful adjunct of his patent rights, a limited power to exclude others from competition in nonstaple goods. A patentee may sell a nonstaple article himself while enjoining others from marketing that same good without his authorization. By doing so, he is able to eliminate competitors and thereby to control the market for that product. Moreover, his power to demand royalties from others for the privilege of selling the nonstaple item itself implies that the patentee may control the market for the nonstaple good; otherwise, his "right" to sell licenses for the marketing of the nonstaple good would be meaningless, since no one would be willing to pay him for a superfluous authorization.

Rohm & Haas' conduct is not dissimilar in either nature or effect from the conduct that is thus clearly embraced within § 271(d). It sells propanil; it authorizes others to use propanil; and it sues contributory infringers. These are all protected activities. Rohm & Haas does *not* license others to sell propanil, but nothing on the face of the statute requires it to do so. To be sure, the sum effect of Rohm & Haas' actions is to suppress competition in the market for an unpatented commodity. But as we have observed, in this its conduct is no different from that which the statute expressly protects.

The one aspect of Rohm & Haas' behavior that is not expressly covered by § 271(d) is its linkage of two protected activities—sale of propanil and authorization to practice the patented process—together in a single transaction. Petitioners vigorously argue that this linkage, which they characterize pejoratively as "tying," supplies the otherwise missing element of misuse. They fail, however, to identify any way in which this "tying" of two expressly protected activities results in any extension of control over unpatented materials beyond what § 271(d) already allows. Nevertheless, the language of § 271(d) does not explicitly resolve the question when linkage of this variety becomes patent misuse. In order to judge whether this method of exploiting the patent lies within or without the protection afforded by § 271(d), we must turn to the legislative history.

B

Petitioners argue that the legislative materials indicate at most a modest purpose for § 271. Relying mainly on the committee reports that accompanied the "Act to Revise and Codify the Patent Laws" (1952 Act), 66 Stat. 792, of which § 271 was a part, petitioners assert that the principal purpose of Congress was to "clarify" the law of contributory infringement as it had been developed by the courts, rather than to effect any significant substantive change. They note that the 1952 Act undertook the major task of codifying all the patent laws in a single title, and they argue that substantive changes from recodifications are not lightly to be inferred. See United States v. Ryder, 110 U.S. 729, 739–740, 4 S.Ct. 196, 201, 28 L.Ed. 308 (1884). They further argue that, whatever the impact of § 271 in other respects, there is not the kind of "clear and certain signal from Congress" that should be required for an extension of patent privileges. See Deepsouth Packing Co. v. Laitram Corp., 406 U.S. 518, 531, 92 S.Ct. 1700, 1708, 32 L.Ed.2d 273 (1972). We disagree with petitioners' assessment. In our view, the relevant legislative materials abundantly demonstrate an intent both to change the law and to expand significantly the ability of patentees to protect their rights against contributory infringement. .   .   .

C

Other legislative materials that we have not discussed bear as well on the meaning to be assigned to § 271(d); but the materials that we have culled are exemplary, and they amply demonstrate the intended scope of the statute. It is the consistent theme of the legislative history that the statute was designed to accomplish a good deal more than mere clarification. It significantly changed existing law, and the change moved in the direction of expanding the statutory protection enjoyed by patentees. The responsible congressional committees were told again and again that contributory infringement would wither away if the misuse rationale of the *Mercoid* decisions remained as a barrier to enforcement of the patentee's rights. They were told that this was an undesirable result that would deprive many patent holders of effective protection for their patent rights. They were told that Congress could strike a sensible compromise between the competing doctrines of contributory infringement and patent misuse if it eliminated the result of the *Mercoid* decisions yet preserved the result in *Carbice*. And they were told that the proposed legislation would achieve this effect by restricting contributory infringement to the sphere of nonstaple goods while exempting the control of such goods from the scope of patent misuse. These signals cannot be ignored. They fully support the conclusion that, by enacting §§ 271(c) and (d), Congress granted to patent holders a statutory right to control nonstaple goods that are capable only of infringing use in a patented invention, and that are essential to that invention's advance over prior art.

We find nothing in this legislative history to support the assertion that respondent's behavior falls outside the scope of § 271(d). To the contrary, respondent has done nothing that would extend its right of control over unpatented goods beyond the line that Congress drew. Respondent, to be sure, has licensed use of its patented process only in connection with purchases of propanil. But propanil is a *nonstaple* product, and its herbicidal property is the heart of respondent's invention. Respondent's method of doing business is thus essentially the same as the method condemned in the *Mercoid* decisions, and the legislative history reveals that § 271(d) was designed to retreat from *Mercoid* in this regard.

There is one factual difference between this case and *Mercoid:* the licensee in the *Mercoid* cases had offered a sublicense to the alleged contributory infringer, which offer had been refused. Seizing upon this difference, petitioners argue that respondent's unwillingness to offer similar licenses to its would-be competitors in the manufacture of propanil legally distinguishes this case and sets it outside § 271(d). To this argument, there are at least three responses. First, as we have noted, § 271(d) permits such licensing but does not require it. Accordingly, petitioners' suggestion would import into the statute a requirement that simply is not there. Second, petitioners have failed to adduce any evidence from the legislative history that the offering of a license to the alleged contributory infringer was a critical factor in inducing Congress to retreat from the result of the *Mercoid* decisions. Indeed, the *Leeds & Catlin* decision, which did not involve such an offer to license, was placed before Congress as an example of the kind of contributory infringement action the statute would allow. Third, petitioners' argument runs contrary to the long-settled view that the essence of a patent grant is the right to exclude others from profiting by the patented invention. If petitioners' argument were accepted, it would force patentees either to grant licenses or to forfeit their statutory protection against contributory infringement. Compulsory licensing is a rarity in our patent system, and we decline to manufacture such a requirement out of § 271(d).

IV

Petitioners argue, finally, that the interpretation of § 271(d) which we have adopted is foreclosed by decisions of this Court following the passage of the 1952 Act. They assert that in subsequent cases the Court has continued to rely upon the *Mercoid* decisions, and that it has effectively construed § 271(d) to codify the result of those decisions, rather than to return the doctrine of patent misuse to some earlier stage of development. We disagree.

The cases to which petitioners turn for this argument include some that have cited the *Mercoid* decisions as evidence of a general judicial "hostility to use of the statutorily granted patent monopoly to extend the patentee's economic control to unpatented products." United States v. Loew's, Inc., 371 U.S. 38, 46, 83 S.Ct. 97, 107, 9 L. Ed.2d 11 (1962). These decisions were not directly concerned with the doctrine of contributory infringement, and they did not require the Court to evaluate § 271(d) or its impact on the holdings in *Mercoid*. Like other cases that do not specifically mention those decisions, they state the general thrust of the doctrine of patent misuse without attending to its specific statutory limitations.

In another case, Deepsouth Packing Co. v. Laitram Corp., 406 U.S. 518, 92 S.Ct. 1700, 32 L.Ed.2d 273 (1972), the Court dealt only with the scope of direct infringement under § 271(a). The question under consideration was whether a patent is infringed when unpatented elements are assembled into the combination outside the United States. The Court held that such assembly would not have constituted direct infringement prior to the enactment of § 271(a), and it concluded that enactment of the statute effected no change in that regard. The Court cited *Mercoid I* for the well established proposition that unless there has been direct infringement there can be no contributory infringement. Again, the Court did not have occasion to focus on the meaning of § 271(d).

The only two decisions that touch at all closely upon the issues of statutory construction presented here are Aro Mfg. Co. v. Convertible Top Co., 365 U.S. 336, 81 S.Ct. 599, 5 L.Ed.2d 592 (1961) (*Aro I*) and Aro Mfg. Co. v. Convertible Top Co., 377 U.S. 476, 84 S.Ct. 1526, 12 L.Ed.2d 457 (1964) (*Aro II*). These decisions emerged from a single case involving an action for contributory infringement based on the manufacture and sale of a specially cut fabric designed for use in a patented automobile convertible top combination. In neither case, however, did the Court directly address the question of § 271(d)'s effect on the law of patent misuse.

The controlling issue in *Aro I* was whether there had been any *direct* infringement of the patent. The Court held that purchasers of the specially cut fabric used it for "repair" rather than "reconstruction" of the patented combination; accordingly, under the patent law they were not guilty of infringement. Since there was no direct infringement by the purchasers, the Court held that there could be no contributory infringement by the manufacturer of the replacement tops. This conclusion rested in part on a holding that § 271(c) "made no change in the fundamental precept that there can be no contributory infringement in the absence of a direct infringement." Id., at 341, 81 S.Ct., at 602. It in no way conflicts with our decision.

As petitioners observe, *Aro I* does quote certain passages from the *Mercoid* decisions standing for the proposition that even single elements constituting the heart of a patented combination are not within the scope of the patent grant. In context, these references to *Mer-*

coid are not inconsonant with our view of § 271(d). In the course of its decision, the Court eschewed the suggestion that the legal distinction between "reconstruction" and "repair" should be affected by whether the element of the combination that has been replaced is an "essential" or "distinguishing" part of the invention. Id., at 344, 81 S.Ct., at 603. The Court reasoned that such a standard would "ascrib[e] to one element of the patented combination the status of patented invention in itself," and it drew from the *Mercoid* cases only to the extent that they described limitations on the scope of the patent grant. In a footnote, the Court carefully avoided reliance on the misuse aspect of those decisions. Accordingly, it had no occasion to consider whether or to what degree § 271(d) undermined the validity of the *Mercoid* patent misuse rationale.

Aro II is a complicated decision in which the Court mustered different majorities in support of various aspects of its opinion. After remand from *Aro I*, it became clear that the Court's decision in that case had not eliminated all possible grounds for a charge of contributory infringement. Certain convertible top combinations had been sold without valid license from the patentee. Because use of these tops involved direct infringement of the patent, there remained a question whether fabric supplied for their repair might constitute contributory infringement notwithstanding the Court's earlier decision.

Aro II decided several questions of statutory interpretation under § 271. First, it held that repair of an unlicensed combination was direct infringement under the law preceding enactment of § 271, and that the statute did not effect any change in this regard. Like the constructions of § 271(a) in *Aro I* and *Deepsouth Packing Co.*, this conclusion concerns a statutory provision not at issue in this case.

Second, the Court held that supplying replacement fabrics specially cut for use in the infringing repair constituted contributory infringement under § 271(c). The Court held that the specially cut fabrics, when installed in infringing equipment, qualified as nonstaple items within the language of § 271(c), and that supply of similar materials for infringing repair had been treated as contributory infringement under the judicial law that § 271(c) was designed to codify. It also held that § 271(c) requires a showing that an alleged contributory infringer knew that the combination for which his component was especially designed was both patented and infringing. We regard these holdings as fully consistent with our understanding of § 271(c). In any event, since petitioners have conceded contributory infringement for the purposes of this decision, the scope of that subsection is not directly before us.

Third, the Court held that the alleged contributory infringer could not avoid liability by reliance on the doctrine of the *Mercoid* decisions. Although those decisions had cast contributory infringement into some doubt, the Court held that § 271 was enacted "for the express purpose . . . of overruling any blanket invalidation of the [contributory infringement] doctrine that could be found in the *Mercoid* opinions." 377 U.S., at 492, 84 S.Ct., at 1535. Although our review of the legislative history finds a broader intent, it is not out of harmony with *Aro II's* analysis. The Court explicitly noted that a defense of patent misuse had not been pressed. Accordingly, its discussion of legislative history was limited to those materials supporting the observation, sufficient for purposes of the case, that any direct attack on the contributory infringement doctrine in its entirety would be contrary to the manifest purpose of § 271(c). Since the Court in *Aro II* was not faced with a patent misuse defense, it had no occasion to consider other evidence in the hearings relating to the scope of § 271(d).

Finally, in a segment of the Court's opinion that commanded full adherence of only four Justices, 377 U.S., at 493–500, 84 S.Ct., at 1535–1539, it was stated that an agreement in which the patentee had released some purchasers of infringing combinations from liability defeated liability for contributory infringement with respect to replacement of convertible tops after the agreement went into effect. The plurality rejected the patentee's attempt to condition its release by reserving "rights in connection with future sales of replacement fabrics." Id., at 496, 84 S.Ct., at 1537. It relied on the *Carbice* and *Mercoid* decisions, as well as United States v. Loew's, Inc., supra, for the proposition that a patentee "cannot impose conditions concerning the unpatented supplies, ancillary materials, or components with which the use [of a patented combination] is to be effected." 377 U.S., at 497, 84 S.Ct., at 1538. This statement is qualified by the circumstances to which it applied. Because the Court already had determined in *Aro I* that replacement of worn-out convertible top fabric constituted a permissible repair of the combination, the agreement sought to control an unpatented article in the context of a noninfringing use. The determination that the agreement defeated liability does not reflect resort to the principles of patent misuse; rather it betokens a recognition that the patentee, once it had authorized use of the combination, could not manufacture contributory infringement by contract where under the law there was none.

Perhaps the quintessential difference between the *Aro* decisions and the present case is the difference between the primary use market for a chemical process and the replacement market out of which the *Aro* litigation arose. The repair-reconstruction distinction and its legal consequences are determinative in the latter context, but are not controlling here. Instead, the staple-nonstaple distinction, which *Aro I* found irrelevant to the characterization of replacements, supplies the controlling benchmark. This distinction ensures that the patentee's right to prevent others from contributorily infringing his patent affects only the market for the invention itself. Because of this significant difference in legal context, we believe our interpretation of § 271(d) does not conflict with these decisions.

V

Since our present task is one of statutory construction, questions of public policy cannot be determinative of the outcome unless specific policy choices fairly can be attributed to Congress itself. In this instance, as we have already stated, Congress chose a compromise between competing policy interests. The policy of free competition runs deep in our law. It underlies both the doctrine of patent misuse and the general principle that the boundary of a patent monopoly is to be limited by the literal scope of the patent claims. But the policy of stimulating invention that underlies the entire patent system runs no less deep. And the doctrine of contributory infringement, which has been called "an expression both of law and morals," *Mercoid I,* 320 U.S., at 677, 64 S.Ct., at 277 (Frankfurter, J., dissenting), can be of crucial importance in ensuring that the endeavors and investments of the inventor do not go unrewarded.

It is, perhaps, noteworthy that holders of "new use" patents on chemical processes were among those designated to Congress as intended beneficiaries of the protection against contributory infringement that § 271 was designed to restore. We have been informed that the characteristics of practical chemical research are such that this form of patent protection is particularly important to inventors in that field. The number of chemicals either known to scientists or disclosed by existing research is vast. It grows constantly, as those engaging in "pure" research publish their discoveries.[23] The number of these chemicals that have known uses of commercial or social value, in contrast, is small. Development of new uses for existing chemicals is thus a major component of practical chemical research. It is extraordinarily expensive. It may take years of unsuccessful testing before a chemical having a desired property is identified, and it may take several years of further testing before a proper and safe method for using that chemical is developed.

Under the construction of § 271(d) that petitioners advance, the rewards available to those willing to undergo the time, expense, and interim frustration of such practical research would provide at best a dubious incentive. Others could await the results of the testing and then jump on the profit bandwagon by demanding licenses to sell the unpatented, nonstaple chemical used in the newly developed process. Refusal to accede to such a demand, if accompanied by any attempt to profit from the invention through sale of the unpatented chemical, would risk forfeiture of any patent protection whatsoever on a finding of patent misuse. As a result, noninventors would be almost assured of an opportunity to share in the spoils, even though they had con-

---

23. As of March 1980, the Chemical Registry System maintained by the American Chemical Society listed in excess of 4,848,000 known chemical compounds. The list grows at a rate of about 350,000 per year. The Society estimates that the list comprises between 50% and 60% of all compounds that ever have been prepared. See Brief for American Chemical Society as *Amicus Curiae* 4–5.

tributed nothing to the discovery. The incentive to await the discoveries of others might well prove sweeter than the incentive to take the initiative oneself.

Whether such a regime would prove workable, as petitioners urge, or would lead to dire consequences, as respondent and several *amici* insist, we need not predict. Nor do we need to determine whether the principles of free competition could justify such a result. Congress' enactment of § 271(d) resolved these issues in favor of a broader scope of patent protection. In accord with our understanding of that statute, we hold that Rohm & Haas has not engaged in patent misuse, either by its method of selling propanil, or by its refusal to license others to sell that commodity. The judgment of the Court of Appeals is therefore affirmed.

It is so ordered.

[The dissenting opinion of Mr. Justice White is summarized in Note 1, below.]

NOTES

1. Justice White, joined by Justices Brennan, Marshall and Stevens, dissented from the Court's decision in *Rohm & Haas*. According to White, the Supreme Court had for decades, "denied relief from contributory infringement to patent holders who attempt to extend their patent monopolies to unpatented materials used in connection with patented inventions. The Court now refuses to apply this 'patent misuse' principle in the very area in which such attempts to restrain competition are most likely to be successful." 100 S.Ct. 2601, 2626, 2627, 65 L.Ed.2d 696, 729. In White's view, the Court misread section 271(d). "The plain language of section 271(d) indicates that respondent's conduct is not immunized from application of the patent misuse doctrine. Section 271(d) does not define conduct that constitutes patent misuse; rather it simply outlines certain conduct that is not patent misuse." 100 S.Ct. 2601, 2631, 2632, 65 L.Ed.2d 696, 735–736.

2. In Brulotte v. Thys Co., 379 U.S. 29, 85 S.Ct. 176, 13 L.Ed.2d 99, 143 U.S.P.Q. 264 (1964), defendants, hop farmers, had bought from plaintiff, patent owner, hop picking machines that incorporated several of plaintiff's patented devices. Under the purchase agreement, the buyers were to pay royalties based upon the quantities of crops harvested over a seventeen-year period. The contract period exceeded the life of all of the patents. Alleging patent misuse, defendants refused to pay royalties accruing both before and after expiration of the patents' statutory term.

The Supreme Court, in an opinion by Justice Douglas, ruled that defendants could not be held for royalties accruing after the expiration of the last of the patents. The defect in the seventeen-year license, Douglas wrote, was that it extended the patent monopoly beyond the point required by the Constitution's "limited times" provision, and by negative implication from the patent statute, to be free from monopoly restraint. Reasoning that if contractual devices of this sort were tolerated, "the free market visualized for the post-expiration period would be subject to monopoly influences that have no proper place there," the Court struck down the contract rule applied by the state courts as "unlawful *per se*." 379 U.S. 29, 32–33, 85 S.Ct. 176, 179, 180.

Does *Rohm & Haas* in any way limit the *Brulotte* logic? To what extent had *Brulotte* already been limited by the Court's 1979 decision in Aronson v. Quick Point, p. 64, above?

3. Can a patent licensee defend an action for nonpayment of royalties by asserting that the licensed patent is invalid? It has long been held that licensees are privileged to stop paying royalties if a third party proves that the patent is invalid. But, where the licensee itself sought to challenge validity, the doctrine of licensee estoppel traditionally barred the defense. Automatic Radio Mfg. Co. v. Hazeltine Research, Inc., 339 U.S. 827, 70 S.Ct. 894, 94 L.Ed. 1312, 85 U.S. P.Q. 378 (1950). Thus in Adkins v. Lear, Inc., 67 Cal.2d 882, 891, 64 Cal.Rptr. 545, 435 P.2d 321, 156 U.S.P.Q. 258 (1967), the California Supreme Court recognized that "one of the oldest doctrines in the field of patent law establishes that so long as a licensee is operating under a license agreement he is estopped to deny the validity of his licensor's patent in a suit for royalties under the agreement. The theory underlying this doctrine is that a licensee should not be permitted to enjoy the benefit afforded by the agreement while simultaneously urging that the patent which forms the basis of the agreement is void."

The Supreme Court granted certiorari in Lear v. Adkins to "reconsider the validity of the *Hazeltine* rule in the light of our recent decisions emphasizing the strong federal policy favoring free competition in ideas which do not merit patent protection, Sears, Roebuck v. Stiffel Co., 376 U.S. 225 (1964); Compco Corp. v. Day-Brite Lighting, Inc., 376 U.S. 234 (1964)." 395 U.S. 653, 89 S.Ct. 1902, 23 L.Ed. 2d 610, 162 U.S.P.Q. 1 (1969). The first part of Justice Harlan's opinion for the Court traced *Hazeltine's* "clouded history" to conclude that "the uncertain status of licensee estoppel in the case law is a product of judicial efforts to accommodate the competing demands of the common law of contracts and the federal law of patents. On the one hand, the law of contracts forbids a purchaser to repudiate his promises simply because he later becomes dissatisfied with the bargain he has made. On the other hand, federal law requires that all ideas in general circulation be dedicated to the common good unless they are protected by a valid patent. When faced with this basic conflict in policy, both this Court and courts throughout the land have naturally sought to develop an intermediate position which somehow would remain responsive to the radically different concerns of the two different worlds of contract and patent. The result has been a failure. Rather than creative compromise, there has been a chaos of conflicting case law, proceeding on inconsistent premises." 395 U.S. 653, 668, 89 S.Ct. 1902, 1910.

It was the practical marketplace effects of licensee estoppel that convinced the Court that *Hazeltine* should be overruled. "A patent, in the last analysis, simply represents a legal conclusion reached by the Patent Office. Moreover, the legal conclusion is predicated on factors as to which reasonable men can differ widely. Yet the Patent Office is often obliged to reach its decision in an ex parte proceeding, without the aid of the arguments which could be advanced by parties interested in proving patent invalidity. Consequently, it does not seem to us to be unfair to require a patentee to defend the Patent Office's judgment when his licensee places the question in issue, especially since the licensor's case is buttressed by the presumption of validity which attaches to his patent. Thus, although licensee estoppel may be consistent with the letter of contractual doctrine, we cannot say that it is compelled by the spirit of contract law, which seeks to balance the claims of promisor and promisee in accord with the requirements of good faith.

"Surely the equities of the licensor do not weigh very heavily when they are balanced against the important public interest in permitting full and free competition in the use of ideas which are in reality a part of the public domain. Licensees may often be the only individuals with enough economic incentive to challenge the patentability of an inventor's discovery. If they are muzzled, the public may continually be required to pay tribute to would-be monopolists without need or justification. We think it plain that the technical requirements of contract doctrine must give way before the demands of the public interest in the typical situation involving the negotiation of a license after a patent has issued." 395 U.S. 653, 670–671, 89 S.Ct. 1902, 1911.

Lear answered some questions but left others open. The decision made clear that the licensee was not required to pay royalties while it was litigating the patent's validity. But if the licensee prevails, can it recover the royalties it paid *before* challenging the patent? See Troxel Mfg. Co. v. Schwinn Bicycle Co., 465 F.2d 1253, 1260, 175 U. S.P.Q. 65 (6th Cir. 1972). ("The public interest is protected adequately under *Lear* without imposing on the patent holder the obligation to refund royalties paid under the license of a patent procured and asserted in good faith.") 489 F.2d 968 (6th Cir. 1973), cert denied, 416 U.S. 939, 94 S.Ct. 1940, 40 L.Ed.2d 289 (1974). Must the licensee withhold royalty payments, and risk termination of its license, before it can challenge the patent's validity? See Warner-Jenkinson Co. v. Allied Chem. Corp., 567 F.2d 184, 193 U.S.P.Q. 753 (2d Cir. 1977).

Does *Lear* allow licensees under consent decrees to later attack the patent involved? Compare Kraly v. National Distillers & Chem. Corp., 502 F.2d 1366, 183 U.S.P.Q. 79 (7th Cir. 1974) with Schlegel Mfg. Co. v. U.S.M. Corp., 525 F.2d 775, 187 U.S.P.Q. 417 (6th Cir. 1975), cert. denied, 425 U.S. 912, 96 S.Ct. 1509, 47 L.Ed.2d 763, 189 U.S.P.Q. 384 (1976). Licensees under settlement agreements? See

Aro Corp. v. Allied Witan Co., 531 F.2d 1368, 190 U.S.P.Q. 392 (6th Cir. 1976), cert. denied 429 U.S. 862, 97 S.Ct. 165, 50 L.Ed.2d 140, 191 U.S.P.Q. 751 (1976).

Can a patent owner avoid *Lear* by drafting its license agreements to convey not only patent rights but also rights to related knowhow in the hope that, if the patent is invalidated, the knowhow will support the royalty payments? See Finnegan, International Patent and Know-How Licensing, Industrial Property, Sept. 1976 at 225. What are the implications for *Lear* of Aronson v. Quick Point, p. 64 above?

See generally, McCarthy, "Unmuzzling" the Patent Licensee: Chaos in the Wake of Lear v. Adkins, 45 Geo.Wash.L.Rev. 429 (1977).

3. REMEDIES

BROADVIEW CHEM. CORP. v. LOCTITE CORP.

United States District Court, D. Connecticut, 1970.
311 F.Supp. 447, 164 U.S.P.Q. 419.

BLUMENFELD, District Judge.

On June 19, 1968, 159 U.S.P.Q. 80, after a hearing, Broadview was found in civil contempt for having violated a consent decree by selling "Sta-Lok," an anaerobic sealant, made by it from admittedly infringing formulae of Loctite's concededly valid patents. Loctite was held entitled to recover damages and attorney's fees and costs incurred in prosecuting the motions for contempt. The amount of the award for those items, and for damages resulting from the infringement was left open pending attempted accord between the parties.

They have been unable to reach agreement as to the amount of costs and attorney's fees to be awarded, and disagree as to the appropriate measure and amount of damages. Agreed statements of fact and briefs in support of their respective positions have been submitted and at a hearing counsel limited themselves to arguments on the effect to be given to the agreed statements. No further evidence was offered at the hearing.

Damages

The first question considered is what damages Loctite has proved. At the outset, it is well to remember that this is an action for civil contempt and not directly one for patent infringement. In civil contempt proceedings, the general rule is that damages may be awarded in the form of a fine payable to the party injured by the acts of the contemnor, and are to be remedial and compensatory, not punitive, in nature. . . .

. . . Since this is a civil contempt proceeding, the court is not bound by the statutory provision, 35 U.S.C.A. § 284, relating to damages for patent infringement. . . . However, since that statute relates to the subject matter underlying the contempt and both parties refer the court to it, it is not inappropriate to utilize it to measure the damages in this case.

The parties have advanced two theories as to the measure of damages. Plaintiff Loctite urges the court to adopt the so-called "lost profits" theory under which the injured party is awarded damages on the basis of the profits it would have made had it made the sales which the infringer made in contempt of the order not to infringe. Defendant, on the other hand, would have the court adopt the "reasonable royalty" measure whereby the contemnor is required to pay a reasonable royalty on the infringing sales.

It has been held in this circuit that in order to recover lost profits in patent infringement cases, "[t]he holder of the patent must show that he would have made the sales if the infringer had not." Power Specialty Co. v. Connecticut Light & Power Co., 80 F.2d 874, 875, 28 U.S.P.Q. 321, 322 (2d Cir. 1936). Similarly, the court in Electric Pipe Line, Inc. v. Fluid Systems, Inc., 250 F.2d 697, 116 U.S. P.Q. 25 (2d Cir. 1957), while allowing lost profits, was careful to point out that the findings of fact "justify the conclusion that *but for* Electric Pipe's infringement, Fluid Systems would have made all these installations." Id. at 699, 116 U.S.P.Q. at 27 (emphasis added). See also American Safety Table Co. v. Schreiber, 415 F.2d 373, 163 U.S.P.Q. 129 (2d Cir. 1969), where lost profits were awarded on the basis of a special master's finding that "but for defendants' sale . . . purchasers would have bought from plaintiff in order to supply their need. . . ." Id. at 378, 163 U.S.P.Q. at 132.

In deciding whether the lost profits measure should be applied in this case, one factor to support its applicability is that there were no other sources of supply. There were only two manufacturers of these unique patented anaerobic sealants, Loctite and Broadview. Consequently, if those who bought them from Broadview would have bought them from someone else, they had nowhere to turn but to Loctite.

Although recognizing that "[t]here is no presumption that appellant would have sold its devices to those who purchased the infringing articles," the court in Oil Well Improvements Co. v. Acme Foundry & Mach. Co., 31 F.2d 898, 901 (8th Cir. 1929), nevertheless observed:

> "The cost of either device was negligible in comparison to its saving to the customer so it may be assumed, practically to a certainty, that those of that class who bought the infringement would have bought the appellant's device *(it being the only other one on the market)* if they had not bought the infringement." (Emphasis added).

Arguing that this still does not necessarily establish that they would have bought from Loctite, Broadview calls attention to deposition testimony of an independent marketing consultant that the same results from the use of anaerobic sealants can be obtained by using "mechanical techniques for fastening. . . . Examples are clamps, clamping if you will, welding or brazing, lock washers, lock nuts. . . ." But anaerobic sealant is unique not only in its composition, but also in the way it accomplishes the desired fastening. Indeed, Broadview's consultant also testified that his investigation disclosed "no other products that get the same results in the same way." Manufacturers who use one or more of the alternative ways of getting the same result may be potential customers who can be persuaded to change to anaerobic sealants, but it is likely that Broadview's customers who bought its "Sta-Lok" had either never used the alternative methods or had already made the switch to an anaerobic sealant. And it is worth noting that users of anaerobic sealants are manufacturers for whom a change to another method would most likely require a considerable change in their own manufacturing methods. Anaerobic sealants are not shelf items in a neighborhood hardware store; they are sold through distributors or manufacturers' representatives. In a less compelling situation, the court in Continuous Glass Press Co. v. Schmertz Wire Glass Co., 219 F. 199 (3d Cir.), cert. denied, 238 U.S. 623, 35 S.Ct. 661, 59 L.Ed. 1494 (1915), thought that the "but for" rule would be satisfied, stating at 206:

> "There is no doubt that, if the defendant had not manufactured the glass in question, the complainant would have produced and sold to its own profit an equal amount, for the complainant and the defendant at that time were the only manufacturers of this product."

If Broadview had sold its sealants at prices substantially lower than Loctite's, that might militate against a finding that Loctite would have made the same sales; but the fact is that the prices at which Broadview sold the infringing sealants were almost identical, for each grade, to Loctite's prices. Thus, what appears to me to be a high price policy strengthens the conclusion that Broadview's customers would have bought from Loctite if Broadview had not made the sales. Customers were willing to pay the price.

I do not understand that satisfaction of the "but for" rule requires the injured party to negate *all possibilities* that the purchasers would not have bought a different product, or that the proof must be convincing beyond a reasonable doubt. Insofar as sales of the sealants to customers for use in the United States are concerned, I find that in all reasonable probability Loctite would have made the sales had Broadview not made them. Some of Broadview's sales were to customers for use abroad. Since these must be considered separately, an analysis of the sales is in order.

Sales by Broadview

The total sales of anaerobic sealants by Broadview from February 14, 1967, the date of the consent decree, to April 21, 1969, when Broadview ceased selling the infringing sealants, may be divided into two classes. One class consists of sales in the United States for use there (hereafter "domestic sales"); the other, of sales for ultimate use in foreign countries (hereafter "foreign sales").

Domestic Sales

Domestic sales, allowing for returns prior to April 21, 1969, amounted to $164,490.00. Broadview contends that this figure must be reduced by (1) material thereafter "returned or in process of being returned" in the amount of $34,187.62, and also by (2) "Estimated Material to be Returned" in the amount of $26,850.00. Loctite, naturally, takes the position that there should be no deduction for any returns after the decree, arguing that these were the likely result of Broadview's own wrong in violating the decree. However, consistent with my conclusion that Loctite would have sold those goods "but for" Broadview's sale of them, I consider that customers who did in fact return Broadview's infringing sealants without using them were then likely to become customers of Loctite.

The "Estimated Material to be Returned" calculated as of August 1969 stretches the somewhat vague concept of "Material in the Process of Being Returned" to the point where it is too elusive to be accepted in mitigation of damages. Accordingly, I find that domestic sales by Broadview in violation of the decree of February 14, 1967, amounted to $130,302.38.

Lost Profits

Over a period of 2½ years, from October 1, 1966, through March 31, 1969, Loctite's total sales of its anaerobic sealants amounted to approximately $7,750,000. It was well represented throughout the market, and its manufacturing facilities and personnel could have handled the additional volume of some $277,000 (foreign and domestic) sold by Broadview from February 14, 1967, through April 21, 1969 without any increase in administrative, market development, advertising, or research and development expenses. Very little increase in expense for district managers would have been entailed. The selling expenses listed by Loctite as "Variable" (travel and entertainment, incentives and commissions) were likely to have increased in direct proportion to increased sales. This increase, based on past figures would have been about 6.6% of the increase in sales. Allowing generously also for a likely increase in other expenses, such as telephones, auto depreciation of salaried district managers, labmobile and training schools, I find that the increase in Loctite's business by the amount of infringing sales Broadview made would have been carried out at an added expense of no more than 20.2% of those sales. Adding to that the cost of goods sold, which amounted to 19.8% of the sales, Loctite would have realized a profit of 60%. As damages for domestic sales of infringing products by Broadview, Loctite is entitled to recover 60% of $130,302.38, or $78,181.43. Since this amount was unliquidated, no interest is added.

Foreign Sales

Computing the amount of sales for use abroad (although technically some of those sales were completed in the United States), in the same way that domestic sales were figured, I find that Broadview sold $112,480.00 of infringing products from February 14, 1967, through April 21, 1969. Deducting the amount of "Known Material Returned and in Process of Being Returned" consisting of $1,047.91, Broadview is liable for damages attributable to sales of $111,432.09. Not only would Loctite face more than one foreign competitor, but other factors inherent in the protection of patent rights in foreign countries are such that I am not persuaded that there was a reasonable probability that Loctite would have made those sales "but for" the sale of them by Broadview. Without sufficient proof that foreign sales would have been made by Loctite but for Broadview's sales for use abroad, damages resulting from those sales should be measured by a reasonable royalty.

According to Broadview's Financial Statements, it made a gross profit for the calendar years 1967 and 1968 of approximately 59% and 58% respectively. Although it sustained a net loss because of high legal fees, those expenses would not be attributable to a license to make and sell Loctite's anaerobic sealants. There would be a substantial benefit from a license in the acquisition thereby of manufacturing knowhow. (In this connection, it is instructive to note that Loctite's cost of goods sold was less than one-half of Broadview's when both are measured as a percent of gross sales.) Moreover, the benefits of Loctite's advertising and research would inure to a licensee. True, selling expenses would be incurred, but the protection afforded by Loctite's patent would serve to keep prices up. Loctite earns 36.6% on its own, after cost of goods, selling expenses, administrative expenses and research and development expenses (only $\frac{1}{4}$ of which are expensed).

Since there was no established license fee, the extent of the sales by Broadview, the uniqueness of the sealant, and the facts outlined above are sufficient for ascertainment of a royalty rate to be used as a measure of damages. The lack of express testimony or the testimony of plaintiff's expert are not binding on me any more than it would be on a jury. It is my opinion, and I find that damages for foreign sales should be based on a royalty rate of 20%. Accordingly, Loctite is entitled to recover the additional amount of $22,286.42 with interest at the rate of 6% from June 19, 1968, the date of the contempt decree, from Broadview as damages from its foreign sales of infringing anaerobic sealants.

Increased Damages

There was an element of turpitude involved in the conduct of Broadview in reselling, and in making and selling more of the very sealants which it had agreed were infringements of Loctite's patents. That conduct appears to have been reckless of the consequences to itself, as well as of injury inflicted upon Loctite. However, to the extent that double or treble damages serve a punitive purpose, they may not be awarded in a civil contempt proceeding.

There is also another circumstance which stays me from increasing the damages up to three times the amount awarded for Broadview's foreign sales. The authority to increase damages, 35 U.S.C.A. § 284, supra note 1, is part of the statutory scheme to afford protection to those inventions which the Government has found deserving of a patent. Thus, where it has become necessary to subject the patent to the scrutiny of the court in an adversary proceeding to vindicate it, the public interest has been satisfied. Here, the rights sought to be protected are those which the parties arrived at by bargain and embodied in the consent decree. They thereby withheld full adversary inquiry into the validity of the patent. Furthermore, Loctite initiated this proceeding for contempt, although it could have brought a separate action for infringement. Thus, the issues before the court, as perceptively noted by the United States Court of Appeals for the Second Circuit, were not whether Broadview infringed, but whether it violated the terms of the consent decree. Broadview Chem. Corp. v. Loctite Corp., 406 F.2d 538, 543, 544, 160 U.S.P.Q. 449, 452, 453 (2d Cir.), cert. denied, 394 U.S. 976, 89 S.Ct. 1472, 22 L.Ed.2d 755, 161 U.S.P.Q. 832 (1969).

Principles of equity fully support the damages awarded in this matter, but since the statutory authority of 35 U.S.C.A. § 284, although a helpful guideline, is still one step removed from direct applicability to this case, I do not resort to it to increase damages.

Since an award for double or treble damages in a patent infringement suit is remedial rather than penal, it is more properly utilized in those cases where the actual injury may be elusive of proof, than in this case where full discovery has been allowed and had on the question of damages. If there was anything more which Loctite may have suffered, it was open to it to get the proof.

Attorney's Fees and Costs

The Court of Appeals affirmed the judgment in this case to the extent that it awarded to Loctite its costs and attorney's fees attendant. Their purpose is "not to punish the defendant for his offense, but to compensate the plaintiff for his injuries. . . ." Doroszka v. Lavine, 111 Conn. 575, 578, 150 A. 692–93 (1930).

Loctite has submitted an itemized list of expenses, including attorney's fees, totaling $27,194.76. Broadview challenges only the reasonableness of the items making up that amount. I find the amount submitted for each item reasonable, except that one item on the list is not a recoverable attorney's fee or expense. Loctite has included $2,539.03 representing counsel fees and expenses attributable to the efforts of its house counsel on this case. I consider this to be a regular cost of doing business.

Loctite is awarded $24,655.73 costs and attorney's fees to be paid by Broadview.

To sum up, Loctite is awarded unliquidated damages in the amount of $78,181.43 for Broadview's infringing domestic sales; $22,286.42, with interest at the rate of 6% from June 19, 1968, as damages for Broadview's infringing foreign sales; and $24,655.73 costs and attorney's fees incurred in the prosecution of the contempt action.

NERNEY v. NEW YORK, N. H. & H. R. CO.

Circuit Court of Appeals, Second Circuit, 1936.
83 F.2d 409, 29 U.S.P.Q. 456.

MANTON, Circuit Judge.

The patent in suit No. 1,665,862 relates to a hand brake used on railroad cars. Heretofore a decree had been entered after a defense conducted by the Ajax Handbrake Company, enjoining the appellant from the infringement of this patent. The appellant then had fifteen thousand cars equipped with the Ajax brakes, and the court found these infringed. An appeal was taken from the original decree, but was dismissed upon a licensing agreement reached by the patentee, the Ajax manufacturer, and the railroad. The permanent injunction issued restrained the appellant "from further infringing said Letters Patent, and from, directly or indirectly, making or causing to be made, or using or causing to be used, or selling or causing to be sold, or offering for sale, or advertising for sale, or contributing to the manufacture, use or sale by others, of any brake or apparatus embodying the invention specified in the said claims of the said Letters Patent No. 1,665,862 and particularly the aforesaid Ajax brake, and from, directly or indirectly, infringing said Letters Patent in any way or manner whatsoever; exempting from said injunction, however, all the aforesaid Ajax brakes heretofore purchased by defendant, and all Ajax brakes licensed under the said Sauvage patent. . . ."

Thereafter, in the ordinary course of its business, the appellant was called upon to handle cars of other railroads coming to its line for transportation which were equipped with Equipco brakes. It is conceded that the Equipco brake infringes and also that the only use of it by appellant is on those connecting cars fitted with it. This type of brake was not on its own freight cars. Appellee thereupon brought on a motion asking for a supplemental injunction to restrain appellant from infringing the patent by the use of the Equipco hand brake. After a hearing, on affidavits, the court granted the application and entered a supplemental injunction, first announcing, however, that the Equipco brake was structurally equivalent to the Ajax brake and that the original injunction covered this type of brake. The supplemental injunction in the phrases of the original injunction restrained the use of Equipco hand brakes specifically and directed appellant to notify all class 1 railroads of the United States, and particularly the Pennsylvania Railroad Company, from which it received cars equipped with such Equipco brakes, to refrain from sending or delivering to it or onto its trackage any railroad cars equipped with such hand brakes, and it further ordered that appellant should refuse to accept or receive or move on its trackage any cars of the other railroads equipped with such brakes unless and until noninfringing hand brakes were substituted therefor on such cars.

The affidavits submitted on the motion show that appellant had fifty-three interchange points at which it received cars from other railroads, a total of two or three thousand cars daily at such points. The affidavits make clear the hardship to which appellant would be subjected by the injunction issued. It would be a very serious and exacting task to detect cars so equipped and to eliminate them. It would require extra inspectors at these points, cause loss and delay in emptying and reloading cars found to be equipped with the offending device, and there would be a loss of traffic because of routing around appellant's line. There is a conflict as to the number of cars so received equipped with the Equipco brake. Appellee argues that the injury and inconvenience would be slight, stating that only five cars monthly would be found to infringe. If this be true, the appellee would obtain very little benefit from the injunction. It does appear, however, that a greater number of infringing cars are presented for interchange; sixty having been noted as arriving at the Cedar Hill yards in one week.

The practice of picking up a connecting carrier's car and hauling it over the railroad's own lines for a specific per diem rental to the railroad owning the car is recognized as a necessity to practical shipment of freight.   .   .   .   The railroads sending cars over appellant's lines cannot be expected to select those which do not infringe. Appellee suggests that appellant can install noninfringing brakes on the incoming cars. This they would have no lawful right to do, as the cars are owned by other companies, and, moreover, they should not be expected to bear this expense when the car may be on their lines only for a short time.

If the appellees desired to have the injury of infringement by the Equipco brake enjoined, they might properly proceed against the manufacturers or against the companies owning the cars fitted with such brakes as the proper remedy. Indeed, it does not appear that many railroads are using this type of brake; the Pennsylvania seemingly being the chief offender. In Di Giovanni v. Camden Fire Ins. Ass'n, 296 U.S. 64, 71, 56 S.Ct. 1, 80 L.Ed. 47, the court pointed out that a remedy in equity may be denied where it would inconvenience the defendant beyond the compensating convenience to the plaintiff. An injunction in a patent case is not always granted as a matter of course, and the balance of convenience may dictate its denial. In the City of Milwaukee v. Activated Sludge, Inc., 69 F.2d 577 (C.C.A. 7), the court vacated an injunction against the use of an infringing system of sewerage disposal where its grant would have caused harm by relegating the city to dumping its sewerage in Lake Michigan. There the refusal was based on the line of cases denying injunctive relief where it was not absolutely essential to the patentee and caused the infringing defendant irreparable damages. Where it appears that a much greater injury will be done to the infringer than a benefit to the patentee, the court may, within its equity power, grant an accounting only and deny injunctive relief. And where, as in Hoe v. Boston Daily Advertising Corporation, 14 F. 914 (C.C.Mass.), it is recognized that the only real advantage to a plaintiff in granting the injunction would be to strengthen its position in negotiating a settlement, an injunction should not issue. In Dun v. Lumbermen's Credit Ass'n, 209 U.S. 20, 28 S.Ct. 335, 52 L.Ed. 663, 14 Ann.Cas. 501, an attitude against an unconscionable demand for an injunction was pointed out. There a copyright was violated by the inclusion of some protected material in a book embodying much independent and noninfringing material. An injunction was denied, and the plaintiffs were remitted to their remedy at law. The same principle should and does apply to patent infringement. Indeed, no case is made out of a benefit to this appellant by the use of brakes installed on cars of other carriers and no willful conduct in responding to the invitation to haul such cars is claimed. In American Cotton-Tie Supply Co. v. McReady, 1 Fed.Cas. page 631, No. 295 (C.C.S.D.N.Y.), where a steamship company was enjoined from receiving infringing goods for shipment, there seemed to be an element of willfulness in the company's refusal to divulge the names of the shippers sending the infringing material. This was a direct aid to the infringers. Campbell Printing-Press Mfg. Co. v. Manhattan R. Co., 49 F. 930 (C.C.S.D.N.Y.), seems likewise to have involved a willful infringement.

An equitable remedy should be tempered to cause no inconvenience to the public who are served by carriers. Here is no coercive force applied to carriers sending cars to appellant. To enjoin it from receiving cars with the Equipco brakes is to use it as an instrument to coerce the infringing owners with great inconvenience to itself and to the public.

It is urged that this appeal should be dismissed because this type of brake was embraced in the original decree. As above indicated, there are facts here which bear upon the appropriateness of enjoining receipt of the Equipco brake equipped cars. These consequences were neither pleaded nor proved in the cause resulting in the original decree which dealt chiefly with the Ajax brake, many of which were owned by the appellant. While it is true that the original injunction enjoined the use of infringing hand brakes in general terms broad enough to cover the brake now considered, the language used should be restricted to the issue there considered.

The complaint in the action pleads infringement by the use of the Ajax brakes. Although it is broad enough to cover receipt of cars equipped with Ajax brakes from other lines, the answer admits the use of Ajax brake equipment on appellant's cars, but nothing was presented on the issue here involved, receipt of infringing connecting cars. The final decree entered contained no direct reference to the acceptance of cars equipped with infringing brakes. This issue was not presented and not covered until the supplemental injunction was ordered. Therefore the appeal was properly allowed.

The supplemental decree will be reversed, and injunction denied, but an accounting ordered.

Decree reversed.

NOTES

1. An injunction for the remainder of the patent's life is awarded almost as a matter of course, and will be withheld only for traditional equitable reasons: laches, estoppel or, as in *Nerney,* disproportionate harm to the public interest. Disproportionate harm to the *infringer* will only rarely justify denial of injunctive relief. One typical case for denial is where the infringer does not directly compete with the patent owner and has innocently invested substantial amounts in the manufacture of the patented subject matter. See Electric Smelting & Aluminum Co. v. Carborundum Co., 189 F. 710 (C.C. W.D.Pa.1900), rev'd on other grounds, 203 F. 976 (3d Cir.), cert. denied 231 U.S. 754, 34 S.Ct. 323, 58 L.Ed. 467 (1913).

A claimant's use of its patents to violate the antitrust laws is the most frequently, and successfully, asserted ground for denying the injunctive remedy. Less compelling evidence of injury to the public interest may justify only postponement of relief. In Ransburg Electro-Coating Corp. v. Ford Motor Co., 245 F.Supp. 308, 146 U.S.P.Q. 436, 457 (S.D.Ind.1965), the court recognized that, "The plaintiff has been and will in the future be irreparably damaged unless the defendant is enjoined from unlicensed use of the plaintiff's patents," but ruled that, "the public interest requires that the defendant be accorded sufficient time to effect an orderly changeover in its painting installations without disrupting the economy of the country and of a substantial segment of the population of the United States. The court finds that such orderly changeover can be made within six (6) months time with a minimum of damage to others."

2. Unlike permanent injunctions, preliminary injunctions are sparingly granted. Aside from the customary showing that he will be irreparably harmed unless the preliminary injunction issues, the patent owner must establish title, validity and infringement to an extent variously described as "beyond question" or "without reasonable doubt." Underlying this judicial reluctance is the fear that "the granting of temporary injunctive relief on the basis of incomplete facts may often settle the ultimate issues immediately and cause irreparable injury to the enjoined party. If a temporary injunction is unwarranted, a few years will probably elapse before final determination that the injunction was improvidently granted. By this time, the alleged infringer's loss of competitive advantage over the patentee may be incapable of repair by money damages." Note, Injunctive Relief in Patent Infringement Suits, 112 U.Pa.L.Rev. 1025 (1964).

See generally, Dorr & Duft, Patent Preliminary Injunctive Relief, 60 J.P.O.S. 597 (1978).

Uniroyal Inc. v. Daly-Herring Co., 294 F.Supp. 754, 161 U.S.P.Q. 506 (E.D.N.C.1968), is in many ways typical. Defendant had raised substantial questions concerning both the patent's validity and its infringement. There was no prior adjudication of the patent to confirm its validity, and the other evidence on this issue—widespread public acquiescence in the patent—was unconvincing. The court noted, too, that defendant was financially responsible and had "offered to post a bond in an amount equal to the bond posted by plaintiff in connection with the temporary restraining order." Although these factors alone would probably have dictated the decision reached, the court also rested its denial of preliminary relief on the presence of two unusual factors. Plaintiff's hands were unclean as he had "applied for the temporary restraining order . . . as a matter of timing," when defendant's exposure to financial injury was greatest; second, "the present case is duplicative of and represents only a part of the entire controversy" pending before another court. Several of the same factors were present, and a contrary result reached, in Norwich Pharmacal Co. v. International Brokers, Inc., 159 U.S.P.Q. 417 (N.D.Ga.1968).

3. The statutory and decisional trend in the assessment of damages has been away from formulae that require lengthy accountings and toward more economical methods of computation. Before 1946, when the damages provision was amended to substantially its present form, the successful claimant was allowed to choose for his award between the amount of damages he suffered and the amount of profits earned by the infringer. To discover which was the greater, he could require judicial determination of both amounts. "Because ascertainment of the amount of the infringer's gain, which was necessary in virtually all cases, often involved complex factual issues, the courts frequently directed that these issues be determined by a master in an accounting proceeding. It was largely the general dissatisfaction with protracted and expensive accountings that led Congress to amend the statute in 1946." Note, Recovery in Patent Infringement Suits, 60 Colum.L.Rev. 840, 841 (1960).

Originally devised by courts reluctant to award only nominal damages where the successful claimant was unable to prove either actual damages or the infringer's profits, the reasonable royalty measure was introduced into the statute in 1922 and, under the present act, represents the floor of recovery. As *Broadview* indicates, a reasonable royalty can be assessed not only for an entire infringement but, if the case requires, for aspects of an infringement not compensated by the other measures of damages. For example, while the lost profit measure was facilely applied to sales in the United States, where Broadview was the sole competitor, it was inapt in the context of the more competitive foreign market, and the reasonable royalty measure was applied to this branch of the infringement.

With the 1946 amendment's elimination of infringer's profits as an alternative measure of recovery, reasonable royalty has emerged as the measure most frequently employed. Infringer's profits have, however, retained some relevance to the computation of damages, chiefly as a factor in the determination of reasonable royalty. For an extensive sampling of reasonable royalties awarded in the years 1928–1956, see, Wilson & Lewis, Elements of Recovery in a Patent Infringement Suit, 42 J.P.O.S. 742, 772 (1960). "Reasonable royalty" should be distinguished from "established royalty" which is an independent measure of damages. An established royalty is ascertainable when the right infringed has been licensed by the patent owner to others at a uniform royalty rate. See, for example, Trio Process Corp. v. L. Goldstein's Sons, Inc., 612 F.2d 1353, 204 U.S.P.Q. 881 (3d Cir. 1980).

4. Collateral awards—increased damages, attorney's fees and costs—are awarded sparingly and are generally reserved for cases involving some degree of bad faith. Although it is sometimes said that double or treble damages are intended to be remedial, they are typically awarded in cases in which the infringer wilfully or recklessly disregarded the patent's validity or did not cooperate in the conduct of the litigation. See, e. g., Russell Box Co. v. Grant Paper Box Co., 203 F.2d 177, 97 U.S.P.Q. 19 (1st Cir. 1953).

Interest awards, too, are used to penalize bad faith infringement. Ordinarily, where recovery is measured by reasonable royalty or lost profits, interest is computed from the date that the court assesses damages. If it is shown, however, that the infringer acted unfairly, the interest may be computed from a time prior to the assessment of damages. See, for example, Mathey v. United Shoe Mach. Corp., 54 F.Supp. 694, 61 U.S.P.Q. 79 (D.Mass.1944) (unfair price competition), and Sampson-United Corp. v. F. A. Smith Mfg. Co., 68 U.S.P.Q. 266 (W.D.N.Y.1946) (infringement continued after receipt of notice of infringement and of decisions in other suits sustaining the infringed patent).

The provision for award of attorney's fees "to the prevailing party" is designed to deter not only wilful infringers but vexatious patent owners as well. In Algren Watch Findings Co. v. Kalinsky, 197 F.2d 69, 93 U.S.P.Q. 490 (2d Cir. 1952), the court, after inferring bad faith from the deficiencies in claimant's proof, affirmed the dismissal of the patent owner's claim and the award to defendant of $2,500 attorney's fees. Proof that a defeated opponent acted unconscionably is not always a sufficient predicate for recovery, and not every successful party is a "prevailing" party. In one case, an award of $500,000 attorneys' fees to claimant, Union Carbide, was set aside on the ground that it was not the prevailing party. "After years of litigation it prevailed only on four claims, under the doctrine of equivalents, out of a total of 29 claims. It lost all process claims. It can hardly be said that Union Carbide was the prevailing party and Lincoln the losing party." Union Carbide Corp. v. Graver Tank & Mfg. Co., Inc., 345 F.2d 409, 145 U.S.P.Q. 240, 242 (2d Cir. 1965).

5. Relief by declaratory judgment figured prominently in the earlier phases of the Loctite-Broadview litigation. Battle was joined in 1964 when Broadview sought a declaratory judgment that five Loctite sealant patents were invalid or not infringed by 32 sealant compositions then being manufactured by Broadview. Loctite counterclaimed for infringement of the patents in issue. Over two and one-half years later the action was settled by a consent decree entered upon Broadview's concession that three of the five Loctite patents were valid and infringed by 30 of the Broadview compositions. Subsequently, Loctite charged that, in violation of the consent decree, Broadview was marketing new sealants substantially similar to the old, infringing compositions. Agreeing, the district court found Broadview in contempt and decreed that "For each future violation of the Consent Decree the violating persons shall pay to Loctite Corporation $2,000." The contempt ruling was affirmed by the court of appeals as to all but two of the nine new Broadview compositions. Broadview Chem. Corp. v. Loctite Corp., 406 F.2d 538, 160 U.S.P.Q. 449 (2d Cir. 1969), cert. denied 394 U.S. 976, 89 S.Ct. 1472, 22 L.Ed. 2d 755.

Undaunted, Broadview devised yet another line of sealant compositions and sought a declaratory judgment that they did not infringe the Loctite patents. Acknowledging that a controversy sufficient to meet the jurisdictional requirements of the Declaratory Judgment Act, 28 U.S.C.A. § 2201, was probably present, the district court nonetheless declined to entertain the action. Among the reasons given by the court were that "apart from the possibility of a penalty for violation of the injunction, the financial interest at stake is small," and that it would be imprudent to employ the court "as a testing ground for such prolific chemists." Broadview Chem. Corp. v. Loctite Corp., 162 U.S.P.Q. 366 (1969).

The circuit court reversed. "It is our conclusion that the following facts required the trial court to entertain jurisdiction and to issue a declaratory judgment: (1) the *in terrorem* effect, in the event Loctite's position were sound, of the $2,000 penalty applicable not only to the appellant but also to anyone who, with notice of the injunction, participated in a sealant transaction with Broadview; . . . (3) the amount of infringement damages normally recoverable together with, in this particular case, the probability of increased damages for willful infringement; and (4) a liberal interpretation has been given to charges of infringement in patent cases for the purpose of taking jurisdiction in declaratory judgment actions. . . . Although the patents in suit here have been declared valid, the amplitude of the area they affect has been interpreted differently by both parties and remains undetermined. In view of the staggering damages resulting from a mistake on the part of Broadview or of its customers, Broadview will be compelled to abandon the manufacture and sale of anaerobic sealants, even though the Broadview products may be outside of the area affected by the Loctite patents." 417 F.2d 998, 1001, 163 U.S.P.Q. 455 (2d Cir. 1969).

The Court also thought declaratory relief was compelled by Loctite's letter-writing campaign informing customers of the consent decree and of Loctite's readiness to bring actions against customers under the decree. Apparently the court relied for this ground upon the frequent use of declaratory judgments in clearer cases of patent aggression, beginning with two of the earliest applications of the federal Declaratory Judgment Act, Lionel Corp. v. De Filippis, 11 F.Supp. 712, 26 U.S.P.Q. 234 (D.C.N.Y.1935); Zenie Bros. v. Miskind, 10 F. Supp. 779, 25 U.S.P.Q. 153 (D.C.N.Y.1935). See, for a particularly careful application of the justiciability requirement, Sweetheart Plastics, Inc. v. Illinois Tool Works, Inc., 439 F.2d 871, 168 U.S.P.Q. 737 (1st Cir. 1971). See generally, O'Rourke, Do Unto Others Before They Do Unto You or: Current Trends in Declaratory Judgments, 57 J.P.O.S. 541 (1975).

6. Damages are recoverable only from the time that the infringer has notice of the subsisting patent. Notice is typically given by the mark, "Patented" or "Pat.," along with the patent number, placed on articles manufactured or sold under the patent. Absent marking, the requisite notice can be given directly—orally or in writing—and, at the latest, by commencement of the infringement action.

Section 292 proscribes both counterfeit marking and false marking. The motive of the first paragraph's counterfeit marking provision, like that of unfair competition law, is to protect against public deception as to the source of goods. The false marking provisions of the next two paragraphs guard against public deception of another sort, and their motive stems from patent, rather than unfair competition, policy: to free the marketplace of unwarranted monopoly effects.

Section 292's predecessors provided exclusively for a qui tam action. The section now makes false and counterfeit marking an ordinary federal criminal offense and, in subsection (b), retains the qui tam action as a supplementary method for enforcement. Rarely is the informer plaintiff entirely disinterested. In Brose v. Sears, Roebuck & Co., 455 F.2d 763, 172 U.S.P.Q. 454 (5th Cir. 1972), an appeal from dismissal of a qui tam action, the court observed that, "As is true in nearly all of the relatively few qui tam informer actions brought in the past one and a quarter century this one is used as a weapon in the arsenal of patent litigation."

D. INFRINGEMENT

See Statute Supplement 35 U.S.C.A. §§ 281–282, 288, 290, 293.

CREWS, PATENT CLAIMS AND INFRINGEMENT

Dynamics of the Patent System 128, 133 (W. Ball Ed.1960).*

In the subject of patent claims and infringement we all know that what you do is take the copy of the patent and the copy of the accused device and you read the claims and if the claims read, there is infringement, and if the claims do not read there is not infringement. There is a little more to it than that. The little more I think, reminds me somewhat of the law of evidence. You take a course in evidence in law school and you spend the first five minutes learning the rules of evidence and the next two years trying to learn the exceptions to the hearsay rule. And it is really the exceptions to the rule of simply reading the claims on the device that we are concerned with in considering the question of patent claims and infringement.

. . . .

So in any and every question of infringement, the prior art makes a difference and must be looked at. What difference it makes depends upon the difference between the patent, the prior art and the patent, the difference between the patent and the accused structure and the difference between the prior art and the accused structure. All must be considered and it is impossible to have any sound opinion on the question of whether or not a claim of a patent is infringed, in my opinion, unless all are considered. Of course, what that means as a practical matter, is that since you never know all the prior art, you never know when another patent will turn up; it may be a little closer than anything you know of; you can do the best you can with what you have, but like so many questions of patent law, we have to advise our clients that it is a field of uncertainty. It depends so much on subjective analysis and subjective appraisal, that you cannot advise with great confidence that any patent is valid or invalid or is infringed or is not infringed.

EIBEL PROCESS CO. v. MINNESOTA & ONTARIO PAPER CO., 261 U.S. 45, 43 S.Ct. 322, 67 L.Ed. 523 (1923). TAFT, C. J.: In administering the patent law the court first looks into the art to find what the real merit of the alleged discovery or invention is and whether it has advanced the art substantially. If it has done so, then the court is liberal in its construction of the patent to secure to the inventor the reward he deserves. If what he has done works only a slight step forward and that which he says is a discovery is on the border line between mere mechanical change and real invention, then his patent, if sustained, will be given a narrow scope and infringe-

* Copyright 1960 by Villanova University.

ment will be found only in approximate copies of the new device. It is this differing attitude of the courts toward genuine discoveries and slight improvements that reconciles the sometimes apparently conflicting instances of construing specifications and the finding of equivalents in alleged infringements. In the case before us, for the reasons we have already reviewed, we think that Eibel made a very useful discovery which has substantially advanced the art. His was not a pioneer patent, creating a new art; but a patent which is only an improvement on an old machine may be very meritorious and entitled to liberal treatment. Indeed, when one notes the crude working of machines of famous pioneer inventions and discoveries, and compares them with the modern machines and processes exemplifying the principle of the pioneer discovery, one hesitates in the division of credit between the original inventor and the improvers; and certainly finds no reason to withhold from the really meritorious improver, the application of the rule *"ut res magis valeat quam pereat,"* which has been sustained in so many cases in this Court.

GRAVER TANK & MFG. CO., INC. v. LINDE AIR PRODUCTS CO.

Supreme Court of the United States, 1950.
339 U.S. 605, 70 S.Ct. 854, 94 L.Ed. 1097, 85 U.S.P.Q. 328.

Mr. Justice JACKSON delivered the opinion of the Court.

Linde Air Products Co., owner of the Jones patent for an electric welding process and for fluxes to be used therewith, brought an action for infringement against Lincoln and the two Graver companies. The trial court held four flux claims valid and infringed and certain other flux claims and all process claims invalid. 75 U.S.P.Q. 231. The Court of Appeals affirmed findings of validity and infringement as to the four flux claims but reversed the trial court and held valid the process claims and the remaining contested flux claims. 167 F.2d 531. We granted certiorari, 335 U.S. 810, 69 S.Ct. 50, 93 L.Ed. 366, and reversed the judgment of the Court of Appeals insofar as it reversed that of the trial court, and reinstated the District Court decree. 336 U.S. 271, 69 S.Ct. 535, 93 L.Ed. 672. Rehearing was granted, limited to the question of infringement of the four valid flux claims and to the applicability of the doctrine of equivalents to findings of fact in this case.

At the outset it should be noted that the single issue before us is whether the trial court's holding that the four flux claims have been infringed will be sustained. Any issue as to the validity of these claims was unanimously determined by the previous decision in this Court and attack on their validity cannot be renewed now by reason of limitation on grant of rehearing. The disclosure, the claims, and the prior art have been adequately described in our former opinion and in the opinions of the courts below.

In determining whether an accused device or composition infringes a valid patent, resort must be had in the first instance to the words of the claim. If accused matter falls clearly within the claim, infringement is made out and that is the end of it.

But courts have also recognized that to permit imitation of a patented invention which does not copy every literal detail would be to convert the protection of the patent grant into a hollow and useless thing. Such a limitation would leave room for—indeed encourage— the unscrupulous copyist to make unimportant and insubstantial changes and substitutions in the patent which, though adding nothing, would be enough to take the copied matter outside the claim, and hence outside the reach of law. One who seeks to pirate an invention, like one who seeks to pirate a copyrighted book or play, may be expected to introduce minor variations to conceal and shelter the piracy. Outright and forthright duplication is a dull and very rare type of infringement. To prohibit no other would place the inventor at the mercy of verbalism and would be subordinating substance to form. It would deprive him of the benefit of his invention and would foster concealment rather than disclosure of inventions, which is one of the primary purposes of the patent system.

The doctrine of equivalents evolved in response to this experience. The essence of the doctrine is that one may not practice a fraud on a patent. Originating almost a century ago in the case of Winans v. Denmead, 15 How. 330, it has been consistently applied by this Court and the lower federal courts, and continues today ready and available for utilization when the proper circumstances for its application arise. "To temper unsparing logic and prevent an infringer from stealing the benefit of an invention" a patentee may invoke this doctrine to proceed against the producer of a device "if it performs substantially the same function in substantially the same way to obtain the same result." Sanitary Refrigerator Co. v. Winters, 280 U.S. 30, 42, 50 S.Ct. 9, 13, 74 L.Ed. 147. The theory on which it is founded is that "if two devices do the same work in substantially the same way, and accomplish substantially the same result, they are the same, even though they differ in name, form, or shape." Machine Co. v. Murphy, 97 U.S. 120, 125, 24 L.Ed. 935. The doctrine operates not only in favor of the patentee of a pioneer or primary invention, but also for the patentee of a secondary invention consisting of a combination of old ingredients which produce new and useful results, although the area of equivalence may vary under the circumstances. The wholesome realism of this doctrine is not always applied in favor of a patentee but is sometimes used against him. Thus, where a device is so far changed in principle from a patented article that it performs the same or a similar function in a substantially different way, but nevertheless falls within the literal words of the claim, the doctrine of equivalents may be used to restrict the claim and defeat the patentee's action for infringement. In its early development, the doctrine was usually applied in cases involving devices where there was equivalence in mechanical components. Subsequently, however, the same principles were also applied to compositions, where there was equivalence between chemical ingredients. Today the doctrine is applied to mechanical or chemical equivalents in compositions or devices.

What constitutes equivalency must be determined against the context of the patent, the prior art, and the particular circumstances of the case. Equivalence, in the patent law, is not the prisoner of a formula and is not an absolute to be considered in a vacuum. It does not require complete identity for every purpose and in every respect. In determining equivalents, things equal to the same thing may not be equal to each other and, by the same token, things for most purposes different may sometimes be equivalents. Consideration must be given to the purpose for which an ingredient is used in a patent, the qualities it has when combined with the other ingredients, and the function which it is intended to perform. An important factor is whether persons reasonably skilled in the art would have known of the interchangeability of an ingredient not contained in the patent with one that was.

A finding of equivalence is a determination of fact. Proof can be made in any form: through testimony of experts or others versed in the technology; by documents, including texts and treatises; and, of course, by the disclosures of the prior art. Like any other issue of fact, final determination requires a balancing of credibility, persuasiveness and weight of evidence. It is to be decided by the trial court and that court's decision, under general principles of appellate review, should not be disturbed unless clearly erroneous. Particularly is this so in a field where so much depends upon familiarity with specific scientific problems and principles not usually contained in the general storehouse of knowledge and experience.

In the case before us, we have two electric welding compositions or fluxes: the patented composition, Unionmelt Grade 20, and the accused composition, Lincolnweld 660. The patent under which Unionmelt is made claims essentially a combination of alkaline earth metal silicate and calcium fluoride; Unionmelt actually contains, however, silicates of calcium and magnesium, two alkaline earth metal silicates. Lincolnweld's composition is similar to Unionmelt's, except that it substitutes silicates of calcium and manganese—the latter not an alkaline earth metal—for silicates of calcium and magnesium. In all other respects, the two compositions are alike. The mechanical methods in which these compositions are employed are similar. They are identical in operation and produce the same kind and quality of weld.

The question which thus emerges is whether the substitution of the manganese which is not an alkaline earth metal for the magnesium which is, under the circumstances of this case, and in view of the technology and the prior art, is a change of such substance as to make the doctrine of equivalents inapplicable; or conversely, whether under the circumstances the change was so insubstantial that the trial court's invocation of the doctrine of equivalents was justified.

Without attempting to be all-inclusive, we note the following evidence in the record: Chemists familiar with the two fluxes testified that manganese and magnesium were similar in many of their reactions. There is testimony by a metallurgist that alkaline earth metals are often found in manganese ores in their natural state and that they serve the same purpose in the fluxes, and a chemist testified that "in the sense of the patent" manganese could be included as an alkaline earth metal. Much of this testimony was corroborated by reference to recognized texts on inorganic chemistry. Particularly important, in addition, were the disclosures of the prior art, also contained in the record. The Miller patent, No. 1,754,566, which preceded the patent in suit, taught the use of manganese silicate in welding fluxes. Manganese was similarly disclosed in the Armor patent, No. 1,467,825, which also described a welding composition. And the record contains no evidence of any kind to show that Lincolnweld was developed as the result of independent research or experiments.

It is not for this Court to even essay an independent evaluation of this evidence. This is the function of the trial court. And, as we have heretofore observed, "To no type of case is this . . . more appropriately applicable than to the one before us, where the evidence is largely the testimony of experts as to which a trial court may be enlightened by scientific demonstrations. This trial occupied some three weeks, during which, as the record shows, the trial judge visited laboratories with counsel and experts to observe actual demonstrations of welding as taught by the patent and of the welding accused of infringing it, and of various stages of the prior art. He viewed motion pictures of various welding operations and tests and heard many experts and other witnesses." 336 U.S. 271, 274–275, 69 S.Ct. 535, 537, 93 L.Ed. 672.

The trial judge found on the evidence before him that the Lincolnweld flux and the composition of the patent in suit are substantially identical in operation and in result. He found also that Lincolnweld is in all respects equivalent to Unionmelt for welding purposes. And he concluded that "for all practical purposes, manganese silicate can be efficiently and effectually substituted for calcium and magnesium silicates as the major constituent of the welding composition." These conclusions are adequately supported by the record; certainly they are not clearly erroneous.

It is difficult to conceive of a case more appropriate for application of the doctrine of equivalents. The disclosures of the prior art made clear that manganese silicate was a useful ingredient in welding compositions. Specialists familiar with the problems of welding compositions understood that manganese was equivalent to and could be substituted for magnesium in the composition of the patented flux and their observations were confirmed by the literature of chemistry. Without some explanation or indication that Lincolnweld was developed by independent research, the trial court could properly infer that the accused flux is the result of imitation rather than experimentation or invention. Though infringement was not literal, the changes which avoid literal infringement are colorable only. We conclude that the trial court's judgment of infringement respecting the four flux claims was proper, and we adhere to our prior decision on this aspect of the case.

Affirmed.

Mr. Justice BLACK, with whom Mr. Justice DOUGLAS concurs, dissenting.

I heartily agree with the Court that "fraud" is bad, "piracy" is evil, and "stealing" is reprehensible. But in this case, where petitioners are not charged with any such malevolence, these lofty principles do not justify the Court's sterilization of Acts of Congress and prior decisions, none of which are even mentioned in today's opinion.

The only patent claims involved here describe respondent's product as a flux "containing a major proportion of alkaline earth metal silicate." The trial court found that petitioners used a flux "composed principally of manganese silicate." Finding also that "manganese is not an alkaline earth metal," the trial court admitted that petitioners' flux did not "literally infringe" respondent's patent. Nevertheless it invoked the judicial "doctrine of equivalents" to broaden the claim for "alkaline earth metals" so as to embrace "manganese." On the ground that "the fact that manganese is a proper substitute . . . is fully disclosed in the specification" of respondent's patent, it concluded that "no determination need be made whether it is a known chemical fact *outside* the teachings of the patent that manganese is an equivalent. . . ." Since today's affirmance unquestioningly follows the findings of the trial court, this Court necessarily relies on what the specifications revealed. In so doing, it violates a direct mandate of Congress without even discussing that mandate.

R.S. § 4888, as amended, 35 U.S.C.A. § 33, provides that an applicant "shall particularly point out and distinctly claim the part, improvement, or combination which he claims as his invention or discovery." We have held in this very case that this statute precludes invoking the specifications to alter a claim free from ambiguous language, since "it is the claim which measures the grant to the patentee." Graver Mfg. Co. v. Linde Co., 336 U.S. 271, 277, 69 S.Ct. 535, 538, 93 L.Ed. 672. What is not specifically claimed is dedicated to the public. For the function of claims under R.S. § 4888, as we have frequently reiterated, is to exclude from the patent monopoly field all that is not specifically claimed, whatever may appear in the specifications. Today the Court tacitly rejects those cases. It departs from the underlying principle which, as the Court pointed out in White v. Dunbar, 119 U.S. 47, 51, 7 S.Ct. 72, 74, 30 L.Ed. 303, forbids treating a patent claim "like a nose of wax which may be turned and twisted in any direction, by merely referring to the specification, so as to make it include something more than, or something different from what its words express. . . . The claim is a statutory requirement, prescribed for the very purpose of making the patentee define precisely what his invention is; and it is unjust to the public, as well as an evasion of the law, to construe it in a manner different from the plain import of its terms." Giving this patentee the benefit of a grant that it did not precisely claim is no less "unjust to the public" and no less an evasion of R.S. § 4888 merely because done in the name of the "doctrine of equivalents."

In seeking to justify its emasculation of R.S. § 4888 by parading potential hardships which literal enforcement might conceivably impose on patentees who had for some reason failed to claim complete protection for their discoveries, the Court fails even to mention the program for alleviation of such hardships which Congress itself has provided. 35 U.S.C.A. § 64 authorizes reissue of patents where a patent is "wholly or partly inoperative" due to certain errors arising from "inadvertence, accident, or mistake" of the patentee. And while the section does not expressly permit a patentee to expand his claim, this Court has reluctantly interpreted it to justify doing so. Miller v. Brass Co., 104 U.S. 350, 353–354, 26 L.Ed. 783. That interpretation, however, was accompanied by a warning that "Reissues for the enlargement of claims should be the exception and not the rule." Id. at 355. And Congress was careful to hedge the privilege of reissue by exacting conditions. It also entrusted the Patent Office, not the courts, with initial authority to determine whether expansion of a claim was justified, and barred suits for retroactive infringement based on such expansion. Like the Court's opinion, this congressional plan adequately protects patentees from "fraud," "piracy," and "stealing." Unlike the Court's opinion, it also protects businessmen from retroactive infringement suits and judicial expansion of a monopoly sphere beyond that which a patent expressly authorizes. The plan is just, fair, and reasonable. In effect it is nullified by this decision undercutting what the Court has heretofore recognized as wise safeguards. One need not be a prophet to suggest that today's rhapsody on the virtue of the "doctrine of equivalents" will, in direct contravention of the Miller case, supra, make enlargement of patent claims the "rule" rather than the "exception."

Whatever the merits of the "doctrine of equivalents" where differences between the claims of a patent and the allegedly infringing product are de minimis, colorable only, and without substance, that doctrine should have no application to the facts of this case. For the differences between respondent's welding substance and petitioners' claimed flux were not nearly so slight. The claims relied upon here did not involve any mechanical structure or process where invention lay in the construction or method rather than in the materials used. Rather they were based wholly on using particular materials for a particular purpose. Respondent's assignors experimented with several metallic silicates, including that of manganese. According to the specifications (if these are to be considered) they concluded that while several were "more or less efficacious in our process, we prefer to use silicates of the alkaline earth metals." Several of their claims which this Court found too broad to be valid encompassed manganese silicate; the only claims found valid did not. Yet today the Court disregards that crucial deficiency, holding those claims infringed by a composition of which 88.49% by weight is manganese silicate.

In view of the intense study and experimentation of respondent's assignors with manganese silicate, it would be frivolous to contend that failure specifically to include that substance in a precise claim was unintentional. Nor does respondent attempt to give that or any other explanation for its omission. But the similar use of manganese in prior expired patents, referred to in the Court's opinion, raises far more than a suspicion that its elimination from the valid claims stemmed from fear that its inclusion by name might result in denial or subsequent invalidation of respondent's patent.

Under these circumstances I think petitioners had a right to act on the belief that this Court would follow the plain mandates of Congress that a patent's precise claims mark its monopoly boundaries, and that expansion of those claims to include manganese could be obtained only in a statutory reissue proceeding. The Court's ruling today sets the stage for more patent "fraud" and "piracy" against business than could be expected from faithful observance of the congressionally enacted plan to protect business against judicial expansion of precise patent claims. Hereafter a manufacturer cannot rely on what the language of a patent claims. He must be able, at the peril of heavy infringement damages, to forecast how far a court relatively unversed in a particular technological field will expand the claim's language after considering the testimony of technical experts in that field. To burden business enterprise on the assumption that men possess such a prescience bodes ill for the kind of competitive economy that is our professed goal.

The way specific problems are approached naturally has much to do with the decisions reached. A host of prior cases, to some of which I have referred, have treated the 17-year monopoly authorized by valid patents as a narrow exception to our competitive enterprise system. For that reason, they have emphasized the importance of leaving business men free to utilize all knowledge not preempted by the precise language of a patent claim. E. g., Sontag Stores Co. v. Nut Co., 310 U.S. 281, and cases there cited. In the Sontag case Mr. Justice McReynolds, speaking for a unanimous Court, said in part: "In the case under consideration the patentee might have included in the application for the original patent, claims broad enough to embrace petitioner's accused machine, but did not. This 'gave the public to understand' that whatever was not claimed 'did not come within his patent and might rightfully be made by anyone.'" Id. at 293.

The Court's contrary approach today causes it to retreat from this sound principle. The damages retroactively assessed against petitioners for what was authorized until today are but the initial installment on the cost of that retreat.

Mr. Justice DOUGLAS, dissenting.

The Court applies the doctrine of equivalents in a way which subverts the constitutional and statutory scheme for the grant and use of patents.

The claims of the patent are limited to a flux "containing a major proportion of alkaline earth metal silicate." Manganese silicate, the flux which is held to infringe, is not an alkaline earth metal silicate. It was disclosed in the application and then excluded from the claims. It therefore became public property. It was, to be sure, mentioned in the specifications. But the measure of the grant is to be found in the claims, not in the specifications. The specifications can be used to limit but never to expand the claim.

The Court now allows the doctrine of equivalents to erase those time-honored rules. Moreover, a doctrine which is said to protect against practicing "a fraud on a patent" is used to extend a patent to a composition which could not be patented. For manganese silicate had been covered by prior patents, now expired. Thus we end with a strange anomaly: a monopoly is obtained on an unpatented and unpatentable article.

STRAUSSLER v. UNITED STATES

United States Court of Claims, 1961.
290 F.2d 827, 129 U.S.P.Q. 480.

JONES, Chief Judge.

This is a suit for infringement of United States Letters Patent 2,398,057 issued to the plaintiff on April 9, 1946, and disclosing a propulsion device for amphibious motor-driven vehicles. The plaintiff claims that the defendant has infringed this patent by the manufacture of such military amphibious equipment as the "Otter," the "Duck," and the T–46E–1 cargo carrier. The defendant has not answered the complaint, but under Rule 51(b) has moved for summary judgment on the grounds that the plaintiff is barred from asserting infringement under the doctrine of file-wrapper estoppel. The facts are as follows:

On May 19, 1943, the plaintiff, a British subject, filed an application for a United States patent on certain features of a propulsion device for amphibious vehicles which he alleged he had invented. Stating only the most important elements, the device included, in a somewhat linear arrangement, a drive shaft, a driving clutch member, a driven clutch member, a propeller shaft and a propeller. The drive shaft and the propeller shaft were linked together by a hinge directly over the two clutch members in such a way that the propeller shaft and the attached propeller could be raised and lowered. Further, since the hinge was placed directly over the clutch members, raising the propeller shaft disengaged the two clutch members and terminated the transmission of power from the drive shaft through the clutch and the propeller shaft to the propeller. Similarly, when the propeller shaft was lowered the clutch members would engage and motive power could be transmitted to the propeller. The arrangement was said to be useful for powering amphibious vehicles. In deep water, the propeller would be driven and would function precisely as a ship's propeller. In shallow water or on land, the propeller and its shaft could be raised out of possible contact with the ground.

In a modification of this basic combination the plaintiff disclosed that the propeller shaft could comprise two sections connected by a universal joint. Thus modified, the entire propeller shaft could be lowered into position, the clutch members engaged and power transmitted to spin the propeller. In addition, and at the same time, the propeller and the distal part of the propeller shaft could be swung laterally. The driver, by swinging the propeller from side to side, could effectively steer the vehicle in the water much in the manner that a small fishing boat may be steered by swinging the outboard motor. In sum, then, the propeller shaft could be swung up and down, in and out of driving engagement, and from side to side for steering. The arrangement of the two pivot points relative to the vehicle was not alleged to be significant. In this regard the plaintiff stated the following in the last paragraph of the original specification as filed:

> The invention is not confined to the relative arrangements of the vertical and horizontal pivotal axes as described above, for by modifying the construction and arrangement of the parts they may be transposed so that the horizontal pivotal axis is arranged aft of the vertical pivotal axis. With such a modified form the universal shaft coupling would be arranged with its centre in line with the vertical pivotal axis but forwardly of the dog clutch which would be located immediately beneath the horizontal pivotal axis. Also as will be understood the construction of the casing would be modified accordingly and the universal shaft coupling will connect the forward section of the propeller shaft to the rear end of the shaft *g*. Further only the rear section of the propeller shaft would be swung upwardly when the propeller is lifted for land use of the vehicle.

The pivot permitting vertical swing of the shaft could be closest to the end of the vehicle with the pivot permitting lateral swing aft [modification I] or the pivot positions could be reversed [modification II].

The plaintiff originally filed six claims with his patent application. Claims 1, 2, and 6 were drawn broadly to the combination described first above, that is, to the device wherein the propeller shaft could only be moved up and down. Claims 3, 4, and 5 were dependent on claim 1 but were drawn to include the additional element which permitted lateral swing as in modification I. None of the claims was specifically drawn to the arrangement of elements which was described by the plaintiff in the last paragraph of the original specification (quoted above) and which we have called modification II.

In the first action on the application, the patent examiner rejected claims 1, 2, 3, and 6 as fully met by prior art. Claims 4 and 5 were rejected as based on subject matter not fully illustrated or described, but the examiner stated that these claims "appear to be clear of the art." Furthermore, the examiner stated that the arrangement of elements which was described in the last paragraph of the original specification "must also be illustrated or else all reference to the same must be eliminated from the disclosure."

The plaintiff responded to the first Patent Office action by cancelling all six of the original claims and substituting claims 7 and 8. Again, neither of these two claims was drawn specifically to modification II. The examiner in the second Patent Office action stated that the new claims were allowable and repeated his requirement either for illustration or cancellation of modification II. Plaintiff did not supply the additional drawings but instead asked that all mention of modification II be stricken from the specification. With this amendment, all of the examiner's objections were overcome and the patent was issued. Claims 7 and 8 of the application became claims 1 and 2 of the patent. They are as follows:

> 1. In an amphibious motor driven vehicle, a vehicle body, a driving clutch member mounted in said body, a propeller shaft, a propeller carried by said shaft, a casing rotatably receiving said shaft, a driven clutch member carried by said shaft, and means mounting said casing to swing about a horizontal axis on said body whereby the driven clutch member may be swung into engagement with the driving clutch member with the propeller occupying an operative position and out of engagement with the driving clutch member with the propeller assuming an elevated inoperative position.

> 2. An amphibious vehicle as claimed in claim 1 wherein said propeller shaft is composed of two sections coupled by a universal joint, the casing including front and rear sections, the front casing section being connected with the mounting means and the rear section being movable about a vertical axis passing through said universal joint.

Sometime after October 11, 1953, within 6 years of the date of filing of the complaint in this case, the defendant manufactured several amphibious vehicles which embodied a propulsion device similar to the one disclosed by the plaintiff in his patent. The plaintiff claims that the defendant's device is equivalent in all respects to his patented device and that the defendant has infringed his patent. The defendant contends that its device is identical to modification II, which the plaintiff originally described in his patent application, but since the plaintiff struck all mention of this modification from his application in response to rejections by the Patent Office, he is now estopped from asserting that the defendant's device lies within the scope of the patent claims.

Whether the claims of the patent read directly on the defendant's propulsion device, or whether this device is the equivalent of the plaintiff's patented device are questions of fact, and will not be decided on this motion. The issue for determination now is whether the plaintiff is estopped from claiming that the defendant's device, an admitted modification of the plaintiff's patented device, lies within the scope of the claims of the patent because the plaintiff failed to illustrate this modification in his patent application, because he struck all mention of this modification from his application, and because he accepted the patent with this deletion.

Estoppel in patent law is simply an application of familiar equitable principles to the technique of Patent Office prosecution and patent infringement litigation.. A person in an infringement suit may not take a position inconsistent with the one he maintained before the Patent Office in the proceedings which led to the issuance of his patent. The defendant in a thorough brief emphasizes the frequently recited rules that where an applicant for a patent, in response to rejections by the Patent Office, amends his application by cancelling entire claims or objectionable features of claims, or by introducing new elements of limitation into the claims, the claims as allowed must be interpreted with reference to those claims which have been cancelled or rejected. Allowed claims may not be construed to have the same meaning which they would have had without amendment. A patentee may not resort to the doctrine of equivalents to recapture claims which he has surrendered by amendment, and he is estopped by the file wrapper to contend for such construction of the claims as would have the effect of disregarding the amendment. While we do not dispute the value of these rules in guiding the proper construction of amended claims, we do not believe they apply in the instant case.

The claims which the plaintiff submitted with his patent application did not mention the specific arrangement of elements of modification II. Six claims were filed originally. Three claims covered the basic combination and three claims included an additional element (a universal joint) in the propeller shaft. Following a rejection by the patent examiner, these claims were cancelled and two new claims were submitted. One claim again covered the basic combination and one claim included additionally the universal joint in the propeller shaft between the clutch and the propeller. No claim was ever filed, and of course no claim was ever cancelled, which was drawn specifically to the combination we have designated as modification II. The only reference to modification II was in the original specification.

The defendant would have us treat the cancellation of part of the specification as equivalent to the cancellation of a claim, and would extend the rules stated above to the situation before us now. It does not appear to us, however, that the conditions which require careful vigil over the development of the claims apply equally to the specification. The scope of the patent monopoly must be ascertainable with a high degree of certainty or the patent will frustrate rather than promote the progress of science and the useful arts. The claims become of utmost importance, for they are of the nature of metes and bounds and describe for the world the area of the invention beyond which no one may go without trespassing. . . . People naturally rely on the wording of the claims. They are also entitled to rely on language deliberately excluded from the claims because this tends to indicate what the inventor has agreed his invention is not.

The specification serves a purpose different from the claims; it does not necessarily measure the invention. It must only disclose an operative embodiment of the invention in such a manner that one having ordinary skill in the art will be taught how to utilize the invention. 35 U.S.C.A. § 112.

When the nature of the case admits, an applicant for a patent shall furnish drawings. 35 U.S.C.A. § 113. However, the Patent Act does not require the specification to contain an illustrated description of every possible infringing device in order that a patentee be protected against future infringement.

Of course, a patentee in an infringement suit may not claim as his invention that which he has specifically disclaimed in the patent specification regardless of the scope of the allowed claims. Furthermore, a patentee is bound by even self-imposed limitations which he notes in the specification. But we do not believe that cancelling a part of the specification referring to an optional arrangement of elements in a patentable combination, as an alternative to filing additional drawings, has the effect of a disclaimer or a limitation of the claims.

In this case nothing was amended, cancelled, or withdrawn to avoid an art rejection directed specifically to modification II. We think it cannot fairly be said that the plaintiff is trying to recapture claims which he has surrendered by amendment. There is nothing on which an estoppel can be based. Any other decision would carry the doctrine of file-wrapper estoppel beyond the limits set out in the previous cases and beyond what we believe fairness to the parties requires. The prosecution of an application before the Patent Office is a complicated proceeding where the penalties for misstatements and omissions must frequently be stringent. We do not believe it would further the objectives of the Patent Act or serve any other useful purpose to bar the plaintiff in this suit by attaching overriding significance to the cancellation of material from the specification, an act heretofore commonplace in patent prosecution.

The claims of the patent are entitled to be read in the light of the specification as it is without specifically excluding from their scope an arrangement of elements as in modification II.

We do not now determine whether the claims of the patent read directly on the defendant's propulsion device, or whether this device is the equivalent of the plaintiff's patented device. These still remain questions of fact on which the parties are entitled to make their proofs.

The defendant's motion for summary judgment will be denied.

CREWS, PATENT CLAIMS AND INFRINGEMENT

Dynamics of the Patent System 128, 139–140 (W. Ball Ed. 1960).*

In other words, if you go to the Patent Office and are required to restrict your claim by the prior art, and you come out with a narrower claim than when you went in and then you try to interpret it to be infringed by a device you are accusing, you cannot, of course, give it in the court the interpretation that you had to read out of it in order to get it allowed by the Patent Office. But suppose the Patent Office does not make you amend your claim. Then when the prior art is shown under this decision, the District Court, or the courts, will do exactly what the Patent Office would have done if this particular prior art had been cited during the prosecution. Since the Patent Office would not have allowed the claim, the courts said, we will hold that the claim cannot be read on the accused device, and it is not infringed. In other words, you have a doctrine of file wrapper estoppel, but does the doctrine of file wrapper estoppel mean anything? What difference does it make whether your claim is limited by the Patent Office by reason of the prior art that is cited there, when if you get into the courts and the same prior art is cited against you, the court says this claim must be held to be limited in exactly the same manner in which we think it would have been limited if this art had been cited in the Patent Office. The doctrine of file wrapper estoppel does not seem to have any significance when looked at in that light. And yet in actual practice, the doctrine is a doctrine of tremendous importance. If you have two alleged infringing devices in one case, you have limited your claims in the Patent Office in order to assert a limitation and you are now trying to read it out. Your chances of success in court are practically nil. However, if you do not have that limitation and that art was not cited by the Patent Office, your chances of success in court are, in my opinion, very much greater.

NOTES

1. Does the label, "patent," possess more than jurisdictional consequence? What interests are served by a system that makes no threshold distinction between "weak," "intermediate" and "strong"

* Copyright 1960 by Villanova University.

patents, leaving these and finer qualitative distinctions to judicial determination of infringement? In one case in which decision on a patent's validity was avoided by a finding that, if valid, it had not
been infringed, Judge Jerome Frank concurred, contending that, "we
should also hold the patent invalid." Weak patents like the one in
suit, he argued, may constitute "vicious Zombis"; the majority decision left the patentee "free to sue others as alleged infringers, putting
them to the expense—notoriously great in patent suits—of defending
themselves." Aero Spark Co., Inc. v. B. G. Corp., 130 F.2d 290, 54
U.S.P.Q. 348 (2d Cir. 1942).

Recall the statistics, at page 449 above, on the relative inclination among circuit courts to sustain patents. Do figures on validity
holdings present only half the story? The judicial conclusion that
underlies a finding of invalidity need not be far different from the
conclusion implicit in a finding that a patent is valid but not infringed.

2. At least at the time of its origin, in Winans v. Denmead, 15
How. 330, 56 U.S. 330, 14 L.Ed. 717 (1853), elastic application of the
doctrine of equivalents was clearly proper: "The doctrine of equivalents is an inheritance from that period during which the patent statutes required the patent claim merely to 'specify and point out' the
invention protected. At that time, claims were usually of the 'as
shown and described' variety, importing into the claim the text of the
specification and the drawing. 'Interpretation' of patent claims was
then the rule; the courts were called upon to determine the actual
extent of the invention, and it is obvious that the doctrine of equivalents was then continually necessary as a routine rule of the patent
law. Today, patent applicants are required to 'particularly point out
and distinctly claim' their inventions and patent claims are now recognized as definitions of the scope of the patent—word fences which
exclude the public from the patented invention but also leave open
that public domain which the patent may not protect. So long as a
claim of a modern patent is not ambiguous, that claim is certainly
the measure of the patentee's monopoly under all normal situations,
and it now appears futile to contend that the claim may be expanded
by the doctrine of equivalents or any other doctrine every time that
the claim fails to encompass that which is used by a potential infringer." Note, The Doctrine of Equivalents Revalued, 19 Geo.Wash.L.
Rev. 491–492 (1951).

One conclusion to be drawn from this historical analysis is that,
under present practice, the doctrine of equivalents should be available
only in cases of ambiguous claims and, then, only as an interpretive
tool. Aside from whether the application in *Graver* was historically
correct, it was probably excessive in terms of the range of equivalents
commonly applied. Can you reconcile the expansionist views of
Graver with the antimonopoly bias of the court's contemporaneous
decisions respecting the standard of patentability?

3. Subsequent developments in the protracted *Graver* litigation illustrate the close relationship between the doctrine of equivalents and file wrapper estoppel. Union Carbide & Carbon Corp. v. Graver Tank & Mfg. Co., Inc., 196 F.2d 103, 93 U.S.P.Q. 137 (7th Cir. 1952), involved review of a judgment holding Graver in contempt for marketing a new flux series in violation of the injunction that had issued under the Supreme Court's mandate in the principal case. Union Carbide—Linde's parent—had argued in the contempt proceeding that Graver's new series, no less than its old, infringed flux claims, 18, 20, 22, 23. Specifically, it charged that the fraction of silicates in Graver's compositions—between 24% and 41% by plaintiff's count—was substantially equivalent to the "major proportion of silicates" protected by plaintiff's patent claims.

The court of appeals ruled that, by its concessions in the Patent Office, plaintiff was estopped from maintaining that a fraction of less than 50% is equivalent to a "major proportion". "We suspect, however, that plaintiff's failure previously to advance its present definition of 'a major proportion' was due to the realization that such a concession would place in serious question the validity of the claims". In argument to the examiner, plaintiff had distinguished an anticipating reference on the ground that it contained only a "minor proportion of silicates"—between 20% and 33%. Reversing the judgment below, the court of appeals noted: "The question arises, however, as to the validity of its [the doctrine of equivalents'] application where the doctrine of estoppel is properly invoked. While we find no case where this question has been discussed, we think it obvious that there are instances where both doctrines cannot be given effect because of their inconsistency."

4. Is file wrapper estoppel a true estoppel? The answer may have procedural consequence. In General Instrument Corp. v. Hughes Aircraft Co., 399 F.2d 373, 158 U.S.P.Q. 498 (1st Cir. 1968), patentee prevailed in the district court on a finding that the accused composition fell within his claims under the doctrine of equivalents. On appeal, defendant asserted the doctrine of file wrapper estoppel for the first time. Agreeing that file wrapper estoppel applied, the court of appeals reversed. "Were this doctrine only that of 'estoppel' and nothing more, we would be inclined to treat this as a defense which, not having been asserted below, is deemed waived. But this doctrine is more. 'It is a rule of patent construction consistently observed that a claim in a patent as allowed must be read and interpreted with reference to claims that have been cancelled or rejected, and the claims allowed cannot by construction be read to cover what was thus eliminated from the patent.' Schriber-Schroth v. Cleveland Trust Co., 311 U.S. 211, 220–221, 47 U.S.P.Q. 345, 348–349 (1940)."

A patentee's cancellation or amendment of claims at the examiner's instance will form the basis for file wrapper estoppel even though the examiner may have been in error. Should the estoppel be applied with respect to arguments or representations to the examiner, short of amendment or cancellation, made in the hope of obtaining allowance? All but the Second Circuit appear inclined to give some estoppel effect to attorneys' Patent and Trademark Office remarks. Judge Learned Hand's staunch opposition to their admission probably explains the Second Circuit position. See Catalin Corp. of America v. Catalazuli Mfg. Co., 79 F.2d 593, 27 U.S.P.Q. 371 (2d Cir. 1935). See generally, Rowland, The Interplay of the Doctrines of Equivalents and File Wrapper Estoppel, 29 Geo.Wash.L.Rev. 917 (1961).

5. The general tests of infringement announced in *Graver* represent only part of the picture. Specific tests, oriented to the particular type of subject matter in suit, also play a role.

Because patent claims for compositions of matter can be distinctly characterized in terms of their ingredients' nature and proportions, infringement consists of replication of the ingredients in substantially the same proportions. For a process patent, it is the series of steps comprising the process that is central. Replication of every step in substantially the same operative order constitutes infringement. See, for example, Engelhard Indus., Inc. v. Research Instrumental Corp., 324 F.2d 347, 139 U.S.P.Q. 179 (9th Cir. 1963). And, in the case of a machine or device, it is substantial similarity in the means, mode and results of operation that infringes. See, for example, Nickerson v. The Bearfoot Sole Co., Inc., 311 F.2d 858, 136 U.S.P.Q. 96 (6th Cir. 1962). For a discussion of some special problems in determining infringement of chemical compositions see Sears, The Markush Patent Claim and Its Relation to the Doctrine of Equivalents, 27 Geo.Wash. L.Rev. 327 (1959).

6. Can a patent owner who has once suffered a finding of invalidity relitigate the patent's validity in another action against another infringer? Until 1971, the answer was that, under the mutuality of estoppel doctrine, he could. That year, the Supreme Court decided Blonder-Tongue Laboratories, Inc. v. University of Illinois Foundation, 402 U.S. 313, 91 S.Ct. 1434, 28 L.Ed.2d 788, 169 U.S.P.Q. 513, overturning the rule of Triplett v. Lowell, 297 U.S. 638, 56 S.Ct. 645, 80 L.Ed. 949, 29 U.S.P.Q. 1 (1936) "to the extent it forecloses a plea of estoppel by one facing a charge of infringement of a patent that has once been declared invalid." 402 U.S. 313, 350, 91 S.Ct. 1434, 1453, 1454.

The Court's decision drew in part on the contemporary erosion of the mutuality of estoppel doctrine in other fields. Also, in the Court's opinion, the doctrine's cost—to plaintiffs, defendants and courts facing recurrent litigation over the same issue—far outweighed its benefits. "Some courts have frankly stated that patent litigation can present issues so complex that legal minds, without appropriate grounding in science and technology, may have difficulty in reaching decision. . . . Assuming a patent case so difficult as to provoke a frank admission of judicial uncertainty, one might ask what reason there is to expect that a second District Judge or Court of Appeals would be able to decide the issue more accurately." Finally, "when these judicial developments are considered in the light of our consistent view—last presented in Lear, Inc. v. Adkins—that the holder of a patent should not be insulated from the assertion of defenses and thus allowed to exact royalties for the use of an idea that is not in fact patentable or that is beyond the scope of the patent monopoly granted, it is apparent that the uncritical acceptance of the principle of mutuality of estoppel expressed in Triplett v. Lowell is today out of place." 402 U.S. 313, 349–350, 91 S.Ct. 1434, 1453, 1454.

The Court ruled that an alleged infringer's plea of estoppel would not entirely bar the patent owner from a second hearing. "Rather the patentee-plaintiff must be permitted to demonstrate, if he can, that he did not have a 'fair opportunity procedurally, substantively and evidentially to pursue his claim the first time.' " The Court gave some examples of the facts to be found in determining whether the patentee had enjoyed a fair opportunity: "If the issue is nonobviousness, appropriate inquiries would be whether the first validity determination purported to employ the standards announced in Graham v. John Deere Co., whether the opinions filed by the District Court and the reviewing court, if any, indicate that the prior case was one of those relatively rare instances where the courts wholly failed to grasp the technical subject matter and issues in suit; and whether without fault of his own, the patentee was deprived of crucial evidence or witnesses in the first litigation."

Recall that *Blonder-Tongue* was decided against a background of circuit courts applying widely divergent standards of invention. See page 449 above. If the Supreme Court could not harmonize the circuits, as it had tried to do in *John Deere*, then at the least it could confine the patent owner's strategy of suing in one circuit after another until it found a court charitably disposed to patents. But, did the Court tip the strategic advantage too far in favor of accused infringers? After *Blonder-Tongue*, the patent owner must choose his first forum with care, since a finding of invalidity there will virtually bar later lawsuits elsewhere. Presumably, the patent owner will choose the most convenient forum that is also known for its hospitality to patents. But, say that it is the *infringer* who chooses the forum, through the vehicle of a declaratory judgment action. How can the patentee avoid the declaratory judgment action—by not threatening suit—and at the same time steer clear of a laches defense?

Will an initial determination of a patent's *validity* bar nonparticipants in the litigation from subsequently asserting the patent's invalidity? Or, is comity the only constraint? See Boutell v. Volk, 449 F.2d 673, 171 U.S.P.Q. 668 (10th Cir. 1971); Columbia Broadcasting System, Inc. v. Zenith Radio Corp., 391 F.Supp. 780, 185 U.S.P.Q. 662 (N.D.Ill.1975). ("A prior finding of validity should be given as much weight as possible consistent with the dictates of due process. Without violating due process, a court can require a defendant to prove that a factual or legal error occurred in the previous adjudication of validity or that the previous litigation was incomplete in some material aspect.") 391 F.Supp. 386. See Kidwell, Comity, Patent Validity and The Search for Symmetry: Son of Blonder-Tongue, 57 J.P.O.S. 473 (1975).

Kahn, Blonder-Tongue and the Shape of Future Patent Litigation, 53 J.P.O.S. 581 (1971), canvasses the Court's opinion for difficult questions left unanswered. On the decision generally, see Smith, The Collateral Estoppel Effect of a Prior Judgment of Patent Invalidity: Blonder-Tongue Revisited, (pts. 1, 2, 3) 55 J.P.O.S. 285, 363, 436 (1973), and Halpern, Blonder-Tongue: A Discussion and Analysis, (pts. 1–2) 53 J.P.O.S. 761 (1971), 54 J.P.O.S. 5 (1972).

III. COPYRIGHT LAW

Copyright law began in England with the printing press. Within a decade after William Caxton founded his press at Westminster in 1476, the Crown sought to control the new art through royal grants of patents for printing. In 1557 control was largely transferred to the printers themselves with the formation of the Stationers' Company to prosecute printers who published seditious matter or who infringed others' licensed works. Through a series of Star Chamber decrees, royal proclamations and legislation, censorship and the regulation of piracy became inseparable. As Benjamin Kaplan observed, "copyright has the look of being gradually secreted in the interstices of the censorship." B. Kaplan, An Unhurried View of Copyright 4 (1967).

As censorship declined at the end of the seventeenth century, the Stationers petitioned Parliament for aid. The response was the Statute of Anne, 8 Ann., c. 19 (1709), the first English copyright act. The Statute established a copyright term of 14 years from the date of publication, renewable once, and provided for fines and forfeiture of infringing copies. The Stationers' role under the statute was limited to registering titles and accepting deposits of copyrighted works.

The English copyright system was adopted in the American colonies. On May 2, 1783, the Continental Congress passed a resolution urging "the several States .   .   .   to secure to the authors or publishers of any new books   .   .   .   the copy right of such books. .   .   ." See U.S. Copyright Office, Copyright Enactments, Bull. No. 3, p. 1 (1973). All the states but Delaware complied, most with laws modeled on the Statute of Anne. The first federal copyright law, the Act of May 31, 1790, was also closely patterned after the English Statute. The Act's original subject matter, charts and books, was gradually expanded as new economic interests and technologies pressed for recognition. Prints were added in the Act of 1802, musical compositions in the Act of 1831, photographs and negatives in the Act of 1865, paintings, drawings, chromos, and statuary in the Act of 1870, and motion pictures in the Act of 1912, the last expansion of coverage until sound recordings were added in 1971.

Despite these expansions in coverage, the Copyright Act remained wedded to the technology of Caxton's printing press, a creaky anachronism in the face of the mid-twentieth century communications revolution. Efforts to revise the 1909 Act began in 1955 when Congress voted funds to support research into the issues to be resolved by a new law. The research effort culminated in a 1961 Report of the Register of Copyrights on the General Revision of the U. S. Copyright Law, 87th Cong., 1st Sess. The Report provided the impetus for the First Draft General Revision Bill, H.R. 11947 and S. 3008, 88th Cong., 2d Sess., introduced in 1964. Revisions, hearings, more revisions and more hearings followed. On February 19, 1976, the Senate passed a much worn and traveled revision bill, S. 22. On September 22, 1976 the House passed a slightly different version. A conference report ironing out the differences was adopted by both houses on September 30, 1976. On October 19, 1976, President Ford signed the bill into law. The law, P.L. 94–553, came into effect for most purposes on January 1, 1978.

The efforts to revise the 1909 Copyright Act stimulated some good writing on copyright law and policy. Thirty-five studies initiated by the Copyright Office, and reprinted in Studies on Copyright (Arthur Fisher Memorial Ed. 1963), examine a variety of topics within the reform context. Provocative views are also expressed in Copyright Law Revision, Report of the Register of Copyrights on the General Revision of the U.S. Copyright Law, 87th Cong., 1st Sess. (1961); Supplementary Report of the Register of Copyrights on the General Revision of the U.S. Copyright Law: 1965 Revision Bill; and Second Supplementary Report of the Register of Copyrights on the General Revision of the U.S. Copyright Law (1975). H.R.Rep.No. 94–1476, 94th Cong., 2d Sess. (1976) and House Conf.Rep.No.94– 1733, 94th Cong., 2d Sess. (1976), are the authoritative legislative sources interpreting the 1976 Act. Debate on the floor of the House of Representatives appears at pp. H–10872 through H–10911 of the Congressional Record, Vol. 122, #144 (Daily ed., September 22, 1976).

Several law review symposia were published in the wake of the Act's passage. See 24 U.C.L.A.L.Rev. 951 (1977); 25 Bull.Copyr.Soc. 191 (1977); 1979 U.Ill.L.Forum 337; 22 N.Y.L.School L.Rev. 471 (1977). Gorman, An Overview of the Copyright Act of 1976, 126 U. Pa.L.Rev. 856 (1978) offers a thoughtful introduction to the Act.

On the early history of copyright, see L. Patterson, Copyright in Historical Perspective (1968); B. Bugbee, Genesis of American Patent and Copyright Law (1967); R. Bowker, Copyright: Its History and Its Law (1912). For purposes of general reference, M. Nimmer, Copyright (1978) is helpful. A. Latman, Howell's Copyright Law (1979) is a good, short handbook. The Bulletin of the Copyright Society of the United States of America regularly publishes interesting articles and summaries of judicial, legislative and administrative developments in the United States and abroad. Copyright literature has also been enriched by the Nathan Burkan Memorial Competition; award-winning student papers in the competition are published in an annual volume by the competition's sponsor, The American Society of Composers, Authors and Publishers.

A Note on the Cases in this Chapter. Many of the cases in this chapter were decided under, and contain references to, the 1909 Act. The 1909 Act is reprinted in the Statute Supplement. A chart aligning sections of the 1909 Act with counterpart provisions of the 1976 Act also appears in the Supplement.

A. REQUIREMENTS FOR PROTECTION

1. FORMALITIES

See Statute Supplement 17 U.S.C.A. §§ 401–412, 601, 701–710.

a. NOTICE

PETER PAN FABRICS, INC. v. MARTIN WEINER CORP.

United States Court of Appeals, Second Circuit, 1960.
274 F.2d 487, 124 U.S.P.Q. 154.

HAND, Circuit Judge.

This is an appeal from a preliminary injunction, granted by Judge Herlands, forbidding the defendant to copy an ornamental design, printed upon cloth. The plaintiffs—which for the purposes of this appeal are to be regarded as one—and the defendant are both "converters" of textiles, used in the manufacture of women's dresses. A "converter" buys uncolored cloth upon which he prints ornamental designs, and which he then sells to dressmakers. The plaintiffs bought from a Parisian designer a design, known as "Byzantium," which it registered as a "reproduction of a work of art," (§ 5(h) of Title 17 U.S. Code) and for which the Copyright Office issued Certificate No. H. 7290. This design they print upon uncolored cloth, sold in bolts to dressmakers. The cloth, so "converted," bears upon its edge at each repetition of the design printed "notices" of copyright which are concededly adequate under the Copyright Law. The buyers of the bolts cut the cloth into suitable lengths and use it to make women's dresses; but in doing so, they either altogether cut off the selvage which bears the notices, or else they sew the adjacent edges of the cloth together at the seams in such a way that the notices are not visible unless the seams are pried, or cut, apart, or unless the dress is turned inside out. The appeal raises two questions: (1) whether the defendant has in fact copied so much of the registered design as to infringe the copyright; and (2) whether the design was dedicated to the public, because it was sold without adequate notice of copyright as required by § 10 of the statute.

The test for infringement of a copyright is of necessity vague. In the case of verbal "works" it is well settled that although the "proprietor's" monopoly extends beyond an exact reproduction of the words, there can be no copyright in the "ideas" disclosed but only in their "expression." Obviously, no principle can be stated as to when an imitator has gone beyond copying the "idea," and has borrowed its "expression." Decisions must therefore inevitably be ad hoc. In the case of designs, which are addressed to the aesthetic sensibilities of an observer, the test is, if possible, even more intangible. No one disputes that the copyright extends beyond a photographic reproduction of the design, but one cannot say how far an imitator must depart from an undeviating reproduction to escape infringement. In deciding that question one should consider the uses for which the design is intended, especially the scrutiny that observers will give to it as used. In the case at bar we must try to estimate how far its overall appearance will determine its aesthetic appeal when the cloth is made into a garment. Both designs have the same general color, and the arches, scrolls, rows of symbols, etc. on one resemble those on the other though they are not identical. Moreover, the patterns in which these figures are distributed to make up the design as a whole are not identical. However, the ordinary observer, unless he set out to detect the disparities, would be disposed to overlook them, and regard their aesthetic appeal as the same. That is enough; and indeed, it is all that can be said, unless protection against infringement is to be denied because of variants irrelevant to the purpose for which the design is intended.

The second question is whether the plaintiffs have forfeited their copyright. As we have said, there is no question that the bolts of cloth were adequately marked to comply with § 10, for a notice was "affixed to each copy . . . offered for sale"; and, it appeared at intervals along the selvage, so that no one using the cloth could avoid seeing it. However, although the notices served the purpose of advising those who bought, or dealt with, the bolts, they did not give adequate notice to those who bought, or wore, dresses made of the cloth, for, when not altogether cut off, they were so placed as to be most unlikely to be detected. Section 21 of the act provides that the "omission by accident or mistake of the prescribed notice from a particular copy or copies shall not invalidate the copyright"; but the effective suppression of this mark on dresses is neither accidental nor mistaken; and sales with a deliberate omission of notice will forfeit the copyright. Therefore, if we construe the words of § 10 with relentless literalism, dresses made out of the "converted" cloth may be said to be "offered for sale" without any effective notice. In support of such an interpretation it may be argued that the doctrine, expressio unius, exclusio alterius, would apply: that is to say, since Congress made only "omission by accident or mistake" an excuse we must not enlarge the exemption.

On the other hand, it is a commonplace that a literal interpretation of the words of a statute is not always a safe guide to its meaning. Indeed, in extreme situations this doctrine has been carried so far that language inescapably covering the occasion has been disregarded when it defeats the manifest purpose of the statute as a whole. We need not go so far in the case at bar. In the first place it is hard to see how "notice" can be said to be "affixed" to a "design" when it is incorporated into it; the copyrighted "work" will itself be changed, even though the change be so immaterial as not to impair the aesthetic appeal of the "design." Be that as it may, we do not hold that in no circumstances will it be possible to "affix notice" upon a "design" which will be still visible when the cloth has been made up into a garment. We do hold that at least in the case of a deliberate copyist, as in the case at bar, the absence of "notice" is a defence that the copyist must prove, and that the burden is on him to show that "notice" could have been embodied in the design without impairing its market value. The defendant asserts that this can be done but it has offered no evidence that it can be. Whatever may be shown at the trial, upon this record we hold that the "design" should be protected, pendente lite.

Order affirmed.

FRIENDLY, Circuit Judge (dissenting).

I regret that I cannot join in the judgment of the Court. I would reverse.

Section 10 of the Copyright Act, 17 U.S.C.A. § 10, provides that "Any person entitled thereto by this title may secure copyright for his work by publication thereof with the notice of copyright required by this title; and such notice shall be affixed to each copy thereof published or offered for sale in the United States by authority of the copyright proprietor." The question is whether plaintiffs met the second requirement.

Admittedly, the notice of copyright is not "affixed to each copy" of the copyrighted design on the dresses manufactured and sold by the purchasers that bought cloth from plaintiffs. Indeed, whether the notice remains affixed to any copy is fortuitous, since, as was conceded at the bar, plaintiffs cannot practically obtain any commitments from the manufacturers in this regard. I do not read the Court's opinion as questioning that the manufacturers make and sell the dresses in this manner "by authority of the copyright proprietor." Such sales were the very purpose of the purchases of the cloth; plaintiffs knew that the notices would generally be cut off; and I read § 10 as using "authority" in the broad sense of permission and not as requiring any technical agency relationship. It is unnecessary to debate whether the conversion of the designs into dresses was a republication; for it was an offer for sale unless we deny those words the sense they have in everyday speech. I take it no one would question that an authorized offer for sale occurred if the purchasers, with plaintiffs' acquiescence, regularly cut off the selvage bearing the copyright notice and sold the cloth in strips; I think there was no less such an offer when the purchasers cut off the selvage and sold the cloth in dresses.

I am not altogether clear whether my brothers say that the sale of the dresses was not an offer for sale with the authority of the copyright proprietor or that it was such an offer but that notice need not be affixed if this was not feasible. The latter construction seems borne out by the suggestion that plaintiffs will be denied a final decree if defendant proves that notice could have been affixed to each copy of the design in the dresses without impairing the market value; for, unless the sale of the dresses is within § 10, plaintiffs are under no requirement to have the notice affixed. In any event the result is plain enough. Plaintiffs receive copyright protection for enabling a multitude of ladies to be caparisoned in the purple of "Byzantium" although the copyright notices, instead of being "affixed to each copy" of the design on the dresses, pile up in the cutting rooms. It is of no moment that the Court now grants protection only pendente lite. For the record makes it evident that designs such as plaintiffs' are anything but Byzantine in longevity—indeed, the moving affidavit gives this one but a few months of life—and in litigation of this sort the preliminary rather than the final injunction is the thing.

I could reconcile the majority's result with the language of § 10 if, but only if, there were clear evidence that the dominant intention of Congress was to afford the widest possible copyright protection whereas the notice requirement was deemed formal or at least secondary. I find nothing to support such a stratified reading of § 10. The notice requirement goes back to almost the earliest days of copyright under the constitutional grant, Act of April 29, 1802, ch. 36, 2 Stat. 171; its essentiality has been emphasized by the highest authority, Mifflin v. R. H. White & Co., 1903, 190 U.S. 260, 23 S.Ct. 769, 47 L.Ed. 1040, Mifflin v. Dutton, 1903, 190 U.S. 265, 23 S.Ct. 771, 47 L. Ed. 1043; Louis Dejonge & Co. v. Breuker & Kessler Co., 1914, 235 U.S. 33, 37, 35 S.Ct. 6, 59 L.Ed. 113 and when Congress has wished to make an exception, it has known how to do so, see 17 U.S.C.A. § 21. The notice requirement serves an important public purpose; the copyright proprietor is protected so long and only so long as he gives effective warning to trespassers that they are entering on forbidden ground. And if the statutory requirement of notice has not been met, it is immaterial whether a particular defendant had actual knowledge of a claim of copyright or not.

I realize that the view I hold may seriously impair the use of copyright to prevent piracy in an area where this has been recognized to be rampant for thirty years, Cheney Bros. v. Doris Silk Corp., 2 Cir., 1929, 35 F.2d 279, certiorari denied, 1930, 281 U.S. 728, 50 S.Ct. 245, 74 L.Ed. 1145, and probably for much longer, since it may not be practicable to affix the notice to an inside seam on every repetition of the design. It can be argued also that this is to insist on a useless formality since, though there is reason for requiring notice on each copy of a book, one notice on a dress is as good as ten. But, as was held by the Supreme Court in Dejonge, it is not for the courts to say that something less than the statutory requirement will serve. Congress has not accompanied the broadening of the subjects of copyright in § 5 with a relaxation of the notice requirement of § 10, except as it has simplified the form of notice for certain subjects in § 19 and has saved against accidental omission in § 21. Nothing gives me warrant for belief that Congress would be content with the proprietor's simply affixing the copyright notice to each copy as it leaves him, when, as here, he knows that almost every notice will be removed before the copyrighted reproductions reach their intended market. As said in Louis Dejonge & Co. v. Breuker & Kessler, supra, 235 U.S. at page 37, 35 S.Ct. at page 6, "The appellant is claiming the same rights as if this were one of the masterpieces of the world, and he must take them with the same limitations that would apply to a portrait, a holy family, or a scene of war." To be sure, the precise defect held fatal in Dejonge is not present here since the notice was on "each copy" as it left plaintiffs, but Mr. Justice Holmes' admonition remains pertinent. So also, while I do not contend decision to be controlled by National Comics Publications, Inc. v. Fawcett Publications, Inc., 2 Cir., 1951, 191 F.2d 594, 600, 601, opinion clarified, 198 F.2d 927, Deward & Rich, Inc. v. Bristol Sav. & Loan Corp., 4 Cir., 1941, 120 F.2d 537, and Advertisers Exchange, Inc. v. Anderson, 8 Cir., 1944, 144 F.2d 907, these cases are at least closer than those relied on by the District Court in holding for plaintiffs. Perhaps my brothers are right in thinking that Congress wished literal compliance with § 10 to be excused under such circumstances as here; but the voice so audible to them is silent to me.

b. REGISTRATION AND DEPOSIT

WASHINGTONIAN PUB. CO. v. PEARSON

Supreme Court of the United States, 1939.
306 U.S. 30, 59 S.Ct. 397, 83 L.Ed. 470, 40 U.S.P.Q. 190.

Mr. Justice McREYNOLDS delivered the opinion of the Court.

By this suit, instituted in the District of Columbia, March 8, 1933, petitioner seeks an injunction, damages, etc., because of alleged unauthorized use of a magazine article copyrighted under Act March 4, 1909 (Ch. 320, 35 Stat. 1075; U.S.C.A., Title 17). Pertinent portions of the statute are in the margin.

The trial court sustained petitioner's claim and directed ascertainment of profits, damages, etc. The Court of Appeals ruled that, as copies of the magazine had not been *promptly* deposited in the Copyright Office as directed by § 12, the action could not be maintained. It accordingly reversed the decree of the trial court and remanded the cause.

The record discloses—

December 10, 1931, petitioner published an issue of "The Washingtonian," a monthly magazine, and claimed copyright by printing thereon the required statutory notice. Fourteen months later, February 21, 1933, copies were first deposited in the Copyright Office and a certificate of registration secured. This suit followed, March 8, 1933.

In August, 1932, Liveright, Inc., published and offered for general sale a book written by two of the respondents and printed by another, which contained material substantially identical with an article contained in The Washingtonian of December, 1931. The usual notice claimed copyright of this book. August 26, 1932, copies were deposited in the Copyright Office and certificate of registration issued.

Respondents concede that petitioner secured upon publication a valid copyright of The Washingtonian. But they insist that although prompt deposit of copies is not prerequisite to copyright, no action can be maintained because of infringement prior in date to a tardy deposit. Counsel assert—"The very foundation of the right to maintain an action for infringement is deposit of copies and registration of the work. Neither of these has the slightest bearing upon the creation of the copyright itself under Section 9. That is obtained merely by publication with notice as required by the Act." Also, "If copies were not deposited promptly after publication the opportunity to comply with the requirement of promptness was gone forever as to that particular work."

Petitioner submits that under the statute *prompt* deposit of copies is not prerequisite to an action for infringement; and that under the facts here disclosed deposit before suit was enough.

The Act of 1909 is a complete revision of the copyright laws, different from the earlier Act both in scheme and language. It introduced many changes and was intended definitely to grant valuable, enforceable rights to authors, publishers, etc., without burdensome requirements; "to afford greater encouragement to the production of literary works of lasting benefit to the world."

Under the old Act deposit of the work was essential to the existence of copyright. This requirement caused serious difficulties and unfortunate losses. The present statute (§ 9) declares—"Any person entitled thereto by this Act may secure copyright for his work by publication thereof with the notice of copyright required by this Act [§ 18]; . . ." And respondents rightly say "It is no longer necessary to deposit anything to secure a copyright of a published work, but only to publish with the notice of copyright." . . .

Although immediately upon publication of The Washingtonian for December, 1931, petitioner secured copyright of the articles therein, respondents maintain that through failure promptly to deposit copies in the Copyright Office the right to sue for infringement was lost. In effect, that the provision in § 12 relative to suits should be treated as though it contained the words "promptly," also "unless" instead of "until," and read—No action or proceeding shall be maintained for infringement of copyright in any work *unless* the provisions of this Act with respect to the deposit of copies *promptly* and registration of such work shall have been complied with.

Plausible arguments in support of this view were advanced by the Court of Appeals. We think, however, its adoption would not square with the words actually used in the statute, would cause conflict with its general purpose, and in practice produce unfortunate consequences. We cannot accept it.

Petitioner's claim of copyright came to fruition immediately upon publication. Without further notice it was good against all the world. Its value depended upon the possibility of enforcement.

The use of the word "until" in § 12 rather than "unless" indicates that mere delay in making deposit of copies was not enough to cause forfeiture of the right theretofore distinctly granted.

Section 12 provides "That after copyright has been secured by publication of the work with the notice of copyright as provided in section nine of this Act, there shall be promptly deposited in the copyright office" two copies, etc. The Act nowhere defines "promptly," and to make the continued existence of copyright depend upon promptness would lead to unfortunate uncertainty and confusion. The great number of copyrights annually obtained is indicated by note 3, supra. The difficulties consequent upon the former requirement of deposit before publication are pointed out in the Committee Report. These would be enlarged if whenever effort is made to vindicate a copyright it would become necessary to show deposits were made promptly after publication especially since there is no definition of "promptly."

The penalty for delay clearly specified in § 13 is adequate for punishment of delinquents and to enforce contributions of desirable books to the Library. To give § 12 a more drastic effect would tend to defeat the broad purpose of the enactment. The Report of the Congressional Committee points out that forfeiture after notice and three months' further delay was thought too severe by some. Nowhere does it suggest approval of the much more drastic result now insisted upon by respondents.

Read together as the Committee which reported the bill said they should be, §§ 12 and 13 show, we think, the Congress intended that prompt deposit when deemed necessary should be enforced through actual notice by the register; also that while no action can be maintained before copies are actually deposited, mere delay will not destroy the right to sue. Such forfeitures are never to be inferred from doubtful language.

This view is in accord with the interpretation of somewhat similar provisions of the English Copyright Act.

The challenged decree must be reversed. The cause will be remanded to the District Court.

Reversed.

[The opinion of Mr. Justice BLACK, dissenting, is omitted.]

B. KAPLAN, THE REGISTRATION OF COPYRIGHT

Study No. 17, Subcommittee on Patents, Trademarks, and Copyrights,
Senate Committee on the Judiciary, 86th Cong., 2d Sess.
35–36, 41 (Comm.Print 1960).

1. Record Material

The chief record material flowing into the Copyright Office in consequence of the various provisions of the act consists of applications for original registration and works (or substitutes) deposited therewith; applications for renewal of copyright; assignments and related documents; notices of use and notices of intention to use.

The records of the Copyright Office are built fundamentally upon this submitted material. Library of Congress collections are fed from the deposited copies. .   .   .

3. Examination of Applications and Deposits

When applications are received in the Copyright Office, the Examining Division scrutinizes them together with the accompanying deposited copies. The check is for compliance with law, but the examiner does not and cannot investigate at large; he generally confines himself to the application and the deposited copies; occasionally, when put on inquiry by this internal examination, he may go elsewhere to relevant records of the Copyright Office. He is certainly not expected to check whether the work duplicates a previously copyrighted work or a work in the public domain. He checks for adequacy of the notice of copyright; agreement in dates, names, etc., between the application and the deposited copies; propriety of the "class" in which copyright is claimed; evident copyrightability of the work, and some other matters. The various forms of letters sent to claimants calling attention to errors spotted by the examiners, and usually soliciting corrections by the claimants, are revealing of the kind of examination that is conducted, as is section 202.2 of the Copyright Office regulations, listing common defects in the notice.

The Register has stated that an examiner is expected to deal with about 40 registrations per day. With respect to perhaps 15 percent of the applications correspondence with the claimant becomes necessary. As to rejections, the Register's annual report for fiscal 1957 says:

> Approximately 3 percent of the applications filed during the fiscal year were rejected. .   .   . Most rejections were in connection with published works lacking notice of copyright, uncopyrightable items, and works other than books, periodicals, or musical compositions, although many renewal applications had to be rejected because of untimely filing (p 2).

Reasons are given for rejections and claimants are permitted to present arguments in writing and orally. There is no formally established procedure by which a claimant or other interested party can secure review of a decision within the Copyright Office; but apparently informal "appeal" lies to the Chief or Assistant Chief of the Examining Division, with final resort to the Register. The policy of the Office, as we have seen, is to be liberal in registering claims.

Assignments and related instruments appearing on their face to relate to copyrights and to be properly executed are not checked but are immediately recorded. Renewal applications are checked and in ordinary cases will not be registered unless original registration has been accomplished.

When a claimant files his application and makes deposit he is in effect submitting himself to an official determination of whether he has complied with the law. The check carried out by the Examining Division is a means of enforcing both formal and substantive requirements including provisions or standards governing notice, copyrightability, manufacturing, import, etc. As a practical matter this check is perhaps the chief official instrument of law enforcement. Were it not for administrative surveillance "at the source," a considerable number of works belonging in the public domain would circulate with notice of copyright inhibiting access to the works. In many cases the check serves to advise or warn claimants about legal requirements with which they are then quite willing to comply. The fact that applications are officially examined puts a certain pressure on claimants to examine and attempt to comply with the law before attempting registration.

Administrative examination of claims to copyright is however far from complete. It is necessarily limited in the great majority of cases to a check of obvious points arising on the claimants' ex parte submissions. Invalid claims may slip by; and when they do, they carry a kind of official imprimatur which may itself operate unjustly in creating a preserve that is practically effective although legally unjustified.

The Copyright Office policy of registering doubtful claims can be objected to on the ground that it fosters "monopolies" which are in last analysis illegal. On the other side, objection has been voiced to any administrative decisions of invalidity. As these decisions are not conclusive on the courts, it has been argued that the Office should abandon the whole effort to examine claims and register all claims as such, so that the contentions of interested parties regarding particular works will be disclosed of record, giving users and others a better basis for deciding how they should act.

NOTES

1. The present Act continues the basic positions on formalities reflected in the *Peter Pan* and *Washingtonian* decisions. Failure to affix proper copyright notice at the required time still results in forfeiture. Registration and deposit continue to be permissive. At the same time, the Act has adjusted these formalities, relaxing some and tightening others. The earlier requirement that copyright notice comply with technical, sometimes arbitrary, requirements for content and position has been replaced with a looser, more reasonable standard, and the Act excuses omission of copyright notice in a wide range of circumstances. New inducements to registration and deposit have been added, and the sanction of forfeiture for failure to comply with the Register's demand for deposit has been dropped.

2. What purposes do copyright notice and the forfeiture sanction serve? One long-time observer has noted: "Assuming that certain formalities may be desirable, it is fair to question whether the penalty of absolute forfeiture of all property rights in the work is a

proper or necessary sanction. The only purpose of a copyright notice or registration is to warn a user that the owner of the work has not authorized its reproduction without special permission. It is submitted that a notice of copyright is not the only means of placing a user on notice; that registration of a claim of copyright would serve an equal, if not a more effective purpose; and that in any event omission of the notice or failure to register should not be a defense to anyone who is not an 'innocent' infringer." Letter of Herman Finkelstein, May 7, 1958, printed in Appendix to Doyle, Cary, McCannon & Ringer, Notice of Copyright, Study No. 7, Subcomm. on Patents, Trademarks, and Copyrights, Sen. Comm. on the Judiciary, 86th Cong., 2d Sess. 60 (1960).

Another perceived benefit of copyright notice is that "[i]t identifies the copyright owner . . . and it shows the date of publication." H.R.Rep.No.94–1476, 94th Cong., 2d Sess. at 143 (1976). How important is it to know the date of publication in a system that generally measures the term of copyright not from the date of publication (as was the case under the 1909 Act), but rather by the life of the author plus 50 years? Will a proper copyright notice under the present Act invariably identify the owner and date of first publication? See section 404(a). To be sure, a prospective user may find the answer to these and other questions about a work's provenance when he examines the owner's registration in the Copyright Office— *if* the owner has registered.

What underlies the widespread assumption in the United States that copyright formalities are necessary or proper? Few other countries have a notice requirement or, indeed, require formalities generally. See generally, Note, Reappraisal of the Notice Requirement in Copyright, 8 U.C.L.A.L.Rev. 703 (1961).

3.   The Second Circuit has set the pace for judicial liberalization of copyright notice formalities. *Peter Pan* is typical in its effort to align the purposes of copyright notice with commercial realities in the copyright industries. The effort at alignment is not always successful. For example, the test stated in the last paragraph of Judge Hand's *Peter Pan* opinion—whether notice can be embodied in a design without impairing its market value—may sound good, but is it sound? What is there in the purpose of copyright notice, or in the statutory text, to support such a test? Would this test enable fine artists to leave notice off their works on the ground that it impairs the work's market value? Aesthetic value? Is the test administrable?

Would attention in *Peter Pan* to the distinct purposes served by copyright notice in the wholesale market for converted textiles and the retail market for finished dresses have produced a better decision? What inference are retail consumers most likely to draw from a copyright notice appearing on finished goods? Compare the two-market rationale that Judge Hand formulated in a trademark case, Bayer v. United Drug Company, page 306 above.

4. *Omission of Notice.* Under the new Act, like the old, copyright will be lost if copies or phonorecords of a work are published without the required notice. The new Act does, however, significantly ease the conditions for compliance that previously obtained. The ringing message of the House Report, heard clearly by at least one court, is that "[o]ne of the strongest arguments for revision of the present statute has been the need to avoid the arbitrary and unjust forfeitures now resulting from unintentional or relatively unimportant omissions or errors in the copyright notice." H.R.Rep.No. 94–1476, 143, quoted in P. Kaufman, Inc. v. Rex Curtain Corp., 203 U.S.P.Q. 859, 860 (S.D.N.Y.1978). Section 405 accomplishes this aim by adopting some of the meliorative approaches pioneered in the Second Circuit and by introducing some innovations of its own.

Section 405(c) generalizes *Peter Pan's* approach to copyright notices that will inevitably be removed in the course of manufacture by providing that protection will not be lost "by the removal, destruction, or obliteration of the notice, without the authorization of the copyright owner, from any publicly distributed copies or phonorecords." Section 405(a)(1) follows another Second Circuit approach by saving copyright if "the notice has been omitted from no more than a relatively small number of copies or phonorecords distributed to the public." The House Report states that the phrase, "relatively small number," is "intended to be less restrictive than the phrase 'a particular copy or copies' now in section 21." H.R.Rep.No.94–1476, 147.

Section 405(a)(2) is entirely new, offering a five-year *locus poenitentiae* for publication without notice if the work is registered in the interim and an effort is made to place notice on copies distributed in the United States after the omission has been discovered. Although the Act's use of the word "discovered" might be read to imply a requirement that the omission be unintended, the House Report states that the omission may be deliberate and that "the reason for the omission has no bearing on the validity of copyright." H.R.Rep.No. 94–1476, 147. If so, when is an advertent omission "discovered," so that remedial affixation is required?

What is the result under the Act if notice is omitted without the authority of the copyright owner? Section 405(c) says that the copyright's validity will be unaffected if notice, having once been affixed, is later removed without the owner's consent. Section 405(a)(3) embodies Learned Hand's suggestion that copyright will not be lost if the notice is omitted in violation of an agreement conditioning authorization to publish on proper affixation of the statutory notice. According to Hand, if a licensee agreed to affix notice, but did not, his publication could not be viewed as authorized by the owner, and so would not forfeit the owner's copyright. National Comics Publications, Inc. v. Fawcett Publications, Inc., 191 F.2d 594, 90 U.S. P.Q. 274 (2d Cir. 1951). Section 405(a)(3)'s condition is more rigorous than Hand's, requiring a "writing" and that the writing be "express." It is less rigorous in not requiring that the omitter be a licensee.

Note that, under sections 401(a) and 402(a), for the notice requirement to apply the work must be published "by authority of the copyright owner." Can the owner's "authority" be rested on an oral or implied, rather than a written and express, condition that notice be affixed? If so, is section 405(a)(3) unintended surplusage? Section 405(c), which refers to "authorization," makes no mention of "express" or "written". What of the relationship between sections 401 and 402 and section 405(a) suggested by the House Report's statement that "[t]he consequences of omissions or mistakes with respect to the notice are far less serious under the bill than under the present law, and section 405(a) makes doubly clear that a copyright owner may guard himself against errors or omissions by others if he makes use of the prescribed notice an express condition of his publishing licenses." H.R.Rep.No.94–1476, 144.

5. *Name of Copyright Owner.* Section 401(b)(3)'s permission to substitute for the full name of the copyright owner "an abbreviation by which the name can be recognized, or a generally known alternative designation of the owner," embodies the contemporary trend of decision.

In Herbert Rosenthal Jewelry Corp. v. Grossbardt, 436 F.2d 315, 168 U.S.P.Q. 193 (2d Cir. 1970), the only notice appearing on plaintiff's jewelled bee pin consisted of the letters, "HR," within a diamond and an encircled "C" imprinted on the back of a wing. Noting that "there have been numerous holdings that the use of a well-advertised or widely known trademark or trade name on the copyrighted article itself will suffice," Judge Friendly conceded that "[O]n the specific question whether mere initials can constitute an acceptable substitute . . . the decisions are not so clear." 436 F.2d 315, 318. The court finally rested its decision for plaintiff on "HR"'s trademark status. "[W]e stress the evidence that Rosenthal has used HR as a trade name or mark since 1945, that it applied for trademark registration on June 1, 1962 and received it on Jan. 29, 1963 (barely three months after the first bee was sold)." 436 F.2d 315, 318.

Grossbardt stopped short of a possibly more extensive holding. "We thus have no occasion to consider the correctness of the statement in Dan Kasoff, Inc. v. Novelty Jewelry Co., 309 F.2d 745, 135 U.S.P.Q. 234 (2d Cir. 1962), that an infringer aware of the existence of copyright is in no position to assert insufficiency of the notice." 436 F.2d 315, 319. Judge Friendly underscored his reservations about *Kasoff* a year later in Puddu v. Buonamici Statuary, Inc., 450 F.2d 401, 171 U.S.P.Q. 709 (2d Cir. 1971). "Although Professor Nimmer states that even illegible notices may be good 'as against infringers who managed to decipher them or who should have been put on inquiry by the illegible printing, or who had actual notice of the plaintiff's copyright,' Nimmer, Copyright § 90.4, only three of the seven decisions cited can be said to support this proposition." 450 F.2d 401, 405.

Whose name should appear as the "owner of copyright"? What consequences flow from use of the wrong name? Of the wrong date? See section 406.

6. *Position of Notice.* For certain classes of works, the 1909 Act specified exactly where notice was to appear. For example, in the case of books and other printed publications, notice was to appear upon the "title page or the page immediately following." Failure to comply with the position requirements forfeited copyright as completely as if notice had been entirely omitted.

Some courts were relentless in their insistence on punctilio. In Booth v. Haggard, 184 F.2d 470, 87 U.S.P.Q. 141 (8th Cir. 1950), the court concluded that the cover of plaintiff's book, bearing the phrase "1948–49, Kossuth County, Iowa, TAM Service," was the book's title page, and not page 3 which contained a full page of printed text bearing, at the top, the words "The 1948–1949 Rural TAM, For Kossuth County, Iowa." The copyright notice, "Copyright 1948, R. C. Booth Enterprises, Harlan, Iowa," appeared at the bottom of page 3. The court held that plaintiff's notice was deficient for not appearing on the title page or the page immediately following.

The present Act replaces this niggling approach with the simple and comprehensive requirement in sections 401(c) and 402(c) that notice shall be affixed to copies or placed on phonorecords in such manner and location "as to give reasonable notice of the claim of copyright." Once again, decisions from the Second Circuit under the 1909 Act, together with guidelines issued by the Register of Copyrights, can be expected to add some content to the newly relaxed, functional standard. See, for example, Scarves by Vera, Inc. v. United Merchants & Mfrs., Inc., 173 F.Supp. 625, 121 U.S.P.Q. 652 (S.D. N.Y.1959).

7. What constitutes a "copy" for purposes of section 401(a)'s requirement that copyright notice be placed "on all publicly distributed copies from which the work can be visually perceived, either directly or with the aid of a machine or device"? Answers, easy in the case of a one-volume novel or single sheet musical composition, are more difficult for other types of subject matter. For example, in the case of a strip of gift wrapping paper bearing twelve reproductions, arranged side by side, of a holly, mistletoe and spruce sprig cluster, what constitutes the copy—each of the twelve paintings or each strip of wrapping paper? In DeJonge & Co. v. Breuker & Kessler Co., 235 U.S. 33, 35 S.Ct. 6, 59 L.Ed. 113 (1914), in which plaintiff had affixed one copyright notice per strip, Justice Holmes agreed with the courts below that "the notice must be repeated on each of the twelve squares, although they did not present themselves as separate squares on the continuous strip." 235 U.S. 33, 36, 35 S.Ct. 6.

Holmes answered appellant's assertion that "it is overtechnical to require a repetition of the notice upon every square in a single sheet that makes a harmonious whole," with the observation that "[t]his argument tacitly assumes that we can look to such larger unity as the sheet possesses. . . . The protected object does not gain more extensive privileges by being repeated several times upon one sheet of paper, as any one would recognize if it were the Gioconda. The appellant is claiming the same rights as if this work were one of the masterpieces of the world, and he must take them with the same limitations that would apply to a portrait, a holy family, or a scene of war." 235 U.S. 33, 36–37, 35 S.Ct. 6.

Is the *DeJonge* rule defensible? Administrable? Does the present Act's definition of "copies" in section 101 offer any aid to the copyright owner who wants to avoid repetitive notices? Would the authority or rationale of section 404(a), which allows a single copyright notice for a collective work consisting of many contributions, aid the owner? Should section 101's definition of collective work (one "in which a number of contributions constituting separate and independent works in themselves are assembled into a collective whole") be taken literally or is it limited by the examples given—"a periodical issue, anthology, or encyclopedia"?

Once again, courts may choose to follow the lead of the Second Circuit's revolt against formalism. The fabric design considered in H. M. Kolbe Co., Inc. v. Armgus Textile Co., 315 F.2d 70, 137 U.S.P. Q. 9 (2d Cir. 1963), consisted of a checkerboard pattern created by the repetition of clusters of purple roses. Plaintiff printed copyright notice on the selvage down one side of the fabric at sixteen-inch intervals. Rejecting defendant's argument "that the statute required one notice for each rose square of Kolbe's design," the court held that "the 'work' or 'reproduction of a work of art' which Kolbe sought to copyright was not merely the single rose square from which its textile design was created. It was rather the composite design itself, which depends for its aesthetic effect upon both the rose figure and the manner in which the reproductions of that figure are arranged in relation to each other upon the fabric." 315 F.2d 70, 72. *DeJonge* was distinguished in a footnote: "Because the component picture rather than the total design was the copyrighted 'work,' the Supreme Court held that each reproduction of the picture within the design required a notice of copyright."

The court recognized, however, that this did not dispose of the brunt of defendant's argument. "Because of the continuous nature of the composition design printed on Kolbe's fabric there are conceptual difficulties inherent in determining the limits of the protected 'work,' and the number of 'copies' thereof contained in a bolt of the printed fabric." The court rested its eventual determination that notice at 16-inch intervals was sufficient upon two practical grounds. First, the basic pattern, formed by a single revolution of the roller that embodied the master pattern, was sixteen inches in length. Second, "textiles are normally sold by the bolt at wholesale, in units of a yard at retail. By repeating its notice of copyright every 16 inches on the length of its printed fabric, therefore, Kolbe affixed at least one statutory notice to each smallest commercial unit by which its product is normally sold." 315 F.2d 70, 72–73.

8. In a sense, the justice of Washingtonian v. Pearson was poet-ic: the decision was against Drew Pearson and Robert S. Allen, co-authors of The Nine Old Men (1936).

Washingtonian was promptly followed by the introduction of a bill, initiated by the Register of Copyrights, defining the post-publication period in which deposit was to be made—60 days for works published in the United States, 120 days for those published abroad. A late deposit would bar the copyright proprietor from recovering damages accruing between the end of the deposit period and the date of deposit. Failure to deposit within six months would forfeit the copyright. H.R.5319, 76th Cong. 1st Sess. (1939). Congress did not act on the bill.

Washingtonian's central premise is restated in the deposit and registration provisions of the present Act. Section 407(a) requires deposit of two copies of the work's best edition within three months of publication, but makes clear that deposit is not a condition of copyright protection. Indeed, under section 407(d) the sanctions for failure to deposit will only be felt if the Register makes a demand for deposit. Section 408(a), subheaded "Registration Permissive," even more boldly states the *Washingtonian* premise that "registration is not a condition of copyright protection." At the same time, the Act offers several inducements to early registration. Registration will save copyright protection for a work published without notice [section 405(a)(2)] or with an erroneous name in the notice [section 406(a)(1)]. Also, registration provides prima facie evidence of the copyright's validity [section 410(c)] and increases the array of remedies on infringement [section 412].

What connections, if any, are there between the Act's system of private incentives to deposit and register, and the public welfare functions served by deposit and registration? The public purpose of deposit is to supply the Library of Congress' collection of works published in the United States. The public purpose of registration is to provide a paper record enabling title to copyright to be searched so that licenses and assignments can be negotiated.

9. The outlines of the Register's authority over applications for copyright have been sketched in several judicial decisions and opinions of the Attorney General. Bouvé v. 20th Century Fox Film Corp., 122 F.2d 51, 50 U.S.P.Q. 338 (D.C.Cir. 1941) authoritatively described the Register's role: "It seems obvious . . . that the Act establishes a wide range of selection within which discretion must be exercised by the Register in determining what he has no power to accept. The formula which he must apply is a more diffi-

cult one than that of the Recorder of Deeds, upon which appellee relies by way of analogy. Nor would there seem to be any doubt that
the Register may refuse to issue a certificate of registration until the
required fee is paid, and until other formal requisites of the Act have
been satisfied." 122 F.2d 51, 53–54. Even amicus curiae concedes
that the Register may properly refuse to accept for deposit and registration 'objects not entitled to protection under the law.' " 122 F.
2d 51, 53. Section 410(a) and (b) confirms this general view of the
Register's authority.

Under the 1909 Act, a copyright owner could not bring an infringement action until the claim to copyright had been registered.
If the Register refused registration, an infringement suit had to await
the copyright owner's success in a direct action against the Register.
Vacheron & Constantin-Le Coultre Watches, Inc. v. Benrus Watch
Co., 260 F.2d 637, 119 U.S.P.Q. 189 (2d Cir. 1958). Section 411(a) of
the present Act reverses the *Vacheron* rule, allowing the applicant to
institute an infringement action if the "deposit, application and fee
required for registration have been delivered to the Copyright Office
in proper form and registration has been refused." The copyright
owner must give notice of the action and a copy of the complaint to
the Register, who is then allowed to intervene.

Copyright owners, particularly in fast-paced industries like newspaper and periodical publication, sometimes need an injunction within
days of publication and cannot abide the delay that the registration
process entails. Does section 411(a) allow them to bring an infringement action notwithstanding the absence of registration? Compare
sections 410(d) and 411(b).

2. ORIGINALITY

SHELDON v. METRO-GOLDWYN PICTURES CORP., 81 F.2d
49, 28 U.S.P.Q. 330 (2d Cir.), cert. denied 298 U.S. 669, 56 S.Ct. 835,
80 L.Ed. 1392 (1936), L. HAND, J.: We are to remember that it
makes no difference how far the play was anticipated by works in the
public demesne which the plaintiffs did not use. The defendants appear not to recognize this, for they have filled the record with earlier
instances of the same dramatic incidents and devices, as though, like
a patent, a copyrighted work must be not only original, but new.
That is not however the law as is obvious in the case of maps or com-
pendia, where later works will necessarily be anticipated. At times,
in discussing how much of the substance of a play the copyright protects, courts have indeed used language which seems to give countenance to the notion that, if a plot were old, it could not be copyrighted. But we understand by this no more than that in its broader outline a plot is never copyrightable, for it is plain beyond peradventure
that anticipation as such cannot invalidate a copyright. Borrowed
the work must indeed not be, for a plagiarist is not himself pro tanto
an "author"; but if by some magic a man who had never known it

were to compose anew Keats's Ode on a Grecian Urn, he would be an "author," and, if he copyrighted it, others might not copy that poem, though they might of course copy Keats's. Bleistein v. Donaldson Lithographing Co., 188 U.S. 239, 249, 23 S.Ct. 298, 47 L.Ed. 460. But though a copyright is for this reason less vulnerable than a patent, the owner's protection is more limited, for just as he is no less an "author" because others have preceded him, so another who follows him, is not a tort-feasor unless he pirates his work. If the copyrighted work is therefore original, the public demesne is important only on the issue of infringement; that is, so far as it may break the force of the inference to be drawn from likenesses between the work and the putative piracy. If the defendant has had access to other material which would have served him as well, his disclaimer becomes more plausible.

BLEISTEIN v. DONALDSON LITHOGRAPHING CO.

Supreme Court of the United States, 1903.
188 U.S. 239, 23 S.Ct. 298, 47 L.Ed. 460.

Mr. Justice HOLMES delivered the opinion of the court.

This case comes here from the United States Circuit Court of Appeals for the Sixth Circuit by writ of error. It is an action brought by the plaintiffs in error to recover the penalties prescribed for infringements of copyrights. The alleged infringements consisted in the copying in reduced form of three chromolithographs prepared by employes of the plaintiffs for advertisements of a circus owned by one Wallace. Each of the three contained a portrait of Wallace in the corner and lettering bearing some slight relation to the scheme of decoration, indicating the subject of the design and the fact that the reality was to be seen at the circus. One of the designs was of an ordinary ballet, one of a number of men and women, described as the Stirk family, performing on bicycles, and one of groups of men and women whitened to represent statues. The Circuit Court directed a verdict for the defendant on the ground that the chromolithographs were not within the protection of the copyright law, and this ruling was sustained by the Circuit Court of Appeals. Courier Lithographing Co. v. Donaldson Lithographing Co., 104 Fed.Rep. 993.

There was evidence warranting the inference that the designs belonged to the plaintiffs, they having been produced by persons employed and paid by the plaintiffs in their establishment to make those very things. It fairly might be found also that the copyrights were taken out in the proper names. One of them was taken out in the name of the Courier Company and the other two in the names of the Courier Lithographing Company. The former was the name of an unincorporated joint stock association formed under the laws of New York, Laws of 1894, c. 235, and made up of the plaintiffs, the other a trade variant on that name.

Finally, there was evidence that the pictures were copyrighted before publication. There may be a question whether the use by the

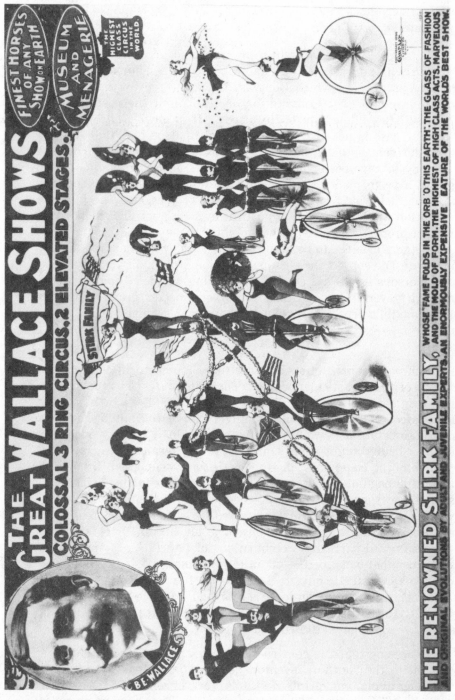

Poster in Bleistein v. Donaldson Lithographing Co.

defendant for Wallace was not lawful within the terms of the contract with Wallace, or a more general one as to what rights the plaintiffs reserved. But we cannot pass upon these questions as matter of law; they will be for the jury when the case is tried again, and therefore we come at once to the ground of decision in the courts below. That ground was not found in any variance between pleading and proof, such as was put forward in argument, but in the nature and purpose of the designs.

We shall do no more than mention the suggestion that painting and engraving unless for a mechanical end are not among the useful arts, the progress of which Congress is empowered by the Constitution to promote. The Constitution does not limit the useful to that which satisfies immediate bodily needs. It is obvious also that the plaintiffs' case is not affected by the fact, if it be one, that the pictures represent actual groups—visible things. They seem from the testimony to have been composed from hints or description, not from sight of a performance. But even if they had been drawn from the life, that fact would not deprive them of protection. The opposite proposition would mean that a portrait by Velasquez or Whistler was common property because others might try their hand on the same face. Others are free to copy the original. They are not free to copy the copy. The copy is the personal reaction of an individual upon nature. Personality always contains something unique. It expresses its singularity even in handwriting, and a very modest grade of art has in it something irreducible, which is one man's alone. That something he may copyright unless there is a restriction in the words of the act.

If there is a restriction it is not to be found in the limited pretensions of these particular works. The least pretentious picture has more originality in it than directories and the like, which may be copyrighted. The amount of training required for humbler efforts than those before us is well indicated by Ruskin. "If any young person, after being taught what is, in polite circles, called 'drawing,' will try to copy the commonest piece of real *work*,—suppose a lithograph on the title page of a new opera air, or a woodcut in the cheapest illustrated newspaper of the day—they will find themselves entirely beaten." Elements of Drawing, 1st ed. 3. There is no reason to doubt that these prints in their *ensemble* and in all their details, in their design and particular combinations of figures, lines and colors, are the original work of the plaintiffs' designer. If it be necessary, there is express testimony to that effect. It would be pressing the defendant's right to the verge, if not beyond, to leave the question of originality to the jury upon the evidence in this case, as was done in Hegeman v. Springer, 110 Fed.Rep. 374.

We assume that the construction of Rev.Stat. § 4952, allowing a copyright to the "author, inventor, designer, or proprietor   .   .   . of any engraving, cut, print   .   .   . [or] chromo" is affected by the act of 1874, c. 301, § 3, 18 Stat. 78, 79. That section provides that "in the construction of this act the words 'engraving,' 'cut' and 'print' shall be applied only to pictorial illustrations or works connected with the fine arts." We see no reason for taking the words "connected with the fine arts" as qualifying anything except the word "works," but it would not change our decision if we should assume further that they also qualified "pictorial illustrations," as the defendant contends.

These chromolithographs are "pictorial illustrations." The word "illustrations" does not mean that they must illustrate the text of a book, and that the etchings of Rembrandt or Steinla's engraving of the Madonna di San Sisto could not be protected to-day if any man were able to produce them. Again, the act however construed, does not mean that ordinary posters are not good enough to be considered within its scope. The antithesis to "illustrations or works connected with the fine arts" is not works of little merit or of humble degree, or illustrations addressed to the less educated classes; it is "prints or labels designed to be used for any other articles of manufacture." Certainly works are not the less connected with the fine arts because their pictorial quality attracts the crowd and therefore gives them a real use—if use means to increase trade and to help to make money. A picture is none the less a picture and none the less a subject of copyright that it is used for an advertisement. And if pictures may be used to advertise soap, or the theatre, or monthly magazines, as they are, they may be used to advertise a circus. Of course, the ballet is as legitimate a subject for illustration as any other. A rule cannot be laid down that would excommunicate the paintings of Degas.

Finally, the special adaptation of these pictures to the advertisement of the Wallace shows does not prevent a copyright. That may be a circumstance for the jury to consider in determining the extent of Mr. Wallace's rights, but it is not a bar. Moreover, on the evidence, such prints are used by less pretentious exhibitions when those for whom they were prepared have given them up.

It would be a dangerous undertaking for persons trained only to the law to constitute themselves final judges of the worth of pictorial illustrations, outside of the narrowest and most obvious limits. At the one extreme some works of genius would be sure to miss appreciation. Their very novelty would make them repulsive until the public had learned the new language in which their author spoke. It may be more than doubted, for instance, whether the etchings of Goya or the paintings of Manet would have been sure of protection when seen for the first time. At the other end, copyright would be denied to pictures which appealed to a public less educated than the judge. Yet if they command the interest of any public, they have a commercial value—it would be bold to say that they have not an aesthetic and educational value—and the taste of any public is not to be treated with contempt. It is an ultimate fact for the moment, whatever may be our hopes for a change. That these pictures had their worth and their success is sufficiently shown by the desire to reproduce them without regard to the plaintiffs' rights. We are of opinion that there was evidence that the plaintiffs have rights entitled to the protection of the law.

The judgment of the Circuit Court of Appeals is reversed; the judgment of the Circuit Court is also reversed and the cause remanded to that court with directions to set aside the verdict and grant a new trial.

Mr. Justice HARLAN, with whom concurred Mr. Justice McKENNA, dissenting.

Judges Lurton, Day and Severens, of the Circuit Court of Appeals, concurred in affirming the judgment of the District Court. Their views were thus expressed in an opinion delivered by Judge Lurton: "What we hold is this: That if a chromo, lithograph, or other print, engraving, or picture has no other use than that of a mere advertisement, and no value aside from this function, it would not be promotive of the useful arts, within the meaning of the constitutional provision, to protect the 'author' in the exclusive use thereof, and the copyright statute should not be construed as including such a publication, if any other construction is admissible. If a mere label simply designating or describing an article to which it is attached, and which has no value separated from the article, does not come within the constitutional clause upon the subject of copyright, it must follow that a pictorial illustration designed and useful only as an advertisement, and having no intrinsic value other than its function as an advertisement, must be equally without the obvious meaning of the Constitution. It must have some connection with the fine arts to give it intrinsic value, and that it shall have is the meaning which we attach to the act of June 18, 1874, amending the provisions of the copyright law. We are unable to discover anything useful or meritorious in the design copyrighted by the plaintiffs in error other than as an advertisement of acts to be done or exhibited to the public in Wallace's show. No evidence, aside from the deductions which are to be drawn from the prints themselves, was offered to show that these designs had any original artistic qualities. The jury could not reasonably have found merit or value aside from the purely business object of advertising a show, and the instruction to find for the defendant was not error. Many other points have been urged as justifying the result reached in the court below. We find it unnecessary to express any opinion upon them, in view of the conclusion already announced. The judgment must be affirmed." Courier Lithographing Co. v. Donaldson Lithographing Co., 104 Fed.Rep. 993, 996.

I entirely concur in these views, and therefore dissent from the opinion and judgment of this court. The clause of the Constitution giving Congress power to promote the progress of science and useful arts, by securing for limited terms to authors and inventors the exclusive right to their respective works and discoveries, does not, as I think, embrace a mere advertisement of a circus.

Mr. Justice McKENNA authorizes me to say that he also dissents.

DONALD v. ZACK MEYER'S T.V. SALES AND SERV.

United States Court of Appeals, Fifth Circuit, 1970.
426 F.2d 1027, 165 U.S.P.Q. 751, cert. denied 400 U.S. 992, 91
S.Ct. 459, 27 L.Ed.2d 441.

GOLDBERG, Circuit Judge.

In this infringement suit a maker of business forms seeks copyright protection for a common legal form. The characters in this drama are O. W. Donald, the copyright claimant; Moore Business Forms, Inc., the alleged infringer; and Zack Meyer's T.V. Sales and Service, the innocent bystander. Act I of this play ended when the trial court found for Donald. We rewrite the script and reverse.

In 1961 Donald registered with the copyright office the following paragraph:

"Agreement"

"For value received, the undersigned jointly and severally promise to pay to the Dealer, or order, the unpaid balance shown on this invoice according to the agreed terms. Title to said Chattel, described hereon by model, make and serial number, is hereby retained, or transferred to Dealer until Customer has paid in cash all amounts owing said Dealer. Customer shall not misuse, secrete, sell, encumber, remove or otherwise dispose of or lose possession of said Chattel. There is no outstanding lien, mortgage, or other encumbrance against said Chattel. Should Customer fail to pay its indebtedness when due, or breach this contract, the entire unpaid balance shall at once become due and payable, and Dealer may without notice or demand, by process of law, or otherwise, take possession of said Chattel wherever located and retain all monies paid thereon for use of said Chattel. This Agreement may be assigned."

This language, known as the "Agreement," was printed at the bottom of standard invoice forms which Donald printed and sold to television dealers and repairmen. Moore began using this language on its forms when one of its customers ordered a set of invoices and specifically requested that this language be included on the forms. The customer apparently had clipped the requested language from a form prepared by Donald. Subsequently, when Zack Meyer ordered invoice forms from Moore, Moore copied the language that its previous customer had requested.

Upon discovering Zack Meyer's forms, Donald brought suit against Moore and Zack Meyer, claiming that their use of the language contained in the "Agreement" infringed Donald's copyright. The trial court, while expressing doubt concerning the originality of the "Agreement," found that Donald had a valid copyright on the language used by Moore and that Moore had infringed Donald's copyright by printing and selling the offending forms. The court enjoined Moore from any future infringement and assessed the costs of suit against Moore as required by 17 U.S.C.A. § 116. Finding that Zack

Meyer had nothing whatever to do with the selection of language in the forms supplied by Moore, the court held that Zack Meyer was not liable for any copyright infringement and had been unnecessarily joined as a party defendant by Donald. Zack Meyer's counsel fees were divided equally between Moore and Donald.

Moore has appealed from the decision of the trial court, claiming that Donald's copyright is invalid for lack of originality. We agree.

It is too plain to be denied that the "Agreement" is nothing more than an ordinary conditional sales contract or chattel mortgage agreement, an instrument familiar to even the most inexperienced legal practitioner. It is the type of contract which has been published in numerous form books, many of which are themselves copyrighted.

Plaintiff, a non-lawyer who stated that he studied law for approximately one year, has denied that he used these prior works in preparing the "Agreement." However, considering the technical difficulties involved in drafting such a form, plaintiff's limited legal education, and his obvious access to and knowledge of these forms from his uncompleted legal studies, we have no doubt that plaintiff either consciously or unconsciously availed himself of these prior works while drafting the "Agreement." Moreover, the striking similarity in arrangement, order, and wording between plaintiff's "Agreement" and the standard forms is sufficient to compel a finding that plaintiff used these earlier works.

Neither the existence of these earlier forms nor Donald's use of them, however, necessarily renders his paragraph ineligible for copyright protection. It is settled law that to obtain a valid copyright, as distinguished from a patent, the applicant need not show that the material in question is unique or novel; it need only be original. Thus a work may be protected by copyright even though it is based on a prior copyrighted work or something already in the public domain if the author, through his skill and effort, has contributed a distinguishable variation from the older works. In such a case, of course, only those parts which are new are protected by the new copyright.

In determining the amount of originality required it is frequently stated that the standards are minimal and that in copyright law "originality means little more than a prohibition against copying." Gelles-Widmer Co. v. Milton Bradley Co., [313 F.2d 143]. Nevertheless, something more than merely refraining from outright copying is required before a new variation on an old work has sufficient originality to be copyrightable. The author must add "some substantial not merely trivial originality." Chamberlin v. Uris Sales Corp., 2 Cir. 1945, 150 F.2d 512, 513, 65 U.S.P.Q. 544, 545; the variation must be meaningful and must result from original creative work on the author's part. Amsterdam v. Triangle Publications, Inc., 3 Cir. 1951, 189 F.2d 104, 89 U.S.P.Q. 468; Smith v. George E. Muehlebach Brewing Co., W.D.Mo.1956, 140 F.Supp. 729, 110 U.S.P.Q. 177. As the court said in Smith,

" 'Originality' in the above context means that the material added to what is in the public domain, must have aspects of 'novelty' and be something more than a trivial addition or variation. If what is added does not itself give some value to a public domain composition, or serve some purpose other than to merely emphasize what is present and subsisting in the public domain, it is not entitled to copyright." 140 F.Supp. at 731, 110 U.S.P.Q. at 178.

In the case before us we search in vain for the requisite originality in plaintiff's "Agreement." The "Agreement" contains nothing of substance which resulted from Donald's creative work. The order and arrangement of the subject matter in the "Agreement" are identical with several forms suggested in prior works. The word arrangement used, while not identical, is at most only a paraphrase of various portions of earlier forms, and in copyright law paraphrasing is equivalent to outright copying. The plaintiff did no original legal research which resulted in a significant addition to the standard conditional sales contract or chattel mortgage forms; he merely made trivial word changes by combining various forms and servilely imitating the already stereotyped language found therein. In fact it may be fairly assumed that such variations in language as did occur in plaintiff's "Agreement" were deliberately insignificant, for he plainly wanted a valid conditional sales contract or chattel mortgage, and validity was an attribute which the earlier forms had been proved through use to have.

In Amsterdam v. Triangle Publications, Inc., supra, the Third Circuit faced a claim to copyright protection in a similar situation. The plaintiff in that case had used several existing maps but little independent original research of his own to prepare a map upon which he claimed a copyright. In denying his map copyright protection from a claimed infringement, the court, adopting the language of the trial court, said:

"To make his map, the plaintiff had to determine only what information he was going to use from other maps, the emphasis to be given to that information and the coloring scheme and symbols he was going to use. When he finished, his map by comparison was a new map that contained some information that was not on any one of his base maps but was collectively on all of these maps.

"Is this exercise of judgment and discretion by the plaintiff the type of original work that is intended to be protected by the Copyright Act? I think not.

.   .   .

"The presentation of ideas in the form of books, movies, music and other similar creative work is protected by the Copyright Act. However, the presentation of information available to everybody, such as is found on maps, is protected only when the publisher of the map in question obtains originally some of that information by the sweat of his own brow. Almost anybody could combine the information from several maps onto one map, but not everybody can go out and get that information originally and then transcribe it into a map.

"The plaintiff's reputation as a qualified map maker cannot make copyrightable maps for him. He, or his agents, must first do some original work, get more than an infinitesimal amount of original information. With no reflection whatsoever upon the plaintiff's ability as a map maker or upon other maps published and copyrighted by the plaintiff, it seems to me that the plaintiff's map entitled 'Map of Delaware County, Pa.' is, for lack or (sic) original work, not subject to copyright." 189 F.2d at 106, 89 U.S.P.Q. at 469.

In the case before us Donald has contributed nothing more than the map maker in Amsterdam. While the "Agreement" is not identical to any single existing form, the substance of each sentence can be found in an earlier form. Thus, like the map in Amsterdam, Donald's form is nothing more than a mosaic of the existing forms, with no original piece added. The Copyright Act was not designed to protect such neglible efforts. We reward creativity and originality with a copyright but we do not accord copyright protection to a mere copycat. As one noted authority has observed, "to make the copyright turnstile revolve, the author should have to deposit more than a penny in the box." B. Kaplan, An Unhurried View of Copyright 46 (1966). In our case not even the proverbial penny has been placed in the box. Indeed the box is virtually empty. We hold, therefore, that Donald's copyright is invalid for lack of originality. Having concluded that Donald's "Agreement" was not subject to copyright, we think it goes without saying that Moore's use of the form language was not an infringement.

The only remaining questions concern the assessment of costs and attorney's fees. The trial court assessed the costs of suit against the losing party, Moore, as required by 17 U.S.C.A. § 116. Since we have reversed the trial court's determination on the merits, Donald, the losing party, must pay the costs as required by statute. An award of attorneys' fees is discretionary under § 116, and the trial court exercised this discretion by directing that Donald and Moore pay their own counsel fees. We see no reason to disturb this determination. The counsel fees incurred by Zack Meyer were divided by the trial court equally between Donald and Moore. We think, however, that the entire amount of this expense must be assessed against Donald. Moore has already been put to the expense of defending an infringement suit against an invalid copyright claim. It was Donald who unnecessarily joined Zack Meyer as a party defendant, and it is Donald who should bear the expense for this error.

Reversed.

GORMAN, COPYRIGHT PROTECTION FOR THE COLLEC-
TION AND REPRESENTATION OF FACTS, 76 Harv.L.Rev. 1569–
1571 (1963).* In literary or artistic works, the three components of
the intellectual product—the ideas, their patterning, and their ultimate
expression—are generally all originated by the author. While the
author's broad ideas must be left in the public domain free for all to
use, his patterning of those ideas and mode of expression are copyrightable. As distinguished from literary or artistic works, there is a class
of publication which involves only the gathering of facts or their representation in language or picture. Included in that class—which will be
denoted "fact works"—are maps, news and historical accounts, directories, advertising art, photographs, and a closely related type of production, legal and business forms. In these works the author's raw materials are objective data, and his unique contribution is to gather these
facts and to express them in language or visual images so ordered as to
be intelligible and useful to others. The pattern and expression are basically mechanical and do not reflect the personality of the author. In
maps, for example, they are lines and shapes the relations of which
are determined by geographical configuration; in directories, they
are terse entries simply organized. What the copyright monopoly
here protects is not a product whose social value is its mark of personality or individuality, but the effort, time, expense, and, in certain
cases, the skill employed in performing a task which does not require
special intellectual competence.

Despite the significant difference between the elements protected
in fact works and in creative works, courts have nonetheless used the
same terms and same tools of analysis in dealing with both types of
copyright. Judicial practice in this field has been characterized by
opinions which fail to evince a conscious appreciation of the broad
policies of benefit to the author and the public which underlie the
copyright monopoly and which vary with different types of intellectual enterprise. This article seeks to clarify the differences between
the two broad classes of copyrightable works, as well as distinctions
between the various types of fact works, and to determine how these
differences affect the application of our copyright law.

At the outset, however, it must be recognized that the law of
copyright, which avowedly protects expression only, may not be the
ideal vehicle for the protection of fact works, the value of which is
generally attributable to the labor they embody rather than their
mode of expression. Where it is clear that it is labor, effort, and expense that is sought to be protected, the most apt body of protective
principles might be found in that branch of the law of unfair competition dealing with misappropriation. But this is a relatively new and
difficult area of the law, which the courts approach but gingerly.
They tend to turn first to copyright law, on which this article focuses, and apply those well-defined principles whenever possible. There

* Copyright © 1963 by The Harvard Law
Review Association.

is nothing improper about this tactic because the basic goal of both
the law of copyright and the law of unfair competition is the protection of intellectual endeavor; the former branch of law is designed
merely to protect expression, while the latter is designed directly to
protect the business advantage derived from that intellectual endeav-
or. Some overlap between the law of copyright and of unfair competition must therefore be expected; the doctrine of fair use is the perfect example. The only complaint that might be leveled at the
courts is their occasional use of traditional copyright language and
concepts in a distorted manner so as to regulate a class of intellectual
enterprise which is appropriate for regulation only by unfair competition principles, if at all.

NOTES

1. Does *Zack Meyer's* follow the originality test announced in
Bleistein? The test that Learned Hand propounded in *Sheldon*?
Does *Bleistein* square with the *Sheldon* test? It is some measure of
the *Sheldon* test that, in a long career deciding copyright cases, Judge
Hand never once found that a work was insufficiently original to
qualify for copyright protection.[n]

Consider the result that application of the *Sheldon*, *Bleistein* and
Zack Meyer's tests would produce in the following case. Plaintiff,
who executed a scaled-down reproduction of Rodin's "Hand of God"
that is identical to the Rodin piece in all respects save size and configuration of base, now seeks to enjoin defendant from producing and
distributing exact copies of its reproduction. Defendant answers that
because plaintiff admittedly copied the Rodin work, which is in the
public domain, the reproduction necessarily fails the originality test.
In Alva Studios, Inc. v. Winninger, 177 F.Supp. 265, 123 U.S.P.Q. 487
(S.D.N.Y.1959), the court held plaintiff's reproduction to be original
in light of the "great skill and originality" required to "produce a
scale reduction of a great work with exactitude." 177 F.Supp. 265,
267.

Compare L. Batlin & Son, Inc. v. Snyder, 536 F.2d 486, 189 U.S.
P.Q. 753 (2d Cir. 1976), cert. denied 429 U.S. 857, 97 S.Ct. 156, 50 L.
Ed.2d 135, 191 U.S.P.Q. 588, in which a plastic model of an antique
cast iron "Uncle Sam" bank was held to be unoriginal. The plastic
model differed from the prototype in size and details. Among other
differences, "the carpetbag shape of the plastic bank is smooth, the
iron bank rough; the metal bank bag is fatter at its base; the eagle
on the front of the platform in the metal bank is holding arrows in
his talons while in the plastic bank he clutches leaves." 536 F.2d
486, 489. In the court's judgment, the "complexity and exactitude
. . . involved [in Alva v. Winninger] distinguishes that case amply from the one at bar." 536 F.2d 486, 491–492. From this, the
court easily turned the proof of differences between the plastic model

n. I am grateful to Professor Douglas
Baird, of the University of Chicago
Law School, for this observation,
made in his unpublished study, *The
Copyright Decisions of Learned
Hand.*

and the cast iron prototype *against* the copyright claimant: "[t]hus concededly the plastic version is not, and was scarcely meticulously produced to be, an exactly faithful reproduction." 536 F.2d 486, 492.

Are the results in *Alva* and *Batlin* just the opposite of what they should be? The copyright claimant in *Alva* presumably invested more painstaking effort than the copyright claimant in *Batlin*. Is the purpose of copyright to induce investment in the production of works that exactly copy public domain works, or production of works that embody expressive differences?

What are the "narrowest and most obvious limits," referred to in *Bleistein*, within which courts may judge a work's relative artistic worth? To put the question in the terms of the Justice Holmes' reasoning, at what point do judgments on artistic worth rendered by persons trained only to the law—or by anyone, for that matter— cease to be "a dangerous undertaking"?

What support is there in copyright principle for Benjamin Kaplan's suggestion, alluded to in *Zack Meyer's*, that "to make the copyright turnstile revolve, the author should have to deposit more than a penny in the box"? 462 F.2d 1026, 1031. Is there behind all of these originality cases a practical concern that to allow copyright for even the most meager efforts will enable greedy proprietors to stifle competition through the threat of lawsuits?

2. *"Novelty" and "Originality."* Novelty has two uses in the determination of originality, both sharply limited. The first use of novelty is properly made in cases in which plaintiff contends that he has not copied from other sources. Even if his work, like the work of Judge Hand's hypothetical poet in *Sheldon*, exactly replicates a prior work, he will be entitled to copyright if he can show that he did not copy from the prior work. The improbability that exact replication will occur absent copying creates a practically irrebuttable presumption that the copyright claimant copied from the prior source. Novelty in these cases enables proof through inference that the claimant did not draw his work from prior sources.

Alfred Bell & Co. v. Catalda Fine Arts, Inc., 191 F.2d 99, 90 U.S. P.Q. 153 (2d Cir. 1951), is the kind of case in which the second use of novelty is properly made. There the originality of plaintiff's mezzotint engravings of paintings by old masters was upheld on the ground that "[t]here is evidence that they were not intended to and did not, imitate the paintings they reproduced. But even if their substantial departures from the paintings were inadvertent, the copyrights would be valid. A copyist's bad eyesight or defective musculature, or a shock caused by a clap of thunder, may yield sufficiently distinguishable variations. Having hit upon such a variation unintentionally, the 'author' may adopt it as his and copyright it." 191 F.2d 99, 104–105. In cases like this, in which copying is either admitted or, as in Hand's Keats example, is irrebuttably self-evident, the court looks for new matter, for some variation from previous works, not to break the inference of copying, for copying is assumed, but rather to find some copyrightable—uncopied—component in claimant's work.

Should novelty enjoy even this limited role? Copyright law possesses none of the search mechanisms for determining novelty that have grown up around patent law's novelty and nonobviousness requirements. The few recorded and largely vain efforts at introducing prior art on the issue of copyright novelty only dramatize copyright law's incapacity to measure novelty systematically. See for example Hollywood Jewelry Mfg. Co. v. Dushkin, 136 F.Supp. 738, 107 U.S. P.Q. 354 (S.D.N.Y.1955) (introduction of expired design patents to rebut the originality of plaintiff's copyrighted jewelry).

The point was apparently lost on Justice Douglas who, dissenting from the Court's denial of certiorari in Lee v. Runge, 404 U.S. 887, 92 S.Ct. 197, 30 L.Ed.2d 169, 171 U.S.P.Q. 322 (1971), suggested that the lower court had erred in holding that "[t]he standard of 'novelty' urged by appellants is applicable to patents, but not copyrights. The copyright standard is one of 'originality' . . . Runge v. Lee, 441 F.2d 579, 169 U.S.P.Q. 388 (9th Cir. 1971)." Giving a constitutional dimension to patent law's novelty requirement, Douglas argued that "no reason can be offered why we should depart from the plain import of this grant of congressional power and apply more lenient constitutional standards to copyrights than to patents. . . . To create a monopoly under the copyright power which would not be available under the patent power would be to betray the common birthright of all men at the altar of hollow formalisms." 404 U.S. 887, 890, 891, 92 S.Ct. 197, 199, 200.

3.   No serious student of copyright law can afford to miss reading the entire of Professor Gorman's article excerpted above. Assuming that there is a "difference between the elements protected in fact works and in creative works," does it necessarily follow that different analytical tools are required for the administration of each type? Is the assumed difference one of kind or degree? Consider which of the following is a fact work and which a nonfact work: a map, a photograph, a trompe l'oeil painting, an impressionist painting, an abstract expressionist painting.

Treatment of maps has been the most problematic area, with Amsterdam v. Triangle Publications, Inc., 189 F.2d 104, 89 U.S.P.Q. 468 (3d Cir. 1951), relied on in *Zack Meyer's*, usually cast as the villain of the piece. There, plaintiff contended that its county map, consisting of information compiled at the expense of "considerable time and effort," and obtained almost exclusively "from maps already in existence, although none of this information had been published previously on any one map," was copyrightable and infringed by defendant's publication of a map of the county. Acknowledging defendant's concession that it had copied plaintiff's map, the court of appeals ruled that plaintiff's map was not sufficiently original to qualify for copyright protection. First "the location of county lines, township lines and municipal lines is information within the public domain, and is not copyrightable." Second, "the presentation of information available to everybody, such as is found on maps, is protected only when the publisher of the map in question obtains originally some of that information by the sweat of his own brow. . . . He, or his agents, must first do some original work, get more than an infinitesimal amount of original information." 189 F.2d 104, 106.

Whicher, Originality, Cartography and Copyright, 38 N.Y.U.L. Rev. 280 (1963) traces *Amsterdam's* first, "public domain," point to a line of careless dicta initiated by Andrews v. Guenther Pub. Co., 60 F.2d 555 (S.D.N.Y.1932). According to Whicher, the earlier, authoritative opinions of Story and Hand refute the point entirely. On the second, "sweat of the brow" point, Professor Gorman notes that "It is no doubt true that most of the early cases dealing with map copyright referred to the requirement of original effort in exploring, surveying, making inquiries, and drafting the map solely on the basis of one's own investigations." But, he points out, "it is essential to realize that these courts were not speaking of the requisites to procuring copyright; their language was not meant to be descriptive of the sort of efforts that would achieve the minimum 'originality' to be protected by law. The courts were merely stating that the defendant in the cases before them had not engaged in enough original work to prevent a finding of infringement. This distinction between the effort necessary to avoid infringement and that necessary to procure copyright is indispensable to a clear understanding of copyright problems. It seems clear that the *Amsterdam* court either failed to draw the distinction or thought it immaterial." 76 Harv.L.Rev. 1572–73.

Although it has attracted a wide following, *Amsterdam* has also been rejected by some courts. In United States v. Hamilton, 583 F.2d 448, 200 U.S.P.Q. 14 (1978), the Ninth Circuit Court of Appeals turned to some earlier cases to reject *Amsterdam's* direct observation rule. In the court's view, "[e]xpression in cartography is not so different from other artistic forms seeking to touch upon external realities that unique rules are needed to judge whether the authorship is original." 583 F.2d 448, 451. Thus, the court ruled that "elements of compilation which amount to more than a matter of trivial selection may, either alone or when taken into consideration with direct observation, support a finding that a map is sufficiently original to merit copyright protection." 583 F.2d 448, 452.

4. The originality requirement closely parallels the rule that copyright protects expression, but not ideas. A journalist who writes a factual account of a well known event may be denied protection either on the ground that the idea is unprotectable or on the ground that his expression lacks originality. A court choosing the first ground would say that facts are like ideas and thus are unprotectable. A court choosing the second ground would concede the protectability of facts but conclude that the author's expression is so close to the facts themselves as to be unoriginal.

The originality requirement and the rule declining protection for ideas may also intersect and justify opposing results. If a researcher uncovers and reports a previously undisclosed historical fact, a court inclined to allow recovery can do so by pointing to the fact that the researcher's work was original—the product of some independent effort and not copied from any other written source. A court inclined against recovery can rely instead on the rule that ideas are unprotectable—no matter how new they are or how much effort was involved in unearthing them.

This interplay between the originality requirement and the idea-expression distinction is most evident in cases involving historical facts. In Hoehling v. Universal City Studios, 618 F.2d 972, 205 U.S. P.Q. 681 (2d Cir. 1980), the court rejected plaintiff's claim that defendants had unlawfully scavenged exhaustively researched information and original interpretations of fact from his book, *Who Destroyed the Hindenburg?*. The interpretation, "whether or not it originated with Mr. Hoehling, is not protected by his copyright and can be freely used by subsequent authors." As to the facts uncovered through Hoehling's research, these also were in the public domain. "Accordingly, there is little consolation in relying on cases in other circuits holding that the fruits of original research are copyrightable." 618 F.2d 972, 979.

One of the "rejected cases in other circuits" was Miller v. Universal City Studios, Inc., 460 F.Supp. 984, 200 U.S.P.Q. 232 (S.D.Fla. 1978). Plaintiff there claimed that defendant's television film infringed his journalistic account of a Florida kidnapping that had stirred national attention. The court upheld the jury verdict of more than $200,000, rejecting defendant's argument that the jury had improperly been instructed on the copyrightability of research. In the court's view, "the law is clear that research can be copyrightable." Drawing on cases that found the requisite originality in original research, the court used the fact of originality to sidestep the idea-expression issue: "The court views the labor and expense of the research involved in the obtaining of those uncopyrightable facts to be intellectually distinct from those facts and more similar to the expression of the facts than to the facts themselves." 460 F.Supp. 984, 987.

Can you find any flaw in the *Universal* court's reasoning? In the reasoning of the *Hoehling* court?

3.   STATUTORY SUBJECT MATTER

See Statute Supplement 17 U.S.C.A. §§ 101–105.

COPYRIGHT LAW REVISION, H.R.REP.NO.94–1476

94th Cong., 2d Sess. 51–57 (1976).

Section 102.   General Subject Matter of Copyright

"Original Works of Authorship"

The two fundamental criteria of copyright protection—originality and fixation in tangible form—are restated in the first sentence of this cornerstone provision. The phrase "original works of author-ship," which is purposely left undefined, is intended to incorporate without change the standard of originality established by the courts under the present copyright statute. This standard does not include requirements of novelty, ingenuity, or esthetic merit, and there is no intention to enlarge the standard of copyright protection to require them.

In using the phrase "original works of authorship," rather than "all the writings of an author" now in section 4 of the statute, the committee's purpose is to avoid exhausting the constitutional power of Congress to legislate in this field, and to eliminate the uncertain-ties arising from the latter phrase. Since the present statutory lan-guage is substantially the same as the empowering language of the Constitution, a recurring question has been whether the statutory and the constitutional provisions are coextensive. If so, the courts would be faced with the alternative of holding copyrightable some-thing that Congress clearly did not intend to protect, or of holding constitutionally incapable of copyright something that Congress might one day want to protect. To avoid these equally undesirable results, the courts have indicated that "all the writings of an author" under the present statute is narrower in scope than the "writings" of "authors" referred to in the Constitution. The bill avoids this dilem-ma by using a different phrase—"original works of authorship"—in characterizing the general subject matter of statutory copyright pro-tection.

The history of copyright law has been one of gradual expansion in the types of works accorded protection, and the subject matter af-fected by this expansion has fallen into two general categories. In the first, scientific discoveries and technological developments have made possible new forms of creative expression that never existed be-fore. In some of these cases the new expressive forms—electronic music, filmstrips, and computer programs, for example—could be re-garded as an extension of copyrightable subject matter Congress had already intended to protect, and were thus considered copyrightable from the outset without the need of new legislation. In other cases, such as photographs, sound recordings, and motion pictures, statutory enactment was deemed necessary to give them full recognition as copyrightable works.

Authors are continually finding new ways of expressing them-selves, but it is impossible to foresee the forms that these new expres-sive methods will take. The bill does not intend either to freeze the scope of copyrightable subject matter at the present stage of commu-nications technology or to allow unlimited expansion into areas com-pletely outside the present congressional intent. Section 102 implies neither that that subject matter is unlimited nor that new forms of expression within that general area of subject matter would neces-sarily be unprotected.

The historic expansion of copyright has also applied to forms of expression which, although in existence for generations or centuries, have only gradually come to be recognized as creative and worthy of protection. The first copyright statute in this country, enacted in 1790, designated only "maps, charts, and books"; major forms of expression such as music, drama, and works of art achieved specific statutory recognition only in later enactments. Although the coverage of the present statute is very broad, and would be broadened further by the explicit recognition of all forms of choreography, there are unquestionably other areas of existing subject matter that this bill does not propose to protect but that future Congresses may want to.

Fixation in Tangible Form.

As a basic condition of copyright protection, the bill perpetuates the existing requirement that a work be fixed in a "tangible medium of expression," and adds that this medium may be one "now known or later developed," and that the fixation is sufficient if the work "can be perceived, reproduced, or otherwise communicated, either directly or with the aid of a machine or device." This broad language is intended to avoid the artificial and largely unjustifiable distinctions, derived from cases such as White-Smith Publishing Co. v. Apollo Co., 209 U.S. 1 (1908), under which statutory copyrightability in certain cases has been made to depend upon the form or medium in which the work is fixed. Under the bill it makes no difference what the form, manner, or medium of fixation may be—whether it is in words, numbers, notes, sounds, pictures, or any other graphic or symbolic indicia, whether embodied in a physical object in written, printed, photographic, sculptural, punched, magnetic, or any other stable form, and whether it is capable of perception directly or by means of any machine or device "now known or later developed."

Under the bill, the concept of fixation is important since it not only determines whether the provisions of the statute apply to a work, but it also represents the dividing line between common law and statutory protection. As will be noted in more detail in connection with section 301, an unfixed work of authorship, such as an improvisation or an unrecorded choreographic work, performance, or broadcast, would continue to be subject to protection under State common law or statute, but would not be eligible for Federal statutory protection under section 102.

The bill seeks to resolve, through the definition of "fixation" in section 101, the status of live broadcasts—sports, news coverage, live performances of music, etc.—that are reaching the public in unfixed form but that are simultaneously being recorded. When a football game is being covered by four television cameras, with a director guiding the activities of the four cameramen and choosing which of their electronic images are sent out to the public and in what order, there is little doubt that what the cameramen and the director are doing constitutes "authorship." The further question to be considered is whether there has been a fixation. If the images and sounds to be broadcast are first recorded (on a video tape, film, etc.) and then transmitted, the recorded work would be considered a "motion picture" subject to statutory protection against unauthorized reproduction or retransmission of the broadcast. If the program content is transmitted live to the public while being recorded at the same time, the case would be treated the same; the copyright owner would not be forced to rely on common law rather than statutory rights in proceeding against an infringing user of the live broadcast.

Thus, assuming it is copyrightable—as a "motion picture" or "sound recording," for example—the content of a live transmission should be regarded as fixed and should be accorded statutory protection if it is being recorded simultaneously with its transmission. On the other hand, the definition of "fixation" would exclude from the concept purely evanescent or transient reproductions such as those projected briefly on a screen, shown electronically on a television or other cathode ray tube, or captured momentarily in the "memory" of a computer.

Under the first sentence of the definition of "fixed" in section 101, a work would be considered "fixed in a tangible medium of expression" if there has been an authorized embodiment in a copy or phonorecord and if that embodiment "is sufficiently permanent or stable" to permit the work "to be perceived, reproduced, or otherwise communicated for a period of more than transitory duration." The second sentence makes clear that, in the case of "a work consisting of sounds, images, or both, that are being transmitted," the work is regarded as "fixed" if a fixation is being made at the same time as the transmission.

Under this definition "copies" and "phonorecords" together will comprise all of the material objects in which copyrightable works are capable of being fixed. The definitions of these terms in section 101, together with their usage in section 102 and throughout the bill, reflect a fundamental distinction between the "original work" which is the product of "authorship" and the multitude of material objects in which it can be embodied. Thus, in the sense of the bill, a "book" is not a work of authorship, but is a particular kind of "copy." Instead, the author may write a "literary work," which in turn can be embodied in a wide range of "copies" and "phonorecords," including books, periodicals, computer punch cards, microfilm, tape recordings, and so forth. It is possible to have an "original work of authorship" without having a "copy" or "phonorecord" embodying it, and it is also possible to have a "copy" or "phonorecord" embodying something that does not qualify as an "original work of authorship." The two essential elements—original work and tangible object—must merge through fixation in order to produce subject matter copyrightable under the statute.

Categories of Copyrightable Works

The second sentence of section 102 lists seven broad categories which the concept of "works of authorship" is said to "include." The use of the word "include," as defined in section 101, makes clear that the listing is "illustrative and not limitative," and that the seven categories do not necessarily exhaust the scope of "original works of authorship" that the bill is intended to protect. Rather, the list sets out the general area of copyrightable subject matter, but with sufficient flexibility to free the courts from rigid or outmoded concepts of the scope of particular categories. The items are also overlapping in the sense that a work falling within one class may encompass works coming within some or all of the other categories. In the aggregate, the list covers all classes of works now specified in section 5 of title 17; in addition, it specifically enumerates "pantomimes and choreographic works".

Of the seven items listed, four are defined in section 101. The three undefined categories—"musical works," "dramatic works," and "pantomimes and choreographic works"—have fairly settled meanings. There is no need, for example, to specify the copyrightability of electronic or concrete music in the statute since the form of a work would no longer be of any importance, nor is it necessary to specify that "choreographic works" do not include social dance steps and simple routines.

The four items defined in section 101 are "literary works," "pictorial, graphic, and sculptural works," "motion pictures and audiovisual works", and "sound recordings." In each of these cases, definitions are needed not only because the meaning of the term itself is unsettled but also because the distinction between "work" and "material object" requires clarification. The term "literary works" does not connote any criterion of literary merit or qualitative value: it includes catalogs, directories, and similar factual reference, or instructional works and compilations of data. It also includes computer data bases, and computer programs to the extent that they incorporate authorship in the programmer's expression of original ideas, as distinguished from the ideas themselves.

Correspondingly, the definition of "pictorial, graphic, and sculptural works" carries with it no implied criterion of artistic taste, aesthetic value, or intrinsic quality. The term is intended to comprise not only "works of art" in the traditional sense but also works of graphic art and illustration, art reproductions, plans and drawings, photographs and reproductions of them, maps, charts, globes, and other cartographic works, works of these kinds intended for use in advertising and commerce, and works of "applied art." There is no intention whatever to narrow the scope of the subject matter now characterized in section 5(k) as "prints or labels used for articles of merchandise." However, since this terminology suggests the material object in which a work is embodied rather than the work itself, the bill does not mention this category separately.

In accordance with the Supreme Court's decision in Mazer v. Stein, 347 U.S. 201 (1954), works of "applied art" encompass all original pictorial, graphic, and sculptural works that are intended to be or have been embodied in useful articles, regardless of factors such as mass production, commercial exploitation, and the potential availability of design patent protection. The scope of exclusive rights in these works is given special treatment in section 113, to be discussed below.

The Committee has added language to the definition of "pictorial, graphic, and sculptural works" in an effort to make clearer the distinction between works of applied art protectable under the bill and industrial designs not subject to copyright protection. The declaration that "pictorial, graphic, and sculptural works" include "works of artistic craftsmanship insofar as their form but not their mechanical or utilitarian aspects are concerned" is classic language: it is drawn from Copyright Office regulations promulgated in the 1940's and expressly endorsed by the Supreme Court in the *Mazer* case.

The second part of the amendment states that "the design of a useful article .   .   .   shall be considered a pictorial, graphic, or sculptural work only if, and only to the extent that, such design incorporates pictorial, graphic, or sculptural features that can be identified separately from, and are capable of existing independently of, the utilitarian aspects of the article." A "useful article" is defined as "an article having an intrinsic utilitarian function that is not merely to portray the appearance of the article or to convey information." This part of the amendment is an adaptation of language added to the Copyright Office Regulations in the mid-1950's in an effort to implement the Supreme Court's decision in the *Mazer* case.

In adopting this amendatory language, the Committee is seeking to draw as clear a line as possible between copyrightable works of applied art and uncopyrighted works of industrial design. A two-dimensional painting, drawing, or graphic work is still capable of being identified as such when it is printed on or applied to utilitarian articles such as textile fabrics, wallpaper, containers, and the like. The same is true when a statue or carving is used to embellish an industrial product or, as in the *Mazer* case, is incorporated into a product without losing its ability to exist independently as a work of art. On the other hand, although the shape of an industrial product may be aesthetically satisfying and valuable, the Committee's intention is not to offer it copyright protection under the bill. .   .   .

Enactment of Public Law 92–140 in 1971 marked the first recognition in American copyright law of sound recordings as copyrightable works. As defined in section 101, copyrightable "sound recordings" are original works of authorship comprising an aggregate of musical, spoken, or other sounds that have been fixed in tangible form. The copyrightable work comprises the aggregation of sounds and not the tangible medium of fixation. Thus, "sound recordings" as copyrightable subject matter are distinguished from "phonorecords," the latter being physical objects in which sounds are fixed. They are also distinguished from any copyrighted literary, dramatic, or musical works that may be reproduced on a "phonorecord."

As a class of subject matter, sound recordings are clearly within the scope of the "writings of an author" capable of protection under the Constitution, and the extension of limited statutory protection to them was too long delayed. Aside from cases in which sounds are fixed by some purely mechanical means without originality of any kind, the copyright protection that would prevent the reproduction and distribution of unauthorized phonorecords of sound recordings is clearly justified.

The copyrightable elements in a sound recording will usually, though not always, involve "authorship" both on the part of the performers whose performance is captured and on the part of the record producer responsible for setting up the recording session, capturing and electronically processing the sounds, and compiling and editing them to make the final sound recording. There may, however, be cases where the record producer's contribution is so minimal that the performance is the only copyrightable element in the work, and there may be cases (for example, recordings of birdcalls, sounds of racing cars, et cetera) where only the record producer's contribution is copyrightable.

Sound tracks of motion pictures, long a nebulous area in American copyright law, are specifically included in the definition of "motion pictures," and excluded in the definition of "sound recordings." To be a "motion picture," as defined, requires three elements: (1) a series of images, (2) the capability of showing the images in certain successive order, and (3) an impression of motion when the images are thus shown. Coupled with the basic requirements of original authorship and fixation in tangible form, this definition encompasses a wide range of cinematographic works embodied in films, tapes, video disks, and other media. However, it would not include: (1) unauthorized fixations of live performances or telecasts, (2) live telecasts that are not fixed simultaneously with their transmission, or (3) filmstrips and slide sets which, although consisting of a series of images intended to be shown in succession, are not capable of conveying an impression of motion.

On the other hand, the bill equates audiovisual materials such as filmstrips, slide sets, and sets of transparencies with "motion pictures" rather than with "pictorial, graphic, and sculptural works." Their sequential showing is closer to a "performance" than to a "display," and the definition of "audiovisual works," which applies also to "motion pictures," embraces works consisting of a series of related images that are by their nature, intended for showing by means of projectors or other devices.

Nature of Copyright

Copyright does not preclude others from using the ideas or information revealed by the author's work. It pertains to the literary, musical, graphic, or artistic form in which the author expressed intellectual concepts. Section 102(b) makes clear that copyright protection does not extend to any idea, procedure, process, system, method of operation, concept, principle, or discovery, regardless of the form in which it is described, explained, illustrated, or embodied in such work.

Some concern has been expressed lest copyright in computer programs should extend protection to the methodology or processes adopted by the programmer, rather than merely to the "writing" expressing his ideas. Section 102(b) is intended, among other things, to make clear that the expression adopted by the programmer is the copyrightable element in a computer program, and that the actual processes or methods embodied in the program are not within the scope of the copyright law.

Section 102(b) in no way enlarges or contracts the scope of copyright protection under the present law. Its purpose is to restate, in the context of the new single Federal system of copyright, that the basic dichotomy between expression and idea remains unchanged.

MAZER v. STEIN

Supreme Court of the United States, 1954.
347 U.S. 201, 74 S.Ct. 460, 98 L.Ed. 630, 100 U.S.P.Q. 325.

Mr. Justice REED delivered the opinion of the Court.

This case involves the validity of copyrights obtained by respondents for statuettes of male and female dancing figures made of semivitreous china. The controversy centers around the fact that although copyrighted as "works of art," the statuettes were intended for use and used as bases for table lamps, with electric wiring, sockets and lamp shades attached.

Respondents are partners in the manufacture and sale of electric lamps. One of the respondents created original works of sculpture in the form of human figures by traditional clay-model technique. From this model, a production mold for casting copies was made. The resulting statuettes, without any lamp components added, were submitted by the respondents to the Copyright Office for registration as "works of art" or reproductions thereof under § 5(g) or § 5(h) of the copyright law, and certificates of registration issued. Sales (publication in accordance with the statute) as fully equipped lamps preceded the applications for copyright registration of the statuettes. Thereafter, the statuettes were sold in quantity throughout the country both as lamp bases and as statuettes. The sales in lamp form accounted for all but an insignificant portion of respondents' sales.

Petitioners are partners and, like respondents, make and sell lamps. Without authorization, they copied the statuettes, embodied them in lamps and sold them.

Statuette in Mazer v. Stein.

The instant case is one in a series of reported suits brought by respondents against various alleged infringers of the copyrights, all presenting the same or a similar question. Because of conflicting decisions, we granted certiorari. In the present case respondents sued petitioners for infringement in Maryland. Stein v. Mazer, 111 F. Supp. 359. Following the *Expert* decision and rejecting the reasoning of the District Court in the Rosenthal opinion, both referred to in the preceding note, the District Court dismissed the complaint. The Court of Appeals reversed and held the copyrights valid. Stein v. Mazer, 204 F.2d 472. It said: "A subsequent utilization of a work of art in an article of manufacture in no way affects the right of the copyright owner to be protected against infringement of the work of art itself." Id., at 477.

Petitioners, charged by the present complaint with infringement of respondents' copyrights of reproductions of their works of art, seek here a reversal of the Court of Appeals decree upholding the copyrights. Petitioners in their petition for certiorari present a single question:

"Can statuettes be protected in the United States by copyright when the copyright applicant intended primarily to use the statuettes in the form of lamp bases to be made and sold in quantity and carried the intentions into effect?

"Stripped down to its essentials, the question presented is: Can a lamp manufacturer copyright his lamp bases?"

The first paragraph accurately summarizes the issue. The last gives it a quirk that unjustifiably, we think, broadens the controversy. The case requires an answer, not as to a manufacturer's right to register a lamp base but as to an artist's right to copyright a work of art intended to be reproduced for lamp bases. As petitioners say in their brief, their contention "questions the validity of the copyright based upon the actions of the respondents." Petitioners question the validity of a copyright of a work of art for "mass" production. "Reproduction of a work of art" does not mean to them unlimited reproduction. Their position is that a copyright does not cover industrial reproduction of the protected article. Thus their reply brief states:

"When an artist becomes a manufacturer or a designer for a manufacturer he is subject to the limitations of design patents and deserves no more consideration than any other manufacturer or designer."

It is not the right to copyright an article that could have utility under §§ 5(g) and (h) that petitioners oppose. Their brief accepts the copyrightability of the great carved golden saltcellar of Cellini but adds:

"If, however, Cellini designed and manufactured this item in quantity so that the general public could have salt cellars, then an entirely different conclusion would be reached. In such case, the salt cellar becomes an article of manufacture having utility in addition to its ornamental value and would therefore have to be protected by design patent."

It is publication as a lamp and registration as a statue to gain a monopoly in manufacture that they assert is such a misuse of copyright as to make the registration invalid.

No unfair competition question is presented. The constitutional power of Congress to confer copyright protection on works of art or their reproductions is not questioned. Petitioners assume, as Congress has in its enactments and as do we, that the constitutional clause empowering legislation "To promote the Progress of Science and useful Arts, by securing for limited Times to Authors and Inventors the exclusive Right to their respective Writings and Discoveries," Art. I, § 8, cl. 8, includes within the term "Authors" the creator of a picture or a statue. The Court's consideration will be limited to the question presented by the petition for the writ of certiorari. In recent years the question as to utilitarian use of copyrighted articles has been much discussed.

In answering that issue, a review of the development of copyright coverage will make clear the purpose of the Congress in its copyright legislation. In 1790 the First Congress conferred a copyright on "authors of any map, chart, book or books already printed." Later, designing, engraving and etching were included; in 1831 musical compositions; dramatic compositions in 1856; and photographs and negatives thereof in 1865.

The Act of 1870 defined copyrightable subject matter as:
".   .   . any book, map, chart, dramatic or musical composition, engraving, cut, print, or photograph or negative thereof, or of a painting, drawing, chromo, *statue, statuary, and of models or designs intended to be perfected as works of the fine arts.*" (Emphasis supplied.)

The italicized part added three-dimensional works of art to what had been protected previously. In 1909 Congress again enlarged the scope of the copyright statute. The new Act provided in § 4:

"That the works for which copyright may be secured under this Act shall include all the writings of an author."

Some writers interpret this section as being coextensive with the constitutional grant, but the House Report, while inconclusive, indicates that it was "declaratory of existing law" only. Section 5 relating to classes of writings in 1909 read as shown in the margin with subsequent additions not material to this decision. Significant for our purposes was the deletion of the fine-arts clause of the 1870 Act. Verbal distinctions between purely aesthetic articles and useful works of art ended insofar as the statutory copyright language is concerned.

The practice of the Copyright Office, under the 1870 and 1874 Acts and before the 1909 Act, was to allow registration "as works of the fine arts" of articles of the same character as those of respondents now under challenge. Seven examples appear in the Government's brief amicus curiae. In 1910, interpreting the 1909 Act, the pertinent Copyright Regulations read as shown in the margin. Because, as explained by the Government, this regulation "made no reference to articles which might fairly be considered works of art although they might also serve a useful purpose," it was reworded in 1917 as shown below. The amicus brief gives sixty examples selected at five-year intervals, 1912–1952, said to be typical of registrations of works of art possessing utilitarian aspects. The current pertinent regulation, published in 37 C.F.R., 1949, § 202.8, reads thus:

> "*Works of art (Class G)—(a) In General.* This class includes works of artistic craftsmanship, in so far as their form but not their mechanical or utilitarian aspects are concerned, such as artistic jewelry, enamels, glassware, and tapestries, as well as all works belonging to the fine arts, such as paintings, drawings and sculpture. . . ."

So we have a contemporaneous and long-continued construction of the statutes by the agency charged to administer them that would allow the registration of such a statuette as is in question here.

This Court once essayed to fix the limits of the fine arts. That effort need not be appraised in relation to this copyright issue. It is clear Congress intended the scope of the copyright statute to include more than the traditional fine arts. Herbert Putnam, Esq., then Librarian of Congress and active in the movement to amend the copyright laws, told the joint meeting of the House and Senate Committees:

> "The term 'works of art' is deliberately intended as a broader specification than 'works of the fine arts' in the present statute with the idea that there is subject-matter (for instance, of applied design, not yet within the province of design patents), which may properly be entitled to protection under the copyright law."

The successive acts, the legislative history of the 1909 Act and the practice of the Copyright Office unite to show that "works of art" and "reproductions of works of art" are terms that were intended by Congress to include the authority to copyright these statuettes. Individual perception of the beautiful is too varied a power to permit a narrow or rigid concept of art. As a standard we can hardly do better than the words of the present Regulation, § 202.8 supra, naming the things that appertain to the arts. They must be original, that is, the author's tangible expression of his ideas. Such expression, whether meticulously delineating the model or mental image or conveying the meaning by modernistic form or color, is copyrightable. What cases there are confirm this coverage of the statute.

The conclusion that the statutes here in issue may be copyrighted goes far to solve the question whether their intended reproduction as lamp stands bars or invalidates their registration. This depends solely on statutory interpretation. Congress may after publication protect by copyright any writing of an author. Its statute creates the copyright. It did not exist at common law even though he had a property right in his unpublished work.

But petitioners assert that congressional enactment of the design patent laws should be interpreted as denying protection to artistic articles embodied or reproduced in manufactured articles. They say:

> "Fundamentally and historically, the Copyright Office is the repository of what each claimant considers to be a cultural treasure, whereas the Patent Office is the repository of what each applicant considers to be evidence of the advance in industrial and technological fields."

Their argument is that design patents require the critical examination given patents to protect the public against monopoly. Attention is called to Gorham Co. v. White, 14 Wall. 511, interpreting the design patent law of 1842, 5 Stat. 544, granting a patent to anyone who by "their own industry, genius, efforts, and expense, may have invented or produced any new and original design for a manufacture. . . ." A pattern for flat silver was there upheld. The intermediate and present law differs little. "Whoever invents any new, original and ornamental design for an article of manufacture may obtain a patent therefor, . . ." subject generally to the provisions concerning patents for invention. § 171, 66 Stat 805. As petitioner sees the effect of the design patent law:

> "If an industrial designer can not satisfy the novelty requirements of the design patent laws, then his design as used on articles of manufacture can be copied by anyone."

Petitioner has furnished the Court a booklet of numerous design patents for statuettes, bases for table lamps and similar articles for manufacture, quite indistinguishable in type from the copyrighted statuettes here in issue. Petitioner urges that overlapping of patent and copyright legislation so as to give an author or inventor a choice between patents and copyrights should not be permitted. We assume petitioner takes the position that protection for a statuette for industrial use can only be obtained by patent, if any protection can be given.

As we have held the statuettes here involved copyrightable, we need not decide the question of their patentability. Though other courts have passed upon the issue as to whether allowance by the election of the author or patentee of one bars a grant of the other, we do not. We do hold that the patentability of the statuettes, fitted as lamps or unfitted, does not bar copyright as works of art. Neither the Copyright Statute nor any other says that because a thing is patentable it may not be copyrighted. We should not so hold.

Unlike a patent, a copyright gives no exclusive right to the art disclosed; protection is given only to the expression of the idea—not the idea itself. Thus, in Baker v. Selden, 101 U.S. 99, 25 L.Ed. 841, the Court held that a copyrighted book on a peculiar system of book-keeping was not infringed by a similar book using a similar plan which achieved similar results where the alleged infringer made a different arrangement of the columns and used different headings. The distinction is illustrated in Fred Fisher, Inc. v. Dillingham, 298 F. 145, 151, when the court speaks of two men, each a perfectionist, independently making maps of the same territory. Though the maps are identical, each may obtain the exclusive right to make copies of his own particular map,. and yet neither will infringe the other's copyright. Likewise a copyrighted directory is not infringed by a similar directory which is the product of independent work. The copyright protects originality rather than novelty or invention—conferring only "the sole right of multiplying copies." Absent copying there can be no infringement of copyrights. Thus, respondents may not exclude others from using statuettes of human figures in table lamps; they may only prevent use of copies of their statuettes as such or as incorporated in some other article. Regulation § 202.8, supra, makes clear that artistic articles are protected in "form but not their mechanical or utilitarian aspects." See Stein v. Rosenthal, 103 F.Supp. 227, 231. The dichotomy of protection for the aesthetic is not beauty and utility but art for the copyright and the invention of original and ornamental design for design patents. We find nothing in the copyright statute to support the argument that the intended use or use in industry of an article eligible for copyright bars or invalidates its registration. We do not read such a limitation into the copyright law.

Nor do we think the subsequent registration of a work of art published as an element in a manufactured article, is a misuse of the copyright. This is not different from the registration of a statuette and its later embodiment in an industrial article.

"The copyright law, like the patent statutes, makes reward to the owner a secondary consideration." United States v. Paramount Pictures, 334 U.S. 131, 158, 68 S.Ct. 915, 929, 92 L.Ed. 1260. However, it is "intended definitely to grant valuable, enforceable rights to authors, publishers, etc., without burdensome requirements; 'to afford greater encouragement to the production of literary [or artistic] works of lasting benefit to the world.' " Washingtonian Co. v. Pearson, 306 U.S. 30, 36, 59 S.Ct. 397, 400, 83 L.Ed. 470.

The economic philosophy behind the clause empowering Congress to grant patents and copyrights is the conviction that encouragement of individual effort by personal gain is the best way to advance public welfare through the talents of authors and inventors in "Science and useful Arts." Sacrificial days devoted to such creative activities deserve rewards commensurate with the services rendered.

Affirmed.

Opinion of Mr. Justice DOUGLAS, in which Mr. Justice BLACK concurs.

An important constitutional question underlies this case—a question which was stirred on oral argument but not treated in the briefs. It is whether these statuettes of dancing figures may be copyrighted. Congress has provided that "works of art," "models or designs for works of art," and "reproductions of a work of art" may be copyrighted (17 U.S.C.A. § 5); and the Court holds that these statuettes are included in the words "works of art." But may statuettes be granted the monopoly of the copyright?   •

Article I, § 8 of the Constitution grants Congress the power "To promote the Progress of Science and useful Arts, by securing for limited Times to Authors .   .   .   the exclusive Right to their respective Writings. .   .   ." The power is thus circumscribed: it allows a monopoly to be granted only to "authors" for their "writings." Is a sculptor an "author" and is his statue a "writing" within the meaning of the Constitution? We have never decided the question.

Burrow-Giles Lithographic Co. v. Sarony, 111 U.S. 53, 4 S.Ct. 279, 28 L.Ed. 349, held that a photograph could be copyrighted.

Bleistein v. Donaldson Lithographing Co., 188 U.S. 239, 23 S.Ct. 298, 47 L.Ed. 460, held that chromolithographs to be used as advertisements for a circus were "pictorial illustrations" within the meaning of the copyright laws. Broad language was used in the latter case, ".   .   . a very modest grade of art has in it something irreducible, which is one man's alone. That something he may copyright unless there is a restriction in the words of the act." 188 U.S., at 250, 23 S.Ct. at page 300. But the constitutional range of the meaning of "writings" in the field of art was not an issue either in the Bleistein case nor in Woolworth Co. v. Contemporary Arts, 344 U.S. 228, 73 S.Ct. 222, 97 L.Ed. 276, recently here on a writ of certiorari limited to a question of damages.

At times the Court has on its own initiative considered and decided constitutional issues not raised, argued, or briefed by the parties. Such, for example, was the case of Continental Bank v. Rock Island R. Co., 294 U.S. 648, 667, 55 S.Ct. 595, 601, 79 L.Ed. 1110, in which the Court decided the constitutionality of § 77 of the Bankruptcy Act though the question was not noticed by any party. We could do the same here and decide the question here and now. This case, however, is not a pressing one, there being no urgency for a decision. Moreover, the constitutional materials are quite meager (see Fenning, The Origin of the Patent and Copyright Clause of the Constitution, 17 Geo.L.J. 109 [1929]; and much research is needed.

The interests involved in the category of "works of art," as used in the copyright law, are considerable. The Copyright Office has supplied us with a long list of such articles which have been copyrighted—statuettes, book ends, clocks, lamps, door knockers, candlesticks, inkstands, chandeliers, piggy banks, sundials, salt and pepper shakers, fish bowls, casseroles, and ash trays. Perhaps these are all "writings" in the constitutional sense. But to me, at least, they are not obviously so. It is time that we came to the problem full face. I would accordingly put the case down for reargument.

ESQUIRE, INC. v. RINGER

United States Court of Appeals, District of Columbia Circuit, 1978.
591 F.2d 796, 199 U.S.P.Q. 1, cert. denied 440 U.S. 908, 99 S.Ct. 1217, 59
L.Ed.2d 456, reh. denied 441 U.S. 917, 99 S.Ct. 2019, 60 L.Ed.2d 389.

Before BAZELON, LEVENTHAL and ROBINSON, Circuit Judges.

Opinion for the Court filed by Circuit Judge BAZELON.

Concurring opinion filed by Circuit Judge LEVENTHAL.

BAZELON, Circuit Judge:

This case presents the question whether the overall shape of certain outdoor lighting fixtures is eligible for copyright as a "work of art." The Register of Copyrights determined that the overall shape or configuration of such articles is not copyrightable. The district court disagreed, and issued a writ of mandamus directing the Register to enter the claim to copyright. Esquire, Inc. v. Ringer, 414 F. Supp. 939 (D.D.C.1976). For the reasons expressed below, we reverse.

I.

Although the issues involved are fairly complex, the facts may be briefly stated. Appellee, Esquire, Inc. (Esquire) submitted three applications to the Copyright Office for registration of what it described as "artistic design[s] for lighting fixture[s]." Photographs accompanying the applications showed stationary outdoor luminaries or floodlights, of contemporary design, with rounded or elliptically-shaped housings. The applications asserted that the designs were eligible for copyright protection as "works of art." 17 U.S.C.A. § 5(g).

The Register of Copyrights (Register) refused to register Esquire's claims to copyright. The principal reason given was that Copyright Office regulations, specifically 37 C.F.R. § 202.10(c) (1976), preclude registration of the design of a utilitarian article, such as lighting fixtures, "when all of the design elements . . . are directly related to the useful functions of the article. . . ." The fixtures, according to the Register's analysis, did not contain "elements, either alone or in combination, which are capable of independent existence as a copyrightable pictorial, graphic, or sculptural work apart from the utilitarian aspect." Esquire twice requested reconsideration of its copyright applications, and was twice refused.

Lighting Fixture in Esquire, Inc. v. Ringer.

Esquire then filed suit in the district court, seeking a writ of mandamus directing the Register to issue a certificate of copyright for its lighting fixture designs. This time, Esquire met with success. The court, per Judge Gesell, concluded that registration was compelled by Mazer v. Stein, 347 U.S. 201, 74 S.Ct. 460, 98 L.Ed. 630 (1954), where the Supreme Court upheld the copyright of statuettes intended to be mass-produced for use as table lamp bases. The district court reasoned that to uphold the issuance of the copyrights in *Mazer*, but deny Esquire's applications, would amount to affording certain copyright privileges to traditional works of art, but not to abstract, modern art forms. The court went on to find that "[t]he forms of the articles here in dispute are clearly art" and concluded that they were "entitled to the same recognition afforded more traditional sculpture." 414 F.Supp. at 941. The court also suggested that registration of Esquire's designs was compelled by prior "interpretative precedent." Id. This appeal followed.

The heart of the controversy in this case involves, in the district court's words, an "elusive semantic dispute" over the applicable regulation, 37 C.F.R. § 202.10(c). We have divided our analysis of this dispute into two parts: Part II considers whether the Register adopted a permissible interpretation of the regulation; Part III, whether the regulation, as interpreted, was properly applied to the facts presented by Esquire's applications.

II.

A.

Section 5(g) of the Copyright Act of 1909, 17 U.S.C.A. § 5(g), indicates that "[w]orks of art; models or designs for works of art" are eligible for copyright. The terse language of the statute is more fully elaborated in regulations drafted by the Register pursuant to Congressional authorization.[9] The provision at issue, 37 C.F.R. § 202.10(c), provides as follows:

(c) If the sole intrinsic function of an article is its utility, the fact that the article is unique and attractively shaped will not

---

9. "Subject to the approval of the Librarian of Congress, the Register of Copyrights shall be authorized to make rules and regulations for the registration of claims to copyright as provided by this title." 17 U.S.C.A. § 207. See also 17 U.S.C.A. § 702.

The Register has promulgated regulations, codified currently in 37 C.F.R. § 202.10, to clarify the parameters of copyrightable "works of art." The general definition of "works of art," § 202.10(a), was adopted in 1948. It evidences a concern—pervasive in this area—to distinguish between "works of art" eligible for copyright, and functional or utilitarian articles not so eligible.

Works of Art (Class G)

(a) General. This class includes published or unpublished works of artistic craftsmanship, insofar as their form but not their mechanical or utilization aspects are concerned, such as artistic jewelry, enamels, glassware, and tapestries, as well as works belonging to the fine arts, such as paintings, drawings and sculpture.

37 C.F.R. § 202.10(a).

Section 202.10(b) was enacted after the Supreme Court's decision in Mazer v. Stein, supra. This regulation embodies the principle, affirmed in *Mazer*, that commercial use does not disqual-

qualify it as a work of art. However, if the shape of a utilitarian article incorporates features, such as artistic sculpture, carving, or pictorial representation, which can be identified separately and are capable of existing independently as a work of art, such features will be eligible for registration.

The parties have advanced conflicting interpretations of § 202.10(c). The Register interprets § 202.10(c) to bar copyright registration of the overall shape or configuration of a utilitarian article, no matter how aesthetically pleasing that shape or configuration may be. As support for this interpretation, the Register notes that the regulation limits copyright protection to features of a utilitarian article that "can be identified separately and are capable of existing independently as a work of art." The Register argues that this reading is required to enforce the congressional policy against copyrighting industrial designs, and that it is supported by the continued practice of the Copyright Office and by legislative history.

Esquire on the other hand, interprets § 202.10(c) to allow copyright registration for the overall shape or design of utilitarian articles as long as the shape or design satisfies the requirements appurtenant to works of art—originality and creativity. Esquire stresses that the first sentence of § 202.10(c) reads in its entirety, "If the *sole* intrinsic function of an article is its utility, the fact that the article is unique and attractively shaped will not qualify it as a work of art." Esquire maintains that it designed its lighting fixtures with the intent of creating "works of modernistic form sculpture," and therefore that their *sole* intrinsic function is not utility. Esquire also contends that the language of § 202.10(c) referring to "features   .   .   . which can be identified separately and are capable of existing independently as a work of art" is not inconsistent with its interpretation. In effect, Esquire asserts that the *shape* of the lighting fixtures is the "feature" that makes them eligible for copyright as a work of art. Esquire argues that its reading of § 202.10(c) is required by the decisions of the Supreme Court in Mazer v. Stein, 347 U.S. 201, 74 S.Ct. 460, 98 L.Ed. 630 (1954) and Bleistein v. Donaldson Lithographing Co., 188 U.S. 239, 23 S.Ct. 298, 47 L.Ed. 460 (1903).

---

ify an otherwise registrable work of art from copyright protection.

(b) In order to be acceptable as a work of art, the work must embody some creative authorship in its delineation or form. The registrability of a work of art is not affected by the intention of the author as to the use of the work, the number of copies reproduced, or the fact that it appears on a textile material or textile product. The potential availability of protection under the design patent law will not affect the registrability of a work of art, but a copyright claim in a patented design or in the drawings or photographs in a patent application will not be registered after the patent has been issued.

37 C.F.R. § 202.10(b).

B.

We conclude that the Register has adopted a reasonable and well-supported interpretation of § 202.10(c).

The Register's interpretation of § 202.10(c) derives from the principle that industrial designs are not eligible for copyright. Congress has repeatedly rejected proposed legislation that would make copyright protection available for consumer or industrial products. Most recently, Congress deleted a proposed section from the Copyright Act of 1976 that would have "create[d] a new limited form of copyright protection for 'original' designs which are clearly a part of a useful article, regardless of whether such designs could stand by themselves, separate from the article itself." [13] In rejecting proposed Title II, Congress noted the administration's concern that to make such designs eligible for copyright would be to create a "new monopoly" having obvious and significant anticompetitive effects.[15] The issues raised by Title II were left for further consideration in "more complete hearings" to follow the enactment of the 1976 Act.

In the Register's view, registration of the overall shape or configuration of utilitarian articles would lead to widespread copyright protection for industrial designs. The Register reasons that aesthetic considerations enter into the design of most useful objects. Thus, if overall shape or configuration can qualify as a "work of art," "the whole realm of consumer products—garments, toasters, refrigerators, furniture, bathtubs, automobiles, etc.—and industrial products designed to have aesthetic appeal—subway cars, computers, photocopy-

---

13. H.R.Rep.No.1476, 94th Cong., 2d Sess. 50 (1976), U.S.Code Cong. & Admin.News 1976, pp. 5659, 5663. The report explains that

> [t]he Committee chose to delete Title II in part because the new form of design protection provided by Title II could not truly be considered copyright protection and therefore appropriately within the scope of copyright revision.

Id.

15. The Register's brief illustrates the problems involved in allowing copyright of the shape of utilitarian articles.

> There are several economic considerations that Congress must weigh before deciding whether, for utilitarian articles, shape alone, no matter how aesthetically pleasing, is enough to warrant copyright protection. First, in the case of some utilitarian objects, like scissors or paper clips, shape is mandated by function. If one manufacturer were given the copyright to the design of such an article, it could completely prevent others from producing the same article. Second, consumer preference sometimes demands uniformity of shape for certain utilitarian articles, like stoves for instance. People simply expect and desire certain everyday useful articles to look the same particular way. Thus, to give one manufacturer the monopoly on such a shape would also be anticompetive [sic]. Third, insofar as geometric shapes are concerned, there are only a limited amount of basic shapes, such as circles, squares, rectangles and ellipses. These shapes are obviously in the public domain and accordingly it would be unfair to grant a monopoly on the use of any particular such shape, no matter how aesthetically well it was integrated into a utilitarian article.

Brief for Appellant at 18–19.

ing machines, typewriters, adding machines, etc.—must also qualify as works of art."

Considerable weight is to be given to an agency's interpretation of its regulations. "[T]he ultimate criterion is the administrative interpretation which becomes of controlling weight unless it is plainly erroneous or inconsistent with the regulation." Bowles v. Seminole Rock & Sand Co., 325 U.S. 410, 414, 65 S.Ct. 1215, 1217, 89 L.Ed. 1700 (1945). This is particularly so if an administrative interpretation relates to a matter within the field of administrative expertise and has been consistently followed for a significant period of time. The Register's interpretation of § 202.10(c) reflects both administrative expertise and consistent application.

The regulation in question attempts to define the boundaries between copyrightable "works of art" and noncopyrightable industrial designs. This is an issue of longstanding concern to the Copyright Office, and is clearly a matter in which the Register has considerable expertise.

Whether the Register's interpretation has been consistently followed for a significant period of time is somewhat less clear. Since the Copyright Office does not publish opinions explaining registration decisions, there is little evidence bearing directly on this point. What evidence exists, however, indicates that the Register's construction has been followed consistently. The district court suggested, without elaboration, that prior registration decisions create an "interpretative precedent" favoring Esquire's position. But we think this confuses the *test* employed by the Copyright Office in evaluating the copyrightability of utilitarian articles with the *results* that obtained after the test was applied. The register's test requires the application of subjective judgment, and given the large volume of copyright applications that must be processed there may be some results that are difficult to square with the denial of registration here. But this does not mean that the Register has employed different standards in reaching these decisions. The available evidence points to a uniform and longstanding interpretation of § 202.10(c), and accordingly this interpretation is entitled to great weight.

The Register's interpretation of § 202.10(c) finds further support in the legislative history of the recently enacted 1976 Copyright Act. Although not applicable to the case before us, the new Act was designed in part to codify and clarify many of the regulations promulgated under the 1909 Act, including those governing "works of art." Thus, the 1976 Act and its legislative history can be taken as an expression of congressional understanding of the scope of protection for utilitarian articles under the old regulations. "Subsequent legislation which declares the intent of an earlier law is not, of course, conclusive . . . . But the later law is entitled to weight when it comes to the problem of construction." Federal Housing Administration v. The Darlington, Inc., 358 U.S. 84, 90, 79 S.Ct. 141, 145, 3 L.Ed.2d 132 (1958).

The House Report indicates that the section of the 1976 Act governing "pictorial, graphic and sculptural works" was intended "to draw as clear a line as possible between copyrightable works of applied art and uncopyrighted works of industrial design." The Report illustrates the distinction in the following terms:

> . . . although the shape of an industrial product may be aesthetically satisfying and valuable, the Committee's intention is not to offer it copyright protection under the bill. Unless the shape of an automobile, airplane, ladies' dress, food processor, television set, or any other industrial product contains some element that, physically or conceptually, can be identified as separable from the utilitarian aspects of that article, the design would not be copyrighted under the bill. The test of separability and independence from "the utilitarian aspects of the article" does not depend upon the nature of the design—that is, *even if the appearance of an article is determined by aesthetic (as opposed to functional) considerations, only elements, if any, which can be identified separately from the useful article as such are copyrightable.* And even if the three dimensional design contains some such element (for example, a carving on the back of a chair or a floral relief design on silver flatware), *copyright protection would extend only to that element, and would not cover the over-all configuration of the utilitarian article as such.*

H.R.Rep. No. 1476, 94th Cong., 2d Sess. 55 (1976), U.S.Code Cong. & Admin.News 1976, p. 5668 (emphasis added).

This excerpt is not entirely free from ambiguity. Esquire could arguably draw some support from the statement that a protectable element of a utilitarian article must be separable "physically *or conceptually*" from the utilitarian aspects of the design. But any possible ambiguity raised by this isolated reference disappears when the excerpt is considered in its entirety. The underscored passages indicate unequivocally that the overall design or configuration of a utilitarian object, even if it is determined by aesthetic as well as functional considerations, is not eligible for copyright. Thus the legislative history, taken as congressional understanding of existing law, reinforces the Register's position.

The legislative history of the 1976 Act also supports the Register's practice of ascribing little weight to the phrase "sole intrinsic function." As noted above, Esquire contends that as long as the overall shape of a utilitarian article embodies *dual* intrinsic functions—aesthetic and utilitarian—that shape may qualify for registration. But the new Act includes a definition of "useful article," referred to by the House Report as "an adaptation" of the language of § 202.10(c), H.R.Rep. No. 1476, supra n. 13, at 54, U.S.Code Cong. & Admin.News 1976, p. 5668, which provides:

> A 'useful article' is an article having *an* intrinsic utilitarian function that is not merely to portray the appearance of the article or to convey information.

17 U.S.C.A. § 101 (emphasis added). In deleting the modifier "sole" from the language taken from § 202.10(c), the draftsmen of the 1976 Act must have concluded that the definition of "useful article" would be more precise without this term. Moreover, Congress may have concluded that literal application of the phrase "sole intrinsic function" would create an unworkable standard. For as one commentator has observed, "[t]here are no two-dimensional works and few three-dimensional objects whose design is absolutely dictated by utilitarian considerations."

C.

The district court basically ignored the foregoing considerations. Instead, it advanced two reasons for rejecting the Register's interpretation of § 202.10(c) as a matter of law. It concluded, first, that the register's construction was inconsistent with the Supreme Court's decision in Mazer v. Stein, 347 U.S. 201, 74 S.Ct. 460, 98 L.Ed. 630 (1954). Second, it found that the Register's interpretation amounted to impermissible discrimination against abstract modern art. We respectfully disagree on both counts.

We are unable to join in the district court's broad reading of Mazer v. Stein, supra. The principle issue in *Mazer* was whether objects that are concededly "works of art" can be copyrighted if incorporated into mass-produced utilitarian articles. The Register had issued copyright certificates for the statuettes of Balinese dancing figures created with the intent to reproduce and sell them as bases for table lamps. The Court noted that the "long-continued construction of the statutes" by the Copyright Office permitted registration of the statuettes as "works of art." 347 U.S. at 213, 74 S.Ct. at 468. It then concluded that there was "nothing in the copyright statute to support the argument that the intended use or use in industry of *an article eligible for copyright* bars or invalidates its registration." Id. at 218, 74 S.Ct. at 471 (emphasis added).

The issue here—whether the overall shape of a utilitarian object is "an article eligible for copyright"—was not addressed in *Mazer*. In fact, under the Register's interpretation of § 202.10(c), the dancing figures considered in *Mazer* would clearly be copyrightable. The statuettes were undeniably capable of existing as a work of art independent of the utilitarian article into which they were incorporated. And they were clearly a "feature" segregable from the overall shape of the table lamps. There is thus no inconsistency between the copyright upheld in *Mazer* and the Register's interpretation of § 202.10(c) here.

The district court's second conclusion is somewhat more problematical. The court found, in effect, that that Register's interpretation of § 202.10(c) amounted to impermissible discrimination against designs that "emphasize line and shape rather than the realistic or the ornate   . . . ." 414 F.Supp. at 941.

We agree with the district court that the Copyright Act does not enshrine a particular conception of what constitutes "art." Id. As Justice Holmes noted in Bleistein v. Donaldson Lithographing Co., 188 U.S. 239, 251, 23 S.Ct. 298, 300, 47 L.Ed. 460 (1903), " [i]t would be a dangerous undertaking for persons trained only to the law to constitute themselves final judges of the worth of pictorial illustrations .   . .." Neither the Constitution nor the Copyright Act authorizes the Copyright Office or the federal judiciary to serve as arbiters of national taste. These officials have no particular competence to assess the merits of one genre of art relative to another. And to allow them to assume such authority would be to risk stultifying the creativity and originality the copyright laws were expressly designed to encourage. Id. at 251–52, 23 S.Ct. 298.

But in our view the present case does not offend the nondiscrimination principle recognized in *Bleistein*. *Bleistein* was concerned only with conscious bias against one form of art—in that case the popular art reflected in circus posters. Esquire's complaint, in effect, is that the Register's interpretation of § 202.10(c) places an inadvertent burden on a particular form of art, namely modern abstract sculpture. We may concede, for present purposes, that an interpretation of § 202.10(c) that bars copyright for the overall design or configuration of a utilitarian object will have a disproportionate impact on designs that exhibit the characteristics of abstract sculpture. But we can see no justification, at least in the circumstances of this case, for extending the nondiscrimination principle of *Bleistein* to include action having an unintentional, disproportionate impact on one style of artistic expression. Such an extension of the nondiscrimination principle would undermine other plainly legitimate goals of copyright law—in this case the congressional directive that copyright protection should not be afforded to industrial designs.

At oral argument, Esquire proposed for the first time a test which it claimed would respect the principle disfavoring the copyright of industrial designs, and yet would not impose a differential burden on modernistic art forms. Esquire suggested that the overall design or configuration of a utilitarian article should be copyrightable as a work of art if its shape is original and creative, and it exhibits "a sufficient quantity of intellectual labor" to distinguish it from everyday industrial designs. However, Esquire was unable to cite any authority in support of this proposed test. Moreover, such a test would pose obvious administrative difficulties, and would appear to thrust the Copyright Office and the courts into the very role Esquire argues so forcefully against—as overseers of the relative "worth" or value of different forms of art. Accordingly, we find no basis for requiring the Register to consider Esquire's belated suggestion.

III.

Given that the Register adopted an appropriate interpretation of § 202.10(c), the question remains whether the regulation was properly applied to the materials presented by Esquire's copyright claims.

In general, the Copyright Act "establishes a wide range of selection within which discretion must be exercised by the Register in determining what he has no power to accept." Bouvé v. Twentieth Century-Fox Film Corp., supra, 74 U.S.App.D.C. at 273, 122 F.2d at 53. Here, the application of the regulation to the facts presented by Esquire's copyright applications unquestionably involved the exercise of administrative discretion.

When the question of the application of the regulation was raised at oral argument, Esquire took the position that its copyright applications should be read as requesting registration for only *part* of a utilitarian object. Specifically, Esquire maintained that it sought registration for the *housing* of each fixture, not for the design of the entire lighting assembly—including base, housing, electrical fixture, and light bulb. But Esquire's applications were not so limited. Each characterized the work for which registration was sought as an "artistic design for lighting fixtures." The photographs accompanying the applications portrayed both housings and bases for the lighting fixtures. No lesser feature was singled out as being that for which registration was sought. On the basis of these submissions, the Register could quite reasonably conclude that Esquire was claiming a copyright for the overall design of its outdoor lighting fixtures. The denial of registration in these circumstances did not amount to an abuse of discretion.

For the aforesaid reasons, the decision of the district court is

Reversed.

[Concurring opinion of LEVENTHAL, Circuit Judge, omitted.]

NOTES

1.   Could petitioner's argument in *Mazer*, that respondent's intention to use his work commercially disqualified it from protection, have been simply disposed of on the authority of *Bleistein*, page 670 above? The circuit court decision reversed in *Bleistein* had held that "if a chromolithograph or other print, engraving, or picture has no other use than that of a mere advertisement, and no value aside from this function, it would not be promotive of the useful arts, within the meaning of the constitutional provision to protect the 'author' in the exclusive use thereof, and the copyright statute should not be construed as including such a publication .   .   .   it must follow that a pictorial illustration designed and useful only as an advertisement, and having no intrinsic value other than its function as an advertisement, must be .   .   .   without the obvious meaning of the constitution." 104 F. 990, 993 (6th Cir. 1900).

Would the circuit court—or the Supreme Court—have reached a different result if it had recognized that promotion of the progress of "science," rather than of "useful arts," is the province of copyright? See page 1, note 2, above.

2. The present Act's definition of "pictorial, graphic and sculptural works" substantially repeats the definition given in 37 C.F.R. § 202.10(c), considered in Esquire v. Ringer. The House Committee added this language to the Senate version of the revision bill, S.22, 94th Cong. 1st Sess., after the district court's decision in *Esquire* allowed registration of the lighting fixtures.

What lies behind the widespread belief that industrial designs should not be copyrightable? The belief antedates, and survived the rebuff in, Mazer v. Stein. Is it that this subject matter is better suited for design patent protection and that design patent law should therefore be the exclusive arbiter of protection? Courts have rejected such claims of exclusivity when design patent overlaps trademark protection. See pages 352–353, above. And the House Report, excerpted above, specifically acknowledges that the availability of design patent protection should not bar copyright.

Does the rule denying copyright to industrial designs make any sense? The copyright law elsewhere embraces such patently utilitarian subject matter as computer programs, instruction manuals and science texts. Is there any reason to distinguish between two-dimensional, verbal works of utility, and three-dimensional, visual works? If the concern is that copyright for industrial designs will permit a monopoly over their functional use, would a better solution be to allow registration, as is done with computer programs and instruction manuals, but take care to administer rights in the subject matter so that function is not protected? Does the functional-nonfunctional distinction employed in unfair competition law, page 128, offer a better solution?

As noted in *Esquire*, a separate title of the copyright revision bill aimed at protecting industrial designs was dropped, in part to facilitate passage of the main bill. "This measure was originally introduced by Chairman Edwin Willis of the House Judiciary Subcommittee in 1957, and received active consideration in both Houses during the early 1960's. It passed the Senate as separate legislation on three occasions, in 1962, 1963, and 1966. It was reintroduced in the 90th and 91st Congresses, and on December 10, 1969, the Senate Subcommittee conjoined it with the general copyright revision bill, reporting it as Title III of S. 543. As a separate title of S. 1361 of the 93d Congress, 1st Sess., and now of S. 22, the design legislation has passed the Senate on two additional occasions." H.R.Rep.No.94–1476, 94th Cong. 2d Sess. 49–50 (1976). Bills to amend the Copyright Act to provide for the protection of original, "ornamental designs of useful articles," have since been introduced. See H.R. 2706, 4530, 96th Cong., 1st Sess. (1979).

Reread the next-to-last paragraph of Judge Bazelon's opinion in *Esquire*. Does it—or Mazer v. Stein—suggest a relatively easy way to circumvent the rule against copyright for industrial designs?

3. When the Print and Label Law, 18 Stat. 79 (1874), was being enacted, the Librarian of Congress managed to fob off responsibility

for the registration of labels on the Patent Office, apparently because "he regarded [them] as beneath the dignity of literature proper." Howell, The Copyright Law 27 (3d Ed. 1952). Copyright for labels and prints was handled by the Patent Office's Trademark Division until 1940 when, by act of Congress, jurisdiction was transferred to the Register of Copyrights, 53 Stat. 1142 (1939). See Derenberg, Commercial Prints and Labels: A Hybrid in Copyright Law, 49 Yale L.J. 1212 (1940); Kupferman, Copyright Protection for Commercial Prints and Labels, 33 So.Cal.L.Rev. 163 (1960). See generally, Allen, Advertising Protection Through Copyright, 2 Ariz.L.Rev. 230 (1960).

Copyright for labels inevitably intersects unfair competition and trademark protection. In keeping these two areas separate, courts sometimes follow the test for copyrightability stated in Higgins v. Keuffel, 140 U.S. 428, 11 S.Ct. 731, 35 L.Ed. 470 (1891): "To be entitled to a copyright the article must have by itself some value as a composition, at least to the extent of serving some purpose other than as a mere advertisement or designation of the subject to which it is attached." 140 U.S. 431.

In Alberto-Culver Co. v. Andrea Dumon, Inc., 466 F.2d 705, 175 U.S.P.Q. 194 (7th Cir. 1972), the lower court had relied on this test to find that the entire face side of plaintiff's feminine hygiene spray container was copyrightable. Further, "on the back side, the colored art work and the connecting phrase 'is the most personal sort of deodorant' was copyrightable and is valid. The remaining language on the back side is purely descriptive or deals with directions and cautions. As this language has no separate value as composition or an extension of the original art work, it was not copyrightable and is not valid." 466 F.2d 705, 711.

The Seventh Circuit Court of Appeals agreed in all respects but one: "the phrase 'most personal sort of deodorant' is not subject to copyright protection." In the court's view, the phrase was "merely a 'short phrase or expression' which hardly qualifies as an 'appreciable amount of original text'" as is required for copyrightability. Further, "this phrase is just as descriptive as the rest of the text. The ingenuity and creativity reflected in the development of the product itself does not give appropriate descriptive language, such as 'personal sort of deodorant,' any separate value as a composition or as an extension of a work of art. We conclude that this ordinary phrase is not subject to copyright protection." 466 F.2d 705, 711.

4.   Should copyright be withheld if a work is seditious, libelous, fraudulent or obscene? Courts have sometimes refused to protect such works on the ground that to do otherwise would contravene the constitutional purpose "to promote the progress of . . . science."

Mitchell Bros. Film Group v. Cinema Adult Theatre, 604 F.2d 852, 203 U.S.P.Q. 1041 (5th Cir. 1979), cert. denied, 445 U.S. 917, 100 S.Ct. 1277, 63 L.Ed.2d 601 (1980), may mark a turning point for decision in the area. In an action brought by the copyright proprietors of the motion picture, "Behind the Green Door," the district court ruled for defendant infringers who had asserted as an affirmative defense that the movie was obscene and that plaintiffs were barred from relief under the unclean hands doctrine. The court of appeals reversed. In an extensive and closely-reasoned opinion, the court held that neither the Copyright Act nor the Constitution's copyright clause required that protection be withheld because of obscene content.

The court looked first at the Copyright Act and found nothing to suggest a congressional intent to withhold copyright from obscene subject matter. Indeed, "the history of content-based restrictions on copyrights, trademarks and patents suggests that the absence of such limitations in the Copyright Act of 1909 is the result of an intentional policy choice and not simply an omission." 604 F.2d 852, 854. The court noted that on the few occasions that Congress introduced content-based restrictions into the Act, it later removed them. By contrast, Congress has placed express content restrictions in the Trademark Act (prohibiting registration of "immoral, deceptive or scandalous matter," see page 353, above) and the Patent Act (requiring utility, see page 485, above). 604 F.2d 852, 855. The court was particularly concerned that to deny copyright "to works adjudged obscene by the standards of one era would frequently result in lack of copyright protection (and thus lack of financial incentive to create) for works that later generations might consider to be not only nonobscene but even of great literary merit." Among the works "held in high regard today," but "adjudged obscene in previous eras" are: Edmund Wilson's Memoirs of Hecate County, Henry Miller's Tropic of Cancer and Tropic of Capricorn, Erskine Caldwell's God's Little Acre, D. H. Lawrence's Lady Chatterley's Lover and Theodore Dreiser's An American Tragedy. 604 F.2d 852, 857.

To the argument that copyright protection for obscene works would violate the constitutional limit on Congress's copyright power, "to promote the progress of science and useful arts," the court answered that, while Congress could indeed "require that each copyrighted work be shown to promote the useful arts (as it has with patents,) it need not do so." Instead, Congress could put "promotion of science and useful arts" in a larger frame, and "conclude that the best way to promote creativity is not to impose any governmental restrictions on the subject matter of copyrightable works." 604 F.2d 852, 860.

Mitchell relied in part on Belcher v. Tarbox, 486 F.2d 1087, 180 U.S.P.Q. 1 (9th Cir. 1973), which had refused to withhold copyright protection because of the subject matter's allegedly fraudulent content. "There is nothing in the Copyright Act to suggest that the courts are to pass upon the truth or falsity, the soundness or unsoundness, of the views embodied in a copyrighted work. The gravity and immensity of the problems, theological, philosophical, economic and scientific, that would confront a court if this view were adopted are staggering to contemplate. It is surely not a task lightly to be assumed, and we decline the invitation to assume it." 486 F.2d 1087, 1088.

If *Mitchell* and *Belcher* had reached contrary conclusions, would any problems be raised by the fact that obscenity and fraud are typically determined by reference to local community standards and state laws that vary across the country?

For an early study of the general issue, see Rogers, Copyright and Morals, 18 Mich.L.Rev. 390 (1920). See also, Phillips, Copyright in Obscene Works: Some British and American Problems, 6 Anglo-American L.Rev. 138 (1977); Note, The Obscenity Defense in Actions to Protect Copyright, 46 Fordham L.Rev. 1037 (1978); Note, 74 Colum.L.Rev. 1351 (1974); Note, 51 Denver L.J. 621 (1974).

5. To what extent does the following Copyright Office Regulation, 37 C.F.R. § 202.1, exclude subject matter on the basis of content rather than form? Would it be preferable for the Copyright Office to register all the listed forms of subject matter and leave it to the courts to determine the extent to which the subject matter is original and infringed?

§ 202.1 Material not subject to copyright

The following are examples of works not subject to copyright and applications for registration of such works cannot be entertained:

(a) Words and short phrases such as names, titles, and slogans; familiar symbols or designs; mere variations of typographic ornamentation, lettering or coloring; mere listing of ingredients or contents;

(b) Ideas, plans, methods, systems, or devices, as distinguished from the particular manner in which they are expressed or described in a writing;

(c) Blank forms, such as time cards, graph paper, account books, diaries, bank checks, scorecards, address books, report forms, order forms and the like, which are designed for recording information and do not in themselves convey information;

(d) Works consisting entirely of information that is common property containing no original authorship, such as, for example: Standard calendars, height and weight charts, tape measures and rulers, schedules of sporting events, and lists or tables taken from public documents or other common sources.

6. Which of the following three formulations do you think best answers Justice Douglas' query in *Mazer* as to the meaning of the constitutional term, "Writings:"

(a) The traditionally held view is that a work is a writing if it reflects some degree of intellectual labor and is embodied in tangible form. The quantum of intellectual labor may be minimal. Although no decision squarely holds that a writing must be in tangible form, courts have widely assumed the constitutional bearing of this second requisite. Under the tangibility requirement, a spontaneous dramatic performance, a broadcast sporting event or an ad libbed narrative would not constitute writings, while their respective reduction in tangible form to a play, movie or book would. Contemplate the practicalities of litigation—problems of proof, particularly—and then consider why there is no authoritative decision on the question. Is the tangible form requirement drawn from the Constitution or from expedience?

(b) Under another formulation, a writing consists of "any intellectual conception of an author expressed in a way that communicates it to others." Note, Study of the Term "Writings" in the Copyright Clause of the Constitution, 31 N.Y.U.L.Rev. 1263 (1956).

(c) Finally, one court faced with the question found "it sensible to say that the constitutional clause extends to any concrete, describable manifestation of intellectual creation; and to the extent that a creation may be ineffable, we think it ineligible for protection against copying simpliciter under either state or federal law." Columbia Broadcasting System, Inc. v. DeCosta, 377 F.2d 315, 320, 153 U.S.P.Q. 649 (1st Cir. 1967), cert. denied 389 U.S. 1007, 88 S.Ct. 565, 19 L.Ed. 2d 603.

What does the present Act add to, or subtract from, these formulations?

B. RIGHTS AND REMEDIES

1. RIGHTS

See Statute Supplement 17 U.S.C.A. §§ 106–118, 201–205, 302–305, 602–603, 801–810.

a. THE NATURE OF COPYRIGHT

BAKER v. SELDEN

Supreme Court of the United States, 1879.
101 U.S. 99, 25 L.Ed. 841.

Mr. Justice BRADLEY delivered the opinion of the court.

Charles Selden, the testator of the complainant in this case, in the year 1859 took the requisite steps for obtaining the copyright of a book, entitled "Selden's Condensed Ledger, or Bookkeeping Simplified," the object of which was to exhibit and explain a peculiar system of book-keeping. In 1860 and 1861, he took the copyright of several other books, containing additions to and improvements upon the said system. The bill of complaint was filed against the defendant, Baker, for an alleged infringement of these copyrights. The latter, in his answer, denied that Selden was the author or designer of the books, and denied the infringement charged, and contends on the argument that the matter alleged to be infringed is not a lawful subject of copyright.

The parties went into proofs, and the various books of the complainant, as well as those sold and used by the defendant, were exhibited before the examiner, and witnesses were examined on both sides. A decree was rendered for the complainant, and the defendant appealed.

The book or series of books of which the complainant claims the copyright consists of an introductory essay explaining the system of book-keeping referred to, to which are annexed certain forms or blanks, consisting of ruled lines, and headings, illustrating the system and showing how it is to be used and carried out in practice. This system effects the same results as book-keeping by double entry; but, by a peculiar arrangement of columns and headings, presents the entire operation, of a day, a week, or a month, on a single page, or on two pages facing each other, in an account-book. The defendant uses a similar plan so far as results are concerned; but makes a different arrangement of the columns, and uses different headings. If the complainant's testator had the exclusive right to the use of the system explained in his book, it would be difficult to contend that the defendant does not infringe it, notwithstanding the difference in his form of arrangement; but if it be assumed that the system is open to the public use, it seems to be equally difficult to contend that the books made and sold by the defendant are a violation of the copyright of the complainant's book considered merely as a book explanatory of the system. Where the truths of a science or the methods of an art are the common property of the whole world, any author has the right to express the one, or explain and use the other, in his own way. As an author, Selden explained the system in a particular way. It may be conceded that Baker makes and uses account-books arranged on substantially the same system; but the proof fails to show that he has violated the copyright of Selden's book, regarding the latter merely as an explanatory work; or that he has infringed Selden's right in any way, unless the latter became entitled to an exclusive right in the system.

The evidence of the complainant is principally directed to the object of showing that Baker uses the same system as that which is explained and illustrated in Selden's books. It becomes important, therefore, to determine whether, in obtaining the copyright of his books, he secured the exclusive right to the use of the system or method of book-keeping which the said books are intended to illustrate and explain. It is contended that he has secured such exclusive right, because no one can use the system without using substantially the same ruled lines and headings which he has appended to his books in illustration of it. In other words, it is contended that the ruled lines and headings, given to illustrate the system, are a part of the book, and, as such, are secured by the copyright; and that no one can make or use similar ruled lines and headings, or ruled lines and headings made and arranged on substantially the same system, without violating the copyright. And this is really the question to be decided in this case. Stated in another form, the question is, whether the exclusive property in a system of book-keeping can be claimed, under the law of copyright, by means of a book in which that system is explained? The complainant's bill, and the case made under it, are based on the hypothesis that it can be.

It cannot be pretended, and indeed it is not seriously urged, that the ruled lines of the complainant's account-book can be claimed under any special class of objects, other than books, named in the law of copyright existing in 1859. The law then in force was that of 1831, and specified only books, maps, charts, musical compositions, prints, and engravings. An account-book, consisting of ruled lines and blank columns, cannot be called by any of these names unless by that of a book.

There is no doubt that a work on the subject of book-keeping, though only explanatory of well-known systems, may be the subject of a copyright; but, then, it is claimed only as a book. Such a book may be explanatory either of old systems, or of an entirely new system; and, considered as a book, as the work of an author, conveying information on the subject of book-keeping, and containing detailed explanations of the art, it may be a very valuable acquisition to the practical knowledge of the community. But there is a clear distinction between the book, as such, and the art which it is intended to illustrate. The mere statement of the proposition is so evident, that it requires hardly any argument to support it. The same distinction may be predicated of every other art as well as that of book-keeping. A treatise on the composition and use of medicines, be they old or new; on the construction and use of ploughs, or watches, or churns; or on the mixture and application of colors for painting or dyeing; or on the mode of drawing lines to produce the effect of perspective,—would be the subject of copyright; but no one would contend that the copyright of the treatise would give the exclusive right to the art or manufacture described therein. The copyright of the book, if not pirated from other works, would be valid without regard to the novelty, or want of novelty, of its subject-matter. The novelty of the art or thing described or explained has nothing to do with the validity of the copyright. To give to the author of the book an exclusive property in the art described therein, when no examination of its novelty has ever been officially made, would be a surprise and a fraud upon the public. That is the province of letters-patent, not of copyright. The claim to an invention or discovery of an art or manufacture must be subjected to the examination of the Patent Office before an exclusive right therein can be obtained; and it can only be secured by a patent from the government.

The difference between the two things, letters-patent and copyright, may be illustrated by reference to the subjects just enumerated. Take the case of medicines. Certain mixtures are found to be of great value in the healing art. If the discoverer writes and publishes a book on the subject (as regular physicians generally do), he gains no exclusive right to the manufacture and sale of the medicine; he gives that to the public. If he desires to acquire such exclusive right, he must obtain a patent for the mixture as a new art, manufacture, or composition of matter. He may copyright his book, if he pleases; but that only secures to him the exclusive right of printing and publishing his book. So of all other inventions or discoveries.

The copyright of a book on perspective, no matter how many drawings and illustrations it may contain, gives no exclusive right to the modes of drawing described, though they may never have been known or used before. By publishing the book, without getting a patent for the art, the latter is given to the public. The fact that the art described in the book by illustrations of lines and figures which are reproduced in practice in the application of the art, makes no difference. Those illustrations are the mere language employed by the author to convey his ideas more clearly. Had he used words of description instead of diagrams (which merely stand in the place of words), there could not be the slightest doubt that others, applying the art to practical use, might lawfully draw the lines and diagrams which were in the author's mind, and which he thus described by words in his book.

The copyright of a work on mathematical science cannot give to the author an exclusive right to the methods of operation which he propounds, or to the diagrams which he employs to explain them, so as to prevent an engineer from using them whenever occasion requires. The very object of publishing a book on science or the useful arts is to communicate to the world the useful knowledge which it contains. But this object would be frustrated if the knowledge could not be used without incurring the guilt of piracy of the book. And where the art it teaches cannot be used without employing the methods and diagrams used to illustrate the book, or such as are similar to them, such methods and diagrams are to be considered as necessary incidents to the art, and given therewith to the public; not given for the purpose of publication in other works explanatory of the art, but for the purpose of practical application.

Of course, these observations are not intended to apply to ornamental designs, or pictorial illustrations addressed to the taste. Of these it may be said, that their form is their essence, and their object, the production of pleasure in their contemplation. This is their final end. They are as much the product of genius and the result of composition, as are the lines of the poet or the historian's periods. On the other hand, the teachings of science and the rules and methods of useful art have their final end in application and use; and this application and use are what the public derive from the publication of a book which teaches them. But as embodied and taught in a literary composition or book, their essence consists only in their statement. This alone is what is secured by the copyright. The use by another of the same methods of statement, whether in words or illustrations, in a book published for teaching the art, would undoubtedly be an infringement of the copyright.

Recurring to the case before us, we observe that Charles Selden, by his books, explained and described a peculiar system of book-keeping, and illustrated his method by means of ruled lines and blank columns, with proper headings on a page, or on successive pages. Now, whilst no one has a right to print or publish his book, or any material part thereof, as a book intended to convey instruction in the art, any person may practise and use the art itself which he has described and illustrated therein. The use of the art is a totally different thing from a publication of the book explaining it. The copyright of a book on book-keeping cannot secure the exclusive right to make, sell, and use account-books prepared upon the plan set forth in such book. Whether the art might or might not have been patented, is a question which is not before us. It was not patented, and is open and free to the use of the public. And, of course, in using the art, the ruled lines and headings of accounts must necessarily be used as incident to it.

The plausibility of the claim put forward by the complainant in this case arises from a confusion of ideas produced by the peculiar nature of the art described in the books which have been made the subject of copyright. In describing the art, the illustrations and diagrams employed happen to correspond more closely than usual with the actual work performed by the operator who uses the art. Those illustrations and diagrams consist of ruled lines and headings of accounts; and it is similar ruled lines and headings of accounts which, in the application of the art, the book-keeper makes with his pen, or the stationer with his press; whilst in most other cases the diagrams and illustrations can only be represented in concrete forms of wood, metal, stone, or some other physical embodiment. But the principle is the same in all. The description of the art in a book, though entitled to the benefit of copyright, lays no foundation for an exclusive claim to the art itself. The object of the one is explanation; the object of the other is use. The former may be secured by copyright. The latter can only be secured, if it can be secured at all, by letters-patent. . . .

Another case, that of Page v. Wisden (20 L.T.N.S. 435), which came before Vice-Chancellor Malins in 1869, has some resemblance to the present. There a copyright was claimed in a cricket scoring-sheet, and the Vice-Chancellor held that it was not a fit subject for copyright, partly because it was not new, but also because "to say that a particular mode of ruling a book constituted an object for a copyright is absurd."

These cases, if not precisely in point, come near to the matter in hand, and, in our view, corroborate the general proposition which we have laid down. . . .

The conclusion to which we have come is, that blank account-books are not the subject of copyright; and that the mere copyright of Selden's book did not confer upon him the exclusive right to make and use account-books, ruled and arranged as designated by him and described and illustrated in said book.

The decree of the Circuit Court must be reversed, and the cause remanded with instructions to dismiss the complainant's bill; and it is so ordered.

WARNER BROS. PICTURES, INC. v. COLUMBIA BROADCASTING SYSTEM, INC.

United States Court of Appeals, Ninth Circuit, 1954.
216 F.2d 945, 104 U.S.P.Q. 103, cert. denied 348 U.S. 971, 75 S.Ct.
532, 99 L.Ed. 756, 105 U.S.P.Q. 518.

STEPHENS, Circuit Judge.

Dashiell Hammett composed a mystery-detective story entitled "The Maltese Falcon" which was published serially, and each installment was copyrighted by the publisher. Subsequently, Alfred A. Knopf, Inc., entered into a contract with the author to publish the work in book form, Knopf published the book and, in accord with the terms of the contract, copyrighted it.

In 1930, after publication in book form and after publication of all installments of the first serial thereof, Knopf and Hammett, designated as "Owners", for a consideration of $8,500.00, granted certain defined rights in and to The Maltese Falcon (called "writings" in the agreement) to Warner Bros., as "Purchaser". Coincidentally, Knopf executed an instrument to Warner called "Assignment of Copyright" for a nominal consideration. The text of the "assignment" shows on its face that it is not an assignment of the copyright but that it is a grant to Warner of specified rights to the use of the writings in The Maltese Falcon. Both the contract between Hammett-Knopf and Warner, and the "assignment" from Knopf, purport to grant to Warner certain defined and detailed exclusive rights to the use of The Maltese Falcon "writings" in moving pictures, radio, and television.

By the common law, the author of a writing possesses the sole and exclusive right to publish it, but upon and after the first publication the writing may be published by anyone including the author, since the writing has gone into the public domain. The copyright statute extends the author's sole and exclusive right in accordance with its terms and provisions. In other words, it reserves the writing from the public domain for the effective period of the copyright. What we have just said is what is meant by courts when they say: "When the copyright comes in, the common law right goes out."

No question as to the legality of the copyright on The Maltese Falcon or to its continuing effectiveness through all times in suit, or to its complete beneficial ownership by Hammett and Knopf together, is in issue. Therefore, at the effective moment of the grants by Hammett and Knopf to Warner, the latter became possessed of the sole and exclusive right to the writing which is within the copyright, less all limiting terms of the grants. The grants are limited to defined uses in motion pictures, talking pictures, radio, and television.

It is claimed by Warner that it acquired the exclusive right to the use of the writing, The Maltese Falcon, including the individual characters and their names, together with the title, "The Maltese Falcon", in motion pictures, radio, and television. The use of the title is not in issue, since the grant to Warner specifically includes it.

It is the position of Hammett and the other defendants, all of whom claim some interest under him, that the rights acquired by Warner are those specifically mentioned in the conveying or granting instruments, and that the exclusive right to the use of the characters and/or their names were not mentioned as being granted; that the instruments, properly construed, do not convey any exclusive right to the use of characters with or without names, hence Hammett could use them in other stories. However, if, by reason of the silence in the instruments as to such claimed rights, the instruments should be held to be ambiguous on this point, the custom and practice demonstrate that such rights are not customarily parted with by authors, but that characters which are depicted in one detective story together with their names are customarily retained and used in the intricacies of subsequent but different tales.

Hammett did so use the characters with their names and did contract with others for such use. In 1946 he used The Maltese Falcon characters including Sam Spade, the detective and the leading character in the Falcon, by name, and granted to third parties the sole and exclusive right, except their use in the Falcon, to use that character by name (later orally enlarged to include other characters of the Falcon) in radio, television, and motion pictures. Under such claimed rights, radio broadcasts of "Adventures of Sam Spade", including "The Kandy Tooth" were broadcast in weekly half-hour episodes from 1946 to 1950.

Warner claims infringement of copyright and "unfair use and competition" by such re-use and, as well, for infringement of parts of the story and the whole of the writing inclusive of characters and their names. Hammett and the other defendants deny infringement or unfair use and competition on any count, and Hammett requests the court to declare his rights in the premises. Knopf is a nominal party asking and claiming nothing, and is made a plaintiff under the right granted Warner in the Hammett-Knopf-Warner contract.

The trial court denied relief to Warner, declared Hammett's rights, and assessed costs against Warner, who appeals.

The instruments under which Warner claims were prepared by Warner Bros. Corporation which is a large, experienced moving picture producer. It would seem proper, therefore, to construe the instruments under the assumption that the claimant knew what it wanted and that in defining the items in the instruments which it desired and intended to take, it included all of the items it was contracting to take. We are of the opinion that since the use of characters and character names are nowhere specifically mentioned in the agreements, but that other items, including the title, "The Maltese Falcon", and their use are specifically mentioned as being granted, that the character rights with the names cannot be held to be within the grants, and that under the doctrine of *ejusdem generis*, general language cannot be held to include them. As was said in Phillip v. Jerome H. Remick & Co., S.D., N.Y., Op.No. 9,999, 1936, "Such doubt as there is should be resolved in favor of the composer. The clearest language is necessary to divest the author of the fruits of his labor. Such language is lacking here."

The conclusion that these rights are not within the granting instruments is strongly buttressed by the fact that historically and presently detective fiction writers have and do carry the leading characters with their names and individualisms from one story into succeeding stories. This was the practice of Edgar Allen Poe, Sir Arthur Conan Doyle, and others; and in the last two decades of S. S. Van Dine, Earle Stanley Gardner, and others. The reader's interest thereby snowballs as new "capers" of the familiar characters are related in succeeding tales. If the intention of the contracting parties had been to avoid this practice which was a very valuable one to the author, it is hardly reasonable that it would be left to a general clause following specific grants. Another buttressing fact is that Hammett wrote and caused to be published in 1932, long after the Falcon agreements, three stories in which some of the leading characters of the Falcon were featured, and no objection was voiced by Warner. It is also of some note that the evidence shows that Columbia, long subsequent to the conveying instruments, dickered with Warner for the use of the Falcon on its "Suspense" radio program and, failing in its efforts, substituted "The Kandy Tooth" which uses the Falcon characters under license of Hammett. Warner made no claim against Columbia at or reasonably soon afterward. The conclusion we have come to, as to the intention of the parties, would seem to be in harmony with the fact that the purchase price paid by Warner was $8,500.00, which would seem inadequate compensation for the complete surrender of the characters made famous by the popular reception of the book, The Maltese Falcon; and that the intention of the parties, inclusive of the "Assignment", was not that Hammett should be deprived of using the Falcon characters in subsequently written stories, and that the contract, properly construed, does not deprive Hammett of their use.

Up to this point we have discussed the points at issue by construing the contract and by seeking the intention of the parties to it, and we have concluded that the parties never intended by their contract to buy and sell the future use of the personalities in the writing.

It will now be profitable to consider whether it was ever intended by the copyright statute that characters with their names should be under its protection.

The practice of writers to compose sequels to stories is old, and the copyright statute, though amended several times, has never specifically mentioned the point. It does not appear that it has ever been adjudicated, although it is mentioned in Nichols v. Universal Pictures Corp., 2 Cir., 1930, 45 F.2d 119. If Congress had intended that the sale of the right to publish a copyrighted story would foreclose the author's use of its characters in subsequent works for the life of the copyright, it would seem Congress would have made specific provision therefor. Authors work for the love of their art no more than other professional people work in other lines of work for the love of it. There is the financial motive as well. The characters of an author's imagination and the art of his descriptive talent, like a painter's or like a person with his penmanship, are always limited and always fall into limited patterns. The restriction argued for is unreasonable, and would effect the very opposite of the statute's purpose which is to encourage the production of the arts.

It is our conception of the area covered by the copyright statute that when a study of the two writings is made and it is plain from the study that one of them is not in fact the creation of the putative author, but instead has been copied in substantial part exactly or in transparent re-phrasing to produce essentially the story of the other writing, it infringes.

It is conceivable that the character really constitutes the story being told, but if the character is only the chessman in the game of telling the story he is not within the area of the protection afforded by the copyright. The subject is given consideration in the Nichols case, supra, 45 F.2d at page 121 of the citation. At page 122 of 45 F. 2d of the same case the court remarks that the line between infringement and non-infringement is indefinite and may seem arbitrary when drawn; nevertheless it must be drawn.

We conclude that even if the Owners assigned their complete rights in the copyright to the Falcon, such assignment did not prevent the author from using the characters used therein, in other stories. The characters were vehicles for the story told, and the vehicles did not go with the sale of the story.

We turn to the consideration of general infringement. It is agreed that a story entitled "The Kandy Tooth" is the closest to The Maltese Falcon, and from a practical standpoint if the Tooth does not infringe the Falcon, there has been no infringement.

We have set out in notes 7 and 8 at the end of this opinion, short summations of the two works. There is a sameness in the tricks of spinning out the yarn so as to sustain the reader's suspense as to hinted mystery, and there is a similarity in the two stories in that there is a long complicated search for a lost article of fabulous value. The searches are filled with complications, fatalities, and moral delinquencies by characters in name, description, and action of some similarities. The script of the Tooth was not composed by Hammett and, except for a few expressions, is not written in the Hammett literary style.

We see no clear error in the trial court's holding that the similarities of the two stories do not go to the degree of constituting practically the same story. There is no textual copying; the mystery of the Tooth and the suspense to the reader would not be dulled through his having read the Falcon. In a phrase, they are different stories though of the same general nature.

Unfair Use and Competition

Warner claims the radio broadcasts, "The Adventures of Sam Spade" and the "Suspense" broadcast of "The Kandy Tooth", and others, wherein the characters of the Falcon were used by name and their peculiarities, constituted unfair use and competition. The trial court found against such contention and we think the conclusion does not constitute clear error.

It is patent that the characters of The Maltese Falcon could not fairly be used in such a manner as to cause the Falcon to be materially lessened in its commercial worth by degrading or cheapening them so that the public would not be interested in their capers. They could not be used in such a manner as to deceive the public or to "palm off" to the public the idea that they were really witnessing The Maltese Falcon when they viewed showings of the other stories. We think there was no reversible error in the court's conclusions on these points.

Although we have thought it necessary to arrive at some conclusions not entirely in accord with those of the district court, or to arrive at like conclusions through somewhat different reasoning, nevertheless we commend a reading of that court's opinion and notation of authorities cited. We are in complete accord with the order of the district court that the plaintiffs-appellants take nothing, and that defendants-appellees recover their costs.

The judgment in accordance with this opinion will settle all of the issues of the case, including all of Hammett's interest in the subject matter under Warner's claims. There is no justiciable controversy between Hammett and Knopf, the nominal plaintiff. It follows that no useful purpose could be served by considering Hammett's prayer for a declaration of his rights and his counterclaim for a declaratory judgment is therefore dismissed and the judgment running to him on it is reversed. Otherwise, the judgment is affirmed.

Reversed and affirmed in part.

GROVE PRESS, INC. v. GREENLEAF PUB. CO.

United States District Court, E.D. New York, 1965.
247 F.Supp. 518, 147 U.S.P.Q. 99.

BARTELS, District Judge.

This is an action against the defendants based upon an alleged copyright infringement of the copyright on a book by Jean Genet, a well known author, published by Editions Gallimard Et Cie in Paris in the French language, entitled "Journal du Voleur" ("The Thief's Journal"), and also a copyright upon an excerpt therefrom published in an anthology in the English language in the United States. The plaintiffs include the author and owner of the copyright and those claiming license and contractual rights with respect thereto, and the defendants include the publisher, its officers, and also the printers and distributors of the accused publication. Both parties move for a partial summary judgment pursuant to Rule 56, Fed.Rules Civ.Proc., 28 U.S.C.A., seeking a determination as to the merits of the infringement questions based upon the undisputed facts, leaving by agreement the other issues, if any, such as proof of damages, profits, attorneys' fees, etc., for future consideration. Jurisdiction is founded on 28 U.S.C.A. § 1338(a) and §§ 101 and 112 of the Copyright Act (hereinafter referred to as "the Act"), 17 U.S.C.A. §§ 101 and 112.

Pertinent Facts

The controversy revolves around five books:

1. The genesis of "The Thief's Journal" begins on June 16, 1949 with its publication in France and in French under the title "Journal du Voleur." This edition (hereinafter sometimes referred to as "the underlying work") contained a legend following the title page reading:

> "Tous droits de traduction, de reproduction et d'adaptation reservés pour tous les pays, y compris l'U.R.S.S.
> © 1949 Editions Gallimard."

Defendants concede the validity of the 1949 copyright. On July 7, 1965, as a prerequisite to this suit, the plaintiffs registered this copyright in the United States under Section 13 of the Act, 17 U.S.C.A. § 13.

2. On October 21, 1952, an English translation of a portion of "The Thief's Journal", which Genet and Gallimard had licensed plaintiff Bernard Frechtman to make, was published in the United States by The New American Library of World Literature, Inc. in an anthology entitled "New World Writing Second Mentor Selection." This excerpt, which consisted of five pages (hereinafter sometimes referred to as the "N.A.L. copyright") contained the following legend on the back of the title page:

> "A section from The Thief's Journal Copyright, 1952, by Bernard Frechtman"

Registration of this copyright was made in the United States on November 12, 1952. Defendants admit the validity of the 1952 copyright.

3. In 1954 an English translation (hereinafter sometimes referred to as "the Olympia edition") by Frechtman of the complete "Journal du Voleur" was published in France by The Olympia Press under license from Genet. The following legends appear in the proper places on the Olympia edition:

> "Published in agreement with the Librairie Gallimard.
>
> Journal du Voleur was first published in 1949 in a privately printed edition of four hundred copies. A slightly modified version was published in the same year by the Librairie Gallimard. The present translation follows the original and only complete text, though it incorporates a few footnotes which the author added to the later edition.
>
> Copyright 1954 by B. Frechtman and The Olympia Press, Paris"

and on the back cover page the following appears:

> "Not to be sold in the U.S.A. or U.K."

No application for United States registration of copyright and no attempt to secure ad interim protection pursuant to 17 U.S.C.A. §§ 22 and 23 were made for the Olympia edition.

4. On November 16, 1964, plaintiff Grove Press, Inc., acting pursuant to an exclusive license granted by Genet on October 19, 1959, published for distribution in the United States and Canada another English translation (hereinafter referred to as "the Grove edition") made by Frechtman. All copies of the Grove edition contained the following legends on the back of the title page:

> "Copyright © 1964 by Grove Press, Inc.
>
> All Rights Reserved
>
> Originally published by Librairie Gallimard in Paris, France under the title Journal du Voleur, copyright © 1949 by Librairie Gallimard."

Registration of this copyright in the United States was made on January 26, 1965. Defendants do not contest the validity of this copyright and plaintiffs assert no claim of infringement as to this publication except insofar as Grove Press sues as a licensee of Jean Genet.

5. In 1965 defendants published, distributed and sold in the United States an English translation of "Journal du Voleur" which had been produced by photocopying the Olympia edition. Upon this work (hereinafter referred to as "the Greenleaf edition") the following legends appear:

> "This edition follows the original text of the Olympia Press edition, published in Paris; it is complete and unabridged." (on the back of the first page)
>
> "translated from the French by Bernard Frechtman" (on the title page)

special contents this edition copyright, © 1965 by The Greenleaf Publishing Company" (on the back of the title page)

None of the plaintiffs has authorized the publication of the Greenleaf edition. Defendants rest their authority to copy upon the theory that the Olympia edition, including the N.A.L. excerpt, was in the public domain.

Notwithstanding the extensive and detailed contentions and arguments of both sides, the issues may be reduced to the fundamental question of whether Greenleaf infringed either the N.A.L. copyright or the 1949 copyright, or both. To the extent that this involves an adjudication of the effect upon the underlying work of an English translation first published in a foreign country without copyright registration in the United States and without seeking *ad interim* protection, it appears to be an issue of first impression. At all events, no authorities have been cited or found squarely in point.

The N.A.L. Copyright

The first question posed involves the alleged infringement of the N.A.L. copyright. The issue raised is whether this copyright lost its vitality by its incorporation in the Olympia and Grove work. Each party argues that Bentley v. Tibbals, 2 Cir. 1915, 223 F. 247, is decisive in its favor. In Bentley a British citizen secured in 1906 a copyright in the United States of a book entitled "Bentley's Telegraph Cyphers," the now famous international telegraphic code. In 1907 he published in London a larger book entitled "Bentley's Complete Phrase Code" containing a substantial amount of the "Cyphers" together with additional matter. For that work he secured a British copyright, on the title page of which appeared the following statement:

> "This Code includes the Telegraph Cyphers entered according to act of Congress in the year 1906, by E. I. Bentley in the office of the Librarian of Congress at Washington, D.C. All rights reserved. Entered at Stationer's Hall." (p. 250)

Bentley then sold, both in the United Kingdom and in the United States, copies of this larger book which was uncopyrighted. Tibbals copied the exact "Complete Phrase Code" in the same size and color, and sold this book under the title "Bentley's Complete Phrase Code". This publication Bentley claimed infringed his 1906 copyright of "Bentley's Telegraph Cyphers," the essential features of which were embodied in the larger work. Tibbals contended that Bentley by importing and selling the larger work in the United States, lost his right of protection to anything contained therein and "that the publication of parts of a copyrighted book as parts of an uncopyrighted book involves an abandonment of the copyright." The Court denied the injunction, grounding its decision upon the fact that there was nothing in the larger work which would identify "the copyrighted from the uncopyrighted matter," stating:

> "In our opinion one who so embodies copyrighted with uncopyrighted matter that one reading his work cannot distinguish between the two has no right to complain if the book is republished by third parties." (p. 256)

It is true that the Court in the course of its opinion, called attention to the fact that the larger book was imported by the copyright owner and implicitly referred to this difference in citing United Dictionary Company v. G. & C. Merriam Company, 1908, 208 U.S. 260, 28 S.Ct. 290, 52 L.Ed. 478. Plaintiffs rely upon this distinction in support of their position that the Bentley ruling is not applicable to the facts in this case. The premise of the Bentley decision, however, was not the nature of the importation but the failure of identification.

Here, unlike Bentley's publication, neither the Olympia nor the Grove publication contained any notice that the copyrighted N.A.L. excerpt was included anywhere in the respective publications. But even if such notice had been imprinted on the title page of either edition, no one by an inspection of either work could have identified which portion was the N.A.L. excerpt and which was not. The fragment was completely submerged and unidentified in both versions. Thus, if there was any copying of the N.A.L. excerpt from the Olympia and the Grove editions, it did not constitute a copyright infringement. In essence, the same conclusion was reached by this Court in denying the plaintiffs' application for a preliminary injunction.

The 1949 Copyright (the underlying work)

A more serious and subtle issue is raised by the alleged infringement of the 1949 copyright on the original French language work involving the nature of a translation and the effect of its dedication.

Jean Genet's original story published in the French language, was copyrighted in 1949 and there is no question that that copyright still subsists. Frechtman's English translation published in France in 1954, followed the original and only complete text of the 1949 publication. While it bore the inscription "Copyright 1954 by B. Frechtman and The Olympia Press, Paris," it concededly did not comply with the *ad interim* protection provided by Sections 22 and 23 of the Act, 17 U.S.C.A. §§ 22 and 23, and for the purpose of this decision, it will be assumed arguendo that it fell within the public domain.

The Greenleaf edition "follows the original text of the Olympia Press edition, published in Paris" as it was "translated from the French by Bernard Frechtman". The query is, what did Greenleaf copy when it copied this English translation. Defendants assert that physically all they copied was an uncopyrighted English translation and nothing more, that they did not copy the copyrighted book which was a 1949 French language work, and that when Frechtman failed to obtain copyright protection for his English translation in France of the 1949 French language work, that translation which was with the consent of the author, of necessity included Genet's novel and the novel as thus translated was automatically dedicated to the public. They argue, therefore, that the accused book could not have infringed the 1949 copyright.

Discussion

Resolution of the problem involves the interpretation of the basic concept of copyright protection upon which reasonable men in this case might differ. The essential purpose of the copyright law is to grant valuable and enforceable rights to composers, authors, publishers, and others without imposing burdensome requirements and at the same time to require a notice of the copyright to be affixed to each copy of the work, to protect the innocent from the penalties of infringement. The Court is thus confronted with the question of whether Frechtman's English translation published abroad without *ad interim* protection destroyed the author's copyright protection in his literary composition.

Section 7 of the Act, 17 U.S.C.A. § 7, reads as follows:

"Compilations or abridgements, adaptations, arrangements, dramatizations, *translations*, or other versions of works in the public domain or of copyrighted works when produced with the consent of the proprietor of the copyright in such works, or works republished with new matter, shall be regarded as *new works subject to copyright* under the provisions of this title: *but the publication of any such new works shall not affect the force or validity of any subsisting copyright upon the matter employed or any part thereof*, or be construed to imply an exclusive right to such use of the original works, or to secure or extend copyright in such original works." (Emphasis supplied)

The above section permits the copyright of a translation of a work in the public domain or of a copyrighted work with the consent of the owner without permitting the publication of such "new work" to affect the validity of the existing copyright upon the matter employed in such translation. If the work translated is in the public domain, of course no consent of the copyright owner is required. The pertinence of the section is only to demonstrate the fact that a translation can be copyrighted separate and apart from a copyrighted work without affecting the subsisting copyright. The copyright of the translation is not mandatory under the section to preserve the copyright on the underlying work.

Keeping in mind the purpose of the Act, the Court is compelled to reject the defendants' interpretation of the effect of Greenleaf's copying Frechtman's translation as too literal, mechanical and unrealistic. It is obvious that Greenleaf copied not only the words of Frechtman, the translator, but also the content and meaning of those words as created in Jean Genet's original biographical story. This creation included the entire plot, scenes, characters and dialogue of the novel, i. e., the format and pattern. Greenleaf copied two things, (1) the words and (2) the story. Frechtman's reproduction of the novel in another language was permitted by the author but this did not constitute a consent that reproduction by others could be accomplished without Genet's authority if Frechtman failed to copyright his derivative work. The fact that it was unnecessary for Greenleaf to obtain Frechtman's consent did not automatically make it unnecessary for Greenleaf to obtain the consent of the copyright owner. It is an old story that reproductions of a copyrighted article cannot be made without the consent of the creator. Illustrative of this principle is Mr. Justice Holmes' decision holding that an attempt to reproduce the copyrighted story of "Ben Hur" by moving pictures of scenes dramatizing the work, constituted an infringement of the author's copyright, wherein he remarked:

> "But if a pantomime of Ben Hur would be a dramatizing of Ben Hur, it would be none the less so that it was exhibited to the audience by reflection from a glass, and not by direct vision of the figures,—as sometimes has been done in order to produce ghostly or inexplicable effects. *The essence of the matter in the case last supposed is not the mechanism employed, but that we see the event or story lived."* Kalem Company v. Harper Brothers, 1911, 222 U.S. 55, 61, 32 S.Ct. 20, 21, 56 L.Ed. 92. (Emphasis supplied)

The query is, what does a copyright of a novel include? Does it cover only the form of communication or the mechanism employed, or does it also embrace the pattern of the story? The essence of a novel or any other story for that matter, is the plot, plan, arrangement, characters and dialogue therein contained and not simply its form of articulation. "In truth, every author of a book has a copyright in the plan, arrangement and combination of his materials, and in his mode of illustrating his subject, if it be new and original in its substance." Emerson v. Davies, D.Mass.Cir. 1845, 8 Fed.Cas. 615, 619 (Case No. 4,436). While this does not mean that the abstract idea of the novel or play alone is protected, it does mean that the particular pattern employed in arranging and expressing that idea is entitled to protection. It may be difficult sometimes to distinguish whether the idea or plot alone is being employed or whether the pattern is being copied, but the line must be drawn. In the opinion of Professor Nimmer: " . . . it would seem that any authorized publication of a derivative work must necessarily also constitute a publication of the basic work upon which it is based." Nimmer on Copyright (1965) § 57.1, p. 220. The translation does not insulate the original story from copyright infringement even though the translation itself may be uncopyrighted. Like any other derivative work, the translation is separate and apart from the underlying work and a dedication to the public of the derivative work did not without more, emancipate the pattern of the underlying work from its copyright. The essence of the matter, as Mr. Justice Holmes observed, is that "we see the event or story lived" and that story is copyrighted. Kalem Company v. Harper Brothers, supra.

Each party relies heavily upon the case of G. Ricordi & Co. v. Paramount Pictures, Inc., 2 Cir. 1951, 189 F.2d 469, cert. denied, 1951, 342 U.S. 849, 72 S.Ct. 77, 96 L.Ed. 641. It is appropriate therefore to examine its facts. The work involved there was "Madame Butterfly," the original novel having been written in 1897 by John Luther Long and copyrighted. Thereafter Long licensed David Belasco to write a play based upon the novel under the same name, which was not copyrighted until 1917. In 1901 Long and Belasco granted Ricordi rights to make a Libretto for an opera of Belasco's play "founded on the original theme", written by Long; "the said Libretto and all rights therein, dramatic or otherwise, to be the exclusive property of" Ricordi. Under this grant Puccini composed the opera upon which Ricordi secured both the original and renewal copyright. In 1925 Long obtained a renewal of the copyright on his novel and in 1932 Long's administrator granted Paramount the motion picture rights therein. No renewal was ever obtained of the copyright on Belasco's play. Ricordi claimed to be the exclusive owner of the motion picture rights in the novel, based upon the original agreement with Long and Belasco and his renewal copyright of the opera.

The Court of Appeals in reversing judgment in favor of Ricordi, held that the play was in the public domain and both parties were free to make a motion picture version thereof; that Paramount had the exclusive motion picture rights in the novel and therefore plaintiff could not make general use thereof for a motion picture version of its opera, and that plaintiff had the exclusive motion picture rights in the opera and Paramount could make no use of the opera in a motion picture version of the novel.

Upon a petition for clarification as to the meaning of the Court's statement that "When the copyright expired, the play was property in the public demesne   .   .   ." (p. 471), the Court clarified its holding in these words:

> "What the petitioner desires is an express statement that only the new matter which Belasco's play added to Long's novel came into the public demesne upon the expiration of Belasco's copyright. It is implicit in the opinion as a whole that what is dedicated to the public as a condition of obtaining a copyright is only such matter as is copyrightable, but to avoid any possible cavil we will amend the above quoted sentence to read as follows: 'When the copyright expired, the copyrightable new matter in the play was property in the public demesne, since the record discloses no renewal of the copyright.'" (p. 472)

While that case involved a renewal of copyright, the differentiation between dedicating the underlying work and the derivative work to the public is the same in both cases.

Defendants claim that Ricordi simply means that the stage play was in the public domain and the screen play was not because it was a new version of the original novel; and similarly in this case, that while the Frechtman translation was in the public domain, no other translation of the 1949 French work could be made without Genet's permission. They argue from this comparison that they had a right to copy the Frechtman translation in the same manner as anyone could copy Belasco's stage play. This is a false and distorted view because it ignores the fact that the only thing placed in the public domain in the Ricordi case was the *new matter* in the play upon which the original copyright had expired. The Court held that the "Madame Butterfly" novel could not be employed for any purpose without the consent of the proprietor or the licensee of the copyright, and that only the new matter that Belasco had added to Long's novel was dedicated. By parallel reasoning, the only *new matter* that Frechtman added to the Genet novel was his translation and only that could have been dedicated to the public. As a practical matter, new matter which a play adds to a novel might be more discernible or separable than new matter which a translation adds to a story. Both, however, represent a change in the mechanism or medium of expressing the same underlying work, and both are derivatives which may be described as new works under Section 7 of the Act. If the derivative, such as the new matter in a play or the new matter added by different mediums of thought conveyance or communication represented by translation, cannot be used without copying part or all of the copyrighted underlying work, then the consent of the proprietor of that copyright must be obtained.

Defendants, however, have not been charged with violating the copyright law by an unauthorized translation of the underlying work. What the defendants did was to copy a translation which they allege was not copyrighted. The fact that the copying of the original story was accomplished indirectly through copying of a translation of the original was nonetheless copying. Unauthorized copying may be effected either directly or indirectly; thus copying from a copy is no less an infringement than copying from the original copyrighted work. In Wihtol v. Crow, 8 Cir. 1962, 309 F.2d 777, the plaintiff had composed a song which he had first copyrighted in 1935 and later incorporated in a new version which he also copyrighted in 1944. The defendant unauthorizedly incorporated the 1944 version of the song (which included the 1935 copyright) in a new arrangement of his own. While he copied only one song, it was held that he had infringed both of plaintiff's copyrights. By analogy, an infringement of an underlying copyright may likewise occur by copying an uncopyrighted translation of a copyrighted original since the underlying copyright might not be disclosed in either case.

A postscript should be added. Defendants have placed considerable emphasis upon the fact that the Olympia edition did not obtain *ad interim* protection. While this is true and by hypothesis placed this edition in the public domain, it does not follow that such failure by the publisher or translator should be fatal to the copyright on the pattern of the underlying work unless the author has consented to such dedication. Here it is admitted that Librairie Gallimard and The Olympia Press executed a contract under which Gallimard granted Olympia the right to publish the translation of "The Thief's Journal" in all countries "provided he sells it neither in England nor in the United States (the above edition to carry the notation 'Not to be sold in the USA and the United Kingdom')". Accordingly, a legend was placed on the back cover page on all copies of the Olympia edition reading: "Not to be sold in U.S.A. or U.K." There was, in addition, a prominent copyright notice placed upon the Olympia edition which notified the world that it followed the original and only complete text of the publication in 1949 by Librairie Gallimard.

While this legend and notice might not have been sufficient to protect the translation, it was ample notice that the Olympia edition was only a translation which was not to be sold in the United States and that accordingly there might be a copyright on the underlying work. At all events, the above contract and the legends placed upon the Olympia edition were sufficient to establish that there was no consent on the part of the author to dedicate his underlying work to the public. It cannot therefore be claimed that he abandoned his copyright on the 1949 French edition. To impose upon the author the duty to see that the Olympia edition obtained *ad interim* protection in the United States in order that his own copyright on the pattern of the underlying work might survive, would appear to be imposing upon the author an unnecessarily burdensome requirement. As far as the public is concerned, it was placed upon sufficient notice to inquire as to any copyright on the underlying work. In the reverse situation a notice of copyright on the derivative work has been held sufficient to protect both the derivative as well as the underlying work. In Nom Music, Inc. v. Kaslin, 2 Cir. 1965, 343 F.2d 198, the Court remarked:

"In part because of the statutory equation of a derivative work with a 'new work,' it has been held that the notice need give only the date and owner of the copyright in the derivative work, *leaving the reader to his own devices in ferreting out this information as to the original.*" (p. 200) (Emphasis supplied)

Consequently, it is clear enough that as far as affixing a copyright notice is concerned, the copyright on the underlying work is not dependent upon the copyright on the derivative or new work.

The conclusion, therefore, is that the defendants' publication and sale within the United States of Frechtman's English translation of "Journal du Voleur" accomplished by photocopying the Olympia edition, constitutes an infringement of Jean Genet's 1949 copyright published by Gallimard and registered under Section 13 of the Act.

Since the determination of the quantum of damage as well as the parties entitled thereto and the parties liable therefor, have by agreement been deferred for a subsequent hearing, summary judgment will be entered for such of the plaintiffs as shall be subsequently determined to have an interest as either copyright owner or licensee of the 1949 copyright, against the defendant Greenleaf and such of the other defendants as may be subsequently determined to have participated in infringing said copyright and for the amount of damages to be subsequently determined. Settle order on two (2) days' notice.

NOTES

1. Did Baker v. Selden hold that plaintiff's subject matter was not copyrightable? That, though copyrightable, plaintiff had no rights in it as against the sort of use being made by defendant? That, although plaintiff had rights in the work, they were not infringed by defendant's work? The case has been cited as authority for each of these three propositions. With the first proposition, compare the discussion above of the copyrightability of fact works. With the third, compare the discussion below of infringement generally.

Baker's second proposition, if taken to hold that copyright secures no right to use, obviously goes too far. Although the Copyright Act, unlike the Patent Act, nowhere grants a blanket right to use, each of its many specific rights necessarily connotes some specific use. The question in any case is whether the use for which the copyright owner seeks protection is one that the law secures for his type of work.

Consider, for example, Scholz Homes, Inc. v. Maddox, 379 F.2d 84, 154 U.S.P.Q. 197 (6th Cir. 1967), in which plaintiff accused defendant of copying his architectural plans and of building a house from them. The court distinguished two cases that had "considered and rejected the contention that copyrighted plans were infringed merely by constructing buildings according to those plans" and concluded that "even if the holder of a copyright of architectural plans cannot prevent others from building according to those plans, he might still retain the exclusive right to their duplication." 379 F.2d 84, 85.

Noting that *Baker* would seem to go farther than the two distinguished cases and permit even the copying of plans, the court suggested that "perhaps the most promising method of avoiding this difficulty is to argue that copyrighted architectural plans should be treated differently from copyrighted books, and that the principles enunciated in *Baker* should therefore be held inapplicable. . . . It is far less obvious that architectural plans are prepared for the purpose of instructing the general public as to how the depicted structure might be built. Rather, they are often prepared so that they may be used in the building of unique structures, or at least structures limited in number. If the copyright statute protected merely against the vending of plans instead of against their unauthorized use, it would therefore fail to afford a form of protection architects might strongly desire. This protection would most effectively be provided by holding the unauthorized construction of a building according to a copyrighted plan to be an infringement; if *Baker* is followed to the extent of holding that the possession of the copyright in the plans gives no exclusive right to construct the building, then protection could be provided by declaring the making of unauthorized copies of the plans to be an infringement." 379 F.2d 84, 86.

For a more straightforward declaration that the copying of architectural plans constitutes infringement, see Imperial Homes Corp. v. Lamont, 458 F.2d 895, 173 U.S.P.Q. 519 (5th Cir. 1972).

2. In *Grove Press,* what *was* forfeited by publication of the Olympia edition? If the court had reached the opposite result, would a subsequent, unauthorized translation of the Olympia edition into French have been held to infringe the copyright in the underlying work—the original, 1949 French publication of *Journal du Voleur?* Given the dilemma, do you think that the court found the best way out?

What warrant is there for the court's assertion that it is "unnecessarily burdensome" to require copyright proprietors to see that their licensees comply with copyright formalities? Recall that decisions under the 1909 Act had imposed such a duty on copyright proprietors as a condition to maintaining copyright. See page 664, above. What are the implications for cases like *Grove Press* of the fact that the new Act has relaxed the policing requirement?

In resolving cases like *Grove Press,* in which one work continues to be protected by copyright while a connected work is in the public domain, should it be important to know *why* the second work is in the public domain? The Olympia edition was in the public domain because of failure to comply with a statutory formality. Should the court have reached a different result if the edition was in the public domain because the initial copyright term had expired and not been renewed? If the term had been renewed and the renewal period had expired?

Another way out of the *Grove* dilemma is suggested by a perspective on Ricordi v. Paramount different from the one afforded by *Grove*: "The court in *Grove Press* viewed *G. Ricordi* as based on the theory that derivative works have independent lives only as to new matter added by the derivation; when any derivative work enters the public domain, it dedicates only the original matter added by the derivation, not the basic work itself or additions made by other derivative works. This interpretation is too broad. The licensing agreement between Long and Belasco was only for the course of the original copyright term of Long's novel. When that term expired in 1925, Belasco no longer had the contractual rights to use the underlying novel; his right was, therefore, confined to only the "new matter" he had added. Belasco's subsequent failure to secure renewal on his play copyright could therefore only forfeit his rights in the new matter. Thus, the issue of the effect upon the underlying work of forfeiture of a derivative work whose license is still in force was not touched upon in *G. Ricordi,* which does not control the present case.

"In *Grove Press*, the infringement consisted of making an exact copy of the dedicated derivative work in the same communications medium for which the forfeited work had been licensed by the underlying proprietor. Since the derivative work is separately copyrightable under section 7, it might be considered a wholly 'independent entity,' so that the underlying work would arguably merge into the derivative work to the extent that the underlying proprietor licensed the derivative work. Thus, when the derivative work falls into the public domain, it would carry the underlying work with it as to that particular medium. This argument points up the fact that it seems analytically difficult to say that Frechtman's words are in the public domain, yet unavailable for identical reproduction." Note, 79 Harv.L. Rev. 1718 (1966).*

3. What did Warner Brothers v. C.B.S. hold with respect to the copyrightability of characters? Would Hammett and Knopf have had an action if Warner Brothers—or anyone else, for that matter—later used the Sam Spade character in dramas unrelated to the *Maltese Falcon*? Some courts have dismissed the part of the opinion dealing with copyrightability as dicta. See, for example, Columbia Broadcasting System v. DeCosta, 377 F.2d 315, 153 U.S.P.Q. 649 (1st Cir. 1967), cert. denied 389 U.S. 1007, 88 S.Ct. 565, 19 L.Ed.2d 603, 156 U.S.P.Q. 719. The language was, however, taken seriously as "an alternative rationale" by a district court in the Ninth Circuit. Concluding that "the *Warner Bros.* holding did not purport to shut the door entirely on protection for characters," the district court found enough room in the decision to protect Mickey Mouse and other cartoon characters in the Disney clan. Walt Disney Productions v. Air Pirates, 345 F.Supp. 108, 113, 174 U.S.P.Q. 463 (N.D.Cal.1972). On appeal, the Ninth Circuit Court of Appeals observed that characterization of the language as dicta or as an alternate holding would "not affect the result in the case." The central reason was that "while many literary characters may embody little more than an unprotected idea, a comic book character, which has physical as well as conceptual qualities, is more likely to contain some unique elements of expression. Because comic book characters therefore are distinguishable from literary characters, the *Warner Brothers* language does not preclude protection of Disney's characters." 581 F.2d 751, 755, 199 U.S.P.Q. 769 (1978), cert. denied 439 U.S. 1132, 99 S.Ct. 1054, 59 L. Ed.2d 94 (1979).

For a literary character to obtain the degree of definition necessary to sustain copyright protection it may have to be elaborated through a series of works over a period of time. Yet, copyright is traditionally thought to attach to individual works, not to personae that may emerge from an aggregate of works. How, then, does one prove infringement of a literary character? To what work or works does one point as the object of infringement? Does this suggest that, in limiting protection to situations in which "the character really constitutes the story being told," the *Warner Brothers* court was only responding to the practicalities of proof? If a character that is developed through a series of books can be protected, to what extent will the character be free for all to use if one of these books falls into the public domain? See National Comics Publications, Inc. v. Fawcett Publications, Inc., 191 F.2d 594, 90 U.S.P.Q. 274 (2d Cir. 1951). Compare Grove Press v. Greenleaf, above.

What sources other than copyright offer shelter for characters? In Columbia Broadcasting System, Inc. v. DeCosta, 377 F.2d 315, 153 U.S.P.Q. 649 (1st Cir. 1967), protection under state law misappropriation doctrine was held to be preempted under the authority of *Sears* and *Compco,* pp. 130 and 133 above. Would 17 U.S.C.A. § 301 require a similar result today? Do the more traditional unfair competition doctrines of passing off and dilution offer possibilities for protection without the risk of preemption? See DeCosta v. Columbia Broadcasting System, Inc., 520 F.2d 499, 186 U.S.P.Q. 305 (1st Cir. 1975) cert. denied 423 U.S. 1073, 96 S.Ct. 856, 47 L.Ed.2d 83 (1976). What of federal trademark law? See Frederick Warne & Co., Inc. v. Book Sales, Inc., 481 F.Supp. 1191, 1196, 205 U.S.P.Q. 444 (S.D.N.Y. 1979). ("The fact that a copyrightable character or design has fallen into the public domain should not preclude protection under the trademark laws so long as it is shown to have acquired independent trademark significance, identifying in some way the source or sponsorship of the goods.")

See generally, Brylawski, Protection of Characters—Sam Spade Revisited, 22 Bull. Copyright Soc'y 77 (1974); Umbreit, A Consideration of Copyright, 87 U.Pa.L.Rev. 932 (1939); Kellman, The Legal Protection of Fictional Characters, 25 Brooklyn L.Rev. 3 (1958); Note, The Protection Afforded Literary and Cartoon Characters Through Trademark, Unfair Competition, and Copyright, 68 Harv.L. Rev. 349 (1954).

4. The Copyright Act assigns specific rights to different classes of subject matter. For example, the Act gives the exclusive right of public performance to several types of works, but not to sound recordings. 17 U.S.C.A. § 106(4); § 114(a). In each case, the rights given are thought to balance the incentive needed to stimulate the desired level of investment against the public's interest in free access to the specific type of subject matter.

Apart from the statute's differential allocation of rights, different types of subject matter will enjoy different rights simply by reason of their nature. Courts and commentators have frequently observed that characters depicted in cartoons and other visual formats receive far more immediate and complete protection than verbally depicted characters. This divergence in protection is not the result of any careful or principled act of balancing. It is simply that a cartoon character can be sketched quickly, completely and eternally with just a few lines within a single frame, while literary characters must be described in hundreds of pages before they obtain sufficient definition for a charge of infringement to be taken seriously.

Finer distinctions also exist in the rights given to different types of subject matter. Architectural plans and cartoon characters are both works of visual art. Copyright in architectural plans does not give the proprietor any right against use of the plans to put up a building. By contrast, copyright in cartoon characters has been held to extend to dramatic presentations and the production of dolls or other three-dimensional products based on them. See, for example, Hill v. Whalen & Martell, Inc., 220 F. 359 (2d Cir. 1914) (Mutt and Jeff); Fleischer Studios, Inc. v. Ralph A. Freundlich, Inc., 73 F.2d 276 (2d Cir. 1934) (Betty Boop). Can you find a basis for distinguishing between the results reached for these two classes of visual art?

5. Keeping in mind that rights will vary with the type of subject matter in issue, how would you decide the following cases:

Plaintiff, which has compiled and published a booklet of forms, "Standard Documents of the American Institute of Architects," seeks damages from defendant who has made and used six copies of one form and delivered them to contractors with whom he was dealing. See American Institute of Architects v. Fenichel, 41 F.Supp. 146, 51 U.S.P.Q. 29 (S.D.N.Y.1941).

Plaintiff, which has secured copyright in a work described as "Bridge Approach—The drawing shows a novel bridge approach to unsnarl traffic congestion," seeks damages from defendant which allegedly used the work in its "design, plan, construction and operation of the Approach to Cross Bay Parkway Bridge." See Muller v. Triborough Bridge Auth., 43 F.Supp. 298, 52 U.S.P.Q. 227 (S.D.N.Y.1942).

Plaintiff, owner of copyright in a series of books that expound a system of shorthand, claims infringement by defendant's work which contains a substantial portion of the system together with plaintiff's "expression of the mode and manner of teaching it." See Brief English Systems, Inc. v. Owen, 48 F.2d 555, 9 U.S.P.Q. 20 (2d Cir. 1931).

Plaintiff, owner of rights to "Rapid Contract Bridge," charges infringement by defendant's publication in its newspaper of a problem substantially similar to one appearing in plaintiff's book. See Russell v. Northeastern Pub. Co., 7 F.Supp. 571, 23 U.S.P.Q. 123 (D.Mass.1934).

Plaintiff, copyright proprietor of two college physics texts containing problems—without answers—based on the textual material, seeks an injunction against defendant's publication of a book containing solutions to the problems. See Addison-Wesley Pub. Co. v. Brown, 223 F.Supp. 219, 139 U.S.P.Q. 47 (E.D.N.Y. 1963).

What other facts would you want to know in formulating your answers to these questions?

b. Statutory Rights

COPYRIGHT LAW REVISION, H.R.REP.NO.94–1476

94th Cong., 2d Sess. 61–65 (1976).

Section 106.   Exclusive Rights in Copyrighted Works

General Scope of Copyright

The five fundamental rights that the bill gives to copyright owners—the exclusive rights of reproduction, adaptation, publication, performance, and display—are stated generally in section 106.   These exclusive rights, which comprise the so-called "bundle of rights" that is a copyright, are cumulative and may overlap in some cases.   Each of the five enumerated rights may be subdivided indefinitely and, as discussed below in connection with section 201, each subdivision of an exclusive right may be owned and enforced separately.

The approach of the bill is to set forth the copyright owner's exclusive rights in broad terms in section 106, and then to provide various limitations, qualifications, or exemptions in the 12 sections that follow.   Thus, everything in section 106 is made "subject to sections 107 through 118," and must be read in conjunction with those provisions.

The exclusive rights accorded to a copyright owner under section 106 are "to do and to authorize" any of the activities specified in the five numbered clauses.   Use of the phrase "to authorize" is intended to avoid any questions as to the liability of contributory infringers. For example, a person who lawfully acquires an authorized copy of a motion picture would be an infringer if he or she engages in the business of renting it to others for purposes of unauthorized public performance.

Rights of Reproduction, Adaptation, and Publication

The first three clauses of section 106, which cover all rights under a copyright except those of performance and display, extend to every kind of copyrighted work.   The exclusive rights encompassed by these clauses, though closely related, are independent;   they can generally be characterized as rights of copying, recording, adaptation, and publishing.   A single act of infringement may violate all of these rights at once, as where a publisher reproduces, adapts, and sells copies of a person's copyrighted work as part of a publishing venture.   Infringement takes place when any one of the rights is violated: where, for example, a printer reproduces copies without selling them or a retailer sells copies without having anything to do with their reproduction. The references to "copies or phonorecords," although in the plural, are intended here and throughout the bill to include the singular (1 U.S.C.A. § 1).

Reproduction.—Read together with the relevant definitions in section 101, the right "to reproduce the copyrighted work in copies or phonorecords" means the right to produce a material object in which the work is duplicated, transcribed, imitated, or simulated in a fixed form from which it can be "perceived, reproduced, or otherwise communicated, either directly or with the aid of a machine or device." As under the present law, a copyrighted work would be infringed by reproducing it in whole or in any substantial part, and by duplicating it exactly or by imitation or simulation. Wide departures or variations from the copyrighted work would still be an infringement as long as the author's "expression" rather than merely the author's "ideas" are taken. An exception to this general principle, applicable to the reproduction of copyrighted sound recordings, is specified in section 114.

"Reproduction" under clause (1) of section 106 is to be distinguished from "display" under clause (5). For a work to be "reproduced," its fixation in tangible form must be "sufficiently permanent or stable to permit it to be perceived, reproduced, or otherwise communicated for a period of more than transitory duration." Thus, the showing of images on a screen or tube would not be a violation of clause (1), although it might come within the scope of clause (5).

Preparation of Derivative Works.—The exclusive right to prepare derivative works, specified separately in clause (2) of section 106, overlaps the exclusive right of reproduction to some extent. It is broader than that right, however, in the sense that reproduction requires fixation in copies or phonorecords, whereas the preparation of a derivative work, such as a ballet, pantomime, or improvised performance, may be an infringement even though nothing is ever fixed in tangible form.

To be an infringement the "derivative work" must be "based upon the copyrighted work," and the definition in section 101 refers to "a translation, musical arrangement, dramatization, fictionalization, motion picture version, sound recording, art reproduction, abridgment, condensation, or any other form in which a work may be recast, transformed, or adapted." Thus, to constitute a violation of section 106(2), the infringing work must incorporate a portion of the copyrighted work in some form; for example, a detailed commentary on a work or a programmatic musical composition inspired by a novel would not normally constitute infringements under this clause.

Use in Information Storage and Retrieval Systems.—As section 117 declares explicitly, the bill is not intended to alter the present law with respect to the use of copyrighted works in computer systems.*

Public Distribution.—Clause (3) of section 106 establishes the exclusive right of publication: The right "to distribute copies or phonorecords of the copyrighted work to the public by sale or other transfer of ownership, or by rental, lease, or lending." Under this provision the copyright owner would have the right to control the

---

* See Statute Supplement, P.L. 96–517,
§ 10(b) amending 17 U.S.C.A. § 117.
[Ed.]

first public distribution of an authorized copy or phonorecord of his work, whether by sale, gift, loan, or some rental or lease arrangement. Likewise, any unauthorized public distribution of copies or phonorecords that were unlawfully made would be an infringement. As section 109 makes clear, however, the copyright owner's rights under section 106(3) cease with respect to a particular copy or phonorecord once he has parted with ownership of it.

Rights of Public Performance and Display

Performing Rights and the "For Profit" Limitation.—The right of public performance under section 106(4) extends to "literary, musical, dramatic, and choreographic works, pantomimes, and motion pictures and other audiovisual works and sound recordings" and, unlike the equivalent provisions now in effect, is not limited by any "for profit" requirement. The approach of the bill, as in many foreign laws, is first to state the public performance right in broad terms, and then to provide specific exemptions for educational and other nonprofit uses.

This approach is more reasonable than the outright exemption of the 1909 statute. The line between commercial and "nonprofit" organizations is increasingly difficult to draw. Many "non-profit" organizations are highly subsidized and capable of paying royalties, and the widespread public exploitation of copyrighted works by public broadcasters and other noncommercial organizations is likely to grow. In addition to these trends, it is worth noting that performances and displays are continuing to supplant markets for printed copies and that in the future a broad "not for profit" exemption could not only hurt authors but could dry up their incentive to write.

The exclusive right of public performance is expanded to include not only motion pictures, including works recorded on film, video tape, and video disks, but also audiovisual works such as filmstrips and sets of slides. This provision of section 106(4), which is consistent with the assimilation of motion pictures to audiovisual works throughout the bill, is also related to amendments of the definitions of "display" and "perform" discussed below. The important issue of performing rights in sound recordings is discussed in connection with section 114.

Right of Public Display.—Clause (5) of section 106 represents the first explicit statutory recognition in American copyright law of an exclusive right to show a copyrighted work, or an image of it, to the public. The existence or extent of this right under the present statute is uncertain and subject to challenge. The bill would give the owners of copyright in "literary, musical, dramatic, and choreographic works, pantomimes, and pictorial, graphic, or sculptural works", including the individual images of a motion picture or other audiovisual work, the exclusive right "to display the copyrighted work publicly."

Definitions

Under the definitions of "perform," "display," "publicly," and "transmit" in section 101, the concepts of public performance and public display cover not only the initial rendition or showing, but also any further act by which that rendition or showing is transmitted or communicated to the public. Thus, for example: a singer is performing when he or she sings a song; a broadcasting network is performing when it transmits his or her performance (whether simultaneously or from records); a local broadcaster is performing when it transmits the network broadcast; a cable television system is performing when it retransmits the broadcast to its subscribers; and any individual is performing whenever he or she plays a phonorecord embodying the performance or communicates the performance by turning on a receiving set. Although any act by which the initial performance or display is transmitted, repeated, or made to recur would itself be a "performance" or "display" under the bill, it would not be actionable as an infringement unless it were done "publicly," as defined in section 101. Certain other performances and displays, in addition to those that are "private," are exempted or given qualified copyright control under sections 107 through 118.

To "perform" a work, under the definition in section 101, includes reading a literary work aloud, singing or playing music, dancing a ballet or other choreographic work, and acting out a dramatic work or pantomime. A performance may be accomplished "either directly or by means of any device or process," including all kinds of equipment for reproducing or amplifying sounds or visual images, any sort of transmitting apparatus, any type of electronic retrieval system, and any other techniques and systems not yet in use or even invented.

The definition of "perform" in relation to "a motion picture or other audio visual work" is "to show its images in any sequence or to make the sounds accompanying it audible." The showing of portions of a motion picture, filmstrip, or slide set must therefore be sequential to constitute a "performance" rather than a "display", but no particular order need be maintained. The purely aural performance of a motion picture sound track, or of the sound portions of an audiovisual work, would constitute a performance of the "motion picture or other audiovisual work"; but, where some of the sounds have been reproduced separately on phonorecords, a performance from the phonorecord would not constitute performance of the motion picture or audiovisual work.

The corresponding definition of "display" covers any showing of a "copy" of the work, "either directly or by means of a film, slide, television image, or any other device or process." Since "copies" are defined as including the material object "in which the work is first fixed," the right of public display applies to original works of art as well as to reproductions of them. With respect to motion pictures and other audiovisual works, it is a "display" (rather than a "performance") to show their "individual images nonsequentially." In addition to the direct showings of a copy of a work, "display" would include the projection of an image on a screen or other surface by any method, the transmission of an image by electronic or other means, and the showing of an image on a cathode ray tube, or similar viewing apparatus connected with any sort of information storage and retrieval system.

Under clause (1) of the definition of "publicly" in section 101, a performance or display is "public" if it takes place "at a place open to the public or at any place where a substantial number of persons outside of a normal circle of a family and its social acquaintances is gathered." One of the principal purposes of the definition was to make clear that, contrary to the decision in Metro-Goldwyn-Mayer Distributing Corp. v. Wyatt, 21 C.O.Bull. 203 (D.Md.1932), performances in "semipublic" places such as clubs, lodges, factories, summer camps, and schools are "public performances" subject to copyright control. The term "a family" in this context would include an individual living alone, so that a gathering confined to the individual's social acquaintances would normally be regarded as private. Routine meetings of businesses and governmental personnel would be excluded because they do not represent the gathering of a "substantial number of persons."

Clause (2) of the definition of "publicly" in section 101 makes clear that the concepts of public performance and public display include not only performances and displays that occur initially in a public place, but also acts that transmit or otherwise communicate a performance or display of the work to the public by means of any device or process. The definition of "transmit"—to communicate a performance or display "by any device or process whereby images or sound are received beyond the place from which they are sent"—is broad enough to include all conceivable forms and combinations of wired or wireless communications media, including but by no means limited to radio and television broadcasting as we know them. Each and every method by which the images or sounds comprising a performance or display are picked up and conveyed is a "transmission," and if the transmission reaches the public in any form, the case comes within the scope of clauses (4) or (5) of section 106.

Under the bill, as under the present law, a performance made available by transmission to the public at large is "public" even though the recipients are not gathered in a single place, and even if there is no proof that any of the potential recipients was operating his receiving apparatus at the time of the transmission. The same principles apply whenever the potential recipients of the transmission represent a limited segment of the public, such as the occupants of hotel rooms or the subscribers of a cable television service. Clause (2) of the definition of "publicly" is applicable "whether the members of the public capable of receiving the performance or display receive it in the same place or in separate places and at the same time or at different times."

TWENTIETH CENTURY MUSIC CORP. v. AIKEN

Supreme Court of the United States, 1975.
422 U.S. 151, 95 S.Ct. 2040, 45 L.Ed.2d 84, 186 U.S.P.Q. 65.

Mr. Justice STEWART delivered the opinion of the Court.

The question presented by this case is whether the reception of a radio broadcast of a copyrighted musical composition can constitute copyright infringement, when the copyright owner has licensed the broadcaster to perform the composition publicly for profit.

I

The respondent George Aiken owns and operates a small fast-service food shop in downtown Pittsburgh, Pennsylvania, known as "George Aiken's Chicken." Some customers carry out the food they purchase, while others remain and eat at counters or booths. Usually the "carry-out" customers are in the restaurant for less than five minutes, and those who eat there seldom remain longer than 10 or 15 minutes.

A radio with outlets to four speakers in the ceiling receives broadcasts of music and other normal radio programing at the restaurant. Aiken usually turns on the radio each morning at the start of business. Music, news, entertainment, and commercial advertising broadcast by radio stations are thus heard by Aiken, his employees, and his customers during the hours that the establishment is open for business.

On March 11, 1972, broadcasts of two copyrighted musical compositions were received on the radio from a local station while several customers were in Aiken's establishment. Petitioner Twentieth Century Music Corp. owns the copyright on one of these songs, "The More I See You"; petitioner Mary Bourne the copyright on the other, "Me and My Shadow." Petitioners are members of the American Society of Composers, Authors and Publishers (ASCAP), an association that licenses the performing rights of its members to their copyrighted works. The station that broadcast the petitioners' songs was licensed by ASCAP to broadcast them. Aiken, however, did not hold a license from ASCAP.

The petitioners sued Aiken in the United States District Court for the Western District of Pennsylvania to recover for copyright infringement. Their complaint alleged that the radio reception in Aiken's restaurant of the licensed broadcasts infringed their exclusive rights to "perform" their copyrighted works in public for profit. The District Judge agreed, and granted statutory monetary awards for each infringement. 356 F.Supp. 271. The United States Court of Appeals for the Third Circuit reversed that judgment, 500 F.2d 127, holding that the petitioners' claims against the respondent were foreclosed by this Court's decisions in Fortnightly Corp. v. United Artists, 392 U.S. 390, 88 S.Ct. 2084, 20 L.Ed.2d 1176, and Teleprompter Corp. v. CBS, 415 U.S. 394, 94 S.Ct. 1129, 39 L.Ed.2d 415. We granted certiorari.

II

The Copyright Act of 1909, 35 Stat. 1075, as amended, 17 U.S.C. A. § 1 et seq., gives to a copyright holder a monopoly limited to specified "exclusive" rights in his copyrighted works. As the Court explained in Fortnightly Corp. v. United Artists, supra:

> "The Copyright Act does not give a copyright holder control over all uses of his copyrighted work. Instead, § 1 of the Act enumerates several 'rights' that are made 'exclusive' to the holder of the copyright. If a person, without authorization from the copyright holder, puts a copyrighted work to a use within the scope of one of these 'exclusive rights,' he infringes the copyright. If he puts the work to a use not enumerated in § 1, he does not infringe." 392 U.S. at 393–395, 88 S.Ct., at 2086.

Accordingly, if an unlicensed use of a copyrighted work does not conflict with an "exclusive" right conferred by the statute, it is no infringement of the holder's rights. No license is required by the Copyright Act, for example, to sing a copyrighted lyric in the shower.

The limited scope of the copyright holder's statutory monopoly, like the limited copyright duration required by the Constitution, reflects a balance of competing claims upon the public interest: creative work is to be encouraged and rewarded, but private motivation must ultimately serve the cause of promoting broad public availability of literature, music, and the other arts. The immediate effect of our copyright law is to secure a fair return for an "author's" creative labor. But the ultimate aim is, by this incentive, to stimulate artistic creativity for the general public good. "The sole interest of the United States and the primary object in conferring the monopoly," this Court has said, "lie in the general benefits derived by the public from the labors of authors." Fox Film Corp. v. Doyal, 286 U.S. 123, 127, 52 S.Ct. 546, 547, 76 L.Ed. 1010. . . . When technological change has rendered its literal terms ambiguous, the Copyright Act must be construed in light of this basic purpose.

The precise statutory issue in the present case is whether Aiken infringed upon the petitioners' exclusive right, under the Copyright Act of 1909, 17 U.S.C.A. § 1(e), "[t]o perform the copyrighted work publicly for profit." We may assume that the radio reception of the musical compositions in Aiken's restaurant occurred "publicly for profit." The dispositive question, therefore, is whether this radio reception constituted a "performance" of the copyrighted works.

When this statutory provision was enacted in 1909, its purpose was to prohibit unauthorized performances of copyrighted musical compositions in such public places as concert halls, theaters, restaurants, and cabarets. An orchestra or individual instrumentalist or singer who performs a copyrighted musical composition in such a public place without a license is thus clearly an infringer under the statute. The entrepreneur who sponsors such a public performance for profit is also an infringer—direct or contributory. But it was never contemplated that the members of the audience who heard the composition would themselves also be simultaneously "performing," and thus also guilty of infringement. This much is common ground.

With the advent of commercial radio, a broadcast musical composition could be heard instantaneously by an enormous audience of distant and separate persons operating their radio receiving sets to reconvert the broadcast to audible form. Although Congress did not revise the statutory language, copyright law was quick to adapt to prevent the exploitation of protected works through the new electronic technology. In short, it was soon established in the federal courts that the broadcast of a copyrighted musical composition by a commercial radio station was a public performance of that composition for profit—and thus an infringement of the copyright if not licensed. In one of the earliest cases so holding, the Sixth Circuit Court of Appeals said:

> "While the fact that the radio was not developed at the time the Copyright Act . . . was enacted may raise some question as to whether it properly comes within the purview of the statute, it is not by that fact alone excluded from the statute. In other words, the statute may be applied to new situations not anticipated by Congress, if, fairly construed, such situations come within its intent and meaning. . . . While statutes should not be stretched to apply to new situations not fairly within their scope, they should not be so narrowly construed as to permit their evasion because of changing habits due to new inventions and discoveries.
>
> . . .
>
> "A performance, in our judgment, is no less public because the listeners are unable to communicate with one another, or are not assembled within an inclosure, or gathered together in some open stadium or park or other public place. Nor can a performance, in our judgment, be deemed private because each listener may enjoy it alone in the privacy of his home. Radio broadcasting is intended to, and in fact does, reach a very much larger number of the public at the moment of the rendition than any other medium of performance. The artist is consciously addressing a great, though unseen and widely scattered, audience, and is therefore participating in a public performance." Jerome H. Remick & Co. v. American Automobile Accessories Co., 5 F.2d 411, 411–412. . . .

If, by analogy to a live performance in a concert hall or cabaret, a radio station "performs" a musical composition when it broadcasts it, the same analogy would seem to require the conclusion that those who listen to the broadcast through the use of radio receivers do not perform the composition. And that is exactly what the early federal cases held. "Certainly those who listen do not perform, and therefore do not infringe." Jerome H. Remick & Co. v. General Electric Co., 16 F.2d at 829. "One who manually or by human agency merely actuates electrical instrumentalities, whereby inaudible elements that are omnipresent in the air are made audible to persons who are within hearing, does not 'perform' within the meaning of the Copyright Law." Buck v. Debaum, 40 F.2d 734, 735 (S.D.Cal.1929).

Such was the state of the law when this Court in 1931 decided Buck v. Jewell-LaSalle Realty Co., 283 U.S. 191, 51 S.Ct. 410, 75 L.Ed. 971. In that case the Court was called upon to answer the following question certified by the Eighth Circuit Court of Appeals: "Do the acts of a hotel proprietor, in making available to his guests, through the instrumentality of a radio receiving set and loud speakers installed in his hotel and under his control and for the entertainment of his guests, the hearing of a copyrighted musical composition which has been broadcast from a radio transmitting station, constitute a performance of such composition within the meaning of 17 U.S.C.A. Sec. 1(e)?" The Court answered the certified question in the affirmative. In stating the facts of the case, however, the Court's opinion made clear that the broadcaster of the musical composition was not licensed to perform it, and at least twice in the course of its opinion the Court indicated that the answer to the certified question might have been different if the broadcast itself had been authorized by the copyright holder.

We may assume for present purposes that the Jewel-LaSalle decision retains authoritative force in a factual situation like that in which it arose. But, as the Court of Appeals in this case perceived, this Court has in two recent decisions explicitly disavowed the view that the reception of an electronic broadcast can constitute a performance, when the broadcaster himself is licensed to perform the copyrighted material that he broadcasts. Fortnightly Corp. v. United Artists, 392 U.S. 390, 88 S.Ct. 2084, 20 L.Ed.2d 1176; Teleprompter Corp. v. CBS, 415 U.S. 394, 94 S.Ct. 1129, 39 L.Ed.2d 415.

The language of the Court's opinion in the Fortnightly case could hardly be more explicitly dispositive of the question now before us:

> "The television broadcaster in one sense does less than the exhibitor of a motion picture or stage play; he supplies his audience not with visible images but only with electronic signals. The viewer conversely does more than a member of a theater audience; he provides the equipment to convert electronic signals into audible sound and visible images. Despite these deviations from the conventional situation contemplated by the framers of the Copyright Act, broadcasters have been judicially treated as exhibitors, and viewers as members of a theater audience. Broadcasters perform. Viewers do not perform. Thus, while both broadcaster and viewer play crucial roles in the total television process, a line is drawn between them. One is treated as active performer; the other, as passive beneficiary." 392 U.S., at 398–399, 88 S.Ct., at 2088 (footnotes omitted).

The Fortnightly and Teleprompter cases, to be sure, involved television, not radio, and the copyrighted materials there in issue were literary and dramatic works, not musical compositions. But, as the Court of Appeals correctly observed, "[i]f Fortnightly, with its elaborate CATV plant and Teleprompter with its even more sophisticated and extended technological and programming facilities were not 'performing,' then logic dictates that no 'performance' resulted when the [respondent] merely activated his restaurant radio." 500 F.2d, at 137.

To hold in this case that the respondent Aiken "performed" the petitioners' copyrighted works would thus require us to overrule two very recent decisions of this Court. But such a holding would more than offend the principles of *stare decisis*; it would result in a regime of copyright law that would be both wholly unenforceable and highly inequitable.

The practical unenforceability of a ruling that all of those in Aiken's position are copyright infringers is self-evident. One has only to consider the countless business establishments in this country with radio or television sets on their premises—bars, beauty shops, cafeterias, car washes, dentists' offices, and drive-ins—to realize the total futility of any evenhanded effort on the part of copyright holders to license even a substantial percentage of them.[12]

And a ruling that a radio listener "performs" every broadcast that he receives would be highly inequitable for two distinct reasons. First, a person in Aiken's position would have no sure way of protecting himself from liability for copyright infringement except by keeping his radio set turned off. For even if he secured a license from ASCAP, he would have no way of either foreseeing or controlling the broadcast of compositions whose copyright was held by someone else. Secondly, to hold that all in Aiken's position "performed" these musical compositions would be to authorize the sale of an untold number of licenses for what is basically a single public rendition of a copyrighted work. The exaction of such multiple tribute would go far beyond what is required for the economic protection of copyright owners, and would be wholly at odds with the balanced congressional purpose behind 17 U.S.C.A. § 1(e):

> "The main object to be desired in expanding copyright protection accorded to music has been to give to the composer an adequate return for the value of his composition, and it has been a serious and a difficult task to combine the protection of the composer with the protection of the public, and to so frame an act that it would accomplish the double purpose of securing to the composer an adequate return for all use made of his composi-

---

12. The Court of Appeals observed that ASCAP now has license agreements with some 5,150 business establishments in the whole country, 500 F.2d 127, 129, noting that these include "firms which employ on premises sources for music such as tape recorders and live entertain- ment." Id., at 129 n. 4. As a matter of so-called "policy" or "practice," we are told, ASCAP has not even tried to exact licensing agreements from commercial establishments whose radios have only a single speaker.

tion and at the same time prevent the formation of oppressive monopolies, which might be founded upon the very rights granted to the composer for the purpose of protecting his interests." H.R.Rep.No.2222, 60th Cong., 2d Sess., 7 (1909).

For the reasons stated in this opinion, the judgment of the Court of Appeals is affirmed.

It is so ordered.

Mr. Justice BLACKMUN, concurring in the result.

My discomfort, now decisionally outdated to be sure, with the Court's opinion and judgment is threefold:

1. My first discomfort is factual. Respondent Aiken hardly was an innocent "listener," as the Court seems to characterize him throughout its opinion and particularly on page 162. In one sense, of course, he was a listener, for as he operated his small food shop and served his customers, he heard the broadcasts himself. Perhaps his work was made more enjoyable by the soothing and entertaining effects of the music. With this aspect I would have no difficulty.

But respondent Aiken installed four loudspeakers in his small shop. This, obviously, was not done for his personal use and contentment so that he might hear the broadcast, in any corner he might be, above the noise of commercial transactions. It was done for the entertainment and edification of his customers. It was part of what Mr. Aiken offered his trade and it added, in his estimation, to the atmosphere and attraction of his establishment. Viewed in this light, respondent is something more than a mere listener and is not so simply to be categorized.

2. My second discomfort is precedential. Forty-four years ago, in a unanimous opinion written by Mr. Justice Brandeis, this Court held that a hotel proprietor's use of a radio receiving set and loudspeakers for the entertainment of hotel guests constituted a performance within the meaning of § 1 of the Copyright Act, 17 U.S.C.A. § 1. Buck v. Jewell-LaSalle Realty Co., 283 U.S. 191, 51 S.Ct. 410, 75 L.Ed. 971 (1931). For more than 35 years the rule in Jewell-LaSalle was a benchmark in copyright law and was the foundation of a significant portion of the rather elaborate licensing agreements that evolved with the developing media technology. Seven years ago the Court, by a 5–1 vote, and with three Justices not participating, held that a community antenna television (CATV) station that transmitted copyrighted works to home subscribers was not performing the works, within the meaning of § 1 of the Copyright Act. Fortnightly Corp. v. United Artists, 392 U.S. 390, 88 S.Ct. 2084, 20 L.Ed.2d 1176 (1968). The divided Court only briefly noted the relevance of Jewell-LaSalle and announced that that decision "must be understood as limited to its own facts." Id., at 396–397, n. 18. I have already indicated my disagreement with the reasoning of Fortnightly and my conviction that it, rather than Jewell-LaSalle, is the case that should be limited to its facts. Teleprompter Corp. v. CBS, 415 U.S. 394, 415, 94 S.Ct. 1129,

1141, 39 L.Ed.2d 415 (1974) (dissenting opinion.) I was there concerned about the Court's simplistic view of television's complications, a view perhaps encouraged by the obvious inadequacies of an ancient copyright act for today's technology. A majority of the Court, however, felt otherwise and extended the simplistic analysis rejected in Jewell-LaSalle, but embraced in Fortnightly, to even more complex arrangements in the CATV industry. Teleprompter Corp. v. CBS, supra.

I had hoped, secondarily, that the reasoning of Fortnightly and Teleprompter would be limited to CATV. At least in that context the two decisions had the arguably desirable effect of protecting an infant industry from a premature death. Today, however, the Court extends Fortnightly and Teleprompter into radio broadcasting, effectively overrules Jewell-LaSalle, and thereby abrogates more than 40 years of established business practices. I would limit the application of Teleprompter and Fortnightly to the peculiar industry that spawned them. Parenthetically, it is of interest to note that this is precisely the result that would be achieved by virtually all versions of proposed revisions of the Copyright Act. See, e. g., § 101 of S. 1361, 93d Cong., 2d Sess., which sought to amend 17 U.S.C.A. § 110(5). See also §§ 48(5) and (6) of the British Copyright Act of 1956, 4 & 5 Eliz. 2, c. 74, which distinguishes between the use of a radio in a public place and "the causing of a work or other subject-matter to be transmitted to subscribers to a diffusion service."

Resolution of these difficult problems and the fashioning of a more modern statute are to be expected from the Congress. In any event, for now, the Court seems content to continue with its simplistic approach and to accompany it with a pragmatic reliance on the "practical unenforceability," ante, at 162, of the copyright law against persons such as George Aiken.

3. My third discomfort is tactical. I cannot understand why the court is so reluctant to do directly what it obviously is doing indirectly, namely, to overrule Jewell-LaSalle. Of course, in my view, that decision was correct at the time it was decided, and I would regard it as good law today under the identical statute and with identical broadcasting. But, as I have noted, the Court in Fortnightly limited Jewell-LaSalle "to its own facts" and in Teleprompter ignored its existence completely by refusing even to cite it. This means, it seems to me, that the Court did not want to overrule it, but nevertheless did not agree with it and felt, hopefully, that perhaps it would not bother us anymore anyway. Today the Court does much the same thing again by extracting and discovering great significance in the fact that the broadcaster in Jewell-LaSalle was not licensed to perform the composition. I cannot join the Court's intimation, ante, at 160— surely stretched to the breaking point—that Mr. Justice Brandeis and the unanimous Court for which he spoke would have reached a contrary conclusion in Jewell-LaSalle in 1931 had that broadcaster been licensed. The Court dances around Jewell-LaSalle, as indeed it must,

for it is potent opposing precedent for the present case and stands stalwart against respondent Aiken's position. I think we should be realistic and forthright and, if Jewell-LaSalle is in the way, overrule it.

Although I dissented in Teleprompter, that case and Fortnightly, before it, have been decided. With the Court insisting on adhering to the rationale of those cases, the result the Court of Appeals and the Court reaches here is compelled. Accepting the precedent of those cases, I concur in the result.

Mr. Chief Justice BURGER, with whom Mr. Justice DOUGLAS joins, dissenting.

In Fortnightly Corp. v. United Artists, 392 U.S. 390, 402, 88 S.Ct. 2084, 2091, 20 L.Ed.2d 1176 (1968), Mr. Justice Fortas observed that cases such as this call "not for the judgment of Solomon but for the dexterity of Houdini." There can be no really satisfactory solution to the problem presented here, until Congress acts in response to longstanding proposals. My primary purpose in writing is not merely to express disagreement with the Court but to underscore what has repeatedly been stated by others as to the need for legislative action. Radio today is certainly a more commonplace and universally understood technological innovation than CATV, for example, yet we are, basically, in essentially the same awkward situation as in the past when confronted with these problems. We must attempt to apply a statute designed for another era to a situation in which Congress has never affirmatively manifested its view concerning the competing policy considerations involved.

Yet, the issue presented can only be resolved appropriately by the Congress; perhaps it will find the result which the Court reaches today a practical and equitable resolution, or perhaps it will find this "functional analysis" too simplistic an approach, and opt for another solution.

The result reached by the Court is not compelled by the language of the statute; it is contrary to the applicable case law and, even assuming the correctness and relevance of the CATV cases, Fortnightly, supra, and Teleprompter, supra, it is not analytically dictated by those cases. In such a situation, I suggest, "the fact that the Copyright Act was written in a different day, for different factual situations, should lead us to tread cautiously here. Our major object . . . should be to do as little damage as possible to traditional copyright principles and to business relationships, until the Congress legislates and relieves the embarrassment which we and the interested parties face." Fortnightly, supra, at 404 (Fortas, J., dissenting).

As the Court's opinion notes, ante, at 160, in Buck v. Jewell-La-Salle Realty Co., 283 U.S. 191, 51 S.Ct. 410, 75 L.Ed. 971 (1931), answering a precisely phrased certified question, the Court construed the Copyright Act in a manner which squarely conflicts with what is held today. Congress, despite many opportunities, has never legislatively overruled Buck, supra. It was not overruled in Fortnightly but treated "as limited to its own facts." 392 U.S., at 396–397, n. 18, 88 S.Ct., at 2087. Even assuming the correctness of this dubious process of limitation, see Fortnightly, supra, 392 U.S. at 405, 88 S.Ct. at 2092 (Fortas, J., dissenting); Teleprompter, supra, 415 U.S. at 415, 94 S. Ct. at 1141 (Blackmun, J., dissenting); Buck is squarely relevant here since the license at issue expressly negated any right on the part of the broadcaster to further license performances by those who commercially receive and distribute broadcast music. Moreover, even accepting, *arguendo*, the restrictive reading given to Buck by the Court today, and assuming the correctness of Fortnightly and Teleprompter in the CATV field, it is not at all clear that the analysis of these latter cases supports the result here. Respondent was more than a "passive beneficiary." Fortnightly, supra, 392 U.S. at 399, 88 S.Ct. at 2089. He took the transmission and used that transmission for commercial entertainment in his own profit enterprise, through a multispeaker audio system specifically designed for his business purposes. In short, this case does not call for what the Court describes as "a ruling that a radio listener 'performs' every broadcast that he receives . . . ." ante, at 2047. Here, respondent received the transmission and then put it to an independent commercial use. His conduct seems to be controlled by Buck's unequivocal holding that:

> "One who hires an orchestra for a public performance for profit is not relieved from a charge of infringement merely because he does not select the particular program to be played. Similarly, when he tunes in on a broadcasting station, for his own commercial purposes, he necessarily assumes the risk that in so doing he may infringe the performing rights of another." 283 U.S. at 198–199, 51 S.Ct. at 412.

In short, as Mr. Justice DOUGLAS observed in the Teleprompter case: "The Court can read [sic] the result it achieves today only by 'legislating' important features of the Copyright Act out of existence." 415 U.S., at 421, 94 S.Ct. at 1145. In my view, we should bear in mind that "[o]ur ax, being a rule of law, must cut straight, sharp, and deep; and perhaps this is a situation that calls for the compromise of theory and for the architectural improvisation which only legislation can accomplish." Fortnightly, supra, 392 U.S. at 408, 88 S.Ct. at 2093 (Fortas, J., dissenting).

MURA v. COLUMBIA BROADCASTING SYSTEM, INC., 245 F. Supp. 587, 147 U.S.P.Q. 38 (S.D.N.Y.1965). LEVET, J.: 7. On or about March 14, 1955, certificates of registration of claims to copyright in works of art were issued to plaintiff by the United States Copyright Office for the mouse hand puppet, register No. 7927, for the pig hand puppet, register No. 7926, and for the rooster hand puppet, register No. 7922. The plaintiff has not sold or assigned her rights in said copyrights. . . .

9. On October 12, 1957, defendants broadcast a television image of plaintiff's pig puppet and of plaintiff's rooster puppet on the Cap-

tain Kangaroo program for approximately 35 seconds. No express permission was given by plaintiff to defendants to use the puppets. A kinescope or film recording of the program was made by CBS but never used for any commercial purpose. In October 1957, kinescope or film recordings constituted the only means of making copies of live television broadcasts.

10. On the October 12, 1957 program, as shown in Exhibit 7, the pig hand puppet and the rooster hand puppet were manipulated as hand puppets with the accompaniment of a barn dance recording, which was subordinate and incidental to the principal action of Captain Kangaroo and of a Mr. Green Jeans, a rural character, demonstrating a certain musical invention. The puppets were not featured as the principal objects of attention. . . .

The rights accorded the plaintiff as the owner of a copyrighted "work of art" include "the exclusive right: (a) To print, reprint, publish, copy, and vend the copyrighted work. . . ." 17 U.S.C. A. § 1.

In this action it is clear that defendants have not manufactured, sold or even used an article simulating any one of plaintiff's copyrighted puppets. Rather, the defendants used genuine puppets in a television show. The plaintiff claims this use as an infringement of her copyright.

The specific question therefore is whether that use constituted a copying. The commonly accepted definition of "a copy" appears in the old English case, West v. Francis, 5 Barn. & Ald. 743, which was cited with approval by the Supreme Court in White-Smith Music Pub. Co. v. Apollo Co., 209 U.S. 1, 17, 28 S.Ct. 319, 323, 52 L.Ed. 655 (1908): "A copy is that which comes so near to the original as to give to every person seeing it the idea created by the original." Certainly no three dimensional objects were reproduced. Was the presentation on the television program, by an image reproduction of a transitory and impermanent nature, a copying of the puppets? Weil, author of American Copyright Law, well stated:

> "It would seem that a copy involves the conception that it must have some degree of permanency or the maxim de minimis would apply. Thus, while the making of a single copy may be infringement, if this copy were destroyed almost as soon as made, as for example, if a vaudeville artist drew with colored chalks, or if a verse were cast upon a screen through a stereopticon, it may be doubted whether such a temporary production could fairly be called a copy." (p. 406)

It is obvious that a copyright of a work of art may be infringed by reproduction of the *object* itself. Home Art Inc. v. Glensder Textile Corp., 81 F.Supp. 551 (S.D.N.Y.1948) (oil painting reproduced in scarf); Leigh v. Gerber, 86 F.Supp. 320 (S.D.N.Y.1949) (painting reproduced by publication without consent in a magazine). Tiffany Productions, Inc. v. Dewing, 50 F.2d 911 (D.Md.1931) (projection of photoplay on screen without copyright owner's permission). This, however, is not the nature of the "copying" here alleged. Here the puppets were not reproduced.

The evanescent reproduction of a hand puppet on a television screen or on the projected kinescope recording of it is so different in nature from the copyrighted hand puppet that I conclude it is not a copy. I find no violation of plaintiff's copyright here under the circumstances of this case. There was no copying of the copyrighted puppets.

Nevertheless, even if we were to assume that the projection on television of the hand puppets was an infringement, the defense of fair use is applicable. Fair use is at best a "troublesome question." MacDonald v. Du Maurier, 144 F.2d 696, 701 (2d Cir. 1944). Every case depends on its own facts.

The puppets were sold by plaintiff without any contractual limitations as to use. The use complained of here was of the type for which the puppets were intended and was reasonable. It can hardly be contended, for example, that if a copyright owner of a film sells the film without a stipulated condition as to its use that the purchaser is forbidden to *exhibit* the film merely because it is copyrighted.

Commentators agree that among the most important factors bearing on whether a use is a fair one, perhaps *the* most important, is whether the use tends to interfere with the sale of the copyrighted article. Here, if anything, the exhibition on television would stimulate sales of the hand puppets rather than prejudice them. Further, the "copies" complained of here could not be used as a substitute for the original work. In addition, these hand puppets were not the principal attraction on the television programs. Rather, their use was incidental. Nor can any intent to pirate be found here.

I conclude that the use of the hand puppets on the Captain Kangaroo Show was fair.

GOLDSTEIN, PREEMPTED STATE DOCTRINES, INVOLUNTARY TRANSFERS AND COMPULSORY LICENSES: TESTING THE LIMITS OF COPYRIGHT *

24 U.C.L.A.L.Rev. 1107, 1127–1135 (1977).

Of the thirteen sections defining the new law's statutory rights, four impose compulsory licenses. Section 111 specifies the conditions and fees under which cable television operators may transmit copyrighted materials without the consent of the copyright proprietor. Sections 115 and 116 prescribe the conditions and fees for recording musical compositions or performing them on jukeboxes without consent. Section 118 introduces compulsory licensing into the context of public broadcasting. Chapter 8 creates a Copyright Royalty Tribunal to oversee the administration of these provisions and to review and adjust the compulsory fees.

Like other systems of private property, copyright law is founded on the notion that privately bargained prices are preferable to publicly administered rates. Why, then, did Congress so warmly embrace the questionable economics of compulsory licensing? The most likely reason is consensus politics, not market economics. Faced with a welter of contending industrial and regulatory interests, Congress sought compromise positions lying somewhere between exclusive rights and no rights at all.[83] In the circumstances, it is a hard question whether the decision for compulsory licensing was correct. A closer look at the new provisions and at their possible investment effects is needed.

A. *Compulsory Licenses in the New Act*

In a sense, compulsory licenses are as old as equity's discretion to withhold injunctions when issuance of the decree would harm the defendant disproportionately to the plaintiff's benefit. By allowing defendants in these cases to continue their invasion of property rights upon payment of damages, courts substitute their estimate of appropriate compensation for the figure that the parties would have arrived at privately. This result has been reached in real property cases and in patent cases. Compulsory licensing of patents has also been specifically authorized by statute in narrowly defined sets of circumstances. In all these situations, the compelled license fees are set individually for the particular parcel or invention involved so that the owner's reward is proportioned to the perceived value of his real property or invention.

The compulsory license provisions of the new copyright statute depart from this individualized approach by pegging their compulsory fees to a fixed rate. As a consequence, the royalties to be paid are uniform regardless of the work's individual market value. Some room for differentiated compensation does exist under the new law. Section 115 multiplies its uniform rate by the number of records distributed by the compulsory licensees, connecting total license fees to market appeal. Sections 111, 116 and 118, though generally undiscriminating, do leave some room for differentiation at the point at which fees are distributed to the copyright proprietors.

---

83. The Register of Copyrights, Barbara Ringer, has perceptively traced a recurrent theme in the political evolution of contemporary copyright law. The process begins with the exploitation of a new technological development expanding the use of copyrighted works. Next comes the question whether the new use constitutes copyright infringement; the discovery that "the 1909 copyright statute and the cases interpreting it contain no answers, only analogies;" and then an action for copyright infringement. Because the allegedly infringing activities have become widespread, and because the 1909 Act is considered inapposite, courts "reluctantly hold against the copyright owner and urgently call upon Congress to do its duty and reform an archaic and unjust statute." Caught between the traditionally protected interests of creators and the pressures exerted by representatives of the newly emergent user industries, Congress is politically compelled to compromise. "Now, and even more in the future, the compromises seem likely to consist of compulsory licensing." Ringer, Copyright and the Future of Authorship, 101 Lib.J. 229, 231 (1976).

1. Section 111: Cable Transmission

Section 111 resolves the question of cable television's liability for retransmitting copyrighted programs originated by broadcast stations. The question, twice considered by the Supreme Court, occupied an important place on the copyright revision agenda from the outset. Section 111 is the product of many compromises and, more explicitly than any other aspect of the new law, commits its operation to assumptions about industry structure and regulation. The provision can be understood only against its industrial and regulatory background.

The earliest cable television systems consisted of prominently placed antennae connected by coaxial cable to the homes of subscribers in the surrounding area. The sole purpose of these early facilities was to provide television signals to areas that had been physically cut off from television.

Under the prevailing business arrangements in the broadcast industry, television stations, networks and copyright proprietors all stood to gain, not lose, from this new service. Television stations and networks get their revenues from advertisers and, roughly speaking, advertisers will pay more as the size of the audience delivered by a station increases. The interests of copyright proprietors generally coincide with the interests of the television stations and networks they license to carry their programs. As broadcast markets, and advertising revenues, expand, so do the prices at which broadcasters bid for copyrighted programs.

Cable quickly outgrew its early role, and broadcasters and copyright proprietors soon perceived the new medium's larger implications. By the 1960's cable systems were importing the broadcast signals of distant independent stations into markets that were already served by the three networks and by independent stations. In some communities cable also served to improve the quality of local signals already being received or originated programming on its own. The new services moved cable well beyond its initial role of expanding television markets and increasing broadcasters' revenues. Cable now competed with local broadcasters, capturing portions of their markets with programs received at no cost to the cable systems. Broadcasters, and the copyright proprietors who supplied them with programming, began to complain.

The Federal Communications Commission responded erratically to the question of liability of cable systems for distant signal importation. In 1966, seven years after it refused to take jurisdiction on the ground that cable did not interfere with broadcast television, the Commission asserted jurisdiction and imposed stringent limits on cable's freedom to import distant signals into the one hundred largest television markets. However, these regulations were soon suspended and, after a series of abortive proposals, the Commission in 1972 settled on the regulatory approach that is followed today. Under this approach, cable systems are required to serve a public utility function in carrying local signals and are permitted to carry a prescribed complement of distant signals. It is this approach that forms the basis for section 111's compulsory license provisions.

The basic approach of the present FCC regulations, and of section 111's compulsory licensing provisions, is embodied in the regulations' division between signals that a cable system is required to carry and those that it may, but not must, carry. Essentially, local signals fall into the category of "must carry," and distant signals into the category of "may carry," with the precise number of signals in each category assigned to a cable system determined by a calculus of technical and economic factors. For example, the number of distant signals that a system may import will vary with the size of the television market in which it is situated. Distant signal carriage is further limited by exclusivity rules under which, for example, a system may not import a program if a local network station is carrying the same program at the same time.

Because, in part, the fortunes of copyright proprietors are tied to those of broadcasters, the FCC's compromise between broadcasters and cable operators is also a compromise between copyright proprietors and cable operators. Section 111 takes the logic of this compromise as its starting point. Section 111(c) provides that "secondary transmissions to the public by a cable system of a primary transmission made by a broadcast station licensed by the Federal Communications Commission" shall be subject to compulsory licensing "where the carriage of the signals comprising the secondary transmission is permissible under the rules, regulations, or authorizations of the Federal Communications Commission." In short, retransmission of "must carry" and "may carry" signals falls within the statute's compulsory license.

Section 111 refines the logic of the FCC regulations in its method for computing the fees to be paid by any cable system under the compulsory license. Under a formula prescribed in section 111(d), fees are tied to the number of distant signal "equivalents" carried and to the gross receipts derived by the system from providing secondary transmissions. As gross receipts and number of distant signal equivalents increase, so do the compulsory license fees levied. Once royalties are received by the Copyright Office, and administrative costs deducted, aggregate royalties for the period are to be distributed to copyright proprietors in proportions determined by the Copyright Royalty Tribunal. Michael Botein, a close observer of cable-copyright issues, has aptly observed that the "failure to relate copyright consumption to copyright compensation points up Section 111's highly regulatory aspects."

Outside this basic regulatory scheme, section 111 specifies the circumstances under which secondary transmissions will be completely exempted from copyright liability, and those under which there will be full liability. Full liability is imposed for willful or repeated transmissions where the carriage of signals is not permissible under

FCC rules or where the cable operator fails to comply with the prescribed compulsory licensing procedures; for retransmission of non-broadcast primary transmissions, such as programs originated by another cable system; for transmission of Canadian and Mexican signals outside prescribed zones; and for transmission of foreign signals generally. Cable systems are also subject to full copyright liability if they substitute other program materials for the advertised messages carried by the primary transmitter. And, with narrow exceptions, full liability exists by definition where the cable system's transmission is not simultaneous with the primary transmission.

2. Section 115: Phonorecords

Section 115 updates section 1(e) of the 1909 Act, the provision that introduced compulsory licensing into copyright. Under section 1(e), once a copyright owner permits his composition to be recorded, anyone else may, without his authority, record the composition upon payment of a statutorily prescribed royalty.

The new law differs from the old in several respects. Section 1(e)'s royalty rate, two cents for each record manufactured by the compulsory licensee, has been altered by the new law to 2.75 cents per work or .5 cents per minute of playing time, whichever is greater. The new royalty is to be figured on the basis of the number of phonorecords actually distributed by the compulsory licensee and not, as under the 1909 Act, on the basis of number of records manufactured. Section 115(a)(1) premises compulsory licensing on the first authorized distribution of phonorecords by the copyright owner, rather than on the making or licensing of the first recording, as under the 1909 law. Another part of section 115(a)(1) restricts the compulsory license to the making of phonorecords primarily for distribution to the public for private use. This presumably excludes compulsory licensing for specialized production for commercial uses such as background music systems and broadcast and jukebox operations.

3. Section 116: Jukeboxes

The 1909 Act exempted jukebox uses of musical compositions by providing that the "reproduction or rendition of a musical composition by or upon coin operated machines shall not be deemed a public performance for profit unless a fee is charged for admission to the place where such reproduction or rendition occurs." Almost as soon as it was enacted, the jukebox exemption became the target of proposals ranging from outright repeal and imposition of full copyright liability to variations on the compulsory licensing theme. The resolution reached by section 116 is imposition of an annual compulsory fee of eight dollars per unit on jukebox operators.

The mechanics of section 116's compulsory license are simple. Upon payment of the eight dollar royalty to the Copyright Office, the Register of Copyrights issues a certificate which the operator is then required to place on the jukebox. The fees collected are to be distributed annually upon claims submitted to the Copyright Royalty Tribunal. Section 116(c)(4) expressly provides for different means for allocating payments as between individual claimants and performing rights societies. Like the royalty rates fixed in the other compulsory licensing provisions, the eight dollar jukebox fee is open to review and adjustment by the Copyright Royalty Tribunal created by Chapter 8.

4. Section 118: Public Broadcasting

Section 118 authorizes the Copyright Royalty Tribunal to prescribe rates for the use by public broadcasters of published nondramatic musical works and pictorial, graphic and sculptural works. Within thirty days of the President's announcement of initial appointments to the Tribunal, the Tribunal is to initiate proceedings to determine the "reasonable terms and rates" on which these uses can be made. The Tribunal is to publish terms and rates within six months of the notice of initiation of proceedings. The Tribunal's adoption of fixed rates and terms will not bar broadcasters and copyright proprietors from entering into negotiated agreements although, of course, private negotiations will unavoidably be colored by the availability of the compelled alternative. Section 118 further limits private discretion by requiring that voluntarily negotiated agreements be filed with the Copyright Office in order to be given effect.

Section 118, as enacted, marks a retreat from the terms first proposed in a predecesor bill introduced by Senator Charles Mathias, Jr., in the ninety-third Congress. The Mathias Bill would have given public broadcasters a compulsory license to broadcast nondramatic literary works as well as nondramatic musical works and pictorial, graphic, or sculptural works. The bill would have authorized the Copyright Royalty Tribunal to establish reasonable fees "for public television and radio broadcasts by public broadcasting entities." The bill also provided for distribution of royalties deposited with the Register of Copyrights. Faced with sharp resistance from the Register of Copyrights and from organizations and individuals representing authors and publishers and producers of audiovisual works objecting to the inclusion of nondramatic literary works, the House Committee withdrew to the more limited coverage now embodied in section 118.

Congress' purpose in enacting section 118 was to encourage agreements, yet provide a mechanism ensuring the availability of copyrighted materials on terms satisfactory to the broadcasters. The provision reflects the judgment that public broadcasting is different from commercial enterprises "due to such factors as the special nature of programming, repeated use of programs, and, of course, limited financial resources." While the House Committee Report artfully states that copyright owners should not be required to subsidize public broadcasting, it cannot obscure the fact that, whatever the source, it is in fact a subsidy that section 118 confers on public broadcasters.

NOTES

1. Does section 110(5) endorse or discredit the result and rationale of Twentieth Century Music Corp. v. Aiken? The legislative history suggests that it does a little of both. When the Senate passed S. 22, containing the present language of section 110(5), the Committee Report noted that the "exemption would not apply where broadcasts are transmitted by means of loudspeakers or similar devices in such establishments as . . . quick-service food shops of the type involved in Twentieth Century Music Corp. v. Aiken." 122 Cong.Rec. 2835 (Feb. 6, 1976). The exemption passed the House with a minor amendment, the House Committee observing that the *Aiken* facts, though within the exemption, represented its "outer limit." H.R. Rep.No.94-1476, p. 87. The Conference Committee restored the Senate language but adopted the House Committee's more expansive reading of the exemption:

> "It is the intent of the conferees that a small commercial establishment of the type involved in Twentieth Century Music Corp. v. Aiken, 422 U.S. 151 (1975), which merely augmented a home-type receiver and which was not of sufficient size to justify, as a practical matter, a subscription to a commercial background music service, would be exempt. However, where the public communication was by means of something other than a home-type receiving apparatus, or where the establishment actually makes a further transmission to the public, the exemption would not apply." House Conf.Rep.No.94-1733, 94th Cong., 2d Sess. 75 (1976).

What economic justification is there for the exemption of performances like those involved in *Aiken*? Is it so obvious that, given a clear definition of its members' rights, ASCAP would not have entered into an "evenhanded" licensing program? Are the transaction costs of extending licenses to "countless business establishments" in fact as high as the *Aiken* court supposed them to be? Say that ASCAP devised a two-tier licensing structure under which, for one fee, a radio broadcaster would receive the usual blanket license and, for a somewhat higher fee, it would receive a license allowing listeners like Aiken to retransmit its broadcasts. What incentives would broadcasters have to pay the higher fee? Note that broadcasters make their living from advertising, and that advertisers pay according to the size of the broadcast audience reached.

Is it really a problem that "even if he secured a license from ASCAP," the retailer "would have no way of either foreseeing or controlling the broadcast of compositions whose copyright was held by someone else"? How do broadcasters avoid this same exposure? See page 809, below, discussing the role of ASCAP and its companion licensing organizations, BMI and SESAC.

Would it really be so bad if the alternative to an exemption was Aiken's "keeping his radio set turned off"? Was the complaint addressed to the presence of the radio set or the four loudspeakers attached to it? What does the Conference Report mean when it conjures an establishment "not of sufficient size to justify, as a practical matter, a subscription to a commercial background music service"?

2.   Would *Mura* have been decided differently under the present Act? Section 106(5) confers the exclusive right "in the case of literary, musical, dramatic, and choreographic works, pantomimes, and pictorial, graphic, or sculptural works, including the individual images of a motion picture or other audiovisual work, to display the copyrighted work publicly."

What are the limits of this new statutory right? Can an artist who has sold a painting prevent a buyer from displaying the work publicly? See section 109(b) which reflects the House Committee's intention "to preserve the traditional privilege of the owner of a copy to display it directly, but to place reasonable restrictions on the ability to display it indirectly in such a way that the copyright owner's market for reproduction and distribution of copies would be affected. Unless it constitutes a fair use under section 107, or unless one of the special provisions of section 110 or 111, is applicable, projection of more than one image at a time, or transmission of an image to the public over television or other communication channels, would be an infringement for the same reasons that reproduction in copies would be." H.R.Rep.No.94–1476, 94th Cong. 2d Sess. 80 (1976).

3.   Was *Mura* correct to suggest that plaintiff might have restricted the display by imposing "contractual limitations as to use" at the time the puppets were sold? The power to condition a first sale of an item with a servitude restricting its subsequent use would certainly seem to inhere in the right to vend, secured by section 1(a) of the 1909 Act, and in the right to distribute, secured by section 106(3) of the present Act. Yet this power is limited by the first sale doctrine, embodied in section 27 of the 1909 Act and section 109(a) of the present Act, entitling the owner of any lawfully made copy or phonorecord "to sell or otherwise dispose of the possession of that copy or phonorecord." The question to be resolved within this framework is, what kind of servitude can the copyright owner lawfully impose as part of the first sale?

In Bobbs-Merrill Co. v. Straus, 210 U.S. 339, 28 S.Ct. 722, 52 L. Ed. 1086 (1908), the question for decision was "does the sole right to vend . . . secure to the owner of the copyright the right, after a sale of the book to a purchaser, to restrict future sales of the book at retail, to the right to sell it at a certain price per copy, because of a notice in the book that a sale at a different price will be treated as an infringement, which notice has been brought home to one undertaking to sell for less than the named sum?" 210 U.S. 339, 350, 28 S.Ct. 722, 726. The Court answered that it did not, and ruled that defendant was free to sell authorized copies of plaintiff's work for 89 cents a copy, notwithstanding the presence in each copy, immediately below the copyright notice, of the legend: "The price of this book at retail is $1.00 net. No dealer is licensed to sell it at a less price, and a sale at a less price will be treated as an infringement of the copyright."

The Court took pains to distinguish the situation before it from the one that would have obtained had patent rights been in issue, or had plaintiff contracted with wholesalers or retailers respecting price, but it did not fully explicate its reasons for rejecting plaintiff's argument that the Act's provision for a right to vend "vested the whole field of the right of exclusive sale in the copyright owner; that he can part with it to another to the extent that he sees fit, and may withhold to himself, by proper reservations, so much of the right as he pleases." 210 U.S. 339, 349, 28 S.Ct. 722, 725, 726. Because the Court viewed the Act's main purpose as being "to secure the right of multiplying copies of the work," it apparently envisioned the right to vend as auxiliary and thus more limited. 210 U.S. 339, 351, 28 S.Ct. 722, 726.

4. The offending use of a copyrighted work will sometimes neighbor, but not fall expressly within, one of copyright's prescribed rights. *Mura* involved such a situation. So, more frequently, do cases involving the right to adapt a copyrighted work to other uses. These cases pose a difficult balance: on the one hand, giving substance to Congress' definition of an exclusive right; on the other, enforcing the principle of free alienability of goods that is the essence of the first sale doctrine.

In C. M. Paula Co. v. Logan, 355 F.Supp. 189, 177 U.S.P.Q. 559 (N.D.Tex.1973), plaintiff claimed that its exclusive rights to copy, vend and adapt the copyrighted designs on its greeting cards were infringed when defendant purchased the cards at retail, transferred the designs from the cards to ceramic plaques, and then sold the plaques. Since each plaque that defendant sold required "the purchase and use of an individual piece of artwork marketed by the plaintiff," the court ruled that neither the right to vend nor to copy had been violated. 355 F.Supp. 189, 191. The court also held that the right to adapt had not been infringed, observing that defendant's activities fell short of those involved in National Geographic Soc'y v. Classified Geographic, 27 F.Supp. 655 (D.Mass.1939). *National Geographic* had held that plaintiff's adaptation right was infringed when defendant removed selected articles from issues of the *National Geographic* and reassembled and rebound them with its own index. The *National Geographic* court ruled that defendant's extensive reworking of purchased magazines went well beyond the consumer freedom permitted by the first sale doctrine and invaded the plaintiff's exclusive right to make other versions of its copyright works.

See generally, Nolan, All Rights Not Reserved After the First Sale, 23 Bull. Copyright Soc'y 76 (1975).

5. The rights that attach to sound recordings are closely circumscribed. Section 114(a) restates the basic message of section 106 that copyright in sound recordings includes the right to reproduce, to

prepare derivative works, and to distribute, but not the right to perform or display. Section 114(b) further limits sound recordings to a right against exact replication or dubbing. Imitations of the sound recording or slight alterations—conduct that would infringe other kinds of works—are permitted.

Section 114(d) represents a compromise on the performance right issue, calling for the Register of Copyrights to file a report on the wisdom of performance rights for sound recordings. The Register's report, submitted to Congress on January 3, 1978, and supplemented on March 13, 1978, contained a strong recommendation that "section 114 be amended to provide performance rights, subject to compulsory licensing, in copyrighted sound recordings and that the benefits of this right be extended both to performers (including employees for hire) and to record producers as joint authors of sound recordings." In part, the Register rested her recommendation on the view that the "lack of copyright protection for performers since the commercial development of records has had a drastic and destructive effect on both the performing and recording arts." 43 Fed.Reg. 11773–4, March 21, 1978. The Register's recommended legislation is paralleled in H.R. 237, 96th Cong. 1st Sess. (Jan. 15, 1979) proposing a "Performance Rights Amendment of 1977."

For another view on performance rights, see Bard & Kurlantzick, A Public Performance Right in Recordings: How to Alter the Copyright System Without Improving It, 43 Geo.Wash.L.Rev. 152 (1974).

6.   Section 115 of the present Act attempts to resolve the more troublesome questions that had arisen under its predecessor in the 1909 Act, 17 U.S.C.A. § 1(e). Section 115(a)(1) carries forward the Act's distinction between "musical works" and "sound recordings" and makes clear "that a person is not entitled to a compulsory license of copyrighted *musical works* for the purpose of making an unauthorized duplication of a musical *sound recording* originally developed and produced by another." H.R.Rep.No.94–1476, 108 [Emphasis added]. Also, section 115(a)(2) was "intended to recognize the practical need for a limited privilege to make arrangements of music being used under a compulsory license, but without allowing the music to be perverted, distorted, or travestied." H.R.Rep.No.94–1476, 109.

Section 115 does nothing to shake the earlier commitment to compulsory licensing for phonorecords. In section 1(e) Congress had sought to mediate between contemporary demands for a mechanical reproduction right and expressed fears that an exclusive right would permit one firm, the Aeolian Company, to monopolize recording rights to popular music, "and by controlling these copyrights monopolize the business of manufacturing and selling music producing machines, otherwise free to the world." H.R.Rep.No.2222, 60th Cong. 2d Sess. 4 (1909).

In the years since its passage, section 1(e) was the object of numerous proposals for modification or outright repeal, most significantly in the 1961 Report of the Register of Copyrights. The Register subsequently revised his opinion: "During the discussion following issuance of the [1961] Report, it became apparent that record producers, small and large alike, regard the compulsory license as too important to their industry to accept its outright elimination." Copyright Law Revision, Part 6, Supplementary Report of the Register of Copyrights, 1965 Revision Bill 53 (1965). Earlier proposals had called for removal of compulsory licensing from the Copyright Act and for its ad hoc administration by the Federal Trade Commission, H.R. 3456, 77th Cong. 1st Sess. (1941), or the Federal Communications Commission, H.R. 10633, 75th Cong. 3d Sess. (1938).

The economic arguments advanced for and against the compulsory licensing provision are shaky at best. The one systematic appraisal of section 1(e)'s place in the economics of the record industry indicates that institutional divisions in the industry and the fugitive nature of the success that attends popular compositions, taken together, make it extremely unlikely that elimination of the compulsory license scheme would be attended by new monopoly effects. Blaisdell, The Economic Aspects of the Compulsory License, Study No. 6, Subcommittee on Patents, Trademarks and Copyrights, Senate Committee on the Judiciary, 86th Cong. 1st Sess. 91, 109 (1960).

7. What justification generally is there for compulsory licensing of copyrights? Congress' anxiety over extending exclusive rights into unfamiliar circumstances clearly played a role in its adoption of the compulsory licensing provisions of sections 111, 115, 116 and 118. One concern was that the delays traditionally encountered in negotiations for copyright licenses would seriously hamper the new, fast-paced technologies for transmission of copyrighted works.

Although compulsory licensing will doubtless reduce transaction delays, other means exist for easing transactions without intruding so deeply into market processes. Thus, because the photocopying question was resolved without resort to compulsory licensing, publishers and photocopiers quickly began to negotiate blanket licenses through clearinghouse mechanisms similar to those used by ASCAP and BMI, see page 784, note 5, below.

To be sure, the Act's compulsory license provisions do allow some differentiation in returns. In the case of recorded musical compositions, and less directly in the case of jukeboxes, cable television and educational broadcasting, license fees are tied to frequency of use, giving the copyright investor some economic incentive to gamble on creating popular works. Also, the effects of the compulsory licensing provisions are not nearly as dramatic as they would be if the Act had subjected all works to complete compulsory licensing. No work under the present Act will be completely surrounded by compulsory licenses. Dramatic, literary and pictorial works enjoy a wide array of exclusive rights, and returns to these rights can be expected to balance the investment effects of forced licensing for cable transmission and educational broadcasts.

For background on section 111, see Botein, The New Copyright Act and Cable Television—A Signal of Change, 24 Bull. Copyright Soc'y 1 (1976). On the evolution, problems, and prospects of the Copyright Royalty Tribunal, see Brylawski, The Copyright Royalty Tribunal, 24 U.C.L.A.L.Rev. 1265 (1977). See also Besen, Manning & Mitchell, Copyright Liability for Cable Television: Compulsory Licensing and the Coase Theorem, 21 J. L. & Econ. 67, 68 (1978).

c. FAIR USE

MEEROPOL v. NIZER, 560 F.2d 1061, 1063, 1064, 1068–1072, 195 U.S.P.Q. 273 (2d Cir. 1977), cert. denied 434 U.S. 1013, 98 S.Ct. 727, 54 L.Ed.2d 756. SMITH, J.: ["Appellants are the natural children of Julius and Ethel Rosenberg. Their parents were executed in June 1953 after conviction for conspiring to transmit information relating to the national defense to the Soviet Union. Appellees Louis Nizer ("Nizer"), Doubleday & Co., Inc. ("Doubleday") and Fawcett Publications, Inc. ("Fawcett") are the author and publishers respectively of an account of the events surrounding the Rosenberg trial entitled The Implosion Conspiracy, published in 1973. Plaintiffs-appellants alleged that Nizer incorporated in his book substantial portions of copyrighted letters written by Ethel and Julius Rosenberg without authorization and that this use constituted infringement of their statutory and common-law copyright."]

Fair use has been defined as:

a privilege in others than the owner of the copyright to use the copyrighted material in a reasonable manner without his consent, notwithstanding the monopoly granted to the owner by the copyright.[8]

The doctrine offers a means of balancing the exclusive right of a copyright holder with the public's interest in dissemination of information affecting areas of universal concern, such as art, science, history, or industry. Its application has been termed among "the most troublesome in the whole law of copyright." 2 M. Nimmer Copyright, § 145 (1976), quoting Dellar v. Samuel Goldwyn, Inc., 104 F.2d 661, 42 U.S.P.Q. 164 (2d Cir. 1939). Justice Story in an early case addressing the fair use defense which involved alleged infringement of copyrighted letters of George Washington remarked that "Patents and copyrights approach nearer than any other class of cases belonging to forensic discussions, to what may be called the metaphysics of the law, where the distinctions are, or at least may be very subtle and refined, and sometimes, almost evanescent." Folsom v. Marsh, 9 F. Cas. 342, 344 (C.C.D.Mass.1841) (No. 4901). It is thus not surprising that the application of the fair use doctrine to the facts of this case confronts us with difficult and complex issues.

---

8. Rosemont Enterprises, Inc. v. Random House, Inc., 366 F.2d 303, 306, 150 U.S.P.Q. 715, 718–719 (2d Cir. 1966), cert. denied 385 U.S. 1009, 87 S.Ct. 714, 17 L.Ed.2d 546, 152 U.S.P.Q. 844, quoting Ball, The Law of Copyright and Literary Property, 260 (1944).

The line which must be drawn between fair use and copyright infringement depends on an examination of the facts in each case. It cannot be determined by resort to any arbitrary rules or fixed criteria. The Copyright Revision Act of October 19, 1976, P.L. 94–553, 90 Stat. 2541 (1976), which will take effect January 1, 1978, codifies the fair use doctrine in § 107. Section 107 is intended to restate the existing judicial doctrine of fair use, not to change, narrow or enlarge it. The text of 17 U.S.C.A. § 107 is as follows:

Notwithstanding the provisions of section 106, the fair use of a copyrighted work, including such use by reproduction in copies or phonorecords or by any other means specified by that section, for purposes such as criticism, comment, news reporting, teaching (including multiple copies for classroom use), scholarship, or research, is not an infringement of copyright. In determining whether the use made of a work in any particular case is a fair use the factors to be considered shall include—

(1) the purpose and character of the use, including whether such use is of a commercial nature or is for nonprofit educational purposes;

(2) the nature of the copyrighted work;

(3) the amount and substantiality of the portion used in relation to the copyrighted work as a whole; and

(4) the effect of the use upon the potential market for or value of the copyrighted work.

The court below applied these criteria in order to determine whether the fair use defense was available to defendants. It held that to succeed on a summary judgment motion defendants had to show that no genuine issues of fact "had to be tried." 417 F.Supp. 1206, 1208, 191 U.S.P.Q. 350, 352–353. It found that factual issues raised by plaintiffs were either not in dispute or were such that even if resolved in plaintiffs' favor they would not affect the fair use question. We must disagree. We think fair use not established as a matter of law and that genuine issues of fact exist precluding the grant of summary judgment for defendants.

Relying on Rosemont Enterprises, Inc. v. Random House, Inc., 366 F.2d 303, 150 U.S.P.Q. 715 (2d Cir. 1966), the court held that the definition of an historical work for the purpose of the fair use doctrine is a very broad one, and that The Implosion Conspiracy fell within this definition. Rosemont involved the use of copyrighted material about Howard Hughes published in Look Magazine in a subsequent biography of Hughes. The court there found that this use fell within the fair use doctrine. Biographers, it held, customarily refer to and utilize earlier works dealing with the subject of the biography and occasionally quote directly from their works. The fact that the Hughes biography was perhaps not a profound work did not deprive it of the fair use privilege as a book of historical interest. Whether or not an author also has a commercial motive in publishing the work was held irrelevant to the availability of the fair use defense. In Rosemont, however, only two direct quotations had been copied. The Implosion Conspiracy includes verbatim portions of 28 copyrighted letters. Rosemont involved the use of copyrighted statements concerning the actions of a biographical subject, not as here the use of verbatim letters written by the subject. In addition, it appears that the fair use defense was upheld in Rosemont at least in part because the court found that the plaintiff there was acting in bad faith seeking to prevent the publication of a legitimate biography of Howard Hughes.

We agree that the mere fact that Nizer's book might be termed a popularized account of the Rosenberg trial lacking substantial scholarship and published for commercial gain, does not, standing alone, deprive Nizer or his publishers of the fair use defense. For a determination whether the fair use defense is applicable on the facts of this case, however, it is relevant whether or not the Rosenberg letters were used primarily for scholarly, historical reasons, or predominantly for commercial exploitation. The purpose and character of the use of the copyrighted material, the nature of the copyrighted work, and amount and substantiality of the work used, and its effect upon the potential market for the copyrighted material are factors which must be evaluated in concert. If the effect on the market by an infringing work is minimal, for example, far greater use may be privileged than where the market value of the copyrighted material is substantially decreased. Similarly, where use is made of underlying historical facts such use will be entitled to complete freedom but it is otherwise if there is verbatim copying of original, copyrighted material. "The fair use privilege is based on the concept of reasonableness and extensive verbatim copying or paraphrasing of material set down by another cannot satisfy that standard." Rosemont Enterprises, Inc. v. Random House, Inc., supra, 366 F.2d 310, 150 U.S.P.Q. 721–722.

A key issue in fair use cases is whether the defendant's work tends to diminish or prejudice the potential sale of plaintiff's work. The fact that the Rosenberg letters have been out of print for 20 years does not necessarily mean that they have no future market which can be injured. The market for republication or for sale of motion picture rights might be affected by the infringing work. Here the court concluded that plaintiffs might be able to prove damages at trial but held this fact irrelevant. The court also conceded that the qualitative impact of the copied material presented an issue as to which reasonable men might disagree even though the basic quantity of the infringement and the surrounding circumstances were undisputed. The court admitted that the ultimate resolution of these issues turned on the subjective judgment of the trier of fact. The court then proceeded to hold that the use of the letters in The Implosion Conspiracy was entitled to the fair use defense because it found the use of copyrighted letters by Nizer to be insubstantial. "The letters .   .   ." it held, "do not in any sense form a major part of defendants' work." Id. at 1213, 191 U.S.P.Q. at 356–357. We disagree.

It was error to hold that as a matter of law the fair use defense was available to defendants when the purpose for which the letters were included in the book and the effect of the use of the copyrighted letters on their future market were in dispute. The determination whether the use under these circumstances was substantial should have been made by the trier of fact in the light of all relevant facts. In holding that the use here was insubstantial, the court distinguished Folsom v. Marsh, supra, 9 F.Cas. 342, the only American case which has addressed the verbatim copying of copyrighted historical letters. Justice Story denied the fair use defense in Folsom because he found that George Washington's letters formed a substantial part of the allegedly infringing biography. He held that there could be no fair use of letters in an historical work "if the value of the original is sensibly diminished or the labors of the original author are substantially appropriated. "[Letters] may be inserted as a sort of distinct and mosaic work, into the general texture of the second work, and constitute the peculiar excellence thereof, and then it may be a clear piracy." Id. at 348. Justice Story is quite explicit about the policy underlying copyright protection for personal letters.

> What descendant or representative of the deceased author would undertake to publish at his own risk and expense, any such papers; and what editor would be willing to employ his own learning and judgment, and researches, in illustrating such work, if the moment they were successful, and possessed the substantial patronage of the public, a rival bookmaker might republish them, either in the same, or in a cheaper form, and thus either share with him, or take from him the whole profits.

Id. at 347.

Defendants-appellees reprinted verbatim portions of 28 copyrighted letters, a total of 1957 words. Although these letters represent less than one percent of The Implosion Conspiracy, the letters were prominently featured in promotional material for the book. The fact that the letters were quoted out of chronological order, many undated, without indication of elisions or other editorial modifications is relevant to a determination of the purpose for their use and the necessity for verbatim quotations for the sake of historical accuracy.

The availability of the fair use defense depends on all the circumstances surrounding the use of copyrighted material. This court has repeatedly stressed

> that "on a motion for summary judgment the court cannot try issues of fact; . . . it must resolve all ambiguities and draw all reasonable inferences in favor of the party against whom summary judgment is sought, . . . with the burden on the moving party to demonstrate the absence of any material factual issue genuinely in dispute. . . ."

Frey Ready-Mixed Concrete v. Pine Hill Concrete Mix Corp., 554 F.2d 551, slip op. 3369, 3375 (2d Cir. May 6, 1977), citing Heyman v. Commerce & Industry Insurance Co., 524 F.2d 1317, 1319–20 (2d Cir. 1975). See also Time, Inc. v. Bernard Geis Associates, 293 F.Supp. 130, 159 U.S.P.Q. 663 (S.D.N.Y.1968); Berlin v. E. C. Publications, Inc., 329 F.2d 541, 141 U.S.P.Q. 1 (2d Cir.), cert. denied, 379 U.S. 822, 85 S.Ct. 46, 13 L.Ed.2d 33, 143 U.S.P.Q. 464 (1964). Summary judgment on the issue of fair use was granted in Time, Inc. v. Bernard Geis and in the Berlin case, but there were no relevant facts in dispute in either case. In Berlin it was clear that the infringing parody had neither the effect nor the intent of fulfilling the demand for the original work, and that no greater amount had been appropriated than necessary. In Time, Inc. v. Bernard Geis it was likewise undisputed that there was little or no injury to the copyright owner, and the court found that the infringing book was not bought because it contained a copyrighted photograph of the Kennedy assassination at issue in that case. 293 F.2d 146, 159 U.S.P.Q. 675–676. In the case before us it has been conceded that plaintiffs might have incurred damages, and there is a dispute between the parties as to the purpose of and necessity for including verbatim letters in the book. For the sole purpose of the summary judgment motion all parties conceded that appellants held a valid copyright for the Death House Letters. This issue, as well as the fair use question, remains in dispute however.

Appellants are entitled to an opportunity to introduce evidence on the issues of the purpose of the use and of damages. Whether or not there has been substantial use which would deprive appellees of the fair use defense is a decision which must be made by the trier of fact after all the evidence has been introduced. We hold that it was error to uphold the fair use defense as a matter of law as to all defendants. As to Nizer and Doubleday it also was error to uphold the defense in the alternative on factual findings, in the absence of evidence on the question of damages. We therefore reverse the grant of summary judgment as to all defendants and remand so that appellants can be given the opportunity to introduce evidence on all aspects of the fair use defense.

ENCYCLOPAEDIA BRITANNICA EDUCATIONAL CORP. v. CROOKS

United States District Court, W.D. New York, 1978.
447 F.Supp. 243, 197 U.S.P.Q. 280.

CURTIN, District Judge.

The plaintiffs are three corporations engaged in the business of producing, acquiring, and licensing educational motion picture films. On October 19, 1977 the plaintiffs filed this copyright infringement suit against the Board of Cooperative Educational Services of Erie County [BOCES], a nonprofit corporation organized under the Education Law to provide educational services to the public schools in Erie County. The complaint alleges that BOCES has videotaped a number of their copyrighted films without their permission and distributed the copies to the school districts for delayed viewing by the students. The plaintiffs demand that the defendants be enjoined from videotaping copyrighted films and they seek both actual and statutory damages for past infringement. They also request an award of costs and fees, and the surrender or destruction of all infringing copies of the films.

At the time of filing the complaint, the plaintiffs moved for a temporary restraining order to prevent the destruction of the existing videotapes and records pertaining to the tapes in BOCES' possession pending a final decision in the case, and also to obtain accelerated discovery privileges. This motion was granted by the court, upon the plaintiffs' agreement to post a $10,000 bond to indemnify the defendants against possible loss. Both parties proceeded to engage in preliminary discovery.

The case is now before the court on the plaintiffs' motion for a preliminary injunction. The plaintiffs seek to temporarily enjoin the defendants from videotaping plaintiffs' copyrighted motion pictures from television broadcasts, recopying the videotapes, distributing these tapes to the school districts, displaying the copies in classrooms, and transmitting the videotaped films to the schools over closed-circuit television cables. A hearing on the motion was held on December 27, 1977, at which the attorneys agreed not to call witnesses in connection with the motion but to rely on filed affidavits, exhibits, memoranda of law, depositions, and oral argument.

All three of the plaintiffs are engaged in the business of producing, acquiring, and licensing educational audiovisual materials. Although the percentage varies among the three, all derive substantial income from the sale and licensing of copyrighted educational motion pictures, both to television networks and to educational institutions. Each of the plaintiffs owns copyrights to some of the films on which this infringement suit is based.

Since 1969, plaintiff Learning Corporation of America [LCA] has been entering into licensing agreements with BOCES for the purchase of 16-millimeter prints of educational films. In 1975, its revenues from BOCES reached a peak of $12,676.25, but declined to $1,703.75 by 1977. Some of the films on which LCA's infringement claim is based have been the subject of licensing agreements. Neither of the other two plaintiffs has at any time entered into licensing agreements with BOCES.

BOCES was created under § 1958 of the New York Education Law for the purpose of providing educational services and specialized instruction on a cooperative basis to the school districts within its geographic district. The Erie County BOCES services twenty-one school districts, including over one hundred separate schools. The focus of this lawsuit is one of BOCES' services, its practice of videotaping educational programs from television broadcasts and distributing the tapes to the schools for delayed viewing in the classrooms.

BOCES admits that it has been videotaping television programs of educational value since 1966. Since 1968, it has been openly distributing catalogs to the teachers within the twenty-one school districts which describe the available programs and provide ordering instructions. Each of the educational films involved in this lawsuit has been listed in one of BOCES' catalogs as available to the schools.

When a program of educational value is broadcast on television, BOCES makes a master videotape of the entire film. The vast majority of films it tapes are broadcast by the local public broadcasting channel, WNED-17, but some also are broadcast by commercial stations. The catalog describes the programs and provides that if a teacher wants to order a copy, the school district must supply BOCES with sufficient blank videotape and allow two weeks for processing.

When a school files a written request for a videotape, BOCES copies the master onto the blank tape and delivers the copy to the requesting school. BOCES holds the master in its videotape library for varying periods of time before erasure. The copies are viewed by the students in the classroom, and in most instances then are returned to BOCES for erasure and reuse in videotaping other programs. However, BOCES does not require the schools to return the tapes. A few of the school districts keep the copies for their own videotape libraries. BOCES also does not monitor the use of the tapes by the schools, but presumes they are used solely for educational purposes. Copies are distributed only to schools within its twenty-one school districts and then only upon written request. Copies are supplied to the schools at cost, and no admission is charged to the students.

With the exception of the 1974–75 school year, BOCES has records of the number of copies made of each particular television program. These records show that the volume of copying is substantial. During the 1976–77 school year, for instance, BOCES duplicated approximately ten thousand videotapes. BOCES has not kept records of the number of times a copy has been displayed in the classroom or the ultimate disposition of the tapes.

According to the defendants' affidavits, this program is a significant component of the instructional support services provided by BOCES, and is relied upon by the teachers in planning their school curricula. Since many of the programs are televised when classes are not in session or at times that do not coincide with coverage of the subject in a particular course of study, it is claimed that the students cannot view these programs unless videotapes are available. In order to provide this service, BOCES has invested a considerable amount of money in videotape equipment, which has an estimated replacement cost of one-half million dollars. BOCES has between five and eight full-time employees working to provide the service. The defendants claim that if the program is discontinued, public education would be greatly disrupted.

All three of the plaintiffs have been aware that educational institutions were videotaping their copyrighted television programs for some time. Time-Life has had knowledge of this practice since at least 1972, and LCA and Encyclopaedia Britannica have known since 1973. The Association of Media Producers, a trade organization to which all three of the plaintiffs belong, has been negotiating with the National School Board Association and other representatives of educational institutions in an attempt to define what constitutes fair use in the area of videotaping educational programs. These negotiations are still in progress, and no compromise has yet been reached.

BOCES' practices came to LCA's attention approximately in December 1976, when it received a copy of the BOCES videotape catalog. The catalog was thereafter supplied to the other two plaintiffs, and this action was commenced.

The plaintiffs' theory of infringement is straightforward. As the copyright owners of the films in question, they claim that they have the exclusive rights under federal copyright law to copy and perform the films. These exclusive rights were infringed by BOCES each time it videotaped one of the films off the air without permission and again each time it distributed a copy of a tape to a requesting school for performance in the classroom. They argue that in copyright infringement actions, irreparable harm is presumed once a prima facie case of infringement is established, and that therefore they are entitled to preliminary injunctive relief.

BOCES admits that it has videotaped the plaintiffs' copyrighted films without paying license fees or obtaining permission, but opposes the motion on three grounds. First, it raises the fair use doctrine as a defense and argues that noncommercial videotaping of television programs off the air for purposes of delayed viewing in the classroom is not a copyright infringement. Second, BOCES argues that the plaintiffs are barred by the doctrines of laches and estoppel from obtaining preliminary relief. Finally, it contends that any presumption of irreparable harm is rebutted by the existence of a clear measure of damages provided by the plaintiffs' licensing agreements, coupled with BOCES' records of the number of copies it has produced. In the post-argument papers, BOCES makes the additional claim that most of the television programs videotaped by BOCES were purchased by the local educational channel, WNED-TV, with state funds, and that these appropriations were made to WNED for the purpose of providing instructional broadcasts for the public schools at no cost to the schools. BOCES argues that the plaintiffs are seeking to force the state to pay twice for the use of their films and that the appropriations would not have been made if the instructional programs could not be utilized by the schools through videotaping. Although BOCES voluntarily stopped distributing tapes to the schools when the suit was commenced, it claims that this has caused a substantial hardship to the educational institutions served and wishes to reinstate its program.

As a general rule, a motion for preliminary relief should be granted only upon a clear showing of either probable success on the merits and possible irreparable injury or sufficiently serious questions going to the merits to make them a fair ground for litigation and a balance of hardships tipping in the plaintiff's favor. In copyright infringement cases, however, the standard is less rigorous. It is well established that "[a] copyright holder in the ordinary case may be presumed to suffer irreparable harm when his right to the exclusive use of the copyrighted material is invaded." American Metropolitan Enterprises v. Warner Brothers Records, 389 F.2d 903, 905, 157 U.S. P.Q. 69, 70–71 (2d Cir. 1968). Because injury normally can be presumed, the plaintiff in a copyright case is entitled to a preliminary injunction even without a detailed showing of irreparable harm if the plaintiff demonstrates probable success on the merits or a prima facie case of infringement. Wainwright Securities, Inc. v. Wall Street Transcript Corp., 588 F.2d 91, 94, 194 U.S.P.Q. 401, 402–403 (2d Cir. 1977), cert. denied 434 U.S. 1014, 98 S.Ct. 730, 54 L.Ed.2d 759, 196 U.S.P.Q. 864 (1978).

I.

Turning first to the question of irreparable injury, the plaintiffs claim that BOCES' videotaping is depriving them of licensing fees and is irreparably impairing their market for educational films. They point out that BOCES could readily avoid any disruption in its educational services pending a final decision in this case by entering into licensing agreements with the plaintiffs for the copying and performance of their copyrighted films. They contend that these licenses would provide a ready measure of damages, payable out of the $10,000 bond should BOCES ultimately prevail.

BOCES contends that the presumption of irreparable harm in copyright infringement cases can be rebutted by showing that monetary damages would provide full compensation for any infringement. They claim that the plaintiffs' licensing agreements, taken in conjunction with BOCES' records of the number of videotapes being made, provide a clear measure of damages, and that therefore preliminary relief is inappropriate.

I find that the plaintiffs' showing of irreparable harm is sufficiently detailed to meet the standard enunciated in Wainwright. The plaintiffs allege that BOCES' practices threaten to destroy or substantially impair their market for educational films. This claim, if true, encompasses injury beyond lost licensing fees, which cannot readily be reduced to monetary terms. Moreover, BOCES does not keep records of the number of times each film is displayed in the schools, and it does not guarantee return of the videotapes. Absent such records and guarantees, the licensing agreements would not provide a clear measure of damages caused by distributing copies of the films to the schools.

II.

The question of probable success on the merits poses a more troublesome issue. Educational institutions have been videotaping television broadcasts for strictly educational purposes for some time. The legality of such copying has never been determined, either by the courts or by the legislature. The problem of accommodating the competing interests of both educators and film producers raises major policy questions which the legislature is better equipped to resolve. However, Congress has not as yet provided a legislative solution to the problem, but has left the issue to the courts.[2]

I assume for purposes of this motion that the plaintiffs are the copyright owners of the films providing the basis for this lawsuit, and that BOCES has videotaped and distributed copies of these films without the plaintiffs' permission, either by license agreements or otherwise. This squarely raises the issue of infringement.

Section 1 of the Copyright Act of 1909 declares that a copyright owner shall have the exclusive rights to copy the copyrighted work and to exhibit or perform it publicly. Infringement of these rights entitles the copyright owner to injunctive and monetary relief. Substantially the same general provisions were reenacted by Congress in

---

2. The Copyright Revision Act of 1976, Act of Oct. 19, 1976. Pub.L.No. 94–553, 90 Stat. 2541, codified in 17 U.S.C.A. §§ 101–810, makes extensive changes in the copyright law, many of which were designed to address issues raised by rapidly changing technology. Several isolated problems regarding the use of copyrighted works by educators are resolved by the new legislation. See, e. g., 17 U.S.C.A. § 110(1) (allowing teachers engaged in "face-to-face teaching activities" to use copyrighted works under certain well-defined circumstances); id. § 504(c)(2) (exempting teachers acting in good faith and with the reasonable belief that their use was fair from statutory liability for infringement). For a more detailed discussion of these provisions, see Comment, "Education and the Copyright Law," 46 Ford.L.Rev. 91 (1977). The Act also mentions videotaping in several limited contexts. See, e. g., id. § 108(f)(3) (allowing libraries to videotape newscasts for distribution to educators and researchers); id. § 118(d)(3) (allowing nonprofit institutions to videotape certain noncommercial television broadcasts for use in face-to-face-teaching activities within seven days of the broadcast). However, the Act does not address the question of whether off-the-air video-

taping of copyrighted motion pictures for classroom use is an infringement. The legislative history clearly demonstrates Congress' intent to leave the problem to the courts pending further negotiations between the film industry and educators aimed at developing guidelines to protect the interests of both groups. The House Report, urging the interest groups to continue their discussions, states:

The problem of off-the-air taping for nonprofit classroom use of copyrighted audiovisual works incorporated in radio and television broadcasts has proved to be difficult to resolve. The Committee believes that the fair use doctrine has some limited application in this area, but it appears that the development of detailed guidelines will require a more thorough exploration than has thus far been possible of the needs and problems of a number of different interests affected, and of the various legal problems presented. Nothing in section 107 or elsewhere in the bill is intended to change or prejudge the law on the point.

H.R.Rep.No.94–1476, 94th Cong., 2d Sess. 71–72 (1976), reprinted in [1976] USCC&AN 5659, 5685.

the Copyright Revision Act of 1976, which applies to any alleged infringements occurring on or after January 1, 1978.

Viewed solely in reference to the copyright law, BOCES' videotaping activities would seem to constitute a blatant violation of the plaintiffs' exclusive rights to copy and perform their films. However, the statutory language is qualified by the judicial doctrine of "fair use." Although the doctrine is a defense to claims of copyright infringement, its application nevertheless must be considered in determining the existence of a prima facie case for purposes of preliminary relief.

The fair use doctrine was developed by the courts as a means of balancing the public's interest in the development of arts, science, and history with the copyright owner's exclusive rights. It has been defined as "a privilege in others than the owner of a copyright to use the copyrighted material in a reasonable manner without his consent, notwithstanding the monopoly granted to the owner . . . ." Rosemont Enterprises v. Random House, 366 F.2d 303, 306, 150 U.S.P.Q. 715, 718–719 (2d Cir. 1966), cert. denied, 385 U.S. 1009, 87 S.Ct. 714, 17 L.Ed.2d 546, 152 U.S.P.Q. 844 (1967), quoting Ball, Copyright and Literary Property 260 (1944).

Although the line between infringement and fair use of copyrighted material depends on the facts of each case the courts have given primary consideration to four factors in determining whether a given use is fair. Congress has codified these four factors in § 107 of the Copyright Revision Act of 1976. Section 107 is intended to restate and not to change existing doctrine of fair use. . . .

BOCES argues that videotaping educational programs off the air for delayed viewing by students constitutes a fair use of plaintiffs' films and that therefore the plaintiffs have not shown probable success on the merits in their application for preliminary relief. In support of its position, BOCES relies on Williams & Wilkins Co. v. United States, 487 F.2d 1345, 180 U.S.P.Q. 49 (Ct.Cl.1973), aff'd by an equally divided court, 420 U.S. 376, 95 S.Ct. 1344, 43 L.Ed.2d 264, 184 U.S.P.Q. 705 (1975), the leading case in the application of the doctrine to noncommercial copying. Due to the difficulty and complexity of the issues raised by BOCES' defense, a detailed examination of Williams & Wilkins is in order.

In Williams & Wilkins, a major publisher of medical journals sued a federal medical research organization and its library for copyright infringement of four of its journals. The claim was based on the defendants' admitted practice of photocopying articles from medical journals at the request of medical researchers and practitioners who used the articles for professional purposes The defendants also supplied copies of journal articles to other libraries and research institutions as part of an inter-library loan program. The copying for individual requesters was massive in scope, involving ninety-three thousand articles in the year 1970 alone and requiring four full-time employees to fill the requests. The copying for the inter-library loan program also was substantial. However, the defendants normally restricted copying on individual requests to a single copy of a single article and to articles of less than fifty pages. Requests from other institutions were filled in most cases only if the article was at least five years old or not published in one of approximately one hundred widely available medical journals. An excessive number of requests from a given individual or institution would not be honored. In all cases, the requests were for professional, nonprofit purposes, but no monitoring took place of the use to which the copies were put, and copies were not returned to the library.

After an extensive trial, the trial judge found that the plaintiff's copyrights had been infringed. A sharply divided panel of the Court of Claims reversed, and an equally divided Supreme Court affirmed.

Judge Davis, writing for the four-judge majority on the Court of Claims, applied the four factors described above, and concluded that the defendants' copying was a fair use. The court's conclusion was based on three primary considerations:

> First, plaintiff has not in our view shown, and there is inadequate reason to believe, that it is being or will be harmed substantially by these specific practices of NIH and NLM; second, we are convinced that medicine and medical research will be injured by holding these particular practices to be an infringement; and, third, since the problem of accommodating the interests of science with those of the publishers (and authors) calls fundamentally for legislative solution or guidance, which has not yet been given, we should not, during the period before congressional action is forthcoming, place such a risk of harm upon science and medicine.

Id. at 1354, 180 U.S.P.Q. at 55.

The analysis used by the Court of Claims in Williams & Wilkins is instructive in comparing the two cases and in deciding the issues presented here. The purpose and character of the use, which is the first factor considered by the courts in determining whether a given use is fair, is similar in both cases. Both sets of defendants have been providing services on a strictly noncommercial basis to a limited class of requesters for the purpose of promoting two traditionally favored areas of endeavor: science and education. Although the plaintiffs argue that a distinction should be drawn between the two uses because scientific research is more creative than education, there is no support for this distinction in the case law. As to the first factor, the parallels between the two cases are strong.

But as to the factors of the substantiality of the copying and the effect of the copying on the copyright owner's market, the two cases are distinguishable. In Williams & Wilkins, the requests normally were limited to single articles of fifty pages or less. In this case, the entire copyrighted film is being reproduced. Although the medical library did copy entire articles, each of which could be considered a discrete whole, there is nevertheless a significant difference between copying an article out of a medical journal and reproducing an entire copyrighted work. In the latter case, the potential impact on the copyright owner's market is much greater because the reproduction is interchangeable with the original. The substantiality and extent of BOCES' copying clearly exceeds that of the medical libraries.

As to the impact on the copyright owner's market, the court must assume for purposes of this motion that BOCES' practices have had or will have a substantial effect on the plaintiffs. In Williams & Wilkins, in contrast, the court found the effect on the market to be minimal. Id. at 1357–59, 180 U.S.P.Q. at 57–59. This difference in economic impact between the two cases arises out of their different procedural postures. The Williams & Wilkins decision followed a full trial on the merits. After the plaintiff had an opportunity to demonstrate the effect of the photocopying on the market for medical journals, the court concluded that it had failed to show that it would be substantially harmed by the defendants' practices. Here, in contrast, the case arises on the plaintiffs' motion for preliminary relief. The question of the effect of BOCES' videotaping on the plaintiffs' market for educational films has not yet been tried. Although BOCES has made a noteworthy attempt to show through preliminary discovery that the plaintiffs have not suffered any economic loss or impairment of their market, the plaintiffs' affidavits contain allegations to the contrary. These allegations raise substantial questions of fact, which can be decided only after a full trial record has been developed. Since the burden of establishing fair use is on the defendant and since the plaintiff in a copyright case is presumed to suffer irreparable injury, the court must assume for purposes of this motion that the plaintiffs are capable of proving their allegations.

A final distinguishing factor between this case and Williams & Wilkins is BOCES' ability to avoid disruption of classroom services by entering into licensing agreements with the plaintiffs pending resolution of this case. One of the three considerations cited as controlling by the court in Williams & Wilkins was the injury to medical research that would result if the court found copyright infringement. Here, any injury can be avoided pending a final decision, and the plaintiffs' bond provides a ready source of recovery should BOCES ultimately prevail.

The scope of BOCES' activities is difficult to reconcile with its claim of fair use. This case does not involve an isolated instance of a teacher copying copyrighted material for classroom use but concerns a highly organized and systematic program for reproducing videotapes on a massive scale. BOCES had acquired videotape equipment worth one-half million dollars, uses five to eight full-time personnel to carry out its program, and makes as many as ten thousand tapes per year. For the last twelve years, these tapes have been distributed throughout Erie County to over one hundred separate schools.

Considering all of these factors, I find that the plaintiffs have established a prima facie case entitling them to preliminary relief. As

BOCES points out, the applicability of the defense of fair use raises numerous questions of fact which cannot be resolved without a full trial on the merits. At this stage in the proceedings, I find that the substantiality of the copying and the possible impact on the market for education films tip the balance in favor of the plaintiffs, out-weighing BOCES' noncommercial, educational purpose in copying the films.

In its post-argument papers, BOCES raises the additional claim that most of the television programs which it videotaped were pur-chased by WNED-TV with state funds, and that these appropriations were made to WNED for the purpose of providing instructional broadcasts for the public schools at no cost to the schools. BOCES argues that the plaintiffs are seeking to force the state to pay twice for the use of their films and that the appropriations would not have been made if the instructional programs could not be utilized by the schools through videotaping. At this time, the record does not con-tain sufficient information pertaining to this claim to defeat the plaintiffs' application for preliminary relief. This possible defense should be developed at trial.

III.

The final point to be addressed is BOCES' contention that the plaintiffs' laches in bringing this motion bars their claim for prelimi-nary relief.

Although the plaintiffs may have been aware for some time of the practice of some educational institutions of videotaping their copyrighted films, on the present record it appears that the plaintiffs had no knowledge of BOCES' practices until December of 1976 and therefore could not have sued BOCES until that time. Their delay in raising the infringement question in the courts, caused at least in part by their attempts to reach an out-of-court compromise solution to a difficult and complex problem, should be commended rather than condemned.

As to the ten-month delay between the time that the plaintiffs received BOCES' catalogs and the time that they filed a complaint against BOCES, I recognize that the organization and planning of a lawsuit involving multiple plaintiffs and substantial legal claims re-quire time. On the present record, I am not willing to find that the ten-month delay was so excessive as to preclude preliminary relief.

The cases cited by the defendant are readily distinguishable from this case because they involved substantial questions of fact as to whether the defendant had in fact copied the plaintiff's copyrighted material. These disputes decreased the likelihood that the plaintiffs would succeed on the merits, rendering preliminary relief less appro-priate than in cases such as this where the copying is admitted.

IV.

The plaintiffs have established their entitlement to preliminary relief. Accordingly, I direct that BOCES be enjoined from videotaping the plaintiffs' educational films or programs off the public airwaves. If this order unduly disrupts educational plans, BOCES can obtain licenses from the plaintiffs for use of the films. As to films which have already been videotaped and are incorporated into the curricula of the BOCES' school districts, however, I find that the public interest would be served if BOCES is allowed to continue distributing such tapes to the schools. The interests of the plaintiffs will be adequately protected if BOCES, in cooperation with the school districts, implements a plan to monitor the use of the tapes in the schools and to require their return and erasure within a specified time period.

The parties are directed to meet with the court on March 3, 1978 at 9:00 a. m. to frame an order complying with this decision.

So ordered.

WALT DISNEY PRODUCTIONS v. AIR PIRATES, 581 F.2d 751, 753, 756–758, 199 U.S.P.Q. 769 (9th Cir. 1978). CUMMINGS, J.: ["The individual defendants have participated in preparing and publishing two magazines of cartoons entitled "Air Pirates Funnies." The characters in defendants' magazines bear a marked similarity to those of plaintiff. The names given to defendants' characters are the same names used in plaintiff's copyrighted work. However, the themes of defendants' publications differ markedly from those of Disney. While Disney sought only to foster "an image of innocent delightfulness," defendants supposedly sought to convey an allegorical message of significance. Put politely by one commentator, the "Air Pirates" was "an 'underground' comic book which had placed several well-known Disney cartoon characters in incongruous settings where they engaged in activities clearly antithetical to the accepted Mickey Mouse world of scrubbed faces, bright smiles and happy endings." It centered around "a rather bawdy depiction of the Disney characters as active members of a free thinking, promiscuous, drug ingesting counterculture." Note, Parody, Copyrights and the First Amendment. 10 U.S.F.L.Rev. 564, 571, 582 (1976)."]

Defendants do not contend that their admitted copying was not substantial enough to constitute an infringement, and it is plain that copying a comic book character's graphic image constitutes copying to an extent sufficient to justify a finding of infringement. Defendants instead claim that this infringement should be excused through the application of the fair use defense, since it purportedly is a parody of Disney's cartoons.

At least since this Court's controversial ruling in Benny v. Loew's Inc., 239 F.2d 532, 112 U.S.P.Q. 11 (9th Cir. 1956), affirmed by an equally divided Court, 356 U.S. 43, 78 S.Ct. 667, 2 L.Ed.2d 583, 116 U.S.P.Q. 479, the standards for applying the fair use defense in parody cases, like the standards for applying fair use in other contexts, have been a source of considerable attention and dispute. As a general matter, while some commentators have urged that the fair use defense depends only on whether the infringing work fills the demand for the original this Court and others have also consistently focused on the substantiality of the taking.

In inquiring into the substantiality of the taking, the district court read our Benny opinion to hold that any substantial copying by a defendant, combined with the fact that the portion copied constituted a substantial part of the defendant's work, automatically precluded the fair use defense. That such a strict reading of Benny was unjustified is indicated first by the fact that it would essentially make any fair use defense fruitless. If the substantiality of the taking necessary to satisfy the first half of that test is no different from the substantiality necessary to constitute an infringement, then the Benny test would be reduced to an absurdity, covering any infringement except those falling within the much-criticized and abandoned exception for cases in which the part copied was not a substantial part of the defendant's work.

The language in Benny concerning the substantiality of copying can be given a reading much more in keeping with the context of that case and the established principles at the time of that case if the opinion is understood as setting a threshold that eliminates from the fair use defense copying that is virtually complete or almost verbatim. It was an established principle at the time of Benny that such verbatim copying precluded resort to the fair use defense. Moreover, the Benny facts presented a particularly appropriate instance to apply that settled principle. As the Benny district court found, Benny's "Autolight" tracked the parodied "Gas Light" in almost every respect: the locale and period, the setting, characters, story points, incidents, climax and much of the dialogue all were found to be identical. In this context, Benny should not be read as taking the drastic step of virtually turning the test for fair use into the test for infringement. To do otherwise would be to eliminate fair use as a defense except perhaps for those infringers who added an extra act at the end of their parody.

Thus Benny should stand only as a threshold test that eliminates near-verbatim copying. In the absence of near-verbatim copying, other courts have analyzed the substantiality of copying by a parodist by asking whether the parodist has appropriated a greater amount of the original work than is necessary to "recall or conjure up" the object of his satire. Berlin v. E. C. Publications, Inc., 329 F.2d 541, 141 U.S.P.Q. 1 (2d Cir. 1964), certiorari denied, 379 U.S. 822, 85 S.Ct. 46, 13 L.Ed.2d 33, 143 U.S.P.Q. 464.

In order to facilitate application of either the Benny threshold test or the Berlin test, it is important to determine what are the relevant parts of each work that are compared in analyzing similarity. Plaintiff assumes in its brief that the graphic depiction, or pictorial illustration, is separately copyrightable as a component part, so that a verbatim copy of the depiction alone would satisfy the Benny test. Defendants proceed on the assumption that comparing their characters with plaintiff's involves a comparison not only of the physical image but also of the character's personality, pattern of speech, abilities, and other traits. Apparently this issue has not been addressed previously, and neither position is without merit. On the one hand, since an illustration in a book or catalogue can be copyrighted separately it might follow that an illustration in a comic strip is entitled to the same protection by virtue of Section 3 of the former Copyright Act. On the other hand, to a different extent than in other illustrations, a cartoon character's image is intertwined with its personality and other traits, so that the "total concept and feel" (Roth Greeting Cards v. United Card Co., 429 F.2d 1106, 1110, 166 U.S.P.Q. 291, 294 (9th Cir. 1970)) of even the component part cannot be limited to the image itself.

We need not decide which of these views is correct, or whether this copying was so substantial to satisfy the Benny test, because it is our view that defendants took more than is allowed even under the Berlin test as applied to both the conceptual and physical aspects of the characters. In evaluating how much of a taking was necessary to recall or conjure up the original, it is first important to recognize that given the widespread public recognition of the major characters involved here, such as Mickey Mouse and Donald Duck, in comparison with other characters very little would have been necessary to place Mickey Mouse and his image in the minds of the readers. Second, when the medium involved is a comic book, a recognizable caricature is not difficult to draw, so that an alternative that involves less copying is more likely to be available than if a speech, for instance, is parodied. Also significant is the fact that the essence of this parody did not focus on how the characters looked, but rather parodied their personalities, their wholesomeness and their innocence.[15] Thus arguably defendants' copying could have been justified as necessary more easily if they had paralleled closely (with a few significant twists) Disney characters and their actions in a manner that conjured up the particular elements of the innocence of the characters that were to be satirized. While greater license may be necessary under those circumstances, here the copying of the graphic image appears to have no other purpose than to track Disney's work as a whole as closely as possible.

Defendants' assertion that they copied no more than necessary appears to be based on an affidavit, which stated that "the humorous

15. In making this distinction, we do not regard it as fatal, as some courts have done (see e. g., Walt Disney Productions v. Mature Pictures Corp., 389 F.Supp. 1397, 186 U.S.P.Q. 48 (S. D.N.Y.1975)), that the "Air Pirates" were parodying life and society in addition to parodying the Disney characters. Such an effect is almost an inherent aspect of any parody. To the extent that the Disney characters are not also an object of the parody, however, the need to conjure them up would be reduced if not eliminated.

effect of parody is best achieved when at first glance the material appears convincingly to be the original, and upon closer examination is discovered to be quite something else". The short answer to this assertion, which would also justify substantially verbatim copying, is that when persons are parodying a copyrighted work, the constraints of the existing precedent do not permit them to take as much of a component part as they need to make the "best parody." Instead, their desire to make the "best parody" is balanced against the rights of the copyright owner in his original expressions. That balance has been struck at giving the parodist what is necessary to conjure up the original, and in the absence of a special need for accuracy that standard was exceeded here. By copying the images in their entirety, defendants took more than was necessary to place firmly in the reader's mind the parodied work and those specific attributes that are to be satirized.

Because the amount of defendant's copying exceeded permissible levels, summary judgment was proper. While other factors in the fair use calculus may not be sufficient by themselves to preclude the fair use defense, this and other courts have accepted the traditional American rule that excessive copying precludes fair use.

NOTES

1. Section 107, although it purports only to "restate the present judicial doctrine of fair use, not to change, narrow, or enlarge it in any way," H.R.Rep.No.94–1476, 66, in fact gives the defense a clarity and cohesiveness it never previously possessed. To be sure, the several purposes and factors referred to in section 107 have been mentioned in fair use decisions over the years, but they never received the uniform and systematic treatment offered by section 107. Courts historically treated the favored purposes differently and assigned vastly different weights to each of the four factors. One example of this diversity is the different approaches to substantiality of appropriation taken in *Air Pirates,* Benny v. Loews, *Crooks* and *Williams & Wilkins.*

While section 107's comprehensive ingathering of the fair use factors previously mentioned in judicial decisions may aid courts in future decisions, the section's failure to discriminate among these factors may also mislead them. For example, the market effects test— section 107's fourth factor—though mentioned by courts, can hardly be more than a rhetorical flourish, for the test is entirely circular. Whether a use will affect "the potential market for or value of the copyrighted work" necessarily turns on whether the use will be proscribed. Thus, if copyright in a work is considered to include the right to reprint the work in biographies, to make videotapes for classroom use, or to make parodies of it, then allowing these uses without license will necessarily interfere with the copyright proprietor's ability to license these uses to others, impairing the potential market for or value of the copyrighted work. It is no surprise that the market effects test has won more adherents among commentators than among courts that must make concrete findings in deciding real cases. See Hayes, Classroom "Fair Use": A Reevaluation, 26 Bull. Copyright Soc'y 101, 110–112 (1978).

2. From the time that section 107 was first proposed, debate centered on the status of classroom copying, particularly photocopying, of copyrighted works. According to the House Report, the House Committee resisted educators' proposals for " 'a specific exemption freeing certain reproductions of copyrighted works for educational and scholarly purposes from copyright control.' " The Committee did, however, recognize " 'a need for greater certainty and protection for teachers.' " One step toward meeting this need was section 504(c), "to provide innocent teachers and other nonprofit users of copyrighted material with broad insulation against unwarranted liability for infringement." H.R.Rep.No. 94–1476, 66–67.

As another step in the direction of certainty, the House Committee encouraged education and trade groups to agree on joint guidelines for permissible classroom uses. The effort bore fruit. On March 19, 1976 educator groups, the Authors League, and the Association of American Publishers reached an *Agreement on Guidelines for Classroom Copying in Not-For-Profit Educational Institutions with Respect to Books and Periodicals*. The *Guidelines* cover unlicensed copying in the form both of single copies made by teachers for their own use, and multiple copies made for classroom use. Under the *Guidelines* a teacher may, for research or teaching purposes, make a single copy of a chapter from a book, an article from a periodical or newspaper, a short story, essay or poem, or a chart, graph, diagram, drawing, cartoon or picture. The *Guidelines* impose more rigorous and detailed standards of "brevity," "spontaneity" and "cumulative effect" for multiple copies for classroom use. H.R.Rep.No. 94–1476, 68–70.

The House Committee accepted these, and counterpart *Guidelines* for educational uses of music, as "a reasonable interpretation of the minimum standards of fair use. Teachers will know that copying within the *Guidelines* is fair use." H.R.Rep.No.94–1476, 72. The House and Senate Conferees also accepted the *Guidelines* "as part of their understanding of fair use." House Conf.Rep.No.94–1733, 94th Cong. 2d Sess. 72 (1976).

3. In Benny v. Loew's, discussed in the *Air Pirates* case above, the copyrighted work in issue was "Gaslight," a motion picture produced by plaintiff and starring Charles Boyer, Ingrid Bergman and Joseph Cotton. The infringing work was "Autolight," a fifteen-minute segment of Jack Benny's half-hour television show, starring Benny and Barbara Stanwyck.

Comparison of the two works led Judge Carter to the findings:

"(1) that the locale and period of the works are the same; (2) the main setting is the same; (3) the characters are generally the same; (4) the story points are practically identical; (5) the development of the story, the treatment (except that defendants' treatment is burlesque), the incidents, the sequences of events, the points of suspense, the climax are almost identical and finally, (6) there has been a detailed borrowing of much of the dialogue with some variation in wording. There has been a substantial taking by defendants from the plaintiffs' copyright property."

"If this was the ordinary plagiarism case," the court concluded, "without the defense of burlesque as a fair use, it would be crystal clear, under the controlling authorities, that there had been access, a substantial taking and therefore infringement." Loew's, Inc. v. Columbia Broadcasting System, Inc., 131 F.Supp. 165, 171–172 (S.D.Cal. 1955).

Judge Carter rested his refusal to exempt defendant's burlesque on several grounds. He found that the attempted exemption "has been the subject of several decisions and has been disposed of, not by determining whether the alleged infringing use was parody or burlesque, but by ascertaining whether it amounted to a taking of substantial, copyrightable material. In other words, a parodized or burlesqued taking is treated no differently from any other appropriation." Carter drew an interesting comparison to a case involving a directory: "Defendants have transposed the work, from the serious to the comic vein. This is analogous to the situation in Leon v. Pacific Telephone & Telegraph Co., 9 Cir. 1947, 91 F.2d 484, when defendant took plaintiff's copyrighted telephone book and inverted the list from an alphabetical one to a numerical one."

Judge Carter had the opportunity to refine his views on parody, burlesque and fair use in a case he decided later that same year, Columbia Pictures Corp. v. National Broadcasting Co., 137 F.Supp. 348, 107 U.S.P.Q. 344 (S.D.Cal.1955). Ruling that defendant's broadcast of a parody, "From Here to Obscurity," did not infringe plaintiff's rights in its motion picture, "From Here to Eternity," he noted that "this case tests the general principle and dictum in Loew's. . . . Unlike Loew's here there was a taking of only sufficient to cause the viewer to recall and conjure up the original. This is a necessary element of burlesque." If, as has been suggested, Columbia Pictures represents a withdrawal from the position staked out in Loew's, the change made little difference to the Loew's defendants who had by then taken their appeal to the Ninth Circuit Court of Appeals. Seventeen days after Judge Carter's decision in Columbia, the circuit court released its decision affirming his disposition of Loew's, 239 F. 2d 532 (1956). The Ninth Circuit decision was affirmed by an evenly divided, 4–4, Supreme Court, 356 U.S. 43 (1958).

To be excused, must the parody directly concern the copyrighted work, or may it use the copyrighted work merely as the vehicle for a critique of cultural, social or political institutions generally? Does the approach offered in footnote 15 of Air Pirates resolve the issue satisfactorily? See also Elsmere Music, Inc. v. National Broadcasting Co., Inc., 623 F.2d 252, 207 U.S.P.Q. 277 (2d Cir. 1980).

The questions raised by Judge Carter's opinions in the *Loew's* and *Columbia Pictures* cases are considered in Netterville, Copyright and Tort Aspects of Parody, Mimicry and Humorous Commentary, 35 So.Calif.L.Rev. 225 (1962); Selvin, Parody and Burlesque of Copyrighted Works as Infringement, 6 Bull. Copyright Soc'y 53 (1958); Rossett, Burlesque as Copyright Infringement, 9 ASCAP Copyright L. Symposium 1 (1956). See generally, Light, Parody, Burlesque and the Economic Rationale for Copyright, 11 Conn.L.Rev. 615 (1979).

4. Section 108 exempts a wide range of reproduction activities by libraries and archives—from copying for archival purposes, covered by subsections (b) and (c), to photocopying for users, covered by subsections (d) and (e). It was the permission to photocopy for users that produced the most intricate drafting and the greatest controversy, focussed primarily on subsection (g). As originally proposed in the Senate, section 108(g) sought to quell publisher's fears that libraries would effectively compete with them through the "systematic reproduction" of copyrighted works. Librarians argued that the restriction went too far and would seriously jeopardize interlibrary loan activities. In response, the House added the proviso that now appears at the end of section 108(g)(2)—"nothing in this clause prevents a library or archives from participating in interlibrary arrangements that do not have, as their purpose or effect, that the library or archives receiving such copies or phonorecords for distribution does so in such aggregate quantities as to substitute for a subscription to or purchase of such work."

What constitutes "aggregate quantities" for purposes of the proviso? The most authoritative answer can be found in guidelines that were agreed upon by the principal library, publisher and author organizations shortly before the law was enacted. The guidelines, embodied in the Conference Report, provide, for example, that "aggregate quantities" shall mean "(a) with respect to any given periodical (as opposed to any given issue of a periodical), filled requests of a library or archives . . . within any calendar year for a total of six or more copies of an article or articles published in such periodical within five years prior to the date of the request." House Conf. Rep.No.94-1733, 94th Cong. 2d Sess. 72 (1976).

The National Commission on New Technological Uses of Copyright Works (CONTU) played a key role in bringing the parties together to frame the photocopying guidelines. It also contributed to the agenda for section 108's future, offering suggestions to aid the Register of Copyrights in designing the first five-year study of the section's operation, mandated by section 108(i). "The research effort should attempt to determine the impact of copying fees on the health of the publishing industry, with special emphasis on the publication of scientific, technical, and medical journals. In particular, the study should attempt to determine: (1) whether the imposition of copying fees contributes to the viability of individual journal titles; (2) what impact, if any, the imposition of copying fees has on journal subscriptions and library acquisitions; and (3) what information concerning the use of individual journal titles and their contents is provided by the numbers of photocopies for which payments are made." CONTU, Final Report 50 (1978).

CONTU's Final Report also provides a superb overview of the law and practice of photocopying in the United States and elsewhere. Circular R21, Reproduction of Copyrighted Works by Educators and Librarians (1978), published by the Copyright Office, collects and analyzes many of the relevant documents. See also, Treece, Library Photocopying, 24 U.C.L.A.L.Rev. 1025 (1977).

5. The problem of transaction delays played an important role in the evolution and statutory embodiment of fair use doctrine. One of the concerns in Williams & Wilkins v. United States was that the delay and other costs involved in locating copyright proprietors and negotiating with them for licenses to photocopy protected materials would seriously inhibit medical research activities. The Senate Report recommended that "workable clearance and licensing procedures be developed" for library photocopying practices not authorized by the new law. S.Rep.No.94–473, 94th Cong. 1st Sess. 71 (1975).

The Copyright Clearance Center, a not-for-profit corporation, was organized in 1977 to help users and publishers overcome the problem of transaction costs. On or after January 1, 1978, publications registered with the Center will typically state a copying permission fee on the first page of each article published together with the following notice:

> The appearance of the code at the bottom of the first page of an article in this Journal indicates the copyright owner's consent that copies of the article may be made for personal or internal use, or for personal or internal use of specific clients. This consent is given on the condition, however, that the copier pay the stated per-copy fee through the Copyright Clearance Center, Inc., P.O. Box 765, Schenectady, New York 12301 for copying beyond that permitted by Sections 107 or 108 of the U. S. Copyright Law. This consent does not extend to other kinds of copying, such as copying for general distribution, for creating new collective works or for resale.

The copying organization is expected periodically to remit payment for all copies made, and the Center will then distribute payments among publishers.

See generally, Copyright Clearance Center, Handbook for Libraries and Other Organizational Users Which Copy from Serials and Separates: Procedures for Using the Programs of the Copyright Clearance Center, Inc. (1977); Spilhaus, The Copyright Clearance Center, 9 Scholarly Publishing 143, 145 (1978). For a description of the operations of suppliers of authorized photocopies, like University Microfilms International and The National Technical Information Service, see National Commission on New Technological Uses of Copyrighted Works, Final Report, 61–65 (1978).

6. What connections are there between the fair use defense and the first amendment's free speech and press principles? *Air Pirates* rejected defendants' arguments that the "First Amendment should bar any liability for their parody because otherwise protected criticism would be discouraged." Recognizing that there is "of course some tension between the First Amendment and the Copyright Act," the court concluded that because defendants "could have expressed their theme without copying Disney's protected expression," their first amendment challenge should be dismissed. 581 F.2d 751, 758–759.

See Goldstein, Copyright and the First Amendment, 70 Colum.L. Rev. 983 (1970); Nimmer, Does Copyright Abridge the First Amendment Guarantees of Free Speech and Press? 17 U.C.L.A.L.Rev. 1180 (1970); Patterson, Private Copyright and Public Communication: Free Speech Endangered, 28 Vand.L.Rev. 1161 (1975); Denicola, Copyright and Free Speech: Constitutional Limitations on the Protection of Expression, 67 Cal.L.Rev. 283 (1979).

7. What are the political justifications and economic effects of fair use? The political justification for excusing criticism, comment and news reporting is substantial, resting squarely on free speech and press principles. Fair use avoids the threat of injunctive relief and the delay encountered in seeking copyright permission, both of which could improperly stifle free and open debate. At the same time, the economic impact of fair use in this area is probably small. Even if copyright proprietors actively sought to license critical and limited journalistic uses of their works, the returns would probably be much smaller than the returns from other direct and subsidiary uses.

Is there any political justification for excusing teaching, scholarship and research uses? What is the likely economic effect of excusing these uses? Is it probable that publishers will lower their investment in the development of materials for educational markets? If classroom users will not repay the copyright proprietor's investment in a work, who will? Will the cost be repaid in the form of implicit subsidies coming from other, noneducational users? What if the copyrighted work is a text, or other instructional tool that has a small noneducational market? See generally, P. Goldstein, Changing the American Schoolbook: Law, Politics and Technology, 67–70 (1978).

8. How would you dispose of the fair use defense raised in each of the following cases:

(a) Plaintiff, an institutional research and brokerage firm, prepares in-depth analytical reports on approximately 275 industrial, financial, utility and railroad corporations. Defendant publishes abstracts of these copyrighted research reports in its newspaper. See Wainwright Securities, Inc. v. Wall Street Transcript Corp., 558 F.2d 91, 194 U.S.P.Q. 401 (2d Cir. 1977), cert. denied 434 U.S. 1014, 98 S. Ct. 730, 54 L.Ed.2d 759 (1978).

(b) Plaintiff publishes the New York Times and the New York Times Index and operates a computer data bank consisting of a subject index to the New York Times. Access to data in the computer is obtained through key words, of which approximately 350,000 are personal names. Defendants are in the process of publishing a 22-volume personal name index to the annual New York Times Index. Defendants compile their index by culling all personal names that appear as headings in the New York Times Index; after each name, they cite the pages in the New York Times Index on which the name appears. See New York Times Co. v. Roxbury Data Interface, Inc., 434 F.Supp. 217, 194 U.S.P.Q. 371 (D.N.J.1977).

(c) Plaintiff publishes the periodical, *TV Guide*. Defendant publishes a television supplement to the Sunday edition of its newspaper. In one of defendant's television advertisements for its supplement, an actor displays the cover of an issue of *TV Guide* for a few seconds. Plaintiff charges that the use violates the exclusive right to display its copyrighted work. See Triangle Publications, Inc. v. Knight-Ridder Newspapers, Inc., 626 F.2d 1171, 207 U.S.P.Q. 977 (5th Cir. 1980).

(d) Plaintiffs own the copyrights to motion pictures produced for theatrical release and for television broadcast. Individuals use videotape recorders to copy plaintiffs' copyrighted works off the air. Defendants include the producer and distributor of a videotape recorder; retail stores selling the videotape recorder; an advertising agency that promotes sales of the recorder; and an individual who uses the videotape recorder in his home to copy plaintiffs' broadcast material. See Universal City Studios, Inc. v. Sony Corp. of America, 480 F.Supp. 429, 203 U.S.P.Q. 656 (C.D.Cal.1979).

d. DURATION, OWNERSHIP AND TRANSFER

COPYRIGHT LAW REVISION, H. R. REP. NO. 94–1476

94th Cong., 2d Sess. 120–129 (1976).

Section 201. Ownership of Copyright

Initial Ownership

Two basic and well-established principles of copyright law are restated in section 201(a): that the source of copyright ownership is the author of the work, and that, in the case of a "joint work," the coauthors of the work are likewise coowners of the copyright. Under the definition of section 101, a work is "joint" if the authors collaborated with each other, or if each of the authors prepared his or her contribution with the knowledge and intention that it would be merged with the contributions of other authors as "inseparable or interdependent parts of a unitary whole." The touchstone here is the intention, at the time the writing is done, that the parts be absorbed or combined into an integrated unit, although the parts themselves may be either "inseparable" (as the case of a novel or painting) or "interdependent" (as in the case of a motion picture, opera, or the words and music of a song). The definition of "joint work" is to be contrasted with the definition of "collective work," also in section

101, in which the elements of merger and unity are lacking; there the key elements are assemblage or gathering of "separate and independent works . . . into a collective whole."

The definition of "joint works" has prompted some concern lest it be construed as converting the authors of previously written works, such as plays, novels, and music, into coauthors of a motion picture in which their work is incorporated. It is true that a motion picture would normally be a joint rather than a collective work with respect to those authors who actually work on the film, although their usual status as employees for hire would keep the question of coownership from coming up. On the other hand, although a novelist, playwright, or songwriter may write a work with the hope or expectation that it will be used in a motion picture, this is clearly a case of separate or independent authorship rather than one where the basic intention behind the writing of the work was for motion picture use. In this case, the motion picture is a derivative work within the definition of that term, and section 103 makes plain that copyright in a derivative work is independent of, and does not enlarge the scope of rights in, any pre-existing material incorporated in it. There is thus no need to spell this conclusion out in the definition of "joint work."

There is also no need for a specific statutory provision concerning the rights and duties of the coowners of a work; court-made law on this point is left undisturbed. Under the bill, as under the present law, coowners of a copyright would be treated generally as tenants in common, with each coowner having an independent right to use or license the use of a work, subject to a duty of accounting to the other coowners for any profits.

Works Made for Hire

Section 201(b) of the bill adopts one of the basic principles of the present law: that in the case of works made for hire the employer is considered the author of the work, and is regarded as the initial owner of copyright unless there has been an agreement otherwise. The subsection also requires that any agreement under which the employee is to own rights be in writing and signed by the parties.

The work-made-for-hire provisions of this bill represent a carefully balanced compromise, and as such they do not incorporate the amendments proposed by screenwriters and composers for motion pictures. Their proposal was for the recognition of something similar to the "shop right" doctrine of patent law: with some exceptions, the employer would acquire the right to use the employee's work to the extent needed for purposes of his regular business, but the employee would retain all other rights as long as he or she refrained from the authorizing of competing uses. However, while this change might theoretically improve the bargaining position of screenwriters and others as a group, the practical benefits that individual authors would receive are highly conjectural. The presumption that initial ownership rights vest in the employer for hire is well established in American copyright law, and to exchange that for the uncertainties of the shop right doctrine would not only be of dubious value to employers and employees alike, but might also reopen a number of other issues.

The status of works prepared on special order or commission was a major issue in the development of the definition of "works made for hire" in section 101, which has undergone extensive revision during the legislative process. The basic problem is how to draw a statutory line between those works written on special order or commission that should be considered as "works made for hire," and those that should not. The definition now provided by the bill represents a compromise which, in effect, spells out those specific categories of commissioned works that can be considered "works made for hire" under certain circumstances.

Of these, one of the most important categories is that of "instructional texts." This term is given its own definition in the bill: "a literary, pictorial, or graphic work prepared for publication with the purpose of use in systematic instructional activities." The concept is intended to include what might be loosely called "textbook material," whether or not in book form or prepared in the form of text matter. The basic characteristic of "instructional texts" is the purpose of their preparation for "use in systematic instructional activities," and they are to be distinguished from works prepared for use by a general readership.

Contributions to Collective Works

Subsection (c) of section 201 deals with the troublesome problem of ownership of copyright in contributions to collective works, and the relationship between copyright ownership in a contribution and in the collective work in which it appears. The first sentence establishes the basic principle that copyright in the individual contribution and copyright in the collective work as a whole are separate and distinct, and that the author of the contribution is, as in every other case, the first owner of copyright in it. Under the definitions in section 101, a "collective work" is a species of "compilation" and, by its nature, must involve the selection, assembly, and arrangement of "a number of contributions." Examples of "collective works" would ordinarily include periodical issues, anthologies, symposia, and collections of the discrete writings of the same authors, but not cases, such as a composition consisting of words and music, a work published with illustrations or front matter, or three one-act plays, where relatively few separate elements have been brought together. Unlike the contents of other types of "compilations," each of the contributions incorporated in a "collective work" must itself constitute a "separate and independent" work, therefore ruling out compilations of information or other uncopyrightable material and works published with editorial revisions or annotations. Moreover, as noted above, there is a basic distinction between a "joint work," where the separate elements merge into a unified whole, and a "collective work," where they remain unintegrated and disparate.

The bill does nothing to change the rights of the owner of copyright in a collective work under the present law. These exclusive rights extend to the elements of compilation and editing that went into the collective work as a whole, as well as the contributions that were written for hire by employees of the owner of the collective work, and those copyrighted contributions that have been transferred in writing to the owner by their authors. However, one of the most significant aims of the bill is to clarify and improve the present confused and frequently unfair legal situation with respect to rights in contributions.

The second sentence of section 201(c), in conjunction with the provisions of section 404 dealing with copyright notice, will preserve the author's copyright in a contribution even if the contribution does not bear a separate notice in the author's name, and without requiring any unqualified transfer of rights to the owner of the collective work. This is coupled with a presumption that, unless there has been an express transfer of more, the owner of the collective work acquires "only the privilege of reproducing and distributing the contribution as part of that particular collective work, any revision of that collective work, and any later collective work in the same series."

The basic presumption of section 201(c) is fully consistent with present law and practice, and represents a fair balancing of equities. At the same time, the last clause of the subsection, under which the privilege of republishing the contribution under certain limited circumstances would be presumed, is an essential counterpart of the basic presumption. Under the language of this clause a publishing company could reprint a contribution from one issue in a later issue of its magazine, and could reprint an article from a 1980 edition of an encyclopedia in a 1990 revision of it; the publisher could not revise the contribution itself or include it in a new anthology or an entirely different magazine or other collective work.

Transfer of Ownership

The principle of unlimited alienability of copyright is stated in clause (1) of section 201(d). Under that provision the ownership of a copyright, or of any part of it, may be transferred by any means of conveyance or by operation of law, and is to be treated as personal property upon the death of the owner. The term "transfer of copyright ownership" is defined in section 101 to cover any "conveyance, alienation, or hypothecation," including assignments, mortgages, and exclusive licenses, but not including nonexclusive licenses. Representatives of motion picture producers have argued that foreclosures of copyright mortgages should not be left to varying State laws, and that the statute should establish a Federal foreclosure system. However, the benefits of such a system would be of very limited application, and would not justify the complicated statutory and procedural requirements that would have to be established.

Clause (2) of subsection (d) contains the first explicit statutory recognition of the principle of divisibility of copyright in our law.

This provision, which has long been sought by authors and their representatives, and which has attracted wide support from other groups, means that any of the exclusive rights that go to make up a copyright, including those enumerated in section 106 and any subdivision of them, can be transferred and owned separately. The definition of "transfer of copyright ownership" in section 101 makes clear that the principle of divisibility applies whether or not the transfer is "limited in time or place of effect," and another definition in the same section provides that the term "copyright owner," with respect to any one exclusive right, refers to the owner of that particular right. T..e last sentence of section 201(d)(2) adds that the owner, with respect to the particular exclusive right he or she owns, is entitled "to all of the protection and remedies accorded to the copyright owner by this title." It is thus clear, for example, that a local broadcasting station holding an exclusive license to transmit a particular work within a particular geographic area and for a particular period of time, could sue, in its own name as copyright owner, someone who infringed that particular exclusive right.

Subsection (e) provides that when an individual author's ownership of a copyright, or of any of the exclusive rights under a copyright, have not previously been voluntarily transferred, no action by any governmental body or other official or organization purporting to seize, expropriate, transfer, or exercise rights of ownership with respect to the copyright, or any of the exclusive rights under a copyright, shall be given effect under this title.

The purpose of this subsection is to reaffirm the basic principle that the United States copyright of an individual author shall be secured to that author, and cannot be taken away by any involuntary transfer. It is the intent of the subsection that the author be entitled, despite any purported expropriation or involuntary transfer, to continue exercising all rights under the United States statute, and that the governmental body or organization may not enforce or exercise any rights under this title in that situation.

It may sometimes be difficult to ascertain whether a transfer of copyright is voluntary or is coerced by covert pressure. But subsection (e) would protect foreign authors against laws and decrees purporting to divest them of their rights under the United States copyright statute, and would protect authors within the foreign country who choose to resist such covert pressures.

Traditional legal actions that may involve transfer of ownership, such as bankruptcy proceedings and mortgage foreclosures, are not within the scope of this subsection; the authors in such cases have voluntarily consented to these legal processes by their overt actions —for example, by filing in bankruptcy or by hypothecating a copyright.

Section 202.   Distinction Between Ownership of Copyright and Material Object

The principle restated in section 202 is a fundamental and important one: that copyright ownership and ownership of a material object in which the copyrighted work is embodied are entirely separate things. Thus, transfer of a material object does not of itself carry any rights under the copyright, and this includes transfer of the copy or phonorecord—the original manuscript, the photographic negative, the unique painting or statue, the master tape recording, etc.—in which the work was first fixed. Conversely, transfer of a copyright does not necessarily require the conveyance of any material object.

As a result of the interaction of this section and the provisions of section 204(a) and 301, the bill would change a common law doctrine exemplified by the decision in Pushman v. New York Graphic Society, Inc., 287 N.Y. 302, 39 N.E.2d 249 (1942). Under that doctrine, authors or artists are generally presumed to transfer common law literary property rights when they sell their manuscript or work of art, unless those rights are specifically reserved. This presumption would be reversed under the bill, since a specific written conveyance of rights would be required in order for a sale of any material object to carry with it a transfer of copyright.

Section 203.   Termination of Transfers and Licenses

The Problem in General

The provisions of section 203 are based on the premise that the reversionary provisions of the present section on copyright renewal (17 U.S.C.A. § 24) should be eliminated, and that the proposed law should substitute for them a provision safeguarding authors against unremunerative transfers. A provision of this sort is needed because of the unequal bargaining position of authors, resulting in part from the impossibility of determining a work's value until it has been exploited. Section 203 reflects a practical compromise that will further the objectives of the copyright law while recognizing the problems and legitimate needs of all interests involved.

Scope of the Provision

Instead of being automatic, as is theoretically the case under the present renewal provision, the termination of a transfer or license under section 203 would require the serving of an advance notice within specified time limits and under specified conditions. However, although affirmative action is needed to effect a termination, the right to take this action cannot be waived in advance or contracted away. Under section 203(a) the right of termination would apply only to transfers and licenses executed after the effective date of the new statute, and would have no retroactive effect.

The right of termination would be confined to inter vivos transfers or licenses executed by the author, and would not apply to transfers by the author's successors in interest or to the author's own bequests. The scope of the right would extend not only to any "transfer of copyright ownership," as defined in section 101, but also to nonexclusive licenses. The right of termination would not apply to "works made for hire," which is one of the principal reasons the definition of that term assumed importance in the development of the bill.

Who Can Terminate a Grant

Two issues emerged from the disputes over section 203 as to the persons empowered to terminate a grant: (1) the specific classes of beneficiaries in the case of joint works; and (2) whether anything less than unanimous consent of all those entitled to terminate should be required to make a termination effective. The bill to some extent reflects a compromise on these points, including a recognition of the dangers of one or more beneficiaries being induced to "hold out" and of unknown children or grandchildren being discovered later. The provision can be summarized as follows:

1. In the case of a work of joint authorship, where the grant was signed by two or more of the authors, majority action by those who signed the grant, or by their interests, would be required to terminate it.

2. There are three different situations in which the shares of joint authors, or of a dead author's widow or widower, children, and grandchildren, must be divided under the statute: (1) The right to effect a termination; (2) the ownership of the terminated rights; and (3) the right to make further grants of reverted rights. The respective shares of the authors, and of a dead author's widow or widower, children, and grandchildren, would be divided in exactly the same way in each of these situations. The terms "widow," "widower," and "children" are defined in section 101 in an effort to avoid problems and uncertainties that have arisen under the present renewal section.

3. The principle of per stirpes representation would also be applied in exactly the same way in all three situations. Take for example, a case where a dead author left a widow, two living children, and three grandchildren by a third child who is dead. The widow will own half of the reverted interests, the two children will each own 16⅔ percent, and the three grandchildren will each own a share of roughly 5½ percent. But who can exercise the right of termination? Obviously, since she owns 50 percent, the widow is an essential party, but suppose neither of the two surviving children is willing to join her in the termination; is it enough that she gets one of the children of the dead child to join, or can the dead child's interest be exercised only by the action of a majority of his children? Consistent with the per stirpes principle, the interest of a dead child can be exercised only as a unit by majority action of his surviving children. Thus, even though

the widow and one grandchild would own 55½ percent of the reverted copyright, they would have to be joined by another child
or grandchild in order to effect a termination or a further transfer of reverted rights. This principle also applies where, for example, two joint authors executed a grant and one of them is
dead; in order to effect a termination, the living author must be
joined by a per stirpes majority of the dead author's beneficiaries. The notice of termination may be signed by the specified owners of termination interests or by "their duly authorized
agents," which would include the legally appointed guardians or
committees of persons incompetent to sign because of age or
mental disability.

When a Grant Can Be Terminated

Section 203 draws a distinction between the date when a termination becomes effective and the earlier date when the advance notice
of termination is served. With respect to the ultimate effective date,
section 203(a)(3) provides, as a general rule, that a grant may be
terminated during the 5 years following the expiration of a period of
35 years from the execution of the grant. As an exception to this basic 35-year rule, the bill also provides that "if the grant covers the
right of publication of the work, the period begins at the end of 35
years from the date of publication of the work under the grant or at
the end of 40 years from the date of execution of the grant, whichever term ends earlier." This alternative method of computation is
intended to cover cases where years elapse between the signing of a
publication contract and the eventual publication of the work.

The effective date of termination, which must be stated in the
advance notice, is required to fall within the 5 years following the
end of the applicable 35- or 40-year period, but the advance notice itself must be served earlier. Under section 203(a)(4)(A), the notice
must be served "not less than two or more than ten years" before the
effective date stated in it.

As an example of how these time-limit requirements would operate in practice, we suggest two typical contract situations:

Case 1: Contract for theatrical production signed on September
2, 1987. Termination of grant can be made to take effect between
September 2, 2022 (35 years from execution) and September 1, 2027
(end of 5 year termination period). Assuming that the author decides to terminate on September 1, 2022 (the earliest possible date)
the advance notice must be filed between September 1, 2012 and September 1, 2020.

Case 2: Contract for book publication executed on April 10,
1980; book finally published on August 23, 1987. Since contract covers the right of publication, the 5-year termination period would begin on April 10, 2020 (40 years from execution) rather than April 10,
2015 (35 years from execution) or August 23, 2022 (35 years from
publication). Assuming that the author decides to make the termina-

tion effective on January 1, 2024, the advance notice would have to be served between January 1, 2014, and January 1, 2022.

Effect of Termination

Section 203(b) makes clear that, unless effectively terminated within the applicable 5-year period, all rights covered by an existing grant will continue unchanged, and that rights under other Federal, State, or foreign laws are unaffected. However, assuming that a copyright transfer or license is terminated under section 203, who are bound by the termination and how are they affected?

Under the bill, termination means that ownership of the rights covered by the terminated grant reverts to everyone who owns termination interests on the date the notice of termination was served, whether they joined in signing the notice or not. In other words, if a person could have signed the notice, that person is bound by the action of the majority who did; the termination of the grant will be effective as to that person, and a proportionate share of the reverted rights automatically vests in that person. Ownership is divided proportionately on the same per stirpes basis as that provided for the right to effect termination under section 203(a) and, since the reverted rights vest on the date notice is served, the heirs of a dead beneficiary would inherit his or her share.

Under clause (3) of subsection (b), majority action is required to make a further grant of reverted rights. A problem here, of course, is that years may have passed between the time the reverted rights vested and the time the new owners want to make a further transfer; people may have died and children may have been born in the interim. To deal with this problem, the bill looks back to the date of vesting; out of the group in whom rights vested on that date, it requires the further transfer or license to be signed by "the same number and proportion of the owners" (though not necessarily the same individuals) as were then required to terminate the grant under subsection (a). If some of those in whom the rights originally vested have died, their "legal representatives, legatees, or heirs at law" may represent them for this purpose and, as in the case of the termination itself, any one of the minority who does not join in the further grant is nevertheless bound by it.

An important limitation on the rights of a copyright owner under a terminated grant is specified in section 203(b)(1). This clause provides that, notwithstanding a termination, a derivative work prepared earlier may "continue to be utilized" under the conditions of the terminated grant; the clause adds, however, that this privilege is not broad enough to permit the preparation of other derivative works. In other words, a film made from a play could continue to be licensed for performance after the motion picture contract had been terminated but any remake rights covered by the contract would be cut off. For this purpose, a motion picture would be considered as a "derivative work" with respect to every "preexisting work" incorporated in it, whether the preexisting work was created independently or was prepared expressly for the motion picture.

Section 203 would not prevent the parties to a transfer or license from voluntarily agreeing at any time to terminate an existing grant and negotiating a new one, thereby causing another 35-year period to start running. However, the bill seeks to avoid the situation that has arisen under the present renewal provision, in which third parties have bought up contingent future interests as a form of speculation. Section 203(b)(4) would make a further grant of rights that revert under a terminated grant valid "only if it is made after the effective date of the termination." An exception, in the nature of a right of "first refusal," would permit the original grantee or a successor of such grantee to negotiate a new agreement with the persons effecting the termination at any time after the notice of termination has been served.

Nothing contained in this section or elsewhere in this legislation is intended to extend the duration of any license, transfer or assignment made for a period of less than thirty-five years. If, for example, an agreement provides an earlier termination date or lesser duration, or if it allows the author the right of cancelling or terminating the agreement under certain circumstances, the duration is governed by the agreement. Likewise, nothing in this section or legislation is intended to change the existing state of the law of contracts concerning the circumstances in which an author may cancel or terminate a license, transfer, or assignment.

Section 203(b)(6) provides that, unless and until termination is effected under this section, the grant, "if it does not provide otherwise," continues for the term of copyright. This section means that, if the agreement does not contain provisions specifying its term or duration, and the author has not terminated the agreement under this section, the agreement continues for the term of the copyright, subject to any right of termination under circumstances which may be specified therein. If, however, an agreement does contain provisions governing its duration—for example, a term of fifty years—and the author has not exercised his or her right of termination under the statute, the agreement will continue according to its terms—in this example, for only fifty years. The quoted language is not to be construed as requiring agreements to reserve the right of termination.

Sections 204, 205. Execution and Recordation of Transfers

Section 204 is a somewhat broadened and liberalized counterpart of sections 28 and 29 of the present statute. Under subsection (a), a transfer of copyright ownership (other than one brought about by operation of law) is valid only if there exists an instrument of conveyance, or alternatively a "note or memorandum of the transfer," which is in writing and signed by the copyright owner "or such owner's duly authorized agent." Subsection (b) makes clear that a notarial or consular acknowledgment is not essential to the validity of any transfer, whether executed in the United States or abroad. However, the subsection would liberalize the conditions under which certificates of acknowledgment of documents executed abroad are to be accorded prima facie weight, and would give the same weight to domestic acknowledgments under appropriate circumstances.

The recording and priority provisions of section 205 are intended to clear up a number of uncertainties arising from sections 30 and 31 of the present law and to make them more effective and practical in operation. Any "document pertaining to a copyright" may be recorded under subsection (a) if it "bears that actual signature of the person who executed it," or if it is appropriately certified as a true copy. However, subsection (c) makes clear that the recorded document will give constructive notice of its contents only if two conditions are met: (1) the document or attached material specifically identifies the work to which it pertains so that a reasonable search under the title or registration number would reveal it, and (2) registration has been made for the work. Moreover, even though the Register of Copyrights may be compelled to accept for recordation documents that on their face appear self-serving or colorable, the Register should take care that their nature is not concealed from the public in the Copyright Office's indexing and search reports.

The provisions of subsection (d), requiring recordation of transfers as a prerequisite to the institution of an infringement suit, represent a desirable change in the law. The one- and three-month grace periods provided in subsection (e) are a reasonable compromise between those who want a longer hiatus and those who argue that any grace period makes it impossible for a bona fide transferee to rely on the record at any particular time.

Under subsection (f) of section 205, a nonexclusive license in writing and signed, whether recorded or not, would be valid against a later transfer, and would also prevail as against a prior unrecorded transfer if taken in good faith and without notice. Objections were raised by motion picture producers, particularly to the provision allowing unrecorded nonexclusive licenses to prevail over subsequent transfers, on the ground that a nonexclusive license can have drastic effects on the value of a copyright. On the other hand, the impracticalities and burdens that would accompany any requirement of recordation of nonexclusive licenses outweigh the limited advantages of a statutory recordation system for them.

ROHAUER v. KILLIAM SHOWS, INC.

United States Court of Appeals, Second Circuit, 1977.
551 F.2d 484, 192 U.S.P.Q. 545, cert. denied, 431 U.S. 949,
97 S.Ct. 2666, 53 L.Ed.2d 266.

FRIENDLY, Circuit Judge.

This well briefed and argued appeal raises a question of copyright law of first impression. The question is of considerable importance despite the small amount of money here at stake. The issue is this: When the author of a copyrighted story has assigned the motion picture rights and consented to the assignee's securing a copyright on motion picture versions, with the terms of the assignment demonstrating an intention that the rights of the purchaser shall extend through a renewal of the copyright on the story, does a purchaser which has made a film and obtained a derivative copyright and renewal copyright thereon infringe the copyright on the story if it authorizes the performance of the copyrighted film after the author has died and the copyright on the story has been renewed by a statutory successor under 17 U.S.C.A. § 24, who has made a new assignment of motion picture and television rights? As has been so often true in cases arising under the Copyright Act of 1909, neither an affirmative nor a negative answer is completely satisfactory. A court must grope to ascertain what would have been the thought of the 1909 Congress on an issue about which it almost certainly never thought at all. In returning an affirmative answer to the question posed, Judge Bauman recognized that the negative would not be illogical, see 379 F.Supp. at 727. While we recognize that an affirmative answer likewise is by no means illogical, we believe a negative answer is more in keeping with the letter and purposes of the statute as best we can discern them.

There is no dispute about the facts. Sometime before May 15, 1925, Edith Maude Hull (Mrs. Hull), a British subject, wrote a novel entitled "The Sons of the Sheik." The novel was published in the United States about that time by Small, Maynard & Co., Inc., which obtained a United States copyright, assigned by it to Mrs. Hull in November 1925. By an instrument dated December 7, 1925, Mrs. Hull, as Seller, for a consideration of $21,000, granted, sold and assigned to Joseph H. Moskowitz, as Purchaser, all the motion picture rights to the story for the entire world, "together with the sole and exclusive right to make motion picture versions thereof," to secure copyright on the films, and to "vend, exhibit, exploit and otherwise dispose of the same." The Seller agreed "to renew or procure the renewal of the copyrights" in the story prior to their expiration and thereupon to assign to the Purchaser the motion picture rights for the renewal term.[2]

---

2. The appellants concede that because of Mrs. Hull's death before the accrual of the right to a renewal of the United States Copyright in the novel, they could not obtain specific enforcement of this agreement in respect of such copyright; they rely on the clause as demonstrating the in-

Pursuant to this agreement, a highly successful silent motion picture entitled "The Son of the Sheik," starring Rudolph Valentino, was produced and released for exhibition in the United States in 1926. On August 24, 1926, the picture was registered in the Copyright Office by and in the name of Feature Productions, Inc., an assignee of Moskowitz. This copyright was renewed on March 18, 1954, in the name of Artcinema Associates, Inc., the then proprietor of the copyright; the renewal copyright was sold in 1961 to Gregstan Enterprises, Inc., a corporation headed by Paul Killiam, and was assigned by Gregstan to the defendant Killiam Shows, Inc. (hereafter Killiam) in 1968.

Mrs. Hull died in 1943. On May 22, 1952, the United States copyright in the novel was renewed in the name of her daughter, Cecil Winstanley Hull (Miss Hull), a party plaintiff herein, the author's sole surviving child. On May 6, 1965, Miss Hull assigned to plaintiff Rohauer all of her "right, title and interest (if any) in and to the motion picture and television rights of every kind and character throughout the world and in all languages" to "Sons of the Sheik." Rohauer paid 446 pounds 10 shillings (then the equivalent of $1250) for this assignment.

On July 13, 1971, the motion picture was shown on television station WNET, owned by defendant Educational Broadcasting Corporation (hereafter Broadcasting) and operating on Channel 13 in the New York metropolitan area. The videotape required for this exhibition was made by Broadcasting from a print of the film made available to it by Killiam. No license had been obtained from plaintiffs Rohauer or Miss Hull, although Rohauer's attorney had informed an officer of Killiam in 1966 of his assignment from Miss Hull and had advised that any showing of the picture would constitute an infringement. Similar notice was given by Rohauer's counsel to Broadcasting the day before the first television showing. After this action was commenced the film was shown twice more on Channel 13.

The plaintiffs claimed and the District Court held, 379 F.Supp. 723 (S.D.N.Y.1974), that upon the expiration of the original term of the copyright in the novel and Miss Hull's succession to the renewal term, all rights of defendants and their predecessors to authorize the exhibition of the motion picture terminated. Defendants-appellants contend that while after the expiration of the original term of the copyright in the novel and the daughter's succession, no new motion picture versions could lawfully be made on the basis of the 1925 grant from Mrs. Hull, their predecessors and they were entitled to renew the copyright on a film already made and copyrighted and to authorize its exhibition.

tention of the parties, which appellees do not dispute, that the Purchaser should be entitled to the motion picture rights both for the original and for any renewal term.

I.

In endeavoring to answer the question here posed, we turn first to the words of the statute. Derivative copyright is provided for in 17 U.S.C.A. § 7, which states in pertinent part:

> Compilations or abridgments, adaptations, arrangements, dramatizations, translations, or other versions of works in the public domain or of copyrighted works when produced with the consent of the proprietor of the copyright in such works . . . shall be regarded as new works subject to copyright under the provisions of this title; but the publication of any such new works shall not affect the force or validity of any subsisting copyright upon the matter employed or any part thereof, or be construed to imply an exclusive right to such use of the original works, or to secure or extend copyright in such original works.

Section 24 of title 17 begins by stating that "[t]he copyright secured by this title shall endure for twenty-eight years from the date of first publication." An initial proviso states that in several cases there enumerated, including "any work copyrighted . . . by an employer for whom such work is made for hire," the proprietor of the copyright shall be entitled to renewal and extension for a further twenty-eight year term. The problem here arises from a second proviso, stating in pertinent part:

> That in the case of any other copyrighted work . . . the author of such work, if still living, or the widow, widower, or children of the author, if the author be not living, . . .
> shall be entitled to a renewal and extension of the copyright in such work for a further term of twenty-eight years when application for such renewal and extension shall have been made to the copyright office and duly registered therein within one year prior to the expiration of the original term of copyright . . .

The thrust of the portion of § 7 down to the semicolon—and it is a strong thrust—is rather clear. Doubtless aware, even in those simpler days, that new versions of copyrighted works might involve a degree of intellectual effort and expense quite as great as or considerably greater than the contribution of the author of the underlying work, Congress provided that derivative works "shall be regarded *as new works subject to copyright under the provisions of this title*" (emphasis supplied); plaintiffs-appellees do not dispute that the current proprietor of such a copyright, if the work was originally copyrighted as a work "made for hire", is entitled to effect a renewal of the derivative copyright under § 24.

When we look to the second half of the sentence, taking the subjects in reverse order, we find that defendants-appellants are not attempting "to secure or extend copyright" in Mrs. Hull's original work. Likewise they do not assert that Killiam's derivative copyright implies "an exclusive right to such use of the original works";

they concede that any such exclusive right would rest on the agreement of December 7, 1925 and at least implicitly that any such exclusivity, as distinguished from a right of continued use, terminated with the original term of the copyright on the novel. Likewise, they do not assert that the publication of the derivative work has any effect on the "validity" of any subsisting copyright. Plaintiffs say, however, that defendants' acts do affect the "force" of Miss Hull's renewal copyright on the novel, since the defendants are invading their exclusive right under § 1 of the Copyright Act to make copies of the work; to "make any other version thereof, if it be a literary work; to dramatize if it be a nondramatic work"; to make any "transcription or record" of the underlying work from which it might be exhibited or produced in whole or part; and to perform the work in public for profit. Each exhibition of the Valentino film presumably thus constitutes a "dramatization" of the underlying story exclusively reserved to plaintiffs, and an unauthorized "copying" of the underlying story. On a parity of reasoning, creation of any new prints of the film presumably amounts to manufacturing a new "transcription or record" of the underlying novel. In addition, the Authors League of America, Inc. argues in its amicus brief that the "force" of the renewal copyright on an underlying work includes the proprietor's right to "refrain from vending or licensing" and "simply . . . to exclude others from using his property," Fox Film Corp. v. Doyal, 286 U.S. 123, 127 (1932), including preventing any public exhibition for profit of the derivative work.

Defendants answer that sufficient "force" is given to the renewal copyright on the novel if it is held to prevent any new or "second generation" derivative works, without going to the extent of holding that the owner of the derivative copyright may not "print, reprint, publish, copy, and vend the copyrighted work" represented by the derivative copyright, along with others whom the new owner of the underlying copyright may license to make derivative works not infringing the "new matter" added by the owner of the derivative copyright.

A legislative history of the 1909 Copyright Act edited and compiled by E. Fulton Brylawski and Abe Goldman which became available only late in 1976,[4] after this appeal had been argued, indicates to us that the "force or validity" clause of § 7 has no bearing on the problem here at issue. . . .

II.

Turning to the precedents, we do not find that any of the Supreme Court decisions discussed at length in the briefs, has any real bearing on the issue here before us, either in holding or in opinion. All these cases were concerned with the relative rights of persons claiming full assignment or ownership of the renewal term of an underlying copyright. None involved the question here presented of ef-

---

4. Legislative History of the 1909 Copyright Act (E. Brylawski & A. Goldman, eds.) (Fred B. Rothman & Co. 1976).

fecting a proper reconciliation between the grant of derivative copyright in § 7 and the final proviso of § 24 with respect to renewals of underlying copyrights.

Appellees contend that even if this be so, the question here at issue has been settled in their favor by lower court decisions, notably Fitch v. Shubert, 20 F.Supp. 314 (S.D.N.Y.1937); G. Ricordi & Co. v. Paramount Pictures, Inc., 189 F.2d 469 (2 Cir.), cert. denied, 342 U. S. 849, 72 S.Ct. 77, 96 L.Ed. 641 (1951); and Sunset Securities Company v. Coward McCann, Inc., 297 P.2d 137 (Dist.Ct. of Appeal 2d Dist. 1956), vacated, 47 Cal.2d 907, 306 P.2d 777 (1957). Apart from the fact that none of these cases except Ricordi would bind us as a precedent, we do not find that any of them decided the question here at issue.

The Fitch case involved a dispute between the plaintiff Richard W. Fitch who, as next of kin of the author Clyde Fitch, had obtained a renewal copyright after Clyde Fitch's death on a play called "Barbara Frietchie, The Frederick Girl," and the defendants who had produced a musical version of the play, known as "My Maryland." Clyde Fitch had died intestate without widow or child in 1909, years before the expiration in 1928 of the original term of the copyright in the play. His interest in the initial term passed first to his mother and, after her death, by her bequest to the Actors' Fund of America. In 1925, contemplating the production of an operetta based on "Barbara Frietchie" the Shuberts negotiated a license agreement with the Actors' Fund; the operetta was first produced in 1927, and was leased by the Shuberts for amateur performances over many years thereafter. In 1927 Richard Fitch renewed the copyright on the play and, after the Shuberts had mounted another production, sued them in 1937 for infringement. Although the ultimate holding was that the defendants had acquired a license from the plaintiff by direct dealings with him in the renewal term, Judge Patterson did say, 20 F.Supp. at 315,

> [I]t is clear that the plaintiff acquired a new and independent right in the copyright, free and clear of any rights, interests, or licenses attached to the copyright for the initial term . . . .
> It is evident therefore that all rights which the defendants acquired in 1925 to use the Fitch play as the basis of a musical operetta expired when the copyright for the original term expired in 1928 and when a new grantee appeared as owner of the Fitch play for the renewal term.

However, this was said in a case where without dispute the original license agreement was limited to the first term; not only did the license agreement make no reference to renewal rights, but no one could have meant it to do so. The Shuberts had not obtained the license agreement from an author who could contemplate renewal, but from a charitable grantee after the author's death, when the renewal rights had passed by statute to the next of kin surviving at the end of the original term.

Ricordi was a suit by G. Ricordi & Co. for a declaratory judgment against Paramount Pictures, Inc. The case involved the story, play and opera entitled "Madame Butterfly." The novel was written in 1897 by John Luther Long, published that year in Century Magazine and copyrighted by the Century Company. In 1900 David Belasco wrote a play with the consent of the copyright owner which, however, was not copyrighted until 1917. In 1901 Long and Belasco entered into a contract with Ricordi giving it the exclusive right to make a libretto for an opera of Belasco's dramatic version of Madame Butterfly. In 1904 Ricordi copyrighted the famous opera composed by Puccini and subsequently secured an assignment from Puccini's son of the renewal copyright therein. In 1925 Long obtained a renewal of the copyright on his novel and in 1932, subsequent to Long's death, his administrator granted the motion picture rights therein to Paramount. In the same year, with the Belasco play still in its first copyright term, Paramount obtained from the trustee of Belasco's will an assignment of the motion picture rights to the play; no renewal of the copyright in the play was ever effected. Ricordi sought a declaration that it was entitled to make a motion picture of the opera free from any interference by Paramount. This court, speaking through Judge Swan for a particularly distinguished bench including Judge Learned Hand and Judge Frank, held that Ricordi was not entitled to so broad a declaration. Ricordi's renewal copyright in the opera extended only to so much of the opera as was "a new work." Hence it was not entitled to make general use of the novel for a motion picture version of its opera but was restricted for that purpose to what was copyrightable as new matter in its operatic version.

Ricordi is not determinative here, however, for a fundamental reason: the original 1901 agreement between Long, Belasco, and Ricordi did not purport to run beyond the original term of Long's copyright on the novel. Ricordi neither sought nor obtained operatic rights in the renewal term of the novel in the 1901 agreement, or in any other negotiation. To conclude that the renewal term of a copyright is a new estate free from previous licenses is one thing when, as in Ricordi, the parties have never bargained for renewal rights, and another when, as in the case of Mrs. Hull and Joseph Moskowitz, the assignment agreement explicitly included rights to the derivative work during the renewal term.

We find even less helpful to the plaintiffs the decisions previously cited in the California case of Sunset Securities Company v. Coward McCann, Inc. For whatever it may be worth, the opinion of the District Court of Appeal is favorable to the defendants and the reversal by the California Supreme Court was on the grounds of contract rather than of copyright law.

The short of the matter is that we have been cited to no case holding that the inability of an author to carry out his promise to effect a renewal of a copyright because of his death prior to the date for obtaining renewal terminates *as a matter of copyright law* the right of a holder of a derivative copyright to continue to publish a derivative work copyrighted before the author's death on which the copyright was thereafter renewed. It is equally true that we have been cited no case upholding such a right.

With arguments based on the "force or validity" clause of § 7 eliminated by the legislative history, we do not believe, despite language in the cases to the effect that the proprietor of a derivative copyright is "protected" only as to the "new matter" conceived by him and that a statutory successor obtains a "new estate" in the underlying copyright, that the vesting of renewed copyright in the underlying work in a statutory successor deprives the proprietor of the derivative copyright of a right, stemming from the § 7 "consent" of the original proprietor of the underlying work, to use so much of the underlying copyrighted work as already has been embodied in the copyrighted derivative work, as a matter of copyright law. That view is only a slight extension of this court's decision in Edmonds v. Stern, 248 F. 897 (2 Cir. 1918). There the purchaser of a song, having copyrighted it with the consent of the composer, prepared an operetta and copyrighted an orchestral medley based on the operetta which utilized, among other things, the notes of the song. Later the purchaser assigned the copyright in the song back to the composer. The court held, as an alternate ground of decision, that the reassignment would not deprive the proprietor of the copyright of the score of the right to sell copies of the medley since, as Judge Hough said, 248 F. at 898,

> The two things [the song and the orchestral score] were legally separate, and independent of each other; it makes no difference that such separate and independent existence might to a certain extent have grown out of plaintiff's consent to the incorporation of his melody in the orchestration. When that consent was given, a right of property sprang into existence, not at all affected by the conveyance of any other right.

So here when the purchaser from Mrs. Hull embodied her story in a motion picture which was copyrighted under § 7, the vesting of the renewal right of the story in her daughter did not affect the property right in the copyrighted derivative work. . . .

To such extent as it may be permissible to consider policy considerations, the equities lie preponderantly in favor of the proprietor of the derivative copyright. In contrast to the situation where an assignee or licensee has done nothing more than print, publicize and distribute a copyrighted story or novel, a person who with the consent of the author has created an opera or a motion picture film will often have made contributions both literary, musical and economic as great as or greater than the original author. As pointed out in the Bricker article, ["Renewal and Extension of Copyright"], 29 S.Cal. L.Rev. at 33, the purchaser of derivative rights has no truly effective way to protect himself against the eventuality of the author's death before the renewal period since there is no way of telling who will be the surviving widow, children or next of kin or the executor until that date arrives. To be sure, this problem exists in equal degree with respect to assignments or licenses of underlying copyright, but in such cases there is not the countervailing consideration that large and independently copyrightable contributions will have been made by the transferee. As against this, the author can always protect his heirs by imposing a contractual limit upon the assignment. It is true that this might not be practicable from a business standpoint in cases where the assignment was made shortly before the expiration of the initial term, but those are the very cases where the inequity of terminating the transferee's rights with respect to so much of the underlying work as is embodied in the derivative work is the greatest.

We find recognition of these policy considerations in §§ 203(b)(1) and 304(c)(6)(A) of the recently enacted copyright revision bill, 90 Stat. 2541 (1976). In connection with a new plan whereby copyright in any work created on or after January 1, 1978 or created before that date but not then yet published or copyrighted shall, with certain exceptions, run for the life of the author plus 50 years, with any grant of a transfer or license subject to a right of termination between the 35th and 40th year of the grant; and the renewal term of any existing copyright is extended for another 19 years subject to a right of termination of any transfer or license at the end of the 28th year of the renewal term over a like period of five years, Congress expressly provided:

> A derivative work prepared under authority of the grant before its termination may continue to be utilized under the terms of the grant after its termination, but this privilege does not extend to the preparation after the termination of other derivative works based upon the copyrighted work covered by the terminated grant.

§§ 203(b)(1), 304(c)(6)(A). While it is true that this proviso was part of a package which extended the temporal rights of authors (but also of their assignees) and that the proviso thus does not deal with the precise situation here presented, we nevertheless regard it as evidence of a belief on the part of Congress of the need for special protection for derivative works. We agree, of course, that provisions of the new Act cannot be read as varying clear provisions of the 1909 Act in cases to which the new Act does not apply. However, the present situation fits rather well under Judge Lumbard's language in Goodis v. United Artists Television, Inc., 425 F.2d 397, 403, 165 U.S. P.Q. 3, 7 (2 Cir. 1970):

> Our decision today is that the result which the proposed legislation would compel is not precluded in any way by the decisions rendered under the present Copyright Act. As discussed earlier, the "problem" with which the proposed legislation deals is one which exists because of judicial dicta rendered in cases not apposite to the factual situation before us in this case.

For these reasons we hold that the licensing by Killiam of exhibition of the film already copyrighted and its exhibition by Broadcasting did not violate the renewal copyright.   - •

In view of this holding we have no occasion to pass on the various affirmative defenses raised by appellants and rejected by the District Court. There are two principal ones. Plaintiff Rohauer is alleged to come into court with unclean hands since he frequently exhibited the movie prior to 1965 without obtaining a license either from Miss Hull or from the proprietors of the motion picture copyright. The other is a defense of res judicata based upon a judgment of the District Court for the Southern District of Iowa in an action by Rohauer against another licensee of Killiam which the latter defended, where the court dismissed the complaint because of Rohauer's refusal to submit to discovery, Rohauer v. Eastin-Phelan Corporation, Civ. 72–25–D (S.D.Iowa, Feb. 7, 1974), aff'd, 499 F.2d 120 (8 Cir. 1974). If we were obliged to rule on these defenses, we would regard them as warranting somewhat more consideration than did the district judge. The judgment is reversed with instructions to dismiss the complaint.

NOTES

1.   On sections 203 and 304(c), the present Act's termination provisions, see Curtis, Caveat Emptor in Copyright: A Practical Guide to the Termination-of-Transfers Provisions of the New Copyright Code, 25 Bull. Copyright Soc'y 19 (1977); Stein, Termination of Transfers and Licenses Under the New Copyright Act: Thorny Problems for the Copyright Bar, 24 U.C.L.A.L.Rev. 1141 (1977). For more general background, see Curtis, Protecting Authors in Copyright Transfers: Revision Bill § 203 and the Alternatives, 72 Colum.L.Rev. 799 (1972).

For extensive analysis of the questions raised by Rohauer v. Killiam Shows, see Mimms, Reversion and Derivative Works Unde the Copyright Acts of 1909 and 1976, 25 N.Y.L.School L.Rev. 595 (1980); Note, Rohauer v. Killiam Shows, Inc. and the Derivative Work Exception to the Termination Right: Inequitable Anomalies Under Copyright Law, 52 So.Calif.L.Rev. 635 (1979).

2.   One of the present Act's main innovations is to alter the duration of copyright from a term measured by 28 years from the date of publication, with a renewal period of 28 years, to a term measured by the life of the author plus 50 years. The change brings United States law into line with the copyright terms of most other nations. The most vexing question raised by the new term stems from the fact that it attaches federal copyright from the moment of a work's creation rather than its publication. What has become of state common law copyright which traditionally protected works from creation to publication? Some answers to the question are considered at pages 213 to 232 above. The new copyright term also raises some less thorny questions.

(a) *If the copyright term is measured by the "life of the author," how is the term measured when a work has more than one author?* Section 302(b) provides that where two or more authors prepare a joint work, the copyright will last for a term measured by the life of the last surviving author plus 50 years. The rule obviously requires careful attention to the Act's definition of "joint work."

(b) *How is the term measured for anonymous or pseudonymous works, or works made for hire, whose author is not known or, as a corporation, enjoys an indeterminate life?* Section 302(c)'s response to these situations is to approximate an author's life plus 50 years with a term of 75 years from the year of a work's first publication or 100 years from the year of its creation, whichever expires first. If, before the end of this term, the identity of the anonymous or pseudonymous author is revealed in Copyright Office records, the copyright will last for the standard life plus 50 term.

(c) *How, as a practical matter, will prospective users be able to determine the life and death facts that will tell them whether a work is in or out of copyright?* Section 302(d) gives the copyright owner, or anyone having an interest in the copyright, the opportunity to record in the Copyright Office a statement of the date of the author's death, or a statement that the author is still living. Why should the owner record? Section 302(e) provides that if, after 75 years from first publication or 100 years from a work's creation, whichever expires first, a prospective user obtains a certified report from the Copyright Office that its records disclose nothing to indicate that the author of the work is living or died less than 50 years before, the prospective user becomes entitled to the benefit of a presumption that the author has been dead for at least 50 years. Good faith reliance on the report constitutes a complete defense to any action for infringement.

(d) *What of works created and copyrighted before the Act's effective date, January 1, 1978?* Section 304 divides its treatment of these works between those that are in their first copyright term on January 1, 1978 and those that are in their renewal term, or registered for renewal, before January 1, 1978. For copyrights in their first term on January 1, 1978, section 304(a) retains the previous 28-year copyright term, allows renewal, but changes the renewal term from the previous 28-year term to 47 years. Effectively, this creates a total term of 75 years from publication, establishing parity between works protected under the old Act and works created after January 1, 1978 and protected under the new Act. Section 304(b) establishes parity for works already in their renewal term on January 1, 1978 by automatically extending the renewal term to 75 years from the date copyright was originally secured.

(e) *What of works created, but not under statutory copyright, before January 1, 1978?* The revisors recognized that there may be many unpublished works that have been in existence for a long time —centuries even—and whose authors are long since dead. Thus, they provided in section 303 that these works are to enjoy the same term as works created after January 1, 1978, but added that copyright in this class of works will in any event not expire before December 31, 2002, thus assuring at least 25 years of protection. As an inducement to publication, section 303 also provides that if the work is published on or before December 31, 2002, the term will be extended through December 31, 2027.

See generally, Cohen, Duration, 24 U.C.L.A.L.Rev. 1180 (1977).

3. Section 24's renewal scheme was among the more problematic parts of the old Act. These provisions promise to create problems for many years to come, for section 304(a) perpetuates the renewal scheme for works in their first copyright term before January 1, 1978. The House Report explains: "A great many of the present expectancies in these cases are the subject of existing contracts, and it would be unfair and immensely confusing to cut off or alter these interests." H.R.Rep.No.94–1476, 94th Cong. 2d Sess. 139 (1976).

The opacity of the renewal provisions no doubt explains the attention that the Supreme Court lavished on them in a trio of decisions, Fred Fisher Music Co., Inc. v. M. Witmark & Sons, 318 U.S. 643, 63 S.Ct. 773, 87 L.Ed. 1055, 57 U.S.P.Q. 50 (1943); De Sylva v. Ballentine, 351 U.S. 570, 76 S.Ct. 974, 100 L.Ed. 1415, 109 U.S.P.Q. 431 (1956); and Miller Music Corp. v. Charles N. Daniels, Inc., 362 U.S. 373, 80 S.Ct. 792, 4 L.Ed.2d 804, 125 U.S.P.Q. 147 (1960).

The question for decision in Fisher v. Witmark was, "Does the Copyright Act nullify an agreement by an author, made during the original copyright term, to assign his renewal?" 318 U.S. 643, 647, 63 S.Ct. 773, 774, 775. Justice Frankfurter rested his negative answer upon an extensive review of the pre-1909 legislation, which did not restrict assignability, and of the legislative history of the 1909 Act, which indicated an intent to continue the earlier position. "Neither the language nor the history of the Copyright Act of 1909 lend support to the conclusion that the 'existing law' prior to 1909, under which authors were free to assign their renewal interests if they were so disposed, was intended to be altered." 318 U.S. 643, 656, 63 S.Ct. 773, 778, 779.

Another tenet of existing law incorporated in the 1909 Act was that, before expiration of the initial 28-year term, the author's interest in the renewal term is contingent and will vest in him or his assignee only if the author is alive when the initial term expires. If the author is not alive, rights to the renewal term vest in the "widow, widower, or children of the author" or, if they are not alive, in the other individuals designated by section 24. De Sylva v. Ballentine considered whether for these purposes, "the widow and children take as a class, or in order of enumeration." 351 U.S. 570, 572, 76 S.Ct. 974, 975, 976. Acknowledging that "the matter is far from clear," it held for the first proposition. The Court left open, however, "the question of what are the respective rights of the widow and child in the copyright renewals, once it is accepted that they both succeed to the renewals as members of the same class." 351 U.S. 570, 582, 76 S.Ct. 974, 980, 981. For the assumption that the widow and children are to share equally, see Bartok v. Boosey & Hawkes, Inc., 523 F.2d 941, 942 n. 2, 187 U.S.P.Q. 529, 530 n. 2 (2d Cir. 1975).

Miller v. Daniels involved a mix of the issues raised in *Witmark* and *De Sylva* and found Justice Frankfurter, who wrote the *Witmark* opinion, and Justice Harlan, who wrote the *De Sylva* opinion, in dissent, and Justice Douglas, who dissented in *Witmark* and concurred in *De Sylva*, delivering the majority opinion. The question in *Miller* differed from the question in *Witmark* in one detail: "The question for decision is whether by statute the renewal rights accrue to the executor in spite of a prior assignment by his testator." 362 U.S. 373, 374, 80 S.Ct. 792, 794. Taking the *Witmark* assumption— that if the author expires before the initial term, the widow or widower and children take regardless of the *inter vivos* transfer—together with petitioner's concession—"that where the author dies intestate prior to the renewal period leaving no widow, widower, or children, the next of kin obtain the renewal copyright free of any claim founded upon an assignment made by the author in his lifetime"—the Court concluded: "We fail to see the difference in this statutory scheme between widows, widowers, children, or next of kin on the one hand and executors on the other. . . . Section 24 reflects, it seems to us, a consistent policy to treat renewal rights as expectancies until the renewal period arrives. When that time arrives, the renewal rights pass to one of the four classes listed in § 24 according to the then-existing circumstances." 362 U.S. 373, 375–378, 80 S.Ct. 792, 794–796.

4. The origins of section 201(e), voiding involuntary governmental transfers of copyright, can be traced to the Soviet Union's announced adherence to the Universal Copyright Convention in February, 1973. The Soviet move, initially hailed as a long overdue acceptance of "responsibility toward the authors and other creators of works distributed and performed in the Soviet Union," was soon perceived as a possible device for tightening control over the circulation abroad "of literature which does not meet with Communist approval." 119 Cong.Rec. 9387 (Mar. 26, 1973). In March 1973, prodded by the Author's League of America, Senator McClellan introduced S. 1359, the predecessor to section 201(e). S. 1359 provided that any copyright would "remain the property of the author . . . regardless of any law, decree or other act of a foreign state or nation which purports to divest the author or said other persons of the United States copyright in his work." S. 1359, 93rd Cong., 1st Sess. (1973).

Section 201(e), by invalidating domestic as well as foreign involuntary transfers, offers a symmetry that is missing from S. 1359. Does section 201(e) threaten to interfere with accustomed practices in domestic copyright industries? An involuntary transfer occurs any time a mortgage on a copyright interest is foreclosed. Involuntary transfers are also implicit in the power of federal and state governments to take individual copyrights under eminent domain. Section 201(e) may also unintentionally disrupt techniques employed by other nations to mediate between the interests of citizen and state. For example, in the interest of broad public access to copyrighted works, Brazil's Civil Code art. 660 (1968), provides that "if the owner of a published work refuses to authorize new editions thereof, the Union and any of its States may, after indemnification, expropriate the work for reasons of public utility." Would expropriation on the ground that the author has suppressed publication constitute a voluntary or an involuntary transfer? To call it a voluntary transfer would offend the clear language of section 201(e). To call it an involuntary transfer would reinforce suppression, something that section 201(e) intended to eliminate.

Was section 201(e) really needed to combat repressive practices? How effective is copyright as a tool for suppressing political views? Can copyright be enlisted to enjoin news reports and commentary describing a work's dissident themes? What of the idea-expression distinction? The fair use defense? See generally, Goldstein, Preempted State Doctrines, Involuntary Transfers and Compulsory Licenses: Testing the Limits of Copyright, 24 U.C.L.A.L.Rev. 1107, 1123–1127 (1977).

5. New technologies offer copyright owners an unprecedented opportunity for the wide and rapid dissemination of their works. These technologies also create the problem of policing widely dispersed uses. One answer to the challenge has been to finesse it, as Congress did in section 111 providing for compulsory licensing of cable transmissions. Another, more flexible response is the copyright clearinghouse, organized to administer market transactions quickly and at low cost. The Copyright Clearance Center, which clears photocopying fees between publishers and users, is one example of the clearinghouse technique. See page 784, above.

The history of the American Society of Composers, Authors and Publishers (ASCAP) indicates some of the structural benefits and costs of the clearinghouse technique. ASCAP was formed in 1914 when, with the decline of sheet music sales and the rise of radio and other vehicles for public performance, popular composers foresaw the need to organize for the exploitation and enforcement of their performance rights. ASCAP was organized as a nonprofit association of composers, authors and publishers that would pool the non-dramatic ("small") performance rights to its members' musical compositions for licensing to users engaged in nondramatic public performances for profit. The Society's repertory would be licensed on a bulk basis and the royalties collected would be apportioned among members according to a schedule that accounted for both the general character and standing of the works and the average number of times the works of each member were performed. By 1980 ASCAP's pool consisted of the small performance rights to approximately 3,000,000 compositions and the Society had a membership of approximately 6,000 music publishing companies and 16,000 composers. Although radio and television networks and stations are the Society's major licensees, restaurants, dance halls, hotels and wired music facilities like Muzak also take licenses.

ASCAP's success invited both competition and antitrust regulation. Competition came from Broadcast Music, Inc. (BMI), formed by broadcasters in 1939 for the purpose of contracting with writers and publishers to clear performance fees through blanket licensing on their behalf. BMI has proved to be a strong rival. As of 1980, BMI was affiliated with or represented 10,000 publishers and 20,000 authors and composers, and had a repertory of about 1,000,000 compositions. Together with ASCAP, it controls the small performance rights to virtually all domestic copyrighted musical compositions.

ASCAP's antitrust exposure was in significant part resolved by a consent decree entered in March, 1941, terminating Justice Department charges filed earlier that year. The 1941 decree was amended in 1950 and 1960 to relax the Society's membership requirements, adjust voting rights and distribute revenues on a more objective basis, to broaden the licensing choices available to licensees and to impose compulsory licensing and judicial determination of reasonable royalties in the event that an applicant and ASCAP are unable to agree. Members were also given the unrestricted right to license their own works to users unwilling to take the blanket license. BMI, too, is governed by an antitrust consent decree.

Blanket licensing is crucial to the success of performing rights clearinghouses. But, taken literally, blanket licensing involves price-fixing. The point was not lost on the Columbia Broadcasting System, a major licensee of ASCAP and BMI. In 1969 C.B.S. filed suit against both organizations, charging them with Sherman Act violations—among them, that the blanket license was an illegal price-fixing device. The District Court dismissed the complaint on the ground that C.B.S. could have obtained licenses from individual members and that there was no coercion to take the blanket license. Columbia Broadcasting System, Inc. v. American Soc'y of Composers, Authors & Publishers, 400 F.Supp. 737, 187 U.S.P.Q. 431 (S.D.N.Y. 1975). The Second Circuit Court of Appeals reversed, ruling that the blanket licenses constituted price-fixing, illegal per se under the Sherman Act. 562 F.2d 130, 195 U.S.P.Q. 209 (1977). The Supreme Court reversed, holding that the rule of reason rather than the per se rule applied, and remanded to the Court of Appeals to determine whether blanket licensing violated the rule of reason. Broadcast Music, Inc. v. Columbia Broadcasting System, Inc., 441 U.S. 1, 99 S.Ct. 1551, 60 L.Ed.2d 1, 201 U.S.P.Q. 497 (1979). On remand, the Court of Appeals held that, under the rule of reason test, blanket licensing did not violate the Sherman Act. Columbia Broadcasting System, Inc. v. American Soc'y of Composers, Authors and Publishers, 620 F. 2d 930, 205 U.S.P.Q. 880 (1980).

On the C.B.S. antitrust litigation, see Cirace, CBS v. ASCAP: An Economic Analysis of a Political Problem, 47 Fordham L.Rev. 277

(1978); Hartnick, From Black to White—A Comment on Broadcast Music, Inc.—American Society of Composers, Authors and Publishers v. Columbia Broadcasting System, Inc., 27 Bull. Copyright Soc'y 1 (1979); Note, CBS v. ASCAP: Performing Rights Societies and the Per Se Rule, 87 Yale L.J. 783 (1978); Note, The Middleman as Price Fixer: Columbia Broadcasting System, Inc. v. American Society of Composers, Authors & Publishers, 91 Harv.L.Rev. 488 (1977).

The antitrust background generally is considered in Timberg, The Antitrust Aspects of Merchandising Modern Music: The ASCAP Consent Judgment of 1950, 19 L. & Contemp.Prob. 294 (1954); Garner, United States v. ASCAP: The Licensing Provisions of the Amended Final Judgment of 1950, 23 Bull. Copyright Soc'y 119 (1975). The ASCAP consent decrees appear at C.C.H. 1940–43 Trade Cases ¶ 56,104 (1941); 1950–51 Trade Cases ¶ 62,595 (1950); 1960 Trade Cases ¶ 69,612. The BMI consent decrees appear at C.C. H. 1940–43 Trade Cases ¶ 56,096 (1941); C.C.H. 1966 Trade Cases ¶ 71,941.

On the distinction between "small" and "grand" performing rights, see Perrone, Small and Grand Performing Rights? (Who Cared Before "Jesus Christ Superstar"), 20 Bull. Copyright Soc'y 19 (1972).

And, for general background on A.S.C.A.P., B.M.I. and a third licensing organization, S.E.S.A.C., see Finkelstein, Public Performance Rights in Music and Performance Right Societies, 7 Copyright Problems Analyzed 69 (1951); Goldstein, Copyright and the First Amendment, 70 Colum.L.Rev. 983, 1050–1055 (1970); Finkelstein, The Composer and the Public Interest—Regulation of Performing Right Societies, 19 L. & Contemp.Prob. 275 (1954).

2.   REMEDIES

See Statute Supplement 17 U.S.C.A. §§ 412, 502–510.

COPYRIGHT LAW REVISION, H.R.REP. NO. 94–1476

94th Cong., 2d Sess. 160–164 (1976).

Section 502.   Injunctions

Section 502(a) reasserts the discretionary power of courts to grant injunctions and restraining orders, whether "preliminary," "temporary," "interlocutory," "permanent," or "final," to prevent or stop infringements of copyright. This power is made subject to the provisions of section 1498 of title 28, dealing with infringement actions against the United States. The latter reference in section 502(a) makes it clear that the bill would not permit the granting of an injunction against an infringement for which the Federal Government is liable under section 1498.

Under subsection (b), which is the counterpart of provisions in sections 112 and 113 of the present statute, a copyright owner who has obtained an injunction in one State will be able to enforce it against a defendant located anywhere else in the United States.

Section 503.   Impounding and Disposition of Infringing Articles

The two subsections of section 503 deal respectively with the courts' power to impound allegedly infringing articles during the time an action is pending, and to order the destruction or other disposition of articles found to be infringing. In both cases the articles affected include "all copies or phonorecords" which are claimed or found "to have been made or used in violation of the copyright owner's exclusive rights," and also "all plates, molds, matrices, masters, tapes, film negatives, or other articles by means of which such copies of phonorecords may be reproduced." The alternative phrase "made or used" in both subsections enables a court to deal as it sees fit with articles which, though reproduced and acquired lawfully, have been used for infringing purposes such as rentals, performances, and displays.

Articles may be impounded under subsection (a) "at any time while an action under this title is pending," thus permitting seizures of articles alleged to be infringing as soon as suit has been filed and without waiting for an injunction. The same subsection empowers the court to order impounding "on such terms as it may deem reasonable." The present Supreme Court rules with respect to seizure and impounding were issued even though there is no specific provision authorizing them in the copyright statute, and there appears no need for including a special provision on the point in the bill.

Under section 101(d) of the present statute, articles found to be infringing may be ordered to be delivered up for destruction. Section 503(b) of the bill would make this provision more flexible by giving the court discretion to order "destruction or other reasonable disposition" of the articles found to be infringing. Thus, as part of its final judgment or decree, the court could order the infringing articles sold, delivered to the plaintiff, or disposed of in some other way that would avoid needless waste and best serve the ends of justice.

Section 504.   Damages and Profits

In General

A cornerstone of the remedies sections and of the bill as a whole is section 504, the provision dealing with recovery of actual damages, profits, and statutory damages. The two basic aims of this section are reciprocal and correlative: (1) to give the courts specific unambiguous directions concerning monetary awards, thus avoiding the confusion and uncertainty that have marked the present law on the subject, and, at the same time, (2) to provide the courts with reasonable latitude to adjust recovery to the circumstances of the case, thus avoiding some of the artificial or overly technical awards resulting from the language of the existing statute.

Subsection (a) lays the groundwork for the more detailed provisions of the section by establishing the liability of a copyright infringer for either "the copyright owner's actual damages and any additional profits of the infringer," or statutory damages. Recovery of actual damages and profits under section 504(b) or of statutory damages under section 504(c) is alternative and for the copyright owner to elect; as under the present law, the plaintiff in an infringement suit is not obliged to submit proof of damages and profits and may choose to rely on the provision for minimum statutory damages. However, there is nothing in section 504 to prevent a court from taking account of evidence concerning actual damages and profits in making an award of statutory damages within the range set out in subsection (c).

Actual Damages and Profits

In allowing the plaintiff to recover "the actual damages suffered by him or her as a result of the infringement," plus any of the infringer's profits "that are attributable to the infringement and are not taken into account in computing the actual damages," section 504(b) recognizes the different purposes served by awards of damages and profits. Damages are awarded to compensate the copyright owner for losses from the infringement, and profits are awarded to prevent the infringer from unfairly benefiting from a wrongful act. Where the defendant's profits are nothing more than a measure of the damages suffered by the copyright owner, it would be inappropriate to award damages and profits cumulatively, since in effect they amount to the same thing. However, in cases where the copyright owner has suffered damages not reflected in the infringer's profits, or where there have been profits attributable to the copyrighted work but not used as a measure of damages, subsection (b) authorizes the award of both.

The language of the subsection makes clear that only those profits "attributable to the infringement" are recoverable; where some of the defendant's profits result from the infringement and other profits are caused by different factors, it will be necessary for the court to make an apportionment. However, the burden of proof is on the defendant in these cases; in establishing profits the plaintiff need prove only "the infringer's gross revenue," and the defendant must prove not only "his or her deductible expenses" but also "the element of profit attributable to factors other than the copyrighted work."

Statutory Damages

Subsection (c) of section 504 makes clear that the plaintiff's election to recover statutory damages may take place at any time during the trial before the court has rendered its final judgment. The remainder of clause (1) of the subsection represents a statement of the general rates applicable to awards of statutory damages. Its principal provisions may be summarized as follows:

1. As a general rule, where the plaintiff elects to recover statutory damages, the court is obliged to award between $250 and $10,000. It can exercise discretion in awarding an amount

within that range but, unless one of the exceptions provided by clause (2) is applicable, it cannot make an award of less than $250 or of more than $10,000 if the copyright owner has chosen recovery under section 504(c).

2. Although, as explained below, an award of minimum statutory damages may be multiplied if separate works and separately liable infringers are involved in the suit, a single award in the $250 to $10,000 range is to be made "for all infringements involved in the action." A single infringer of a single work is liable for a single amount between $250 and $10,000, no matter how many acts of infringement are involved in the action and regardless of whether the acts were separate, isolated, or occurred in a related series.

3. Where the suit involves infringement of more than one separate and independent work, minimum statutory damages for each work must be awarded. For example, if one defendant has infringed three copyrighted works, the copyright owner is entitled to statutory damages of at least $750 and may be awarded up to $30,000. Subsection (c)(1) makes clear, however, that, although they are regarded as independent works for other purposes, "all the parts of a compilation or derivative work constitute one work" for this purpose. Moreover, although the minimum and maximum amounts are to be multiplied where multiple "works" are involved in the suit, the same is not true with respect to multiple copyrights, multiple owners, multiple exclusive rights, or multiple registrations. This point is especially important since, under a scheme of divisible copyright, it is possible to have the rights of a number of owners of separate "copyrights" in a single "work" infringed by one act of a defendant.

4. Where the infringements of one work were committed by a single infringer acting individually, a single award of statutory damages would be made. Similarly, where the work was infringed by two or more joint tort feasors, the bill would make them jointly and severally liable for an amount in the $250 to $10,000 range. However, where separate infringements for which two or more defendants are not jointly liable are joined in the same action, separate awards of statutory damages would be approp iate.

Clause (2) of section 504(c) provides for exceptional cases in which the maximum award of statutory damages could be raised from $10,000 to $50,000, and in which the minimum recovery could be reduced from $250 to $100. The basic principle underlying this provision is that the courts should be given discretion to increase statutory damages in cases of willful infringement and to lower the minimum where the infringer is innocent. The language of the clause makes clear that in these situations the burden of proving willfulness rests on the copyright owner and that of proving innocence rests on the infringer, and that the court must make a finding of either willfulness or innocence in order to award the exceptional amounts.

The "innocent infringer" provision of section 504(c)(2) has been the subject of extensive discussion. The exception, which would allow reduction of minimum statutory damages to $100 where the infringer "was not aware and had no reason to believe that his or her acts constituted an infringement of copyright," is sufficient to protect against unwarranted liability in cases of occasional or isolated innocent infringement, and it offers adequate insulation to users, such as broadcasters and newspaper publishers, who are particularly vulnerable to this type of infringement suit. On the other hand, by establishing a realistic floor for liability, the provision preserves its intended deterrent effect; and it would not allow an infringer to escape simply because the plaintiff failed to disprove the defendant's claim of innocence.

In addition to the general "innocent infringer" provision clause (2) deals with the special situation of teachers, librarians, archivists, and public broadcasters, and the nonprofit institutions of which they are a part. Section 504(c)(2) provides that, where such a person or institution infringed copyrighted material in the honest belief that what they were doing constituted fair use, the court is precluded from awarding any statutory damages. It is intended that, in cases involving this provision, the burden of proof with respect to the defendant's good faith should rest on the plaintiff.

Sections 505 Through 509. Miscellaneous Provisions on Infringement and Remedies

The remaining sections of chapter 5 of the bill deal with costs and attorneys' fees, criminal offenses, the statute of limitations, notification of copyright actions, and remedies for alteration of programming by cable systems.

Under section 505 the awarding of costs and attorney's fees are left to the court's discretion, and the section also makes clear that neither costs nor attorney's fees can be awarded to or against "the United States or an officer thereof."

Four types of criminal offenses actionable under the bill are listed in section 506: willful infringement for profit, fraudulent use of a copyright notice, fraudulent removal of notice, and false representation in connection with a copyright application. The maximum fine on conviction has been increased to $10,000 and, in conformity with the general pattern of the Criminal Code (18 U.S.C.A.), no minimum fines have been provided. In addition to or instead of a fine, conviction for criminal infringement under section 506(a) can carry with it a sentence of imprisonment of up to one year. Section 506(b) deals with seizure, forfeiture, and destruction of material involved in cases of criminal infringement.

Section 506(a) contains a special provision applying to any person who infringes willfully and for purposes of commercial advantage the copyright in a sound recording or a motion picture. For the first such offense a person shall be fined not more than $25,000 or imprisoned for not more than one year, or both. For any subsequent offense a person shall be fined not more than $50,000 or imprisoned not more than two years, or both.

Section 507, which is substantially identical with section 115 of the present law, establishes a three-year statute of limitations for both criminal proceedings and civil actions. The language of this section, which was adopted by the act of September 7, 1957 (71 Stat. 633), represents a reconciliation of views, and has therefore been left unaltered. Section 508, which corresponds to some extent with a provision in the patent law (35 U.S.C.A. § 290), is intended to establish a method for notifying the Copyright Office and the public of the filing and disposition of copyright cases. The clerks of the Federal courts are to notify the Copyright Office of the filing of any copyright actions and of their final disposition, and the Copyright Office is to make these notifications a part of its public records.

Section 509(b) specifies a new discretionary remedy for alteration of programming by cable systems in violation of section 111(c)(3): the court in such cases may decree that, "for a period not to exceed thirty days, the cable system shall be deprived of the benefit of a compulsory license for one or more distant signals carried by such cable system." The term "distant signals" in this provision is intended to have a meaning consistent with the definition of "distant signal equivalent" in section 111.

Under section 509(a), four types of plaintiffs are entitled to bring an action in cases of alteration of programming by cable systems in violation of section 111(c)(3). For regular copyright owners and local broadcaster-licensees, the full battery of remedies for infringement would be available. The two new classes of potential plaintiffs under section 501(d)—the distant-signal transmitter and other local stations—would be limited to the following remedies: (i) discretionary injunctions; (ii) discretionary costs and attorney's fees; (iii) any actual damages the plaintiff can prove were attributable to the act of altering program content; and (iv) the new discretionary remedy of suspension of compulsory licensing.

SHELDON v. METRO-GOLDWYN PICTURES CORP.

Supreme Court of the United States, 1940.
309 U.S. 390, 60 S.Ct. 681, 84 L.Ed. 825, 44 U.S.P.Q. 607.

Mr. Chief Justice HUGHES delivered the opinion of the Court.

The questions presented are whether, in computing an award of profits against an infringer of a copyright, there may be an apportionment so as to give to the owner of the copyright only that part of the profits found to be attributable to the use of the copyrighted material as distinguished from what the infringer himself has supplied, and, if so, whether the evidence affords a proper basis for the apportionment decreed in this case.

Petitioners' complaint charged infringement of their play "Dishonored Lady" by respondents' motion picture "Letty Lynton," and sought an injunction and an accounting of profits. The Circuit Court of Appeals, reversing the District Court, found and enjoined the infringement and directed an accounting. 2 Cir., 81 F.2d 49. Thereupon the District Court confirmed with slight modifications the report of a special master which awarded to petitioners all the net profits made by respondents from their exhibitions of the motion picture, amounting to $587,604.37. D.C., 26 F.Supp. 134, 136. The Circuit Court of Appeals reversed, holding that there should be an apportionment and fixing petitioners' share of the net profits at one-fifth. 2 Cir., 106 F.2d 45, 51. In view of the importance of the question, which appears to be one of first impression in the application of the copyright law, we granted certiorari.

Petitioners' play "Dishonored Lady" was based upon the trial in Scotland, in 1857, of Madeleine Smith for the murder of her lover,—a *cause célèbre* included in the series of "Notable British Trials" which was published in 1927. The play was copyrighted as an unpublished work in 1930, and was produced here and abroad. Respondents took the title of their motion picture "Letty Lynton" from a novel of that name written by an English author, Mrs. Belloc Lowndes, and published in 1930. That novel was also based upon the story of Madeleine Smith and the motion picture rights were bought by respondents. There had been negotiations for the motion picture rights in petitioners' play, and the price had been fixed at $30,000, but these negotiations fell through.

As the Court of Appeals found, respondents in producing the motion picture in question worked over old material; "the general skeleton was already in the public demesne. A wanton girl kills her lover to free herself for a better match; she is brought to trial for the murder and escapes." But not content with the mere use of that basic plot, respondents resorted to petitioners' copyrighted play. They were not innocent offenders. From comparison and analysis, the Court of Appeals concluded that they had "deliberately lifted the play"; their "borrowing was a deliberate plagiarism." It is from that standpoint that we approach the questions now raised.

Respondents contend that the material taken by infringement contributed in but a small measure to the production and success of the motion picture. They say that they themselves contributed the main factors in producing the large net profits; that is, the popular actors, the scenery, and the expert producers and directors. Both courts below have sustained this contention.

The District Court thought it "punitive and unjust" to award all the net profits to petitioners. The court said that, if that were done, petitioners would receive the profits that the "motion picture stars" had made for the picture "by their dramatic talent and the drawing power of their reputations." "The directors who supervised the production of the picture and the experts who filmed it also contributed in piling up these tremendous net profits." The court thought an allowance to petitioners of 25 per cent. of these profits "could be justly fixed as a limit beyond which complainants would be receiving profits in no way attributable to the use of their play in the production of the picture." But, though holding these views, the District Court awarded all the net profits to petitioners, feeling bound by the decision of the Court of Appeals in Dam v. Kirk La Shelle Co., 2 Cir., 175 F. 902, 903, 41 L.R.A.N.S., 1002, 20 Ann.Cas. 1173, a decision which the Court of Appeals has now overruled.

The Court of Appeals was satisfied that but a small part of the net profits was attributable to the infringement, and, fully recognizing the difficulty in finding a satisfactory standard, the court decided that there should be an apportionment and that it could fairly be made. The court was resolved "to avoid the one certainly unjust course of giving the plaintiffs everything, because the defendants cannot with certainty compute their own share." The court would not deny "the one fact that stands undoubted," and, making the best estimate it could, it fixed petitioners' share at one-fifth of the net profits, considering that to be a figure "which will favor the plaintiffs in every reasonable chance of error."

First. Petitioners insist fundamentally that there can be no apportionment of profits in a suit for a copyright infringement; that it is forbidden both by the statute and the decisions of this Court. We find this basic argument to be untenable.

The Copyright Act in § 25(b) provides that an infringer shall be liable—

> "(b) To pay to the copyright proprietor such damages as the copyright proprietor may have suffered due to the infringement, as well as all the profits which the infringer shall have made from such infringement, . . . or in lieu of actual damages and profits, such damages as to the court shall appear to be just, . . ."

We agree with petitioners that the "in lieu" clause is not applicable here, as the profits have been proved and the only question is as to their apportionment.

Petitioners stress the provision for recovery of "all" the profits, but this is plainly qualified by the words "which the infringer shall have made from such infringement." This provision in purpose is cognate to that for the recovery of "such damages as the copyright proprietor may have suffered due to the infringement." The purpose is thus to provide just compensation for the wrong, not to impose a penalty by giving to the copyright proprietor profits which are not attributable to the infringement.

Prior to the Copyright Act of 1909, there had been no statutory provision for the recovery of profits, but that recovery had been allowed in equity both in copyright and patent cases as appropriate equitable relief incident to a decree for an injunction. That relief had been given in accordance with the principles governing equity jurisdiction, not to inflict punishment but to prevent an unjust enrichment by allowing injured complainants to claim "that which, *ex aequo et bono,* is theirs, and nothing beyond this." Livingston v. Woodworth, 15 How. 546, 560, 14 L.Ed. 809. Statutory provision for the recovery of profits in patent cases was enacted in 1870. The principle which was applied both prior to this statute and later was thus stated in the leading case of Tilghman v. Proctor, 125 U.S. 136, 146, 8 S.Ct. 894, 899, 31 L.Ed. 664:

> "The infringer is liable for actual, not for possible gains. The profits, therefore, which he must account for, are not those which he might reasonably have made, but those which he did make, by the use of the plaintiff's invention; or, in other words, the fruits of the advantage which he derived from the use of that invention, over what he would have had in using other means then open to the public and adequate to enable him to obtain an equally beneficial result. If there was no such advantage in his use of the plaintiff's invention, there can be no decree for profits, and the plaintiff's only remedy is by an action at law for damages."

In passing the Copyright Act, the apparent intention of Congress was to assimilate the remedy with respect to the recovery of profits to that already recognized in patent cases. Not only is there no suggestion that Congress intended that the award of profits should be governed by a different principle in copyright cases but the contrary is clearly indicated by the committee reports on the bill. .   .   .

We shall presently consider the doctrine which has been established upon equitable principles with respect to the apportionment of profits in cases of patent infringement. We now observe that there is nothing in the Copyright Act which precludes the application of a similar doctrine based upon the same equitable principles in cases of copyright infringement.

Nor do the decisions of this Court preclude that course. Petitioners invoke the cases of Callaghan v. Myers, 128 U.S. 617, 9 S.Ct. 177, 32 L.Ed. 547, and Belford v. Scribner, 144 U.S. 488, 12 S.Ct. 734, 740, 36 L.Ed. 514. In the *Callaghan* case, the copyright of a reporter of judicial decisions was sustained with respect to the portions of the books of which he was the author, although he had no exclusive right in the judicial opinions. On an accounting for the profits made by an infringer, the Court allowed the deduction from the selling price of the actual and legitimate manufacturing cost. With reference to the published matter to which the copyright did not extend, the Court found it impossible to separate the profits on that from the profits on the other. And in view of that impossibility, the defendant, being responsible for the blending of the lawful with the unlawful, had to abide the consequences, as in the case of one who has wrongfully produced a confusion of goods. A similar impossibility was encountered in Belford v. Scribner, a case of a copyright of a book containing recipes for the household. The infringing books were largely compilations of these recipes, "the matter and language" being "the same as the complainant's in every substantial sense," but so distributed through the defendants' books that it was "almost impossible to separate the one from the other." The Court ruled that when the copyrighted portions are so intermingled with the rest of the piratical work "that they cannot well be distinguished from it," the entire profits realized by the defendants will be given to the plaintiff.

We agree with the court below that these cases do not decide that no apportionment of profits can be had where it is clear that all the profits are not due to the use of the copyrighted material, and the evidence is sufficient to provide a fair basis of division so as to give to the copyright proprietor all the profits that can be deemed to have resulted from the use of what belonged to him. Both the Copyright Act and our decisions leave the matter to the appropriate exercise of the equity jurisdiction upon an accounting to determine the profits "which the infringer shall have made from such infringement."

Second. The analogy found in cases of patent infringement is persuasive. There are many cases in which the plaintiff's patent covers only a part of a machine and creates only a part of the profits. The patented invention may have been used in combination with additions or valuable improvements made by the infringer and each may have contributed to the profits. In Elizabeth v. American Nicholson Pavement Co., 97 U.S. 126, 142, 24 L.Ed. 1000, cited in the *Callaghan* and *Belford* cases, supra, it had been recognized that if a separation of distinct profit derived from such additions or improvements was shown, an apportionment might be had. . . .

The principle as to apportionment of profits was clearly stated in the case of Dowagiac Mfg. Co. v. Minnesota Moline Plow Co., 235 U.S. 641, 35 S.Ct. 221, 59 L.Ed. 398,—a case which received great consideration. The Court there said:

"We think the evidence, although showing that the invention was meritorious and materially contributed to the value of the infringing drills as marketable machines, made it clear that their value was not entirely attributable to the invention, but was due in a substantial degree to the unpatented parts or features. The masters and the courts below so found and we should hesitate to disturb their concurring conclusions upon this question of fact, even had the evidence been less clear than it was.

"In so far as the profits from the infringing sales were attributable to the patented improvements they belonged to the plaintiff, and in so far as they were due to other parts or features they belonged to the defendants. But as the drills were sold in completed and operative form the profits resulting from the several parts were necessarily commingled. It was essential therefore that they be separated or apportioned between what was covered by the patent and what was not covered by it, for, as was said in Westinghouse Co. v. Wagner Co., supra, (225 U.S. 615, 32 S.Ct. 694, 56 L.Ed. 1222, 41 L.R.A.,N.S., 653): 'In such case, if plaintiff's patent only created a part of the profits, he is only entitled to recover that part of the net gains.' " Id., 235 U. S. 646, 35 S.Ct. 223, 59 L.Ed. 398.

In the *Dowagiac* case, we again referred to the difficulty of making an exact apportionment and again observed that mathematical exactness was not possible. What was required was only "reasonable approximation" which usually may be attained "through the tesimony of experts and persons informed by observation and experience." Testimony of this character was said to be "generally helpful and at times indispensable in the solution of such problems." The result to be accomplished "is a rational separation of the net profits so that neither party may have what rightfully belongs to the other." Id., 235 U.S. p. 647, 35 S.Ct. at page 223, 59 L.Ed. 398.

We see no reason why these principles should not be applied in copyright cases. Petitioners cite our decision in the trade-mark case of Hamilton-Brown Shoe Co. v. Wolf Bros. Co., 240 U.S. 251, 36 S.Ct. 269, 60 L.Ed. 629, but the Court there, recognizing the rulings in the *Westinghouse* and *Dowagiac* cases, found on the facts that an apportionment of profits was "inherently impossible." The burden cast upon the defendant had not been sustained. .   .   .

Petitioners stress the point that respondents have been found guilty of deliberate plagiarism, but we perceive no ground for saying that in awarding profits to the copyright proprietor as a means of compensation, the court may make an award of profits which have been shown not to be due to the infringement. That would be not to do equity but to inflict an unauthorized penalty. To call the infringer a trustee *ex maleficio* merely indicates "a mode of approach and an imperfect analogy by which the wrongdoer will be made to hand over the proceeds of his wrong." Larson Co. v. Wrigley Co., 277 U.S. 97, 99, 100, 48 S.Ct. 449, 72 L.Ed. 800. He is in the position of one who has confused his own gains with those which belong to another. He "must yield the gains begotten of his wrong." Duplate Corp. v. Triplex Co., 298 U.S. 448, 457, 56 S.Ct. 792, 796, 80 L.Ed. 1274. Where there is a commingling of gains, he must abide the consequences, unless he can make a separation of the profits so as to assure to the injured party all that justly belongs to him. When such an apportionment has been fairly made, the copyright proprietor receives all the profits which have been gained through the use of the infringing material and that is all that the statute authorizes and equity sanctions.

Both courts below have held in this case that but a small part of the profits were due to the infringement, and, accepting that fact and the principle that an apportionment may be had if the evidence justifies it, we pass to the consideration of the basis of the actual apportionment which has been allowed.

Third. The controlling fact in the determination of the apportionment was that the profits had been derived, not from the mere performance of a copyrighted play, but from the exhibition of a motion picture which had its distinctive profit-making features, apart from the use of any infringing material, by reason of the expert and creative operations involved in its production and direction. In that aspect the case has a certain resemblance to that of a patent infringement, where the infringer has created profits by the addition of non-infringing and valuable improvements. And, in this instance, it plainly appeared that what respondents had contributed accounted for by far the larger part of their gains.

Respondents had stressed the fact that, although the negotiations had not ripened into a purchase, the price which had been set for the motion picture rights in "Dishonored Lady" had been but $30,000. And respondents' witnesses cited numerous instances where the value, according to sales, of motion picture rights had been put at relatively small sums. But the court below rejected as a criterion the price put upon the motion picture rights, as a bargain had not been concluded and the inferences were too doubtful. The court also ruled that respondents could not count the effect of "their standing and reputation in the industry." The court permitted respondents to be credited "only with such factors as they bought and paid for; the actors, the scenery, the producers, and directors and the general overhead."

The testimony showed quite clearly that in the creation of profits from the exhibition of a motion picture, the talent and popularity of the "motion picture stars" generally constitutes the main drawing power of the picture, and that this is especially true where the title of the picture is not identified with any well-known play or novel. Here, it appeared that the picture did not bear the title of the copyrighted play and that it was not presented or advertised as having any connection whatever with the play. It was also shown that the picture had been "sold," that is, licensed to almost all the exhibitors as identified simply with the name of a popular motion picture actress before even the title "Letty Lynton" was used. In addition to the drawing power of the "motion picture stars," other factors in creating the profits were found in the artistic conceptions and in the expert supervision and direction of the various processes which made possible the composite result with its attractiveness to the public.

Upon these various considerations, with elaboration of detail, respondents' expert witnesses gave their views as to the extent to which the use of the copyrighted material had contributed to the profits in question. The underlying facts as to the factors in successful production and exhibition of motion pictures were abundantly proved, but, as the court below recognized, the ultimate estimates of the expert witnesses were only the expression "of their very decided opinions." These witnesses were in complete agreement that the portion of the the profits attributable to the use of the copyrighted play in the circumstances here disclosed was very small. Their estimates given in percentages of receipts ran from five to twelve per cent; the estimate apparently most favored was ten per cent as the limit. One finally expressed the view that the play contributed nothing. There was no rebuttal. But the court below was not willing to accept the experts' testimony "at its face value." The court felt that it must make an award "which by no possibility shall be too small." Desiring to give petitioners the benefit of every doubt, the court allowed for the contribution of the play twenty per cent. of the net profits.

Petitioners are not in a position to complain that the amount thus allowed by the court was greater than the expert evidence warranted. Nor is there any basis for attack, and we do not understand that any attack is made, upon the qualifications of the experts. By virtue of an extensive experience, they had an intimate knowledge of all pertinent facts relating to the production and exhibition of motion pictures. Nor can we say that the testimony afforded no basis for a finding. What we said in the *Dowagiac* case is equally true here,—that what is required is not mathematical exactness but only a reasonable approximation. That, after all, is a matter of judgment; and the testimony of those who are informed by observation and experience may be not only helpful but, as we have said, may be indispensable. Equity is concerned with making a fair apportionment so that neither party will have what justly belongs to the other. Confronted with the manifest injustice of giving to petitioners all the profits made by the motion picture, the court in making an apportionment was entitled to avail itself of the experience of those best qualified to form a judgment in the particular field of inquiry and come to its conclusion aided by their testimony. We see no greater difficulty in the admission and use of expert testimony in such a case than in the countless cases involving values of property rights in which such testimony often forms the sole basis for decision.

Petitioners also complain of deductions allowed in the computation of the net profits. These contentions involve questions of fact which have been determined below upon the evidence and we find no ground for disturbing the court's conclusions.

The judgment of the Circuit Court of Appeals is

Affirmed.

Mr. Justice McREYNOLDS took no part in the decision of this case.

BREFFORT v. I HAD A BALL CO.

United States District Court, S.D. New York, 1967.
271 F.Supp. 623, 155 U.S.P.Q. 391.

MANSFIELD, District Judge.

This action for infringement of plaintiffs' copyright in a musical play entitled "Impasse de la Fidelite" ("Impasse" herein) was tried for six days to a jury, which returned a verdict in the sum of $19,000 damages against defendants Chodorov and Kipness, the author and producer, respectively of the infringing musical play "I Had a Ball," a verdict for $14,000 profits against Chodorov, and a verdict in favor of defendants The I Had a Ball Company, Lawrence, and Freeman, the latter two being the writers of the songs and lyrics for "I Had a Ball."

Plaintiffs now move for (1) permanent injunctive relief, and (2) reasonable attorneys fees, pursuant to Title 17 U.S.C.A. § 116. The prevailing defendants, on the other hand, move for an award to them of attorneys' fees under the same section and for reasonable expenses pursuant to Rule 37(c), F.R.Civ.P., because of the plaintiffs' alleged denial of facts requested under Rule 36, F.R.Civ.P., to be admitted.

Plaintiffs' Application for Injunctive Relief

At the outset of trial it was stipulated between the parties that the record of the jury trial would be accepted as the basis for determination of equitable relief. That record, coupled with the jury's verdict, convinces the Court that in accordance with Title 17 U.S.C.A. § 101 a permanent injunction should issue restraining the defendants Chodorov and Kipness from further infringing plaintiffs' copyright in "Impasse," including a restraint against further performance of "I Had a Ball," at least as long as it remains substantially in its present form, which infringes plaintiffs' copyrighted work. The injunction should not, however, extend to the independent rendition of music or lyrics of "I Had a Ball," or preclude their being performed or used other than as an integral part of the musical play "I Had a Ball."

The jury's verdict against Chodorov and Kipness, in the light of the Court's instructions and the record before it, implicitly represents a finding, which the Court adopts and independently makes, that the plaintiff Alexandre Breffort was the author and co-owner with the plaintiff Societe de Participations Theatrales of a valid United States copyright in "Impasse," which was infringed by these two defendants' production and performance of the musical play "I Had a Ball." The copyright protected the plaintiffs' original arrangement and expression of ideas in "Impasse," including the plaintiffs' development of the plot, of characters, of sequences of scenes and incidents, and of the interplay of characters, which possessed originality.

The jury's verdict was amply supported by substantial credible evidence. There is no question about the fact that prior to their production and performance of the infringing work Chodorov and Kipness not only had access to "Impasse" but pursuant to an agreement with Arthur Lesser, holder of an option from the plaintiffs, embarked upon doing an English adaption of it, upon which Chodorov worked for some months with the aid of Lawrence and Freeman, after Chodorov had seen Breffort's composition performed in Paris and received the text from him. After this extensive access Chodorov, again with the aid of Lawrence and Freeman, wrote the infringing work which was produced by Kipness and performed on Broadway, in Detroit, and in Phildelphia. Both musical plays were read in toto to the Court and jury and were the subject of extensive testimony by the defendants and experts offered by both sides.

Viewing the proof as a whole, and independently determining the weight and credibility to be extended to the testimony, the Court finds that to the ordinary observer there appears to be a substantial similarity of expression in material portions of both works, and that "I Had a Ball" infringes copyrightable material in "Impasse." Although a finding of irreparable injury may not be essential to the issuance of injunctive relief, the proof here leads me to conclude that it would be difficult to measure the damages that might flow from any future infringement of plaintiffs' play, which had substantial value before it was infringed by Chodorov and Kipness.

Defendants oppose injunctive relief, arguing that it is not warranted for the reasons that although plaintiffs asserted their claim of infringement in November 1964, at the commencement of the six-month Broadway run of "I Had a Ball," and commenced suit shortly thereafter, plaintiffs did not press their claim for injunctive relief until trial in 1967, two years later; that there is no real probability or threat of continuing or additional infringements, since the defendants' production and performance of the infringing work was not a financial success; and that the 16 songs and lyrics written by the defendants Lawrence and Freeman, which are incorporated into the play, were not found to infringe the songs and lyrics of "Impasse." On the other hand, the record shows that it was not until approximately two years after abandonment of their work on an English adaption of plaintiffs' play that Chodorov and Kipness apparently resurrected plaintiffs' arrangement and dressed it in a modified suit of clothes to produce the infringement.

Against this background, and the existence of proof providing ample grounds for the inference that the infringement represented calculated and deliberate conduct, as distinguished from an unwitting or negligent misuse, the plaintiffs should not be required to assume the risk that these two defendants will not repeat such infringement or engage in similar conduct in the future. In addition to protecting the plaintiffs against such risk, the issuance of a permanent injunction does not threaten any substantial harm to any legitimate interests of the defendants, particularly since it will not bar independent performance of the songs and lyrics involved.

Plaintiffs' Application for Award of Attorneys' Fees

Section 116 of the Copyright Statute (Title 17 U.S.C.A. § 116) authorizes the Court in the exercise of its discretion to award "to the prevailing party a reasonable attorney's fee as part of the costs." It represents a departure from the normal practice of not permitting assessment of attorneys' fees as costs, which is designed to insure the availability of our courts to all alike by not rendering them prohibitive to the poor through imposition of heavy costs. For this reason an award of counsel fees is considered in the nature of a penalty which the Court has the discretionary power to impose on the losing party, and the statute has been "sparingly used and the amounts awarded modest." Orgel v. Clark Boardman Co., 301 F.2d 119, 2 A.

L.R.3d 1203 (2d Cir.), cert. denied, 371 U.S. 817, 83 S.Ct. 31, 9 L.Ed. 2d 58 (1962). Accordingly the considerations prompting an award of fees to a successful plaintiff must of necessity differ from those determining whether a prevailing defendant is entitled to such an award. The purpose of an award of counsel fees to a plaintiff is to deter copyright infringement. In the case of a prevailing defendant, however, prevention of infringement is obviously not a factor; and if an award is to be made at all, it represents a penalty imposed upon the plaintiff for institution of a baseless, frivolous, or unreasonable suit, or one instituted in bad faith.

In the present case an award of a reasonable attorney's fee to the plaintiffs as part of the costs to be assessed against the defendants Chodorov and Kipness is both appropriate and in keeping with the purpose of 17 U.S.C.A. § 116. The infringement represented deliberate conduct on their part, undertaken with knowledge of the plaintiffs' copyright in the musical play "Impasse," after it had been entrusted to them for the very purpose of developing an English adaption capable of being performed on the United States stage.

The factors to be considered in determining the amount of the attorney's fee to be awarded to plaintiffs are well established. The subject matter and legal questions in the present case were complicated. Successful prosecution of the suit by the plaintiffs required from the outset specialized legal skill of a superior order which is possessed by plaintiffs' attorneys, who are specialists in the field of copyright and trademark practice. Counsel were required, among other things, to view the play in Philadelphia, to read numerous drafts of both works, to consult at length with co-counsel and plaintiffs' French attorneys, to conduct extensive pretrial discovery (including argument of motions and the taking of depositions), to research difficult questions of law and fact, to consult with expert witnesses, to prepare and submit trial memoranda and requests to charge, to conduct a jury trial which extended over a period of six days, to prepare briefs and affidavits for argument of post-trial motions, and generally to supervise the handling of a demanding piece of litigation. All this work involved expenditure of 475 hours on the part of plaintiffs' counsel, most of it by the partner in charge of the case.

After taking into consideration all of these factors, together with the fact that plaintiffs prevailed and were awarded verdicts in the amounts indicated above, the Court finds that an attorney's fee in the sum of $12,500 is reasonable and directs that the said sum be awarded as additional costs against the defendants Chodorov and Kipness in the following proportions: $9,000 to be assessed against the defendant Chodorov and $3,500 to be assessed against the defendant Kipness. This allocation takes into consideration the fact that Chodorov, as the author of the non-lyrical text of "I Had a Ball," was the principal infringer.

Application of Defendants The I Had a Ball Company, Lawrence and Freeman for Attorneys' Fees Pursuant to Title 17 U.S.C.A. § 116

The application of the above-named defendants for an award of a reasonable attorney's fee to them as prevailing defendants is denied. Plaintiffs' claim against them does not fall in the category of actions instituted unreasonably, capriciously or in bad faith, which are to be discouraged through assessment of attorneys' fees as a penalty. Far from being groundless, the claim was supported by evidence warranting its submission to the jury, at least as the basis for an inference of contributory infringement. There was proof that Lawrence and Freeman had worked with Chodorov in 1961 and 1962 in his preparation of the English adaption of "Impasse"; and that a little more than one year later they performed similar services in Chodorov's writing of "I Had a Ball." Although they testified that their assistance was limited to writing songs and lyrics, none of which infringed the songs and lyrics of "Impasse," there was testimony by Freeman that he had been furnished by Chodorov with an outline of "Impasse" and by Lawrence that he may have given Chodorov suggestions as to the script. Chodorov testified by deposition that after their work on the adaption of "Impasse" Lawrence and Freeman "kicked around" and discussed with him ideas for "I Had a Ball" and "what direction it should take," suggesting "facets of a character," with their collaboration merging and melding. Furthermore plaintiffs contended that some of the lyrics were substantially similar to non-lyrical material found in "Impasse."

Thus an issue of fact arose as to whether Lawrence and Freeman participated in the creation of any of the infringing material found in "I Had a Ball," and this issue was sufficiently meritorious to warrant its being submitted to the jury. Against this background an award of attorneys' fees to them under Title 17 U.S.C.A. § 116 will not be made since the effect of such a penalty would be to inhibit the submission of legitimate issues for resolution by the Court. The situation here is quite different from that found in decisions cited by Lawrence and Freeman, where awards of attorneys' fees were granted against plaintiffs who had instituted groundless suits. In Burnett v. Lambino, 206 F.Supp. 517 (S.D.N.Y.1962), for instance, the court found that "the asserted claim of infringement was so demonstrably lacking in merit that bringing it was clearly unreasonable." To the same general effect is Mailer v. RKO Teleradio Pictures, Inc., 332 F. 2d 747 (2d Cir. 1964), where plaintiffs' claim was found to be "unreasonable". . . .

Motion of Defendants Lawrence and Freeman for Reasonable Expenses Pursuant to Rule 37(c), F.R.Civ.P.

Acting under Rule 36, F.R.Civ.P., counsel for Lawrence and Freeman, during the pretrial discovery phases of the lawsuit, served the following requests for admission upon the plaintiffs:

"1. The musical score of defendants' production of 'I Had a Ball' was not copied or derived from the musical score of any version of 'Impasse de la Fidelite' and does not in any way infringe upon or violate the copyright or any other rights of plaintiffs in the musical score of 'Impasse de la Fidelite.'

"2. The songs and the lyrics of the songs in defendants' production of 'I Had a Ball' were not copied or derived from any of the songs and lyrics of songs of any version of 'Impasse de la Fidelite' and do not in any way infringe or violate the copyright or any other rights of plaintiffs in the songs and lyrics of 'Impasse de la Fidelite'."

Upon plaintiffs' motion objecting to the requests, Judge Tenney upheld the requests to the extent of requiring plaintiffs to answer "whether the songs and lyrics of defendants' work were not copied from plaintiffs' work," but held that the plaintiffs should not be required to answer that portion of the requests calling upon them "to admit that defendants' work does not infringe upon theirs, as that request appears to call for a mixture of opinion and conclusion of law and is improper" (S.D.N.Y. April 19, 1965).

Thereupon plaintiffs denied the truth of the matter set forth in the foregoing requests as so modified. The trial record discloses that plaintiffs' denials were justified. At trial Lawrence and Freeman both testified that in writing the song "Think Beautiful" for "I Had a Ball" they had "inadvertently" used 16 bars of music identical to those found in the song "Pas de Raison" in "Impasse," and they conceded that an additional 16 bars were very similar. It further appears that the denials were asserted in good faith by plaintiffs' counsel, since he expressed a willingness to enter into a stipulation setting forth the facts and issues in more detail, but this procedure was apparently not found acceptable to defendants' counsel.

In any event the amount of time and effort required to prove that except for the small amount of music referred to above there was no copying of the music and lyrics of "Impasse," would be minimal, in view of the obvious dissimilarity between the music in both plays. Although a substantially greater amount of time and services were required to prepare Lawrence and Freeman with respect to the question of whether they were contributory infringers, their preparation and presentation of proof on this latter issue could not have been avoided through requests for admission, short of a voluntary dismissal of plaintiffs' suit against them. For the reasons indicated above plaintiffs were not unreasonable in pressing the issue of contributory infringement and the evidence warranted submission of it to the jury. Accordingly, the motion of the defendants Lawrence and Freeman for reasonable expenses pursuant to Rule 37(c), F.R.Civ.P., is denied.

Submit order.

NOTES

1. In a handful of short, bold strokes, section 504 resolved several questions that had grown up around the old Act's provisions for monetary awards. One question, whether the 1909 Act intended awards for damages and profits to be cumulative or alternative, had

found the two major copyright circuits sharply divided. Compare Thomas Wilson & Co. v. Irving J. Dorfman Co., 433 F.2d 409, 167 U. S.P.Q. 417 (2d Cir. 1970), cert. denied 401 U.S. 977, 91 S.Ct. 1200, 28 L.Ed.2d 326, 169 U.S.P.Q. 65 (cumulative) with Sid & Marty Krofft Television Productions, Inc. v. McDonald's Corp., 562 F.2d 1157, 196 U.S.P.Q. 97 (9th Cir. 1977) (alternative). Section 504(b) strikes a balance between the Second Circuit's deterrent approach and the Ninth Circuit's compensatory approach by allowing the copyright owner to recover actual damages and any of the infringer's profits "not taken into account in computing the damages." Thus, if as one element of damages the copyright owner recovers the profits it would have made on sales lost to the infringer, it can only recover the infringer's profits to the extent that they exceed the owner's lost profits.

Section 504(c), allowing the copyright owner to elect statutory damages, resolves earlier questions about the circumstances in which statutory damage awards were discretionary and the circumstances in which they were mandatory. As to apportionment, section 504 confirms the approach taken in Sheldon v. M. G. M. The section also attempts to define the limits on statutory damages for multiple infringements. Compare Robert Stigwood Group Ltd. v. O'Reilly, 530 F.2d 1096, 189 U.S.P.Q. 453 (2d Cir. 1976), cert. denied 429 U.S. 848, 97 S.Ct. 135, 50 L.Ed.2d 121.

Yet, section 504 leaves some old questions unanswered and raises several new questions of its own. In computing net profits, what items should the infringer be permitted to prove as "deductible expenses": Some proportion of overhead for its entire operation? The cost of capital invested in the infringing venture? Taxes on income from the infringing venture? Commissions paid and specific losses incurred in connection with the venture? What interplay, if any, is there between the new provisions on damages and profits and the infringer's burden of proof respecting allocation of profits? How expansively should "work" be defined for purposes of section 504(c)(1)? Does the last sentence of that subsection provide a sufficient guide? What of the *DeJonge* test, p. 666, above?

2. Preliminary injunctions are far more freely available to copyright owners than to patent or trademark owners. Generally, a copyright owner will be entitled to preliminary relief upon making a prima facie case of the copyright's validity and infringement. Demonstration of irreparable harm, though helpful, is usually not necessary. Compare Rushton Co. v. Vitale, 218 F.2d 434, 436, 104 U.S.P. Q. 158 (2d Cir. 1955) ("When a prima facie case for copyright infringement has been made, plaintiffs are entitled to a preliminary injunction without a detailed showing of danger of irreparable harm"), with American Metropolitan Enterprises of New York, Inc. v. Warner Brothers Records, Inc., 389 F.2d 903, 905, 157 U.S.P.Q. 69 (2d Cir. 1968) ("A copyright holder in the ordinary case may be presumed to suffer irreparable harm when his right to the exclusive use of the copyrighted material is invaded."). See generally Latman, Prelimi-

nary Injunctions in Patent, Trademark and Copyright Cases, 60 Trademark Rep. 506 (1970).

What considerations weigh for and against such liberality in giving threshold relief? Is it a matter for concern that the injunction is directed against conduct that in other contexts might be protected under the first amendment's free speech and press guarantees? If the underlying concern is that the eventual monetary award, coupled with a permanent injunction, will not make the copyright owner whole, would it be better to adjust the statute's damages schedule to a more realistic scale and, possibly, introduce treble damages? Is there anything about the behavior of copyright industries or the solvency of copyright infringers that distinguishes them for these purposes from patent and trademark infringers?

Should the tests for preliminary relief be more closely attuned to the equities and hardships of particular copyright industries? Compare, for example, the situation of fabric designers, whose designs go out of fashion quickly and are even more quickly appropriated by competitors, with the situation of the writer who claims that his story or script outline is being appropriated by defendant motion picture producer in the course of a multimillion dollar production. What are the relative costs of delay to the parties in these two situations? Does it matter that, while the ultimate award of defendant's profits will be apportioned to the benefits gained from use of plaintiff's work, a preliminary injunction will not cut nearly so fine and will effectively halt *all* of defendant's production activity?

C. INFRINGEMENT

See Statute Supplement 17 U.S.C.A. § 501.

ARNSTEIN v. PORTER, 154 F.2d 464, 68 U.S.P.Q. 288 (2d Cir. 1946). FRANK, J.: The principal question on this appeal is whether the lower court, under Rule 56, properly deprived plaintiff of a trial of his copyright infringement action. The answer depends on whether "there is the slightest doubt as to the facts."

In applying that standard here, it is important to avoid confusing two separate elements essential to a plaintiff's case in such a suit: (a) that defendant copied from plaintiff's copyrighted work and (b) that the copying (assuming it to be proved) went so far as to constitute improper appropriation.

As to the first—copying—the evidence may consist (a) of defendant's admission that he copied or (b) of circumstantial evidence —usually evidence of access—from which the trier of the facts may reasonably infer copying. Of course, if there are no similarities, no amount of evidence of access will suffice to prove copying. If there is evidence of access and similarities exist, then the trier of the facts must determine whether the similarities are sufficient to prove copying. On this issue, analysis ("dissection") is relevant, and the testimony of experts may be received to aid the trier of the facts. If evidence of access is absent, the similarities must be so striking as to preclude the possibility that plaintiff and defendant independently arrived at the same result.

If copying is established, then only does there arise the second issue, that of illicit copying (unlawful appropriation). On that issue (as noted more in detail below) the test is the response of the ordinary lay hearer; accordingly, on that issue, "dissection" and expert testimony are irrelevant.

In some cases, the similarities between the plaintiff's and defendant's work are so extensive and striking as, without more, both to justify an inference of copying and to prove improper appropriation. But such double-purpose evidence is not required; that is, if copying is otherwise shown, proof of improper appropriation need not consist of similarities which, standing alone, would support an inference of copying.

1. LITERATURE

NICHOLS v. UNIVERSAL PICTURES CORP.

United States Circuit Court of Appeals, Second Circuit, 1930.
45 F.2d 119, 7 U.S.P.Q. 84.

L. HAND, Circuit Judge.

The plaintiff is the author of a play, "Abie's Irish Rose," which it may be assumed was properly copyrighted under section five, subdivision (d), of the Copyright Act, 17 U.S.C.A. § 5(d). The defendant produced publicly a motion picture play, "The Cohens and The Kellys," which the plaintiff alleges was taken from it. As we think the defendant's play too unlike the plaintiff's to be an infringement, we may assume, arguendo, that in some details the defendant used the plaintiff's play, as will subsequently appear, though we do not so decide. It therefore becomes necessary to give an outline of the two plays.

"Abie's Irish Rose" presents a Jewish family living in prosperous circumstances in New York. The father, a widower, is in business as a merchant, in which his son and only child helps him. The boy has philandered with young women, who to his father's great disgust have always been Gentiles, for he is obsessed with a passion that his daughter-in-law shall be an orthodox Jewess. When the play opens the son, who has been courting a young Irish Catholic girl, has already married her secretly before a Protestant minister, and is concerned to soften the blow for his father, by securing a favorable impression of his bride, while concealing her faith and race. To accomplish this he introduces her to his father at his home as a Jewess, and lets it appear that he is interested in her, though he conceals the marriage. The girl somewhat reluctantly falls in with the plan; the father takes the bait, becomes infatuated with the girl, concludes that they must marry, and assumes that of course they will, if he so decides. He calls in a rabbi, and prepares for the wedding according to the Jewish rite.

Meanwhile the girl's father, also a widower, who lives in California, and is as intense in his own religious antagonism as the Jew, has been called to New York, supposing that his daughter is to marry an Irishman and a Catholic. Accompanied by a priest, he arrives at the house at the moment when the marriage is being celebrated, but too late to prevent it, and the two fathers, each infuriated by the proposed union of his child to a heretic, fall into unseemly and grotesque antics. The priest and the rabbi become friendly, exchange trite sentiments about religion, and agree that the match is good. Apparently out of abundant caution, the priest celebrates the marriage for a third time, while the girl's father is inveigled away. The second act closes with each father, still outraged, seeking to find some way by which the union, thus trebly insured, may be dissolved.

The last act takes place about a year later, the young couple having meanwhile been abjured by each father, and left to their own resources. They have had twins, a boy and a girl, but their fathers know no more than that a child has been born. At Christmas each, led by his craving to see his grandchild, goes separately to the young folks' home, where they encounter each other, each laden with gifts, one for a boy, the other for a girl. After some slapstick comedy, depending upon the insistence of each that he is right about the sex of the grandchild, they become reconciled when they learn the truth, and that each child is to bear the given name of a grandparent. The curtain falls as the fathers are exchanging amenities, and the Jew giving evidence of an abatement in the strictness of his orthodoxy.

"The Cohens and The Kellys" presents two families, Jewish and Irish, living side by side in the poorer quarters of New York in a state of perpetual enmity. The wives in both cases are still living, and share in the mutual animosity, as do two small sons, and even the respective dogs. The Jews have a daughter, the Irish a son; the Jewish father is in the clothing business; the Irishman is a policeman. The children are in love with each other, and secretly marry, apparently after the play opens. The Jew, being in great financial straits, learns from a lawyer that he has fallen heir to a large fortune from a great-aunt, and moves into a great house, fitted luxuriously. Here he and his family live in vulgar ostentation, and here the Irish boy seeks out his Jewish bride, and is chased away by the angry father. The Jew then abuses the Irishman over the telephone, and both become hysterically excited. The extremity of his feelings makes the Jew sick, so that he must go to Florida for a rest, just before which the daughter discloses her marriage to her mother.

On his return the Jew finds that his daughter has borne a child; at first he suspects the lawyer, but eventually learns the truth and is overcome with anger at such a low alliance. Meanwhile, the Irish family who have been forbidden to see the grandchild, go to the Jew's house, and after a violent scene between the two fathers in which the

Jew disowns his daughter, who decides to go back with her husband, the Irishman takes her back with her baby to his own poor lodgings. The lawyer, who had hoped to marry the Jew's daughter, seeing his plan foiled, tells the Jew that his fortune really belongs to the Irishman, who was also related to the dead woman, but offers to conceal his knowledge, if the Jew will share the loot. This the Jew repudiates, and, leaving the astonished lawyer, walks through the rain to his enemy's house to surrender the property. He arrives in great dejection, tells the truth, and abjectly turns to leave. A reconciliation ensues, the Irishman agreeing to share with him equally. The Jew shows some interest in his grandchild, though this is at most a minor motive in the reconciliation, and the curtain falls while the two are in their cups, the Jew insisting that in the firm name for the business, which they are to carry on jointly, his name shall stand first.

It is of course essential to any protection of literary property, whether at common-law or under the statute, that the right cannot be limited literally to the text, else a plagiarist would escape by immaterial variations. That has never been the law, but, as soon as literal appropriation ceases to be the test, the whole matter is necessarily at large, so that, as was recently well said by a distinguished judge, the decisions cannot help much in a new case. Fendler v. Morosco, 253 N.Y. 281, 292, 171 N.E. 56. When plays are concerned, the plagiarist may excise a separate scene, or he may appropriate part of the dialogue. Then the question is whether the part so taken is "substantial," and therefore not a "fair use" of the copyrighted work; it is the same question as arises in the case of any other copyrighted work. But when the plagiarist does not take out a block in situ, but an abstract of the whole, decision is more troublesome. Upon any work, and especially upon a play, a great number of patterns of increasing generality will fit equally well, as more and more of the incident is left out. The last may perhaps be no more than the most general statement of what the play is about, and at times might consist only of its title; but there is a point in this series of abstractions where they are no longer protected, since otherwise the playwright could prevent the use of his "ideas," to which, apart from their expression, his property is never extended. Nobody has ever been able to fix that boundary, and nobody ever can. In some cases the question has been treated as though it were analogous to lifting a portion out of the copyrighted work, but the analogy is not a good one, because, though the skeleton is a part of the body, it pervades and supports the whole. In such cases we are rather concerned with the line between expression and what is expressed. As respects plays, the controversy chiefly centers upon the characters and sequence of incident, these being the substance.

We did not in Dymow v. Bolton, 11 F.(2d) 690, hold that a plagiarist was never liable for stealing a plot; that would have been flatly against our rulings in Dam v. Kirk La Shelle Co., 175 F. 902, 41 L.R.A.(N.S.) 1002, 20 Ann.Cas. 1173, and Stodart v. Mutual Film Co.,

249 F. 513, affirming my decision in (D.C.) 249 F. 507; neither of which we meant to overrule. We found the plot of the second play was too different to infringe, because the most detailed pattern, common to both, eliminated so much from each that its content went into the public domain; and for this reason we said, "this mere subsection of a plot was not susceptible of copyright." But we do not doubt that two plays may correspond in plot closely enough for infringement. How far that correspondence must go is another matter. Nor need we hold that the same may not be true as to the characters, quite independently of the "plot" proper, though, as far as we know, such a case has never arisen. If Twelfth Night were copyrighted, it is quite possible that a second comer might so closely imitate Sir Toby Belch or Malvolio as to infringe, but it would not be enough that for one of his characters he cast a riotous knight who kept wassail to the discomfort of the household, or a vain and foppish steward who became amorous of his mistress. These would be no more than Shakespeare's "ideas" in the play, as little capable of monopoly as Einstein's Doctrine of Relativity, or Darwin's theory of the Origin of Species. It follows that the less developed the characters, the less they can be copyrighted; that is the penalty an author must bear for marking them too indistinctly.

In the two plays at bar we think both as to incident and character, the defendant took no more—assuming that it took anything at all—than the law allowed. The stories are quite different. One is of a religious zealot who insists upon his child's marrying no one outside his faith; opposed by another who is in this respect just like him, and is his foil. Their difference in race is merely an obbligato to the main theme, religion. They sink their differences through grandparental pride and affection. In the other, zealotry is wholly absent; religion does not even appear. It is true that the parents are hostile to each other in part because they differ in race; but the marriage of their son to a Jew does not apparently offend the Irish family at all, and it exacerbates the existing animosity of the Jew, principally because he has become rich, when he learns it. They are reconciled through the honesty of the Jew and the generosity of the Irishman; the grandchild has nothing whatever to do with it. The only matter common to the two is a quarrel between a Jewish and an Irish father, the marriage of their children, the birth of grandchildren and a reconciliation.

If the defendant took so much from the plaintiff, it may well have been because her amazing success seemed to prove that this was a subject of enduring popularity. Even so, granting that the plaintiff's play was wholly original, and assuming that novelty is not essential to a copyright, there is no monopoly in such a background. Though the plaintiff discovered the vein, she could not keep it to herself; so defined, the theme was too generalized an abstraction from what she wrote. It was only a part of her "ideas."

Nor does she fare better as to her characters. It is indeed scarcely credible that she should not have been aware of those stock figures, the low comedy Jew and Irishman. The defendant has not taken from her more than their prototypes have contained for many decades. If so, obviously so to generalize her copyright, would allow her to cover what was not original with her. But we need not hold this as matter of fact, much as we might be justified. Even though we take it that she devised her figures out of her brain de novo, still the defendant was within its rights.

There are but four characters common to both plays, the lovers and the fathers. The lovers are so faintly indicated as to be no more than stage properties. They are loving and fertile; that is really all that can be said of them, and anyone else is quite within his rights if he puts loving and fertile lovers in a play of his own, wherever he gets the cue. The plaintiff's Jew is quite unlike the defendant's. His obsession is his religion, on which depends such racial animosity as he has. He is affectionate, warm and patriarchal. None of these fit the defendant's Jew, who shows affection for his daughter only once, and who has none but the most superficial interest in his grandchild. He is tricky, ostentatious and vulgar, only by misfortune redeemed into honesty. Both are grotesque, extravagant and quarrelsome; both are fond of display; but these common qualities make up only a small part of their simple pictures, no more than any one might lift if he chose. The Irish fathers are even more unlike; the plaintiff's a mere symbol for religious fanaticism and patriarchal pride, scarcely a character at all. Neither quality appears in the defendant's, for while he goes to get his grandchild, it is rather out of a truculent determination not to be forbidden, than from pride in his progeny. For the rest he is only a grotesque hobbledehoy, used for low comedy of the most conventional sort, which any one might borrow, if he chanced not to know the exemplar.

The defendant argues that the case is controlled by my decision in Fisher v. Dillingham (D.C.) 298 F. 145. Neither my brothers nor I wish to throw doubt upon the doctrine of that case, but it is not applicable here. We assume that the plaintiff's play is altogether original, even to an extent that in fact it is hard to believe. We assume further that, so far as it has been anticipated by earlier plays of which she knew nothing, that fact is immaterial. Still, as we have already said, her copyright did not cover everything that might be drawn from her play; its content went to some extent into the public domain. We have to decide how much, and while we are as aware as any one that the line, wherever it is drawn, will seem arbitrary, that is no excuse for not drawing it; it is a question such as courts must answer in nearly all cases. Whatever may be the difficulties a priori, we have no question on which side of the line this case falls. A comedy based upon conflicts between Irish and Jews, into which the marriage of their children enters, is no more susceptible of copyright than the outline of Romeo and Juliet.

The plaintiff has prepared an elaborate analysis of the two plays, showing a "quadrangle" of the common characters, in which each is represented by the emotions which he discovers. She presents the resulting parallelism as proof of infringement, but the adjectives employed are so general as to be quite useless. Take for example the attribute of "love" ascribed to both Jews. The plaintiff has depicted her father as deeply attached to his son, who is his hope and joy; not so, the defendant, whose father's conduct is throughout not actuated by any affection for his daughter, and who is merely once overcome for the moment by her distress when he has violently dismissed her lover. "Anger" covers emotions aroused by quite different occasions in each case; so do "anxiety," "despondency" and "disgust." It is unnecessary to go through the catalogue for emotions are too much colored by their causes to be a test when used so broadly. This is not the proper approach to a solution; it must be more ingenuous, more like that of a spectator, who would rely upon the complex of his impressions of each character.

We cannot approve the length of the record, which was due chiefly to the use of expert witnesses. Argument is argument whether in the box or at the bar, and its proper place is the last. The testimony of an expert upon such issues, especially his cross-examination, greatly extends the trial and contributes nothing which cannot be better heard after the evidence is all submitted. It ought not to be allowed at all; and while its admission is not a ground for reversal, it cumbers the case and tends to confusion, for the more the court is led into the intricacies of dramatic craftsmanship, the less likely it is to stand upon the firmer, if more naive, ground of its considered impressions upon its own perusal. We hope that in this class of cases such evidence may in the future be entirely excluded, and the case confined to the actual issues; that is, whether the copyrighted work was original, and whether the defendant copied it, so far as the supposed infringement is identical.

The defendant, "the prevailing party," was entitled to a reasonable attorney's fee (section 40 of the Copyright Act [17 U.S.C.A. § 40]).

Decree affirmed.

2. MUSIC

JEWEL MUSIC PUB. CO. v. LEO FEIST, INC.

United States District Court, S.D. New York, 1945.
62 F.Supp. 596, 66 U.S.P.Q. 282.

CONGER, District Judge.

Suit for copyright infringement. Plaintiff complains that defendant by its musical composition "Drummer Boy" has infringed the copyright of plaintiff's musical composition "Carnival in Cotton Town." Defendant denies the infringement.

The words and music of "Carnival in Cotton Town" were written some time prior to December 30, 1936, by Jules Loman and Lou Ricca, who transferred all their right, title and interest in and to said song to the plaintiff who had the song copyrighted under the copyright laws of the United States on or about December 30, 1936.

From that date on plaintiff has been the sole proprietor of all rights, title and interest in and to the copyright in said musical composition.

Defendant's song was written and composed by Roger Edens at Los Angeles, California, in the early part of 1940.

At that time Roger Edens was in the employ of Metro-Goldwyn-Mayer Corporation as an arranger and composer. As originally written this song was to be and was included as a musical number of a picture put out by Metro-Goldwyn-Mayer entitled "Strike up the Band." The leads in this picture were Judy Garland (who sang the song) and Mickey Rooney (who did a drum specialty in connection therewith).

Subsequently and some time during the year 1940, defendant published and had the song "Drummer Boy" copyrighted and defendant is now the owner of said copyright.

Both by deposition and by testimony at the trial, Roger Edens denied that he ever knew the authors of plaintiff's song or that he had ever seen or heard the song, "Carnival in Cotton Town."

Both plaintiff and defendant are music publishers.

Both compositions are of the popular variety.

Plaintiff's song has a verse and a chorus. Defendant's song has only one verse or one chorus. Defendant insists that it has neither verse or chorus; plaintiff insists that it has a chorus only. It seems to me that it does not make any difference what it is called. It is at least the entire composition with which we are concerned. It is only the chorus of plaintiff's song which it is claimed was infringed. This chorus and defendant's composition follow the usual pattern for popular pieces of this type. It is of the A.A.B.A. structure. Each letter represents an eight bar part. The melodic theme as contained in the first A part is repeated in the other A parts. The B part is different and is interposed as a variation by way of contrast to the A parts. The chorus of plaintiff's song has 32 bars of which 24 are A parts and 8 bars of the B variety.

Defendant's composition has 36 bars, the first 32 of which follow the conventional A.A.B.A. structure with a coda (additional ending) of six bars.

Plaintiff's contention is that defendant's composition infringes both the words and music of the chorus of plaintiff's.

As far as the lyrics are concerned, I hold that there has been no infringement. There is nothing in the evidence to indicate that the writer of defendant's song copied the lyrics of "Carnival in Cotton Town" and used them in his song. There is not even sufficient similarity of words to create a suspicion. The real question centers around the music.

Plaintiff's contention is that the A parts of defendant's composition are the infringing parts. There is no claim that the B part of defendant's composition infringes or is even similar to the B part of plaintiff's chorus.

For the purpose of inquiring into the similarity of the pertinent parts of these two songs, it will only be necessary to compare the first A part, in as much as the other A parts are practically identical with the first A.

First, however, I should refer to the over-all similarity.

Both compositions are in the same key—C minor.

Both are written in the same tempo—4/4 fox trot.

There is a similarity in rhythm. When these compositions are played, the similarity is marked and quite apparent, even to one with no particular musical ability.

Briefly I will now compare the first A part of each composition.

Melody

1st bar

The first two notes are not similar. The third and fourth are similar.

2nd bar

The four notes are identical.

3rd bar

Identical with first bar.

4th bar

Identical with second bar.

5th bar

Identical except for a slight difference in syncopation.

6th bar

The first note is different. The second two notes are the same. The last beat and a half is different.

7th and 8th bars

The melodies in both songs return again to C minor, the first notes in both seventh bars and the last of both eighth bars being the same.

As to the actual identity of the first A part (repeated in the others), there is an identity of melodic notes in the 2nd, 4th and 5th bars; the 4th bar being a repetition of the 2nd bar and the 5th contains one note repeated.

Harmony

The harmonic structure in both songs is basically the same. It is a rather common harmony structure. Nothing unusual about it. It is nothing more than one would expect, in as much as the harmony follows the melody.

As I look at the over-all picture, the similarities and identities in the component parts which go to make up the music of a song, and the effect of similarity when the two pieces are played, I have arrived at the conclusion expressed by one of plaintiff's experts (Greenfield): "There is enough similarity throughout to warrant questioning."

With this in mind I have examined the issue of access. This is always most important in these cases. Similarity, even a striking similarity, may be arrived at honestly. It is extremely difficult for one to say that similarity alone spells piracy or theft. This is very well illustrated in Haas v. Leo Feist, Inc., et al., D.C., 234 F. 105, 107. In that case the court decided that there was infringement proved because of (1) a parallelism between the two songs which to the ear of the judge, passed the bounds of mere accident, (2) a real and actually proven opportunity for access.

Judge Hand in writing the opinion stated:

"It is said that such similarities are of constant occurrence in music, and that little inference is permissible."

He then proceeded to state that perhaps he should not take them (the similarities) as enough except for the opportunity proved, the habits of the writer of the infringing song shown in other instances, and the serious question of his credibility.

Plaintiff's song was published in December, 1936. 4,000 professional copies were printed and were distributed to various broadcasting stations, artists, etc.

6,000 copies were printed for sale of which 5,626 were sold.

1,000 orchestrations were printed and 168 sold. 198 band arrangements were sold through a third party.

Plaintiff's song was written to be used in connection with the Cotton Carnival held at Memphis in December, 1938. The testimony is a bit hazy as to just what publicity the song got in connection with that event. There is testimony that the song was put out too late to associate with the Cotton Carnival in 1938, and that the phonograph companies refused to record it.

The song was used on a number of occasions in broadcast performances of the Columbia Broadcasting System and the National Broadcasting Company. Most of this was in 1938. In most instances these broadcasts were country wide. There were electrical transcriptions made for General Motors (Chevrolet) and Coca Cola and these were used in broadcasts on some occasions.

In addition one may conclude from the evidence that shortly after its publication, a copy of plaintiff's song was sent to the music department head of the motion picture studio, in whose employ the writer of defendant's song was, and to whose musical library he resorted frequently in arranging and adapting music for pictures.

This is a general picture of the activity of plaintiff's song. After all it was not a success. Certainly it was not a financial success. Practically all of the pianoforte copies were sold in 1938. In 1939 there were only 11 copies sold.

After 1938 there was no real demand for the song. The president of plaintiff corporation testified that they started to "work" the song in 1938 a little but after that they made no effort to do so.

The burden of proof on this issue of access is upon the plaintiff: I feel that the plaintiff has not met this burden. The proof of actual access falls far short of that which I believe is required. The writer of defendant's song has testified that he has no recollection of ever having heard plaintiff's song and that he never saw it prior to composing "Drummer Boy." There is nothing in plaintiff's evidence to convincingly indicate otherwise. As I said in Allen v. Walt Disney Productions, D.C., 41 F.Supp. 134, 136, to so find "I would again have to indulge in speculation, conjecture and suspicion." Of course, having so found against plaintiff on this question of access, that does not end the matter.

Access may be inferred. For a discussion of this point, see Allen v. Walt Disney Productions, supra. After all this brings us back to the fundamental issue of this case. Is the similarity of the two so great and so convincing that one may say that piracy exists and is found? If the answer is in the affirmative, then of course it necessarily follows that access may be inferred.

We have a situation here which does not merit the conclusion reached by Judge Hand in Fred Fisher, Inc. v. Dillingham, D.C., 298 F. 145, 147. There we find the composition "Dardanella," a most popular number. The infringing song was written by one "who had necessarily known it, as a musician knew it." Further the similarity between the two pieces was in the accompaniment of the chorus or refrain of the infringing song which had in part an absolute identity with the accompaniment of the verse though not the chorus of "Dardanella." The court stated:

". . . Not only is the figure in each piece exactly alike, but it is used in the same way. . . . Further, the defendants have been able to discover in earlier popular music neither this figure, nor even any 'ostinato' accompaniment whatever."

In that case there was no proof of actual access, but it was inferred by reason of the facts which I have set forth above.

The relationship of the two songs here are not in any way comparable with the two songs in the Dardanella case. Plaintiff's song never had any real vogue. There is no reason to infer that the writer of defendant's song ever heard "Carnival in Cotton Town." There is nothing unique about plaintiff's song. There is nothing unusual or out of the ordinary in plaintiff's composition. As a matter of fact there is no particular musical skill displayed in either of these compositions. It seems to me that the two songs here involved are in the category of the two songs involved in Darrell v. Joe Morris Music Co., 2 Cir., 113 F.2d 80.

I quote from that case for the reason that it is most pertinent because of similarity of facts and because the conclusion reached and the reasons therefor coincide with my views here:

"The strength of the plaintiff's case lies in the substantial identity of a sequence of eight notes in his song and theirs; and indeed, that hardly does justice to the similarity between the two, because the sequence reappears in each song so frequently as to constitute the greater part of each. This makes the two, when rendered, so much alike to the ear, that the supposed piracy appears almost inevitable. Nevertheless, we are not convinced that that conclusion is inescapable. The showing of access was not very persuasive. . . . We have already said in Arnstein v. [Edward B.] Marks Music Corporation, 2 Cir., 82 F.2d 275, that such simple, trite themes as these are likely to recur spontaneously. . . . It must be remembered that, while there are an enormous number of possible permutations of the musical notes of the scale, only a few are pleasing; and much fewer still suit the infantile demands of the popular ear. Recurrence is not therefore an inevitable badge of plagiarism."

The above question expresses in better language than I have at my command, just how I feel about the two songs before me.

Similarity or identity must create more than a suspicion of piracy. They must establish piracy with reasonable certainty. The evidence here of similarity and identity has not so convinced me.

Each of these compositions has its own personality. Plaintiff's composition is of the swing type. The words and music are indicative of a happy carnival spirit.

Defendant's song is really a drum specialty. Roger Edens has testified that he was instructed to prepare a composition for Mickey Rooney, so that he could use his drum specialty. The composition of the piece so indicated. In the melodic line 22 bars are a repetition of the same note, to indicate the beat of a drum and the piece is to be played "with steady tempo."

I am unable to arrive at a definite conclusion as to the source of defendant's composition. On the examination before trial, Edens testified that it was hard to state from what source he got his inspiration. He rather intimated it might be from a negro jubilee song.

On the trial, however, he stated his composition was patterned after an old Indian ceremonial dance "Hako."

I was not too favorably impressed by this latter explanation of the source of defendant's song. At any rate it is not material to definitely find just where Edens got his inspiration, as long as it was not from plaintiff's piece. All that one might say is that defendant's composition is written in the minor mode and resembles in character and rhythm a number of the negro jubilee and spiritual type of songs that were played before me during the trial.

I was very much impressed with the similarity between the two songs here involved and an old, and at one time very popular song "Lulu's Back in Town."

Testimony on the part of defendant tended to show that certain parts of this composition were substantially similar to the basic part of plaintiff's composition. When played before me in court the similarity between all three songs was marked and apparent. I mention this not for the purpose of suggesting that this song "Lulu's Back in Town" might have been the source of either plaintiff's or defendant's song, but to indicate how similarity in songs of this type may easily and innocently be arrived at.

Defendant is entitled to a judgment dismissing the complaint and for judgment in its favor to be settled on notice.

3.   VISUAL ARTS

NOVELTY TEXTILE MILLS, INC. v. JOAN FABRICS CORP.

United States Court of Appeals, Second Circuit, 1977.
558 F.2d 1090, 195 U.S.P.Q. 1.

GURFEIN, Circuit Judge:

This is an appeal from an order of the District Court for the Southern District of New York (Werker, D. J.) denying plaintiff's motion for a preliminary injunction against the continued use by defendant of a fabric design which it allegedly copied from plaintiff's fabric design. The complaint charges copyright infringement under 17 U.S.C.A. §§ 101, 112 and 116 and seeks a permanent injunction, impoundment and destruction of the allegedly infringing copies, and damages. Jurisdiction is based on 28 U.S.C.A. § 1338(a).

I

The basic facts as found by the court below are not in dispute. Plaintiff Novelty Textile Mills, Inc. ("Novelty") and defendant Joan Fabrics Corporation ("Joan") both manufacture upholstery fabrics which they sell in competition with each other to furniture manufacturers. Novelty created Style 253 during the latter part of 1975 and copyrighted it. It was first displayed to the trade in January, 1976. The fabric sold well and was delivered to furniture manufacturers in commercial quantities beginning in March, 1976. Several manufacturers exhibited display models of their furniture, upholstered with Style 253 fabric, at a regional furniture trade market held in April, 1976 at High Point, North Carolina. At that time both the sales and design personnel of defendant Joan viewed plaintiff's Style 253 and learned that there was a substantial demand for this type of design, known as "bias" or "argyle" plaid, among its customers.

Joan's management thereafter determined that it too should offer a collection of bias plaid upholstery fabrics. Its designers were instructed to make such a collection and were told "to avoid any infringement of fabrics manufactured by others." Subsequently five bias plaid designs were made by its designers and used in the manufacture of Joan's fabrics.

After the introduction of these Joan fabric designs, the sales of Novelty's Style 253 declined precipitously. The president of Novelty testified that its continuing loss in sales amounted to approximately $11,000 per week. He attributed this loss to the introduction of the Joan designs.

Within two months Novelty instituted this lawsuit and moved for a preliminary injunction. The District Court after an evidentiary hearing, as noted, denied the motion. This appeal followed.

II

In order to prove infringement a plaintiff must show ownership of a valid copyright and copying by the defendant. Novelty's ownership and the validity of its copyright are not disputed for the purpose of this motion. This leaves the issue of whether Joan copied Novelty's design. Since direct evidence of copying is rarely, if ever, available, a plaintiff may prove copying by showing access and "substantial similarity" of the two works. Here Joan not only admits access, but also the actual viewing by its designers of Novelty's Style 253 before its own designs were produced.

The District Court found, however, that there was no substantial similarity because certain differences in the works "would be apparent to a furniture manufacturer, or for that matter to a consumer seriously contemplating purchase of a couch covered with one or another of the fabrics."

"Substantial similarity" is to be determined by the "ordinary observer" test. Judge Learned Hand in defining this test stated there is substantial similarity where "the ordinary observer, unless he set out to detect the disparities, would be disposed to overlook them, and regard their aesthetic appeal as the same." Peter Pan Fabrics, Inc. v. Martin Weiner Corp., 274 F.2d 487, 489 (2d Cir. 1960). More recently this court formulated the test as "whether an average lay observer would recognize the alleged copy as having been appropriated from the copyrighted work." Ideal Toy Corp. v. Fab-Lu Ltd., 360 F. 2d 1021, 1022 (2d Cir. 1966). And, of course, by definition "[t]he copying need not be of every detail so long as the copy is substantially similar to the copyrighted work." Comptone Co. v. Rayex Corp., 251 F.2d 487, 488 (2d Cir. 1958).

We have viewed the fabrics presented in the District Court. While it is true that "[t]he test for infringement of a copyright is of necessity vague", Peter Pan Fabrics, Inc. v. Martin Weiner Corp., supra, 274 F.2d at 489, it is clear to us that Joan's Fleetwood Spice is "substantially similar" to Novelty's Cane 253 and, in fact, to our "lay" eyes, is almost identical.[5] And "[a]s we have before us the same record, and as no part of the decision below turned on credibility, we are in as good a position to determine the question as is the district court." Concord Fabrics, Inc. v. Marcus Bros. Textile Corp., 409 F.2d 1315, 1317 (2d Cir. 1969). We conclude that plaintiff has established a prima facie case of infringement as to Fleetwood Spice.

Plaintiff has also alleged that other Joan Fabrics infringe Style 253. The District Court, after determining that the two above fabrics (which were thought to present plaintiff's best case) were not substantially similar, did not make individual findings with regard to these other fabrics. In light of our determination, we remand for consideration of whether these other fabrics are also substantially similar to Style 253.[6]

The question remains whether Novelty is entitled to a preliminary injunction with respect to Fleetwood Spice or other Joan fabrics which the District Court on remand may find to be substantially similar to Style 253. In Houghton Mifflin Co. v. Stackpole Sons, Inc., 104 F.2d 306, 307 (2d Cir.), cert. denied, 308 U.S. 597, 60 S.Ct. 131, 84 L.Ed. 499 (1939), this court stated that "it is settled in copyright cases that, if the plaintiff makes a prima facie showing of his right, a preliminary injunction should issue." Much later in another fabric

5. As the District Court found, both fabrics use brown and camel or beige on a light-colored background to form a plaid design consisting of intersecting diamonds with an interior dimension of approximately four inches. And in each fabric, one series of diamonds is formed by a stripe which is somewhat broader than the other. When the Joan Fleetwood Spice fabric is placed over a portion of the Novelty fabric, the design, dimensions and colors match-up and the appearance is of one fabric.

6. Appellant has alleged that if Fleetwood Spice infringes Style 253, then at least some of Joan's other fabrics also infringe because they are simply expressions of the Fleetwood design in different colors. Indeed, testimony offered by Joan appears to concede that differences in the appearance of some of the Joan fabrics result essentially from variations in color and texture of yarn, rather than differences in a black and white rendering of the design. However, some of the color variations create such different effects that the ordinary observer might not consider them similar.

There thus arises the issue of whether a fabric infringes a copyrighted design when it employs the black and white outline of a design that is copied from a copyrighted design but expresses that outline in colors so different from those used in the fabric of the copyrighted design that no substantial similarity results. While recognizing that there may be color combinations, beyond the simple use of primary or calico colors, which may themselves be the subject of copyright as a work of art, it is the writer's view that, once a copyrighted design is found to have been copied, mere changes in the color scheme on the copied design would ordinarily not protect the defendant from a claim of infringement. Indeed, no such claim has been made on this appeal, nor has the question been briefed. Moreover, we have found no precedent or commentary on the question.

However, since we are not unanimous on this point nor on the appropriateness of deciding it on this record, we suggest that the District Court take proof of precisely what was granted registration as a work of art to determine whether color was an ingredient of the copyright granted. The District Court will, in the first instance, have to determine the legal implications that flow from the facts found with respect to the fabrics subject to the remand.

design case we stated that "[a]n injunction pending the outcome of trial . . . should issue if plaintiff can show a reasonable probability of prevailing on the merits." Concord Fabrics, Inc. v. Marcus Bros. Textile Corp., supra, 409 F.2d at 1317. And recently Chief Judge (then Judge) Kaufman in Robert Stigwood Group Ltd. v. Sperber, 457 F.2d 50, 55 (2d Cir. 1972), reaffirmed the statement made in American Metropolitan Enterprises of New York, Inc. v. Warner Bros. Records, Inc., 389 F.2d 903, 905 (2d Cir. 1968), that:

> "[a] copyright holder in the ordinary case may be presumed to suffer irreparable harm when his right to the exclusive use of the copyrighted material is invaded."

Here there is not even a need for a presumption of harm because the undisputed evidence shows that after the introduction of Joan's fabrics into the market, Novelty's sales declined by $11,000 a week. Consequently, we think that more than a sufficient showing has been made to require the issuance of a preliminary injunction.

For the foregoing reasons, we reverse the order of the District Court and remand for the issuance of an injunction with respect to Fleetwood Spice and a determination of whether the other Joan fabrics alleged to infringe Style 253 are "substantially similar," and therefore, on the facts of this case, should also be preliminarily enjoined.

Reversed and remanded with instructions.

MANSFIELD, Circuit Judge (concurring and dissenting):

I concur in Judge Gurfein's carefully reasoned opinion, except for its remand of a portion of the case to the district court to determine whether color is an ingredient of the copyright and to dispose of the balance of the infringement claims. In my view the color scheme should be treated as one of the elements of the copyrighted design and, since we are in as good a position as the district court to resolve the infringement issue, we should hold that Novelty's Style 253 is not infringed by any of the alleged infringing fabrics produced by Joan other than its "Fleetwood Spice" and "Sand."

The subject of Novelty's Certificate of Copyright is a textile design consisting of an upholstery fabric woven in a common Argyle or bias plaid, using a combination of brown and camel or beige colors on a light background. When the alleged infringing Joan fabrics were laid alongside Novelty's copyrighted design No. 253, "Cane," at a distance of approximately 20 feet in the court, it was readily apparent to ordinary lay observers, i. e., the members of this panel, that Joan's "Fleetwood Spice" and CK–0028 (entitled "Sand"), which were produced after it had access to Novelty's 253, were substantially similar to 253.

Of course all Argyle or bias plaids are somewhat similar, consisting of diamonds in stripes, which may vary in width, shading, spacing, mesh composition, and color. At a distance of 15 feet or more the similarity between Novelty's 253, on the one hand, and the two infringing Joan plaids, on the other, was substantial, not solely because of the shading, spacing, composition, and juxtaposition of the diamonds and stripes, but principally because of the identical color scheme which lent the same overall effect to the designs. The general impression from a distance is described by Judge Gurfein:

> "When the Joan fabric is placed over a portion of the Novelty fabric, the design, dimensions and *colors* match up and the appearance is of one fabric." (Emphasis supplied).

However, a closer comparison of the fabrics (at a distance of two to five feet) reveals several marked differences, which were noted by Judge Werker. The stripes are of differing widths, compositions and dimensions, which are clearly discernible. One main cross-bar, for instance, consists of strands solidly woven together on Novelty's "Cane" to form a bar ⅞" wide, whereas the bars (or multiple bars) similarly situated on Joan's "Fleetwood Spice" consists of a series of separate strands, each of which except the middle two are totally separated from one another, measuring 1¼" in width. Moreover, when one turns to the other allegedly infringing Joan fabrics, samples of which have been furnished to us by the parties, it will be noted that, quite aside from the differences observed by Judge Werker, the fabrics produced by Joan in other color combinations and with different shading and accent to the lines, mesh and stripes, are not substantially similar to Novelty's 253, even at a distance of 15 feet or more.

The majority express doubt as to whether color or color schemes should constitute part of a copyrighted design and remand the case to the district court for further consideration of that issue after briefing by the parties. I believe this is unnecessary. If color did not constitute an integral element of copyrighted design, we have already gotten off on the wrong foot. As already noted, the similarity of colors between the copyrighted Novelty design and the two Joan designs found to infringe was an influential factor. If the copyright extended only to the 253 design in black and white, we should have limited ourselves to a comparison of the alleged infringing designs with Novelty's 253 in black and white, which in my view would lead us, upon duplicating in black and white the courtroom comparison made by us, to hold that the designs were not substantially similar.

Our courtroom comparison, therefore, implicitly recognizes that where (as here) a design is registered in a particular colorway rather than in black and white, that colorway is part of the copyrighted design. We have previously sanctioned consideration of color as a factor in determining whether there has been infringement of a copyrighted design. See Soptra Fabrics Corp. v. Stafford Knitting Mills, 490 F.2d 1092, 1094 (2d Cir. 1974), and decisions cited therein, including Scarves by Vera v. United Merchants and Manufacturers, 173 F.Supp. 625, 627 (S.D.N.Y.1959). Although we have never ruled as a matter of law on the issue, it seems to me that if color is to be taken into consideration for infringement purposes, it must inevitably be considered as an element of the copyrighted subject matter.

In short, what Novelty copyrighted was its plaid design in a brown, beige and white color combination. In this well-plowed field of Argyle and bias plaids, it obviously did not gain protection against the manufacture of all similar textile plaids, even though some might be produced by persons who had access to its copyrighted design. In my view it gained copyright protection for the overall effect or impression created by the particular combination of lines, space, juxtaposition, shading *and color scheme*. Whether another manufacturer could avoid infringement by changing the color scheme would depend in a particular case on how important the color scheme was in the overall effect or impression of the design. Obviously if the design consisted merely of a simple red square or circle with dots, a change by the copier from red to green would be of great importance. On the other hand, if the design were an intricate or unusual one, as the court noted in *Soptra,* a mere change in color would be insufficient to avoid infringement.

Since I believe the applicable principles are clear and that nothing would be gained by further prolongation of this case, I would rule now that, except for the "Fleetwood Spice" and "Sand" designs, there was no infringement of Novelty's 253 and to that extent affirm the decision of the district court.

J. MUCHA, ALPHONSE MUCHA

135–136 (1969).*

The Paris World Exhibition of 1900 was the pinnacle of the era of Art Nouveau. By then its influence had spread so widely that it was impossible to tell what came directly from Mucha, what was plagiarism and what was simply created in the same spirit. The entrance to the Paris métro at the Place de l'Etoile, designed by Guimard, features the typical Mucha Moorish arch in the shape of an omega, which my father even adapted as his monogram. Yet this does not mean that Guimard, whose Castel Beranger is a show-piece of Art Nouveau architecture, surreptitiously copied Mucha or vice versa. Lalique also used my father's designs; at other times creating in the same spirit, he arrived at very similar results. It is perhaps unique in the history of art that a single artist has so impressed his unmistakable imprint on a style. But since his contribution became public property, it was no longer of importance who was the originator. The supreme master became the style, and the other artists complied with it. Even today we see that the more unanimously some temporary fashion is accepted, the less important its origin becomes. The fashion becomes an expression of its time. Naturally there were obvious plagiarisms.

"My art, if I may call it that, crystallised. It was en vogue. It spread to factories and workshops under the name of 'style Mucha'

* New York: Humanities Press, Inc., 1967.

and at the exhibition a whole lot of objects were removed to prevent infringement of copyright. This was a safeguard for the manufacturers—but the weeding out was done at my expense, because I was the one who had to go to the storerooms to identify fakes, and I got nothing out of it. And there were many fakes—even the main pavilion was not without my ornamentation, figures and flowers. Needless to say, nobody paid any fines over to me; they were collected by the manufacturers and the publishers. But in any case that was not the point. I simply deplored the precious time it cost me."

GROSS v. SELIGMAN

United States Circuit Court of Appeals, Second Circuit, 1914.
212 F. 930.

Appeal from the District Court of the United States for the Southern District of New York.

This cause comes here upon appeal from an order of the District Court, Southern District of New York, enjoining defendant from publishing a photograph. The suit is brought under the provisions of the Copyright Act. One Rochlitz, an artist, posed a model in the nude, and therefrom produced a photograph, which he named the "Grace of Youth." A copyright was obtained therefor; all the artist's rights being sold and assigned to complainants. Two years later the same artist placed the same model in the identical pose, with the single exception that the young woman now wears a smile and holds a cherry stem between her teeth. He took a photograph of this pose, which he called "Cherry Ripe"; this second photograph is published by defendants, and has been enjoined as an infringement of complainant's copyright.

LACOMBE, Circuit Judge (after stating the facts as above). This is not simply the case of taking two separate photographs of the same young woman.

When the Grace of Youth was produced a distinctly artistic conception was formed, and was made permanent as a picture in the very method which the Supreme Court indicated in the Oscar Wilde Case (Burrow-Giles Company v. Sarony, 111 U.S. 53, 4 Sup.Ct. 279, 28 L.Ed. 349) would entitle the person producing such a picture to a copyright to protect it. It was there held that the artist who used the camera to produce his picture was entitled to copyright just as he would have been had he produced it with a brush on canvas. If the copyrighted picture were produced with colors on canvas, and were then copyrighted and sold by the artist, he would infringe the purchaser's rights if thereafter the same artist, using the same model, repainted the same picture with only trivial variations of detail and offered it for sale.

Of course when the first picture has been produced and copyrighted every other artist is entirely free to form his own conception of the Grace of Youth, or anything else, and to avail of the same young woman's services in making it permanent, whether he works with pigments or a camera. If, by chance, the pose, background, light, and shade, etc., of this new picture were strikingly similar, and if, by reason of the circumstance that the same young woman was the prominent feature in both compositions, it might be very difficult to distinguish the new picture from the old one, the new would still not be an infringement of the old because it is in no true sense a *copy* of the old. This is a risk which the original artist takes when he merely produces a likeness of an existing face and figure, instead of supplementing its features by the exercise of his own imagination.

It seems to us, however, that we have no such new photograph of the same model. The identity of the artist and the many close identities of pose, light, and shade, etc., indicate very strongly that the first picture was used to produce the second. Whether the model in the second case was posed, and light and shade, etc., arranged with a copy of the first photograph physically present before the artist's eyes, or whether his mental reproduction of the exact combination he had already once effected was so clear and vivid that he did not need the physical reproduction of it, seems to us immaterial. The one thing, viz., the exercise of artistic talent, which made the first photographic picture a subject of copyright, has been used not to produce another picture, but to duplicate the original.

The case is quite similar to those where indirect copying, through the use of living pictures, was held to be an infringement of copyright.

The eye of an artist or a connoisseur will, no doubt, find differences between these two photographs. The backgrounds are not identical, the model in one case is sedate, in the other smiling; moreover the young woman was two years older when the later photograph was taken, and some slight changes in the contours of her figure are discoverable. But the identities are much greater than the differences, and it seems to us that the artist was careful to introduce only enough differences to argue about, while undertaking to make what would seem to be a copy to the ordinary purchaser who did not have both photographs before him at the same time. In this undertaking we think he succeeded.

The order is affirmed.

NOTES

1. As noted in *Arnstein,* similarities between plaintiff's and defendant's works may be adduced for any of three distinct points. First, because copying rarely involves conduct that will attract the attention of witnesses, it is typically proved by inference rather than directly; evidence of similarities between plaintiff's and defendant's works, taken together with evidence of defendant's access to plaintiff's work, may yield the inference that defendant copied from plaintiff's work. Second, because access, like copying can rarely be

proved directly, evidence of similarities between plaintiff's and defendant's works is also admitted as an inferential substitute for direct proof of access. The third use of similarities is in the determination whether the proved copying invades plaintiff's protected ground.

With respect to similarity's two inferential uses, should a more extensive showing of similarity be required when there is no direct proof of access than when there is? What of the so-called "inverse ratio" rule espoused by at least one federal district court, Morse v. Fields, 127 F.Supp. 63, 66, 104 U.S.P.Q. 54 (S.D.N.Y.1954): "When access is established a lesser degree of similarity is required." The rule was subsequently rejected by Judge Clark in Arc Music Corp. v. Lee, 296 F.2d 186, 187, 131 U.S.P.Q. 338 (2d Cir. 1961): "We fear that counsel with that semantic proclivity natural to our profession have allowed themselves to be seduced by a superficially attractive apothegm which upon examination confuses more than it clarifies. The logical outcome of the claimed principle is obviously that proof of actual access will render a showing of similarities entirely unnecessary." Is it?

2. What assumptions underlie the rules governing proof of copying? Absent direct evidence of copying, expert testimony is allowed because of the technical nature of the question. Just as too many surface similarities might mislead the lay factfinder into concluding that defendant copied plaintiff's subject matter, so strong surface dissimilarities might improperly lead to the opposite conclusion. The expert eye or ear can discern more subtle, structural clues.

What assumptions underlie the rules governing proof of unlawful appropriation? Why do courts in resolving this issue look to the reactions of ordinary readers, listeners or observers? Is it that "the copyright [act], like all statutes, is made for plain people; and that copying which is infringement must be something 'which ordinary observation would cause to be recognized as having been taken from' the work of another"? Dymow v. Bolton, 11 F.2d 690, 692 (2d Cir. 1926). Or do courts more properly weigh this proof as evidence of the extent to which consumers would substitute the accused work for the copyrighted work? To what extent does this inquiry coincide with the inquiry under section 107 into the "effect of the use upon the potential market for or value of the work"?

If the question is the extent that one work substitutes for another, how should courts define "work"? Definition is easy enough when defendant has borrowed all the elements that make up an entire novel, play, painting or musical composition. But what if defendant has copied only a part of a larger work—a few paragraphs or lines of dialogue, a detail of a painting or a few bars of music? Should it make a difference that the fragment is exactly replicated or only paraphrased? Are there any helpful parallels between proofs on appropriation in copyright and proofs on consumer confusion in trademark law?

3.   The presence of common errors in plaintiff's and defendant's work offers virtually irrefutable proof that defendant copied from plaintiff.   Where defendant's map, like plaintiff's, contains sixteen misspellings and locates a river on the wrong side of a main highway, or defendant's "Fighting Yank" doll has the same misplaced right thumbnail as plaintiff's "G.I. Joe," the aberrations are just too extended to be explained as coincidence.   See General Drafting Co. v. Andrews, 37 F.2d 54, 4 U.S.P.Q. 72 (2d Cir. 1930); Hassenfeld Bros., Inc. v. Mego Corp., 150 U.S.P.Q. 786 (S.D.N.Y.1966).   Defendant's only plausible excuse is that the error appeared in a common source, presumably copied by both plaintiff and defendant.

A study of fifty-two cases involving common errors revealed that, of the eight cases in which plaintiff had clearly inserted the error as a trap for the unwary copier, seven cases involved directories and one case involved a catalogue.   Thus, in American Travel & Hotel Directory Co. v. Gehring Pub. Co., 4 F.2d 415 (S.D.N.Y.1925), plaintiff listed several nonexistent hotels in its hotel directory.   The author of the study observed: "My sympathies, however, are with the weary traveler who late at night tries to locate one of the trap hotels."   Taylor, Common Errors as Evidence of Copying, 22 Bull. Copyright Soc'y 444, 448 (1975).   Should the law encourage this use of fictitious information in works that purport to offer facts?

4.   The idea-expression distinction was shaped in the crucible of cases involving literary works.   One of the more troublesome aspects of the distinction is that it seeks to apply identical principles to subject matter that frequently lies far afield of literary works.   Problematic differences exist even within individual arts.   For example, in Franklin Mint Corp. v. National Wildlife Art Exchange, Inc., 575 F.2d 62, 197 U.S.P.Q. 721 (3d Cir. 1978), cert. denied 439 U.S. 880, 99 S.Ct. 217, 58 L.Ed.2d 193, 199 U.S.P.Q. 576, the court observed that "in the world of fine art, the ease with which a copyright may be delineated may depend on the artist's style.   A painter like Monet when dwelling upon impressions created by light on the facade of the Rouen Cathedral is apt to create a work which can make infringement attempts difficult.   On the other hand, an artist who produces a rendition with photograph-like clarity and accuracy may be hard-pressed to prove unlawful copying by another who uses the same subject matter and the same technique.   A copyright in that circumstance may be termed 'weak,' since the expression and the subject matter converge.   In contrast, in the impressionist's work, the lay observer will be able to differentiate more readily between the reality of subject matter and subjective effect of the artist's work." 575 F.2d 62, 65.

In Kepner-Tregoe, Inc. v. Carabio, 203 U.S.P.Q. 124 (E.D.Mich. 1979), the court took unusual care to attempt some relevant distinctions between literary works and instructional materials.   One was that "in teaching, a noticeable style is a hindrance.   Two simple and straightforward explanations of an economic law or principle must bear a close resemblance, so greater similarity must be allowed."   203

U.S.P.Q. 124, 132. Another was that, in a literary work, plot, theme, character and the "total concept and feel of the work," are important. "There is an unlimited variety which may be invented. Authors are not confined. In addition, there is no societal interest in many variants on a single theme or plot, nor is there the likelihood that by extending broad protection, entry to the market for literary works will be foreclosed. But with respect to the useful arts, there is a societal interest in having many offer the art in the marketplace. Our economy functions best under competition. And, if many can present variants on the copyrighted material, we hope that advances in its teaching will result. As a consequence, more similarity between two works of a commercial and useful character is required to find infringement than between two literary works." 203 U.S.P.Q. 124, 131. The court concluded that although plaintiff had a "thin" copyright, defendant had infringed it "in certain minor respects." 203 U.S.P.Q. 124, 132.

Is the *Kepner-Tregoe* approach preferable to, or different from, the rule that when an idea and its expression are inextricably connected, the expression is not protectable? See page 675, above. How would *Kepner-Tregoe* resolve fact work infringement claims? What if the copyrighted work is a scientific paper from which the accused work—a novel—borrows literary elements? See Musto v. Meyer, 434 F.Supp. 32, 196 U.S.P.Q. 820 (S.D.N.Y.1977), aff'd without opinion 598 F.2d 609 (2d Cir.).

5. Although plaintiff must, to prevail, prove that defendant copied his work, he need not prove that the copying was intentional. One who copies an overheard tune or another's copy of a copyrighted work is liable even if he has no knowledge that the work is covered by copyright. The reason for the rule, given in De Acosta v. Brown, 146 F.2d 408, 63 U.S.P.Q. 311 (2d Cir. 1944), cert. denied 325 U.S. 862, 65 S.Ct. 1197, 89 L.Ed. 1983, is that "the protection accorded literary property would be of little value if it did not go against third persons, or if, it might be added, insulation from payment of damages could be secured by a publisher by merely refraining from making inquiry." 146 F.2d 408, 412. Learned Hand dissented in *De Acosta*. "If my brothers are right, a publisher must be prepared to respond in damages to any author who can prove that the publisher has incorporated, however innocently, and at whatever remove, any part of the author's work. If that possibility were to hover over all publication, it would, I believe, be a not negligible depressant upon the dissemination of knowledge." 146 F.2d 408, 413.

The Copyright Act ameliorates the strict liability principle through an adjustment of remedies. Section 504(c)(2) reduces the floor for statutory damages if the "infringer was not aware and had no reason to believe that his or her acts constituted an infringement of copyright," and remits statutory damages entirely in certain circumstances if the infringer believed that its use was fair under the terms of section 107. Do these remedial limitations sufficiently answer Judge Hand's concerns?

Should the rule of strict liability be made to depend upon the innocent infringer's ability to insure against errors and omissions, or to contract for indemnity from the knowing infringer? One form of agreement used in the book publishing trade provides:

> The Author represents and warrants that he has full power to enter into this agreement; that he will use all reasonable care to ensure that the work as submitted is innocent and without matter that is libelous or injurious or otherwise actionable or that will infringe any copyright, proprietary right at common law, or any right of privacy; that if it should be necessary for him to incorporate in the work any material, illustrations, or text that has been published or is the property of others, he will incorporate such material only with the knowledge and consent of the Publisher and will furnish to the Publisher such releases as the Publisher may deem necessary. The Author agrees that he and his legal representatives will indemnify and hold the Publisher harmless from any claim, suit, proceeding, or prosecution, including the reasonable costs of defense (or any resulting liability, loss, expense, or damage), asserted or instituted by reason of publication or sale of the work and arising from the lack of reasonable care or intentional act of the Author. The Author hereby authorizes the Publisher to defend any and all suits and proceedings that may be brought against it arising out of the publication of the work; provided, however, that the Author will not be liable for any amount which the Publisher has agreed to pay in settlement of any such suit or proceeding unless the Author shall consent to such settlement.

What changes to this language would you advise Author to propose? How would you advise Publisher?

To what extent does the rule of strict liability undercut the traditional rationale for the copyright notice requirement?

6. As new technologies emerge for the dissemination of copyrighted works so, obviously, have the occasions for infringement. A less obvious, but far more significant aspect of the new information technologies is their tendency to push accountability for infringement away from centralized, easily policed institutions and toward users who are more diffuse and harder to reach. In a world in which everyone with access to a photocopy machine is his own publisher, and in which everyone with access to a home videotape recorder is his own movie exhibitor, copyright owners cannot hope to recover all of their damages and lost profits from centralized corporate publishers and television networks.

Should copyright law impose liability on these dispersed copyists? On those institutions that, by reason of size or position, can contract with, or otherwise govern and spread costs among, these users? What would the consequence be of holding libraries or school systems liable for all of the copying that is done on their photocopy machines? Of holding the manufacturers of video recorders liable for the home copying of televised programs and motion pictures?

The two main doctrinal vehicles for imposing liability in these circumstances are contributory infringement and vicarious liability. Should these doctrines, if employed, be tempered by the modification of other copyright rules, such as the rule of strict liability?

Contributory Infringement. "One who, with knowledge of the infringing activity, induces, causes or materially contributes to the infringing conduct of another, may be held liable as a 'contributory' infringer." Gershwin Pub. Corp. v. Columbia Artists Management, Inc., 443 F.2d 1159, 1162, 170 U.S.P.Q. 182 (2d Cir. 1971). In *Gershwin* the court gave as an example, the decision in Screen Gems-Columbia Music, Inc., v. Mark-Fi Records, Inc., 256 F.Supp. 399, 150 U. S.P.Q. 523 (S.D.N.Y.1966) where "the district court held that an advertising agency which placed non-infringing advertisements for the sale of infringing records, a radio station which broadcast such advertisements and a packaging agent which shipped the infringing records, could each be held liable as a 'contributory' infringer if it were shown to have had knowledge, or reason to know, of the infringing nature of the records. Their potential liability was predicated upon 'the common law doctrine that one who knowingly participates or furthers a tortious act is jointly and severally liable with the prime tort-feasor. . . .' " 256 F.Supp. 399, 403.

Vicarious Liability. "When the right and ability to supervise coalesce with an obvious and direct financial interest in the exploitation of copyrighted materials—even in the absence of actual knowledge that the copyright monopoly is being impaired, the purposes of the copyright law may be best effectuated by the imposition of liability upon the beneficiary of that exploitation." Shapiro, Bernstein & Co. v. H. L. Green Co., 316 F.2d 304, 307, 137 U.S.P.Q. 275 (2d Cir. 1963).

Defendant in *Green*, the H. L. Green Co., operated a chain of retail stores. In twenty-three of these stores, defendant Jalen operated a phonograph record concession and sold, without H. L. Green's knowledge, unlicensed recordings of plaintiffs' copyrighted compositions. The extent of Green's supervisory power and direct financial interest were obvious from the face of its license agreement with Jalen: "Jalen and its employees were to 'abide by, observe and obey all rules and regulations promulgated from time to time by H. L. Green Company, Inc. . . .' Green, in its 'unreviewable discretion', had the authority to discharge any employee believed to be conducting himself improperly. Jalen, in turn, agreed to save Green harmless from any claims arising in connection with the conduct of the phonograph record concession. Significantly, the licenses provided that Green was to receive a percentage—in some cases 10%, in others 12%—of Jalen's gross receipts from the sale of records, as its full compensation as licensor." 316 F.2d 304, 306.

From this, the court concluded that "the imposition of *vicarious* liability in the case before us cannot be deemed unduly harsh or unfair. Green has the power to police carefully the conduct of its concessionaire Jalen; our judgment will simply encourage it to do so, thus placing responsibility where it can and should be effectively exercised. Green's burden will not be unlike that quite commonly imposed upon publishers, printers, and vendors of copyrighted materials." 316 F.2d 304, 308 (Emphasis in original).

D. RIGHTS BEYOND COPYRIGHT: MORAL RIGHT

SARRAUTE, CURRENT THEORY ON THE MORAL RIGHT OF AUTHORS AND ARTISTS UNDER FRENCH LAW, 16 AM.J. COMP.L. 465–467, 480–481 (1968).* In French law the concept of literary and artistic rights involves two elements.

The first is analogous to the English-speaking countries' copyright. It is a property right, and consists of a temporary monopoly over the exploitation of protected works. It assures the author of the exclusive right to control the reproduction and the performance or exhibition of his creation.

The second element is the "moral" right. It includes non-property attributes of an intellectual and moral character which give legal expression to the intimate bond which exists between a literary or artistic work and its author's personality; it is intended to protect his personality as well as his work. . . .

Until this moment of disengagement, the work is an expression of the artist's personality and remains strictly his own. No one can claim any right to it whatsoever. It is a rough draft, a design which the artist may modify or destroy at will. He alone can determine from the moment when his plan has been realized, when his work is completed, when he feels that he can, without injuring his reputation, reveal it to the public and surrender his rights over it to a third party.

Once this decision is made, the work is separated from the artist; it falls into commerce, becomes the subject of transactions. It is published, exhibited, performed. But the artist still retains certain rights over the work. In some cases he retains the right to suppress it if he is no longer satisfied with it; in all instances he retains the right to demand that he be recognized as its author, that his name be associated with it, and, above all, that the work be neither abridged nor distorted.

Thus the moral right is generally composed of four aspects:

(1) The right of disclosure (*divulgation*);

Then, after the work has been made public and the author's rights to it have been transferred:

(2) The right to withdraw or disavow;

(3) The right of paternity—i. e., the right to have one's name and authorship recognized;

(4) The right of integrity of the work of art. . . .

As we have seen, Article 6 of the law of March 11, 1957 recognizes the author's right to insist that the integrity of his work be respected. This right has always been acknowledged by the courts. It does not arise until, after completion, the work has been put on the market by the author, has been sold, or has been made the subject of contracts of publication or performance. From that time on the author has the right to insist that its integrity must not be violated by measures which could alter or distort it.

This principle is unquestioned and its practical application presents few theoretical difficulties. A case in point is the recent decision of the Court of Cassation on July 6, 1965, which affirmed a decision rendered by the Paris Court of Appeals of May 30, 1962. Both Courts found in favor of the painter Bernard Buffet, who maintained that the refrigerator he had decorated was an indivisible artistic unit, and opposed the sale of any of the elements of the ornamentation separately from the others.

An extremely delicate problem does, however, arise in one situation. This is the problem of protecting the integrity of a work when the author has authorized its adaptation to a different medium, as in the case of the adaptation of an opera or a ballet for the theatre or the cinema. The problem here is to ascertain to what extent the right of the author of the original work can insist on its integrity, when this claim conflicts with creative freedom of the adapter, as the author of a work which purports to be equally original. How may a conflict between two equally valid moral rights be resolved?

TREECE, AMERICAN LAW ANALOGUES OF THE AUTHOR'S "MORAL RIGHT"

16 Am.J.Comp.L. 487, 494–496, 499–500 (1968).*

M. Sarraute has described the moral right in French law as serving authors and artists not only during the period of creation but after a work is made public. The moral right confers, he states, a paternity right—the right to have authorship acknowledged; a right to the integrity of the work—the right that a work not be mutilated; and a right of withdrawal—the right to withdraw from the public, upon equitable terms, a work that has been made public.

American law has, relatively speaking, a callous disregard for the paternity rights of creative persons. Section 26 of the Copyright Act provides that "the word 'author' shall include an employer in the case of works made for hire." Under a "work made for hire" arrangement the person whose mind generates the creative process can be regarded as a mere employee and his employer, perhaps a corporation, can be regarded as the "author." The "work for hire" arrangement severs completely the relation between the creator and ownership of his work. An employee who creates for hire can scarcely be concerned with an author's right in American law to have his authorship acknowledged, for by Congressional ipse dixit the author label has been shifted beyond his grasp.

An author or artist who retains his identity by avoiding the employee pitfall still finds that under American law he can compel one who publishes his work to communicate his authorship only if he can point to a clause in a contract binding the publisher in question to identify the author when exploiting the work. In Vargas v. Esquire, Inc., the artist Vargas produced a number of drawings for Esquire magazine, transferred to Esquire all of his rights in the drawings and then failed in an attempt to compel Esquire to attribute authorship to him when his drawings were published. The court stated that the artist had no basis for bringing suit, having failed to extract from Esquire an enforceable promise to attribute authorship.

Granz v. Harris shows that a contract between creator and distributor is the repository of all that American law recognizes in the way of paternity rights. Granz sold defendant's assignor three record masters. The assignor agreed to use at all times the phrase "presented by Norman Granz" in distributing records cut from the masters. The court, in the course of an opinion ruling upon other points, stated that ordinarily the defendant could present records made from the Norman Granz masters without informing the public of Norman Granz's connection with the product, but stated that in this case to omit a reference to Norman Granz would breach the contract. . . .

Whether American law protects an author whose work has been garbled is, of course, another question. M. Sarraute assures us that in France, under the moral right doctrine, an author or artist can command respect for the integrity of his work. The right to the integrity of the work picks up where the right of disclosure leaves off, and assures the creator that his work will not be altered or destroyed.

Otto Preminger produced the most celebrated attempt yet to persuade an American court to save an artistic work from mutilation. Preminger tried to enjoin Columbia Pictures from distributing his picture "Anatomy of a Murder" to television stations under agreements permitting or calling for cuts in the picture and permitting or calling for interruption of the picture for commercial messages.

Preminger and Carlyle Productions, as owners of all rights in the picture, could in licensing television rights by contract confer on the licensee the right to edit, cut, and interrupt the picture. Similarly, they could elicit from the licensee a promise not to edit, cut or interrupt the picture for commercial messages. In the actual case Preminger gave Columbia Pictures television rights in a contract that did not speak of cuts or interruptions, although Columbia apparently consented not to cut the film while, of course, insisting on the right to interrupt the telecast for commercial messages. The court ruled that Preminger, having failed to cover clearly the issue of cuts and interruptions in the contract, must have given to Columbia Pictures whatever the custom of the industry regarded as comprised by the phrase "television rights." In the context of custom, said the court, one who receives television rights, unfettered, receives the right to interrupt for commercials and to make minor cuts to accommodate time segment requirements.

In dictum the court suggested that if Preminger's 161 minute feature were cut to 53 minutes or even to 100 minutes such cuts would amount to mutilation, and Preminger would be entitled to injunctive relief. Judge Rabin, dissenting, buttressed the majority's dictum on cuts by stating that a producer has a common law right to have the picture shown as he produced it—especially where a contract requires that the producer be identified by name in television screenings. Judge Rabin also held the view that unlimited interruptions for commercials might conceivably result in a presentation of an uncut version of the film that would offend against a producer's common law right to an "unmutilated screening." . . .

The third element in M. Sarraute's recital of the post-publication protection available under the French droit moral is the right of withdrawal or renunciation. It confers upon an author who is party to a publishing contract a power to withdraw a work, upon compensating the publisher, if a work has been overcome by history or by a developing artistic style.

M. Sarraute says the power of withdrawal is neither well-established nor very useful in France; it is safe to say that it is not established at all in the United States. In America an author or artist cannot take back a published work, even on a trademark theory. Gene Autry, the western star, argued unsuccessfully to the Ninth Circuit that an exhibition on television of his old films depicting him in outmoded garb mouthing trite phrases injured his present career. The court refused to allow Autry's claim, saying it involved a risk inherent in the performer's art. Samuel Clemens, imaginative even when acting through attorneys, attempted to enjoin the publication of a collection of his works written under the Mark Twain pen name by asserting that he had an exclusive right, analogous to a trademark right, to use the nom de plume. Clemens lost. The court ruled that anyone can publish public domain material and designate its author, whether the author uses a true name or a nom de plume.

GILLIAM v. AMERICAN BROADCASTING COMPANIES, INC.

United States Court of Appeals, Second Circuit, 1976.
538 F.2d 14, 192 U.S.P.Q. 1.

LUMBARD, Circuit Judge.

Plaintiffs, a group of British writers and performers known as "Monty Python," appeal from a denial by Judge Lasker in the Southern District of a preliminary injunction to restrain the American Broadcasting Company (ABC) from broadcasting edited versions of three separate programs originally written and performed by Monty Python for broadcast by the British Broadcasting Corporation (BBC). We agree with Judge Lasker that the appellants have demonstrated that the excising done for ABC impairs the integrity of the original work. We further find that the countervailing injuries that Judge Lasker found might have accrued to ABC as a result of an injunction at a prior date no longer exist. We therefore direct the issuance of a preliminary injunction by the district court.

Since its formation in 1969, the Monty Python group has gained popularity primarily through its thirty-minute television programs created for BBC as part of a comedy series entitled "Monty Python's Flying Circus." In accordance with an agreement between Monty Python and BBC, the group writes and delivers to BBC scripts for use in the television series. This scriptwriters' agreement recites in great detail the procedure to be followed when any alterations are to be made in the script prior to recording of the program.[2] The essence of this section of the agreement is that, while BBC retains final

---

2. The Agreement provides:

V. When script alterations are necessary it is the intention of the BBC to make every effort to inform and to reach agreement with the Writer. Whenever practicable any necessary alterations (other than minor alterations) shall be made by the Writer. Nevertheless the BBC shall at all times have the right to make (a) minor alterations and (b) such other alterations as in its opinion are necessary in order to avoid involving the BBC in legal action or bringing the BBC into disrepute. Any decision under (b) shall be made at a level not below that of Head of Department. It is however agreed that after a script has been accepted by the BBC alterations will not be made by the BBC under (b) above unless (i) the Writer, if available when the BBC requires the alterations to be made, has been asked to agree to them but is not willing to do so and (ii) the Writer has had, if he so requests and if the BBC agrees that time permits if rehearsals and recording are to proceed as planned, an opportunity to be represented by the Writers' Guild of Great Britain (or if he is not a member of the Guild by his agent) at a meeting with the BBC to be held within at most 48 hours of the request (excluding weekends). If in such circumstances there is no agreement about the alterations then the final decision shall rest with the BBC. Apart from the right to make alterations under (a) and (b) above the BBC shall not without the consent of the Writer or his agent (which consent shall not be unreasonably withheld) make any structural alterations as opposed to minor alterations to the script, provided that such consent shall not be necessary in any case where the Writer is for any reason not immediately available for consultation at the time which in the BBC's opinion is the deadline from the production point of view for such alterations to be made if rehearsals and recording are to proceed as planned.

authority to make changes, appellants or their representatives exercise optimum control over the scripts consistent with BBC's authority and only minor changes may be made without prior consultation with the writers. Nothing in the scriptwriters' agreement entitles BBC to alter a program once it has been recorded. The agreement further provides that, subject to the terms therein, the group retains all rights in the script.

Under the agreement, BBC may license the transmission of recordings of the television programs in any overseas territory. The series has been broadcast in this country primarily on non-commercial public broadcasting television stations, although several of the programs have been broadcast on commercial stations in Texas and Nevada. In each instance, the thirty-minute programs have been broadcast as originally recorded and broadcast in England in their entirety and without commercial interruption.

In October 1973, Time-Life Films acquired the right to distribute in the United States certain BBC television programs, including the Monty Python series. Time-Life was permitted to edit the programs only "for insertion of commercials, applicable censorship or governmental . . . rules and regulations, and National Association of Broadcasters and time segment requirements." No similar clause was included in the scriptwriters' agreement between appellants and BBC. Prior to this time, ABC had sought to acquire the right to broadcast excerpts from various Monty Python programs in the spring of 1975, but the group rejected the proposal for such a disjoined format. Thereafter, in July 1975, ABC agreed with Time-Life to broadcast two ninety-minute specials each comprising three thirty-minute Monty Python programs that had not previously been shown in this country.

Correspondence between representatives of BBC and Monty Python reveals that these parties assumed that ABC would broadcast each of the Monty Python programs "in its entirety." On September 5, 1975, however, the group's British representative inquired of BBC how ABC planned to show the programs in their entirety if approximately 24 minutes of each 90 minute program were to be devoted to commercials. BBC replied on September 12, "we can only reassure you that ABC have [sic] decided to run the programmes 'back to back,' and that there is a firm undertaking not to segment them."

ABC broadcast the first of the specials on October 3, 1975. Appellants did not see a tape of the program until late November and were allegedly "appalled" at the discontinuity and "mutilation" that had resulted from the editing done by Time-Life for ABC. Twenty-four minutes of the original 90 minutes of recording had been omitted. Some of the editing had been done in order to make time for commercials; other material had been edited, according to ABC, because the original programs contained offensive or obscene matter.

In early December, Monty Python learned that ABC planned to broadcast the second special on December 26, 1975. The parties be-

gan negotiations concerning editing of that program and a delay of
the broadcast until Monty Python could view it. These negotiations
were futile, however, and on December 15 the group filed this action
to enjoin the broadcast and for damages. Following an evidentiary
hearing, Judge Lasker found that "the plaintiffs have established an
impairment of the integrity of their work" which "caused the film or
program . . . to lose its iconoclastic verve." According to Judge
Lasker, "the damage that has been caused to the plaintiffs is irreparable by its nature." Nevertheless, the judge denied the motion for
the preliminary injunction on the grounds that it was unclear who
owned the copyright in the programs produced by BBC from the
scripts written by Monty Python; that there was a question of
whether Time-Life and BBC were indispensable parties to the litigation; that ABC would suffer significant financial loss if it were enjoined a week before the scheduled broadcast; and that Monty Python had displayed a "somewhat disturbing casualness" in their pur-
suance of the matter.

Judge Lasker granted Monty Python's request for more limited
relief by requiring ABC to broadcast a disclaimer during the December 26 special to the effect that the group dissociated itself from the
program because of the editing. A panel of this court, however,
granted a stay of that order until this appeal could be heard and permitted ABC to broadcast, at the beginning of the special, only the
legend that the program had been edited by ABC. We heard argument on April 13 and, at that time, enjoined ABC from any further
broadcast of edited Monty Python programs pending the decision of
the court.

I

In determining the availability of injunctive relief at this early
stage of the proceedings, Judge Lasker properly considered the harm
that would inure to the plaintiffs if the injunction were denied, the
harm that defendant would suffer if the injunction were granted, and
the likelihood that plaintiffs would ultimately succeed on the merits.
We direct the issuance of a preliminary injunction because we find
that all these factors weigh in favor of appellants.

There is nothing clearly erroneous in Judge Lasker's conclusion
that any injury suffered by appellants as a result of the broadcast of
edited versions of their programs was irreparable by its nature.
ABC presented the appellants with their first opportunity for broadcast to a nationwide network audience in this country. If ABC adversely misrepresented the quality of Monty Python's work, it is likely that many members of the audience, many of whom, by defendant's admission, were previously unfamiliar with appellants, would
not become loyal followers of Monty Python productions. The subsequent injury to appellants' theatrical reputation would imperil their
ability to attract the large audience necessary to the success of their
venture. Such an injury to professional reputation cannot be measured in monetary terms or recompensed by other relief.

In contrast to the harm that Monty Python would suffer by a denial of the preliminary injunction, Judge Lasker found that ABC's relationship with its affiliates would be impaired by a grant of an injunction within a week of the scheduled December 26 broadcast. The court also found that ABC and its affiliates had advertised the program and had included it in listings of forthcoming television programs that were distributed to the public. Thus a last minute cancellation of the December 26 program, Judge Lasker concluded, would injure defendant financially and in its reputation with the public and its advertisers.

However valid these considerations may have been when the issue before the court was whether a preliminary injunction should immediately precede the broadcast, any injury to ABC is presently more speculative. No rebroadcast of the edited specials has been scheduled and no advertising costs have been incurred for the immediate future. Thus there is no danger that defendant's relations with affiliates or the public will suffer irreparably if subsequent broadcasts of the programs are enjoined pending a disposition of the issues.

We then reach the question whether there is a likelihood that appellants will succeed on the merits. In concluding that there is a likelihood of infringement here, we rely especially on the fact that the editing was substantial, i. e., approximately 27 percent of the original program was omitted, and the editing contravened contractual provisions that limited the right to edit Monty Python material. It should be emphasized that our discussion of these matters refers only to such facts as have been developed upon the hearing for a preliminary injunction. Modified or contrary findings may become appropriate after a plenary trial.

Judge Lasker denied the preliminary injunction in part because he was unsure of the ownership of the copyright in the recorded program. Appellants first contend that the question of ownership is irrelevant because the recorded program was merely a derivative work taken from the script in which they hold the uncontested copyright. Thus, even if BBC owned the copyright in the recorded program, its use of that work would be limited by the license granted to BBC by Monty Python for use of the underlying script. We agree.

Section 7 of the Copyright Law, 17 U.S.C.A. § 7, provides in part that "adaptations, arrangements, dramatizations . . . or other versions of . . . copyrighted works when produced with the consent of the proprietor of the copyright in such works . . . shall be regarded as new works subject to copyright. . . ." Manifestly, the recorded program falls into this category as a dramatization of the script, and thus the program was itself entitled to copyright protection. However, section 7 limits the copyright protection of the derivative work, as works adapted from previously existing scripts have become known, to the novel additions made to the underlying work, and the derivative work does not affect the "force or validity" of the copyright in the matter from which it is derived.

Thus, any ownership by BBC of the copyright in the recorded program would not affect the scope or ownership of the copyright in the underlying script.

Since the copyright in the underlying script survives intact despite the incorporation of that work into a derivative work, one who uses the script, even with the permission of the proprietor of the derivative work, may infringe the underlying copyright. See Davis v. E.I. duPont deNemours & Co., 240 F.Supp. 612, 145 U.S.P.Q. 258 (S. D.N.Y.1965) (defendants held to have infringed when they obtained permission to use a screenplay in preparing a television script but did not obtain permission of the author of the play upon which the screenplay was based).

If the proprietor of the derivative work is licensed by the proprietor of the copyright in the underlying work to vend or distribute the derivative work to third parties, those parties will, of course, suffer no liability for their use of the underlying work consistent with the license to the proprietor of the derivative work. Obviously, it was just this type of arrangement that was contemplated in this instance. The scriptwriters' agreement between Monty Python and BBC specifically permitted the latter to license the transmission of the recordings made by BBC to distributors such as Time-Life for broadcast in overseas territories.

One who obtains permission to use a copyrighted script in the production of a derivative work, however, may not exceed the specific purpose for which permission was granted. Most of the decisions that have reached this conclusion have dealt with the improper extension of the underlying work into media or time, i. e., duration of the license, not covered by the grant of permission to the derivative work proprietor. Appellants herein do not claim that the broadcast by ABC violated media or time restrictions contained in the license of the script to BBC. Rather, they claim that revisions in the script, and ultimately in the program, could be made only after consultation with Monty Python, and that ABC's broadcast of a program edited after recording and without consultation with Monty Python exceeded the scope of any license that BBC was entitled to grant.

The rationale for finding infringement when a licensee exceeds time or media restrictions on his license—the need to allow the proprietor of the underlying copyright to control the method in which his work is presented to the public—applies equally to the situation in which a licensee makes an unauthorized use of the underlying work by publishing it in a truncated version. Whether intended to allow greater economic exploitation of the work, as in the media and time cases, or to ensure that the copyright proprietor retains a veto power over revisions desired for the derivative work, the ability of the copyright holder to control his work remains paramount in our copyright law. We find, therefore, that unauthorized editing of the underlying work, if proven, would constitute an infringement of the copyright in that work similar to any other use of a work that exceeded the license granted by the proprietor of the copyright.

If the broadcast of an edited version of the Monty Python program infringed the group's copyright in the script, ABC may obtain no solace from the fact that editing was permitted in the agreements between BBC and Time-Life or Time-Life and ABC. BBC was not entitled to make unilateral changes in the script and was not specifically empowered to alter the recordings once made; Monty Python, moreover, had reserved to itself any rights not granted to BBC. Since a grantor may not convey greater rights than it owns, BBC's permission to allow Time-Life, and hence ABC, to edit, appears to have been a nullity.

ABC answers appellants' infringement argument with a series of contentions, none of which seems meritorious at this stage of the litigation. The network asserts that Monty Python's British representative, Jill Foster, knew that ABC planned to exclude much of the original BBC program in the October 3 broadcast. ABC thus contends that by not previously objecting to this procedure, Monty Python ratified BBC's authority to license others to edit the underlying script.

Although the case of Ilyin v. Avon Publications, Inc., 144 F.Supp. 368, 373, 110 U.S.P.Q. 356, 359 (S.D.N.Y.1956), may be broadly read for the proposition that a holder of a derivative copyright may obtain rights in the underlying work through ratification, the conduct necessary to that conclusion has yet to be demonstrated in this case. It is undisputed that appellants did not have actual notice of the cuts in the October 3 broadcast until late November. Even if they are chargeable with the knowledge of their British representative, it is not clear that she had prior notice of the cuts or ratified the omissions, nor did Judge Lasker make any finding on the question. While Foster, on September 5, did question how ABC was to broadcast the entire program if it was going to interpose 24 minutes of commercials, she received assurances from BBC that the programs would not be "segmented." The fact that she knew precisely the length of material that would have to be omitted to allow for commercials does not prove that she ratified the deletions. This is especially true in light of previous assurances that the program would contain the original shows in their entirety. On the present record, it cannot be said that there was any ratification of BBC's grant of editing rights. ABC, of course, is entitled to attempt to prove otherwise during the trial on the merits.

ABC next argues that under the "joint work" theory adopted in Shapiro, Bernstein & Co. v. Jerry Vogel Music, Inc., 221 F.2d 569, 105 U.S.P.Q. 178 (2d Cir. 1955), the script produced by Monty Python and the program recorded by BBC are symbiotic elements of a single production. Therefore, according to ABC, each contributor possesses an undivided ownership of all copyrightable elements in the final work and BBC could thus have licensed use of the script, including editing, written by appellants.

The joint work theory as extended in Shapiro has been criticized as inequitable unless "at the time of creation by the first author, the second author's contribution [is envisaged] as an integrated part of a single work," and the first author intends that the final product be a joint work. Furthermore, this court appears to have receded from a broad application of the joint work doctrine where the contract which leads to collaboration between authors indicates that one will retain a superior interest. In the present case, the screenwriters' agreement between Monty Python and BBC provides that the group is to retain all rights in the script not granted in the agreement and that at some future point the group may license the scripts for use on television to parties other than BBC. These provisions suggest that the parties did not consider themselves joint authors of a single work. This matter is subject to further exploration at the trial, but in the present state of the record, it presents no bar to issuance of a preliminary injunction.

Aside from the question of who owns the relevant copyrights, ABC asserts that the contracts between appellants and BBC permit editing of the programs for commercial television in the United States. ABC argues that the scriptwriters' agreement allows appellants the right to participate in revisions of the script only prior to the recording of the programs, and thus infers that BBC had unrestricted authority to revise after that point. This argument, however, proves too much. A reading of the contract seems to indicate that Monty Python obtained control over editing the script only to ensure control over the program recorded from that script. Since the scriptwriters' agreement explicitly retains for the group all rights not granted by the contract, omission of any terms concerning alterations in the program after recording must be read as reserving to appellants exclusive authority for such revisions.

Finally, ABC contends that appellants must have expected that deletions would be made in the recordings to conform them for use on commercial television in the United States. ABC argues that licensing in the United States implicitly grants a license to insert commercials in a program and to remove offensive or obscene material prior to broadcast. According to the network, appellants should have anticipated that most of the excised material contained scatological references inappropriate for American television and that these scenes would be replaced with commercials, which presumably are more palatable to the American public.

The proof adduced up to this point, however, provides no basis for finding any implied consent to edit. Prior to the ABC broadcasts, Monty Python programs had been broadcast on a regular basis by both commercial and public television stations in this country without interruption or deletion. Indeed, there is no evidence of any prior broadcast of edited Monty Python material in the United States. These facts, combined with the persistent requests for assurances by the group and its representatives that the programs would be shown intact belie the argument that the group knew or should have known that deletions and commercial interruptions were inevitable.

Several of the deletions made for ABC, such as elimination of the words "hell" and "damn," seem inexplicable given today's standard television fare. If, however, ABC honestly determined that the programs were obscene in substantial part, it could have decided not to broadcast the specials at all, or it could have attempted to reconcile its differences with appellants. The network could not, however, free from a claim of infringement, broadcast in a substantially altered form a program incorporating the script over which the group had retained control.

Our resolution of these technical arguments serves to reinforce our initial inclination that the copyright law should be used to recognize the important role of the artist in our society and the need to encourage production and dissemination of artistic works by providing adequate legal protection for one who submits his work to the public. We therefore conclude that there is a substantial likelihood that, after a full trial, appellants will succeed in proving infringement of their copyright by ABC's broadcast of edited versions of Monty Python programs. In reaching this conclusion, however, we need not accept appellants' assertion that any editing whatsoever would constitute infringement. Courts have recognized that licensees are entitled to some small degree of latitude in arranging the licensed work for presentation to the public in a manner consistent with the licensee's style or standards. That privilege, however, does not extend to the degree of editing that occurred here especially in light of contractual provisions that limited the right to edit Monty Python material.

II

It also seems likely that appellants will succeed on the theory that, regardless of the right ABC had to broadcast an edited program, the cuts made constituted an actionable mutilation of Monty Python's work. This cause of action, which seeks redress for deformation of an artist's work, finds its roots in the continental concept of droit moral, or moral right, which may generally be summarized as including the right of the artist to have his work attributed to him in the form in which he created it.

American copyright law, as presently written, does not recognize moral rights or provide a cause of action for their violation, since the law seeks to vindicate the economic, rather than the personal, rights of authors. Nevertheless, the economic incentive for artistic and intellectual creation that serves as the foundation for American copyright law, cannot be reconciled with the inability of artists to obtain relief for mutilation or misrepresentation of their work to the public on which the artists are financially dependent. Thus courts have long granted relief for misrepresentation of an artist's work by relying on theories outside the statutory law of copyright, such as contract law, Granz v. Harris, 198 F.2d 585 (2d Cir. 1952) (substantial cutting of original work constitutes misrepresentation), or the tort of unfair competition, Prouty v. National Broadcasting Co., 26 F.Supp. 265, 40 U.S.P.Q. 331 (D.C.Mass.1939). Although such decisions are clothed in terms of proprietary right in one's creation, they also properly vindicate the author's personal right to prevent the presentation of his work to the public in a distorted form. See Gardella v. Log Cabin Products Co., 89 F.2d 891, 895–96, 34 U.S.P.Q. 145, 148–150 (2d Cir. 1937); Roeder, The Doctrine of Moral Right, 53 Harv.L.Rev. 554, 568 (1940).

Here, the appellants claim that the editing done for ABC mutilated the original work and that consequently the broadcast of those programs as the creation of Monty Python violated the Lanham Act § 43(a), 15 U.S.C.A. § 1125(a). This statute, the federal counterpart to state unfair competition laws, has been invoked to prevent misrepresentations that may injure plaintiff's business or personal reputation, even where no registered trademark is concerned. It is sufficient to violate the Act that a representation of a product, although technically true, creates a false impression of the product's origin. See Rich v. RCA Corp., 390 F.Supp. 530, 185 U.S.P.Q. 508 (S.D.N.Y. 1975) (recent picture of plaintiff on cover of album containing songs recorded in distant past held to be a false representation that the songs were new).

These cases cannot be distinguished from the situation in which a television network broadcasts a program properly designated as having been written and performed by a group, but which has been edited, without the writer's consent, into a form that departs substantially from the original work. "To deform his work is to present him to the public as the creator of a work not his own, and thus makes him subject to criticism for work he has not done." Roeder, supra, at 569. In such a case, it is the writer or performer, rather than the network, who suffers the consequences of the mutilation, for the public will have only the final product by which to evaluate the work. Thus, an allegation that a defendant has presented to the public a "garbled," distorted version of plaintiff's work seeks to redress the very rights sought to be protected by the Lanham Act, 15 U.S.C.A. § 1125(a), and should be recognized as stating a cause of action under that statute. See Autry v. Republic Productions, Inc., 213 F.2d 667, 101 U.S.P.Q. 478 (9th Cir. 1954); Jaeger v. American Intn'l Pictures, Inc., 330 F.Supp. 274, 169 U.S.P.Q. 668 (S.D.N.Y.1971), which suggests the violation of such a right if mutilation could be proven.

During the hearing on the preliminary injunction, Judge Lasker viewed the edited version of the Monty Python program broadcast on December 26 and the original, unedited version. After hearing argument of this appeal, this panel also viewed and compared the two versions. We find that the truncated version at times omitted the climax of the skits to which appellants' rare brand of humor was leading and at other times deleted essential elements in the schematic development of a story line.[12]   We therefore agree with Judge Lasker's conclusion that the edited version broadcast by ABC impaired the integrity of appellants' work and represented to the public as the product of appellants what was actually a mere caricature of their talents. We believe that a valid cause of action for such distortion exists and that therefore a preliminary injunction may issue to prevent repetition of the broadcast prior to final determination of the issues.[13]

III

We do not share Judge Lasker's concern about the procedures by which the appellants have pursued this action.   The district court indicated agreement with ABC that appellants were guilty of laches in not requesting a preliminary injunction until 11 days prior to the broadcast.   Our discussion above, however, suggests that the group did not know and had no reason to believe until late November that editing would take place.   Several letters between BBC and Monty Python's representative indicate that appellants believed that the programs would be shown in their entirety.   Furthermore, the group did act to prevent offensive editing of the second program immediately after viewing the tape of the first edited program.   Thus we find no undue delay in the group's failure to institute this action until they were sufficiently advised regarding the facts necessary to support the action.   In any event, ABC has not demonstrated how it was prejudiced by any delay.

Finally, Judge Lasker denied a preliminary injunction because Monty Python had failed to join BBC and Time-Life as indispensable parties.   We do not believe that either is an indispensable party. ABC argues that joinder of both was required because it acted in good faith pursuant to its contractual rights with Time-Life in broadcasting edited versions of the programs, and Time-Life, in turn, relied

12.   A single example will illustrate the extent of distortion engendered by the editing.   In one skit, an upper class English family is engaged in a discussion of the tonal quality of certain words as "woody" or "tinny." The father soon begins to suggest certain words with sexual connotations as either "woody" or "tinny," whereupon the mother fetches a bucket of water and pours it over his head.   The skit continues from this point.   The ABC edit eliminates this middle sequence so that the father is comfortably dressed at one moment and, in the next moment, is shown in a soaken condition without any explanation for the change in his appearance.

13.   Judge Gurfein's concurring opinion suggests that since the gravamen of a complaint under the Lanham Act is that the origin of goods has been falsely described, a legend disclaiming Monty Python's approval of the edited version would preclude violation of that Act.   We are doubtful that a few words could erase the indelible impression that is made by a television broadcast, especially since the viewer has no means of comparing the truncated version with the complete work in order to determine for himself the talents of plaintiffs. Furthermore, a disclaimer such as the one originally suggested by Judge Lasker in the exigencies of an impending broadcast last December, would go unnoticed by viewers who tuned into the broadcast a few minutes after it began.

We therefore conclude that Judge Gurfein's proposal that the district court could find some form of disclaimer would be sufficient might not provide appropriate relief.

upon its contract with BBC. Furthermore, ABC argues, BBC must be joined since it owns the copyright in the recorded programs.

Even if BBC owns a copyright relevant to determination of the issues in this case, the formalistic rule that once required all owners of a copyright to be parties to an action for its infringement has given way to equitable considerations. In this case, the equities to be considered under Fed.R.Civ.P. 19(a) strongly favor appellants. Monty Python is relying solely on its copyright in the script and on its rights as an author. No claim is being made that Monty Python has rights derived from the copyright held by another. One of the parties is an English corporation, and any action that appellants, a group of English writers and performers, might have against that potential defendant would be better considered under English law in an English court.

Complete relief for the alleged infringement and mutilation complained of may be accorded between Monty Python and ABC, which alone broadcast the programs in dispute. If ABC is ultimately found liable to appellants, a permanent injunction against future broadcasts and a damage award would satisfy all of appellants' claims. ABC's assertion that failure to join BBC and Time-Life may leave it subject to inconsistent verdicts in a later action against its licensors may be resolved through the process of impleader, which ABC has thus far avoided despite a suggestion from the district court to use that procedure. Finally, neither of the parties considered by ABC to be indispensable has claimed any interest in the subject matter of this litigation. See Fed.R.Civ.P. 19(a)(2).

For these reasons we direct that the district court issue the preliminary injunction sought by the appellants.

GURFEIN, Circuit Judge, concurring.

I concur in my brother Lumbard's scholarly opinion, but I wish to comment on the application of Section 43(a) of the Lanham Act, 15 U.S.C.A. § 1125(a).

I believe that this is the first case in which a federal appellate court has held that there may be a violation of Section 43(a) of the Lanham Act with respect to a common-law copyright. The Lanham Act is a trademark statute, not a copyright statute. Nevertheless, we must recognize that the language of Section 43(a) is broad. It speaks of the affixation or use of false designations of origin or false descriptions or representations, but proscribes such use "in connection with any goods or services." It is easy enough to incorporate trade names as well as trademarks into Section 43(a) and the statute specifically applies to common law trademarks, as well as registered trademarks. Lanham Act § 45, 15 U.S.C.A. § 1127.

In the present case, we are holding that the deletion of portions of the recorded tape constitutes a breach of contract, as well as an infringement of a common-law copyright of the original work. There is literally no need to discuss whether plaintiffs also have a claim for relief under the Lanham Act or for unfair competition under New York law. I agree with Judge Lumbard, however, that it may be an exercise of judicial economy to express our view on the Lanham Act claim, and I do not dissent therefrom. I simply wish to leave it open for the District Court to fashion the remedy.

The Copyright Act provides no recognition of the so-called droit moral, or moral rights of authors. Nor are such rights recognized in the field of copyright law in the United States. If a distortion or truncation in connection with a use constitutes an infringement of copyright, there is no need for an additional cause of action beyond copyright infringement. An obligation to mention the name of the author carries the implied duty, however, as a matter of contract, not to make such changes in the work as would render the credit line a false attribution of authorship.

So far as the Lanham Act is concerned, it is not a substitute for droit moral which authors in Europe enjoy. If the licensee may, by contract, distort the recorded work, the Lanham Act does not come into play. If the licensee has no such right by contract, there will be a violation in breach of contract. The Lanham Act can hardly apply literally when the credit line correctly states the work to be that of the plaintiffs which, indeed it is, so far as it goes. The vice complained of is that the truncated version is not what the plaintiffs wrote. But the Lanham Act does not deal with artistic integrity. It only goes to misdescription of origin and the like.

The misdescription of origin can be dealt with, as Judge Lasker did below, by devising an appropriate legend to indicate that the plaintiffs had not approved the editing of the ABC version. With such a legend, there is no conceivable violation of the Lanham Act. If plaintiffs complain that their artistic integrity is still compromised by the distorted version, their claim does not lie under the Lanham Act, which does not protect the copyrighted work itself but protects only against the misdescription or mislabelling.

So long as it is made clear that the ABC version is not approved by the Monty Python group, there is no misdescription of origin. So far as the content of the broadcast itself is concerned, that is not within the proscription of the Lanham Act when there is no misdescription of the authorship.

I add this brief explanation because I do not believe that the Lanham Act claim necessarily requires the drastic remedy of permanent injunction. That form of ultimate relief must be found in some other fountainhead of equity jurisprudence.

NOTES

1. Does *Gilliam* suggest that United States copyright law offers a more commodious shelter for moral right than was previously thought? Was the court effectively saying that the right to make a truncated or otherwise edited version inheres in the right to make derivative works, today secured by section 106(2)? To what extent

must this right yield to the freedom of parody sanctioned by section 107?

Compare *Gilliam's* analysis with the concern for moral right reflected in section 115(a)(2), and in H.R. 288, 96th Cong. 1st Sess. (Jan. 15, 1979), which would have added a new subsection (d) to section 113 providing that "independently of the author's copyright in a pictorial, graphic, or sculptural work, the author or the author's legal representative shall have the right, during the life of the author and fifty years after the author's death, to claim authorship of such work and to object to any distortion, mutilation, or other alteration thereof, and to enforce any other limitation recorded in the Copyright Office that would prevent prejudice to the author's honor or reputation."

2. To what extent has state law protection of moral rights been preempted under section 301 of the Copyright Act? While the objects of state law in protecting an author's moral rights may differ from the economic objects of copyright, the state law may nonetheless extend an "equivalent right" over the "subject matter of copyright" and thus be preempted under section 301. Would a state law permitting authors to recall their copyrighted works conflict with section 109? What of state enforcement of contractual limitations against a transferee from the author or artist? A distant transferee? A noncontracting third party? See page 213 to 232 above.

3. Moral right doctrine is considered generally in Diamond, Legal Protection for the "Moral Rights" of Authors and Other Creators, 68 Trademark Rep. 244 (1978); Merryman, The Refrigerator of Bernard Buffet, 27 Hastings L.J. 1023 (1976); Roeder, The Doctrine of Moral Right: A Study of the Law of Artists, Authors and Creators, 53 Harv.L.Rev. 554 (1940); Strauss, The Moral Right of the Author, 4 Am.J. of Comp.L. 506 (1955); Katz, The Doctrine of Moral Right and American Copyright Law—A Proposal, 24 S.Calif.L.Rev. 375 (1951). G. Michaelides-Nouaros, Le Droit Moral de l'Auteur (1935) is the authoritative work.

Intersections between moral right and copyright are explored in Note, An Author's Artistic Reputation Under the Copyright Act of 1976, 92 Harv.L.Rev. 1490 (1979) and Note, Moral Rights and 'the Compulsory License for Phonorecords, 46 Brooklyn L.Rev. 67 (1979). *Gilliam* is noted in 125 U.Pa.L.Rev. 611 (1977).

An economic counterpart to the doctrine of moral right is closely appraised in Price, Government Policy and Economic Security for the Artist: The Case of The Droit de Suite, 77 Yale L.J. 1333 (1968). See also, Note, Artists' Resale Royalties Legislation: Ohio House Bill 808 and a Proposed Alternative, 9 U.Toledo L.Rev. 366 (1978); Note, A Proposal for National Uniform Art-Proceeds Legislation, 53 Indiana L.J. 129 (1977).

Part Four

INTELLECTUAL PROPERTIES IN
THE MARKETPLACE

―――

I. ANTITRUST

―――

A. PATENTS

WOOD, PATENTS, ANTITRUST AND PRIMA
FACIE ATTITUDES

50 Va.L.Rev. 571, 573–76 (1964).*

Judicial attitudes toward the patent-antitrust issue may, for convenience of review, be divided arbitrarily into three generic periods. During the early part of this century the response of the courts to the efforts by patent owners to safeguard their own manufacturing and marketing opportunities by imposing limitations on use by others was favorable. Limitations were generously sustained on the theory that the patentee, in selectively waiving any portion of his exclusive rights, could do so on such terms as he chose to prescribe. Illustrative of such judicial paternalism toward patent exploitation was Henry v. A. B. Dick Co., [224 U.S. 1 (1912)] an infringement action in which the Supreme Court sustained a restriction in connection with the sale of patented mimeograph machines whereby they could be used only with supplies made by the patentee. This decision was overruled five years later in Motion Picture Patents Co. v. Universal Film Manufacturing Co., [243 U.S. 502 (1917)] in which the Court noted that since A. B. Dick Congress had enacted section 3 of the Clayton Act "as if in response to that decision." However, the Court's narrow holding was that the patent law conferred no power upon the patentee to limit the use of a patented article in such fashion, and it did not reach any antitrust questions. The stage was thus set for the clarification of the Court's position which appeared almost a decade later in United States v. General Electric Co. [272 U.S. 476 (1926)]. In that case, Mr. Chief Justice Taft, speaking for a unanimous Court, approved license limitations "normally and reasonably adapted to secure the pecuniary reward for the patentee's monopoly," and consequently upheld a patent license which required, among other things, that the licensee sell the licensed product at a price stipulated by the licensor. The opinion applied a rule of reason, which was expressed in the following terms:

> One of the valuable elements of the exclusive right of a patentee is to acquire profit by the price at which the article is sold. The higher the price, the greater the profit, unless it is prohibitory. When the patentee licenses another to make and vend, and retains the right to continue to make and vend on his own account, the price at which his licensee will sell will necessarily affect the price at which he can sell his own patented goods. It would seem entirely reasonable that he should say to the licensee, "Yes, you may make and sell articles under my patent, but not so as to destroy the profit that I wish to obtain by making them and selling them myself."

During this same period it was also accepted that a license provision which limited the use of a patent to a certain field or within a specified territory or restricted the production of the patented product by the licensee could be imposed because the benefits secured thereby to the patentee were "reasonably within the reward which the patentee by the grant of the patent is entitled to secure." Thus, for example, in General Talking Pictures Corp. v. Western Electric Co., [305 U.S. 124 (1938)] the Supreme Court upheld patent licenses which limited the licensee's manufacture and sale of vacuum tube amplifiers to the noncommercial field.

A second phase in the patent-antitrust relationship was entered in the late thirties with the boom in antitrust enforcement, which held as a part of its conceptual core that the patent system was a major obstacle to effective enforcement of the Sherman Act. It was at this time that the Temporary National Economic Committee inaugurated hearings focused on abusive or illegal patent practices in some industries, and a few years later, the Truman and Kilgore Committees commenced investigations of international cartels and patent practices as they affected national defense.

There can be no doubt that license limitations had been used in some instances as a cloak of legitimacy to cover concerted price fixing and other restrictive arrangements intended to insulate an industry from the rigors of competition. Witness, for example, the *Gypsum* and *New Wrinkle* cases, decided during this period. In *Gypsum*, [United States v. U.S. Gypsum Co., 333 U.S. 364 (1948)] patent licenses setting minimum resale prices had been granted to the principal manufacturers of gypsum board. There was evidence that the licensees had undertaken to encourage others to accept similar licenses. The Government broadly charged that the licensing agreements were part of a conspiracy to fix prices on both patented and unpatented board, to curtail production of unpatented board, and to impose other restraints on competition. The Supreme Court invalidated the agreements primarily on the ground that "price fixing licenses made in knowing concert" violated the Sherman Act. In *New Wrinkle*, [United States v. New Wrinkle Inc., 342 U.S. 371 (1952)] the

Court held that an arrangement whereby patent holders pooled their patents in a holding company which was empowered to issue patent licenses with minimum price provisions to be operative when twelve of the producers of wrinkle finishes subscribed to the minimum price came within the purview of section 1 of the Sherman Act.

The great surge of antitrust prosecutions involving patents also reached into section 2 of the Sherman Act. The *Hartford-Empire* case [Hartford-Empire Co. v. United States, 323 U.S. 386 (1945)], decided in 1945, is a classic. There competing glass manufacturers had, over a period of time, brought their patents for glass-making machinery together in a pool under the control of Hartford-Empire, a patent holding company. The Government's charge that Hartford-Empire had used the combined strength of the patents to exclude new entrants and to control the supply and prices of glassware was found to be true and this conduct was held a violation of section 2.

It is difficult to quarrel with the Supreme Court's disposition of specific cases decided during this period, but the sweep of the Court's language in some opinions helped feed the fires of continuous conflict between patent practices and antitrust. Looking at what the Court said rather than concentrating on what the Court did on the basis of the facts before it, one might have concluded that antitrust was most surely anti-patent. Moreover, at times the Court seemed on the threshold of yielding to the unfavorable patent climate and condemning license limitations as per se improper.

HEYMAN, PATENT LICENSING AND THE ANTITRUST LAWS—A REAPPRAISAL AT THE CLOSE OF THE DECADE

14 Antitrust Bull. 537–541, 543, 551 (1969).*

The close of the decade would seem an appropriate time to attempt an assessment of the state of compatibility or conflict between the patent system and the antitrust laws in respect of patent licensing. It would be very pleasant if one could only announce that the courts have offered us a clear and concise statement of the areas of compatibility and conflict. Unfortunately such is not the case, and further, the scene is cloudier today than ever and filled with warnings of further conflict.

The right given to a patentee is one to exclude others, for a limited period, from making, using or selling his invention. Yet, the value of such invention to the general public will only be realized by use of such invention by the patentee or by his permitting others to acquire the right to use the invention by purchase of, or license under, the patent. It is upon such sale or licensing and the attaching of ancillary restrictive conditions thereto that potential incompatibility or conflict between the antitrust laws and the patent system arises. It is at this point that one must determine whether the agreement of sale or license and the conduct of the patentee and his purchaser, or licensees, in respect thereof violate the antitrust laws or give rise to patent misuse.

It is unquestioned that the dissemination of technical information and innovation through the patent system and the sale and licensing of patented inventions, can and does promote competition and is to that extent clearly compatible with the antitrust laws. It has been suggested that the legality of the acquisition of patent rights by license or sale should be determined solely under the general law governing legality of contracts including the antitrust laws. Certainly in the '60's, this has been the approach of the courts and it has been developing in this fashion for some substantial period. The attitude of the courts with respect to a variety of ancillary conditions or restrictions attaching to and arising out of patent licensing and acquisition has changed from one of approbation to that of a critical view of all such ancillary conditions or restrictions with the courts requiring that such conditions or restrictions be demonstrated not to inhibit competition in violation of the antitrust laws. . . .

The attitude of the government in testing the propriety of licensing practices and provisions has been stated to be:

"First is the particular provision justifiable as necessary to the patentee's exploitation of his lawful monopoly? Second, are less restrictive alternatives which are more likely to foster competition available to the patentee? Where the answer to the first question is no and to the second yes, we will consider bringing a case challenging the restriction involved."

With such attitudes in mind we will review the status of (I) "tying," "exclusive dealing," and "package licensing" arrangements; (II) interchange of patent rights by cross-licensing, patent "pools" and grantbacks; and (III) the applicability of Section 7 of the Clayton Act and the Robinson-Patman Act to licensing or acquisition of patents.

I

A. *"Tying" Arrangements.* The so-called "tying" arrangement is one in which the licensor of a patent requires that the licensee, as condition for the grant of the license, either purchase or otherwise deal or not deal with specific property of the patentee or others which is not the subject of the patent grant in question and is prohibited by Section 1 of the Sherman Act and Section 3 of the Clayton Act. In United States v. Loew's Inc., [371 U.S. 38 (1962)] the Court found there to be virtual per se illegality arising from a "tying" arrangement where the tying product was patented or copyrighted. The Court noted that tying agreements serve hardly any purpose beyond suppression of competition, forcing buyers into giving up the purchase of substitutes for the tied product and destroying free access of competing suppliers of the tied product to the consuming market. The Court reaffirmed its finding in Northern Pacific Railway Co. v. United States [356 U.S. 1 (1958)] that tying arrangements are unreasonable whenever a party has sufficient economic power with respect to the tying product to appreciably restrain free competition in the market for the tied product where a substantial amount of interstate commerce is affected. The Court found that "[The] requisite economic power is presumed when the tying product is patented or copyrighted. . . ." but stopped short of a finding of absolute per se illegality where the tying product is patented or copyrighted, noting: "There may be rare circumstances in which the doctrine we have enunciated under § 1 of the Sherman Act prohibiting tying arrangements involving patented or copyrighted tying product is inapplicable." However, the Court stated that it would be difficult to conceive of such a case. A very few cases have carved out extremely limited instances where "tying" arrangements involving patented products may not be considered per se illegal.

In Susser v. Carvel Corporation, [332 F.2d 505 (2d Cir. 1964)] the Court, with a strong dissent by Judge Lumbard, did not find that the *Loew's* case had established a rule of per se illegality where the tying product was patented, and the majority limited the holding in *Loew's* to its facts, i. e., block-booking of films. It was persuaded in large part by the fact that Carvel's market dominance was only 1% in the area under consideration and the alleged need to maintain the goodwill of the trademark involved. . . .

It appears that the risk involved in introducing any appearance of a "tying" arrangement into a license agreement far outweighs any conceivable benefit that might be derived therefrom, and that only in very unusual instances will the "business justification" or "single product" tests be of value to avoid the virtual per se illegality of "tying" arrangements.

B. *"Exclusive Dealing" Arrangements.* This practice involves restrictions on the licensee in the form of a prohibition against dealing in equipment or products that compete with the patented device. In Zenith Radio Corp. v. Hazeltine Research, Inc., [395 U.S. 100 (1969)] the Supreme Court made clear that such restrictions inherent in exclusive dealing arrangements are a misuse of the patent and stated:

> "Among other restrictions upon him, he may not condition the right to use his patent on the licensee's agreement to purchase, use, or sell, or not to purchase, use, or sell, another article of commerce not within the scope of his patent monopoly."

In Berlenbach v. Anderson and Thompson Ski Co., [329 F.2d 782 (9th Cir. 1964)] the Court found the mere existence of an exclusive dealing arrangement to be a misuse of the patent which would disable a patentee from enforcing its license agreement. The Court did make clear that in order to establish that such an arrangement was a violation of Section 3 of the Clayton Act, it would be necessary to meet the test of a substantial lessening of competition. . . .

C. *"Package Licensing" Arrangements.* This practice among others, involving the licensor's conditioning the license of one patent upon the licensee's agreeing to take a license under other of licensor's patents was condemned in Ethyl Gasoline Corp. v. United States, [309 U.S. 436 (1940)]. Though it is clear that one can voluntarily take a license under a number of patents, a patent misuse will be found where one compels his licensee to take a license under a number of patents. Such compulsory package licensing was held to be a misuse in American Securit Co. v. Shatterproof Glass Corp. [268 F.2d 769 (3d Cir. 1959)].

In Hazeltine Research, Inc. v. Zenith Radio Corp., [388 F.2d 25 (7th Cir. 1967)] the Court, while noting with approval the licensor's variable royalty schedule which was contingent upon the number of patents licensed, found Hazeltine's conduct in repeatedly offering the full package of patents to Zenith to be economically coercive. The pricing of the patents in the license was such as to coerce licensee into taking the full package.

There is undoubtedly a very close relationship between package licensing cases and tying agreements. The tied products are patents themselves, and compulsory package licensing of patents certainly falls within the prohibition of the block-booking cases such as United States v. Loew's Inc. . . .

II

Interchange of Patent Rights by Cross-Licensing,
Patent "Pools" and Grant-Backs

Restrictive cross-licensing intended for its anticompetitive effect, particularly where coupled with other restrictive conditions, as to pricing or production limitations, is a violation of the antitrust laws. Further, the development of patent "pools" via various cross-licensing arrangements throughout an industry with the intent of such pooling arrangements to exclude competition, will not be countenanced. In Zenith Radio Corp. v. Hazeltine Research, Inc., the Court found that the effect of certain pooling of patents was intended to restrict or prevent Zenith from entering certain foreign markets.

In United States v. Singer Mfg. Co., [374 U.S. 174 (1963)] cross-licensing agreements between American, Italian and Swiss sewing machine manufacturers designed to obtain and enforce certain United States patents pursuant to a scheme to divide world markets and suppress foreign competition in the United States was found to be a per se violation of Sections 1 and 2 of the Sherman Act.

It seems clear that the cross-licensing of patents in and of itself is not a misuse of patent rights. What is condemned are agreements between owners of patents to limit cross-licenses to themselves and not to license others. Clearly the "pooling" of patents and cross-licensing which are open equally to the public on the same terms, do not fall within the interdiction of the antitrust laws or the doctrine of patent misuse.

The acquisition of patent rights by virtue of a grant-back arrangement has been the subject of critical comment. Mr. McLaren has stated:

> "For example, we contemplate challenging under Section 1 of the Sherman Act patent licenses which require an assignment grant-back of all improvement patents. It is our view that the right to a non-exclusive license back on improvements may be a legitimate provision in the licensing of a basic patent but that a grant-back requirement tends unduly to extend the patent monopoly and to stifle research and development efforts on the part of licensees, contrary to the public interest."

Since the use of grant-back arrangements to illegally dominate and control an industry are certainly a violation of the antitrust laws, Mr. McLaren is not addressing himself to such a situation. There is no question as to the impropriety of such activities. Rather, his attack is upon exclusive grant-back provisions in and of themselves as a potential instrument for stifling competition. In attempting to establish exclusive grant-back provisions without any other factors involved as a per se patent misuse, Mr. McLaren will have to overcome Transparent-Wrap Machine Corp. v. Stokes & Smith Co. [329 U.S. 637 (1946)].

While Mr. McLaren would appear to have a strong position with respect to an exclusive grant-back which extends for the life of the licensed patent, his position would not seem to be as strong where the exclusive grant-back is for a limited period of years. It would be hoped that when the courts take up his challenge they will set forth guidelines which will delineate the metes and bounds of proper use of grant-back provisions.

III

A. The Applicability of Section 7 of the Clayton Act to the Acquisition of Patent Rights by Purchase or License

A corporation may by acquisition of patents either through its own patented developments or by purchasing or licensing under patents of others place itself in a position where it secures patent control in an industry. When a corporation reaches a dominant position in an industry either by virtue of its control of certain patent rights or its dominant marketing and manufacturing position, what is the effect of Section 7 upon future acquisition of patent rights by that corporation? The unanswered question for the next decade is the extent to which Section 7 of the Clayton Act will be used in connection with the acquisition of patent rights by purchase or license in such an instance. Mr. Turner has suggested that the significant reach of the antitrust laws in the future with respect to patent licensing will almost certainly be under this Section.

Section 7 provides that ". . . no corporation . . . shall acquire the whole or any part of the assets of another corporation . . . where . . . the effect of such acquisition may be substantially to lessen competition or to tend to create a monopoly." The threshold question is whether a patent can be considered an "asset" within the terms of this statute and whether a patent license may also be considered an "asset." Mr. Turner has indicated that he believes that both the patent and an exclusive license under a patent are assets within the meaning of Section 7 of the Clayton Act.

In United States v. Columbia Pictures Corp., [189 F.Supp. 153 (S.D.N.Y.1960)] the Court held that a licensee under a non-assignable exclusive fourteen-year license for television use of movie films, acquired assets as defined by Section 7. The Court stated:

> "As used here, the words 'acquire' and 'assets' are not terms of art or technical legal language. In the context of this statute, they are generic, imprecise terms encompassing a broad spectrum of transactions whereby the acquiring person may accomplish the acquisition by means of purchase, assignment, lease, license, or otherwise. The test is pragmatic. The final answer is not in the dictionary.

> The statute imposes no specific method of acquisition. It is primarily concerned with the end result of a transfer of a sufficient part of the bundle of legal rights and privileges from the transferring person to the acquiring person to give the transfer economic significance and the proscribed adverse 'effect.'

> The broad sweep to be given to the term 'acquire' is also suggested by the circumstance that the following words are unrestricted, i. e., 'the whole or any part of the assets.' Nothing could be more unqualified than the words 'any part.' Those words likewise must be given a liberal interpretation.

> Consistent with the broadly-drawn language is the word 'assets.' It is not a word of art, nor is it given a built-in definition by statute. As used in this statute, and depending upon the factual context, 'assets' may mean anything of value."

In United States v. Lever Brothers Company, [216 F.Supp. 887 (S.D.N.Y.1963)] the Court held that:

> "It appears clear, however, that a trademark may be a very valuable asset of a company; patents may be valuable assets of a company; . . . ."

Certainly under these cases, patents, trademarks and copyrights are assets within the ambit of Section 7 and under the reasoning of the Court in the *Columbia Pictures* case, licenses, even non-exclusive licenses of patents could be considered assets. Certainly, depending upon who acquires the non-exclusive license, such as where one of the acquiring parties has a dominant position in a line of commerce, such an acquisition of a non-exclusive license could substantially lessen competition in violation of Section 7.

It would seem clear that the acquisition of a patent from a private inventor would not come within the ambit of Section 7 and yet, a small research corporation whose stock in trade is the development of new products or processes and obtaining patents thereon, might be effectively precluded from obtaining its just reward for development of these patented inventions by virtue of Section 7. It would seem a frequent occurrence that certain inventions will be of interest only to certain corporations having a dominant position in a field and who because of the capital investment needed in a particular area would be the only party desirous of obtaining a license under a given patent. Thus, small corporate patent owners not having the capital to enter a given field would not be able to exploit their patents by licensing the dominant party in a given field. The effect of such a situation would be an undesirable limitation on the dissemination of technical information, leaving the patent owner with the right only to exclude others from making, using or selling.

It has been contended that a non-exclusive license may avoid the effect of Section 7 since a non-exclusive license is not a transfer of patent rights but is merely a promise not to sue. The language of the Court in the *Columbia Pictures* case is contrary to this position and it would seem clear that the right to practice under a patent is in fact an asset of the corporation, and it would be extremely difficult to justify escaping the provision of Section 7 merely because the license in question was non-exclusive.

Certainly it would seem clear that the "failing company" doctrine and other theories that have been devised to justify an acquisition under Section 7 would apply to permit a company dominant in a field to acquire a license where, to prevent such an acquisition, would leave the patent owner unable to market or in other ways exploit the invention because of the great capital costs involved. However, it would be necessary to demonstrate that there was no other available market for the patent rights other than the company in question, in order to avoid the ambit of Section 7.

<h2 style="text-align:center">SELECTED BIBLIOGRAPHY</h2>

General Views. Bowman, Patent and Antitrust Law: A Legal and Economic Appraisal (1973); Nordhaus & Jurow, Patent-Antitrust Law (1961); Report of the Attorney General's National Committee To Study the Antitrust Laws, c. 5 (1955); Wood, Patents and Antitrust Law (1942); McGee, Patent Exploitation: Some Economic and Legal Problems, 9 J.L. & Econ. 135 (1966); Bowes, Patent Law Reform and the Expansion of Provisions Related to Licensing, 8 Loyola U.L.J. 279 (1977); Adelman & Jaress, Patent-Antitrust Law: A New Theory, 17 Wayne L.Rev. 1 (1971); Van Cise, Antitrust Laws and Patents, 52 J.P.O.S. 776 (1970); McCarthy, A Patent Licensing Policy for Minimizing Antitrust and Misuse Risks, 46 J.P.O.S. 547 (1964); Turner, The Patent System and Competitive Policy, 44 N.Y. U.L.Rev. 450 (1969); Symposium, Patents, Know-How and Antitrust, 28 U.Pitt.L.Rev. 145 (1966).

Specialized Topics. Adelman & Juenger, Patent-Antitrust: Patent Dynamics and Field of Use Licensing, 50 N.Y.U.L.Rev. 273

(1975); Comment, The Validity of Grant-Back Clauses in Patent Licensing Agreements, 42 U.Chi.L.Rev. 733 (1975); Goller, Competing, Complementary and Blocking Patents: Their Role in Determining Antitrust Violations in the Areas of Cross-Licensing, Patent Pooling and Package Licensing, 50 J.P.O.S. 723 (1968); Corbett, Licensing and Tie-In Sales: How Far Can the Seller Go? 9 Antitrust Bull. 701 (1964); Murchison, Patent Acquisitions and the Antitrust Laws, 45 Tex.L.Rev. 663 (1967); Gibbons, Field Restrictions in Patent Transactions: Economic Discrimination and Restraint of Competition, 66 Colum.L.Rev. 423 (1966); Wheeler, A Reexamination of Antitrust Law and Exclusive Territorial Grants by Patentees, 119 U.Pa.L.Rev. 642 (1971); Note, Regulation of Patent License Royalty Rates Under the Antitrust Laws, 65 Mich.L.Rev. 1631 (1967); Furth, Price Restrictive Patent Licenses Under the Sherman Act, 71 Harv.L.Rev. 815 (1958); Compulsory Licensing of Patents by the Federal Trade Commission, 59 Nw.L.Rev. 543 (1964).

B. COPYRIGHTS

NOTE, THE MISUSE DEFENSE IN COPYRIGHT ACTIONS

37 N.Y.U.L.Rev. 916–917, 920–926 (1962).*

In 1909, when the concept of an author's exclusive right to his work was first translated into legislation, the fear was voiced that such a monopoly would conflict with the prohibitions of the antitrust laws. Now more than half a century later, with revision of the copyright grant under consideration, the interplay between that monopoly and the antimonopoly statutes still poses significant questions. A particularly troublesome problem for the copyright holder arises when his own antitrust violation is used as a defense to his claim of copyright infringement or his action for breach of contract involving copyrighted material. What begins as a simple tort or contract action may be transformed by the defendant's plea of misuse of copyright into a hearing on the antitrust issue. If the defendant succeeds on this issue, the plaintiff may find that he has lost his copyright grant.

The defense of misuse of copyright is in fact three defenses, each meriting separate consideration. First, there is the claim that the plaintiff has used his grant to gain exclusive rights beyond those which the Copyright Act has given him. This defense obviously is based upon a limitation inherent in the grant itself. It is available to the defendant in both legal and equitable actions upon a showing that the plaintiff has extended his legally created monopoly beyond the bounds of the Copyright Act. Proof that the plaintiff is violating the letter of the antitrust laws or is harming the defendant through the misuse is unnecessary.

Second, there is the antitrust defense whereby the defendant seeks to establish that the plaintiff's violation of the antitrust laws automatically precludes his obtaining relief for the patent or copyright infringement. The violation may be wholly unrelated to the subject matter of the litigation, and the defendant need not show special harm as a consequence of the violation. This defense is based upon a propensity of the courts to uphold the public interest in punishing violations of the antitrust laws and a judicial reluctance to approve a violation of the law in even the most indirect manner.

Finally, there is the "unclean hands" defense, an equitable doctrine which denies one who is himself a wrongdoer access to a court of equity. This defense is proper when the plaintiff is not using his grant in conformity with the Copyright Act or is using it in violation of the antitrust laws. Moreover, there are two further requirements: that the plaintiff's wrongful conduct grow out of the transaction which gives rise to his request for relief, and that the defendant be specially harmed by that conduct. It can be seen, therefore, that the unclean hands defense is in effect a special instance of either of the two other misuse defenses. The long history of the defense as a rule of equity has, however, prevented its merger with those defenses. For this reason it is considered a separate defense, and in those special instances where it is applicable the defendant invariably has at his disposal at least two defenses to the copyright or patent action.

While the misuse defenses have enjoyed their greatest success in patent litigation, they are frequently raised in actions concerning copyrighted material, particularly in cases involving the music and motion picture industries where combination is most common. But unlike the patent cases, the copyright infringement decisions indicate a reluctance to accept the antitrust violation as a per se defense to an infringement suit. Where this particular misuse defense has been recognized as a possible bar to an infringement suit, its applicability has been determined by weighing the gravity of the harm resulting from the antitrust violation against that resulting from the infringement, a test unknown to the patent cases. The existence of such a test leads to the speculation that in contract actions involving copyrighted material, the traditional concepts of collateral and inherent illegality may not be applied with the rigor that has characterized their application in the past. . . .

In copyright law, as in patent law, a wrongful extension of the plaintiff's right to exclusive control will prevent him from successfully maintaining an infringement suit. Also, prosecutions under the antitrust laws will not be prevented solely because the subject matter of the concerted activity under scrutiny is copyrighted. In United States v. Paramount Pictures, Inc., [334 U.S. 131 (1948)] the Supreme Court acknowledged that the copyright owner may choose his own customers and contract for the distribution of his property, but stated that "no such absolute right exists where its exercise will involve an extension of a copyright monopoly or an unreasonable interference with competition in the distribution and exhibition of motion pictures."

Winning acceptance for the antitrust violation as a *defense* to a copyright infringement suit, however, has been considerably more difficult. In fact, a showing by the defendant that the plaintiff is violating the antitrust laws will not, without more, relieve the defendant of the consequences of his infringement. In one of the earliest cases dealing with this matter, Scribner v. Straus, [130 F. 389 (S.D. N.Y.1904)] a district court summarily dismissed the defendant's argument that the plaintiff be denied relief for the copyright infringement because of an alleged antitrust violation. The reason for such a conclusion has been found to lie in an analogy to contract law. A contract which on its face contains terms making the agreement an illegal conspiracy is unenforceable. If, however, the conspiracy is only collateral to the contract, the contract is enforceable. In copyright law, according to the analogy, if the plaintiff's unlawful activity has not affected the defendant to an infringement suit, then such activity is only collateral to the subject matter of the suit. Consequently, the plaintiff should prevail, since the collateral defense of an antitrust violation should not be permitted to destroy the statutory right. The leading case in the area, M. Witmark & Sons v. Pastime Amusement Co., [298 F. 470 (E.D.S.C.1924)] expressly relied on the analogy to contract law in rejecting the antitrust defense.

In refusing to permit the antitrust defense in suits for copyright infringement, courts have also resorted to analogies between the copyright and other private property. For example, in Harms v. Cohen, [279 F. 276 (E.D.Pa.1922)] the court, in rejecting the antitrust defense, said:

> If he [the defendant] can set up an unlawful combination as a defense against his infringement of the copyright, then any one who wrongfully trespasses upon or takes the property of another may set up as a defense that the property was being held and used by a member of an unlawful combination in carrying out the purposes of that combination.

So well established were these analogies that while the antitrust policy defense was attaining recognition in patent infringement suits, courts faced with similar defenses in copyright actions were disposing of them summarily. "The defense alleged is not available to a defendant in an action for infringement of a copyright."

What accounts for the recognition of the defense of a plaintiff's antitrust violation in a patent infringement case and not in a copyright infringement case? One possible explanation is that the disparity stems from the markedly dissimilar fact patterns in which the questions arise.

In the copyright cases, the alleged antitrust violation is most likely to be related to the plaintiff's dealings with others, giving rise to the claim that he is a member of an illegal conspiracy. In the patent cases, the defendant's charge usually is that the plaintiff alone is licensing improperly or seeking control of nonpatented articles. But since in both situations there is an antitrust violation, a more fundamental answer is required. Such an answer lies in an examination of the differences between the two grants themselves. First, a patent more effectively removes a work from the public, and for this reason management of the grant may invite closer public control. There can be no innocent infringement of an invention, but two persons who independently arrive at the same result may both copyright their work. Second, while both grants seek to insure creativity by securing private rewards for a limited time, the public has an additional and more direct interest in the patent grant. Unlike the copyrightee, the patentee may often secure greater rewards by exploiting his invention as a secret process. But the public interest lies in early disclosure of the invention so that others may improve on it and in that way advance scientific progress. Finally, the antitrust policies have long been more prominent in patent litigation than in copyright litigation because patents are used more often in large industries, thereby enhancing the possibility that commerce will be affected. As important as these distinctions are, it would nevertheless be difficult to use them to suggest that a violation of the antitrust laws may never serve as a defense to a copyright infringement suit.

In M. Witmark & Sons v. Jensen, [80 F.Supp. 843 (D.Minn. 1948)] the court expressly declined to decide whether an antitrust violation alone would bar the plaintiff's copyright infringement suit. In that case the defendant claimed that the American Society of Composers, Authors and Publishers (ASCAP) was engaged in the practice of licensing music synchronization rights to motion picture producers, who placed the songs on soundtracks. It was further claimed that ASCAP then required that exhibitors obtain licenses to perform the music already on the track. The effect was much like that in *Morton Salt*, [Morton Salt Co. v. G. S. Suppiger Co., 314 U.S. 488 (1942)] for in order to use the copyrighted music the exhibitors first had to secure a license from the grantee on another aspect of his work. The court found that the plaintiff was subverting copyright policy, as well as violating the antitrust laws, and denied relief. It noted:

> However free plaintiffs and their associates in ASCAP may have been from any design or intent to extend their copyright monopoly, or however beneficial it may be for them to carry on their business in this manner, or however inconvenient it may be for them to function otherwise, such facts and circumstances will not permit them to enlarge their lawful monopoly.

It is significant that in this case, unlike the cases already considered in which the plaintiff was simply accused of belonging to an illegal conspiracy, the court's attention was directed to copyright policy, and only incidentally to the concurrent violation of the antitrust laws. Under both a conspiracy and a tie-in, a plaintiff is striving to gain more effective control of the market than his copyright originally gave him. But *copyright* policy is not offended by a conspiracy of copyright owners to do together what they may do alone.

Apart from instances of tying, where it is recognized that both the copyright and antitrust policies are offended, the antitrust defense has recently found a new role in copyright actions. This role was fashioned by the Second Circuit in Alfred Bell & Co. v. Catalda Fine Arts, Inc. [191 F.2d 99 (2d Cir. 1951)]. In this case a British print dealer brought an action for the infringement of the copyright on his mezzotints. The defendant alleged that the plaintiff was part of a conspiracy to fix prices and limit production of the prints. The lower court adhered to the argument that the antitrust remedies were exclusive and refused to acknowledge the alleged violation as being at all material in an infringement suit. In affirming, the Second Circuit rejected the notion that a violation of the antitrust laws was never a defense to a copyright infringement action. Instead, it fashioned a balancing test for determining the propriety of permitting the antitrust defense. Initially, the court recognized that it was faced with conflicting policies. The policy of the Copyright Act, not undermined by setting prices and the limiting of production, directed that the piracy of the protected material be enjoined. On the other hand, antitrust policy, with its objective the prohibition of restraints of trade, favored refusing to enjoin the infringement. After considering the "comparative innocence or guilt of the parties, the moral character of their respective acts, the extent of the harm to the public interest, the penalty inflicted on the plaintiff if . . . [relief were denied]," the court ruled that copyright considerations outweighed antitrust considerations and enjoined the infringement. All cases following *Catalda* which have balanced the subversive effects of infringement on copyright and antitrust policy have resulted in rejections of the misuse defense.

In the most recent consideration of the matter, United Artists Associated v. NWL Corp., [198 F.Supp. 953 (S.D.N.Y.1961)] the court refused to strike an antitrust misuse defense, but recognized a need to look beyond the pleadings and engage in a delicate balancing of competing public policies. The defendant was the operator of two community antenna systems. He charged that the plaintiff, the assignee of various film copyrights, was violating the antitrust laws by block-booking the films to television stations. The district court felt that *Catalda* was applicable, even though on its facts *NWL* more closely resembled the line of decisions holding that an antitrust violation was no defense to an action for copyright infringement. In *Catalda* the user of prints could well have been harmed by a conspiracy to fix prices and limit production. But in *NWL* only the television stations could have suffered from a policy of block-booking and the defendant was not a station owner. *NWL* thus confirms the notion suggested in *Catalda* that while an antitrust violation is not a per se defense to a charge of copyright infringement, all antitrust violations may result in forfeiture of copyright if the gravity and consequences of the violation outweigh those of the infringement. As in *Morton Salt*, the fact that the defendant-infringer has not been harmed by the plaintiff's unlawful activities is immaterial.

SELECTED BIBLIOGRAPHY

Taubman, Copyright and Antitrust (1960); Zelnick, The Relationship of Copyright and Antitrust Statutes, 7 Antitrust Bull. 331 (1962); Timberg, Copyright and Antitrust, 26 Bull. Copyright Soc'y 349 (1979); Cassady, Impact of the *Paramount* Decision on Motion Picture Distribution and Price Making, 31 So.Calif.L.Rev. 150 (1958); Timberg, The Antitrust Aspects of Merchandising Modern Music: The ASCAP Consent Judgment of 1950, 19 Law & Contemp. Prob. 294 (1954); ASCAP and the Antitrust Laws, 1959 Duke L.J. 258 (1959); Fine, Misuse and Antitrust Defenses to Copyright Infringement Actions, 17 Hastings L.J. 315 (1965); Lewis, The Defense of Misuse in Copyright Actions, 41 Denver L.J. 30 (1964).

For a discussion of the antitrust problems encountered by copyright clearinghouses, see page 810, above.

C. TRADEMARKS

NOTE, ANTITRUST PROBLEMS IN TRADEMARK FRANCHISING

17 Stan.L.Rev. 926–940 (1965).*

The increase in trademark and trade name licensing, or "franchising" as it is sometimes called, is easily accounted for: owners of established marks have found that authorization of a licensee to use the mark on products manufactured or processed by the licensee provides royalty income to the licensor with a minimum capital commitment. Licensing has a variety of competitive effects. Individuals who may not otherwise do so are induced to enter production by being given the opportunity to take advantage of the licensor's technological experience and marketing methods. It has also been asserted that licensing allows a group of "small" producers to compete against "large" producers. Consumer choice is also increased since licensing stimulates the production of a greater variety of products. Licensing may, however, have adverse competitive effects through discouraging innovation by either the licensor or the licensee, discouraging entry of new firms in a field where the trademark is well established, or disrupting a "local" market with a well advertised trademark and thus causing smaller companies to fail.

A conceptual rationale for licensing is provided by the prevailing theory that a trademark represents primarily a "guarantee of quality" and not exclusively an "origin of source." Under the "guaranty" theory the function of the trademark is to assure the consumer of a consistent level of product quality, rather than simply to designate the source of the product. The Lanham Act provides for registration of a mark used in interstate commerce by its owner. Section 5 states that where a mark is used by "related companies" such use inures to the benefit of the registrant. A "related company" is one that is controlled by the registrant "in respect to the nature and quality of the goods or services in connection with which the mark is used." This requirement of quality control is generally thought to have been necessary for a valid license at common law and is consistent with the "guaranty" theory of trademarks.

Under the guise of "quality control" the licensor often attempts to control the retail price of the goods produced under the trademark license, to impose exclusive dealing arrangements on the licensee, to divide territories among licensees, or to require that the licensee purchase some or all of the latter's raw material requirements from the licensor or sources approved by the licensor. .   .   .

Tying Arrangements

A tying arrangement exists when, as a condition of the license of the mark, the licensee agrees to purchase his raw materials (components which are subject to further licensee processing or manufacture) only from the licensor or sources approved by the licensor. The evils of tying arrangements are that they restrict buyer choice and discourage entry of new suppliers into the market for the tied product. This is true whether the licensor sells the tied component or designates suppliers from whom the licensee must purchase. .   .   .

Thus, in the absence of quality considerations, tying represents an economic choice by the licensor. The sole factor in this choice is economic benefit to the licensor, whether in the form of "rebates" where the licensor designates suppliers or "royalties" where the licensor sells the tied component. This form of licensor benefit, however, does not serve the purposes of quality control; it protects neither the consumer nor the licensor's mark.

Under the Sherman Act tying is illegal per se where a " 'not insubstantial' amount of interstate commerce is affected" and "a party has sufficient economic power with respect to the tying product to appreciably restrain free competition in the market for the tied product.   .   .   ." Under section 3 of the Clayton Act, tying is illegal per se "when the seller enjoys a monopolistic position in the market for the 'tying' product, *or* if a substantial volume of commerce in the 'tied' product is restrained.   .   .   ." The precise meaning of "sufficient economic power" is uncertain, but one meaning given it is "distinctiveness" of the tying product. Arguably a trademark provides the required "distinctiveness." However, in the recent case of Susser v. Carvel Corp., [332 F.2d 505 (2d Cir. 1964)] a majority of the Court of Appeals for the Second Circuit rejected this approach, stating that a trademark must "satisfy the market dominance" test and that the evidence showed that the Carvel trademark was not such a mark.

In *Susser* the plaintiffs, licensees of a soft ice cream trademark and trade name and lessees of defendant licensor's patented dispensing machines, were required to purchase the basic ice cream mix and toppings from suppliers designated by the licensor. The licensees could not sell other products without licensor approval. The plaintiffs also claimed that the defendant was fixing resale prices and sought treble damages, contending that these restrictions constituted per se violations of "the antitrust laws." A unanimous court affirmed the district court's finding that the licensees had the right to determine retail prices and held that the licensor was not required to permit his licensees to sell other products. The court split on the tying provision. The majority upheld the restriction on the ground that the evidence indicated that the licensor did not have sufficient power with respect to the tying product—the Carvel trademark—and that an insubstantial amount of commerce was involved. The majority rejected the argument that the patented dispensing machines created an irrebuttable presumption of market control with regard to the machines, relying on judicial statements that a patent creates a prima facie presumption of market control. This latter presumption was said to be rebutted by evidence which indicated that the licensees accounted for only one per cent of the retail sales in the relevant market. The dissenter concluded that the presumption of economic power in patents and copyrights should be extended to the Carvel trademark and that a not insubstantial amount of commerce was involved.

Both opinions stated that tying may be justified as reasonably necessary to protect a trademark. The majority said in dictum that specifications of the mix and toppings could not be reasonably supplied to the four hundred franchisees and that the costs of inspection were decreased significantly by specifying suppliers whose output of the tied products could be easily supervised. However, the dissent thought that the evidence regarding the justification was inconclusive and that the necessity of defendant's practice of supplier designation to protect its trademarks was negated by a competing ice cream chain's practice of allowing independent purchases by its licensees under its own specifications.

Challenges under the antitrust laws to tying arrangements for the purchase of raw materials in licensing contracts are relatively new, and the decisions are far from uniform. Judicial opinion ranges from blanket approval to outright condemnation. In Anchor Serum Co. v. FTC, [217 F.2d 867 (7th Cir. 1954)] the defendant licensor contended that requiring the licensees to purchase their drug requirements from it was necessary to assure proper use and protection of its trade name. In reply, the court stated:

A short answer to the contention on this score is that § 3 makes no provision or exception for such contingencies. . . . Petitioner's contention on this point, if adopted, would permit an easy avoidance of § 3. Nothing more would be required by the contracting parties, irrespective of the effect which their contract might have upon competition, than that there be included in the contract the right or privilege on the part of the purchaser to use the trade name of the seller.

An intermediate position relies on the *Standard Oil* [Standard Oil Co. v. United States, 337 U.S. 293, 69 S.Ct. 1051, 93 L.Ed. 1371 (1949)] dictum that tying may be permissible where the "specifications for a substitute would be so detailed that they could not practicably be supplied." While this approach gives flexibility, it is arguable that the gain in certainty and the consequent protection afforded competing sellers of the tied product achieved by imposing a quantitative substantiality test on tying arrangements far outweigh the protection of the legitimate interests in the "rare" cases when specifications would be so detailed that they could not practicably be supplied.

From the standpoint of the businessman, two rationales for tying can be asserted. The first is that tying is necessary to insure proper quality control. This rationale, however, requires an examination of the interests protected by the statutory quality control requirement. A nonlicensing trademark owner can vary the quality of the components in the final product or change the techniques of production, but he usually will not market trademarked goods with varying qualities at approximately the same time. The interest of the public, to the extent trademarks are relied on as a guarantee of quality and as a basis for informed consumer choice, is therefore "served so long as the licensing program results in no more variation in product standards than the owner could have engendered himself."

The licensor's interest in uniformity of quality arises out of a desire to preserve and expand the consumer's reliance on his mark. The licensor's interests in consistent quality should be the same in any licensing situation, whether a "celebrity" mark is licensed, the licensing parties are related by equity interests, or a "collective mark" is used.

It is questionable whether a licensee has any interest in maintaining consistent quality even in market areas controlled by that licensee. If the licensee seeks to capitalize on past buyer experience with the product or on buyer desire generated by *informative*, as against persuasive group advertising, a level of quality consistent with that of other licensees will be sought by the licensee. Thus it may be that tying arrangements are not necessary where the licensee desires product uniformity because the licensee will adhere to the licensor's instructions voluntarily. Nevertheless, a tying agreement would be required to protect the consumers' reliance interest and the licensor's integrity interest where the difference between the cost of tied materials from approved sources and that of similar components from nonapproved sources exceeds the benefits anticipated from consumer purchases induced by consumer reliance on consistency of quality of the marked product. . . .

There are many alternatives that will assure the licensor the benefit of quality control without the need for tying arrangements. For example, the licensor may allow independent purchase by the licensee in accord with the licensor's specifications, followed by the licensor's post-production control through inspection prior to sale or through submission of samples. Postpurchase control, however, may increase significantly the licensor's costs and may delay sale. Moreover, this arrangement may be unsatisfactory to the licensing parties if the end product fails to meet the licensor's standards and cannot be marketed under the licensing agreement.

Another variation involving independent purchase by the licensee would be to permit the licensor to cancel the franchise agreement in the event the goods produced under the license did not meet the licensor's standards. This kind of agreement has been upheld as satisfying the substantive quality control requirements. However, the licensor may have difficulty recruiting licensees when the licensing agreement allows cancellation on short notice.

A third variation of the independent purchase approach is to require that the licensee give a signed warranty of quality to the consumer. As is the franchise cancellation provision, however, this method is "after-the-fact" control in that the reliance interest of the consumer on consistent quality has not been served in the event of variation. Such variation may lead to adverse consumer reaction which would damage the licensing parties' interest in maintaining the integrity of the mark.

A basic assumption underlying each of these suggested alternatives to tying arrangements is that the specifications can be practicably met. In Susser v. Carvel Corp. the court remarked that the texture and taste of an ice cream cone was "insusceptible of precise verbalization" and the fact that "Carvel was able to specify this to its source of supply . . . does not show that administration could be confided to 400 dealers." The majority also noted that one of the specifications imposed on the approved topping suppliers was the purchase of fruits at crop site. It is not clear whether the licensor has the burden of establishing that the specifications could not be furnished to the licensees without harming the interests of the consumers and the licensor. At the least the burden of production should be on the licensor to show the specifications that are claimed to make tying necessary.

One technique by which the licensor could control the quality of the end product would be to allow the licensee to purchase components through a list of suppliers approved by the licensor. The licensor would furnish specifications to inquiring suppliers; the suppliers would later submit samples to the licensor for approval. The licensor's inspection of the submitted samples would have to be conducted in good faith; at a minimum the licensor would have to show the grounds on which the samples were rejected. Such "good faith" need not require more than that the justifying goal in fact motivate the action. Under the foregoing analysis the licensor's legitimate interest in tying extends only to considerations of quality and not to considerations of price; decisions based on price should be left to the licensee.

It is suggested that this alternative, requiring submission of samples to the licensor for his good-faith approval, is a more acceptable alternative to quality control than the tying arrangement. It would allow the licensor to achieve quality control without unreasonable expense and would leave the licensee and the suppliers free to resolve contractual matters unrelated to quality of the components.

Resale Price Maintenance

Resale price maintenance prohibits price cutting by the licensee and thus precludes the consumer from receiving through price reductions economies resulting from competitive distribution. Resale price maintenance provisions in franchise agreements are unlawful per se unless protected by applicable state fair trade laws. In some instances, however, the licensor "suggests" a retail price through widespread price advertising or by supplying priced promotional literature to the licensee. These suggested retail prices are not illegal where the licensor can show that the individual licensee has the right to determine retail price.

As justification for prescribing licensees' retail prices, licensors assert that the goodwill surrounding their trademarked products will be lost if the products are subject to price reductions. But it does not follow that uniformity of price is a legitimate licensor interest merely because uniformity of quality is. If the licensor believes that price publication is necessary to elicit buyer interest or to inform the buyer, then the advertising literature should state clearly that the price is subject to local variance.

Exclusive Dealing Arrangements

Exclusive dealing arrangements, common in franchising, involve agreements by the licensees to handle only the licensed product and other products approved by the licensor. These restrictions increase the difficulty of entry by a new dealer into the field and reduce the ability of the licensees to satisfy consumer preferences by dispensing a variety of products. If dealer entry is made more difficult the consumer may also be adversely affected by having to pay higher prices.

Under the oft-criticized *Standard Stations* test such arrangements violate section 3 of the Clayton Act whenever they foreclose competition "in a substantial share of the line of commerce affected." The *Standard Stations* test was modified, however, in *Tampa Electric* [Tampa Electric Co. v. Nashville Coal Co., 365 U.S. 320, 81 S.Ct. 623, 5 L.Ed.2d 580 (1961)]. There the Supreme Court posed a three-pronged test which takes into account the relative strength of the parties, the proportionate volume of commerce involved, and the probable immediate and future effects which preemption of that share of the market might have on effective competition therein.   In *Tampa Electric* the Court held that the plaintiff-vendor coal company was entitled to enforce its twenty-year requirements contract with defendant-vendee utility where the contract preempted 0.77 per cent of the relevant market.   In support of its holding the Court emphasized the economies of requirements contracts and the interest of the vendee in an assured source of supply.

Under the *Tampa Electric* approach a number of factors are relevant in assessing the competitive effect of an exclusive dealing contract.   Some of these are: The proportion of business done by licensees subject to the arrangement, the status of the licensor using the arrangements and the degree of competition within the industry, the extent to which other suppliers are also using the device, the duration of the arrangement and the rapidity of product and price changes within the industry, the likelihood that competitors may be able to establish their own distribution outlets or obtain new independent dealers to handle their products, the effect of the arrangement in reducing the costs of the licensor using it, the extent to which the arrangement significantly reduces licensee costs when accompanied by a requirements contract, the likelihood of vertical integration if exclusive dealing is banned, the extent to which weaker competitors can fortify their market position against more secure rivals, and the extent to which new entrants can gain a foothold through the assurance of a set volume of business.

Exclusive dealing arrangements are justified on the ground that they induce an independent dealer to assert his maximum sales effort and tend to foster dealer loyalty, thereby promoting competition rather than hindering it.   In the franchising context the danger that the sale of other nonlicensed products by the licensee may tend to confuse the consumer and thus dilute the usefulness of the mark has persuaded the courts to uphold this type of restriction.   The likelihood of confusion is greatest where the franchisee operates an outlet bearing a licensed trade name and also sells physically similar products which compete with the trademarked product.   Confusion will be least likely where the licensee under an independent trade name produces and markets a physically distinct product unrelated to the product produced under the licensed mark.   Thus, in addition to economic factors, a court should consider the likelihood of consumer confusion in the varying licensing situations, taking into account the buyer's expertness and the ability of the licensing parties to minimize confusion through disclosure.   Consumer confusion, rather than the possibility that consumers will purchase a competing product from the licensee, should be the object of the court's inquiry.

Territorial Limitations

Territorial limitations are vertically imposed geographical limits on the licensee's area of permissible sales.   The distinction between a territorial limitation and an exclusive franchise—one with an agreement by the licensor not to license another producer in a given licensee's territory—is difficult to draw. Often licensing agreements grant an "exclusive right" to use the licensed mark in a given territory. This should be considered a territorial limitation since the licensee can maintain an action for damages upon invasion of that area by another licensee.

Territorial limitations, also common in trademark licenses, restrict intrabrand competition and thus tend to result in higher prices for the product. In White Motor Co. v. United States [372 U.S. 253, 83 S.Ct. 696, 9 L.Ed.2d 738 (1963)] the Supreme Court reversed a summary judgment in favor of the Government, holding that a trial was required to determine whether territorial limitations should be considered unlawful per se. Mr. Justice Douglas, writing for the Court, stated that

> this is the first case involving a territorial restriction in a *vertical* arrangement; and we know too little of the actual impact of both that restriction and the one respecting customers to reach a conclusion on the bare bones of the documentary evidence before us.

Territorial limitations may stimulate dealer participation and investment and will induce licensees to concentrate on developing their sales territories. In a trademark context territorial limitations serve the additional purpose of aiding the licensor in tracing customer complaints to a particular licensee.

The effectiveness of the restraint to accomplish these purposes is dependent upon the amount of extra-territorial selling by the licensee. Usually the sanction for such cross-selling is a "profit pass-over," calling for payment by the cross-selling licensee of some or all of his profit to the licensee whose territory was invaded. The purpose of the profit pass-over is to deter cross-selling and also to reimburse the local licensee for any postsales servicing he may have to perform. Thus, the competition barrier presented to intrabrand competition "is no greater than the required payment over."

It is likely that the quality control aspect of trademark licenses, viz., tracing defective trademarked items, can be achieved through a coding system on the item produced under the license. This would be effective especially in the case of durable consumer goods. The other general business purposes of territorial limitations can probably be achieved through an "area-of-primary-responsibility" clause in the licensing agreement which allows the licensor to terminate the franchise of a licensee who does not adequately present and promote the product in his designated area.

FLINN, BASIC ANTITRUST PROBLEM AREAS AND THEIR SIGNIFICANCE FOR TRADEMARK OWNERS AND PRACTITIONERS

67 Trademark Reporter 225, 275–279 (1977).*

Clearly an exclusive sales area provision is intended to and will in fact protect the favored dealer from at least some intrabrand competition, even if there are dealers with the same brand in other neighboring areas. Indeed, depending upon the kind of product and how far customers will travel to buy it, an exclusive sales area may totally insulate the dealer from intrabrand competition. For example, a franchised candy dealer with an exclusive territory of five miles' radius may have no competition in that brand because consumers will not travel more than a mile or two to buy a box of candy. And yet, notwithstanding this inevitable diminution, if not elimination, of intrabrand competition resulting from an exclusive sales area grant, Mr. Justice Fortas in the much-debated Schwinn decision declared that such restraints are lawful if no other restrictions are involved and competitive products are readily available. [United States v. Arnold Schwinn & Co., 388 U.S. 365, 87 S.Ct. 1856, 18 L.Ed. 2d 1249 (1967).]

On a related issue, however, Schwinn reached a negative and, at the time, unexpected conclusion. In reliance upon the supposed common law prohibition of restraints on alienation, the Court held for the first time that territorial and customer limitations imposed by a manufacturer upon the resale of its goods by both its distributors and franchised retailers were per se violations of Section 1 of the Sherman Act. Proceeding on the premise that those who purchase goods (whether or not trademarked) must be free to resell them "where and to whomever they choose," the decision precluded a supplier from limiting his distributors' sales to specified areas or to designated or "franchised" retailers even though the same supplier could unilaterally restrict his own direct sales to such customers and in such areas as he chose. Consequently, Schwinn made it impossible for a supplier to insulate one customer to whom he had granted an exclusive franchise in an area from intrabrand competition by confining other customers located in neighboring areas to whom he also sold.

In the ten years after it was decided, Schwinn was the subject of much criticism from different sources, even including some government enforcement officials. Its seeming emphasis upon dealer freedom and intrabrand competition above all else was repeatedly questioned. It was urged that, while dealer freedom and intrabrand competition may be valid competitive objectives, they are not so regardless of the price.

The attainment of those objectives should at least be consonant with other equally valid competitive objectives, certainly including the fostering of effective interbrand competition which must exist, as has been suggested in discussing exclusive franchises, before there can be any meaningful intrabrand competition beneficial to consumers, or, indeed, any dealers willing to compete in the distribution of the same brand of product. More specifically, some restrictions upon untrammeled dealer freedom and intrabrand competition can be necessary in particular circumstances to create, promote or preserve interbrand competition. Such circumstances include at least those situations discussed above in analyzing the competitive rationale for treating exclusive territorial grants or franchises by rule-of-reason rather than per se standards.

Before Schwinn, suppliers often made the granting of an exclusive sales area or franchise more attractive as an inducement to the handling of their goods and as a means of attaining the most effective competition in their distribution by also prohibiting each dealer from reselling outside his exclusive territory into that of any other dealer. Obviously, however, Schwinn's prohibition of such vertical restrictions diluted the complete territorial insulation available under such arrangements, at least where the nature of the business was such that a dealer, even though located outside, could sell into or attract customers from another dealer's exclusive sales area. As noted, there are instances where dealers will refuse to invest the time, effort and capital necessary to represent a supplier without at least the limited protection of an exclusive sales area. There are also other instances where dealers will be unwilling to risk such investment without the complete protection against intrabrand competition afforded by a vertical territorial restriction imposed upon other dealers.

. . . .

The dispute which has raged for ten years over Schwinn and its implications now appears to be resolved. After the basic preparation of this article and shortly before publication, the Supreme Court has just overruled the per se holding in Schwinn. In affirming a decision by the Ninth Circuit in the Sylvania case that location clauses (provisions by which a supplier restricts his dealer or franchisee to reselling his product only from a specified location) should be measured by the rule-of-reason, a majority of five Justices, "unable to find a principled basis for distinguishing" such provisions from the territorial and customer resale restrictions banned by Schwinn, has concluded "that the per se rule stated in Schwinn must be overruled." [Continental T.V., Inc. v. GTE Sylvania, Inc., 433 U.S. 36, 97 S.Ct. 2549, 53 L.Ed.2d 568 (1977).] Noting, inter alia, that "vertical restrictions promote interbrand competition by allowing the manufacturer to achieve certain efficiencies in the distribution of his products" in a variety of circumstances such as those discussed earlier in this article, the majority concluded that "interbrand competition . . . is the primary concern of antitrust law" and that "when interbrand competition exists . . . it provides a significant check on the exploitation of intrabrand market power because of the ability of consumers to substitute a different brand of the same product." Consequently, the Court held, the promotion of interbrand competition attainable by vertical restrictions renders inappropriate the application of any per se rule, a standard proper only when challenged practices have such a "pernicious effect on competition and lack . . . any redeeming virtue" as to be "conclusively presumed to be unreasonable and therefore illegal without elaborate inquiry as to the precise harm they have caused or the business excuse for their use."

SELECTED BIBLIOGRAPHY

Timberg, Trade-Marks, Monopoly, and the Restraint of Competition, 14 Law & Contemp.Prob. 323 (1949); LeBlanc, Antitrust Ramifications of Trademark Licensing and Franchising, 53 Trademark Rep. 519 (1963); Bisgaier & Price, Quality Control and the Antitrust Laws in Trademark Licensing, 53 Trademark Rep. 1130 (1963); Rudnick, The Sealy Case: The Supreme Court Applies the Per Se Doctrine to a Hybrid Distribution System for Trademarked Bedding Products, 57 Trademark Rep. 459 (1967); The Antitrust Defense in Trademark Infringement Actions, 45 Va.L.Rev. 94 (1959); Trademark Cancellation and Unenforceability—Use of a Trademark in Violation of the Anti-Trust Laws, 32 N.Y.U.L.Rev. 1002 (1957); McCarthy, Trademark Franchising and Antitrust: The Trouble With Tie-Ins, 58 Calif.L.Rev. 1085 (1970); Quality Control and the Antitrust Laws in Trademark Licensing, 72 Yale L.J. 1171 (1963); Rudnick, The Franchisor's Dilemma: Can He Satisfy the Legal and Commercial Requirements of a Trademark Licensing System Without Exposing Himself to Other Legal Risks, 56 Trademark Rep. 621 (1966).

II. FEDERAL INCOME TAXATION

In addition to the sources cited below, you may wish to consult J. Bischel, Taxation of Patents, Trademarks, Copyrights, and Know-How (1974); Patent Law Association of Chicago, Patent, Trademark and Copyright Tax Guide (1965); Finnegan & McCarthy, The Impact of the United States Tax Laws on International Technology Transfer: An Overview and Some Suggestions for Minimizing the Bite, 60 J.P. O.S. 407 (1978); Note, A Comparison of the Tax Treatment of Authors and Inventors, 70 Harv.L.Rev. 1419 (1957); and Duke, Foreign Authors, Inventors, and the Income Tax, 72 Yale L.J. 1093 (1963).

A. PATENTS

MORREALE, PATENTS, KNOW–HOW AND TRADEMARKS: A TAX OVERVIEW

29 Tax Lawyer 553–567 (1976).*

Self-Developed Patents

Business-related expenditures for the self-development of patents are deductible. Alternatively, these expenditures can be amortized under section 174(b), but only until a patent issues. In many situations, it is not known at the time the expenditures are incurred whether a patent or other depreciable property will ultimately result. Deferred expense treatment under a section 174(b) election terminates once a patent issues, at least insofar as the deferred expense amount allocable to the patent is concerned. The balance in the deferred expense account attributable to the patent becomes the tax basis of the patent and is amortizable over its useful life.

Fixed Price Sales

A fixed price sale of a patent generally will give rise to capital gain or loss when, as is usually the case, the patent constitutes section 1231 property or a capital asset in the hands of the seller. Gain realized to the extent of depreciation deductions taken since 1961, however, will be recaptured as ordinary income. Any capital gain will be long-term if the seller held the patent or underlying invention for more than six months[o] or if the seller is a "holder" under section 1235(b). The holding period of an invention begins when it is acquired or when it is actually reduced to practice.

A patent purchaser can amortize the price of the patent over its remaining useful life, which is ordinarily the remaining statutory life, 17 years less the time already expired, for a United States patent. Ordinarily, it is difficult to persuade the Service that a shorter period is appropriate, unless the patent becomes valueless. Patent amortization

[o]. Now one year. 26 U.S.C.A. § 1222. (Ed.)

or license payment deductions are depreciation deductions under section 167.   Thus, if depreciated patents are later sold, gain realized upon the sale will be recaptured as ordinary income to the extent of depreciation deductions taken since 1961.

Patent Licenses

Intellectual property rights are frequently transferred under a license agreement where payments are contingent in whole or part upon the licensee's sales, production volume, or the like.   Licenses are a preferred vehicle for the transfer of intellectual property rights, primarily because of the difficulty of valuing such rights.

1. *Corporate Licensors*

The most common and important licensing tax problem is determining whether a license should be characterized as a sale.   Sale characterization ordinarily means that payments received by the licensor will result in capital gain or loss.   Licenses are typically long and complex instruments with clauses defining, restricting, and limiting the rights of the parties.   Normally, intellectual property agreements are called "license agreements."   Historically, the term "license" has ordinarily meant a right to use only.   A licensor seeking sale treatment might prefer to use sale or assignment language.   The tax treatment will, of course, be governed by the substance of the transaction regardless of the form or name of the agreement.

A patent license will produce capital gains only if it transfers an undivided interest in a patent or "all substantial rights" to a patent which have any significant value at the date of transfer.   This basic tax rule has been developed largely by case law interpretations of the sale or exchange provisions of the Code, and since 1954 by analogy to section 1235, which deals specifically with the sale or exchange of patents by individuals.   Patents grant rights only in the country of their issuance, and thus, "all substantial rights" means rights within that country.   The form of payments is irrelevant to the capital gains determination; it no longer matters whether payments are contingent upon sales, use, or the like.

Ordinarily, an *exclusive* license to make, use, and sell under a patent, for a term at least equal to the remaining statutory life of the patent, produces capital gains.   A nonexclusive license produces ordinary income, as is usually the case with a "sole" license, i. e., where a licensor grants exclusive rights against everyone but himself.

2. *Imputed Interest*

Even if a license produces capital gains, seven percent of deferred payments may be treated as ordinary income under the imputed interest provisions of section 483, which apply to indefinite payments such as contingent license payments.   Section 483(f)(4) excepts only "payments made pursuant to a transfer described in section 1235(a) (relating to sale or exchange of patents)."   Most substantial licenses are granted by corporate licensors, and because section 1235 does not apply to corporations, section 483 presents a serious obstacle to total capital gains treatment. Moreover, because most licenses are long-term and payments are often greatest several years after the license grant, the amount of section 483 interest can be very substantial.

Section 483 also presents a serious obstacle to total capital gains treatment for individual licensors. The Service position is that section 483 applies unless a license is *governed* by section 1235. Consistently rejecting this view, however, the courts have held that section 483 does not apply to *patent* licenses by *individuals,* on the ground that they are exempt under section 483(f)(4) because they are "described" in section 1235(a).

Individual Inventors

Section 1235 provides special rules for individual patent licensors who qualify as "holders" under section 1235(b). The purposes underlying the enactment of section 1235 were to provide additional incentives to individual inventors, to remove the distinctions that had developed between professional and amateur inventors, and to make clear that sale treatment may result even where contingent payments are payable over the life of a patent.

An *individual* can qualify as a holder whether or not he is in the business of selling patents. To qualify, an individual must be the inventor or must have financed the invention before actual reduction to practice and must not be the employer of the inventor nor be related to the inventor within the meaning of section 1235(d).

A patent license by a holder to an unrelated party will ordinarily produce long-term capital gain if the license transfers all substantial rights to a patent or an undivided interest therein. The major advantages of section 1235 qualification are exemption from section 483 imputed interest, exemption from any holding period requirement, and avoidance of any potential "holding for sale" problem.

For a patent holder who does not meet the technical requirements of section 1235, e. g., because he licenses a "related person," the government view is that the license can still produce capital gains under the general "sale or exchange" capital gain provisions of the Code. In 1966, however, the Tax Court held that section 1235 is a holder's *exclusive* route to capital gains treatment, at least if payments are contingent or payable over a period generally coterminous with a licensee's use of the patent.[35] The Tax Court has since indicated that it will probably maintain this view notwithstanding the Service's continuing position to the contrary.[36] The government's position seems justified by the language of section 1235, which does not give any indication that it is intended to be a holder's exclusive route

35. Myron C. Poole, 46 T.C. 392, 404–05 (1966), acq., 1966–2 C.B. 6, as to the deductibility by transferee corporation of increased royalties.

36. See Ray E. Omholt, 60 T.C. 541, 547 n.7 (1973), acq., 1974–2 C.B. 4; Lan Jen Chu, 58 T.C. 598, 608 n. 1 (1972), aff'd 486 F.2d 696 (1st Cir. 1973); William W. Taylor, 29 T.C.M. 1488, 1494 (1970).

to sale or exchange treatment. The legislative history provides some support for both positions, however, and arguably favors the Tax Court position. For planning purposes, a holder is thus best advised to try to qualify the transaction under section 1235.

License Restrictions in General

License restrictions are responsible for most tax litigation and often result in ordinary income because "all substantial rights" have not been transferred. The Service has adopted a narrow view as to the scope of restrictions that may be imposed without producing ordinary income. The government position, applicable to section 1235 and non-section 1235 licenses, is set forth in the section 1235 regulations and may be summarized as follows:

(1) A grant of "all substantial rights to a patent" does *not* include a license that:

(a) is limited geographically within the country of issuance; or

(b) is limited in duration by the terms of the agreement to a period less than the remaining life of the patent; or

(c) grants rights to a grantee, in fields of use within trades or industries, that are less than all the rights covered by the patent which exist and have value at the time of the grant; or

(d) grants less than all of the claims or inventions covered by a patent which exist and have value at the time of the grant; or

(e) includes the retention of a right to terminate the transfer at will.

(2) Restrictions that *may* be imposed include the retention of:

(a) legal title for the purpose of securing performance or payment; and

(b) rights that are "not inconsistent with the transfer of ownership," such as the retention of a security interest, or a reservation in the nature of a condition subsequent, e. g., forfeiture on account of nonperformance.

(3) Retained rights that may or may not be substantial, depending upon the circumstances of the whole transaction, are:

(a) retention of an absolute right to prohibit sublicensing or subassignment; and

(b) failure to convey the right to use or to sell.

The Tax Court has adopted a much more liberal view as to the scope of license restrictions that may be imposed without producing ordinary income, while the circuit courts have varied in their treatment of the issue. The following is a discussion of some of the more common restrictions and the current state of the authorities on their tax consequences.

1. *Geographic Restrictions*

A licensor may prefer to restrict the territorial scope of a license to the area in which a licensee has a well-established business. The total value of licensed rights can often be enhanced by territorial divisions. A territorial restriction creates a serious ordinary income risk, however.

The Service view is that a license produces ordinary income if limited geographically to less than the country of patent issuance—provided that rights to the territory not granted have significant value at the date of license. Support for capital gains treatment for such a license, however, can be found in the historic patent assignment case, Waterman v. MacKenzie.[43] In addition, the Tax Court allowed capital gains treatment for such a license as early as 1955,[44] and has recently held invalid the regulations' geographical restriction provision.[45] Most of the circuit courts have not definitively spoken, but if the "field of use" trend of decisions (discussed below) is followed, most circuit courts seem likely to uphold the government's position, with the result that a geographical restriction or a field of use restriction will ordinarily produce ordinary income.

2. *Field of Use Restrictions*

A field of use restriction limits the scope of a license grant to a particular industrial field of use or application. For example, a licensee might be granted the right to make, use, and sell a licensed invention, useful as a drive train clutch device, in the marine field only and not in the automotive field. As in the case of geographic restrictions, a licensor can often increase the total value of his rights by this type of restriction, but in so doing can again create a very serious ordinary income risk.

The Service position has long been that a license produces ordinary income if it includes a field of use restriction and if the rights to any field of use not licensed have any significant value at the date of the license. Prior to the 1954 enactment of section 1235, the Government lost several decisions on this issue in situations where the fields of use retained had no established value at the date of license. The taxpayer was also successful in the first case decided under the 1954 Code,[50] after which the section 1235 regulations were amended to provide that field of use restrictions produce ordinary income. The Tax Court has twice held this provision invalid, but was reversed on both occasions, by the Sixth and Ninth Circuits.[52]

---

43. 138 U.S. 252, 11 S.Ct. 334, 34 L.Ed. 923 (1891). Although *Waterman* was not a tax case, it is a leading historic case dealing with the issue of whether a license should be treated as a sale or as an assignment.

44. Vincent A. Marco, 25 T.C. 544 (1955), nonacq., 1956–2 C.B. 10, acq., 1958–2 C.B. 6.

45. Estate of George T. Klein, 61 T.C. 332 (1973), rev'd, 507 F.2d 617 (7th Cir.), cert. denied, 421 U.S. 991, 95 S.Ct. 1998, 44 L.Ed.2d 482; Vincent

B. Rodgers, 51 T.C. 927 (1969), acq., 1973–2 C.B. 2 (result only).

50. William S. Rouverol, 42 T.C. 186 (1964), nonacq., 1965–2 C.B. 7. The legislative history is ambiguous. See H.R.Rep.No.1337, 83d Cong., 2d Sess. 279 (1954); S.Rep.No.1622, 83d Cong., 2d Sess. 438 (1954).

52. Albert A. Mros v. Commissioner, 493 F.2d 813 (9th Cir. 1974) (per curiam), rev'g 30 T.C.M. 519; Thomas L. Fawick v. Commissioner, 463 F.2d 655 (6th Cir. 1971), rev'g 52 T.C. 104.

3. *Successive Licenses*

A license may grant less than all rights relating to an underlying patent. For example, there may have been a prior grant by the licensor or the licensor may not have owned all rights to the patent in the first place. Such "successive licenses" create a serious ordinary income risk, particularly if the granting licensor previously granted another license.

The regulations under section 1235 provide:

The term "all substantial rights" to a patent means all rights (*whether or not then held by the grantor*) which are of value *at the time the rights to the patent* (or an undivided interest therein) *are transferred;* . . .

The government's litigating position appears to be that a license, with the exception of a license of an undivided interest, produces ordinary income if a licensor previously granted rights having any significant value, at least if the previously-granted rights have any significant value at the date of the subsequent license. On the other hand, the regulations have been interpreted by some courts and commentators to mean that only the rights held by a licensor at the time of a subsequent grant are significant, and thus, that a license may produce capital gains even if a licensor granted prior valuable licenses. In summary, a successive licensor has a chance under the case law for capital gains treatment on the second license, particularly if he grants all substantial rights *he* ever had.

Employee or Stockholder Licensors

1. *Employee Licensors*

An employee may license invention rights he conceived during employment to either his employer or, occasionally, an unrelated party (with the employer often sharing in the payments). This is a fairly common occurrence, even though an employer often has some rights to employee inventions without need for a license by reason of an employment contract or common law doctrines of shop rights or alter ego. An employee license may create some ordinary income risk, but the case law is generally favorable to employee licensors. Thus, an employee license structured to produce capital gains will usually do so unless the employee was hired specifically and primarily to invent.

Employee licenses present two potential ordinary income problems: (1) a successive transfer issue, because an employer typically already has some invention rights, and (2) a compensation issue.

In *Mros*, the Tax Court expressly declined to follow the Sixth Circuit reversal of its decision in *Fawick*. It may be that the First Circuit would also deny capital gains treatment for a field of use license. See Redler Conveyor Co. v. Commissioner, 303 F.2d 567, 569 (1st Cir. 1962) (dictum), aff'g 20 T.C.M. 371. A license of a "separate invention" which is part of a single "multi-invention" patent may arguably produce capital gains. See Merck & Co. v. Smith, 261 F.2d 162 (3d Cir. 1958). But see Reg. § 1.-1235-2(b)(1)(iv).

The former has generally not been troublesome; when raised by the Government, it is usually dismissed on the ground that when the transfers took place is irrelevant as long as they were to the same party.

The key inquiry under the compensation issue, of course, is to determine whether the license payments are in return for services or for the license of invention rights. Most courts focus on whether the employee was "hired to invent," generally concluding that he was not and that the payments are therefore not for services. Thus, if an employee was hired for skills other than those of an inventor, capital gains treatment should be upheld, particularly if his inventing activities were only incidental to other duties for which he was paid reasonable compensation. Besides the terms of hire and the specific activities engaged in by an employee, other factors pertinent to this issue include: whether payments depend upon production, sales or use by, or value to, the employer of the rights licensed; language in any employment contract; and the treatment of payments by the employee and employer for withholding tax purposes.

2. Stockholder Licensors

A major stockholder patent licensor faces an additional tax hurdle. If he and/or certain family members own more than eighty percent in value of a licensee corporation's stock (a "controlling stockholder"), an outright sale or license will generally trigger ordinary income under section 1239. The application of section 1239 may be avoided in some cases, however, if an invention is licensed before a patent issues.

Section 1239 provides that gain realized upon a sale or exchange by a controlling stockholder will be taxed as ordinary income if the property sold is "of a character" subject to depreciation in the hands of the corporation. A patent is depreciable if it is used in a trade or business or held for the production of income. Thus, a controlling stockholder patent license which otherwise qualifies as a sale or exchange will produce ordinary income.

A controlling stockholder license before patent issuance, however, may produce capital gains. A patent *application* is nondepreciable because it has no readily ascertainable useful life. Thus, a controlling stockholder license of an invention to a domestic corporation before patent issuance, whether the invention turns out to be patentable or not, should produce capital gains. Exploitation after patent issuance of the licensed invention by the controlled corporation, usually an operating company, can in turn result in depreciation deductions against ordinary operating or licensing income.

In light of the section 1239 exposure, a controlling stockholder license or sale should preferably take place before a patent application is filed, or if an application has been filed, before notices of allowance of important claims have been received from the Patent and Trademark Office. This approach has been sanctioned by both the First and Sixth Circuits in *Lan Jen Chu* and *Davis*, respectively.[68]   Although both circuits indicated that the results reached in these cases may be undesirable from a tax policy point of view, it was concluded that any reform would have to come from Congress.   If, however, a licensor has received any notices of allowability of significant claims prior to transfer, a court may treat the application as sufficiently "matured" to be regarded as property "of a character" subject to depreciation, thus subjecting the transfer to section 1239.

Finally, section 1239 applies only to transfers by *individual* controlling stockholders.   If and when the tax benefits of a *Lan Jen Chu*-type transfer are eliminated, another possible way to produce capital gains may appear, i. e., establishing a corporation, perhaps a Subchapter S corporation, to develop, hold, and sell an invention to a sister corporation.

Patent Licensees

Because a patent has a useful life which can be estimated with reasonable accuracy, a *patent* licensee can deduct license payments regardless of whether a license produces capital gains or ordinary income.   Capital gains license payments represent a reasonable estimate of depreciation charges for a purchased (licensed) patent, and ordinary income license payments represent ordinary and necessary business deductions for the business use of property.   The theory supporting deductibility is important because if a licensee later sells or assigns his rights, *depreciation* deductions may be subject to ordinary income recapture.

II.   KNOW–HOW

The term "know-how" refers to any compilation of information used in a business that gives the user an opportunity to gain an advantage over competitors who do not know about or use such information.   Thus, it includes not only secret processes, formulae, and other traditional trade secrets, but also customer lists, drawings, design manuals, operating instructions, and the like.

Self-Developed Know-How

Business-related expenditures for the self-development of know-how are currently deductible [77] or, if research or experimental related,[78] they are amortizable over a period of at least five years, at the election of the taxpayer.[79]   Except for start-up situations, most taxpayers currently deduct know-how expenditures.

68.   Davis v. Commissioner, 491 F.2d 709 (6th Cir. 1974) (per curiam), aff'g 31 T.C.M. 1155; Lan Jen Chu v. Commissioner, 486 F.2d 696 (1st Cir. 1973), aff'g 58 T.C. 598; accord, Vincent W. Eckel, 33 T.C.M. 147 (1974). But see Estate of Stahl v. Commissioner, 442 F.2d 324 (7th Cir. 1971), aff'g in part and rev'g in part 52 T.C. 591.

77.   I.R.C. §§ 162, 174(a); Reg. § 1.-174–2(a)(1) and (3).

78.   Reg. § 1.174–2(a)(1) defines research or experimental expenditures.

79.   I.R.C. § 174(b).   Amortization, on a straight-line basis, begins with the month in which a taxpayer first realizes benefits from the expenditures,

A frequent problem area involves whether a taxpayer has sufficient business activity to support deductibility or amortization. Section 174 entitles a taxpayer to deduct or amortize research or experimental expenditures "incurred . . . in connection with his trade or business. . . ." Thus, section 174 arguably requires a somewhat less developed "business" to justify deductibility than section 162, which requires that a taxpayer be engaged "in carrying on" a trade or business.

There has been considerable litigation as to whether expenditures deducted or amortized under section 174 were incurred in connection with a taxpayer's business or were incurred preparatory to any "business existence" so as to preclude either deductibility or amortization. This issue has been particularly troublesome where the taxpayer is an individual inventor or financier. A recent Supreme Court case, Snow v. Commissioner, [416 U.S. 500, 94 S.Ct. 1876, 40 L.Ed.2d 336 (1974)] is particularly interesting in this connection. Rejecting the view of both the Sixth Circuit and the Tax Court, the Supreme Court permitted a section 174 deduction to an individual investor in a tax shelter limited partnership which engaged in research and development work on a new type of trash burner. Given *Snow* and the Supreme Court's emphasis therein on the Congressional policy underlying section 174, i.e., to provide an incentive for small and growing businesses to engage in a search for new products and inventions, the Service and the courts are likely to be less strict in requiring that the taxpayer have an actual going business to justify deductibility or amortization under section 174.

Fixed Price Sales

Sales of know-how will produce capital gains as long as the know-how constitutes property and is a capital asset in the hands of the seller. The apparent Service position is that only know-how that is secret and protectible against disclosure, at least in significant part, can qualify as "property" within the meaning of section 1221. The courts, however, ordinarily take a less restrictive view of whether know-how constitutes property, and it would appear that know-how need not necessarily be a trade secret in order to qualify as property. For example, a valuable process known only to a few companies in a large industry should be treated as property, as should an indexed compilation of technical information relating to a process known by several companies. Finally, in a combined transfer of patents and know-how, the know-how may be so incidental or ancillary to the patent as to be deemed to have taken on the "property" character of the transferred patent.

A purchaser of know-how cannot deduct or amortize any portion of the purchase price because know-how does not have a reasonably

---

which is ordinarily the month in which he first puts the property to "an income producing use." Reg. § 1.174–4(a)(3). As noted above, research and experimental expenditures related to depreciable property, e. g., a patent, can be deducted under section 174(a), but they can be amortized under section 174(b) only until a patent issues.

determinable useful life. A deduction against ordinary income can be taken only if the know-how becomes demonstrably worthless and is abandoned by the purchaser.

Know-How Licenses

1. Capital Gains Treatment

A know-how license, like a patent license, will produce capital gains only if all substantial rights to the know-how (and presumably an undivided interest therein) which have any significant value at the date of license are transferred. Thus, ordinarily an exclusive license to make, use, and sell under know-how for a term at least equal to its remaining useful life, e. g., until such time that it becomes public knowledge, will produce capital gains, except to the extent of imputed interest under section 483.

The tax rules previously summarized in connection with patent licensors, except for the section 1235 rules, apply as well to know-how licensors. For example, know-how licenses that include a field of use or geographic restriction, within a particular country, create very serious ordinary income risks. The following is a discussion of certain other tax aspects which are particularly significant in the know-how licensing area.

2. Right to Prevent Unauthorized Disclosure, Term, and After-Acquired Know-How

A "substantial right" relating to confidential know-how is the right to prevent unauthorized disclosure. In order to assure capital gains, this right should be explicitly transferred.

Because know-how has an indeterminate useful life, a know-how license must be either perpetual or last until the know-how no longer has any significant commercial value, e.g., until it becomes public knowledge and is no longer protectible under the laws of the licensed territory.

A know-how license, like a patent license, should allow for more than a six-month holding period for grants of subsequently developed improvements. A know-how license should also clearly state that the initial grant is of know-how acquired or developed during a specific period of time or before a specific date, e.g., before the license date; otherwise, a license may be viewed as merely a continuing commitment to develop and furnish know-how and related technical assistance.

3. Know-How Licensees

If a know-how license produces ordinary income, e. g., a nonexclusive license, a licensee can deduct the license payments as business expenses. On the other hand, if a know-how license produces capital gains, a licensee *cannot* deduct license payments, either currently or through amortization, because licensed (purchased) know-how has no reasonably determinable useful life. Such a licensee will be entitled to an ordinary income deduction only if the know-how becomes demonstrably worthless and is abandoned.

SELECTED BIBLIOGRAPHY

Note, Capital Gains Treatment on Proceeds from Patent Transfers, 34 Mo.L.Rev. 98 (1969); Note, The Exclusive Nature of Internal Revenue Code Section 1235: A Forgotten Congressional Policy, 31 Wash. & Lee L.Rev. 715 (1964); Cooper, How a Corporation Can Get Capital Gains When Licensing Inventions and Know-How, 24 J.Taxation 334 (1966); Capital Gains Treatment of Patent Transfers, 17 Western Res.L.Rev. 844 (1966); Farber, Capital Gains—"Transfer . . . of Property Consisting of All Substantial Rights to a Patent," 47 J.P.O.S. 981 (1965); Lawlor, Tax Treatment of Patent Costs, 39 J.P.O.S. 900 (1957); Blaustein, Planning for Maximum Depreciation by Proper Treatment of Patent Acquisitions, 31 J.Taxation 340 (1969); Meyer & Hickey, Taxation of Contingent Payments of the Sale of a Patent, 14 IDEA 497 (1970); Dunn, Tax Considerations in Patent Assignments and Licenses Between Related Corporations, 16 Tax.L.Rev. 315 (1961).

B. COPYRIGHTS

HALPER, DEALINGS IN COPYRIGHT AND LITERARY PROPERTY

3 A.P.L.A. Quarterly Journal 1!–15; 17; 20–23 (1975).*

The creative person (or other copyright proprietor) generally attempts to take advantage of the same tax benefit provisions as other taxpayers. He would like to report as much of his income as possible as capital gains. If his income has reached appropriate levels, he may wish to invoke the maximum placed on the tax on earned income or avail himself of the benefits of income averaging. Upon his death, he would like, if possible, to protect his family from the double burdens of an estate tax and an income tax on the residual income from his works. He may also wish for all or part of his creative efforts to be exploited through a corporate entity. Each of these aspirations is a subject in and of itself. Oversimplification would result from assuming to cover all these areas in detail in the short space allotted. Accordingly, only the highlights will be touched upon.

Copyright Property and the Capital Gain Provisions

The income tax laws have long attempted to ameliorate the burden of a progressive income tax that taxes at the point of sale or exchange increases in the value of property that may have taken place over extended periods of time. Special tax treatment is thus afforded to gains from the sale or exchange of capital assets and certain depreciable property used in a trade or business held for more than six months.¹' By specific exclusion in the statutory definition of the term "capital asset", these reduced effective rates of tax are not

* Reprinted with permission of the American Patent Law Association.   p. Now one year. 26 U.S.C.A. § 1222. (Ed.)

available for "a copyright, a literary, musical, or artistic composition, a letter or memorandum, or similar property, held by—

    (A) a taxpayer whose personal efforts created such property,

    (B) in the case of a letter, memorandum, or similar property, a taxpayer for whom such property was prepared or produced, or

    (C) a taxpayer in whose hands the basis of such property is determined, for purposes of determining gain from a sale or exchange, in whole or part by reference to the basis of such property in the hands of a taxpayer described in subparagraph (A) or (B)".[3]

Subsection (A) of § 1221(3) effectively prevents the creative person from achieving capital gain on the transfer of copyright works he has created. The provisions of (C) prevent a donee of the creator from enjoying a tax advantage not available to the creator. Thus, a family member is effectively prevented by subsection (C) from achieving capital gain in a transaction that would have produced ordinary income for the creator. For transferees not covered by § 1221(3) there are no specific statutory rules on the possibility of achieving capital gain on a sale or exchange of copyright property.

Prior to 1950 and the enactment of § 1221(3) there was no specific exclusion of copyright or literary property in the Internal Revenue Code definition of the term capital asset. The non-professional author or composer was able to treat gains from the exploitation of his works as capital gain if the sale or exchange and holding period requirements of the statute were met. These requirements had their own built-in pitfalls, but at least there was hope for the amateur. The professional, even before 1950, was precluded from capital gain treatment on income from the exploitation of his works; his works were considered held by him primarily for sale to customers in the ordinary course of business and thereby excluded from the definition of a capital asset even prior to the 1950 amendment.

The popular impetus for the enactment of § 1221(3) of the Internal Revenue Code was the large capital gain achieved by President Eisenhower—an amateur author—on the publication of his memoirs. This event fanned the feeling of the Internal Revenue Service and the tax law writers in Congress that the work product of the author, composer or creative person is integrally wound up in the performance of personal services. Personal service income has traditionally been ordinary income not entitled to capital gain treatment. It is an interesting commentary on the priorities of our times that the patented work product of the inventor is afforded special treatment under our tax laws by way of capital gains, whereas the work product of the author, composer or other creative person is subject to taxation at ordinary rates.

3. I.R.C. §§ 1221(3), 1231(b)(1)(C).

A theatrical production, radio program, newspaper cartoon strip or any other property eligible for protection (whether under statute or common law) are considered by the Regulations to be "similar property" to a copyright, a literary, musical or artistic composition and are excluded from the definition of capital asset when held by the creator or one using his basis for purposes of computing gain.[9] The Commissioner's interpretation of excluded property has been further expanded by the Court of Claims to cover all types of artistic works which are products of personal efforts and skill. Specifically, the Court denied capital gains treatment in a sale by the creator of the format for the radio program quiz show "Take It Or Leave It", even though the format had been declared not subject to copyright by the Copyright Office.[10]

Recognizing that the exclusion from capital gains for creative property sold by the creator was based upon the nature of the creator's input—personal services—the Commissioner has agreed to capital gain treatment on the sale of copyrighted motion picture films by a corporate producer. In a Revenue Ruling that has been superseded on other grounds, the Commissioner stated:[11]

> "Many corporations, including some whose stock is widely held and traded on established stock exchanges, create copyrights as well as other property described in paragraph (3) of section 1221. The property created by these corporations is not considered to be created by the personal efforts of a taxpayer where all of the costs and expenses are paid for by the corporation at the current going rate for the services rendered. The production of each of the films in the instant case involved a multiplicity of skills and abilities, the combined efforts of numerous individuals of various backgrounds and trades, and the use of substantial amounts of capital. Thus, no single individual may be said to have created by his personal efforts the films in question or a property in the films."

This ruling is significant in that it recognizes that the corporate producer who uses input from varied individuals may be able to achieve a capital gain that the individual creative person cannot. The producer must, of course, circumvent all the other problems of achieving capital gain, such as the possibility that he is holding pictures primarily for sale in the ordinary course of business.

For the holder of copyright property other than the creator or one using his basis for purposes of gain, capital gain is available if the other requirements of the Code are met. The transfer must be tantamount to a sale. If something less than the entire bundle of rights held by the transferor is transferred, there may not be a "sale". The Commissioner now recognizes that a copyright may be divided so that

9. Regs. § 1.1221–1.

10. Cranford v. U. S., 338 F.2d 379 (Ct. of Claims, 1964).

11. Rev.Rul. 55–706, CB 1955–2, p. 300. Superseded on other grounds by Rev.Rul. 62–141, CB 1962–2, p. 182.

a transfer may be considered a sale if there is a grant of the exclusive right to exploit the copyrighted work throughout the life of the copyright in a particular medium. A transfer of less would be considered a grant of a license and not a sale. Thus, a copyright proprietor could sell publishing rights to one purchaser and achieve capital gain and retain other rights for sale to a different purchaser.

The Commissioner has also recognized that for a transfer to qualify as a sale, the consideration received by the transferor does not have to be in a lump sum. It may be in the nature of a royalty measured by a percentage of the receipts from the sale, performance, exhibition or publication of the copyrighted work or be measured by the number of copies sold, performances given or exhibitions made of the copyrighted work. The royalty may be payable over a period generally coterminous with the grantee's use of the copyrighted work. Additionally, of course, the proprietor must have held the asset for more than six months.[q]

Maximum Tax on Earned Income

In an effort to reduce the pressure for the use of tax loopholes and to forestall the development of new methods of tax avoidance, the Tax Reform Act of 1969 introduced the concept of a maximum tax on earned income. It is questionable that the stated objectives were met to any substantial degree but the provision may reduce the tax bite of the creative person who has a high income. The term "earned income" is intended to include wages, salaries, professional fees and other compensation for personal services. Covered would be payments made to a creative person directly for personal services performed, royalties for the use of a work created by the personal efforts of the creative person and proceeds from the sale by the creative person of the work product of his personal efforts.

The maximum tax on earned income for years after 1971 is 50%. The general effect of the statute is to tax earned income at the regular rates of tax until the first bracket over 50% (currently $38,000 for single taxpayers and $52,000 for joint returns), at which point the balance of earned income which would otherwise fall into brackets exceeding 50% is taxed at the 50% rate. Taxable income which does not qualify as earned income is then taxed at the regular rates at the tax bracket into which it would fall when added to the earned income. A simple example of the computation is as follows:

Taxpayer A who is single with no dependents has a total taxable income after deductions of $60,000, of which $50,000 is earned taxable income. His tax would be computed as follows:

(a) On the 1st $38,000 of earned taxable income which falls in the 50% and lower tax brackets, a tax at normal rates of $13,290

q. Now one year. 26 U.S.C.A. § 1222.
(Ed.)

(b) On the earned taxable income which falls
in brackets in excess of 50% ($50,000
less $38,000) or $12,000, a tax at the
50% rate of 6,000

(c) Tax on the balance of taxable income
computed as follows:
Normal tax on $60,000 .... $26,390
Less: Normal tax on $50,000 ETI 20,190
Normal tax on the $10,000 ordinary tax-
able income falling between the $60,000
and $50,000 6,200

(d) Total Tax $25,490

For a single taxpayer with earned taxable income of $100,000 and no offsets for tax preferences, the maximum tax on earned income would result in a tax savings of $8,800. . . .

Income Averaging

Another tool the creative person may use to reduce his tax burden is income averaging. Averaging is generally worthwhile for taxpayers with wide fluctuations in taxable income over relatively short periods of time. If the individual's adjusted taxable income for the year in question is at least $3,000 more than 120% of the average adjusted taxable income for the four years prior to the computation year, he may avail himself of income averaging. Once the income is qualified for averaging, the $3,000 figure is unimportant and the entire excess in the computation year over 120% of the average base period adjusted taxable income is subject to averaging. One-fifth of the income subject to averaging is taxed at the first rate brackets after the non-averageable income. The tax rate on that one-fifth is then multiplied by five to obtain the tax on the income subject to averaging. Tax savings is achieved by the taxing of all income subject to averaging at the first brackets above the non-averageable income.

Taxpayers who avail themselves of income averaging may not take advantage of the alternative tax on long-term capital gains and the 50% maximum tax on earned income. . . .

Depreciation

A reasonable allowance for depreciation is allowed as a deduction from gross income for (1) property used in a trade or business and (2) property held for the production of income.[40] Creative property may fall into either (1) or (2). For the publisher or movie distributor the copyright or similar property he owns is being used in his trade or business of publishing or movie distribution, as the case may be. For the heir of an author or songwriter who owns a copyright and is receiving royalties in a passive capacity without being in the publishing or music business, the copyright property is being held for the production of income. The Commissioner's Regulations recognize this and specifically provide "If an intangible asset is known from ex-

---

40. I.R.C. § 167(a).

perience or other factors to be of use in the business or in the production of income for only a limited period, the length of which can be estimated with reasonable accuracy, such an intangible asset may be the subject of a depreciation allowance. Examples are patents and copyrights." [41]

The amount which may be depreciated over the useful life of the copyright property is its cost or other basis. For the purchaser cost is relatively easily defined as the purchase price paid including, in the case of property purchased subject to a mortgage indebtedness, the amount of the mortgage debt. Basis for the heir would be the value at the date of death (or alternate valuation date six months thereafter if elected by the executor). For purposes of computing gain, a donee would generally use the donor's basis plus any gift taxes paid.

If the useful life of a copyrighted property cannot otherwise be determined, it would be depreciated over the life of the original term of copyright, 28 years.[r] Because there is not a very great percentage of renewal in the copyright field, a taxpayer would be reasonably safe in using the original term as the starting point for determining useful life. If it can be established that the particular copyrighted work being depreciated is of a nature that its useful life (generally the period it will be productive of income) is less than the copyright term, that lesser period may be used for purposes of computing depreciation.

Normally, the method of depreciation would be the "straight line" where the cost or basis of the copyright property less its estimated salvage value is deductible in equal annual amounts over the period of the estimated useful life of the copyright property. In the movie industry, the Internal Revenue Service has approved the use of the income forecast method to depreciate motion picture films.[48] Under this method a particular year's depreciation is determined by multiplying the tax basis of the film (less salvage value) by a fraction, the numerator of which is the net receipts produced by the film during the taxable year and the denominator of which is the total amount of net receipts projected for the film's useful life (including actual income realized to date). In determining the projected receipts from the film, it may be necessary to include projected receipts from television distribution in addition to anticipated receipts from theatre exhibition and other exploitation.[49]

The theory of the income forecast method is that the owner of a motion picture should be able to depreciate the picture based upon the flow of income from the film rather than upon the passage of time. Thus, since in most instances the bulk of the receipts from the exploitation of a film are derived in the early years of its useful life,

41. Regs. 1.167(a)–3.

r. Now life plus 50 years. See page 805, above. (Ed.)

48. Rev.Rul. 60–358, 1960–2 CB 68, as amplified by Rev.Rul. 64–273, 1964–2 CB 62.

49. Rev.Proc. 71–29, Note 1971–2 CB 568.

the income forecast method results in a substantial portion of the film's cost being written off over a relatively short period of time. Under the income forecast method, the forecast must be based on conditions existing at the end of each tax year. If after the initial forecast has been made it is found that projected net receipts were overestimated, the forecast should be revised for the purpose of computing later years' depreciation.

The ability to take large depreciation deductions over short periods of time have made motion pictures a popular tax sheltered investment vehicle in recent years. The investment in a motion picture also may qualify for the investment tax credit. Up to 7% of a taxpayer's depreciation base in a motion picture may be claimed as a credit directly against his tax liability.

Transfers to a Controlled Corporation

The creative person may wish to reduce his tax burden by transferring his creative properties to a corporation which he controls. The transfer of property in exchange for a controlling interest in the corporation's stock would not be taxable. By using a corporate entity to exploit his work product, the creative person may be able to take advantage of many of the employee benefit provisions available to corporate employees, one of the most attractive of which is the qualified retirement program. Contributions to such a plan have the effect of deferring the taxation on income until termination of employment, retirement or death. Benefits from such plans paid after the employee's death and to the extent attributable to contributions made by the corporation on the employee's behalf would be exempt from Federal estate tax.

The Internal Revenue Service has a formidable array of tools to combat any attempts by a creative person to use a corporate entity to convert into capital gain income that would have been ordinary income had it been received by the creative person in his individual capacity. The collapsible corporation rules were enacted in response to a practice in the motion picture industry whereby producers, directors and leading actors would organize a corporation for the production of a single motion picture. Working for modest salaries the picture would be completed on a low cash budget. Upon completion of the motion picture the corporation would then be liquidated with the shareholders reporting a capital gain for the difference between their cash investment in the corporation's stock and the value of the completed picture. The effect would be to convert the exhibition proceeds, which would have been reported as ordinary income by the corporation (or the shareholders had they operated in noncorporate form from the outset), into capital gain. The basic principle of the collapsible corporation rules is to tax a shareholder at ordinary income rates on the proceeds of a sale, exchange or liquidation of his shares.

Another tool available to the Commissioner is the special tax on the undistributed income of personal holding companies. Personal holding companies are generally corporations controlled by a limited number of shareholders who derive a large percentage of their income from specified sources, including copyright royalties from shareholder created works. The Commissioner may also attempt to use the provisions of § 532(a) which impose a special tax on the accumulated earnings of any corporation which is formed or availed of for the purposes of avoiding the income tax on its shareholders by permitting its earnings and profits to accumulate instead of being distributed. These provisions are beyond the scope of this limited treatment and are merely mentioned to highlight some of the problems which must be considered when the creative person attempts to exploit his works through the use of a corporate entity.

Conclusion

We have seen that the attorney representing the creative person who maintains an awareness of the content of the provisions of the tax law has an opportunity for reducing the tax burdens that fall on his successful client. Although denied the special treatment granted inventors whereby a patented work product may give rise to capital gain for the creator, there still remains substantial opportunity for a softening of the impact of the Federal income tax through proper planning. The individual creative person may compute his tax using income averaging or the maximum tax on earned income. Substantial income tax savings may be achieved by heirs and the estates of creative people or copyright proprietors who during their lifetime have considered the effects of the rules dealing with income in respect of a decedent. Finally, for those willing to forego the casual comfort of handling business through one's own personal checking account, the corporate form has its own blend of interesting avenues for creative tax planning.

SELECTED BIBLIOGRAPHY

Mott, Authors' Tax Problems—A Summary of the Provisions of the Internal Revenue Code, 22 Fed.B.J. 148 (1962); Symposium, Artists and Authors—Estate Planning and Administration, 14 Real Prop., Probate and Trust J. 45 (1979); Pilpel, Tax Aspects of Copyright Property, in Copyright Problems Analyzed (Kupferman Ed. 1966); Taxation of Copyright Income Under the 1954 IRC, 1960 Wash.U.L.Q. 195; Linton, Tax Problems With Television Properties: Films, Copyrights and Property Rights, 26 J.Taxation 240 (1967).

C. TRADEMARKS

MORREALE, PATENTS, KNOW–HOW AND TRADEMARKS: A TAX OVERVIEW

29 Tax Lawyer 568–571 (1976).*

Self-Developed Trademarks and Trade Names

Most significant business-related trademark or trade name expenditures, such as promotional and advertising expenditures, are currently deductible as ordinary and necessary business expenses, even if they relate to a trademark or trade name with an indefinite commercially useful life.

Section 177 provides, however, that a taxpayer must elect to amortize certain types of trademark and trade name expenditures over not less than five years; absent an election, such expenditures are neither deductible nor amortizable. For example, expenditures for legal services and name searches relating to filing and prosecuting an application for federal or state registration of a mark, and for legal services incurred in an infringement proceeding or in the defense of a mark, should be amortized. Unless a taxpayer *elects* to amortize this type of expenditure, he will be entitled to an ordinary income deduction for the expenditures only if he abandons the trademark as worthless.

Sales of Trademarks and Trade Names

A trademark is "property" within the meaning of section 1221, and almost always represents a capital asset in the hands of a seller. Thus, trademark sales produce capital gains. The purchaser, however, ordinarily cannot deduct *or amortize,* under section 177 or any other provision, any portion of the purchase price, because a trademark does not have a readily determinable useful life. This is true even if payments are for the purpose of protecting or expanding a previously owned trademark, or for an agreement to discontinue the use of a trademark if the effect of such an agreement is the purchase of a trademark. Thus, a deduction against ordinary income can be taken only if a purchased trademark becomes demonstrably worthless and is abandoned by the purchaser.

Trade names and service marks are not ordinarily sold except as part of a sale of an entire business. Payments purportedly for the transfer of a trade name or service mark incident to the sale of a business will generally not be treated separately for tax purposes. Such payments would instead usually be regarded as attributable to a component of residual goodwill, ordinarily representing capital gains to a seller and nondeductible payments to a purchaser. If the purchase price includes contingent payments, however, section 1253, discussed below, may trigger ordinary income, and the payments may, in turn, become deductible by the purchaser. The Service position is that section 1253 applies to any amount attributable to the transfer of a trademark or trade name incident to the transfer of a business. Thus, in the common situation where the sale of a business includes a transfer of trademarks and a trade name, and the price includes "earn-out" payments contingent upon sales or gross income of the purchaser, the Service may treat all of the contingent payments as ordinary income.

Trademark Licenses

1. Trademark Licensors

During the 1950's and 1960's there was considerable litigation, particularly in the franchise area, as to whether a trademark or franchise transfer produced capital gains. The courts differed widely in cases that often involved quite similar agreements. Section 1253, added by the Tax Reform Act of 1969, was enacted in large part to add a measure of certainty to this area.

Unfortunately for trademark licensors, the certainty established by section 1253 is that most trademark licenses will now produce ordinary income. Section 1253 applies to trademark licenses entered into or renewed after December 31, 1969. Section 1253(a) provides:

> *General Rule.*—A transfer of a franchise, trademark or trade name shall not be treated as a sale or exchange of a capital asset if the transferor retains any significant power, right, or continuing interest with respect to the subject matter of the franchise, trademark or trade name.

If a trademark licensor retains quality control rights, or if a license provides for *significant* contingent payments, *all* license payments will be ordinary income, i. e., in either case a "significant power, right or continuing interest" will have been retained. A trademark licensor almost always retains product quality control rights, because such rights usually must be retained for trademark law reasons absent an affiliation between the licensor and licensee. Moreover, a substantial portion of trademark license payments are usually contingent upon sales of trademarked products. Most trademark licenses therefore produce ordinary income.

There is a limited exception to ordinary income treatment for *noncontingent* trademark license payments if the contingent payments are not a "substantial element" of total estimated payments. Contingent payments will not be deemed to represent a substantial element if their estimated total amount is fifty percent or less of total estimated license payments. If total estimated contingent payments exceed fifty percent, all payments, including lump-sum or fixed payments, are taxed as ordinary income.

2. Trademark Licensees

The corollary to section 1253 treatment of trademark licensors is that trademark licensees can now usually deduct license payments. Thus, a trademark licensee can generally deduct or amortize trademark license payments that, for whatever reason, represent ordinary income to the licensor.

If a license produces ordinary income because of section 1253, contingent payments are treated as deductible under section 162 rather than under section 167. This result follows even where the licensed trademark rights have a determinable useful life, e. g., under a license with a fixed term. Accordingly a subsequent disposition by a licensee (for example, by assignment or sublicense) of rights under such a license should not result in depreciation recapture on account of prior deductions of contingent payments. Amortizable fixed amounts, however, are probably not currently deductible under section 162.

SELECTED BIBLIOGRAPHY

Kegan, Tax Treatment of Transfers of Trademark and Trade Secret Rights, 3 A.P.L.A.Q.J. 46 (1975); Cohan, Income Tax Considerations in Trademarks and Unfair Competition, 51 Trademark Rep. 866 (1961); Kragen & Pearce, Tax Problems in the Trademark and Trade Name Field, 44 Calif.L.Rev. 511 (1956); Kragen, Tax Aspects of Trademarks (And Patents), 58 Trademark Rep. 810 (1968); Mann, Tax Treatment of Trademark Litigation Expenses, 55 Trademark Rep. 39 (1965); Meyer & Creed, Trademarks and Taxes, 8 IDEA 377 (1964).

Part Five

INTERNATIONAL PROTECTION: THE CONVENTIONS

I. COPYRIGHT

See Statute Supplement 17 U.S.C.A. § 104.

RINGER, THE ROLE OF THE UNITED STATES IN INTERNATIONAL COPYRIGHT—PAST, PRESENT, AND FUTURE

56 Georgetown L.J. 1050, 1051–1064 (1968).*

Historical Background

The Origins of International Copyright

Copyright as a legal concept originated in the form of direct sovereign grants of monopolies during the Renaissance as a response to the needs created by the invention of movable type. During the Age of Reason, copyright in the form of national statutory protection developed as part of the growth of organized publishing industries. Similarly, international copyright appears to have been a response to the Industrial Revolution; the expanding technology in communications necessitated reciprocal protection of works between countries.

At first, international copyright protection was the exception rather than the rule. National copyright laws usually denied protection to works originating in other countries, and such exceptions as existed were derived from bilateral treaties negotiated between particular countries on the basis of strict reciprocity. Domestic printers and publishers were unwilling to give up their ready markets for unauthorized reprints, but the local "piratical" copies were cheap in quality as well as price. Foreign authors had ample reason to complain of the mutilation of their works and the loss of royalties in other countries. National authors "found that their interests were prejudiced by the abundant publication and sale of unauthorized foreign works at cheap prices."

European attitudes toward this situation first began to change around the middle of the 19th century. In 1852 France extended copyright protection to all works, foreign and domestic alike, and while this generous gesture did not set a pattern, it accelerated the movement toward a multilateral copyright system. The Association Litteraire et Artistique Internationale (ALAI) was formed in Paris and took the lead in seeking ways to establish an international union of countries pledged to the protection of authors' rights.

* © 1968 Georgetown Law Journal Association.

918

Development of The Berne Convention

A conference held under ALAI auspices in Berne in 1883 marked the end of the discussion phase and the beginning of actual work on what became the Berne Convention of 1886. The goals of the conference were: "(1) The study of the legislative enactments affecting literary property in all civilized countries; (2) the study of important points of these enactments with a view to unification and the foundation of a union for the protection of literary property; (3) the drawing up of certain articles, clear and concise, setting forth the principles that are most likely to be accepted by the various powers and which should constitute the text of a universal convention."

A draft convention prepared by the ALAI was discussed at the 1883 conference, and the government of Switzerland agreed to circulate it to "all civilized countries." The Swiss president's letter of transmittal emphasized the "imperative necessity" of protecting the rights of writers and artists in international relations. He stated that previous agreements were "far from protecting the author's rights in a uniform, efficacious, and complete manner" and that the problem was "connected with the divergency of national laws, which the conventional regime ha[d] necessarily been obliged to take into account."

Intergovernmental conferences considering the draft convention were held at Berne in 1884, 1885, and 1886, the last comprising a full diplomatic conference at which the final instrument was signed. The original Berne Convention of September 9, 1886, was a modest beginning; nevertheless, it was the first truly multilateral copyright treaty in history, and it established some important basic principles. Rather than reciprocity ("I'll protect your works, but only to the extent you protect my works"), the Berne Convention adopted the principle of national treatment ("I'll protect your works to the same extent I protect my own works, if you promise to do the same"). The convention set up a "Union for the protection of authors over their literary and artistic works" consisting of the contracting states, and established a requirement that among Union members the right of translation had to be protected for a minimum of ten years.

The original Berne Convention provided that rights enjoyed under it "shall be subject to the accomplishment of the conditions and formalities prescribed by law in the country of origin of the work, and must not exceed in the other countries the term of protection granted in the said country of origin." In the successive revisions of the Convention, the minimum requirements governing protection have been substantially expanded. A Berne Union member accepting the Brussels text of 1948, which is the latest revision now in effect, must, with some exceptions, accord protection to the works of other member countries without requiring compliance with any formalities, during the life of the author and fifty years after his death. The Convention provides specific minimum requirements with respect to the protection of certain exclusive rights, most notably the so-called "moral rights" of the author. Any country that now wants to join the Berne Union must obligate itself to grant a very high level of copyright protection.

The original Berne Union consisted of 14 countries. The present membership comprises 58 countries that have adhered to one or more of the Berne revisions; one country is still bound by the Berlin revision of 1908, 14 countries are bound by the Rome text of 1928, and 43 countries are bound by the Brussels revision of 1948. On July 14, 1967, a new revision of the Berne Convention was signed at Stockholm, but as yet it has not been ratified or acceded to by any country. The Stockholm revisions, notably the new "Protocol Regarding Developing Countries," mark a substantial departure from the high level of copyright protection that hitherto has been characteristic of the Berne Convention. The implications of the Stockholm Act for international copyright in general and the United States in particular will be examined more closely below.

International Copyright in the United States Before World War II

For a century after enactment of the first United States copyright statute in 1790, only published works by citizens and residents of the United States could secure statutory copyright protection. For a century, the United States was exceptionally parochial in copyright matters, not only denying any protection to the published works of nonresident foreign authors, but actually appearing to encourage piracy. Common law protection for unpublished works regardless of the nationality of their authors was cold comfort at a time when publication was the only profitable way to disseminate a work. "Under such circumstances, other nations were understandably reluctant to protect American works."

Literary piracy, particularly of British works, became common in the 19th century, and efforts began in the United States in the 1830's to secure an "international copyright law." In 1837 Henry Clay, as chairman of a Senate select committee, submitted a report strongly recommending enactment of international copyright legislation. "In principle," he said, "the committee perceives no objection to considering the republic of letters as one great community, and adopting a system of protection for literary property which should be common to all parts of it." Clay's report was accompanied by a bill intended to extend U.S. copyright protection to British and French authors under rigorous conditions. The Clay bill was reintroduced several times between 1837 and 1842, but never reached a vote.

There followed more than a half-century of agitation for international copyright protection in the United States. Efforts to conclude a bilateral copyright treaty with Great Britain failed, and legislation to extend U.S. copyright protection to foreign authors attracted strong opposition, principally by American printing and publishing interests who believed that their livelihood depended upon cheap reprints of English books. They demanded that the extension of U.S.

copyright to foreign works be conditioned on compliance with a requirement of manufacture in this country.

The legislative phase of the international copyright movement in the United States began shortly after the Civil War and finally achieved success in the International Copyright Act of March 3, 1891. During much of this same period the Berne Convention of 1886 was under gestation, and its development was well known to those interested in international copyright in the United States. Yet U.S. government representatives refrained from participating directly in the development of the Convention, under circumstances that leave many questions unanswered.

The prevailing official attitude was summarized in a letter sent by Secretary of State Bayard on June 29, 1886, in response to a Swiss note inviting U.S. participation in the final diplomatic conference. Secretary Bayard stated that the question of international copyright pending before Congress had not advanced far enough in the legislative channel to enable the Executive to act with the assurance of congressional approval, and that the pendency of measures in Congress made it impracticable for the United States to appoint a plenipotentiary to attend the conference at Berne for the purpose of signing the proposed convention. The American government's attitude toward the project was "merely one of expectancy and reserve," favoring the plan in principle but without determinate views as to the shape it should assume. It was "unprepared to suggest modifications which might conform the convention to the legislation which Congress may hereafter deem appropriate." Secretary Bayard specifically held out the possibility of future accession to the convention "should it become expedient and practicable to do so," thus echoing President Cleveland's message to Congress on December 8, 1885. This possibility was also reflected in the language of the International Copyright Act of 1891:

> That this act shall apply to a citizen or subject of a foreign state or nation when such foreign state or nation permits to citizens of the United States of America the benefit of copyright on substantially the same basis as its own citizens; or when such foreign state or nation is a party to an international agreement which provides for reciprocity in the granting of copyright, by the terms of which agreement the United States may, at its pleasure, become a party to such agreement.

The compromise that made the Act of 1891 possible was the introduction of a requirement of domestic manufacture for "a book, photograph, chromo, or lithograph." Under section 4956 of the Act, copyright could be secured only by making registration before publication and by depositing two copies of the work on or before the date of publication anywhere. Moreover, in the case of books and certain graphic works, the two copies had to be manufactured in the United States.

The requirements of the 1891 "manufacturing clause" were so rigid that they made the extension of copyright protection to foreigners illusory. Acts were passed in 1904 and 1905 in an effort to liberalize the clause by giving foreigners extra time to comply with the manufacturing requirement, and finally, in 1906, Congress undertook work on a general revision of the U.S. copyright laws. This revision effort was at its peak when, on October 14, 1908, a major conference for revision of the Berne Convention was held in Berlin. The United States was invited to attend with "full freedom of action," but the delegate, Thorvald Solberg, the Register of Copyrights, was sent as an observer only. Mr. Solberg explained to the Conference that the United States found it impracticable to send a delegate authorized to commit it to actual adhesion to the Berne Convention since some of the questions to be discussed there were pending before the Congress and premature action at the Convention might embarrass the legislative branch of the Government.

The original Berne Convention of 1886 had allowed member countries to impose certain formalities, such as notice, registration, and domestic manufacture, as conditions of copyright. This was changed by article 4 of the Berlin revision of 1908, which provided without qualification that "the enjoyment and exercise of these rights shall not be subject to the performance of any formality." This made it impossible for the United States to join the Berne Union without substantial changes in its domestic law.

In 1909, the year after the Berlin revision abolished formalities in international copyright, Congress passed a complete revision of the United States copyright law. The Act of March 3, 1909, which was essentially the same as the present American copyright law, retained rather rigid notice formalities, and, while further liberalizing the manufacturing provisions, retained the basic requirement of domestic manufacture as a condition of copyright in English-language books and periodicals. American adherence to the Berne Convention thus became impossible unless Congress could be persuaded to change the law again, but this obviously was unfeasible in the immediate future. Active U.S. participation in the development and revision of the Berne Convention in its nascent stages might not have avoided this result, but it might have prevented the paths from diverging so sharply.

The 1909 Act continued the provision of the 1891 statute under which the President is empowered to proclaim the existence of bilateral copyright relations between the United States and particular foreign countries. This system has proved cumbersome and ineffective in comparison with the simplicity, certainty, and other advantages offered by multilateral arrangements. In fact, efforts to achieve adherence to the Berne Convention began less than 15 years after the enactment of the 1909 statute; following the First World War, the increasing use of American works in other countries brought with it a demand that the United States adhere to the Berne Convention. Beginning in 1922, a series of bills for this purpose was introduced in Congress.

The history during the 1920's and 1930's of the combined legislative programs to obtain general revision of the copyright law and U. S. adherence to the Berne Convention makes painful reading. One commentator attributed the total failure of both these programs to the effort to link them together, pointing out that "the development of radio and motion picture technology during the 1920's introduced new interests into the orbit of intellectual properties, and made more difficult the task of securing agreement on proposals to effect a general revision of the copyright law." On the other hand, a motion picture attorney felt that the United States never adhered to Berne "primarily because it contains concepts which are foreign to our concepts of copyright, such as copyright without formalities, protection of moral rights, retroactivity and also because of the requirement of our manufacturing clause."

Whatever the reason for the failure of these legislative programs, the United States had become an exporter in the copyright trade, and something had to be done. It did not take American copyright owners long to discover an attractive loophole that has come to be known as the "backdoor to Berne." By the simple device of simultaneous publication of an American work in the United States and in a country which was a Berne Union member, such as Canada, a work became entitled to protection throughout the Berne Union without any corresponding obligations on the United States to protect Berne works. This practice of simultaneous publication became extremely widespread, and provoked resentment that is surprising only in its relative mildness. In 1914 the Berne Union adopted a retaliatory protocol under which member countries could, if they chose, limit the protection of nonmember authors under certain conditions, and there were cases in which the existence of true simultaneous publication was decided on narrow grounds.

In 1928 the Berne Convention was revised at Rome, and the level of protection was again raised. In an effort to induce the United States to join the Union, however, the Rome Convention permitted nonmembers to adhere to the Berlin text of 1908 until August 1, 1931. Strenuous efforts in Congress to meet this deadline were unsuccessful; although Senate approval of the Rome version was prematurely obtained in 1935, it was immediately withdrawn. Another major effort sponsored by a committee formed under the auspices of an American organization related to the League of Nations resulted in the introduction of a bill in 1940, but it died in committee.

Inter-American Conventions

Efforts to develop multilateral copyright arrangements in the Americas began in the 1880's, at about the same time the Berne Convention and the United States International Copyright Act were being formed. These efforts produced a series of Pan-American copyright conventions, but for all practical purposes the United States is a member of only one of them, the Buenos Aires Convention of 1910. It has failed to accept the later revisions adopted at Havana in 1928 and at Washington in 1946, which are more closely analogous to the principles of the Berne Convention.

Under the Buenos Aires Convention a work is protected in a member country if it has been copyrighted in another member country and bears a form of copyright notice. Since no legislation implementing it has ever been enacted, the conditions and extent of protection under this convention remain somewhat unclear in the United States. Furthermore, during the past twenty years there has been an unmistakable trend away from regional conventions and in favor of worldwide copyright arrangements, and the Universal Copyright Convention has superseded the Pan-American conventions in many cases.

The Universal Copyright Convention

After the Second World War it became even more imperative for the Berne Union and the United States to reach an accommodation. The failure of the United States to offer foreign works the level of copyright protection generally available throughout the Berne Union gave rise to indignation, which was intensified by the practice of American copyright owners' taking full advantage of Berne protection in other countries. The situation grew worse with the emergence of the United States as the leading exporter of copyrighted works in the world. As one commentator has said, "Consideration was given to attracting the Americas into Berne, but member countries refused to tolerate their own retrogression for the simple expediency of attracting the American countries." The postwar situation was urgent, but it seemed clear at that time that the Berne countries would refuse to lower protection sufficiently to attract American adherence and that further efforts by the United States to join the Berne Union would be futile. The approach that was adopted represented a compromise: a new "common denominator" convention that was intended to establish a minimum level of international copyright relations throughout the world, without weakening or supplanting the Berne Convention. The Universal Copyright Convention, as it came to be called, was sponsored by UNESCO, and one of the leaders in its development was the United States.

Advocates of international copyright protection began once again to lay the groundwork for altering the domestic law in the United States while concomitantly devising universal agreement that would appeal to all countries committed to the promotion of cultural interchange. Furthermore, "vigorous leaders appeared in the United States among the champions of international copyright, and organizations of creators, producers, and consumers of literary works became alerted to the[se] questions."

The landmark Universal Copyright Convention was signed at Geneva on September 6, 1952, and, following the required 12 ratifications, took effect on September 16, 1955. The United States was one of the first signatories to ratify it. The most significant provisions of the Convention can be summarized as follows:

1. *Adequate and Effective Protection.* Under article I, the contracting states are obliged to "provide for the adequate and effective protection of the rights of authors and other copyright proprietors. . . ."

2. *National Treatment.* Article II provides that the "published works of nationals of any Contracting State and works first published in that State shall enjoy in each other Contracting State the same protection as that other State accords to works of its nationals first published in its own territory." There is a similar provision for unpublished works.

3. *Formalities.* Article III, which represents the great compromise of the U.C.C., provides that the formal requirements, such as notice, registration, and manufacture, of a contracting state's copyright law are satisfied with respect to foreign U.C.C. works "if from the time of first publication all of the copies of the work . . . bear the symbol © accompanied by the name of the copyright proprietor and the year of first publication placed in such manner and location as to give reasonable notice of claim of copyright."

4. *Duration of Protection.* Another major compromise is embodied in article IV of the U.C.C. The minimum term, subject to various detailed qualifications and exceptions, is to be either 25 years from the death of the author or from the date of first publication.

5. *Translation Rights.* The U.C.C., in article V, requires contracting states to give exclusive translation rights to foreign U.C.C. authors for at least seven years; thereafter a rather cumbersome compulsory licensing system can be established.

6. *Nonretroactivity.* Under article VII a contracting state is not obliged to protect works that are permanently in its public domain on the date the Convention becomes effective in that state.

7. *Berne safeguard clause.* An enormously important provision of the U.C.C. is found in article XVII and the "Appendix Declaration" attached to it. These provide, in effect, that no Berne country can denounce the Berne Convention and rely on the U.C.C. in its copyright relations with Berne Union members.

Thus, at least in comparison with the 1948 Brussels revision of the Berne Convention, the Universal Copyright Convention represents a rather low-level copyright arrangement, resembling in many ways the original 1886 Berne text.

The minimum requirements as to exclusive rights are extremely modest, being limited to providing "adequate and effective protection" and translation rights which can be subject to compulsory licensing. The requirements as to minimum duration of protection are also very permissive, and a system of copyright notice is actually sanctioned as a substitute for other formalities. It is therefore understandable that Berne Union members regarded the U.C.C. as a retrogressive step, and insisted on safeguarding the Berne Convention from the danger of being undermined by the defection of Berne members to the U.C.C.

Developments, 1952–1967

U.S. Ratification of the Universal Copyright Convention

Getting the United States to ratify the Universal Copyright Convention and to enact the statutory revisions necessary to implement it was more of an accomplishment than the development of the U.C. C. itself. That there was opposition goes without saying, but it was neutralized or overcome in a remarkably short time. On August 31, 1954, President Eisenhower signed Public Law 743 which conformed the indigenous copyright law to the Convention, and on November 5, 1954, he signed the instrument of ratification of the U.C.C. itself.

Since the Universal Copyright Convention was to a considerable extent tailored to meet the requirements of existing United States law, the changes necessary to implement it were, for the most part, technical. The most important alteration involved a complete waiver of all formalities as to deposit, registration, manufacture, and importation for foreign U.C.C. works, as long as the copies of the work bore the notice of copyright prescribed by the Convention. As a practical matter, this has removed the manufacturing requirement for the majority of English language works of foreign authorship and has induced a much greater use of copyright notices on foreign works.

Current Status of the U.C.C.

In general, the Universal Copyright Convention has been a genuine success. It has been ratified or acceded to by 55 countries, nearly as many as belong to the Berne Union. It has vastly simplified the international copyright relations of the United States with other countries and of other countries with the United States, and it has brought some newly independent or developing countries into the international copyright community on terms that they found acceptable.

For some time after the U.C.C. came into effect, it appeared to have achieved a reasonably harmonious coexistence with the Berne Union. There was some acrimony between the two secretariats, but the governing bodies of the two conventions began holding their meetings together, and there was some talk of working toward a merger that would raise the level of U.C.C. protection. However, the emergence of newly independent countries seeking to import foreign educational materials on favorable terms began to impair this accord in the late 1950's and the problem reached crisis proportions by 1967.

HADL, TOWARD INTERNATIONAL COPYRIGHT REVISION, REPORT ON THE MEETINGS IN PARIS AND GENEVA, SEPTEMBER 1970

18 Bull. Copyright Soc'y 183–189, 207–208 (1971).*

International copyright was plunged into crisis in 1967 at the Stockholm Intellectual Property Conference. One of the objectives of this Conference was the revision of the Berne Convention including special provisions for the benefit of developing countries. These provisions were annexed to the draft text of the Convention as a Protocol Regarding Developing Countries (hereafter, "Protocol", or "Stockholm Protocol"). During the Conference, however, it became apparent that the developing countries were not satisfied with the concessions proposed in the draft text. Led by India, they were able to orchestrate a chorus of protest which sought much wider gains. The developed countries, unprepared for this onslaught and without strong leadership, found themselves in disarray and unable to silence the developing countries. As a result, the final text of the Protocol adopted by the Conference gave developing countries very broad and uncontrolled privileges with respect to works copyrighted in Berne Union countries. For the most part, these privileges were considered unacceptable by the developed countries.

The Stockholm victory won by the developing countries proved, however, to be a hollow one. They had left one loophole, namely, the provision that unless a developed country agreed to accept the Stockholm Protocol, it could not be bound by it. To this day, no major developed country has ratified or acceded to the Stockholm Protocol, and none is expected to do so in the future. In the aftermath of Stockholm what became apparent was that the developing countries had won the opening battle, but they had not won the war.

For their part, the developing countries were not without recourse against the refusal of the developed countries to accept the Stockholm Protocol. They had two substantial weapons in their arsenal. First, they could renounce their international copyright obligations completely by withdrawing from the UCC and Berne Convention. Second, they could alter their membership in the two major multilateral copyright conventions by resigning from one but maintaining membership in the other. At this point, the existence of two different copyright conventions with different levels of protection and a large overlap in membership created added complexities to the crisis produced by the Stockholm Protocol.

The UCC, to which the United States is a party, is characterized chiefly by the principle of national treatment: even if a country's domestic legislation provides for relatively low-level protection, it can still belong to the UCC. The Berne Convention requires its parties to provide a specified minimum of copyright protection for other Berne works in their domestic legislation, and that minimum establishes a standard providing for a high level of copyright protection.

The situation is further complicated by the fact that the original Berne Convention of 1886 has been revised a number of times and there are, as a result, several different "Berne texts," each providing for different standards of protection. Protection in Berne Convention countries will vary depending upon which text the particular country has accepted. Moreover, some of the texts permit reservations on particular points, and others do not. In addition, the UCC contains the so-called "Berne safeguard clause"—Article XVII and its Appendix Declaration—a provision prohibiting a Berne Convention country from denouncing Berne and relying on the UCC for protection of its works in Berne union countries. Thus, under this clause, a country resigning from the Berne Union but remaining in the UCC would continue to have obligations under the UCC, but would have no protection for its own works under either convention.

Under these circumstances, the developing countries wishing to leave the Berne Convention for the lower level UCC were frustrated by the existence of the "Berne safeguard clause." To remove this difficulty, they launched a counter-offensive designed to suspend the effectiveness of the "Berne safeguard clause." They argued that without such a suspension their only practical alternative was denunciation of both major copyright conventions. The latter prospect was not appealing to the developed countries, despite their displeasure with the Stockholm Protocol.

It was with this background that the Register of Copyrights announced to a meeting of the IGCC and Berne Permanent Committee in December, 1967, that it would be impossible for the United States to join the Berne Convention if it had to accept the Stockholm Protocol, and that he viewed with very great concern the confusion and erosion in standards of international copyright protection resulting from the Stockholm Conference. He urged that the representatives of both developed and developing countries join together to restudy the whole international copyright situation, including practical ways of meeting the needs of developing countries.

Underlying the Register's remarks were two policy goals. The first was to renegotiate the concessions for developing countries contained in the Stockholm Protocol. The second was to maintain the structure of international copyright and the balance between the two major multilateral copyright conventions. In both of these he had to overcome the opposition of the developing countries. In the second, he also had to persuade some of the developed countries, members of the Berne Union, that Stockholm did not justify a reorganization of the international copyright system. In their view, Stockholm proved the danger to the developed countries of keeping the developing countries in the Berne Convention. The clear answer was to pave the way for the renunciation of Berne in favor of the UCC by suspension of the "Berne safeguard clause."

Time was needed, however, to review the ramifications of Stockholm and to consider new policies. Thus, it was early 1969 before the curtain rose on the next act of the diplomatic melodrama. At this point the representatives were ready to accept the suggestion made by the Register in December, 1967. The IGCC and Berne Permanent Committee adopted resolutions establishing an International Copyright Joint Study Group, and upon the invitation of the United States, agreed that the Joint Study Group would meet in Washington in September, 1969.

At that meeting, attended by representatives from twenty-five countries, a proposal to end the international copyright crisis was presented and adopted. Dubbed the "Washington Recommendation," this proposal called for the simultaneous revision of both the UCC and Berne Convention to achieve the following objectives:

(1) In the UCC the level of protection would be improved by the adoption of certain minimum rights. These would include the rights of reproduction, public performance, and broadcasting. At the same time, special provisions would be included in the UCC for the benefit of developing countries. Finally, the "Berne safeguard clause" would be suspended to permit developing countries to leave the Berne Convention without penalty under the UCC.

(2) In the Berne Convention, the Protocol would be separated from the Stockholm Act and, in turn, the developing countries would be able to substitute the special provisions included for their benefit in the UCC. This would mean that the developing countries could remain in the Berne Convention and would not be forced to exercise the option provided by the suspension of the "Berne safeguard clause." As a protective measure, it was provided that the Stockholm Protocol could not be separated from the Stockholm text until such time as France, Spain, the United Kingdom and the United States had ratified the revised text of the UCC. Furthermore, developing countries would be relieved of the obligation to pay assessments to the Berne Union if they continued their membership after the new revision.

The Washington Recommendation won the general support of all the countries that attended the meeting. While it was a sound proposal on paper, the unresolved question was whether it could be implemented successfully. The meetings that have taken place since then have all addressed themselves to this problem.

In December, 1969, the IGCC and Berne Permanent Committee met to consider the results of the Washington meeting. With the exception of France, they agreed that the preparations for revision of each Convention should be made "in accordance with the considerations stated in the preamble to the Washington Recommendation and the specific recommendations contained therein, including, in particular, the recommendation that the Universal Copyright Convention and the Berne Convention be revised in revision conferences to be held at the same time and place. . . . ." In addition they scheduled several preparatory meetings to consider draft texts.

Pursuant to these arrangements, two Ad Hoc Preparatory Committees met in Paris and Geneva in May, 1970. Based largely upon a proposal for revision of the UCC submitted by the United States, draft texts were prepared for the two conventions. As contrasted with the trend represented by the Stockholm Protocol, several important demands of the developing countries were abandoned at this meeting. These included the concessions respecting the term of copyright, the exclusive right of broadcasting, and the broad right to restrict the protection of literary and artistic works for "teaching, study and research in all fields of education." Accordingly, the concessions for developing countries were limited to restricting the rights of translation and reproduction. The major negotiations in May concerned these points.

The draft texts produced in May were then circulated to governments and interested international non-governmental organizations. As recommended by the resolutions adopted in December, 1969, the IGCC and Berne Permanent Committee met in extraordinary sessions in September, 1970, to consider the draft texts and to make final preparations for the revision conferences. . . .

Conclusion

The international copyright crisis started by the Stockholm Protocol seems headed for a successful resolution. At Stockholm, the developing countries had won concessions relating to the term of copyright, the rights of broadcasting, translation and reproduction. They had also gained broad power to restrict the protection of literary and artistic works for "teaching, study and research in all fields of education." The possible economic benefits from all of these concessions were further enhanced by exceptionally loose provisions concerning the export of copies made under compulsory licenses and royalty payments.

In the final texts of the draft Conventions adopted by the two Committees, the concessions relating to the term of copyright and the right of broadcasting have been eliminated. The broad power to restrict the protection of literary and artistic works for "teaching, study and research in all fields of education" has also disappeared. The export of copies made under compulsory licenses has been prohibited and the payment provisions and standards for determining royalties have been improved considerably. Furthermore, the translation and reproduction provisions are now more realistic and generally represent the kind of concessions which the copyright owners in the developed countries are ready and willing to make.

Moreover, the level of protection in the UCC has been improved by the introduction of certain minimum rights. This will guarantee a minimum level of protection in the UCC which had previously been subject, under the national treatment standard, to any level the particular country wished to set.

With respect to maintaining the equilibrium between the two Conventions, the final texts carry out the thrust of the Washington Recommendation by duplicating the concessions for developing countries in each Convention. While some substantive differences exist because of differences in structure, they should not lead to a wholesale defection by developing countries from the Berne Convention to the UCC. Thus, the Berne Convention will continue to maintain its historic role of improving the level of copyright protection throughout the world, and the United States can continue to look with hope upon the day when it may become a member.

Given the results of the September, 1970 meetings, it would seem that the chances are good for successful diplomatic conferences next July. As contrasted with the Stockholm situation, the developing countries have moderated their demands, the developed countries have had an affirmative program, there have been careful preparations beforehand, firm leadership, and the discussions have taken place in a more rational and less emotionally charged atmosphere. All of these are the ingredients for success, and the United States has contributed substantially to each of them.

NOTES

1. With amendments, the 1970 draft texts of the UCC and Berne Convention were adopted at the Paris conferences. The revised UCC was signed at Paris on July 24, 1971 by the United States and twenty-five other member countries. The United States ratified the Paris revision in September, 1972. The UCC and Berne revisions came into force on July 10, 1974.

For background on the Paris revisions and the relationships between the UCC and Berne, see Olian, International Copyright and the Needs of Developing Countries: The Awakening at Stockholm and Paris, 7 Cornell Int'l L.J. 81 (1974); Ulmer, International Copyright After the Paris Revisions, 19 Bull.Copyright Soc'y 263 (1972); Johnson, The Origins of the Stockholm Protocol, 18 Bull.Copyright Soc'y 91 (1970); Schrader, Analysis of the Protocol Regarding Developing Countries, 17 Bull.Copyright Soc'y 160 (1970); Nimmer, Implications of the Prospective Revisions of the Berne Convention and the United States Copyright Law, 19 Stan.L.Rev. 499 (1967); Mott, The Relationship Between the Berne Convention and the Universal Copyright Convention, 11 IDEA 306 (1967).

2. On February 27, 1973, the Soviet Union announced its intention to adhere to the UCC, effective May 27, 1973. Some repercussions in the United States are discussed at page 808, above.

See generally, J. Baumgarten, US–USSR Copyright Relations Under the Universal Copyright Convention (1973); M. Boguslavsky, Copyright in International Relations: International Protection of Literary and Scientific Works (N. Poulet, trans., D. Catterns, ed. 1979); Maggs, New Directions in US–USSR Copyright Relations, 68 Am.J. Int'l L. 391 (1974).

3. *Selected Bibliography.* A. Bogsch, The Law of Copyright Under the Universal Convention (3d Ed.1963); Ulmer, The Protection of Performing Artists, Producers of Sound Recordings, and Broadcasting Organizations: A Study in International and Comparative Law (Secretan & Dunne, Eds.1957); Universal Copyright Convention Analyzed (Kupferman & Foner Eds.1955).

Dawid, Basic Principles of International Copyright, 21 Bull.Copyright Soc'y 1 (1974); Gabay, The United States Copyright System and the Berne Convention, 26 Bull.Copyright Soc'y 202 (1979); Ringer & Flacks, Applicability of the Universal Copyright Convention to Certain Works in the Public Domain in their Country of Origin, 27 Bull.Copyright Soc'y 157 (1980).

Dubin, The UNESCO Universal Copyright Convention, 1952 Wis.L.Rev. 493; Schulman, Another View of Article III of the Universal Copyright Convention, 1953 Wis.L.Rev. 297; Sargoy, UCC Protection in the United States: The Coming Into Effect of the Universal Copyright Convention, 33 N.Y.U.L.Rev. 811 (1958); Henn, The Quest for International Copyright Protection, 39 Cornell L.Q. 43 (1953); Sherman, The Universal Copyright Convention: Its Effect on United States Law, 55 Colum.L.Rev. 1137 (1955).

Dittrich, The Practical Application of the Rome Convention, 26 Bull.Copyright Soc'y 287 (1979); Ulmer, The Rome Convention for the Protection of Performers, Producers of Phonograms and Broadcasting Organizations, 10 Bull.Copyright Soc'y 90, 165, 219 (1962–1963).

The annual Jean Geiringer Memorial Lectures on International Copyright Law, published regularly in the Bulletin of the Copyright Society, provide a variety of perspectives on contemporary international problems.

II. PATENT

See Statute Supplement 35 U.S.C.A. §§ 119, 351–376.

VERNON, THE INTERNATIONAL PATENT SYSTEM AND FOREIGN POLICY

Study No. 5, Subcommittee on Patents, Trademarks and Copyrights, Senate Committee on the Judiciary, 85th Cong., 1st Sess. 1–4 (1957).

A. The Nature of the System

In November 1957, the 45 signatories of the International Convention for the Protection of Industrial Property will assemble in Lisbon to consider whether the convention should be amended. This will be the first such meeting since 1934. Since the convention represents the principal agreement defining the rights of inventors who patent in foreign countries, the meeting will afford the first opportunity in nearly a quarter of a century for a full-dress review of international patent relations.

The international convention is 1 of 3 elements which go to make up what we have called the "international patent system." The other 2 elements are the national patent laws of the sovereign States, and the practices which involve the use of foreign patents in international trade and investment.

The national patent laws of the various sovereign governments of the world, to the extent that they have a common theme, grant patentees the right to prevent others in the grantor government's jurisdiction from making and selling the object or from using the process which is the subject of the patent. But the right is circumscribed in a variety of ways from one jurisdiction to the next. To begin with, the duration of the patent grant varies from country to country; in the United States, the patent's life is 17 years, while in other countries it may be as little as 5 years for "little patents" or as long as 20. In addition, different countries exclude different types of product from the patent grant. Finally, national concepts of patent "abuse" and penalties for misuse, such as compulsory licensing, revocation, and dedication, are also varied.

These different national patent laws have been ingeniously linked together by the International Convention for the Protection of Industrial Property. The treaty, now in its 74th year, includes among its 45 signatory nations every major industrialized nation of the free world and a few in the Soviet orbit. In substance, the convention deals essentially with the rights to which patentees in any signatory country may be entitled under the national patent laws of the other signatories. Only 3 or 4 of its main provisions, however, need be considered here.

The great achievement of the treaty, from the point of view of inventors and investors, is the fact that its signatories have agreed to grant patent treatment to nationals or residents of other signatory countries equal to the treatment they grant their own nationals. Adopted in 1883, this was an extraordinary provision for its time. It eliminated the possibility of discrimination against foreigners and excluded a pattern of international patent relations based on reciprocity, that is, on the principle that foreigners were entitled to get in other countries only as much as their governments gave to foreigners at home. Instead, this unusual convention represented the "open" form of international agreement, extending its provisions to any nation which was willing to give nondiscriminatory patent rights to foreigners.

The practice of granting national treatment to foreigners is sensible on many counts, for reasons whose applicability extend beyond the confines of this paper. The practice has proved particularly appropriate as regards patents. For one thing, a considerable proportion of the world's patentholders are corporations; and the "nationality" of a corporation—the question whether or not it is a "foreigner" for purposes of domestic law—revolves largely around certain fictions and ordinarily depends not upon the identity of the natural persons who created the corporation but upon the nation under whose corporate statutes such persons have chosen to place their enterprise. Thus a Swedish corporation organized by United States nationals would be regarded as an entity of Swedish nationality for the purposes of Swedish patent law.

The convention goes further in securing foreigners' rights. It provides that a prospective patentee who has filed his application in any signatory country and who is entitled to the convention's protection has a period of 1 year in which to apply for patent protection in any other convention jurisdiction. This provision has extensive implications. For in the absence of some such provision, the inventor of a product or a process in country A, having duly made a patent application in his own country, might well find that country B was unwilling to consider him entitled to claim a patent in that country; country B might insist, for instance, that the first introducer of the invention in its territory was the eligible patentee, or it might even insist that no patent was issuable at all if the invention was already being publicly used in country A. This 1-year priority provision, therefore, greatly increases the probability that an applicant will acquire a legal monopoly not only in his own nation but also in other signatory countries.

The international convention grants still another right to the patentee. The convention provides that once a patent has been granted on the basis of the priority provisions of the convention, the subsequent invalidation of the patent by the original granting nation will not of itself affect the validity of patents granted elsewhere on the same invention. This means that even if it were later determined that the patent in the first country of application should never have been granted—either because the invention had been developed previously or because the subject matter of the patent was eventually determined to be lacking in inventiveness or on any other grounds on which the courts may invalidate patents—the patents proliferated in other countries on the basis of the convention's priority rights remain unaffected by their invalidation in the original country of issue. To be sure, the facts which led to invalidation in the first country, when adduced by the proper party in the proper courts of other nations, might eventually invalidate these counterpart patents. But in the absence of some such action, these patents must be allowed to continue to stand.

Another feature of the convention which has a direct bearing on this review is its provisions with respect to the compulsory licensing of patents. The institution of the patent grant was originally devised partly as a means by which the sovereign might reward his favorites and partly as a device for stimulating domestic industry. This latter philosophy—this emphasis on the development of domestic industry —had pervaded many early patent laws and had led quite logically to provisions which required the patentee to "work" his patent in the jurisdiction where the patent was granted. To this end, for example, some patent laws had automatically withdrawn the grant whenever the patentee imported his product into the country; other laws obliged the patentee, on pain of losing his grant, to "work" the patent in some stated period, either by actually producing the product or using the process within the jurisdiction, or by some other statutory test.

The international convention has put various restraints on the scope of these "working" provisions. It prohibits the cancellation of a patent when the action is based simply on the fact that the relevant product had been imported into the jurisdiction. Moreover the convention prevents its signatories from taking any steps to compel "working" in the first 3 years after a patent is issued; thereafter, the convention binds its signatories to resort initially to compulsory *licensing* at reasonable royalties, rather than to cancellation of the patent grant, as a remedy under the "working" provisions or indeed for any other patent "abuse" under their respective laws. Cancellation is permitted only as a final remedy, after the compulsory licensing technique has been tried for at least 2 years and has failed. These compulsory licensing provisions of the convention, it is evident, have altered the complexion of the patent grant from one designed primarily to stimulate domestic industry to one in which the foreign patentee has an increased chance of producing where he chooses and retaining his patent monopoly.

A third element of the international patent system is the body of practices by which patentees use their foreign patent rights in international trade and investment. There are few generalizations about the practices of foreign patentees which are not subject to major qualifications. Yet it is fair to say that a foreign patentee is usually subject to different forces and motivations in the strategy of patent use from those of his domestic counterpart. A foreign patentee, by hypothesis, is the recipient of a monopoly grant covering an area which is not his principal locus of operation. This means that a license granted by him for the use of the patent is less likely to create direct and immediate competition for his own production than would be the case for patent licenses in his home territory. The fact that the patent applies to a foreign market means also that there are frequently limitations on the value of the patent grant to its owner arising out of the inaccessibility of the foreign market in which he has the patent monopoly.

BENSON, THE IMPACT OF THE PATENT COOPERATION TREATY (PCT) AND THE EUROPEAN PATENT CONVENTION (EPC) ON U.S. PRACTITIONERS

60 Journal of the Patent Office Society 118–126 (1978).

Back in the mid-1960s President Johnson appointed a special commission to study the United States patent system. One of the recommendations of this commission was that "the United States promote direct interim steps towards the ultimate goal—a universal patent including harmonization of patent practices." As a direct result of this recommendation, the United States Government, along with some other countries, asked the United International Bureau for the Protection of Intellectual Property (BIRPI) to develop a proposal that would meet the recommendation of the Presidential Commission. Specifically, they were asked to draft a proposal that would (a) simplify the procedures in filing foreign patent applications corresponding to the basic initially filed patent application, (b) reduce the cost of obtaining patents in foreign countries, (c) promote more uniform national laws relating to procurement and enforcement of patents and (d) improve the patent systems in countries that did not have a patent examination system.

The first proposal from BIRPI came out in February of 1967 and called for a system of international cooperation that included a uniform format for patent applications, a centralized searching system and a preliminary examination which could result in the issuance of what was then called "a certificate of patentability." This proposal then became the basic document from which the various drafts of the proposed Patent Cooperation Treaty were drawn. The negotiations for the Patent Cooperation Treaty culminated in a diplomatic conference in June of 1970 at which conference the Patent Cooperation Treaty was signed by some 26 countries.

A lot has been written about the various provisions of the Patent Cooperation Treaty and I will not go into them in detail except to outline the principal provisions. First the form and content of the international applications would be accepted by all countries who participate in the Patent Cooperation Treaty. Secondly, the PCT called for searching authorities which would have to have minimum prior art documentation for their searches. The PCT defined minimum standards of patentability against which the applications would be examined. In the first phase, or Chapter I, of the Patent Cooperation Treaty a prior art search would be conducted and a search report issued to the applicant. In the second phase of the Patent Cooperation Treaty, referred to as Chapter II, a preliminary examination would be conducted with the prior art actually being applied to the claimed invention. The PCT applicant has the right to amend his application, including the claims, to distinguish from the art cited by the searching authority and as applied during the examination phase. At the end of this procedure, copies of the application together with the search report would be forwarded to the national offices of the countries the applicant had designated. The national patent offices of the designated countries are responsible for finally issuing a patent. After the patent is issued, it is to be enforced in each country strictly in accordance with the national laws of that country.

Immediately after the Patent Cooperation Treaty was signed, the common market countries reopened negotiations relative to a European patent and a common market patent. The Common Market Patent Convention providing for a single patent for all of the EEC countries has been signed but now must be ratified by all the member countries before coming into force. The negotiations leading to the European Patent Convention continued through 1973 at which time a number of European countries signed what is now known as the "European Patent Convention." The European Patent Convention contains a large number of clauses which were extracted almost verbatim from the Patent Cooperation Treaty and are completely compatible with that Treaty. In accordance with the European Patent Convention, initial proceedings take place in the European Patent Office in Munich, but the prior art searches are conducted in the branch of the European Patent Office at The Hague. The proceedings in the European Patent Convention include not only a preliminary search but a complete examination against a specific standard of invention for all applications filed in the European Patent Office. Upon completion of the examination stage and a determination of patentability, a copy of the patent application is transferred to the Patent Office in each of the individual countries that were designated in the original application. The application is then translated (if required) and issued as a patent. In effect, then, although you file a single patent application in the European Patent Office and prosecute it through to completion in that office, the result is that you have as many separate and distinct patents as the countries that were designated in the original application. As in the Patent Cooperation Treaty, patents in the European Patent Convention are enforced in each individual country strictly in accordance with the national laws of that country. A number of countries in the European community have amended or are planning to amend their patent laws to bring them into conformity with specific provisions set forth in the European Patent Convention.

Both the European Patent Convention and the Patent Cooperation Treaty become operational in June of 1978. As we look at it today, we will soon have two additional systems that we can utilize for obtaining patent protection for our clients' inventions. It will be interesting to measure the results from these treaties against the goal that was set forth in the mid-1960s. Have we really developed systems that will simplify the filing and obtaining of patents in various foreign countries at less cost? Will the new systems promote or encourage more uniform laws in various countries? Have we set up a system in which the less developed countries can participate and thereby significantly upgrade the patent systems in those countries? I think that we have met at least some of these goals, although only time will tell if there is sufficient use of the new system to achieve the goals. Furthermore, there is a good bit of controversy over whether or not the cost of obtaining patents through the new systems will be less than going the conventional country-by-country route.

A U.S. practitioner, especially those representing multinational companies who market their products or license their technology worldwide, must take a hard look at these systems to determine whether or not they are applicable to the inventions of his clients. Like any other new system which becomes available, there will be a period of experimentation during which we will become familiar with the system and we cannot expect perfect results immediately. However, I think both the PCT and European Patent Convention will be suitable vehicles that can be used for protecting inventions for those who plan to obtain patents in more than a few countries. As of now, Belgium, West Germany, France, Luxembourg, the Netherlands, Switzerland and Great Britain have adhered to the European Patent Convention. However, 7 more countries are expected to ratify the Convention in 1978, including Italy, Norway and Sweden. About 20 countries are expected to be party to the Patent Cooperation Treaty by June 1, 1978, including the United States, Great Britain, West Germany, France, Switzerland, Brazil and Russia. Japan and Austria are expected to join by the end of 1978.

Most American corporations, I believe, will look upon the European Patent Convention as the most significant of the two treaties at this time because the European Patent Convention procedures provide a full examination system. Furthermore, almost all of the significant industrialized countries of Europe either have already ratified the European Patent Convention or are expected to do so by the end of this year.

On the other hand, the U.S. has reserved under Chapter II of the PCT. Hence, U.S. applicants can only take advantage of the search phase of PCT. Therefore, even though such significant non-European countries as Russia, Brazil and Japan have or are expected to ratify the PCT, it will have less appeal to U.S. citizens and corporations, at least initially, than the European Patent Convention. The PCT does have the flexibility of permitting a U.S. applicant to file an international application in the U.S. Patent and Trademark Office under PCT and designate filing in national offices of European countries either directly via PCT or through the European Patent Convention.

Now let's look at some of the potential advantages of using the new systems.

The most significant advantage is the additional time provided before a final decision has to be made on the filing of individual applications in the different countries. In accordance with PCT, the applicant has eight additional months beyond the year provided by the Paris Convention, plus a preliminary search report on which to base the decision on whether to complete the filings in the designated countries. Under Article 27(7) and Rule 4.7, an applicant does not need to appoint a national attorney or agent until processing of the application has started in the designated national Patent Office. In practice, appointment of the associate attorney or agent can be delayed until the 20th month following the filing date of the international application. Under the European Patent Convention, you will not only have the preliminary search, but you will have a complete examination of the claimed invention against the prior art and the application will be prosecuted through to the point of allowance. In both PCT and the European Patent Convention, the applicant has the opportunity to amend the claims and the specification of the application.

If, under either system, the applicant decides that his invention is not patentable or that the protection he is likely to obtain is not valuable, he can withdraw his designations of countries and does not have to complete the filing of the applications in individually designated countries. Of course, if he has not yet appointed agents, he saves the initial "opening the file" type of charge that agents usually make. The possibility of changing the decision of filing additional applications has a very significant bearing on the potential cost of using either PCT or the European Patent Convention. For example, if in one case out of ten the applicant is able to make a better decision which results in not filing applications in initially designated countries, he could save more money than the additional costs he has incurred in using either the PCT or the European Patent Convention.

Another significant advantage is that the applications in the United States, the Patent Cooperation Treaty and the European Patent Convention can all be prepared in exactly the same format. The form and content of an application, if it meets the standards of the Patent Cooperation Treaty, must be accepted in the European Patent Convention and in all of the countries which have adhered to either the European Patent Convention or the Patent Cooperation Treaty. The format includes the drawings, the description of the invention, the claims and the typing which, in accordance with the new system, is 1½ spaced typing. As you know, under the present system many countries have different requirements for drawings, formalities in the application, paper size and type spacing. Although this may appear to be trivia, it all takes time which increases costs.

The fact that PCT and European Patent Convention applications, in the initial stages, can all be prepared and prosecuted in the English language is an advantage for those of us who do not have good command of a second and third language. This avoids at least some of the problems encountered in translations.

Another significant advantage, at least from our point of view, is the savings in valuable attorney time by using the international system. Simply being able to prosecute a single patent application through to issuance, such as in the European Patent Convention, before having to embark on the prosecution of patent applications in other countries, is a significant advantage. For example, an amendment in a patent application in the European Patent Convention automatically applies to all of the patent applications that will be filed based on that international application thus eliminating the need to make duplicate amendments. Furthermore, the arguments made to distinguish the invention from the prior art will automatically be part of the file in all applications filed in the designated countries. Thus, instead of attempting to prosecute patent applications on the same invention in four or five or more countries simultaneously, the attorney will have the opportunity to go through one complete prosecution before he has to spend any time on the applications filed in other countries. Furthermore, assuming that the European Patent Convention operates as expected, there will be no requirement for further prosecution of a patent application when it is filed in the other countries. However, some countries may require a translation of the entire application into their native language. The present rules require that the claims in each patent be translated into the other official languages of the treaty.

Another advantage of both the PCT and the European Patent Convention which will be available to all of us, even those that do not use the system, is the periodic publication of an Official Journal containing an abstract of all patents issued through either the European Patent Convention or the Patent Cooperation Treaty.

Let's now consider some of the possible disadvantages of using either one of the international patent systems. First and foremost, of course, is the question of cost. There is no question, but the cost of filing and prosecuting a patent application in either the PCT or the European Patent Convention is going to be considerably more than in any individual country. At one time, it was projected that filing through the PCT would be a cost savings if the applicant intended to file patent applications in three or more countries. Later studies seem to indicate that the break even point is higher than that. Furthermore, some of the quotations of costs coming in from associates abroad indicate that the overall cost in the European Patent Office is going to be substantially more than we originally anticipated. However, the costs that are being quoted are primarily the Patent Office and associate fees and do not take into account the savings in attorney time or the potential savings due to the applicant being in a position to make a better judgment as to whether or not to finally file the applications in the designated countries. Therefore, any such study should be carefully scrutinized and the quoted costs of filing through either of the international systems should be measured against some of the other potential cost-saving features of the treaties before a final decision is made that the system is prohibitively expensive.

Other potential disadvantages of using the system is the argument that you are placing all of your eggs in a single basket. It is pointed out that if you go the individual country route in Europe, you are certain to get patents issued in some countries even if you can't get them in the difficult examination countries such as Switzerland and Germany. While this may be true, I think that you have to consider the potential value of such patents to your client. I am sure that when it comes to enforcing patents in the European community, the courts are going to inquire as to whether or not the patent was prosecuted through the European Patent Office or whether or not it went directly through the national offices. Thus, even if the national standard of patentability is not harmonized with the European Patent Convention standard by national legislative action, the national courts of the European Patent Convention member countries are likely to achieve some harmonization. This will be especially true in countries that do not maintain an examination system.

NOTES

1. PCT filings in the United States have fallen far below original expectations. One writer reports that, as against estimates "that 9900 PCT applications would be filed in the United States Receiving Office during the first year of operations, and that this figure would rise to 17,000 the second year," in fact "only 636 applications were filed in the U.S. during the first year, and that after 18 months, an additional 664 applications had been filed." And, as of July 23, 1980, "the date of this writing, the United States Receiving Office has assigned serial numbers up to 900 for 1980. . . . These actual figures indicate an upswing in PCT acceptance, but are still far below initial projections." Winner, Practical Effects of the Patent Cooperation Treaty and the European Patent Convention on Domestic Technology Management and Patent Practice, 62 J.P.O.S. 419, 421 (1980).

For additional background on the PCT, see Maassel & Turowski, PCT Implementation—Effect on Filing and Procedures, 59 J.P.O.S. 208 (1977).

2. Treaty obligations have significantly shaped the transfer of technology from developed to developing nations. Since at least the late 1970's, the developing countries (called the "Group of 77") have pressed for changes in the Paris Convention to accommodate their special economic position. A February, 1980 diplomatic conference,

intended to iron out substantive disagreements between the developed and developing countries, instead "bogged down in a bitter dispute over voting rules which finally were adopted, over the objection of the U.S., on Saturday, March 1." Statement of the Patent and Trademark Office, reprinted in 470 Patent, Trademark, Copyright Journal A-5 (March 13, 1980).

    3. *Selected Bibliography.* S. Ladas, Patents, Trademarks and Related Rights: National and International Protection (1975); G. Bodenhausen, Guide to the Application of the Paris Convention for the Protection of Industrial Property as Revised at Stockholm in 1967 (1968); Baxter, World Patent Law and Practice (1968); Lang, Foreign Patent Laws, with Comparative Analysis (Wade Ed. 1968); Lignac, Foreign Patent Applications (1969).

    Note, International Patent Cooperation, 20 Stan.L.Rev. 1000 (1968); O'Brien, Our International Patent Program, 48 J.P.O.S. 283 (1966); Meller, Toward a Multinational Patent System, 44 J.P.O.S. 227 (1962); Goldsmith, Patent Protection for United States Inventions in the Principal European Countries—Existing Systems, 6 B.C. Ind. & Com.L.Rev. 533 (1965).

III. TRADEMARK

See Statute Supplement 15 U.S.C.A. § 1126.

FRAYNE, HISTORY AND ANALYSIS OF TRT

63 Trademark Reporter 422–437 (1973).*

Background

The problem for which the Trademark Registration Treaty (TRT) is an intended solution is one which has beset the manufacturer or trader engaged in international commerce since trademarks began to assume importance in such commerce, a period of approximately the last one hundred fifty years, beginning some time after the first flowering of the Industrial Revolution. That problem has its roots in the territoriality of trademark law (in which respect, of course, trademark law does not differ from nearly every other field of law). Businessmen find trademarks to be commercially valuable, and desire to preserve to themselves the exclusive use of their trademarks in every country in which they trade or might trade. To accomplish this end, they find it necessary to seek protection in each country separately, complying with the law of each country. National law varies greatly but, in general, it is necessary or highly advisable to register trademarks with a public body, usually the Registry of Trademarks administered by the Patent Office. To register, the international businessman is forced to meet different procedural and substantive requirements in every country, to complete a bewildering variety of different forms in different languages, to cope with different and sometimes unintelligible systems of classifications of goods, to submit electro-types and prints differing in size and number, and to pay disparate official fees in a plethora of currencies. After registration has been obtained, its assignment, licensing or renewal is again subject to differences in national treatment. Perhaps most painful of all, the international businessman's inability to cope directly with all of these differences compels him to retain, in each country in which he desires protection, trademark attorneys or agents to do the necessary, against payment, of course, of a reasonable professional fee for the unravelling of the mysteries of national law.

All of this entails a good deal of bother and expenditure of money, neither of which is very attractive to the international business community.

The seed of subsequent attempts to solve the problem may be found in the Paris Convention for the Protection of Industrial Property (1883), usually called simply the International Convention. The basic principle of the International Convention was "national treatment" in each country for the nationals of all other member countries. There was, however, an Article 6 (now Article 6 quinquies), the famous "telle-quelle" provision, which required each member country to register the trademark of a national of another member country "just as" it was registered in the home country. The immediate purpose of the "telle-quelle" provision was to overcome national differences in the form of the matter deemed registrable as a trademark; for example, one of the obstacles which this provision sought to overcome was the requirement of Russian law at the time that all word trademarks be spelt in the Cyrillic alphabet. Beyond the desire to deal with this kind of problem, however, the "telle-quelle" provision embodied a certain philosophy which was relevant to the more general problem described above. It was the thought that, save for certain specific exceptions touching upon the fundamentals of national trademark law, and stated explicitly in Article 6, a national of a member country of the International Convention should have the right to "extend" his national protection to other member countries. This principle was rooted in a sentiment akin to the "full-faith-and-credit" clause of our Constitution: whatever any member country had done to protect a trademark officially by way of registration, would be recognized by all of the others if at all possible under national law. Hence, Article 6 of the International Convention made the first breach in the hermetically sealed compartments of national law, but premised that breach upon the principle of respect by all member countries for the official acts of any; or, put more crudely, upon the principle of the mutual solidarity of all national bureaucracies.

The seed planted by the "telle-quelle" provision of the International Convention grew into the first full-fledged effort at a solution of the problem, the Madrid Arrangement for the International Registration of Trademarks (1891), usually known as the "Madrid Arrangement." The Madrid Arrangement institutionalized and systematized the underlying philosophy of the "telle-quelle" provision. Under the Madrid Arrangement, a national of a member country having obtained a registration in that country could request his national Patent Office to forward such national registration to the International Bureau created by the International Convention, with a request that the same form the basis for an International Registration; and that International Registration would have the force of a national registration in every member country for as long, if properly renewed, as the home registration subsisted. This system took two important steps forward as compared with the "telle-quelle" provision of the International Convention. First, the trademark owner's home registration could be extended to other member countries without a multiplicity of national filings. Second, a sort of procedural presumption in favor of protection was created: whereas in the ordinary situation, a national filing does not result in a registration unless specifically granted, under the Madrid Arrangement an International Registration automatically had the force of a national registration unless specifically refused by the national administration within a term of twelve months.

Naturally, the underlying philosophy of the Madrid Arrangement dictated that the International Registration would be strictly co-extensive and co-existent with the home registration, a concept which is now called "dependency" upon the home registration. The International Registration could not be obtained until the home registration had issued, covered exactly the same mark and goods, and died with the home registration. This opened the possibility for a third party to destroy the International Registration in all member countries through a successful attack on the basic home registration, a device later dubbed "Central Attack." This system provided a powerful but erratic weapon: powerful, because if available it destroyed the International Registration everywhere regardless of the merits of the cases of the litigants in all countries but the home country; erratic, because it was available only if the attacker had superior rights in the registrant's home country.

From fairly early in the life of the Madrid Arrangement, it became evident that it created a great deal of "deadwood" on the International Register, marks neither in use nor likely to be used, and that this "deadwood" formed a substantial obstacle to the ever more difficult search for new trademarks. This phenomenon, called in more recent years "proliferation," resulted from the absence of restraints at the two points where these might have been applied: at the national registration level (where the dependency mechanism of the Madrid Arrangement would have made restraints automatically effective internationally), and at the International Registration level. Nationally, most countries party to the Madrid Arrangement did not, until recent years, practice examination, have an opposition procedure, have user requirements before or after registration, or limit the number of goods or classes that might be covered by one registration; thus, the national registration basis for an International Registration was easily and broadly established and maintained. At the International Registration level, the Madrid Arrangement, until the 1957 Nice Revision came into force in December 1965, automatically extended protection to all member countries, and did not impose any limitation upon, or demand extra payment for, the inclusion of any number of goods or classes.

The United States never adhered to the Madrid Arrangement. Our reluctance to join sprang from two causes. First, our domestic legislation would, under the dependency rule of the Madrid Arrangement, place our nationals at a considerable disadvantage, since they could not establish the necessary United States registration basis until after actual use of the trademark in commerce subject to the regulation of Congress, and successful traverse through the examination and opposition process, and then only for a narrowly defined specification of goods. Second, there was considerable apprehension of the proliferation problem, the possible flooding of our Register with marks of no or little real commercial importance. For similar reasons, other Western Hemisphere countries have been reluctant to join; Brazil, Cuba and Mexico, which had actually joined, subsequently withdrew. Thus, the Madrid Arrangement remained essentially a European agreement, although even there it did not include the United Kingdom and the Scandinavian countries.

The members of the Madrid Arrangement, although generally satisfied with its workings, were not unaware of these defects, and did wish to make it more attractive to non-members. The 1957 Nice Revision took certain important steps. While dependency upon a basic home registration was left intact as a condition precedent to the International Registration, it was moderated as a condition subsequent for its maintenance: five years after the grant of an International Registration, it would become entirely independent of the home registration. Further, member countries were given the option (which nearly all have since exercised) of stating that they would not be covered by an International Registration unless the registrant specifically named them, and paid an additional fee. Finally, additional fees were imposed for all classes covered by an International Registration beyond the first three.

These changes did not seem to non-member countries to go far enough, and suggestions were made in 1969, particularly by the United States, for a more drastic revision. As a result, in December 1969 the World Intellectual Property Organization (WIPO) circulated a statement containing a list of possible further changes that might be made in the Madrid Arrangement.

There ensued in April 1970 the first of a series of WIPO-sponsored Conferences of (Government) Experts in Geneva. At that first conference, where the United States delegation was led by former Commissioner of Patents, William E. Schuyler, Jr., a deadlock quickly developed between non-member countries, and particularly the United States, on the one hand, and member countries of the Madrid Arrangement on the other. The United States wished to have complete abolition of dependency. Member countries, with the exception of Germany, wished to retain dependency at least as a condition precedent: in part, probably because it belonged to the traditional philosophy of the Madrid Arrangement; in part, because dependency provided one of the few restraints upon proliferation and constituted a sort of preliminary "sieve" which might preserve non-examining member countries from a flood of International Registrations emanating, for example, from the United States, whose examining system would thus do the work of that lacking in most member countries; and in part because of the member countries' attachment to a system of central attack, which seemed most difficult to provide for excepting in conjunction with dependency upon a home registration.

There were differences on other points also. Non-member countries wished separate fees to be payable for each country named and for each class named, both as a restraint on proliferation, and to meet the financial burden which would be imposed upon examining countries. Member countries preferred the simpler and cheaper system of the Madrid Arrangement. Non-member countries were generally favorable to international filings directly with WIPO; several member countries preferred retention of a requirement for filing through the home Patent Office. Non-member countries were skeptical, at best, of the possibility of a central attack system; most member countries were insistent upon its necessity. Some non-members, like the United States, were pleased by a WIPO proposal that international filings provide for the possibility of meeting the special requirements of certain countries (specifically, that a declaration alleging use in commerce must be filed with every international application naming the United States). Member countries were highly critical of any provision incorporating into the Madrid Arrangement recognition of the specific requirements of certain countries and, in particular, clearly indicated their opposition to the United States requirement for use in commerce as a precondition to registration; in their eyes, this requirement, to which the United States and Canada alone among the major countries of the world still adhere, would place their nationals at a comparative disadvantage in relation to American and Canadian nationals who would be confronted with no such difficulty when naming member countries in international applications.

At the end of the April 7, 1970 Conference, Commissioner Schuyler suggested that to break the impasse, the United States would consider submitting to the Executive Committee of the Paris Union a proposal for an agreement for the International Registration of Trademarks, capable of meeting the needs of all Paris Union members, in other words, a suggestion of an entirely new agreement, distinct from the Madrid Arrangement.

A recital of developments at the ensuing six further conferences in Geneva, and of their arguments, discussions, confrontations, etc., would fill volumes, and delight the heart of none but a professional historian. Suffice it to say that, by the time the Diplomatic Conference opened in Vienna on May 17, 1973, the following results had been achieved:

A new Treaty would be drafted, containing basically the provisions desired by non-member countries of the Madrid Arrangement but designed to co-exist with the Madrid Arrangement and to detract as little as possible from the viability of the continued existence of the Madrid Arrangement among its present members.

The new Treaty, in one of its rare substantive provisions, would require member countries not to refuse, nor to cancel for a number of years, International Registrations, on the ground that the marks covered thereby had not been used.

The latter provision, concerning which more is said below, is clearly aimed at the United States and at the elimination of that part of our law which foreigners find most obnoxious. Since that part of our law happens also to be at the very root of our entire Common Law of trademarks, the provision obviously presents us with a certain challenge. There is no doubt, however, that in the history of the negotiations leading to TRT, this provision was the essential consideration for the agreement of the members of the Madrid Arrangement countries to participate in the drafting of a new Treaty for which, with the major exception of Germany, they do not care, and which they fear would imperil the survival of their much-loved Madrid Arrangement.

The great fights having been fought in the preparatory conferences in Geneva, the May-June 1973 Vienna Diplomatic Conference produced few major changes in the text of TRT, but a host of lesser amendments, not unimportant but not basic to the TRT scheme. From the standpoint of the United States, there were two major debates.

The first dealt with the critical provision requiring member states to suspend their user requirements for a given term of years. A stalemate had developed on whether that term should be three years or five years. A compromise had been reached at one of the last Geneva Conferences, whereby that term would be three years, but extendible to five under certain circumstances. In Vienna, the United States delegation deemed it necessary to insist upon three years without possibility of an extension. This produced great opposition on the part of a number of other delegations, who thought that we had, in the vernacular, "welshed" on a deal. Nevertheless, the United States stood firm and indicated that the chances of ratification of the Treaty by the Senate would be poor unless the term were strictly limited to three years. On that argument, our position won the day.

Second, there was an unforeseen proposal by Brazil on behalf of the "developing countries," insisting upon special benefits to these countries in view of their economic inferiority vis-a-vis the developed countries. Specifically, Brazil proposed that the nationals of developing countries be entitled, for a number of years, to obtain International Registrations, without requiring such developing countries to adhere to TRT and thus be capable of designation in an International Registration by nationals of member countries. The United States delegation thought this proposal devoid of merit and quite unrelated to the needs of developing countries. To our surprise, however, we found that other developed countries such as Great Britain and Germany were ready to agree on some compromise language. Accordingly, the final text of TRT contains a complicated Article 40, under which for certain (extendible) terms, nationals of non-member developing countries will be entitled to obtain International Registrations.

There was also, somewhat unexpectedly, a great "non-fight" at Vienna. Throughout all of the conferences leading up to the Vienna Diplomatic Conference, the question of Central Attack had been the subject of prolonged and sometimes acidulous debate. Complex proposals had been submitted by WIPO, Switzerland, the Netherlands and Belgium. In the absence of the simple mechanism of dependency upon a home registration, none of these substitute proposals was found workable or acceptable to a majority. At no time, however, did any of the proponents of Central Attack formally abandon their quest, or indicate their willingness, however reluctant, to do without a Central Attack system if necessary. There was some expectation, therefore, that new proposals, or renewed efforts to gain acceptance of earlier proposals, would be made at the Vienna Diplomatic Conference. That this did not happen may indicate that the proponents of Central Attack have bowed to reality; or it may indicate that they have written off TRT as an instrument to which they can adhere, and will make do with the Madrid Arrangement. Time will tell.

Thus was the Trademark Registration Treaty born: conceived in the clash of sharply differing opinions, and characterized by radical mutations from the properties of its ancestor, the Madrid Arrangement, mutations which are certain to put to the test the adaptability of the intended adoptive parents.

The Provisions of TRT

Before noting in detail the provisions of TRT, it is important to be clear in one's mind as to the essential nature of the Treaty. Despite its name, which can easily be misunderstood, TRT does not create a true International Registration. Such a legal creature, which indeed has been proposed in a number of responsible quarters, would have required one substantive law of trademarks, applicable in all member countries; supra-national administrative and juridical institutions capable of administering and interpreting such law, and adjudicating under it; and an International Registration having the same force and the same significance in every member country. This, a true supra-national trademark, would supersede national law and national institutions and represent, in the field of trademarks, a large surrender of national sovereignty. There is much to commend such a concept as an ultimate goal, at least for nations whose economies are sufficiently unified to constitute one market. Indeed, the supra-national mark is not merely a dream, but is already a reality for some countries: the Benelux mark is a true International Registration for the three countries involved, and the European trademark, if and when it comes to pass, will be a true International Registration for the nine countries of the European Common Market. The concept, however, does not yet seem warranted for the seventy-nine member countries of the Paris Union to whom adherence to TRT will be open (TRT being a special arrangement under Article 19 of the International Convention).

Thus TRT, like the Madrid Arrangement, is essentially a filing treaty. The supra-national character of TRT is exhausted at the filing stage (although, it will be seen, "filing" should be understood to include not merely filing for International Registrations, but also filing for later designations, assignments, changes of name, restrictions of specifications of goods, and renewals). A formally correct filing results in recordal on the International Register, and thereafter national law takes over, with the single major exception, mentioned above, of the suspension of national user requirements for a certain term of years. The International Registration when granted is but a bundle of national rights. The form of TRT is substance, but its substance is form: or, to speak in less Delphically oracular terms, while the language of TRT is frequently that of substantive trademark law, in fact it is concerned, with one major and a few minor exceptions, with the formalities of filing.

The principal provisions of TRT may be set forth as follows:

(1) International Registrations may be obtained by nationals or residents of member countries independent of any home registration (but member states have the option of requiring persons who are both nationals and residents of that state to file nationally before filing internationally).

(2) Applications may be filed directly with the International Bureau of WIPO in Geneva, in either English or French.

(3) International Applications may claim the priority date of an earlier national application within the six-month term established by the International Convention.

(4) International Applications must identify goods with reasonable precision, and according to the International Classification of Goods.

(5) International Applications must specifically name each TRT member state to be covered ("Designated State"). An interesting feature of TRT is "self-designation"; that is, an international applicant may designate his own home country, and indeed only his home country. Thus, depending upon his circumstances, an American trademark owner may well choose to obtain the equivalent of a United States registration by filing in Geneva rather than in Washington.

(6) Each International Application is subject to an international filing fee, presently set at 400 Swiss francs. In addition, there is payable a fee for each Designated State which, at the option of the Designated State, may be 100% of the national fees payable; this State Designation fee may vary according to the number of classes covered.

(7) After examination of the International Application for formalities, the International Bureau grants an International Registration, whose date is the filing date of the International Application.

(8) The International Bureau publishes the International Registration, and notifies the National Patent Office of each Designated State. At this point, TRT mostly leaves the stage, and national law takes over.

(9) The International Registration immediately has the effect, in each Designated State, of a national application and in due course thereafter, unless refused, has also the effect of a national registration in that State.

(10) After publication of the International Registration, each Designated State carries out its internal examination, and/or opens its opposition procedure, pursuant to national law. Each such State is granted a period of fifteen months (eighteen months in the case of certification marks) within which to notify the International Bureau of a refusal, or possible refusal, of the International Registration. The notification must include all grounds, including oppositions, for the refusal or possible refusal. Unless such notification is made within the fifteen (eighteen) months from the date of publication, the International Registration automatically gains national registration effect in the Designated State.

(11) Each Designated State may refuse on any ground established by national law, provided that such ground not be inconsistent with any provision of TRT, the International Convention, and in particular Article 6 quinquies (telle-quelle provision). As previously noted, TRT provides that the International Registration may not be refused on the ground that the mark has not been used anywhere. The "telle-quelle" provision also limits, but within generous boundaries, the grounds for refusal.

(12) Unless refused, an International Registration has in each Designated State an independent life as a national registration, and subject in almost all respects to national law. But it cannot be canceled for nonuse during at least the first three years and its renewable life span is ten years. The text leaves entirely to national law the legal rights flowing from a registration, although it is obvious that the expectation of TRT is that some substantive rights are created by registration.

(13) After the grant of an International Registration, the registrant may at any time during its life apply to designate additional States; these "later designations" are treated, mutatis mutandis, in the same fashion as the original International Application.

(14) The International Registration may be assigned, and the assignment recorded at the International Bureau. Recordal at the International Bureau has the effect of recordal with the Patent Office of each Designated State, but each such State may refuse the said effect on any ground provided by national law. Similarly, changes of name may be recorded with the International Bureau with national effect, but the Patent Office of each Designated State may require proof satisfactory to it of the change of name.

(15) Another provision relating to assignments permits the international registrant to assign the International Registration for some of the goods only, and/or for some of the Designated States only. This raises the interesting possibility of the virtual atomization of an International Registration. As to the separate alienability of rights in Designated States, it must be remembered that this is entirely consistent with the "bundle of national rights" nature of an International Registration; as to the divisibility of the goods, it remains open to Designated States to reject an assignment when the same would re-

sult in ownership of the International Registration by different parties in respect of goods which that State deems similar for trademark purposes.

(16) Renewal of an International Registration for ten-year periods is automatic in all Designated States, upon filing of the proper form with, and payment of the correct fee to, the International Bureau.

(17) An International Registration may be canceled, in each Designated State, on any ground established by national law, save for the limitation imposed by the normal three-year suspension of user requirements.

(18) An important provision, inserted at the insistence of the United States delegation, permits national law to state that no infringement action may be brought on the registration of an unused trademark; the action lies in a Designated State only after continuing use has commenced in that State, and damages are limited to the period subsequent to the commencement of such continuing use. Several things may be said concerning this provision. First, this provision is normally significant during only the first three years (or five in some States) of the life of an International Registration, which thereafter may be canceled for nonuse. Second, it does not touch upon other rights, such as oppositions and cancellation actions, which may be grounded upon an International Registration. Third, it may well prove to be a booby-trap for the unwary subsequent user, as the rights of the registrant, after continuing use has commenced, go back to the International Registration date. On the whole, the utility and wisdom in purely practical terms of this provision may be questioned, but there is no doubt that it represents a psychologically important gesture of respect to the Common Law concept that exclusionary rights to a trademark may be exercised only as an incident of its use.

(19) Provision is made for the absorption by an International Registration of the rights deriving from an earlier Madrid Arrangement or national registration in a given Designated State; and, conversely, provision is made for the possibility of a national application claiming the rights deriving from an earlier International Registration.

Prospects and Problems

. . .

Is Proliferation a Real Danger?

Proliferation had been a problem under the old Madrid Arrangement. TRT does contain just about all of the built-in "anti-proliferation" measures that could be devised, and which are absent from the original Madrid Arrangement: the obligation to name each country and class separately, and to pay corresponding fees for each. This will be some deterrent against proliferation, but hardly a decisive one.

Further, the danger of proliferation, if defined as the increase in the number of filings and registrations, cannot be evaluated on the same basis for every country. The United States, alone among the major countries, at present is the possessor of a powerful "anti-proliferation" weapon, the requirement for use of a trademark in commerce prior to filing. This requirement has a double inhibitory effect. First, and most obviously, a prospective United States resident applicant must go to the trouble and expense of making interstate use (genuine and commercial, if he hopes for a valid registration) before he can even file. Second, and more subtle, is the fact that a person who has made use of a trademark in the United States by that fact acquires Common Law rights; a federal registration, despite its very considerable advantages, is not necessary to establish ownership. Ironically, the small regional manufacturer or merchant who might most benefit from a federal registration is probably less aware of such benefits and less prone to go to the trouble and expense of a federal application than his larger competitors; while great corporations who market nationally build up such extensive Common Law rights that a federal registration is frequently deemed unnecessary.

Statistics disclose the anti-proliferative effect of our law both upon domestic business enterprises and foreign ones. The United States, as the largest market and most productive economy in the world, may reasonably be thought to offer a correspondingly favorable climate to trademarks. And yet, this fact is not reflected in the filing figures. In the year 1970, the United States Patent Office received a total of 33,326 trademark applications. This is about the same as the number filed in Brazil, 1½ times that filed in France, slightly more than 1½ times the number filed in West Germany, about twice the number filed in the United Kingdom, and—surprisingly—only about 15% more than the 26,968 filed in Spain. One almost hesitates to mention the statistics for Japan, all of whose economic figures in recent years seem to have been made in the Land of Oz: 139,367 in 1970, or more than four times the total filed in the United States.

The 1970 figures for filing by foreigners are equally striking. There were 3,053 such applications in the United States. That same year, that number was exceeded by the non-national filings in the following countries: Argentina, Belgium, Brazil, Canada, Chile, China (Taiwan), Denmark, France, West Germany, Italy, Japan, Mexico, South Africa, Sweden, Great Britain and Venezuela.

It is unimaginable that the huge and wealthy United States market is less attractive to trademark owners, both domestic and foreign, than those of the countries named in the preceding two paragraphs. Only a few of the named countries are party to the Madrid Arrangement. The explanation for the disparity of the figures must, therefore, lie in the inhibitory effect of our requirement for use as a condition to filing.

The conclusion, therefore, must be that TRT will bring about a great increase in the number of filings, and of registrations, in the United States: in part (for both United States nationals and non-nationals), because of the facility of filing under TRT, but in greater part, for United States nationals, because of the elimination of use as a pre-condition to filing and, for the first three years, as a condition to the maintenance of the registration. Under TRT, therefore, we must reconcile ourselves to a considerably greater number of registrations on our Register than at present, registrations which, moreover, do not reflect Common Law rights.

Thus the internal TRT safeguards against proliferation, while good in themselves, cannot be relied upon by the United States to prevent a large increase in the number of filings and registrations in this country. Our reliance must be upon our own domestic law, and while we cannot under TRT remove unused trademarks from the Register for at least the first three years, it is to be hoped that among the many other changes in our legislation which would ensue from our ratification of TRT, there would be included much more stringent procedures for the removal from the Register of trademarks unused after three years from the date of registration.

Still, TRT cannot be simultaneously criticized for providing negligible benefits to nationals of member countries, and for leading to proliferation. If the benefits are negligible, there will be no proliferation. If there is proliferation, it can only be because TRT is attractive to many trademark owners.

NOTES

1. The Trademark Registration Treaty was signed in Vienna in June, 1973 by the United States and seven other nations. The treaty is to enter into force six months after ratification by five countries. Early in December 1979, the Deputy Commissioner of Patents and Trademarks reported that the TRT had not yet been ratified by the required number of countries. "This has not happened yet because most of the world is waiting to see whether the United States, which took the initiative in drafting the treaty, will officially accept the final text." 460 Pat., TM & Copyright J. A-7 (Jan. 3, 1980).

Will it be necessary for domestic legislation implementing the TRT to depart substantially from current, basic principles of United States trademark law? To what extent have the Lanham Act and decisions under it already departed from strict insistence on the use requirement? On implementation problems and prospects, see Frayne, History and Analysis of TRT, 63 Trademark Rep. 429, 437–447 (1973). Cudek, TRT Impact on United States Statutory and Common Law, 63 Trademark Rep. 501 (1973); Pattishall, The Proposed Trademark Registration Treaty and its Domestic Import, 62 Trademark Rep. 125 (1972).

See generally, Symposium, 63 Trademark Rep. 421 (1973); Hack, The TRT—Does It Need Modification?, 62 Trademark Rep. 134

(1972). On the pros and cons of adherence to the Madrid Agreement, see generally, Symposium, Should the United States Adhere to the Madrid Agreement?, 56 Trademark Rep. 289 (1966).

2. *Selected Bibliography.* S. Ladas, Patents, Trademarks and Related Rights: National and International Protection (1975); E. Offner, International Trademark Protection (1965); European Trademark Law and Practice (P.L.I. Ed. 1971).

Waelbroeck, Trademark Problems in the European Common Market, 54 Trademark Rep. 333 (1964); Ulmer, The Law of Unfair Competition and the Common Market, 53 Trademark Rep. 625 (1963); Ladas, Trademark Agreements in the Common Market, 52 Trademark Rep. 1153 (1962); Lippmann, American Business Interests and a Uniform Common Market Trademark Law, 12 Am.J. Comp.L. 255 (1963); Weiser, Recent EEC Antitrust Activity Relating to Exclusive Distributorships and Trademarks, 55 Trademark Rep. 863 (1965).

Offner, The Benelux Trademark Convention, 54 Trademark Rep. 102 (1964); McAuliffe, Consideration of Inter-American Conventions, 52 Trademark Rep. 25 (1962); Beier & Reimer, Preparatory Study for the Establishment of a Uniform International Trademark Definition, 45 Trademark Rep. 1266 (1955); Ebb, Current Problems of American Companies That Permit Use of Their Corporate Names and Trademarks Overseas, 20 Buffalo L.Rev. 147 (1970).

*

INDEX

References are to pages

ABANDONMENT
Patent, 476
Trademark, 323, 381–382

ACCOUNTING FOR PROFITS
See Profits

ADMINISTRATIVE PROCEDURES
Copyright, 658–662, 668–669
Patent, 557–568, 574–576
Trademark, 355–359

ADVERTISING
Ideas, 43
Trademark, 19–28, 292, 299–300
Unfair competition, 94

ANTITRUST
Copyright, 881–886
Patent, 872–881
Trademark, 886–896

APPEALS
Patent, 574
Trademark, 358

ARCHITECTURAL PLANS
Common law copyright, 206–209
Copyright, 732–733

ATTORNEY FEES
Copyright, 823–828
Patent, 630
Trade secrets, 159–160
Trademark, 394–395

CABLE TELEVISION
Copyright, 754–756

CERTIFICATION MARKS
See Trademark

CHARACTERS
Copyright, 718–722, 734–736, 777–780
Unfair competition, 735

COLLECTIVE MARKS
See Trademark

COMMON LAW COPYRIGHT
Generally, 195–241
Architectural plans, 206–209
Conversations, 234–239

COMMON LAW COPYRIGHT—Cont'd
Derivative works, 211–212
Letters, 239–240
Preemption, 195–196, 213–232
Right of privacy, 232–241
Theory of protection, 197–212

COMPULSORY LICENSE
Copyright, 752–757, 761–763
Trademark, 384–385

COMPUTER PROGRAMS
Patent, 507–525

CONSTITUTION
Commerce clause, 1
Copyright clause, 1, 712–713
Federal system, 2
Patent clause, 1
Preemption, 2

CONTRIBUTORY INFRINGEMENT
Copyright, 854
Patent, 591–592, 597–616

CONVERSATIONS
Copyright, 234–239

COPYRIGHT
Antitrust, 881–886
Architectural plans, 732–733
Attorney fees, 823–828
Cable television, 754–756
Characters, 718–722, 734–736, 777–780
Common errors, 851
Compulsory license, 752–757, 761–763
Contributory infringement, 854
Conversations, 234–239
Copy, 666–668
Damages, 812–815, 828–829
Deposit, 658–662, 668
Derivative works, 211–212, 723–732, 733–734
Display, 759
Fact works, 679–680, 682–684
Fair use, 763–786
First amendment, 785
First sale, 759–760
Formalities, 654–669
Functionality, 699–709
Functions of, 9–15, 28, 29–30
History, 652–653

COPYRIGHT—Cont'd
Immoral content, 710–712
Income taxation, 907–914
Industrial designs, 699–709
Infringement, 830–855
Injunctions, 811–812, 829–830
International protection, 919–932
Jukeboxes, 756–757
Jurisdiction, 269–275
Labels, 709–710
Letters, 239–240
Moral right, 855–871
Notice, 195–210, 654–658, 662–668
Novelty, 681–682
Obscene content, 710–712
Originality, 669–684
Performance, 758–759
Performing rights societies,
    ASCAP, 809–811
    BMI, 810–811
    SESAC, 811
Phonorecords, 756, 761–762
Photocopying, 781, 783–784
Preemption, 195–196, 213–232, 426
Profits, 812–815, 828–829
Public broadcasting, 757
Registration, 658–662, 668
Remedies, 811–830
Renewal, 807–808
Requirements,
    Formalities, 654–669
    Originality, 669–684
Satire, 781–783
Sound recordings, 228, 760–761
Statutory damages, 813–815
Strict liability, 852–853
Subject matter, 684–713
Substantial similarity, 849–850
Term, 786–807
Transfers, 786–805, 808–809
Utility, 699–709
Vicarious liability, 854–855
"Writings," 712–713

CORRESPONDENCE
See Letters

COVENANT NOT TO COMPETE
See Trade Secrets

CUSTOMER LIST
See Trade Secrets

DAMAGES
Copyright, 812–815, 828–829
Ideas, 60–62
Patent, 629–630
Statutory, see Statutory Damages
Trade secrets, 159–160
Trademark, 393–394
Unfair competition, 95

DECLARATORY JUDGMENT
See Declaratory Relief

DECLARATORY RELIEF
Patent, 631–632

DERIVATIVE WORKS
Common law copyright, 211–212
Copyright, 723–732, 733–734

DESIGN PATENT
    Generally, 526–542
Double patenting, 532–540
Functionality, 542
Nonobviousness, 540–542
Relation to trademark, 352–353

DILUTION
    See also Trademark; Unfair Competi-
        tion
Trademark, 369–377
Unfair competition, 101–107, 114–115

DISTINCTIVENESS
Right of publicity, 257–258
Trademark, 293–325, 346

DOCTRINE OF EQUIVALENTS
See Patent

ESTOPPEL
Collateral, 649–651
File wrapper, 641–646, 648–649
Licensee, 617–619

FACT WORKS
Copyright, 679–680, 682–684

FAIR USE
Copyright, 763–786
Trademark, 382–384

FEDERAL TRADE COMMISSION
See Trademark

FILE WRAPPER ESTOPPEL
See Patent

FIRST AMENDMENT
Copyright, 785
Right of publicity, 259–268

FUNCTIONALITY
Copyright, 699–709
Design patent, 542
Trademark, 351–352
Unfair competition, 128–130, 138–139

IDEAS
    Generally, 33–70
Brokers, 44–45
Concreteness, 60
Damages, 60–62
Novelty, 59–60

IDEAS—Cont'd
Patent protection, 31
Preemption, 64–70, 223
Remedies, 60–62
Theories of protection, 45–64
  Contract implied in fact, 58–59
  Express contract, 57–58
  Property, 56–57
  Quasi contract, 59
Waiver forms, 43–44, 62–64

IMMORAL CONTENT
Copyright, 710–712
Patent, 492–493
Trademark, 353–354

INCOME TAX
Copyright, 907–914
Patent, 897–907
Trademark, 915–917

INDUSTRIAL DESIGN
Copyright, 699–709

INFRINGEMENT
Copyright, 830–855
Patent, 633–651
Trademark, 395–418

INJUNCTIONS
Copyright, 811–812, 829–830
Patent, 628–629
Trade secrets, 158–159
Trademark, 395
Unfair competition, 94–95

INTERFERENCES
Patent, 476, 576
Trademark, 356–357

INTERNATIONAL PROTECTION
Copyright, 918–932
Patent, 933–942
Trademark, 288–290, 943–955

**INTERNATIONAL TRADE COMMIS-
SION**
Patent, 574

JURISDICTION
See Copyright; Patent; Trademark;
  Unfair Competition

LABELS
Copyright, 709–710
Trademark, 339–346

LETTERS
Copyright, 239–240

MENTAL PROCESSES
See Patent

MENTAL STEPS
See Patent

MISAPPROPRIATION
Preemption, 140, 223
Record piracy, 6
Right of publicity, 255–256
Sound recording, 227–228, 257–258
Unfair competition, 107–113, 115–116

MISREPRESENTATION
Common law theory, 71–80, 91–92
Federal law, 91, 230–231
Moral right, 859–870
Trademark, 418–421, 426–428

MORAL RIGHT
See Copyright

NAME AND LIKENESS
See Privacy, Right of; Publicity, Right
  of

NOTICE
Copyright, 195–210, 654–658, 662–668
Patent, 632
Trademark, 394

NOVELTY
Copyright, 681–682
Ideas, 59–60
Patent, 454–463, 472, 478–485
Plant patent, 556
Trade secrets, 156

ORIGINALITY
Copyright, 669–684
Patent, 494–496

PARODY
See Satire

PASSING OFF
Preemption, 223

PATENT
Abandonment, 476
Aggression, 590–591
Alternative systems, 31–32
Antitrust, 872–881
Appeals, 574
Attorney fees, 630
Collateral estoppel, 649–651
Computer programs, 507–525
Conception, 477
Contributory infringement, 591–592, 597–
  616
Damages, 629–630
Declaratory relief, 631–632
Design patents, 526–542
Doctrine of equivalents, 634–641, 647–648
Double patenting, 532–540
Experimental use, 464–472, 476

References are to pages

PATENT—Cont'd

File wrapper estoppel, 641–646, 648–649
Functions of, 15–19, 28, 31
History, 430–431
Ideas, 31
Income taxation, 897–907
Infringement, 633–651
Injunctions,
  Permanent, 628
  Preliminary, 628–629
Interest awards, 630
Interferences, 476, 575–576
International protection, 933–942
International Trade Commission, 574
Jurisdiction, 269–275
Licensee estoppel, 617–619
Mental processes, 525–526
Mental steps, 525–526
Micro-organisms, 497–507
New use, 526
Nonobviousness, 540–542
Notice, 632
Patent and Trademark Office, 452–453
Plant patents, 543–556
Printed publication, 473–474
Reasonable royalty, 629–630
Reconstruction, 585–589
Reduction to practice, 477, 493
Reissue, 574–575
Relation to trade secrets, 192, 194
Relation to trademark, 306–307
Remedies, 619–632
Repair, 585–589

Requirements,
  Nonobviousness,   432–454,   478–485,
    569–573
  Novelty, 454–463, 472, 478–485
  Operability, 493
  Originality, 494–497
  Statutory bars, 454
  Subtests of invention, 451–452
  Utility, 485–494
Subject matter, 497–556
Suppression, 587–589
Term, 590
Treble damages, 630
Utility patents, 497–526

PATENT AND TRADEMARK OFFICE
  See, also Patent; Trademark
Patent applications, 557–568, 574–576
Trademark registration, 355–359

PATENT APPLICATION
See Patent and Trademark Office

PERFORMING RIGHTS SOCIETIES
See Copyright

PERSONAL NAMES
Trademark, 318–321, 323
Unfair competition, 118–128

PHONORECORDS
Copyright, 756, 761–752

PHOTOCOPYING
Copyright, 781, 783–784

PLANT PATENT
  Generally, 543–556
Novelty, 556
Statutory bar, 556
Subject matter, 555

PLANT VARIETY PROTECTION
Generally, 557

PLANTS
See Plant Patent; Plant Variety Protection

PREEMPTION
Common law copyright, 195–196, 213–232
Constitutional, 2, 228–230
Copyright, 7, 426, 871
Ideas, 64–70, 223
Misappropriation, 140, 223
Passing off, 223
Right of publicity, 267–268
State trademark law, 223–224
Trade secrets, 175–194, 224
Unfair competition, 128–140, 223

PRELIMINARY INJUNCTION
Copyright, 829–830
Patent, 628–629

PRINCIPAL REGISTER
See Trademark

PRIVACY, RIGHT OF
Common law copyright, 232–241
Name and likeness, 257–259
Publicity compared, 255–256

PRODUCT SIMULATION
Trademark, 350–351
Unfair competition, 128–140

PROFITS
Copyright, 812–815, 828–829
Trade secrets, 159–160
Trademark, 393–394
Unfair competition, 95

PUBLIC BROADCASTING
Copyright, 757

PUBLIC DOMAIN
Role of, 7–8

PUBLICATION
Common law copyright, 195–212
Copyright, 195–212
Printed, patent law, 473–474

PUBLICITY, RIGHT OF
Duration, 255–257
First amendment, 259–268
Misappropriation rationale, 255–256
Name and likeness, 257–259
Preemption, 267–268
Privacy rationale, 255–256
Survival, 255–257
Theory of protection, 242–259
Unfair competition rationale, 255–256

REASONABLE ROYALTY
Patent, 629–630
Trade secrets, 159–160

RECORD PIRACY
See Misappropriation; Phonorecords;
   Sound Recordings

REDUCTION TO PRACTICE
See Patent

REISSUE
Patent, 574–575

REMEDIES
   See also Damages; Injunctions; Prof-
     its
Copyright, 811–830
Ideas, 60–62
Patent, 619–632
Trade secrets, 158–160
Trademark, 387–395
Unfair competition, 94–95

RENEWAL
Copyright, 807–808
Trademark, 357–358

REVERSE ENGINEERING
Trade secrets, 157–158

RIGHT OF PRIVACY
See Privacy, Right of

RIGHT OF PUBLICITY
See Publicity, Right of

SATIRE
Copyright, 781–783
Trademark, 383

SECONDARY MEANING
Trademark, 322
Unfair competition, 83–84

SERVICE MARKS
See Trademark

SHOP RIGHTS
See Trade Secrets

SOUND RECORDINGS
Copyright, 228, 760–761
Misappropriation, 257–258
State protection, 227–230

STATUTORY DAMAGES
Copyright, 813–815

SUPPLEMENTAL REGISTER
See Trademark

SUPPRESSION
Copyright, 808–809
Patent, 587–589

SURVEYS
Trademark, 411–415, 417

TERM
Copyright, 805–808
Patent, 590
Trademark, 357–358

TERRITORIAL RIGHTS
Trademark, 359–369, 378–380
Unfair competition, 96–100

TRADE SECRETS
Accounting for profits, 159–160
Administrative handling, 161–162
Attorney fees, 159–160
Covenant not to compete, 162–175
Customer list, 173–174
Injunctions, 158–159
Novelty, 156
Preemption, 6, 175–194, 224
Reasonable royalty, 159–160
Relation to patents, 192, 194
Remedies, 158–160
Reverse engineering, 157–158
Secrecy requirement, 156–157
Shop rights, 173
Theory of protection, 141–162

TRADEMARK
Abandonment, 323, 381–382
Administrative procedures, 355–359
Advertising, 292, 299–300
Antitrust, 886–896
Attorney fees, 394–395
Cancellation, 357, 385–386
Certification marks, 331–339
Collateral use, 92–94
Collective marks, 331–339
Common law, 421–425, 428–429
Compulsory license, 384–385
Concurrent use, 356, 378–380
Damages, 393–394
Deceptive terms, 323–325
Design patent, 306–307, 352–353

TRADEMARK—Cont'd
Dilution, 369–377
Distinctiveness, 346
Examination, 355–356
Fair use, 382–384
"Family" of marks, 380–381
Federal Trade Commission, 307, 384–385
Functions of, 19–28, 30–31
Generic terms, 300–304, 305–308, 323
Geographic terms, 293–297, 311–317
History, 276–278
Immoral content, 353–354
Income tax, 915–917
Incontestability, 385–386
Infringement, 395–418
Injunctions, 395
Interferences, 356–357
International protection, 288–290, 943–955
Jurisdiction, 269–275
"Merely descriptive" marks, 308–311
Misrepresentation, 230–231, 418–421, 426–428
Notice, 394
Oppositions, 356
Patent and Trademark Office, 355–359
Personal names, 318–321, 323
Principal register, 355–359
Profits, 393–394
Remedies, 387–395
Renewal, 357–358
Requirements,
    Affixation, 284–287, 291–292
    Distinctiveness,
        Generally, 293–325
        Common law, 293–308
        Statutory, 308–325
    Secondary meaning, 322
    Use, 279–292
    Use in commerce, 290–291
Satire, 383
Service marks, 325–331
State law, 223–224
Subject matter,
    Color, 346–347
    Expired design patents, 352–353
    Expired utility patents, 306–307, 351-352
    Firm name, 349
    Functional features, 351–352
    Ingredients, 348–349
    Labels, 339–346
    Location, 347–348
    Packages, 350–351
    Slogan, 349

TRADEMARK—Cont'd
Suggestive terms, 297–299, 323–324
Supplemental register, 322, 354–355
Surveys, 411–415, 417
Term, 357–358
Territorial rights, 359–369, 378–380
Transfers, 382
Unfair competition compared, 90–91
Utility patent, 306–307, 351–352

TRADEMARK REGISTRATION
See Patent and Trademark Office

TRANSFER
Copyright, 786–805, 808–809
Trademark, 382

UNFAIR COMPETITION
    See also Misrepresentation; Trademark
    Generally, 71–140
Accounting for profits, 95
Characters, 735
Damages, 95
Dilution, 101–107, 114–115
Functionality, 128–130, 138–139
Injunctions, 94–95
Jurisdiction, 269–275
Misappropriation, 107–113, 115–116
Passing off, 80–83
Patent aggression, 590–591
Personal names, 118–128
Preemption, 128–140, 223
Product simulation, 128–140
Remedies, 94–95
Right of publicity, 255–256
Secondary meaning, 83–84
Territorial rights, 96–100
Trademark compared, 90–91
Use, 84–88

USE
Experimental, 464–472, 476
In commerce, 290–291
Patent law, 473
Trademark, 279–292
Unfair competition, 84–88, 95

UTILITY
Copyright, 699–709
Patent, 485–494

UTILITY PATENT
See Patent

VICARIOUS LIABILITY
Copyright, 854–855